CW01456776

THE OXFORD HANDBOOK OF

HIGHER EDUCATION IN THE ASIA-PACIFIC REGION

THE OXFORD HANDBOOK OF

HIGHER EDUCATION IN THE ASIA-PACIFIC REGION

Edited by

DEVESH KAPUR, LILY KONG, FLORENCE LO, AND DAVID M. MALONE

OXFORD
UNIVERSITY PRESS

OXFORD
UNIVERSITY PRESS

Great Clarendon Street, Oxford, OX2 6DP,
United Kingdom

Oxford University Press is a department of the University of Oxford.
It furthers the University's objective of excellence in research, scholarship,
and education by publishing worldwide. Oxford is a registered trade mark of
Oxford University Press in the UK and in certain other countries

© Oxford University Press 2023

The copyright in the Editor's contribution to the Work remains vested in the Editor.

The moral rights of the authors have been asserted

First Edition published in 2023
Impression: 1

All rights reserved. No part of this publication may be reproduced, stored in
a retrieval system, or transmitted, in any form or by any means, without the
prior permission in writing of Oxford University Press, or as expressly permitted
by law, by licence or under terms agreed with the appropriate reprographics
rights organization. Enquiries concerning reproduction outside the scope of the
above should be sent to the Rights Department, Oxford University Press, at the
address above

You must not circulate this work in any other form
and you must impose this same condition on any acquirer

Published in the United States of America by Oxford University Press
198 Madison Avenue, New York, NY 10016, United States of America

British Library Cataloguing in Publication Data
Data available

Library of Congress Control Number: 2022942573

ISBN 978–0–19–284598–6

DOI: 10.1093/oxfordhb/9780192845986.001.0001

Printed and bound by
CPI Group (UK) Ltd, Croydon, CR0 4YY

Links to third party websites are provided by Oxford in good faith and
for information only. Oxford disclaims any responsibility for the materials
contained in any third party website referenced in this work.

Contents

List of Figures   xi
List of Tables   xv
List of Contributors   xix

Introduction   1
    DEVESH KAPUR, LILY KONG, FLORENCE LO, AND DAVID M. MALONE

PART I HISTORY

1. History of Higher Education in Asia-Pacific   31
    DEANE NEUBAUER

PART II GOALS, GROWTH, AND MASSIFICATION

2. From Elite Higher Education to Massification: The Asia-Pacific
   Experience   47
    MALCOLM TIGHT

3. Employment and Labor Markets   66
    ROSLYN CAMERON AND JOHN BURGESS

4. Productive Workers or Better Citizens?   93
    ARNOUD DE MEYER

PART III WHO LEARNS?

5. Access   115
    PROMPILAI BUASUWAN AND ARISARA LEKSANSERN

6. Gender in Higher Education in the Asia-Pacific Region: Vertical
   Progress, Horizontal Segregation, and a Leaky Pipeline   134
    ELIZABETH M. KING

PART IV WHAT: CONTENT AND LEARNING IN HIGHER EDUCATION

7. The Relationship Between Credentials and Learning: A Focus on International Educational Value and Distinction   159
JOHANNA L. WATERS

8. Liberal Arts and Sciences Education for the Twenty-First Century in Asia   173
MIKIKO NISHIMURA

9. STEM Field Demand and Educational Reform in Asia-Pacific Countries   189
AKI YAMADA

10. The Ranking Game   210
WILLIAM YAT WAI LO AND RYAN M. ALLEN

11. Professional Education: Models and Issues   228
SHENG-JU CHAN AND HUA-CHI CHOU

PART V HOW AND WHO?

12. Quality Regulation in Higher Education in Asia-Pacific: Roles of Quality Assurance and National Qualification Frameworks   249
ANGELA YUNG CHI HOU, I-JUNG GRACE LU, KAREN HUI JUNG CHEN, AND CHAO YU GUO

13. Internationalization and Education-Related Mobility in Asia-Pacific Universities   268
K. C. HO, RAVINDER SIDHU, AND BRENDA S. A. YEOH

14. Internationalization and Mobility: Providers, Academic Collaborators, and Recognition of Qualifications   289
CHRISTOPHER S. COLLINS AND ALEXANDER H. JONES

15. Education Hubs in the Asia-Pacific   306
KRIS OLDS

16. Open University Systems   330
MELINDA DELA PEÑA BANDALARIA AND ALEXANDRA IVANOVIC

17. MOOCs in Asia: Promise Unfulfilled or Promise Realized?   356
HELEN FARLEY

PART VI COSTS: WHO PAYS?

18. Public Financing   379
XI WANG AND W. JAMES JACOB

19. Private Philanthropy in Higher Education in Asia   402
SWEE-SUM LAM

20. Student Loans in Practice: Benefits and Pitfalls of Loans Schemes in Asia   423
ADRIAN ZIDERMAN

PART VII CONSEQUENCES AND CHALLENGES

21. Returning Talent   451
RENNIE J. MOON

22. Asia as a Producer of Knowledge   464
YOUNGSUK CHI AND JOHN VAN ORDEN

23. Asian Higher Education as Soft Power?   500
JACK T. LEE

24. Higher Education and Nationalism in the Asia-Pacific   514
CHRISTOPHER D. HAMMOND

25. Lifelong Learning as a Globally Diffused Policy Discourse in Asia   534
HONGXIA SHAN AND ZHENG REN

PART VIII COUNTRY STUDIES

26. China: Historical and Contemporary Development of Higher Education   553
WENQIN SHEN AND WANHUA MA

27. Elite Universities in China   574
LAN XUE, ZHEN YU, AND ZHOU ZHONG

28. India: History and Thrust of Overall Higher Education and
    Research Patterns   592
    NIRAJA GOPAL JAYAL

29. Private Universities in India: New Dawn or False Dawn?   612
    PRATAP BHANU MEHTA

30. Japan: The Changing Role of Higher Education for Nation-Building   629
    AKIYOSHI YONEZAWA

31. Japan: Challenges in Internationalization of its Higher Education
    Sector   651
    MIKI SUGIMURA AND SHINOBU YUME YAMAGUCHI

32. Higher Education in the Republic of Korea   670
    JANG WAN KO

33. Singapore: The Making of Higher Education in an Asian
    Education Hub   692
    S. GOPINATHAN AND MICHAEL H. LEE

34. Higher Education in Hong Kong: Recent Developments and
    Challenges   714
    JIN JIANG

35. Australia: History versus Geography in an Evolving National System   735
    ANTHONY WELCH

36. Education for All? Higher Education at a Crossroads in Aotearoa
    New Zealand   755
    KATHRYN A. SUTHERLAND AND STEPHEN J. MARSHALL

37. Indonesia: The Politics of Equity and Quality in Higher Education   774
    CHIARA LOGLI AND HERMIN INDAH WAHYUNI

38. Higher Education in Malaysia   798
    CHANG DA WAN

39. Privatized Higher Education in Thailand: In Pursuit of Legitimacy
    and Profitability   815
    PRACHAYANI PRAPHAMONTRIPONG KANWAR AND FLORENCE LO

40. Higher Education in Myanmar   837
    MARIE LALL, CAMILLE KANDIKO HOWSON, AND AYE AYE TUN

41. Philippine Higher Education: A Case for Public–Private
Complementarity in the Next Normal   856
MARIA CYNTHIA ROSE BAUTISTA, VICENTE PAQUEO,
AND ANICETO ORBETA JR.

Index   879

Figures

0.1	Growth in tertiary education in Asia, 2000–2019	6
0.2	Massification in Asia has come at much lower levels of income	7
4.1	Percentage enrollment in tertiary education of eligible students for selected countries	95
5.1	Correlation of GER and GDP per capita	118
5.2	Percentage of enrollment in tertiary education in private institutions	125
5.3	Official development assistance flows for scholarship by sector and type of study	127
6.1	Gross enrollment rates in tertiary education of females and males, by world region	136
6.2	Gross tertiary education enrollment rates in the Asia-Pacific region, by gender	137
6.3	Gender inequality in gross enrollment rates	138
6.4	Gender equality in enrollment and female share of faculty in tertiary education	141
6.5	Gender distribution of non-agricultural occupations in the Asia-Pacific region	150
8.1	Development of liberal education programs in Asia	177
11.1	Triangle of coordination	232
11.2	Triangle of coordination of professional education	242
15.1	Offshore campus development worldwide, 1921–2020	312
15.2	Share of major importing countries in 1990, 2000, 2010, and 2020	313
15.3	Number of international branch campuses per city (as at 2000)	314
15.4	Pacific Asia: the 25 largest urban areas by population, 2010	318
15.5	Models for the globalization of higher education	323
18.1	Public vs. private percentage of spending on tertiary education, latest year available	383
18.2	Government expenditure on education as a share of GDP in selected Asian countries in 2018	383

18.3   Government expenditure per tertiary student in selected Asian countries,
       latest year available   384

18.4   General higher education institution student entrants in 1995–2018   390

18.5   Number of general higher education intuitions in 1995–2018   391

18.6   Governmental expenditure on education as percentage of GDP   391

18.7   Expenditures on tertiary education as a percentage of government
       expenditures on education in Vietnam, 2008–2013   394

19.1   Donations in China   411

19.2   Donations by sector and source in Singapore, 2018   411

22.1a GDP vs. GERD in Asia, four countries/regions, 2009–2018   467

22.1b GDP vs. GERD in Asia, six countries/regions, 2009–2018   467

22.2a Total publication output, four countries/regions, 2009–2018   469

22.2b Total publication output, seven countries/regions, 2009–2018   469

22.3a GERD ($M USD, PPP) vs. publication output, global
       countries/regions, 2009   471

22.3b GERD ($M USD, PPP) vs. publication output, global
       countries/regions, 2009   471

22.4   Publications per GERD ($M USD, PPP) from 2009–2018   472

22.5   Publications per researcher in Asia, 2009–2018   474

22.6   Percentage of publications from 2009 to 2018 written in a language
       other than English in each country/region   475

22.7   Field-weighted citation impact of top Asian knowledge producers,
       2009–2018   479

22.8a Change in publication output and FWCI, 2009–2018   481

22.8b Change in publication output and FWCI, 2009–2018   481

22.9   Comparing Asian regions' relative activity by discipline, 2009–2018   483

22.10 Breakdown of East Asia's FWCI by subject area, 2009–2018   485

22.11 Comparing Asian region's Relative Activity Index (RAI) by discipline,
       2009–2018   486

22.12 Breakdown of South Asia's FWCI by subject area, 2009–2018   487

22.13 Percentage of total publications receiving patent citations, 2009–2018
       (EPO, JPO, USPTO)   488

22.14 Total patent citations accrued by research from the top Asian knowledge
       producers, 2009–2018 (EPO, JPO, USPTO), disaggregated according to
       publication field of research   490

22.15   Percentage of patent citations to publications from each country by
sector of publication authors, 2009–2018 (EPO, JPO, USPTO),
all six disciplines included   490

22.16a Triadic patent count among top Asian knowledge producers,
2009–2018 (USPTO, EPO, and JPO), all six disciplines included   492

22.16b Triadic patent count among top Asian knowledge producers,
2009–2018 (USPTO, EPO, and JPO)   492

22.17   Number of patents vs. technology relevance, 2008–2019
(Triadic patents filed at EPO, USPTO, and JPO)   494

24.1   A conceptualization of forms and types of nationalisms   516

24.2   Top-down and bottom-up nationalism   517

26.1   Number of newly approved TNHE activities   559

26.2   The ratio of tuition to overall revenue in different colleges and
universities and its changes   567

27.1   Number of China's universities in QS top 1000 ranking   583

27.2   Spatial distribution of China's DWC universities   584

30.1   Number of newly enrolled students in higher education, graduates
from secondary education (1960–2020) and 18-year-old population
(estimated 1960–2040)   635

30.2   Number of newly enrolled students by gender (four-year undergraduate
and junior colleges, 1970–2020)   637

31.1   Number of inbound international students to Japan, 1983–2019   654

31.2   Short-term outbound students from Japan, 2009–2018   660

31.3   Number of Japanese universities offering double degree programs and
number of outgoing and incoming students participating in double
degree programs   662

32.1   Trends of national scholarship   679

32.2   Internationalization policies and the number of international students
in Korea   682

34.1   Pathway to post-secondary education   718

34.2   Recurrent government expenditure on post-secondary education in
Hong Kong, 2007–2019   719

34.3   Number of full-time undergraduate students, 2008–2019   723

34.4   Expansion of higher education in Hong Kong, East Asia and the
Pacific, and the world   724

34.5   Non-local enrollment of self-financed and UGC-funded programs
from 2011/12 to 2018/19   729

35.1   Public and private expenditure on higher education,
       selected countries, 1999   739

35.2   Participation rates by gender, 1989–2017   741

35.3   Higher education participation rates, by equity group, 2016   742

35.4   Asian-born academics, Australian universities, by place of birth, 2015   747

36.1   International students studying in NZ tertiary institutions by
       country of citizenship, 2009–2019   761

36.2   International students studying in NZ universities by country
       of citizenship, 2009–2019   762

38.1   Gender Parity Index for tertiary education in Malaysia, 1979–2018   803

39.1   Legitimacy of private and public institutions in the Thai higher
       education marketplace   821

39.2   Thai higher education enrollment, both private and public, 1995–2020   822

39.3   Government budget expenditure on higher education, 2005–2021   828

39.4   The MHESI annual budget expenditure by type, fiscal year 2021   829

41.1   Higher education enrollment comparison between the Philippines,
       regional peers and the average of middle-income countries   860

41.2   Percentage of STEM graduates in higher education, 2016   861

41.3   Net enrollment rate in higher education by income decile, 2019   863

41.4   Distribution of enrollment in public and private HEIs, by income
       decile, 2019   864

41.5   Number of SUCs established by year of legislation   872

41.6   First year college enrollment in public and private HEIs, 2011–2019   874

Tables

0.1   The domestic education system matters overwhelmingly for most
students in Asia   18

3.1   The demographic profile of the region   70

3.2   The economic capacity and drivers of higher education   71

3.3   Highest educational attainment by the population aged 25 years and
over (male and female)   72

3.4   Industries identified for growth, employment through
Industry 4.0, and 4IR   83

5.1   Enrollment in tertiary education in Asia   116

5.2   Government expenditure on tertiary education   126

6.1   Percentage of male and female tertiary graduates in STEM areas of study   139

6.2   Gender inequality (F/M) in tertiary education, by wealth quintile   146

6.3   Female researchers as percentage of total researchers, by field and
place of employment   151

9.1   R&D spending by country: total and percentage of GDP   193

9.2   PISA science and math, top rankings, 2018   196

9.3   TIMSS 8th grade science and math, top rankings, 2019   197

10.1   Leading global university systems with indicator weights   214

11.1   Different models of professional education in Asia   241

12.1   A comparison between QA and QF in terms of characteristics   254

12.2   Summary of the number of QA agencies in the Asia-Pacific region   256

12.3   Development of national qualification frameworks of ASEAN states   258

12.4   The lead units responsible for regulating higher education quality
in Asia-Pacific   259

13.1   The flow of tertiary international students to selected countries
in Asia and Australia, 2019   270

14.1   Top ten origin and destination countries, 2017   299

14.2   Tertiary-level Asian students' flow to destination countries   300

15.1   Percentage urban and rate of urbanization of the world, by geographic
       region, selected periods, 1950–2050   317

16.1   Single-mode distance teaching universities in Asia   339

18.1   Journal citation ranking and documents produced by country, 1998,
       2008, and 2018   380

18.2   Public tertiary funding trends as a percentage of government
       expenditure on education, 2003 to the latest year available   382

18.3   Maximum tuition fees at public HEIs according to every discipline
       from academic years 2015 to 2021 in Vietnam   395

19.1   Asia and the Pacific countries in the Global Philanthropy
       Environment Index   406

19.2   Top 10 ranked Asia-Pacific Universities in the QS world university
       ranking 2020   413

19.3   Some Asia-Pacific universities and their endowments   416

20.1   Private rates of return to higher education: selected Asian countries
       with loans schemes   425

20.2   Loans scheme objective and coverage   426

20.3   Loans scheme funding source and loans allocation   430

20.4   Measures and sanctions against default   434

20.5   Loan repayment: collection alternatives and repayment mechanisms   436

20.A.1 Asian loans schemes: general description   446

21.1   Net number of immigrants per period by development group
       and region, 1950–2020   452

22.1   Top engineering and technology topics by publication count,
       East Asia, 2009–2018   484

26.1   Structure of higher education funding source, 1994–2017   563

29.1   Private enrollments in selected countries   613

29.2   Requirements for setting up private universities: three examples   615

30.1   Higher education institutions and student enrollment, 2020   630

30.2   Higher education institutions and student enrollment, 1945   634

32.1   Historical development of the number of HEIs and student enrollment   673

32.2   The number of international students by degree programs   684

32.3   Top five countries of origin for international students and faculty, 2019   685

33.1   Distribution of R&D spending in Singapore, 1999–2018   698

33.2   International rankings of Singapore universities, 2016–2021   699

33.3   Government recurrent expenditure on higher education, 1998–2018   699

33.4   Government recurrent expenditure on higher education per student,
       1998–2018   699

34.1   Degree-awarding HEIs in Hong Kong   715

34.2   The funding sources of HKU, 2018–2019 and 2003–2004   721

35.1   Student fees by disciplinary band, 2020   740

35.2   ASEAN private overseas post-secondary and higher education
       students, 1976–1984   744

35.3   International student enrollments, higher education, 2002–2019   745

37.1   Indonesian higher education institutions in 2019   776

37.2   Gross attendance ratio indicators in Indonesian higher education in 2017   779

37.3   Graduation indicators in Indonesian higher education in 2018   780

37.4   International mobility in tertiary education in ASEAN middle-income
       countries in 2018   784

37.5   International mobility in tertiary education in Indonesia in 2017   785

38.1   Enrollment and number of institutions, 2008 and 2018   801

38.2   Ethnic proportion in Malaysian public universities, 1966–2013   802

39.1   Types of HEIs in Thailand, 2020   817

39.2   Comparison of private and public higher education growth in Thailand   819

39.3   Graduates by employment status and type of HEIs, overall, 2018   826

40.1   Number and type of higher education institutions under the ministries   839

40.2   Students in higher education in Myanmar, 2017–2018   840

41.1   Composition and enrollment of higher education institutions   859

41.2   Some quality indicators   861

41.3   Participation rate of persons 17–24 years old in higher education: poorest
       vs. "richest," 1999, 2014, 2016, 2017, and 2019   863

Contributors

Ryan M. Allen, Chapman University

Aye Aye Tun, Private Consultant

Melinda dela Peña Bandalaria, University of the Philippines Open University

Maria Cynthia Rose Bautista, University of the Philippines

Prompilai Buasuwan, Kasetsart University

John Burgess, Torrens University

Roslyn Cameron, Torrens University

Sheng-Ju Chan, National Chung Cheng University

Karen Hui Jung Chen, National Taipei University of Education

Youngsuk Chi, Elsevier

Hua-Chi Chou, Higher Education Evaluation and Accreditation Council of Taiwan

Christopher S. Collins, Azusa Pacific University

Helen Farley, University of Southern Queensland

S. Gopinathan, The HEAD Foundation

Chao Yu Guo, National Chengchi University

Christopher D. Hammond, The University of Tokyo

K. C. Ho, National University of Singapore

Angela Yung Chi Hou, National Chengchi University

Camille Kandiko Howson, Imperial College London

Alexandra Ivanovic, United Nations University

W. James Jacob, FamilySearch International

Niraja Gopal Jayal, King's College London

Jin Jiang, Hong Kong Baptist University

Alexander H. Jones, Roberts Wesleyan College

Prachayani Praphamontripong Kanwar, University at Albany-State University of New York

Elizabeth M. King, Brookings Institution

Jang Wan Ko, Sungkyunkwan University

Marie Lall, University College London

Swee-Sum Lam, National University of Singapore and Asia Pastoral Institute, Singapore

Jack T. Lee, University of Edinburgh

Michael H. Lee, The Chinese University of Hong Kong

Arisara Leksansern, Mahidol University

Florence Lo, United Nations University

William Yat Wai Lo, The Education University of Hong Kong

Chiara Logli, Honolulu Community College

I-Jung Grace Lu, Tunghai University

Wanhua Ma, Peking University

Stephen J. Marshall, Victoria University of Wellington

Pratap Bhanu Mehta, Princeton University

Arnoud De Meyer, Singapore Management University

Rennie J. Moon, Yonsei University

Deane Neubauer, University of Hawaii at Manoa

Mikiko Nishimura, International Christian University

Kris Olds, University of Wisconsin-Madison

Aniceto Orbeta Jr., Philippine Institute of Development Studies

John Van Orden, Elsevier

Vicente Paqueo, Philippine Institute of Development Studies

Zheng Ren, Beihang University

Hongxia Shan, University of British Columbia

Wenqin Shen, Peking University

Ravinder Sidhu, University of Queensland

Miki Sugimura, Sophia University

Kathryn A. Sutherland, Victoria University of Wellington

Malcolm Tight, Lancaster University

Hermin Indah Wahyuni, Center for Southeast Asia Social Studies (CESASS), Gadjah Mada University

Chang Da Wan, Universiti Sains Malaysia

Xi Wang, University of Pittsburgh

Johanna L. Waters, University College London

Anthony Welch, University of Sydney

Lan Xue, Tsinghua University

Aki Yamada, Tamagawa University

Shinobu Yume Yamaguchi, United Nations University

Brenda S. A. Yeoh, National University of Singapore

Akiyoshi Yonezawa, Tohoku University

Zhen Yu, Beijing Normal University

Zhou Zhong, Tsinghua University

Adrian Ziderman, Bar-Ilan University

INTRODUCTION

DEVESH KAPUR, LILY KONG, FLORENCE LO, AND DAVID M. MALONE

1. WHY THIS HANDBOOK?

SINCE the turn of the millennium, it has become clear that the Asia-Pacific region[1] is economically (although no longer demographically) the fastest-growing continent in the world and is likely to remain so for some time, despite the setback of the COVID-19 pandemic. The Asia-Pacific's share of the world's gross domestic product (GDP) doubled from 15 percent to 30 percent between 1970 and 2017 and is projected to account for half of global GDP by 2050. If measured by purchasing power parity, the region already accounted for 42.6 percent of global GDP in 2017, up from 30.1 percent in 2000 (Asian Development Bank, 2018).

Asia dominated the world economy for most of human history until the end of the seventeenth century when Europe (and later the United States) became the dominant economic powers, riding on the Enlightenment and the Scientific and Industrial Revolutions. However, over the past half century, Japan and the East Asia "tigers"—Hong Kong, Singapore, South Korea, and Taiwan—were the first countries in Asia to catch up with the West, joining and then surpassing the two "Western" countries in the Asia-Pacific region—Australia and New Zealand.[2]

Their rise, however, has been overshadowed by China's extraordinary take-off following the country's introduction of market-oriented reforms in the late 1970s. With South-East and South Asia also growing rapidly, with over half the world's population and three of the world's five largest economies, Asia is also poised to home half of the world's middle class—a class that is both the driver and the product of higher education.

These developments have also, indeed primarily, created considerable opportunity for the growth of higher education in most Asian countries. The economic benefits of this massive expansion appear manifestly obvious, whether for the teeming numbers of seriously aspirational young Asians and their families, the companies that seek to hire them, or their countries' economic competitiveness. But there are also potential social

---

[1] The Asia-Pacific region refers to East, South, and South-East Asia and Australasia (excluding Central Asia and the Middle East).

[2] South Korea surpassed Australia in overall GDP as of 2009.

and political payoffs in addition to socialization effects. Idle (primarily male) youth between the ages of roughly 18 and 25 have often been the demographic most willing to confront state authority in the streets. Enrolling large numbers from this cohort in higher education redirects their energies. Nonetheless, universities are also places where students organize to challenge the status quo, as has been widely observed worldwide.[3]

But beneath this surface reality are swirling undercurrents that raise a host of questions, from its effects on individuals to its impacts on regions, from knowledge creation to innovation and creativity, and from economics to geopolitics. Expectedly, many of these questions are intrinsic to higher education anywhere. However, what is distinctive about the Asia-Pacific region is the sheer scale and rate of growth. Even as governments in many Asian countries have encouraged or at least tolerated the nearly wild-cat growth of the higher education sector, they have had to grapple with quality-control challenges while building structures and an ethos that also respects academic freedom.

The explosion in higher education has followed on the heels of burgeoning demand resulting from multiple factors: demographic momentum in the college-age population, one that is more motivated and, in some cases, better prepared for higher education; a swelling middle class (expected to cross 3 billion people by 2030); rapid urbanization; and technological change that has made growth more skill intensive and has raised the skill premium, and thereby the demand for higher education.

The quality of a country's system of higher education may be seen as a gauge both of its current level of national development and of its future economic prospects. It is therefore natural that the putative "Asian Century" should generate interest in the region's higher education systems, which, on the one hand share common characteristics—a fixation with credentials and engineering, high technology, and business degrees (especially among male students)—while on the other hand are also highly differentiated, not only across countries but also within.

In the region's poorest countries, which upon independence sometimes inherited one or several universities as a colonial legacy, very little reinvestment has been made. Indeed, in several cases—in South Asia, Myanmar, and the Philippines—the modest colonial inheritance has failed to serve as a springboard. Picturesque campuses attracting teeming throngs of students have little to offer them in these instances. Classes are too large, the curriculum sometimes hopelessly outdated, and the academic staff poorly trained and mostly discouraged. Children of the elite often go to study overseas at

---

[3] The University of Rangoon was a cockpit for young Burmese seeking independence of the country from Great Britain (achieved in 1948) and subsequently a range of governments experienced challenges in controlling its students in years such as 1988 and 1991, with most undergraduate programs closed altogether between 1996 and 2013. This proved economically counterproductive in terms of workforce preparedness to integrate and power a more dynamic economy. Chapter 40 on Myanmar details numerous ups and downs of higher education in the country, also touching on its troubled current situation. And Thailand, a middle-income country, particularly its capital, Bangkok, has experienced similar, recurring student unrest over the past decades.

regional hubs or higher education magnets such as Singapore, Hong Kong, or the United Arab Emirates (UAE), when they do not favor Europe, North America, Australia, or New Zealand. While some lower-income countries of the region do have high-quality outliers (e.g., the Lahore University of Management Sciences in Pakistan), this tells us little about the quality of education imparted by the median institution.

While the large *cross-country variance* in higher education in the Asia-Pacific region seems obvious, the large *within-country variance* is less visible, especially in countries that remain lower-income on average. India, for example, has high-quality non-university affiliated research institutions and high-quality federal institutions (such as the Indian Institutes of Technology) now joined by a new generation of high-quality private universities, operating largely on the North American model.[4] Yet, for the most part, STEM (science, technology, engineering, and mathematics) and professional fields do better than the "liberal arts," which face multiple political pressures, as Nishimura and Mehta discuss in their respective Chapters 8 and 29. However, as Jayal indicates in Chapter 28, most students face dismal offerings, with only a few federal universities being the exception to this rule. The patchy quality at best of the bulk of institutions, public and private, remains distressing and is a barrier to economic transition to higher income brackets, both individually and nationally.

The study of international trends in higher education is not at all new. Indeed, a number of global and regional expert groups have emerged in this field, such as SEAMEO RIHED (Southeast Asian Ministers of Education Organization Regional Institute for Higher Education Development) in Bangkok, as have several centers of excellence elsewhere, including the University of Toronto's Ontario Institute for Studies in Education, the Center for International Higher Education at Boston College, and the Institute of Education at London's University College.

2. AIMS OF THIS HANDBOOK

As the economically fastest growing and most populous continent, Asia increasingly matters in every substantive area of human endeavor. A better understanding of its higher education achievements, failings, potential, and structural limitations is imperative. International organizations, such as the Asian Development Bank, Organisation for Economic Co-operation and Development (OECD), and World Bank, have issued occasional reports on the topic but they tend to be narrow in purpose—rooted in national statistics that often lag behind reality—and are hesitant to report too critically against any particular country. These reports, their length notwithstanding, too often tell us very little, although they carry some comparative value. We should note that beyond

---

[4] Examples include Ahmedabad, Ashoka, Azim Premji, BITS, Jindal, Kreya, Plakshya, and Shiv Nadar universities.

rapidly overtaken headline figures, the usable data on higher education in Asia from which policy analysis can be derived is notoriously weak, delayed, and unreliable. The richest vein of expertise in this field is likely to be fostered by country or disciplinary specialization.

Our aim has been to devote chapter-length essays to a number of significant or particularly interesting countries, and more than one chapter to several countries of particular significance in the Asia-Pacific region (China, India, and Japan); and to document cross-cutting trends relating, for example, to: the trilemma as governments juggle to manage the tensions between competing claims of access, accessible cost, and quality; the balance between teaching and research; the links between labor markets (demand) and higher education (supply); preferred fields of study and their consequences; the rise of the research university in Asia; the lure of institutions of international reputation within the region; new education technologies and their effects; and trends in government policy within the wider region but also in sub-regions.

Due consideration was given to select authors from the Asia-Pacific region, particularly local authors for country-specific chapters. This poses some challenges since many authors are not native-English speakers. While this made editing a time-consuming endeavor, we strongly believe that the volume's credibility hinges in part on carrying the voices of a complement of authors from the region. Varying degrees of analysis accompany description and documentation, in part reflecting differing levels of comfort with the English language, but the voices are authentic and experienced within the respective national contexts.

In selecting authors for this publication, the editors made a conscious decision to invite local experts where possible and to ensure gender parity across our lead authors, which we have managed to achieve.

3. HISTORY

While we tend to think of higher education as a Western import, with roots going back to medieval Europe and the rise of the modern research university in the nineteenth century along the lines of the German Humboldtian model, Asia too had Buddhist and Confucian learning traditions that have a long history, especially in the two civilizational states, China and India. As Deane Neubauer recounts in Chapter 1, "History of Higher Education in Asia-Pacific," it was Asia's encounter with Western imperialism and colonialism between the sixteenth and nineteenth centuries that marked the onset of the current higher education system in the region. This is supported by Wenqin Shen and Wanhua Ma, in Chapter 26 on "China: Historical and Contemporary Development of Higher Education," where they provide a historical overview of the development of higher education in China, dating back to a tradition of higher learning in the Shang dynasty of 1800 BC. Mehta also reports in Chapter 29 on "Private Universities in India: New Dawn or False Dawn?" that "universities like Nalanda, Vikramshila, and

Taxila in the Indian subcontinent housed tens of thousands of students and were zones of cosmopolitan cultural, scientific and intellectual exchange."

Japan had a distinctive trajectory, with its program of *datsu-A* (脱亞, "leaving Asia"), an idea first floated within Japan in 1855, and an emphasis on higher education as an instrument of nation-building in the late Meiji period, as Akiyoshi Yonezawa shows in Chapter 30 on "Japan: The Changing Role of Higher Education for Nation-Building." But it was only in the aftermath of decolonization and the rise of new independent states across the region (with exceptions like Australia, Japan, and New Zealand), and concomitant social, economic, and political changes, that the region's higher education systems grew from small elite systems to progressive massification. The expansion of higher education institutes and attendance in the post-colonial era is clearly demonstrated in the case of India, as Niraja Gopal Jayal reports in Chapter 28 on "India: History and Thrust of Overall Higher Education and Research Patterns" that "since independence, the number of degree-awarding universities has increased 52 times, the number of colleges has increased approximately 84 times, and student enrollment has gone up 178 times." Nonetheless, colonial (or in the case of pre-war Japan) legacies continue to shape higher education in these countries, and a number of India's most successful universities and specialized research centers trace their lineage back to colonial times, while the first of its famed Indian Institutes of Technology dates back only to 1951, and the enviably very successful Indian Institutes of Management to 1961.

4. GOALS, GROWTH, AND MASSIFICATION

The role of higher education and universities varies both across and within the region. In low- and middle-income countries such as Indonesia, Malaysia, and Thailand their primary goal is to raise the skills of the population, i.e., to build the human capital that can absorb ideas from advanced economies, rather than to generate new knowledge. In more advanced economies, such as Australia, Singapore, and South Korea, higher education is seen as a key driver of innovation and national competitiveness. However, the middle-income giants, notably China and India, have had to run on both legs, and the resulting "massification," while providing a ladder of social mobility, has inevitably led to trade-offs between cost and quality, engendering fears that elite universities are simply reproducing existing social hierarchies, as demonstrated by Lan Xue, Zhen Yu, and Zhou Zhong in Chapter 27 on "Elite Universities in China."

The focus on higher education's instrumental role, in particular training skilled labor for a growing economy and promoting and advancing research and innovation, risks losing sight of the normative role of higher education, whether helping to foster better citizens or fairer and more resilient societies, as discerned by Arnoud De Meyer in Chapter 4 on "Productive Workers or Better Citizens?" Can Asia pursue these academic and economic goals without collateral damage to other valued goals of social equity and political stability?

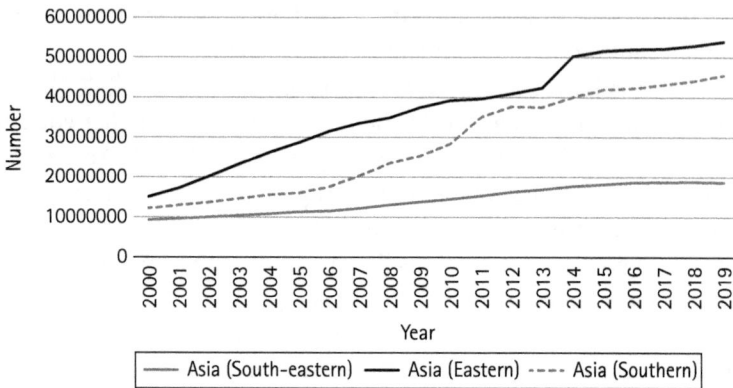

FIGURE 0.1 Growth in tertiary education in Asia, 2000–2019

Figure 0.1 shows that the huge growth of higher education in Asia reflects both shifts in underlying goals as well as changes in the economy and society. The number of students enrolled in higher education in Asia rose from 38 million in 2000 to 118 million in 2019 (with another couple of million in Australia and New Zealand). These changes were largely driven by massive increases in East Asia (led by China) and South Asia (led by India), although even the numbers in South-East Asia doubled.

In the early post-war years higher education was seen as integral to nation-building. Low income levels meant that government funding was key and with low levels of literacy and secondary schooling, the demand for tertiary education was limited. In recent decades, rising incomes, a demographic bulge in secondary education, and a growing services sector have driven large increases in the demand for higher education. The resulting shift from elite to mass higher education has led to "massification," a trajectory clearly illustrated in the case of South Korea in Chapter 32, "Higher Education in the Republic of Korea," by Jang Wan Ko.

The different meanings and implications attached to elite, mass, and universal higher education are examined by Malcolm Tight in Chapter 2, "From Elite Higher Education to Massification: The Asia-Pacific Experience." However, there appear to be three features of massification of higher education in Asia that are distinctive from the Western experience. First, the expansion of higher education in Asia has come at much lower levels of income compared to most Western countries and Japan (Figure 0.2). If we examine the per capita income (PCI) of the United States when its gross enrollment ratio (GER) was the same as China's and India's, it was three times that of China when its GER was 51 percent (China's GER in 2019) and seven times more than India's when its GER was 26 percent. Similarly, China's PCI when it achieved India's current GER (in 2012) was $6,316—three times India's.

A second implication that follows is that because the expansion of higher education has come at lower income levels, these countries have less public finance capacity to fund it—and hence there is a greater reliance on the private sector to finance it. This is attested in many of the country chapters, particularly in the case of Thailand

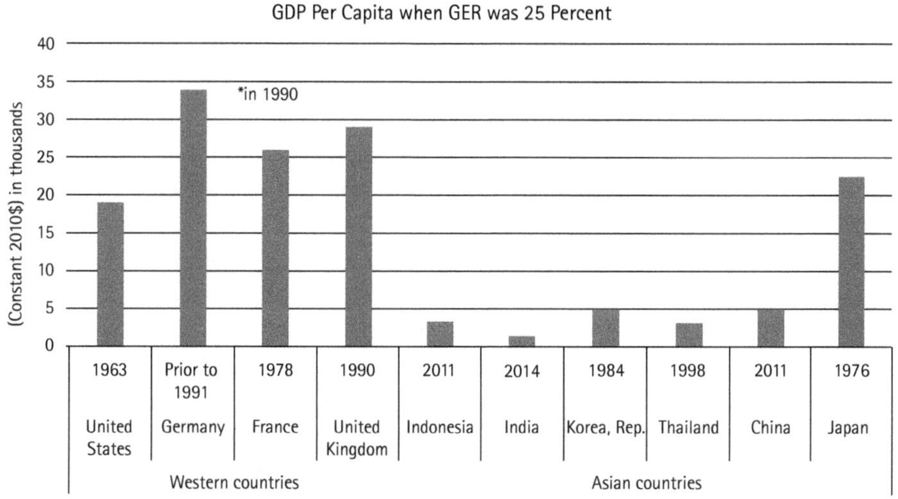

GDP Per Capita when GER was 25 Percent

FIGURE 0.2 Massification in Asia has come at much lower levels of income

(Chapter 39), as illustrated by Prachayani Praphamontripong Kanwar and Florence Lo on "Privatized Higher Education in Thailand: In Pursuit of Legitimacy and Profitability." Third, the much faster *rate* of expansion—in contrast to a much longer period in the West—inevitably has implications for quality and equity, as demonstrated by Chiara Logli and Hermin Indah Wahyuni in "Indonesia: The Politics of Equity and Quality in Higher Education" (Chapter 37).

But why has higher education grown much more rapidly in Asia than in the West when they were at similar levels of income? Partly this is due to different economic structures and hence demand in labor markets, which is discussed in Chapter 3 by Roslyn Cameron and John Burgess on "Employment and Labor Markets." For most people, higher education is the pathway to better jobs. In the early 1980s, a Chinese university official proclaimed to students who had been lined up, "University is a single-plank bridge [that] separates those who will always wear cotton plimsolls and those who study hard and then one day may get to wear leather shoes."[5] This meritocratic mentality still rings true for many Asian families who are willing to invest in the education of their children as a pathway out of poverty.

The supply structures of higher education evolve in response to changing employment prospects and the evolution of labor markets. This in turn is a function of the race between education and technology which goes back to Jan Tinbergen (1974), who posited that technological change is continually raising skill requirements while education's job is to supply those rising skill levels. A knowledge-based society requires ever more levels of skill, be it critical thinking, problem-solving, or creativity. In

[5] James Kynge, "Chaos vs control: China's communists and a century of revolution," *Financial Times*, June 26, 2021.

conditions of rapid technological change, technology "gets ahead" of education, the skill premium will tend to rise, and those with greater education will see relatively greater gains in income and widening income inequality (Goldin and Katz, 2010; Autor et al., 2020). New programs are introduced to respond, from professional degrees (Sheng-Ju Chan and Hua-Chi Chou, Chapter 11 on "Professional Education: Models and Issues") to liberal arts (Mikiko Nishimura, Chapter 8 on "Liberal Arts and Sciences Education for the Twenty-First Century in Asia").

The goals of higher education have shifted as well. Higher education was initially seen as the training of elites but also as "a great equalizer of the conditions of men," as Horace Mann declared in 1848. But in today's world it is both a ladder of social mobility and also a sorting and screening mechanism that has emerged as the great divider, including, but not limited to, a divider among genders (Elizabeth M. King, Chapter 6 on "Gender in Higher Education in the Asia-Pacific Region: Vertical Progress, Horizontal Segregation, and a Leaky Pipeline").

How do different countries in the Asia-Pacific region view the wider societal function of higher education? In Chapter 4, Arnoud De Meyer discusses the motivations behind national interests in investing in higher education and whether there is a contradictory or complementary role in fostering productive workers versus better citizens. De Meyer examines this question in competing tensions and objectives, including nation-building, national identity, or lifelong learning, specifically in the context of Japan, China, Singapore, Thailand, and India. In his conclusion, he formulates four major policy tools to overcome potential trade-offs that could produce both productive works and better citizens.

However, the mechanisms that link "better citizens" and "nation-building" are somewhat unclear. Is higher education a mechanism of nation-building by influencing and molding the minds of young people or is it to use their skills for nation-building projects? Does nation-building here refer to state-building—staffing bureaucracies, building roads, strengthening military technologies—or does it refer to infusing a sense of nationalism or patriotism? Or is it to raise national competitiveness through its role in innovation? At the individual level as well, there are questions regarding what exactly higher education does. It raises human capital but is it knowledge, skills, habits, abilities, judgment, or creativity possessed by an individual? Or, is it mainly credentials? How is all this further complicated by global rankings, with their own criteria that shape how universities view or distort their missions? In various country chapters in this volume, and in a dedicated chapter by William Yat Wai Lo and Ryan M. Allen (Chapter 10 on "The Rankings Game"), the universities' response to global rankings is further elaborated upon.

5. WHO LEARNS?

Increasing access is one of the critical challenges facing higher education. In Chapter 5 on "Access," Prompilai Buasuwan and Arisara Leksansern discuss the sensitive issue of access. How have higher education systems in Asia tried to promote access whether from lower-income groups, marginalized social groups, or less represented regions, especially rural populations? What is the role of affirmative action and how have these policies differed? In Asian multi-ethnic countries such as Malaysia and Indonesia, in particular, equitable access to higher education has vast socio-political and socio-economic ramifications.

Chang Da Wan describes in Chapter 38 on "Higher Education in Malaysia" an effective, but controversial, government policy between 1971 to 2002 imposing an ethnic quota of 55:45 Bumiputera (Malays and indigenous people) to non-Bumiputera student enrollment at public universities to address significant underrepresentation of Bumiputera students. While the quota seemingly solved one aspect of the accessibility issue, it became increasingly entrenched, leading many minority-group students to seek higher education overseas at much higher costs to their families and promoting a brain drain with many students choosing not to return. It also led to the growth of private higher education institutions in Malaysia and a stark divergence in academic pathways among students, with public universities predominantly Bumiputera and private universities largely non-Bumiputera (Lee, 2017). While access has increased and conflict diffused, its implications for national integration are more questionable.

However, most of what we know about access is from gross enrollment data. While certainly a starting point, it is not unlikely that widening access may simply be channeled to lower-quality institutions. Access could vary enormously across different groups between elite universities and the median university or between professional degree programs versus humanities. Furthermore, enrollment data may hide very different rates of graduation, reliable figures on which rarely exist.

Buasuwan and Leksansern also point to an often ignored, but crucial factor shaping access. Enrollment and then completion in secondary education is a *sine qua non* for access to higher education. If rural students pass secondary school exams at lower rates than their urban counterparts, their access will be automatically lower. While in principle national university entrance exams (such as China's *gaokao*, South Korea's *suneung*, or India's entrance tests to its professional programs) were meant to create a level playing field, the fierce competition has created a vast coaching industry whose costs are onerous for lower-income students and their ability to compete, thereby proscribing access.

One of the biggest divides in access in Asia (and worldwide) has been around gender. This gap has been narrowing but not in all countries or in all fields. With the deck still stacked against women in labor markets, how has gender equality in higher education evolved? In Chapter 6, Elizabeth M. King describes the trends and patterns of gender-disaggregated tertiary education indicators and labor force and occupational data in the Asia-Pacific, focusing on the determinants of tertiary education enrollment and choice of program. King presents findings that corroborate the overall picture of unprecedented vertical educational progress but also evidence about gender inequality mediated by income, ethnicity, place of residence, and social norms. Furthermore, horizontal segregation reveals systematic differences in the fields of study pursued by female and male students and creates a broader issue of what King describes as a "leaky pipeline"—a serious loss of talent in the labor markets of the region because female graduates, especially in the STEM fields, are not able to find jobs that are commensurate to their academic expertise and performance and to their career aspirations.

An important mechanism of increasing access to higher education is Open University (OU) systems, which is examined by Melinda dela Peña Bandalaria and Alexandra Ivanovic in Chapter 16, "Open University Systems." OUs provide non-traditional tertiary systems of learning, skills programs, and non-degree forms of learning. They complement traditional universities, and have been important in broadening access to millions of underserved populations in the Asia-Pacific region. As access becomes a less pressing challenge in the region, and with increasing life expectancy and rapid skill obsolescence, OUs offer the possibility of better providing "lifelong learning" than traditional universities.

Access is usually seen as a one-shot event—a person either gets into college or does not. However, a different lens on access is offered over the life cycle. In Chapter 25 on "Lifelong Learning as a Globally Diffused Policy Discourse in Asia," Hongxia Shan and Zheng Ren provide an overview of the development of lifelong learning in Asia, and how it differs from the dominant lifelong learning discourse in the West. Specifically, they focus on major problems that lifelong learning is intended to address, the kind of society that is imagined through the adoption of lifelong learning, the patterns of movement in lifelong learning, and the international actors driving the move towards lifelong learning in Asia. The chapter raises important questions around issues of power, control, and capacity of participation in the diffusion of lifelong learning as a global policy discourse.

6. What: Content and Learning in Higher Education

If the evidence of higher levels of enrollment and greater access in higher education in Asia is unequivocal, whether this tells us more about credentialing or learning is less so. The trade-off between credentials and learning is addressed by Johanna Waters in Chapter 7 on "The Relationship Between Credentials and Learning: A Focus on International Educational Value and Distinction." Are they substitutes or complements? Do employers treat credentials as a form of educational signaling of an individual's intrinsic abilities (cognitive, perseverance) to get into a selective college and navigate through the college maze (grades)? But what credentials matter? Is it the reputation of the educational institution or the content of the education?

Waters argues that overseas credentials confer internationally valuable cultural capital, which matters more than learning per se. While this might be so, the reality is that the vast majority of students in higher education get educated domestically, i.e., domestic credentialing is far more important for the vast majority of students. And given the reputation of flagship institutions of many Asian countries such as the University of Tokyo in Japan, Seoul National University in South Korea, the National University of Singapore, Tsinghua University and Peking University in China, or the Indian Institutes of Technology in India, credentials from these institutions carry strong signals for employers both within the country but increasingly outside as well.

Indeed, empirical analyses of Chinese students studying overseas find that while returnee postgraduates get salary premiums (relative to domestic postgraduates), this is largely due to the superior skills gained from overseas education rather than from any "signaling" effect (Du et al., 2021). But these gains vanish for those who obtain bachelor's degrees overseas relative to local bachelor's degree recipients. Du et al. (2021) suggest that Chinese students and their families are best served when the students obtain a local undergraduate degree and then go overseas for graduate training.

Skill obsolescence and newer forms of higher education delivery are also resulting in changes in types of certification, such as "certificates" or "micro-credentials." It is also likely that the importance of credentials varies across occupations. For professions, such as medicine and law, one cannot practice the profession without the credential. But becoming an entrepreneur does not require formal credentialing.

In Chapter 8, Mikiko Nishimura examines another aspect of credentialing in her analysis of how the liberal arts and sciences have fared in higher education across the Asia-Pacific. Her chapter raises difficult questions about the state of the liberal arts (broadly defined) in Asia. Is it that society (and parents) see the liberal arts as a poor cousin of STEM? Or is the social and political environment in Asia simply less conducive considering that a liberal mode of learning which respects diversity and pluralism requires an attitude that questions the status quo and existing power structure? Given the hyper-knowledge economy and the high-speed, cross-border mobility of ideas and services in our globalized world, Nishimura argues for the importance of higher education institutes in embracing the liberal educational imperatives of critical thinking, creativity, and civic engagement which have become part of the practical needs of the labor market in Asia and beyond.

More than half a century ago, an internal report of the University of Chicago laid out its vision of a liberal arts university: "A university faithful to its mission will provide enduring challenges to social values, policies, practices, and institutions. By design and by effect, it is the institution which creates discontent with the existing social arrangements and proposes new ones. In brief, a good university will be unsettling."[6] But can this vision be realized in the absence of a broadly liberal polity, one where social hierarchies and political power can be critically challenged?

In Chapter 9 on "STEM Field Demand and Educational Reform in Asia-Pacific Countries," Aki Yamada examines Asia's compulsive preoccupation with STEM

---

[6] The Kalven Committee Report to the University of Chicago faculty in 1967.

and its drivers, the training of STEM personnel, and knowledge creation in STEM, i.e., which fields in STEM get more emphasis. The chapter raises several questions. First, what does STEM include—and exclude—and with what consequences? For instance, the social sciences are generally not included within the STEM umbrella in Asia, while in the West they generally are. Indeed, in the United States across all S&E highest degrees, social sciences is the most common degree followed by engineering (NSF, 2022), perhaps one reason why Asia lags in this field of knowledge. What are the consequences of a possible overemphasis on STEM and the relative neglect of other fields of knowledge?

A second issue relates to the role of STEM higher education in workforce development. The reality is that the vast majority of STEM students do not go into research; indeed, after some years the majority do not even work in STEM occupations. So why is there so such emphasis on STEM in Asia? Do the degrees signal general cognitive skills (such as problem-solving) or specific capabilities (such as proficiency with specialized software)? Or, is it just that non-STEM education is perceived as the default option for those who could not make the STEM cut, and hence the fact that students selecting into STEM is a positive in and of itself?

Third, Chapter 9 makes a strong case for the strengths of STEM in Asia, especially for workforce development. However, it raises a larger puzzle: why is it that in the twenty-first century when STEM has mushroomed in Asia, Asian universities have produced so few winners of top prizes in the sciences, whether the Nobel, Abel, Turing, Marconi, or Kavli Prizes? What does this very modest record tell us about creativity in STEM fields in Asia?

Another feature of Asian higher education that has evolved since the start of the twenty-first century has been the rise in the profile and rankings of a number of leading Asian universities (National University of Singapore; University of Hong Kong; University of Beijing; Tsinghua University, and Fudan University of Shanghai are some examples). These are increasingly challenging, and even overtaking, the leading Japanese universities, which have traditionally dominated the global and regional rankings of Asian tertiary institutions. The growing obsession with university rankings in Asia, as elsewhere, while a useful spur to competition, in fact conceals as much as it reveals—rankings tell us nothing about the vast majority of higher education institutions in Asia and within individual countries.

One consequence of the "rankings game," the subject of Lo and Allen's Chapter 10, is that it has further amplified the STEM thrust in Asia. The authors argue that as late development and developmental states, Asian countries regard internationalization of higher education as a way to enhance national competitiveness and catch up and compete with the advanced Western nations. Governments in the Asia-Pacific region have sharply increased funding into their elite universities, expressly with the aim of achieving boasting rights on international league tables.

The aspirational aim of building "world-class universities," together with the reality that others are doing the same, has very likely spurred stronger efforts. International rankings have also pushed regulators to develop domestic rankings. But all of this does raise the question of whether the criteria for these rankings are necessarily appropriate for individual countries.

First, drawing from Goodhart's Law (formulated in the context of inflation targeting), which states that when a measure becomes a target it ceases to be an appropriate measure, the focus on rankings is less about improving the average quality of higher education per se, and more about what it takes to improve the select few in the list. While the top few are showered with resources, the vast majority must struggle, making higher education systems more unequal. Equity has been further undermined because the major global university ranking systems—Academic Ranking of World Universities (ARWU) (produced by the Shanghai Ranking Consultancy), Times Higher Education, and Quacquarelli Symonds—give measures of internationalization significant weight, while access (for instance to students from poor families or to a country's socially marginalized groups) is quite simply absent.

Additionally, playing the rankings game may be constricting scholarly diversity given that the data for the measurement in ranking systems draws heavily from English-language sources. This homogenizing effect perversely reinforces Western benchmarks even as Asian countries seek to build their own distinctive systems. Knowledge production that emphasizes local relevance gets short shrift, since such research output is much more difficult to place in leading international journals, the very ones that matter most for rankings. Whether the region's universities can muster the self-confidence to shift their focus from imitating the West to charting their own course and thus nudge changes in the ranking systems themselves remains an open question. But wider tensions in contemporary international relations may convince some to try.

Another important aspect related to the content of higher education—professional education—is examined by Chan and Chou in Chapter 11. From accounting to architecture, from business schools to public policy schools, and from law, engineering, and medicine to nursing, professional education is also the most lucrative niche in higher education and has become a big business. The chapter examines different "models" of professional education in the region, driven by the contending forces of state authority, professional bodies, and market-oriented pressures. In the face of increasing internationalization and transnational mobility of professionals, the authors raise a number of issues that may need to be addressed in the development of professional education in the region, including a common measure for quality education through a standardized qualification framework and mutual recognition for domestic accreditation and licensing.

But a larger structural challenge looms for professional education. As increasingly capable technologies—from telepresence to artificial intelligence—proliferate, the "practical expertise" of professionals (accountants, architects, doctors, lawyers, teachers) is likely to be available much more widely and at much lower costs (Susskind and Susskind, 2017). If, as a result, returns to professional education fall, the high costs of professional education will face increasing pressure as well.

7. How and Who?

The massification of higher education in the Asia-Pacific region has required an enormous supply response, with growing diversity of institutions, sources of funding, and students. Although the absolute amounts of public funding and public institutions have grown, its share has declined.

Since the early 2000s, private higher education has been the fastest-growing sector of higher education. Government promotion of private providers in higher education and the growth of private higher education are much more significant in Asia than in other regions of the world. Across Asia, nearly 40 percent of higher education students are enrolled in private institutions; about four-fifths of the students in the Republic of Korea and Japan, nearly three-fifths in Cambodia, Indonesia, and the Philippines, two-thirds in India, and two-fifths in Bangladesh are enrolled in private institutions. This has led to rising student debt, with serious implications relative to the types of jobs available and the creation of a political economy of young and anxious debtors pressuring universities to help them secure decent jobs after graduation. While governments in many countries have for years pressured universities to aspire to social and economic relevance, this largely produced a focus on applied research and expanding access. But rising costs of private and even sometimes public education have made employability worthy of higher education credentials an increasingly important, and, in several Asian countries, elusive goal.

Not surprisingly, this shift towards private institutions and household funding to finance higher education has increased demand for accountability in the sector, and in turn for more (and better) regulation, the subject of Chapter 12 on "Quality Regulation in Higher Education in Asia-Pacific: Roles of Quality Assurance and National Qualification Frameworks" by Angela Yung Chi Hou, I-Jung Grace Lu, Karen Hui Jung Chen, and Chao Yu Guo.

The issue of regulation in higher education needs to be understood within the larger context of a shift in the state's role from production to regulation, with less emphasis on direct control to a steering and balancing role, in most Asian countries. But the issue of "quality regulation" raises multiple questions. What exactly is quality relative to higher education? Is it about student academic achievement, research output, labor market outcomes—or all of them? Who are the regulators in higher education and who do they regulate? Is there a super-regulator for all types of higher education or are there different regulators for the different professions, distance education, etc.? What are their responsibilities? How much political and managerial autonomy do regulators enjoy and what is the administrative separation between agencies and existing ministerial structures? And what are the instruments available to them to force actions by the regulated entities? Indeed, the best predictor of quality of a higher education institution is selectivity with regard to student intake. The regulatory apparatus that shapes national college entrance exams implicitly exercises considerable regulatory power by shaping one of the most crucial factors that affect quality: selection. A related question applies to legislative bodies when they turn their attention to higher education. When is legislation lacking, and when is it too abundant and issued too frequently, as in some South-East Asian countries?

In Chapter 12, Hou et al. focus on qualification frameworks (QFs) as a mechanism of regulation. Currently, more than a third of countries in the region lack a national qualification framework. While all ASEAN countries have them, advanced countries in East Asia, including China, Japan, Taiwan, and South Korea, do not. Despite this, as Maria Cynthia Rose Bautista, Vicente Paqueo, and Aniceto Orbeta Jr. observe in Chapter 41 on "Philippine Higher Education: A Case for Public–Private Complementarity in the Next Normal," highly uneven quality persists among Philippine higher education institutions as a result of liberal government policies that promote the establishment of higher education institutes to attain massification—without the necessary levers to close poorly performing institutions. Only 29 percent of higher education institutions in the Philippines have undergone voluntary accreditation and the stark contrast between the very low average passing rates of graduates (36–40 percent) and the 90–100 percent passing rates of graduates at the few elite higher education institutions merely reflect the wide disparity in their quality. This raises questions about how crucial QFs are for quality regulation. Furthermore, there is little evidence that QFs mattered in the development of higher education in the twentieth century in much of the West, and within its great universities in particular. It seems more likely, that QFs and quality assurance agencies (QAAs) matter much more in raising quality in countries with weak oversight administrations and self-regulatory capacity.

International student mobility has grown significantly over the past two decades. The number of foreign students in tertiary education programs worldwide rose from 2 million in 1998 to 5.3 million in 2017. Although international students account for only 4 percent of total enrollment in bachelor's programs, they represent 22 percent of enrollment in doctoral programs. Students from Asia form the largest group of international students enrolled in tertiary education programs, representing 56 percent of all mobile students across the OECD in 2017. More than 60 percent converge on four countries: the United States, the United Kingdom, Canada, and Australia.

Increasingly, however, student mobility has been shifting from a largely unidirectional South–North to a multi-directional dynamic, encompassing new sending and hosting countries. For example, the rise of Singapore as an educational hub has been vertiginous and the rise in foreign student numbers in Australia may have been too large and occurred too fast to provide adequate quality assurance.

Furthermore, an emerging trend in international student mobility is to study abroad but close to home. The expansion of higher education systems in Asian countries, and their aspiration to become educational hubs, has resulted in a marked increase in the number of international students in Asia. In 2011, about half a million international students were pursuing a higher education degree in the region, double the number in 2005, and since then the number has again doubled. With more Asian colleges offering internationally recognized degree programs in English at more affordable cost than institutions in many Western countries, and political apprehensions, students are moving to new higher education hubs in Asia. The richer countries in the region—Japan, South Korea, Hong Kong, and Singapore—have better institutions but their declining fertility rate is both reducing the supply of outgoing international students while increasing the demand for students from abroad. The growing intra-Asia mobility of students led, in 2018, to the establishment of the Asia-Pacific Regional Convention on the Recognition of Qualifications in Higher Education, better known as the Tokyo Convention, along the lines of the Lisbon Convention in Europe. And a new aspirant to this pattern may be Malaysia, where quasi-privatization of the formerly state-financed (and often high-quality) universities suggests a need to attract many more high fee-paying foreign students, on top of those already attending branches of UK and Australian universities established in Malaysia.

Until recently, Japan had been the major host country in the region attempting to leverage its excess university capacity, generated by excessive expansion and a stagnant and more recently, declining, demography to attract international students. As detailed by Miki Sugimura and Shinobu Yume Yamaguchi in chapter 31 on "Japan: Challenges in Internationalization of its Higher Education Sector," the country has implemented a series of internationalization policies since the 1980s to promote the flow of students and researchers by developing innovative international programs such as joint or double degrees both internally and with other countries and promoting collaboration with international higher education institutions. While the Japanese government successfully attained its national goal to increase the number of inbound international students to 300,000 by 2020 a year early, 27 percent of such students actually attend Japanese language schools instead of higher education institutions. Japanese higher education programs continue to lack the global competitiveness to attract much of the top talent due to pervasive language barriers, lack of integration support, and limited employment opportunities for foreign students. This inward orientation of the Japanese higher education sector is evident in the growing reluctance of Japanese students to study abroad fueled by a lack of incentive or reward relative to employability in Japan and a general sense of comfort (rather, in many cases, than stimulation) in Japanese student life.

Africa has been a particular focus for Chinese universities with the government funding tens of thousands of scholarships for students from Africa, reflecting a big push for China to develop closer economic and political links with the continent. Just as the United States used scholarships such as the Fulbright Fellowship as an instrument of "soft power," countries in the region, especially Japan and China, are attempting to do the same, although the real cost levels of doing so are higher for Japan and Korea per foreign student than for still middle-income China.

Meanwhile, at globally competitive levels, the long-established primacy of Japan (and to a lesser extent, Australia) has been successfully challenged by both Singapore and Hong Kong, while leading Chinese institutions are rising fast on the strength of very sizable government investment in them. However, political upheaval in Hong Kong and the severe disruptions caused by COVID-19, require considerable caution on what lies ahead. The falling rankings of universities in Japan arise from a complex mix of circumstances: declining demographics; a cash-strapped national government juggling many spending priorities; an imperative to contain the ballooning national debt; and constant trimming of government financial allocations to universities—other than those splashily announced for highly targeted purposes, generally supporting the natural sciences—while blocking tuition rises (which would be politically unpopular).[7]

As noted above, international education has become a highly profitable market for institutional aspirants with the right strategies. These actors can be regionally focused (as several Australian universities are in Asia and the Middle East) or fully global with the rise of the "multiversity" (e.g., NYU and its twelve campuses on multiple continents, including a degree-granting one in Shanghai—with some students traveling among these different campuses). As reported by Anthony Welch in Chapter 35 on "Australia: History versus Geography in an Evolving National System," Australia, since the mid-1990s, has capitalized on higher education provision to private international students as a marketable industry, which has provoked serious criticism over perceptions of dilution in academic quality and overreliance on international student fees to sustain operations and research. The vulnerability in the business model of Australian higher education has been underscored dramatically in recent years with the COVID-19 pandemic preventing international students arriving onshore. The direct impact of the higher education industry on the Australian economy has been further undermined by political tensions with China, the largest contributor of international students to Australia, comprising 40 percent of all onshore international students.

The notion of a range of "business models" underpinning higher education institutions, while always a reality, would have been considered a vulgar prism through which to examine universities some decades ago. More recently, however, attracting international students and researchers has emerged as an important component of higher education business models. In countries dominated by state systems and relatively few or no private universities, the issue of business models would not have arisen. But today, particularly in light of growing competition for the best students and faculty, it is important to highlight variations in national models and how individuals choose among them.

The internationalization of higher education and much-enhanced student mobility has intensified and benefited from globalization, but this high-end phenomenon conceals a great deal of higher education that is not globalized, as evident in the data in Table 0.1. In almost all major Asian countries, students going abroad to study represent barely 1–2 percent of those studying within the domestic education system. Nonetheless, the numbers are still substantial enough that any serious interruption of that flow, as could be the case with China, would seriously impact the bottom lines of

---

[7] Japan's contemporary younger generation is less interested in (or cannot afford) higher education abroad to nearly the extent that its parents and sometimes grandparents did. It prefers the domestic "national", formerly "imperial", universities such as those of Tokyo, Kyoto, and Tohoku, while also favouring certain private ones such as Waseda and KEIO, both in Tokyo, the latter two rightly admired mostly for teaching quality.

Table 0.1 The domestic education system matters overwhelmingly for most students in Asia

Country	Students abroad	Outbound mobility ratio	Students hosted	Inbound mobility ratio
Australia	13,319	0.8	444,514	8.0
Bangladesh	50,004	1.6	–	–
China	993,367	2.2	201,177	0.4
India	375,055	1.1	47,424	0.1
Indonesia	49,900	0.6	7,677	0.1
Japan	31,903	0.8	182,748	4.7
Singapore	23,752	–	51,756	–
South Korea	101,774	1.8	84,749	2.8
Vietnam	108,527	1.9	7,250	0.4

Source: UNESCO.

many universities and faculties in receiving countries (one, and probably the principal, reason that former US President Donald Trump, wound up qualifying his initial ban on all foreign students early in the COVID-19 crisis as of March 2020).

However, student mobility is just one face of internationalization of higher education. A framework for understanding the different modalities of international higher education can be drawn from the four distinct modes for supplying cross-border services under the General Agreement on Trade in Services (GATS) of the World Trade Organization (WTO). Mode 1 entails cross-border delivery without physical movement (for instance through MOOCs—Massive Open Online Courses). Mode 2, "Consumption Abroad," involves the movement of students from one country to another to obtain education services. Mode 3, "Commercial Presence," occurs when an institution based in one country establishes an overseas branch to deliver higher education in another. And Mode 4 occurs through the "Presence of Natural Persons," via the temporary movement of education service providers such as faculty and other education personnel from one country to another.

The most familiar is Mode 2—students going abroad for education. In Chapter 13, "Internationalization and Education-Related Mobility in Asia-Pacific Universities," K. C. Ho, Ravinder Sidhu, and Brenda S. A. Yeoh shed light on the diverse trends in student mobility in the Asia-Pacific region. While Australia is the preferred destination in the Asia-Pacific region, China has edged beyond Japan as the second most preferred destination. But as a percentage of higher education students in the country, New Zealand, Singapore, and Taiwan are the leaders.[8] The steep decline in fertility in East Asia (China,

---

[8] For a country that is otherwise so well organized, official data on Singapore's higher education system, such as GER, or outward and inward mobility ratios, is surprisingly hard to find.

Hong Kong, Japan, South Korea, and Taiwan) as well as several countries in South-East Asia (Singapore and Thailand), together with already high GERs and low immigration rates, means that for these countries, their higher education systems will shrink unless they can attract foreign students. But many of these will be from lower-income countries in the region, who can only afford to come if the costs are low or subsidized.

A complementary look at internationalization and mobility in the region is offered by Christopher S. Collins and Alexander H. Jones in Chapter 14 on "Internationalization and Mobility: Providers, Academic Collaborators, and Recognition of Qualifications." They argue that student mobility has been bolstered by regional agreements on cross-border education and recognition of qualifications, in particular the Asia-Pacific Regional Convention on the Recognition of Qualifications in Higher Education. China's University Alliance of the Silk Road (UASR), established in 2015 and believed to involve 150 universities across 38 countries, possibly offers a distinctive "internationalization with Chinese characteristics" pathway (Peters, 2020).

Institutional mobility is apparent in the growth of international branch campuses, though these are fraught with challenges of differences in institutional and political cultures, as well as the sheer financial undertaking that they require. The examples of Yale-NUS College, Duke Kunshan University, and New York University Abu Dhabi are instructive. Consequently, more common than overseas physical campuses, commercial presence (Mode 3) is expanding through greater dual (or joint) degrees, twinning, franchised and validated programs, and distance/open-learning programs. However, institutional and student mobility have been much easier to measure than their effects.

Technology has enabled the rapid rise of Mode 1—cross-border delivery of higher education services without physical movement. Governments and educators are seeking to leverage new technologies to rein in rising costs. For many in the region, this currently means online or distance learning. Asia has more than seventy open universities, while in China one in ten degree-level students are taking part in online learning. Students of Indira Gandhi National Open University alone account for 20 percent of all tertiary learners in India. Governments are funding professors at their elite flagship institutions to develop online teaching materials to benefit students in lower-ranked institutions. With smartphone and 4G systems increasingly ubiquitous (and 5G systems rolling out rapidly), distance education has become a means to expand access while controlling spiraling costs in higher education. But how do its graduates fare?

In Chapter 17 on "MOOCs in Asia: Promise Unfulfilled or Promise Realized?," Helen Farley sheds light on the rise of MOOCs. While distance learning had a long history in Asia (see Chapter 16 on "Open University Systems"), the providers were mainly internal. MOOCs are a specific form of distance learning that provide web-based and online learning and are poised to reshape the landscape of higher education, especially in lower- and middle-income countries in Asia. Already by 2013, one in five enrollments from the major providers of MOOCs courses (Coursera, edX, and Udacity) were from Asia and by 2016, enrollments from India lagged only behind those from the United States and Brazil.

Farley points to two factors that distinguish MOOCs in Asia. First, the region's population embraces emerging technologies very willingly. Second, unlike MOOCs in the West, governments of many Asian countries have been proactive in supporting MOOC initiatives to increase access to higher education and improve the quality of instruction. They have made concerted efforts to develop MOOCs within the country and make them integral to the formal education systems.

Yet there remain numerous hurdles. A robust ICT infrastructure needs to be in place, which is not the case for many of the region's lower-income countries and populations. Even when this exists, political compulsions have led several countries (China notably, but also Myanmar and Vietnam) to build firewalls that limit access to overseas MOOCs. Language is another barrier, especially to access overseas MOOCs. However, the COVID-19 pandemic has accelerated trends in virtual learning and is likely to give a further fillip to MOOCs in the region. And MOOCs work primarily for those who can shut themselves off in a room conducive to study, a luxury, indeed an impossibility, for so many in poorer developing countries.

Another feature of the internationalization of higher education is the emergence and growth of international research networks. However, although there was a more than eightfold increase in the percentage of international collaborative papers (from 3 to 24.7 percent) in the past forty years, the opposite was true for most Asian countries. The region's scientific powerhouses (in terms of publications)—China, India, South Korea, and Japan—are all ranked at the bottom (Hu et al., 2020).

The massive expansion in higher education raises the question of the spatial sites of learning. Do students go to where higher education institutions exist or are educational institutions going to where students are? Are particular cities in the region becoming higher education magnets? Kris Olds examines these questions in Chapter 15 on "Education Hubs in the Asia-Pacific" through the lens of four key "Ps"—patterns, processes, politics, and policies. His chapter raises the question of whether higher education generates agglomeration economies and if so, what are its implications for inequality?

Complementing this chapter is S. Gopinathan and Michael H. Lee's chapter on "Singapore: The Making of Higher Education in an Asian Education Hub" (Chapter 33), which examines Singapore's higher education policies to invest in the development of "world-class" institutions and position itself as a regional education hub supporting, attracting, and retaining local and foreign talent. The resulting success cannot be viewed in isolation but in parallel with the broader government strategy of utilizing universities to serve as vital agents for enabling post-industrial economic growth by nurturing R&D capabilities and upgrading the workforce so as to make Singapore a vibrant, knowledge-intensive, innovative, and entrepreneurial economy.

But such a strategy is not without political risk. Any system of finite capacity that takes in more foreign students will crowd out at least some domestic students, leading to resentment. Such tensions become particularly pronounced in times of economic stress and downturns, as resentments turn to ire directed at foreigners.

The chapters on internationalization are hopeful about the normative possibilities of internationalization, believing that these mobilities could well "open up new possibilities for establishing regional sociabilities and solidarities" and that concurrently, the institutional citizenship of universities could shift from national to global.

The optimistic view of internalization is facing some reality checks as the convulsive effects of COVID-19 and the rise of nationalism are harbingers of a bumpy road ahead. At one level, the links between higher education and soft power seem self-evident. Five hundred and seventy current or former heads of foreign governments have studied in America on US government-supported programs like Fulbright. Yet there is also the reality that despite the dominance of China and the United States in higher education-related international mobility—China as the biggest source of international students and the United States as the biggest destination—there can be little doubt that the soft power is morphing into hard power. "America First" and the "Chinese Dream" are in direct competition as both countries have become much more nationalist. These issues are discussed in Chapter 23 on "Asian Higher Education as Soft Power?" by Jack T. Lee and in Chapter 24 on "Higher Education and Nationalism in the Asia-Pacific" by Christopher D. Hammond.

Worldwide higher education has expanded massively in recent decades and paradoxically or, perhaps because, nationalism has also been on the rise. While higher education was always seen as part of a country's soft power, it is also emerging as battleground of hard power. How has this played out in Asia?

In 2018, China shut down 234, or one-fifth, of its international university partnerships. With top universities in China rewriting charters that emphasize "the comprehensive leadership of the Communist Party" as part of the party leadership's bid to strengthen ideological control, Sino-foreign joint venture universities and other collaborations with Western universities especially come under pressure. Conversely, the United States, for example, has tightened rules for Chinese visa holders in some STEM fields. Reports in Australia and Britain, both major recipients of Chinese students, have warned of inappropriate research collaboration with China. Do these signal a new wariness of internationalization in higher education? Or will Asia be different?

Christopher D. Hammond, in Chapter 24, posits six ways in which nationalism and higher education can intersect. The first four intersections—nation-building, national "brand" promotion and soft power, nationalism and internationalization, and global rankings and status competition—represent "top-down" policies and practices of the state in its attempt to shape and constrain the activities of universities. This segues to the fifth intersection on constraints on academic freedom which explores the "bottom-up" influence of student-led activism and the utilization of university campuses as physical spaces for mobilizing social change, activities which are frequently tied up either in support of or opposition to various nationalist causes. The final intersection looks to cyberspace, and the issues surrounding the rise of misinformation and targeted nationalist extremism that has implications for university educators and policymakers.

8. COSTS: WHO PAYS?

The capacity to establish high-quality universities or upgrade existing ones requires considerable resources relative to the overall state allocations for education, which can be startlingly low in Asia, as is the case, somewhat surprisingly, in Indonesia and in India. In parliaments, and until recently, in international development circles, the highest priority was placed on primary schooling and then secondary teaching institutions. Funding for tertiary education was rarely prioritized, and then typically in favor of the STEM fields. This is still the case, but a more sophisticated understanding of tertiary education has gradually developed, alongside some appreciation of disciplinary diversity. Further, while the Millennium Development Goals simply called for universal access to primary education, the Sustainable Development Goals, by contrast, advance a number of nuances, including the notion of "high-quality" education at all levels.

The expanding scale and scope as well as shifting priorities of higher education are inevitably reflected in the sources of funds as well as the allocation of resources across academic disciplines (among professional education, basic sciences, or liberal arts). In the higher education field, international organizations (IOs) tend to study the distinction between "public" (or "state") universities and "private" ones closely. This distinction, arising out of a prescriptive instinct within IOs, often reveals a policy preference for private expansion of the field. But this can be misleading. In Asia, as elsewhere, taxpayers pick up the bill for many of the government tax-breaks and other incentives offered (whether openly or not) to "private" institutions (owned or run, in some instances, by relatives or close friends of those in government), implicit or explicit guarantees on education loans, and indeed, directly or indirectly subsidizing foreign education institutions on their soil. Private money also flows into public institutions in some countries.

When higher education was the purview of elites, expenditures—both public and private—were relatively modest. As it moved to massification, overall expenditures grew. And with the rise of the research university, the shift from teaching to knowledge production further increased the financial requirements of higher education. As Akira Arimoto, a former Japanese university president asserts, public funding and investment are often key requirements and predictors for the development of successful research universities. Thus, large economies with higher per capita incomes are closely correlated with high research productivity.[9]

In Chapter 18 on "Public Financing," Xi Wang and W. James Jacob examine national and subnational policies on public higher education funding in the region. Several different data lenses exist to understand levels and trends in public financing of higher education: for example, public expenditure on education as a percentage of

---

[9] In dialogue with two of this volume's editors in July 2021. Japan's research funding, more than in several other industrialized countries, often springs from the private sector and takes place within private sector teams and in their labs.

GDP and as percentage of total government spending; the share of tertiary education in public expenditures on education and the distribution between levels of education; and expenditures per student. Then there are issues relating to the distribution of these expenditures between elite/flagship universities and the object of expenditures, from student scholarships to research to salary support to capital expenditures. Is public expenditure on higher education aimed at funding providers or financing students? An examination of what policies exist in providing financial assistance and ensuring access to some of the most disadvantaged groups (e.g., indigenous communities, ethnic minorities, refugees, and low socio-economic status populations) is also highlighted in select country cases, including Chapter 36 by Kathryn A. Sutherland and Stephen J. Marshall on "Education for All? Higher Education at a Crossroads in Aotearoa New Zealand."

Given the pressures on government budgets, several innovations in public financing have emerged, beyond direct budgetary support. Grants of land have served as endowments. While Cambridge and Oxford in the United Kingdom have a combined land portfolio of 126,000 acres, the United States pioneered land grant universities in 1862, when each state received 30,000 acres of federal land (itself largely grabbed from Native Americans) for each member of the Senate and House of Representatives it had in Congress at the time.[10]

More recently, governments have also deployed financial engineering. Given historically low interest rates, higher education institutions are seeking recourse to bond markets, often with implicit government guarantees. Specialized credit institutions have been set up to leverage funds from the market for capital projects in tertiary education which are serviced through internal accruals. And in some cases, they have resorted to tax code provisions to incentivize private philanthropy.

As wealth increases in the region, a growing trend in private philanthropy in the higher education sector has developed across middle- and high-income countries, an issue examined by Swee-Sum Lam in Chapter 19, "Private Philanthropy in Higher Education in Asia." In principle, the growing trend of philanthropy in higher education creates the potential for Asia-Pacific universities to systematically deepen their financial sustainability. However, developing large endowments is a long-term process. Of the 110 universities in the world with endowments exceeding 1 billion dollars, the United States has 100 and the rest of the world combined has just 10. Of these, three are in Europe (two in England and one in France), one is in Saudi Arabia, while the Asia-Pacific region has five (NUS and NTU in Singapore; Kyoto and Osaka universities in Japan; and University of Melbourne in Australia).

While private philanthropy certainly holds out much potential, it is still a long way from complementing government funding and student fees to sustain and grow core programs in higher education. Just four universities in Asia—which together account

[10] In cases where insufficient public land was available, states received land scrip, or certificates of entitlement to such public lands. Money from the sale of this land or land scrip was to be used to support endowments.

for about 0.2 percent of students in higher education in the region—have investment incomes (on endowments) exceeding 5 percent of annual expenditure. Moreover, the concentration of private philanthropy in elite universities risks further amplifying the gap between the privileged "world-class" and the median university (Callahan, 2017; Giridharadas, 2018).

Increasingly, a large part of higher education is self-financed (by students and their families), a subject examined by Adrian Ziderman in Chapter 20, "Student Loans in Practice: Benefits and Pitfalls of Loans Schemes in Asia." The increasing financial burden has led governments to create loans schemes that help students pay for the costs of education and then repay with the higher incomes resulting from their enhanced skills and human capital. These loans schemes vary considerably in their objectives, design, practice, and outcome from Australia's pioneering contingent income loans (replicated to some degree in Japan, New Zealand, and South Korea) to India's public student loans guarantee programs.

While there is little doubt that these schemes have facilitated large increases in enrollments (especially in private higher education institutions), overall loans recovery is below (and in many cases well below) long-term financial viability. A more troubling inadvertent outcome may be that it has incentivized the entry of relatively high-cost, poor-quality private higher education institutions that leave students with large debt obligations and repayment hardship resulting from sub-standard qualifications with poor labor market prospects.[11]

9. CONSEQUENCES AND CHALLENGES

With more students studying internationally, another facet of internationalization is explored in Rennie J. Moon's discussion of "Returning Talent" in Chapter 21. A key factor animating discussions on returning talent is concern about the "brain drain"—the seeming loss of a country's best and brightest (Kapur and McHale, 2005). While there is recognition that the "stay" and "return" binaries have been, at least partly, replaced by "brain circulation," the effects depend on the magnitudes and selectivity of returnees on different parameters (e.g., gender or research productivity or political attitudes). How do return rates vary by country of education, field of study, and level of study? In general, return rates of doctoral students and researchers tend to be lower than those of undergraduate students. They are also affected by economic and political conditions in countries of origin and destination. Students from countries with weaker economic conditions tend to display higher stay rates in economically more developed countries than their peers from other economically developed countries.

[11] This is increasingly the case with graduate studies as well, even in elite universities. See Melissa Korn and Andrea Fuller, "'Financially hobbled for life': The elite master's degrees that don't pay off," *Wall Street Journal*, July 8, 2021.

Moon's chapter examines how governments in the region have been attempting to increase return rates with varying success. Growing geopolitical rivalries, visa policies, and lower outward mobility in the aftermath of the COVID-19 pandemic are all likely to impact returning talent. In the case of Hong Kong, will rising political tensions and the erosion of free speech and academic freedom intensify the "brain drain" phenomenon, or will it be able to retain its status as an international city with long-standing "world-class" universities to attract and retain talent? In Chapter 34 on "Higher Education in Hong Kong: Recent Developments and Challenges," Jin Jiang maintains an optimistic view that "brain drain" may nevertheless result in "brain circulation" or "brain bridging" as a result of transnational synergies and that Hong Kong has great potential to leverage its uniquely "privileged position" as a bridge connecting the international academic community to mainland China.

For Myanmar, however, "brain drain" is only an option for the rich and upper class who can afford to send their children abroad, mostly after the country opened up after 2012. As it continues to deal with over seventy years of political and civil unrest, Myanmar's higher education system has slowly decayed despite domestic attempts to re-form the higher education sector and the recent support of international aid and assist-ance. Amid the ongoing coup of February 2021, Marie Lall, Camille Kandiko Howson, and Aye Aye Tun, the authors of Chapter 40 on "Higher Education in Myanmar," de-scribe the continued challenges facing Myanmar and its recovery that will be key to the future aspirations of its higher education sector. But while the Myanmar country study rightly points to well-known deficits in its higher education provision, the unhappy political dynamics and economic conditions in the country dating back nearly to inde-pendence have been fairly unique within the Asia-Pacific region, particularly in terms of the long-lasting nature of the stresses and strains involved.

Myanmar, of course, is a sad outlier case in a region that is both hugely aspirational and has been overwhelmingly successful in acting and delivering on its aspirations. One need only think of Vietnam's success in overcoming the ravages of twenty-five years of devastating wars on its territory between roughly 1950 and 1975, or the so-called "basket-case" that Bangladesh was thought to be after its independence in 1971, on many indicators now outperforming others in its neighborhood.

In Chapter 22, Youngsuk Chi and John Van Orden examine "Asia as a Producer of Knowledge." What are the implications of increased growth in research and innovation in Asia for global knowledge? Data on scholarly publications—in terms of both the quantity and the impact of publications—shows a rapid increase, led by China, followed by India, Japan, and South Korea. This rapid growth has been driven both by much-expanded funding and strong incentives to publish. Gross expenditure on research and development (GERD)—which includes money allocated to funding academic research as well as by private businesses on R&D—varies from less than 0.5 percent of GDP to nearly 4.5 percent of GDP in different parts of Asia, the latter a truly impressive score.

Although Japan and South Korea rank among the top countries in Asia in terms of their GERD as a percentage of GDP, they conversely rank among the lowest in terms of publication output per $m GERD. This is because a much larger fraction of research expenditures in both countries are from the private sector, while research expenditures through higher education are among the lowest among industrialized countries. However, when it comes to quality of publications Hong Kong, Singapore, Australia, and New Zealand are in the top tier and also are the most efficient in terms of publications on a per researcher basis. The chapter raises the possibility that Asia's growth in publications and research resources could result in the region supplanting the United States and Europe as the global center of science and technology in future decades.

One issue that is common to places as distinct as Myanmar and Hong Kong, which occupy polar extremes in their quality of higher education, is a common worry and a common cause: academic freedom and its relationship with the governing political regime. Academic freedom has been declining sharply in Hong Kong, even well before China imposed the national security law there in 2020, bringing it close to China, which according to one study (Kinzelbach et al., 2021) has one of the lowest academic freedom rankings in Asia. If this trend continues, the more Hong Kong becomes integrated into China's polity, the less it will be an academic "bridge" to China.

This raises another set of questions about the nature of academic freedom itself. What does it entail and why does it matter? Studies of academic freedom (see for instance Kinzelbach et al., 2021) suggest that academic freedom in Asia is less than in Africa and Latin America, even though their universities are considerably weaker in a broader sense.[12] One obvious implication is that there is no axiomatic relationship between university rankings and academic freedom rankings (taking both sets of rankings at face value). Countries like Nepal and Indonesia rank higher in academic freedom than Singapore and China, but there is simply no question of how much academic heft the latter have compared to the former. Japan, Taiwan, and South Korea are outliers in Asia in that their higher education systems are ranked quite highly in academic freedom and host some well-regarded universities as well.

Does this imply that academic freedom, while a valued core concept underlying the very idea of the university, may not matter much for the sorts of factors that make for a "good" university, however "good" is defined, including as measured in university rankings? The answer is likely to depend on the meanings and measurements of academic freedom. Western concepts are rooted more in the classical liberal ideas of "negative freedoms," the freedom from coercion, whether from the state, religious groups. or other elites. But if academic freedom also includes positive freedoms—the ability to do something—which requires resources and capabilities, then the answer might be quite different, whether across countries, institutions, or disciplines.

This issue is likely to become more salient as geostrategic tensions among the three principal military powers of our time, China, the Russian Federation and the United

[12] As with university rankings, there are now rankings of academic freedom across countries. One such index—the Academic Freedom Index (AFi)—includes the freedom to research and teach; freedom of academic exchange and dissemination; institutional autonomy; campus integrity; and freedom of academic and cultural expression. Since it is an expert coded index (and hence subjective) with plausible but arbitrary weights, its findings are suggestive at best.

States, each of them active players on Asia's strategic map, increase. Adding to these geostrategic strains, this volume was developed during an unprecedented global crisis stemming from the COVID-19 pandemic, which has amplified the uncertainties facing higher education's future in Asia-Pacific.

While university strategists might prefer to ignore these worrying trends, they would be wise not to. In all likelihood, universities will be greatly affected by them. Higher education is uniquely positioned to build international bridges to a shared humanity. But politics—domestic and international—has its own logic. If so, international student mobility and cross-border research collaborations are likely to suffer, at least relative to the rosy projections of even a few years ago. On the other hand, these crises have accelerated the diffusion of new educational technologies as well as improved programming options. As a result, virtual learning is emerging as a viable supplement, a definite "second best" to many of the students compelled to adopt it, but a major improvement for many others.

Understanding these complex realities is part of the promise of higher education. Whether higher education lives up to its promise may not determine, but will surely shape the future of the Asia-Pacific region.

References

Asian Development Bank (2018). *Key Indicators for Asia and the Pacific 2018*, 49th Edition. http://dx.doi.org/10.22617/FLS189512-3

Autor, D., Goldin, C., and Katz, L. F. (2020). "Extending the race between education and technology." *AEA Papers and Proceedings*, 110, 347–351.

Callahan, D. (2017). *The Givers: Wealth, Power, and Philanthropy in a New Gilded Age.* New York: Knopf.

Du, Z., Sun, Y., Zhao, G., and Zweig, D. (2021). "Do overseas returnees excel in the Chinese labour market?" *The China Quarterly*, 247, 875–897.

Giridharadas, A. (2018). *Winners Take All: The Elite Charade of Changing the World.* New York: Knopf.

Goldin, C. and Katz, L. F. (2010). *The Race between Education and Technology.* Cambridge, MA: Belknap Press.

Hu, Z., Tian, W., Guo, J., and Wang, X. (2020). "Mapping research collaborations in different countries and regions: 1980–2019." *Scientometrics*, 124, 729–745.

Kapur, D. and McHale, J. (2005). *Give Us Your Best and Brightest: The Global Hunt for Talent and Its Impact on the Developing World.* Washington, DC: Center for Global Development and Brookings Institution.

Kinzelbach, K., Saliba, I., Spannagel, J., and Quinn, R. (2021). *Free Universities: Putting the Academic Freedom Index into Action.* Berlin: Global Public Policy Institute.

Lee, H.-A. (2017). *Majority Affirmative Action in Malaysia: Imperatives, Compromises and Challenges.* Ottawa: Global Center for Pluralism.

National Science Board, National Science Foundation. 2022. Higher Education in Science and Engineering. Science and Engineering Indicators 2022. NSB-2022-3. Alexandria, VA. https://ncses.nsf.gov/pubs/nsb20223/

Peters, M. A. (2020). "China's Belt and Road Initiative: Reshaping global higher education." *Educational Philosophy and Theory*, 52, 586–592.

Susskind, R. and Susskind, D. (2017). *The Future of the Professions: How Technology Will Transform the Work of Human Experts*. New York: Oxford University Press.

Tinbergen, J. (1974). "Substitution of graduate by other labour." *Kyklos*, 27/2, 217–226.

PART I

HISTORY

CHAPTER 1

HISTORY OF HIGHER EDUCATION IN ASIA-PACIFIC

DEANE NEUBAUER

1. HISTORICAL PRECEDENTS FOR HIGHER EDUCATION IN ASIA

THE history of higher education in Asian societies as an organized social activity extends back literally for thousands of years, in one form or another. Buddhist and Confucian learning traditions served to educate ruling elites and the sophisticated bureaucracies that served them. Situated initially within India and China these knowledge traditions diffused, and transformed, and reformed many times over within the context of the societies in which they were located. Overall, this phenomenon can be viewed as a "precursor" to Western influences, creating a "knowledge framework" which persists to this day in complex residual practices and beliefs.

Buddhism flourished in India from its initial emergence in present-day Nepal until the collapse of the Pala dynasty in the twelfth century. Earlier expansions extended its presence across much of Asia, coming to have an enduring presence in such distant locales as China, Korea, Japan, and South-East Asia. Within India and South-East Asia, Buddhist ashrams became centers of learning and sources for both the creation and extension of knowledge. (Asia Sentinel, 2011). From the establishment of the school in Pushpagiri in the third century CE, to that of Nalanda in the fifth century and subsequently Vikramashila in the ninth, these entities operated as the earliest known universities. Vikramashila, as one of the largest Buddhist universities had over 1,000 students and 100 teachers (Scharfe, 2002a, 2002b).

The extension of Buddhism across such a wide expanse of cultures, territories, and peoples led, not surprisingly, to an equally wide diversity of centers for the instruction and inculcation of knowledge, most of which would not be recognized by later notions of a university. Perhaps the most enduring of these has been the tradition that reached a high and stable point in Japan from its introduction in 552 CE, where monasteries came to develop as significant teaching institutions that persisted over centuries.

Organized education in China, much scholarship suggests, may be the oldest in the world with scholars tending to date it from the establishment by Confucius of a private academy in the fourth century BCE, while other elements can be traced back as far as the Spring and Autumn Periods (770 BCE to 403 BCE) of the Eastern Zhou dynasty (1046 BCE to 256 BCE) (Wu and Zha, 2018). The linkage during the Han dynasty (206 BCE to 220 CE) of Confucian education with the civil service examination system provided higher education in China with a highly developed structure and the means of perpetuation, unique in the world for many centuries. As Hayhoe points out, outgrowths of the Song dynasty academies of classical learning which had emerged to codify and perpetuate the basic learning traditions, "grew up from [private] libraries and Buddhist monasteries" which allowed scholarship to be pursued outside the constraints of the imperial bureaucracy and its dominant examination system (Hayhoe, 2001, p. 327, cited in Wu and Zha, 2018). This was mainly because the higher education system in effect at the point of the Opium War in 1840 served to usher in an entire subsequent era of higher education development in China.

2. COLONIALIZATION AND THE EXTENSION OF EUROPEAN INFLUENCE

Throughout Asia the process of Western exploration and subsequent colonialization insinuated an essentially European style of education throughout the region with results that would persist through the decades and centuries as these areas progressed through diverse colonial structures and histories, culminating in various ways with a fundamental redefinition of national power and identities at the conclusion of World War II. Within this broad time frame, extending essentially from the sixteenth through the middle of the twentieth centuries, England, Portugal, and Spain vied with each other, along with France in Indo-China and the Dutch in Indonesia, for regional power and dominance, to be joined by the United States in the latter half of the nineteenth century. This politics and economics of discovery and exploitation also served as the vehicle for extending the varied dimensions of the Industrial Revolution to the region, as well as Western educational notions (centered on literacy and numeracy).

Perhaps most famously, the British experience in the overall colonialization of the Indian subcontinent best illustrates how European notions of education in general and higher education in particular were an integral component of the imperializing experience. The domination of the East India Company from its inception as the ruler of the country from 1601 created a governing context in which efforts to establish all of education were essentially opposed until 1793 when two clauses were added to the company's charter document that permitted the sending out of schoolmasters to the country.

Higher education as an official governmental policy was not permitted until 1835 on the recommendation of Lord William Bentinck, the governor general, whose framing of the policy would dominate Indian education for the subsequent century, leading to the transfer in 1858 of higher education policy from the East India Company to the British Crown. In their earliest manifestations Indian universities engaged in almost no teaching or research, their primary role being that of serving as examination bodies for skills gained at lower levels of education.

The "opening" of Asian higher education to the West occurred variously and differentially with renewed emphasis from the major political and social revolutions of the eighteenth and nineteenth centuries, which accompanied the powerful but complex imperatives of the Industrial Revolution. Coupled with outgrowths of Western colonialization that took place in a variety of forms across Asia during the previous two centuries, these served to frame higher education as a "social good" with novel utilitarian values. This was perhaps nowhere more emphatically the case than within the Meiji Restoration in Japan as of 1868, following the country's forced opening to US trade interests. Viewed in this context, higher education as a social practice continued as an essential vehicle for developing a "national" educated bureaucratic class dedicated to the creation and maintenance of state power within a legitimated hierarchical social and economic structure. These functions of higher education had been introduced through other parts of Asia, especially in China and South-East Asia, as essential components of the extended development of colonialism with its associated need to develop a hybridized bureaucratic and commercial class equipped to handle the economic, social, and political demands of colonialism—especially, again, with the highly intrusive advent of industrialized production and consumption from the mid-nineteenth century onward.

While Japan was not colonialized, its basic social structure was significantly impacted by multiple Western contacts initiated by the visitation of United States Admiral Perry to Edo in 1853. As singly important as this event was, for over a century and a half preceding that event, Japan had been significantly influenced by Jesuit missionaries who had been introduced to the country along with Portuguese traders and who established various religious schools. During the Edo period and especially that of the Tokugawa regime (1600–1867), Japan became unified as a national political entity and within the attendant influence of Confucianism developed a training program for bureaucrats serving the Shogunate. These elements set the stage, as it were, for the even greater transformative events of the Meiji period and its introduction of Western modalities, including that for its basic education system, and a national university structure significantly influenced by the logic and modalities of the German university—a system that would largely remain in place until superseded by the "Americanization" of its higher education system following World War II.

Other elements of Asian higher education either proceeded along the differentiated paths of colonialism as it progressively developed over an extended period from the advent of the seventeenth century through World War II, or as in the definitive case of Thailand, which was able to escape colonialization, through a context defined by its own national development. The first instance is perhaps best illustrated by the case of the Philippines in which religious orders, both Augustinians and Franciscans, established its first schools and universities in the sixteenth century, an activity that was supported by a "feeder" system of schools distributed throughout the islands, and included the creation of the oldest university in the Philippines and indeed the whole of Asia, the University of Santo Thomas, established by the Dominican order in 1621 (Chuong, 2018). The creation of a free basic educational system by the central government in 1863 set the stage for the expansion of higher education into a system following the defeat of the Spanish colonial regime and the establishment of the First Republic of the Philippines in 1898 (Estioko, 1994). In the subsequent period, leading up to World War II, the overall effort within the Philippines focused on the establishment of an educational system at pre-university levels, embedded into which were the goals of creating a national language, achieving adult literacy, and promoting vocational education. The expansion of higher education as a unique factor in national development would not fully take place until the post-World War II period (Teaching and Education, 2020).

Throughout the "rest" of Asia and especially South and South-East Asia, higher education—with the singular exception of Thailand—was also a consequence of extensions of colonial power, especially within French Indo-China, India, British Burma, Malaya, and Singapore. The National University of Singapore, which would grow into a public research university of world-class standing in the post-World War II period, was established in 1905 as the Straits Settlements and Federated Malay States Government Medical School, and as such may be viewed as an exemplar of the colonial higher education model. Higher education in Malaysia would not be established until the creation of the University of Malaya in 1959 (Arokiasamy, 2011), while that in Myanmar, then Burma, dates back to the creation of Yangon College in 1884, affiliated with Calcutta University of India. In Indonesia, the Dutch colonial administration created a medical and law school in Jakarta in the late nineteenth century along with an engineering institute in Bandung and an agricultural center in Bogor, but the development of what would emerge as the quality centers of Indonesian higher education, including Gadjah Mada University in Yogyakarta, would not be developed until the post-war period (Nizam, 2006).

Education traditions in India date prior to the Christian era with the emergence of Indian religions, mathematics, and logic within both early Hindu and Buddhist centers of learning. During the Middle Ages, Islamic education also came to be distributed throughout the Indian subcontinent (Blackwell, 2004). The Jesuits introduced Western higher education to India with the founding of St Paul's College in Goa in 1542, an institution that was to become famous for its extensive library. In 1857 three Central universities were established at Calcutta, Bombay, and Madras with twenty-seven affiliated colleges. By 1947 there were nineteen universities in India, to be followed by a remarkable expansion of the overall higher education system post-independence, and based on ISCED enrollment data to become in contemporary times one of the largest higher education systems in the world (UGCNETPAPER1, 2020).

Pakistan followed quite a different course in developing its higher education system following its independence. Taking place within the post-war period, it was characterized by a few universities which proved of indifferent value. A crisis throughout the system led to an overall reorganization subsequent to 2001, leading to the establishment of a Higher Education Commission, with results that some scholars have characterized as "extraordinary," citing supporting data of large numbers of scholars participating in development programs, including extensive engagement of scholars in foreign PhD programs along with major upgrades for laboratories and ICT, rehabilitated facilities, expanded research support, and "one of the best digital libraries in the region" (Hayward, 2020, p. 45). This fundamentally remapped system has proved better able to provide effective undergraduate education, and research and training within its leading universities while supporting a college system that has expanded both participation and skills (Hayward, 2020). This relatively positive view is contested, however, by other sources such as the World Bank, which asserts that "The research environment in Pakistan is still very much dominated by inadequate and irrelevant research activities" (World Bank, 2019).[1]

Australia created universities in the nineteenth century: the University of Sydney (1850), the University of Melbourne (1853) and the University of Adelaide (1874). After the country was federated in 1901, the University of Queensland and the University of Western Australia were added, in 1909 and 1911 respectively. University participation remained low throughout the period leading up to World War II, with but six universities and two university colleges accounting for a combined enrollment of somewhat over 14,000, of which slightly in excess of 10,000 were degree students (Breen, 2002).

New Zealand embarked on its higher education experience with the establishment of the University of Otago in 1869 by the Otago Provincial Council, which was transitioned into the University of New Zealand in 1870 to reflect national rather than provincial interests. It was followed by Auckland University College in 1883 and Victoria University College in 1889. As such, these early universities were both small and tightly bound to Great Britain, to which, for example, examination papers were provided to be marked until the beginning of World War II. Overall, in both countries, higher education was relatively small in scope and significantly informed by its ties to Great Britain (Pollock, 2020).

3. POST-WORLD WAR II: A REGIONAL SYSTEM DEVELOPS

World War II, in almost all respects, served as a powerful vehicle of transition for both the concept and actuality of higher education. The post-war period ushered in (or

---

[1] This view is supported as well by Pervez Hoodbhoy (2009).

extended) the widespread phenomenon of decolonialization (in various forms across the multiple regions of Asia) providing a tension within most Asian societies between the need to develop some form of national education while at the same time generating both an institutional structure for presumptive quality higher education, and its progressive massification. This motive force, as it were, came to take place within multiple contexts of fundamental social, economic, and political reform and restructuring. One powerful example of this was Japan's creation of a "new" political-economic framework within the country from the mid-1950s onward as it restructured both its economy and society, much influenced by the occupation of US forces and the availability of capital, to become one of the primary transformative economic powers in the world. By 1970 it would rank as the second largest economy in the world, having created a model for economic development that would be widely pursued and emulated in Asia during subsequent decades (Zhu, 2007).

As the complex forces of decolonialization and revolution played out across Asia, the resulting social changes became powerful expectations that formerly "subject peoples" within these emergent post-war societies could claim and have access to higher education experiences as pathways to social acceptance and effective participation. Country after country was to undergo variously shaped, engineered, and articulated processes of social change. Both as a fundamental tool, and a critical element of social legitimation, gaining access to higher education was perceived as having a wide range of desirable instrumental outcomes, and as such, fueled in a variety of ways the emergence of higher education policy and subsequent developments across the region.

Specifically, in India, China, Korea, Indonesia, and Vietnam, national conflicts of differing forms, length, and intensity brought to power representatives of new social elements; one aspect of which was their history of having been in the main denied effective prior access to higher education. As new regimes took shape in the 1940s and 1950s, the extension of literacy, schooling, and higher education quickly followed apace, the latter tied directly and importantly to the linkages between schooling, higher education, and economic development. This period of approximately two and a half decades would come to be subsequently recognized as the "ramp up" to the progressive economic integration of the world, especially what would come to be viewed as the "Global North," within the complex constructs of neoliberalism and globalization (Barnet and Müller, 1974; Harvey, 1990; Steger, 2003; Gills and Thompson, 2006). As the Global North would in the subsequent three decades come to be viewed as the fundamental driver of global economic development, the Global South would stand, in contradistinction, as constituted by those areas striving to leave behind the complex legacies of colonialization and war.

Education, and specifically higher education, became a focused national policy throughout the region, viewed as an essential step in the creation and promotion of economic development and as a necessary step in the process of legitimating the emergence of new leadership groups within society. Within much of South-East Asia and East Asia (but not South Asia) a process developed that would be replicated and extended throughout the remainder of the century, consisting essentially of three stages.

In the first, promising individuals (who in the contemporary lexicon would come to be termed "talents") would be recruited, largely with national subsidies, to be "sent out" to the "developed" world for higher education training and (importantly) certification. Initially, a disproportionate fraction of this "outflow" would be to the United States, and later with the post-war recovery of Europe, to there as well, with the goal of generating a "new professoriate" that would help create and staff the aspiring and expanding Asian systems of higher education. In the second stage, and as an essential component within the separate processes of a movement toward massification, existing institutions of higher education would be staffed and built out even as the institutional structures of higher education were significantly expanded across populations and regions. In the third stage, as these systems of national higher education were developed, the dynamics of the second stage would begin to shift as the national supply of "trained academics" gained sufficient critical mass to sustain systematic expansion, which would then lead to a "mature" third stage in subsequent decades in which the purposive mobility of both students and faculty would become an essential part of the radically extended and developed higher education structures of countries throughout the region with such countries coming to function as designated "attractors" in their own right of those seeking higher education opportunities of high quality.

4. THE CONTEMPORARY PERIOD

The complex dynamics of a continually expanding system of higher education would lead in the latter three decades of the century and into the twenty-first century, with much differentiation across the individual countries constituting the region, in the clear direction of what Martin Trow would establish as the progression from elite to mass to universal access to higher education (Trow, 2006). Famously, Trow distinguished this progression as proceeding through three distinct phases—the elite stage in which a higher education system was both designed for and accommodated less than 15 percent of the "eligible cohort"; the massification stage representing the provision of higher education for 15–50 percent of such eligible populations; and a universal stage in which a society—moving in the direction of rapid social and technological change—would continually seek to make some form of higher education available to all. As essential elements of this process, Trow acknowledged the transformations in the role of traditional elite universities to significantly expand their functions especially in regard to the extent and quality of their research endeavors. However, even more important were the overall social impacts the transformation of traditional universities brought, including their expansion into higher education systems with a primary charge from national governments of facilitating continued economic development.

These underlying structures and motive purposes would play out differentially across the Asia-Pacific region, even as the national structures within which they were taking place followed differential processes of post-war reconstruction (e.g., Korea and

Vietnam), post-revolution institutionalization (e.g., China), post-colonial emergence (e.g., India, Pakistan, Sri Lanka, Malaysia), and varied pathways into the emergent structures of globalization (e.g., Japan, Singapore, Hong Kong, Australia, New Zealand). Whereas the varied dynamics of progressive globalization would dominate and continue to shape higher education throughout all of Asia in the decades following the 1970s, in the decade between 2010 and 2020 the continued progress toward a "mature globalization" was interrupted by various forms of a resurgent nationalism, such that by the middle of the decade academic conferences throughout the world had begun to emerge seeking to explore the phenomenon by detailing its dynamics and implications for global education.[2]

Over this extended period of five decades as national systems of higher education moved through the varied stages identified by Trow and the complex processes of differentiated national development in the context of continued global interdependence, three essential "elements" were established as extended properties of higher education systems throughout the region: issues of quality and the attendant movement toward both national and international accreditation, rankings, and the focused pursuit of international students. In all of higher education throughout the world, issues of creating and then maintaining quality at all levels of development is a central concern, rising to critical levels of concern when systems are rapidly expanded (for whatever reasons). In these decades as nations invested heavily in the creation of their own higher education systems, largely from the conviction that doing so was/is essential for economic development, issues of the quality being developed within such systems became critical (Neubauer and Gomes, 2017). Typically, following initial efforts to build out either historical flagship institutions and/or develop new, specialized institutions of science or technology, national systems were created in a context of aligning institutions through a combination of mission and specific considerations of the levels of quality they were meant to achieve and sustain. Nowhere was this more extended, ambitious, or engaged than in China in which after a massive expansion of higher education in the 1980s, the process had produced a proliferation of institutions of questionable quality across the country. Two policies, 985 and 211, were introduced in the 1990s to create linked systems of institutions framed within explicit sets of goals, at the center of which ample resources and missions were invested to produce results that could meet international standards of excellence. By the end of the twentieth century, policies with similar goals were employed in one fashion or another in India, the Philippines, Japan, South Korea, Malaysia, Hong Kong, Taiwan, Indonesia, Australia, and New Zealand

---

[2] Note in this regard the November 2017 "International Conference on Globalism vs Nationalism" co-presented by the World Academy of Art and Science, the European Academy of Sciences and Arts, The Global Roundtable, and the Montenegrin Academic of Sciences and Arts. Topics included mass immigration, free trade, global super-state, the belief that all races and cultures should blend into a mono-race and mono-culture, opposition to mass immigration, the notion of sovereign ethno-states for all people, etc.

leading to the creation of "tiered" systems in which institutions could be differentiated by their relative quality and the resources dedicated to produce it.

While such revolutionary national efforts were fashioned and executed within policy frameworks in which notions of quality, research, and contributions to national economic development were largely inseparable, the actual measurements and articulations of quality have been more problematic, wherein the specific quality assurance organizations of individual nations, having been largely modeled after those of Europe and the United States, emerged in practice with a lesser impact than initially intended. (See in this regard a review of higher education quality in China: Liu, 2018.) Overall, across the countries of the region we have witnessed some version of a "quest for quality" in which the greatest efforts and resources have been focused on a set of elite institutions which stand at the top of structures of greater massification in which central elements of quality tend invariably to decline with efforts to provide higher education opportunities to larger numbers of students.

As is well known and remarked, this dual tendency within the region for national higher education systems to take the form of hierarchical structures of quality has been reinforced and expanded by the global system of institutional ranking. Whereas such a system had existed within higher education circles for some time, largely focused on European and North American universities, its explosive expansion within an Asian context dates from the development of the ranking system devised by Shanghai Jiaotong University in 2003 which led to new and vastly extended uses within Asia by providing empirical measures (however biased in terms of the attributes they were intended to measure and the indicators employed to obtain ranking scores). In its necessarily reductionist modality, it has proved extraordinarily popular throughout the region, supplying as Marginson and Sawir would frame it in 2011, a highly desired (if radically simplified) "currency" for higher education institutions competing in what had become an increasingly intense global marketplace. Over the past two decades, the variety of uses for ranking systems has grown significantly and they now operate within various countries as integral components of national budgetary processes.

Creating and maintaining a significant number of cross-border students has come to be an explicit goal of many countries in the region. In several, the overall demographics of the country in which the university-age population is declining have confronted governments with the uncomfortable choice of either accepting that the overall per-student cost will continue to rise with declining enrollments, or taking significant steps to promote and sustain cross-border higher education flows. By the decade of 2010, the recruitment of international students, both from within the whole of the Asia-Pacific region and outside, had become an essential element within the political economy of many nations. Within Australia, national universities were given the mandate of raising something in the order of 20 percent of their budget through the recruitment of international students, at both graduate and undergraduate levels. By 2018 international students accounted for over half of all university enrollments, primarily drawn from China, India, and Nepal (van Onselen, 2019). In a slightly different case in point, China had developed the recruitment of foreign students, especially those from Africa, as an inseparable part of its One Belt One Road policy. In 2019, the Ministry of Education announced a total of 492,185 international students enrolled, the largest number of international students of any country in the world (China Education Center, 2019).

Viewed across the whole of the region, the mobility of international higher education represents the quest for different goals depending on the country involved. For some, for example, Australia and New Zealand, the dynamic is an explicit effort to monetize the relative quality of its higher education institutions.

5. THE FUTURE

As this volume is being developed, the world has been engulfed in the unprecedented and largely unexpected crisis of the COVID-19 pandemic, the extraordinary dimensions of which have confounded most of our predictions concerning the future of higher education in Asia fashioned over the preceding months. Even without this extraordinary event, the future of higher education in Asia and, indeed, throughout the world, was entering a period of extended uncertainty framed by three interrelated factors: global demography, the growth of artificial intelligence (AI) in the context of the emergent Fourth Industrial Revolution, and the complex uncertainties of global climate change. Each of these macro-factors will be touched on in the chapters that follow. Here, let me simply point to several dimensions of these structural change factors that will impinge on all of higher education.

Even before the onset of the global pandemic, the "nature" of Asian populations was being increasingly framed by a progressive aging of multiple populations and a resultant lowering of fertility rates, most particularly those of Singapore, South Korea, Japan, and China, but also to a lesser degree those of Thailand, Taiwan, and Hong Kong. Indeed, from a high in the early 1960s, birth rates globally have declined with only sub-Saharan Africa providing evidence of a rapidly growing younger population suitable for conventional movement into higher education over the coming two decades (World Bank, 2020). Throughout the rest of the world, the dynamics of movement into Trow's stage of massification have been and will continue to be impacted by relatively rapid aging and lowered fertility. Even as the phenomenon of a declining higher education-aged population fuels much of the regional efforts to generate national higher education enrollments through external recruitment (and the resources that were an essential part of that effort), aging as a structural factor is combining with the dynamics of the emergent Fourth Industrial Revolution and the pandemic to reframe this future.

Increasing numbers of scholarly volumes are seeking to outline the dynamics propelling the Fourth Industrial Revolution (4th AI) characterized by the extraordinary growth of AI and its impacts, current and future, on the purposes and nature of higher education. Foremost among these, it would appear, are predictions about the impacts that AI will have on current jobs and employment practices, assumptions about which fundamentally underlie the structural bases of most higher education current activities and planning throughout the region. While quite expectedly, estimates vary about the impacts of AI on contemporary societies and their current job structures (which in turn overwhelmingly frame most higher education strategic planning, including that of advanced technology-focused institutions), some well-regarded projections suggest that as many as 40 percent of current jobs could disappear over the next decade or so (Seldon, 2018; Susskind, 2020).[3] Irrespective of any other strategic imperatives that could/will face higher education over the coming decade(s), dealing with the range of challenges and dislocations presented by the Fourth Industrial Revolution will demand types of responses that are just beginning to be perceived within higher education institutions and related policy entities.

Both of these broad structural factors of progressive aging and the growth of AI were, of course, well underway prior to the onset of the pandemic, which as a "once in a century" event presents a wide array of unpredictable consequences. Here I wish only to emphasize that this will undoubtedly significantly affect the trajectories that higher education will take in the coming months and years and which have not been "foreseen" within a framework in which "the future" emerges in various anticipated ways from a careful consideration of the past. One is the confounding demographic impacts of the pandemic, given that it will likely spread differentially across the globe in various waves and presumably impact older generations more than younger ones—a contrary outcome of the current demographic structures of the region as indicated above involving progressively aging populations. Indeed, the International Monetary Fund has begun to publish projections both of the overall decline in global wealth from the pandemic but also future population declines over the coming three to five decades (IMF, 2020). The other is the cyclical nature of pandemics in which even with the creation of effective vaccines, one can expect widespread social disruptions including in travel (thereby radically affecting current notions of the international exchange of students and the role they play in higher education funding structures), and in the complex routines of social distancing. As witnessed in the early days of the pandemic, these were incompatible with in-place, face-to-face instruction across all levels of education with profound negative effects on higher education institutions at all levels of quality. As many had foreseen a future in which "virtual communication" would become an increasing part of conventional higher education engagement, what we have recently witnessed suggests that this "revolution" is already upon us and will continue to have unpredicted consequences.

Finally, the economic disruptions of the pandemic are unpredictable but in general can be expected to be significant, and potentially unprecedented. As such they will, in turn, significantly impact governmental revenues as well as private incomes. Within one frame of estimations in the United States, for example, informed largely by the enduring impacts on public higher education institutions of the financial crisis of 2008–2009, early predictions are that many higher education institutions, perhaps 20 percent, may indeed be forced to close (Capatides, 2020). A similar early analysis of

---

[3] See especially ch. 9 of Susskind (2020), entitled "Education and Its Limits."

higher education in the United Kingdom conducted by *London Economics* states baldly that: "Initial estimates of the economic impact of the pandemic are worse than *anything the UK has ever experienced*—and deteriorating steadily" (London Economics, 2020). Unpredictable as the range of possible outcomes is in this current context, one unescapable conclusion is that accepted financial structures and expectations that have been established as the basis for planning higher education endeavors across the region will be subject to urgent and significant revision based on how individual countries engage and survive the dislocating effects of the pandemic.

REFERENCES

Arokiasamy, A. R. A. (2011). "An analysis of globalization and higher education in Malaysia." *Australian Journal of Business and Management Research*, 1/9, 73–81.

Asia Sentinel (2011). "Diffusion of Hindu and Buddhist institutions and values to Southeast Asia and China." August 2. https://www.asiasentinel.com/p/diffusion-hindu-buddhist-insti tutions-values-southeast-asia-china, accessed March, 10, 2020.

Barnet, R. and Müller, H. (1974). *Global Reach: The Power of the Multinational Corporations.* New York: Simon & Schuster.

Blackwell, F. (2004). *India: A Global Studies Handbook*. Santa Barbara, CA: ABC-CLIO.

Breen, J. (2002). "Higher education in Australia: Structure, policy, debate." http://nihongo.mon ash.edu/aused/aused.html, accessed April 22, 2020.

Capatides, C. (2020). "Colleges across the U.S. brace for impacts as the coronavirus batters their already tenuous financial ground." https://www.cbsnews.com/news/us-colleges-coro navirus-impact-finances/, accessed April 30, 2020.

China Education Center (2019). "Education in China." https://www.chinaeducenter.com/en/ cedu.php, accessed April 30, 2020.

Chuong, D. Van (2018). "Education in Southeast Asia from the second half of the 19th century to the early 20th century." *US-China Educational Review B*, 8/4, 141–146.

Estioko, L. R. (1994). *History of Education: A Filipino Perspective*. Manila: LOGOS Publications.

Gills, B. and Thompson, W. R. (eds.) (2006). *Globalization and Global History.* New York: Routledge.

Harvey, David. (1990). *The Condition of Post Modernity: An Inquiry into the Origins of Cultural Change*. Oxford: Blackwell Publishers.

Hayhoe, R. (ed.) (1984). *Contemporary Chinese Education*. Armonk, NY: M. E. Sharpe.

Hayward, F. (2020). *Transforming Higher Education in Asia and Africa: Strategic Planning and Policy*. Albany, NY: SUNY Press.

Hoodbhoy, P. (2009). "Pakistan's higher education system: What went wrong and how to fix it." *The Pakistan Development Review*, 48/4 Pt. 2, 581–594.

International Monetary Fund (2020). *IMF Data Mapper.* https://www.imf.org/external/ datamapper/NGDP_RPCH@WEO/OEMDC/ADVEC/WEOWORLD, accessed April 27, 2020.

Liu, Z. M. (2018). Production and Education Integration: From "Integration" to "Integration". China Higher Education, No. 2, 24–25.

London Economics (2020). *Impact of the Covid-19 Pandemic on University Finances: Report for the University and College Union*. https://www.ucu.org.uk/media/10871/LE_report_on_

covid19_and_university_finances/pdf/LEreportoncovid19anduniversityfinances, accessed April 27, 2020.

Marginson, S. and Sawir, E. (2011). "Interrogating global flows in higher education." *Globalization, Societies and Education*, 3/3, 281–310.

Neubauer, D. E. and Gomes, C. (eds.) (2017). *Quality Assurance in Asia-Pacific Universities: Implementing Massification in Higher Education*. Cham: Palgrave Macmillan.

Nizam (2006). "Indonesia." In UNESCO (ed.), *Higher Education in South-East Asia*. Bangkok: UNESCO, 35–68.

Pollock, K. (2020). "Tertiary education: Universities before 1990." In *Te Ara: The Encyclopedia of New Zealand*. http://www.TeAra.govt.nz/en/tertiary-education/page-1, accessed April 22, 2020.

Scharfe, H. (2002a). "From monasteries to universities." In *Education in Ancient India*. Leiden: Brill, 131–165.

Scharfe, H. (2002b). "From temple schools to universities." In *Education in Ancient India*. Leiden: Brill, 166–193.

Seldon, A., with Oladimeji Abidoye (2018). *The Fourth Education Revolution: Will Artificial Intelligence Liberate or Infantilize Humanity*. Buckingham: University of Buckingham Press.

Steger, M. B. (2003). *Globalization: A Very Short Introduction*. Oxford: Oxford University Press.

Susskind, D. (2020). *A World Without Work*. New York: Henry Holt and Company.

Teaching and Education (2020). "A history of the system of education in the Philippines: Its implication for the present generation." https://www.teacherph.com/history-system-education-philippines/, accessed April 21, 2020.

Trow, M. (2006). "Reflections on the transition from elite to mass to universal access: Forms and phases of higher education in modern societies since WW II." In J. J. F. Forest and P. G. Altbach (eds.), *International Handbook of Higher Education, Part One: Global Themes and Global Challenges*. Dordrecht: Springer, 243–280.

UGCNETPAPER1 (2020). "Evolution of higher learning and research in post independence India." https://ugcnetpaper1.com/higher-education-regulatory-framework, accessed October 21, 2020.

Van Onselen, L. (2019). "Australian universities double down on international students." *Macrobusiness*, November 1. https://www.macrobusiness.com.au/2019/11/australian-universities-double-down-on-international-students/, accessed April 30, 2020.

World Academy of Art and Science (2017). "International Conference on Globalism vs Nationalism." http://www.worldacademy.org/conference-page/international-conference-globalism-vs-nationalism, accessed April 30, 2020.

World Bank (2019). *Higher Education Development in Pakistan*. Washington, DC: World Bank.

World Bank (2020). Birth rate data. https://data.worldbank.org/indicator/SP.DYN.CBRT.IN, accessed April 25, 2020.

Wu, H. and Zha, Q. (2018). "Chinese higher education, History of." In M. A. Peters (ed.), *Encyclopedia of Educational Philosophy and Theory*. Singapore: Springer Nature.

Zhu, Z. (2007). *Understanding East Asia's Economic Miracles*. Ann Arbor, MI: Association for Asian Studies.

PART II

GOALS, GROWTH, AND MASSIFICATION

FROM ELITE HIGHER EDUCATION TO MASSIFICATION

The Asia-Pacific Experience

MALCOLM TIGHT

1. INTRODUCTION

THIS chapter reviews the experience of the Asia-Pacific region in moving from elite to mass higher education participation and beyond. This experience is reviewed in the context of the broader global experience, where the North American higher education systems took the lead, followed somewhat later by many European systems. The Australian and New Zealand systems, included within the Asia-Pacific region, were also relatively early in making the transition to mass higher education, something which not all Asian systems have yet done.

The chapter starts by considering the meanings attached to elite, mass, and universal higher education, and their place in higher education research, practice, and policy. It then considers the historical development of higher education in the region, before examining the recent experience of massification—i.e., the transition to mass higher education—and how it has played out in particular systems. In conclusion, some reflections on likely future directions are offered.

In writing (and reading) this chapter, two main limitations must be acknowledged. First, the Asia-Pacific region is a huge and complex area, so a chapter-length discussion of the development of its higher education systems must necessarily be an overview. Second, this overview rests wholly on the English language literature; while this is a growing and substantial literature, it does bring in its own biases, most notably the idea that the English-speaking countries are global leaders in most significant developments, including, of course, the massification of higher education.

2. Elite, Mass, and Universal Higher Education

An American researcher, Trow (1970, 1973; see also Tight, 2019a), is widely credited for setting out the early thinking on mass higher education. Working in the United States, the first higher education system to allow and achieve mass participation, but with a keen comparative interest, particularly concerning the United Kingdom, he suggested the following definitions:

- "elite" higher education systems enrolled less than 15 percent of the age group;
- "mass" higher education systems enrolled between 15 percent and 50 percent of the age group;
- "universal" higher education systems enrolled over 50 percent of the age group.

While the break points may seem somewhat arbitrary, and others might prefer to use different labels, this typology has been widely accepted and applied.

Trow (1973, pp. 6–7) explained the distinction between elite, mass, and universal systems of higher education in the following fashion:

> the old institutions cannot expand indefinitely; they are limited by their traditions, organizations, functions, and finance. In European countries, it is likely that an increased enrollment in higher education beyond about 15 percent of the age grade requires not merely the further expansion of the elite university systems, but the rapid development of mass higher education through the growth of popular non-elite institutions. Mass higher education differs from elite higher education not just quantitatively but qualitatively … if the transition is made successfully the system is then able to develop institutions that can grow without being transformed until they reach about 50 percent of the age grade. Beyond that, and thus far only in the United States, large sections of the population are sending nearly all their sons and daughters to some kind of higher education, and the system must again create new forms of higher education as it begins to move rapidly toward universal access.

He recognized that, in a mass higher education system, the vast majority of students could not expect to attend Oxford, Harvard, or the equivalent, but would be accommodated by less well-funded and lower-status institutions, including, in the United States, community colleges, and, in the United Kingdom, further education colleges. In other words, while all students would be receiving an education at a higher level, they would be getting different sorts of higher education, or, in his own phrase, "some kind of higher education."

Returning to the theme twenty-six years later, Trow (1999) argued that, while his thesis had stood the test of time, the means by which it might be met were now more diverse, with the impact of information technology (through online learning) now very strong. Writing in the same year, Altbach noted that: "Mass higher education has become the international norm at the end of the 20th century" (1999, p. 107), with most developed and developing countries at least aspiring to engage the majority of their citizens in some form of higher education. Of course, Trow and Altbach were not the only researchers writing about mass higher education, with others, including McConnell (1973), Neave (1985), and Teichler (1998) also prominent.

With the passage of time, some of the terms used and the foci of interest have subtly changed; this is a common occurrence in any field. Thus, rather than talk simply about mass higher education, the rather ugly term "massification" has come into use to signify the process undergone to achieve mass higher education. And, instead of then anticipating a further expansion to universal higher education, the discussion has now turned to what happens "post-massification" or in "high participation systems" (Marginson, 2016a, 2016b). In this, of course, there is an implicit suggestion that mass and/or universal higher education may not necessarily be a total success.

We should, of course, be cautious about applying a model developed in a particular context—North America and other Western developed economies—globally. The social, cultural, and economic histories of the Asia-Pacific region are rather different, and most of the countries in this region are not in a position equivalent to that of the United States fifty or sixty years ago. In an increasingly globalized world, however, it may also be the case that the pressures to expand higher education are impacting earlier, more widely, and for different reasons.

3. PAST

Four key points will be emphasized about the early development of higher education in the Asia-Pacific region. First, it was early in a literal sense; though the development of the modern university is traced to medieval Europe (Ridder-Symoens, 1992), higher learning and its associated institutions were to be found before then in early Asian civilizations such as those of the Middle East, India, and China.

Second, while the Asia-Pacific region is vast, highly populated, and far from homogeneous, some commonalities may be noted. Most notably, in East Asia, there are several Confucian nations or areas—Japan, Korea, China, Hong Kong, Taiwan, Singapore, Vietnam—which share a heritage that stresses, among other matters, the importance of family and education, and respect for elders and teachers.

Third, as with the rest of the non-European world, the countries of the Asia-Pacific region have been subject to centuries of colonialism and neo-colonialism. The sources have been variously American, British, Chinese, Dutch, French, German, Japanese, Portuguese, Russian, and Spanish, and the impacts upon higher education provision and development have been significant.

Fourth, nowhere in the Asia-Pacific region made the transition to mass higher education as early as America; indeed, in most countries throughout the world this has only occurred during the last few decades.

In most Asia-Pacific countries, higher education—in its modern form—does not have a lengthy history. Thus, in Malaysia and Singapore, formerly British colonies, "The University of Malaya was established in 1949 in Singapore and in 1959 the university started an autonomous division in Kuala Lumpur which became a separate entity in 1962" (Lee, 2015, p. 107). Similarly, in Hong Kong, another British colony now returned to China: "Before the 1970s, higher education in Hong Kong was mainly provided by two local universities: The University of Hong Kong and The Chinese University of Hong Kong" (Wan, 2011, p. 115). These are fairly typical British colonial arrangements, with national universities being established in the run-up to independence (Ashby and Anderson, 1966).

In India, yet another former British colony, which used to incorporate what are now the separate states of Pakistan and Bangladesh, the pre-independence higher education system was strongly influenced by the University of London, an "examining" university which operated internationally as well as nationally (Bell and Tight, 1993). As Datta (2017, p. 147) argues: "The dominant characteristic of the Indian university system is its orientation towards examination at the expense of teaching and research," which he links to its continuing quality issues.

In other countries, the colonial/neo-colonial heritage is more complex; Taiwan, for example, betrays Japanese, Chinese, and American traces:

> Higher education provision in Taiwan does not have a long history. During the period of the Japanese occupation, from 1894 to 1945, there was only one university (Taipei Imperial University), and a few special schools. After the Nationalist Government withdrew from Mainland China to Taiwan, the number of institutions increased to one university and three colleges. However, higher education did not expand significantly until the 1960s. (Wang, 2003, p. 261)

China itself, having endured lengthy periods of interference by several foreign powers in the nineteenth and twentieth centuries, and massive turbulence as it re-established its independence, is an even more complex case:

> In 1922 it adopted the American model, and this dominated the Chinese higher education system until 1949. By then China had 205 higher education institutions ... with a total enrolment of 117,000 students. In 1952 all the higher education institutions, including the 60 private ones, were brought under the jurisdiction of the communist government, and the Soviet model was adopted ... From 1958 to 1960 the number of universities and colleges, as well as student enrolments, increased drastically. More than 100 new higher education institutions were established, and total enrolments increased to 961,623 in 1960 from 441,181 in 1957. Yet this attempt to expand higher education failed ... and the number of higher education institutions was reduced to 407 in 1963 from 1,289. (Bai, 2006, pp. 129–130)

Despite its very different pattern of governance, the post-war experience of the Japanese higher education system, and indeed some of the nomenclature adopted, has striking similarities with that of China:

> The dramatic expansion of Japanese higher education was initiated in the late 1950s when Japan started its New Long-Term Economy Plan with the purpose of doubling its citizens' income. By 1963, Japan's enrollment had reached 15% of the age-cohort, indicating that its higher education had entered into the phase of mass higher education … the gross enrollment in higher education … increased from 15.5% in 1963 to 51.6% of the age-cohort in 1985. (Huang, 2015, p. 30)

Japan was, therefore, in the lead in East Asia in the move from elite to mass higher education:

> The mass higher education threshold … had been reached by the late 1960s in Japan, the early 1970s in Taiwan, and the early 1980s in South Korea. These growth patterns generally reflect economic growth patterns in the three societies, with Japan in the lead, followed by Taiwan, then South Korea. (Hayhoe, 1995, p. 300)

Australia, another former British colony, transitioned relatively early to mass higher education. Its higher education system was also relatively old, having been initiated at the same time as the English system was expanding away from the Oxford/Cambridge duopoly:

> The Australian higher education system originated in the latter half of the nineteenth century. In 1913, the total number of students across six universities amounted to 4,172, compared to an estimated national population in 1913 of around 4.8 million people. By 1976, a further 12 universities had been created and approximately 290,000 domestic students were enrolled. In 1996, this figure had more than doubled to 580,906 … seeing a further increase to 733,352 in 2006, with total enrolments (boosted by a large increase in overseas students) rising to 984,146 in that year. (Pitman et al., 2015, p. 610)

In the post-colonial and post-World War II period, the role of higher education in the Asia-Pacific region has largely been to contribute to nation-building, and also to regional parity within nations, through economic and social development. As is evident, a range of higher education models have been adopted, including, but not limited to, American, British, French, and Soviet.

The most significant difference between countries, however, has been in terms of the role of the private sector in higher education, which has been substantial in countries like Japan and Korea, but minimal in others like Australia and China. This has been linked, of course, to the role of central government in overseeing higher education policy and to concerns with the quality of provision.

4. PRESENT

The experience of massification of higher education in the Asia-Pacific countries has, unsurprisingly, been closely related to their relative development and wealth:

> In this region, the upper income countries such as Japan, South Korea and Australia have achieved universal higher education with gross enrolment ratios over 50% while the middle income countries such as Malaysia, Thailand, Philippines … have achieved mass higher education with gross enrolment ratios ranging from 20 to 50%. As for the low income countries such as Indonesia, Vietnam and Cambodia, the tertiary gross enrolment ratios are below 20% with education remaining at the elite stage. (Lee, 2015, p. 105; see also Organisation for Economic Co-operation and Development, 2019; UNESCO Institute for Statistics, 2014)

Comparative analyses of the recent development of higher education systems in the Asia-Pacific region have emphasized both differences and commonalities in national experiences. Taking the former first, in a relatively early comparative analysis, Hayhoe (1995, pp. 300–301) drew attention to "four broad parameters":

> First, the degree to which female students are able to achieve equal participation is perhaps the most fundamental issue in terms of social equity. Second, the degree of emphasis on the basic and applied sciences … indicates the extent to which modern-ization is seen as a technocratic process or as one of broader social and cultural trans-formation. Third, the success with which 4-year academic programs are balanced by an appropriate emphasis on short-cycle programs … may well reflect the character of links between higher education and the economic and employment systems. Finally, the level of private higher education reflects familial support as well as governmental policy.

Other parameters might, of course, be added to these four, including: the role of part-time and online provision alongside full-time provision; the role of foreign institutions in providing higher education, both within and beyond the Asia-Pacific region; the sig-nificance of postgraduate and research education; and (somewhat fleshing out Hayhoe's fourth parameter) the issue of who bears the costs for higher education participation.

Turning to the commonalities in experience, Marginson (2011, p. 587) emphasizes the influence of the Confucian heritage, which infuses thinking in nations throughout a major part of East Asia:

> The Confucian Model rests on four interdependent elements: (1) strong nation-state shaping of structures, funding and priorities; (2) a tendency to universal tertiary participation, partly financed by growing levels of household funding of tu-ition … (3) "one chance" national examinations that mediate social competition and university hierarchy and focus family commitments to education; (4) accelerated

public investment in research and "world-class" universities. The Model has downsides for social equity in participation, and in the potential for state interference in executive autonomy and academic creativity.

The Confucian model is a significant development from the Confucian heritage, which long predates massification and had little if any role in bringing it about. This model offers a powerful structure for higher education expansion, combining the benefits (and disbenefits) of state authoritarianism with family duty. It contrasts with what we might call the liberal (or perhaps now the neoliberal) model found in Western Europe and North America, where state oversight and funding combine with institutional autonomy, academic freedom, and individualization, with the last of these more emphasized as the responsibility for funding is increasingly transferred to the student (Tight, 2019b).

The massification of higher education in the Asia-Pacific region has not, of course, been achieved unproblematically; such a large-scale change inevitably raises issues wherever it is attempted. Mok and his co-authors have been particularly critical in this respect:

> the massification of higher education has not necessarily led to more occupational opportunities for youth or opportunities for upward social movement, particularly since the significant changes in the global labour market after the 2008 global financial crisis. On the contrary, the intensification of "positional competition" among college graduates seems to reflect growing social inequality. (Mok, 2016, p. 51; see also Mok et al., 2016; Mok and Jiang, 2018)

Massification has had deleterious impacts upon the academic profession as well as on students, most notably in terms of workload (Mok, 2015). Indeed, national systems of higher education have suffered from the effects of overly rapid massification: "the rapid pace of massification carried with it a heavy price. Efforts to supply capacity within a short time frame to steadily increasing numbers of students quickly revealed the fragility of national systems to do so while at the same time maintaining even minimal standards of quality and effectiveness" (Jiang et al., 2018, p. 1).

Jiang et al.'s point about standards of quality and effectiveness is key, as expansion in participation has often taken place without significant changes to underlying practices and delivery. Thus, Huang (2017, p. 523), in a comparative study of the shift from mass to universal higher education in China and Japan, noted that: "with the advancement of higher education enrollment rates from the mass phase to the phase of universal access … remarkable changes do not necessarily happen to all aspects of curriculum and instruction and academics' role in these activities." Such tensions can soon become unsustainable, as institutions and academics continue to try to implement existing practices in a radically changed environment.

It is also the case that, even with the powerful influence of the Confucian model, many vestiges of colonialism and neo-colonialism may still be found in higher education structures and practices throughout the region. They may be seen, for example, in the continuing prevalence of the American model in the Japanese and Korean systems, and in the remaining influence of the British model (or models) in India, Hong Kong, and Malaysia. In addition, the world-class university model which so many governments aim to emulate is, in essence, that of the American research university (Mohrman et al., 2008).

A more contemporary, and perhaps more insidious, influence of this kind, however, is that of transnational higher education. This is where higher education opportunities are provided by institutions based in other countries—such as Australia, the United Kingdom, and the United States—through branch campuses, which may be operated in liaison with local institutions. At present, English language provision remains dominant in transnational higher education, and is also an increasing practice in "national" higher education institutions. Some Asian countries, such as China and Singapore, are themselves becoming hubs for transnational students, and this trend is likely to continue.

Even with the massification of higher education throughout much of the Asia-Pacific region, it remains the case that many students from this region either go abroad (within or beyond the region) to receive their higher education or gain it by attending branch campuses of foreign universities in their own countries. Sufficient higher education capacity of sufficient quality is not yet available throughout East Asia.

The experience of massification is, of course, somewhat different in the various countries that make up the Asia-Pacific region. Critical assessments are available on the largest and most developed, and thus most researched, of these.

4.1   Australia

Australia is as atypical as any nation in the Asia-Pacific region, forming an outpost—along with New Zealand—of Western society implanted upon the indigenous population.

Pitman (2014, p. 348) draws attention to how the massification of higher education has been linked to quality concerns within Australian policy:

> the discursive relationship between mass higher education and higher education quality shifted from conceptualising quality as a function of economic productivity, through educational transformation and academic standards, to market competition and efficiency. Throughout, the student was more often positioned as a servant towards higher education quality, rather than its benefactor.

The positioning of the student as simply an input to (or output of) the system is far from being unique to Australia, however, despite the oft-repeated mantras of, on the one hand, the student as consumer, or, on the other, the student voice. The processes involved in delivering mass higher education efficiently and successfully can be somewhat opposed to those needed for enhancing the individual student experience.

Pitman et al. (2015), in analyzing Australian national data for the period 2009–2011, offer a more optimistic perspective. They focus their analysis on widening participation and academic achievement: "Our analysis reveals that, whilst widening access results in more students with lower levels of academic achievement entering higher education, this does not necessarily equate to a lowering of educational quality" (Pitman et al., 2015, p. 609). However, one might not expect major changes to be evidenced over a short, three-year, period, while there are necessarily many other intervening factors— such as student support arrangements, changes in assessment practices, and varied expectations—which might have influenced the findings.

4.2 China

China now hosts the largest higher education system in the region, and, by some measures, in the world as a whole. Its recent massification dates to a policy decision taken in 1999, but has come with problems, not least graduate unemployment (Bai, 2006; Shi, 2015). The wish to create not just a mass higher education system, but also a number of world-class universities, has caused tensions in a highly bureaucratic and centrally driven system:

> While massification of higher education is an important indication of the great stride in China's higher education, the ... strategic plan to build up world-class universities reflects that China is ... seeking to achieve a breakthrough in quality higher education. However, the ambitious state is both a driving force and a constraint for China's higher education. Although the heavy investment from the state has provided [the] necessary financial condition[s] for China's universities to catch up with the top universities in the world, the accompanying administrative control has led to bureaucratization ... which has handicapped severely the autonomy of universities and the development of their innovation and uniqueness. (Ngok, 2008, p. 562)

Zha (2011; see also Zhou and Zha, 2010) concurs in noting that "China's current 'success' in higher education is limited to quantitative success in access" (p. 766). Zha argues that massification is "mainly benefitting a small proportion who study in the more selective universities" (p. 766), concluding that: "The Chinese model ... manifests some strength and attraction in relation to the efficiency of mobilizing and utilizing public and private resources to push for higher education growth, yet the inner constraints with respect to social equity and human potential fulfilment are serious" (p. 766). Again, we see that massification and the quality of the student experience do not necessarily go hand in hand.

Li (2012; see also Li, 2009) carried out a nationwide survey of twelve Chinese universities to assess the student experience of massification, noting that:

> particular policy interventions need to be directed towards how to achieve greater equity of access and success; how to improve curricular and teaching offerings; how

to provide stronger career guidance on campus for students; and how to further enhance the openness of universities to the global community with particular emphasis
on private universities, on students majoring in natural sciences or technologies, and
on students with limited family educational attainments and socio-economic status.
(Li, 2012, p. 472)

Most of these conclusions, of course, could also be (and have been) applied to many
other higher education systems, in the Asia-Pacific region and worldwide. The point
regarding the lack of "openness of universities to the global community" is, however, rather more specific, but essential to the desired achievement of world-class universities.
The emphasis on students "majoring in natural sciences or technologies," while
understandable, makes clear that the aim of national policy is directional as much as
supportive.

Unsurprisingly, therefore, many students in China, as in other countries, remain
skeptical regarding how they have benefited from mass participation:

The massification of higher education has increased college access and in general
enhanced the extent of equity and equality in society. Nonetheless, the situation has
become far more complex as returns of education have flattened out recently and social mobility has slowed down in general. University students have started to doubt
the ability of higher education to improve their competitiveness in the job market.
This, in turn, has led to a wide dissatisfaction with higher education development in
China. (Mok and Wu, 2016, p. 77)

Clearly, the Chinese higher education system is the one in the Asia-Pacific region that
will be most closely watched globally for future developments.

4.3 Hong Kong

Hong Kong, while a relatively small higher education system, has been highly influential
in recent decades in research terms in the Asia-Pacific area (Horta et al., 2015; Kim et al.,
2017), and has been much studied. It took a particular approach to the massification of
higher education, one that was arguably very close to Trow's expectations:

Hong Kong has moved from elite to mass post-secondary education in a very short
space of time and at little cost to the Government. Most of this spectacular expansion
in participation has come through enrolments in 2 year associate degrees in recently
founded community colleges, which have self-financing status. The achievement has
been clouded by complaints from associate degree graduates that the articulation
envisaged by the government is not working; so they are unable to obtain places for
undergraduate degrees in UGC [University Grants Committee]-funded universities.
The value of an associate degree as a suitable terminal award for employment in a
knowledge-based economy is yet to be clearly established. (Kember, 2010, p. 167)

The system was meant to operate much like that in the United States, with efficient transfer of suitable students from two-year colleges to four-year universities, but clearly has yet to achieve this.

As in mainland China, recent expansion, to take Hong Kong into a "post-massification era," has arguably been achieved at the expense of the quality of the higher education experience:

> The higher education sector in Hong Kong was reformed in the twenty-first century, and within a period of 5 years the post-secondary participation rate for the 17–20 age group doubled to 66 per cent. This ushered the higher education sector in Hong Kong into a post-massification era … Lack of articulation opportunities [designed to aid the movement from higher education to employment], the quality of education, and educated unemployment are the key challenges ahead. (Wan, 2011, p. 127)

Again, as in mainland China, the widening of participation resulting from massification has yet to overcome the handicaps faced by those from low socio-economic status backgrounds:

> the massification of higher education in Hong Kong has … failed to enhance social mobility in the city … [it] has taken on a partial privatisation model in which expansion occurs almost exclusively in the private sector. As a result, publicly funded degree programmes have remained highly selective and are increasingly biased towards wealthy students. In the process, graduates from self-financed programmes are severely disadvantaged in terms of employability despite their investment. (Lee, 2016, pp. 27–28)

The key difference between the Hong Kong and Chinese experience of massification to date has been, of course, the significant involvement of the private sector in the former. In both systems, however, the children of the elites continue to dominate recruitment to the highest-regarded institutions.

4.4 India

The Indian higher education system is second only to that of China in terms of its overall size, but confronts a rather different set of issues. While large, it has only recently become "massified":

> There has been a veritable explosion in numbers. From a small base of about 20 universities and a couple of lakhs [100,000s] of students, the system has grown to an enormous size with nearly one thousand universities, 40,000 colleges, and about ten thousand stand-alone institutions, with about 37 million students and about 1.5 million teachers … With such a large network of institutions, the Indian system

became the second largest higher education system in the world ... [and] is about to enter the phase of massification of higher education. (Tilak, 2020, p. 55)

Within this vast system, while there are pockets of excellence and innovation, there are continuing problems with equity of access, shortage of teachers, public funding, poor institutional governance and overall quality of provision (Carnoy and Dossani, 2013; Altbach, 2014). As a consequence, the private sector has grown rapidly in recent years (Jayaram, 2004; Gupta, 2008).

While the Indian economy faces major upskilling and reskilling challenges, analyses indicate that higher education makes a significant contribution:

when a larger share of workers in a particular sector has a college or university-level technical education or vocational education in technical fields, there is a positive impact on firm performance in those sectors. Further, higher education in a general field seems to consistently benefit the organised manufacturing sector. (Sangita, 2021, p. 122)

What is needed, therefore, is greater investment in the Indian higher education system as a whole.

Unlike several of the other Asian-Pacific systems considered in this section, the Indian higher education system does not attract many foreign students (Kumar, 2015), and does not as yet offer a model for possible emulation elsewhere.

4.5 Japan

Japan is similar to Hong Kong and Korea, in that massification has been achieved largely through the expansion of the private sector of higher education (Yonezawa and Baba, 1998). This is not to say that the public sector has been unaffected, and this impact is likely to increase as Japanese higher education moves through the post-massification phase:

Given that the drive towards post-massification is accelerating in most countries, problems as yet unexperienced will emerge. Government will no longer be able to match society's demands for higher education with a relatively abundant finance ... In the near future, the demand for accountability from taxpayers will be strong enough to convert national universities to performance funding and oblige them to change their administrative structure. (Reiko, 2001, pp. 289–290)

The expectation was that Japanese universities would adopt the more managerial practices already found in American, British, and Australian universities, among others. While this is happening, the Japanese higher education system remains relatively isolated from the rest of the world, with only limited exchanges of students and staff.

Looked at from a historical perspective, the growth in participation in Japanese higher education has not been a story of smooth and continued growth. Huang (2012) identified the period from the late 1970s to the mid-1980s as a time of suspended growth. The expansion of participation in higher education may, therefore, be spasmodic, strongly influenced by the underlying state of the economy.

4.6 Singapore

Singapore, like Hong Kong, is a small but forward-thinking society which has placed great emphasis on the development of its higher education system. While Hong Kong necessarily now sees its future within the much larger Chinese system, Singapore seeks to place itself internationally. Thus, as well as providing high-quality higher education to large numbers of its own citizens, it aspires to become a regional or global hub which, like Australia, attracts large numbers of students from other countries (Lee, 2002; Tan, 2004; Mok, 2008, 2012):

> Since the mid-1990s ... the government has constantly demonstrated its strong determination to develop the state or publicly-funded universities into the ones whose academic standards, research quality, resource endowment, and managerial efficiency can be comparable with world renowned higher education institutions ... The government's commitment is to develop Singapore as a regional education hub capable of drawing in talented non-local students as well as fee-paying students to study and eventually settle and work in the city-state. (Gopinathan and Lee, 2011, p. 292)

Lo (2014) argues that these policies have been implemented through neoliberal managerialism, and that "quality assurance has been used as an instrument to reshape the higher education landscape in Singapore" (p. 263). Singapore is similar to China, therefore, in its application of detailed national planning to higher education, though the approaches taken and the underlying political ideologies are very different.

4.7 Taiwan

The expansion of the Taiwanese higher education system from the 1990s onwards placed considerable pressure on the labor market:

> the massification of higher education in Taiwan ... promised bright prospects for students, parents, industries and higher education institutions. The massification had positive effects in terms of upgrading the industrial structure and maintaining regional competitiveness. At the individual level, the pressure of access to higher education substantially improved by providing extra places. Nevertheless, this process posed challenges for the career development of the younger generation. High-end job vacancies seem nowadays limited in Taiwan, which has led to declining wage levels, because of the overprovision of master's and doctoral courses. (Chan and Lin, 2015, p. 31; see also Chuang and Hu, 2012)

In addition, massification has been observed to have deleterious consequences for higher education institutions, including their resourcing and quality:

> The problems created by the expansion of higher education in many countries, including Taiwan ... include the uneven allocation of resources, tuition discrepancies between public and private HEIs [higher education institutions], severe competition in the face of declining student enrollments, and increasing concerns about issues involving educational quality ... Taiwan's university enrollment rate can be seen as one of the highest in Asia, but the distribution of resources has been increasingly geared toward privileged groups in a few public universities. (Chou and Wang, 2012, p. 18)

Among the positive consequences observed, however, have been declines in the gender disparity in recruitment between different disciplines; notably in the traditionally male STEM (science, technology, engineering, mathematics) and traditionally female humanities disciplines (Chang and ChangTzeng, 2020; see also Wang, 2012).

Rather like in mainland China, the emphasis in higher education policy in Taiwan has now moved on, with entrepreneurial and technological developments to the fore:

> All in all, the Taiwan case has clearly shown how the massification of higher education has affected social and economic development of Taiwan. The quest for [the] entrepreneurial university and attempts to advance technology in higher education may not satisfactorily tackle the consequences of over-supply of university graduates without proper and well-coordinated measures between economic development and massification of higher education. (Mok et al., 2013, p. 277)

It may be, of course, that the expectations placed on universities and colleges in some systems are just too high and/or disparate.

5. Future(s)?

The Asia-Pacific region has traveled far in terms of the massification of higher education over the last few decades. In seeking to draw general conclusions from this experience, as we move on through what some have called the "Asian Century," some speculation is in order. At the same time, however, we must repeat the caution about the size and heterogeneity of the region, and recognize that alternative futures are possible for higher education in different countries.

First, we may place the Asia-Pacific experience in the international context and ask how it compares to that in other parts of the world. Here the absence of a single homogeneous Asia-Pacific experience is clear, and a good deal of variety is evident. Some countries or systems, such as Australia, Japan, and South Korea, have forged ahead in terms of massification, following the lead of the United States. Others, such as China, have taken massive strides more recently to catch up; while still others have yet to achieve mass higher education.

While massification of higher education in the Asia-Pacific region came after that in North America and Western Europe—with the exception of Australia and New Zealand—it has paralleled developments in the rest of Europe and Latin America, and remains ahead of progress in much of Africa and the Middle East. Globalization and internationalization have ensured that higher education systems in different parts of the world are increasingly interconnected. Where the Asia-Pacific region has differed from the Western world, and particularly Western Europe, has been in the greater role of both central government in driving massification and of private sector institutions in delivering it.

Second, another characteristic of the Asia-Pacific region which stands out is the continuing role of transnational higher education. As well as delivering mass participation in higher education at home, several Asia-Pacific nations, most notably China, continue to send large numbers of their citizens abroad to receive their higher education. Whether this will prove to be a long-term trend is debatable, as it is noticeable that some Asia-Pacific nations, including China, Malaysia, and Singapore, are also seeking to become higher education hubs that will themselves attract students, primarily from less-developed nations.

Third, we may ask what happens post-massification as Asia-Pacific higher education systems continue to develop? Based on their experience to date, and that of other systems that have already experienced post-massification, three developments seem likely:

- expansion of postgraduate education and research (UNESCO Institute for Statistics, 2014);
- the continuance of an elite sub-system—patronized by the better off, better connected, and better educated—within the massified higher education systems; and
- continued efforts at establishing world-class universities within the leading systems.

Interestingly, these three developments appear mutually compatible, even supportive; but they are somewhat in contradiction to the underlying aims of mass higher education, notably in terms of widening participation and increasing social equity and opportunities.

Perhaps we have to accept that discrimination, in terms of educational ability and/ or achievement, is at the heart of higher education, even when provision is open to and accommodates the great majority of the population. Unless we adopt truly draconian policy measures, the extent to which higher education can operate as a means for social inclusion and advancement is limited.

It is possible, of course, that the Asia-Pacific region, or at least some of its component nations, may take a different route, or routes, to that of other systems that have already entered the post-massification stage. The early indications do not, however, bear this out. It may be that massification and post-massification—signifying the move from the craft to the industrial delivery of higher education—have an undeniable logic of their own.

References

Altbach, P. (1999). "The logic of mass higher education." *Tertiary Education and Management*, 5/2, 107–124.

Altbach, P. (2014). "India's higher education challenges." *Asia Pacific Education Review*, 15, 503–510.

Ashby, E. and Anderson, M. (1966). *Universities: British, Indian, African. A Study in the Ecology of Higher Education*. London: Weidenfeld & Nicolson.

Bai, M. (2006). "Graduate unemployment: Dilemmas and challenges in China's move to mass higher education." *China Quarterly*, 185, 128–144.

Bell, R. and Tight, M. (1993). *Open Universities: A British Tradition?* Buckingham: Open University Press.

Carnoy, M. and Dossani, R. (2013). "Goals and governance of higher education in India." *Higher Education*, 65, 595–612.

Chan, S.-J. and Lin, L.-W. (2015). "Massification of higher education in Taiwan: Shifting pressure from admission to employment." *Higher Education Policy*, 28, 17–33.

Chang, D.-F. and ChangTzeng, H.-C. (2020). "Patterns of gender parity in the Humanities and STEM programs: The trajectory under the expanded higher education system." *Studies in Higher Education*, 45/6, 1108–1120.

Chou, P. and Wang, L.-T. (2012). "Who benefits from the massification of higher education in Taiwan?" *Chinese Education and Society*, 45/5–6, 8–20.

Chuang, C.-P. and Hu, J.-H. (2012). "Employment of college graduates in the era of universalized higher education." *Chinese Education and Society*, 45/5–6, 45–58.

Datta, S. (2017). *A History of the Indian University System: Emerging from the Shadows of the Past*. London: Palgrave Macmillan.

Gopinathan, S. and Lee, M. (2011). "Challenging and co-opting globalisation: Singapore's strategies in higher education." *Journal of Higher Education Policy and Management*, 33/3, 287–299.

Gupta, A. (2008). "International trends and private higher education in India." *International Journal of Educational Management*, 22/6, 565–594.

Hayhoe, R. (1995). "An Asian multiversity? Comparative reflections on the transition to mass higher education in East Asia." *Comparative Education Review*, 39/3, 299–321.

Horta, H., Jung, J., and Yonezawa, A. (2015). "Higher education research in East Asia: Regional and national evolution and path dependencies." *Higher Education Policy*, 28, 411–417.

Huang, F. (2012). "Higher education from massification to universal access: A perspective from Japan." *Higher Education*, 63, 257–270.

Huang, F. (2015). "Higher education development in Japan." In J. Shin, G. Postiglione, and F. Huang (eds.), *Mass Higher Education Development in East Asia: Strategy, Quality and Challenges*. Cham: Springer, 27–42.

Huang, F. (2017). "The impact of mass and universal higher education on curriculum and instruction: Case studies of China and Japan." *Higher Education*, 74, 507–525.

Jayaram, N. (2004). "Higher education in India: Massification and change." In P. Altbach and T. Umakoshi (eds.), *Asian Universities: Historical Perspectives and Contemporary Challenges*. Baltimore, MD: Johns Hopkins University Press, 85–112.

Jiang, J., Mok, K.-H., and Neubauer, D. (2018). "The nature of higher education massification throughout the Asia-Pacific region. In D. Neubauer, K.-H. Mok, and J. Jiang (eds.), *The Sustainability of Higher Education in an Era of Post-Massification*. London: Routledge, 1–7.

Kember, D. (2010). "Opening up the road to nowhere: Problems with the path to mass higher education in Hong Kong." *Higher Education*, 59, 167–179.

Kim, Y., Horta, H., and Jung, J. (2017). "Higher education research in Hong Kong, Japan, China and Malaysia: Exploring research community cohesion and the integration of thematic approaches." *Studies in Higher Education*, 42/1, 149–168.

Kumar, S. (2015). "India's trade in higher education." *Higher Education*, 70, 441–467.

Lee, M. (2002). "A tale of two cities: Comparing higher education policies and reforms in Hong Kong and Singapore." *Australian Journal of Education*, 46/3, 255–286.

Lee, M. (2015). "Higher education in Malaysia: National strategies and innovative practices." In J. Shin, G. Postiglione, and F. Huang (eds.), *Mass Higher Education Development in East Asia: Strategy, Quality and Challenges*. Cham: Springer, 105–118.

Lee, S.-Y. (2016). "Massification without equalisation: The politics of higher education, graduate employment and social mobility in Hong Kong." *Journal of Education and Work*, 29/1, 13–31.

Li, J. (2009). "Fostering citizenship in China's move from elite to mass higher education: An analysis of students' political socialization and civic participation." *International Journal of Educational Development*, 29, 382–398.

Li, J. (2012). "The student experience in China's revolutionary move to mass higher education: Institutional challenges and policy implications." *Higher Education Policy*, 25, 453–475.

Lo, W. (2014). "Think Global, Think Local: the changing landscape of higher education and the role of quality assurance in Singapore." *Policy and Society*, 33, 263–273.

McConnell, T. (1973). "Beyond the universities: The movement towards mass higher education in Britain." *Higher Education*, 2/2, 160–171.

Marginson, S. (2011). "Higher education in East Asia and Singapore: Rise of the Confucian model." *Higher Education*, 61, 587–611.

Marginson, S. (2016a). "The worldwide trend to high participation higher education: Dynamics of social stratification in inclusive systems." *Higher Education*, 72/4, 413–434.

Marginson, S. (2016b). "High participation systems of higher education." *Journal of Higher Education*, 87/2, 243–271.

Mohrman, K., Ma, W., and Baker, D. (2008). "The research university in transition: The emerging global model." *Higher Education Policy*, 21/1, 5–27.

Mok, K.-H. (2008). "Singapore's global education hub ambitions: University governance change and transnational higher education." *International Journal of Educational Management*, 22/6, 527–546.

Mok, K.-H. (2012). "The rise of transnational higher education in Asia: Student mobility and studying experiences in Singapore and Malaysia." *Higher Education Policy*, 25, 225–241.

Mok, K.-H. (2015). "Higher education transformations for global competitiveness: Policy responses, social consequences and impact on the academic profession in Asia." *Higher Education Policy*, 28, 1–15.

Mok, K.-H. (2016). "Massification of higher education, graduate employment and social mobility in the greater China region." *British Journal of Sociology of Education*, 37/1, 51–71.

Mok, K.-H. and Jiang, J. (2018). "Massification of higher education and challenges for graduate employment and social mobility: East Asian experiences and sociological reflections." *International Journal of Educational Development*, 63, 44–51.

Mok, K.-H., Wen, Z., and Dale, R. (2016). "Employability and mobility in the valorisation of higher education qualifications: The experiences and reflections of Chinese students and graduates." *Journal of Higher Education Policy and Management*, 38/3, 264–281.

Mok, K.-H. and Wu, A. (2016). "Higher education, changing labour market and social mobility in the era of massification in China." *Journal of Education and Work*, 29/1, 77–97.

Mok, K.-H., Yu, K.-R., and Ku, Y.-W. (2013). "After massification: The quest for entrepreneurial universities and technological advancement in Taiwan." *Journal of Higher Education Policy and Management*, 35/3, 264–279.

Neave, G. (1985). "Elite and mass higher education in Britain: A regressive model?" *Comparative Education Review*, 29/3, 347–361.

Ngok, K. (2008). "Massification, bureaucratization and questing for 'world-class' status: Higher education in China since the mid-1990s." *International Journal of Educational Management*, 22/6, 547–564.

Organisation for Economic Co-operation and Development (2019). *Education at a Glance 2019*. Paris: OECD.

Pitman, T. (2014). "Reinterpreting higher education quality in response to policies of mass education: The Australian experience." *Quality in Higher Education*, 20/3, 348–363.

Pitman, T., Koshy, P., and Phillimore, J. (2015). "Does accelerating access to higher education lower its quality? The Australian experience." *Higher Education Research and Development*, 34/3, 609–623.

Reiko, Y. (2001). "University reform in the post-massification era in Japan: Analysis of government education policy for the 21st century." *Higher Education Policy*, 14, 277–291.

Ridder-Symoens, H. de (ed.) (1992). *A History of the University in Europe, Volume 1: Universities in the Middle Ages*. Cambridge: Cambridge University Press.

Sangita, S. (2021). "Higher education, vocational training and performance of firms." *Margin: The Journal of Applied Economic Research*, 15/1, 122–148.

Shi, X. (2015). "The path toward mass higher education in China." In J. Shin, G. Postiglione, and F. Huang (eds.), *Mass Higher Education Development in East Asia: Strategy, Quality and Challenges*. Cham: Springer, 63–88.

Tan, J. (2004). "Singapore: Small nation, big plans." In P. Altbach and T. Umakoshi (eds.), *Asian Universities: Historical Perspectives and Contemporary Challenges*. Baltimore, MD: Johns Hopkins University Press, 175–197.

Teichler, U. (1998). "Massification: A challenge for institutions of higher education." *Tertiary Education and Management*, 4/1, 17–27.

Tight, M. (2019a). "Mass higher education and massification." *Higher Education Policy*, 32/1, 93–108.

Tight, M. (2019b). "The neoliberal turn in higher education." *Higher Education Quarterly*, 73/3, 273–284.

Tilak, J. (2020). "Dilemmas in reforming higher education in India." *Higher Education for the Future*, 7/1, 54–66.

Trow, M. (1970). "Reflections on the transition from mass to universal higher education." *Daedalus*, 99/1, 1–42.

Trow, M. (1973). *Problems in the Transition from Elite to Mass Higher Education*. Berkeley, CA: Carnegie Commission on Higher Education.

Trow, M. (1999). "From mass higher education to universal access: The American advantage."
  Minerva, 37, 303–328.
UNESCO Institute for Statistics (2014). *Higher Education in Asia: Expanding Out, Expanding
  Up. The Rise of Graduate Education and University Research*. Paris: UNESCO.
Wan, C. (2011). "Reforming higher education in Hong Kong towards post-massification: The
  first decade and challenges ahead." *Journal of Higher Education Policy and Management*, 33/
  2, 115–129.
Wang, H.-H. (2012). "The dilemma and solutions for the conflicts between equality and excel-
  lence in the massification of higher education in Taiwan." *Chinese Education and Society*, 45/
  5–6, 82–98.
Wang, R.-J. (2003). "From elitism to mass higher education in Taiwan: The problems faced."
  Higher Education, 46, 261–287.
Yonezawa, A. and Baba, M. (1998). "The market structure for private universities in Japan: How
  has Japan achieved mass higher education in the private sector?" *Tertiary Education and
  Management*, 4/2, 145–152.
Zha, Q. (2011). "China's move to mass higher education in a comparative perspective."
  Compare, 41/6, 751–768.
Zhou, G. and Zha, Q. (2010). "The transformation of China's key science and technology
  universities in the move to mass higher education." *Frontiers of Education in China*, 5/4,
  531–557.

CHAPTER 3

··

EMPLOYMENT AND LABOR MARKETS

··

ROSLYN CAMERON AND JOHN BURGESS

According to global projections, in the next 20 to 30 years labour markets will continue to experience rapid shifts in skills demand. Whilst traditional forms of education will continue to play an important role in building core skills, support for lifelong learning will smooth the transition from education to work, promote ongoing education and training engagement and increase the uptake of different jobs through re-skilling and upskilling. (APEC, 2017b, p. 7)

1. INTRODUCTION

The world is experiencing unprecedented challenges including social, economic, and environmental mega trends many of which are driven by accelerating globalization and rapid developments in technologies associated with the Fourth Industrial Revolution (4IR) and the onset of Industry 4.0. Since the beginning of 2020 the world has seen a global health pandemic (COVID-19) which has added a level of complexity to these mega trends and caused huge challenges to health systems and impacted every aspect of economies worldwide. Labor markets and the higher education sector are not immune and the impacts are far reaching and evolving as the world rides this crisis curve. These mega trends are a strong impetus for redesigning the demand for certain skills, knowledge competencies, and capabilities and reshaping the design of work and how organizations choose to operate. This adds greater complexity and dynamism to labor markets resulting in demand for mobile, highly skilled workers to meet these demands.

According to the ILO (2018), the dynamic Asia-Pacific region has experienced robust economic growth over the last two decades with the world's lowest rates of unemployment in general, and lowest unemployment rates for youth. This has been a result of high labor productivity (output per worker) which has seen flow-down effects of economic benefits to general populations and standards of living. "The region has both the world's largest proportion of workers in the working-age population and the world's lowest unemployment rate" (ILO, 2018, p. xi). Nonetheless, this data can be misleading and masks deep structural challenges. There remains a long road ahead in dealing with decent work deficits which needs to be a focus for the future as the region strives for inclusive growth. An added level of complexity is the mixed data across countries and subregions. The seven key labor market trends identified by the ILO are as follows:

- Asia and the Pacific as a region (globally) has the most people working, relative to the working-age population.
- Labor force participation rates among the older population and youth are high in Asia and the Pacific.
- While the regional unemployment rate remains low, unemployment among youth and among workers with secondary and tertiary education remains a challenge.
- Many workers remain close to poverty or are in vulnerable employment, and access to decent jobs remains a challenge for many people.
- Not all wage and salaried employment in the Asia-Pacific region is decent work.
- Gender inequality in the world of work remains an issue of primary concern.
- Structural transformation has been fast in the region, with employment moving from agriculture mainly into services and only to some extent into industry (ILO, 2018, pp. xv–xvi).

Quality higher education plays a crucial role in producing a baseline of sustainable skilled professional human capital to fuel these regional economies. According to the Asian Development Bank, "investing in higher education will help developing Asian countries build high-income economies, with the innovation, knowledge, and technology needed to thrive in an interconnected, competitive world" (Asian Development Bank, 2011, p. v).

This chapter explores employment and labor markets within the broad regional scope of the Asia-Pacific region which includes East, South, and South-East Asia. We have endeavored to cover these regions with our analysis of the labor market within and across these regions. The chapter is structured into four main sections:

- The Asia-Pacific region: diverse economies, demographics, and labor markets
- Mega trends impacting the future of work and employment: regional strategies
- Higher education and the labor market: graduate unemployment, underemployment, and employability
- Strategic responses to generating work-ready graduates across the region.

2. THE ASIA-PACIFIC REGION: DIVERSE ECONOMIES, DEMOGRAPHICS, AND LABOR MARKETS

This section will address the diversity within the region in terms of economic development, demography, educational attainment, and education participation. The focus will be on the trends of higher education participation, and higher education internationalization. The 2019 *World Development Report* (World Bank, 2019) highlights the strategic and developmental importance of developing human capital through education, health, and social support programs. It emphasizes the importance of investing in education, including tertiary education, to realize personal and community development goals. On average the returns for investing in tertiary education are around 16 percent globally, but with differences across nations, regions, courses, and universities (World Bank, 2019). Across the globe the gross tertiary education enrollment ratio is 37 percent (the percentage enrolled in tertiary education of the relevant age group) and the expenditure on tertiary education (as a percentage of public expenditure on education) is 22 percent. Within East Asia and the Pacific, the respective percentages are 44 and 17; in South Asia they are 23 and 21 (World Bank, 2019).

The economies in the Asia-Pacific are diverse in terms of size, living standards, and economic structure. Within the region, China and India are two of the largest economies by gross domestic product (GDP) and population. In terms of living standards, Japan, Singapore, and Australia are ranked as among the wealthiest global economies on a GDP basis. At the other end of the spectrum are small and poor countries such as Nepal, Timor Leste, and Laos which face high rates of poverty and illiteracy, and low investment in human capital. In terms of the national economic structure the range includes those economies with relatively large agricultural sectors (Indonesia and Cambodia), those with relatively large manufacturing sectors (Taiwan and South Korea), and those with large service sectors (Singapore and Australia) (World Bank, 2019).

Fundamentally the demand for higher education is driven by demographic and economic conditions (OECD, 2018). The demographics encompass the numbers and shares of the population of the age group between 18 and 24, as this is the cohort that typically enters tertiary education. A conditional factor is meeting entry conditions, and this entails meeting literacy standards and completing secondary education. However, there are emerging trends towards increasing participation in education across all age groups globally and within the region (World Bank, 2012, 2019). This reflects increasing participation and completion rates for secondary education, improved literacy, and the expansion in the tertiary education sector. There is also an increasing demand for postgraduate and adult education and improved access to tertiary education through online programs for adults with employment and caring responsibilities (OECD, 2018).

The state and structure of the economy impacts the demand for tertiary education in several ways. First, the wealthier the economy, the greater the demand for tertiary education. Education is a normal good, and as the community becomes wealthier more families can afford to finance participation in tertiary education. Second, and linked to the first reason, more students can afford to participate in and complete secondary education, thus being able to transit into tertiary education; and finally, the better paying jobs in certain professions require a tertiary education as an entry condition into those professions (OECD, 2018).

However, there are caveats to the above conditions. The distribution of income and wealth will determine the capacity to participate in secondary and tertiary education. Unless there are offsetting state funded places for higher education, those in the bottom end of the income/wealth distribution will not be able to afford the financial and opportunity costs associated with higher education participation. In the region there are several countries with a large share of the population living in poverty. According to the Asian Development Bank (2018) the following counties have more than 20 percent of their population living below national poverty standards: India (21.2 percent); Pakistan (24.3 percent); and the Philippines (21.6 percent). The second condition is that of equitable access; there may be situations where gender, location, or ethnicity may be a barrier to participation (OECD, 2018). Finally, there is capacity, that is the number and quality of higher education institutions, the costs and funding of higher education, and the admissions systems (Bekhradnia and Beech, 2017). In emerging, relatively poor economies, there may not be the financial capacity to support higher education; consequently there is a physical limit to participation. For example, Timor Leste, Papua New Guinea, and Nepal have few universities.

What follows is a brief overview of those demographic and economic conditions across the Asia-Pacific region that contribute to driving the demand for higher education. This will be followed by an overview of higher education participation and internationalization across the region.

Within the region are the two most populous nations globally, India and China. Large numbers of youth will potentially require large numbers of places in higher education. It is the large youth cohort and improved living standards in China and India that are driving the regional demand for higher education since it is students from China and India that dominate international student numbers in the region (OECD, 2019a, 2019b). The demographic profile indicates the current and future demand for places in higher education. Table 3.1 outlines population growth and profiles from ESCAP (2018) by three regions: East/North Asia, South-East Asia, and South/South-West Asia.

Apart from India and China, the region also contains other nations with large populations of 200 million plus (Pakistan, Indonesia). In absolute terms there will be large numbers of those in the age profile range, currently and in the future, who will potentially participate in higher education. In terms of the population share within the child age group (0–14 years), several nations stand out by having relatively large shares (20 percent plus), indicating a future increase in potential demand for higher education places. This applies to Indonesia, Malaysia, the Philippines, India, and Nepal. Across the

Table 3.1 The demographic profile of the region

Region/country	Pop. (m)	Pop. growth %	Median age	Share 0–14 yrs %	Share 15–24 yrs %
E/N Asia					
China	1415	0.4	37	17.6	16.6
Japan	127	-0.2	46	12.8	9.3
South Korea	51	0.3	34	13.4	12.1
SE Asia					
Indonesia	266	1.0	28	27.0	16.9
Malaysia	32	1.3	27	24.0	18.0
Philippines	106	1.5	24	31.5	19.0
Singapore	6	1.4	40	17.0	12.5
Thailand	69	0.2	37	13.0	13.7
Vietnam	96	1,0	30	16.9	14.7
S/SW Asia					
India	1354	1.1	26	27.4	18.2
Bangladesh	116	1.0	26	27.8	17.0
Nepal	29	1.1	23	30.2	21.3
Pakistan	200	1.9	22	19.0	19.0
Pacific					
Australia	25	1.3	37	19.1	12.5
New Zealand	5	0.9	37	19.8	13.5

Source: ESCAP (2018).

region the population is aging due to improved living standards, declining birth rates, and improved health conditions. For China, Japan, Thailand, and Korea the population is forecasted to decline. However, for all other countries the population will increase.

Accessing higher education in general requires the completion of secondary schooling. In turn the transition to higher education will be determined by access, funding, and the expected return from finishing a degree or qualification. Across the region the literacy, higher education completion, and participation in higher education rates are very uneven. The wealthier the country, the more likely that the state and individuals are able to afford funding private and public higher education. However, the greater the unemployment rate, the greater the share in the informal economy, and the lower the labor force participation rate, there is either less opportunity or less incentive to participate in higher education. Table 3.2 presents these indicators in countries presented in alphabetical order.

From Table 3.2 those countries with relatively high GDP per capita (US$30,000 plus) can be found in North-East Asia, the Pacific and Singapore (as an exception in

Table 3.2 The economic capacity and drivers of higher education

Nation	GDP US$b	GDP pc US$'000	Unempl % M F	LFPR % M F	Informal empl share M F	High skill share % M F
Australia	1480	58.1	5.7 5.8	82.5 70.8	–	18.0 20.1
Bangladesh	343	2.1				
China	15740	10.7	N.a. N.a.	84.3 70.3	–	N.a N.a.
India	3260	2.3	4.1 7.7	82.0 28.5	70.3 75.7	8.1 1.8
Indonesia	1210	4.4	5.7 5.4	85.8 52,5	77.3 80.2	5.6 4.8
Japan	5500	43.4	3.4 2.8	85.0 66.4	–	27.1 21.1
Korea	1740	34.0	3.8 3.6	76.4 55.9	–	47.2 29.3
Malaysia	401	12.4	2.9 3.4	81.1 52.8	–	11.8 11.7
Nepal	33	1.1	2.6 3.4	88.4 83.2	98.8 99.4	7.9 4.1
New Zealand	224	46.6	4.8 5.5	83.3 73.7	–	14.9 16.9
Pakistan	283	1.2	5.0 9.9	85.7 25.7	71.0 75.2	6.9 2.1
Philippines	389	3.5	6.6 5.8	80.9 52.6	–	12.9 12.7
Singapore	391	67.0	2.7 2.9	82.6 65.9	–	27.4 24.1
Thailand	4547	7.8	0.2 0.2	85.8 70.0	–	6.8 8.9
Vietnam	282	2.9	2.3 2.0	86.9 79.9	–	7.4 7.0

Source: WEF 2017 (– is either 0 or unknown); IMF (2019).

GDP (current US$ billion).

GDP per capita, US$ 000 (nominal GDP in US S\$ divided by population)/(Female, male labor force participation rate (LFPR), age 15–64 (%).

Adult unemployment (as % of female, male labor force). Adult unemployment refers to the share of the labor force aged 15–64 that is without work but available for and seeking employment.

Workers in informal employment (as % of total female, male employment). Informal employment refers to workers holding informal jobs, whether employed by formal sector enterprises, informal sector enterprises, or as paid domestic workers by households.

High skill share of labor force (%). Measures the proportion of a country's working-age population with a tertiary degree (ISCED 5–8) that engages actively in the labor market, either by working or looking for work.

South-East Asia). The male labor force participation rates are similar across the region, but there are great differences in the female participation rate. Very low rates (60 percent or less) relative to men are found in India, Indonesia, Malaysia, Pakistan, and the Philippines. Low rates of labor force participation are related to institutional, cultural, family, and labor market conditions. In these countries females perform family and care duties, and participate in agriculture and in the rural economy. However, it means that

for females, tertiary education is either difficult to access (low literacy rates, low participation in secondary education, poverty and rural locations) or the opportunities for jobs
for females post-graduation are limited. A high informal sector employment share as in
India, Indonesia, Nepal, and Pakistan suggests that in those countries, formal education
qualifications typically associated with the formal labor market are not required. Finally,
the high skill share of the workforce, the share with post-secondary qualifications, is
relatively low (less than 10 percent), in India, Indonesia, Nepal, Pakistan, and Thailand.
This again suggests that in order to access jobs, post-secondary credentials are not
required. In contrast, Japan, Korea, and Singapore have a relatively high skill workforce
share that results in relatively higher participation rates in tertiary education in order to
gain access to skilled jobs. Table 3.3 depicts percentages (male and female) for highest
educational attainment for countries presented in alphabetical order.

From Table 3.3 it can be seen that the patterns of educational attainment across the
adult population follow the patterns of development. Those countries with relatively
high GDP per capita have relatively high rates of attainment in tertiary education.

Table 3.3 Highest educational attainment by the population aged 25 years and over (male and female)

Country, year	No schooling % M F	Completed primary % M F	Completed secondary % M F	Bachelor's degree % M F
Australia 2018	0.2 0.4	6.2 6.0	35.5 24.4	20.4 26.2
Bangladesh 2018	25.9 33.7	14.9 14.6	15.4 14.6	7.1 3.7
China 2010	3.5 9.8	24.7 31.6	15.4 11.6	3.7 2.7
India 2011	30.0 52.9	15.1 12.5	21.3 12.2	11.5 6.7
Indonesia 2018	3.4 7.5	26.9 28.1	28.2 21.1	8.8 8.8
Japan 2010	0.1 0.1	N.a. N.a.	38.3 41.4	25.1 10.1
Malaysia 2016	4.1 8.1	19.8 19.7	38.0 36.9	8.8 10.7
Nepal 2011	37.4 66.4	17.3 10.3	10.3 4.9	5.1 1.6
New Zealand 2016	N.a. N.a.	3.4 2.8	20.4 25.7	20.2 24.7
Pakistan 2017	34.8 59.6	14.8 10.1	22.1 15.2	8.4 5.2
Philippines 2017	1.9 2.1	25.5 23.7	N.a. N.a.	12.9 18.3
South Korea 2015	1.2 5.8	7.0 12.5	37.6 34.7	22.8 20.8
Singapore 2018	N.a. N.a.	6.2 6.7	16.4 19.0	34.0 29.4
Thailand 2018	3.4 5.7	21.6 19.4	15.5 12.4	11.2 14.2
Vietnam 2009	4.2 8.9	24.6 31.6	16.1 11.3	7.6 5.9

Source: UNESCO (2020), Share of population by educational attainment, population 25 years and
above (N.a. – unknown or not available).

Those emerging economies in South-East Asia (Malaysia, Thailand, Indonesia, and the Philippines) have mid-range rates of participation in tertiary education as compared to Japan, Korea, Australia, Singapore, and New Zealand.

South-West Asia (Nepal, Bangladesh, India, and Pakistan) has a relatively high share of the population without educational attainment and relatively low attainment in tertiary education. The gender divide in educational qualifications is also apparent for these countries.

International student enrollments have increased globally over the past two decades. Within the OECD, the number of enrollments increased from 2 to 5 million between 1998 and 2017 (OECD, 2018). Students from Asia are the largest group of international students globally, and at all levels of education with India and China together accounting for around 40 percent of the international student population (OECD, 2018). English-speaking nations, apart from Japan, are major destinations for international students, and two-thirds of Asian international students are located in Australia, Canada, the USA, the UK, and Japan (OECD, 2018). (See UNESCO's 2014 report on higher education, and Chapter 14 in the present volume for further details and discussion on internationalization within the region.)

3. Mega Trends Impacting the Future of Work and Employment: Regional Strategies

The emerging interest and policy activities around skilling for the future, the changing nature of work and the 4IR/Industry 4.0 will be the central themes of this section. It draws on research being undertaken by international organizations and multinational economic bodies (e.g., ILO, World Economic Forum, APEC, and OECD). Reports, statistics, and research will inform this section of the chapter based on identified "mega trends" impacting the future of work. These include: demographic changes; climate change and resource depletion; socio-political shifts, widening inequality, and changing consumer patterns; emergence of new business models, transition to the green economy, and the adoption of 4IR/Industry 4.0 technologies. For the latter the key technological developments include:

Digitalization/digital disruption	Robotics or Robotic Process Automation (RPA)
Artificial intelligence (AI)	Natural language processing (NLP)
Machine learning	Blockchain
Internet of Things (IoT)	Big data science/analytics

The OECD (2018) identified three major challenges: environmental, social, and economic. The latter has a significant impact on labor markets and the provision of higher education to help address some of these trends/challenges. The OECD summarizes aspects of these economic challenges as follows:

> Scientific knowledge is creating new opportunities and solutions that can enrich our lives, while at the same time fuelling disruptive waves of change in every sector. Unprecedented innovation in science and technology, especially in bio-technology and artificial intelligence, is raising fundamental questions about what it is to be human. It is time to create new economic, social and institutional models that pursue better lives for all. (OECD, 2018, p. 3)

The Asia-Pacific region comprises large and diverse economies with some at the frontiers of digital transformations and others very underdeveloped and globally outdated. Higher education plays a key role in addressing these mega trends and ensuring the region has graduates who are work ready, skilled, and professionally educated to embrace and deal with these large-scale trends.

The ILO in its report *Skills and the Future of Work* (ILO, 2019d) is concerned with how mega trends are impacting the future of work across the Asia and Pacific region and aims to connect the themes of "skills," "future of work," and "inclusive growth," by bringing together the UN Sustainable Development Goals of Quality Education (SDG 4), Decent Work (SDG 8), Eliminating Poverty (SDG 1), and Gender Equality (SDG 5). The report states that, "the emerging characteristics of future labour markets are more fluid (rapid change), unforeseeable, less secure and technology driven" (ILO, 2019d, p. 3; see also ESCAP, 2019).

Oxford Economics and CISCO (2018) undertook an examination of the impact of AI on workers in six of ASEAN's largest economies (ASEAN-6): Indonesia, Malaysia, the Philippines, Singapore, Thailand, and Vietnam. Their economic modeling was focused upon the "new technology scenario" to provide an evidence base for regional stakeholders and policymakers to prepare for the technology future of the region (Oxford Economics and CISCO, 2018). The report concluded:

> *Over the next decade, both existing and new technologies will be applied to business activity in increasingly innovative and diverse ways.* From ASEAN's professional and financial services hubs to its agricultural sectors, and every industry in between, AI-enabled technologies are set to deliver substantial productivity gains. If these opportunities can be seized, substantial benefits await the ASEAN economy, and the prosperity of the region.
>
> *But for many workers, this shift will bring about significant life changes, as they are forced to adapt their skills or face the threat of redundancy.* New technologies precipitate a shift in the nature of work, by altering the balance between man and machine in performing different tasks. (Oxford Economics and CISCO, 2018, p. 11, emphasis in original)

Higher education in the Asia-Pacific region has a key role to play in ensuring the region is equipped with the educational capacity and provision to assist the region through this new digital evolution across all its economic sectors.

The World Economic Forum's recent report *Jobs of Tomorrow: Mapping Opportunity in the New Economy* (WEF, 2020), takes an in-depth look at the emerging labor market and explores the emergence of new jobs and future shifts in professions and skill needs (WEF, 2020, p. 4). The mega trends driving this include: the 4IR and Industry 4.0, demographic changes, industrial transitions, and associated changes in consumer needs. Combined, these trends will provide opportunities for millions of new jobs and at the same time will create unequal opportunities for others in low-skilled occupations and jobs where the new technologies will displace these workers already experiencing structural inequality (WEF, 2020, p. 5). It is not only the advances in digital technologies that will drive this growth but also strong "human" factors resulting in seven key clusters of new professions. The WEF (2020) report identifies these seven professional clusters along with 96 new jobs and categorizes these as either high-volume jobs or lower-volume jobs. The professional clusters are: Sales and Content Production; Marketing; People and Culture; Product Development; Engineering; Cloud Computing; and Data and AI. The high-volume jobs include jobs such as: Artificial Intelligence Specialists, Medical Transcriptionists, Data Scientists, Customer Success Specialists and Full Stack Engineers. Lower-volume jobs with the highest growth include: Landfill Biogas Generation System Technicians, Social Media Assistants, Wind Turbine Service Technicians, Green Marketers, and Growth Hackers. Overall, the growth is highest in care roles and lowest in green jobs and professions (WEF, 2020, p. 4). The skill sets needed for these new jobs for the emerging new economy are contained in five skill clusters: "Business Skills, Specialized Industry Skills, General and Soft Skills, Tech Baseline Skills and Tech Disruptive Skills" (WEF, 2020, p. 4) while technical skills in digital technologies are required for other professions. As a result of this report the WEF has also created a platform for driving strategies towards these new jobs and professions. The platform is a "Reskilling Revolution" to support new opportunities for many in the global labor market over the next decade.

The ILO has produced a report entitled *Preparing for the Future of Work: National Policy Responses in ASEAN+6* (2019c) which focused on ten ASEAN countries and six key trading partners (+6). The ten ASEAN countries are: Brunei Darussalam, Cambodia, Indonesia, Lao People's Democratic Republic, Malaysia, Myanmar, the Philippines, Singapore, Thailand, and Vietnam. The "+6" countries are: Australia, China, India, Japan, New Zealand, and the Republic of Korea. The report focuses upon three mega trends: technological change, demographic change, and environmental and climate change. A key foundation driving the report is the ILO's Centenary Declaration that "calls for 'a human-centred approach for the future of work' that focuses on increasing investment in people's capabilities, in the institutions of work and in productive employment and decent work" (ILO, 2019c, p. iii). The report examines the policies, strategies, initiatives, and plans related to the three mega trends. A key finding from the report is that there is "one common feature found among many countries in the region: labour market issues are found to be treated as an afterthought in most of the national policy documents reviewed, especially those linked to 'Industry 4.0' where economic interests often trump social considerations" (ILO, 2019c, p. iii; see also ILO, 2019a, 2019b).

In support of this argument is a recent economic working paper from the Asian Development Bank which focused upon education, skills, and lifelong learning in the era of the fourth technological revolution. Several issues are identified including declining productivity for older workers due to technological advancements and associated job polarization. Kim and Park (2020) refer to these in terms of the need for re-skilling and retraining of existing workers and how this will drive future education, skills, and life-long learning policies. In light of this they argue for a major rethink of education and skills training: "we should acknowledge the necessity for lifelong learning of workers. Formal education can no longer be the major focus for policymakers to improve worker productivity. Instead, workers and governments must recognize the importance of learning and acquiring skills throughout a worker's life" (Kim and Park, 2020, p. 1).

Tay and Tijaja (2017) addressed global mega trends for ASEAN nations and asserted that "Despite a growing body of literature addressing global megatrends, there is little reference made to the ASEAN-specific context" (2017, p. iii). The authors view these mega trends within the context of the ASEAN integration agenda and the ASEAN Economic Community (AEC) Blueprint 2025. Issues addressed in the collection include: regional integration in context with global mega trends; opportunities for the ASEAN region in terms of the digital economy and advances in technology; ASEAN approaches to people-centered and orientated economic communities; ASEAN approaches to sustainable development and environmental protection; and the wave of urbanization across the region.

Regional strategies to address impacts of many of these mega trends are crucial to developing labor markets to meet these challenges. Higher education has a significant role to play to ensure a supply of graduates that can help to build strong economies to address these trends. The *APEC Education Strategy 2016–2030* will be central to this discussion.

3.1   APEC Education Strategy and Associated Initiatives

The rationale for the *APEC Education Strategy 2016–2030* is summarized as follows:

> In an increasingly interconnected and globally competitive environment, there is a need for an overarching framework for engagement in education and training and lifelong learning to help APEC economies share information and best practices, address common challenges and leverage regional expertise to best effect. (APEC, 2017a, p. 2)

The strategy aims to foster educational cooperation between the APEC economies to increase workforce participation and participation in education and life-wide learning, all of which assists in meeting the social and economic needs of the participating countries. The objectives of the APEC Strategy are threefold (APEC, 2017a, p. 3):

1. Enhance and align competencies to the needs of individuals, societies and economies.
2. Accelerate innovation.
3. Increase employability.

Each objective has a set of action items and many if not all of them have a direct link to the higher education and vocational education and training (VET) sectors. An important group within APEC, the Human Resource Development Working Group (HRDWG), plays a key role in implementing these objectives and related actions. The group was formed in 1990 to ensure the building of human capacity through initiatives in education and labor by means of regional collaboration and aimed at economic growth that is sustainable. The working group is guided by three objectives:

1. Develop 21st century knowledge and skills for all
2. Integrate human resources development into the global economy
3. Address the social dimensions of globalization. (APEC, 2019)

To ensure these objectives are met, a set of three networks are in place:

- The **Capacity Building Network** (CBN), which focuses on skills development, human resource management and vocational training through crosscutting collaboration to facilitate 21st century talents, enhance employability and provide quality employment.
- The **Education Network** (EDNET), which focuses on fostering strong and vibrant learning systems across APEC member economies, promoting quality and equitable education to enable people of all ages to meet the challenges of rapid change in today's world through enhancing competencies, accelerating innovation and increasing employability.
- The **Labour and Social Protection Network** (LSPN), which focuses on fostering strong and flexible labour markets and strengthening social protection, including social safety nets, through evidence-based interventions, collaboration, technical co-operation and the provision of labour market and social protection information and analysis to address sustainable human resource development across APEC member economies. (APEC, 2019)

Another APEC initiative is the *Framework on Human Resources Development in the Digital Age* (APEC, 2017c). The Framework is also in the hands of the HRDWG and is to be implemented from 2017 to 2025. The three priority areas are: the future of work in the digital age and labor market policy implications; skills education and training; and social protection.

Reports on the outcomes of these initiatives are not currently available and the onset of the global COVID-19 pandemic which began early in 2020 may be a key inhibitor to their progress. The HRDWG last met in February 2020. However, the LSPN held a special session on COVID-19 on September 2020. On 20 November 2020, the 27th APEC Economic Leaders meeting was held which issued the 2020 Kuala Lumpur Declaration. The Declaration is squarely focused upon COVID-19 economic recovery and safeguarding health in the region.

4. TERTIARY EDUCATION AND THE LABOR MARKET: GRADUATE UNEMPLOYMENT, UNDEREMPLOYMENT, AND EMPLOYABILITY

> Adults with higher proficiency in literacy, numeracy and problem solving in technology-rich environments tend to have better outcomes in the labour market than their less-proficient peers. They have greater chances of being employed and, if employed, of earning higher wages. (OECD, 2016, p. 17)

> Transition between education and employment is one of the main obstacles facing youth of the region, especially those from South and South-West Asia, South-East Asia and the Pacific. (United Nations, 2010)

4.1 Higher Education

Completing a university degree is not a guarantee for employment that is well paid or a career. Throughout the region there is a challenge for graduates, their families, and universities to translate the completion of a degree program into a career. The challenges associated with moving from graduation to a job and a career have been captured under the umbrella term of "graduate work readiness" (GWR). Several authors have discussed the origins and conceptualization of GWR (Caballero and Walker, 2010; Tran, 2015; Burgess et al., 2018; Prikshat et al., 2019). The manifestation of GWR challenges is apparent as a result of the increase in graduate unemployment and underemployment (Burgess et al., 2018, p. 3). There is evidence that graduates are not directly transitioning into career jobs linked to their fields of study, but are experiencing post-graduation underemployment in part-time and temporary work, or they are being employed in jobs that do not require graduate qualifications (ILO, 2013). In its report on global employment trends for youth, the ILO (2013) highlighted the systemic high rates of unemployment and underemployment for youth and young adults globally (Burgess et al., 2018, p. 4). Despite ongoing economic growth, and claimed shortages of skilled labor, and despite increasing participation in post-secondary education, labor market problems persist among graduates. Obtaining a degree is no longer a sufficient entry condition for accessing a decent job (ILO, 2013), where a decent job incorporates minimum income, career advancement, and regular employment (ILO, 2013). In a recent *Human Capital Report*, the WEF (2016) argued that youth unemployment and underemployment is an impediment to national and global development and depresses the private and social returns from investing in education. Addressing the challenges of graduate transition and graduate work readiness is a national and global imperative. Despite the growing participation in tertiary education, more graduates are finding it difficult to access regular employment. The concept of transitional labor markets captures the process of moving in and out of the labor market (Schmidt, 1995). For those transitioning into the labor market, such as from schooling and university, from full-time childcare, and from military to civilian jobs, the transition process can be challenging (Burgess et al., 2018). Access to jobs may be limited by a lack of work experience, an absence of support networks, distance barriers (i.e., not being located in proximity to jobs), and not having the required skills and credentials to fill job vacancies.

Graduates are faced with such transitional labor market challenges. An important challenge identified in the GWR literature is that of skill mismatch (ILO, 2013). Graduates may face three barriers to a successful job search. First, they may have credentials or a degree in an area in which there are no job vacancies. Typically, a degree requires three or more years of study. While there may have been job prospects when the degree started, these may have dissipated by the time of the degree completion. There could be cyclical changes, such as a downturn in the economy, and structural changes, such as technological and organizational change resulting in job displacement. Second, they may be overqualified for existing jobs. The indications are that over education and credentialism, or excessive investment in education, is increasing (ILO, 2013). The third challenge is that although they possess a degree, they do not possess the skills required by employers to fill job vacancies. Degrees typically impart technical and analytical skills, but they may not impart other skills that are required to access a job. These skills incorporate soft and attitudinal skills such as effective communication, IT skills, and teamwork and innovation (Nankervis et al., 2019).

The absence of key skills in graduates results in two challenges: skills shortage and graduates not being job or work ready. Throughout the region, both GWR and skill shortages coexist (Dhakal et al., 2019a). There are skilled job vacancies, but graduates cannot access jobs (Dhakal et al., 2019b). This contradiction captures the discourse on GWR. The investment, enrollments in, and graduates from higher education increase, but graduates do not have the portfolio of skills required to access jobs. The conceptualization of GWR in the literature is used to identify the gap in skills or competencies that graduates possess and those skills and competencies that are required to meet existing job vacancies (Tran, 2015). The degree may satisfy technical requirements for a job, but it may not provide other necessary skills, especially soft skills (Montague, 2013). Following a review of the literature on the skills that graduates require to access employment, Nankervis et al. (2019) identified common skill requirements: teamwork, cognitive, self-management, political, technology, system thinking, leadership, innovation, communication, and creativity. The challenge for universities within the region, and for governments funding public education, is to develop processes that support the acquisition of these necessary skills and improve employability.

Within the literature, GWR has been challenged in terms of its foundations and conceptualization (Rothwell and Rothwell, 2017). There are three issues that are contestable. First, the foundations of and purpose of a university. Should graduates be expected to have very specific and essentially vocational skill sets, or should graduates have generic skill sets? Second, the supply-side orientation of GWR; the problems associated with GWR are the consequence of failings by graduates and tertiary education institutions. Third, the vagueness of GWR as there are many attributes or competencies that are required within different industries and occupations, and these cannot be captured with a degree structure.

On the third point above, the number and type of skills required depend upon the structure of the economy and the skill content and requirement of jobs. In their review of skill needs in Asia, Nankervis et al. (2019) highlighted the different sets of skill requirements associated with different stages of economic development and different industry structures. GWR attributes are not universal but are very contextually dependent on the structure of the economy and the state of the economy.

What are the graduate work readiness challenges in the region? While the Asia-Pacific region is the most populous globally and contains 60 percent of the world's youth population (United Nations, 2010), there are high unemployment rates (over 10 percent) for youth (15–24 years of age) in Australia, Indonesia, Korea, Malaysia, New Zealand, Pakistan, and Indonesia. Nankervis et al. (2019) reported high rates of graduate unemployment in the region of over 20 percent, six months after graduation in Malaysia, Indonesia, and Taiwan. Underemployment of graduates is also a challenge in Australia, with over 30 percent of graduates unable to access a full-time job within six months of graduation. For many graduates the period following graduation often involves short-term and part-time employment, or employment in jobs that do not require a degree for entry.

What are the skill challenges in the region? In a survey of nine countries in the AP region, Dhakal et al. (2019c) noted that the national skill shortages had to be viewed against the background of large migrant labor flows within the region. In some countries like Nepal and Lao, skilled shortages were exacerbated by large outflows of labor. In other countries such as Singapore and Australia, skill shortages were alleviated by migrant labor. In the lower-income countries the skill shortages were in agriculture and construction (Laos, Nepal). Construction appeared as a skill shortage sector across nearly all countries, including Singapore and Australia. Manufacturing labor shortages were present in Taiwan, Vietnam, and India. For these listed industries, the majority of occupations did not require a tertiary degree. In general, it is those professional services that require a degree for job entry, and services skill shortages, including tourism, health and professional services, were present in Indonesia, Singapore, Australia, and Taiwan.

In terms of graduate employability, the QS World University Rankings (2019) constructs a graduate employability index that is a composite of several indicators: employer reputation; alumni outcomes; graduate employment; partnerships with employers; and employer–student connections. This provides a measure of employment and engagement with potential employers. For 2019 the ranking of universities globally revealed that 27 out of the top 100 universities were in the Asia-Pacific region. Nationally, the number of universities represented came from Australia (8); Japan (6); China (5); Korea (4); New Zealand (1); Singapore (1); Hong Kong (1); and Taiwan (1). The top 20 universities globally included 2 from Australia, 2 from China, and 1 each from Hong Kong and Japan. There are 280 institutions listed for the region "Asia" which includes the Middle East on the QS webpage. Unfortunately, this makes any further analysis of QS ranking results cumbersome and time-consuming.

Who is responsible for addressing GWR challenges? In their assessment of the key stakeholders linked to improving GWR, Nankervis et al. (2019, p. 35) suggest that: "graduate work-readiness encompasses individuals' characteristics, attributes and skills, which are then collectively transformed into the human and social capital which meet the productivity demands of employers, and more broadly, the social and economic aspirations of their governments and societies." From their analysis of stakeholder interests they suggest that stakeholder salience is important, that is, the ability to enact changes to and affect outcomes of GWR. On this basis they argue that there are three key stakeholder groups: employers as the source of graduate demand; government as the source of funding and policy responsibility for education, labor market matching and human capital development; and tertiary institutions, as the responsible authority for educating graduates. While there are other stakeholders, notably students and their families, Nankervis et al. (2019) argue that salience, or the power to influence processes and outcomes in the short term, rests with the three identified stakeholders. The stakeholder groupings are not homogeneous in their views, interests, or responsibilities. For example, employers include a range of businesses, sectors, ownership, and exposure to graduates.

What are some of the innovative regional schemes in place to address GWR? In their review of GWR programs in nine Asia-Pacific economies, Dhakal et al. (2019c) highlighted the national programs that are in place to support skills development and improve GWR. In Vietnam there is a national fund for employment to support initiatives in the VET and university sector to develop curriculum and improve training to support employability. In India there is the Indian Technical Education Quality Improvement Project, a joint venture between the national government and the World Bank, to improve the quality of education and training in engineering institutes. Malaysia has a national graduate employment enhancement program to improve skill and competencies and provide work experience. The Singapore SkillsFuture Program enables graduates from polytechnics to join work placement programs with participating employers.

Universities are under pressure competitively, and demonstrating their ability to fill skill gaps in the economy is one way to demonstrate their relevance to potential students and funding bodies. Governments are assessing output (graduates; employment) rather than inputs (enrollments) for funding purposes; and there are assessment, degree accreditation and rating agencies, national and international, that incorporate graduate employability and graduate skills into their rankings of programs, degrees, faculties, and universities (Tran, 2015).

Across the region the challenges of GWR have been recognized and are being addressed. In Australia universities are building employability criteria into their courses and programs, reporting employability metrics and developing closer relationships (advisory, placements, traineeships) with industry and successful alumni. The QS World University Rankings (2019), cited above, is an example of the application of graduate skill and employment attributes to rate programs and universities. In a competitive national and international environment, employability is used to enhance reputation and standing, and to attract students into programs (Burgess et al., 2018).

4.2 Technical, Vocational Education, and Training

The technical, vocational education, and training (TVET) sector also plays a major role in regional skills development and training primarily in trade-based skills and qualifications. However, the outputs for these efforts are often not as would be hoped:

> Developing Asia and the Pacific provides a rich array of technical and vocational education and training (TVET) experiences, but too often these have recorded only modest results. On the whole, training and skills development systems in developing member countries are not fully equipped to produce graduates with competencies that are aligned to the needs of the labor market. Still, there is much to be learned from past and current TVET programs as countries work to make improvements in this important subsector. (ADB, n.d., https://www.adb.org/what-we-do/sectors/education/overview/tvet)

The Asian Development Bank (ADB) has sponsored several country-based studies on the role of TVET in the region and the most recent includes a compilation of articles from across the Asia-Pacific region titled: *Anticipating and Preparing for Emerging Skills and Jobs: Key Issues, Concerns and Prospects* (Panth and Maclean, 2020). The compilation places responses to the 4IR as central to the brief of education, not only in educating the youth but in training for new skills and reskilling and upskilling existing workforces. The editors also refer to a trend in the last two decades referred to as the "vocationization" of secondary education whereby preparedness for vocational work and employment is increasingly becoming part of secondary education (Panth and Maclean, 2020).

In terms of TVET across the region some of the key issues for countries include: in the Philippines a focus on skills mismatches to ensure job-ready graduates (Dernbach, 2020); industry partnerships as a means of creating a responsive TVET in New Zealand (Williams, 2020); targeting priority sectors (IT-ITeS sector) in India (Bhattacharjee and Chakrabarti, 2015; Madan, 2020); and TVET system improvements such as TVET teacher training to improve TVET in China (Maruyama, 2020). Other examples include the garment industry in Bangladesh. The ADB is working with the Bangladeshi government by partnering with the booming garments industry and other high priority areas to assist in training almost 400,000 young people across Bangladesh through the ADB-supported Skills for Employment Investment Program (SEIP). It is anticipated that 800,000 people will be trained by 2024 (ADB, n.d., https://www.adb.org/news/videos/new-skills-better-future-bangladesh).

A recent report from the ADB (2021) titled *Reaping the Benefits of Industry 4.0 through Skills Development in High-Growth Industries in Southeast Asia* has identified key industries for four nations in the South-East Asia region that are summarized in Table 3.4. The aim of the report is to "provide policy makers with research and evidence-based solutions for skills and talent development to strengthen the countries' readiness for a transition to 4IR" (ADB, 2021, p. vi). The report acknowledges that the 4IR will result in job losses through automation; however, new jobs will also emerge and growth and employment have been identified for certain industries in, for example, Cambodia, Indonesia, Philippines, and Vietnam (see Table 3.4). The key to improving prosperity through these industries will be investment in skills and training and closer partnerships between the private and public sectors.

The report made the following five key recommendations: develop 4IR transformation road maps for key sectors; develop industry-led TVET programs targeting skills for 4IR; upgrade training delivery through 4IR technology in classrooms and training facilities; develop flexible and modular skills certification programs; and formulate

Table 3.4 Industries identified for growth, employment through Industry 4.0, and 4IR

Country	Industry 1	Industry 2	% of employers who believe impact of 4IR technologies may be greater than 25% in next 5 years
Cambodia	Tourism	Garments	19% for tourism 12% for garments
Indonesia	Food & beverage manufacturing	Automotive manufacturing	52% for F&B manufacturing 76% for automotive manufacturing
Philippines	Information technology – business process outsourcing (IT–BPO)	Electronics	63% for IT-BPO 55% for electronics
Viet Nam	Agro-processing	Logistics	31% for agro-processing 41% for logistics

Source: Adapted from ADB (2021, p. xiv).

new approaches and measures to strengthen inclusion and social protection under 4IR (ADB, 2021, pp. xvi–xvii).

4.3 Overeducation

Overeducation and mismatch in the labor market occurs when there is an over-supply of qualified workers which outpaces the demand for those educated workers. Overeducation can have major implications for graduate wages/incomes, the mobility of graduates, and the productivity of nations. Leuven and Oosterbeek (2011) refer to this as "overschooling" and explore this phenomenon through economics literature in a US-based context. They look at overschooling in relation to a set of theories: human capital theory (wages are determined solely by education level and not related to jobs); career mobility theory (commencing a job lower than one's educated ability in anticipation of a higher probability of significant promotion opportunities); theory of job competition (highest-ranked workers are assigned to the highest-ranked job and crowding out of lower educated workers); signaling and screening theory (overinvestment in schooling); preferences (individuals acquire more education than is needed to maximize their overall lifetime income); and search and frictions (highly skilled workers transitioning in unskilled jobs while looking for better skilled jobs).

Xing et al. (2018) examined the increased rates of Chinese graduate unemployment and linked this to the Chinese expansion of higher education, which they refer to as the "supply shock of higher education expansion" (p. 181). They found that two major factors assisted in reducing graduate unemployment rates, given this higher education expansion. These were: to reduce the barriers to mobility for graduates and increase investments in local economies to create more opportunities for graduates. Wu and Wang (2018) investigated wage loss caused by overeducation (wage penalty), again in China, and take the perspective of what overeducation means in a developing nation. They refer to a common finding in the literature that "overeducated employees typically earn more than individuals employed in the same job that have the required level of education but less than individuals with the same level of education who are employed in a job that matches their education. Returns to overeducation are generally half to two-thirds of the returns to required education" (Wu and Wang, 2018, p. 207). The resulting mismatches, crowding out of less educated workers, and resulting skills underutilization of highly educated workers is a crucial issue for national human capital policies. In the case of China this is especially significant when the "human capital per head in China is only a fifth of the United States and a quarter of Canada" (Wu and Wang, 2018, p. 216). A very recent study by Zheng et al. (2021) also firmly places its focus within the context of an ever-expanding higher education sector in China. They refer to an estimate of an expansion over the next two decades to 2040, as being ten times what it is today. Their novel study found that approximately half of the online job seekers in China are overeducated by about two years or more, commensurate with a 5 percent wage penalty; however, STEM and business graduates from high-ranking universities were less likely to be overeducated and were more likely to enjoy a wage premium (Zheng et al., 2021, p. 1).

5. Strategic Responses to Generating Work-Ready Graduates across the Region

> We live in a rapidly changing world with diverse demands and challenges. Governments are increasingly looking to universities to produce human resources with the right kind of capacities, skills and knowledge to meet 21st century needs. They also call on universities to facilitate the shift to knowledge-based economy and high-technology through effective linkages between research and industry to ensure that their countries have a competitive edge in the global market. (UNESCO, 2012, preface)

Universities and the higher education sector in general play a crucial role in not only generating research-informed innovation and stimulation within economies but also supplying these economies with the human capital to drive the necessary shift to high-technology knowledge economies. A key challenge for higher education and TVET lies in being able to produce work-ready graduates that have the necessary knowledge, skills, and competencies to ensure this economic shift has momentum. These challenges are being played out against a backdrop of increasing enrollments in higher education and growing unemployment rates for these graduates. This section will explore national approaches to improving graduate employability and will draw upon examples of tertiary education responses towards tackling issues related to graduate employability.

As mentioned above in section 3, the *APEC Education Strategy 2016–2030* has three objectives, the third being employability. Under this objective are three associated actions: (1) promotion of collaboration between government, higher education and TVET institutions, business and education and training stakeholders; (2) development of twenty-first-century competencies for work and entrepreneurship; and (3) smoothing the transition from education to work (APEC, 2017a). The APEC Education Strategy shows that there is regional attention being paid to employability with the impetus being the growth in higher education enrollments and increasing rates of youth unemployment. This is set against a backdrop of increasing pressure on tertiary education institutions to supply regional human capital needs to ensure economic growth and to keep up with rapid technological change.

In the *Graduate Employability in Asia* report (UNESCO, 2012), UNESCO has also identified graduate employability as an issue for the region. The report was the result of a coordinated study of university graduates from three selected Asian countries—Indonesia, Malaysia, and the Philippines—with funding from Japanese Funds-in-Trust and UNESCO, Jakarta. Two of the case studies in the report are Malaysian based (the second Malaysian case study looked specifically at ICT graduates). The focus was first degree undergraduates who were 0–12 months out from graduation and the report analyzed their respective employability. Employability in this case of this report included:

- Communication skills
- Logical, analytical, and problem-solving skills
- Personality, confidence, and integrity
- Flexibility and adaptability
- Innovation and creativity
- Team spirit (see Nankervis et al., 2019, and Prikshat et al., 2019 for more detailed competencies/typologies/models of graduate employability and work readiness).

These attributes and competencies need to be contextualized within individual characteristics, personal circumstances, and external factors including macro trends, labor market conditions, and associated recruitment factors. As such, many factors are in play and key stakeholders include tertiary education institutions, labor market policymakers, students, employers, and sector bodies.

As discussed in the previous section, oversupply and unemployment rates remain an issue and can be exacerbated by graduate job preferences for working in private versus public sectors. The report findings point to inconsistent/disparate perspectives from key stakeholders. "Graduates generally believed their education and skills were sufficient. The universities considered their students to be well prepared for the transition to the workplace. Unfortunately, the employers concluded that new graduates lacked vital skills for employment, citing unrealistic expectations and demands for higher salaries as examples" (UNESCO, 2012, p. 3).

Employers are not only in search of high grades for prospective employees' academic studies but also look for the "++ factors." These factors are related to attitudes and qualities including motivation and many of the employability factors listed above. Entrepreneurship, work-based placements, and internships were identified as ways to increase employability.

As mentioned earlier, the study by Dhakal and colleagues concerning the challenge for GWR includes a comparative analysis across nine Asia-Pacific nations and Mauritius (Dhakal et al., 2019c). A key analytical technique employed a comparison of the Human Development Index (HDI) and the Human Capital Index (HCI) between the countries. Not surprisingly, they found a large disparity between the countries with India, Indonesia, and Vietnam having low rates for both indicators and developed countries like Singapore and Australia having high rankings. The countries with the widest gaps between the two indices were Indonesia, Vietnam, and Thailand. The recommendation for these countries is more investment in human capital development through educational policies and practices (Dhakal et al., 2019c). They conclude: "addressing the wicked challenge of GWR is likely to be much more effective with concerted policy emphasis on stakeholder engagement than without it" (Dhakal et al., 2019c, p. 251). (See also Dhakal et al., 2019c, pp. 249–250, for snapshots of innovative GWR initiatives across the region covered by this sample of Asia-Pacific nations.)

6. CONCLUSION

We conclude this chapter with a summation of the challenges and opportunities for higher education across the region in meeting the labor market imperatives for technology-driven knowledge economies of the future. As Warner (2011, p. 384) points out, the "sheer variation of geography, population, economies, [and] labour markets" results in uneven impacts of globalization across the Asia-Pacific economies. Nonetheless, we have drawn upon data, research, and position papers/reports from transnational, regional, and global financial institutions to paint a picture of employment and labor markets that reflects the diversity of the region and synthesizes the labor market imperatives and challenges the region is experiencing and is likely to experience over the next decade. We have examined the diversity of the region's economies, demographics, and labor market and addressed the mega trends impacting the region and strategic educational responses to this. We also explored the relationship between higher education and the labor market and the associated issues of graduate work readiness, employment, and unemployment and employability.

Societies across the globe are changing rapidly and profoundly due to a complex interplay of mega trends. This combines with specific Asia-Pacific regional demographics, diverse levels of economic development, and structural pressures to create a highly complex world to navigate in striving for sustainable economic development. The challenges of rapid rates of globalization and the almost sonic speed of technological developments, advances, innovations, and broad applications, need to be addressed head on through quality and responsive higher education. In an "increasingly volatile, uncertain, complex and ambiguous world, education can make the difference as to whether people embrace the challenges they are confronted with or whether they are defeated by them" (OECD, 2018, p. 3). According to UNESCO, the contributions of higher education to economic development are undeniable and play out in three ways: "(i) producing and accumulating human capital; (ii) generating, disseminating, and applying knowledge; and (iii) innovating and inventing new information and technology" (UNESCO, 2012, p. 1).

The accelerating shift to high-technology industries and an information technology economy requires sustained human resource development and training. Therefore, an appropriate higher education system is critical for preparing a competent workforce. "A better educated population is more innovative, flexible and able to adapt to structural changes in the economy as its skills can be more readily transferred across sectors" (APEC, 2017a, p. 1). The *APEC Education Strategy 2016–2030* and associated initiatives go some way to addressing many of these issues across the Asia-Pacific region. For graduates there are transitional labor market challenges and another important challenge identified in the GWR literature is that of skill mismatch. Time will tell if these strategies and initiatives along with other complementary policy interventions within countries and across the region lead to real impacts on employment and labor markets. Notwithstanding this, higher education is a major stakeholder in the region for developing human capital to drive and sustain a region riding a tsunami of mega trends.

During the writing of this chapter, the world was experiencing the COVID-19 pandemic with vaccinations being rolled out in many nations and not others, and second and third waves continue to challenge national efforts to contain the pandemic. The COVID-19 pandemic is having massive impacts on societies, economies, global supply chains, global mobility, and humanity in general. Higher education is not immune and has been disrupted, with many of its traditional foundations challenged in ways that could not have been foreseen. What will higher education look like post pandemic?

The ILO and Asian Development Bank (2020) have highlighted the impact that the COVID-19 pandemic is having on youth employment in Asia and the Pacific:

> Young people's employment prospects in Asia and the Pacific are severely challenged as a result of the COVID-19 pandemic. Youth will be hit harder than adults in the immediate crisis and also will bear higher longer-term economic and social costs. Before the pandemic, young people were already facing challenges in the labour market. These are worsened by the COVID-19 crisis, and its multiple effects threaten to create a "lockdown generation" that will feel the weight of this crisis for a long time. (ILO and ADB, 2020, p. vi)

The four hardest-hit sectors in the region (wholesale and retail; manufacturing, rental, and business services; and accommodation and food services) employ almost half of the region's youth and it was estimated that youth unemployment across 13 nations would double by the end of 2020. Solutions to address this include wage subsidies, employment programs, and minimizing educational disruption strategies. Particular concern is for those youth with pre-existing vulnerabilities. Park and Inocencio (2020) pick up on this last point, highlighting the effects that will be felt by those already experiencing economic vulnerabilities through the creation of more polarized wage inequities. They also see the combination of the impacts of COVID-19 and the adoption of technologies as exacerbating these inequities through worker displacement, shorter work hours, and subsequent losses of income. These estimates and predictions provide the region with some unprecedented challenges and may set recent progress back some years. Only when the world emerges from this pandemic will we be able to assess the impact it has had on the adoption of 4IR data-driven technologies in businesses, sectors, economies, and societies.

On a brighter note, the ADB (2021) predicts that those industries and companies that employed 4IR digital technologies during the COVID-19 pandemic in 2020 are more likely to recover faster than those that did not, ensuring greater economic resilience and sustainability. The report recommends strategies to accelerate digital capabilities and transformations through the strengthening of enhanced skills and training using online learning and accompanying skills based "digital platforms, education technology (EdTech), and simulation based learning" (ADB, 2021, p. vii), along with stronger partnerships between the private and public sectors.

References

APEC (2017a). *APEC Education Strategy 2016–2030.* http://mddb.apec.org/Documents/2017/HRDWG/EDNET/17_hrdwg_ednet_003.pdf

APEC (2017b). *2017 APEC Economic Policy Report: Structural Reform and Human Capital Development.* APEC Economic Committee (EC), November, APEC#216-EC-01.2. https://www.apec.org/Publications/2017/11/2017-APEC-Economic-Policy-Report

APEC (2017c). *Framework on Human Resources Development in the Digital Age.* https://www.apec.org/Groups/SOM-Steering-Committee-on-Economic-and-Technical-Cooperation/Working-Groups/Human-Resources-Development/Framework

APEC (2019). *Human Resources Development.* https://www.apec.org/Groups/SOM-Steering-Committee-on-Economic-and-Technical-Cooperation/Working-Groups/Human-Resources-Development

Asian Development Bank (2011). *Higher Education Across Asia: An Overview of Issues and Strategies.* https://www.adb.org/sites/default/files/publication/29407/higher-education-across-asia.pdf

Asian Development Bank (2018). *Key Indicators for Asia and the Pacific 2018.* Manila: ADB.

Asian Development Bank (2021). *Reaping the Benefits of Industry 4.0 through Skills Development in High-Growth Industries in Southeast Asia: Insights from Cambodia, Indonesia, the Philippines, and Viet Nam.* https://www.adb.org/publications/benefits-industry-skills-development-southeast-asia

Bekhradnia, B. and Beech, D. (2017). *Demand for Higher Education to 2030.* Report 105. London: Higher Education Policy Institute.

Bhattacharjee, S. and Chakrabarti, D. (2015). "Investigating India's competitive edge in the IT-ITeS sector." *IIMB Management Review,* 27/1, 19–34. https://doi.org/10.1016/j.iimb.2015.01.003

Burgess, J., Cameron, R., Dhakal, S., and Brown, K. (2018). "Introduction: Applicant work-readiness and graduate employability challenges in the Asia Pacific." In R. Cameron, S. Dhakal, and J. Burgess (eds.), *Transitions from Education to Work: Workforce Ready Challenges in the Asia Pacific.* Abingdon: Routledge, 3–15.

Caballero, C. and Walker, A. (2010). "Work readiness in graduate recruitment and selection: A review of current assessment methods." *Journal of Teaching and Learning for Graduate Employability,* 1/1, 13–25.

Dernbach, A. (2020). "Philippine experience in dual training system." In B. Panth and R. Maclean (eds.), *Anticipating and Preparing for Emerging Skills and Jobs: Key Issues, Concerns and Prospects.* Singapore: Springer, 101–108.

Dhakal, S., Prikshat, V., Burgess, J., and Nankervis, A. (2019). "Conclusion: The future for transition from graduation to work in the Asia Pacific and beyond." In S. Dhakal, V. Prikshat, A. Nankervis, and J. Burgess (eds.), *The Transition from Graduation to Work: Challenges and Strategies in the Twenty-First Century Asia Pacific and Beyond.* Singapore: Springer, 255–263.

Dhakal, S., Prikshat, V., Nankervis, A., and Burgess, J. (2019). "An introduction to the transition from graduation to work: Challenges and strategies in the Asia Pacific and beyond." In S. Dhakal, V. Prikshat, A. Nankervis, and J. Burgess (eds.), *The Transition from Graduation to Work: Challenges and Strategies in the Twenty-First Century Asia Pacific and Beyond.* Singapore: Springer, 3–14.

Dhakal, S., Prikshat, V., Nankervis, A., and Burgess, J. (2019). "Challenges and strategies of transition from graduation to work in the post-2020 Asia Pacific and beyond: A comparative analysis of nine countries." In S. Dhakal, V. Prikshat, A. Nankervis, and J. Burgess (eds.), *The Transition from Graduation to Work: Challenges and Strategies in the Twenty-First Century Asia Pacific and Beyond*. Singapore: Springer, 241–254.

ILO (2013). *Global Employment Trends for Youth 2013: A Generation at Risk*. Geneva: ILO.

ILO (2018). *Asia-Pacific Employment and Social Outlook 2018: Advancing Decent Work for Sustainable Development*. Geneva: ILO. https://www.ilo.org/asia/publications/labour-markets/WCMS_574709/lang--en/index.htm

ILO (2019a). *Labour Market Access: A Persistent Challenge for Youth around the World*. Geneva: ILO.

ILO (2019b). *From School to Work: An Analysis of Youth Labour Market Transitions*. Geneva: ILO.

ILO (2019c). *Preparing for the Future of Work: National Policy Responses in ASEAN+6*. Geneva: ILO. http://www.ilo.int/wcmsp5/groups/public/---asia/---ro-bangkok/---sro-bangkok/documents/publication/wcms_717736.pdf

ILO (2019d). *Skills and the Future of Work*. Geneva: ILO. https://www.ilo.org/asia/publications/skills-fow/lang--en/index.htm

ILO and ADB (2020). *Tackling the COVID-19 Youth Employment Crisis in Asia and the Pacific*. Bangkok and Manila: International Labour Organization and Asian Development Bank. https://www.adb.org/sites/default/files/publication/626046/covid-19-youth-employment-crisis-asia-pacific.pdf

IMF (2019). *World Economic Outlook*. Washington, DC: International Monetary Fund.

Kim, J. and Park, C.-Y. (2020). *Education, Skill Training, and Lifelong Learning in the Era of Technological Revolution*. ADB Economic Working Papers Series No. 606. https://www.adb.org/sites/default/files/publication/559616/ewp-606-education-skill-training.pdf

Leuven, E. and Oosterbeek, H. (2011). "Overeducation and mismatch in the labor market." In E. Hanushek, S. Machin, and L. Woessmann (eds.), *Handbook of the Economics of Education*, Volume 4. Amsterdam: North Holland, 283–326

Madan, A. (2020). "Gram Tarang: Skills development for priority sectors in India." In B. Panth and R. Maclean (eds.), *Anticipating and Preparing for Emerging Skills and Jobs: Key Issues, Concerns and Prospects*. Singapore: Springer, 125–132.

Maruyama A. (2020). "TVET system reform and development in the PRC." In B. Panth and R. Maclean (eds.), *Anticipating and Preparing for Emerging Skills and Jobs: Key Issues, Concerns and Prospects*. Singapore: Springer, 143–152.

Montague, A. (2013). "Review of Australian higher education: an Australian policy perspective." *Policy Futures in Education*, 11/6, 671–687.

Nankervis, A., Prikshat, V., and Dhakal, S. (2019). "Mapping stakeholders of graduate work-readiness (GWR)." In S. Dhakal, V. Prikshat, A. Nankervis, and J. Burgess (eds.), *The Transition from Graduation to Work: Challenges and Strategies in the Twenty-First Century Asia Pacific and Beyond*. Singapore: Springer, 31–42.

OECD (2018). *The Future of Education and Skills Education 2030: The Future We Want*. Paris: OECD. https://www.oecd.org/education/2030-project/contact/E2030_Position_Paper_(05.04.2018).pdf

OECD (2019a). *Education at a Glance: OECD Indicators*. Paris: OECD.

OECD (2019b). *Education at a Glance: Country Note, India. OECD Indicators*. Paris: OECD. https://www.oecd.org/education/education-at-a-glance/EAG2019_CN_IND.pdf

Oxford Economics and CISCO (2018). *Technology and the Future of ASEAN Jobs: The Impact of AI on Workers in ASEAN's Six Largest Economies.* https://www.cisco.com/c/dam/global/en_ sg/assets/csr/pdf/technology-and-the-future-of-asean-jobs.pdf

Panth, B. and Maclean R. (2020). "Introductory overview: Anticipating and preparing for emerging skills and jobs: Issues, concerns, and prospects." In B. Panth and R. Maclean (eds.), *Anticipating and Preparing for Emerging Skills and Jobs: Key Issues, Concerns and Prospects.* Singapore: Springer, 1–10.

Park, C.-Y. and Inocencio, A. M. (2020). *COVID-19, Technology and Polarizing Jobs.* Asian Development Bank Briefs No. 147. https://www.adb.org/sites/default/files/publication/ 623036/covid-19-technology-polarizing-jobs.pdf

Prikshat, V., Nankervis, A., Burgess, J. and Dhakal, S. (2019). "Conceptualising graduate work-readiness: Theories, concepts and implications for practice and research." In S. Dhakal, V. Prikshat, A. Nankervis, and J. Burgess (eds.), *The Transition from Graduation to Work: Challenges and Strategies in the Twenty-First Century Asia Pacific and Beyond.* Singapore: Springer, 15–30.

QS World University Rankings 2019 (2019). https://www.topuniversities.com/university-rankings/world-university-rankings/2019

Rothwell, A. and Rothwell, F. (2017). "Graduate employability: A critical oversight." In M. Tomlinson and L. Holmes (eds.), *Graduate Employability in Context: Theory, Research and Debate.* London: Palgrave Macmillan, 41–64.

Schmid, G. (1995). Economic and Industrial Democracy, 16/3, 429–456. In Tay, S. S. C. and Tijaja, J. P. (eds.) (2017). *Global Megatrends: Implications for the ASEAN Economic Community.* Jakarta: ASEAN Secretariat.

Tran, T. T (2015). "Enhancing graduate employability and the need for university enterprise collaboration." *Journal of Teaching and Learning for Graduate Employability,* 7/1, 58–71.

UNESCO (2012). *Graduate Employability in Asia.* Bangkok: UNESCO Bangkok. https:// unesdoc.unesco.org/ark:/48223/pf0000215706

UNESCO (2014). *Higher Education in Asia: Expanding Out, Expanding Up.* Montreal: UNESCO.

United Nations (2010). *ESCAP Regional Overview: Youth in Asia and the Pacific.* New York: United Nations.

United Nations, Economic and Social Commission for Asia and the Pacific (ESCAP) (2018). *ESCAP Population Data Sheet 2018.* New York: United Nations.

United Nations, Economic and Social Commission for Asia and the Pacific (ESCAP) (2019). *Asia and the Pacific SDG Progress Report 2019.* New York: United Nations. https://www. unescap.org/publications/asia-and-pacific-sdg-progress-report-2019

Warner, M. (2011). "Globalization, labour markets and human resources in Asia-Pacific economies: An overview." *The International Journal of Human Resource Management,* 13/3, 384–398.

Williams, J. (2020). "Industry-led training and apprenticeships: The New Zealand model." In B. Panth and R. Maclean (eds.), *Anticipating and Preparing for Emerging Skills and Jobs: Key Issues, Concerns and Prospects.* Singapore: Springer, 117–124.

World Bank (2012). *Putting Higher Education to Work: Skills and Research for Growth in East Asia.* World Bank East Asia and Pacific Regional Report. Washington, DC: WorldBank.http://siteresources.worldbank.org/EASTASIAPACIFICEXT/Resources/226300-1279680449418/7267211-1318449387306/EAP_higher_education_fullreport.pdf

World Bank (2019). *The World Development Report 2019: The Changing Nature of Work*. Washington, DC: World Bank.

World Economic Forum (2016). *The Human Capital Report 2016*. Geneva: WEF.

World Economic Forum (2020). *Jobs of Tomorrow: Mapping Opportunity in the New Economy*. Geneva: WEF.

Wu, N. and Wang, Q. (2018). "Wage penalty of overeducation: New micro-evidence from China." *China Economic Review*, 50, 206–217.

Xing, C., Yang, P., and Li, Z. (2018). "The medium-run effect of China's higher education expansion on the unemployment of college graduates." *China Economic Review*, 51, 181–193.

Zheng, Y., Zhang, X., and Zhu, Y. (2021). "Overeducation, major mismatch, and return to higher education tiers: Evidence from novel data source of a major online recruitment platform in China." *China Economic Review*, 66, 101584.

CHAPTER 4

···

PRODUCTIVE WORKERS OR BETTER CITIZENS?

···

ARNOUD DE MEYER

1. INTRODUCTION

WHY do countries invest in higher education? Is it to produce a workforce of well-educated and highly skilled employees and professionals that can serve the economy? Or do they have other objectives such as building a national identity and creating the social capital that any well-functioning society needs? It is probably both and even more than that. But as the title of this chapter provocatively suggests, there may be a trade-off or even a contradiction between some of these objectives.

To answer this question, I will first analyze four reasons why Asian governments have significantly invested in higher education over the last thirty years. Higher education grooms teachers and professionals needed in an ever more sophisticated economy and society. It also responds to the variegated expectations of young citizens and supports innovation in the economy. It may also help in building the nation. And, more recently, higher education has become a significant contributor to continuing education in societies where we live longer and will likely work longer.

Are there contradictions or conflicts between these objectives? Do, for example, the preferences of young citizens match or diverge from the demands of the economy and society? Will these preferences align with building the nation? After providing my analysis in the second section on the potential contradictions and complementarities between these objectives, I will formulate in the third section, based on a few simplified cases, some policy tools to overcome or at least accommodate the potential contradictions and reinforce the complementarities.

There is of course an important caveat. Higher education is only one component of a country's schooling system and it is normally well integrated within the whole education system. The other components such as pre-schooling, primary and secondary education, technical education, skills education, etc. contribute as well and sometimes even more to some of the objectives that I describe here for higher education. The focus of this chapter is on the specific contributions made by higher education and the trade-offs to be handled.

2. The Role of Higher Education in Asia?

What is the specific role of higher education in Asian societies? In a 2011 report on higher education in Asia, the Asian Development Bank posits that higher education contributes to national development in three principal ways (Asian Development Bank, 2011). First, it prepares the primary and secondary teachers, who shape the dimensions and quality of the overall education system of a country. As such, higher education is a significant part of the overall education system and it helps in the creation of a virtuous cycle to improve the preparedness of future graduates to enter the labor market. Second, higher education institutions educate the high-level technical and administrative personnel needed in society, government, and business, including highly skilled workers and professionals. Third, universities may operate as incubators for innovation and creative thinking needed for an economically competitive society.

These three contributions are all somewhat market-driven: they see the system of higher education as a supplier of employees and a source of innovation to support the economic development of a country. There is indeed strong evidence that higher education is an effective tool to stimulate the development of a country's gross domestic product (GDP). According to a report published by the OECD in 2015, access to higher education and providing systems to enhance the mastery of sophisticated skills can boost GDP by an average of 28 percent per year in low-income countries and 16 percent per year in high-income countries for the next eighty years (Hanushek and Woessmann, 2015).

Beyond this market-driven objective, higher education has an important secondary role in responding to the variegated aspirations of a growing group of young citizens and providing them with opportunities for social mobility. Enrollment in higher education in Asia has increased significantly from the late 1980s onwards. Figure 4.1 shows the increase in tertiary school enrollment from 1990 to 2018 as a percentage of all eligible children, i.e., for those who have completed education at secondary level in a select group of countries. Since 1990, this percentage has grown in China from 3 percent to about 50 percent and in India from about 6 percent to 28 percent. The highest growth has been in South Korea where the percentage enrollment in tertiary education has grown from 36.5 percent to close to 95 percent. Considering that these countries have also seen a significant increase in their population over the same period, the absolute number of students in tertiary education has grown very rapidly.

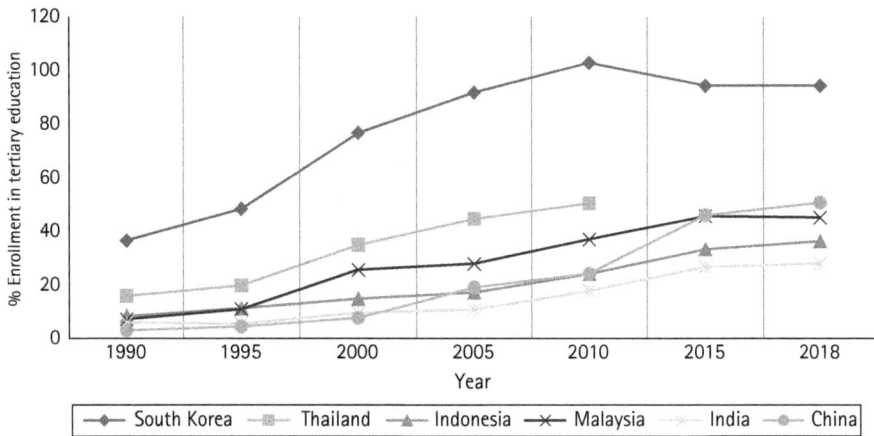

FIGURE 4.1 Percentage enrollment in tertiary education of eligible students for selected countries

Source: UNESCO (2012).

This significant increase has primarily been the result of growth in population, increasing cohort participation rates, and of the perceived importance of advanced education. Marginson (2011) noted that countries and cultures with a strong Confucian tradition and a Sinicized civilization attach great importance to education as a means of enhancing a person's worth and career. Education is a means for moving up the social ladder, for moving from a lower social stratum to a higher economic status, by helping citizens to better jobs (UNESCO, 2012). To accommodate this demand, new universities had to be created and existing ones had to expand, pools of new faculty members had to be developed by introducing graduate programs to prepare instructors, and private higher education providers have been given licenses to operate.

For many governments, such as those of Japan, South Korea, Singapore, and Australia, expanding postgraduate education (research Master's and PhD programs) had an important additional benefit. Universities and their postgraduate education programs were expected to grow into centers of research to yield positive economic returns to the country. Hence, expanding postgraduate education was viewed as a means of enhancing a country's competitiveness, and the need to respond to citizens' expectations and the economic development of a country.

Higher education traditionally has a third objective, which can be defined as building social capital for the country, or in a variant of it, "nation-building." In its description of the benefits of education, the 2008 report from the OECD on tertiary education mentions external (non-private) benefits of tertiary education or education externalities (Santiago et al., 2008). In an overview of the literature, McMahon (2004) mentions that some of the more frequently cited non-economic externalities include more political stability and a higher involvement of citizens in political institutions, a positive impact on the environment, a faster diffusion of new technologies, reduced inequality, and positive health effects.

Some of these assertions require further research. Greater political stability as a consequence of investing in higher education may not apply under all types of regimes. And while higher education has contributed to social mobility, it may have led to greater economic inequality for those who did not benefit from higher education. Indeed the quantitative empirical evidence of such positive externalities for the society is limited. There are a few studies that can be used as a proxy and that support the role of higher education in engaging citizens and improving societies. For example, in the United States, those with a post-secondary education tend to give twice as much time to community services activities (NCES, 1995). Whereas in Ireland, Healy (2005) observed that tertiary graduates were seven times more likely to volunteer in the community than those with only secondary education. In the United Kingdom, Bynner and Egerton (2001) found that there is a positive link between tertiary education and participation in community affairs, political processes, egalitarian attitudes, parenting, and voluntary work. While empirical evidence for Asia is not yet widely available, a 2017 study by the Singapore Institute for Policy Studies (IPS) found that educational status is associated with diversity in social networks which, in turn, strengthens social capital, trust, national identity, and national pride (Chua et al., 2017).

A nation-building role through education, or the construction of a national identity, where people develop a strong sense of belonging to the nation and are willing to contribute to its development, is perhaps more prevalent and important in emerging countries or countries which were created relatively recently. There may be less of a need for it in a country like Japan, which has a strong and long-standing identity. But in younger countries such as Singapore, or countries which are a merger of different cultures, ethnicities, and languages, such as Indonesia, Malaysia, India, and to some extent, mainland China, there may be a more pronounced need for higher education to contribute to nation-building. In India, nation-building and in particular, the narrative around the shaping of India through the colonial and post-colonial struggle has been given top priority in education in general and tertiary education in particular. As another example, Malaysia's national philosophy of education states that:

> Education in Malaysia is an on-going effort towards further developing the potential of individuals in a holistic and integrated manner, so as to produce individuals who are intellectually, spiritually, emotionally and physically balanced and harmonious, based on a firm belief in and devotion to God. Such an effort is designed to produce Malaysian citizens who are knowledgeable and competent, who possess high moral standards, and who are responsible and capable of achieving high level of personal well-being as well as being able to contribute to the harmony and betterment of the family, the society and the nation at large. (KPM, 2020)

Malaysia has also attempted to promote multicultural citizenship (Saravanamuttu, 2019). Organic ethnic mixing at the universities proved insufficient, as there is a general tendency for ethnic groups to find their own comfort zones outside of campuses in places like monocultural restaurants, churches, mosques or temples. Therefore, there was a major top-down policy decision in the early 2000s to introduce an ethnic relations module or university course to promote cross-cultural learning. After some teething problems, a well-crafted compulsory module has been in use by all universities since 2006. Though some observers describe this effort to bridge ethnic differences at universities as "too little, too late," it does illustrate how higher education can be considered to be a policy tool to develop social capital. In a stronger critique, Saravanamuttu (2019) noted that while the course led to some ethnic mingling and social learning, the module had too many students to be effective and that it was hard to find competent lecturers. Ultimately, students were not interested in it and lecturers showed little passion.

Thus, one could summarize that until now the development of higher education in Asia has had three broad objectives: responding to the needs of the society for a highly skilled workforce, offering choices to an ever more sophisticated group of young citizens for pursuing their interests and careers, and developing social capital to build a nation.

Recently, a fourth role has arisen and that is shaping lifelong or continuing education. Institutes of higher education have always been providers of courses for continuing education, e.g., professional updates in medicine or engineering. As Frey and Osborne (2013) have argued, jobs have been partially automated and destroyed or redefined because of the influence of fast evolving digitalization. People now live longer and may have to remain longer in the workforce. They may switch jobs several times during their career, or switch careers altogether, and may need additional education. The new challenge posed by the growing demand for continuing education is well illustrated by the needs in mainland China alone. In January 2021, McKinsey published an extensive report on the need to reskill China (Manyika et al., 2021). The report posits that China needs to achieve three labor force transitions in the next decade: up to 220 million workers or 36 percent of the workforce may need to switch occupations; 516 billion hours or 87 days per worker will be displaced due to automation; and 330 million migrant workers are at risk of being automated. Taking into account these approximate figures, the report forewarns the sheer size of the task of reskilling through continuing education.

But with a few exceptions, such as in business schools, adult training and education was often seen in Asia as a marginal activity for institutes of higher learning and it was left to private initiative, the unions, or specialized government institutions. Asia's universities did not have an elaborate set of extension programs that provided degree and non-degree programs for adult learners, often providing small-scale evening and weekend programs, as is the case for many universities in the United States. There, these programs are often as large as the full-time undergraduate programs of the university. In the future, Asian universities may or may not develop equally large continuing education programs, but they have in my opinion a core role to play in designing the curricula and the organization of credentialing.

Therefore, universities throughout Asia are challenged to play a key role as anchors in the development of high-quality continuing education and lifelong learning. They may not be the providers of all this education, but they are challenged by policymakers to re-envision education, including higher education. Universities are not limited anymore to education for a typical age group of young adults between 17 and 28 years old, but they will have to develop standards and curricula for adult education that can guide the providers of such courses. Students will be moving in and out of universities over a longer time in their career and life. Institutions of higher learning will have to articulate and experiment with new models and approaches across a lifelong learning system.

It will be clear that the importance and relevance of these four different objectives will differ from one country to another. Indeed, in any analysis of higher education issues across Asia Pacific, one cannot generalize. The region includes the People's Republic of China and India, the two countries with the largest populations in the world, and other large developing countries like Indonesia or Vietnam, along with a few small ones like the Lao People's Democratic Republic or Mongolia. It includes some of the most affluent like Japan, the Republic of Korea, Brunei, the Republic of Singapore, Australia, and New Zealand, several middle-income countries that have the ambition to move up the ladder like Malaysia and Thailand, and some of the poorest economies in the world like Cambodia and Myanmar. It includes one of the fastest growing higher education systems in China and at least two that are already downsizing because of declining birth rates, i.e., Japan and the Republic of Korea. There are wide variations in the circumstances facing higher education in the region and important differences in the capacity of governments to respond to the challenges posed by the growth of higher education. Depending on their specific situation, countries will choose their own weighted combination of these four objectives and even add additional ones, idiosyncratic to their situation. And, as we have described elsewhere for Singapore, their choices will evolve over time (De Meyer and Ang, 2021).

3. POTENTIAL CONTRADICTIONS BETWEEN THE OBJECTIVES OF HIGHER EDUCATION

The provocative question raised by the title of this chapter is whether there may be a contradiction or trade-off between the goal of building a nation or educating "better citizens" and the goal of educating "productive workers." Obviously, this raises the question what is a "better citizen"? The answer will no doubt be situational and differ from one country to another and from one political regime to another. But for the purpose of this chapter, I define better citizens as citizens who have a stronger sense of national identity and are prepared to invest in nation-building. Or by extension of this trade-off, are there conflicts between the four goals described in the previous section? To explore this let us analyze a few examples.

3.1 Responding to Economic Imperatives versus Building a National Identity

Building an education system that develops the nation and strengthens the national identity may potentially be in conflict with educating middle and higher management, professionals and technical experts to operate in a global economy. For example, the development of a more international outlook for business or engineering students, which is required to compete in a global economy, may lead to lower loyalty toward national interests.

An interesting example of this was the development of the Global Schoolhouse initiative in Singapore. This was a project initiated by the Singapore government in the early 2000s to attract foreign institutions of higher education to set up subsidiaries in Singapore, with the intention of rapidly grooming a highly educated workforce for Singapore's fast developing knowledge economy. At that time, a significant number of young Singapore citizens were leaving the country to study overseas with many of them opting to stay abroad at the completion of their studies. This outflow and potential loss of local talent was negative to the economy and needed to be halted. Thus, offering more options for higher education through the creation of campuses of foreign institutions in Singapore was a way of discouraging young Singaporeans from going overseas to pursue their education.

The Global Schoolhouse initiative was also an interesting attempt to develop an economic strategy that mixed public and private supply and collaboration on education and research. Through the increase in the total number of students in Singapore, it was envisaged that the education sector could fuel economic growth. The then Minister for Trade and Industry, George Yeo, said in 2003 (Ng and Tan, 2010):

> This will be a growth market for us. If we can double or triple the number of international students in Singapore to 100,000 or 150,000, there will be all kinds of spin-offs for our economy. Our shops, restaurants and housing rental market will all benefit. More than that, these students when they return home will expand our international network.

It was believed that existing institutions would not be able to ramp up fast enough to produce the number of graduates needed, and that the local pool of talent was not big enough to cope with the knowledge-based needs of the industry. By attracting foreign students and faculty, they would be able to contribute to the human capital needed for the knowledge-based activities. For example, when INSEAD's Asia Campus was created in Singapore, the Economic Development Board expressed hope that graduates from its MBA program would stay on to work or create companies in Singapore.

But did this fit with the goals of nation-building? Fairly soon it appeared that there was tension between the intention to engineer a market economy for tertiary education and the ambition to contain higher education within the parameters defined by the government. Sidhu et al. (2016) have argued that the unintended consequence of the Global Schoolhouse initiative was to re-engineer the institution of citizenship, transforming it into a transient, self-sufficient, innovative, entrepreneurial identity, committed to self-betterment. But this market-driven objective created tensions within the Singapore society. Indeed, an unintended consequence of the rapid increases in foreign students was that they hoped if not expected to get jobs in Singapore. Thus, they started competing with Singaporean citizens in the labor market, and this competition became more intense during and after the global financial crisis of 2008.

Given these (and other) tensions, the government decided to adjust its plans. The original target of 150,000 full fee-paying students was never reached. In early 2020, there were less than 75,000 foreigners studying in Singapore, though this is still a significant number given the proportion of the total student population in Singapore. In order to allay the concerns of Singaporean citizens, the government decided to impose stricter quotas on foreign undergraduate students. As it regularly happens in Singapore when a program does not meet expectations, the concept of the Global Schoolhouse was quietly dropped after 2013. The goal of attracting overseas institutions to set up base in Singapore moved from having a volume target towards a quality target. By early 2020, several foreign institutions who originally signed up for the program ceased operations, though business schools like INSEAD, ESSEC, EDHEC, and Australian universities, like James Cook University and Curtin University, have stayed and developed new activities and thrive.

3.2 Catering for the Preferences of Young Citizens versus Responding to Economic Needs

Another source of potential tension is whether the aspirations of 18-year-old citizens are aligned with the economic needs of the country? Free choice in choosing education can lead to a paucity of graduates with a STEM background. The preferences of young citizens to pursue university studies may lead to an oversupply of university graduates and a shortage of skilled technicians, with undergraduate underemployment as a consequence. For example, the underemployment or even unemployment of a significant group of graduates in the Republic of Korea is well known. In 2019, the general press referred to jobless college graduates as Korea's "latest big export" (Yang and Kim, 2019). Lim and Lee (2019) recognized that graduate unemployment is a complex issue with various structural problems such as prolonged low economic growth; college graduates' selective job-seeking activities and their reluctance to lower expectations; and mandatory military service for young Korean men. But one of the main reasons is a mismatch between the supply of and demand for college graduates in the labor market, where the disciplines chosen by graduates do not match the needs of the economy. This is exacerbated by the increase in Korea's overall education level where, as we saw earlier (Figure 4.1), the percentage of enrollment in tertiary institutions for qualifying young people is close to 95 percent. Perhaps there are just too many graduates for what the country needs.

3.3 How Does One Groom Better Citizens?

What does it take to groom better citizens? Will this require a portfolio of courses on the country's issues, be it political or cultural? Will it require rewriting history books in a perspective that supports the national narrative as in India? And if so, will such education lead to a trade-off with deeper specializations in technical subjects that are needed for employment in industry or with economic agencies? Or will such courses develop a critical attitude that may be in conflict with the expectations of the current political leadership? During the turbulent protests in Hong Kong in 2019, some blamed the liberal studies curriculum in the high schools for the radicalization of Hong Kong's youth. Yet, that mandatory civics course had been a hallmark of the curriculum in Hong Kong for many years. The objective is to groom better citizens who are more engaged with society. These courses are an investment in social capital for the society but may conflict with the market orientation of higher education.

3.4 Grooming Young Citizens versus Retraining Mid-Career Professionals

This is another example of potential contradiction between the traditional role of a university and its investment in lifelong learning and continuing education. Elsewhere we pointed out three general challenges for the implementation of continuing education by institutions of higher learning (De Meyer and Ang, 2021).

First, universities in Asia (and elsewhere) do not know enough about andragogy, or how adults learn. There is insufficient knowledge about how adults acquire skills and knowledge, as opposed to how 20-year-old students learn and acquire skills and knowledge. The current pedagogical methods that were developed for young adults are not adapted to older learners. There are some interesting studies on adult learning (Jarvis and Griffin, 2003) that showed a negative correlation between aging and the ability to learn in a traditional way and the differences in crystallized and fluid intelligence between younger and older people. These studies inform us that in order to be successful in continuing education, education providers need to address multiple factors including the different methods of learning that are appropriate to the different ages and work experience, and the motivation of the older people to learn. Other implications of these studies are related to the admissions criteria especially on how to judge past work experience as a guide for admissions to adult programs instead of classical admission processes.

Second, how willing and prepared are the faculty of research-oriented universities to engage in adult learning? Universities in Asia offer a different mix of full-time tenure track faculty, practice and education track faculty, adjunct lecturers and facilitators. No doubt, practice faculty and adjunct lecturers are well placed to work with adult learners who are in the workforce and have a lot of experience. But, if and when continuing education becomes a core activity of the universities, the core tenure track faculty should be prepared to engage in it. In reviewing why some of the top graduate business schools like INSEAD, Harvard Business School, the Wharton Business School, or London Business School have been successful in adult learning, especially in the executive development programs, I observed that this is partially due to the commitment of their best research faculty to these programs. It is also encouraging to see that some top researchers have responded well to the call to create MOOCs (massive open online courses) with private providers such as Coursera and others.

Third, what kind of operating model do universities need to organize continuing education? Close and deep collaboration with employers is deemed essential. But to what extent should employers have a say over the design of the program curricula and credentialing? Universities may have to implement the credentialing of micro-credits and develop stackable courses. What would be the ideal model—a retail model for open enrollment programs or a business-to-business (B2B) model where the universities collaborate with large companies to educate their workforce? These questions will require a lot more research into the role of Asia's universities in continuing education.

Finally, universities that traditionally cater to young adults in their twenties have a role that goes beyond teaching disciplines. They offer a more complete student development by organizing a wide range of character-developing activities and often provide pastoral care. That would not be the necessary role of a university that targets mid-career adults who wish to attend courses simply to reorient themselves into new career tracks.

4. A Few Examples of Policy Choices

How have countries in Asia managed some of these contradictions? There is quite rich material provided by OECD and ADB, and I will just highlight here a few salient characteristics on how some of them have done so.

4.1 Japan: Reinventing the System

The first case is that of Japan, which has a very established and mature system of universities. A very specific feature of the system of higher education is that the

Constitution of Japan stipulates that every citizen shall be entitled to equal opportunities to receive education in accordance with concerned laws and according to his or her ability (MEXT, 2011). This seems to favor the choice of citizens to get an education according to their preferences and capabilities over other objectives. It also emphasizes social inclusivity. Therefore, more than 50 percent of Japanese high school graduates attend university and more than 70 percent pursue some form of higher education.

Japan's universities were initiated on a Western model, the original Von Humboldt University, with some adjustments to fit it with the Japanese context. One specific characteristic is that access to universities is determined by a national exam that is organized only once a year, and that determines to a large extent which university one can join. Access is almost exclusively based on academic merits.

Another characteristic is that until the 1990s, the labor market for good quality graduates was dominated by companies offering lifetime employment and organizing internal training programs for their employees. Companies did not value the difference between an undergraduate and a graduate degree. Graduate schools in Japan were underdeveloped and largely only for those students who wanted to pursue an academic or a research career. As companies organized continuing education and training internally, universities did not engage in it (Newby et al., 2009).

A third characteristic is the importance of private universities in education. The top research-based universities are largely government institutions, the exceptions being Waseda and Keio University. But close to 80 percent of students attend private universities, many of which prepare students for professional roles. There is thus, more than in many other countries, a natural division of tasks between the public and the private system. The top national universities and two private universities engage in research, and prepare the elite for government and business, thus supporting nation-building. The vast majority of private universities engage in preparing students for jobs in the economy. The potential contradiction between objectives for higher education is thus solved by a division of tasks between the public and the private education sector.

The economic stagnation of Japan following the asset price bubble of the early 1990s forced significant change. The OECD review of tertiary education in Japan (Newby et al., 2009) makes the point that the organization of the university sector and its relationship with the Ministry of Education (MEXT) had to respond to many significant changes. The authors mention that there is "a new political context marked by sustained public budgetary pressures and an anti-regulatory orientation, which, in combination, constrain the possibility of funding increases to tertiary education, while at the same time challenging the traditional role of the Ministry vis-à-vis higher education institutions" (Newby et al., 2009, p. 22). There is also "a new demographic context [i.e., declining birth rates], which poses a serious challenge to the continued viability of many private institutions, and challenges of efficiency within the public sector institutions" (Newby et al., 2009, p. 22). On top of that, there is "a new global context" including the commercial and diplomatic opportunity of "cross-border flows of students," "new/alternative providers (within a new, somewhat liberalized regulatory environment)," "the challenge of international competition in research so as to be internationally competitive with respect to the recruitment and retention of high-impact researchers, and to provide the basis ... for knowledge-based innovation ... [and] facing this competition within an environment pressured by international research rankings that expose domestic institutions to international benchmarking" (Newby et al., 2009, p. 22). Finally, there is a "new labour market context": the proportion of employees who are part-time or short-term workers has risen significantly. Therefore, "students and employers appear to be developing somewhat different expectations of higher education" which has to "provide employability skills and a stronger vocational orientation" (Newby et al., 2009, p. 22).

In order to have a university sector that could cope with this changing context, the Koizumi government created in 2004 what was described as a "big bang" in higher education. The main feature of this change was a change in governance, whereby national universities were corporatized and the roles of the president and the board of directors (with external representation) were strengthened. The aim was to make the universities more agile, more responsive to their environment, more innovative and entrepreneurial and more competitive. With more autonomy for universities, the relationship with MEXT had to change. The Ministry had to take more of a steering role and needed to develop a reliable system of quality control. Quality reviews cover, of course, every aspect of the running of the universities, but in the high-level list of checkpoints produced by MEXT (2011) two stand out in the context of this chapter. It expects universities to be clear about the goals that the university sets itself, and whether those goals are set with sufficient consideration for the expectations of the stakeholders, e.g., students, faculty, and the local environment in which the university operates. It also requires that there are sufficient full-time teachers assigned to the subjects that are deemed as priority areas for MEXT. In other words, the government has decentralized the management of the trade-offs between different objectives for the universities to the institutions themselves. MEXT expects that this exercise of decentralization and quality control will lead to a higher diversity among the institutions.

In 2017 the Japanese government introduced an additional policy reform aimed at improving the academic capacity, administrative efficiency, and social contributions of the national universities. Funding schemes were tied to organizational restructuring including the closing of departments with low enrollments. However, it appears that the institutions saw this series of reforms as another government directive, which interfered with their internal decision-making. The reform clearly sent mixed messages and contributed to a political struggle between the government and the universities.

Other changes that have taken place in view of the changing labor market for graduates in Japan are the growth of graduate schools and a slow but steady process of universities engaging in continuing education. The government also implemented a set of actions and accompanying funding to stimulate the internationalization of a selected group of universities.

4.2 Mainland China: Building Scale Rapidly through Central Governance

A second interesting example is that of mainland China. The current system of universities in China is relatively young. Many of the established universities can trace their origins back to the late nineteenth or early twentieth century. But the reality is that they had to be rebuilt from 1977 onwards, after the end of the Cultural Revolution, when there were less than 50,000 university students. Currently there are close to 3,000 universities with more than 20 million students enrolled. These numbers indicate the vast challenge of building the biggest system of higher education in the world, almost from scratch, in less than forty-five years.

The challenge for the system of universities faced by the Chinese authorities is

> the dilemma faced by many [rapidly evolving] countries of simultaneously seeking to expand the quantity of tertiary education, widen access and improve quality, within a tight fiscal constraint. But China faces this dilemma on an unprecedented scale in terms of student numbers and timeframes. China also has to meet particular challenges, on the one hand, arising from pressures to respond to rapidly rising student and parental aspirations for tertiary education as a means to upward social mobility, and on the other hand, reflecting the realities of absorptive limits and uneven price signals of labour markets in the rapidly transforming economy. (Gallagher et al., 2009, p. 6)

China has managed the development of its universities through comprehensive five-yearly planning processes at the national level. These plans translate into investment priorities for growth in capacity at the university level. But these centralized planning requirements regarding enrollment numbers and how universities are organized can sit at odds with the demands and social pressures at the local level. Gallagher et al. (2009) further point out that

> extensive decentralisation of administrative arrangements allows for gaps in provision, inequities in access, barriers to learning pathways, and worrying differences in the quality of learning experiences and outcomes. At the same time, various aspects of tertiary education are regulated centrally at a level of detail, and through a one-size-fits-all approach, that can reduce institutional flexibility, innovation and differentiation. Considerable scope exists for improving policy coherence and planning coordination and reducing regulatory prescriptiveness. (Gallagher et al., 2009, p. 8)

This tension between central planning based on the country's overall needs and the local social pressures has not been solved yet.

Another feature of how the central government attempts to steer the system of higher education is its focus on a relatively small group of universities that it wants to compete at the top international level. The 211 project (1995), the 985 project (1998), and the Double First-Class University Plan (2015) were all comprehensive plans to transform a limited group of elite Chinese universities and their individual faculty departments into world-class research institutions.

4.3 Singapore: Seeking Complementarities Rather Than Contradictions

A third example is that of Singapore, where the participation ratio for each generation of young adults has increased from 5 percent in the late 1980s to more than 40 percent today. Like China, Singapore has seen simultaneous growth in size and quality. The portfolio of the six Singapore universities is a relatively recent one. Before 1990, there was only one, mainly teaching-oriented, university. In thirty years, the country has added five new universities of which several have by today been recognized as high-quality institutions on a global level.

The three objectives in building the university system were nation-building, developing an appropriate workforce for an evolving economy, and providing diversity in tuition so that an ever more sophisticated group of young citizens could pursue their own interests and study according to their own rhythm (De Meyer and Ang, 2021). How was the complementarity between these objectives achieved?

First, it promoted a system of governance described as "autonomous" universities. As in Japan, the government corporatized universities and placed a lot more authority in the hands of the president and the board in the early 2000s. But to mitigate the risks entailed in this autonomy, there was a system of performance and policy contracts in place where MOE and the universities develop an understanding about what is expected from them. Several observers have mentioned that the system was implemented faster and perhaps more successfully than in Japan or Korea. Additionally, the system of yearly reporting and five-yearly quality control was notably an important factor in the successful development of the university system.

Second, there is a strong and evolving alignment between the management of the economic development of the country and the requirements imposed on universities. Over the last thirty years, Singapore's economy evolved from a production economy over a knowledge-based economy into an innovation-based economy. This evolution was translated in the creation and evolution of the incumbent and new universities, which received significant amount of financial resources for research and development.

Finally, since 2015 the government has launched a massive project on continuing education, under the name of SkillsFuture, which forced universities to reflect on their role in continuing education, not as a marginal source of revenues, but on how they can really help shape the conceptual framework for continuing education.

4.4 Thailand: The Need for Continuity

Another interesting example is Thailand, which has used higher education as a tool to help the country move to an industrialized economy. Its system of higher education has evolved in line with many of the other ASEAN countries as it graduates toward a middle-income economy. Quality of education at elite institutions in Thailand has been high and some observers have expressed the opinion that in principle its education system could evolve into a highly performing one. However, this hinges on the condition that the appropriate policy changes are implemented (Michael and Trines, 2018). The country currently faces several issues that have an impact on its universities and tertiary education in general. Political instability in the country over the last twenty years, ensuing economic sluggishness, and a very rapidly aging society have created new challenges for the university system.

In response to these challenges and trends, Thailand needs to accelerate the upskilling of its people. The country actually has a relatively low-skilled labor force compared to its neighbors in ASEAN, and because of the rapidly aging population faces a severe shortage of highly skilled labor and professionals. Therefore, it has invested heavily in improving and modernizing its education system and its universities in particular. One of the initiatives of previous governments were changes designed to internationalize the Thai education system, such as a relaxation of visa rules to attract more foreign teachers, the harmonization of credentialing with ASEAN partner countries, and an increase of English-language programs.

But reform has not been easy. Thailand has had no fewer than twenty different education ministers from 2001 to 2018. Despite relatively high government spending on education since the military takeover in 2014, the coup interrupted important education reforms and led to a change in priorities. Under the current government, for example, there is a higher emphasis on communicating the values promulgated by Prime Minister Prayuth Chan-ocha, such as "correctly understanding democracy with the monarchy as head of the state, discipline and respect for the law and elders." The 2020 street protests led by students might suggest that this effort has not led to its desired outcomes. This example shows that beyond policy proposals and initiatives there is a need for continuity in implementation.

4.5 India: A New "Statement of Intent"

India's new National Educational Policy 2020, announced at the end of July 2020, is an interesting statement of how the government wants to steer higher education in a new direction (Ministry of Human Resource Development, 2020). The government wants to readjust and revamp higher education to meet the need for a creative, multidisciplinary, and highly skilled workforce for employment. Its primary objective is to improve the quality of universities and colleges, and thus improve employability of the educated workforce, as well as to reduce overspecialization and early streaming of students. Its secondary objective is to reduce the fragmentation of higher education by transforming higher education institutions into large multidisciplinary universities and colleges with at least 3,000 students each. This would have the added benefit of creating vibrant communities of scholars and peers, breaking down silos and enabling students to become well-rounded across different disciplines. Another objective is to move toward

a holistic education with less rote learning, and an increased emphasis on communication, discussion, debate, and research, among others. Other objectives include focusing
on internationalization and promoting India as a global study destination; improving
teacher education; including professional education as an integral part of the overall
higher education; promoting high-quality research; and simplifying the regulatory regime to eliminate disjunction of regulatory efforts. A new regulatory authority will be
set up to regulate in a light, tight, and facilitative manner.

At this stage it is too early to evaluate how much will really change. But it appears that
in the trade-off between nation-building and responding to the needs for productive
citizens, the new policies favor the latter. This example illustrates well that the trade-offs
between different objectives, and how they are handled, may evolve over time.

5. Discussion

In the introduction I started with the question whether there is a trade-off between
grooming better citizens, or citizens that contribute to nation-building, and responding
to the market demands for graduates. Through some of the examples I tried to show
that the trade-offs are real and difficult to bridge. But it is possible to overcome them.
Reflecting on the examples I provided in the previous section, I formulate four major
policy tools that can help overcome the different trade-offs that I alluded to earlier in
this chapter.

First, and in my opinion, most important, the organization and consistent implementation of a good and appropriate governance system is essential. As was the case in
both Japan and Singapore, greater autonomy and ample independence for universities
to manage their institutions may lead to more agility in the institutions and to more diversity within the system at large. Better governance systems will lead to better managed
institutions that can respond flexibly to changing demands in the environment.
Institutions that can determine their own strategy will develop competitive behavior
and differentiate themselves from other institutions. Ultimately, such differentiation
will lead to more diversity and more choice for students.

The proposed simplification of India's regulatory framework points in the same direction. But the quality of implementation is essential. The tension that exists in China and
to some extent in Thailand between centralization and decentralized autonomy is far
from helpful in the implementation of a clear portfolio of objectives.

Second, the trade-offs are easy to overcome when there is sufficient diversity in the
system. Whether it is diversity by design, as in Singapore, or through autonomy, as in
Japan, or through the focus on top institutions as in both Japan and China, such diversity enables society to respond to different objectives through differentiation between
institutions. Of course, this diversity needs to be communicated by both the government and the institutions of higher learning to the general public and the students

in particular. Therefore, enhancing the quality and quantity of information provided to young applicants, thus influencing their choices, is needed.

Third, the trade-offs may be eased by increasing the cohort participation rate, i.e., have more young citizens attending higher education. With numbers come the means to increase diversity. And by having a higher cohort participation rate there is also an opportunity to promote social capital and nation-building activities through enhancing and managing co-curricular activities.

Finally, a clear alignment between different departments in government, stakeholders in society, and institutions of higher education is needed. The respective ministries of education have an important role in coordinating and steering. But it is the needs of society as a whole and the citizens that need to be reflected in the objectives for higher education. A "whole-of-government" approach is needed.

6. CONCLUSION

We started this chapter with the question whether there are contradictions between the different objectives of higher education in Asia. Can nation-building go hand in hand with responding to the rising needs for highly skilled workers in the economy? Will the dreams of young citizens about what they want to study match the needs of society? The answer is yes: there are trade-offs to be made and there are potential contradictions. But as we have shown in some of the short examples, one can manage these trade-offs quite well through good governance, the creation of diversity in the system, and a whole-of-government approach. We also observed that how these trade-offs are managed may evolve over time. Having a long-term vision on the required dynamics in the system of higher education is imperative to a holistic governmental approach to higher education investment that produces both productive workers and better citizens.

REFERENCES

Asian Development Bank (2011). *Higher Education across Asia: An Overview of Issues and Strategies*. Manila: ADB.

Bynner, J. and Egerton, M. (2001). *The Wider Benefits of Higher Education*. London: Institute of Education, University of London. https://dera.ioe.ac.uk//5993/, accessed April 16, 2020.

Chua, V., Tan, E. S., and Koh, G. (2017). *A Study on Social Capital in Singapore*. Singapore: Institute for Policy Studies. https://lkyspp.nus.edu.sg/docs/default-source/ips/study-of-social-capital-in-singapore.pdf, accessed November 10, 2020.

De Meyer, A. with Ang, J. (2021). *Building Excellence in Higher Education: Singapore's Experience*. London: Routledge.

Frey, C. B. and Osborne, M. A. (2013). *The Future of Employment: How Susceptible Are Jobs to Computerisation?* Oxford: Oxford Martin School, University of Oxford. https://www.

oxfordmartin.ox.ac.uk/downloads/academic/The_Future_of_Employment.pdf, accessed February 20, 2020.

Gallagher, M., Hasan, A., Canning, M., Newby, H., Saner-Yiu, L., and Whitman, I. (2009). *OECD Reviews of Tertiary Education: China*. Paris: OECD.

Hanushek, E. A. and Woessmann, L. (2015). *Universal Basic Skills: What Countries Stand to Gain*. Paris: OECD. http://www.oecd.org/education/universal-basic-skills-9789264234833-en.htm, accessed March 20, 2020.

Healy, T. J. (2005). *In Each Other's Shadow: What Has Been the Impact of Human and Social Capital on Life Satisfaction in Ireland?* Dublin: University College.

Jarvis, P. and Griffin, C. (2003). *Adult and Continuing Education*. London: Routledge.

Kementerian Pendidikan Malaysia (KPM) (2020). *National Education Philosophy*. https://www.moe.gov.my/en/dasarmenu/falsafah-pendidikan-kebangsaan, accessed April 17, 2020.

Lim, J. and Lee, Y. (2019). "Exit duration and unemployment determinants for Korean graduates." *Journal for Labour Market Research*, 53/5. https://doi.org/10.1186/s12651-019-0255-2, accessed April 16, 2020.

McMahon, W. W. (2004). "The social and external benefits of education." In G. Johnes and J. Johnes (eds.), *International Handbook on the Economics of Education*. Cheltenham, UK and Northampton, MA, USA: Edward Elgar Publishing, 211–259.

Manyika, J., Smit, S., and Woetzel, J. (2021). *Reskilling China: Transforming the World's Largest Workforce into Lifelong Learners*. McKinsey Global Institute. https://www.mckinsey.com/featured-insights/china/reskilling-china-transforming-the-worlds-largest-workforce-into-lifelong-learners, accessed January 15, 2021.

Marginson, S. (2011). "Higher education in East Asia and Singapore: Rise of the Confucian model." *Higher Education*, 61, 587–611.

Michael, R. and Trines, S. (2018). "Education in Thailand." *World Education News + Reviews*, February 6. https://wenr.wes.org/2018/02/education-in-thailand, accessed April 20, 2020.

Ministry of Education, Culture, Sports, Science and Technology (MEXT) (2011). *Higher Education in Japan*. Higher Education Bureau. https://www.mext.go.jp/en/policy/education/highered/title03/detail03/__icsFiles/afieldfile/2012/06/19/1302653_1.pdf, accessed April 20, 2020.

Ministry of Human Resource Development (2020). *National Education Policy 2020*. https://www.education.gov.in/sites/upload_files/mhrd/files/NEP_Final_English_0.pdf, accessed January 26, 2021.

NCES (National Centre for Education Statistics) (1995). *The Condition of Education 1995*. Washington, DC: US Department of Education.

Newby, H., Weko, T., Breneman, D., Johanneson, T., and Maasen, P. (2009). *OECD Reviews of Tertiary Education: Japan*. Paris: OECD.

Ng, P. T. and Tan, C. (2010). "The Singapore global schoolhouse: An analysis of the development of the tertiary education landscape in Singapore." *International Journal of Educational Management*, 4/3, 178–188.

Santiago, P., Tremblay, K., Basri, E., and Arnal, E. (2008). *Tertiary Education for the Knowledge Society, Volume 1: Special Features: Governance, Funding, Quality*. Paris: OECD.

Saravanamuttu, J. (2019). "Educational diversity, social learning and multicultural citizenship: The Malaysian experience." *Higher Education in Southeast Asia and Beyond*, 6, 15–17.

Sidhu, R., Ho, K. C., and Yeoh, B (2016). "The global schoolhouse: Governing Singapore's knowledge economy aspirations." In S. Marginson, S. Kaur, and E. Sawir (eds.), *Higher Education in the Asia-Pacific*. Berlin: Springer Verlag, 255–272.

UNESCO (2012). *Graduate Employability in Asia*. UNESCO Bangkok. https://unesdoc.unesco.org/ark:/48223/pf0000215706, accessed November 10, 2020.

Yang, H. and Kim, C. (2019). *South Korea's Latest Big Export*. https://www.reuters.com/article/us-southkorea-jobs-kmove-insight/south-koreas-latest-big-export-jobless-college-gradua tes-idUSKCN1SI0QE, accessed April 16, 2019.

PART III

WHO LEARNS?

CHAPTER 5

···

ACCESS

···

PROMPILAI BUASUWAN AND
ARISARA LEKSANSERN

IN recent decades, higher education as a whole throughout Asia-Pacific has grown rapidly, although at different stages of development (Collins and Buasuwan, 2017; Sánchez and Singh, 2018). This expansion of higher education throughout the region, to some extent reflects the global commitment to Article 26 of the Universal Declaration of Human Rights (UN General Assembly, 1948):

> Everyone has the right to education. Education shall be free, at least in the elementary and fundamental stages. Elementary education shall be compulsory. Technical and professional education shall be made generally available and higher education shall be equally accessible to all on the basis of merit.

When describing higher education expansion, the most popular terms are proposed by Trow (1970, 1973, 1999): "elite," "mass," and "universal" higher education. "Elite" here refers to higher education when a maximum of 15 percent are enrolled; "mass" refers to when a maximum of 50 percent are enrolled; and "universal" refers to when more than 50 percent are enrolled (UNESCO, 2014).

Across the world, the massification process has meant a greater number of students being enrolled in higher education. By 2030, 414.2 million people are expected to be enrolled in higher education, a rise of 314 percent compared to worldwide enrollment in 2000. Only five years later, in 2035, the number of students enrolled in higher education globally is expected to exceed 590 million (Calderon, 2018) and may reach the 50 percent threshold of "high-participation systems" (HPS) in the coming generations (Marginson, 2016).

Asia has the largest number of student enrollments in higher education (HE) in the world (Calderon, 2018). Table 5.1 shows that tertiary education is increasing throughout Asia, with the largest share in Eastern and South-Eastern Asia. However, despite rapid growth of higher education participation in Asia, levels of participation differ among countries both within regions and within countries, where individuals experience some form of

Table 5.1 Enrollment in tertiary education in Asia

Indicator	Enrollment in tertiary education, all programs, both sexes (number)					
Year	2013	2014	2015	2016	2017	2018
Country						
World	200,583,509	213,025,355	217,626,607	220,187,114	222,657,154	223,671,873
Asia (Western)	9,766,481	10,614,641	11,274,308	11,958,498	12,522,988	12,512,228
Asia (Central and Southern)	39,070,379	41,539,385	43,386,544	43,716,266	44,722,854	46,118,168
Asia (Central)	1,568,016	1,509,355	1,455,338	1,430,619	1,449,055	1,459,212
Asia (Southern)	37,502,363	40,030,030	41,931,206	42,285,647	43,273,799	44,658,956
Asia (Eastern and South-eastern)	59,269,010	67,864,876	69,712,745	70,540,881	70,831,387	70,457,831
Asia (Eastern)	42,391,187	50,193,867	51,555,192	51,984,456	52,145,643	51,771,665
Asia (South-eastern)	16,877,823	17,671,008	18,157,554	18,556,425	18,685,744	18,686,166

Source: http://data.uis.unesco.org.

inclusion or exclusion. Although access to higher education is considered a key compo-nent of any right-based conception, the expansion of availability of higher education in the region has yet to offer equal access to every individual.

Although there is an explicit link between higher education and economic growth and that private returns to tertiary education are the highest among all educational levels (Sánchez and Singh, 2018), making higher education available to all does require political will and is accompanied by massive costs. The HE expansion seen in many countries in Asia-Pacific has predominantly been driven by human capital as it plays an important role in national economic competition. Nwadiani (2012, p. 17) opined that "the tendency to relate educational provisions to national development arose from the popularization of education as an unexplained residual in national cum economic de-velopment equations." However, to ensure national growth that is inclusive, there is a need to examine how increases in enrollment and completion correlate with different axes of inequalities. Thus, it is not just about expansion but about access, equality, and quality of higher education so that each citizen of the country can lead a meaningful life or is at least able to ensure a decent standard of living (Bordoloi, 2018). Although Asian countries have seen a rapid increase in overall participation and gender disparities are being overcome to some extent, issues of fair access and quality remain.

This chapter aims to address the inclusion and exclusion of those who have access to HE within the changing landscape of the Asia-Pacific region's shift from elite to mass education in terms of axes of inequalities—gender, class, socially marginalized groups as ethnicity/religion/caste, rural–urban, and regional. It begins with an examination of what access means, who has access to higher education and to what quality, and in particular the question of whether growing enrollments and access have come at the cost of quality. The structural features of HE systems in Asia that shape access will be discussed, e.g., enrollment and completion in secondary education, as a *sine qua non* for access to HE. The instruments and the effectiveness of instruments used to improve access in HE in this region will be evaluated using McCowan's (2016) "Three dimensions of equity of access to higher education."

1. Access to HE Participation: What, Who, and to What?

This section discusses the meaning of access and the nature of participation in Asia-Pacific HE, with special attention to who has access to HE and to what, and how access has been changing as HE systems in the region shift from elite to mass education. Since access is correlated with different axes of inequality—gender, class, socially marginalized groups as ethnicity/religion/caste, rural–urban, and regional—changing access in some of these dimensions will also be discussed.

The term "access" typically refers to the ways in which educational institutions and policies ensure—or at least strive to ensure—that students have equal and equitable opportunities to take full advantage of their education. Increasing access generally requires educational institutions to provide additional services or remove any actual or potential barriers that might prevent some students from equitable participation in certain courses or academic programs (https://www.edglossary.org/access/). Access to higher education is commonly defined as "the ability of people from all backgrounds to access higher education on a reasonably equal basis" (Usher and Medow, 2010; Wang, 2011; Clifford et al., 2012). This definition implies that students of all backgrounds are given equal opportunity to access higher education, regardless of their geographical region, rural versus urban environment, social class, type of school, gender or ethnicity (Fields, 1980) and that they must be adequately prepared for the system to be accessible (Usher and Medow, 2010; Wang, 2011).

Based on Trow's classification of HE expansion, as of 2018–2019, higher education in Asia-Pacific is now universal in developed countries like Australia, New Zealand, Singapore, Republic of Korea, Hong Kong, and China (http://data.uis.unesco.org), with China, India, and Indonesia seeing the largest increases in number of enrollments. India's tertiary sector is still an elite one according to Trow's classification, however, despite India having the second largest increase, from 5 million in 1990 to 34 million in 2018, with a gross enrollment ratio of 28 percent. Meanwhile, many developed countries in Asia-Pacific like Singapore and South Korea have experienced a decrease in HE enrollment, largely due to the change in population structure towards an aging society.

While some countries like Thailand, the Philippines, and Vietnam are experiencing a slight decline in tertiary participation, probably largely due to demographic changes, other countries like Malaysia and Indonesia are expected to enroll some of the world's largest number of university students (Songkaeo and Yeong, 2016).

Figure 5.1 shows that HE participation is linked to levels of economic development. Countries with low economic development, such as Pakistan, Cambodia, Lao PDR, Sri Lanka, and Myanmar, have low levels of HE participation. However, the expansion seen in many countries that has meant a shift from elite to mass education and to universal education, reflects the fact that HE is moving away from being an elite system and that to some extent, the global commitment that "education shall be equally accessible to all on the basis of merit" is being met. However, expansion of HE participation does not guarantee *fair access*: based on evidence from the global map of equity, Atherton et al. (2016) have concluded that inequality in access to HE prevails. The expansion of availability of higher education in the region has not guaranteed equal access to higher education for every individual, especially to equal quality higher education.

Access to higher education differs not only among countries but also within countries, where certain individuals or groups may experience various forms of exclusion. These inequalities in terms of accessing HE are complex and do not exist in isolation from other *economic, political, or policy* contexts. These complexities lie in the

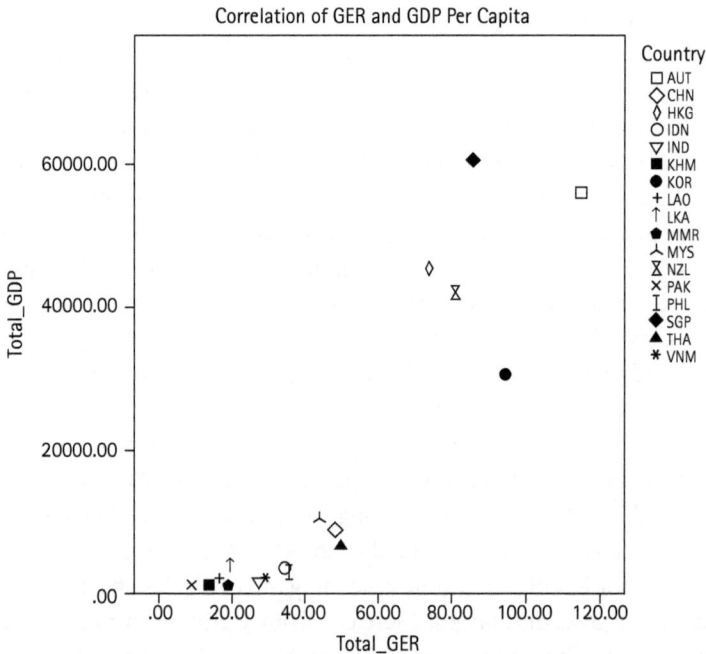

FIGURE 5.1 Correlation of GER and GDP per capita

Source: http://data.uis.unesco.org.

intersectionality, albeit incongruent, of various dimensions of equity such as gender and class, groups, social marginalization because of ethnicity/religion/caste, being first-generation college students, or rural–urban and regional inequalities.

Based on the data available, as measured by UNESCO's Gender Parity Index (GPI), most countries in Asia-Pacific have GPI for first entry to tertiary programs that exceeds 1 except for India that is 0.98 as of 2018. This trend also reflects predictions made by the OECD that if the rate of women becoming more numerous than men in higher education continued, "the inequalities to the detriment of men would be well entrenched at the aggregate level in 2025" (Vincent-Lancrin, 2008, p. 266). India, a country traditionally and historically driven by principles of inequality and social hierarchy through the religious values of the caste system, has successfully improved gender disparity in access to higher education and its GPI has now almost reached 1. In 1950, there were 13 females enrolled for every 100 males; in 2017–2018 this number rose to 91. While Sri Lanka and Myanmar, low-income countries with low levels of HE participation, have the highest GPI with more females having access to HE, the Republic of Korea, Pakistan, and Cambodia respectively, have GPI below 1, which means that in these countries, the HE system still favors males over females. However, although South Korea is one of the world's most educated countries, contributing to the nation's economic rise over the past seventy years (Mani and Trines, 2018) and has dramatically reduced the gender gap in college enrollment (Cha, 2017), gender inequality in HE prevails, as GPI remains below 1. Historically, higher education in South Korea served to support the class structure, social status, and male dominance but recently, the gender gap has been reduced. As Cha (2017) comments, higher education in Korea is no longer seen as a privilege and has come close to becoming mass education.

However, access to higher education does not only mean being admitted to a college or university: more importantly, access implies the successful completion of a degree. Despite increases in the enrollment of women in tertiary education, the female educational attainment rate of Bachelor's degree or equivalent, remains far below that of males even in developed countries like Australia, New Zealand, and Singapore. Whereas in most countries, young men are more likely than young women to lack an upper secondary qualification and women are also more likely to have obtained a tertiary qualification, in India, 58 percent of young men and 70 percent of young women did not attain upper secondary education, while 16 percent of young men and 12 percent of young women attained a tertiary qualification (OECD, 2019b). This implies that women have a lower success rate of attainment than men.

Inequality of access is more complex when gender, socio-economic, ethnicity, and locality dimensions are combined. In China, 67 percent of 25- to 34-year-olds are expected to enter tertiary education for the very first time, which is slightly higher than the OECD average of 65 percent (OECD, 2019a). However, although higher education will soon approach universal levels, according to Trow's classification, rural–urban and socio-economic inequalities remain (Guo and Guo, 2016). Furthermore, China has a hierarchical higher education structure with about 10 percent of research-oriented universities at the top, 40 percent of local public institutions in the middle, and the remaining higher vocational colleges and private universities (Huang, 2019) at the bottom. Students from higher socio-economic family backgrounds, from better high schools and from urban areas, are more likely to be admitted into the more prestigious colleges (Jia and Ericson, 2016). This kind of stratification, however, is not unique to China but can be seen throughout Asia (Collins and Buasuwan, 2017; Sánchez and Singh, 2018). For example, similar inequalities can be seen in Myanmar where, according to 2014 census data, far higher numbers of urban females enroll in higher education than males and 68 percent of young people from the richest quintile attain tertiary educational level, compared to only 1.2 percent of young people in the poorest quintile. Also, rural-based ethnic young people are least likely to achieve similar education outcomes compared to their Bamar urban counterparts (Kandiko Howson and Lall, 2020).

During the past decade, India has made considerable achievements in higher education. If higher education enrollments are a function of income, by that standard, India's higher education enrollment ratio is considerably *higher* than would be warranted for its income level. Yet as elsewhere in the region, socio-economic and geographic inequalities still exist (Vani, 2016). In countries with high HE participation like Indonesia, the Philippines, and Thailand, income level seems to be a condition for females in rural areas to have access to higher education, as almost 80 percent of the gross attendance ratio of females in rural areas are from the richest quintile. This implies that greater access in terms of gender can widen the urban–rural gap and that the expansion in access to higher education may predominantly benefit the rich (Ilie and Rose, 2016). An implication can be drawn that in developing countries in this region, a cost–benefit approach to access is prioritized, based on wealth, geographic distribution, and gender, since education is seen as an investment good that profits the receiver.

Access inequalities based on class and gender have been extensively discussed but more recently, other dimensions of inequality are receiving increasing attention, disability being an obvious example. In this regard, there has been improvement in access to HE for students with disabilities in Asia-Pacific. In Korea, for example, following the implementation of the special admissions policy, there has been an increase in the number of high school students with disabilities entering college. In 2017, of 7,734 (15.4 percent) high school graduates with disabilities, 1,191 were enrolled in two-year and four-year colleges (3.9 percent in special schools, 11.9 percent in special classrooms, and 49.4 percent in regular classrooms), which is 2.5 times more than the university enrollment rates of 2001 (Korean Ministry of Education, 2017 cited in Kim and Kim, 2019). However, research indicates that students with disabilities experience difficulties adjusting to college life (K. Kim, 2015; Seo, 2010), and hence, drop-out rates are far higher.

More complex dimensions of inequality that are barriers to widening participation in HE are being explored. Despite the achievements in terms of access, the stratification of higher educational systems differs widely (Sánchez and Singh, 2018). Overall, there has been a reduction in gender inequality of access to HE and some improvements in terms of the axes of inequality, namely socio-economic circumstances, social class, ethnicity, and locality. However, increasing access to HE participation does not guarantee equal opportunity of access and factors such as human capability, parent's education, school performance, values towards education, job opportunities, and group membership, can also affect access in complex ways.

While overall expansion can be viewed as impressive in the region, it may be interesting to investigate what quality of education students have access to, especially when society perceives the institutional processes of high quality to be determined by student selectivity (or rejection rates) of the institution. Although several international organizations have visualized the role of quality as a mechanism to improve access (UNESCO, 2005), quality and access are often viewed as being conflictual (Tan and Decena, 2015). Most top-ranked universities in both developing and developed countries are very selective, require high tuition fees, and are located in the city, and so are inaccessible to average and low-income students, especially those who reside in rural areas. The University of the Philippines, for example, has created a reputation for being of high quality so that a rejection rate of over 80 percent is accepted by society. By contrast, in countries with declining number of student enrollments in higher education, like Thailand, the quality of top-ranked universities, as determined by student selectivity, is being compromised by the quest for student admissions.

Growing evidence indicates that the rapid increase of access to higher education over the past two decades has come at a tremendous cost of a severe and pervasive decline in academic quality. Final outcomes of the educative process will only be of quality if the inputs and processes that lead to them are of quality. Furthermore, the enrollment explosion that is prevailing over standards has raised concerns from stakeholders regarding the employability skills of graduates. Tremendous growth in school enrollment, as a movement toward universal basic education, might have a domino effect on higher education participation, which has led to calls for a higher quality of education at the tertiary level (Tan and Decena, 2015). While the private sector has filled the void to higher education participation in some respects, it is unclear whether all qualified students have access to quality higher education. In India, for example, the private sector is expected to achieve a target of 30 percent in providing contributions to higher education participation by 2020, set by the government. However, due to issues of quality where unemployability of graduates is a cause of concern, private institutes are not able to attract high-ranking students (Tiwari, 2013).

Study programs that students choose and have access to, also reflect another complex dimension of inequality. Although the available data are for a limited number of countries and therefore it is hard to generalize any trends, a recent review of higher education in Asia by the Asian Development Bank shows that despite growing enrollments in higher education (Asian Development Bank, 2011), several countries have a limited number of students in science and technology subject areas (STEM). In the West it has been observed that access has been greater in non-STEM fields, and within STEM, greater in the biological sciences than in physical sciences or engineering. In Asia, a contrast can be seen between developed and developing countries and access is quite diverse, especially within sub-regions. In China, engineering students form the largest group (33.4 percent), followed by those studying administration and management

(18.1 percent) (Huang, 2019). More than one-third of students in China major in the fields of science, technology, engineering, and mathematics (OECD, 2019a). South Korea has a quite balanced enrollment in diverse disciplines, but like China, the largest enrollment is in engineering (22.67 percent in 2017). This is followed by arts and humanities (16.16 percent in 2017), business administration (14.66 percent in 2017), and health (13.17 percent in 2017). Among countries in South-East Asia, the most popular subject is business administration. Cambodia has the largest proportion (37.45 percent in 2018), followed by Thailand (32.23 percent in 2016). Engineering is nonetheless also very popular, with 24.25 percent of students studying engineering (2017) in Malaysia, 18.82 percent in Vietnam (2017), 16.95 percent in the Philippines (2018), and 14.16 percent in Thailand (2017).

Enrollment in the social sciences is generally low in the region, mostly below 10 percent, with the exception of India where 32.45 percent of students enrolled in social science degrees (in 2018), followed by natural sciences (17.05 percent in 2018) and engineering (12.28 percent in 2018). The country with the largest proportion of arts and humanities students is Myanmar (23.97 percent in 2018), followed by the USA (16.90 percent in 2017) and South Korea (16.16 percent in 2017). Recent data reported by Varghese (2015) on areas of study in this region, tracking changes between 2006 and 2010, divides countries into three clusters. The most popular programs of study in Cluster 1 (Hong Kong, Macao, Japan, Republic of Korea, Singapore) in 2006 were in science technology and health services. For example, 41 percent of students in Hong Kong, 46 percent in Korea, and 34 percent in Japan chose STEM subject areas. Macao is a notable exception in this group, where humanities and social sciences accounted for nearly four-fifths of enrollments. In Cluster 2 (Brunei Darussalam, China, India, Indonesia, Iran, Lao PDR, Malaysia, the Philippines, Sri Lanka, Thailand, Timor-Leste, Vietnam) and Cluster 3 (Afghanistan, Bangladesh, Bhutan, Cambodia, Maldives, Myanmar, Nepal, Pakistan) the STEM subject areas account for a lower share of enrollment, except in Iran where the share of students in STEM is around 49 percent. Cambodia has a very unbalanced disciplinary structure, with 66 percent of students graduating in social science, business, or law. These trends are seen to continue in 2010, although there seems to be an increased preference for STEM subject areas in many more countries in 2010 than in 2006.

A key reason why increasing the number of graduates in science and technology is seen as so important is that they are widely expected to lead the way to innovation and economic growth and development. Even during the current coronavirus crisis, most countries in the developed world try to protect investment in STEM as a strategy to come out of the crisis. Another reason is that employment opportunities are expanding in those sectors and require a degree in these subject areas. Meanwhile, private universities in Asia generally offer courses in lower cost study programs such as business and education, at the expense of higher cost programs in science, technology, medicine, and engineering.

In terms of gender and STEM, data available at UIS UNESCO (online) shows that as of 2020, there are stark male–female differences in the choice of subjects. In general, more women students are found in the social sciences, education, arts and humanities, and health and welfare disciplines, while a higher proportion of male students choose STEM subjects, e.g., engineering, ICT, and agriculture. A report on the subject choices of women in Japan shows that while women account for 43 percent of total enrollment in all subjects (except medical and agricultural fields), only 14 percent of those students choose STEM subjects, whereas they constitute 66 percent of enrollment in the humanities (Tanikawa, 2013). More recent data (2013–2018) from UIS UNESCO (online) shows that Japanese females constitute a low percentage in all disciplines, except for health and welfare where over 60 percent of students were female.

It can be concluded that the rapid expansion of HE in the Asia-Pacific region reflects a global commitment to education for all to support worldwide economic competitiveness. Clearly there has been a movement from elite to massification and towards universal higher education. Yet different countries are at different stages of development and in many of them, ethnicity, locality, wealth, and gender inequalities interact to increase the gap (Ilie and Rose, 2016). In addition, not only are there differences of access in specific disciplines in Asian HE, especially between the non-STEM fields, but also in gender differences in the choice of subjects. Due to limited data, it is not possible to generalize patterns of differences in terms of accessing specific disciplines in this region, but it might be that the differences identified can be linked to different stages of economic development and directions. It points to the need for further investigations as to the extent of differences within countries on the axes of gender, socio-economic status, values, and ethnicity.

2. INSTRUMENTS USED TO IMPROVE ACCESS TO HE

Many countries, informed by the current neoliberalism perspective, have adopted policies and instruments that position the state as a facilitator of market forces (Friedman, 1962) in improving access to HE. Legal action is required for enforcement to ensure that higher education is inclusive of every individual in society.

Affirmative action, a policy to ensure that an individual's race, sex, color, religion, or ethnicity are taken into account to increase equal opportunities provided to an underrepresented segment of society, is widely adopted in many countries as an instrument to increase access in HE. However, laws regarding quotas and affirmative action vary widely from nation to nation. In India, for example, a caste system society, Article 46 of the national Constitution states that the state "shall promote with special care the educational and economic interests of weaker sections of the people and in particular of the Scheduled Caste and Scheduled Tribes and shall protect them from social injustice and all forms of exploitation." Under the country's Affirmative Action Policy, various facilities for educational development provided to special care groups are in two forms: material and non-material. Material facilities include scholarships and freeships, financial incentives for girls, hostel boarding provision, books and research fellowships. Non-material facilities include remedial coaching, developing language skills, pre-exam coaching for medical, engineering, and administrative services, and reservation of seats in admission with their population proportion (Wankhede, 2006).

Affirmative Action in Korea came into effect in 2006 as an active measure designed to improve deeply rooted discriminatory practices against women. The Convention on the Elimination of All Forms of Discrimination against Women (CEDAW) ensures appropriate measures to eliminate discrimination against women and operates as the basis for equal rights with men in the field of education; as a result, the rate of female enrollment is now over 45 percent (Cha, 2017). In China, there is Affirmative Action in education for minority nationalities. Some universities set quotas for minority (non-Han) student intake. Further, minority students enrolled in ethnic minority-oriented specialties (e.g., language and literature programs) are provided with scholarships and/or pay no tuition and are granted a monthly stipend. By contrast, Malaysia provides Affirmative Action to the ethnic majority because in general, the Malays have lower incomes than the Chinese, who have traditionally been involved in businesses and industries, but who were also general migrant workers.

Vietnam, a highly populated country with many ethnic minorities, most of whom reside in underdeveloped areas, has introduced two policies in the legal system with regards to ensuring human rights and HE access. They are (1) regional priority policy and bonus points and (2) the procedure of checking the political and moral qualities of students (e.g., family relationship, political and moral dispositions) before being accepted. These legal initiatives aim to create equality of opportunity for every student to register their names for any university and to increase the chance to access university study for all ethnic groups (Le, 2017).

The emergence of private institutions is also an instrument that is improving access to higher education. In many Asian countries, growth in enrollment has placed a strain on public higher education institutions, with financial resources to state institutions not growing at the same pace as enrollment. This is leading to a growth in private institutions in response to increased demand for places in some contexts (Ilie and Rose, 2016). This rapid growth has arisen largely due to the disparity between governments' capacity and the increasing demand for higher education, as a result of increasing the numbers of high school graduates that leads to a demand for more higher education (ADB, 2002; Welch, 2007, 2011). Expansion of private HEIs has also largely been influenced by neo-liberalism where market-driven identities and values are legitimized by states (Giroux, 2004). Also, with the influence of human capital theory on global economic competition, states have massified the HE system and welcomed the private sector to take part in providing HE access.

As can be seen from Figure 5.2, in many countries in Asia-Pacific, such as Korea, Japan, Cambodia, India, and the Philippines, most students are enrolled in private institutions. In Korea, 80 percent of students in Bachelor's programs were enrolled in independent private institutions in 2017, the highest proportion among OECD countries and well above the OECD average of students enrolled in both government dependent

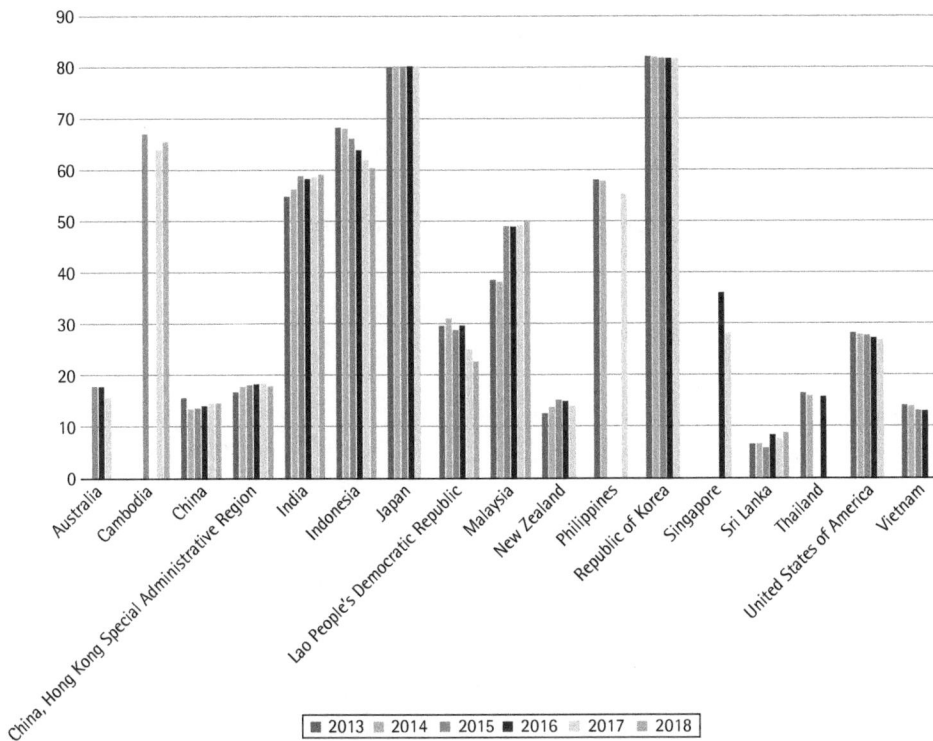

FIGURE 5.2 Percentage of enrollment in tertiary education in private institutions

Source: http://data.uis.unesco.org.

and independent private institutions (29 percent). The pattern of privatization in many countries is mainly due to excess demand and is providing a less competitive alternative to elite state HEIs. Expansion of low- and middle-income (LMI) contexts has been aided by a large private sector (Brewis, 2019). However, this might not be the case for Korea where private institutions share the vast majority of HE enrollment, yet remain quite competitive with comparatively high quality when compared to public institutions. Korea spends more on education than the OECD average from primary to tertiary levels of education. Private expenditure is significantly higher than public expenditure at tertiary level (OECD, 2019c). Also, in Indonesia, there are examples of private HEIs that are differentiated to provide specialized and high-quality HE with links to specific industries (see Brewis, 2019). In Japan, approximately 75 percent of all universities are private, according to a government agency (the Promotional and Mutual Aid Corporation for Private Schools of Japan), and 160 of the total 542 four-year private universities now have lower student enrollments than the enrollment quota (*teiin*) approved by the Ministry of Education (Akabayashi, 2006).

Table 5.2 indicates that government expenditure on tertiary education as a percentage of GDP is associated with level of economic income. New Zealand, Australia, and the USA have the highest percentage of government expenditure followed by Japan, Korea,

Table 5.2 Government expenditure on tertiary education (% to GDP)

Indicator	Government expenditure on tertiary education as a percentage of GDP (%)					
Time	2014	2015	2016	2017	2018	2019
Country						
Australia	1.37066	1.53259	1.41548	1.28691	–	–
Indonesia	0.49494	0.56622	–	–	–	–
Japan	0.75	–	0.63	0.64		
Lao People's Democratic Republic	0.40578	–	–	–	–	–
Malaysia	–	–	1.11148	0.98193	0.95662	0.9466
Myanmar	–	–	–	0.23549	0.28413	0.28265
New Zealand	1.58286	1.62023	1.52699	1.49767	–	–
Pakistan	0.55049	0.6039	0.66667	0.64109	–	–
Republic of Korea	–	0.89206	0.886	0.89297	–	–
Singapore	–	–	0.9889	0.81771	0.87305	–
United States of America	1.36459	1.36599	1.21082	1.45485	–	–

Source: http://data.uis.unesco.org.

and Singapore. However, overall in the Asia-Pacific region there has been a declining trend in government expenditure on tertiary education during the past two decades. Public funding to support HE participation has shifted from public institutions to supporting students through student loans and scholarship programs. Although student loans have increased, with the increased opportunity for students to participate in HE the proliferation of fee-charging universities has increased financial pressure on students and their families, to the point that the majority of university students in the Asia-Pacific region now attend private, not public, institutions.

As seen in Figure 5.3, there has been a slightly increasing trend in scholarships provided by donor countries and other aid providers to countries such as Indonesia, Vietnam, Cambodia, Myanmar, India, and China. However, since the data only indicates expenditure on students from the given beneficiary country to study abroad, it does not indicate the number of students being supported. However, it could be inferred that economic development to promote welfare in developing countries may contribute to the increased participation in higher education in this region.

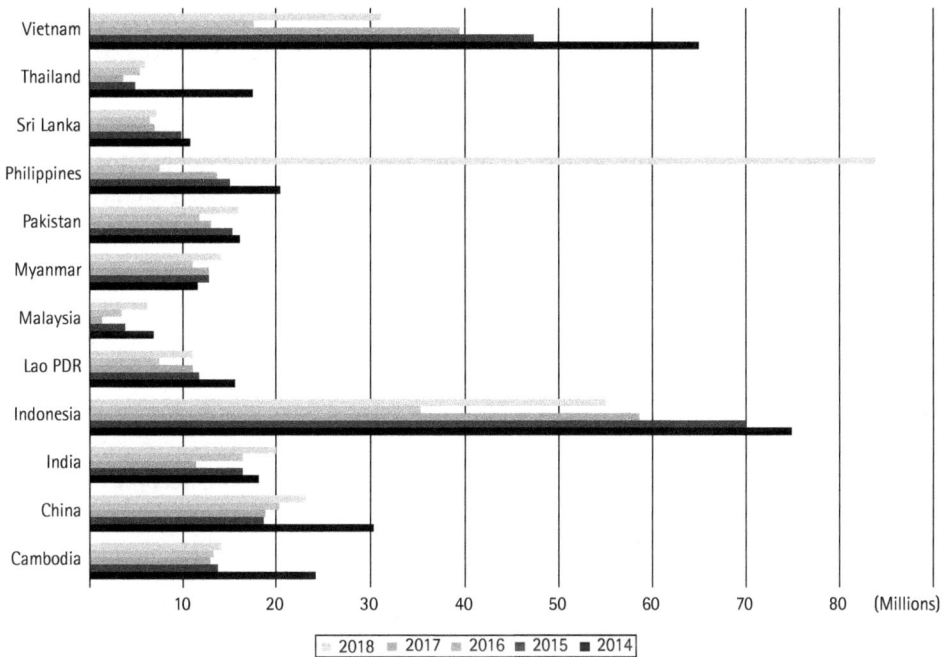

Vietnam
Thailand
Sri Lanka
Philippines
Pakistan
Myanmar
Malaysia
Lao PDR
Indonesia
India
China
Cambodia

10   20   30   40   50   60   70   80   (Millions)

2018   2017   2016   2015   2014

FIGURE 5.3 Official development assistance flows for scholarship by sector and type of study

Source: http://data.uis.unesco.org.

Open university and online or distance programs have an increasing role in providing access to HE, especially for students who cannot afford to live away from home and where access to educational institutions is limited. In Myanmar, an increase in distance programs has contributed to a dramatic increase in HE participation. HE institutions are state-financed and accept students depending on their grades. Those who cannot afford to live away from home study in the world's largest distance program consisting of poor-quality programs (Kandiko Howson and Lall, 2020). In India, state-run open universities have emerged to cater for the needs and demands of the people of the respective states in which they are established, so that everyone irrespective of caste, class, religion, sex, place, occupation, etc., can benefit from higher education. The National Knowledge Commission (NKC) of India stated that, "Open and distance education enabled and delivered through information and communication technology (ICT) holds the promise to address the questions of access, and provide new, alternative forms of capacity building" (NKC, 2009, p. 4). Fourteen state open universities, and more than 112 Directorates of Distance Education attached to conventional universities, have been established across India. In fact, open and distance learning (ODL) accounts for about 12 percent of the total enrollment in the segment of higher education and has contributed substantially towards the rise of the gross enrollment ratio (GER) of India, which is 24.5 percent. The most significant contribution of ODL in higher education is that it provides more opportunities to female learners to educate themselves and have a dignified life in society. For instance, women enrolled in higher education through distance learning make up 46.03 percent whereas in regular study, women's share is 45 percent (All India Survey of Higher Education, 2015–2016) (Bordoloi, 2018).

Due to demographic changes of becoming an aging and aged society, many countries such as Singapore, Thailand, Taiwan, Japan, and South Korea are experiencing a shortfall of student enrollment, which means that universities, whether they are private or public institutions, local or foreign institutions, currently compete for student enrollment. Studying abroad is an emerging trend in terms of the increase in access to HE in Asia. In 2017, 2 percent of Chinese tertiary students studied abroad, on par with the OECD average (OECD, 2019a). Many countries in Asia, especially in East Asia, which has the greatest number of world-class universities and an emphasis on STEM disciplines, where HE has reached massification level and there is a decline in HE enrollment, are turning to China and other neighboring countries, where there is excess demand for HE access. International cooperation in HE, therefore, has become a strategy for this region in terms of improving access (Postiglione, 2020).

3. EFFECTIVENESS OF INSTRUMENTS USED TO IMPROVE ACCESS TO HE

This section will explore the effectiveness of the instruments used to improve access in terms of equality and quality, by employing McCowan's "Three dimensions of equity of access to higher education" (2016) which are: availability (sufficient places in HEIs proportionate to the age cohort); accessibility (fair procedure for entering and accessing HE); and horizontality (consistent quality across HEIs rather than stratification) as a framework of analysis. These three dimensions, however, intersect and cannot be investigated entirely independently.

The instruments that countries in this region have used to address access have meant a rapid expansion of higher education, so that the share of the Asia-Pacific region in the global expansion of HE is higher than in other regions. Although this expansion is impressive, it has also brought many challenges. Clearly, increased access to HE depends on the availability of HEIs.

Although affirmative actions have been taken by many states in Asia-Pacific countries to promote equality and to ensure that no one is denied access to education, various studies have found there are unintended disadvantages to this policy. Studies show that Affirmative Action has certainly contributed to the progression of marginalized groups (Wankhede, 2006; Kim and Kim, 2019; Mahlangu, 2020). However, making special provisions for specific discriminated groups of society can result in new forms of discrimination and lead to quality deficiencies (Wankhede, 2006; Zhou and Hill, 2009; Lee, 2012; Mahlangu, 2020). In India, for example, special reservations of seats for admission to scheduled castes and tribes under their Affirmative Action Policy, has led to regional and caste-to-caste imbalances (Wankhede, 2006). Affirmative Action in Malaysia has also had adverse effects on education quality and employment (Lee, 2012). The growing importance of education quality adversely affects Bumiputera graduates, who predominantly enroll in less well-regarded domestic public institutes, whose access is facilitated by quotas and who are highly dependent on the public sector, compared to non-Bumiputera domestic graduates, who compete more intensely for admission and are more likely to attain positions in the private sector. Location of tertiary institution, a proxy for quality, and racial preference in selection processes, also have an impact on occupational outcomes (Lee, 2012).

During the 1990s there was a significant growth in private HE institutions in many developing countries throughout Asia-Pacific, which has resulted in the massification of HE. Through the privatization of HE, the burden of cost in HE participation is transferred from states to students and parents through market mechanisms. Asia-Pacific countries with high participation rates of tertiary education have been very susceptible to this trend. In South Korea, for example, where 90 percent of young people enroll in higher education, nearly 81 percent of which is private, the educational debt in 2013 had increased by 12 percent, or twice the pace of consumer debt. Similarly, in Japan, where 76 percent of high school graduates pursue tertiary education, with over 78 percent of them at private institutions with high tuition fees and loan-only policies, financing has exacerbated the debt burden (Asadullah and Chan, 2019). Privatization measures in both public and private universities reduce the pressure on governments to fund higher education. While this may be a welcome change, in the absence of targeted interventions to subsidize those from lower socio-economic backgrounds, various studies have found this is increasing inequalities among present and future generations (e.g., Vani, 2016; Sánchez and Singh, 2018; Brewis, 2019).

In addition, most private universities offer courses in market-friendly subject areas at the undergraduate, diploma, or certificate levels. In many instances, private universities operate in poor conditions—poor state of infrastructure, less qualified teachers, etc. Although the development of private higher education institutions has the potential to increase access, as seen in many developing countries, it often comes at the expense of quality (Botello, 2019; Kandiko Howson and Lall, 2020). Open universities and online education are also instruments used to increase availability and allow more access to HE, yet the issue of quality has also been raised in this regard. While there is a need to encourage the private sector, including open and distance education, there is also a need to regulate it so as to provide quality education at relatively affordable prices (Varghese, 2015).

Many countries in Asia-Pacific face the dilemma of achieving universal HE participation on the one hand and pursuing the status of having world-class universities on the other. Classifying universities into a more hierarchical structure is a strategy likely to be used by many countries. China, for example, has a small number of top universities, the distribution of which is regionally very unequal. In general, top universities are in urban areas, which means rural students are unlikely to attend. Exacerbating this inequality is the importance of the university entrance examination (*Gaokao*) in controlling access to prestigious universities, the role of provincial student quotas, and the fierce competition for places at top universities. The result is a system that advantages applicants from big eastern cities and provinces and disadvantages students from poorer, inland provinces. This helps to reproduce regional (and economic?) inequalities in China (Hamnett et al., 2018). Furthermore, this hierarchical HE structure is accompanied by unequal distribution of government funding, as more resources are given to top or research-oriented universities as part of the drive towards achieving world-class status. Various studies have also found that minority ethnic groups are less likely to apply and gain places in research-intensive institutions (Gorard et al., 2012; Mahlangu, 2020). Although national examinations to elite universities are a common feature of many countries in this region, admission systems that rely on university entrance examination could widen inequality of access, as it implies that the education system determines which students go to which type of universities and so shapes participation by socio-economic and cultural background.

It can be concluded that HE in Asia-Pacific has had much success in terms of availability and to some extent, accessibility, but not horizontality, in that universities are mostly stratified and not every individual has equal access to quality HE. Strategies and instruments that have been adopted to expand HE and move towards massification have emphasized quantitative measures to increase HE access, such as increasing the availability of HEIs and improving accessibility through scholarships and reservations of seats. Now more attention is being given to quality for inclusive development, so that quality HE is accessible to all. In order to achieve that aim, human capability should be enhanced so that HE can be equally accessed based on merit. More attention, therefore, should be given to the qualitative factors that affect equity of access to HE, such as values and attitudes toward education and job opportunity, learning performance, parental education, test and admission systems, and lastly, the cumulative effects from achievement gaps created from early childhood education through to high school sectors.

4. CONCLUSION

In recent years, there has been an expansion in the availability of HE which has resulted in greater opportunities for access to higher education. Gender disparity has been reduced and students from social classes or groups that were previously excluded are now more included. Cultural heritage, philosophy, politics, history, societal values, conditions of availability, cumulative effects of education achievement gaps, quality, and presence or absence of public funding, shape beliefs about who should and can have access to higher education, which means that who is excluded from higher education is unique in each country. Although economic development has proved to be highly associated with access in this region, inequality is still prevalent and more acute unique to each context, compounded by complex dimensions of gender, income, religious values, cultural heritage, ethnicities, and human capabilities. Although a number of common instruments are used to increase access in HE, the main ones discussed here being privatization, affirmative action, financial support to students, and open and on-line education, how these policies are put into action is contextually specific and thus yields different results at different stages of development. Some initiatives that have proven to increase levels of HE participation may create wider inequality in other dimensions. One of the major challenges in Asia-Pacific HE, therefore, is how to maintain quality and inclusivity of higher education alongside expansion.

REFERENCES

Akabayashi, H. (2006). "Private universities and government policy in Japan." *International Higher Education*, 42. https://doi.org/10.6017/ihe.2006.42.7887

Asadullah, M. N. and Chan, T. (2019). "Asia's student-debt time bomb." *Bangkok Post*. August 12. https://www.bangkokpost.com/business/1728791/asias-student-debt-time-bomb

Asian Development Bank. (2002). Education and Skills: Strategies for Accelerated Development in Asia and the Pacific. Manila: Asian Development Bank.

Asian Development Bank. (2011). *Higher Education across Asia: An Overview of Issues and Strategies*. Manila: ADB.

Atherton, Dumangane, C. and Whitty, G. (2016). *Charting Equity in Higher Education: Drawing the Global Access Map*. London: Open Ideas at Pearson, Pearson.

Bordoloi, R. (2018). "Transforming and empowering higher education through open and distance learning in India." *Asian Association of Open Universities Journal*, 13/1, 24–36.

Botello, R. G. (2019). "Is free tuition the panacea to improve equity in higher education?" Council for Higher Education Accreditation Report, No. 13, April.

Brewis, E. (2019). Quality and Equitable Access: Insights from Indonesia. *International Higher Education*, 99, 12–13. https://doi.org/10.6017/ihe.2019.99.11651

Calderon, A. J. (2018). *Massification of Higher Education Revisited*. https://www.academia.edu/36975860/Massification_of_higher_education_revisited

Clifford, M., Miller, T., Stasz, C., Sam, C., and Kumar, K. (2012). *The Impact of Different Approaches to Higher Education Provision in Increasing Access, Quality and Completion for Students in Developing Countries*. London: EPPI-Centre Social Science Research Unit Institute of Education, University of London.

Cha, S. (2017) "Higher education as a symbol of equal rights in South Korea." In C. Collins, and P. Buasuwan, P. (eds.) *Higher Education Access in the Asia Pacific: Privilege or Human Right?* Cham: Palgrave Macmillan, 23–39

Collins, C. and Buasuwan, P. (eds.) (2017). *Higher Education Access in the Asia Pacific: Privilege or Human Right?* Cham: Palgrave Macmillan.

Fields, G. S. (1980). "Education and income distribution in developing countries: A review of the literature." In T. King (ed.), *Education and Income*. Staff Working Paper 402. Washington, DC: World Bank, 231–315.

Friedman, M. (1962). *Capitalism and Freedom*. Chicago: University of Chicago Press.

Giroux, H. (2004). "Public pedagogy and the politics of neo-liberalism: Making the political more pedagogical." *Policy Futures in Education*, 2/3–4, 494–503.

Gorard, S., See, B., and Davies, P. (2012). *The Impact of Attitudes and Aspirations on Educational Attainment and Participation*. York: Joseph Rowntree Foundation.

Guo, S. and Guo, Y. (2016). *Spotlight on China: Changes in Education under China's Market Economy*. Taipei: Sense Publishers

Hamnett, C., Hua, S., and Bingjie, L. (2018). "The reproduction of regional inequality through university access: The *Gaokao* in China." *Journal Area Development and Policy*, 4/3, 252–270.

Huang, F. (2019). "China's higher education system – 70 years of evolution." *University World News*. https://www.universityworldnews.com/post.php?story=20191001085233566.

Ilie, S. and Rose, P. (2016). "Is equal access to higher education in South Asia and sub-Saharan Africa achievable by 2030?" *Higher Education*, 72, 435–455.

Jia, Q. and Ericson, D. P. (2016). "Equity and access to higher education in China: Lessons from Hunan province for university admissions policy." *International Journal of Educational Development*, 52, 97–110.

Kandiko Howson, C. and Lall, H. M. (2020). "Higher education reform in Myanmar: Neoliberalism versus an inclusive developmental agenda." *Globalisation, Societies and Education*, 18, 2, 109–124.

Kim, K. H. and Kim, J. (2019). "Transition to higher education in South Korea: Current status and issues." *Intervention in School and Clinic*, 55/5, 319–324.

Korean Ministry of Education. (2017). 2017 *Special Education Annual Report*. Sejong, South Korea: Author

Le, T.T. (2017). "Political/ moral dispositions and bonus points: An examination of access to Vietnam higher education." In C. Collins, and P. Buasuwan, (eds.) *Higher Education Access in the Asia Pacific: Privilege or Human Right?* Cham: Palgrave Macmillan, pp. 115–137

Lee, H. A. (2012). "Affirmative action in Malaysia: Education and employment outcomes since the 1990s." *Journal of Contemporary Asia*, 42/2, 230–254.

McCowan, T. (2016). "Three dimensions of equity of access to higher education." *Compare*, 46/4, 645–665.

Mahlangu, V. P. (2020). "Rethinking student admission and access in higher education through the lens of capabilities approach." *International Journal of Educational Management*, 34/2, 450–460.

Mani, D. and Trines, S. (2018). *Education in South Korea*. https://wenr.wes.org/2018/10/education-in-south-korea

Marginson, S. (2016). "The worldwide trend to high participation higher education: Dynamics of social stratification in inclusive systems." *Higher Education*, 72, 413–434.

National Knowledge Commission (NKC) (2009). *Report to the Nation 2006–2009*. New Delhi: National Knowledge Commission, Government of India.

Nwadiani, Mon (2012). "Educational Expectations and Realities: Functional Dilemmas in Education Planning", An inaugural Lecture Series 126, University of Benin.

OECD (2019a). *Education at a Glance 2019: People's Republic of China (China)*. https://www.oecd.org/education/education-at-a-glance/EAG2019_CN_CHN.pdf

OECD (2019b). *Education at a Glance 2019: India*. https://www.oecd.org/education/education-at-a-glance/EAG2019_CN_IND.pdf

OECD (2019c). *Education at a Glance 2019: Korea*. https://www.oecd.org/education/education-at-a-glance/EAG2019_CN_KOR.pdf

Postiglione, G. A. (2020) "International cooperation in East Asian higher education." In A. Al-Youbi et al. (eds.), *Successful Global Collaborations in Higher Education Institutions*, https://doi.org/10.1007/978-3-030-25525-1_4

Sánchez, A. and Singh, A. (2018). "Accessing higher education in developing countries: Panel data analysis from India, Peru, and Vietnam." *World Development*, 109, 261–278.

Seo, S. (2010). "A study of examining the transition-adjustment experiences of five college students with disabilities." *Korean Journal of Rehabilitation Research*, 14, 1, 31–53.

Songkaeo, Thammika, and Loke Hoe Yeong. (2016). *THF Literature Review: Defining Higher Education Issues and Challenges in Southeast Asia/ASEAN within the International Context.* Singapore: The HEAD Foundation.

Tan, J. W. and Decena, R. A. (2015). "Access-quality model in higher education." *NMSCST Research Journal*, 3/1, 157–173.

Tanikawa, M. (2013). "Japan's 'science women' seek an identity." *New York Times*, June 16.

Tiwari, R. (2013). "Role of private sector in Indian higher education." *International Interdisciplinary Research Journal*, 1/2, 75–83.

Trow, M. (1970). "Reflections on the transition from mass to universal higher education." *Daedalus*, 99/1, 1–42.

Trow, M. (1973). *Problems in the Transition from Elite to Mass Higher Education.* Berkeley, CA: Carnegie Commission on Higher Education.

Trow, M. (1999). "From mass higher education to universal access: The American advantage." *Minerva*, 37, 303–328.

UNESCO. (2005). The Total Quality Imperative. EFA Global Monitoring Report.

UNESCO Institute for Statistics (2014). *Global Education Digest: Comparing Education Statistics across the World.* Montreal: UIS.

Usher, A. and Medow, J. (2010). *Global Higher Education Rankings 2010: Affordability and Accessibility in Comparative Perspective.* Toronto: Higher Education Strategy Associates.

Vani, B. (2016). "Measuring inequality of access to higher education in India." *Journal of Quantitative Economics*, 15/2, 241–263.

Varghese, N. V. (2015). *Reshaping of Higher Education in Asia.* Paris: UNESCO.

Vincent-Lancrin, S. (2008). "The reversal of gender inequalities in higher education: An on-going trend." In *Higher Education to 2030.* Volume 1. Paris: OECD. http://www.oecd.org/education/ceri/41939699.pdf

Wang, H. (2011). "Access to higher education in China: Differences in opportunity." *Frontiers of Education in China*, 6/2, 227–247.

Wankhede, G. G. (2006). "Affirmative actions and the scheduled castes: Access to higher education in India." *Advances in Education in Diverse Communities: Research, Policy and Praxis*, 5, 329–342.

Welch, A. R. (2007). "Blurred vision?: public and private higher education in Indonesia." *Higher Education*, 54/5, 665–687.

Welch, A. R. (2011). Higher Education in Southeast Asia: Blurring Borders, Changing Balance, Routledge Research on Public and Social Policy in Asia. New York: Routledge.

Zhou, M. and Hill, A. M. (eds.) (2009). *Affirmative Action in China and the U.S.* New York: Palgrave Macmillan.

CHAPTER 6

....

GENDER IN HIGHER EDUCATION IN THE ASIA-PACIFIC REGION

Vertical Progress, Horizontal Segregation, and a Leaky Pipeline

....

ELIZABETH M. KING

1. INTRODUCTION

....

HIGHER enrollment and completion rates in primary and secondary education have raised enrollment rates at the tertiary level worldwide. This vertical educational progress is evident in the East Asia and Pacific (EAP) countries where the average gross enrollment rate in tertiary education grew from 3.1 percent in 1970 to 46.7 percent in 2017, faster than in most regions of the world. The region came from behind the European Union (EU), Latin America, and the Arab countries, but has overtaken the Arab states and is approaching the average rates in Latin America and the EU. Within EAP, the average enrollment rate in South Asian (SAR) countries trails behind the rest of the countries, but it too has risen in multiples—from 4.3 percent to 23.3 percent.[1]

Diversity within the Asia-Pacific region is particularly evident in tertiary education. Female enrollment exceeds that of males in EAP countries, but not in the countries in

---

[1] The data on gross enrollment rates are extracted from the World Development Indicators (World Bank, 2019). Barro and Lee (2013) have translated enrollment rates into average completed years of schooling (the latest estimates are for 2010). They calculate that 26 countries in the region have seen a more than threefold increase in completed years (equivalent to 4.3 years) over the period 1970–2010. Among women, the increase in average completed years of schooling has been dramatic—more than a sevenfold increase over the period 1970–2010. Excluding the region's richer countries (Australia, Japan, and New Zealand) from this calculation, the average growth over the period was more than eightfold.

South Asia (SAR). A number of factors account for the huge increase in enrollment rates in tertiary education, especially for women: the global push for universal basic education, relatively rapid economic growth, and increased labor force participation rates. This chapter presents the latest gender-disaggregated data on tertiary education indicators and discusses the gender patterns that emerge from those indicators. Gender gaps are largest when they overlap with other sources of disparities such as poverty, residence, and minority status. Thus, while urban women from well-off groups attain similar to or even more tertiary education than men, rural women from poorer population groups lag behind.

The chapter is organized as follows: The next section describes the trends and patterns of gender-disaggregated tertiary education indicators and labor force and occupational data, though several of these indicators are not systematically available from the main sources of comparable data—UNESCO, the World Bank, and the International Labour Organization.[2] The third section reviews the literature on the determinants of tertiary level enrollment and the choice of program in the Asia-Pacific region, and discusses the studies that estimate the relationship between tertiary education and labor market participation. The section also drills down on the employment of women with tertiary education in academia and in research positions. The last section highlights the key findings of the chapter.

2. TRENDS AND PATTERNS
IN GENDER DIFFERENCES

2.1 Vertical Progress in Enrollment Rates

Figure 6.1 compares the regional averages of gross enrollment rates in tertiary education during the period 2013–2018. In many world regions, the female enrollment rate exceeds the male enrollment rate, including in EAP. In 2013, the tertiary enrollment rates in EAP countries were 36.6 and 33.4 percent for women and men, respectively, but women's enrollment rate grew faster, doubling the female edge by 2018. In SAR, women's enrollment rate increased from 21.5 percent in 2013 to 25.8 percent, converging to men's enrollment rate by 2018.[3]

---

[2] I looked for data on the small island countries in the Pacific region in these sources (Fiji, French Polynesia, Kiribati, Marshall Islands, Micronesia, Nauru, New Caledonia, Northern Mariana Islands, Palau, Samoa, Solomon Islands, Tonga, Tuvalu, Vanuatu, and Wallis and Futuna), but only Palau has gender-disaggregated data for enrollment, though only as far back as 2013.

[3] Tertiary education encompasses four levels of education. According to UN categories, ISCED 5 pertains to short-cycle tertiary education; ISCED 6 refers to Bachelor's level, usually involving four years of education; ISCED 7 is the Master's level and equivalent; and ISCED 8 pertains to the Doctoral level. Overall, the gender distribution of graduates by level of tertiary education varies by country. Short-cycle tertiary education (ISCED 5) programs, which are more vocational than academic, are a significant part of the tertiary education system in several countries, indicating a greater diversity in educational offerings in

Females

Males

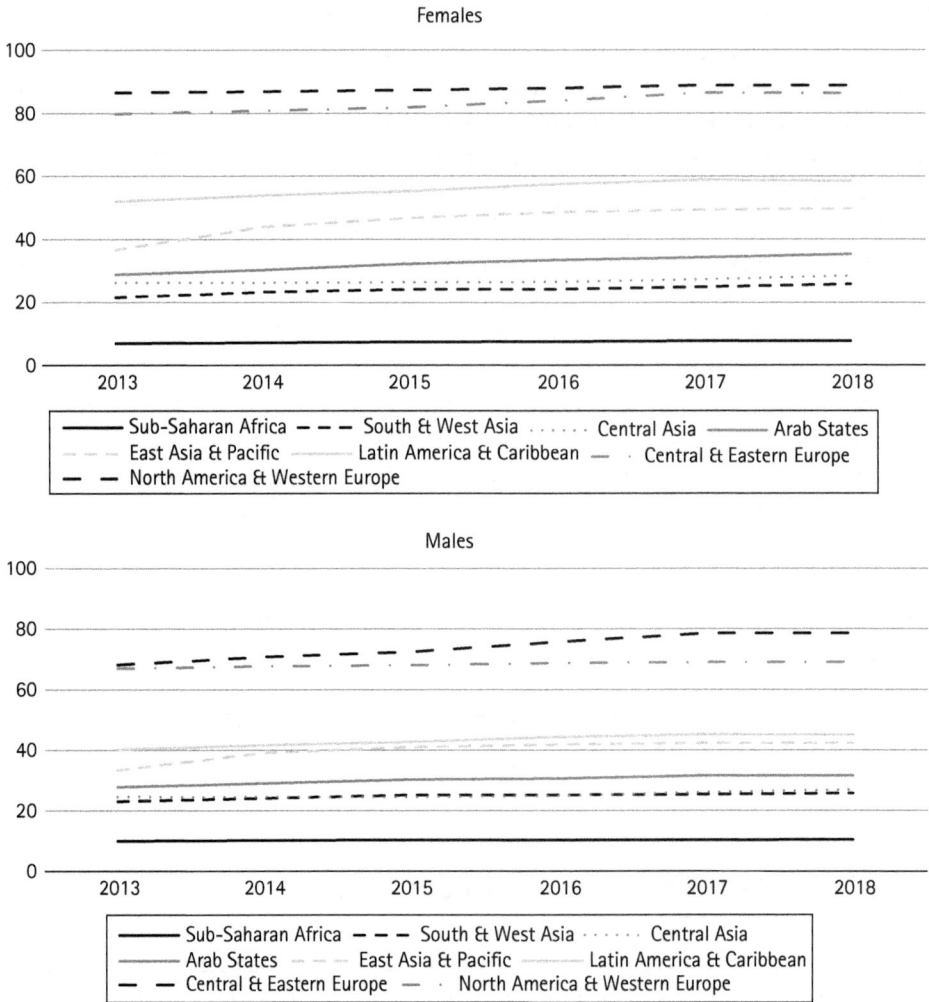

FIGURE 6.1 Gross enrollment rates in tertiary education of females and males, by world region

Data source: Extracted from UIS.Stat, January 2020.

Country data on gross enrollment rates show tremendous variation within the Asia-Pacific region, from just 10 percent in Pakistan to over 100 percent in Australia and South Korea, with the median in the 25 countries with data being about 40 percent. Disaggregating by gender reveals that the size of the gender gap also differs widely

those systems. These programs account for about two-thirds of female graduates and more than one-half of male graduates in Lao PDR, for 60 percent of male graduates and less than one-half of female graduates in Malaysia, and for only a tiny share of female and male graduates in Bangladesh, Myanmar, Mongolia, India, and Nepal. In most of the countries, the largest percentage of graduates, female or male, complete a Bachelor's degree (ISCED 6), and in all countries, less than 20 percent of graduates complete a Master's level (ISCED 7) or higher (ISCED 8), except in Macao (China) in the case of female graduates and in Australia and Myanmar for male graduates where this share is more than 20 percent.

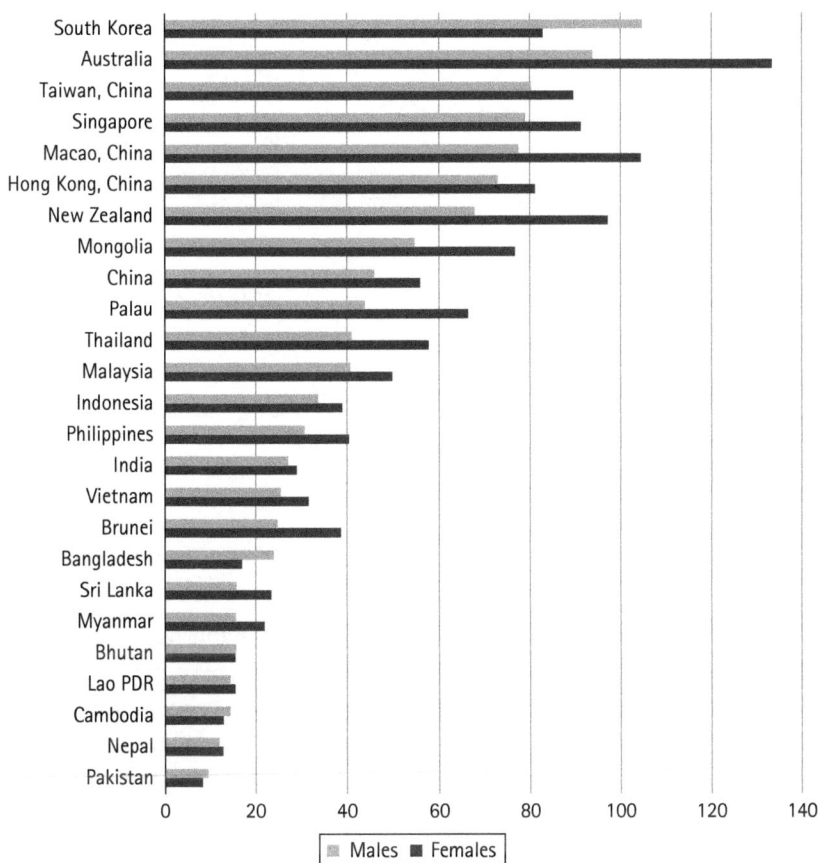

FIGURE 6.2 Gross tertiary education enrollment rates in the Asia-Pacific region, by gender

across countries (Figure 6.2). The gender gap in tertiary education (measured as a male deficit and what some have called a "reverse gender gap") tends to be larger in the high-enrollment countries than in the low-enrollment countries: In Australia, women's gross enrollment rate exceeds men's enrollment by 42 percent; while in Bangladesh, women's gross enrollment rate is only 71 percent of men's enrollment. An exception is South Korea where the tertiary enrollment rate is among the highest in the world but women's enrollment rate is just 79 percent of men's enrollment.

Figure 6.3 which is a scatter plot of the tertiary enrollment rates shows this point more clearly. The plot indicates that 19 of 25 countries have a male deficit, with women's enrollment rate being at least more than 10 percent higher than that of men.[4] Three countries have a female deficit, however, with women's enrollment being 90 percent or

[4] This "reverse gender gap" is not unique to the Asia-Pacific region. In the UK, women in higher education equaled men for the first time in 1992; since then, more women than men have been enrolled in higher education. In the USA, for every two men who get a college degree, three women will do the

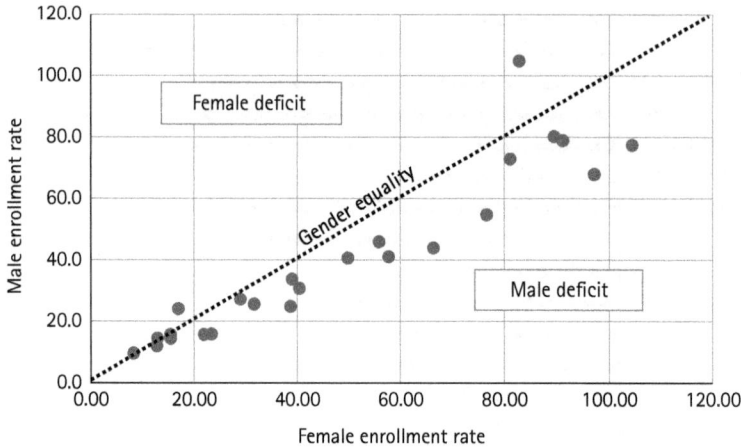

FIGURE 6.3 Gender inequality in gross enrollment rates

Source: Author's calculations using enrollment data extracted from the
World Development Indicators (World Bank, 2020).

less of men's enrollment. Important questions from these patterns are ones that other researchers have raised also about other world regions: Why are young women enrolling in tertiary education in much larger numbers than young men, especially in high-enrollment countries? Are these young women and men attaining the same level of tertiary education and choosing the same field of study? What are the implications of these gender patterns on their future life and work?

2.2 Horizontal Segregation in Areas of Study

Women enrolled in tertiary education are expanding into study programs typically dominated by men, but there remain clear gender differences. Grouping programs into broad categories of STEM (science, technology, engineering, and mathematics) and other fields of study, more males choose STEM fields compared to females (Table 6.1).[5] This gender pattern has been termed "horizonal segregation" (Peng et al., 2017). The highest STEM concentration among males is in Malaysia (57 percent) and the lowest is in Bangladesh (12 percent). The ratio of female to male graduates in STEM areas ranges from a low of 24 percent in Macao (China) to 80 percent in Myanmar. Only in Myanmar, India, Brunei, and Bangladesh do women graduates number more than

same. Even in societies that are known to be more patriarchal, such as Saudi Arabia, women, not men, have become the majority group in tertiary education campuses (Wan, 2018).

  [5] The non-STEM fields of study include arts and humanities, education, business, administration and law, social sciences, journalism and communication, services.

Table 6.1 Percentage of male and female tertiary graduates
in STEM areas of study

	Females	Males
Macao, China (2018)	3.3	14.0
Cambodia (2015)	6.0	22.5
Bangladesh (2018)	8.2	12.4
Australia (2017)	10.2	29.6
Indonesia (2018)	12.4	29.4
Lao PDR (2018)	12.8	32.5
New Zealand (2017)	12.9	32.2
South Korea (2017)	14.4	45.0
Mongolia (2018)	14.4	41.7
Thailand (2016)	15.0	44.3
Vietnam (2016)	15.4	31.2
Philippines (2017)	17.8	44.3
Singapore (2017)	22.6	48.9
Malaysia (2018)	26.2	57.3
India (2018)	26.9	36.6
Myanmar (2018)	31.0	38.8
Brunei (2018)	33.7	48.6

Notes: These are the only countries for which data on tertiary education programs are available from UIS. Unspecified field of study accounts for the residual.

Source: Author's calculation using data from UIS.Stat, February 2020, latest year of available data.

one-half of male graduates in STEM fields, and in no country does the female share equal the male share.[6]

Disaggregating these two broad study areas further, female graduates of STEM programs are more likely than males to complete natural sciences, math and statistics rather than engineering and information and communication technologies (ICT).[7]

---

[6] There are also differences by urban–rural residence, but we do not have data across the countries. In rural India, for example, female students have significantly higher odds of choosing arts and humanities programs as compared with male students, and significantly lower odds that they would choose sciences and engineering (Chakrabarti, 2009).

[7] This underrepresentation of female graduates in the STEM fields of study, especially in engineering, manufacturing, and construction as well as computing but not as much in physical sciences or mathematics and statistics, is similar to findings in European countries (van Langen and Dekkers, 2005).

The significantly smaller percentage of female graduates in ICT programs, compared to male graduates, in several countries (e.g., Brunei, India, Indonesia, Myanmar, New Zealand, the Philippines) suggests that, in the future, young men are going to be relatively better equipped to take advantage of the growing importance of the ICT industry in the region. According to the *World Development Report 2019* on the changing nature of jobs, "technology is reshaping the skills needed for work. The demand for less advanced skills that can be replaced by technology is declining. At the same time, the demand for advanced cognitive skills, socio-behavioral skills, and skill combinations associated with greater adaptability is rising" (World Bank, 2019, p. 6). A World Economic Forum (2016) report states that seven Asia-Pacific countries (Australia, Hong Kong (China), Japan, Republic of Korea, New Zealand, and Singapore) are among the top 20 countries in terms of overall ICT readiness.

There are striking gender differences also within the non-STEM fields, but the patterns do not necessarily align with what might be traditional expectations. In Myanmar, 42 percent of male students complete education programs, compared with 4 percent of female graduates, while 48 percent of females graduate from arts and humanities, compared to less than 1 percent of males. In Cambodia, 40 percent of male graduates have degrees in social sciences and journalism, compared with less than 1 percent of female graduates; 63 percent of females have degrees in business, administration, and law. In India, 28 percent of male students complete arts and humanities programs, as compared with 6 percent of females; 34 percent of female graduates complete social sciences and journalism programs. In the region as a whole, among female graduates in 17 countries, the fields of education, arts and humanities, and business, administration, and law account, on average, for 56 percent, compared with just 30 percent among male graduates. Business, administration, and law as a category accounts for 29 percent of female graduates, as compared with 12 percent of male graduates, and social sciences and journalism account for an average of 10 percent of female graduates and 25 percent of male graduates.

2.3 A Leaky Pipeline in the Academic Profession

The presence of female academics in tertiary education and their positions within those institutions are strong signals about gender equality in tertiary education. In the past two decades, this share has risen in the Asia-Pacific countries from a regional average of 35 percent to just under 50 percent or about gender equality. This average, however, masks wide variation across the countries, with a few countries reaching 50 percent or more and others staying below 20 percent. Superimposing the female share of enrollment on the female share of the faculty in tertiary education institutions by country shows that despite the large number of young women relative to men enrolled in tertiary education, women remain a small proportion of faculty staff in many countries (Figure 6.4). For example, Japan has reached almost gender equality in enrollment (0.94), but its share of female faculty is just 18 percent, the second lowest share in the region. South Korea has also achieved high enrollment rates among women relative to men (0.79), but

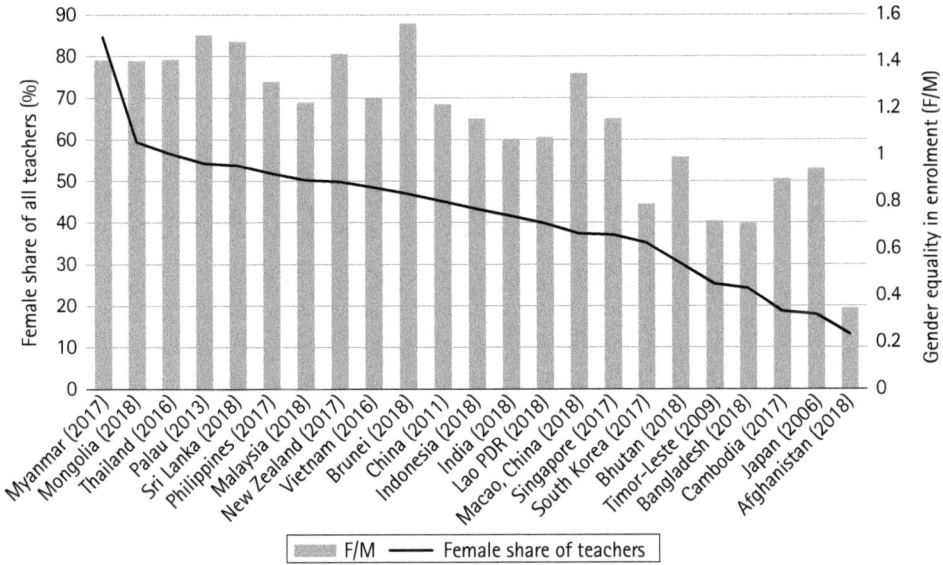

FIGURE 6.4 Gender equality in enrollment and female share of faculty in tertiary education
Source: Author's calculations using data extracted from World Bank Indicators, February 2020, latest year of data.

its share of female academic staff is just 35 percent. By comparison, the average female share in all high-income countries in the world is 42 percent.

Further, women are significantly underrepresented as deans and heads of departments, according to a report of the Association of Pacific Rim Universities (APRU) which surveyed 39 universities in 23 countries (APRU, 2019). On average, women account for 24.3 percent of deans and 24.4 percent of department heads in those universities. In 9 of the 12 Asia-Pacific countries included in the survey, the female share ranges from 9 percent in Japan to 43 percent in India.

Several reasons have been given to explain why more women are not promoted to management in academic institutions in the Asia-Pacific region. First, despite the higher enrollment rates of women, most do not continue beyond a first degree. Men hold the highest tertiary degrees (ISCED 7 and ISCED 8), outnumbering women at those levels of study. Secondly, a behavioral factor works against women's academic career. Men tend to form networking groups within academic institutions while female academics engage less with such groups (Ismail and Rasdi, 2007). Social networks can be important to career advancement, especially for understanding the roles of strategic alliances among colleagues and contacts with external scholars, so not participating in such networks disadvantages women. A study in Malaysia reports the reasons why women participate less in academic networks; women cite lack of funds and support from their institutions to participate in conferences, collaborative work, or any other networking events (Arokiasamy et al., 2011). However, the competing demands for women's time in the home, such as childcare and housekeeping, leave little time for such networking activities: "in crucial moments of their scientific careers, women tend to choose to abandon academia … for reasons outside of the professional realm, citing instead reasons of a private nature" (Cervia and Biancheri, 2017, p. 216). Social norms about gender roles are sticky and women are still the primary caregivers in many societies (King et al., 2021).

3. WHY ARE THERE GENDER DIFFERENCES IN TERTIARY EDUCATION?

This section reviews the empirical literature on the factors that influence tertiary education choices. It focuses on studies on the Asia-Pacific countries, undertaken and published since 2000, that use student-level data from randomized household or labor force surveys to understand how gender influences those choices. The theoretical framework behind these studies is that students consider their ability, aspiration, and preferences, the availability and affordability of supply options, expected returns, and societal norms (especially with respect to gender) in making their choices. The review prioritizes those studies that have estimated the effect of gender per se in these choices, controlling for the effects of other factors. Gender differences in tertiary education indicators are misleading if they are attributed only to gender preferences or norms and are not attributed also to factors such as graduation from upper secondary schools, access to student loans, job opportunities for college-aged youth, and family income. The "raw" gender gaps discussed in the preceding section may be smaller or wider than real gender gaps depending on these other factors. This point implies that the chosen analytical method should be able to delineate the effect not only of gender but also of compounding or confounding factors.[8]

3.1 Gender and Socio-Economic Background

Empirical research in the region, especially in its less developed countries, has centered on attendance and performance in basic and secondary education. Few have estimated the determinants of tertiary education choices and fewer still have examined the factors that lead to gender differences in those choices. The corresponding research on advanced or high-income countries in the region focuses more on the transition to tertiary education, choice of program, and choice of institution to attend, but less on the gender differences in those choices. We review below the findings from relatively recent empirical studies (over the past two decades) that estimate the *marginal effect* of gender, controlling for (or interacted with) socio-economic background, and those that analyze

---

[8] Most of the studies reviewed rely on multivariate regression methods, many of which estimate the direction and size of association rather than causal effects.

medium- to large-scale survey data using multivariate econometric approaches. The principal findings of those studies as they apply to gender are discussed below.

Gender. Studies estimate the probability of participation in tertiary education conditional on the successful completion of upper or senior secondary education; thus, the estimated coefficients show the marginal effects of factors, including gender, irrespective of how those factors have affected a student's journey to tertiary education. Azam and Blom (2008), for example, note that once they condition tertiary education enrollment on the completion of upper secondary education, most of the attainment and enrollment gap attributable to gender in India is reduced but they still obtain a significantly negative coefficient for women (-0.138). Among rural residents, being female means even lower participation (-0.731), controlling for other factors. Chakrabarti (2009) obtains a negative coefficient for women (-0.207), as do Sánchez and Singh (2018) for the state of Andhra Pradesh (-0.62).

In contrast to India, in Indonesia it is men who are less likely than women to attend tertiary education (-0.374), and this negative coefficient is larger for rural men than for urban men (-0.445 vs. -0.309) (Ogawa and Iimura, 2010). In contrast, Rifa'i et al. (2019) obtain a much smaller negative coefficient for men (-0.055). They find that, relative to women, men have a higher propensity to choose diploma programs (ISCED 5) over work, but both genders are equally likely to choose a Bachelor's program (ISCED 6) over work, holding other factors constant. This result is attributed to the higher certification value of a Bachelor's program for women in search of employment. In Vietnam, women are more likely to attend tertiary education than men, controlling for socio-economic background, but this female advantage is much smaller (0.072) (Sánchez and Singh, 2018). Vu et al. (2013) find an even smaller female advantage (0.006) in Vietnam, but Linh et al. (2012) find no significant gender gap after controlling for completing secondary education, suggesting that gender inequality occurs prior to tertiary education.

The study by Diffendal and Weidman (2011) on Mongolia does not use a multivariate approach, but it provides an explanation for why adolescent boys drop out of school before adolescent girls do. In Mongolia, parents allow their daughters to stay in school but push their sons to drop out in order to help ra, sell goods, pan for gold, and do other work to earn income. Also, the country's transition from a centrally planned economy to a market economy has opened new employment opportunities for men, making it possible for them to get relatively high-paying jobs that do not require higher education. The reverse gender gap in education starts in secondary education, with 71.4 percent of male students dropping out at this level.[9]

Gender differences in the choice of area of study, discussed above, are evident even after controlling for socio-economic background. On the supply side, the availability

---

[9] A different explanation is given by Jacob (2002) for the USA where the gross enrollment of females and males was 102 and 76 percent, respectively, in 2017. Conditional on attendance, there are few differences in enrollment status or selectivity of institution between males and females, but most of the gender gap in attendance can be explained by the higher non-cognitive skills of women, controlling for high school achievement.

and quality of options and the ease of admission into the desired programs in tertiary education institutions can explain choice—but the strength of these factors differs by gender (James et al., 1999). On the demand side, the number and salaries of jobs that graduates can command in the labor market attract students. As labor demand continues to shift towards occupations that require higher levels of technical and non-routine skills, it is unlikely that young women will enroll in STEM fields if STEM female graduates are effectively blocked from those appealing and well-paying jobs.

Gender differences in math and science performance at the secondary level also influence the choice of field at the tertiary level, but the 2018 PISA scores in math and science[10] for the Asia-Pacific region indicate that girls performed only slightly less well than boys in eight countries and outperformed boys in five countries. The reasons for their choice of field of study in tertiary education, thus, must be rooted elsewhere. A qualitative study suggests that young women in South Korea who are enrolled in engineering tend to drop out without completing their program for a variety of other reasons: lack of information and absence of mentors at the time when students decide their field of study; negative attitudes toward female engineering students in a male-dominant atmosphere; negative preconceptions about women's physical strength and machine-tooling ability; and lack of assistance from the university during their job search (Youn and Choi, 2015).

Caste, ethnicity, and norms. The marginal effect of gender interacts with other factors such as ethnicity, caste, and household wealth, either intensifying or attenuating it. In India, youths belonging to a Scheduled Caste or Scheduled Tribe background have significantly lower odds of enrolling in higher education compared to other groups in rural areas (Chakrabarti, 2009).[11] There is also considerable regional heterogeneity in this pattern: females of ST/SC background in the states of Bihar, Jharkhand, Orissa, and Rajasthan are more disadvantaged than those residing in Kerala and the North East. These regional differences are due to a combination of "economic backwardness, geographical isolation and shyness of contact with the community at large" that lead to female seclusion in the northern states as compared to the southern states (Chakrabarti, 2009, pp. 373–374). In Kerala, the positive attitudes of parents towards the education of their daughters and the migration of young men to the Middle East have been cited as factors for the gender education imbalance in favor of women (Chanana, 2007).

In Lao PDR, significant disparities stem also from the interactions between a person's gender and geographic location, ethno-linguistic affiliation, and income (King and van de Walle, 2012). In general, urban males from the Lao-Tai majority do better than rural

---

[10] These tests were taken by representative samples of 15-year-olds, many of them just completing lower or junior secondary school.

[11] Chanana (2007, p. 595) emphasizes that "in spite of a very well formulated policy of positive discrimination, the representation of *dalit* and *adivasi* students is not adequate and the proportion of women from among them is negligible. They generally join general education courses and are denied access to elite/courses and institutions."

females from the non-Lao-Tai minority groups. Rural women who are non-Lao-Tai lag farthest behind other population groups, in contrast to Lao-Tai women whose literacy and years of education have converged with those of Lao-Tai men in urban areas, and have achieved nearly the same level in rural areas. In Vietnam, the tertiary education enrollment rate of youth in the Kinh ethnic group is far higher than that of youth from other ethnic groups (18.8 percent vs. 3.4 percent), but studies do not interact this variable with gender in order to obtain a different effect of ethnicity for females and males (Linh et al., 2012; Vu et al., 2013). In all, language diversity as well as poverty and remoteness of residence are effective barriers to higher education for ethnic minorities in many Asian countries, and even as early as basic education (Hall and Patrinos, 2012).

Gender norms not necessarily due to minority affiliation also affect tertiary education choices. In South Korea, for example, parents with higher socio-economic status expect their children to succeed in school more, value autonomy and academic activities more highly, and spend more resources than do parents with low socio-economic status (Shin et al., 2015). In Shaanxi Province of China, college expectations are associated with parents' occupation and college education (Wei et al., 2019). The attitudes and preferences regarding children's academic choices have been attributed to Confucian cultures which emphasize the obligation of parents to children and children's obedience to their parents (Shin et al., 2015).

Parental education, especially the education of the household head, is often regarded as a proxy measure of the socio-economic status and wealth of the family in the absence of more direct measures. In many studies, parental education (and other household characteristics) has also been interpreted as a proxy for parental preferences and family norms regarding education. In India, whether the household head is female has a strikingly different marginal effect on the education of females and males (Chakrabarti, 2009). In the estimates for females, having a female household head is positively associated with tertiary education in urban areas but negatively associated in rural areas; in the estimates for males, having a female head is not statistically significant. These results suggest the importance of older women as role models and mentors to younger women. Whether the household head has higher education affects enrollment differently: the coefficients of this variable are also larger among urban residents than among rural residents, but are not significantly different between males and females. In Indonesia, both father's and mother's education levels are equally significant for daughter's or son's education, controlling for household income (Rifa'i et al., 2019).

Household income and wealth. Data from the Demographic and Health Surveys in Asia-Pacific countries reveal a large gap between the highest education level attained by the richest quintile in the population and that attained by the poorest quintile (Table 6.2). In Pakistan, the fraction of women aged 15–49 with more than secondary education is 0.69 of the proportion of men who do, but this female deficit is much smaller in the richest quintile (0.94) than in the poorest quintile (0.10). In Nepal, Myanmar, and Papua New Guinea, the gender pattern with respect to household wealth is more mixed.

Table 6.2 Gender inequality (F/M) in tertiary education, by wealth quintile

	Total F/M	Q5/Q1
Afghanistan (2015)	0.28	2.7
Cambodia (2014)	0.61	4.19
India (2015)	0.72	2.17
Myanmar (2016)	1.43	0.27
Nepal (2016)	0.68	1.31
Pakistan (2017)	0.69	9.36
Papua New Guinea (2017)	0.75	1.61
Timor Leste (2016)	0.89	1.67

Notes: The data pertain to post-secondary enrollment. Although other countries in the Asia-Pacific region than those listed here have DHS data, the other countries do not have comparable data for men. Vietnam is omitted because its latest survey is at least 10 years older than the other surveys. Q5/Q1 is the gender inequality (F/M) in the richest quintile (Q5) relative to the poorest quintile (Q1). In Papua New Guinea, the proportion of women with more than secondary education in the poorest quintile is zero, so the number shown is Q5/Q2.

Source: Author's calculations using data from Demographic & Health Surveys in each country for latest year.

Household income is significantly and positively associated with tertiary education attendance, controlling for other variables (Chakrabarti, 2009, for India; Ogawa and Iimura, 2010; and Rifa'i et al., 2019, for Indonesia). Chakrabarti's separate estimates for females and males suggest that the marginal effect of household income is larger for daughters than sons. These results are markedly different from the findings of Sánchez and Singh (2018) for the state of Andhra Pradesh in which household income makes no difference for daughters but has a large and significantly positive effect for sons; in other words, in Andhra Pradesh, daughters are not more likely to attend tertiary education in richer than in poorer households, whereas sons in richer households are more likely to do so. Wan (2018) suggests that, in patriarchal Asian cultures, when households are confronted with limited resources, it is expected that sons will receive more of the resources than daughters.

3.2 Characteristics of Tertiary Education Institutions

Students in the Asia-Pacific region have a wide range of enrollment options today as the number of higher education institutions has increased around the region, and students are making choices not only according to their ambition and constraints but also according to specific characteristics of the available institutions—their reputation, breadth and quality of programs offered, availability of student financial support, quality of student–professor interactions, and state of facilities and services. Differences in these characteristics partly explain why some institutions may be more appealing to either male or female students.

Dao and Thorpe (2015) use principal component analysis of data from more than 1,000 students in Vietnam to identify the features that influence student choices. The most important features are facilities and services; types of program offerings; price; offline information provided to prospective students; opinions of family members and friends; online information about the university; the form of communication used by the university; program additions; and type of advertising. The results indicate significant differences between genders. Relative to male students, female students rate the first seven factors above as more important, especially facilities and services. The analysis also indicates that undergraduates are influenced more by the views of parents and siblings whereas postgraduates are affected more by teachers and friends/colleagues. Durdyev and Ihtikar (2018) also find that students are significantly influenced by university-related factors, namely, university reputation and financial opportunities in Cambodia.

In Australia, students' preferred university is most closely linked to their chosen field of study; ease of access from home is the only other institutional consideration that is as important (James et al., 1999). In New Zealand, ease of access from home is also a key determinant of choice, with distance being more of a deterrent among rural male students than among rural females (Callister et al., 2008). In addition, female students are less concerned than male students with the starting salaries for new graduates, what university their friends are planning to attend, and what information technology is used in teaching. Instead, they are more concerned with the atmosphere of the campus and the opportunities for higher degree study.

In sum, tertiary education decisions by prospective students depend on the supply characteristics of academic institutions, so understanding the gender disparities in these preferences would be important for attracting students: "Today's student population wants convenience, a standardised curriculum and good value for their money. Students have become customers for which HEIs must compete. The massification and marketisation of higher education have created a competitive environment that must be addressed in ways many HEIs have not done before" (Taylor et al., 2008, p. 130).

3.3 The Draw of the Labor Market

Returns to tertiary education. None of the empirical studies we reviewed contains a direct measure of the labor market opportunities available to students or graduates; instead, several studies have examined how the aspirations of youths and of their parents or families affect the choices they make. Worldwide estimates of gender differences in returns to education show that the returns to tertiary education are higher than the returns to both primary and secondary education, and that they are higher for women than for men (Montenegro and Patrinos, 2014; Gunewardena et al., 2018). In low- and middle-income EAP countries, the average returns to tertiary education are about equal for men and women and are significantly higher than the returns to secondary education. In SAR countries, these returns are larger and also far larger for women than for men. In fact, the estimated return to tertiary education for women in SAR is the highest among world regions, a result of the rapid growth of employment opportunities for women created by the economic expansion in the region and also their still relatively low tertiary enrollment rates.

A few studies have also argued that social returns are higher for tertiary than for basic education, possibly because of the effect of tertiary education on improving the capacity of a country for innovation and good governance (Birdsall, 1996; Mammen and Paxson, 2000; Malik and Courtney, 2011; Psacharopoulos and Patrinos, 2014). Non-market returns to higher education are expected to differ by gender as well because of their different social and familial roles, although estimates of these non-market returns are relatively rare. Worldwide, women contribute more unpaid work to the care of their children and other family members, so the returns to women's education in terms of a country's human capital development is larger (Becker et al., 2010; King et al., 2021).

Two other studies indicate that academic performance in tertiary education also matters in the labor market. In Vietnam "excellent" graduation status increases earnings by 33 percent, while "good" graduation status increases earnings by only 3.5 percent (Sakellariou and Patrinos, 2000). In nine countries, four of which are Asian countries (China, Lao PDR, Sri Lanka, and Vietnam), multivariate quantile regressions show that tertiary education and cognitive skills are more important for women's earnings especially at the lower end and middle of the earnings distribution (Gunewardena et al., 2018).

Labor force participation. A woman's decision to work for pay involves making trade-offs, a balance between work opportunities and potential wages, and the need and value of her work at home. These trade-offs could lead to her accepting lower wages in return for job flexibility in terms of hours or place of work, even though this flexibility may reduce chances for future promotion or pay raises. She may also turn down a promotion because of the potential conflict with her family responsibilities. This balancing act is made more difficult by norms (and laws) that constrain her mobility and the type of work women are allowed to have. The Asia-Pacific region consists of some of the most modern and liberal cultures as well as some of the most traditional and patriarchal cultures (Asian Development Bank, 2015).

Quite striking is the difference in the labor force participation (LFP) rates of women who have tertiary education and those who have only secondary education. In every country in the region, women's tertiary education is associated with a higher LFP.

A woman with tertiary education in Sri Lanka, for example, is 40 percent more likely to be in the labor force than a woman with just secondary education, and in Pakistan, Bangladesh, and Indonesia, she is about 20 percent more likely. These are large differences. In comparison, the gap in LFP for men who have just secondary education and those with tertiary education is not significantly different, except in Lao PDR and Nepal where men with tertiary education are about 10 percent more likely to be in the labor force.[12]

Occupation and a "leaky pipeline". Do chosen fields of study translate into related occupations for men and women? Elementary occupations, that is, work related to agriculture, fishery, and forestry, dominate employment in low-income countries, but the share of this occupation has been diminishing. In low-income countries, the share of agriculture-related employment is larger for women than for men, and men are more likely than women to be employed as machine operators and assemblers. Services and sales, and craft and trade work account for about the same shares for women and men. In high-income countries, there is a greater balance across the occupational groups—but gender differences are still evident. Work related to craft and trades has become rare for women, replaced by service and sales work and by clerical work, and work as technicians has increased in equal importance for both women and men, all possibly reflecting the growing enrollment of women in higher education. Interestingly, the share of women in management is still far lower than the share of men.

Focusing on non-agricultural work and on the variation in the occupational distribution of women and men in 2019, gender differences in occupations become even clearer (Figure 6.5). While there is diversity in this pattern across countries, the gender differences in the median values are clear. A sizable share of women are professionals and clerical workers while a larger percentage of men are machine operators and assemblers. This occupational distribution is consistent with the reverse gender gap in tertiary education. On the whole, it seems consistent with the gender distribution of the fields of study, but examining specific jobs within occupations by country indicates that eligible women are blocked from certain jobs (a "glass wall"). Sam (2018) finds that being male helps graduates to find a matched job faster by 25 percent than women.

It is noteworthy that the proportion of management positions in the hands of women has increased over the past two decades across the Asia-Pacific region, starting with a (unweighted) regional average of 23 percent in 2000 to 30 percent in 2018. There is wide variation across the countries in this trend. The Philippines stands out with the share of women in management jobs being almost 50 percent, while Pakistan stands out for

[12] ILO data (2018) show that female labor force participation rates have increased from a worldwide average of about 30 percent in 1960 to above 50 percent in 2017. These rates are highest in low-income countries where families cannot afford to have women not work, but they are also high in high-income countries in North America and Europe. Studies find that individuals are able to balance their employment and caregiving when their care responsibilities are not heavy, but much less so when care work involves more than ten hours per week, particularly for women (Do, 2008; Jung, 2012; Liu et al., 2010).

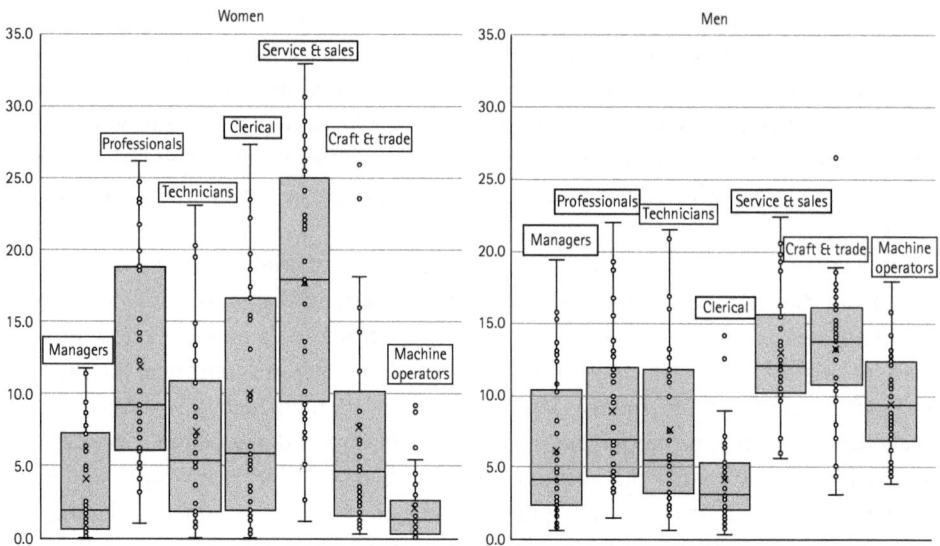

FIGURE 6.5 Gender distribution of non-agricultural occupations in the Asia-Pacific region

Note: These are box-and-whisker plots; median values are indicated by the horizontal bar within each box, and mean values are indicated by "x."

Data source: Author's calculations using data extracted from ILO.Stat, March 2020.

a female share of just 3 percent. And, despite the large numbers of women in Korea and Japan who have tertiary education, similar to the findings for women in academic jobs, women in those two countries account for account for just 11 and 12 percent, respectively, of management jobs, indicating that gender norms do weaken the positive links among tertiary education, employment, occupation, and lifetime earnings.[13]

Lastly, focusing on women with tertiary education and their employment, Table 6.3 presents data on the female share of total researchers by field of R&D and where they are employed. The weak relationship between field of study and occupation has been described as a "leaky pipeline," the phenomenon of progressively fewer women in STEM fields being employed in related fields at each developmental stage, from training to employment (Rosser, 2004). Myanmar is an outlier in this regard, with female researchers accounting for three-fourths of researchers in the natural sciences and engineering, all of them in government and higher education institutions. In Mongolia, the Philippines, Malaysia, and Sri Lanka, women account for about one-half of the total researchers in this field, whereas in Japan and South Korea women's share is less than one-fifth. For instance, Kim and Kim (2015) find that STEM female PhD graduates in Korea are 20 percent less

---

[13] Using survey data from Japan, South Korea, and Taiwan (China), Chang and England (2011) find similar patterns. In Taiwan, a higher percentage of women works in either professional (44 percent) or managerial and administrative (16 percent) positions than in Japan (46 and 10 percent, respectively) or Korea (38 and 7 percent). In Japan too, 36 percent of women are in non-regular (contingent or temporary) jobs, compared with only 8 percent in Korea and 6 percent in Taiwan.

Table 6.3 Female researchers as percentage of total researchers, by field and place of employment

Country/latest year of data	Female share of total researchers (%) by field of R&D		Female share of total researchers by place of employment (%)			
	Natural sciences and engineering	Social sciences and humanities	Business enterprise	Government	Higher education	Private non-profit
Cambodia (2015)	21.6	27.4	9.3	27.7	18.5	34.4
Macao, China (2017)	33.2	44.2	8.6	–	40.1	18.2
Indonesia 2017)			40.0	37.6	46.6	46.9
Japan (2017)	12.7	32.7	9.6	18.5	27.1	15.3
Malaysia (2016)	48.2	50.2	36.0	–	50.9	73.9
Mongolia (2017)	60.6	49.8	27.4	59.6	52.3	–
Myanmar (2017)	75.8	70.8	–	71.2	84.1	–
Pakistan (2017)	36.2	42.3	–	15.0	39.8	–
Papua New Guinea (2016)	32.9	46.9	–	30.5	34.6	18.2
Philippines (2013)	46.4	65.1	43.1	55.0	56.7	60.8
South Korea (2017)	15.8	43.1	16.0	26.1	31.7	28.6
Singapore (2014)			26.1	35.8	33.6	–
Sri Lanka (2015)	45.2	49.4	49.3	46.9	45.4	50.0

Note: This table includes only countries with data since 2000.

Data source: UIS.Stat, extracted 2/2020.

likely to find an academic position than their male peers, net of other factors. With respect to place of employment, government and academia employ the largest shares of female researchers, but this is not the case in Cambodia, Japan, and South Korea. Quite striking is that female researchers account for at least one-half of total researchers in private, non-profit organizations and for more than 40 percent in business enterprises in the Philippines and Sri Lanka.

4. Summary and Conclusions

The Asia-Pacific region is home to a handful of highly educated, high-income countries, several large middle-income countries, and many populous low-income countries, as well as small island states. The region has some of the highest gross enrollment rates in tertiary education—or among the fastest growing enrollment rates—but also some of the lowest. Some of these countries produce the highest-performing students, according to international assessments of students such as PISA and TIMSS, but some produce the lowest-performing students (OECD, 2019). Overlaid on these huge educational contrasts are stunningly diverse social norms about gender roles and behaviors (Duflo, 2012; Ji, 2015). Although young women in most of the Asia-Pacific countries today are drawn to tertiary education in greater numbers than males, a trend shared by other world regions, this overall picture hides large heterogeneity in gender equality that stems from the economic, social, and cultural differences within the region.

The chapter has presented the many facets of gender inequality and has reviewed existing empirical research that estimates the effects of socio-economic factors. The findings corroborate the overall picture of unprecedented vertical educational progress but also evidence of gender inequality. First, data show that gender differences are mediated by income, ethnicity, place of residence, and social norms. Because of the wide diversity of economies and cultures in the region, more such research is warranted on a larger set of indicators and for different population groups. It is not enough to present trends and patterns in gender indicators without considering their relationship to the socio-demographic and economic background of women and men. Second, horizontal segregation is the systematic differences in the fields of study pursued by female and male students. Although the degree of gender segregation varies across the countries in the region, these systematic differences stand out. Finally, the issue of a "leaky pipeline" is about a serious loss of talent in labor markets because female graduates, especially in the STEM fields, are not able to find jobs that are commensurate with their academic expertise, performance, and career aspirations. According to UNESCO (2015), the average share of researchers who are women is 23.4 percent in East Asia and the Pacific and 18.5 percent in South Asia.

This chapter has not discussed what tertiary education systems can do to address gender inequalities and what are the lessons from previous efforts to do so. Winchester et al. (2006) emphasize that such efforts should increase support for female candidates, consider part-time and non-traditional careers, and include more women on promotions committees. Australia's affirmative action policy for universities increased the application rates and success rates for women, and though women remain underrepresented, their share at the professorial level has increased.

To end, here are a few highlights about gender patterns in Asia-Pacific:

- There has been a worldwide boom in female enrollment in tertiary education. This is, in part, a response to the higher returns to tertiary education for women than for men, especially at the lower end and middle of the earnings distribution. Returns are 50 percent higher for women than for men, holding constant socio-economic factors as well as measures of cognitive and socio-emotional skills, in four Asian countries with requisite data (Gunewardena et al., 2018).
- Neither economic nor educational development guarantees gender equality in tertiary education. The legacy of patriarchal gender norms has been persistent

even in the wealthier and more industrialized countries in the region, and in most countries, gender bias overlays discrimination by caste and ethno-linguistic affiliation, creating pockets of severe gender disparities. To achieve greater gender equality in the region, it is important to understand more deeply which women are getting ahead and which are left behind and to target interventions accordingly

- Despite the rising number of female tertiary graduates, women are a small proportion of the faculty and management in higher education institutions, not to mention in private enterprises. The proportion of management positions held by women has increased only modestly in the past decades, and this proportion remains quite small in several countries. Evidence suggests that social norms act on two fronts in this regard: they proscribe women's social and economic roles, ultimately dampening women's career aspirations, and they reduce the willingness to promote women to senior positions and positions of leadership despite their academic attainment.

- Why young men are not enrolling in higher education at rates equal to young women in several countries in the region is a question that also deserves rigorous inquiry. A World Bank study (2012) identifies five weaknesses of higher education systems in the region that may explain why they fail to attract young men: a gap between those institutions and the skill needs of employers; a weak research and technology nexus between higher education institutions and companies; a separation between teaching and research functions of those institutions; a disconnect among higher education institutions themselves and between these institutions and training providers; and a separation between higher education institutions and lower levels of education.

- Male students are choosing STEM fields at much higher proportions than female students; within STEM fields, they dominate engineering, manufacturing, and construction as well as ICT programs. This finding implies that young men are going to be better prepared than young women to take advantage of the growing importance of the ICT industry in the Asia-Pacific region. The ICT industry and ICT-enabled innovations in non-ICT enterprises are expected to continue to fuel economic growth, and future jobs will require both ICT literacy and higher related technical skills. One of the reasons why young women hesitate to choose STEM fields is that female graduates of STEM are not welcome to the same jobs as male graduates. Moreover, the demands of private life often conflict with the needs associated with career advancement. To attract and retain more young women in STEM fields, they need better career and job search support from higher education institutions.

References

Arokiasamy, L., Ismail, M., Ahmad, A., and Othman, J. (2011). "Determinants of career advancement of academics in private institutions of higher learning in Malaysia." In *Proceedings of the 10th International Conference of the Academy of HRD (Asia Chapter)*, 1–11.

Asian Development Bank (2015). *Women in the Workforce: An Unmet Potential in Asia and the Pacific.* Mandaluyong City, Philippines: Asian Development Bank.

Association of Pacific Rim Universities (APRU) (2019). *2019 APRU Gender Gap Report.* Sydney: University of Sydney and the Asia-Pacific Women in Leadership (APWiL) Program.

Azam, M. and Blom, A. (2008). *Progress in Participation in Tertiary Education in India from 1983 to 2004.* Washington, DC: World Bank.

Barro, R. J. and Lee, J. W. (2013). "A new data set of educational attainment in the world, 1950–2010." *Journal of Development Economics*, 104, 184–198.

Becker, G. S., Hubbard, W. H. J., and Murphy, K. M. (2010). "Explaining the worldwide boom in higher education of women." *Journal of Human Capital*, 4/3, 203–241.

Birdsall, N. (1996). "Public spending on higher education in developing countries: Too much or too little?" *Economics of Education Review*, 15/4, 407–419.

Callister, P., Leather, F., and Holt, J. (2008). *Gender and Tertiary Education: Is It Useful to Talk about Male Disadvantage?* Washington, DC: Institute of Policy Studies.

Cervia, S. and Biancheri, R. (2017). "Women in science: The persistence of traditional gender roles. A case study on work–life interface." *European Educational Research Journal*, 16/2–3, 215–229.

Chakrabarti, A. (2009). "Determinants of participation in higher education and choice of disciplines: Evidence from urban and rural Indian youth." *South Asia Economic Journal*, 10/2, 371–402.

Chanana, K. (2007). "Globalisation, higher education and gender: Changing subject choices of Indian women students." *Economic & Political Weekly*, 42/7, 590–598.

Chang, C. F. and England, P. (2011). "Gender inequality in earnings in industrialized East Asia." *Social Science Research*, 40/1, 1–14.

Dao, M. T. N. and Thorpe, A. (2015). "What factors influence Vietnamese students' choice of university?" *International Journal of Educational Management*, 29/5, 666–681.

Diffendal, E. A. and Weidman, J. C. (2011). "Gender equity in access to higher education in Mongolia." In J. C. Weidman and W. J. Jacobs (eds.), *Beyond the Comparative.* Rotterdam: Sense Publishers, 333–353.

Do, Y. K., Norton, E. C., Stearns, S. C., and Van Houtven, C. H. (2015). "Informal Care and Caregiver's Health." *Health Economics* 24/2, 224–37.

Duflo, E. (2012). "Women empowerment and economic development." *Journal of Economic Literature*, 50/4, 1051–1079.

Durdyev, S. and Ihtiyar, A. (2019). "Structural equation model of factors influencing students to major in architecture, engineering, and construction." *Journal of Professional Issues in Engineering Education and Practice*, 145/2, 05018019/1–05018019/19.

Gunewardena, D., King, E. M. and Valerio, A. (2018). *More than schooling: Understanding gender differences in the labor market when measures of skill are available.* Policy Research Working Paper Series No. 8588. Washington, DC: World Bank.

Hall, G. H. and Patrinos, H. A. (eds.) (2012). *Indigenous Peoples, Poverty, and Development.* Cambridge: Cambridge University Press.

International Labour Organization (2018). *Care Work and Care Jobs for the Future of Decent Work.* Geneva: ILO.

Ismail, M. and Rasdi, R. M. (2007). "Impact of networking on career development: Experience of high-flying women academics in Malaysia." *Human Resource Development International*, 10/2, 153–168.

Jacob, B.A. (2002). "Where the boys aren't: Non-cognitive skills, returns to school and the gender gap in higher education." *Economics of Education review*, 21/6, 589–598.

James, R., Baldwin, G., and McInnis, C. (1999). *Which University? The Factors Influencing the Choices of Prospective Undergraduates*. Canberra: Department of Education, Training and Youth Affairs.

Ji, Y. (2015). "Asian families at the crossroads: A meeting of east, west, tradition, modernity, and gender." *Journal of Marriage and Family*, 77/5, 1031–1038.

Kim, K. and Kim, J. K. (2015). "Trends in determinants of entry into the academic career: The case of South Korea, 1980–2010." *PloS One*, 10/10, e0141428. doi:10.1371/journal.pone.0141428

King, E. M., Randolph, H., Floro, M., and Suh, J. (2021). "Demographic, health, and economic transitions and the future care burden." *World Development*, 140, 105371.

King, E. M. and van de Walle, D. (2012). "Laos: Ethnolinguistic diversity and disadvantage." In G. H. Hall and H. A. Patrinos (eds.), *Indigenous Peoples, Poverty, and Development*. Cambridge: Cambridge University Press, 249–303.

Linh, V. H., Thuy, L. V., and Long, G. T. (2012). *Equity and Access to Tertiary Education: The Case of Vietnam*. Vietnam: DEPOCEN Working Paper Series 2012/10. http://www.depocenwp.org

Liu, L., Dong, X. Y., and Zheng, X. (2010). "Parental care and married women's labor supply in urban China." *Feminist Economics*, 16/3, 169–192.

Malik, S. and Courtney, K. (2011). "Higher education and women's empowerment in Pakistan." *Gender and Education*, 23/1, 29–45.

Mammen, K. and Paxson, C. (2000). "Women's work and economic development." *Journal of Economic Perspectives*, 14/4, 141–164.

Montenegro, C. E. and Patrinos, H. A. (2014). *Comparable Estimates of Returns to Schooling around the World*. Policy Research Working Paper Series No. 7020. Washington, DC: World Bank.

OECD. (2019). https://www.oecd.org/pisa/Combined_Executive_Summaries_PISA_2018.pdf

Ogawa, K. and Iimura, K. (2010). "Determinants of access and equity in tertiary education: The case of Indonesia." *Excellence in Higher Education*, 1/1–2, 3–22.

Peng, Y. W., Kawano, G., Lee, E., Tsai, L. L., Takarabe, K., Yokoyama, M., Ohtsubo, H., and Ogawa, M. (2017). "Gender segregation on campuses: A cross-time comparison of the academic pipeline in Japan, South Korea, and Taiwan." *International Journal of Gender, Science and Technology*, 9/1, 3–24.

Psacharopoulos, G. and Patrinos, H. A. (2014). *Returns to Investment in Education: A Review and Further Update*. Washington, DC: World Bank.

Rifa'i, A., Irwandi, I., and Mendy, D. (2019). "Determinants of demand for higher education in Indonesia: Evidence from Indonesia Family Life Survey." *Jurnal Ekonomi Pembangunan: Kajian Masalah Ekonomi dan Pembangunan*, 20/1, 130–140.

Rosser, S. V. (2004). *The Science Glass Ceiling: Academic Women Scientists and the Struggle to Succeed*. New York: Routledge.

Sakellariou, C. N. and Patrinos, H. A. (2000). "Labour market performance of tertiary education graduates in Vietnam." *Asian Economic Journal*, 14/2, 147–165.

Sánchez, A. and Singh, A. (2018). "Accessing higher education in developing countries: Panel data analysis from India, Peru, and Vietnam." *World Development*, 109, 261–278.

Shin, J., Lee, H., McCarthy-Donovan, A., Hwang, H., Yim, S., and Seo, E. (2015). "Home and motivational factors related to science-career pursuit: Gender differences and gender similarities." *International Journal of Science Education*, 37/9, 1478–1503.

Taylor, J., Brites, R., Correia, F., Farhangmehr, M., Ferreira, B., de Lourdes Machado, M., Sarrico, C., and Sá, M. J. (2008). "Strategic enrolment management." *Higher Education Management and Policy*, 20/1, 1–17.

UNESCO (2015). *A Complex Formula: Girls and Women in Science, Technology, Engineering and Mathematics in Asia*. http://unesdoc.unesco.org/images/0024/002457/245717E.pdf

Van Langen, A. and Dekkers, H. (2005). "Cross-national differences in participating in tertiary science, technology, engineering and mathematics education." *Comparative Education*, 41/3, 329–350.

Vu, L. T. H., Le, L. C., and Muhajarine, N. (2013). "Multilevel determinants of colleges/universities enrolment in Vietnam: Evidences from the 15% sample data of population census 2009." *Social Indicators Research*, 111/1, 375–386.

Wan, C.-D. (2018). "Student enrolment in Malaysian higher education: Is there gender disparity and what can we learn from the disparity?' *Compare: A Journal of Comparative and International Education*, 48/2, 244–261.

Wei, Y., Zhou, S., and Yang, X. (2019). "College expectations and choices: Explaining the gaps in college enrollment for high- and low-SES students in China." *International Journal of Educational Development*, 70, 102079. doi.org/10.1016/j.ijedudev.2019.102079

Winchester, H., Lorenzo, S., Browning, L., and Chesterman, C. (2006). "Academic women's promotions in Australian universities." *Employee Relations*, 28/6, 505–522.

World Bank (2012). *Putting Higher Education to Work: Skills and Research for Growth in East Asia*. Washington, DC: World Bank.

World Bank (2019). *World Development Report 2019: The Changing Nature of Work*. Washington, DC: World Bank.

World Economic Forum (2016). *Global Information Technology Report 2016*. Geneva: World Economic Forum.

Youn, J. T. and Choi, S. A. (2015). "Women included engineering education in Korea." *Procedia: Social and Behavioral Sciences*, 174, 1678–1683.

PART IV

....

WHAT

*Content and Learning
in Higher Education*

....

CHAPTER 7

THE RELATIONSHIP BETWEEN CREDENTIALS AND LEARNING

A Focus on International Educational Value and Distinction

JOHANNA L. WATERS

1. INTRODUCTION

EDUCATION has become thoroughly valorized throughout the Asia-Pacific region. It underpins household decision-making and familial and individual sacrifices (Stafford, 1995; Seth, 2002; Waters, 2015). Educational achievement and success represent the "ultimate goal" of many households with young children. And yet, the *meanings* attached to education are often not interrogated. In this chapter, I explore the notion of education from two (sometimes competing) perspectives—that of the acquisition of credentials, on the one hand, and acquiring learning, on the other. Credentials refer to what Bourdieu (1986) has called "institutionalized cultural capital"—the value attributed to attaining a qualification from a particular educational institution, materialized (for example) in a "degree certificate." As will be discussed, for various reasons, educational institutions are *differentially valued*, by students, families, and employers. Such differential value is particularly apparent when considered through the lens of international student mobility, whereby students are choosing where (in the world) to study, often drawing on a set of metrics (such as university rankings) to make their decisions.

Learning, by contrast, is far less tangible. It can be formal (within or attached to an educational institution) or informal (outside or "beyond" the classroom setting), explicit or tacit. The focus on this chapter will be on formal learning, and how this relates (or not) to the process of credentialization. The chapter will interrogate the claim that credentials and learning are increasingly becoming disconnected within (international) higher education, with implications for social mobility and social (in) equalities. This is because some employers are placing emphasis on *where* someone studies (the symbolic distinction attached to the institution) when choosing between particular job candidates and not *what* they have studied or, indeed, *what they know* in terms of the knowledge they have accrued. The institution acts as a form of short-hand or "signaling" to indicate, to potential employers, the "quality" of a job candidate (Spence, 1978).

The link between (formal) learning and credentials has been discussed in the literature on international higher education and the transnational mobilities of students within and outwith the Asia-Pacific region. International student mobility refers to the tendency of young people to seek education outside their home countries. According to the OECD, international student mobility at tertiary level has increased from 0.8 million in the late 1970s to 4.6 million in 2015 and then to 5.6 million in 2018 (OECD, 2020). Academics have also pointed to the significance of student mobility between countries within Asia (Sidhu et al., 2020). China has been and continues to be the most significant "source country" of internationally mobile students whilst, in recent years, also becoming the third largest "host" or "receiver" of international students (Lee, 2020a). Across Asia, however, spanning numerous countries within the region, an increasing number of students are moving outside of their countries or birth or residence for education. Whilst a relatively insignificant phenomenon overall (if total student numbers are taken into account), for some states (such as Singapore, Malaysia, and the Philippines), student mobility has become an important part of national-level economic policy (see Yang, 2016; Koh, 2017; Ortiga, 2017).

The principal conceptual lens through which these developments have been discussed is Pierre Bourdieu's "forms of capital" (1986): (international) education is conceived as "capital"—predominately cultural capital, which is both embodied in the "learner" and institutionalized in the credential-awarding university. The embodied nature of cultural capital can *include* learning. It relates to language ability, but also *accent* and inflection, ways of dressing, ways of holding oneself, sense of humor, as well as types of "knowledge" associated with more formal learning, as captured so well in Ong's (1999) now iconic work on wealthy transnational Chinese migrants. However, credentials, not learning, have emerged as a marker of distinction in (international) higher education. Thus, credentials represent what Bourdieu (1986) has called "institutionalized cultural capital" (see also Bourdieu, 1984). In other words, the value of credentials is directly attached to the distinction held by the degree- or certificate-awarding institution and not the nature, amount, or content of the "learning" that takes place as part of the degree. The implications of this disconnect are that, in some cases, less academically able students are able effectively to "buy" a prestigious, international education and bypass their more stringent and demanding domestic system (Waters, 2006). While only a small percentage of the total student body in many countries are actually able to do this, this small number has a relatively big impact on the private-sector job markets of their home societies when they return, armed with their prestigious international credentials, and find their CVs at the "top of the pile" (Waters, 2008).

In what follows, the chapter first considers the realm where credentials and learning most clearly align, that is, in relation to formal examinations (such as university entrance examinations). I then consider the value attributed to credentials and learning separately, in relation to the literature on international student mobility and the internationalization of higher education.

2. FORMAL EXAMINATIONS, LEARNING, CREDENTIALS, AND CREDENTIALIZATION

Collins (1979) popularized the notion of "the credential society," to indicate (rather ironically and underpinned by critique) the rise of credentialization within higher education. Credentialization refers to the fact that "value" is attached to the credential rather than to the knowledge itself and is often discussed in relation to massification in higher education (also known as the democratization of higher education, as it has become available to the "masses"). This has led to an increased importance being given to the notion of "distinction" (after Bourdieu) and attaining "positional advantage" in the labor market. Countries and institutions within those countries have become increasingly differentiated in terms of the value attached to their credentials. Brown and Souto-Otero (2020) discuss credentials and the role they play within contemporary society in some depth, and it is worth briefly reflecting upon their arguments here. The credential, they argue, acts as a "currency of opportunity" "mediating the relationship between education and occupational destinations" (p. 95). Credentials play a "crucial role in shaping social stratification through their role in recruitment processes" (p. 110). In other words, credentials are linked to jobs/careers which, in turn, are linked to "social class"/"social (im)mobility."

As discussed in Waters (2015), throughout East and South-East Asia, the accumulation of credentials has become a compulsion. Education is what Seth (2002, p. 2) has described (in the South Korean context) as an "intense preoccupation." For many Asian households, education is viewed as a necessity and the only route to social reproduction and social acceptability. Consequently, the literature has documented the degree of sacrifice attached to education: these sacrifices are habitually gendered (Huang and Yeoh, 2005, 2011). It falls on the mother's shoulders to guarantee a child's "success" in their educational pursuits. Sometimes, such sacrifices include transnational migration strategies, as detailed in the literature on "wild geese/kirogi," "parachute kids," "astronaut" families, and "study mothers" (Zhou, 1998; Ho, 2002; Waters, 2003; Huang and Yeoh, 2005; Lee and Koo, 2006; Chew, 2010; Kim, 2010).

At this point, a brief discussion of what is meant by "learning" is required. Here, I am drawing on the work of Jarvis et al. (2003), who make the distinction between learning as a human process of acquiring knowledge and more "institutionalized" definitions of learning that have come to prominence in the past few decades, such as the "learning society" and the "learning organization." Here, the idea of learning as a process, tied to the acquisition of specific knowledge and skills, is more applicable and useful. Learning involves the investment of time and effort by the "holder." Individual learning is one of the most important objectives of contemporary education.

The link between credentials and learning is most clearly seen in relation to formal examinations. In formal exams, students are tested on "what they know," which results in a credential (involving marks, grades, and/or rankings). Such examinations are sometimes called "meritocratic"; yet overwhelmingly, academic scholarship has concluded that education systems (and the outcomes they produce) are "unfair." Students compete for the spoils of education (selective school places, university access, and desirable jobs) that are not on a level playing field. As social theorist Pierre Bourdieu has amply demonstrated, education systems enact a form of "pedagogic violence" against the children of working-class families, through which the reproduction of those in power is guaranteed (Reay, 2018). It is known that children born into less privileged households are not inherently less intelligent than those born into wealthier households, and yet statistically the latter group will be far more likely to "succeed" in the academic arena. Sociologists, anthropologists, and social geographers have been grappling with questions around the causes of these inequalities. Very little work, however, has focused on understanding why people do not, by and large, question the unfairness of this system. To put it another way, why does the concept of educational meritocracy remain such a powerful ideological trope when it is critical, for the maintenance of these systems (and the wider economies that they support), that people believe that the social outcomes they produce are somehow "fair"?

According to the OECD, in meritocratic societies a combination of individual effort and innate "ability" determines income. In many countries around the world, but particularly in East and South-East Asia, the principle of "educational meritocracy" functions as a powerful social glue. Parents across the social divide invest heavily in their children's education, in the hope (what Lauren Berlant (2011) might call a "cruel optimism") that they will succeed. Some countries have imbibed this notion of educational meritocracy more than others. East Asian countries, which are widely seen as the most education-obsessed, exam-driven places in the world, are also frequently described as the most "meritocratic" in nature (Liu, 2016; cf. Waters and Leung, 2017). According to Liu (2013), meritocracy has been a powerful ideology used by the Chinese authorities in the transition to a market-driven economy, particularly in relation to the *Gaokao* (the university entrance examination) (see Liang, 2010).

Interestingly, it is these same countries that "top" international league tables for performance in education. In the latest PISA (Programme for International Student Assessment, OECD) rankings for math and science, East Asian countries took the top five spots (Singapore, Hong Kong, South Korea, Japan, and Taiwan). The UK came 20th, according to this metric, and many recent UK-based policy and media discussions have considered how British education might emulate pedagogy in East Asia. These discussions relate—in part—to notions of educational meritocracy.

Meritocratic education systems are supported by a complex apparatus that includes public examinations which rank, categorize, and label young people. The concept of biopower (after Michel Foucault) may be useful for conceptualizing the role that meritocracy plays in wider structures of governance. Ideas around educational meritocracy can also be related to the consequences of academic "failure" for individuals (in "meritocratic" societies, failure is often "pathologized," as described by T. E. Woronov (2015) in an excellent ethnography of academic failure in China). In other words, such weight is given to "success" in such ostensibly meritocratic education systems, that to fail is described in "life or death" terms by young people themselves and by their wider household unit (Liang, 2010; Waters and Leung, 2017). Therefore, formal examinations which either confer credentials themselves or open the door to opportunities for credential acquisition (such as universities) are one arena where credentials and knowledge imparted through the education system are still closely aligned.

Finally, it is worth touching on the related issue of "failure." The successful accumulation of credentials by some individuals is paralleled by the absence of success for other young people. Academic failure is a "real life" problem, insofar as the majority of young people are confronted with failure of some sort during a prolonged experience of schooling. However, what failure means varies by stage of schooling, and by context. For example, for middle-class students in Hong Kong, failure means being unable to access higher education at a domestic university (Waters, 2008), whilst for privileged (privately educated) UK sixth-formers, failure means being unable to secure a place at either Oxford or Cambridge (Waters and Brooks, 2010) (even though many other so-called "world-class" universities exist within the United Kingdom). Interestingly, in these examples, failure has little to do with the actual learning that has (or has not) taken place. Rather, failure is attached to the ability (or not) to acquire an institutionalized credential.

In parts of Asia-Pacific, young people must confront failure at various stages of schooling. Presently, in Hong Kong, fewer than 30 percent of people sitting the Hong Kong Diploma of Secondary Education are able to study for an undergraduate degree at a domestic university (SCMP, 2018). According to OECD figures, this is one of the lowest percentages amongst advanced economies in the world. The young people that remain are consequently "shut out" of local university courses, with only limited options. Those options include studying at a local continuing education college for a certificate, higher diploma, or associate degree; applying for a degree course overseas (most commonly in North America or Europe); or entering the labor market. For Singapore, the figure representing young people able to access a local university (known as the "cohort participation rate") is around 30 percent. Consequently, whilst learning *may* lead to credentials, this is clearly not inevitably the case. In the next section, I turn to consider, specifically, credentials and how they are ascribed particular *value* on a global stage.

3. VALUE AND CREDENTIALS

The historic value attached to credentials from particular English-speaking countries, on a global stage, has its roots in colonialism and imperialism. As has been described for Hong Kong, teaching and learning in English has become a marker of "distinction" (Chan, 2002; Choi, 2003). Chan (2002) discusses that English language use in Hong Kong's schools goes "beyond pedagogy"—English functions as a marker of distinction—a form of credential, if you will (in this case, to distinguish Hong Kong residents from citizens of the People's Republic of China). It is interesting, however, to consider how countries such as China may be challenging this assumed dominance of former imperial powers, in part through the recent growth in numbers of international students attending universities there (a so-called non-traditional destination country) (Lee, 2020a; Mulvey, 2021).

The emergence of global league tables, which can differ considerably amongst each other in their findings, has also played a role in the creation and maintenance of the value attributed to particular credentials, to which students and families often pay heed (Jöns and Hoyler, 2013). Increasingly, university rankings have been seen as the cornerstone of the marketization and neoliberalization of the higher education sector across several countries, impacting domestic students' decision-making on where to attend university (Hazelkorn, 2015).

In her work on international student mobility, Beech (2019) describes how important university rankings are in determining the choice of study destination for international student informants. Rankings and "reputation" are closely aligned in ensuring institutional cultural capital. Beech (2019) writes: "reputation and quality could therefore be based on two different factors, either the university's performance in contrast to others or alternatively a more generally accepted belief that the [country] ... as a whole could offer a superior degree to what they would find elsewhere" (p. 139). This relates to postcolonial imaginaries, wherein particular countries and regions of the world (notably, "the West") are valued above all others.

University rankings, however, have been shown to be problematic, reinforcing and producing global geographies of valued "knowledge production," which tend to work in favor of former imperial and colonial powers (Jöns and Hoyler, 2013; see Waters and Brooks, 2021) and promote the idea of the "world class university." In a blog posting on global rankings, Olds (2012) observes the following:

> My concern about the term "World University Rankings" relates to the very small number of universities that are ranked relative to the total number of universities around the world that have combined research and teaching mandates. World University Rankings is a term that implies there is a unified field of universities that can be legitimately compared and ranked in an ordinal hierarchical fashion on the basis of some common metrics. (n.p.)

In other words, many universities are *excluded* from "world university rankings," which consequently could be seen to be both misleading and damaging. The point is, however, that students are invariably attracted to particular educational institutions *irrespective of the learning* that those institutions offer. It could be argued, of course, that the prestige of an institution is assumed to attach itself to the quality of knowledge (or learning) imparted also. In the extant literature, however, students rarely discuss the importance of learning when describing their decision-making around (international) higher education (Waters, 2008).

Institutional cultural capital is also tied to particular places. Prazeres et al. (2017) discuss "alternative narratives of distinction" in relation to higher education (p. 114). They argue that international students consider issues of "place" and "lifestyle" when deciding on a study destination (Beech, 2014, 2019; Collins, 2014). Value is ascribed to that place. Notably, learning (or knowledge acquisition) does not feature in these discussions, underlining the disconnect that I am describing.

Cities themselves are thought to generate value for the student. Collins (2014) notes that "International students are often attracted to major cities as higher education folds into future labour market participation and the social and cultural lives of students" (p. 243). They can assume that studying in a particular city will inevitably generate important social capital, which in turn will facilitate them in the process of job seeking (Brooks and Waters, 2018). Thus, students have broader considerations in mind when it comes to deciding where to study. For example, students may have longer-term objectives when it comes to locating their educational experiences, which tie into ideas of life course or life planning (as Shubin (2020) and Xu (2021) have recently claimed) – see also discussions in Favell (2011) and Findlay et al. (2012) around life course and education. These objectives have little to do with the immediacy of learning.

4. LEARNING AND HIGHER EDUCATION

This section will consider academic literature on "learning" within higher education, including work on different types or styles of learning (drawing heavily on Williams' and Baláž's (2014) work on migration and "types of learning"). It will also consider what migrant and international students have reported about different learning styles in different contexts (for example, East Asian students disliking the "rote" learning style that they are exposed to at home, favoring a more expressive and "creative" (in their words) North American and European approach to learning). This difference is often given as a reason for why families migrate for education.

As Waters and Brooks (2021) describe, internationally mobile students—although assumed to be largely concerned with issues around distinction and institutional cultural capital—are sometimes focused on learning. A broad-based liberal arts education, which is offered in many institutions in the United States, may appeal to some international students where it differs considerably from the types of programs available in their home country (Ma, 2020). In Ma's (2020) research, Chinese students studying in the United States articulated the appeal of a more "rounded" education. Perceived "academic culture" might also be decisive, again articulated in Ma's (2020) study, where respondents described an emphasis placed on creativity and critical thinking within learning in the context of a North American degree program. East Asian students studying within a North American system have frequently emphasized their dislike of "rote learning" and preference for (and employers' preference for) more critical thinking skills developed in "the West" (Waters, 2008). Not dissimilar from this, Cairns et al. (2018) have claimed that many European students view the ERASMUS mobility program as an opportunity to engage in "more creative and exploratory forms of learning" (Waters and Brooks, 2021).

Interestingly, there is a growing body of work that has described the increasing appeal of liberal arts courses within East and South-East Asia (e.g., Cheng, 2019). International students in Taiwan, as Roberts et al. (2010) have shown, desired to learn traditional, rather than simplified, Chinese. Waters and Leung (2020) describe something similar in relation to cross-border schooling between Hong Kong and Mainland China, where Mainland parents want their children to access a particular style of learning available over the border. This type of "learning" has as much to do with an expression of cultural identity as it does with knowledge *per se*.

Certain career options demand learning in specific degree subjects, resulting in particular qualifications. Here, we consider the case of Indian students, pursuing medical degrees in China. Yang (2018) considers the experiences of Indian young people from less privileged backgrounds pursuing English-medium degrees in medicine (MBSS) at a provincial university in China. These students are not seeking an education at a globally elite or renowned university but are instead seeking very specific and specialized knowledge in the MBBS (Bachelor of Medicine and Bachelor of Surgery). According to Yang (2018), there was limited evidence that their mobility for education would result in the accumulation of "any meaningful cultural capital." Nevertheless, large numbers of young people from India continue to pursue medical degrees in China—qualifications not available to them "at home" and directly related to a specific and discernible career path.

5. International Higher Education: Valorizing Credentials Over Learning

In this final section, I want to explore the process by which credentials have come to be *valorized over* learning within, specifically, international higher education systems.

In conclusion, I will speculate about the extent to which this trend might be applicable to higher education more broadly (including domestic education). The search for credentials—or the accumulation of institutionalized cultural capital—has been assumed to be a key driver of global flows of international students. There is an interesting geography to these flows—students from Asia represent the majority of globally mobile students, whereas key destination countries, most notably the United States and the United Kingdom, received the greatest number of international students globally. In what follows, I will explore the process by which these credentials *become* valuable and *retain* their value.

British imperial and colonial histories have had a role to play in how and why some education systems have become more ostensibly "valuable" that others. A symbolic importance, with a clear historical basis in colonial governance, has come to be attached to the English language across Asia and the Pacific, but is especially pronounced in places like Malaysia, Singapore, Hong Kong, Taiwan, and South Korea (Koh, 2017). Consequently, more institutionalized cultural capital is attached to universities that teach predominantly in English (Choi, 2003). This is partly where Australian universities have been so successful in recruiting international students from the Asia-Pacific region (and have, in fact, come to depend on these students for their very existence). The United States and United Kingdom are also top "host" destinations for international students globally. In recent years, more European countries are also offering programs taught in the English language, in order to attract the international student market.

International students have, additionally, been seen to attach value to an institution's age and a sense of "tradition." Older universities in the United Kingdom and the United States remain significantly popular amongst international students. Students are attracted by old architecture and rituals (such as college dinners and the wearing of gowns for academic events) (Lee, 2020b). Age and longevity translate into "quality" when it comes to understanding the value attached to credentials conferred by older academic institutions (Jöns, 2007, 2009; Brooks and Waters, 2017; Lee, 2020b). In short, a degree certificate from a particular institution is seen to "open doors" for international students as they enter the labor market. These credentials are portable—they travel and they confer international (not just domestic) cultural capital (Findlay et al., 2012). Western higher education institutions have also been active in marketing their educational programs overseas, facilitated by institutions, such as the British Council, which have a huge global outreach (Sidhu, 2006).

The conferring of internationally valuable cultural capital means that graduates in possession of these credentials have options and increased opportunities when it comes to seeking employment in a global (rather than regional or local) labor market. They possess cosmopolitan cultural capital. They are, as Ong (1999) has written: "not merely engaged in profit making; they are also acquiring a range of symbolic capitals that will facilitate their positioning, economic negotiation, and cultural acceptance in different geographical sites" (pp. 18–19). Education (or the acquisition of credentials, to be more precise) is seen to be a principal way in which families have sought out this "range of symbolic capitals" (Waters, 2008), which is subsequently given recognition by employers in the (international) labor market. As a few studies in the extant literature on international student mobility have suggested, however, far greater emphasis is placed on the symbolic import of educational credentials attached to particular institutions than it is on the knowledge accumulated and learning undertaken by international students during their international educational experiences.

6. CONCLUSIONS

This chapter has considered the relationship between credentials and learning, with a particular focus on international higher education. In theory, credentials and learning should be closely aligned and captured by the umbrella term "education." Formal education systems involve learning and impart terminal credentials: examinations might be considered one indication of how learning and credentials are (in theory, although perhaps not always in practice) closely tied. I have explored, however, how and why learning and credentials have diverged within international higher education—learning is associated with embodied cultural capital, and this can include both formal and informal forms of learning. Increasingly, however, societies (and workplaces within these) are rewarding what are perceived to be valuable "institutional capital," embodied in the university degree. Not just "any" university degree, however, but particular international credentials are bestowed with distinction. This distinction tells employers little about the actual knowledge accrued but instead acts as a form of "signaling"—as a proxy measure of a good potential employee.

The chapter has discussed how and why certain credentials become more highly valued than others, drawing on the literature on international student mobility. As we have seen, colonial legacies, valorizing the English language and certain "centers of knowledge production" and perpetuated by global "league tables" drive international student mobility to certain "destination" countries and institutions (Jöns, 2007; Brooks and Waters, 2011). *Some* students, however, could be conceived to be motivated by learning objectives, and the chapter discussed these briefly here. The examples given included the appeal of Western liberal arts programs, subject-specific programs (such as medical degrees offered in China), and the widespread perception that a Western education develops more critical thinking skills and eschews the types of "rote learning" more commonly found within East and South-East Asia. The chapter has drawn upon literature on international student mobility to argue that the disjunction between credentials and learning is becoming increasingly stark.

The question remains: How applicable are these arguments for understanding domestic (as well as international) higher education systems? The marketization of domestic higher education—the increasing reliance on student fees to fund higher education in certain countries and the need, therefore, to "attract" students—might suggest that students are increasingly more concerned with the institutionalized cultural capital available to them than they are with the content (in terms of "learning") of their degree programs. Universities are utilizing different types of metrics, both internally and nationally (such as student surveys, quality assurance assessments, diversity indices and widening participation goals, research quality, grant income, quality of published outputs, and so on) to rank (and implicitly "value") themselves. And yet, evidence from East Asia suggests that domestic qualifications are still widely preferred over and above their international alternatives. Waters and Leung (2017), for example, discuss how in Hong Kong students and employers within the public sector value and recognize domestic university degrees. Ren (2021) has claimed something similar for the job market in Mainland China. In contrast, international or transnational qualifications, granted by foreign educational providers, are "not recognized" to the same extent (or at all). This could be, in part, related to the relative "learning" achieved domestically—young people are assumed to acquire more relevant and locally contextualized knowledge if attending a local, as opposed to an international, higher education institution (see also Dietz et al., 2015). And this learning is of use in the public sector (in contrast, the private sector has been shown to value international credentials more highly—see Waters, 2006).

Thus, the relationship between credentials and learning is complicated and context dependent and can vary, within the labor market, by sector (public or private). Understanding this relationship—and particularly the tendency towards a disconnect between credentials and learning within international higher education—is important; especially how it relates to social disadvantage and the reproduction of privilege. Ensuring that these two aspects of education are more closely aligned in the labor market (that is, that employers are as concerned with what potential employees know and understand as they are with the university they have attended) might be a first step to a more equitable society.

REFERENCES

Beech, S. E. (2014). Why place matters: Imaginative geography and international student mobility. *Area*, 46/2, 170–177.

Beech, S. E. (2019). *The Geographies of International Student Mobility: Spaces, Places and Decision-Making*. Singapore: Springer.

Berlant, L. (2011). *Cruel Optimism*. Duke University Press.

Bourdieu, P. (1984). *Distinction: A Social Critique of the Judgement of Taste*. Cambridge, MA: Harvard University Press.

Bourdieu, P. (1986). "The forms of capital." In J. G. Richardson (ed.), *Handbook of Theory and Research for the Sociology of Education*. New York: Greenwood Press, 241–258.

Brooks, R. and Waters, J. (2011). *Student Mobilities, Migration and the Internationalization of Higher Education*. Basingstoke: Palgrave Macmillan.

Brooks, R. and Waters, J. (2017). *Materialities and Mobilities in Education*. Abingdon: Routledge.

Brooks, R. and Waters, J. (2018). "Signalling the 'multi-local' university? The place of the city in the growth of London-based satellite campuses, and the implications for social stratification." *Social Sciences*, 7/10, 195.

Cairns, D., Krzaklewska, E., Cuzzocrea, V., & Allaste, A. A. (2018). *Mobility, Education and Employability in the European Union: Inside Erasmus.* Springer.

Chan, E. (2002). Beyond pedagogy: Language and identity in post-colonial Hong Kong. British *Journal of Sociology of Education*, 23/2, 271–285.

Cheng, Y. E. (2019). "Liberal arts educated citizen: Experimentation, subjectification and ambiguous contours of youth citizenship." *Area*, 51/4, 618–626.

Chew, P. G. (2010). "Linguistic capital, study mothers and the transnational family in Singapore." In V. Vaish (ed.), *Globalization of Language and Culture in Asia.* New York: Continuum, 83–105.

Choi, P. K. (2003). "'The best students will learn English': Ultra-utilitarianism and linguistic imperialism in education in post-1997 Hong Kong." *Journal of Education Policy*, 18/6, 673–694.

Collins, F. (2014). "Globalising higher education in and through urban spaces: Higher education projects, international student mobilities and trans-local connections in Seoul." *Asia Pacific Viewpoint*, 55/2, 242–257.

Collins, R. (1979). *The credential society: An historical sociology of education and stratification.* Academic Press.

Dietz, J., Joshi, C., Esses, V. M., Hamilton, L. K., and Gabarrot, F. (2015). "The skill paradox: Explaining and reducing employment discrimination against skilled immigrants." *The International Journal of Human Resource Management*, 26/10, 1318–1334.

Favell, A. (2011). *Eurostars and Eurocities: Free Movement and Mobility in an Integrating Europe.* John Wiley & Sons.

Findlay, A., King, R., Smith, F. Geddes, A., and Skeldon, R. (2012). "World class? An investigation of globalisation, difference and international student mobility." *Transactions of the Institute of British Geographers*, 37/1, 118–131.

Hazelkorn, E. (2015). *Rankings and the Reshaping of Higher Education: The Battle for World-Class Excellence.* Basingstoke: Palgrave Macmillan.

Ho, E. (2002). "Multi-local residence, transnational networks: Chinese 'astronaut' families in New Zealand." *Asian and Pacific Migration Journal*, 111, 145–164.

Huang, S. and Yeoh, B. (2005). "Transnational families and their children's education: China's 'study mothers' in Singapore." *Global Networks*, 5/4, 379–400.

Huang, S. and Yeoh, B. (2011). "Navigating the terrains of transnational education: Children of Chinese 'study mothers' in Singapore." *Geoforum*, 42/3, 394–403.

Jarvis, P., Holford, J., and Griffin, C. (2003). *The theory and practice of learning.* London: Kogan Page.

Jöns, H. (2007). "Transnational mobility and the spaces of knowledge production: A comparison of global patterns, motivations and collaborations in different academic fields." *Social Geography*, 2/2, 97–114.

Jöns, H. (2009). "'Brain circulation' and transnational knowledge networks: Studying long-term effects of academic mobility to Germany, 1954–2000." *Global Networks*, 9/3, 315–338.

Jöns, H. and Hoyler, M. (2013). "Global geographies of higher education: The perspective of world university rankings." *Geoforum*, 46, 45–59.

Kim, J. (2010). "'Downed' and stuck in Singapore: Lower/middle class South Korean wild geese (kirogi) children in Singapore." *Research in Sociology of Education*, 17, 271–311.

Koh, S. Y. (2017). *Race, Education, and Citizenship: Mobile Malaysians, British Colonial Legacies, and a Culture of Migration.* New York: Springer.

Lee, K. H. (2020a). "'I post, therefore I become #cosmopolitan': The materiality of online representations of study abroad in China." *Population, Space and Place*, 26/3, e2297.

Lee, K. H. (2020b). "Becoming a bona fide cosmopolitan: Unpacking the narratives of Western-situated degree-seeking transnational students in China." *Social & Cultural Geography*, 1–19.

Lee, Y. and Koo, H. (2006). "'Wild geese fathers' and a globalised family strategy for education in Korea." *International Development Planning Review*, 28/4, 533–553.

Liang, L. (2010). "Black June." *Education Guardian*, June 29.

Liu, Y. (2016). "The Gaokao as a Meritocratic Selection?." In *Higher Education, Meritocracy and Inequality in China* Singapore: Springer, 85–103.

Ma, Y. (2020). *Ambitious and Anxious: How Chinese College Students Succeed and Struggle in American Higher Education*. New York: Columbia University Press.

Mulvey, B. (2021). "'Decentring' international student mobility: The case of African student migrants in China." *Population, Space and Place*, 27/3, e2393.

OECD (2020). Education at a Glance. Paris: OECD.

Olds, K. (2012) World University Rankings–Time for a Name Change? | GlobalHigherEd. https://www.insidehighered.com/blogs/globalhighered/world-university-rankings-time-name-change, accessed 20/02/2022

Ong, A. (1999). *Flexible Citizenship: The Cultural Logics of Transnationality*. Durham, NC: Duke University Press.

Ortiga, Y. Y. (2017). *Emigration, Employability and Higher Education in the Philippines*. Routledge.

Prazeres, L., Findlay, A., McCollum, D., Sander, N., Musil, E., Krisjane, Z., and Apsite-Berina, E. (2017). "Distinctive and comparative places: Alternative narratives of distinction within international student mobility." *Geoforum*, 80, 114–122.

Reay, D. (2018). "Miseducation: Inequality, education and the working classes." *International Studies in Sociology of Education*, 27/4, 453–456.

Ren, R. (2021) "How Elite Professional Service Firms Recruit Graduates in China." University of Oxford DPhil thesis.

Roberts, A., Chou, P., and Ching, G. (2010). "Contemporary trends in East Asian higher education: Dispositions of international students in a Taiwan university." *Higher Education*, 59/2, 149–166.

SCMP (2018). *Letter*. https://www.scmp.com/comment/letters/article/2165813/why-are-hong-kong-universities-dashing-dreams-so-many-young-people

Seth, M. (2002). *Education Fever: Society, Politics, and the Pursuit of Schooling in South Korea*. Hawai'i: University of Hawai'i Press.

Shubin, S. (2020). "Evaluating the process of cross-European migration: Beyond cultural capital." *Transactions of the Institute of British Geographers*, 45/4, 802–816.

Sidhu, R. (2006). *Universities and Globalization: To Market, To Market*. Totowa, NJ: Laurence Erlbaum Associates.

Sidhu, R. K., Chong, H. K., & Yeoh, B. S. (2019). *Student Mobilities and International Education In Asia: Emotional Geographies of Knowledge Spaces*. Springer Nature.

Spence, M. (1978). "Job market signaling." In P. Diamond and M. Rothschild (eds.), *Uncertainty in Economics*. New York: Academic Press, 281–306.

Stafford, C. (1995). *The Roads of Chinese Childhood: Learning and Identification in Angang*. Cambridge: Cambridge University Press.

Waters, J. L. (2003). "'Satellite kids' in Vancouver: Transnational migration, education and the experiences of lone children." In M. W. Charney, B. S. A. Yeoh, and C. K. Tong (eds.), *Asian Migrants and Education*. Dordrecht: Kluwer Academic, 165–184.

Waters, J. L. (2006). "Geographies of cultural capital: Education, international migration and family strategies between Hong Kong and Canada." *Transactions of the Institute of British Geographers*, 31/2, 179–192.

Waters, J. L. (2008). *Education, Migration and Cultural Capital in the Chinese Diaspora: Transnational Students Between Hong Kong and Canada*. New York: Cambria Press.

Waters, J. (2015). "Educational imperatives and the compulsion for credentials: Family migration and children's education in East Asia." Children's *Geographies*, 13/3, 280–293.

Waters, J., and Brooks, R. (2010). "Accidental achievers? International higher education, class reproduction and privilege in the experiences of UK students overseas." *British Journal of Sociology of Education*, 31/2, 217–228.

Waters, J. and Brooks, R. (2021). *Student Migrants and Contemporary Educational Mobilities*. Cham: Palgrave Macmillan.

Waters, J. L. and Leung, M. W. (2017). "Domesticating transnational education: Discourses of social value, self-worth and the institutionalisation of failure in 'meritocratic' Hong Kong." *Transactions of the Institute of British Geographers*, 422, 233–245.

Waters, J. L., and Leung, M. W. (2020). "Rhythms, flows, and structures of cross-boundary schooling: State power and educational mobilities between Shenzhen and Hong Kong." *Population, Space and Place*, 26/3, e2298.

Woronov, T. (2015). *Class Work*. Stanford University Press.

Williams, A. and Baláž, V. (2014). *International Migration and Knowledge*. Routledge.

Xu, C. L. (2021). "Time, class and privilege in career imagination: Exploring study-to-work transition of Chinese international students in UK universities through a Bourdieusian lens." *Time & Society*, 30/1, 5–29.

Yang, P. (2016). *International Mobility and Educational Desire: Chinese Foreign Talent Students in Singapore*. Springer.

Yang, P. (2018). "Compromise and complicity in international student mobility: The ethnographic case of Indian medical students at a Chinese university." *Discourse: Studies in the Cultural Politics of Education*, 39/5, 694–708.

Zhou, M. (1998). "'Parachute kids' in Southern California: The educational experience of Chinese children in transnational families." *Educational Policy*, 12/6, 682–704.

CHAPTER 8

LIBERAL ARTS AND SCIENCES EDUCATION FOR THE TWENTY-FIRST CENTURY IN ASIA

MIKIKO NISHIMURA

1. INTRODUCTION

THIS chapter will present an overview of the core values of liberal arts and sciences education in Asia and the Pacific, with some examples of recent programs and innovations, and the challenges and transformations deemed necessary in the twenty-first century. With the vast variety in education systems and liberal arts and sciences programs across the Asia-Pacific, this chapter does not attempt to generalize but rather identifies key points for rethinking higher education in the twenty-first-century context. The term "liberal arts" is often misunderstood as excluding sciences in Asia but for the purpose of this chapter, reference to liberal arts includes sciences.

The prolonged debate over liberal arts education versus vocational and professional education does not seem to be relevant anymore in the emerging trend of liberal arts and sciences programs in Asia and the Pacific. Given the hyper-knowledge economy and the high-speed, cross-border mobility of ideas and services in our globalized world, liberal educational imperatives of critical thinking, creativity, and civic engagement have become part of the practical needs of the labor market in Asia and beyond. The pragmatic forms of such programs are often offered in public and private comprehensive research universities as well as in small, US-type private liberal arts colleges in Asia and the Pacific.

Nevertheless, it is true that there still exists some misinterpretation of the division between general knowledge and specialized knowledge, as opposed to interdisciplinarity in the creation of *new* knowledge. We also face a lack of critical inquiry into social change in civic engagement and faculty development to run the curriculum with an open mind rather than a compartmentalized mindset with fear of diversity (Modrowski, 2016; Yonezawa and Nishimura, 2016; Nishimura and Yokote, 2020).

Section 2 of this chapter briefly discusses the historical background of liberal arts education and the current debate on its role and significance. Section 3 discusses the emerging trend of liberal arts and sciences education in Asia and the Pacific. Section 4 illustrates recent innovative examples in Asia and attempts to revisit the core values of liberal arts and sciences education. Section 5 concludes by discussing the implications and challenges faced by liberal arts and sciences education in Asia and the Pacific.

2. Historical Background and the Core Values and Philosophy of Liberal Arts Education

Liberal arts education has its roots in medieval Europe, with the original "seven liberal arts" (i.e., music, arithmetic, geometry, astronomy, grammar, logic, and rhetoric) and their emphasis on rhetoric and eloquence. Liberal arts education gradually evolved from this narrow vision to refer to a more dynamic and practical approach to knowledge creation and its application. With the rise of science and research universities in the nineteenth century, traditional liberal arts education faced the challenge of reforming its more abstract content for practical purposes. A further challenge arose in the early twentieth century which raised questions about humanity in sciences. The mission of liberal arts education then came to be about "deep-going self-discipline and large-visioned ideals" (King, 1917: 14) by questioning the moral emptiness of modern sciences and the lack of intellectual unity in the undergraduate curriculum (King, 1917; Meiklejohn, 1920).

In the United States, liberal arts education expanded its focus in the direction of nurturing ethical, social, and civic attitudes and responsibilities as well as broad-based knowledge (Ferrall, 2011; Chopp et al., 2014; Clark and Jain, 2013; Roth, 2014). In the mid-twentieth century, emphasis was placed on a strong commitment to interdisciplinarity, studying the past in order to understand the present, and providing students with a sense of moral purpose as members of civil society (Buchler, 1954; Summerscales, 1970). Furthermore, philosophical education attempted to "humanize science" as its central task (Dewey, 1958; Hutchins, 1968). Thus, liberal arts education was regarded as a way of nurturing democratic citizens to contribute to society.

More recently, Chopp et al. (2013) have referred to the three pillars of liberal arts education—critical thinking, moral and civic character formation, and intellectual contribution to the improvement of the world. Critical thinking is nurtured by discussion and debate in small groups and interdisciplinary research in a broad context. Moral and civic character is formed by co-curricular activities outside classrooms and community-based activities as well as through interpersonal relations among students and faculty, especially on residential campuses. Furthermore, students are encouraged to engage in various international and intercultural activities, including experiential learning through service-learning and service-research so that they learn how to initiate action over social issues. The Association of American Colleges and Universities (AAC&U) uses the term *liberal education* and not *liberal arts education* as a preferred approach to preparing future leaders for positions of civic responsibility. It does not consider this form of education as merely a subdivision of the college curriculum (e.g., specific disciplines, general education requirements, a simple form of personal development under the guise of *culture* and *refinement*) (Jung, 2016).

Carol Geary Schneider, the former president of AAC&U, states that the core of liberal learning is "global and pluralistic," as expressed in the following text prepared by the AAC&U Board of Directors in 1998:

> Because liberal learning aims to free us from the constraints of ignorance, sectarianism, and myopia, it prizes curiosity and seeks to expand the boundaries of human knowledge. By its nature, therefore, liberal learning is global and pluralistic. It embraces the diversity of ideas and experiences that characterize the social, natural, and intellectual world. To acknowledge such diversity in all its forms is both an intellectual commitment and a social responsibility, for nothing less will equip us to understand our world and to pursue fruitful lives. (Quoted in Schneider, 2016, p. vii)

While many higher education institutions have been integrating liberal arts education or liberal education as an approach to developing well-rounded individuals, flexible and creative ways of thinking, civic engagement, and internationalization, the rising demand for vocational and practical education in an increasingly technologically advanced and competitive global labor market has cast a critical lens on traditional forms of liberal arts colleges and education. The high cost of maintaining small classes, residential campuses, and experiential education has resulted in escalating fees and decreasing enrollment, leading to the decline of many traditional liberal arts colleges in the United States (Breneman, 1994; Ferrall, 2011; Janeksela, 2012; Jung, 2016; Goodwin, 2019). Traditional liberal arts college education has been attacked in the United States as out of touch, elitist, ineffective, and well past relevance (Logan and Curry, 2014; Rowen, 2016). While 120 liberal arts colleges out of 212 (there were 540 in 1987) have been able to retain their original mission, some colleges have disappeared or been forced to offer more vocational courses (Baker et al., 2012).

On the other hand, evidence has accumulated that liberal arts education has an impact on life satisfaction, employment, global experiences, and responsible citizenship as perceived by graduates (Pascarella et al., 2005; Rowen, 2016). Furthermore, as will be seen in the next section, there has been an emerging perspective that liberal arts education provides students with "soft skills" including the ability to think critically, to communicate effectively and efficiently, to synthesize information from various academic and cultural perspectives, and to analyze complex qualitative and quantitative concepts, all of which contribute to twenty-first-century skills and competencies including inter-active use of language and technological tools, interaction in heterogeneous groups, and autonomous action (Rychen and Salganik, 2000; Ananiadou and Claro, 2009; Godwin and Altbach, 2016). Liberal arts education empowers students to expand their intellec-tual, artistic, moral, civic, and scientific capacities as independent thinkers and lifelong learners (Kirby and van der Wende, 2016).

As such, liberal arts education has been the focus of controversies over the role of higher education and its approach to knowledge creation, as well as broader issues of diversity and inclusion, access to higher education, organizational efficiency, and its re-sponse to the labor market.

3. Emergence of Liberal Arts and Sciences Education in Asia and the Pacific: Confusion or Innovation?

The idea of liberal arts education came to Asia from the West in the nineteenth century, when intellectual exchange was translated or reinterpreted. Following World War II, the US type of liberal arts education was introduced into Asia on a larger scale. However, the reception of liberal arts education across countries revealed mixed interpretations of its nature and purpose. The narrowest understanding of traditional liberal arts education was found in colleges or schools of humanities in Taiwan (Yonezawa and Nishimura, 2016). Liberal arts education has also been confused with general education and reinterpreted in the context of comprehensive research universities. For instance, in Japan, general education was taken as an introductory part of four-year undergraduate programs after World War II (Yoshida, 2002). In China, the terms "cultural quality edu-cation" or "education for all-round development" have been used interchangeably with liberal arts education in the highly specialized higher education system (Jiang, 2014; Godwin and Altbach, 2016).

Also notable is the fact that human resource development in contributing towards civil society is extremely thin in higher education systems and liberal arts programs across Japan, South Korea, and China (Yonezawa and Nishimura, 2016). In East Asia, higher education institutions are professionally oriented and serve as the core means of bureaucratic elite training rather than nurturing public values and civic engagement. Although a small number of liberal arts universities have implemented social experi-ential learning such as service-learning programs, following the model of liberal arts colleges in the United States, such programs are often not integrated into the core cur-riculum or offered as credit-bearing courses (Jung et al., 2016). Vocational focus seems evident in other parts of Asia such as India (Modrowski, 2016; Kudtarkar, 2019). Yang (2016) posits that the adaptation of liberal arts education to East Asia reflects an identity crisis whereby East Asian societies that have a strong mindset of playing catch-up with the West focus on Western practicality rather than on the rich traditions of Western civilization.

Several recent publications on liberal arts education including Jung et al. (2016), Kirby and van der Wende (2016), and Nishimura and Sasao (2019) offer intensive discussion on the core values of liberal arts education in the historical context of different regions, introduce best practices of selected liberal arts colleges, and analyze policy and pedagogical guidelines of liberal arts institutes in Asia. Notable features of Asian liberal arts education include a variety of interpretations of the liberal arts education concept and philosophy, a dichotomous view of general versus specialized knowledge, more emphasis on the pragmatic use of liberal education concepts, and a new concept of international liberal arts education with English as the medium of instruction.

A third wave of liberal arts and sciences education has emerged since 2000. As shown in Figure 8.1, Godwin (2013) found that more than 40 percent of the liberal arts education programs in Asia were founded after 2000. Godwin (2015) illustrates that Asia accounts for 12.6 percent (69 programs) of all liberal arts programs in the world, the second-largest share after North America, which accounts for 70.6 percent (386) of the total number of liberal arts programs worldwide. India, Japan, and Hong Kong share half of the programs in Asia (Godwin, 2015). In the Pacific region, there are only seven programs in Australia out of which four have been established after 2000 (Godwin, 2013). Another notable trend is that about 80 percent of the liberal arts programs offered in non-English-speaking countries are conducted in English.

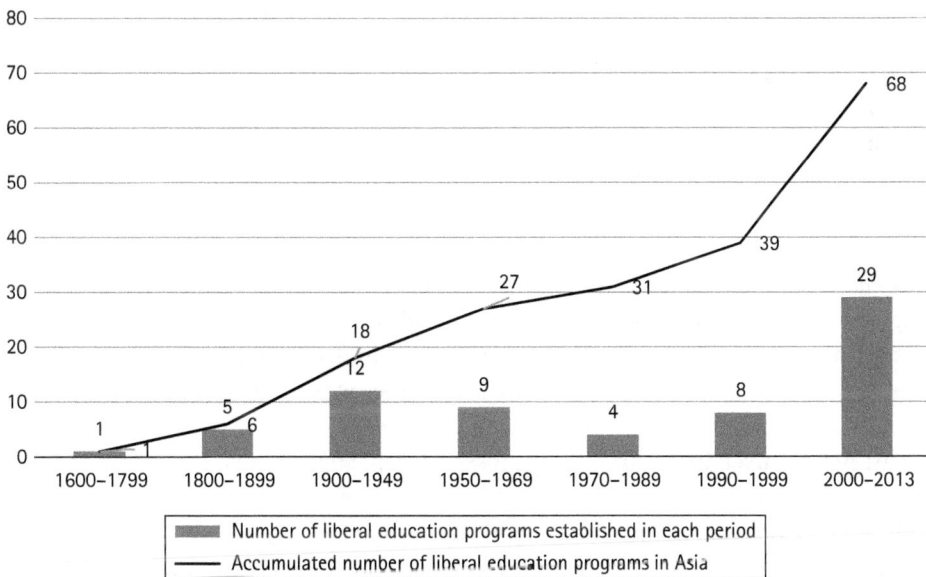

FIGURE 8.1 Development of liberal education programs in Asia

Source: Godwin (2013, p. 127 and p. 327).

Factors for the recent upsurge of liberal arts and sciences education in Asia are three-fold (Ito and Morishima, 2019). First, interdisciplinary perspectives have come to be regarded as an important lens with which to examine complex world issues in light of accelerated globalization. Second, imperatives of liberal arts and sciences education such as critical thinking, creativity, and civic engagement, coincide with a set of widely advocated twenty-first-century skills and competencies as discussed earlier. Third, liberal arts and sciences education has become an emerging business model in the effort to recruit international students in the increasingly competitive global higher education market. As a matter of fact, there are many liberal arts and sciences programs at comprehensive research universities in Asia, while traditional liberal arts colleges with residential campuses are scarce in this region. In addition, China, Hong Kong, and Australia have recently introduced system-wide mandates for more liberal and general education in the higher education curriculum, which has led to an increase in public liberal arts and sciences education in Asia and the Pacific (Godwin, 2013; Godwin and Altbach, 2016).

The recent popular trend of liberal arts and sciences education in Asia is not, however, free from some confusion in practice. There is a persistent and widespread belief in many societies that general education is less academically rigorous than study in specialized subjects and serves a less important function in universities (Yoshida, 2002; Yonezawa and Nishimura, 2016). Under such circumstances, general education is interpreted as a preparatory course for students before they move on to obtaining specialized knowledge. Such a narrow understanding of general education leads to a misunderstanding that liberal arts education is a mere selection of broad subjects necessary for the cultivation of culturally well-informed citizens. What is lost in translation is the original core value of liberal arts education to nurture an individual's holistic development with strong civic-minded engagement and actions. General education is one approach to value all forms of knowledge, to respect alternative viewpoints, to master good logical presentations, and to serve society by solving complex issues.

Market incentives for skills-focus (e.g. English language skills) have largely overridden academic and philosophical debates and ideals, and promote learning *what* as opposed to *how* and *why*. Skills-focus has led to the recent upsurge of international liberal arts programs in Asia as the skill set emphasized by these programs matches the pragmatic views of parents and the general public, particularly with regard to English language skills, soft skills, and analytic and critical thinking skills demanded in the global labor market. Student-centered and inquiry- or discussion-based learning, however, is a relatively new concept to many universities in Asia and may lead to a mixed outcome for liberal learning (Godwin, 2013; Jiang, 2014).

East Asian universities, particularly those in Japan, South Korea, Taiwan, and China, show an increasing interest in liberal arts and sciences education; small, independent dedicated liberal arts colleges and general education programs in both public and private comprehensive research universities have been developed in these countries (Jiang, 2014; Jung et al., 2016). However, liberal arts and sciences education is still marginalized in most parts of Asia and the Pacific and faces a number of challenges including lack of understanding and interest on the part of policymakers, parents, and students, many of whom still show a preference for vocational and professional education. These challenges often result in a lack of integrated policies and limited funding support. Recent trends—a steady decline in the college-age population, increased competition with public research universities, and a growing private education market—have added another challenge especially to small liberal arts colleges that are mostly private and often tuition-dependent. Globalization has brought about changes in higher education, and such often contradictory values as internationality, excellence, equity, and diversity have become more important than ever; yet the neoliberal wave of university rankings and competition over research grants and international students have pushed small liberal arts colleges to the corner and made the core values and outcomes of liberal arts and sciences education less visible (Nishimura, 2014; Kim and Shim, 2019).

In response to these challenges, liberal arts and sciences colleges and programs have undergone a variety of curricular and co-curricular reforms along with rigorous student recruitment strategies in Asia. There are a few interesting examples, such as Yale-NUS College in Singapore, Asian University for Women in Bangladesh, and International Christian University in Japan, that present a transnational and intercultural liberal arts education model in Asia and beyond. These innovative programs are institutionally supported and have a global outlook, as will be presented in the next section.

4. Recent Innovative Examples of Liberal Arts and Sciences Education in Asia

It is often difficult to quantify the success of liberal arts and sciences education. However, outcomes often show as student satisfaction, the promotion rate to higher learning at the graduate school level, and pedagogical innovations and approaches that are theoretically expected to result from successful learning, embedding critical thinking, creativity, and civic engagement through interdisciplinary inquiry. This section presents three recent innovative examples of liberal arts and sciences education in Singapore, Bangladesh, and Japan that demonstrate unique pedagogical innovations by adopting a college-wide approach.

An underlying commonality among the three examples below is that all of them attempt to generate experiential learning to nurture cognitive and non-cognitive skills, attitudes, and behaviors, to critically examine phenomena and values that are taken for granted, and to engage in social issues across borders. Critical thinking, interdisciplinary learning, spontaneous participation with social justice and equity issues, and deep understanding of various cultures and theoretical perspectives are embedded as the core values of liberal arts and sciences education. Liberal arts and sciences education, with its focus on student spontaneity and on flexible and interactive forms of education, aims to develop democratic attitudes in various dialogues and discussions, interdisciplinary and deep critical thinking on various themes, and academic skills for communicating with people from various backgrounds.

4.1 Week 7 Program of Yale-NUS College, Singapore

Yale-NUS College in Singapore has introduced an experiential fieldwork program called the "Week 7 Program" which is jointly organized by faculty and students and takes place in the seventh week of the first term of university. Seven faculty members from different disciplines set a common theme for the course. Previous examples have included "The history of the Chinese village: Agriculture and the future" and "Cultural capital: Museums, narratives of identity, and appreciation" (Khoo and Craig, 2019). For the former theme, faculty members and students of urban studies used a Charrette method to create a rural development plan and held a series of dialogues with various stakeholders in a village for a week. Students were able to deepen their understanding of issues relating to various levels of stakeholders including family, community, market, and the nation-state and build on their education in comparative social studies. For the latter theme, faculty and students visited the national heritage office and museums, deepening their understanding of national strategies for an Asian art hub, as well as economic development strategies. They further examined the role of high culture in the reproduction of social classes by using the concept of cultural capital in a national policy context.

After the Week 7 Program, a one-day symposium is held at which students give three forms of presentation: first, an oral presentation to faculty and students who undertook the program; second, an interview with faculty who did not accompany them in fieldwork for a round of assessment questions and evaluation; and finally, an opportunity to present their learning outcomes creatively by using a booth and classroom space to interact with various audiences.

Khoo and Craig (2019) state that the aim of the Week 7 Program is not merely to link concepts learned in the classroom with practical application, but to nurture twenty-first-century skills such as teamwork, synthesis of various information sources, creation of complex arguments, and communication skills with various stakeholders in society. The Week 7 Program is not the sole education program, but it is regarded as students' first step in experiential learning before other learning opportunities such as field studies, study abroad, language training, internships, etc. Various kinds of institutional support are granted to this program, including student advising, writing support, and pedagogical advice on experiential learning from the Centre for Teaching and Learning and the Writers' Centre. Visiting professors from overseas may join the planning of the Week 7 Program to give an international and diverse touch to the theme as well as strengthening institutional relations across different parts of the world.

4.2 Gender and Diversity at the Asian University for Women, Bangladesh

Asian University for Women (AUW) is the first liberal arts college in South Asia founded for the purpose of fostering female leaders in Asia and the Middle East. AUW targets socio-economically disadvantaged yet high-achieving women in high school and those who have limited opportunities for higher education in their own countries due to gender disparities. AUW is financially supported by international organizations such as the Asian Development Bank, UNESCO, and the World Bank as well as donations from the general public. It also collaborates with non-governmental organizations (NGOs) to identify potential candidates for admission and scholarships to study on campus in Bangladesh. A majority of AUW students are the first generation in their family to go to college.

As many students have limited exposure to diverse views on history and society and limited experience interacting with people from different cultural and religious backgrounds, AUW created the "Access Academy Program" for students to participate in for one year before matriculation into the degree program to learn how to discuss sensitive topics on different cultures and religions, and to reflect on their own identity and diverse viewpoints and values. Furthermore, students can participate in leadership seminars where they are able to learn different styles and qualities of leadership, self-management, professionalism, public speaking, conflict resolution, reformist feminism and activism, civic engagement, and event planning skills.

Once students enter their undergraduate program, they take courses in the core curriculum. The core curriculum consists of five areas, namely ethical inferences, social analysis, writing, science and mathematics, and literature/civilization studies and art. Phillott (2019) notes that gender and diversity is a common theme to each course and that the curriculum aims to reflect on students' lives, society, and experiences, as well as nurturing attitudes and skills for examining concepts, ideas, events, and data. Students are encouraged to develop their own perspectives and studies on gender, culture, and science.

At the end of the first year, students participate in summer projects which involve choosing a theme around which to pursue fieldwork and practical activities. Past themes have included "Accessibility of health loans and health insurance in rural areas of Bangladesh," "An oral history of Zhuan ethnic group and gender equality in Nanning, Guangxi, China," "Factors affecting South and Southeast Asian women in science," and "Observations from the Islamic school for transgender community in Yogyakarta, Indonesia." After returning from their fieldwork, students are required to make oral and poster presentations on the learning outcome.

The impact of the summer project is reported as a positive change in students' reputation among their families and of their communities' perception of women's abilities and competencies (Phillott, 2015). Graduates from AUW go into various fields and industries, including global corporations (20 percent), non-profit sectors such as international organizations and NGOs (26 percent), and government (10 percent). About 15 percent pursue graduate studies in different countries (AUW, n.d.). AUW explores liberal arts and sciences education as a way to propel female leaders beyond national borders to break away from domestic gender structures that perpetuate gender inequality in societies and transform women into leaders who can pursue social change.

4.3 Service-Learning Program of International Christian University, Japan

International Christian University (ICU) is a long-standing liberal arts university and a pioneer in introducing a service-learning program to Japan in 1999. It established the Service-Learning Center in 2002 and initiated the Service-Learning Asia Network (SLAN) with eight universities and one non-profit organization in Asia (i.e., China, Hong Kong, India, Indonesia, the Philippines, South Korea, and Thailand). International service-learning is a form of experiential education that integrates community-led service activities, academic instruction, and intentional reflection in an international or cross-cultural setting (Crabtree, 2008). Service-learning is also a pedagogy designed to transform the role of higher education from an elitist reproduction of privilege and social inequality to one redressing social inequality through civic and community engagement at local and global levels (Nishimura and Yokote, 2020).

After working with SLAN partners for two decades, in 2016, ICU, together with the Center for Community Engagement at Middlebury College in the United States, developed an inbound service-learning program called the Japan Summer Service-Learning (JSSL) to enhance reciprocity in partnership and to overcome the linear development model and "savior complex mentality" in reaching out to the "poor" in Asia. The program is intended to allow a team of students from different countries in Asia and America to examine and experience various contemporary social issues in Japan. JSSL is a short-term (four-week), community-connected, cohort program in the summer tailored for incoming students from the SLAN partner universities, Middlebury College, and ICU. Participating students deepen their understanding of Japanese society by serving together in local communities in both urban and rural areas. ICU students are given three credits for their participation while other universities have their own policies in terms of academic credits and alignment with the curriculum.

A recent evaluative study based on a review of student participants' reports and interviews with stakeholders has demonstrated how the JSSL program fosters students' rich learning and well-being and maintains good relationships with community organizations (Nishimura and Yokote, 2020). The multicultural, reciprocal learning among student groups generated in JSSL added a new reciprocity to the service-learning program framework, generating new questions and a comparative lens on the students' own locality and link between local and global issues. Students repeatedly mentioned learning about themselves through interactions with other students and local community residents, and through being in a different environment. Japanese students learned about their own communities by interpreting the questions posed by international students and the responses from local communities.

Nevertheless, one notable challenge was that a critical perspective on and structural analysis of social inequality and problems were missing from Japanese students' reflection. While citizenship is a major and critical outcome of service-learning in American higher education, it was less prominent at ICU. ICU's approach to service-learning focused on students' whole-person development in the context of Christian philosophy; there was comparatively less discussion about or inquiry into social justice, social change, or democracy. Critical perspectives of service-learning that emerged in the international sphere in the late 2000s did not appear in any curricular student reports, or faculty-led monographs. There was a missing link between student experiences and the intended curriculum that overlooked the focus on revisiting students' own unconscious biases, stereotypical behaviors, and a broader analysis of power within service-learning by critical reflection and reciprocity for social change (Mitchell et al., 2012; Asghar and Rowe, 2017; Atkas et al., 2017).

Another study that examined student reports for international service-learning at ICU also found students' learning outcome to be along the lines of "personal development," "perspective transformation," "interpersonal development," "avoiding stereotyping," "tolerance," and so on (Kuronuma, 2019). While ICU distinctively shows deep conceptions of the meaning of doing service for others, the "others" for, or with whom we serve was vaguely defined (Nishimura and Yokote, 2020). The positionality of students remained unquestioned and the programs did not clearly address social inequality or social justice issues.

This trend is often indicated by other scholars in Asia. The education system in Asia tends to emphasize morality, self-cultivation, and compassion with higher value placed on conformity over critical thinking and social justice (Hoffman, 2015; Sim, 2016). Hence, ICU is currently implementing some reforms to the service-learning curriculum and content, and introducing critical inquiry and positionality into the core part of the service-learning curriculum.

5. CONCLUSION: IMPLICATIONS AND CHALLENGES FOR THE TWENTY-FIRST CENTURY

Unlike the widespread notion that liberal arts and sciences education are more academic than practical or geared towards humanities rather than sciences, the goals of liberal education apply to, and should be addressed across, all fields of study and in all forms of postsecondary learning, including fields considered technical or vocational (Jung,

2016). Liberal learning and technology go hand in hand, as numerous entrepreneurs have avowed (Jung, 2016; Zakaria, 2015). As demonstrated by AAC&U which uses the term *liberal education* rather than *liberal arts* or *liberal arts and sciences education*, higher education in Asia may already see liberal education as a better comprehensive approach, transcending the dichotomy between traditional liberal arts subjects and vocational and professional education. This new hybrid mode of liberal arts and sciences programs requires more research on its implementation, pedagogies, and impact on student learning.

One should be reminded that a liberal mode of learning that respects diversity and pluralism requires an attitude that questions the status quo and existing power structure. Modrowski (2016) indicates that, due partly to the lack of faculty development, unspoken attitudes of defensiveness, a denial of differences, and an avoidance of cultural confrontation exist in liberal arts programs in India. Given the socio-cultural environment in East Asia where individuals are expected to adopt Confucian values and social norms—such as respecting elders and authority, conforming to majority views, and giving priority to collective over personal interests—critical thinking and open and democratic behavior may be difficult to cultivate all at once (Yang et al., 2011). Furthermore, in places where academic freedom is not an a priori given, challenges remain in granting a space for faculty and students to be able to think critically about conventional social and political norms (Godwin and Altbach, 2016; Kirby and van der Wende, 2016). The recent news of the proposed closure of Yale-NUS College in Singapore in 2025 has stimulated public discussion on liberal education and the changing political climate in Asia. The contextual adaptation of liberal education is still underway and requires further profound discussion on the role of higher education in Asia.

Nevertheless, liberal education or liberal arts and sciences education, whatever it is called, shares a few critical and essential aspects across the region. First, it places more importance on interdisciplinarity, as a creation of one's own perspective by understanding and integrating multiple perspectives, than on multidisciplinarity, which merely examines one issue from multiple perspectives with broad knowledge. It is not a mere choice of subjects or width of perspectives but a purpose-driven inquiry that is more important for social innovation and change, and hence in liberal education curricular design.

Second, the diversity and inclusion emphasized in liberal learning are interpreted not as a mere demographic representation of majority and minority groups, as is the case in many higher education institutions in Asia. More emphasis should be put on rich experiential learning in an environment where various minority voices on multiple experiences can be heard with respect for human dignity and inclusion. While a 2015 survey of AAC&U members revealed that 60 percent of institutions reported their general education programs included diversity courses in the United States (Humphreys, 2016), the degree of integration of core values into liberal learning in the curricular design in Asia and the Pacific is questionable and should be investigated further. Furthermore, the practice of diversity on campuses may involve conflicts of interest, resentment, apprehension, emotional stress, and uncomfortable awareness of one's own biases and practices (Nishimura et al., 2019). Working together supportively to move beyond apprehension and silence and towards open dialogue will be required to usher in a culture of diversity and inclusion.

Third, liberal arts and sciences education in the twenty-first century should not be solely a utilitarian mode of international education for global integration or influence with a focus on English as a global medium. Such a shallow global outlook characterizes many programs which go under the label of "liberal arts and sciences education" in Asia, but which lack a vision of liberal learning. The core values should embrace good listening skills and attitudes to multiple voices, critical reflection on one's own epistemology, a positive attitude towards dialogue and new knowledge creation, and strong engagement with social issues as a member of global society.

What is liberal about liberal arts and sciences education in Asia and the Pacific? Liberal arts and sciences education lays the foundation for learning how to interpret, interrogate, or make new knowledge framed in the constructs of various fields (Godwin and Altbach, 2016). For Asian and Pacific higher education institutions to fully embrace the idea of liberal education or liberal arts and sciences education, we need to go beyond the technocratic, market-oriented, or political approach to higher education, and to embrace more philosophically and socially guided ideals for future generations with a vision for and rigor in what we mean by "liberal" learning.

References

Ananiadou, K. and Claro, M. (2009). *21st Century Skills and Competencies for New Millennium Learners in OECD Countries*. OECD Education Working Paper, No. 41. Paris: OECD.

Asghar, M. and Rowe, N. (2017). "Reciprocity and critical reflection as the key to social justice in service learning: A case study." *Innovations in Education and Teaching International*, 54/ 2, 117–125.

Asian University of Women (AUW) (n.d.). *Impact: Our Graduates*. https://asian-university. org/impact/our-graduates/, accessed July 9, 2020.

Atkas, F., Pitts, K, Richards, J. C., and Silova, I. (2017). "Institutionalizing global citizenship: A critical analysis of higher education programs and curricula." *Journal of Studies in International Education*, 21/1, 65–80.

Baker, V. L., Baldwin, R. G., and Makker, S. (2012). "Where are they now? Revisiting Breneman's study of liberal arts colleges." *Liberal Education*, 98/3, 48–53. https:// www.aacu.org/publications-research/periodicals/where-are-they-now-revisiting-breneman%25E2%2580%2599s-study-liberal-arts

Breneman, D. W. (1994). *Liberal Arts Colleges: Thriving, Surviving, or Endangered?* Washington, DC: Brookings Institution.

Buchler, J. (1954). "Reconstruction in the liberal arts." In D. C. Miner (ed.), *A History of Columbia College on Morningside*. New York: Columbia University Press, 48–135.

Chopp, R. (2014). "Remaking, renewing, reimagining: The liberal arts college takes advantage of change." In R. Chopp, S. Frost, and D. H. Weiss (eds.), *Remaking College: Innovation and the Liberal Arts*. Baltimore, MD: Johns Hopkins University Press, 13–24.

Clark, K. and Jain, R. (2013). *The Liberal Arts Tradition: A Philosophy of Christian Classical Education*. Camp Hill, PA: Classical Academic Press.

Crabtree, R. D. (2008). "Theoretical foundations for international service-learning." *Michigan Journal of Community Service Learning*, 15/1, 18–36.

Dewey, J. (1958). *Experience and Nature*. New York: Dover.

Ferrall, V. E. (2011). *Liberal Arts at the Brink*. Cambridge, MA: Harvard University Press.

Godwin, K. A. (2013). "The global emergence of liberal education: A comparative and exploratory study." Boston College Electronic Dissertation. Boston: Boston College.

Godwin, K. A. (2015). "Worldwide emergence of liberal education." *International Higher Education*, 79, 2–4.

Godwin, K. A. and Altbach, P. G. (2016). "A historical and global perspective on liberal arts education." *International Journal of Chinese Education*, 5, 5–22.

Goodwin, A. N. (2019). "The future of liberal arts in higher education: A policy Delphi study." *Educational Perspectives*, 15/1, 13–17.

Hoffman, M. (2015). "What is an education for sustainable development supposed to achieve? A question of what, how, and why." *Journal of Education for Sustainable Development*, 19/2, 213–228.

Humphreys, D. (2016). "Progress and prospects for the reform of undergraduate education." *Liberal Education*, 102/3, 28–35.

Hutchins, R. M. (1968). *No Friendly Voice*. Chicago: University of Chicago Press.

Ito, T. and Morishima, Y. (2019). *Wave of Liberal Arts: Confronting the World without Answers: A Challenge of International Christian University*. Tokyo: Gakken. In Japanese (伊東辰彦・森島泰則（2019）『リベラルアーツという波動—答えのない世界に立ち向かう 国際基督教大学の挑戦』、学研).

Janeksela, G. M. (2012). "The value of a liberal arts education." *Academic Exchange Quarterly*, 16/4, 37–41.

Jiang, Y. G. (2014). *Liberal Arts Education in a Changing Society: A New Perspective on Chinese Higher Education*. Leiden: Brill.

Jung, I. (2016). "Introduction." In I. Jung, M. Nishimura, and T. Sasao (eds.), *Liberal Arts Education and Colleges in East Asia: Possibilities and Challenges in the Global Age*. Singapore: Springer, 1–12.

Jung, I., Nishimura, M., and Sasao, T. (eds.) (2016). *Liberal Arts Education and Colleges in East Asia: Possibilities and Challenges in the Global Age*. Singapore: Springer.

Khoo, H. E. and Craig, T. (2019). "Implementing 'Week 7' at Yale-NUS College, Singapore: A pedagogical experiment beyond disciplinary boundaries." In M. Nishimura and T. Sasao (eds.), *Doing Liberal Arts Education: The Global Case Studies*. Singapore: Springer, 21–29.

Kim, J. and Shim, W.-J. (2019). "What do rankings measure? The U.S. news rankings and student experience at liberal arts college." *The Review of Higher Education*, 42/3, 933–964.

King, H. C. (1917). "What the college stands for." *Association of American Colleges Bulletin*, III/1, 24.

Kirby, W. C. and van der Wende, M. (eds.) (2016). *Experiences in Liberal Arts and Science Education from America, Europe, and Asia: A Dialogue across Continents*. New York: Palgrave Macmillan.

Kudtarkar, S. K. (2019). "Interdisciplinary curriculum and leadership education: The case of FLAME University, India." In M. Nishimura and T. Sasao (eds.), *Doing Liberal Arts Education: The Global Case Studies*. Singapore: Springer, 31–43.

Kuronuma, A. (2019). "Learning outcomes of international service-learning in the Japanese context: The case of International Christian University." Paper presented at the 7th Asia-Pacific Reginal Conference on Service Learning, June 19–21, Singapore.

Logan, J. and Curry, J. (2014). "A liberal arts education: Global trends and challenges." *Christian Higher Education*, 14/1–2, 66–79.

Meiklejohn, A. (1920). *The Liberal College*. Boston, MA: Marshall Jones.

Mitchell, T. D., Donahue, D. M., and Young-Law, C. (2012). "Service learning as a pedagogy of whiteness." *Equity & Excellence in Education*, 45/4, 612–629.

Modrowski, K. A. (2016). "Blending cultures of pedagogy." *International Journal of Chinese Education*, 5, 85–103.

Nishimura, M. (2014). "Practical challenges of globalization and higher education: Implications for a university entrance exam reform." *Educational Research*, 56, 1–11. In Japanese.

Nishimura, M., Kim, A., and Bhatt, B. S. (2019). "Policies and practices of diversity and inclusion in liberal arts colleges." In M. Nishimura and T. Sasao (eds.), *Doing Liberal Arts Education: The Global Case Studies*. Singapore: Springer, 107–120.

Nishimura, M. and Sasao, T. (eds.) (2019). *Doing Liberal Arts Education: The Global Case Studies*. Singapore: Springer.

Nishimura, M. and Yokote, H. (2020). "Service learning as a means to understand socio-economic privilege, inequality, and social mobility." In C. S. Sanger and N. Gleason (eds.), *Diversity and Inclusion in Global Higher Education: Lessons from across Asia*. Singapore: Palgrave Macmillan, 183–207.

Pascarella, E. T., Wolniak, G. C., Seifert, T. A. D., Cruce, T. M., and Blaich, C. F. (2005). "Liberal arts colleges and liberal arts education." *ASHE Higher Education Report*, 31/3, 1–146.

Phillott, A. (2019). Chapter 11: Meeting strategic gender needs: The case of Asian University for Women, Bangladesh. In M. Nishimura & T. Sasao (eds.), *Doing Liberal Arts Education: The Global Case Studies*. Singapore: Springer, 135–145.

Roth, M. S. (2014). *Beyond the University: Why Liberal Education Matters*. New Haven, CT: Yale University Press.

Rowen, C. (2016). So much more than salary: Outcomes research in the liberal arts. *New Direction for Institutional Research*, 169, 51–60.

Rychen, D. S. and Salganik, L. H. (2000). "A contribution of the OECD program definition and selection of competencies: Theoretical and conceptual foundations: Definition and selection of key competencies." Paper presented at the INES (Indicators of Education Systems) General Assembly, September, Chiba, Japan.

Schneider, C. G. (2016). "Foreword." In I. Jung, M. Nishimura, and T. Sasao (eds.), *Liberal Arts Education and Colleges in East Asia: Possibilities and Challenges in the Global Age*. Singapore: Springer, v–vii.

Sim, H. R. (2016). "Global citizenship education in South Korea through civil society organizations: Its status and limitations." *Asian Journal of Education*, 17, 107–129.

Summerscales, W. (1970). *Affirmation and Dissent*. Columbia: Teachers College Press.

Yang, M., Webster, B., and Prosser, M. (2011). "Travelling a thousand miles: Hong Kong Chinese students' study abroad experience." *International Journal of Intercultural Relations*, 35, 69–78.

Yang, R. (2016). "The East–West axis? Liberal arts education in East Asian universities." In I. Jung, M. Nishimura, and T. Sasao (eds.), *Liberal Arts Education and Colleges in East Asia: Possibilities and Challenges in the Global Age*. Singapore: Springer, 27–38.

Yonezawa, A. and Nishimura, M. (2016). "Revisiting key values, roles and challenges of liberal arts education in East Asia." In I. Jung, M. Nishimura, and T. Sasao (eds.), *Liberal Arts Education and Colleges in East Asia: Possibilities and Challenges in the Global Age.* Singapore: Springer, 125–136.

Yoshida, A. (2002). "The curriculum reforms of the 1990s: What has changed?" *Higher Education*, 43/1, 43–63.

Zakaria, F. (2015). *In Defense of a Liberal Education.* New York: W. W. Norton.

CHAPTER 9

STEM FIELD DEMAND AND EDUCATIONAL REFORM IN ASIA-PACIFIC COUNTRIES

AKI YAMADA

1. INTRODUCTION

OVER the last several decades, modern technological advances have resulted in a pervasive integration of science and technology throughout society, contributing towards increased globalization as historical barriers to international travel, commerce, and communication, such as time and cost, have significantly reduced. In turn, increased mobility of talented individuals has given rise to a knowledge-based economy where skills-related knowledge is sought after and can be transferred across national borders. To facilitate technological growth and development, major changes are needed in education, the workplace, and society at large. Workers must increasingly become proficient in Science, Technology, Engineering, and Mathematics (STEM) to become valuable human resources, thus, having a background in STEM will be highly advantageous for roles in innovation. Governments around the world are now seeking to increase the number of technical graduates to ensure continued economic growth through innovation across all business sectors. Many governments see this as the "STEM field crisis," in which the supply of technical skills will be unable to keep up with economic demand. The current demand for STEM workers is primarily based on national interests of securing the talent necessary for maximizing productivity and economic strength through technology and innovation. Thus, it is important to recognize that the modern fears of a "STEM field crisis" do not apply to all fields equally, and this informs how countries are prioritizing STEM field development and competitiveness.

This chapter will examine how the Asia-Pacific region is dealing with the rising demand for STEM expertise and how historical and cultural factors in education affect the potential for STEM development and outcomes in this region. Clearly, the region is vast, and each country is characterized by unique circumstances and goals in relation to the new demand for advanced STEM knowledge, but some commonalities in culture, education systems, and response strategies will be presented and investigated to provide an illustrative view. After providing some background on the growing demand for STEM knowledge and expertise, I posit that many Asian countries already have strong education systems which make them well-positioned to meet the current and predicted economic demands for a highly skilled STEM field workforce. This foundational advantage in Asia is demonstrated through comparative international testing outcomes in math and quality technical graduates from many advanced Asian countries. For the region to maximize its economic potential, we should examine the ways it can increase the quantity and quality of its STEM graduates and workforce, including addressing the significant underrepresentation of women in STEM fields in Asia. Secondly, I highlight the "brain drain" phenomenon, particularly of STEM field students and workers, who migrate to more prosperous Western countries in Europe or North America for better pay or employment opportunities. This "brain drain" phenomenon is a pressing concern for Asian countries, which are now seeking ways to encourage domestic "brain gains." Lastly, I examine the evolution of Asian education systems and how they are being reconfigured to meet the demand for STEM talent with modern global competencies.

2. IMPORTANCE OF STEM IN ASIA AND GLOBALLY

The World Economic Forum (WEF, 2016a) posits that we are now transitioning to a Fourth Industrial Revolution in which technology is increasingly integrated into everyday life, extending human potential, yet blurring the boundaries between technology, its manifestations, and humans at the same time. Soon, developments in AI and robotics will force us to begin interacting with technology in more complex social and psychologically driven ways. The STEM fields play an important role in research and development and drive innovation and cutting-edge industries. STEM fields are becoming indispensable for future jobs and economic competitiveness, and governments worldwide are investing to improve their national competitiveness in these fields. As a leader in STEM fields, it is estimated that at least 50 percent of the United States' economic growth in the last half-century is attributable to STEM driven innovation (US Congress Joint Economic Committee, 2012), and this figure will doubtless grow over time. As advances in technology become increasingly pervasive and integrated into daily life, even jobs outside the STEM sector increasingly require basic proficiency in STEM knowledge (Shin et al., 2015). As such, demand for STEM graduates has risen sharply since their learning outcomes embody the knowledge, skills, and values that are applicable from basic work functionalities to advanced technological needs.

In today's increasingly globalized economy, nations are in fierce competition for STEM field jobs and highly educated workers with technical skills and knowledge. As seen in the Third Industrial Revolution, increased technology usage can improve efficiency, but often at the cost of low-skilled jobs that can be lost to advanced mechanical processes and computing capabilities. According to Frey and Osborne (2013), up to 47 percent of jobs in the United States are at high risk of disappearing due to automation within the next two decades as part of a larger global trend. There is a real concern of an emerging dichotomy in which nations lagging in science and technology infrastructure may be left marginalized, offering mainly low-skilled, poor-paying jobs, while nations with the resources to promote STEM education, skills, and industries will be able to secure a highly-skilled, high-paying economic future for their citizens and residents.

3. Demand for STEM Knowledge in Asia

According to WEF (2016b), Asian countries were among the top producers of recent STEM field graduates, including China (4.7 million), India (2.6 million), Indonesia (206,000), and Japan (195,000). In comparison, the United States accounted for only 568,000 recent STEM graduates, despite its position as a global leader in STEM education and employment opportunities. China's graduation rate in science and engineering has far surpassed that of the United States in the last two decades, while most other Asian countries besides India have remained relatively constant (National Science Foundation, 2020). At the doctoral degree level, China has been trailing the United States only slightly since 2007, with 34,400 Chinese degrees, compared to 39,900 US degrees accredited in 2015. The dominance of China and India among STEM field graduates should come as no surprise, as they are the two most populous countries, combined making up approximately 36 percent of the world population. Nonetheless, it must be recognized that in just the last several decades, with their massification of higher education, India and China have become powerhouses in terms of science and technology degrees conferred. To put this growth in perspective, the National Science Board (NSB, 2008) reports that in 1990 the United States was producing the most graduates with science and engineering as a first university degree with 351,855 graduates, followed by Japan (263,985), China (181,771), and India (176,036). This dramatic shift in supply of STEM field workers and industries to Asia is fully expected to continue through the near future. In 2016, the OECD projected that by 2030, China would produce 37 percent of STEM degrees in OECD and G20 nations, India 26.7 percent, Japan 1.9 percent, Korea 1.6 percent, and the United States 4.2 percent. Even if population size is factored out, NSB (2019) further evidences Asia's strong representation in engineering field degrees as a proportion of all degrees awarded per country in China (32.9 percent), South Korea (22.9 percent), Taiwan (19.5 percent), Japan, (14.8 percent), compared to Western countries like the United States (6.8 percent), and the United Kingdom (8.2 percent). It is worth noting that NSF (2020) shows science and engineering degrees in South Korea, Taiwan, and Japan have plateaued in recent years, indicating their phases of rapid retooling in STEM growth may be over. However, this stagnation does not necessarily align with national policy or prioritization efforts, which still strongly value STEM field education and industries. Due to the low birth rates in these countries, we would not expect a boom in graduates, but there is still a potential shift in the development of human resources further towards the STEM fields. For instance, as noted above, the ratio of Chinese students graduating in STEM fields is significantly higher than in other countries, over double that of Japan, and over four times that of the United States.

Quantitatively, Asian countries evidence very strong output of STEM field graduates, and commitment to industries involving R&D. Though the dramatic rise of China and India's science and engineering graduates is impressive, these numbers alone do not provide any assessment of the skills and value conferred with these degrees. Fundamentally, it must be recognized that the massification of education is relatively new in many of these regions. This leads to questions about the quality of such education pipelines. For example, Loyalka et al. (2021) found that the Computer Science (CS) skills of CS college seniors varied widely, with the United States producing the most competent students by a significant margin when compared to India, China, and Russia, even across both elite and non-elite universities. They suggest that skill gains are attributable to higher-quality teaching and stronger links between education and actual employment. UNESCO Institute for Statistics (2014) notes that because the boom in Asian higher education and STEM field graduates is still recent, many of these education systems are still developing graduate education pipelines that are needed to enhance the quality of future instructors, faculty recruitment, and research programs.

The development of Asia as a major STEM producer has been ongoing over the last century, especially with late industrialization and modernization in many of these countries. Many economies in Asia, particularly the four "Asian Tigers" (South Korea, Taiwan, Singapore, and Hong Kong), have undergone rapid transformation and growth over the last several decades. To varying extents, each has followed the infrastructure and education development patterns that turned post-World War II Japan into the world's second largest economy from 1968 to 2010. Hanna et al. (1996) posited that technological learning and integration of technology into their economies was a contributing factor to the successes of these newly industrialized countries. Dubbed the "East Asian Miracle," the governments of the four Asian Tigers and Japan adopted deliberate measures to promote technological innovation and R&D, while encouraging collaboration among the government, academia, and business sectors. Rather than allow their economic markets to develop naturally, it was the strong planning, effective policy, and synergy between public governance and private industries that aided these countries to become leaders in IT, technological services, and manufacturing (Hanna et al., 1996). Government strategies to build science and technology industries required government intervention, including sheltering businesses from foreign competition with tariffs, financial aid and credit, tax incentives for the private sector, policies to develop human resource talents, and promoting and funding R&D efforts.

South Korea, for example, underwent drastic economic changes after the Korean War in the 1950s, transforming from a poor agricultural nation to one of the top economies in the developing and, eventually, industrialized world. This period of development has been dubbed an "economic miracle" due to its impact and speed. From the 1980s to 1990s, South Korea transitioned towards prioritization of science and technology and R&D, boosting education funding while simultaneously shifting its economy from industrial manufacturing toward IT and innovation (Hong and Choi, 2011). The success of these efforts has led to a continuous cycle of aggressive reinvestment in R&D and education (Shin et al., 2015). South Korea has become the highest domestic R&D investor worldwide, outperforming all other countries as measured by expenditure relative to GDP (see Table 9.1). This shift is evidenced by the rapid rise and successes of major electronics and telecommunication companies and exports in automobiles, integrated circuits, semiconductors, LCD screens, telecommunications, and computers.

Given the comparatively small size and limited natural resources in countries like Singapore, South Korea, and Japan, it is clear how important R&D and innovation are to their economic strength and competitiveness in technological markets and their overall economy. China, which displaced Japan in 2010 to become the world's second largest economy, represents a different case, as it transitioned from a world leader in low-cost industrial manufacturing to technology and innovation. With the largest national population in the world—over 1.4 billion people—China now produces the most STEM graduates per year of any country, conferring approximately 1.7 million degrees in 2015 (NSF, 2020). Historically, protectionist policies, coupled with weak intellectual property enforcement, compelled domestic companies to favor the production of low-tech goods over high-tech innovation and intellectual property. However, China has now become the second largest spender in R&D funds (see Table 9.1) and ranked second in output of high R&D intensive industries in 2018 (NSF, 2020). The country has more than doubled its expenditure in R&D relative to GDP from 0.893 percent to 2.141 percent in 2018, but still lags in its R&D expenditure as a proportion of GDP

Table 9.1 R&D spending by country: total and percentage of GDP

2018 Rank by R&D spending	Country	Spend (USD equivalent)	As % of GDP
1	United States	581,553,000,000	2.84
2	China	554,327,829,310	2.19
3	Japan	176,762,555,530	3.26
4	Germany	137,880,026,160	3.09
5	South Korea	99,625,681,930	4.81
6	India	68,238,350,290	0.65
7	France	66,822,714,160	2.20

Source: Select data from: United Nations Educational, Scientific and Cultural Organization (UNESCO) Institute for Statistics (2020).

compared with other countries in Asia (OECD, 2020a). China was also in the process of improving its national innovation system as described in its 2006 "Medium to Long-Term Plan for the Development of Science and Technology" which aimed to transition the country to an innovation-oriented nation by 2020 with the ambition of becoming the world leader in science and technology by 2050. While many countries in Asia seek to benefit from globalization, China remained insulated from the global technology chain. In response to growing international trade tensions, the government has openly reinforced its preference for self-reliance and domestically driven innovation to further protect itself from global trade instabilities driven by international politics.

Elsewhere in Asia, not all countries have managed to retool their workforces and economies to benefit from the economic imperative of developing STEM skills. Countries like Malaysia, the Philippines, Indonesia, and Vietnam exhibit labor and skills shortages that will become apparent as technology displaces more unskilled labor. Oxford Economics (2018) predicts that among six Association of Southeast Asian Nations (ASEAN) countries (Indonesia, Malaysia, the Philippines, Singapore, Thailand, and Vietnam), technologies ranging from AI and automation to digitization will displace 28 million jobs, affecting 10.2 percent of their workers, by 2028. While some displaced workers may find new emergent jobs stemming from technological changes, 6.6 million workers are estimated to become redundant, and 41 percent of the labor force currently lacks technological skills to transition to new jobs. The International Labour Organization's (2016) ASEAN study reinforces this warning, predicting that up to 56 percent of jobs are at high risk of automation in Cambodia, Indonesia, the Philippines, Thailand, and Vietnam over the next two decades. This change is not limited to Asia but is of greater concern in regions that have not already adopted widespread STEM literacy as a priority for their workforces. Weakness in education outcomes is evidenced by standardized testing results in countries like the Philippines, Indonesia, and Thailand, indicating potential challenges in addressing this emerging skills gap. This global transition towards an increased reliance on technology in most job sectors will necessitate major changes in the knowledge and skills required in the future.

4. STEM Field R&D and Prioritization

The United Nations uses R&D spend and headcount as metrics to help measure the technological capabilities and potential for national innovation as part of its Sustainable Development Goals (United Nations, 2018). Dehmer et al. (2019) posit that R&D efforts have been shifting towards parts of Asia, amidst a larger trend where low-income countries are falling increasingly behind in scientific knowledge and the effects of R&D, which include improved productivity, standards of living, and quality of life. If we consider the top-down industrialization policies among the four Asian Tigers, especially Korea (Hong and Choi, 2011), and Japan, R&D was used to kickstart their economic growth. Similarly, China is now setting R&D spending targets as part of its national goals to transform into an innovation-oriented society. Mathieu and Potterie (2010) further point out that once countries develop strong industries in science and technology, national R&D spending can also be reflective of the strength, capabilities, and organization of a nation's economic structure. Beyond economic impact, STEM fields and their related industries have a critical and cyclical relationship with R&D efforts. UNESCO (2020) provides evidence that Asian countries have become a dominant force in R&D spending. Notably, China, Japan, South Korea, and India are among the highest investors in total R&D spending, though India has underperformed in R&D intensity relative to several smaller countries in Asia such as the Philippines, Singapore, and Hong Kong, for example.

With the recent shift towards prioritization of STEM fields in education and the workplace, it is worth examining how the STEM fields are funded and valued compared with non-STEM fields. UNESCO Institute for Statistics (UIS, 2018) shows that when STEM fields are broken down into categories of natural sciences, engineering and technology, medical and health sciences, and agricultural and veterinary sciences, the headcount for higher education researchers in Vietnam, Singapore, South Korea, the Philippines, Pakistan, and Malaysia is weighted toward engineering and technology and natural sciences, with only Japan showing a distinctly strong focus in medical and health sciences. That data further shows that within Asian higher education Gross Domestic Expenditure on R&D (GERD) spending by field, engineering and technology mostly dominate actual currency spent on R&D in higher education. While the social science fields of study account for significant headcount, funding is largely skewed towards engineering and technology. Across the board, relatively little R&D spending is allocated to non-STEM fields. Because R&D is tied to innovation and economic growth, and the rationalization of STEM workforce demand, these metrics provide insight into the governments prioritization and valuation of specific fields of interest.

5. ASIAN STUDENT PERFORMANCE IN SCIENCE AND MATH

We have touched on the advantage of STEM qualifications in the Asia-Pacific region in terms of workforce and economic development, but each nation's education system is foundational to all those outputs. It is well understood that science and math are essential fields of study for future STEM students and workers. There is also a strong connection with early education that emphasizes science and math education, which forges pathways towards the pursuit of STEM fields in higher education and employment. IES (2020) notes that 8th grade mathematics and science achievement was a strong predictor for graduating college with science and engineering field degrees. Similarly, Wang (2013) found several factors through primary and secondary education which significantly affect pathways for STEM education and careers, including attitudes toward math and toward the capacity to master math. Looking at international standardized testing results helps shed light on the potential for STEM output in the Asia region. The OECD Programme for International Student Assessment (PISA), for example, is one major international testing metric administered to 15-year-old students every three years which focuses on student abilities and functional skills to solve real-world problems. The most recent results continue a trend of Asian countries achieving high rankings (see Table 9.2).

The Trends in International Mathematics and Science Studies (TIMSS) test is another major international education assessment metric run every four years, and provides insight from comparative data between participating countries. The TIMSS testing methodology is based more on academic questions than the PISA, and problems are more aligned toward factual knowledge and short answers. The most recent TIMSS data (2020) also continues a recent trend of Asian countries dominating the top rankings at the 8th grade level (see Table 9.3).

Consistently high-ranking results of Asian countries in TIMSS and PISA testing underscore the point that math and science subjects are a strong focus in Asian education systems. While results are based on test situations, these skills are foundational for STEM fields and prove that Asian countries are well-positioned to meet the demand for STEM field graduates.

Table 9.2 PISA science and math, top rankings, 2018

Ranking	Country	Science	Country	Math
1	B-S-J-Z China*	590	B-S-J-Z China*	591
2	Singapore	551	Singapore	569
3	Macao (China)	544	Macao (China)	558
4	Estonia	530	Hong Kong (China)	551
5	Japan	529	Chinese Taipei	531
6	Finland	522	Japan	527
7	Korea	519	Korea	526
OECD Average	–	489	–	489

* Only four provinces of China were accounted for: Beijing, Shanghai, Jiangsu, and Zhejiang.

Source: Country designations and rankings are provided by the OECD (2019) and limited to participating countries.

Table 9.3 TIMSS 8th grade science and math, top rankings, 2019

Ranking	Science subject	Score	Math subject	Score
1	Singapore	608	Singapore	616
2	Chinese Taipei	574	Chinese Taipei	612
3	Japan	570	Korea, Rep of	607
4	Korea, Rep of	561	Japan	594
5	Russian Federation	543	Hong Kong SAR	578
6	Finland	543	Russian Federation	543

Source: Country designations and rankings are provided by TIMSS (2020) and limited to participating countries.

6. Cultural Commonalities in Asian Education

Many explanations can be advanced to explain the strength of Asia as a region, ranging from societal and cultural views regarding education and occupations, to educational methods and government planning. One such view is that despite having diverse governance and cultures, countries such as China, Taiwan, Japan, Korea, Singapore, and Vietnam all share linkages to Confucian Heritage Culture (CHC), which permeates through to teaching and learning methodologies in these education systems. CHC has also been credited for the rapid economic growth of Asian countries, particularly the four Asian Tigers, in the latter half of the twentieth century. Hawkins characterizes this Confucian pattern of education as being marked by "Confucian traits of self-denial, frugality, fortitude, patience, self-discipline, rote learning, memorization and delayed gratification" (Hawkins, 2008, p. 53). The OECD (2014, p. 90) notes that "[t]he growth of supplementary education in East Asia has had a relatively common trajectory: the broader cultural context of Confucianism, a historical focus on examinations, and a pedagogical tradition that views education as a relatively mechanistic acquisition of canonized knowledge." Emphasis placed on diligence, an extreme work ethic, and rote learning plays an important role in national examination scores, which dictate placement in tertiary and higher education institutions.

East Asian CHC education systems feature a strong culture of testing, commonly thought to originate from a Confucian principle of applied testing and qualifications for public servant positions. Many Asian countries to this day have rigorous testing at various levels of education, culminating in critical university exams. In South Korea, the Suneung national university exam holds sway as do Gaokao in China and the National Center Test in Japan. Societally and culturally, exceptional importance is placed on these tests compared to Western standards, and students are put under extreme pressure to succeed. As a result, in primary and secondary education, students dedicate more time per day to regular schooling, but also commonly enroll in supplemental private schooling and tutoring to prepare further for tests to come. While some critics argue against CHC being a determining factor, Jerrim (2015) studied the performance of students of East Asian extraction living in Australia and found that they continued to outperform their peers significantly, despite being removed from Asian education systems, suggesting a strong cultural component regardless of local environment. Jerrim cites CHC factors such as "the value placed upon education, willingness to invest in out-of-school tuition, instilling a hard-work ethic in their children, [and] high aspirations" (Jerrim, 2015, p. 4). As shown, CHC students tend to have strong potential for STEM studies due to foundational skills in science and math, and they are more predisposed to study in the STEM fields than many of their Western counterparts. UNESCO (2017) notes that self-confidence and self-efficacy beliefs regarding math and sciences are contributing factors to students pursuing STEM fields in the future. Because CHC education systems and many countries in Asia perform well in science and math at the primary and secondary education levels, this could partially explain strong STEM field representation at the tertiary level. While there are inherently many differences between each country, there are still distinctive characteristics that relate to Confucian beliefs, and many other nations have sought to emulate these proven educational methods to further the development of their economies.

While giving credit to the strengths of CHC education, there should be no presumption that non-CHC education pipelines are inferior or producing less capable students and workers. Despite their benefits, the CHC education systems also display many weaknesses. Firstly, they are well known for strong performances at the primary and secondary levels of international testing, but less comparative focus has been given to their tertiary systems. Western universities like Stanford, Oxford, MIT, Cambridge, and Princeton are still recognized as models of higher education, while Asian universities are only recently gaining a foothold in the top university world rankings. Secondly, Confucian education methods involving mass-memorization, rote learning, and teacher-driven instruction are notably inadequate in imparting creativity and critical thinking and are removed from comprehensive learning that aligns education with real-world, problem-solving scenarios. Notably, with advances in technology and automation, formulaic knowledge reproduction is something more easily handled through the assistance of computers, information networks, and AI, while critical thinking, creative application of knowledge, and problem-solving skills are irreplaceable. East Asian education tends to be driven from the top down, with teachers passing knowledge to students in unidirectional lectures, while Western education favors active participation, where teachers and students can be involved in bidirectional dialogues. In Western education, group discussions are common, and students are encouraged to share their own beliefs, present their own identity, and argue points in both oral and written forms. As a result of these differences, critics of Asian education cite a lack of creativity, imagination, critical thinking toward problem-solving, and diminished leadership potential.

As STEM education is being prioritized in part for its capacity to spur innovation, it is believed that strong East Asian test performances do not necessarily translate into real-world outcomes. This critique is something that many Asian education systems seek to address as part of their reform agendas. CHC education systems have long borrowed from the education systems of Western countries like Germany, France, Britain, and the United States in their modernization processes, and most Asian countries' education systems were affected by historical colonialization and foreign influences (Altbach, 1989). This chapter will later examine how Asian education systems are still looking to follow leading Western education patterns and systems in their ongoing reforms.

7. STEM Challenges and Responses in Asia

The new focus on STEM has raised many challenges in the transition to STEM literacy, skills development, and integration of technology within the economy and society. To increase STEM literacy, many countries are now seeking to mobilize underrepresented groups to help fill the demand for STEM education in the workforce, focusing on women and socio-economically underprivileged minority groups. The severe gender disparity across STEM fields is problematic as women are not following the same career pathways as men to high-demand and high-paying STEM field jobs. This is indicative of both socio-cultural biases that push women away from these fields, as well as cases of gender discrimination, pay inequality, and glass ceilings in male dominant workplaces. Consideration should be given to the fact that the overall percentage of women participating in the workforce in Asia is highly variable and influenced by regional social and cultural factors. The World Bank (2021) estimates that among women aged 15 and older, labor force participation rates include: China (63.7 percent), Vietnam (62.3 percent), Japan (54 percent), Korea (54 percent), and India (21 percent), compared to the world average for men (75.8 percent).

According to WEF (2020), the Gender Gap Index which measures gender disparity shows that many Asian countries lag in gender parity in four metrics: (1) economic participation and opportunity; (2) educational attainment; (3) health and survival; and (4) political empowerment in general; not just in STEM education and employment. Scored regionally, where a score of 1 represents equality between genders, Western Europe scored 0.767, East Asia and the Pacific 0.685, and South Asia 0.661. Out of 153 countries, China ranked 106 (0.676), South Korea 108 (0.672), and Japan 121 (0.652). It is useful to note that these are three CHC countries have traditionally been linked to strong patriarchal views and well-defined gender roles that promote men to operate in the public sphere and consign women to household duties. These gender roles also have a role in shaping societal norms of which jobs are perceived as appropriate or desirable for women to pursue. STEM field R&D encompasses both academia and private sector work, so it can also be used as a gauge toward the actual participation of women in these fields. The UNESCO Institute for Statistics (2018) estimates that worldwide, only 28.8 percent of R&D is conducted by female researchers. In the East Asia-Pacific region this ratio drops to 23.4 percent, and in South and West Asia, 18.5 percent. These ratios are especially low in Korea (19.7 percent), Japan (15.7 percent), and India (13.9 percent). For instance, Yoshikawa et al. (2018) point out that in Japan, women have especially low gender representation rates in business R&D, especially in engineering (5 percent) and science fields (13.3 percent).

Globally, and in Asia, higher-level societal issues can shape individual self-selection into STEM field careers by factoring in personal attitudes and self-confidence toward math and science subjects. Lin et al. (2018) and UNESCO (2017) found that math self-efficacy beliefs were shown to significantly affect gender, racial, and ethnic representation in the STEM fields. Consequently, social norms, perceived gender roles, and career stereotypes play a large factor in shaping self-selection into STEM fields even before reaching tertiary education. The education and employment funnel for women entering STEM fields varies significantly from country to country. OECD (2020b) statistics show that fewer women graduate with a bachelor's degree in STEM fields in Japan and Korea, at 15.4 percent and 29.7 percent, respectively, while the OECD average is 31 percent. Concerning Japan, Yoshikawa et al. (2018) attributed workplace underrepresentation of women in STEM to three factors: patriarchy with a strong emphasis on gender roles, prioritization of social collectivism over individuality, and the pervasiveness and strength of social norms in Japanese culture. In other words, married Japanese women who pursue a career over accepting their place in traditionally female roles such as full-time household duties and child-rearing responsibilities are often perceived as selfish. Yet, paradoxically, male colleagues tend to look down on them if they prioritize family commitments over the workplace. Japan's long working hours and normalized over-time, especially in the STEM fields, mean that many women simply cannot fulfill the competing expectations of the workplace and home.

In India, a much different situation prevails where graduation rates of women in STEM are among the highest in the world, but this has not yet converted into female representation in actual employment. According to India's Ministry of Human Resource Development (2019), Indian women accounted for 49.1 percent of Information Technology and 48.7 percent of Computer Engineer undergraduate degrees granted. Yet there is still underrepresentation in the workplace: in the IT employment sector, Ring (2018) estimates that women make up only 34 percent of employees, though this is still better than the US average of 24 percent in 2015. Beyond quantitative representation, a TimesJobs (2020) survey of India's women in tech found that 49 percent plan to change their career, primarily due to gender bias in their fields. This includes hiring discrimination, glass ceilings in their career growth, and pay disparity, among other problems. Such issues are not limited to India and UNESCO (2017) posits that gender differentials are strongly tied to societal biases at all levels, including within the family, education systems, workplace, and media representation. Shifting these entrenched gender stereotypes and deterrents toward women in STEM careers will require substantial long-term efforts spanning the varied stages of upbringing, education, and career development.

With the international demand for STEM researchers and workers, it is readily apparent that the movement of talented individuals and knowledge will affect supply and demand in the global workforce. Increasingly, people possess agency in where they choose to live and work and seek places that can provide the best quality of life, career opportunities, advancement, and compensation. Asian countries have been losing their skilled talent through the "brain drain" phenomenon to Western countries, such as the United States, with its lucrative high-tech industry. According to the Institute of International Education (2019), during the 2018/2019 academic year, among all foreign students in the US, 61 percent of undergraduate students and 74 percent of graduate students came from Asia. In 2017/2018, the top three countries sending international students to the US comprised of China (33 percent, 363,341), India (17.9 percent, 196,271), and South Korea (5 percent, 54,555). Foreign students are often permitted to stay in the United States after graduation through programs such as the Optional Practical Training program, which grants a one-year stay to work in their area of study, with extensions for students in STEM fields. Since 2008, STEM workers have been able to apply for a 17 month extension. This has increased to a 24 month extension in 2016, reflecting the demand for STEM workers in the United States. Similarly, the H-1B visa allows companies to sponsor foreign work visas. This has become problematic for countries like the United States, which has become reliant on a large borrowed international STEM workforce, resulting in domestic concerns about security and future competitiveness. According to an American Immigration Council (AIC, 2017) report, the number of US foreign-born STEM workers has more than doubled in size and percentage. Whereas in 1990, 11.9 percent of the US STEM workforce was foreign born, the number has increased to 24.3 percent in 2015.

As Asian countries have been highly susceptible to "brain drain" with respect to some of their top talent, Asian universities have initiated their own programs to foster domestic talent while attracting international talent at the same time. An examination of China's position in the "brain drain" phenomenon illustrates this problem. To counter international talent outflows, China's 2008 Thousand Talents Plan (TTP) was created primarily to employ incentives to attract elite and successful Chinese entrepreneurs and researchers to return and work in China. Offers to returnees can include matching competitive salaries, securing high amounts of research funding, and other support for top talent. In 2017, it was estimated that China recruited over 7,000 elite individuals through this program (United States Senate, 2019). With intense competition for STEM talent, the TTP has come under scrutiny as a matter of US national security, with fears and allegations that it is being used to facilitate the theft of intellectual property and trade secrets, and siphon away the dividends of US-funded R&D. Of note, most of China's "brain drain" mitigation policies target engineering scientists and technical researchers, with little focus on social scientists, especially amidst restrictions on social science studies that touch on issues seen as sensitive by the Chinese government (Cao, 2008). China's numerous recent policy changes have been largely successful. Cao et al. (2020) note that in 2017 there was an estimated 79 percent return rate of Chinese going abroad, a rate which was as low as 23.4 percent in 2000. However, Zwetsloot et al. (2020, p. 9) found that the recent intention-to-stay rate of Chinese STEM PhD graduates in the US has been very high, ranging from 95 percent in 2000–2005, 91 percent in 2006–2011, and 87 percent in 2012–2017. For comparison, in 2012–2017, the analogous stay rate for Indians was 91 percent, Taiwanese 84 percent, and South Koreans 75 percent. This suggests that despite strong retention efforts like the Chinese TTP, these countries are still at risk of losing their most developed talent to other countries.

Another contributing factor to "brain drain" are local circumstances that can make it difficult for STEM workers in certain fields and with certain qualifications to find work at home. For instance, there are often discrepancies between what higher education provides and what is expected by the public and private sectors that offer employment to new graduates. A key consideration in this "skills gap" is whether graduates can be matched to jobs, and whether their degree, knowledge, and skills translate to the workplace and thus derive satisfactory compensation. In Japan, for example, many Science and Technology (S&T) graduates find it difficult to find work as specialized researchers in the private sector. Ishikawa et al.'s (2015, p. 90) analysis of doctoral graduates found that in a "2007 survey of 924 Japanese companies, more than half report they regularly employ master's graduates, while nearly 70 per cent report they never hire doctoral graduates." In Japan, private sector companies tend to favor hiring new graduates with bachelor's degrees over graduate degrees, with the expectation that they will gain the necessary skills through on-the-job training. Furthermore, Japan's recent decline in STEM competitiveness can be attributed to a lack of attraction to STEM jobs as they are perceived to offer less pay and fewer promotions than analogous jobs in the humanities and social sciences (Ishikawa et al., 2015). This is the opposite of most Western economies like the United States, where the 2017 median income for Science and Engineering workers was $85,390, double the median for US workers overall (NSF, 2020).

As another example, Malaysia's government proposed a New Economic Model (Ministry of Education, 2016) that aimed to create 1.3 million STEM jobs by 2020. However, the ambitious plan pointed to the challenges of a shortage of skilled workers and continuing "brain drain" of local talent seeking better opportunities abroad. This was worsened by low-cost, low-skill, and short-term profit business models favored by the country's private sector, which have led to low levels of R&D and investment in innovation. Shahali et al. (2017) note that three key problems in Malaysia are a lack of interest in science and technology from a young age, a decline in science and math skills as measured by PISA and TIMSS exams, and low-quality and outdated STEM education. Malaysia is now looking to upgrade teaching methods to include project-based material and problem-solving challenges that encourage creativity and critical thinking. This reflects both a desire to improve teacher training and curriculum development, but also raise student interest in learning and understanding the practical applications of STEM.

To counter the "brain drain" phenomenon and factors that limit domestic recruitment, Asian universities are seeking to become more competitive in international rankings to attract foreign talent or "brain gain." Economic improvements in the Asia region and the massification of higher education have resulted in more cross-border education opportunities. Education hubs and prestigious institutions with brand recognition can serve to attract global talent and, even more so, attract regional talent by capturing the attention of those who may not have the opportunity to seek education in top Western universities abroad, or those who simply choose to stay in the region. Countries like Malaysia, Singapore, and Hong Kong have been setting up such education hubs to "develop local talent, attract foreign talent, and repatriate diasporic talent" (Lee, 2014, p. 807). Singapore's Agency for Science Technology and Research (A*STAR) is one such example of a global education hub that concentrates scientific talent and hosts collaborations with highly ranked research centers and universities. Singapore has further embraced the internationalization strategy by supplementing its local recruitment of talent with global recruitment by strengthening its international linkages and seeking to host highly ranked universities with the understanding that diversity and global perspectives are key to creative problem-solving. However, more recently, education hub efforts have been met with resistance at the local level. In such hub states, the large influxes of foreign students being offered scholarships and other benefits are sometimes viewed as competitors for resources, jobs, and educational opportunities. Lo (2018) points out that Singapore's Global Schoolhouse strategy became a political liability with the rise of nationalist sentiments in the public discourse. Similarly, Lo (2018) cites how in the early 2000s, Hong Kong's non-local students rose to 80 percent from mainland China, which in turn stoked anti-mainland China sentiments. With Hong Kong's 2019 anti-government protests and new Chinese national security laws locking down pro-independence thinking, its future as an educational hub accommodating either Western or mainland Chinese students is highly uncertain. These two cases show that while liberal educational policies that have aligned with globalization and commercialization have increased, we are now witnessing how they are highly subject to national politics, and public sentiment that pits local needs against globalization forces.

8. THE NEED FOR REFORM IN ASIAN EDUCATION

This chapter has shown the strengths of Asian education systems, the massive number of STEM graduates being produced in the region, and commitment to technology and innovation. One might jump ahead and ask why the West still dominates world rankings of elite higher education institutions and where are the Asian equivalents of globally recognized tech entrepreneurs, scholars, and Nobel award winners from Asia? These are valid points that indicate challenges that Asian countries are still facing in the development of their STEM potential. When it comes to international awards like the Nobel Prize, Kura et al. (2015) hypothesize that North-East Asians underperform relative to their strengths on paper because they are genetically and culturally predisposed to collectivism over individualism. They posit that traits of high curiosity, individualism, and independent thinking are needed for award-worthy scientific innovation. This can be further linked to a lack of individualism, creativity, and interdisciplinary work in Asian classrooms that stymie innovation in the workforce. We should also consider that when it comes to international recognition and awards, the discourse is inherently Western-centric. This is especially true where English has become the modern lingua franca, such as in international collaboration in the education, research, and business sectors. There are no Asian countries that rank high in English proficiency standards, such as the EF English Proficiency Index. Thus, when considering world rankings, measuring research value through publication citations and business leaders abroad, and other international metrics, Asian countries are at a disadvantage in many regards. These are all issues that Asian higher education is facing and attempting to reform, not just in relation to global competition in the STEM fields.

Along with the Western world, education in Asia has largely shifted towards prioritizing STEM over other areas of study. In Asia, many hold a narrow interpretation of the STEM fields that include mathematics, chemistry, physics, life sciences, computer sciences, and engineering fields, but may exclude the social sciences. Some scholars argue a view that pits STEM and "hard sciences" against non-STEM and "soft sciences" is a false dichotomy. For instance, a wider categorization of the STEM fields would also include social sciences and "soft" sciences such as anthropology, linguistics, psychology, political science, etc. However, regardless, there is recent criticism that higher education funding and government prioritization has become too heavily skewed toward certain STEM fields, weakening many other areas of study, including the social sciences (Kingston, 2015; UIS, 2018; Yang, 2018). For instance, in Japan, humanities and social sciences are sometimes grouped and criticized as "impractical" studies in juxtaposition with the "hard" sciences that a narrow view of the STEM fields encompasses (Kingston, 2015). In 2015, Japan's Minister of Education proposed steps towards abolishing certain social science and humanities organizations in national universities, resulting in backlash from top universities, the business sector, media, general public, and even the Science Council of Japan (ICEF Monitor, 2015). In Taiwan, Yang (2018) points out that there used to be a long history of valuing the humanities and social sciences, but lately that has shifted toward more severe views that equate modernization with STEM, to the detriment of other fields. Such trends are not isolated to Asia, but culturally there is a greater predisposition toward favoring the hard sciences within the STEM fields.

In higher education, it is commonplace that STEM field coursework has become siloed to such an extent that technical subject matter is taught in isolation from other fields. Kelley and Knowles (2016) note that historical STEM reform has often focused on improving education within each field as an isolated area of study, but there is much to be gained by using a comprehensive and integrated approach to learning that involves practical problem-solving. As new technologies become increasingly integrated with everyday life, it is also important for technical workers to be aware of multiple perspectives beyond technical implementation. For instance, there are many interdisciplinary concerns in real-world applications: ethical concerns over data privacy, improving integration of technology through effective and intuitive user design and testing, and creating technologies that are capable of interpreting and acting on human language, behavior, and socio-cultural norms. Thus, while STEM education has traditionally focused on technical skills and knowledge in isolation, "next generation" competencies are more wide-ranging. For instance, many of Japan's leading graduate programs encourage both interdisciplinary and intercultural project-based learning in groups that cut across domestic and international, or engineering and arts backgrounds. Like Japan in this regard, with Korea's shift towards STEM prioritization, universities are transforming their academic structures and curricula to meet demands from outside stakeholders, resulting in new general education and integrated approaches to STEM education (Rhee, 2018; Kang, 2019).

Now, throughout East Asia, educators are undertaking reform to shift the focus from pure STEM education to a broader mix of STEM and non-STEM education, as well as twenty-first-century competencies that encourage the development of communication, problem-solving, teamwork, and global leadership skills. In Western education, these traits and skills, sometimes promoted as "the 4C's"—Critical thinking and problem-solving, Communication, Collaboration, and Creativity and Innovation (National Education Association, 2011)—are commonly developed as soft skills and many Asian education systems including those in Hong Kong, Japan, Singapore, South Korea, and Taiwan are undertaking reform in this direction (Asia Society, 2017). Asian education systems are now diverging from the more limiting aspects of CHC traditions and encouraging active learning methods to develop communication skills and present opportunities for students to acquire and embrace critical thinking capacities (Yamada and Yamada, 2018). Problem-based learning, group work, and open discussion also prepare students for teamwork and leadership that Confucian educational approaches often lack. As technology becomes closely integrated with everyday life, it is important to transition technical learning away from theoretical perspectives and into greater openness to simulation and practice.

9. CONCLUSION

Even before recent global STEM field prioritization, Asian countries attached traditional and cultural values to math and science education. Asian countries like Japan and the four Asian Tigers were late industrializers, and they saw firsthand how the acquisition of Western sciences and technologies was essential to their rapid development. Now, Asia has become well known for its students' overall outstanding record in math and science education, evidenced by PISA and TIMSS results. Furthermore, with the relatively recent massification of higher education in many Asian countries, the region is producing a significant proportion of the world's STEM graduates. National R&D spending in countries like Korea, Japan, Taiwan, and Singapore, and their resulting prominence in tech industries, point to the value and centrality of STEM fields. Faced with today's high demand for STEM talent, Asian students and their respective countries have a solid foundation to build upon.

In today's highly globalized world, STEM graduates around the world have become prized commodities. To prevent further "brain drain," Asian countries are now finding ways to retain and attract new talent through initiatives including diminishing immigration barriers to foreigners, creating education hubs to recruit regionally and internationally, and incentivizing top-tier talent to return from abroad. Furthermore, there are still significant opportunities to increase STEM talent by addressing social and cultural biases that factor into the underrepresentation of women in these fields.

Education in Asia has long been criticized for its reliance on rote learning and lack of student engagement and creativity found in Western classrooms. As part of national STEM policies in Asia, education systems are being retooled to produce higher-quality STEM graduates by reconciling the best aspects of Confucian and Western teaching methods. From both education policy and workforce needs, many Asian countries have identified a need for soft skills in their future technical workforce, such as problem-solving, critical thinking, and the ability to communicate and collaborate effectively across disciplines and borders. It is hoped that soft skills will drive innovation and collaboration, and provide a more holistic integration of technology into society, which will yield economic and social benefits. As we continue to shift towards technologically driven societies, further studies will be needed to reveal the economic and social impacts of these ongoing educational reforms.

REFERENCES

Altbach, P. G. (1989). "Twisted roots: The Western impact on Asian higher education." *Higher Education*, 18, 9–29.

American Immigration Council (2017). *Fact Sheet: Foreign-born STEM workers in the United States.* https://www.americanimmigrationcouncil.org/research/foreign-born-stem-workers-united-states

Asia Society (2017). "Advancing 21st century competencies in East Asian education systems." https://asiasociety.org/files/21st-century-competencies-east-asian-education-systems.pdf

Cao, C. (2008). "China's brain drain at the high end: Why government policies have failed to attract first-rate academics to return." *Asian Population Studies*, 4/3, 331–345.

Cao, C., Baas, J., Wagner, C. S., and Jonkers, K. (2020). "Returning scientists and the emergence of China's science system." *Science and Public Policy*, 47/2, 172–183.

Dehmer, S. P., Pardey, P. G., Beddow, J. M., and Chai, Y. (2019). "Reshuffling the global R&D deck, 1980–2050." *PLoS ONE*, 14/3, e0213801. https://doi.org/10.1371/journal.pone.0213801

Frey, C. B. and Osborne, M. A. (2013). *The Future of Employment: How Susceptible Are Jobs to Computerisation?* https://www.oxfordmartin.ox.ac.uk/downloads/academic/The_Future_of_Employment.pdf

Government of India, Ministry of Human Resource Development (2019). *All India Survey on Higher Education (2018–2019).* aishe.nic.in/aishe/reports

Hanna, N., Boyson, S., and Gunaratne, S. (1996). *The East Asian Miracle and Information Technology: Strategic Management of Technological Learning.* http://documents1.worldbank.org/curated/en/959361468749799964/pdf/multi-page.pdf

Hawkins, J. N. (2008). "Myth or reality? Assessing the validity of the Asian model of education." *Harvard International Review,* 30/3, 52–56.

Hong, S. and Choi, J. (2011). "Success and challenges in managing R&D policy performance in South Korea." *Asian Research Policy,* 2/2, 80–92.

ICEF Monitor (2015). "Japanese government asks universities to close social sciences and humanities faculties." https://monitor.icef.com/2015/09/japanese-government-asks-universities-to-close-social-sciences-and-humanities-faculties/

Institute of Education Sciences (2020). *Stats in brief, June 2020: Health and STEM career expectations and science literacy achievement of U.S. 15-year-old students.* https://permanent.fdlp.gov/gpo154946/2020034.pdf

Institute of International Education (2019). "International student totals by place of origin, 2012/13–2019/10." *Open Doors Report on International Education Exchange.* http://www.iie.org/opendoors

International Labour Organization (2016). *ASEAN in Transformation: The Future of Jobs at Risk of Automation.* https://www.ilo.org/wcmsp5/groups/public/---ed_dialogue/---act_emp/documents/publication/wcms_579554.pdf

Ishikawa, M., Moehle, A., and Fujii, S. (2015). "Japan: Restoring faith in science through competitive STEM strategy." In B. Freeman, S. Marginson, and R. Tytler (eds.), *The Age of STEM: Educational Policy and Practice across the World in Science, Technology, Engineering and Mathematics.* Abingdon: Routledge, 81–101.

Jerrim, J. (2015). *Why Do East Asian Children Perform so Well in PISA? An Investigation of Western-Born Children of East Asian Descent.* https://www.tandfonline.com/doi/pdf/10.1080/03054985.2015.1028525

Kang, N. H. (2019). "A review of the effect of integrated STEM or STEAM (science, technology, engineering, arts, and mathematics) education in South Korea." *Asia Pacific Science Education,* 5. https://doi.org/10.1186/s41029-019-0034-y

Kelley, T. R. and Knowles, J. G. (2016). "A conceptual framework for integrated STEM education." *International Journal of STEM Education,* 3/1, 11. https://doi.org/10.1186/s40594-016-0046-z

Kingston, J. (2015). "Japanese university humanities and social science programs under attack." *The Asia-Pacific Journal,* 13/39, 1–12.

Kura, K., Nijenhuis, J. T., and Dutton, E. (2015). "Why do Northeast Asians win so few Nobel Prizes?" *Comprehensive Psychology,* 4/15, 1–8. https://doi.org/10.2466%2F04.17.CP.4.15

Lee, J. T. (2014). "Education hubs and talent development: Policymaking and implementation challenges." *Higher Education,* 69/6, 807–823. https://link.springer.com/content/pdf/10.1007%2Fs10734-014-9745-x.pdf

Lin, L., Lee, T., and Snyder, L. A. (2018). "Math self-efficacy and STEM intentions: A person-centered approach." *Frontiers in Psychology,* 9.

Lo, W. (2018). "After globalisation: A reconceptualisation of transnational higher education governance in Singapore and Hong Kong." *Higher Education Quarterly,* 72/1, 3–14.

Loyalka, P., Liu, O. L., Li, G. Kardanova, E., Chirikov, I., Hu, S., Yu, N., Ma, L., Guo, F., Beteille, T., Tognatta, N., Gu, L., Ling, G., Federiakin, D., Wang, H., Khanna, S., Bhuradia, A., Shi, Z., and Li, Y. (2021). "Skill levels and gains in university STEM education in China, India,

Russia, and the United States." *Nature Human Behaviour*, 5, 892–904. https://www.nature.com/articles/s41562-021-01062-3

Mathieu, A. and Potterie, B. P. (2010). "A note on the drivers of R&D intensity." *Research in World Economy*, 1/1, 56–65.

Ministry of Education (2016). *Sharing Malaysian Experience in Participation of Girls in STEM Education*. Geneva: UNESCO International Bureau of Education (IBE).

National Education Association (2011). *Preparing 21st Century Students for a Global Society*. http://www.nea.org/assets/docs/A-Guide-to-Four-Cs.pdf

National Science Board (2008). *Science and Engineering Indicators 2008*. https://wayback.archive-it.org/5902/20150818072826/http:/www.nsf.gov/statistics/seind08/c2/c2s5.htm

National Science Board (2019). *Higher Education in Science and Engineering*. https://www.ncses.nsf.gov/pubs/nsb20197/executive-summary

National Science Foundation (2020). *The State of U.S. Science and Engineering 2020*. https://ncses.nsf.gov/pubs/nsb20201

Organisation for Economic Co-operation and Development (2014). *Strong Performers and Successful Reformers in Education: Lessons from PISA for Korea*. https://www.oecd-ilibrary.org/docserver/9789264190672-5-en.pdf

Organisation for Economic Co-operation and Development (2016, August 25). *Tomorrow's scientists: Projected share of graduates with STEM* degrees across OECD and G20 countries in 2030*. https://www.facebook.com/theOECD/photos/where-will-tomorrows-scientists-come-from-compare-countries-grads-wstem-degrees-/10153684760187461/

Organisation for Economic Co-operation and Development (2019). *PISA 2018 Insights and Interpretations*. https://www.oecd.org/pisa/PISA%202018%20Insights%20and%20Interpre tations%20FINAL%20PDF.pdf

Organisation for Economic Co-operation and Development (2020a). *Main Science and Technology Indicators*. http://www.oecd.org/sti/msti.htm

Organisation for Economic Co-operation and Development (2020b). *Compare Your Country: The Pursuit of Gender Equality: An Uphill Battle*. https://www1.compareyour country.org/gender-equality/en/0/215/default

Oxford Economics (2018). *Technology and the Future of ASEAN Jobs: The Impact of AI on Workers in ASEAN's Six Largest Economies*. https://www.oxfordeconomics.com/publica-tion/download/303960

Rhee, B. S. (2018). "Developing the humanities competencies of STEM undergraduate students: New challenges for Korean higher education." In J. Hawkins, A. Yamada, R. Yamada, and W. Jacob (eds.), *New Directions of STEM Research and Learning in the World Ranking Movement: A Comparative Perspective*. Cham: Palgrave Macmillan, 111–126.

Ring, K. (2018). "Women in tech: India leads the way." *451 Research*. https://go.451research.com/women-in-tech-india-employment-trends.html

Shahali, E. H., Ismail, I., and Halim, L. (2017). "STEM education in Malaysia: Policy trajectories and initiatives." *Asian Research Policy*, 8/2, 122–133.

Shin, J. C., Postiglione, G. A., and Huang, F. (eds.) (2015). *Mass Higher Education Development in East Asia: Strategy, Quality, and Challenges*. Springer.

TimesJobs (2020). "Women in tech: Underrepresented | underpaid | undervalued still?" *TJinsite Hiring & Beyond*, 10/3.

Trends in International Mathematics and Science Study (2020). *TIMSS 2018 International Results in Mathematics and Science 2015*. https://timss2019.org/reports/

United Nations (2018). *Technology and Innovation Report 2018: Harnessing Frontier Technologies for Sustainable Development.* https://unctad.org/system/files/official-document/tir2018_en.pdf

United Nations Educational, Scientific and Cultural Organization (2017). *Cracking the Code: Girls' and Women's Education in Science, Technology, Engineering and Mathematics (STEM).* https://unesdoc.unesco.org/ark:/48223/pf0000253479

United Nations Educational, Scientific and Cultural Organization Institute for Statistics (2014). *Higher Education in Asia: Expanding Out, Expanding Up.* http://uis.unesco.org/sites/default/files/documents/higher-education-in-asia-expanding-out-expanding-up-2014-en.pdf

United Nations Educational, Scientific and Cultural Organization Institute for Statistics (2018). *Fact Sheet No. 51: Women in Science.* http://uis.unesco.org/sites/default/files/documents/fs51-women-in-science-2018-en.pdf

United Nations Educational, Scientific and Cultural Organization Institute for Statistics (2020). *Science, Technology and Innovation.* http://data.uis.unesco.org/Index.aspx?DataSetCode=SCN_DS&lang=en

United States Congress Joint Economic Committee (2012). *STEM Education: Preparing for the Jobs of the Future.* https://www.jec.senate.gov/public/_cache/files/6aaa7e1f-9586-47be-82e7-326f47658320/stem-education---preparing-for-the-jobs-of-the-future-.pdf

United States Senate (2019). *Threats to the U.S. Research Enterprise: China's Talent Recruitment Plans.* https://www.hsgac.senate.gov/imo/media/doc/2019-11-18%20PSI%20Staff%20Report%20-%20China's%20Talent%20Recruitment%20Plans.pdf

Wang, X. (2013). "Why students choose STEM majors: Motivation, high school learning, and postsecondary context of support." *American Educational Research Journal,* 50/5, 1081–1121.

World Bank (2021). *Labor Force Participation Rate, Female (% of Female Population Ages 15+).* https://data.worldbank.org/indicator/SL.TLF.CACT.FE.ZS

World Economic Forum (2016a). *What Is the Fourth Industrial Revolution?* https://www.weforum.org/agenda/2016/01/what-is-the-fourth-industrial-revolution/

World Economic Forum (2016b). *Human Capital Report.* https://www.weforum.org/reports/the-human-capital-report-2016

World Economic Forum (2020). *Global Gender Gap Report 2020.* http://www3.weforum.org/docs/WEF_GGGR_2020.pdf

Yamada, A. and Yamada, R. (2018). "The new movement of active learning in Japanese higher education: The analysis of active learning case in Japanese graduate programs." In S. M. Brito (ed.), *Active Learning: Beyond the Future.* London: IntechOpen, 43–58.

Yang, J. C.-C. (2018). "Exploring the relationship between STEM research and world higher education rankings: The case of Taiwan." In J. Hawkins, A. Yamada, R. Yamada, and W. Jacob (eds.), *New Directions of STEM Research and Learning in the World Ranking Movement: A Comparative Perspective.* Cham: Palgrave Macmillan, 43–64.

Yoshikawa, K., Kokubo, A., and Wu, C. (2018). "A cultural perspective on gender inequality in STEM: The Japanese context." *Industrial and Organization Psychology,* 11/2, 301–309.

Zwetsloot, R., Feldgoise, J., and Dunham, J. (2020). *Trends in U.S. Intention-to-Stay Rates of International Ph.D. Graduates across Nationality and STEM Fields.* https://cset.georgetown.edu/wp-content/uploads/CSET-Trends-in-U.S.-Intention-to-Stay-Rates.pdf

CHAPTER 10

··

THE RANKING GAME

··

WILLIAM YAT WAI LO AND RYAN M. ALLEN

1. INTRODUCTION

HIGHER education is increasingly framed in a broad strategy for internationalization, as globalization has reshaped the global landscape of higher education where the operation of universities has transcended national borders. In the context of the knowledge economy, higher education is considered a key component of national competitiveness, as it is important in terms of enhancing a nation's knowledge-producing and talent-attracting capacity. Based on these theoretical understandings of the global nature of higher education, the literature highlights the significance of global competition in understanding contemporary higher education development (see Marginson, 2006; Shahjahan and Morgan, 2016 for the theoretical exploration of such competition for talent in knowledge production).

This chapter analyzes the prevalence of global university rankings within this context of the intensification of global competition in higher education and the associated call for developing world-class universities in Asia. Focusing on the cases of Western Anglophone countries, the literature considers neoliberal ideology and its pro-market practices as important forces driving internationalization of higher education (e.g., Hazelkorn, 2008). According to this neoliberalization thesis, elite universities are differentiated and assigned to establish and maintain a country's status as a global higher education power, while mass universities are responsible for commercial provision of higher education, thereby enlarging the country's share in the global higher education market (Marginson, 2006). Thus, university rankings are seen as an important information tool helping international students choose their destinations and institutions. In a similar vein, partnerships, scholar exchanges, and other international collaborations hinge upon identifying peer partner institutions abroad. The top-ranked universities mostly choose to partner with other highly ranked institutions. Under these conditions, institutions consider their participation in global university rankings as part of their international marketing campaign targeted at multiple actors, both domestically and internationally (Hazelkorn, 2015).

However, this chapter suggests that, different to the neoliberalization thesis, the global competition within the Asian context is largely grounded on the theories of late development and developmental states, which considers higher education internationalization as a way to sustain and enhance national competitiveness. In other words, the national goal of internationalizing higher education is to catch up and compete with the advanced nations. Thus, Asian countries and their universities endeavor to catch up with the standards of the Western academic model, which is perceived to be more advanced. These national desires have eschewed governmental cuts to higher education spending that have dominated Anglo-Western discourse. Instead, governments in the Asian region have poured funding into their universities, especially those on the elite end of the spectrum, with a keen focus on international league table positioning (Deem et al., 2008).

The chapter further explains that such a desire to catch up with Western higher education justifies the region-wide call for building world-class universities. Indeed, several Asian societies (e.g., Mainland China, South Korea, Japan, Taiwan, and Malaysia) encourage their national top universities to pursue an image of a world-class university, with which the universities are able to earn an internationally recognized status and become competitive in the global competition for students, staff, and funding. Then, global university rankings are employed by some of the Asian governments as a policy instrument to measure and monitor the performance of universities and to steer their higher education sectors towards a global standard. Specifically, whilst the model of Western higher education in general and that of the American research-intensive university in particular are widely adopted as a benchmark, university rankings are used to indicate and monitor the gap between Asian universities and their counterparts in the West (Marginson, 2017).

Finally, the chapter illustrates an antinomy of the power of global university rankings. On the one hand, the use of numerical terms in university rankings effectively illustrates a simplified image of world-class university and creates a uniform but open space of competition where universities are provided with a clear pathway to academic and research excellence. On the other hand, given that the data for the measurement in ranking systems are heavily drawn from English-language scientific production (e.g., publishing in indexed English international academic journals), scholarly diversity is significantly narrowed. This homogenizing effect exemplifies the closedness of university rankings. Some literature further conceptualizes such favor to numerical criteria as a form of Western hegemony in higher education (e.g., Marginson, 2009; Lo, 2011). Even under the consideration that ranking culture has manifested locally, global benchmarks still often focus on a Western comparison. On this conceptual basis, the prevalence of university rankings and their strong influence over national higher education policy represent an institutionalization of Western hegemony, which leads to an intensification of hierarchical differentiation and stratification at both national and global levels. As a result, as shown here in the cases of five selected Asian societies, the disparity between institutions within national higher education systems is widened because of the policies of differentiation and fund concentration. At the global level, as the Western hegemony is legitimized, the unequal global higher education landscape is strengthened. However, some changes (e.g., re-emphasizing local relevance and local connection) over the past few years have led to signs of a shift of focus from catching up to the West to combining indigenous and Western knowledge. We suggest that this shift may indicate a new era for Asian universities.

2. PREVALENCE OF THE RANKING GAME

By the early 2000s, domestic rankings such as schemes produced by the *U.S. News & World Report* in the United States and the *Times Good University Guide* in the United Kingdom already dominated their respective sectors, but these kinds of private enterprise league tables lacked impact in Asia. With more heavy-handed state development models, government distinctions and projects resonated more with Asian decision-makers. With the launch of the Academic Ranking of World Universities (ARWU) in 2003, soon followed by *Times Higher Education–QS World University Rankings*, though, the landscape of higher education across the world was forever changed (Hazelkorn, 2015). No longer could universities in the region rely on domestic status symbols related to government connections. Indeed, with the rise of global league tables, Asian universities had a new barometer to measure against regional peers and even Western systems.

The rise of global university rankings in the early 2000s occurred in conjunction with a new global age for international education. This global era saw a dramatic increase in international student mobility, particularly fueled by Chinese students and other Asian neighbors filling classrooms around the world. Likewise, universities in this period created vast networks of research partnerships and joint programs that globally connected scholars, students, and other stakeholders (Altbach, 2013). These global partnerships were exemplified by the rapid growth of transnational higher education in the 2000s. The environment created a race for resources: international students, institutional partners, and elite scholars. So-called world-class class universities could attract all of these resources, and institutions across the globe chased this status lockstep with rankings (Deem et al., 2008).

In addition, research indicates that there is a strong link between the socio-economic development of a country and the rank positions of its universities (M. Li et al., 2011). The World Bank has even promoted the usage of university rankings in its higher education development material (Salmi, 2009). Against this background, global university rankings are used not only as a convenient instrument to identify and monitor the gap between the standards of Asian universities and their Western counterparts, but also as an indicator of the different levels of socio-economic development of countries (Marginson, 2017).

Given the complexity of these global interactions, university rankings became the currency for understanding the sector. Decision-makers could look at a single metric and determine where to recruit students from or which university was worthy of a joint-degree program. Positionality on a league table has turned into the capital that can be used in a competition amongst global peers to determine world-class status (Allen, 2021). In this context of global positional competition, policymakers and university administrators often use performance data generated by ranking agencies to frame decision-making and resource allocation. In this sense, ranking agencies acted as "supra-national agencies," who established standards for monitoring, evaluating, comparing and regulating quality in higher education (Hazelkorn, 2018).

The ranking agencies understand this influence and they profit from it through consultancy services on how institutions can improve positioning. Despite this conflict of interest, university administrators have been willing to pay these consultants for services and plans that often directly benchmark regional or global peers against one another. Asian universities have been fueling the ranking agencies' consultancy wings with desires to catch up with the rest of the world. Nevertheless, higher education leaders and researchers expressed skepticism about the validity and relevance of global rankings. Thus, although the leading ranking schemes have been a commercial success, they needed to constantly struggle for trust and credibility in the higher education sector (Lim, 2018).

One major problem with the ranking game is that it is often seen as a zero-sum game (Marginson, 2014). If a competitor moves up, then another institution moves down. University ranking agencies produce a single metric in which every institution is ordinally ranked sequentially, though there is some variation (see Table 10.1 for criteria and indicators of the leading ranking systems). For instance, in the ARWU, only one university can be ranked at each position from 1 to 100, but the agency creates large bands from 101–150, 151–200, 201–300, and so on through 1000. Moreover, apart from their original global rankings, all of the three leading ranking systems (i.e., ARWU, Quacquarelli Symonds [QS] World University Rankings, and Times Higher Education [THE] World University Rankings) create regional and by-subject rankings, which allow the rankers to include more universities in their league tables. However, the function of ordinal rank increases competition, which is only exacerbated by the yearly nature of the release (Hazelkorn, 2015).

An institution may dramatically fall one year not due to underperformance, but merely because competitors have increased their indicator outputs. University presidents and even government officials have been fired due to these types of falls, such as the high-profile sacking of the University of Malaya's (UM) vice-chancellor due to a drop in the THE ranking that was not even related to changes at the institution, but rather to a tweak in the agency's metric (Salmi, 2009; Hazelkorn, 2015). Further, the threat of this happening sits with these stakeholders every year. There is no running from the rankings. The European Commission attempted to alleviate this jockeying nature of university rankings by introducing a band system league table called Multidimensional Global Ranking of Universities (U-Multirank) (Marginson, 2014). In this scheme,

Table 10.1 Leading global university systems with indicator weights

Criteria	ARWU	%	QS	%	THE	%
Reputational			Employer/ academic reputation surveys	50	Teaching/research reputation surveys	33
Research and bibliometric	Nobel prizes/ medals; Clarivate's highly cited researchers; SSCI/ SCI/ Nature/ science publications	90	Scopus publications/ citations	20	Scopus publications/ citations; research income	42
Internationalization			International faculty/ students	10	International faculty/ students; international collaborations	7.5
University characteristics	Performance relative to size	10	Student-to-faculty ratio	20	Student-to-faculty ratio; doctorate-to bachelor's ratio; doctorates awarded-to-academic staff ratio; institutional income in public–private partnership; Industry income	17.5

Source: Compiled from organizations' websites and categorized by the authors of this chapter.

universities are not ranked ordinally, but rather put in large groups according to various indicators. However, the alternative ranking has had little impact globally, let alone in Asia.

3. Understanding the Ranking Game in the Asian Context

The literature often adopts neoliberalism as the theoretical approach to explain the prevalence of the ranking game within the context of the rapid growth of international higher education trade. From this neoliberal perspective, global university rankings are important, as they substantially influence student choice. In other words, the primary role of rankings is to serve as a consumer information tool providing market information, enhancing market transparency and upholding market accountability (Hazelkorn, 2008). Theoretically, rankings are seen as institutionalization of market principles in the governance of universities. It involves the incorporation of market values and practices into the regulation and organization of universities (Lynch, 2015).

However, the Asian experience provides a different understanding of the role of rankings in the global context. In Asia, university rankings are widely used as a policy instrument by governments and university leaders to measure and monitor the performance of universities in the context of contesting globalization. The performance data provided by university rankings is also used in making decisions and allocating resources (Hazelkorn, 2015). Stepping up specific criteria used in the major global ranking systems becomes an efficient way for universities to earn an internationally recognized status and validate their international stature, thereby gaining more resources. From the governments' perspective, this desire for building globally recognized universities is grounded on the belief that developing higher education is a crucial factor determining the national competitiveness in the age of the knowledge economy (Altbach, 2013). This belief is revealed in the policy texts and supported by the connection between a country's socio-economic development and the rank positions of its universities (see F. Li et al., 2011; M. Li et al., 2011 for the example of China).

The center–periphery model is commonly used in the literature to theoretically explain the eagerness of many Asian countries to climb up university rankings and thus reflect the enhancement of their national competitiveness. Specifically, in this postcolonial theoretical model, peripheral Asian countries are eager to learn from or even copy the perceived more advanced Western higher education model in order to catch up with the core Western countries. This catch-up mentality is further revealed by the quest for establishing world-class universities, which was triggered by the emergence of global university rankings and has become prevalent since the mid-2000s in the region. Consequently, Western research-intensive universities, particularly the prestigious ones, are popularly used by national top universities in Asia as benchmarks to guide their pursuit of world-class status (Shin and Harman, 2009). In short, the post-colonial approach frames the ranking game within the context of the rise of Asia, assuming a direct correlation between developing research universities and enhancing national competitiveness.

Both neoliberal and post-colonial approaches conceptualize the use of rankings in university governance as an application of managerialism, which imposes a performance-driven culture on universities. As a result, a trend of standardization, which emphasizes making outputs, performance, and quality more calculable and comparable, has become prevalent in higher education. Thus, the prevalence of rankings and the associated rise of managerialism can be seen as a process of numerical objectification (Kauppi, 2018). Based on this understanding of the manifestation of managerialism in higher education, the origin of the ranking game refers to the emergence of the global competitive order, which is featured by global capitalism and its neoliberal agenda that identify higher education as a tradable commodity and the structure of the global political economy that can be articulated by the center–periphery explanatory model for higher education (Lo and Hou, 2020).

The strategies for climbing up league tables and building world-class universities have greatly changed the higher education ecosystem in Asia. Given that major ranking systems use the international dimensions of academic impacts and productivity, which mainly refer to publishing and being cited in the international English-language journals listed in the Science Citation Index (SCI) and the Social Science Citation Index (SSCI), as key criteria to assess the performance of universities, a phenomenon of overemphasizing international scientific publications, which is also known as the SCI/SSCI craze, has become common in many Asian higher education systems. Meanwhile, the local dimensions of faculty work are devalued and even marginalized in this process of pursuing world-class excellence (Chou, 2014).

There is a substantial body of literature providing some critical reflections on this pursuit of world-class status (e.g. Allen, 2021; R. Yang, 2019). These reflections reveal and criticize that the world-class university movement simplifies the purpose of Asian universities in its process of copying the Western higher education model and promotes a cultural hegemony. Complying with this hegemony causes a trend of isomorphism, in which indigenous cultural traditions and characteristics of some higher education systems in Asia have been undermined. Thus, this literature emphasizes that Asian societies need to re-establish the connection between universities and local communities, thereby regaining their cultural roots in defining the purposes of universities.

Furthermore, there was (re)stratification in some Asian higher education systems, where policies of differentiation and fund concentration were adopted to facilitate the development of a few elite universities, given the limited government funds (Cheng et al., 2014; Hazelkorn, 2015). Specifically, some Asian governments launched special funding schemes aiming to assist selected universities in improving their research capacity and internationalization profile so as to reach world-class status. These targeted areas align with the criteria used in various ranking schemes. The following are some examples of these stratification, elite-making initiatives from the region.

3.1 Mainland China

Beginning in the mid-1990s, the Chinese government launched several higher education initiatives geared towards improving the nation's standing in the world in terms of higher education. Notably, Mainland China has been one of the most active players on the international higher education landscape in the last 20 years. This contextual factor justified Project 211 in 1995 and later Project 985 in 1998, which funneled substantial funding towards the elite end of the Chinese higher education sector (Song, 2018). The government-backed projects engrained a strict hierarchical status of the sector, with the 39 institutions included in Project 985 at the top, followed by those only included in Project 211. There was further stratification, as nine prestigious universities funded by Project 985 were selected by the government to form the C9 League, an alliance of elite universities, in 2009. The universities included in these government-backed projects have been especially keen on improving international prestige (Huang, 2015).

With strong incentives and funding from the government, Chinese institutions have collectively overtaken most of the world in terms of research output metrics and have rapidly risen in global university rankings (Allen, 2017). Chinese universities formerly created ambitious incentive structures to reward academic production, such as considerable cash rewards for publishing articles in journals listed in SCI and SSCI, both of which are used as an indicator in the ARWU scheme. However, in 2020, the government banned universities from incentivizing their faculty members to publish in these journals (Huang, 2020). Given the rise, the elite Chinese universities now attract scholars, students, and businesses from around the world. In 2015, the government reconceptualized its elite-making projects into the Double First-Class Project, which is a more ambitious strategy compared to those from the 1990s (Peters and Besley, 2018).

3.2 South Korea

In South Korea, the call for developing world-class universities can be put within the context of continued economic growth and the associated rapid higher education expansion in the 1980s and 1990s. By the mid-1990s, South Korea accomplished massification of higher education and began a transformation from a manufacturing economy to a more knowledge-driven sector, putting an emphasis on the development of world-class research universities (Shin, 2012). Thus, in 1999, the government initiated the Brain Korea 21 (BK21) project with the explicit goals of improving the international standing of 10 universities and placing the country among the world's top 10 in terms of knowledge transfer from academia to industry through a massive funding campaign. Overall, the elite universities in the sector saw boosts in their international rank positions, but the funding from BK21 overwhelmingly focused on the hard sciences and technological research (Byun et al., 2013).

With the success of the BK21, the South Korean government launched more elite-making higher education efforts with the World Class University (WCU) project in 2008 and the BK21 PLUS project in 2013. The main goal for the WCU Project was to attract scholars from around the world to South Korean universities through an expansion of programming offerings, including humanities and social science. The funding allowed the top institutions to expand offerings of English language curricula, important for attracting international students, and publications in highly-cited indices, which are mostly published in English. The BK21 PLUS refocused the initiative to foster graduate student (both Master's and doctoral level) research education and output, while moving several universities into the top-200 of global league tables. The efforts have paid off, as South Korea has consistently placed a handful of universities in this desired range on the most popular ranking schemes (Jang et al., 2016).

3.3 Japan

Compared to its neighboring countries like China and South Korea who have been heavily investing in their national top universities to pursue world-class status since the mid-1990s, Japan showed less interest in joining the contest during the period, as its higher education system and universities have been well and long established. However, it felt pressure and took reactive actions, which modeled the elite-making schemes in China and South Korea, in the early 2000s. The first wave of elite-making initiatives include the Twenty-First Century Centers of Excellence in 2002 and the Global Centers of Excellence in 2007. These government-backed projects aimed to selectively fund a few internationally competitive research units and nurture young researchers. Meanwhile, a 10-year project called the World Premier International Center Initiative was launched in 2007 to further increase the government investment in scientific research (Yonezawa and Shimmi, 2015).

The Japanese government later realized the importance of higher education internationalization to the country's international presence, and thus began the second wave of excellence schemes (including the Global 30 in 2009 and the Top Global University Project in 2014). These projects primarily aimed to fund selected universities to increase their degree of internationalization, rather than to invest in research units on their research performance. Nevertheless, the progress in internationalizing higher education remained slow. By launching the Designated National University Project in 2017, the government has further shifted the focus of its excellence initiatives to the socio-economic development of the nation. This latest project therefore requires its six funded universities to link their research and education with promoting social change and industrial innovation (Yonezawa, 2019).

3.4 Taiwan

Taiwan completed its higher education massification and began its elite-making policy in the late 1990s. In 1998, the government rolled out the Program for Promoting Academic Excellence of Universities, aiming to increase the research capacity of the university sector. The launch of the Aim for the Top University Project in 2005 then clearly reflected Taiwan's ambition of building world-class universities. This 10-year project aimed to cultivate at least one university ranked among the world's top 100 within a decade, and develop several global elite research units in some subject areas in five years. Around the same time, the government launched another two projects called the Program for Encouraging Teaching Excellence in Universities and the Program for Developing Exemplary Universities of Science and Technology to improve the teaching quality and applied studies of the funded universities. These competition-based funding schemes have re-stratified the Taiwanese higher education system, in which the 12 funded research intensive universities are considered elite, followed by the teaching- and applied studies-oriented institutions included in the special funding schemes (Lo, 2014).

However, the elite-making schemes are considered unsuccessful, as universities in Taiwan did not significantly rise in major ranking systems within the project period. Meanwhile, these schemes caused an intensification of inter-institutional competition. As a result, the Higher Education Sprout Project was launched in 2017. The project is divided into two parts. The first part includes most universities in Taiwan. Emphasizing universities' social responsibility and diverse development in the sector, this part of the project aims to improve universities' teaching quality and facilitate them to make contributions to their communities. The second part continues to fund universities to pursue world-class excellence. However, compared to the previous elite-making projects, the amount of funding and the number of funded universities have consider- ably decreased (Lo, 2019).

3.5 Malaysia

The world-class university discourse entered Malaysia's higher education policy in the mid-2000s. In 2007, the government launched the National Higher Education Strategic Plan 2020 (NHESP 2020) and its Action Plan 2007–2010 to set the goal of developing Malaysia into a regional education hub by 2020. The hub strategy came with a policy of building world-class universities, intending to enhance the reputation of Malaysia's higher education system. In Action Plan 2011–2015 of the NHESP 2020, the government indicated its ambition of making selected universities among the world's top 100 by 2015. To achieve the goal of building world-class universities, the government identified four institutions as research universities that were provided with extra funding for strengthening their research capacity in 2006. Shortly afterwards, the government initiated the Accelerated Program for Excellence (APEX), which aimed to help a uni- versity achieve world-class status through a government-aided transformation. In 2008, the University of Science Malaysia (USM) was granted the APEX status (Sirat, 2013).

Despite strong government support, the APEX initiative was not successful in making USM significantly rise in global rankings. Meanwhile, the USM management criticized that climbing up league tables was a catch-up game that merely meant to copy the Western higher education model. Thus, they opposed using position in rankings to evaluate their university. Instead, they advocated adopting the concepts of "world's first" and "humaniversity" as alternative benchmarks for success in higher education. The former refers to several discoveries and innovations by USM deemed to be the world's first; the latter stresses such values as inclusiveness and sustainability to humanize universities (Tan and Goh, 2014; Wan et al., 2015). USM's APEX status was renewed in 2014. Though becoming a world-class university remains a goal, climbing up rankings is not included in the plan.

3.6 Implication of the Stratification Initiatives

The significant rise of Asian universities in major ranking systems in recent years shows that the elite-making strategy has successfully boosted the research performance and international reputation of universities from the region. For example, 43 of the world's top 200 are Asian universities according to the QS ranking of 2020. The rise of Asian universities is less obvious in the THE ranking (i.e., 24 of the world's top 200 in 2020). However, THE particularly highlights China's performance, noting that the country is ranked joint six in terms of the number of universities in the top 200. Remarkably, China is a newcomer to this group and did not even appear in the top 10 five years ago. Meanwhile, South Korea has risen from tenth to ninth (Bothwell, 2019). It is noteworthy that the top two universities of Japan and those of Singapore and Hong Kong appear in the world's top 100 in both rankings; the top university of Taiwan is ranked among the top 100 in QS and as the world's top 120 in THE; UM in Malaysia is placed within the top 100 in QS.

On the one hand, the rise of Asian universities has proven a positive association between rankings and resource concentration. On the other hand, the uneven resource allocation can cause negative consequences. Indeed, the academic literature presents strong criticism of the disparity and isomorphism issues brought about by the selection and concentration approach adopted in the elite-making schemes. Disparity within the higher education sector refers to a situation that "rankings are propelling a growing gap between elite and mass higher education with greater institutional stratification and research concentration. (Higher education institutions) which do not meet the criteria or do not have brand recognition will effectively be de-valued" (Hazelkorn, 2007, p. 1). Evidently, while top universities in Japan and Taiwan enjoyed abundant resources to pursue the world-class status, their counterparts in the lower tiers of the system were insufficiently funded to internationalize themselves (Lo, 2014; Yonezawa and Shimmi, 2015). In Mainland China, the funding concentration may have widened the gap between the rich and poor regions, because most elite universities are located in the wealthy eastern coastal region (Gao, 2017).

While the highlighted elite-making policies in the region have led to some impressive results, research also indicates that emphasizing rankings may encourage universities to move resources from educational activities to ranking-oriented activities (e.g., research and publishing) (Kim, 2018). For example, there is a situation of over-attention to research at the expense of teaching, because faculty members, especially younger ones who are hired on a contractual basis, are under enormous pressure to publish in international journals (Tian et al., 2016). This pressure to publish or perish leads to the SCI/SSCI syndrome (Chou, 2014), which reflects that emphasizing highly-cited scientific publications devalues the humanity and soft sciences research and the local/national dimensions of faculty work (e.g., doing applied studies and services and publishing in non-English, non-indexed journals) (Song, 2018; Allen, 2021). This also creates a highly competitive and performative academic culture, which can threaten collegiality in academia (Macfarlane, 2016).

Moreover, the emphasis on international publications also leads to a trend of isomorphism, in which cultural traditions and characteristics of Asian higher education are undermined (Deem et al., 2008). The negative consequences explain why Mainland China prohibited its universities from providing incentives for their faculty staff and students to publish in SCI journals, why Taiwan launched the policy that emphasized the social responsibility of universities and removed its mass higher education sector from the ranking game, and why Malaysia proposed the concepts of world's first and humaniversity as alternative paths. This recent pushback may signal a new, developing relationship between global rankings and the Asian region.

4. ANTINOMY OF THE POWER OF GLOBAL UNIVERSITY RANKINGS

There are two sides of the ranking game forming an antinomy of the power of global university rankings (Marginson, 2009; Lo, 2014). One side sees the function of rankings as an open source, which effectively indicates the path to world-class status. As Kauppi (2018, p. 1755) explains, rankings create "a global unified playing field that includes the best in a quantified, descending interval order" and transform "the implicit criteria of excellence and reputation used hitherto in academia into formal criteria that constitute a numerical global competitive space." He further adds that the performance data provided by ranking exercises is seen as a highly objective form of information that provides players in the global field of higher education with access to a profound level of reality. Consequently, global higher education competition has been increasingly framed in numerical terms (Kauppi, 2018). Indeed, research indicates a close relationship between universities' performance in scientific publishing and their international rank positions (Kivinen et al., 2017). This explains why rankings are widely used as instrumentation for knowledge production and academic reputation, as they provide a global playing field for an open competition for scholarly prestige.

Recent studies suggest that global university rankings reveal and accelerate a long-term shift in academic centrality from Anglo-America to Asia. In particular, the last two decades witnessed the development of knowledge hubs and networks in Asia and an exponential rise of scientific productivity in Mainland China. The constant growth of these knowledge hubs and networks and that of China's research productivity illustrates the emergence of a multipolar and networked pattern, which has been gradually replacing the center–periphery pattern, in the world system of knowledge production (Jöns and Hoyler, 2013). As research capacity that can be expressed in the number of top research universities is closely related to national competitiveness (Altbach, 2013), rankings not only reflect and contribute to the reshaping of the global higher education landscape but also that of the global geopolitical landscape (Hazelkorn, 2018).

However, there are queries about the significance of this potential shift of the academic center. For example, Altbach (2016) calls the current dynamic in China a "glass ceiling [with] feet of clay." The "feet of clay" portion of the critique exemplifies that the mid- to bottom-tier institutions have, in some sense, been left behind due to the fixation with ranking systems that favor the elite. The "glass ceiling" portion of the argument suggests that China's elite universities cannot truly become world-class without the same kinds of academic freedoms found in Western systems, despite rises in the global rankings. The critique has obvious connections to other Asian societies, as the elite-making strategy is widely used in the region and other Asian systems may also face issues in government pressures on research agendas to some degree.

Another side of the ranking game highlights the hegemonic nature and the homogenizing effects of the global rankings. This side of the antimony adopts a post-colonial perspective, from which the Anglo-American paradigm has dominated the discourse on the process of globalization in higher education, thereby leading to the emergence of "a new dependence culture" in academia (Deem et al., 2008). Based on this theoretical approach, global university rankings have become an institution upholding the current Anglo-American academic hegemony in the global field of higher education, as the ranking schemes and their criteria are heavily relied on by academic and research resources (e.g., publishing outlets and bibliometric indices) based in the United States and other Western countries (Marginson, 2009). In other words, the ranking game constitutes "the consolidation of existing asymmetries and monopolies of global power and knowledge" and produces and legitimizes a unipolar global competitive order for higher education (Kauppi, 2018, p. 1751). Recent literature further argues that other criteria (i.e., the degree of internationalization and the number of Nobel laureates) used in leading ranking systems represent a manifestation of whiteness in the global academic field (Estera and Shahjahan, 2019; Stack, 2020). In short, this side of the ranking game produces an institutionalization of the global hegemony, which denotes a coercive appropriation of Western knowledge production. Such coercive power, which is an assertion of the catch-up mentality, is rooted in the historical legacy of European colonialism and contemporary Western supremacy associated with Pax Americana (Lo, 2011; Ordorika and Lloyd, 2014; Shahjahan et al., 2017).

However, some research suggests that the nature of the power of rankings is negotiable rather than hegemonic. For instance, Lim (2018) argues that the influence of rankings is built upon a kind of "weak expertise" that identifies rankings as "the result of a constantly negotiated balance between the relevance, reliability, and robustness of rankers' data and their relationships with their key readers and audiences" (p. 415). Such negotiable nature of rankings reveals that, to a large extent, the global rankings are commercial in nature, despite being used as policy and management tools on the occasion of global competition in higher education. In the context of India, Lim and Øerberg (2017) further note that rankers are willing to accommodate to Indian universities when developing and adjusting the methodologies of their assessments, due to commercial considerations. These findings substantially question the hegemonic nature of rankings.

Furthermore, policymakers and university leaders in peripheral Asian countries have begun to reflect on the emphasis on catching up with the core Western models of research universities. For example, as previously discussed, Mainland China has revised its policies in order to move away from SCI and SSCI measures, although these actions would likely lead to a fall in the rankings (Huang, 2020). Relatedly, in his article in THE, the vice-president of China's Tsinghua University notes that leading Chinese universities will adapt to a development model that is not aimed at catching up, but responds to the needs of their communities, the national development priorities, and critical global issues. He believes that Chinese higher education will demonstrate its own cultural characteristics (B. Yang, 2019). Similar advocacy (i.e., emphasizing cultural roots and missions in higher education development) by university leaders is reported in recent research on other Asian societies (R. Yang, 2019). In sum, these latest developments drive us to rethink the hegemonic power of rankings (Lo and Liu, 2021).

5. Conclusion: A New Era for Asian Universities?

Given the criticism over the competition and oversimplification brought about by the global rankings, research explores the way of toning down the competitive elements and underlining the collaborative ones in ranking exercises. For example, Shin and Toutkoushian (2011) suggest that rankings should develop towards four directions: multidimensional, customer-centered, regional, and discipline-based. These directions are based on a principle that "the real value of 'ranking' is not ranking, but matching" (van der Wende and Westerheijden, 2009, p. 78). Thus, as previously mentioned, U-Multirank was created in Europe, with a goal of overcoming the over-emphasis on research and the convergence caused by the other rankings. Meanwhile, ranking agencies have proliferated the types of league table offerings to include more regional and specialized offerings. For instance, in 2009, QS launched a ranking specifically for the Asian region with altered weights and indicators. Likewise, ARWU also produces a Greater China league table that incorporates universities of Mainland China, Hong Kong, Macau, and Taiwan. Given the rise of a metric regime, international rankings have pushed regulators to develop domestic rankings (e.g., China's Chinese Disciplinary Ranking and India's National Institutional Ranking Framework). However, the impact of these domestic, regional, and specialized rankings has been unclear. On the one hand, the diverse ranking schemes allow universities to create narratives that manipulate their rank positions to promote their own strengths (Heffernan and Heffernan, 2018). On the other hand, when many Asian universities have already reached elite ranks in the more prominent schemes, the secondary regional rankings look less appealing.

The rise of Asian universities in rankings has also led to signs of increased confidence from the elite in the sector. For the past two decades, policies in Asia have been explicit in the goal of catching up to the West and these elite-making policies throughout the region have appeared to work. The top Asian universities and departments now appear in prime positions on the various global league tables and their Western peers have pursued numerous partnerships, providing key recognition from the old hegemonic group to the new risers. As these elite institutions have caught up in the numbers game, they have been trying to combine their traditions with Western knowledge, thereby pursuing research and teaching suited to the unique needs and priorities of their communities (R. Yang, 2019). The announcement that Chinese universities would no longer place emphasis on SCI publications demonstrates this shift of focus in the post catch-up era.

However, although elite universities in Asia have successfully caught up in rankings, strengthening the "clay feet" segment of the systems that had been left behind remains a challenge for many Asian higher education systems. Moreover, both the eagerness to join and win in the ranking game and the argument of tensions caused by the shift in academic centrality reveal an orientation of higher education development that is habitually set out in an East–West dichotomy. This orientation rationalizes the focus of world-class status defined by inclusion and affirmation by Western contexts. Thus, a corollary for what may lay ahead for Asian systems in the post catch-up era is a reorientation that intimates an abandonment of the East–West dichotomous approach and a reconstruction of the worldview that involves a combination of competition and collaboration within and across regions (Lo, 2016). With such a paradigm shift, Asian universities will truly divert attention away from the catch-up game, but will see adherence to the needs of their respective societies.

REFERENCES

Allen, R. M. (2017). "A comparison of China's 'Ivy League' to other peer groupings through university rankings." *Journal of Studies in International Education*, 21/5, 395–411.

Allen, R. M. (2021). "Commensuration of the globalised higher education sector: How university rankings act as a credential for world-class status in China." *Compare: A Journal of Comparative and International Education*, 51/6, 920–938.

Altbach, P. G. (2013). "Advancing the national and global knowledge economy: The role of research universities in developing countries." *Studies in Higher Education*, 38/3, 316–360.

Altbach, P. G. (2016). "Chinese higher education: 'glass ceiling' and 'feet of clay.'" *International Higher Education*, 86, 11–13.

Bothwell, E. (2019). *THE World University Rankings 2020: China Powers Up.* https://www.timeshighereducation.com/world-university-rankings/world-university-rankings-2020-china-powers, accessed March 13, 2020.

Byun, K., Jon, J. E., and Kim, D. (2013). "Quest for building world-class universities in South Korea: Outcomes and consequences." *Higher Education*, 65/5, 645–659.

Cheng, Y., Wang, Q., and Liu, N. C. (eds.) (2014). *How World-Class Universities Affect Global Higher Education*. Rotterdam: Sense Publishers.

Chou, C. P. (ed.) (2014). *The SSCI Syndrome in Higher Education: A Local or Global Phenomenon*. Rotterdam: Sense Publishers.

Deem, R., Mok, K. H., and Lucas, L. (2008). "Transforming higher education in whose image? Exploring the concept of the 'world-class' university in Europe and Asia." *Higher Education Policy*, 21/3, 83–97.

Estera, A. and Shahjahan, R. A. (2019). "Globalizing whiteness? Visually re/presenting students in global university rankings websites." *Discourse: Studies in the Cultural Politics of Education*, 40/6, 930–945.

Gao, C. (2017). "A closer look at China's world class universities project." *The Diplomat*. https://thediplomat.com/2017/09/a-closer-look-at-chinas-world-class-universities-project, accessed March 13, 2020.

Hazelkorn, E. (2007). "How do rankings impact on higher education?" *IMHE Info*, December, 1–4.

Hazelkorn, E. (2008). "Learning to live with league tables and ranking: The experience of institutional leaders." *Higher Education Policy*, 21/2, 193–215.

Hazelkorn, E. (2015). *Rankings and the Reshaping of Higher Education: The Battle for World-Class Excellence* (2nd edition). Basingstoke: Palgrave Macmillan.

Hazelkorn, E. (2018). "Reshaping the world order of higher education: The role and impact of rankings on national and global systems." *Policy Reviews in Higher Education*, 2/1, 4–31.

Heffernan, T. A. and Heffernan, A. (2018). "Language games: University responses to ranking metrics." *Higher Education Quarterly*, 72/1, 29–39.

Huang, F. (2015). "Building the world-class research universities: A case study of China." *Higher Education*, 70/2, 203–215.

Huang, F. (2020). "China is choosing its own path on academic evaluation." *University World News*. https://www.universityworldnews.com/post.php?story=20200225181649179, accessed March 13, 2020.

Jang, D. H., Ryu, K., Yi, P., and Craig, D. A. (2016). "The hurdles to being world class: Narrative analysis of the world-class university project in Korea." *Higher Education Policy*, 29/2, 234–253.

Jöns, H. and Hoyler, M. (2013). "Global geographies of higher education: The perspective of world university rankings." *Geoforum*, 46, 45–59.

Kauppi, N. (2018). "The global ranking game: Narrowing academic excellence through numerical objectification." *Studies in Higher Education*, 43/10, 1750–1762.

Kim, J. (2018). "The functions and dysfunctions of college rankings: An analysis of institutional expenditure." *Research in Higher Education*, 59/1, 54–87.

Kivinen, O., Hedman, J., and Artukka, K. (2017). "Scientific publishing and global university rankings: How well are top publishing universities recognized?" *Scientometrics*, 112/1, 679–695.

Li, F., Zhao, Y., and Morgan, W. J. (2011). "The rate of return to educational investment in China: A comparative commentary." *Education, Knowledge and Economy*, 5/1–2, 45–52.

Li, M., Shankar, S., and Tang, K. K. (2011). "Why does the USA dominate university league tables?" *Studies in Higher Education*, 36/8, 923–937.

Lim, M. A. (2018). "The building of weak expertise: The work of global university rankers." *Higher Education*, 75/3, 415–430.

Lim, M. A. and Øerberg, J. W. (2017). "Active instruments: On the use of university rankings in developing national systems of higher education." *Policy Reviews in Higher Education*, 1/1, 91–108.

Lo, W. Y. W. (2011). "Soft power, university rankings and knowledge production: Distinctions between hegemony and self-determination in higher education." *Comparative Education*, 47/2, 209–222.

Lo, W. Y. W. (2014). *University Rankings: Implications for Higher Education in Taiwan.* Singapore: Springer.

Lo, W. Y. W. (2016). "The concept of Greater China in higher education: Adoptions, dynamics and implications." *Comparative Education*, 52/1, 26–43.

Lo, W. Y. W. (2019). "Taiwan: From 'world-class' to socially responsible." *International Higher Education*, 98, 27–28.

Lo, W. Y. W. and Hou, A. Y.-C. (2020). "A farewell to internationalisation? Striking a balance between global ambition and local needs in higher education in Taiwan." *Higher Education*, 80, 497–510.

Lo, W. Y. W., and Liu, S. Y. (2021). "Are university rankings still important? Perspectives from Greater China." In E. Hazelkorn and M. Georgiana (eds.), *Research Handbook on University Rankings: Theory, Methodology, Influence and Impact.* Cheltenham: Edward Elgar, 278–293.

Lynch, K. (2015). "Control by numbers: New managerialism and ranking in higher education." *Critical Studies in Education*, 56/2, 190–207.

Macfarlane, B. (2016). "Collegiality and performativity in a competitive academic culture." *Higher Education Review*, 48/2, 31–50.

Marginson, S. (2006). "Dynamics of national and global competition in higher education." *Higher Education*, 52/1, 1–39.

Marginson, S. (2009). "Open source knowledge and university rankings." *Thesis Eleven*, 96/1, 9–39.

Marginson, S. (2014). "University rankings and social science." *European Journal of Education*, 49/1, 45–59.

Marginson, S. (2017). "The world-class multiversity: Global commonalities and national characteristics." *Frontiers of Education in China*, 12/2, 233–260.

Ordorika, I. and Lloyd, M. (2014). "International rankings and the contest for university hegemony." *Journal of Education Policy*, 30/3, 385–405.

Peters, M. and Besley, T. (2018). "China's double first-class university strategy: 双一流." *Educational Philosophy and Theory*, 50/12, 1075–1079.

Salmi, J. (2009). *The Challenge of Establishing World-Class Universities.* Washington, DC: World Bank.

Shahjahan, R. A. and Morgan, C. (2016). "Global competition, coloniality, and the geopolitics of knowledge in higher education." *British Journal of Sociology of Education*, 37/1, 92–109.

Shahjahan, R. A., Ramirez, G. B., and Andreotti, V. (2017). "Attempting to imagine the unimaginable: A decolonial reading of global university rankings." *Comparative Education Review*, 61/1, 51–73.

Shin, J. C. (2012). "Higher education development in Korea: Western university ideas, Confucian tradition, and economic development." *Higher Education*, 64, 59–72.

Shin, J. C. and Harman, G. (2009). "New challenges for higher education: Global and Asia-Pacific perspectives." *Asia Pacific Education Review*, 10/1, 1–13.

Shin, J. C. and Toutkoushian, R. K. (2011). "The past, present, and future of university rankings." In J. C. Shin, R. K. Toutkoushian, and U. Teichler (eds.), *University Rankings: Theoretical Basis, Methodology and Impacts on Global Higher Education*. Dordrecht: Springer, 1–16.

Sirat, M. (2013). "Malaysia's world-class university ambition: An assessment." In J. C. Shin and B. M. Kehm (eds.), *Institutionalization of World-Class University in Global Competition*. Dordrecht: Springer, 205–223.

Song, J. (2018). "Creating world-class universities in China: Strategies and impacts at a renowned research university." *Higher Education*, 75/4, 729–742.

Stack, M. (2020). "Academic stars and university rankings in higher education: Impacts on policy and practice." *Policy Reviews in Higher Education*, 4/1, 4–24.

Tan, Y. S. and Goh, S. K. (2014). "International students, academic publications and world university rankings: The impact of globalisation and responses of a Malaysian public university." *Higher Education*, 68/4, 489–502.

Tian, M., Su, Y., and Ru, X. (2016). "Perish or publish in China: Pressures on young Chinese scholars to publish in internationally indexed journals." *Publications*, 4/2, 9.

van der Wende, M. and Westerheijden, D. (2009). "Rankings and classifications: The need for a multidimensional approach." In F. van Vught (ed.), *Mapping the Higher Education Landscape: Towards a European Classification of Higher Education*. Dordrecht: Springer, 71–86.

Wan, C. D., Sirat, M., and Razak, D. A. (2015). "The idea of a university: Rethinking the Malaysian context." *Humanities*, 4/3, 266–282.

Yang, B. (2019). "THE World University Rankings 2020: Time to follow our own star." https://www.timeshighereducation.com/opinion/world-university-rankings-2020-time-follow-our-own-star, accessed March 13, 2020.

Yang, R. (2019). "Turning scars into stars: A reconceptualized view of modern university development in Beijing, Hong Kong, Taipei, and Singapore." *Frontiers of Education in China*, 14/1, 1–32.

Yonezawa, A. (2019). "A new national role for universities, but little funding." https://www.universityworldnews.com/post.php?story=20190121144548216, accessed March 13, 2020.

Yonezawa, A. and Shimmi, Y. (2015). "Transformation of university governance through internationalization: Challenges for top universities and government policies in Japan." *Higher Education*, 70/2, 173–186.

CHAPTER 11

....

PROFESSIONAL EDUCATION
Models and Issues

....

SHENG-JU CHAN AND HUA-CHI CHOU

1. INTRODUCTION

IN addition to the rapid growth of higher education in Asia in recent years, we have seen the expansion of academic disciplines, subjects, and professional training at the university level. These developments have furthered the progress of professional education. Originally, only a few jobs were regarded as professions, such as those of doctor (general practitioner or specialist), pharmacist, nurse, midwife, dental practitioner, architect, and veterinary surgeon. This scope has gradually expanded to include other knowledge domains, such as design, business, engineering, and education. According to Camilleri et al. (2014, p. 24), professional higher education "is a form of higher education that offers a particularly intense integration with the world of work in all its aspects, including teaching, learning, research, and governance and at all levels of the overarching qualifications ... Its function is to diversify learning opportunities, enhance the employability of graduates, offer qualifications, and stimulate innovation for the benefit of learners and society." In other words, the main purposes of professional education are to establish academic independence, integrate higher learning with specific professional work, and limit educational mismatches.

Although the scope of professional education is expanding, limited literature worldwide has addressed professional education at the structural level. Some relevant studies were published before the 1990s (e.g., Kennedy, 1987), but we found almost nothing on this topic in the Asian region. A search for studies of professional education yielded divergent and confusing findings. Most of this literature has addressed professional development in the education field (i.e., teachers' professional development) (Even and Ball, 2009). Another stream of research has considered professionalization within universities for general staff members (Whitchurch, 2010). Other studies have shown that for university faculty, the academic profession is often linked to professional education (Enders, 2007; Teichler et al., 2013). Therefore, the research reported in this chapter investigates how different professional workforces are trained in universities through systematic educational arrangements.

Within this wider context, this study seeks to decipher the different models of professional education in the Asian region. At the same time, the boom in professional education has led to several concerns around the world, such as the role of government, control of quality, and level of education. We use Japan, China, India, and Taiwan as case studies owing to their unique modalities. Two complementary frameworks are used to analyze variations in their models of professional education. Though with greater expansion of professional education, both profession-oriented and academic-oriented degrees are offered simultaneously in these Asian countries/societies (except India), this dual-track approach has been prominent in this region.

2. Origins and Development of Professional Education

From a historical perspective, we assert that the term "profession" has deep roots in the concept of "occupation" or "guild." In the West, certain jobs have traditionally been called professions, as their practitioners are required to possess specialized and specific knowledge and skills, such as in law, medicine, and theology. Apprenticeships were originally the formal route for training practitioners. Apprentices learned from their masters through practice, without systematic planning.

The purposes of professional education are (a) to provide a sufficient workforce for certain professions and (b) to guarantee that practitioners have the necessary knowledge and skills. Professional education is composed of four major elements: the overall knowledge system, the recognition of qualification and the provision of licenses, service to the public community through professional knowledge, and the ethics that regulate the profession's code of conduct (Lin, 2012).

In the twentieth century, professional education began to be gradually incorporated into the formal education system. Around the 1950s and 1960s, some secondary schools and universities introduced professional education courses to their programs, leading to more formal and structured professional education courses. With the expansion of human knowledge and subjects, the list of occupations understood as professions has expanded in the last few decades. To prepare practitioners, the education system in the 1980s began to implement training, education, and placement processes with certain established rules and norms. This marked the beginning of true professional education.

Determining how to provide systematic learning and training to update novices' ability, skills, knowledge, and even attitudes is an essential step in enhancing the professional education system. In a general sense, training and learning should be undertaken by a specific education system in combination with certain components of academic knowledge and practical application. For example, France's *grandes écoles* are well known as practical teaching institutions that cultivate talent in engineering and management. Such arrangements tend to lead to the awarding of certificates, qualifications, or licenses that create a qualified professional workforce with different jobs.

Investigating the nature and definition of a profession, Brante (1990, p. 82) pointed out that "professions are non-manual full-time occupations which presuppose a long, specialized, and tendentiously also scholarly ... training which imparts specific, generalizable and theoretical professional knowledge, often proven by examination." This statement highlights the importance of lengthy training, specific knowledge, and examinations for recognition. Brante noted two preconditions: a profession should be non-manual and full-time. However, these two prerequisites are less applicable today owing to the blurring of the boundary between manual and intellectual activities and the prevalence of part-time workers in professional jobs.

Adopting a similar stance, Camilleri et al. (2014, p. 24) asserted that professional education "is a form of higher education that offers a particularly intense integration with the world of work in all its aspects, including teaching, learning, research, and governance ... Its function is to diversify learning opportunities, enhance the employability of graduates, offer qualifications, and stimulate innovation for the benefit of learners and society." This European report highlighted the primary values of professional education, including further integration into workplaces, the promotion of graduates' employability, and the pursuit of wider public benefits. Investigating the development of professional education in Europe, Camilleri et al. (2014) designed a dual-track framework to decipher the current scenarios of policy and strategy as well as teaching and learning. The core criteria for the policies and strategies implemented by the surveyed European countries covered collaboration with the world of work, the enhancement of job-related skills, competencies, and employability, and regional partnerships (Camilleri et al., 2014, p. 25). In the teaching and learning dimension, particular attention was paid to curriculum development in collaboration with stakeholders, learning outcomes in line with professional requirements and changing work environments, and learning modes with combinations of theory and practice aimed at solving problems in real-world situations (Camilleri et al., 2014, pp. 26–27). The authors recommended that the learning environment include experience of working in real institutions to reflect theory in a practical context. Finally, they stated that the entire program team (including the teaching and administrative staff) should possess a combination of academic expertise and relevant work experience (Camilleri et al., 2014, p. 27). These sub-dimensions of teaching and learning comprise important benchmarking standards that help to illuminate current practices of professional education in Europe. The core goals of this report were to indicate practical applications of study, promote the development of skills and competence, provide practical experiences in the form of internships (placements) and/or work experience, and enhance immersion in enterprises or industries (Camilleri et al., 2014, p. 21). This dual framework of policy and strategy, coupled with teaching and learning serves as a conceptual basis for our research in Asia. It is broadly used to examine how professional education is organized, coordinated, or delivered at the national level.

Although a dual framework can present an overall picture of professional education, a careful review reveals that most studies have focused on the teaching and learning dimensions instead of the policy or structural levels. Wallin et al. (2019) explore the learning experiences of highly experienced professionals through work-based higher education. Considering the development of competence-based learning, Mulder (2017) focuses on how to bridge the gap between the world of work and professional education. A book series published by Springer, entitled *Innovation and Change in Professional Education*, seeks to promote "publications that deal with pedagogical issues that arise in the context of innovation and change in professional education" (Springer, 2020). In other words, the pedagogical dimension of different disciplines is emphasized in these published volumes. Another prominent stream of research on professional education has focused on the issue of identity. For example, Findlow (2012) examines how changes in higher education have affected the identity formation of new academic disciplines. This sociological study pays special attention to how professional identity is associated with these major external factors. Our overall conclusion based on this literature review is that studies have seldom referred to policy or national strategy. Based on the wider context, this chapter aims to explore how major Asian countries/societies organize, construct, or promote professional education at the national level, with reference to structural issues instead of the pedagogical dimension.

3. Conceptual Frameworks for Professional Education

Through exploration of the different models of professional education in Asia, two major conceptual and analytical models were identified. The first is the triangle of coordination in higher education proposed by Clark (1983). The second is drawn from the analysis by Harvey and Mason (2014 [1995]) of the role of professional bodies in monitoring the quality of higher education. The former takes a macro perspective, focusing on the dynamic relationships between the government, market, and academic sectors, while the latter addresses the meso level and examines the unique role of professional bodies. Originally, neither of these frameworks was designed to explain professional education. However, the combination of these two frameworks provides a meaningful angle from which to view the complicated structure of professional education in Asia at the policy and structural levels.

Clark (1983) proposed an innovative model to describe the major forces driving higher education systems, based on a cross-national examination. He pointed to state authority, academic oligarchy, and market forces as the most significant coordinating forces. This model is depicted as a triangle that represents the relative power of each force in a higher education system (Brennan, 2010). For example, as shown in Figure 11.1, state authority is most influential in the former USSR, Sweden, and France, while

State authority

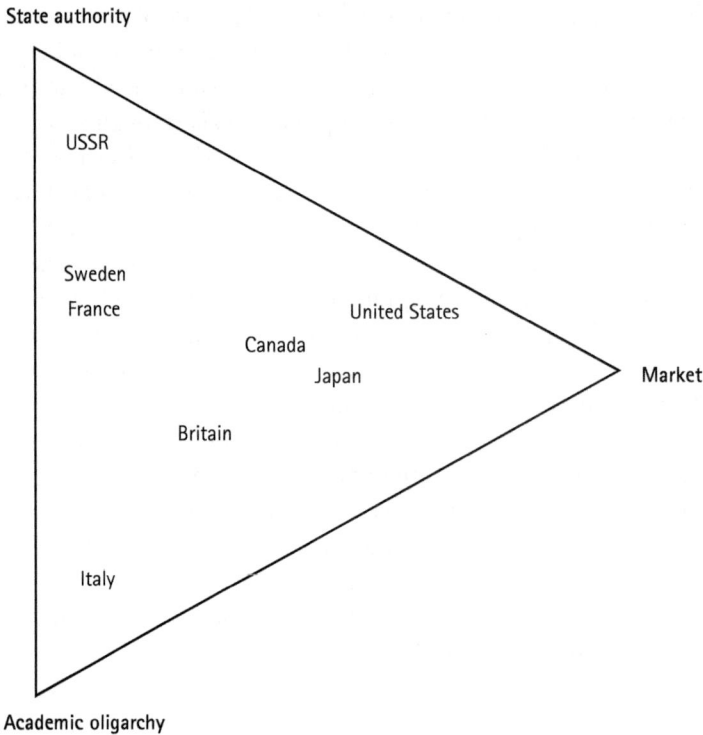

USSR

Sweden
France   United States
                          Canada
                               Japan   Market

                    Britain

Italy

Academic oligarchy

FIGURE 11.1 Triangle of coordination

Source: Clark (1983, p. 143).

market forces are dominant in the United States. Meanwhile, the academic oligarchy tends to prevail in Italy. Different combinations of the three forces lead to different compositions of higher education systems. This comprehensive model is applicable to various aspects of higher education, including financing (Lang, 2017), and is highly relevant to the professional education context studied here.

To explain each of the opposing forces on the triangle further: state authority refers to a range of professional education in different subjects which may be controlled or monitored directly by government departments; academic oligarchy may be represented by a professional body (council) with major constituents from academic or professional communities, such as a legal entity with power authorized by law to carry out its tasks in regulating education in certain disciplines (Harvey and Mason, 2014 [1995]); and market forces enable the free operation of many providers, i.e., higher education institutions to provide professional education without constraints by laws, rules, or professional bodies. In other words, under market forces, institutions are much less bound by the state government and professional bodies with respect to the structure and provision of professional education.

On the basis of this discussion, we replace the term "academic oligarchy" with "professional body" according to Clark's (1983) model to examine our case countries/

societies in Asia, focusing on different models of professional education and in Japan, China, India, and Taiwan.

While state authority and market forces are more commonly understood, a more concise definition of "professional body" is useful in the context of professional education. According to Harvey (2004), "a professional body is a group of people in a learned occupation who are entrusted with maintaining control or oversight of the legitimate practice of the occupation. Professional bodies have, in some countries, a significant role in the oversight of *education* linked to professions." As previously explained, these bodies may be delegated authority by the state through legislation. These buffering bodies have become critical forces determining the content of professional education in many countries. The mandate of a professional body often reflects the mediating role of the government between professional practitioners' communities and the direct influence of their nation state.

For example, Harvey and Mason (2014 [1995]) developed a systematic understanding of the role of professional bodies in British higher education monitoring quality assurance. They proposed that a professional body:

- specifies the requirements for entry into the professional body, including initial educational or professional qualifications;
- identifies requirements for continued membership, including continuing professional membership and work experience; and
- has a set of regulations or code of professional ethics to which members must adhere or risk expulsion from the professional body.

The first two functions are closely related to the operation of professional education in higher education. In principle, a professional body might accredit courses/higher education institutions, validate courses/higher education institutions, provide direct input into curricula, influence curricula, and provide professional qualifications (Harvey and Mason, 2014 [1995]). These tasks illustrate the fundamental definition or scope of professional education. If not specified by a professional body, such tasks could be accomplished by the state authority or market. In the research reported here, these functions were used as analytic tools to examine how professional education is coordinated or controlled within the national context in the selected Asian countries/ societies.

4. Case Studies in Four Asian Countries/Societies

This section studies professional education systems at the national level in Japan, China, India, and Taiwan. Particular attention is directed to governmental approval of the establishment of professional education, course and learning standards, quality assurance/accreditation, qualification and licensing, and codes of conduct/professional ethics.

4.1 Japan: A State-Led Approach

In Japan, professional higher education, which refers specifically to the "professional academic system," including professional graduate schools, professional universities, professional junior colleges, and professional disciplines, was formally proposed in 2003, based on a recommendation in a policy advisory report by the University Council of Japan[1] titled "Measures to enhance and strengthen the function of cultivating advanced professionals with the Graduate School of Professional Degree as the core,"[2] to showcase the different characteristics of universities in a competitive environment. As a result, the School Education Act was amended in 2003, to enable the Ministry of Education, Culture, Sports, Science, and Technology in Japan (MEXT) to regulate the types of professional higher education institutions and the content related to the degree awarded.

4.1.1 *Professional Graduate Schools*

In Japan, professional higher education originated in postgraduate schools. According to Article 2 of the Standards for Establishment of Professional Graduate Schools, "the professional degree programs are designed to develop deep learning and exceptional abilities to take on highly specialized occupations" (MEXT, 2003). To meet the needs of internationally recognized senior professional individuals, MEXT established the professional graduate school system in 2003. The aim of professional graduate schools is not only to teach and research academic theories and their applications, but also to cultivate in-depth and high-quality learning abilities among students (MEXT, 2003). According to Article 5 of the Degree Regulation (学位規則), professional graduate schools in Japan award professional Master's degrees that indicate their areas of specialization. Professional graduate schools focus on eight broad fields: management, accounting, public policy, public health, clinical psychology, law, education, and intellectual property. In 2018, 119 higher education institutions operated 169 professional graduate programs, in which 7,158 students were enrolled. Among them, 2,532 students in the field of management composed the largest group (MEXT, 2019a).

---

[1] The University Council of Japan (大学審議会) is a council established in September 1987 as an advisory body to the MEXT. Its main purpose was to consolidate the infrastructure of higher education in Japan, and it was given the authority to make recommendations to the Minister of MEXT when necessary. Since 2001, the University Council of Japan has been incorporated into the Central Council for Education (中央教育審議会) (Wikipedia, 2020).

[2] 専門職大学院を中核とした高度専門職業人養成機能の充実・強化方策について.

According to the requirements for the establishment of professional graduate schools, the MEXT developed the Standards for Establishing Professional Graduate Schools, which include the length of study of a degree course, faculty, curriculum, credits, and facilities (with additional provisions for the fields of law and education). The length of study for a professional degree is two years (three years for law), and the graduation requirement is at least 30 credits (dissertation is not always required). Depending on the field of study, graduates are qualified to take national examinations in that field; some of them may be exempted from subject tests if they are awarded the degree. The MEXT also has special regulations on the qualifications of faculty in professional graduate schools, stipulating that more than 30 percent of full-time faculty members must be practitioners (20 percent for law and 40 percent for education). Professional graduate schools must establish a Curriculum Coordination Council to organize the degree curriculum in cooperation with the industry and implement it effectively. To ensure the quality of education, according to the School Education Act and its Enforcement Rules, the curriculum and organization operations, teaching staff members, and other research activities of professional graduate schools must be accredited every five years by a professional accreditation agency, such as the National Institution for Academic Degrees and Quality Enhancement of Higher Education (NIAD-QE). Accreditation indicators differ between professional accreditation agencies, but commonly cover the objectives of the program, students, staff, courses, facilities, and internal quality assurance.

4.1.2 *Professional Universities and Junior Colleges*

To cope with a low birth rate, an aging population, and globalization, Japan has adjusted its education system and launched a new system of professional universities and junior colleges to cultivate specialized talents. In addition to professional graduate schools, Japan revised the School Education Act in 2017 to encourage the establishment of professional universities and junior colleges, which began to recruit students in 2019. To date, only 11 institutions (nine universities and two junior colleges) have been recognized to run these programs (MEXT, 2020).

Professional universities and junior colleges have the following main features that differ from those of the general higher education system (MEXT, 2019b):

a. *Educational Content*

Professional universities and junior colleges organize and implement curricula in cooperation with industry. In addition, more than 30–40 percent of course credits are related to internships. For internship courses, a four-year degree course must have more than 20 credits, and a two-year degree course must have more than 10 credits.

b. *Training Period*

There are four-year professional university and two- or three-year professional junior college programs. Professional universities can also adopt a phased curriculum system that divides courses into first and second phases. According to this phased curriculum system, students can obtain employment after completing the first course and then pursue the second course. With recognition of prior learning outcomes, those who have worked for many years might directly enroll in the second phase course, offering a variety of learning methods.

c. *Faculty*

More than 40 percent of the full-time faculty members must be practitioner teachers, and more than 50 percent should be practitioner teachers with research capabilities.

d. *Degree*

Graduates of professional universities receive Bachelor's degrees, and those who graduate from professional junior colleges receive junior college degrees.

e. *Accreditation*

Professional universities and junior colleges, like other institutions of higher education, are accredited at the institutional level every seven years by a recognized quality assurance agency.

4.2 China: Party-State Regulation

To develop economic competitiveness and train application-oriented professionals with a strong professional ability, China introduced a professional degree system in 1990. In 1993, the 14th National Congress of the Communist Party of China issued the Educational Reformation and Development Plan in China (中国教育改革和发展纲要), which established strategic education as a priority for the 1990s. This was an important backdrop against which China implemented a professional degree system. To improve the degree system, the State Council of China (国务院) published the Interim Regulations for the Examination and Approval of the Establishment of Professional Degrees (Professional Degree Regulations) (专业学位设置审批暂行办法) in 1996. The relevant provisions for professional degrees are as follows (State Council of China, 1996):

1. Professional degrees are divided into Bachelor's degrees, Master's degrees, and doctoral degrees, but Master's degrees represent the overwhelming majority.
2. The name of a professional degree is denoted as "XX (professional field) Master's (Bachelor's, doctoral) professional degree," and a professional degree is equivalent to a general degree.

According to the Professional Degree Regulations, the establishment of professional degrees shall be approved by the Academic Degrees Committee of the State Council (ADC; 国务院学位委员会), applied by the relevant governmental ministries or/with universities. The Academic Degrees Committee (ADC) shall also be responsible for establishing national steering committees (全国专业学位研究生教育指导委员会) for different professional degrees, which help to formulate educational programs and evaluation standards. To ensure consistent quality, a university that awards a professional degree must follow the educational guidance of the national steering committee, thus executing relevant regulations with respect to recruiting students, teaching, and degree conferment, and conducting regular evaluation. To promote the acceptance of professional degrees, the law also clearly states that these degrees should gradually be considered as primary qualifications while recruiting a qualified workforce in the corresponding professions.

The recruitment quotas of professional degree programs require permission from jurisdiction ministries (上级主管部门). Some professional degree programs are subject to a quota limit in certain fields. Students who wish to study for a Master's degree must take the national entrance examination for graduate students. The teaching models of professional degrees can be full-time or part-time. The length of study for part-time students is two to four years, and that for full-time students is two to three years. This must include at least one six-month internship. Without work experience, the internship should not last for less than one year.

Most professional degrees awarded in China concentrate on a Master's degree followed by a doctorate degree and a Bachelor's degree. The Master's degree is the mainstream form of professional education in China. There are currently 40 professional Master's degree categories (CADGEI, 2016) including natural sciences, social sciences, and even arts and humanities. In terms of professional doctoral degrees, there are six types: education, veterinary medicine, medicine, stomatological medicine, engineering, and Chinese medicine. Only two universities can offer professional doctoral degree courses in engineering and medicine.

Professional degree evaluation is organized by the State Council and implemented by the China Academic Degrees and Graduate Education Center (CDGDC; 教育部学位与研究生教育发展中心) according to the different subjects of professional degrees. In April 2016, the degree center launched its pilot evaluation of professional degrees, entitled the China University Professional-degree Rankings (CUPR; 专业学位水平评估), in which eight long-standing subjects of professional degrees were selected. In total, 650 professional degree programs were selected to join the ranking exercise, and the results were announced in 2018. The evaluation results were categorized into nine grades among the top 75 percent (CDGDC, 2018).

4.3 India: Professional Bodies Prevail

India's higher education system, one of the largest in the world, has paid special attention to professional education as socially desirable, particularly engineering education. It is known worldwide that the Indian Institutes of Technology (IITs) nurture quality student education in engineering and technologies. This tradition is closely related to the model of professional education in India.

Several disciplinary fields are generally regarded as professions. According to the University Grant Council (UGC) in India, there are 15 professional councils, which are responsible for course recognition, promotion of professional institutions, and provision of grants to undergraduate programs (UGC, 2020). The statutory professional councils include engineering, medicine, teacher education, architecture, law, dental, pharmacy, nursing, and agriculture. A study focusing on professional education in India illustrated the overall structure using examples of technical education, pharmacy education, teacher education, management education, and legal education (Anon., n.d.). This study confirmed that professional education must be recognized and accredited by these statutory bodies in terms of entry, learning environment/process, and even graduation standards. At the same time, Indian professional education centers on the undergraduate and diploma levels, instead of the postgraduate level. To illustrate the detailed operation of professional education in India, we offer technical education (i.e., engineering) as an example.

The All India Council for Technical Education (AICTE) was established as a regulatory body under the AICTE Act, 1987. The council is authorized to take all steps considered appropriate to ensure the coordinated and integrated development of technical education and maintenance of standards. The Council may, among other things, "lay down norms and standards for courses, curricula, physical and instructional facilities, staff patterns, staff qualifications, quality instruction, assessment, and examinations" (UGC, 2020). The AICTE also has the authority to "grant approval for starting new technical institutions and for the introduction of new courses or programs" (UGC, 2020). In other words, this professional council controls the entry channel, learning standards and environments, and faculty quality and instructional facilities at the program and institution levels. Such special arrangements play a critical role in legally distinguishing them from other disciplines or non-professional fields.

The role of the state government is indirect, as legal power is devolved to the AICTE. Its main responsibility is the "preparation of rules and regulations for admission to Engineering Colleges as per the norms of the AICTE" and "conducting entrance exams" (UGC, 2020). The primary aim of the AICTE is to ensure that engineering graduates from any university in India are on par with their counterparts at other universities across the world. Finally, the role of the university lies in promoting the compliance of granting engineering colleges with state policies (including infrastructure and human sources), monitoring academic schedules, performing curriculum design, and conducting periodic inspections. In response to globalization, Indian engineering education is even targeted at providing "skilled people for the outside world, so we can transform our country from a developing nation to a developed nation very easily and quickly" (Anon., n.d.). This assertion suggests that achieving global quality standards is a guiding principle for ensuring professional education.

In summary, India's model of professional education is a devolved professional approach with a light touch from the state government. In contrast, statutory bodies take operational control over certain professional fields by issuing relevant standards, norms, and approvals to make educational quality and graduates' competencies a priority. This is a much more highly regulated model than that of Taiwan, where a free-market style is dominant.

4.4 Taiwan: Free-Market Domination

Unlike its Asian counterparts, Taiwan has very limited regulations and controls by the government and professional bodies with respect to professional education. A strict definition holds that there is only one widely recognized profession: medicine, though more broadly there are several disciplines, including dentistry, architecture, law, teacher education, accounting, and management. However, there are no specific statutory rules or standards governing education in these areas. They are regarded as general areas, like other subjects. The Ministry of Education (MOE) in Taiwan is the sole body regulating the establishment of and entry to specialized programs at the diploma and degree levels. As far as entry is concerned, there are no rules for professional education. Except in the case of medicine, universities can relatively easily gain permission to establish new programs, if they meet the common standards set by the MOE. Therefore, no distinction is made between professional and non-professional subjects. In addition, there is no student quota for certain degree programs. Universities have complete authority to shift quotas across programs to fit their institutional missions and strategies. They also have full responsibility for developing their program (degree) curricula and learning standards.

This low-intervention approach (high market force) grants universities and programs greater autonomy to establish their distinctive niches in the labor market. The only exception in Taiwan is medicine, as this profession has two major thresholds regulated by official bodies. First, only 1,300 students are allowed by the Ministry of Health and Welfare (衛生福利部) to enroll in departments of medicine across Taiwan each year. Second, there are detailed standards and regulations for the education process accredited by the Taiwan Medical Accreditation Council (醫學院評鑑委員會). Furthermore, if medicine graduates wish to practice the profession, a national license must be awarded by the Ministry of Examination (考選部), Examination Yuan (考試院). Some professions also require a license to practice, such as those of attorney, accountant, nutritionist, consultant, and civil engineer. There are more than 100 professions that require official licenses in Taiwan. In other words, back-end control (licensing) is implemented to define the profession by the Ministry of Examination. This process is very different from that of other Asian countries. It is important to note that this national examination tends to have a basic threshold design, rather than being subject to rigid quantity control, to allow more practitioners in the market to compete.

5. COMPARING PROFESSIONAL EDUCATION MODELS IN SELECTIVE ASIAN COUNTRIES/SOCIETIES

Unlike their Western counterparts, two Asian countries examined here (Japan and China) tend to have significant government engagement, while Taiwan and India are different in the relative lack of such. In this section, we synthetically deploy the conceptual tools developed in section 3 to compare the systems in Asia. The different models shown in Table 11.1 are proposed after a systematic examination of the four countries/societies. Broadly, these models can be conceptually identified through two major metrics: whether professional education is controlled, and if so, by whom? Based on the literature review and our empirical case studies, five indicators/phases were identified to examine their variations, leading to different models: entry/establishment, courses and learning standards, quality assurance, qualification and licensing, and code of conduct and professional ethics.

According to Table 11.1, we can categorize the four countries/societies into three models with different features. Clearly, both Japan and China take a strongly government-led approach (top-down approach), while India is mainly dominated by professional councils (horizontal approach). Taiwan is characterized by a mixed-market approach (bottom-up approach). Japan and China tend to be tightly controlled by the government in the form of laws, rules, and regulations, from the entry/establishment of programs/institutions to the acquisition of qualifications. In addition, courses, curricula, learning modalities and standards, facilities, and staff qualifications are rigorously monitored. Regarding quality assurance, a more devolved manner is adopted in Japan through professional accreditors (such as NIAD-QE), while an official bureaucratic system is still in place in China. With respect to the code of conduct/professional ethics, some written protocols exist for certain professional fields. However, the extent to which they are upheld by occupational practitioners in a real-world context is unclear, owing to insufficient information.

The second model is based on Indian practices. Professional councils are the regulatory bodies that control the quality of professional education throughout the system, as indicated by Harvey and Mason (2014 [1995]). Adopting British traditions and practices, greater powers are exercised by professional bodies instead of through direct governmental intervention. However, we also noticed that these regulatory bodies are under the jurisdiction of the UGC. As previously explained, professional councils are composed mainly of members of academic and professional communities. Therefore, in this more horizontal approach, these professional councils have comprehensive authority to address all five important indicators/phases. These regulatory bodies can approve or accredit courses and institutions, regulate detailed learning standards and rules, and award professional qualifications.

The final model is mainly driven by market forces, without specific regulations, norms, or rules defining professional education. The Taiwanese practice indicates an open and penetrable system (except for medical education) where market forces, not the state government or professional council, are the dominant power. The back-end control exercised by the Ministry of Examination (考選部) is implemented by issuing practice qualifications or licenses to certain professions. This demonstrates governmental intervention. However, these are not rigorous, high standards but only guard basic quality. This threshold provides greater autonomy for market operations while recruiting employees.

Table 11.1 Different models of professional education in Asia

	Entry/establishment	Course and learning standards	Quality assurance	Qualification/licensing	Code of conduct/professional ethics
Government-led approach (Japan and China)	Japan: government regulated China: government regulated	Japan: government regulated China: government regulated	Japan: professional accreditors such as NIAD-QE, etc. China: steering committee	Japan: governmental control China: governmental control	Japan: written protocol China: gradually phased into professions
Professional council (India)	Professional councils control	Professional councils control	Professional councils control	Professional councils control	Professional councils control
Mixed-market (Taiwan)	Market (except medicine)	No specific rules	Independent professional accreditors such as HEEACT	Governmental control: Ministry of Examination (考選部)	Loosely implemented, as there is no strong enforcement

State authority

China

Japan

Thailand   Taiwan

Market

Singapore

Australia

India

Professional body

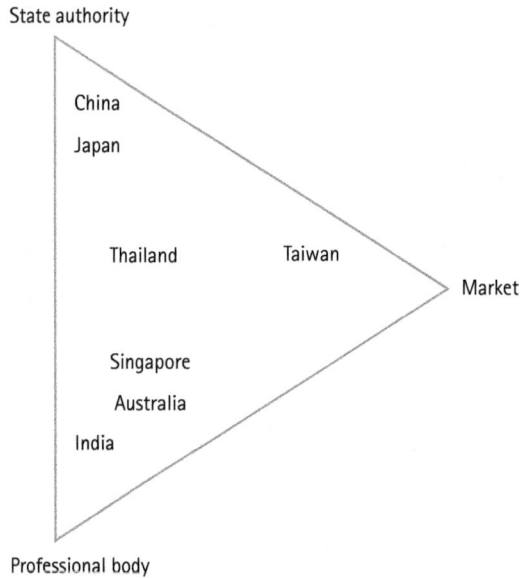

FIGURE 11.2 Triangle of coordination of professional education

While reflecting on the conceptual frameworks, we note that the three models identified here share similarities with Clark's triangle of coordination (1983), introduced earlier in the chapter. In Figure 11.2, we summarize our model, adapted from Clark's, where "professional body" replaces his "academic oligarchy." Our four country/society cases in Asia show how state governments, professional councils, and the market can respectively shape the development of professional education. These different forces define and regulate the scope, content, process, and outcomes of professional education in various ways. They also present diverse patterns of professional education at the national level.

6. Emerging Issues

Our previous model comparison shows that the four Asian countries/societies follow diverse paths in promoting professional education. In the 1980s and 1990s, India and China had already begun to introduce relevant systems, mechanisms, and regulations to secure the quality of professional education. Japan caught up with the trend with several new initiatives, including the recent creation of professional universities and junior colleges in 2017. China even attempted to estimate the quality of such degree programs through ranking exercises. All of these efforts indicate that the three major Asian countries (China, India, and Japan) are keen to build up a more stable and comprehensive professional education system. However, almost no literature in Asia has addressed professional education at the structural level. We are empirically unable to judge whether professional education is improving or not. In what follows, we focus on the evidence we have for a deeper discussion.

With regards to quality control of professional education, Japan, China, and India still place regular control on student entry quotas to maintain graduate quality. In terms of ability to enter into professional education provision, all new providers of professional education must receive governmental approval which will also enable government or professional councils to maintain the overall quality of professional education, and to regulate student numbers and hence outputs for certain professions. Notable measures include detailed guidelines for courses, curricula, learning standards, and environments, regular quality assurance accreditation, and the requirements for continuous professional development. From this perspective, the number of students is not the only way to control the quality of professional education in the selected Asian countries/societies. Many more mechanisms and measures have been introduced to raise educational standards in certain professions.

European reports have shown that most professional education is provided at the Master's level, followed by the doctoral and Bachelor's levels (Camilleri et al., 2014). Our findings were similar for China and Japan, where Master's degrees are predominant in professional education. In India, however, Bachelor's degrees and diplomas are dominant. This is probably due to the demands of the industrial structure in the local market in India. However, if higher social status is socially desirable for professional education, the educational level should be raised to Master's level.

The disciplinary subjects considered to be professional vary substantially between the countries/societies. According to our case studies, China has the widest definition, with more than 40 disciplines included, followed by India, with 15 wider councils. Japan officially recognized only eight areas, with about 7,158 enrolled students, in 2018. We can fairly argue that Japan has the smallest sector of professional education. In Taiwan, if we consider the Ministry of Examination regulations as standards, there are more than 100 specialized qualifications and licenses for certain occupations. This represents a wider scope of professional education.

The trend of increasing professional education will require greater integration with the workplace. This is apparent in the practices of Asian countries/societies, which are currently seeking a greater proportion of learning experiences through internships or more hands-on work prior to admission (Lester, 2009). Further integration or collaboration with industries or enterprises is essential for all areas of professional education in all four of the countries/societies under study here. The educational objective of professional education is to combine academic components with practical skills, promoting employability and distinctive hands-on or practical knowledge (Camilleri et al., 2014). An important area of emphasis is more hands-on experience for teachers. Japan has established standards for the proportion of practitioner teachers in professional education programs. This is an important step towards integrating theory and practice.

Looking to the future, an emerging agenda becomes relevant. The further internationalization of professions will lead to debate on the acceptance of the common qualification framework. Currently, professional education and qualification are mainly valid within national jurisdictions. As a result of internationalization, some professions are challenged by overarching standards or norms applicable to more countries/societies. How will these new needs of transnational mobility affect such areas of professional education? Will international accreditation be more appropriate for these professions? How will Asian national regulations fit into this international development? These wider issues should be addressed in the long run.

7. Conclusions

Despite the very limited research on this topic in Asia, we found that professional education has expanded into several different disciplinary areas over the last two decades. Using four countries/societies as case studies, three major models were identified. In India and especially Japan and China, the state government plays a dominant role, while Taiwan is open to more market forces. This is a very different approach from that of Western societies, where professional bodies/organizations tend to play a greater role in defining and regulating the educational process. This feature highlights the fact that education still falls under the control of the government, even in the case of professional education, such that the government has greater power over the content, scope, and outcomes of professional education.

In addition, there are emerging issues to be addressed in the Asian region, although we have very limited evidence regarding these areas. There is a need to balance the quality and quantity of professional education. Supply-side control still prevails. Therefore, the demand side or outcomes require more quantitative examination. Moreover, further integration with the real world of work is an inevitable learning process. Professional education should have more on-site or clinical learning assisted by practitioner teachers. Finally, the impact of internationalized professions has started to be felt in the educational practices of Asian countries/societies. Therefore, determining how to adopt transnational standards and norms presents a new challenge.

References

Anon. (n.d.). "Growth and workings of professional education in India." https://shodhganga.inflibnet.ac.in/bitstream/10603/70894/8/08_chapter%201.pdf, accessed February 25, 2020.

Brante, T. (1990). "Professional types as a strategy of analysis." In M. Burrage and R. Torsyendahl (eds.), *Professions in Theory and History*. London: Sage Publications, 75–94.

Brennan, J. (2010). "Burton Clark's 'The higher education system: Academic organization in cross-national perspective.'" *London Review of Education*, 8/3, 229–237.

Camilleri, A., Delplace, S., Frankowicz, M., Hudak, R., and Tannhäuser, C. (2014). *Professional Higher Education in Europe: Characteristics, Practice Examples and National Differences*. https://www.eurashe.eu/library/mission-phe/PHE_in_Europe_Oct2014.pdf, accessed March 20, 2020.

China Academic Degrees and Graduate Education Development Center (CDGDC) (2016). *Overview of China University Professional-degree Rankings (CUPR)*. http://www.chinadegr ees.cn/xwyyjsjyxx/2018cpsr/284315.shtml (in Chinese), accessed April 14, 2020.

China Academic Degrees and Graduate Education Development Center (CDGDC) (2018). *Results of China University Professional-degree Rankings (CUPR)*. http://www.chinadegrees. cn/xwyyjsjyxx/2018cpsr/index.shtml (in Chinese), accessed April 14, 2020.

China Academic Degrees and Graduate Education Information (CADGEI) (2016). *An Overview of 40 Professional Master's Degree Programs*. http://www.cdgdc.edu.cn/xwyyjsj yxx/gjjl/szfa/267348.shtml (in Chinese), accessed April 14, 2020.

Clark, B. R. (1983). *The Higher Education System: Academic Organization in Cross-National Perspective*. Berkeley, CA: University of California Press.

Enders, J. (2007). "The academic profession." In J. J. F. Forest and P. G. Altbach (eds.), *International Handbook of Higher Education*, vol. 18. Dordrecht: Springer, 5–21.

Even, R. and Ball, D. L. (eds.) (2009). *The Professional Education and Development of Teachers of Mathematics*. Dordrecht: Springer.

Findlow, S. (2012). "Higher education change and professional-academic identity in newly 'academic' disciplines: The case of nurse education." *Higher Education*, 63, 117–133.

Harvey, L. (2004). "Professional body." http://www.qualityresearchinternational.com/gloss ary/professionalbody.htm, accessed February 3, 2020.

Harvey, L. and Mason, S. with Ward, R. (2014 [1995]). *The Role of Professional Bodies in Higher Education Quality Monitoring*. Birmingham: QHE.

Kennedy, M. M. (1987). Inexact Sciences: Professional education and the development of expertise. *Review of Research in Education*, 13, 133–167.

Lang, D. W. (2017). "Fiscal incentives, Clark's triangle, and the shape and shaping of higher education systems." *Policy Reviews in Higher Education*, 1/2, 112–138.

Lester, S. (2009). "Routes to qualified status: Practices and trends among UK professional bodies." *Studies in Higher Education*, 34/2, 223–236.

Lin, S. K. (2012). "Professional education." http://terms.naer.edu.tw/detail/1678834/ (in Chinese), accessed March 2, 2020.

MEXT (2003). *Standards for Establishment of Professional Graduate Schools*. https://elaws. egov.go.jp/search/elawsSearch/elaws_search/lsg0500/ detail?lawId=41 5M60000080016 (in Japanese), accessed March 15, 2020.

MEXT (2019a). *Brochures for Professional Graduate Schools*. https://www.mext.go.jp/content/ 1236743_005.pdf (in Japanese), accessed March 2, 2020.

MEXT (2019b). *Overview and Features of Professional Universities*. https://www.mext.go.jp/a_ menu/koutou/senmon/index_pc.htm (in Japanese), accessed March 10, 2020.

MEXT (2020). *List of Professional Universities and Junior Colleges*. https://www.mext.go.jp/a_ menu/koutou/senmon/1414446.htm (in Japanese), accessed March 15, 2020.

Mulder, M. (ed.) (2017). *Competence-Based Vocational and Professional Education: Bridging the Worlds of Work and Education*. Cham: Springer International.

Springer (2020). *Innovation and Change in Professional Education*. Book series description. https://www.springer.com/series/6087, accessed January 20, 2020.

State Council of China (1996). *Interim Regulations for the Examination and Approval of the Establishment of Professional Degrees*. http://www.moe.gov.cn/s78/A22/xwb_left/moe_833/ tnull_3445.html (in Chinese), accessed April 14, 2020.

Teichler, U., Arimoto, A., and Cummings, W. (2013). *The Changing Academic Profession: Major Findings of a Comparative Survey*. Dordrecht: Springer.

UGC (2020). *Professional Councils.* https://www.ugc.ac.in/page/Professional-Councils.aspx, accessed March 3, 2020.

Wallin, A., Nokelainen, P., and Mikkonen, S. (2019). "How experienced professionals develop their expertise in work-based higher education: A literature review." *Higher Education,* 77, 359–378.

Whitchurch, C. (2010). "Some implications of 'public/private' space for professional identities in higher education." *Higher Education,* 60, 627–640.

Wikipedia (2020). *The University Council of Japan.* https://ja.wikipedia.org/wiki/%E5%A4%A7%E5%AD%A6%E5%AF%A9%E8%AD%B0%E4%BC%9A (in Japanese), accessed January 22, 2021.

PART V

HOW AND WHO?

CHAPTER 12

QUALITY REGULATION IN HIGHER EDUCATION IN ASIA-PACIFIC

Roles of Quality Assurance and National Qualification Frameworks

ANGELA YUNG CHI HOU, I-JUNG GRACE LU, KAREN HUI JUNG CHEN, AND CHAO YU GUO

1. INTRODUCTION

HIGHER Education in Asia-Pacific has been expanding rapidly since the late 1990s. The total number of higher education providers in Asia-Pacific has increased to 76,387, with more than 115.1 million students enrolled (Calderon, 2018). Furthermore, higher education expenditure has likewise dramatically increased by more than double compared to 10 years ago, particularly in the Asia and Pacific region (OECD, 2017). In order to respond to massification in higher education, as well as to assure the quality of local higher education providers, the establishment of quality assurance systems has become a national agenda concern in most Asian nations.

Since 2000, coupled with the growing economic power of the middle classes, more and more Asian students have chosen to study abroad in search of overseas university education. Traditionally, Western English-speaking countries, such as the United States, United Kingdom, and Australia were the most popular destinations. Yet, with great ambitions to become an education hub, several Asian countries, such as Malaysia, Singapore, China, and Japan strategically attracted international students from neighboring countries (Tan, 2013). It was also found that between a half and three-quarters of international students on Asian campuses come from the other neighboring countries (British Council, 2017). According to UNESCO, China already hosts 178,271 students, Japan 164,338, and Malaysia 122,823 (UNESCO, 2021).

In order to facilitate international student mobility, a regional Qualification References Framework, like the ASEAN Qualification References Framework (AQRF), was developed to accommodate different types of national qualification frameworks within the region. Given Asia's position in the emerging global market and the competition it faces from other regions, having a global outlook has become more and more of a pressing issue. Furthermore, Asian governments have realized that it is increasingly necessary to develop a national qualification framework, supported by a national quality assurance system, in order to ensure overseas qualifications are met (Hou et al., 2017b).

Currently, both quality assurance (QA) and qualification frameworks (QF) are regarded as strong policy tools by governments to either achieve the specific educational goals, or ensure quality of higher education in an either direct or an indirect manner. Despite the fact that QA is strongly connected to local context, some QA agencies supported Asian governments, and engaged in the development of a qualification framework and its implementation, particularly in ASEAN countries. Yet, most East Asian nations without national qualification frameworks mainly rely on external QA systems to ensure and regulate the quality of domestic higher education providers and programs, including Japan, South Korea, and Taiwan (Hou, 2014; Hou et al., 2017b). National college entrance examination systems have significant effects on quality, like quality assurance and qualification frameworks drawing greater attention, but this issue is too huge and complicated in Asia-Pacific to be discussed in this chapter. Thus, the main purpose of this chapter is to explore the impacts of national regulations over higher education providers. The role, function, and interrelations between the two strong quality regulators in Asian nations will then be discussed. The challenges and emerging issues for quality regulation in Asian higher education will be analyzed at the end of the chapter. Three research questions are addressed as follows:

(1) How would Asian governments regulate quality of higher education under neoliberalism?
(2) What are the roles, functions, and interrelations of quality assurance agencies and national qualification frameworks in Asia?
(3) What are the challenges and emerging issues for quality regulation in Asian higher education?

2. Regulations and Governance in Asian Higher Education under Neoliberalism: China, Japan, India, Taiwan, and Malaysia

The relationship between higher education and government has always been connected. Traditionally, the high level of state regulation over higher education is the most common governance model in countries, particular in Asia. As Shin (2018, p. 11) pointed out, "this is particularly true for the stated-centered governance of East Asia," which responds to the argument by van Vught and de Boer (2015, p. 38) that the "state plays a pivotal role in establishing frameworks, objectives, and priorities." Originating from the doctrine of economic efficiency and profit-maximization in the 1980s, the main conceptual idea of neoliberalism is being applied to higher education in order to enhance competitiveness and accountability. At the same time, it has been enacted as "the rule for social and political order" in many nations (Oleksenko et al., 2018, p. 115; Hou et al., 2020). In the late 1990s, neoliberalism, with an emphasis on marketization, privatization, and deregulation with competition as a key characteristic in higher education, was implemented in the national agendas of Asia. Influenced by the new public management theory, several governance reforms were initiated, such as cuts in public funding, incorporation of national universities, competitions for national funding, etc. (Davies and Bansel, 2007; Saunders, 2010). Policymakers interpret neoliberalism as "decreased regulations, increased accountability and more academic autonomy" (Shin, 2018). Scott (2017) identified the changing role of states in a neoliberal turn, a shift from the traditional notion of the post-war "welfare state" with an emphasis on public good to serve as "regulator" and "customer" of higher education. All in all, Olssen and Peters (2005, p. 315) argued that "for neoliberal perspectives, the end goals of freedom, choice, consumer sovereignty, competition and individual initiative, as well as those of compliance and obedience, must be constructions of the state acting now in its positive role through the development of the techniques of auditing, accounting and management," particularly in the emergence of higher education massification.

Higher education in Asia-Pacific has been in the massification phase for the past several decades. Currently, enrollments in Asian higher education have increased by over 50 percent and in East Asia and Pacific, the gross enrollment rate even reached the world average level (Marginson et al., 2011; Calderon, 2018). Due to the variations in demographic and economic development, national higher education systems are vastly different in size and growth. For example, China with a 1.3 billion population has more than 2,900 higher education institutions (HEIs), compared to 1.2 million Timor-Leste with only one public university.

China, Japan, and India with the largest number of HEIs, adopted a centralized approach to regulate higher education in the region. Higher education was highly regulated by the Chinese government. Prior to the 1990s, all HEIs were deemed public sectors under the Department of Education, which featured three characteristics, including "a single system of state ownership, vague responsibilities and obligations between institutions and governments, and resources distributed by the government directly" (Shi and Wu, 2018, p. 58). Without autonomy, internal governance and management in student enrollment, new program offering, senior administrator and staff appointment, and funding allocation were under control of the central government (Hawkins, 2000; Li and Yang, 2011). Since 1993, Chinese higher education reform began as a result of economic growth and increasing global competition. In 1998, the "Law on Higher Education" stipulated that provincial and local governments would engage in higher education regulation, which led to a new focus on decentralization and flexibility.

At the same time, university presidents were authorized to develop institutional policies and strategies and undertake faculty and staff evaluation independently (Cai, 2013; Varghese and Martin, 2013; Wang, 2014). However, the State Council, controlled by the Communist Party, remains very closely involved in governance arrangements and management within all HEIs. The Ministry of Education not only exercises control and regulation over curriculum development and teaching and research activities through various ordinances and documents, but also all appoints presidents and party secretaries in national universities (Zhuang and Liu, 2020).

Like China, the Japanese education system is regulated by the Ministry of Education, Culture, Sports, Science, and Technology (MEXT). There are four types of institutions, namely universities, junior colleges, colleges of technology, and professional training colleges (specialized courses) (Doyon, 2001). In 2019, there were a total of 782 HEIs with 3.6 million students. To enhance university flexibility and autonomy, The Deregulation of University Act was promulgated in 1991, with the aim of decreasing government intervention in such areas as curricula design, credit hour allocations, and academic degree titles. Universities were made responsible for periodic self-assessments to encourage quality and governance improvements. Deregulation brought significant reforms to the national universities, with the status of national universities changing to national university corporations (NUCs) in 2004. The introduction of these market mechanisms gave the NUCs autonomy in terms of university governance and financial and personnel management. Universities were expected to focus on certain core functions: acting as a global research and education center, developing highly professional or wide-ranging human resources, providing a comprehensive liberal arts education, conducting education and research in specific professional fields, serving as community centers for lifelong learning, or making social contributions (Noda et al., 2018). In 2013, MEXT asked national universities to redefine their missions based on objective research, educational evidence, and defined functions (Noda et al., 2018). It was hoped that by clearly defining their missions and goals, universities would be encouraged to be more competitive. However, the universities still need to submit their six-year strategic plan to the government for approval and undergo national evaluation. Due to the fact that education resources remain under control of the national government, institutional autonomy remains limited (Varghese and Martin, 2013; Yamada, 2016; NIAD-QE, 2019).

Higher education in India underwent several phases of transformation and reform. Unlike China and Japan, provinces played a significant role initially in Indian higher education development and evolution. In the colonial period, the system was small and elite and the universities acted as an affiliating body for local colleges but they had a strong link with local governments. After independence, the higher education system evolved to a publicly run system for the elites, yet, the conflict over governance between national government (Central) and the provinces (states) "led to different strategies on funding and regulation" (Carnoy and Dossani, 2013, p. 597). Subsequently, this shared governance model emerged as a key driver of structural change in higher education. During the 1980s, central government started to expand the higher education system by establishing new HEIs and states also licensed new private providers. It was expected that underprivileged groups would have access to higher education. Due to the rapid expansion and liberation after the 1990s, HEIs struggled with insufficient resources, which would not be able to support a good quality of teaching and learning on campus and then led to the problems of low student learning outcomes and graduates' employment (Jayaram, 2013). In response to the over-expansion, the government announced that all universities, besides central universities, needed to be accredited in order to award degrees. Both the National Assessment and Accreditation Council (NAAC) and the National Board of Accreditation (NBA) as the major accrediting bodies are responsible for carrying out accreditation for the HEIs in India (Patil and Pillai, 2015). In 2013, India also published the National Skills Qualifications Framework (NSQF) and set national standards for all levels of education (Ministry of Skill Development and Entrepreneurship, 2020).

Although higher education systems in Taiwan and Malaysia are not as big as in the previously discussed nations, their university quality is recognized worldwide. Over the past decades, the development of higher education in Taiwan was influenced interchangeably by Chinese heritage, Japanese cultures, and American universities. Higher education has always been in the spotlight throughout these social transformations and political system transitions in the Taiwanese context. According to Chou (2015, p. 92), the uniqueness of the system characterized by a combination of Japanese, American, Chinese, and local features indicates "options facing Taiwan in its pursuit of localization and globalization in higher education." After the 1990s, the education system was moving gradually toward a universal system from elitist mode by governmental policies, including inviting private sectors into the field of higher education, adoption of a market-driven management approach, enhancing internationalization, and pursuit of excellence (MOE, 2019a, 2019b). Influenced by neoliberalism, Taiwan HEIs remained regulated by national government in terms of funding and student enrollments but they were encouraged to be internationally competitive.

The Malaysian education system comprises education from pre-school to university. The education structure can be divided into pre-tertiary and tertiary education levels. The governing authority for pre-tertiary education (pre-school to secondary education) is the Ministry of Education Malaysia (MOE), whilst tertiary or higher education is under the jurisdiction of the Ministry of Higher Education Malaysia (MOHE). In order to respond to global trends and international competition, Malaysia published two documents titled *The National Higher Education Strategic Plan 2007–2020 (NHESP)* and *The Malaysia Education Blueprint (Higher Education) 2015–2025 (MEBHE)* to reform the higher education system, particularly through the concept of corporatization of public universities (Wan and Morshidi, 2018). Public universities underwent three phases of transformation from acting federal statutory bodies to corporatized organizations in line with the neoliberal concept. Although universities have been given more autonomy, they are expected to be more accountable than ever.

Singapore, as one of the most vibrant higher education systems in Asia-Pacific, has six autonomous universities, several foreign universities and private HEIs partnering with foreign providers. Like other Asian countries, the Higher Education Group under the Ministry of Education (MOE) controls and regulates all types of higher education providers and oversees policies on higher education and lifelong learning (MOE, 2021, p. 1).

3. Quality Assurance and National Qualification Frameworks in Asian Higher Education as a Policy Tool

Under neoliberalism, QA and national qualification frameworks are regarded as two of the powerful apparatuses by the governments to regulate the quality of HEIs in Asia. Moreover, the expansion of higher education has sped up the development of QA and national qualification frameworks and made them serve specific functions for quality control in higher education (Van Vught and Westerheijden, 1994; Martin and Stella, 2007; Shin, 2018). Due to varying aims and review approaches, quality assurance is often used for measuring university accountability at either institutional or programmatic levels. Vice versa, national qualification frameworks aim to facilitate student mobility and mainly measure individual learning outcomes. In general, QA features onsite visit reviews and an emphasis on institutional effectiveness and effective governance. In contrast, qualification frameworks present their value in reference to international standards. The beneficiaries are higher education institutions and individuals respectively (Table 12.1).

Though the number and the content of quality standards and indicators by governments and national accreditors vary from country to country, learning outcomes are the key elements in the Asian context. For example, Article 17 of the Ordinance of MEXT Japan (2016) required that Japanese universities define and publish three policies

Table 12.1 A comparison between QA and QF in terms of characteristics

	QA	QF
Nature	Governmental / quasi-governmental	Governmental
Objective	Fitness for purposes / diversification	International standards / global recognition
Function / roles	Policy instrument	Policy instrument
Context	Local	Regional / global
Focus	Learning outcomes based	Learning outcomes based
Approach	External review / onsite visit	Documentation review
Beneficiary	Universities	Individual
Impact	University governance and management	Talent mobility and lifelong learning

(a diploma policy, a curriculum policy, and an admissions policy) that emphasize student learning outcomes to clarify their educational goals, processes, and expected learning outcomes in degree programs so that stakeholders can understand the program goals and objectives. The diploma policy in particular, requires that universities clearly define expected learning outcomes that university graduates should achieve (Noda et al., 2020). In Taiwan, the Ministry of Education regulated what students are expected to possess at the time of graduation with a bachelor's degree. Universities define the expected outcome according to the character of the institution. Core competencies refer to professional knowledge and skills that students gain from the professional program they have studied (HEEACT, 2011). Accreditation in particular has encouraged universities to develop clearer concepts of how they apply core competencies and basic literacy in the overall university mission and planning of each program (Noda et al., 2020).

3.1 Quality Assurance

Quality assurance (QA) consisting of internal and external approaches is defined as "a process of establishing stakeholder confidence that provision (input, process and outcomes) fulfills expectations or measures up to threshold minimum requirements" (INQAAHE, 2019, p. 1). "Internal evaluation" focuses on the "process of quality review undertaken within an institution for its own ends." Accordingly, development and management of internal quality assurance systems is "at the discretion of the higher education institution, which usually carries out this mandate in the context of available institutional resources and capacities" (Paintsil, 2016, p. 4). External quality assurance agencies (EQAs), with a "self-critical, objective, and open-minded" character, undertake third-party review activities of HEIs, in order to determine whether the quality of universities "meets the agreed or predetermined standards" (Martin and Stella, 2007, p. 34). Both indeed are so much "two sides of the same coin that the activities are inextricably interrelated" (Vroeijenstijn, 2008, p. 1). Westerheijden et al. (2014, p. 3) pointed out that "the adoption of quality assurance schemes becomes a process of copying instruments and policies that exist elsewhere, or to legitimate political action regardless of its actual effect."

After 2000, most Asian governments started to develop national QA systems to ensure the quality of local higher education providers and programs. Examining the characteristics of Asian QA agencies, it was found that most of the agencies in the region were government funded and acted as a statutory body. Under either direct or indirect governmental control, Asian agencies were considered as extended arms of government. Although most agencies claimed that they have autonomy over review procedures and decisions, they admitted that it was not easy to enhance their level of "autonomy" because of their close affiliation with the government (Jarvis, 2014; Hou et al., 2015). Besides, review standards by QA agencies should either follow national quality standards or be approved by the respective governments. Hence, autonomy and independence remain a considerable challenge for the agencies. The Tertiary Education Quality and Standards Agency (TEQSA) and Malaysian Qualifications Agency (MQA), for example,

Table 12.2 Summary of the number of QA agencies in the Asia-
           Pacific region

Asia-Pacific QA agencies	Number of QA agencies	Number of public QA agencies	Number of private QA agencies
ASEAN	32	12	20
South Asia	11	11	0
East Asia	20	9	11
Central Asia	7	2	5
Pacific	11	10	1
Total	81	44	37

Source: Authors.

were established as governmental agencies under governmental control. TEQSA not only "carried out evaluations of standards and performance to ensure the quality of international education, but also registered providers" throughout a regulatory framework (Rowlands, 2012, p. 101). MQA is a Malaysian governmental organization with six objectives, including implementing the Malaysian Qualifications Framework, developing quality standards and criteria and instruments, undertaking accreditation processes and procedures over higher education providers and programs, facilitating the recognition and articulation of qualifications, and establishing and maintaining the Malaysian Qualifications Register (Parliament of Malaysia, 2007). Singapore is the other case, where the quality assurance system is linked with the workforce of the industry. The Ministry of Education directly supervises and undertakes external review process over six autonomous universities. Those private providers, including international branch campuses, should be accredited and ensured by the Committee for Private Education (CPE) (formerly known as the Council for Private Education) under the Private Education Act 2009 (MOE, 2009). Following the guidelines to improving skills mastery and lifelong learning by SkillsFuture Singapore (SSG) as well as collaborations with quality assurance in Hong Kong, Australia, and the United Kingdom, CPE aims at "uplifting standards in the local private education industry" (SkillsFuture Singapore, 2021).

Since the first QA agency, the Japan University Accreditation Association (JUAA), was established in 1947, there have been an estimated 81 QA agencies and professional accreditors established in Asia, including 44 public and 37 private ones (Table 12.2). Approximately, 39.5 percent of them are located in the ASEAN region, 24.7 percent of all the agencies are in East Asia, and only 13.6 percent are in the Pacific.

3.2 National Qualification Framework

A national qualification framework is defined as an educational system structure, which has a series of instrumental regulatory logics, such as inclusion of all types of higher education providers and developing national standards for all levels of education in terms of learning outcomes (Jarvis, 2014). In other words, a national qualification framework "makes hierarchical distinctions between qualifications and categorizes them by level," in which learners can earn credits and accumulate skills and knowledge in different learning periods and paths (Hanf and Hippach-Schneider, 2005, p. 9).

As a unified and comprehensive system, a national qualification framework demonstrates a further manifestation of government intervention under neoliberalism (Young, 2003). It is often used as a policy instrument for "education system reform in order to connect educational pathways flexibly within the national systems as well as eliminate the barriers to access and progression of learning" (ASEAN, 2017, p. 24). In many countries, a national qualification framework even acts as a quick reference guide on the recognition of foreign qualifications, which would facilitate the mobility of students, workers, and professionals across the regions. Under the Sustainable Development Goals (SDGs), UNESCO emphasized that economic growth, social equity, and sustainability are supposed to be embedded into the function of national qualification frameworks (UNESCO, 2015; Chakroun, 2017).

Up to the present day, 33 Asian nations have developed a national qualification framework. All ASEAN countries completed qualification frameworks, including Malaysia, Indonesia, Thailand, and Cambodia. In contrast, East Asian nations do not have qualification frameworks yet, such as China, Japan, Taiwan, and South Korea. The development of national qualification frameworks in Asia-Pacific may vary in the purposes, content, and the number of levels and descriptors, but the core of all these frameworks is still the learning outcome of the learners. The similarity of using skill, knowledge, and character of the learner as references in defining quality education has been found in many Asian nations. Through the national qualification framework, Asian governments expect to provide a pathway for different types of learning outcome to be recognized, to connect the educational institution and the labor market, and finally to make the qualification system sustainable and become a solid reference for the quality assurance system (Table 12.3).

4. Emerging Issues in Regulating Quality of Higher Education in Asia-Pacific

4.1 Upsurge of State Control over Quality and Accreditation Impacts on Institutions

As discussed above, governments in Asia-Pacific are the leading regulators for higher education institutions (Table 12.4). The Ministries of Education, with different divisions and sectors, regulate all types of higher education institutions and actively engage institutional governance in varying dimensions, including student enrollments, program

Table 12.3 Development of national qualification frameworks of ASEAN states

	Malaysia	Thailand	Indonesia	Philippines	Brunei	Vietnam	Cambodia
Organization responsible	Malaysian Qualifications Agency (2007) LAN 1997	Office of National Education Standards and Assessments 2000	The Indonesian Qualifications National Committee/Komite Nasional Kompetensi Indonesia (IQNC/KNKI)2018	Commission on Higher Education	Brunei National Accreditation Council	MOLISA / MOET / World Bank	National Training Board
Qualifications framework	Malaysian Qualifications Framework	Thai Qualifications Framework	Indonesian National Qualifications Framework	Philippines Qualifications Framework	Brunei National Qualifications Framework	Vietnam National Qualifications Framework	Cambodian Qualifications Framework
Sector coverage	3 –Skills TVET Academic	Higher education	4– Education, Industry, Prior learning, Professional certifications	3– Basic education TVET Higher education	2– School, TVET Higher education	Basic education, TVET and higher education	TVET and higher education
Key features	Levels, level LO descriptors, credits (academic load), pathways, sectors	Levels, LO descriptors, credits	Levels for formal and non-formal education, work related, credits, pathways, professional titles	Level, LO descriptors, credits	Levels, credits, Level LO descriptors	Levels	Levels for formal and non-formal
Levels	8	6	9	8	8	8	8
Learning / competencies domains	8 domains	5 domains Ethical and Moral Development, Knowledge, Cognitive Skills Interpersonal Skills and Responsibility, Analytical and Communication Skills	5 domains Science, knowledge, know-how, skills, affection, competency	5 domains Thinking, behavioral, academic, technical, ethical—defined by disciplines, community of scholars/industry	5 domains knowledge and understanding, applied knowledge and understanding, generic cognitive skills, communication, ICT and numeracy skills, autonomy, accountability and teamwork	–	5 domains Knowledge, cognitive skills; interpersonal skills and responsibility; Communication, Information Technology & Numerical Skills; psychomotor skills;

Source: Authors.

Table 12.4 The lead units responsible for regulating higher education quality in Asia–Pacific

Territories	Central government	Quality assurance agencies
China	Department of Education (Ministry of Education)	Higher Education Evaluation Center
India	Department of Education (Ministry of Education)	National Assessment and Accreditation Council (NAAC) and the National Board of Accreditation (NBA)
Japan	Higher Education Bureau (the Ministry of Education, Culture, Sports, Science, and Technology (MEXT))	National Institution for Academic Degrees and Quality Enhancement of Higher Education (NIAD-QE)
Malaysia	The Department of Higher Education, Department of Polytechnic Education, Department of Community Colleges Education (Ministry of Higher Education Malaysia)	Malaysian Qualification Agency
Indonesia	Directorate General of Higher Education (Ministry of Education, Culture, Research and Technology)	BAN PT
Thailand	Ministry of Education	The Office for National Education Standards and Quality Assessment (ONESQA)
Vietnam	The Tertiary Education Department (Ministry of Education and Training)	CEA VNU-HN in the North, CEA VNU-HCM in the South, CEA-UD in central, Vietnam Association of Universities and Colleges and Vinh University
Taiwan	Department of Higher Education & Department of Technical and Vocational Education (Ministry of Education)	Higher Education Evaluation & Accreditation Council (HEEACT)
Hong Kong	University Grants Committee (Education Bureau)	Quality Assurance Council/ Hong Kong Council for Accreditation of Academic & Vocational Qualifications
Philippines	Commission on Higher Education	The Accrediting Agency of Chartered Colleges and Universities in the Philippines (AACCUP), the Association of Local Colleges and Universities Commission on Accreditation (ALCUCOA), and The Philippine Accrediting Association of Schools, Colleges and Universities (PAASCU)
Singapore	Higher Education Group (Ministry of Education)	Committee for Private Education (CPE)

establishment, funding allocation, university presidential election, etc. In Taiwan, the Ministry of Education is the highest administrative body in charge of national educational policymaking and implementation in order to raise the overall quality of education and the nation's competitiveness (Ministry of Education, 2019a). The Department of Higher Education and Department of Technical and Vocational Education under the Ministry of Education (MOE) are in charge of general and vocational systems respectively. Indonesia and Malaysia are different cases. The Directorate General of Higher Education Indonesia has undergone a transformative process from being merged into the Ministry of Research and Technology (MoRT) in 2014, returning to the Ministry of Education and Culture (Indonesia) in 2019, and renamed as the Ministry of Education, Culture, Research and Technology as of 2021. Currently, the Directorate General of Higher Education is in charge of all types of higher education providers. It is the same as in Malaysia. The Ministry of Higher Education Malaysia (MOHE) was separated from Ministry of Education to form an independent ministry on March 10, 2020. The Department of Higher Education, Department of Polytechnic Education, and Department of Community Colleges Education are responsible for different types of higher education institutions respectively. Yet, non-traditional providers, such as transnational education, for profit providers and distance education, are not all included in the national regulatory framework in Asian nations due to lack of defined standards and criteria over these providers.

Higher education institutions in Asia-Pacific were inevitably affected by accreditation results in varying aspects due to the linkage between accreditation results and resources allocation (Hou et al., 2017a). Moreover, the governments would adopt the accreditation outcomes as the eligibility for applying competitive projects. Throughout the mandatory accreditation process, Asian governments would be able to realize accountability of HEIs on a regular basis. Besides, institutions would use the accreditation outcomes internally to revitalize programs, reallocate resources, and recruit new faculty members. Much literature also demonstrates that QA has both positive and negative impacts on higher education, including its influence on policy decisions and processes, and increased value placed on teaching as a core function of universities, leading to an increased bureaucratization and heavy administrative workload. Most positive consequences occur at the program level (Lemaitre et al., 2011; Hou et al., 2015; Hou et al., 2018).

4.2 Toward a More Diversified Quality Assurance System: A New Approach Launched

Impacted by the new managerialism, HEIs in Asia-Pacific are given more autonomy but also take responsibility for maintaining quality of education. Concurrently, a trend toward diversified quality assurance system apparently emerged in the Asian context (Mok, 2013; Chen and Hou, 2016). Prior to the establishment of national accreditors, local accreditors, including professional accreditors, were set up in Asian countries. To date, half of the Asian nations have more than two accrediting bodies, including Japan, Hong Kong, China, the Philippines and Taiwan (Hou et al., 2015). Under a diversified quality assurance system, universities in some nations would be allowed to select the professional accreditors for their program accreditation, such as business, engineering, and law fields. Yet, the more diversified national QA systems become, the more highly expected it is that HEIs demonstrate their quality, strengthen the internal quality assurance mechanism, and achieve academic excellence (Vanhoof and Van Petegem, 2007).

Notably, self-accreditation is a new approach adopted by several Asian nations, such as Malaysia, Taiwan, and Hong Kong. In Malaysia, for example, institutions are required to be reviewed by the MQA every five years according to two accreditation handbooks, the *Code of Practice for Institutional Audit* (COPIA) for institutional audit and the *Code of Practice for Program Accreditation* (COPPA) for program audit (MQA, 2020a). In 2010, the Ministry of Education Malaysia launched a so called "self-accreditation" policy which allowed universities to review their own programs by organizing a review panel based on the COPIA and COPPA standards. Up to the present, there were more than 20 universities awarded with a self-accrediting status by MQA (MQA, 2020b).

All in all, striking a balance between regulation and autonomy remains a considerable challenge in most nations. Both are, to some extent, a manifestation of confrontation in practice. Accordingly, institutions continue to adhere to the standards of the QA agencies, although they were encouraged to develop their own internal review system, including developing feature standards for program reviews, emphasis on innovations and flexibility in pedagogy, respect for faculty autonomy in research and teaching, etc. Given the fact that institutions still have to inform the general public as to the university's progress in meeting key teaching, research, and public service goals, the government and quality assurance agencies were expected to develop clear standards for institutions to follow. As a result, the key challenge in place for Asian governments and national accreditors is how to avoid another new form of quality regulation.

4.3 Development of Quality Standards from Input-Based to Outcomes-Based Approach

Quality standards and indicators developed by QA agencies set out the priority areas for quality improvement of HEIs. At the developmental phase of QA systems in some nations, the characteristics of standards tend to be input-based with a strong linkage with educational resources in teaching, learning, and research activities (Nguyen et al., 2009). Initially, the input-based standards are set to examine how appropriately and efficiently educational resources are used by universities. As QA systems are growing with maturity, student learning outcomes as well as evidence-based standards become the highlights of the whole review in the next phase. The National Institution for Academic Degrees and Quality Enhancement of Higher Education (NIAD-QE), for example, mainly targeted national and prefectural universities and emphasizes compliance with the 11 evaluation standards in the first cycle (2005–2011), including university mission, education and research structure, academic staff and education support staff, student admissions, academic programs, institutional performance, student support, facilities, internal quality assurance systems, finance, and management. There were several Certified Evaluation and Accreditation (CEA) standard revisions for the second cycle (2012–2018) in response to international trends in QA systems and accountability, with the revised CEA focusing more on learning outcomes, internal QA systems in teaching and learning, and public information disclosure. Similarly, the Higher Education Evaluation and Accreditation Council of Taiwan (HEEACT) Taiwan focused on sufficient resources to conduct teaching and research activities in the first cycle of program and institutional accreditation. At the second cycle, the concept of student learning outcomes penetrated the review activities with four standards, namely, governance and management, resources and support systems, institutional effectiveness, and self-improvement and sustainability (HEEACT, 2018; Hou et al., 2018; Noda et al., 2018).

Besides, Asian QA agencies tended to apply both quantitative and qualitative data to assess a university's performance. In addition to self-assessment report, universities are requested to provide a set of data related to outcome indicators as review references, such as retention rate, graduation rate, student/faculty ratio, employment rate, building and facilities, etc. (Hossler et al., 2001; Noda et al., 2018).

4.4 Divergence between Quality Assurance and Qualification Framework

Emphasis on students' learning outcomes and employability is driving Asian QA agencies to engage the development of national qualification frameworks. Although Asian governments are encouraged to develop a national qualification framework in order to comply with international quality standards and facilitate student mobility, a qualification framework does not closely connect with the QA system in most nations, except Malaysia, Australia, New Zealand, and Hong Kong. As a matter of fact, the convergence of QA and qualification frameworks and its implementation encounter several obstacles owing to limited engagement of higher education stakeholders, lack of confidence in the system, not being embedded into the local context, less transparency, and other factors.

In Malaysia, as a successful case, all programs accredited by MQA should be in compliance with the Malaysia Qualification Framework. According to the Malaysian Qualifications Agency Act, MQA is the agency that leads the development of the qualification framework and undertakes program accreditation and institution reviews in Malaysia. In addition, MQA establishes and maintains a register of programs, qualifications, and higher education providers. It clearly stipulates the dual missions of national quality assurance agencies in Malaysia (Parliament of Malaysia, 2007). Under the ACT, the implementation of the national qualification framework in Malaysia would heavily involve the quality assurance system.

5. CONCLUSION

Over a number of decades, massification, privatization, and marketization have generated and enhanced accessibility to Asian higher education but this process has increased public concern over the quality of institutions and student learning outcomes. Asian governments attempt to regulate higher education providers and ensure quality of teaching and learning activities in varying approaches, particularly quality assurance and qualification frameworks. National accreditors are obligated to monitor colleges and serve as gatekeepers to ensure quality, facilitate agility and responsiveness and promote innovation at the same time. Given the fact that Asian governments attempted to deregulate and corporatize universities under neoliberalism, national states continue to play an influential role for quality control and regulation in higher education governance and management.

Besides, it is argued that QA and a national qualification framework would likely lead to an isomorphism phenomenon in the higher education system. This means that either the qualification framework or quality assurance pressure universities to resemble other well-performing institutions in a constraining way. Whether quality assurance and qualification frameworks will strengthen isomorphism pressures over universities, constrain innovation and diversification, and result in homogenization in the Asian context, remains uncertain.

REFERENCES

ASEAN (2017). *ASEAN Qualification Reference Framework*. Bangkok: ASEAN.
British Council (2017). *10 Trends: Transformative Changes in Higher Education*. London: British Council.
Cai, Y. (2013). "Chinese higher education: The changes in the past two decades and reform tendencies up to 2020." In L. Ferreira and J. A. G. Albuquerque (eds.), *China and Brazil: Challenges and Opportunities*. Campinas: Anablumme, 91–118.
Calderon, A. J. (2018). *Massification of Higher Education Revisited*. RMIT University. https://www.researchgate.net/publication/331521091_Massification_of_higher_education_revisited
Carnoy, M. and Dossani, R. (2013). "Goals and governance of higher education in India." *Higher Education*, 65, 595–612.
Chakroun, B. (2017). "Qualification frameworks in a sustainable development context: Reflections and perspectives." In Cedefop, ETF, UNESCO, and UIL, *Global Inventory of Regional and National Qualifications Frameworks, Volume 1: Thematic Chapters* (pp. 11–20). http://www.cedefop.europa.eu/files/2221_en.pdf

Chen, K. H. J. and Hou, A. Y. C. (2016). "Adopting self-accreditation in response to the diversity of higher education: Quality assurance in Taiwan and its impact on institutions." *Asia Pacific Education Review*, 17/1, 1–11.

Chou, C. P. (2015). "Higher education development in Taiwan." In J. C. Shin, G. A. Postiglione, and F. Huang (eds.), *Mass Higher Education Development in East Asia: Strategy, Quality, and Challenges.* Singapore: Springer, 89–104.

Davies, B. and Bansel, P. (2007). "Neoliberalism and education." *International Journal of Qualitative Studies in Education*, 20/3, 247–259.

Doyon, P. (2001). "A review of higher education reform in modern Japan." *Higher Education*, 41/4, 443–470.

Hanf, G. and Hippach-Schneider, U. (2005). *What Purpose Do National Qualifications Frameworks Serve? A Look at Other Countries.* https://www.bibb.de/dokumente/pdf/a1_bwp_special-edition_hanf_hippach-schneider(1).pdf

Hawkins, J. N. (2000). "Centralization, decentralization, recentralization: Educational reform in China." *Journal of Educational Administration*, 38/5, 442–454.

Higher Education Evaluation & Accreditation Council of Taiwan (HEEACT) (2011). "Is 'basic literacy' different from 'core competencies?'" *Evaluation Bimonthly*, 34. http://epaper.heeact.edu.tw/archive/2011/11/01/5047.aspx

Higher Education Evaluation & Accreditation of Council in Taiwan (HEEACT) (2018). *Institutional Accreditation Handbook.* Taipei, HEEACT.

Hossler, D., Kuh, G. D., and Olsen, D. (2001). "Finding fruit on the vines: Using higher education research and institutional research to guide institutional policies and strategies." *Research in Higher Education*, 42/2, 211–221.

Hou, A. Y. C. (2014). "Quality in cross-border higher education and challenges for the internationalization of national quality assurance agencies in the Asia-Pacific region: Taiwan experience." *Studies in Higher Education*, 39/6, 152–163.

Hou, A. Y. C, Hill, C., Hu, Z., and Lin, L. (2020). "What *is* driving Taiwan government for policy change in higher education after the year of 2016: In search of egalitarianism or pursuit of academic excellence?" *Studies in Higher Education* (online). doi:10.1080/03075079.2020.1744126

Hou, A. Y. C., Ince, M., Tasi, S., and Chiang, C. L. (2015). "Quality assurance of quality assurance agencies from an Asian perspective: Regulation, autonomy and accountability." *Asian Pacific Educational Review*, 16, 95–106.

Hou, A. Y. C., Kuo, C. Y., Chen, K. H. J., Hill, C., Lin, S. R., Chih, J. C. C., and Chou, H. C. (2018). "The implementation of self-accreditation policy in Taiwan higher education and its challenges to university internal quality assurance capacity building." *Quality in Higher Education*, 24/3, 238–259.

Hou, A. Y. C., Lin, S. R., and Chih, C. C. (2017a). "Termination of program evaluation by the Ministry of Education and responses adopted by universities." *Evaluation Bimonthly*, 67, 7–10.

Hou, A. Y. C., Morse, B., and Wang, W. (2017b). "Recognition of academic qualifications in transnational higher education and challenges for recognizing a joint degree in Europe and Asia." *Studies in Higher Education*, 42/7, 1211–1228.

International Network for Quality Assurance Agencies in Higher Education (INQAAHE) (2019). *Analytic Quality Glossary.* http://www.qualityresearchinternational.com/glossary/#s

Jarvis, D. S. L. (2014). "Regulating higher education: Quality assurance and neo-liberal managerialism in higher education—a critical introduction." *Policy and Society*, 33/3, 155–166.

Jayaram, N. (2013). *Higher Education Reform in India: Prospects and Challenges*. http://www.cshe.nagoya-u.ac.jp/seminar/kokusai/jayaram.pdf

Lemaitre, M. J., Torre, D., Zapata, G., and Zentrno, E. (2011). *Impact of Quality Assurance on University Work: An Overview in Seven Ibero-American Countries*. http://www.copaes.org.mx/home/docs/docs_Proyecto_ALFA_CINDA/Impact percent20ofpercent20QApercent20processespercent20inpercent20LApercent20-percent 20Lemaitrepercent20etpercent20al.pdf

Li, M. and Yang, R. (2011). *Design and Management of Higher Education Systems: The Role of Steering Policies and Governance Reforms in the Management of Higher Education in China*. Mimeo. A study sponsored by IIEP-UNESCO.

Malaysia Qualifications Agency (MQA) (2020a). *Code of Practice*. https://www2.mqa.gov.my/qad/v2/copnew.cfm

Malaysia Qualifications Agency (MQA) (2020b). *Self-Accreditation: List of Higher Education Providers*. https://www2.mqa.gov.my/portal_swa/list_PPT_swa.cfm

Marginson, S., Kaur, S., and Sawir, E. (2011). "Global, local, national in the Asia-Pacific." In S. Marginson, S. Kaur, and E. Sawir (eds.), *Higher Education in the Asia-Pacific*. Dordrecht: Springer, 3–34.

Martin, M. and Stella, A. (2007). *External Quality Assurance in Higher Education: Making Choices*. Paris: International Institute for Educational Planning (IIEP) UNESCO.

Ministry of Education (MOE) (2009). *The Private Higher Education Act*. Singapore: MOE.

Ministry of Education (MOE) (2019a). *Education in Taiwan 2019–2020*. Taipei: MOE.

Ministry of Education (MOE) (2019b). *Major Polices*. https://english.moe.gov.tw/lp-48-1.html

Ministry of Education (MOE) (2021). *Organizational Structure: Higher Education Group*. https://www.moe.gov.sg/about-us/organisation-structure/heg

Ministry of Skill Development and Entrepreneurship (MOSDE) (2020). *National Skills Qualifications Framework (NSQF)*. https://www.msde.gov.in/nsqf.html

Mok, K. H. (ed.) (2013). *Centralization and Decentralization: Educational Reforms and Changing Governance in Chinese Societies*. New York: Springer Science & Business Media.

National Institution for Academic Degrees and Quality Enhancement of Higher Education (NIAD-QE) (2019). *Role of NIAD-QE*. https://www.niad.ac.jp/english/en-about/role.html

Nguyen, K. D., Oliver, D. E., and Priddy, L. E. (2009). "Criteria for accreditation in Vietnam's higher education: Focus on input or outcome?" *Quality in Higher Education*, 15/2, 123–134.

Noda, A., Hou, A. Y. C., Shibui, S., and Chou, H. C. (2018). "Restructuring quality assurance frameworks: A comparative study between NIAD-QE in Japan and HEEACT in Taiwan." *Higher Education Evaluation and Development*, 12/1, 2–18.

Noda, A., Sounghee, K., Hou, A. Y. C., Lu, I. I. G., and Chou, H. C. (2020). "The relationships between internal quality assurance and learning outcome assessments: Challenges confronting universities in Japan and Taiwan." *Quality in Higher Education*, 27/1, 59–76.

OECD (2017). *Education at a Glance*. Paris: OECD.

Oleksenko, R., Molodychenko, V., and Shcherbakova, N. (2018). "Neoliberalism in higher education as a challenge for future civilization." *Philosophy and Cosmology*, 20, 113–119.

Olssen, M. and Peters, M. A. (2005). "Neoliberalism, higher education and the knowledge economy: From the free market to knowledge capitalism." *Journal of Education Policy*, 20/3, 313–345.

Paintsil, R. (2016). "Balancing internal and external quality assurance dynamics in higher education institutions: A case study of University of Ghana." Doctoral thesis, University of Oslo.

Parliament of Malaysia (2007). *Malaysian Qualifications Agency Act 2007*. Kuala Lumpur: The Parliament of Malaysia.

Patil, J. and Pillai, L. (2015). "Quality assurance in Indian higher education: Role of NAAC and future directions." In N. V. Varghese and G. Malik (eds.), *India Higher Education Report 2015*. Abingdon: Routledge, 163–188.

Rowlands, J. (2012). "Accountability, quality assurance and performativity: The changing role of the academic board." *Quality in Higher Education*, 18/1, 97–110.

Saunders, D. B. (2010). "Neoliberal ideology and public higher education in the United States." *Journal for Critical Education Policy Studies*, 8/1, 42–77.

Scott, P. (2017). "Global: International higher education and the 'neo-liberal turn.'" In G. Mihut, P. G. Altbach, and H. de Wit (eds.), *Understanding Higher Education Internationalization*. Rotterdam: Sense Publishers, 73–75.

Shi, X. and Wu, Z. (2018). "Paradigm shift of higher education governance in China." In J. C. Shin (ed.), *Higher Education Governance in East Asia*. Singapore: Springer, 55–72.

Shin, J. C. (2018). "Introduction: Incorporation of National Universities and Governance Reforms." In Higher Education Governance in East Asia, edited by J. C. Shin. Singapore: Springer, 1–20.

SkillsFuture Singapore (2021). *About SkillsFuture*. https://www.skillsfuture.gov.sg/About SkillsFuture

Tan, J. (2013). "Introduction." In UNESCO, *The International Mobility of Students in Asia and the Pacific*. Paris: UNESCO, 1–5.

UNESCO (2015). *Education 2030: Incheon Declaration and Framework for Action for the Implementation of Sustainable Development Goal 4*. http://uis.unesco.org/sites/default/files/documents/education-2030-incheon-framework-foraction-implementation-of-sdg4-2016-en_2.pdf

UNESCO (2021). *Global Flow of Tertiary-Level Students*. http://uis.unesco.org/en/uis-student-flow

Van Vught, P. and de Boer, H. (2015). "Governance models and policy instrument." In J. Huisman, H. de Boer, D. D. Dill, and M. Souto-Otero (eds.), *Palgrave International Handbook of Higher Education Policy and Governance*. New York: Palgrave Macmillan, 35–56.

Vanhoof, J. and Van Petegem, P. (2007). "Matching internal and external evaluation in an era of accountability and school development: Lessons from a Flemish perspective." *Studies in Educational Evaluation*, 33/2, 101–119.

Van Vught, F. A. and Westerheijden, D. F. (1994). "Toward a general model of quality assessment in higher education." *Higher Education*, 28, 355–371.

Varghese, N. V. and Martin, M. (2013). *Governance Reforms and University Autonomy in Asia*. Paris: International Institute for Educational Planning (IIEP), UNESCO.

Vroeijenstijn, T. (2008). *Internal and External Quality Assurance: Why Are They Two Sides of the Same Coin?* http://www.eahep.org/web/images/Bangkok/28_panel_ton.pdf

Wan, C. D. and Morshidi, S. (2018). "The evolution of corporatisation of public universities in Malaysia." In J. C. Shin (ed.), *Higher Education Governance in East Asia*. Singapore: Springer, 89–104.

Wang, L. (2014). "Quality assurance in higher education in China: Control, accountability and freedom." *Policy and Society*, 33/3, 253–262.

Westerheijden, D. F., Stensaker, B., Rosa, M. J. & Corbett, A. (2014). "Next generations, catwalks, random walks and arms races: Conceptualizing the development of quality assurance schemes, " *European Journal of Education*, 49/3, 421–434.

Yamada, R. (2016). "Impact of globalization on Japanese higher education policy: Examining government control and quality assurance." In C. S. Collins, M. N. N. Lee, J. N. Hawkins and D. E. Neubauer (eds.), *The Palgrave Handbook of Asia Pacific Higher Education*. New York: Palgrave Macmillan, 409–421.

Young, M. (2003). "National qualifications frameworks as a global phenomenon." In G. Donn and T. Davies (eds.), *Promises and Problems for Commonwealth Qualifications Frameworks*. London and Wellington: Commonwealth Secretariat and NZQA, 94–106.

Zhuang, T. and Liu, B. (2020). "Power landscapes within Chinese universities: A three-dimensional discourse analysis of university statutes." *Cambridge Journal of Education*, 50/5, 639–656.

CHAPTER 13

....

INTERNATIONALIZATION AND EDUCATION-RELATED MOBILITY IN ASIA-PACIFIC UNIVERSITIES

....

K. C. HO, RAVINDER SIDHU,
AND BRENDA S. A. YEOH

1. INTRODUCTION

It is estimated that Asia as a region hosts more than 1 million internationally mobile students, representing some 21 percent of the world's international students in 2017.[1] Traditional senders of international students such as China, Japan, South Korea, Taiwan, and Singapore are actively developing and promoting "world-class" universities and seeking to attract international students and researchers largely from within the region but also beyond. Since the turn of the twenty-first century, there are signs that the patterns of education-related mobility of the twentieth century which established North America and Europe as premier knowledge destinations are being reconfigured, as seen in the rising research reputations of Asian universities, and the increased circulation of students and scholars within the Asia-Pacific region. Where "soft power" with its attendant aspirations of hegemony and competitive advantage may have characterized earlier expression of education-related mobilities, "knowledge diplomacy"—mutual benefits and reciprocal exchanges—is becoming a more important basis for tertiary education movements in the new century (Knight and De Wit, 2018). If there were any doubts about its merits, the urgency for global cooperation demanded by the COVID-19

---

[1] http://data.uis.unesco.org/Index.aspx?queryid=172

pandemic has reinforced the importance of knowledge diplomacy. We return to this point in our concluding comments.

More than a decade after governments and institutional leaders in the Asia-Pacific region introduced concerted internationalization strategies to retain competitive advantage, this chapter explores what has been achieved and what future challenges confront societies and their seats of higher learning in a context of demographic, geopolitical, and environmental changes. This is accomplished through a focus on the broad and diverse collection of activities, people, programs, and networks that constitute education-related mobilities. The chapter explores three interrelated themes. We begin with an outline of the scale and drivers of international student mobilities within Asia, taking higher education as our focus. This is followed by a discussion of the mobilities of researchers—what enables their movements and their unfolding institutional effects. A third and related theme concerns the impact of education-related mobilities in creating economic and civic possibilities at the multiple scales of the university, city, nation-state, and region. In concluding the chapter, we consider the prospects for equity and knowledge diplomacy by new configurations of mobilities in a world where (dis) connections through territorial, virtual, and emotional borders loom large.

2. STUDENT MOBILITY: DIVERSE TRENDS AND LEGACIES

For much of the twentieth century, Asia was largely perceived as a source of international students heading for European and Anglophone study destinations. Its longstanding reputation as a study destination, forged by hosting students and scholars over decades (and centuries in the cases of China and India), was eclipsed by the second half of the twentieth century. However, by the start of the twenty-first century, as Table 13.1 shows, Asia has reinstated its importance as a space of multidirectional student flows.

The statistical compilation in Table 13.1 is based on an approach which focuses on the host country (column 1), ranked according to total number of international students hosted (column 2), top sources of international students as an indication of the diversity of international student sources (columns 3 to 6), and the inward mobility rate as an indication of the share of international students in the total tertiary enrollment (column 7). For the purposes of comparison, Table 13.1 includes Australia (top hosting country with 444,514 students in 2019) and New Zealand (ranked sixth with 52,702 international students hosted in the same year), as they host significant numbers of students from the region.

The top ten host countries may be placed into three tiers, with three countries—Australia, China, and Japan—hosting more than 100,000 international students at the tertiary level in the first tier. UNESCO does not display statistics on Taiwan but this study destination may be added to the first tier as, according to a news source (Taiwan

Table 13.1 The flow of tertiary international students to selected countries in Asia and Australia, 2019

Host country	Total international students	% from top sender (1)	Top sender (1)	Top sender (2)	Top sender (3)	Inward mobility rate
1. Australia	444,514	32	China (143,323)	India (73,316)	Nepal (32,939)	26.5
2. China	201,177	missing	missing	missing	missing	3.6
3. Japan	182,748	46	China (84,101)	Vietnam (34,276)	Nepal (14,462)	4.7
4. South Korea	84,749	61	China (51,349)	Vietnam (7752)	Mongolia (3438)	2.8
5. Malaysia	81,953	14	China (11,713)	Indonesia (8440)	Bangladesh (6904)	6.7
6. New Zealand	52,702	35	China (18338)	India (11,604)	United States (2736)	19.7
7. Singapore	51,756	missing	missing	missing	missing	missing
8. India	47,424	27	Nepal (12,747)	Afghanistan (4,657)	Bangladesh (2057)	0.1
9. China, Hong Kong	42,641	84	China (35,623)	South Korea (1,498)	India (719)	14.3
10. Thailand	31,571	17	China (5,305)	Myanmar (1,896)	Cambodia (1,031)	1.3

Note: Missing data from China on total international students, missing data from Singapore on sending countries and inward mobility rate.

Source: Derived from UNESCO's database (2020) with 2019 as the reference year. http://uis.unesco.org/en/uis-student-flow Global flow of tertiary-level students.

News, 2019), Taiwan attracted 126,997 foreign students in 2018, making it the fourth largest host of international students in Asia and Australasia. In the next tier, Malaysia, South Korea, Singapore, and New Zealand each host between 50,000 and 100,000 international students. The numbers taper off with India, Hong Kong, and Thailand, each hosting under 50,000 international students. In this tier, India features as a center for sub-regional student flows from neighboring countries Nepal, Afghanistan, and Bangladesh as well as an established destination for the Indian-heritage diaspora in South-East Asia.

Apart from absolute numbers of international students, some researchers such as Kosmaczewska and Barczak (2015, p. 67) use the inbound mobility rate (IMR) as a proxy of the attractiveness of a particular country for foreign students. The three countries with the highest IMRs are Australia (26.5 percent), New Zealand (19.7 percent), and Malaysia (6.7 percent) where a commercial strategy is central to higher education policy (as discussed later). Hong Kong's high IMR (14.3 percent) largely stems from students from mainland China (84 percent of all international students) studying in Hong Kong universities. One could argue as Xu (2017, p. 610) has done that such flows should be seen as intra-state student mobility rather than international student mobility. Countries with low IMR such as South Korea (2.8 percent) and Thailand (1.3 percent) are disadvantaged by the hegemony of English in the global market for higher education. In this regard, perhaps the anomaly is India (0.1 percent), where the medium of instruction is English. International students on Indian campuses are attracted to applied science disciplines, in particular the growth areas of information technology, biomedicine and the cultural industries where India enjoys a global reputation. The internationalization of India's economy has also increased investment and trade inflows from Asian multinationals such as those from Korea and Japan. These developments have the potential of rendering India an attractive study destination for regional students interested in acquiring the social, linguistic, and cultural capital associated with an Indian study experience (Pawar et al., 2020, p. 3248). At the same time, while the country counts esteemed universities such as the Indian Institutes of Information Technologies and National Institutes of Technologies, and the affordances of low tuition fees and living costs, Kumar (2015, pp. 441, 458) notes that these advantages tend to be nullified by regulatory and infrastructure problems, safety concerns, and the lack of scholarships to serve as incentives. He observes that some Indian private institutions have the motivation and demonstrable success in attracting foreign students as a source of revenue, but quality and regulatory barriers hinder India from developing a bigger profile in international student recruitment (Kumar, 2015).

Table 13.1 suggests that tertiary student mobility is largely a regional phenomenon. Until the pandemic-related disruptions to cross-border mobility, the largest number of students sent to a regional destination were those from China who went to Australia (143,323). Besides Australia, the other prominent study destinations for Chinese students are Japan (84,101), South Korea (51,345), Malaysia (11,713), Thailand (5,305), and also the Special Administrative Regions of Hong Kong and Macau. India is one of the top source countries for Australia and New Zealand while Vietnam is a main supplier for Japan and South Korea. There are of course exceptions to these inter-regional flows; for example, of significance is the intercontinental movement of American students to New Zealand for short-term programs.

Regional student mobilities are framed by a highly complex set of drivers. At first glance, the relative popularity of Australia, New Zealand, Singapore, Malaysia, India, and Hong Kong as sites for international student flows is underlined by the strong desire among international students from Asian countries to receive an English-medium education. While an important driver of student movements, a closer examination of international student flows in Asia also reveals significant diversity in terms of the scale of movement, drawing attention to the manner in which mobilities are undergirded by regulatory and commercial infrastructures and personal affinities and aspirations (Sidhu et al., 2020). Developed economies such as Hong Kong, Japan, Singapore, South Korea, and Taiwan have also been experiencing rapid declines in fertility and international students potentially provide the critical numbers for their universities to operate at an effective capacity.

Student mobilities range from large-scale movements associated with commercially delivered international education to smaller-scale mobilities accompanying development assistance or aid programs. Before giving attention to the dynamics driving different kinds of student mobilities, we note the importance of cultural affinities and diasporic connections in shaping the textures of mobility flows across the region. Research has largely focused on the instrumental motivations that prompt cross-border study such as perceived advantages related to international education, as well as post-study employment opportunities (see for example, Yeoh et al., 2014; Collins et al., 2017). Less studied are the relations between destination choices and socio-cultural, linguistic, and religious affinities found in diasporic networks. Yet, inter-regional flows may also draw on imaginative ties that are scripted on the basis of shared language, culture, or religion.

For example, students can choose destinations where cultural distance might be more easily mediated, increasing the opportunities for hospitality. Ethnic Koreans from China, Russia, and Mongolia are favored by South Korean immigration and higher education policies and many are attracted to South Korea's universities for undergraduate and postgraduate education (Kong et al., 2010, p. 260). Chinese Malaysians, especially those schooled in Mandarin, are known to choose mainland China and Taiwan as study destinations. As part of a calculated state policy associated with the Cold War, overseas Chinese students from South-East Asia and Hong Kong were given preferential status for university places in Taiwan up until the end of the 1980s. These ties have helped to consolidate networks that endure to the present (Ma, 2014, pp. 124–125). In this sense, the regional character of student mobility holds out new possibilities to produce an emergent sense of regional solidarity. While ethnic, linguistic, and cultural proximities are often important, in other cases, political differences and animosities between neighboring countries can deter educational exchanges. Thus, while the cultural distance between Thailand and Myanmar may be relatively small, a background of political conflict can present difficulties for sojourning Myanmar students in neighboring Thailand (Rhein, 2017, p. 295).

2.1 Commercially Driven International Education

In terms of large-scale recruitment of international students, New Zealand and Australia are unique in the region as they are the most active providers of full-fee-paying commercial education delivered by public institutions. Australia's position at the head of Table 13.1 in terms of having the largest volume of international students is the result of a higher education policy that has privileged commercial provision, drawing on this revenue to finance its universities. Attracting large numbers of international students has been highly lucrative, with international education contributing an estimated

$37.5 billion to Australia's GDP in 2019–2020.[2] Australian universities have the highest student-to-faculty ratio in the region, the result of a deliberate policy by successive Australian governments to steer universities towards marketization so as to reduce their reliance on government funding. Australia is economically dependent on international students and its universities are reliant on revenue from international students to meet operational costs and subsidize research activities (Jayasuriya, 2020). International education is Australia's largest service export and the fourth largest export industry. Income from international student fees accounts for 21–30 percent of university revenue (Hurley and Van Dyke, 2020). The risks of this market-driven approach to financing higher education have been thrown into sharp relief by the COVID-19 pandemic, rendering fragile the income streams of universities (Jayasuriya, 2020). The political and economic structures which have enabled middle-class families from Asia to finance an Australian higher education could be unsettled by the possibilities of declining economic growth. A debt crisis that affects major markets may force tuition prices down with effects on the mission of universities.

Commercialization dynamics in higher education affects student mobility differently in Malaysia (with 81,953 foreign students). There, international students are largely found in English medium programs in the private higher education sector, with smaller numbers of postgraduate students enrolled in selective English medium courses in public universities. The country's public higher education sector has selectively recruited international students from Muslim majority countries in the Middle East and North Africa, Indonesia, and Bangladesh. Its private higher education institutions on the other hand, have focused on providing a low-cost English medium education to regional students (Knight and Sirat, 2011). Neighboring Singapore also has a thriving commercial higher education sector, established through its "Global Schoolhouse" policy blueprint, which attracts demand from both regional and domestic students (Sidhu et al., 2011, 2020).

Branch campuses have been touted as a possible new model of international education. Australia's international branch campuses in Malaysia and Vietnam are considered success stories although it must be noted that the formulae of success in each case invariably rest on local particularities (Sidhu and Christie, 2014). An emerging middle class with the means to pay tuition fees, state and non-state financial support, and access to well-qualified academic labor in-country are all important considerations. A new phenomenon of branch campuses has recently arisen involving provider institutions from outside of the Anglophone Global North. Xiamen University Malaysia is one such example. Here too, success relies on complex (trans)national ties between localities, polities, and cultures. Notwithstanding these successes, a string of failed initiatives point to the international branch campus as a high-risk strategy (Sidhu and Christie, 2014). At the same time, in the event of a reduction in physical mobility across international

---

[2] Department of Education, Skills & Employment (2019), education export income by financial year 2019–2020. https://internationaleducation.gov.au/research/research-snapshots/pages/default.aspx

borders—a possibility in a post-COVID-19 world—branch campuses may see a rise in popularity (Hou et al., 2018).

A different kind of commercial education export involves the franchising or licensing of British and Australia university curricula to overseas private higher education providers. These modes of commercial education have attracted students from neighboring countries to cities like Singapore, Kuala Lumpur, Hong Kong, and Dubai. The provision of a lower-cost English medium higher education has helped to foster the development of "knowledge cities" and "education hubs." These forms of commercial education also open a space for hybrid providers. Private education institutions, for example, may be linked to large conglomerates with other business interests such as real estate and engineering.

2.2 International Education through Development Assistance

Across East Asia, capacity-building and development assistance feature as important drivers of student mobility, in contrast to countries like Australia where the commercial objective of seeking out fee-paying international students has dwarfed development assistance objectives. Bilateral and multilateral development assistance remains an important feature of international education in East Asia with the wealthier countries of Japan, Singapore, South Korea, Taiwan/Chinese Taipei, and China taking the lead as donors. Middle-income countries such as Thailand and Malaysia are also involved in education-related development assistance (Cheng and Sheng, 2015). East Asian public universities, by far and large, receive subsidies to host international students from governments through various development assistance programs (Yang and Ma, 2015).

Ranked second in Table 13.1, China is both a sender and a receiver of students (UNESCO, 2014, pp. 18–20). The country's mission to carve a new position for itself as a world power in the international order of nation-states—its soft power aspirations—articulates with the internationalization strategies of its universities (see also Yang and Ma, 2015). The aim is to increase international student numbers, with the objective that such students have the ability to "understand China and [can] contribute to connecting China to the rest of the world" (Wu, 2019, p. 9). As part of its Education Strategy, China's proposed Belt and Road Initiative can be expected to facilitate regionalization of tertiary education by increasing its attractiveness as a study destination.

As the original vanguard of modernization, and the largest donor of bilateral aid in Asia, Japan and its universities—public and private—are considered attractive options by regional international students (Ishikawa, 2011). The regional reach of the country's multinational corporations helps to produce a perception of scientific and technological expertise, and along with the availability of scholarships for international students makes Japan an attractive study destination. Two key policy goals have also enabled the flows of international students into the country: an official target of attracting

300,000 international students into universities and boosting the number of Japanese universities ranked within "world-class" rankings as indicated on the Top Global Universities platform (Ishikawa, 2011).

On a smaller scale, Singapore prioritizes higher education scholarships to ASEAN (Association of Southeast Asian Nations) applicants, and those from China and India, with a smaller number directed for individuals from the rest of the world. These are offered by various government bodies, universities, and philanthropic foundations.

Multilateral development assistance schemes such as those offered by ASEAN are important drivers of regional education mobility. Such initiatives seek to improve diplomatic ties, capacity-building, and economic exchanges. Examples include regional language learning programs and academic exchange programs fostered through the ASEAN university network (AUN), the ASEAN Graduate Business and Economics Programme, the ASEAN-China Business School Network, and ASEAN Plus Three (Akhir, 2016). While student numbers are currently small, these schemes could be seen as precursors of future trends where a regional bloc provides the rationale and impetus for higher education ties to develop among member countries. Strategically, education-focused partnerships allow partner countries to demonstrate their engagement, commitment and goodwill within their neighborhood. They foster networks that are intended to facilitate people-to-people connections. A diplomatic rationale underpins these schemes: they are designed to inspire international students to form positive impressions of the host country and develop political affinities that support modes of mutual understanding including those in the host country's interests. However, assumptions that students will necessarily act as "ambassadors" to further the interests of the host country deserve critical scrutiny, a point we return to later in the chapter.

2.3 Virtual Learning and the Growth of MOOCs

The acronym MOOC (massive open online courses) describes a new teaching movement that has developed since 2011. While online courses have existed prior to MOOCs, the openness (available to anyone with internet connections) holds out the potential to reach the multitudes—people from all walks of life and in different regions of the world. These features promise a cost-effective and egalitarian alternative to traditional models of higher education learning (Al-Imarah and Shields, 2019). Indeed, the numbers of MOOCs have grown explosively, from 3 modules in October 2011 to 2,090 in December 2014 and 7,465 in June 2017[3] (Chronicle of Higher Education, 2017). We expect the growth to continue in the coming years.

Despite an encouraging growth trajectory, MOOCs face a number of unresolved limitations with consequences for their financial viability in the future. One key problem

---

[3] "The number of massive open online courses is tracked by Class Central, a search engine for online courses and MOOCs. Each course is counted only once, no matter how many times it was offered" (*Chronicle of Higher Education*, August 18, 2017).

is the low completion rates for MOOCs' enrollees. Completion rates are estimated at less than 13 percent (Porter, 2015, p. 8) and have remained sluggish over time (Reich and Ruipérez-Valiente, 2019). Two points are noteworthy in thinking about completion rates. First, as Ebben and Murphy (2014, p. 338) suggest, MOOCs' marketing power rests on cost-free entry, and this feature also allows learners to be selective in deciding which sections of a course and module might be useful to them. From a learning perspective, MOOCs allow users the freedom and flexibility to acquire information that is relevant to them, thus facilitating adult and lifelong learning goals. Second, low completion rates have also been attributed to low levels of user resilience. In the absence of face-to-face, real-time contact, users who have already received higher education and are socialized into a regime of self-regulated learning are more likely to benefit than novice learners (Meinel and Schweiger, 2016, p. 2). The financial sustainability of any MOOC initiative rests on cultivating a balance between these two learner profiles: those who come and go, taking what is relevant, and a smaller population of follow-through users who are more likely to complete courses and pay for certification This latter group of users are sought by MOOC operators to ensure sustainable revenue streams. Current business models involve partnering with high-ranking universities on the premise that brand recognition and course quality will motivate users to pay (Ebben and Murphy, 2014, p. 341; Ivancheva et al., 2020, p. 615). MOOCs' sustainability, put simply, depends upon developing models with the right combination of learners, delivery modes, and business models (Porter, 2015, p. 4). For these reasons, early predictions that MOOCs would disrupt higher education have not been realized (Al-Imarah and Shields, 2019, p. 266).

Selective universities in Asia have used MOOCs as a marketing and profile-building strategy, to draw attention to their specific areas of expertise (Fox, 2016, pp. 160, 170; Jung and Bajracharya, 2016, p. 158). While such modules can reach an international audience, challenges remain as to whether inter-university collaboration based on the MOOCs model can foster regional solidarity in Asia. At one level, the prospect of cooperating to produce core curricula and certification drawing on the strengths of national systems seems attractive. On the other hand, studies of Asian-based MOOCs projects point to the widespread use of English as a medium of instruction, a trend that stands to enhance the hegemonic status of English (Trehan et al., 2017, p. 153; King et al., 2018, p. 5). In summing up, we draw on Toyama's prescient explanatory tool of "amplification" to assess the potential of a MOOCs-driven project of region-making. Toyama (2005, 2015) argues that "technology amplifies underlying human forces." Thus, MOOCs in Asia, if delivered in English, can be expected to amplify benefits for the region's Anglophone, university-educated groups. Because English competencies are unevenly distributed in the region, MOOCs may simply reproduce elite privileges, doing little to alleviate regional socio-economic and educational inequalities. In a context of rising populism and inequality, technology dominated development may even amplify division. Finally, nascent attempts at using MOOCs for region-making to the exclusion of other reciprocally beneficial projects can be expected to amplify existing divisions between the better-resourced higher education systems and those with poor financing and governance structures.

2.4 Embedding Mobility Experiences in Building International Curricula

Regional mobilities are also embedded in, and enabled by the internationalization strategies of Asia's universities. As part of their mission to become international and global, universities, notably those with resources and connections have structured in mobility experiences into their educational programs as part of an approach to "internationalize the curriculum" (Green and Whitsed, 2015). Students have been encouraged to participate in cross-border exchanges, either in institutions of broadly equivalent standing through credit transfer arrangements, or through a looser set of associations between university departments and individual academics. For graduate students, mobility experiences enable them to network with key researchers in their field, to showcase their work and extend their knowledge of techniques and methodologies. Mobility experiences in the Global North are privileged, either by universities or individual students. These developments, positive on the one hand, also risk producing an Anglophone-dominated mode of internationalization in which English language competencies are privileged above other languages and knowledges (Phan, 2013). The prominence of digital learning in mitigating the educational disruptions of the COVID-19 pandemic has prompted the question of whether a MOOCs-delivered internationalized curriculum could facilitate regional sociabilities. Drawing on Toyama's (2005, 2015) idea of amplification, we concede that a MOOCs delivered international education may hold some value for Asia's elite and middling orders. However, in isolation technologically mediated international education is unlikely to foster the broad and enduring solidarities—an Asian cosmopolitanism-from-below—required for political, economic, and social changes.

Some universities are in the enviable position of establishing overseas centers or overseas colleges in targeted cities and countries. Centers act as small satellites for the home campus, a conduit for internships, work integrated learning, and research fieldwork. They are also used for promotional, recruitment and fund-raising activities and for delivering professional development courses in areas where universities claim expertise. Their presence opens up practical and imaginative spaces for program diversifications and curricular innovations. As such, these satellites both sponsor and draw on broader projects of education mobilities.

3. Mobile Researchers and Emerging International Research Networks

Research movements are less studied than student flows but are no less important because of the tangible and intangible benefits and impacts associated with their research networks. Like their counterparts in the Global North, public universities in Asia and Australasia have embarked on improving their research capacities, often as a response to state policies to diversify economic activities towards value-added production. Universities seeking to position themselves as "world-class" have drawn on these projects, adopting a host of strategies used by universities in the Global North where academic capitalism had taken hold.

It is also important that researcher mobility is not portrayed in singular ways, simply as a series of transactional moves for positional competition. Mobile researchers located in collegial collaborative research networks are well-positioned to improve research knowledges. Their varied backgrounds, geographical locations, and experiences, when subject to critical examinations, contestations, and negotiations, stand to produce new insights and capabilities (Lund et al., 2016). In the STEM disciplines, established researchers who move across borders are recognized as "knowledge spill-over agents" providing significant opportunities for experiential learning for emerging researchers in a range of activities from publishing to the broad swathe of projects associated with academic capitalism such as the commercialization of intellectual property and the development of start-ups (Shen, 2018, p. 230).

The statistics compiled for international students are not available for researchers and we use international collaborations as a way of understanding how researchers and their ideas, skillsets and practices move and are generative of further mobilities. In recent years, bibliometric studies of research collaborations have emerged using patents and publications as two key measures. In using these measures to approximate international collaborations, we make three interrelated points. First, such measures not only capture collaborations between researchers but the use of patents as a measure of collaboration also includes partnerships between researchers and companies. In this regard, Crescenzi et al. (2017, p. 733) note that while scientific publications are a useful measure of international collaborations, this indicator downplays the contribution of technology companies. Second, the Schumpeterian thesis—that there are positive correlations between a country's technological capacity and its economic and geopolitical status—has informed the diplomatic, higher education, and R&D policy fields of many countries. While these policy imaginaries might drive researcher mobilities, framing their subsequent patterns, momentum, and destinations, they also raise the specter of greater economic and geopolitical rivalry. And third, following Bubela et al. (2010, p. 29), researchers who develop an appetite for patents and commercial research are less likely to engage in published research. A division of labor between those who engage in patenting activity and those who publish raises longer-term challenges about the link between R&D and the public good.

This short elaboration of publications and patents as bibliometric measures and the strategic motivations behind researchers and companies enables a better appreciation of the sometimes conflicting results that try to measure research collaboration. The measure (publications versus patents) used tends to influence the results. For example, Lee and Haupt (2020) who use publications as a bibliometric measure find growth in US–China collaborations from 2015 to 2019, even in the face of a trade war, accusations of commercial theft, and national security concerns. The study by Tsukada and Nagaoka

(2015. pp. 100–102) which uses international co-inventions (ICIs) in patent applications shows high research productivity in China but a small percentage from international collaboration over time, with a similar trend observed for Japan and South Korea. Thus, patents as a bibliometric indicator require the inclusion of partnerships with companies, and in the East Asian countries the dominant mode is partnership with domestic companies. Thus, what we see from this set of papers is that international collaborations in terms of co-publications may be increasing, suggesting increased mobility between researchers in Asia with other parts of the world. However, commercial-in-confidence and national economic security concerns of the type identified by Lee and Haupt (2020) are co-present, and operate as deterrents to international collaboration for innovation. In a world where national economic security concerns have been heightened, university researchers who work with domestic firms are expected to protect intellectual property and file for patents. Japan and South Korea—home to global conglomerates—have accelerated the push to amplify existing industry–university partnerships with state support (Han and Kim, 2016).

The time period chosen for a study also influences the results. Hu et al. (2020), using co-publication metrics for 1980 to 1984 and 2015 to 2019, noted that China, South Korea, and Japan experienced significant declines in international collaboration size (the number of countries in the publication team). Their analysis suggests that while China produces many papers (ranked fourth in authorship among major publication active countries in the 2015–2019 period), China researchers do so with fewer outsiders compared to the 1980 to 1984 period. The same trend applies for Japan and South Korea. Hu et al. (2020, p. 737) suggest that the rapid development of these countries has turned researchers towards co-nationals for publications.

The pattern which arises for these disparate findings suggests that China and the United States have co-published more together over time (as Lee and Haupt, 2020 suggested). It is important to note that the large numbers are also because co-publication measures include applied and non-applied sciences. Over time from the mid-1980s to 2019, China, while publishing significantly more, has reduced its publication collaboration with other countries, *when ranked against* what other countries (especially European countries where research funds encourage international and regional collaborations) are doing (as Hu et al., 2020 suggested). In patents, China has become even more exclusive, choosing mainly domestic companies for such activities as Tsukada and Nagaoka (2015) have suggested.

In concluding this section, we note that mobile researchers facilitate all kinds of knowledge exchanges from those that are framed by national and institutional projects of competitive advantage, to individual desires to seek positional goods and expand research capabilities. People-to-people collaborations and friendships are also important in creating possibilities for knowledge diplomacy, a point we return to in a later part of this chapter. Mobile students and researchers can release the potential for new imaginaries, knowledges, and capabilities to take hold. As we discuss below, through these mobilities opportunities emerge to refashion the university and its relationship with the cities and regions in which it is placed.

4. Impacts of Education-Related Movements on Cities and Regions

A focus on education-related mobilities reveals the potential for universities to engage the hopes and dreams of new generations of learners and to bring together insight and foresight, knowledge, expertise, and ethical oversight to global, national, and local problems. Students are steered to choose a university not only because of the attractiveness of its programs and research profiles, but also because of the institution's access to entertainment, consumption, recreation and leisure facilities, and opportunities for employability. The arrival of international students potentially changes the urban fabric of cities, reinvigorating retail activities by bringing in demand for particular kinds of housing, food, and other merchandise as well as a broad range of cultural and religious activities and practices. The more visible outcome of international student and scholar mobilities are encounters that enable multicultural mixing, which in the best of scenarios helps to re-mold cities into spaces of intercultural understanding and mutual respect (Bennett et al., 2017, p. 2319). Urban localities and materialities such as shopping precincts, university classrooms, labs and libraries, shared student houses and places of worship, are settings for a range of social practices. From volunteering, to the observances of prayer and ritual, playing sport and participating in student politics, possibilities are opened for difference to be navigated and for conviviality and friendship to emerge (Robertson, 2018). Intercultural mixing outside of co-national friendship groups is often portrayed as an anomaly by the sojourner adjustment literature. According to this well-established body of work, culture shock and language shock lead students to cluster with co-nationals, reducing the possibilities of building enduring intercultural social networks and predisposing students to loneliness (see for example Furnam and Bochner, 1986). More recent work, in contrast, highlights the study sojourn as a series of encounters that enable cosmopolitan sociabilities and friendship networks to develop (Rizvi, 2011). Our own study of interviews with international students drawn from nine campuses in five countries (China, Japan, South Korea, Singapore, and Taiwan) found that while there are clearly many reasons for networks to be formed among co-nationals (Sidhu et al., 2020, pp. 94, 97), international students also find many instances where they form close friendships with local students and other international students through mutual help in assignments, residential living opportunities, and other campus opportunities (Sidhu et al., 2020, pp. 91, 101, 104–105). International students, research suggests, are likely to form friendships with both local and other international students when they share interests, religious beliefs, ethnicity, and language (Gomes et al., 2014; Robertson, 2018; Sidhu et al., 2020). An interesting finding to emerge from this body of work points to international study in potentially strengthening regional relations as students are more likely to establish friendships with other international students from the same region (Gomes et al., 2014).

University teaching and learning plans and internationalization policies are also increasingly paying more attention to facilitating interactions between domestic and international students, both for the purposes of furthering subject-based learning and to enable all students to acquire global graduate competencies such as intercultural skills and capabilities of critical and ethical judgment (Campbell, 2011; Volet and Ang, 2012; Arkoudis et al., 2013). These initiatives are often responding to requirements set by industry and professional bodies for more well-rounded graduates in a context where professionals are expected to work effectively in multicultural teams.

That stated, it must be acknowledged that educational initiatives to produce intercultural understanding are often unevenly rolled out; their success may be compromised by large classes and overcrowded and content-driven curricula. Further and notably, financial pressures on domestic and international students significantly reduce the time both groups might spend on campus as students seek to support themselves through part-time work (Arkoudis et al., 2013). There is hence a need to attend to creating appropriate pedagogical and organizational contexts to further enable intercultural mixing and host/international student relations to flourish (see also Gu et al., 2010; Robertson, 2018; Koh and Harris, 2020).

Universities, cities, and regions have been the sites of a raft of post-industrial strategies to establish service and knowledge economies, often in a bid to reignite economic growth and vitality. Some countries like Australia, New Zealand, and Singapore have introduced policies articulating international education with skilled migration. Australia's policies have been emulated by other OECD countries, even though its effects have been contested. Australia introduced a "2-step migration policy" in 2001 which allowed international students to transition into permanent residents, both as a measure to make its international education sector attractive to students, and also as a means of ensuring the country's attractiveness to skilled migrants. This policy led to a rapid increase in international student enrollments but raised concerns about admissions and progression standards, and declining educational quality and uncertain employment outcomes for newly minted Australian permanent residents (Robertson, 2015). Eight years after its introduction, the policy was moderated, with students and graduates bearing the risks of fallout. However, post-study work rights for former international students remains a policy instrument to make Australia a desirable study destination. The outcomes of this study migration regime though are uneven. While three-quarters of graduates surveyed by an industry body were found to be in full- or part-time employment, only a modest proportion had been able to secure work commensurate with their qualifications (IEAA, 2019). The road to permanent residency, even for those in appropriate employment, has involved long processing times, and onerous language restrictions. International education has been associated with producing a sizable cohort of precariously situated "non-citizens" (Robertson, 2015). Attempts to reconfigure the policy terrain by requiring graduates to obtain employer sponsorship as a safeguard has created other challenges such as subjecting recent graduates to exploitation at the hands of employers (Robertson, 2018).

Outside of Australia, concrete data about the employment outcomes of international students into Pacific Asian campuses is hard to source. Government and industry leaders tend to be positive about the contributions made to the economies of cities and regions by inflows of tertiary educated young people. However, uneven post-study work rights and the large number of private universities in some countries raises the specter of an education-migration nexus that lends itself to labor recruitment. Some graduates who remain in the host country to work have witnessed positive employment outcomes particularly in Japan, while countries like Taiwan facing a tighter labor market for university graduates have stricter after-study work restrictions (Collins et al., 2017). Cities like Singapore with more dynamic urban economies and cosmopolitan culture have emerged as a top after-study work choice not only for international students studying in Singapore, but also from other universities in the region (Ho, 2014, p. 166).

As discussed earlier, at the economic and technological levels, universities are important facilitators of knowledge creation and knowledge transfer spaces, fueled by the movements and embodied encounters of graduate students, postdoctoral fellows, researchers, and professors. Beyond their contributions to inspire innovations in medicine, science, and technology, universities contribute to progressive ideals of rights and justice. Increasingly, across Pacific Asia, universities are discouraged from appearing aloof towards the localities in which they are placed. Young people are increasingly looking to their universities to take a different role from being producer of human capital, to being the conscience of society (Cheng and Jacobs, 2020). More and more institutions are participating in urban programs to address their public service missions (Liu, 2017, p. 138). Mobile graduate students and faculty give weight to these contributions, embodying potentially new practices and philosophies. Ideas germinate in universities and these are transported further afield, mutating as they move into new contexts, in some settings shape-shifting into policies.

The university of the twentieth century was resolutely modernist and nation-centered. In the twenty-first century, universities would do well to address ways of transcending nationalist sentiments that are currently on the rise in many parts of the world. If any doubt existed previously, crises such as the COVID-19 pandemic suggest that economic, medical, social, and environmental problems demand recognition of the mutual interdependencies that bind the people and communities within Pacific Asia and beyond. Educational encounters such as those sponsored by mobile students and researchers prompt dialogue. By broadening imaginative horizons beyond nationalism, education-related mobilities stake out common ground for managing the challenges of economic justice, air, food, water, and energy security, as well as disaster mitigation (Asian Development Bank, 2018; Sidhu et al., 2020).

5. CONCLUSION

Pacific Asia's higher education institutions are caught up in policy deliberations about education's responsibilities for meeting local, national, and regional challenges.

In this concluding section we turn a question posed elsewhere by scholars of internationalization:

> Who could have forecasted that internationalisation would transform from what has been traditionally considered a process based on values of cooperation, partnership, exchange, mutual benefits and capacity building to one that is increasingly characterised by competition, commercialisation, self-interest and status building? (Knight and de Wit, 2018)

Internationalization has moved from the margins of higher education to assuming a central position in the vision and mission of universities worldwide. However, the dominance of economic and political rationales in framing internationalization agendas has militated against a comprehensive, ethical internationalization that fosters diversity, social inclusion, gender equity, and environmental sustainability. Whether through reputation-assembling exercises or outright commodification practices, universities have deferred to varying degrees to the overriding demands of the market, and the effects of these engagements have ranged from the benign to the malignant.

An important and emerging role is for universities to foster knowledge diplomacy—that is, build and strengthen relations between countries and regions—through international higher education (Knight, 2019). Universities have always played vital if understated roles in international relations through their activities—from fellowships to facilitate the movement of influential thinkers and scholars and the granting of honorary degrees to political leaders, to cross-border curriculum development (see Irish, 2015). The pandemic-driven vulnerabilities and disruptions of 2020 have revealed the importance of global cooperation through research and research exchanges to produce public health measures that mitigate the harm caused by the coronavirus.

Although still evolving, the post-COVID-19 context offers a chance to pause and reconsider new possibilities of international higher education. For some, the pandemic is an opportunity to re-purpose universities through virtual learning by making them more accessible to all. Virtual learning, it is argued, will enable new modes of sociality and new forms of pedagogic and cultural exchanges between geographically dispersed universities (Peters et al., 2020). There is the promise of a reduced carbon footprint as fewer people have to travel for work or study although left unexplored is the question of how burgeoning e-waste—currently packed off to poor developing countries where the hazards of recycling are borne by the poorest—will be handled (Morgan, 2015). For others, like Toyama (2015) virtual learning's emancipatory promises deserve interrogation. Technology, they argue, has been a loyal servant of capitalism, and virtual learning will amplify existing inequities, potentially accelerating the relentless march towards the commodification of education. All of these debates point to the indispensable function of universities to make a space to debate the value of things that are not (yet) valued by societies at large (Boulton and Lucas, 2011). It is timely that universities reclaim their creativity and leadership in a world demanding radical solutions to the problems of global interconnectivity.

Many promising starting points can be identified: the United Nations' sustainable development framework—with its focus on "people, planet and prosperity"

(3P framework) is one set of ideas that may open up possibilities for curricular innovations. Through these initiatives, universities can play their part in fostering new ways of knowing and working, ensuring more ethical engagements with non-human worlds. The post-pandemic world requires universities to take seriously the demands of knowledge creation for a changed world.

But the final destination of every progressive project is fraught with the ever-present danger that more of the same will be rolled out. World-class indicators of research productivity may not recognize the new and the bold. There are clear signs that the 3P framework too is susceptible to commercialization, reinstating staggering profits for financial entities under the guise of doing something for the planet and for people (Webber, 2017). Across the Asia-Pacific region, a pervasive technocratic sensibility has invested hope in STEM disciplines, valorizing singular solutions, with effects that are simply unsustainable. In other settings, notably Australasia, universities and their commercially driven modes of international education have supplanted intercultural understanding and "global citizenship." Encounters in classrooms and through the curriculum suggest that divisions based on race, gender, language, and nationhood prevail. In other settings, universities have been conscripted into perpetuating state agendas, largely steeped in the language of competition, hegemony, and fear of being left behind. In other words, international education in its current form can perpetuate the economic, racial, and cultural divisions that have rendered Asia fragile to many colonialisms—external and internal.

Many of the social gains made by half a century of development through compressed modernization are fragile in the face of financial and health crises and climate-related natural disasters. Across the Asia-Pacific region, inequality is on the rise, and the death knell sounds each day for the destruction of habitats and species, producing new and potentially deadly microbes and diseases while displacing people and disrupting livelihoods. A global health and economic crisis like COVID-19 opens a space to re-think the manner in which we have assembled our universities as places of learning and knowledge-making. World-class indicators can only take Asia-Pacific universities so far, as do the attempts to seek inspiration from universities in the Global North. Narrow employability agendas so beloved of governments will need shaking up as we face uncertain futures. Above all, there are pressing questions upon us, as we reconsider the fabric of our being, who we are, and our responsibilities to future generations of species.

References

Akhir, A. M. (2016). "Regional cooperation in education in ASEAN and East Asia." In S. Wajjwalku, K. C. Ho, and O. Yoshida (eds.), *Advancing the Regional Commons in the New East Asia*. New York: Routledge, 96–118.

Al-Imarah, A. A. and Shields, R. (2019). "MOOCs, disruptive innovation and the future of higher education: A conceptual analysis." *Innovations in Education and Teaching International*, 56/3, 258–269.

Arkoudis, S., Watty, K., Baik, C., Yu, X., Borland, H., Chang, S., Lang, I., Lang, J., and Pearce, A. (2013). "Finding common ground: Enhancing interaction between domestic and international students in higher education." *Teaching in Higher Education*, 18/3, 222–235.

Asian Development Bank (2018). *Towards Optimal Provision of Regional Public Goods in Asia and the Pacific.* https://aric.adb.org/pdf/aeir/AEIR2018_theme-chapter-toward-optimal-provision-of-regional-public-goods-in-asia-and-the-pacific.pdf

Bennett, K., Cochrane, A., Mohan, G., and Neal, S. (2017). "Negotiating the educational spaces of urban multiculture: Skills, competencies and college life." *Urban Studies*, 54/10, 2305–2321.

Boulton, G. and Lucas, C. (2011). "What are universities for?" *Chinese Science Bulletin*, 56, 2506–2517.

Bubela, T., Strotmann, A., Adams, R., and Morrison, S. (2010). "Commercialization and collaboration: Competing policies in publicly funded stem cell research?" *Cell Stem Cell*, 7/1, 25–30.

Campbell, N. (2011). "Promoting intercultural contact on campus: A project to connect and engage international and host students." *Journal of Studies in International Education*, 16/3, 205–227.

Cheng, I. and Sheng, J. C. (eds.) (2015). *International Education Aid in Developing Asia Policies and Practices.* Singapore: Springer.

Cheng, Y. and Jacobs, J. (2020). "Urban custodians and hospitable citizens: Citizenship and social actions at two liberal arts universities in Hong Kong and Shanghai." *Space and Polity*, 24/1, 12–29.

Chronicle of Higher Education (2017). "Cumulative growth in number of MOOCs, 2011–2017." *Chronicle of Higher Education*, 63/43.

Collins, F. L., Ho, K. C., Ishikawa, M., and Ma, A. H. S. (2017). "International student mobility and after-study lives: The portability and prospects of overseas education in Asia." *Population, Space and Place*, 23/4, e2029.

Crescenzi, R., Filippetti, A., and Iammarino, S. (2017). "Academic inventors: Collaboration and proximity with industry." *The Journal of Technology Transfer*, 42/4, 730–762.

Ebben, M. and Murphy, J. S. (2014). "Unpacking MOOC scholarly discourse: A review of nascent MOOC scholarship." *Learning, Media and Technology*, 39/3, 328–345.

Fox, R. (2016). "MOOC impact beyond innovation." In C. Ng, R. Fox, and M. Nagano (eds.), *Reforming Learning and Teaching in Asia-Pacific Universities.* Singapore: Springer, 159–172.

Furnam, A. and Bochner, S. (1986). *Culture Shock: Psychological Reactions to Unfamiliar Environments.* London: Methuen.

Gomes, C., Berry, M., Alzougool, B., and Chang, S. (2014). "Home and away: International students and their identity-based social networks in Australia." *Journal of International Students*, 4/1, 2–15.

Green, W. and Whitsed, C. (eds.) (2015). *Critical Perspectives on Internationalising the Curriculum in Disciplines.* Leiden: Brill.

Gu, Q., Schweisfurth, M., and Day, C. (2010). "Learning and growing in a 'foreign' context: Intercultural experiences of international students." *Compare*, 40/1, 7–23.

Han, J. and Kim, J. (2016). "Empirical analysis of technology transfer in Korean universities." *International Journal of Innovation Management*, 20/08, 1640018.

Ho, K. C. (2014). "The university's place in Asian cities." *Asia Pacific Viewpoint*, 55/2, 156–168.

Hou, A. Y. C., Hill, C., Chen, K. H. J., and Tsai, S. (2018). "A comparative study of international branch campuses in Malaysia, Singapore, China, and South Korea: Regulation, governance, and quality assurance." *Asia Pacific Education Review*, 19/4, 543–555.

Hu, Z., Tian, W., Guo, J., and Wang, X. (2020). "Mapping research collaborations in different countries and regions: 1980–2019." *Scientometrics*, 124/31, 729–745.

Hurley, P. and Van Dyke, N. (2020). *Australian Investment in Education: Higher Education.* Melbourne: Mitchell Institute.

IEAA (International Education Association of Australia) (2019). *Economic Opportunities and Outcomes of Post-Study Work Rights in Australia.* https://www.ieaa.org.au/research/post-study-work-rights

Irish, T. (2015). "From international to inter-allied: Transatlantic university relations in the era of the First World War, 1905–1920." *Journal of Transatlantic Studies*, 13/4, 311–325.

Ishikawa, M. (2011). "Redefining internationalization in higher education: Global 30 and the making of global universities in Japan." In D. B. Willis and J. Rappleye (eds.), *Reimagining Japanese Education: Borders, Transfers, Circulations.* Oxford Studies in Comparative Education, 193–224.

Ivancheva, M. P., Swartz, R., Morris, N. P., Walji, S., Swinnerton, B. J., Coop, T., and Czerniewicz, L. (2020). "Conflicting logics of online higher education." *British Journal of Sociology of Education*, 41/5, 608–625.

Jayasuriya, K. (2020). "COVID 10 has revealed a crisis in Australian higher education governance." *Times Higher Education Supplement,* April 24.

Jung, I. and Bajracharya, J. (2016). "Applications of digital technologies in liberal arts institutions in East Asia." In I. Jung, M. Nishimura, and T. Sasao (eds.), *Liberal Arts Education and Colleges in East Asia.* Singapore: Springer, 151–163.

King, M., Pegrum, M., and Forsey, M. (2018). "MOOCs and OER in the Global South: Problems and potential." *The International Review of Research in Open and Distributed Learning*, 19/5. https://doi.org/10.19173/irrodl.v19i5.3742

Knight, J. (2019). "Clarifying misconceptions about knowledge diplomacy." *University Global News,* August 31. https://www.universityworldnews.com/post.php?story=20190816144922180

Knight, J. and De Wit, H. (2018). "What contributions have internationalisation made to higher education?" *University Global News,* October 12. https://www.universityworldnews.com/post.php?story=20181010093946721

Knight, J. and Sirat, M. (2011). "The complexities and challenges of regional education hubs: Focus on Malaysia." *Higher Education*, 62/5, 593–606.

Koh, S. Y. and Harris, A. (2020). "Multicultural reflexivity: University students negotiating 'pockets' and 'strings' of multiculturalism in Malaysia." *Children's Geographies*, 18/6, 712–725.

Kong, D., Yoon, K., and Yu, S. (2010). "The social dimensions of immigration in Korea." *Journal of Contemporary Asia*, 40/2, 252–274.

Kosmaczewska, J. and Barczak, M (2015). "Explaining and measuring attractiveness of different countries: Evidence from the Visegrad group." *Acta Prosperitatis*, 6, 64–74.

Kumar, S. (2015). "India's trade in higher education." *Higher Education*, 70/3, 441–467.

Lee, J. J. and Haupt, J. P. (2020). "Winners and losers in US–China scientific research collaborations." *Higher Education*, 80, 57–74.

Liu, C. (2017). "The tensions of university–city relations in the knowledge society." *Education and Urban Society*, 51/1, 120–143.

Lund, K., Kusakabe, K., Panda, S., and Wang, Y. (2016). "Building knowledge across transnational boundaries: Collaboration and friendship in research." *Emotion, Space and Society*, 20, 18–24.

Ma, A. H. S. (2014). "The development of international student recruitment policies in Taiwan: A 60-year trajectory." *Journal of Studies in International Education*, 18/2, 120–140.

Meinel, C. and Schweiger, S. (2016). "A virtual social learner community: Constitutive element of MOOCs." *Education Sciences*, 6/3, 22.

Morgan, K. (2015). "Is there a future for e-waste recycling?" *Renewable and Sustainable Energy Reviews*. https://www.elsevier.com/atlas/story/resources/is-there-a-future-for-e-waste-recycling-yes,-and-its-worth-billions

Pawar, S. K., Vispute, S., and Wasswa, H. (2020). "Perceptions of international students in Indian higher education campuses." *Qualitative Report*, 25/9, 3240–3254.

Peters, M., Rizvi, F., McCulloch, G., Gibbs, P., Gorur, R., et al. (2020). "Reimagining the new pedagogical possibilities for universities post-Covid-19." *Educational Philosophy and Theory*. https://doi.org/10.1080/00131857.2020.1777655

Phan, L. H. (2013). "Issues surrounding English, the internationalization of higher education and national identity in Asia: A focus on Japan." *Critical Studies in Education*, 54/2, 160–175.

Porter, S. (2015). *To MOOC or Not to MOOC: How Can Online Learning Help to Build the Future of Higher Education?* Waltham, MA: Chandos Publishing.

Reich, J. and Ruipérez-Valiente, J. A. (2019). "The MOOC pivot." *Science*, 363/6423, 130–131.

Rhein, D. (2017). "International higher education in Thailand: Challenges within a changing context." *Journal of Alternative Perspectives in the Social Sciences*, 8/3, 281–298.

Rizvi, F. (2011). "Theorizing student mobility in an era of globalization." *Teacher & Teaching*, 17/6, 693–701.

Robertson, S. (2015). "Contractualization, depoliticization and the limits of solidarity: Noncitizens in contemporary Australia." *Citizenship Studies*, 19/8, 936–995.

Robertson, S. (2018). "Friendship networks and encounters in student-migrants' negotiations of translocal subjectivity." *Urban Studies*, 55/3, 538–553.

Shen, W. (2018). "Transnational research training: Chinese visiting doctoral students overseas and their host supervisors." *Higher Education Quarterly*, 72/3, 224–236.

Sidhu, R. and Christie, P. (2014). "Making space for an international branch campus." *Asia Pacific Viewpoint*, 55/2, 182–195.

Sidhu, R. K., Ho, K. C., and Yeoh, B. S. (2011). "Emerging education hubs: The case of Singapore." *Higher Education*, 61, 23–40.

Sidhu, R. K., Ho, K. C., and Yeoh, B. S. (2020). *Student Mobilities and International Education in Asia: Emotional Geographies of Knowledge Spaces.* Cham: Springer.

Taiwan News (2019). "Foreign students in Taiwan 10% of total university and college students in 2018." *Taiwan News*, February 3. https://www.taiwannews.com.tw/en/news/3631340

Toyama, K. (2005). *Geek Heresy: Rescuing Social Change from the Cult of Technology.* New York: Public Affairs Books.

Toyama, K. (2015). "Why technology will never fix education." *Chronicle of Higher Education*, May 19. https://www.chronicle.com/article/why-technology-will-never-fix-education/

Trehan, S., Sanzgiri, J., Li, C., Wang, R., and Joshi, R. (2017). "Critical discussions on the massive open online course (MOOC) in India and China." *International Journal of Education and Development using ICT*, 13/2, 141–165.

Tsukada, N. and Nagaoka, S. (2015). "Determinants of international research collaboration: Evidence from international co-inventions in Asia and Major OECD countries." *Asian Economic Policy Review*, 10/1, 96–119.

UNESCO Institute for Statistics (2014). *Higher Education in Asia: Expanding Out, Expanding Up: The Rise of Graduate Education and University Research.* UNESCO.

Volet, S. and Ang, G. (2012). "Culturally mixed groups on international campuses: An opportunity for inter-cultural learning." *Higher Education Research & Development*, 31/1, 21–37.

Webber, H. (2017). "Politics of 'leaving no one behind': Contesting the 2030 Sustainable Development Goals agenda." *Globalizations*, 14/3, 399–414.

Wu, H. (2019). "Three dimensions of China's 'outward-oriented' higher education internationalization." *Higher Education*, 77/1, 81–96.

Xu, C. L. (2017). "Mainland chinese students at an elite Hong Kong university: Habitus–field disjuncture in a transborder context." *British Journal of Sociology of Education*, 38/5, 610–624.

Yang, R. and Ma, J. (2015). "China's international aid in education: Development, determinants, and discord." In I. H. Cheng and S. J. Chan (eds.), *International Education Aid in Developing Asia*. Singapore: Springer, 113–130.

Yeoh, B. S., Foong, M., and Ho, K. C. (2014). "International students and the politics of language among 'globalising universities' in Asia." *Knowledge Cultures*, 2/4, 64–89.

CHAPTER 14

INTERNATIONALIZATION AND MOBILITY

Providers, Academic Collaborators, and Recognition of Qualifications

CHRISTOPHER S. COLLINS AND
ALEXANDER H. JONES

1. INTRODUCTION: WHY DOES MOBILITY MATTER?

THE simple moniker, "Asian," can scarcely account for the diversity of culture, economy, size of nation-state, economic power, political orientation, and various histories within it. There are sub-regions, religions, languages, and fluid cultures that cannot be contained by borders. The complexity of the region is marked by the subcategories and the magnitude is marked by the fact that almost three-fifths of the world's population reside in the region. Within the trends and nuances of Asian higher education (or anything else), there is a robust effort in assessing and understanding the portability of ideas, people, currency, and educational degrees. The concept of "mobility" takes on a particularly salient meaning in the broader Asia-Pacific region.

Higher education went through a global phase of massification reflecting the connection between economic growth and the skill development required to meet the demands of the economy. When a nation-state within the vast region of Asia could not develop the skills through their education system, they developed human capital through cross-border education. Other economies in Asia (e.g., Taiwan and Japan), experienced an overproduction of internal capacity for higher education which led to an oversupply when the birth rate began to decline (Neubauer and Hawkins, 2016,

p. 58). Balancing the demand and supply of higher education across borders with diverse languages, cultures, and histories has been a key issue within mobility.

Since the onset of globalization, the question of mobility and portability has been ever-present in higher education. As contemporary conversations regarding border restrictions, such as in the United States, European Union, and across Asia, have intensified, some scholars and policymakers have begun to reassess the impact of policies that enhance mobility (O'Malley, 2019). Global concerns with viruses spreading, displacement, and forced migration have heightened this global reassessment of mobility's effect on systems and outcomes of education. In this chapter, we add to conversations on internationalization by documenting and reflecting on the role of providers, collaborators, and qualifications in an era of increased scrutiny on global mobility.

Appadurai (1996) developed a theory of globalization that illuminates one way in which mobility matters. The anthropologist suggests that the decrease in borders has one of two effects, namely, homogeneity or heterogeneity. The former, Appadurai suggests, is akin to the (North) Americanization of the world. As American knowledge and practice transfer and flow across borders through media, finance, technology, culture, and ideas—what Appadurai terms *scapes*—other localities may be Americanized, for example; there is an imperialistic homogenizing effect of the decrease in borders. To be sure, as Appadurai points out, some localities may be more concerned about Indianization or Indonesianization than they are about Americanization. Regardless, the decrease in rigid borders, and thus the increased ease of mobility, has a homogenizing effect, making individuals more similar despite historical and contemporary differences. "Asian," for example, can function to unify people in an extremely diverse continent.

Conversely, heterogenizing also occurs as knowledge, people, and resources flow globally. This process occurs simultaneously with globalization's homogenizing effects. Appadurai suggests that even with the global flow of cultures, people become more intensely different, at least on the inside. On the outside, practices are adopted that give the impression of a universal culture; but, on the inside, key values and views are reinforced. Indians become more intensely Indian; Chinese become more intensely Chinese; Singaporeans become more intensely Singaporean.

Within higher education, there are therefore a variety of contending motivations and outcomes with internationalization, some of which may be homogenizing, while others are heterogenizing, or reinforcing of differences. The movement of learners influences the thought and action of education providers which gives rise to questions of the transferability of qualifications, market benefits, and the cross-pollination of global knowledges. Is the *movement* of learners in Asia homogenizing—creating similarities, while erasing differences in culture or indigenous knowledge—or heterogenizing? In terms of international branch campuses, the United States and United Kingdom continue to be the biggest "providers," while China, the United Arab Emirates (UAE), Singapore, and Malaysia host the largest numbers of branch campuses (Cross-Border Education Research Team, 2017). In terms of learners, China sends 33 percent of all international students out into the world and another 18 percent come from India

(Cross-Border Education Research Team, 2017). The United States and United Kingdom are the top two hosts for international students, with China increasingly becoming a popular destination. How has the position of Asian nations as recipients of Euro-American values homogenized or heterogenized the region? How has the *Chinaization* of Asia affected higher education? How has the image of Singaporean elites in higher education reinforced and/or erased cultural practices throughout the continent? These are the kinds of questions that must underlie an inquiry into the impact of internationalization in the region.

Globalization is a complex phenomenon to trace. Institutional and student mobility has been much easier to measure than global learning, transferability of knowledge, and their effects. On a global scale, the geographic origin and source of knowledge providers and knowledge consumers have been clear. In the academic canon, the West has self-constructed knowledge production for the consumption of the rest, requiring nearly all tertiary institutions to utilize some variation of a market-oriented framework in their educational systems (Rhoads and Torres, 2006; Bousquet, 2008; Cantwell and Kauppinen, 2014). As Deardorff (2014) has impugned, too often the rhetoric on mobility in education translates to being *globally competitive*. Deardorff and other scholars have thus suggested that global educators should shift to a human-centered (as opposed to market-centered) motivation to build international linkages (Skelly, 2009).

Beyond the movement of international students and branch campuses, there is another evolving system providing regulatory oversight and agreement on cross-border education and recognition of qualifications. In Asia, the 1983, 2011, and 2018 conventions on the recognition of degree qualifications reflect an ongoing effort to enhance the mobility of educational credit and degrees, and therefore promote institutional, student, and knowledge mobility. The most recent legal instrument, the Asia-Pacific Regional Convention on the Recognition of Qualifications in Higher Education (for short, the Tokyo Convention), was enacted in February of 2018 and is an updated effort at transparency, prosperity, stability, and access. Comparing the global sender/provider trends with the regional coverage of the Tokyo Convention will convey different narratives in the competing motivations for and effectiveness of internationalization of higher education. In examining the case study of the Tokyo Convention as a legitimized form of mobility in the region, our reflections seek to document the effectiveness (or lack thereof) of internationalization in higher education.

Fischer (2015, 2019) advanced the notion that international education is a waning trend and wrote, "The elevation of international education blended high-minded ideals and bottom-line concerns. Ultimately, it satisfied neither" (Fischer, 2019). In order to understand whether or not there is a waning trend, depending on the directionality of internationalization, the more critical question of internationalization by and for whom is an important component to define and consider. Internationalization is thus both a method to achieve an objective and an objective in and of itself. The term often refers to policies and/or programs put forth by governments and educational institutions (from executive to department levels) to cultivate international exchanges of research, degree seeking/offering, and other actions under the broad umbrella of education (Altbach, 2016). Though internationalization is not new, there are new market frameworks (e.g., the knowledge economy), universal access, a revolution in information technology, the emergence of English as the primary language of education and communication, and increased global mobility and scrutiny. In light of these components of internationalization, it has become more widespread and more in-depth than in previous centuries. The imperative is driven by rationales ranging from enhancing knowledge collaborations to creating an international brand. The future of internationalization will likely need to address national security, domestic capacity, the use of English, curriculum content, e-learning, and quality assurance/control (Altbach, 2016). These are among the most pressing issues for internationalization in addition to the balance between nationalistic priorities and the compelling, yet complex, motivations for cooperation.

Of the utmost importance for this chapter about providers, collaborators, and accreditors is the question of the effectiveness of substantial tools and programs like the Tokyo Convention. The lens and parameters with which effectiveness may be described will also link back to the question of internationalization for whom. Does the decrease in borders and the enhancement of mobility homogenize or heterogenize? If the explicit goal of the Tokyo Convention is to increase mobility, why does mobility matter? The remainder of the chapter includes (1) an encyclopedic review of the modes of cross-border delivery of education over the past two decades, (2) an in-depth case study examination of the Tokyo Convention, its historical iterations, and the manifest and latent functions of this unique assemblage of providers/collaborators/recognizers, and (3) a conclusion on the effectiveness of the convention as we examine the question, "Why does mobility matter for higher education in Asia?"

2. Modes of Cross-Border Delivery: Adaptation and Updates

The delivery of any good or service across borders operates in different ways, so the World Trade Organization (n.d.) has defined the four primary modes that typically guide conversations of cross-border delivery. The General Agreement on Trade in Services (GATS) operates in the following modes:

(a) from the territory of one Member into the territory of any other Member (Mode 1: Cross border trade);
(b) in the territory of one Member to the service consumer of any other Member (Mode 2: Consumption abroad);
(c) by a service supplier of one Member, through commercial presence, in the territory of any other Member (Mode 3: Commercial presence); and
(d) by a service supplier of one Member, through the presence of natural persons of a Member in the territory of any other Member (Mode 4: Presence of natural persons). (WTO, n.d.)

The first mode does not require the movement of physical persons, which in higher education is referred to as online education or e-learning. Mode 2 identifies the movement of a consumer to a supplier. In the case of education this would be obtaining part or all of your educational credentials outside of your country of origin and/or nationality. Mode 3 concerns the commercial presence of a supplier, for example the establishment of an international branch campus or franchise. This mode gives an institution in the United Kingdom, for example, the ability to establish a branch in China and fully operate with the same name, but under the rules and regulations of the country in which the branch resides. Mode 4 is about the movement of individuals (as opposed to institutions) going to another country to provide a service, which includes professors teaching in another country. This chapter primarily addresses modes 2, 3, and 4.

When the WTO introduced the General Agreement on Trade in Services, there was a high degree of caution about the wisdom of considering higher education as a tradable commodity and what limits that may put on government subsidy (Collins, 2007). However, the impact on the inclusion into GATS has been relatively low. Many Asian countries were part of the agreement and even more joined GATS when following inclusion in the WTO. Even though the actual agreements have not had a significant impact, the conceptual orientation of trade liberalization cultivates a market-oriented perspective with competition for students among a marketplace of providers. The lack of impact is not just limited to the education sector, and Mattoo (2015) suggests that provisions for liberalization have not had their intended effect. Instead, focusing on regulatory flexibility and cooperation (as opposed to a more linear focus on market access) may provide a more nuanced path to understanding the mutual benefits of trade.

In mode 3, there are a variety of options for provider access in education. (1) A *joint or double degree* occurs where institutions in different countries collaborate to offer a program where students earn either a single or multiple degree. (2) Similarly, *twinning arrangements* enable a student to attend two institutions that are partnering to offer part of a degree within a domestic and foreign program. (3) A *franchised* program occurs when a foreign provider delivers the educational program in a domestic institution. (4) A *validated program* occurs in an institution that offers a program that has been "approved" by a foreign institution. (5) *Distance/open-learning* is a course that is offered online or traditionally by a local partner. (6) An *international branch campus* operates in a country outside of its home country.

According to the Cross-Border Education Research Team (2017), there are just over one hundred branch campuses operating throughout Asia. Over 40 of those are in China/Hong Kong and almost half of the campuses throughout the region originate from the United States and United Kingdom. The types of institutions providing branch campuses range from the elite (e.g., the University of Chicago Booth School of Business—Hong Kong Campus, McGill MBA Japan, and RMIT Vietnam) to the very niche (e.g., the Culinary Institute of America in Singapore and the Shanghai Vancouver Film School).

However, in 2018, China shut down 234 (one-fifth) of its international university partnerships. There are compounding pressures that have resulted in universities removing freedom of thought as part of their mission and have prioritized patriotism or economic nationalism over academic independence in newly amended charters in recent months (Fifield, 2019). Fudan, along with Nanjing University, Shaanxi Normal University, and Renmin University are among the top universities in China with newly rewritten charters that emphasize "the comprehensive leadership of the Communist Party" as part of the party leadership's bid to strengthen ideological control over students and teachers. Although the implications of these changes for Sino-foreign joint venture universities and other collaborations with Western universities are theoretical in the short term, the proof of whether or not restrictions on academic freedom are creeping into their China-related activities and collaborations with Chinese universities will soon be revealed.

Wariness of the internationalization of higher education is also apparent among nationalistic powers like the United States. For example, the United States has tightened rules for Chinese visa holders in some STEM fields. A report from the Australian Strategic Policy Institute has warned that collaborations between academic scientists in some Western institutions and People's Liberation Army scientists are providing research findings on artificial intelligence and other areas to "rival militaries." Professors from Harvard, UCLA, and Arkansas have all been arrested for either not disclosing links to China or for conspiring to send military information that breaks international legal standards. Yet, China and the United States continue to collaborate across borders. In 2003, China's Interim Measures for the Administration of Universities and Colleges Engaged in Overseas Education led to the establishment of four overseas education institutions: Soochow University Laos—the first foreign university approved by the Laos Ministry of Education (2012); Xiamen University Malaysia Campus (2015); Yunnan University of Finance and Economics (YUFE) Business School in Bangkok, jointly operated between Yunnan University of Finance and Economics and Thailand's Rangsit University (2014); and Beijing Languages and Cultural University (BLCU) Tokyo College, between BLCU and the Japan ISI Corporation (2015). Beijing Normal University (BNU) Cardiff Chinese College was set up jointly by BNU and Wales's Cardiff University; and Global Innovation Exchange (GIX), a partnership between Tsinghua University and the University of Washington is the first international branch campus established by a Chinese university in the United States.

In addition to globalization and internationalization, regionalization is another important process in Asia and other parts of the world as it includes tacit or semi-formal relationships among institutions and academics and adds more planning, strategy, and formality (Knight 2012). Given the many regions of Asia, there are multiple ways in which cooperative agreements are functioning. As opposed to setting up a campus in another country or sending students abroad, regional cooperation primarily falls within mode 4. The organizations that facilitate the cooperation in the region include the Association of Southeast Asian Nations (ASEAN) and the South Asia Association of Regional Cooperation. While mode 3 is primarily about institutions outside the region establishing a presence in Asia, modes 2 and 4 play a role within regionalization. The role of regionalization also brings up the need for regional quality assurance. The two entities with the largest presence are the Asia-Pacific Quality Network (APQN), which began in 2003 and applies to 53 Asian countries and the ASEAN Quality Assurance Network (AQAN), which began in 2008 and applies to 10 ASEAN countries. Given the complexity across the region, these institutions were designed to build a translation map and portability pathways for degree earners.

For student exchanges, UMAP (University Mobility in Asia-Pacific), the Asia-Pacific Association of International Education, and several others were designed to provide opportunities for a more traditional study away or for international students to study for an entire degree outside of their country (mode 2). Though it is not clear if the association is enhancing the mobility or simply growing alongside mobility, its existence is another signal as to the growing professionalization in international movement. In terms of the portability of education, credit transfer schemes have been developed by UMAP and ASEAN. Both AQAN and APQN are designed to promote cooperation among the national quality assurance agencies in each country across the region. The efforts and organizations to promote regional cooperation are relatively new and issues of quality assurance, qualifications, and degree recognition are ongoing. For instance, China's attempt at leveraging the Belt and Road Initiative via the University Alliance of the Silk Road is thought to involve 150 universities across 38 countries; does this collaboration offer a distinctively Chinese internationalization (Peters, 2020)? As higher education continues to grow, governments as well as colleges and universities are working in multi-contextual frames of reference to determine what goals to try to accomplish.

The multiple modes of cross-border education and the vast size and complexity of the region leave many unanswered questions about how to develop and sustain a common language, framework, or threshold for understanding regional cooperation. The world and higher education are changing so fast, that even developing definitions, metrics, and relationships may need to be modified by the time they are solidified. The purpose and motivation for cross-border activity also need to be analyzed and understood. The primary motivation to set up international branch campuses has been revenue generation and to a lesser degree an attempt to enhance reputation and academic collaboration (Mackie, 2019). However, the compounding complications and rapid change in the Asia-Pacific keep the topics of access, quality, and mobility at the forefront of higher education. As a response to these complexities, the Tokyo Convention is an international/regional instrument that has been revised over many decades to support and sustain the development of structures to address the most urgent needs of higher education in Asia. For the purposes of this chapter, the Tokyo Convention provides a case study by which to explore mechanisms and effects of internationalization.

3. The Case of the Tokyo Convention

There are many mechanisms through which internationalization occurs in Asia and Oceania. One such example is the Tokyo Convention, which we use as a case study to examine the effectiveness of internationalization in the region. Although the Tokyo

Convention has only been signed by eight nations in the region, as a document backed by the United Nations its scope is far-reaching and warrants a critical discussion in this volume as a guiding star for Asia-Pacific's higher education cross-border collaboration. In light of macro-level trends in the region, an examination of the Tokyo Convention's history, manifest/explicit functions, and latent/implicit functions illuminates the goal and impact of mobility in this contentious exemplar.

3.1 The History of the Tokyo Convention

The history of the Tokyo Convention consists of three parts. First, in 1983, the Regional Convention on the Recognition of Studies, Diplomas and Degrees in Higher Education in Asia and the Pacific (UNESCO, 1984) was adopted in Bangkok with three explicit aims, according to Article 2 of the original convention documents. The first aim was to build cooperation for the purposes of peace, international understanding, and to cross-pollinate educational, technological, and scientific potential. The second aim was to harmonize higher education, so as to build similarities and comparability of "credits, subjects of study, certificates, diplomas and degrees, and of the conditions of access to higher education" (Article 2.2.A.iii) across nations. The third and final expressed aim of the 1983 convention was to create a structure whereby national, bilateral, sub-regional, and regional organizations would be linked together. Signed by Australia, Bhutan, China, Korea, India, Indonesia, Lao, Nepal, the Philippines, Vietnam, Sri Lanka, Thailand, Turkey, and the USSR, this convention was ratified, and then entered into force in 1985.

Second, in 2011 in Tokyo, the original Bangkok convention was revisited and revised for the region, entitled the Asia-Pacific Regional Convention on the Recognition of Qualifications in Higher Education (UNESCO, 2012). It maintained much of the original language, with a few amendments. Ultimately, the expressed aim of the Tokyo Convention was about development and peace for the region. However, the cause for the 2011 convention was, in large part, the diversification of higher education in the region: "Conscious of the wide ranging changes in higher education in Asia-Pacific since these Conventions were adopted, resulting in considerably increased diversification within and among national education systems, and of the need to adapt legal instruments and practice to reflect these developments" (UNESCO, 2012, Preamble). Thus, a cursory summary of the 2011 Tokyo Convention is that it recognized the increasing complexity and diversity of higher education in the region, and attempted to alleviate challenges arising from this complexity.

Third, and finally, in 2018 in Korea, the Seoul Statement on the Tokyo Convention (UNESCO, 2018) provided an additional update and interpretation of the previous two major conventions (as well as other smaller gatherings held in Australia and China). The major outcomes of the Seoul Statement situated Asian conversations on mobility and higher education within the Sustainable Development Goals and the United Nations' 2030 Agenda. Further, the Seoul Statement identified how the Tokyo Convention provided "renewed opportunities for Member States to harmonize their recognition" of "policies and practices for greater cross-border mobility of students among countries in the region and beyond" (UNESCO, 2018, p. 1). Authors and signers of the 2018 statement also suggested that quality assurance systems built on trust should be prioritized so as to make this harmonization more efficient. These quality assurance systems, the Seoul Statement proposes, should be based on knowledge and skills achieved, which are measured by learning outcomes that utilize a common language. As one bullet point documents:

> Cross-border mobility programmes can encourage a common understanding of learning outcomes, including in specific subject or discipline areas. Regional collaboration efforts should synergize existing mobility programmes, credit recognition and transfer systems and regional qualifications frameworks so that qualifications and partial studies are better recognized and portable across borders. (UNESCO, 2018, p. 2)

In sum, the original convention in Thailand recognized the need for synergy and harmony—Appadurai's concept of homogeneity—in the region to allow for the cross-border recognition of higher education. With a legal structure that allowed for such harmony, the easing of mobility would allow the region to develop and effectively seek the common good.

In 2011, a new era of mobility, various articles were produced that provided nuance to the original structure. These articles evidenced the complexity and the diversification of higher education since 1983. Clearly, the 2011 iteration of the convention also gave national governments more power in assessing learning (UNESCO, 2012). But, in 2018, as the Seoul Statement documents, synergy, commonality, collaboration, and harmony became the focus once more in a seeming attempt to simplify internationalization. Uniquely, the Seoul Statement sought to accomplish this homogeneity by situating its update in the wider United Nations goals of sustainable development as if to justify or corroborate attempts at inclusivity. Thus, to understand the present-day effectiveness of internationalization as understood by one salient machine (to use the documents' language) in the region, it is important to also understand other international qualifications and conversations about sustainable development and higher education.

3.2 Higher Education and Sustainable Development Goals in Asia

The various iterations of the Tokyo Convention are part of wider global conversations on social change through the conduit of higher education. In the three aforementioned documents, there are two primary factors that have shaped how governments and education secretaries have sought to address the increase of mobility and internationalization. First, the 2011 Tokyo Convention mentions UNESCO's regional conventions in other regions and a 1993 articulation of recognition of qualifications. This 1993 Recommendation on the Recognition of Studies and Qualifications in Higher Education was a worldwide effort:

> Considering that, given the great diversity of the laws, regulations, practices and traditions that determine the organization and functions of higher education systems and institutions, and the diversity of the constitutional, legal and regulatory requirements and arrangements regulating the practice of professions, it is essential, for the purpose of access to and pursuance and completion of higher education and for preparation for the practice of professions, to put into practice policies of evaluation of competence that take into account not only the qualifications obtained but also courses of study taken and skills, knowledge and experience acquired. (UNESCO, 1993, Preamble)

The 1993 Recommendation aimed to guide Member States within their own "national systems and in conformity with their constitutional, legal and regulatory provisions to encourage the competent authorities" to recognize certificates of, qualifications of, and preparation for higher education in other Member States. At a worldwide level, UNESCO provided an impetus for its members to generate mutual recognition.

Second, and more recently, the Sustainable Development Goals (SDGs), which revised the Millennium Development Goals, framed the Seoul Statement (UNESCO, 2018). SDG4 sought inclusivity and equitability in quality education and lifelong learning opportunities. However, most targets and indicators regarding equity in education concern primary and secondary education (see targets that relate to tertiary or post-secondary education in the UN Statistical Commission, 2016).

Because the majority of the indices concern childhood development, the United Nations update reports hardly assess the expansion and impact of higher education. One recent statistic in the Secretary-General's "Progress towards the Sustainable Development Goals" in 2017 highlighted that only $1 billion in scholarships were given to developing nations in 2015, compared to $1.2 billion in 2014, with Australia, France, and the United Kingdom as the largest contributors (United Nations, 2017).

Although it is difficult to trace how the framework of the SDGs has been implemented in Asia, and whether these goals have been enacted, the authors and signers of the Seoul Statement clearly had in mind the SDGs when articulating their rationale for harmony and synergy in internationalization efforts in the region. As the Seoul Statement reads:

> **Affirming** the 2030 Agenda and the Sustainable Development Goals (SDGs), in particular, SDG4 to ensure inclusive and equitable quality education and promote lifelong learning opportunities for all,
> **Inspired** by the SDG4 target 4.b that promotes a substantial expansion of scholarships available to developing countries . . . (UNESCO, 2018)

These macro-level forces of UNESCO's 1993 clarion call to ease borders and the UN's SDGs that set international goals for the expansion of higher education so as to develop underdeveloped or developing regions are important factors in understanding the homogenizing and heterogenizing functions of the Tokyo Convention.

3.3 The Manifest Functions of the Tokyo Convention

Has the Tokyo Convention, as an exemplar of a legitimized and legal impetus to increase mobility, been effective in internationalizing higher education in the region? Explicitly, the manifest function of the Tokyo Convention, and others like it, is to increase mobility by easing restrictions on cross-border recognition of qualifications so as to promote development in the region. According to UNESCO's Institute for Statistics, only four out of the top 10 countries of total number of mobile students worldwide are from East Asia (Table 14.1). However, only four of the top destination countries of mobile students are in the region; and this includes Australia and Russia. Only China and Japan are East Asian countries that are in the top ten of destinations for mobility, while there are no South or Southeast Asian countries. Thus, on a global scale, *although Asia is the source of much of the world's mobility, these students are widely understood to be traveling outside of the region.*

Within the Asia and Oceania region itself, additional data from the UNESCO Institute for Statistics suggest that Japan and Australia are the top recipients of mobile students from other Asian countries. Table 14.2 highlights several Asian countries and their mobile students' top three *Asian* destinations, removing countries from regions outside Asia and Oceania. Thus, when considering interregional mobility, *there are clear and consistent recipients of mobility.*

Table 14.1 Top ten origin and destination countries, 2017

Countries of origin	Destination countries
1. China	1. United States
2. India	2. United Kingdom
3. Germany	3. Australia
4. Republic of Korea	4. France
5. Viet Nam	5. Germany
6. France	6. Russia
7. United States	7. Japan
8. Nigeria	8. Canada
9. Kazakhstan	9. China
10. Saudi Arabia	10. Italy

Source: UNESCO Institute for Statistics. Adapted from https://core.ac.uk/reader/143614920.

Table 14.2 Tertiary-level Asian students' flow to destination countries

Origin country	Top three Asian destination countries
Cambodia	1. Australia (1,054 students) 2. Thailand (1,031) 3. Japan (458)
Malaysia	1. Australia (15,113) 2. Japan (2,439) 3. Russia (1,838)
Thailand	1. Australia (7,427) 2. Japan (3,054) 3. Malaysia (1,516)
India	1. Australia (51,976) 2. New Zealand (12,552) 3. United Arab Emirates (7,395)
China	1. Australia (128,498) 2. Japan (79,375) 3. Korea (44,163)
Indonesia	1. Australia (11,040) 2. Malaysia (10,401) 3. Japan (3,616)
Japan	1. Australia (2,244) 2. Korea (1,455) 3. Malaysia (693)
Korea	1. Japan (13,121) 2. Australia (8,316) 3. Malaysia (1,434)
Timor-Leste	1. Indonesia (1,650) 2. Australia (121) 3. Thailand (55)
Philippines	1. Australia (5,243) 2. New Zealand (1,399) 3. Japan (735)
Singapore	1. Australia (7,864) 2. Malaysia (861) 3. New Zealand (383)

Source: UNESCO Institute for Statistics. Adapted from http://uis.unesco.org/en/uis-student-flow.

A final data point that examines the manifest function of the Tokyo Convention in higher education is in-region collaboration in research. Interested readers can consult Appendix VI of UNESCO's *Higher Education in Asia: Expanding Out, Expanding Up Report* (UNESCO, 2014) that documents specific institutions across nations that collaborate in research by subject. For example, the report documents how Capital Medical University China has grown by 17 percent in its publication rate as it has collaborated with Japan's Kyoto University. Additionally, a recent study documented an eightfold increase in the number of collaborative papers across the world since 1980; however, in Asia, many countries have sufficient capacity and expertise to conduct research independent of other nations (Hu et al., 2020). Exacerbated by the lack of English-language skills, this study suggested that the region is, in general, isolated in terms of cross-border research collaborations.

In sum, has the Tokyo Convention as an exemplar of a legitimized and legal impetus to increase mobility been effective in internationalizing higher education in the region? Though it is difficult to validate the causality of the Tokyo Convention's impact on internationalization, there are at least clear and manifest indicators that the region has seen some growth in the mobility of students. In its manifest functions, the Tokyo Convention appears to at least parallel, if not contribute to, the broad growth and internationalization of higher education in Asia. But, the broader question of internationalization's effect in Asia not only concerns the explicit goals of mobility, but the implicit assumptions about what mobility entails and accomplishes.

3.4 The Latent Functions of the Tokyo Convention

Although the explicit goal of the Tokyo Convention and other similar regulations was to increase mobility and decrease challenges that hinder the cross-pollination of knowledge, people, and resources, there are also implicit functions of the 1983, 2011, and 2018 iterations. Returning to Appadurai's scapes and flows concepts, and thus exploring internationalization as a means and an end, this section illuminates how scholars, educators, and practitioners may examine the latent goals of an internationalization construct such as the Tokyo Convention.

Importantly, in the 1983 Bangkok version of the recognition of qualifications in Asia, there are a few identifiable, though more implicit, goals of the original convention. As the Preamble states, the overall hope of this agreement to simplify international border exchanges through the recognition of degrees across nations was to facilitate "the economic, social, cultural, and technological development of each and all of the countries of the region" (UNESCO, 1984). Further, as the Preamble continues, this agreement, the Member States hoped, would be the catalyst for effectively generating mobility and alleviating unnecessary challenges with an eye toward "the common good." Together, these loaded concepts of development and the common good are ostensibly the two key latent functions of the original convention.

As countries in Asia pursued democracy in the 1980s and 1990s, there was also, for many nations, a pull from a liberal economic agenda. Uniquely, higher education in Asia may rightly be interpreted as a conduit not only of the mobility of knowledge and resource, but of capitalism and cultural homogeneity. Thus, one latent function of the Tokyo Convention is its homogenizing effect. *By implementing a suite of universal learning outcomes, for example, for the purposes of easing mobility and thus promoting the interaction between cultures and peoples, the function of these outcomes can be to restrict knowledge transfer because they attempt to dictate what is learned and how.*

Between 1983 and 2011, there was a clear attempt at diversification of higher education in the region. Although it is unclear whether or not the original convention explicitly catalyzed this heterogeneity, or whether this diversity in systems and structures was influenced by other global streams and flows, there is nevertheless a palpable difference in the first two documents. Whereas the 1983 convention in Bangkok was the genesis of the structure and vision for the easing of mobility in the region, the 2011 version recognized the complexity of the global world, allowing for individual nations to have more power in their recognition of degrees from other countries. Phrases such as "within the Party's territory" and "each Party" were added to the 2011 Tokyo Convention to give more sway to national governments (UNESCO, 2012, Preamble). Other qualifying statements such as, "Each Party shall recognise the qualifications in higher education conferred in another Party, unless a substantial difference can be shown" (UNESCO, 2012, Article VI.1), were likewise added, clearly to support the power of difference across the region. Over the two decades between the two documents that framed internationalization in the region, a complexity was identified; members therefore sought to amend and ameliorate the challenges that came with diversification of the region as mobility increased in the intermediary.

As the Seoul Statement was enacted in 2018, reiterating the goal of commonalities and harmony, these three documents indicate salient perplexities in light of Appadurai's concepts of scapes and homogeneity and heterogeneity. For example, the relationship between opening borders and becoming free-market nations in Asia alongside state-market nations like China within the agreements is a perplexity to explore. Further, the role of economic status and wealth within the cross-pollination of people and resources in the region is another issue for further study. However, in terms of quality assurance and the recognition of qualifications across borders, the drive for "a common understanding of learning outcomes," which is a consistent thread through the three documents, has an important, latent function. Internationalization in Asia and Oceania can seemingly either homogenize or diversify. How the ease of transferability counterintuitively restricts knowledge transfer because there are set learning outcomes to which universities across the region prescribe is an important factor in assessing the effectiveness of internationalization.

Utilizing Appadurai's scapes as a lens through which to dissect and then reconstitute an assessment of mobility offers a unique framework to interpret internationalization. Regarding the Tokyo Convention, instead of asking if it is effective in internationalizing the region, it may be more appropriate to ask, is it pushing the goal of homogeneity or heterogeneity? Further, even if the Tokyo Convention is a great achievement, how exactly is it impacting internationalization in the region—through labor markets, admission to graduate study, government jobs? And why are many Asian countries hesitant to sign up to the accord? Since the Tokyo Convention has yet to galvanize clear alignment throughout the Asia-Pacific region, the relationship between the macro-level international agreements and daily change is murky at best.

4. Conclusion: Asking the Right Question

The case of the Tokyo Convention is one of many legitimized forms of an attempt to internationalize higher education in Asia. In the three iterations of the convention, scholars, practitioners, and policymakers in Asia convened to promote mobility so as to more effectively develop the region for the common good. These, at least, are the expressed and explicit purposes and goals of the Tokyo Convention. Further consideration of the implicit processes and goals of internationalization through Appadurai's concepts of scapes and homogeneity/heterogeneity, however, challenges a surface-level reading of the impact of internationalization. On one hand, one might conclude that the Tokyo Convention, for example, as a conduit of internationalization was and is effective because degrees were transferred, because development indicators were reached, or because mobility increased. On the other hand, if the increase in mobility caused homogeneity, creating a singular kind of Asian citizen concerned with global participation in free-market capitalism, which is one possible and likely outcome of internationalization efforts through the Tokyo Convention, *is it really effective*? If internationalization actually erodes heterogeneity or diversity, is it effective?

Whether or not any particular tool of internationalization delivers on its promise for transparency, mobility, diversity, or coherency will likely depend upon the perspective of the person or agency answering the question. Approaching both the manifest and latent functions of the tools within a sender/receiver paradigm creates a framework for looking across sectors and through explicit purposes. The ways in which people, providers, images, ideas, and finances all move across borders and around the globe provide further insight into the ways in which educational values play a mediating role between social values and contracts (e.g., common good) and market values (e.g. free trade, Sustainable Development Goals). To answer the question of the effectiveness of a tool, which we have demonstrated through a case study on the Tokyo Convention as one such tool, requires a robust understanding of the continuous morphologies of internationalization as a thing (to be commodified, to exert power, to mediate relations, to govern as a core interest of the state).

As scholars and practitioners in Asian higher education examine their own competing frameworks for internationalization, they must examine what they actually mean by internationalization. They must inquire, "Why does mobility matter?" Is it for homogeneity, or heterogeneity? And, if it is indeed for a kind of diversity, what is the threshold for policymakers and scholars in their attempt to heterogenize the world? For internationalization requires a mechanism like the Tokyo Convention that first finds commonality, which is in inverse relationship to difference, to ease the cross-pollination of knowledge, people, and resources. By seeking diversity *through* harmony, an implicit loss of culture and identity may be at stake. Finding the balance between the two is no easy task, and is the ongoing challenge facing internationalization and collaboration in a region with competing economic, political, and social priorities.

References

Altbach, P. G. (2016). *Global Perspectives on Higher Education*. Baltimore: Johns Hopkins University Press.

Appadurai, A. (1996). *Modernity at Large: Cultural Dimensions of Globalization*. Minneapolis: University of Minnesota Press.

Bousquet, M. (2008). *How the University Works: Higher Education and the Low-Wage Nation*. New York: New York University Press.

Cantwell, B. and Kauppinen, I. (eds.) (2014). *Academic Capitalism in the Age of Globalization*. Baltimore: Johns Hopkins University Press.

Collins, C. S. (2007). A general agreement on higher education: GATS, globalization, and imperialism. *Research in Comparative and International Education*, 2/4, 283–296.

Cross-Border Education Research Team (2017, January). *C-BERT Branch Campus Listing*. Data originally collected by Kevin Kinser and Jason E. Lane. Albany, NY. http://cbert.org/branchcampuses.php

Deardorff, D. K. (2014). "Why engage in mobility? Key issues within global mobility: The big picture." In B. Streitwieser (ed.), *Internationalisation of Higher Education and Global Mobility*. Oxford: Symposium Books, 35–42.

Fifield, A. (2019). "In Xi Jinping's China, a top university can no longer promise freedom of thought." *Washington Post*, December 19. https://www.washingtonpost.com/world/asia_pacific/in-xi-jinpings-china-a-top-university-can-no-longer-promise-freedom-of-thought/2019/12/18/59f4d21a-215d-11ea-b034-de7dc2b5199b_story.html

Fischer, K. (2015). "Why a global education doesn't have to mean going abroad." *The Chronicle of Higher Education*. https://www.chronicle.com/article/Why-a-Global-Education/232311, accessed January 2, 2018.

Fischer, K. (2019). "How international education's golden age lost its sheen." *The Chronicle of Higher Education*. https://www.chronicle.com/interactives/2019-03-28-golden-age, accessed March 28, 2019.

Hu, Z., Tian, W., Gyo, J., and Wang, X. (2020). "Mapping research collaborations in different countries and regions: 1980–2019." *Scientometrics*, 124, 729–745.

Knight, J. (2012). "A conceptual framework for the recognition of higher education: Application to Asia." In J. N. Hawkins, K. H. Mok, and D. E. Neubauer (eds.), *Higher Education Regionalization in Asia Pacific*. New York: Palgrave Macmillan, 17–35.

Mackie, C. (2019). "A look into the complex environment of international branch campuses." *World Education News and Reviews*. https://wenr.wes.org/2019/05/the-complex-environment-of-international-branch-campuses

Mattoo, A. (2015). *Services Trade and Regulatory Cooperation. E15Initiative*. Geneva: International Centre for Trade and Sustainable Development (ICTSD) and World Economic Forum. http://www.e15initiative.org/

Neubauer, D. and Hawkins, J. N. (2016). "Prospects for higher education in the midst of globalization." In C. S. Collins, J. Hawkins, M. Lee, and D. E. Neubauer (eds.), *The Palgrave Handbook of Asia Pacific Higher Education*. New York: Palgrave Macmillan, 52–72.

O'Malley, B. (2019). "Global convention on recognising HE qualifications adopted." *University World News*. https://www.universityworldnews.com/post.php?story=201911290546590, accessed March 2, 2020.

Peters, M. A. (2020). "China's belt and road initiative: Reshaping global higher education." *Journal Educational Philosophy and Theory*, 52, 586–592.

Rhoads, R. A. and Torres, C. A. (eds.) (2006). *The University, State, and Market: The Political Economy of Globalization in the Americas*. Stanford, CA: Stanford University Press.

Skelly, J. (2009). "Fostering engagement: The role of international education in the development of global civic society." In R. Lewin (ed.), *The Handbook of Practice and Research in Study Abroad: Higher Education and the Quest for Global Citizenship*. New York: Routledge, 21–32.

UN Statistical Commission (2016). *SDG Indicators: Global Indicator Framework for the Sustainable Development Goals and Targets of the 2030 Agenda for Sustainable Development*. https://sustainabledevelopment.un.org/sdg4, accessed January 2, 2020.

UNESCO (1984). *Regional Convention on the Recognition of Studies, Diplomas and Degrees in Higher Education in Asia and the Pacific*. https://unesdoc.unesco.org/ark:/48223/pf0000059 308.page=14, accessed January 2, 2020.

UNESCO (1993). *Recommendation on the Recognition of Studies and Qualifications in Higher Education*. http://portal.unesco.org/en/ev.php-URL_ID=13142&URL_DO=DO_TOPIC& URL_SECTION=201.html, accessed January 2, 2020.

UNESCO (2012). *Asia-Pacific Regional Convention on the Recognition of Qualifications in Higher Education*. http://portal.unesco.org/en/ev.php-URL_ID=48975&URL_DO=DO_ TOPIC&URL_SECTION=201.html, accessed January 2, 2020.

UNESCO (2014). *Higher Education in Asia: Expanding Out, Expanding Up Report*. http://uis. unesco.org/sites/default/files/documents/higher-education-in-asia-expanding-out-ex-panding-up-2014-en.pdf, accessed February 1, 2020.

UNESCO (2018). *Seoul Statement*. https://bangkok.unesco.org/sites/default/files/assets/arti cle/Education/files/6-seoul-statement.pdf, accessed January 2, 2020.

United Nations (2017). *Report of the Secretary General, Progress towards the Sustainable Development Goals*. https://www.un.org/ga/search/view_doc.asp?symbol=E/2017/66& Lang=E, accessed January 2, 2020.

World Trade Organization (n.d.). *GATS Training Module*. https://www.wto.org/english/trato p_e/serv_e/serv_e.htm, accessed January 5, 2020.

CHAPTER 15

....

EDUCATION HUBS IN THE ASIA-PACIFIC

....

KRIS OLDS

1. INTRODUCTION

....

THIS chapter will explore a range of issues associated with the phenomenon of "education hubs" in the Asia-Pacific region, with a particular focus on Pacific Asia (which I define as East Asia plus South-East Asia). Terms like education hubs, international branch campuses, education cities, or transnational urban education zones are increasingly incorporated into debates about the future of higher education in the Asia-Pacific, as well as in the Arabian Gulf.

Education hubs are associated with academic thinking and public policymaking regarding the changing nature of universities, the evolving nature of the production of knowledge, and new forms of statecraft as countries and regions seek to establish themselves as key nodes, often regionally framed, in the global knowledge economy.

As will be discussed below, literature about education hubs in the Asia-Pacific has tended to focus on hubs that have emerged in Hong Kong, Malaysia, Singapore, and South Korea over the last several decades, with more recent attention on the growing number of hubs in China. Such education hubs, defined as *state-sanctioned transnational education zones*, are concentrated in key cities in the Asia-Pacific. In terms of sheer numbers, the hub "hot spots" are, in ranking order, Singapore, Shanghai, the Hong Kong Special Administrative Region (SAR), and Incheon in South Korea. Singapore dwarfs all of these Asian cities despite the strong efforts of Asian governments to compete with and mimic aspects of the Singaporean development model (cf. Olds, 2007; Sidhu et al., 2011; Kleibert et al., 2020). All of these hubs have emerged in association with structural change in the region, especially that related to growth in a service economy in the Asia-Pacific, the integration of national economies into the global economy via global value chains, massification (the shift of higher education from the education of elites to an increased proportion of populations), the urbanization process, and the development of new technologies, including information and communications technologies. This said, each hub's history, the role of the state in the development process, the nature of foreign universities associated with these hubs, and the nature of domestic–foreign university relations within these hubs vary significantly. All of these themes, and more, will be explored in some detail in the rest of this chapter.

While education hubs are relatively small geographically demarcated spaces considering the size and scale of Asia-Pacific city-regions, they are worth allocating attention to for three main reasons.

First, education hubs are often associated with significant sums of public and private investment. As with all forms of public investment, they generate opportunity costs and frequently lead to the channeling of public funds into supporting what can be risky educational experiments. For example, various ministries and statutory boards in Singapore backed the development of the World Class University in 1998, which subsequently morphed into the Global Schoolhouse program. This initiative provided direct and indirect forms of state support to two well-resourced private universities— Johns Hopkins University (JHU) (est. 1998) and New York University (NYU) (est. 2007)—both of which established commercial presence in Singaporean territory. Yet, by 2015, both universities were gone. The JHU presence—in the field of medicine—was replaced by Duke University, also a private university, and Duke University went on to form what is viewed as a successful joint venture medical school (with the National University of Singapore). In short, education hubs are spaces of experimentation, trial and error, and significant investment.

Second, and on a related note, education hubs matter as they are destabilizing spaces by design. They are experiments, often in the internationalization of higher education, as well as research and development (R&D), that bring together an assemblage of new organizational structures, forms of teaching and learning, technology, infrastructure, and modes of knowledge production. Many are post-colonial spaces as well, where the epistemic communities associated with teaching and learning, as well as research, are guided by independent Pacific Asian states and universities, albeit built on top of the physical and systemic (including linguistic and legal) legacies of earlier colonial eras. And yet, further to this final point, contemporary education hubs in the Asia-Pacific can also be viewed as problematic for many foreign universities that are driven by visions and missions that do not always, or fully, complement those of host states, societies, and universities.

Finally, education hubs are prime examples of initiatives and spaces associated with not just the knowledge economy, but also the "attention economy" (Lanham, 2006). Education hubs are branded spaces, marketized spaces: they are spaces designed to be identifiable by key national, regional, and global stakeholders and powerful organizations, as well as the media. Given this, and the power of slippery metaphors such as "hub," they receive disproportionate attention in comparison to other educational spaces that cannot be as easily represented, or are associated with the mundane yet important education of the majority of students. Indeed, education hubs in the Asia-Pacific (and especially Singapore) have also served as models for other world regions, and vice versa. For example, Education City in Qatar was launched in 1997 and has evolved to become a space for the production of knowledge and expertise regarding future planning for a more diversified post-carbon economy. Each hub has ancillary goals associated with them, including, in the Education City case, a rebalanced workforce with respect to gender (Vora, 2018; Al-Saleh and Vora, 2020; Al-Saleh, 2022).

This chapter is structured around four key "Ps"— patterns, processes, politics, and policies. This is a problematic conceptual division, of course, as the four Ps are all interdependent, but for the sake of a survey-style handbook chapter, I have separated them out to try and shed light on what education hubs are, how they can be made sense of, and what their implications are for higher education in the Asia-Pacific.

Following this introduction, I provide a broad overview of how education hubs have been defined, to date. Definitions matter, for they help us identify phenomena, and in this case, education hubs. In this first substantive section, I will also discuss patterns associated with education hubs in the Asia-Pacific (again, with a focus on Pacific Asia). This is a "40,000 foot" view, and it focuses on patterns associated with hubs or hub-like concentrations of higher education institutions (HEIs) and students.

The next section consists of a discussion of processes associated with education hubs, with a focus on historical foundations of contemporary hubs (universities and colonialism, universities and national development, port cities), the nature of contemporary economic development and the role of universities in city–region development during an era of planetary urbanization. Education hubs are both products of, and enablers of, agglomeration economies in service of the knowledge-based economy. This discussion is structural change-oriented.

The chapter then shifts tack, and focuses on the politics and policies associated with education hubs, with attention to relevant public policy matters, and associated programs. This section will deal with formal and informal policy drivers underlying the emergence and governance of education hubs. Attention will be paid to regulatory change that opens up territory to commercial presence, incentives/subsidies, and infrastructure investment. I also pay significant attention to the nature of the internationalization strategies that bring Asia-Pacific states and foreign HEIs together in the co-production of infrastructure. In short, education hubs are co-constructed— or articulated—"infrastructures" to support the development and expansion of the knowledge-based economy in the region's cities.

Finally, the conclusion will highlight key implications of education hubs, including uneven development and territorial fragmentation, with hubs being driven and drifting to engendering inter-hub network formation patterns at world region and global scales. What does this mean for regional hinterlands and HEIs not linked up to such hubs? This section closes off with a critique of the more commonly adopted definitions of education hubs, and suggests that most literature on education hubs fetishizes foreign (mostly Western) universities and disregards more organic hub-like phenomena, as well as myriad alternative phenomena associated with the production of knowledge in Asia-Pacific universities and city-regions, as well as its multi-level circulation and consumption.

2. Definitions and Patterns

The mainstream concept of "education hubs" was born out of research focused on the internationalization of higher education, itself a stream of literature that came out of discussions, debates, and writings about globalization. Globalization, a "supercomplex series of multicentric, multiscalar, multitemporal, multiform and multicausal forces" (Jessop, 2002, pp. 113–114, cited in Dicken, 2015), generated a series of evolving interdependencies across geographic space. These interdependencies driven by market-oriented ideological change (sometimes crudely labeled "neoliberalism"), unsettled higher education systems, as well as thinking about said systems. These process-oriented changes will be discussed in more detail below. Suffice it to say, the combination of structural and ideological change led states in the Asia-Pacific to open up their territory to the commercial presence of foreign universities (using 1995 General Agreement on Trade in Services (GATS) parlance). More specifically, the GATS delineates four distinct "modes of supplying services":

- **Cross-border supply** covers services flowing from the territory of one member into the territory of another member (e.g., banking or architectural services transmitted via telecommunications or mail);
- **Consumption abroad** refers to situations where a service consumer (e.g., tourist or patient) moves into another member's territory to obtain a service;
- **Commercial presence** implies that a service supplier of one member establishes a territorial presence, including through ownership or lease of premises, in another member's territory to provide a service (e.g., domestic subsidiaries of foreign insurance companies or hotel chains); and
- **Presence of natural persons** consists of persons of one member entering the territory of another member to supply a service (e.g., accountants, doctors, or teachers). The Annex on Movement of Natural Persons specifies, however, that members remain free to operate measures regarding citizenship, residence, or access to the employment market on a permanent basis.[1]

It is the third mode—commercial presence—that was enabled by ideological-cum-regulatory shifts in select parts of the Asia-Pacific, and that subsequently enabled universities to become organizationally mobile such that they could stretch their institutional architectures out across space. Academic and policy observers of the process began observing the articulation of the agendas of select Asia-Pacific states to rapidly build higher education capacity (from the mid-to-late 1990s on) with that of the agendas of internationalizing universities (e.g., Olds, 2007; Sidhu et al., 2011).

---

[1] See https://www.wto.org/english/tratop_e/serv_e/gatsqa_e.htm

There is an abundance of terms linked to "education hubs" including (in alphabetical order):

- Education city;
- Global schoolhouse;
- Innovation hub;
- Knowledge hub;
- Knowledge village;
- Transnational education zones.

These terms broadly mean the same, though the "education hub" term has the most purchase in higher education at this point of history, for good and bad.

But what is an "education hub"?

To date, definitions of education hubs have been relatively narrow, and dominated by the work of Jane Knight, a University of Toronto scholar known for her earlier work on the internationalization of higher education (e.g., Knight, 2004). Jane Knight's most influential definition of education hubs is as follows:

> An education hub is a planned effort to develop a critical mass of local and international actors who are strategically engaged in education, training, knowledge production and innovation initiatives. (Knight, 2011, p. 227)

Other scholars have written about education hubs, but it is Knight's work that has had the most impact in shaping our academic understanding of this phenomenon.

Jack Lee, one of Jane Knight's excellent PhD students, noted that her influential definition of education hub implicitly excludes single institutions and local clusters of HEIs such as the Stanford University innovation ecosystem and the Boston city-region (which encompasses an area with 100+ universities). As Lee reinforces, education hubs are products of "*deliberate planning by a state* to specialise in crossborder education to appeal to both local and international participants" (Lee, 2015a, p. 356, my emphasis). This definition is in alignment with Jason Lane and Kevin Kinser's (2011, p. 82) conceptualization of education hubs as:

> [A] designated region intended to attract foreign investment, retain local students, build a regional reputation by providing access to high-quality education and training for both international and domestic students, and create a knowledge-based economy.

Beecher et al. (2020, p. 88) build on the earlier work of Knight and especially Kinser and Lane (2015) when they define an education hub as a representation of:

> [A] national initiative to create knowledge centers that will support the development of new skills to compete regionally and globally in the knowledge economy.

Education hubs strengthen the development of local and regional human capital by concentrating education, industrial and economic policies that attract foreign expertise. Their primary goals are to educate students, create expertise in their workforce that is valued in the knowledge economy and drive economic prosperity and societal progress by forming strategic partnerships between governments, universities and industries.

And most recently, the German research group TRANSEDU (made up of Jana M. Kleibert, Alice Bobée, Tim Rottleb, and Marc Schulze) builds upon the work of these scholars and has developed a complementary definition to education hub—the "transnational education zone" (TEZ):

> TEZs are designated by governments as territorially defined areas (usually at the level of a city quarter) that host at least two offshore campuses, provide shared infrastructure and market themselves as education hubs or cities. (Kleibert et al., 2020, p. 35)

In all of these cases, the critically important delineators of what hubs are include *formal state action* through the creation of an education hub agenda, which is backed by state largesse and associated regulatory changes, along with policy, program, and projects harnessed to realize the education hub agenda. In addition, education hubs are defined in a way that recognizes, but indeed *requires*, local and national HEIs to collaborate with foreign HEIs within the demarcated space defined as a hub. In short, education hubs are conventionally defined as *state-sanctioned transnational education zones*.

Framed more broadly, the education hub is the perceived deepening and extension of the internationalization of higher education. Knight (2013, p. 375, my emphasis) puts it this way:

> Cross-border education has moved from people mobility (students, faculty, scholars) to programme mobility (twinning, franchise, virtual) and to provider mobility (branch campus) to policy mobility (quality assurance, qualification frameworks, credit systems) and *now to the development of international education hubs*. Education hubs build on and include all these forms of academic mobility but represent a new generation of cross-border education activities where critical mass, co-location and interaction between international and local universities, students, research institutes and private industry are key.

International branch campuses (IBCs), in particular, are viewed as a critical component of education hubs. IBCs are defined as "an entity that is owned, at least in part, by a foreign education provider; operated in the name of the foreign education provider; and provides an entire academic program, substantially on site, leading to a degree awarded by the foreign education provider" (Cross-Border Education Research Team, 2020; also see Hou et al., 2018).

It is clear from research that the growth of IBCs in the Asia-Pacific, and especially Pacific Asia, took off in the 1990s and has continued until the time of writing. As Kleibert et al. note in *Global Geographies of Offshore Campuses* (2020, p. 15):

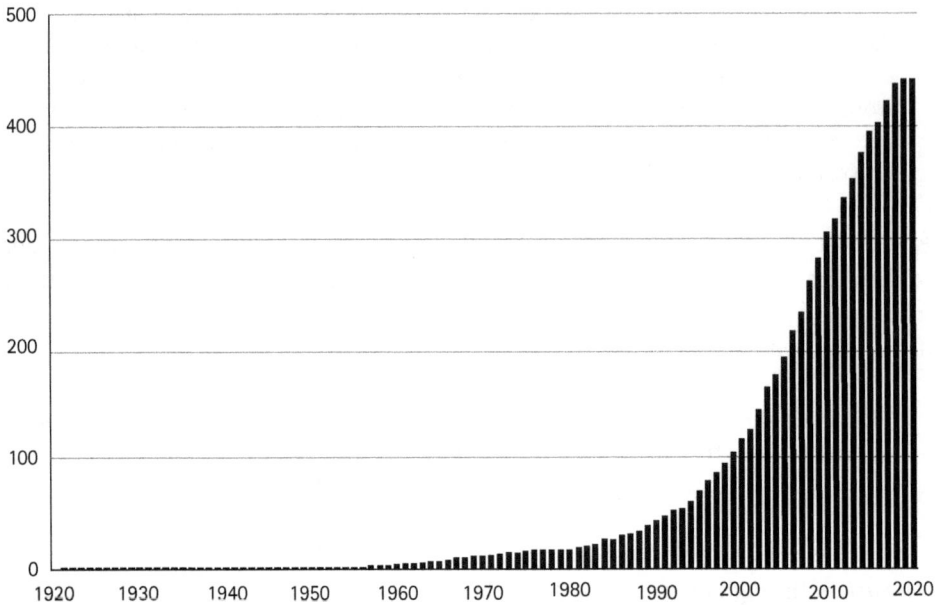

FIGURE 15.1 Offshore campus development worldwide, 1921–2020

Source: Kleibert et al. (2020, p. 15).

The first campus to open was The New School Parsons Paris, an offshore campus from the United States (US) established in France in 1921. The following 70 years were characterised by a minimal increase [in] offshore campuses. Two thirds of the campuses established before 1989 were branches of US universities (22 out of 33 campuses). Growth has accelerated since the end of the Cold War. Over the last 30 years, the number of offshore campuses worldwide has increased by more than 1,000%. The total number of offshore campuses was at 38 in 1989, surpassed 100 in 1999, exceeded 250 in 2009 and rose to more than 440 in 2019.

This growth pattern is captured in Figure 15.1.

It is also important to note, however, that while the growth rate of IBCs is striking and significant, and has helped to drive the growth of education hubs, the rate has evolved and changed over time, going from 9.6 percent (1990–1994) to 11.7 percent (1995–1999) and then gradually declining to 10.0 percent (2005–2009), 6.1 percent (2010–2014), and more recently 2.8 percent (2015–2019). These rates factor in IBC closures as well.

There are distinctive national and regional geographies to IBCs, as is evident in Figure 15.2.

The data in Figure 15.2 suggest that the Asia-Pacific was off the major IBC map until the 2000s when China, Singapore, and Malaysia in Pacific Asia progressively became present in a relative sense. And there was, and continues to be, limited interest in developing IBCs in Australia and New Zealand, largely due to the substantial capacity that exists within the national higher education systems of these two Asia-Pacific countries.

1990

France 9.5%

Canada 9.5%

Germany 7.1%

Spain 4.8%

Other 64.3%

United Kingdom 4.8%

2000

China 10.3%

United Arab Emirates 6.0%

Spain 5.2%

Germany 5.2%

Canada 4.3%

Other 69.0%

2010

United Arab Emirates 12.0%

China 11.3%

Singapore 6.0%

Qatar 4.0%

Other 63.5%

United Kingdom 3.3%

2020

China 14.5%

United Arab Emirates 9.3%

Singapore 4.3%

Malaysia 3.9%

Spain 3.4%

Other 64.6%

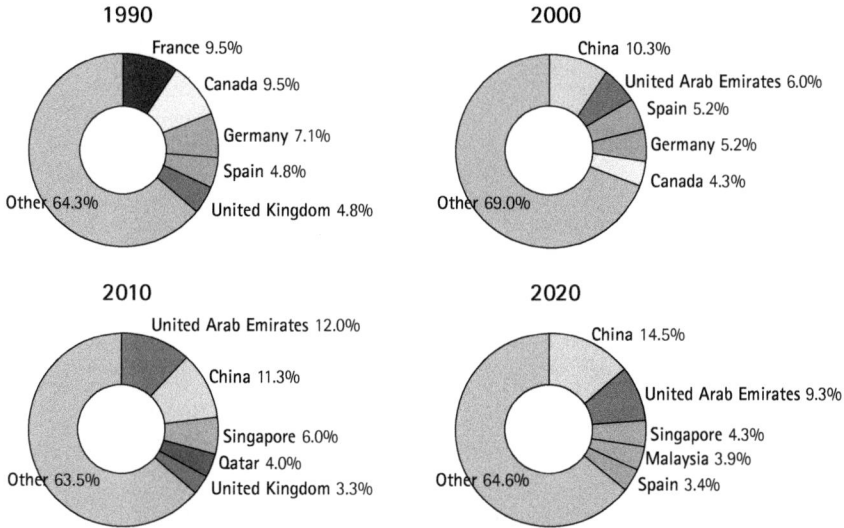

FIGURE 15.2 Share of major importing countries in 1990, 2000, 2010, and 2020

Source: Kleibert et al. (2020, p. 20).

While the concentration of IBCs—educational institutions integral to education hubs as defined in the majority of literature—is very much evident in the Asia-Pacific, education hubs are a subnational phenomenon. Moreover, education hubs have distinctive urban geographies. Figure 15.3, prepared for this chapter on the basis of Cross-Border Education Research Team (C-BERT) data (as at August 2020), visualizes the global urban geographies of IBCs.

The C-BERT data underlying this visualization identifies major clusters[2] of IBCs in six Chinese cities (Shanghai (8); Hong Kong SAR (5); Beijing (3), Dalian (3); Shenzhen (3); Suzhou (3)), one Japanese city (Tokyo), one South Korean city (Incheon), three Malaysian cities (Kuala Lumpur (4); Johor Bahru (4); Shah Alam (3)), and the city-state of Singapore (16).

Beecher et al (2020, p. 81) also note the existence of a secondary education hub in South Korea known as Jeju Global,[3] while Lee (2015b, p. 80) identified Sino Singapore Guangzhou Knowledge City (GKC) that has a goal of attracting "10 world-class universities to this hub" as an additional hub. This latter hub was launched in 2010 and is now known as China-Singapore Guangzhou Knowledge City.[4]

It is helpful to contrast the C-BERT data to the TRANSEDU data that is summarized in their 2020 report *Global Geographies of Offshore Campuses*, for both teams point

---

[2] I define major cluster as *three* or more IBCs in any one Asia-Pacific city. Australia is not included, for example, as Adelaide, Sydney, and the Gold Coast only have one IBC in each of these cities. And the C-BERT data has no entries for New Zealand.

[3] See https://english.jdcenter.com/business/edu/jejuen.cs

[4] See http://www.ssgkc.com/index.asp

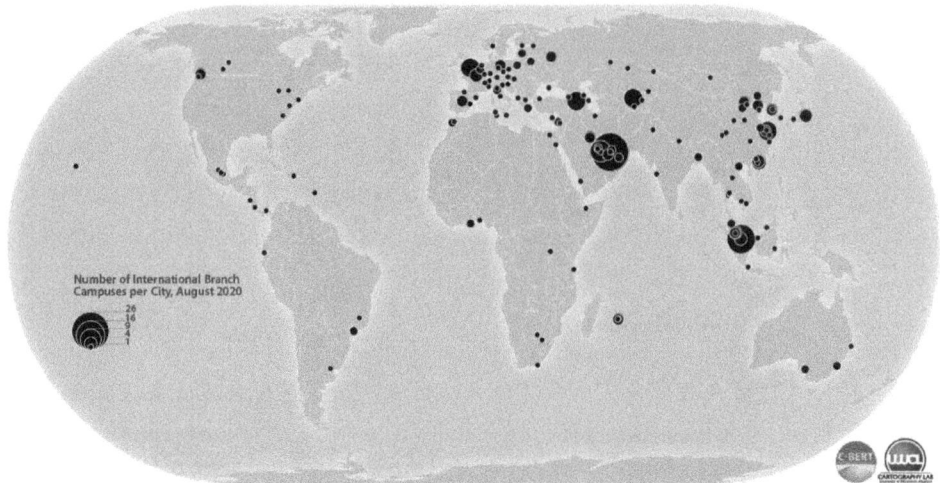

FIGURE 15.3 Number of international branch campuses per city (as at 2000)

Source: Cross-Border Education Research Team (2020).

out broadly similar patterns but have slightly different total numbers in 2020. The TRANSEDU team report suggests Shanghai has 15 IBCs, Singapore 19 IBCs, Kuala Lumpur 10 IBCs, and Suzhou 4 IBCs.

In any case, these are but minor differences, largely driven by definitions and the nature of the research process. What is clear, though, and assuming education hubs are *state-sanctioned transnational education zones*, is that the Asia-Pacific is one of two world regions that are distinguished by the presence of education hubs, with the other being the Arabian Gulf region.

3. Processes and Structural Change

While the patterns associated with the education hubs, as defined in the most prevalent and influential literature, suggest that Pacific Asia is a key site for this educational phenomenon, it is nonetheless important to situate the discussion of such hubs more broadly. Education hubs in Pacific Asia are outcomes of processes and structural change that have impacted not just Asian societies and economies, but also the rest of the world. And in doing so, conditions have emerged that have enabled these hubs to be co-constituted by Pacific Asian states and foreign universities, at this point in history across a huge region with remarkable diversity with respect to society and economy.

Over the course of the last four decades, for example, we have seen:

- The *end of colonialism*, and the beginning and then *end of the Cold War* such that the ideological fractures that once inhibited human mobility across space have been significantly reduced (though not completely).

- The emergence of *English as lingua franca* in many parts of the world in higher education and research circles, especially at the graduate education level.
- Major *demographic change* with a much larger world population (approx. 2 billion in 1925 vs. 7.8 billion in 2020).
- The *enhanced influence of market-oriented ideologies* (which some analysts have deemed "neoliberalism"), which have enabled the emergence of austerity agendas that drive down the proportion of revenue coming from the state, and opened up the higher education sector to managerial approaches (sometimes deemed "corporatization").
- The emergence of *global audit culture*; a broad systemic cultural shift that reflects an uneasy but grudging willingness to compare and be compared, to rank and be ranked.
- Major *technological transformations*, including a variety of technologies that enable higher education systems and the people that make it up to connect, to forge and maintain weak and strong ties, and to compare.
- The *development and restructuring of economies* (local/national/regional/global) with the emergence of regional and global knowledge economies much more dependent upon highly skilled (quaternary sector) labor as well as R&D.
- The emergence of the *global urban era*, such that more than half of the world's population lives in urban areas. Global cities have come to play a key role in acting as the interconnected nodes (that is, command and control centers) of the global economy, while at the same time we have seen huge mega cities emerge, especially in the Global South, and global suburbanization more generally in the Global North and the Global South.
- *Massification*—the structural transformation of higher education so that larger and larger proportions of society attend, and expect to attend, colleges and universities.
- The emergence of *intergovernmental organizations* (e.g., UNESCO, the OECD, the EU) with significant higher education and research mandates.
- The *emergence of new private sector players, public–private partnerships, and public sector spin-offs*. Some of these new players provide higher education services so as to extract profit from the sector, while others seek to serve various stakeholders (both public and private) via consultancies, the media, strategic advice, learning management systems, learning management systems/platforms, and so on.[5]

All of these factors play a role in the development of education hubs worldwide, including in the Asia-Pacific.

Among the more important process-related factors noted above, with respect to the education hub phenomenon, are urbanization and the emergence of regional and global knowledge economies much more dependent upon highly skilled (tertiary and quaternary sector) labor as well as R&D. Both the urbanization process and the development of

---

[5] These themes were raised and debated in a Massive Open Online Course (MOOC) I co-taught with Professor Susan L. Robertson (now based at Cambridge University in the UK). The MOOC (*Globalizing Higher Education and Research for the 'Knowledge Economy*) was run in 2013 and had approximately 18,500 enrolled "students," many of them located in Asia-Pacific cities.

the knowledge economy also depend on, and drive forward, agglomeration tendencies that bring together universities, industries, and government within key city-regions.

Urbanization is an integral driver of the emergence of education hubs, including in the Asia-Pacific and the Arabian Gulf, the two world regions most closely associated with this phenomenon. This is partly because rapid urbanization processes generate a need to enhance capacity within the education sector, including higher education, partly via the import of the HEI mechanism.

As the United Nations (2019a) notes in *World Urbanization Prospects: The 2018 Revision – Key Facts*:[6]

> **The urban population** of the world has grown rapidly since 1950, having increased from 751 million to 4.2 billion in 2018. Asia, despite being less urbanized than most other regions today, is home to 54% of the world's urban population, followed by Europe and Africa (13% each).
>
> **Growth in the** urban population is driven by overall population increase and by the upward shift in the percentage living in urban areas. Together, these two factors are projected to add 2.5 billion to the world's urban population by 2050, with almost 90% of this growth happening in Asia and Africa.
>
> **Just three countries** – India, China and Nigeria – together are expected to account for 35% of the growth in the world's urban population between 2018 and 2050. India is projected to add 416 million urban dwellers, China 255 million and Nigeria 189 million. (emphasis in original)

These patterns are even more striking when presented in tabular format (see Table 15.1).

For example, it is no surprise that education hubs are located within select city-regions in Asia-Pacific countries. Asia, as a whole, has shifted from 32.3 percent urban in 1990 to 49.9 percent in 2018, and is projected to become 66.2 percent urban in 2050 (see Table 15.1). Given the increase in the median level of urbanization in Asia from 1950 to 2018, and the associated growth of the largest urban areas by population (see Figure 15.4), states in the region are under pressure to enhance higher education capacity via the import of HEIs as a complement to the expansion of the domestic higher education system. And key cities are the obvious locations when drawing in foreign HEIs.

This said, while education hubs are being established in select Asia-Pacific cities, they are not necessarily the largest nor the most rapidly expanding cities, with Singapore being the case exemplar. Rather, education hubs are being established in cities that are associated with state-led attempts to expand and diversify the skilled tertiary and quaternary sectors to enhance the nature of the labor force, as well as R&D activity.

The Asia-Pacific, like all world regions, has seen a transformation in labor markets associated with growth of the services sector, including highly skilled employment (Daniels et al., 2005). Between 1991 and 2020, the region's share of high-skilled employment doubled to 15 percent of the overall global labour market, a relatively low

---

[6] See https://population.un.org/wup/Publications/Files/WUP2018-KeyFacts.pdf

Table 15.1 Percentage urban and rate of urbanization of the world, by geographic region, selected periods, 1950–2050

Geographic region	Percentage urban (%)						Rate of urbanization (%)				
	1950	1970	1990	2018	2030	2050	1950–1970	1970–1990	1990–2018	2018–2030	2030–2050
World	29.6	36.6	43.0	55.3	60.4	68.4	1.06	0.80	0.90	0.74	0.62
Africa	14.3	22.6	31.5	42.5	48.4	58.9	2.28	1.68	1.07	1.07	0.99
Asia	17.5	23.7	32.3	49.9	56.7	66.2	1.51	1.54	1.55	1.06	0.78
Europe	51.7	63.1	69.9	74.5	77.5	83.7	1.00	0.51	0.22	0.33	0.38
Latin America and the Caribbean	41.3	57.3	70.7	80.7	83.6	87.8	1.64	1.05	0.47	0.29	0.25
North America	63.9	73.8	75.4	82.2	84.7	89.0	0.72	0.11	0.31	0.25	0.25
Oceania	62.5	70.2	70.3	68.2	68.9	72.1	0.58	0.01	-0.11	0.08	0.23

Source: United Nations (2019b, p. 26).

percentage compared to Europe or the Americas, but a significant increase over time at the intra-regional Asian level (ILO, 2018, p. 5). Moreover, as the ILO carries on, this "upward trend in the share of services employment and of high-skilled employment are projected to continue" (p. 5).

The ILO's (2020) benchmark report—*World Employment and Social Outlook: Trends 2020*—makes a key point about the structural relationship between labor market shifts and Asia-Pacific's urban geographies:

> Within the region, workers in medium- and high-skilled occupations are predominantly located in urban areas ... The employment share of high-skilled occupations reached 26.0 per cent in urban areas in 2019, compared with just 8.8 per cent in rural areas. The employment share of medium-skilled occupations also differs widely between urban and rural areas, standing respectively at 55.3 and 30.0 per cent. The bulk of employment in rural areas (61.2 per cent) is represented by skilled agricultural, fishery and forestry workers and by workers in elementary occupations.
>
> To prepare their countries' labour markets for the use of smart technologies in industries and services, governments in Asia and the Pacific are focusing their policies and programmes on skills development (i.e., for technological upgrading) and on fostering an "innovation ecosystem" ... The emphasis of most countries in the region is on building up a highly skilled workforce through the modernization of vocational education and training programmes, the adoption of "skills roadmaps" for specific sectors, and the establishment of reskilling and upskilling mechanisms. (p. 54)

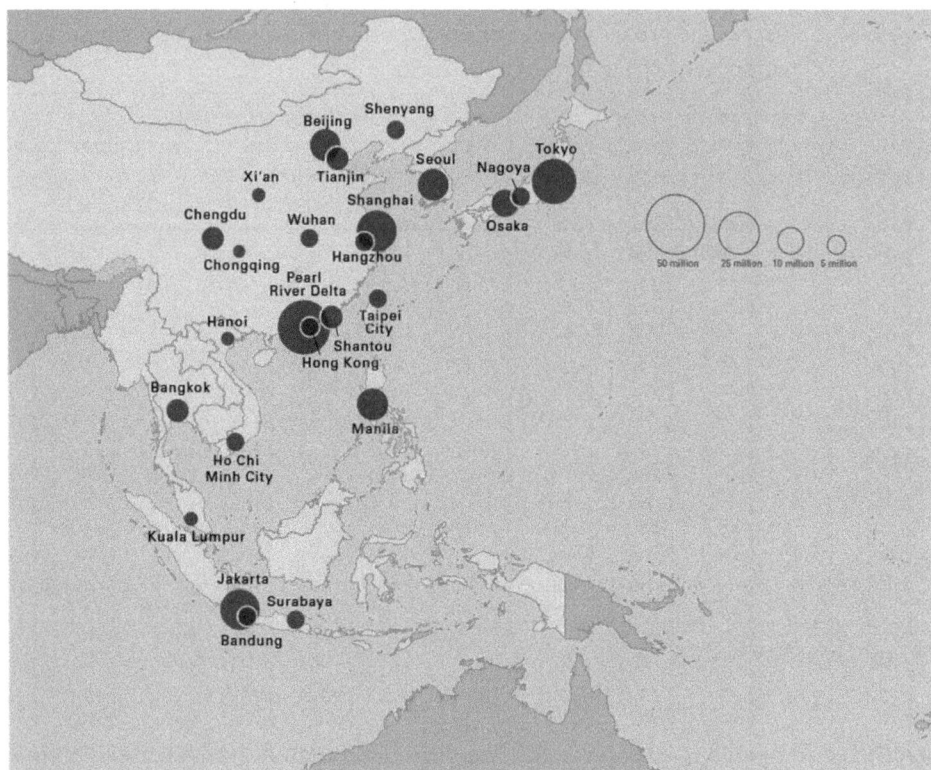

FIGURE 15.4 Pacific Asia: the 25 largest urban areas by population, 2010

Source: World Bank (2015, p. 21).

Education hubs are, then, part and parcel of this structural change towards advanced services and especially high-skilled employment. These hubs reflect state strategies to enhance capacity and facilitate structural change within regional economies and societies, but via institutional change within select urban spaces. And on a related note, education hubs are designed to facilitate university–industry–government linkages (UILs) and synergy, and more innovative development processes at the city-regional scale. The co-presence of national and international HEIs within spatially demarcated urban spaces is supposed to drive forward innovation.

As the Asian Development Bank (2020a) notes, Asia-Pacific states are increasingly cognizant of the concentration of innovation in "select" urban hubs. These hubs are generative of agglomeration economies, which fuel innovation with respect to processes, products, and R&D more generally. And universities—or to be more precise "top-tier universities"—play a key role in this urban ecosystem. The Asian Development Bank (2020c, p. 112) carries on:

> What drives the disproportionate role of cities in Asian innovation? Among a number of potential channels are economies of agglomeration, access to markets

and finance, and the clustering of the different skills that engender innovation. In light of the previous finding that human capital affects innovation, another channel worth exploring is the role of top-tier universities, which tend to be highly concentrated spatially. According to ADB [2020b], modern technology universities are often located near universities and research institutes. Universities, especially the top campuses, are pioneers in exploring the uncharted and leaders in pushing the knowledge frontier. Countries often allocate abundant resources to their top-ranked universities to boost innovation capacity.

Given the above dynamics, we need to conceive of education hubs as *state-sanctioned transnational education zones* that are designed to realize knowledge-driven economy ambitions.

Further information is provided below on the processes and politics associated with the emergence of the above patterns. It is important to keep in mind, however, that the transformation of higher education in the Asia-Pacific is both similar to and different than that unfolding in other world regions. As noted in the Introduction to this handbook, and especially Chapters 13, 14, and 24, these similarities include, firstly, the transformative impact of colonialism and then decolonization upon higher education systems and institutions. This dynamic has left a legacy in most countries that still impacts how universities and colleges (or equivalent) are governed, broadly defined, as well as how national HE systems become integrated.

A second key similarity is the combination of a broad massification agenda to ensure higher proportions of society have been educated so as to participate in the increasingly advanced sectors of the economy. The massification agenda has been spurred on by the integration, albeit differential and ever changing, of Asia-Pacific countries into the world economy. Early influential analyses' development of the so-called new international division of labour (NIDL) were very much focused on Pacific Asia's role in the transformation of global production systems, which were enabled by the development of global infrastructures including container shipping, airports, and so on. This integration required, and requires, knowledgeable workforces, of course, but also increased capacity to conduct R&D, not to mention expertise to shape the regulatory process regarding global integration. Thus, institutions of higher education are charged by the state to play a role in enabling the development of the knowledge-based economy.

4. DEEP INTERNATIONALIZATION AND ARTICULATED INFRASTRUCTURE IN ASIA-PACIFIC CITIES

While structural forces are key drivers of education hubs across the world, including in Asia-Pacific cities, such hubs are de facto co-productions of regional states and internationalizing universities. More specifically, education hubs reflect the articulation of statecraft (in the form of policies, programs, and projects) to construct transnational education spaces and the agency of foreign HEIs as they seek to realize their vision, mission, and developmental agendas. In short, education hubs are co-constructed— or articulated—"infrastructures" to support the development and expansion of the knowledge-based economy in Asia-Pacific cities and countries.

What are infrastructures? For the purposes of this chapter, the burgeoning literature on infrastructure by anthropologists, geographers, and sociologists is useful. The anthropologist Brian Larkin (2013, p. 328) provides perhaps the most lucid definition:

> Infrastructures are built networks that facilitate the flow of goods, people, or ideas and allow for their exchange over space. As physical forms they shape the nature of a network, the speed and direction of its movement, its temporalities, and its vulnerability to breakdown. They comprise the architecture for circulation, literally providing the undergirding of modern societies, and they generate the ambient environment of everyday life.

Keller Easterling's 2014 book, *Extrastatecraft: The Power of Infrastructure Space*, reinforces the important point that infrastructure needs to be broadly defined, and includes not just material phenomenon but also intertwined standards, metrics, and ideas that determine the organization and circulation of people, objects, and content (e.g., curriculum and standards). Similarly, as Christopher Muellerleile (2018, pp. 282–283) emphasizes:

> The relationality of infrastructure also constitutes a unique relationship with territory. The constitutive objects and systems of infrastructure usually facilitate movement across space, or produce connectivity between various commodities, technologies, actors, and institutions.

Thus, education hubs are transnational infrastructural spaces, and reflect the intermingling of Asia-Pacific state agendas to construct the knowledge economy, as noted in the previous section, with internationalizing universities seeking to realize their visions and missions (which vary in nature).

Asia-Pacific states enable education hubs to emerge through a number of actions. First, states in the region transform regulations to enable foreign HEIs to establish commercial presence within national territory. The presence of foreign HEIs is an outcome of an explicit stance to open territory, and enhance capacity, via the import mechanism. This is the third distinct "modes of supplying services" according to GATS—"commercial presence" discussed earlier.

Second, Asia-Pacific states adopt a wide variety of stances on the types of HEIs to target. Some, like Singapore, target top-ranked universities (e.g., MIT, Imperial College, Duke University) to advance graduate education and R&D objectives, while others, like South Korea, target high quality yet less highly ranked universities. For example,

Incheon Global Campus in South Korea now hosts Ghent University (Belgium), George Mason University (USA), The State University of New York (USA), and The University of Utah (USA) (Kliebert et al., 2020). This said, some education hubs also reflect a tiered strategy, with less prestigious universities also being permitted to establish a commercial presence, though they are rarely profiled in public relations-related activities to the hub agenda (Olds, 2007).

Third, Asia-Pacific states adopt a wide variety of stances on the preferential national geographies associated with their hubs. The national geographies of the foreign HEIs in Singapore, for example, are now relatively balanced between Australia, the United Kingdom, the United States, and then France, while the education hubs that the Malaysian state has enabled have been dominated, since the beginning, by the United Kingdom and Australia (Kliebert et al., 2020).

Fourth, Asia-Pacific states incentivize the presence of foreign HEIs via a variety of forms of material support including:

- Time-specific subsidies, often for five years but then phased out.
- Access to national research funding programs, often via collaborative research partnerships with national HEIs, locally and/or regionally based firms, and government research agencies.
- Priority access to built infrastructure, including stand-alone campuses, sites (e.g., labs, offices) within national HEIs, and purpose-built collaborative buildings.
- Funding for human mobility, such that faculty, students, and staff can circulate across global space, engage in dual and joint degrees, acquire new professional skills, and facilitate the transformation of educational structures and systems.

While Asia-Pacific states have pursued the education hub agenda, the actual outcome on the ground in cities will also vary significantly depending on the nature of the internationalization strategy adopted by foreign HEIs.

Since the 2000s, we have seen the development of some new and relatively deep collaborative models of institutional presence in territories outside of universities' main campuses. These new models tend to be research- *and* graduate or professional education-oriented, with relatively strong interdisciplinary inclinations. Some worldwide examples include:

- Cornell Tech in New York City (a Cornell University/Technion–Israel Institute of Technology joint venture).
- Global Innovation Exchange in Seattle (a University of Washington–Tsinghua University joint venture).
- Duke-NUS Medical School in Singapore (a National University of Singapore–Duke University joint venture).
- Lee Kong Chian School of Medicine in Singapore (a Nanyang Technological University–Imperial College London joint venture).

These new models, the ideal according to education hub logic, are formal joint ventures (in full, or in a significant way) vs. stand-alone branch campuses; they involve significant medium-term commitment and investment; they are associated with the development of new purpose-designed buildings and broader institutional infrastructure; they involve the creation of new governance and organizational structures; they involve a concerted effort to produce innovative forms of new knowledge, impact, and sometimes service; and they are located in globalizing cities.

Why has this relatively deep form of internationalization emerged and fueled the development of new forms of higher education infrastructure, including in Asia-Pacific cities? It is certainly the opposite of the "ghost MOU" approach to internationalization where symbolic representations of internationalization are signed but lead to little but the creation of document after document buried in international unit filing cabinets.

Gabriel Hawawini's recent book *The Internationalization of Higher Education and Business Schools: A Critical Review* (2016) is worthy of attention. Hawawini is a professor of finance and former dean of INSEAD (2000–2006). He is the key architect of INSEAD's highly successful transformation into a genuine international business school via a strategic planning process that spurred on INSEAD to refashion its organizational structure in a manner that led to the development of a commercial presence in Pacific Asia (in Singapore) and the Middle East (in Abu Dhabi).

Hawawini's argument is framed by an institutional political economy hat when thinking about the internationalization of higher education. By this I mean he is cognizant of the role of different types of firms and states, as well as variable state–society–economy relations, in shaping the modern knowledge economy. This is a geographically uneven economy, and a very urban one. Given this, and given Hawawini's role as a higher education decision-maker and leader, he confronts what this evolving context means for higher education institutions that are grappling with the internationalization challenge.

In his short but insightful book, Hawawini first outlines what he defines as internationalization (2016, p. 5):

> Internationalization is an ongoing process of change whose objective is to integrate the institution and its key stakeholders (its students and faculty) into the emerging global knowledge economy.

Note the integrative element to this definition, as well as the "emerging" dimension to the global economy. Hawawini then discusses the academic and economic motives for internationalization, as well as the obstacles shaping how the internationalization of higher education can be realized. He then moves on to delineate the organizational model options to realize internationalization. These options can be visualized (see Figure 15.5) to depict the critically important relationship between motives (why internationalize), mechanisms (how to internationalize), and structural change (how to institutionalize internationalization in Asian cities where education hub agendas have been implemented).

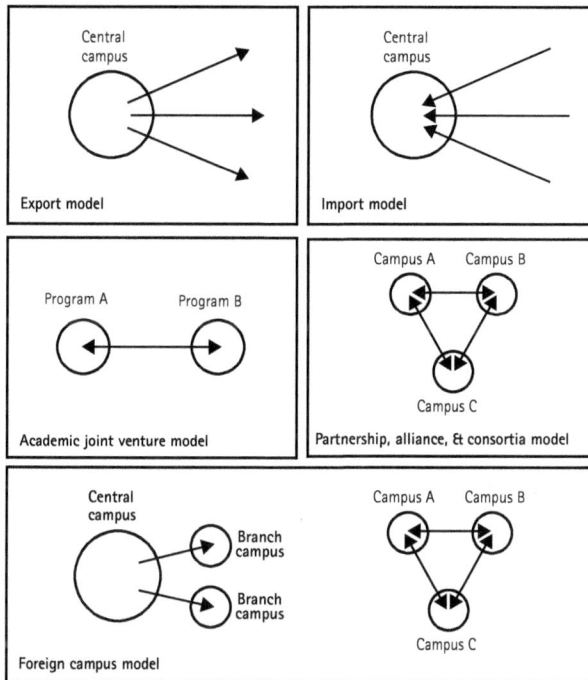

FIGURE 15.5 Models for the globalization of higher education

Source: Derived from Hawawini (2016).

Further to the above models, Hawawini makes the critically important point that the dominant model (the Import model) adopted by most Western universities, including public research universities, is becoming increasingly problematic with respect to the production of regionally and globally relevant knowledge, not to mention educational programming. Why? Economic growth, infrastructure, global production/value chains, and so on are binding together cities and regions, with some regions—such as the Asia-Pacific and the Arabian Gulf—developing as much more important and powerful spaces in their own right. Thus, the creation of solely, or jointly, developed institutional infrastructure in key nodal cities is required to adequately understand what is happening within these regions, how cities and regions are being bound together, and what is needed to develop and circulate relevant forms of knowledge. As Hawawini puts it (2016, pp. 25–26):

> An alternative view is that the global economy is being transformed into an increasingly complex network of interconnected but different economic areas each of which is endowed with the capacity to innovate and create knowledge. According to this multipolar view of the world, knowledge is increasingly being dispersed throughout the globe. In this case learning from the world becomes an imperative, particularly for research-driven higher education institutions. This is why higher education institutions should be present abroad: they need to acquire that dispersed knowledge and meld it together to create new ideas and more advanced knowledge.

Shifts in the spatial structure of economic activity, as well as in emerging growth patterns, are creating new regional economic geographies and political economies and if this is the case, sitting back and resting upon past laurels is not enough if a university seeks to become a "truly global institution" (Hawawini, 2016, p. 76). Committed and aspiring global institutions need to refashion their organizational structures to ensure they can realize their visions and generate an impact. This is, arguably, a key part of the rationale for why highly ranked research HEIs (e.g., Duke University, Imperial College, the University of Chicago) have taken the big step and allocated considerable time, effort, and resources to developing a formal institutional presence in Pacific Asian education hubs like Singapore and Hong Kong. Each university needs to be located within these cities and each has contributed to the development of the infrastructure (broadly defined) needed to become more regionally and globally relevant. They are, as Hawawini puts it, internationalizing "to learn from the world" in order to "create knowledge" in an increasingly "multipolar world."

Hawawini's book should be read in conjunction with other books and articles that focus on particular geographies and sectors. For example, Aihwa Ong's excellent book *Fungible Life: Experiment in the Asian City of Life* (2016) focuses on Singapore and the leading edges of bioscience. Ong's book is a deep dive in the complex role of the state, universities, firms, research stars, and knowledge about genetics in shaping the development of Singapore, in particular, as a key space in the development of scientific knowledge. On the basis of her intensive research, it is clear that universities like Duke and Imperial College seek (and need) to have a formal institutional presence in Singapore, and in association with key national partner universities like NUS and NTU, to enhance their capacity and expertise with respect to societies and economies in the Pacific Asian region. Ong's book, thus, provides insights on the geographical-, historical-, and sectoral-specific developments that these universities are currently navigating via state-sanctioned and governed education hub initiatives.

5. Education Hubs in the Asia-Pacific: Implications and Critique

Education hubs, defined in this chapter as *state-sanctioned transnational education zones*, are deserving of analytical and public policy attention given the resources and attention they are associated with. However, the concept and phenomenon is also problematic and worthy of far more critical assessment.

In terms of the most influential literature about education hubs, definitionally requiring a hub to include "foreign" HEIs (or schools in the case of Jeju Global) fetishizes the power and impact of foreign institutions and downplays the more significant, lasting, and sustainable impact of HEIs born in the Asia-Pacific region. Yes, the commercial presence of foreign universities, usually through the establishment of branch campuses can generate positive impacts in cities and countries in the Asia-Pacific, but it is an open question just how much of an impact foreign universities in the region have had on the production of new forms of innovative knowledge, new skills, and expertise. Indeed no one has ever, to my knowledge, conducted systematic and/or comparative research about how *impactful* foreign universities have been in the Asia-Pacific or at a global scale, in education hubs. There are, of course, individual case studies (e.g., Vora, 2018) but there has been remarkably little light shed upon genuine "value adding" of foreign HEIs within specific cities, countries, and world regions. The IBC phenomenon is also associated with numerous false-starts, closures, failures, rent-seeking behavior, arrogant behavior, and rapid swings in vision and mission. In short, it is problematic when one can bring into existence an *education hub* via the simple criterion of the mere presence of foreign HEIs in Asia-Pacific territory. Are dynamic innovative clusters of Asia-Pacific HEIs that interact with firms, non-profit organizations, and state agencies in city-regions—in countries and geographies that have no foreign HEIs located within them—not education hubs? Of course they are, but scholars have, to date, definitionally erased these types of education hubs from our analytical and public policy imaginations. For example, Melbourne in the Asia-Pacific is a globally significant destination for international students seeking to study in Australia, helping to spur on employment, investment (e.g., in purpose-built student accommodation), and cross-support (via international fees) for the entire university sector, and in particular the STEM fields. But it is not typically deemed an "educational hub" as it hosts no IBCs/TEZs.[7]

Second, and on a related note, terms like IBCs or offshore campuses are useful for creating lists, maps, and so on, but they mask huge differences in size, scale, mission, partnership structure (which many of them have), and capacity. Can one really compare the University of Nottingham, Ningbo (with approximately 8,000 students and 900 staff in 2020), to Singapore-based ESSEC Asia-Pacific which has "welcomed over 5,000 students and managers" over the course of 15 full years (2005–2020)? Many IBCs are housed on one floor of an office tower in cities—hardly a noteworthy presence when it comes to knowledge production, labor market transformation, or economic innovation.

Third, the absence of a formal delineation of an "education hub" (or equivalent) strategy by the state does not necessarily mean that there are not critical masses "of local and international actors who are strategically engaged in education, training, knowledge production and innovation initiatives" (Knight, 2011, p. 227). Shanghai, for example, has been targeted by IBCs since the early 2000s, and is now the third most attractive city in the world for IBCs, following Dubai and then Singapore. And yet the education hubs literature, to date, has not focused on the Shanghai case, while the Dubai and Singapore cases have received abundant attention. This is a problematic lacuna in the education hubs literature due to the expectation that there has to be a formal state-led education hubs development strategy with associated discourse in English.

---

[7] A 2015 report for the Australian Government Department of Education and Training, by Deloitte Access Economics noted "$2.8 billion of international student expenditure has been attributed to Melbourne" in 2014–2015 via the international students this de facto hub draws in (Australian Government Department of Education and Training, 2015, p. 39).

Fourth, is the presence of a blend of local/national and foreign HEIs a critically important dimension to defining education hubs? Or might there be other criteria that better exemplify hub-like innovative activity? For example, some fascinating research has been produced about the distinctive geographies of transnational knowledge production and circulation, and it is often not associated with formal education hubs. This can take the form of international scientific collaboration (as measured via co-authorship of indexed publications), the uneven geographies of R&D expenditure (including HERD expenditure), the evolving geographies of patent production, field-specific production of knowledge (e.g., Kong and Qian, 2017), regional and international co-authorship pipelines (e.g., Adams et al., 2020), and so on.

Fifth, the term "hub" is a metaphor, and metaphors are often political. Metaphors are strategically deployed to structure and interpret events, development processes, development projects, and so on (Kelly, 2001). This leads the human geographer, Trevor Barnes (1996, p. 159), to argue that:

> The more general point is that we must continually think critically about the metaphors we use—where they come from, why they were proposed, whose interests they represent, and the nature of their implications. Not to do so can lead us to be the slaves of some defunct master of metaphors.

So, while metaphors provide "color and entertainment" (Czarniawska-Joerges and Joerges, 1988), are designed to convince, and work (and fail), they also conceal as much, if not more, than they profile. Take Kuala Lumpur Education City (KLEC), for example. KLEC builds upon the successes of Education City Qatar in generating a legible space for the siting of foreign universities in Malaysia, in and around the national capital and the Multimedia Super Corridor. KLEC, though, is primarily a property development vehicle. KLEC's key strategic partner TH Properties Sdn Bhd., a national property development firm is a subsidiary of Lembaga Tabung Haji, an established financial institution. As KLEC noted in 2008 (cited in Olds, 2008):

> TH Properties' most significant development to date is Bandar Enstek. Bandar Enstek is strategically located just 8 minutes from the Low Cost Carrier Terminal (LCCT) and 10 minutes away from the Main Terminal of Kuala Lumpur International Airport (KLIA). It is only 38 minutes from the Kuala Lumpur City Centre via the ERL and a mere 5 minutes from the Sepang F1 Circuit. It is a RM9.2 billion integrated township set over 5,116 acres of prime land. Expected to be fully completed in 2025, Bandar Enstek will be home to 150,000 residents who will enjoy high quality communications infrastructure, fixed and wireless connections included, to support unlimited broadband applications provided by TH Properties' technology partner, Telekom Malaysia Bhd.

Education and property development, or education for property development? How many other education hubs in the Asia-Pacific are in reality for-profit residential or industrial property development vehicles, first and foremost?

In closing, education hubs are important components of higher education change in the Asia-Pacific. Education hubs are deserving of much more scholarly and public policy attention than they have received to date, yet they are equally deserving of far more critical assessment.[8]

REFERENCES

Adams, J., Pendlebury, D., Rogers, G., and Szomszor, M. (2020). *Global Research Report: South and Southeast Asia*. London: ISI Clarivate Analytics. https://clarivate.com/webofsciencegroup/campaigns/south-and-east-asia/

Al-Saleh, D. (In review). "Who will man the rigs when we go? Demographic fever dreams between Qatar and Texas." *Environment and Planning C: Politics and Space.*

Al-Saleh, D. (2022). "'Who will man the rigs when we go' Transnational demographic fever dreams between Qatar and Texas." *Environment and Planning C: Politics and Space*, 39(X), TBD.

Al-Saleh, D. and Vora, N. (2020). "Contestations of imperial citizenship: Student protest and organizing in Qatar's Education City." *International Journal of Middle Eastern Studies*, 52/4, 733–739.

Asian Development Bank (2020a). *Asian Development Outlook 2020 Update: Wellness in Worrying Times*. Manila: Asian Development Bank. https://doi.org/10.22617/FLS200256-3

Asian Development Bank (2020b). *Asia's Journey to Prosperity: Policy, Market, and Technology over 50 Years*. Manila: Asian Development Bank. https://doi.org/10.22617/TCS190290

Asian Development Bank (2020c). *Asian Development Outlook 2020: What Drives Innovation in Asia?* Manila: Asian Development Bank. https://www.adb.org/sites/default/files/publication/575626/ado2020.pdf

Australian Government Department of Education and Training (2015). *The Value of International Education to Australia*. Canberra: Australian Government.

Barnes, T. J. (1996). *Logics of Dislocation: Models, Metaphors, and Meanings of Economic Space*. New York: Guilford Press.

Beecher, B., Streitwieser, B., and Zhou, J. (2020). "Charting a new path toward economic prosperity: Comparing policies for higher education hubs in Hong Kong and South Korea." *Industry and Higher Education*, 34/2, 80–90.

Cross-Border Education Research Team (2020). *C-BERT Branch Campus Listing*. Data originally collected by Kevin Kinser and Jason E. Lane. Albany, NY. http://cbert.org/branchcampuses.php

Czarniawska-Joerges B. and Joerges, B. How to Control Things with Words: Organizational Talk and Control, Management Communication Quarterly. 1988; 2/2: 170–193. doi:10.1177/0893318988002002003

Daniels, P., Ho, K., and Hutton, T. (eds.) (2005). *Service Industries and Asia-Pacific Cities*. New York: Routledge.

[8] Sincere thanks to Lily Kong, Florence Lo, and the entire editorial team who put this wonderful handbook together. COVID-19 related disruptions came fast and steady and I am enormously grateful for their support, input, and abundant patience. I am also very appreciative of the kindness of the C-BERT (especially Kevin Kinser, Jason Lane, and Sarah Zipf) and TRANSEDU (especially Jana Kleibert) research teams who shared their data or reports with me, and with the skilled work of the UW-Madison Cartography Lab mappers (especially Tanya Buckingham and Alicia Iverson) for visualizing C-BERT data. Jack Lee at the University of Edinburgh kindly shared all of his relevant publications with me. Errors of interpretation are mine alone.

Dicken, P. (2015). *Global Shift: Mapping the Changing Contours of the World Economy*. New York: Guilford Press.

Easterling, K. (2014). *Extrastatecraft: The Power of Infrastructure Space*. London: Verso.

Hawawini, G. A. (2016). *The Internationalization of Higher Education and Business Schools: A Critical Review*. Singapore: Springer.

Hou, A. Y.-C., Hill, C., Chen, K. H. J., and Tsai, S. (2018). "A comparative study of international branch campuses in Malaysia, Singapore, China, and South Korea: Regulation, governance, and quality assurance." *Asia Pacific Education Review*, 19/4, 543–555.

ILO (2018). *ILOSTAT Spotlight on Work Statistics*, No. 2, May, pp. 1–11. https://ilo.org/wcmsp5/groups/public/---dgreports/---stat/documents/publication/wcms_629568.pdf

ILO (2020). "World employment and social outlook: Trends 2020." *World Employment and Social Outlook*, 108. https://www.ilo.org/global/research/global-reports/weso/2020/WCMS_734455/lang--en/index.htm

Jessop, B. (2002). *The Future of the Capitalist State*. Cambridge: Polity Press.

Kelly, P. F. (2001). "Metaphors of Meltdown: Political Representations of Economic Space in the Asian Financial Crisis." *Environment and Planning D: Society and Space*, 19/6, 719–742.

Kinser, K. and Lane, J. (2015). "Deciphering 'educational hubs' strategies: Rhetoric and reality." *International Higher Education*, 59, 18–19.

Kleibert, J., Bobée, A., Rottleb, T., and Schulze, M. (2020). *Global Geographies of Offshore Campuses*. Leibniz Institute for Research on Society and Space. http://ibc-spaces.org/wp-content/uploads/2020/08/Global_Geographies_of_Offshore_Campuses-11MB.pdf

Knight, J. (2004). "Internationalization remodeled: Definition, approaches, and rationales." *Journal of Studies in International Education*, 8/1, 5–31.

Knight, J. (2011). "Education hubs: A fad, a brand, an innovation." *Journal of Studies in International Education*, 15/3, 221–240.

Knight, J. (2013). "Education hubs: International, regional and local dimensions of scale and scope." *Comparative Education*, 49/3, 374–387.

Kong, L. and Qian, J. (2017). "Knowledge circulation in urban geography/urban studies, 1990–2010: Testing the discourse of Anglo-American hegemony through publication and citation patterns." *Urban Studies*, 56/1, 44–80.

Lane, J. E. and Kinser, K. (eds.) (2011). *Multinational Colleges and Universities: Leading, Governing, and Managing International Branch Campuses*. San Francisco, CA: Jossey-Bass.

Lanham, R. A. (2006). *The Economics of Attention: Style and Substance in the Age of Information*. Chicago: University of Chicago Press.

Larkin, B. (2013). "The politics and poetics of infrastructure." *Annual Review of Anthropology*, 42, 327–343.

Lee, J. T. (2015a). "Soft power and cultural diplomacy: Emerging education hubs in Asia." *Comparative Education*, 51/3, 353–374.

Lee, J. T. (2015b). "The regional dimension of education hubs: Leading and brokering geopolitics." *Higher Education Policy*, 28/1, 69–89.

Muellerleile, C. (2018). "Calming speculative traffic: An Infrastructural Theory of Financial Markets." *Economic Geography*, 94/3, 279–298.

Olds, K. (2007). "Global assemblage: Singapore, foreign universities, and the construction of a 'global education hub.'" *World Development*, 35/6, 959–975.

Olds, K. (2008). *Education Cities, Knowledge Villages, Schoolhouses, Education Hubs, and Hotspots: Emerging Metaphors for Global Higher Ed*. https://globalhighered.wordpress.com/2008/04/16/metaphors/, accessed September 24, 2020.

Ong, A. (2016). *Fungible Life: Experiment in the Asian City of Life*. Durham, NC: Duke University Press.

Sidhu, R., Ho, K.-C., and Yeoh, B. (2011). "Emerging education hubs: The case of Singapore." *Higher Education*, 61/1, 23–40.

United Nations (2019a). *World Urbanization Prospects: The 2018 Revision – Key Facts*. https://population.un.org/wup/Publications/Files/WUP2018-KeyFacts.pdf

United Nations (2019b). *World Urbanization Prospects: The 2018 Revision*. https://population.un.org/wup/Publications/Files/WUP2018-Report.pdf

Vora, N. (2018). *Teach for Arabia: American Universities, Liberalism, and Transnational Qatar*. Stanford, CA: Stanford University Press.

World Bank (2015). *East Asia's Changing Urban Landscape: Measuring a Decade of Spatial Growth*. Washington, DC: World Bank. https://www.worldbank.org/content/dam/Worldbank/Publications/Urban%20Development/EAP_Urban_Expansion_full_report_web.

CHAPTER 16

··

OPEN UNIVERSITY SYSTEMS

··

MELINDA DELA PEÑA BANDALARIA AND
ALEXANDRA IVANOVIC

1. INTRODUCTION

> Globally, the number of students enrolled in higher education is forecast
> to rise to above 414 million in 2030. The need to increase enrolment will
> be particularly great in the South. Online, Open and Flexible education
> represents a core range of strategies within a variety of contexts, utilising
> media and information and communication technologies (ICT), to con-
> tribute to meeting this growing demand, while ensuring equity, access,
> and quality learning outcomes.
>
> The Paris Message, 2015[1]

THE Paris Message was a set of actions formulated during the Global High Level Policy
Forum in June 2015. The projection emphasized two points: (1) that the increase in enrollment in higher education will be greater in the Global South, where most of the
countries in Asia and the Pacific belong; and (2) that the use of online, open, and flexible education will need to become more widespread to meet the projected enrollment
numbers. With the Asia-Pacific region accounting for almost 60 percent of the world's
population (approximately 4.3 billion people), continued population growth and
attending demand for higher education have created specific challenges for the region
including: the need to improve educational quality and the relevance of curriculum and
instruction, increasing and better utilizing the financial resources available for higher

---

[1] https://iite.unesco.org/files/news/639206/Paris%20Message%2013%2007%202015%20Final.pdf.
Hosted jointly by UNESCO and the International Council for Open and Distance Education, the Global
High Level Policy Forum was attended by more than 150 delegates from 55 countries.

education, and balancing the expansion of access to higher education with equity of access (ADB, 2011).

Governments in the Asia-Pacific region have committed to achieving the United Nations' Sustainable Development Goals (SDGs) by 2030. To meet the objectives of Goal 4.3 to "ensure equal access for women and men to affordable and quality technical, vocational and tertiary education, including university" (UNESCO, n.d.-a), governments will need to invest more in higher education to enable individuals to seize the opportunity to upskill in the twenty-first century—projected to be the "Asian Century" (ICEF Monitor, 2015 as cited by Bandalaria, 2018). There is, therefore, a need to consider non-conventional approaches such as those offered by the Open University (OU) system which can deliver education through open, online, and flexible modes, as proposed in the Paris Message. Moreover, the onset of the COVID-19 pandemic in early 2020 led to significant disruption to traditional tertiary education activities (International Association of Universities, 2020) making accessibility to higher education institutions (HEIs) more important than ever. This presents both challenges and opportunities for the OU system going forward.

Open, online, and flexible education modes are not really new concepts although there are variations in how they are defined and interpreted (Kember and Murphy, 1990; Lewis, 1990; Shurville et al., 2008; Caliksan, 2012). For the purposes of this chapter, open learning or open education can be considered the educational system under which OUs operate, while online learning refers to the mode of delivery through the internet and technology, and flexible learning is a feature of that learning process which provides learners with choices about where, when, and how learning occurs (Shurville et al., 2008). The practice or the system of implementation of these three concepts has evolved over the years, influenced and shaped by different dynamics, including rapidly modernizing information and communication technologies (ICTs); the varying contexts and demands of learners, e.g., mobility; changes in global perspectives about learning, such as more inclusive lifelong learning; and the fast-changing skills demanded by industry.

This chapter presents the imperatives for, and the philosophical underpinnings of, the establishment of OU systems, the development or evolution as practiced or implemented by different OUs in Asia and the Pacific, as well as its potential role in the future of learning and higher education in the region.

2. Harnessing the Potential of Open University Systems

The core philosophy for the development of OU systems is to provide higher education access to marginalized groups in society through open learning practices. Open learning refers to "a student-centered approach to education that removes all barriers to access while providing a high degree of learner autonomy" (Maxwell, 1995, p. 361).

Other widely accepted definitions emphasize the "openness" of this education mode. For instance, the founding chancellor of The Open University in the UK (UKOU), Lord Crowther, defined openness in relation to people, places, methods, and ideas with open learning being a philosophical construct that advocates the removal of constraints and barriers to learning (Kanwar et al., 2016). Daniel (2019) expresses this further as (1) open to people—affordable to all students, (2) open to places—offered ubiquitously as to scale, (3) open to methods—institutions being well-governed and managed, and (4) open to ideas—effectiveness of teaching.

There are currently over 70 Open Universities around the world with student numbers near 30 million, the majority located in Asia and the Pacific region (Contact North, 2018).

2.1   Characteristics of an Open University

Open universities function similarly to traditional or conventional universities—many undertake the major functions of instruction and knowledge creation through research, with some estimating almost 60 percent of OUs having a research focus (DeVries, 2019). However, they engage with society in a non-traditional tertiary system of learning with teaching and learning methods (usually through distance education modalities) that, until the more recent advent of Open Educational Resources (OERs)[2] and the emergence of Massive Open Online Courses (MOOCs),[3] had not always occurred in the conventional classroom.

Open Universities are commonly characterized by the use of distance education modalities, which can cause some confusion. In many countries, like Australia, the term open learning is often used synonymously with "distance education," also known as correspondence education, external study, or off-campus study (Fraser and Deane, 1997). Yet, OUs and distance learning have quite different scopes and objectives—an OU is a type of university offering open admissions to create learning opportunities to large groups of people, whereas distance education is a teaching modality that can be used by both open and conventional universities to provide efficient and inexpensive education to tertiary students who are not physically present at the institution site (Surbhi, 2021). The teaching modality of an OU can be onsite (conventional residential), by distance (including through online learning programs), or dual mode[4]—onsite and through distance learning. While an OU can deliver instructions via distance mode (and most

---

[2] OERs are teaching, learning, and research materials in any medium—digital or otherwise—that reside in the public domain or have been released under an open license that permits no-cost access, use, adaptation, and redistribution by others with no or limited restrictions (UNESCO, n.d.-b).

[3] See Farley's Chapter 17 in this volume.

[4] In this chapter, reference to dual mode means universities that offer on campus and distance education.

of them do), they also offer flexible learning and scheduling (e.g., weekends, evenings) which can be done offline and in person. These features can be challenging to implement in conventional universities given their structures and organizational models, whereas they enable OUs to overcome important barriers to higher education (DeVries, 2019).

Further, being "open to people," the core profile of learners the OU system hopes to target differs from the conventional tertiary system. These targeted learners include those from marginalized social groups (learners with physical barriers, including disabilities; individuals who may not be able to physically attend an onsite university while living in rural and regional areas; or individuals, particularly women, who have not been able to previously enroll in the tertiary system due to social or cultural factors). Other targeted learners include those who may have missed the opportunity to complete tertiary education (school leavers or second chance learners), those who may need to study and work at the same time, and those who seek more flexibility in their education, including adult learners returning to higher education or professionals seeking to upgrade skills or change careers.

Given the different groups targeted by OUs it is no surprise that there is a wide variation in the age of learners at these institutions. Recent trends seem to indicate that the student age profile is getting younger, although with some exceptions, such as South Korea which has seen a decline in the 25- to 39-year-old cohort and an increase in the numbers of older students (Tait, 2018). Females also seem to make up a greater portion of enrolled students at OUs than males (Tait, 2018).

From the learner's perspective, the motivation to undertake study at an OU may not differ significantly from those who attend the more traditional or conventional universities. Some seek formal qualifications through a tertiary degree, while others look to improve skills in specific fields (e.g., learning a programming language), to increase their knowledge and learning (e.g., a course on Chinese calligraphy) or to socialize with peers. However, students who attend OUs are usually dictated by their special circumstances, often due to other commitments or barriers as noted above. In some cases, the programs offered by OUs are cutting edge (such as those that directly respond to the needs of major industries),[5] motivating the learner to choose to attend an OU instead of a conventional university. The flexibility afforded by the OU system also provides greater attraction even to young learners who may want to engage in other activities (e.g., sports competitions, etc.) while studying. In addition to the "open" nature of OUs, catering to the circumstances of learner mobility (ubiquity) is another reason learners choose to attend an OU.

Cost savings for students may also be a consideration, particularly if the delivery mode is by distance education. While tuition fees are often the same or comparable

---

[5] For example, the Open University of China's Education and Training Center established an Artificial Intelligence training program to help meet the soaring needs in this field (OUC Education and Training Center, n.d.). UKOU's Knowledge Media Institute (KMI) is leading a research project using blockchain to verify learners' educational and employment qualifications (Open Blockchain, n.d.).

to some conventional universities, many OUs are subsidized by their governments indicating potential cost savings for students compared to other universities. However, even where tuition fees are similar, reduced costs for students attending an OU are more often due to savings incidental to the course of study itself, such as expenses associated with transportation, and room and board (Educationdata.org, 2021).

2.2 The Evolution of Open Universities

Early initiatives of the OU system were characterized mostly by distance learning or "teaching by correspondence," such as the delivery of educational materials to students by mail, as a strategy to provide access to those who could not participate in the traditional or conventional system of education (Tait, 2008). These early initiatives, still used by many OUs today, emphasized learning by design, assessment, feedback to learners, organized schedules, and learner support. While some of the first institutes that offered an OU system taught through correspondence,[6] these foundational institutions differed in their philosophy and operationalization of an OU system which explains the variations among OUs today.

For example, the University of London's External Study System offered the opportunity for anyone in the United Kingdom to study without a residence requirement, while the University of South Africa (UNISA) was "open uniquely as a higher education institution to people of all ethnicities," providing an opportunity for black South Africans to access higher education, including Nelson Mandela among its alumni (Tait, 2018). UNISA also pioneered the single-mode distance teaching university (DTU) which was later followed by most OUs. Single-mode DTU implements distance education as the only mode of instruction compared to other early distance education institutions, like the University of London, which offered dual-teaching modalities.

However, it was UKOU, established in 1969, that "was considered a breakthrough in higher education," with its impact on the development of single-mode DTU worldwide which has become a "model of imitation and guidance abroad," as seen in most of the large single-mode DTUs established in national jurisdictions, including those in the Asia-Pacific region since the early 1970s (Guri-Rosenblit, 2019). The UKOU's use of the term "open" in its name has also become the norm for other universities providing higher education by correspondence.

---

[6] For example, the University of London in 1826 (Tait, 2008); the Institute for Teaching by Correspondence in Russia in 1850; the Toussaint and Langenscheidt Institute in Berlin in 1856; the Swedish Liber-Hermods Institute, in 1898 (Zadorozhna and Kryms'ka, 2012); and the University of South Africa (UNISA) in 1946 (Tait, 2008).

3. Open University Systems in Asia and the Pacific

The development of the Open University systems in Asia and the Pacific aligns with the observation of Kanwar et al. (2016) that "openness is an evolving concept and that there are degrees of openness in different institutions," which could probably be attributed to the fact that "each particular Open University has its own mission related to the local political and social context in which it works" (Jones et al., 2009). For some, their modality of teaching (most often via distance education) indicates the "openness" of the university, whereas for others it includes both the "openness" of access as well as the modality of educational delivery.

3.1 Teaching Modalities in Open Universities across Asia and the Pacific

3.1.1 *The Single-Mode DTU*

Learning by distance education in Asia and the Pacific can be traced back as far as the late nineteenth century, during the Meiji period in Japan. Due to the absence of formal textbooks, "lecture notes" were the only form of materials given to students to study. Waseda University, Tokyo, enabled students who could not travel to the university to use these printed lecture notes for study and obtain certificates of completion (Aoki, 2010). Later, other OUs used correspondence via postal communication to deliver education. In Australia, the University of Queensland Department of Correspondence Studies, established in 1911, was the first university distance program in the southern hemisphere (White, 1982), closely followed by the Royal Melbourne Institute of Technology (RMIT), which began offering external studies in 1919, and then University of Western Australia in 1921 (Guiton and Smith 1984). Radio correspondence was later added as a mode of teaching during the 1930s (Cunningham et al., 1997). New Zealand's OUs similarly started with correspondence in 1922 before adding radio in 1931 (Stevens and Tate, 1994). Audio and visual instruction via television was a subsequent mode of educational delivery in these and other countries in Asia-Pacific.

In China, distance higher education started in the 1940s through correspondence via postal communication (Li and Chen, 2019). The Tianjin Hongzhuan Broadcast Correspondence University established in 1958, was the first university in the country to add radio as a medium for education (Tianjin Open University, n.d.); distance teaching via television began with the establishment of the Beijing Radio and Television University in the 1960s (Beijing Open University, n.d.). Radio also marked the start of distance education in East Pakistan (now Bangladesh) in 1956 when the Education

Directorate distributed 200 radio receivers to educational institutions for the implementation of distance education (Bangladesh Open University, n.d.)

The 1950s and 1960s saw OUs established in Indonesia and India. In West Java, Indonesia, school broadcasting was "designed for those who could not continue studying due to the geographical barriers and economic problems that were caused by the Indonesian independence war" (Yaumi, 2007). In India, correspondence education started as a supplementary method to meet the growing demand for higher educational opportunities (Panda and Garg, 2019). Specifically, the University of Delhi established the Directorate of Correspondence Courses in 1962 and became the first university in the country to offer correspondence courses at the tertiary level. India's first formal OU was established in 1982, the Andhra Pradesh Open University (APOU), followed in 1985 by the Indira Gandhi National Open University (IGNOU) which was intended to "democratise and increase access to higher education for large sections of the population" (Baggaley and Belawati, 2010, pp. 12–13).

From the 1970s onward, many OUs were established in Asia following the single-mode DTU model of the UKOU, including the Korea National Open University (KNOU), in 1972 (Lim et al., 2019); Allama Iqbal Open University (AIOU) in Pakistan, in 1974 (Awan, 2015); and the Odisha State Open University, a state funded open university in India, which was established recently in 2015 (Panda and Garg, 2019). In almost all countries in the region, OUs were initially established through government initiatives with public funding.

3.1.2 *Dual Modes of Instruction*

The other model, dual mode distance teaching universities,[7] provide mixed programs that are offered either as distance or internal learning programs or both. Open Universities in Australia and New Zealand both follow this dual mode of education delivery. Australia created Open Universities Australia (OUA) in 1993, a higher education consortium of 17 universities providing academic programs through distance education (OUA, 2020). Similar to the model of OUA, the Open University Malaysia (OUM) comprises a consortium of 11 public universities in the country offering degree programs through distance education (OUM, n.d.).

Asia eUniversity offers a new type of dual-mode distance teaching university. Like OUA and OUM, Asia eUniversity consists of a consortium of universities; however, while physically based in Malaysia it is owned by 35 member countries of the Asian Cooperation Dialogue (ACD). The Asia eUniversity collaborates with institutions of higher learning (IHLs) and Training Centers in the ACD member countries to offer quality, accessible, and affordable academic degree and professional training programs (Asia eUniversity, n.d.).

---

[7] Such as the Wawasan Open University (Malaysia) and the Open University of Hong Kong.

3.2 Admission to Open Universities across Asia and the Pacific

Admissions criteria to enter OUs across Asia and the Pacific vary considerably. Some OUs in the region have relatively open admissions systems such as Ramkhamhaeng University of Thailand, which includes students who did not pass the national level entrance exams for conventional universities (Thailand Higher Education, n.d.), while the Indira Gandhi National Open University (IGNOU), India accepts those without secondary qualifications (Perris, 2015). For the Open University China, "admissions were and remain, uniquely open, with the university administering its own entrance examination, credential and enrollment quotas" (Perris, 2015, p. 282).

Other OUs in the region have limited requirements for enrollment, such as the Open University Kaohsiung (Taiwan (ROC), which sets a minimum age limit—"all citizens over 18 are eligible to enrol without requirement of any formal academic record or entrance exam" (Open University Kaohsiung, n.d.), while the OUM (Malaysia) has an open entry system where applicants only need to fulfill the minimum requirements applicable to adults who possess learning experience which can be assessed and matched against the learning outcomes of an academic course (Ali et al., 2006). Admission to Indonesia's Universitas Terbuka still requires a high school certificate or its equivalent, but there is no restriction of age, domicile, or duration of study (Belawati and Bandalaria, 2018).

Other OUs target specific groups. For example, the AIOU (Pakistan) caters to those who have been excluded in the education environment due to physical disabilities and cultural-related reasons. Similarly, the University of the Philippines Open University (UPOU) specifically targets those from marginalized groups, including learners who are physically challenged (Bandalaria, 2020).

3.3 Flexibility in Delivering Instruction through Education Technologies

Most OUs in Asia articulate openness by providing flexibility in the mode of delivering instruction through distance education or technology-enabled instruction. In some cases, flexibility in delivering instructional content is explicitly stated as in the case of OUM, which claims to be the only institution in Malaysia that focuses on open and distance learning (Ahmad and Fadzil, 2002). Similarly, Sukhothai Thammathirat Open University, Thailand, promotes itself as a university without walls and has students from all 76 provinces in the country. The UPOU, in its mission statement, indicates that it will "democratize access to quality tertiary education by delivering instruction through distance education mode" (Bandalaria, 2007). Flexibility offered by OUs can also be offered in relation to scheduling, such as non-fixed registration and semester terms, although some OUs in the region actually follow academic or school calendar years which, rather than being open, can serve as barriers to many learners (Bandalaria, 2018).

3.4   Growth and Development of OUs in Asia and the Pacific

Among the 70 OUs globally, Asia and the Pacific account for approximately two-thirds—45 or 48 according to different sources[8] with almost 19 million learners from single DTUs based on Table 16.1. The massive growth and development of OU systems in Asia may be attributed to the emphasis placed on higher education in the region as a means to improve life and livelihood prospects driving the demand for access to higher education institutions, including those offered by OUs. Also, the rapid population growth rate in the region, especially in South Asia, has worsened poverty and led to increased illiteracy rates (Gu, 1983), further marginalizing those unable to access HEI. This demand has provided imperatives for governments across the region to expand access to education, including tertiary education. By contrast, the developed countries in the region appear to have different imperatives for the establishment of OUs. With one-third of Australians living in rural and regional areas, open universities and distance education learning have been in response to attempts to "equalise educational opportunities" not only for those in the "outback" but also students in urban areas who "opt for the convenience and flexibility of this mode" (Latchem, 2018, pp. 9–10).

By their nature, OUs were created to become large-scale universities (Guri-Rosenblit, 2019). Given Asia's population and the imperatives described above, it should be no surprise that the majority of "mega universities," DTUs that teach over 100,000 students, would be in the Asia-Pacific region. The OUC is the largest university in the world with over 3.6 million students and a network headquartered in Beijing with 44 branches and approximately 3,000 study centers throughout the country, while the IGNOU, KNOU, and AIOU all have students numbering in the millions. This comes with both strengths and challenges. Such large OUs can make significant investments in new technologies and develop high-quality materials but must also balance this with the logistic and pedagogical challenges that come with teaching large numbers of learners (Daniel, 1996 as cited in Guri-Rosenblit, 2019).

---

[8] In 2018, Contact North listed 70 open universities, 45 of which are in Asia (DeVries, 2019), while Kaushik and Dhanarajan (2018) listed 48 Open Universities in Asia, citing ADB (2011) as their source.

Table 16.1 Single-mode distance teaching universities in Asia

Country/territory	No. OUs	Target student body	Total enrollment	Types of programs offered	Percentage of OU enrollment to total HE enrollment	Courses offered
East Asia						
China*	6	Adult learners otherwise without access to HEI higher education; tertiary level students; farmers, disabled people, military officers, and minority groups	4.3 million (2017)	Bachelor's; Associate; non-degree training such as community education, education for the elders, vocational skills training	More than 10.2%	Business, Finance, Economics, Law, Management, Arts, Engineering, Science & Technology (S&T), Education, Humanities, Literature, Information Technology
Hong Kong	1	Working students/part-time students	19,000 (2020)	Bachelor's; postgraduate (PG) degrees (Master's and doctoral)	16.7%	Arts, Social Sciences (SS), S&T Business and Administration, Education and Languages, Nursing and Health
Taiwan	2	Tertiary students and lifelong learners; adult learners	30,000 (2020)	Bachelor's; Associate; BA degree	4.1%	Humanities, SS, Business and Administration, S&T, Arts, Literature and Language, Mass Communication, Law, Education
Japan	1	Adult learners; high school graduates	90,000 (n.d.)	Bachelor's; PG degrees	3.1%	Living and Welfare, Psychology, Education, Society and Industry, Humanities and Culture, Informatics, Nature and Environment
South Korea	1	Adult learners otherwise without access to HE	2,700,000	Bachelor's; PG degrees; non-degree courses	4.1%	Liberal Arts, SS, Natural Sciences, Educational Sciences, Business
South–East Asia						
Indonesia	1	Working adults especially the teachers	300,000 (2020)	Bachelor's; PG degrees	8.3%	Economics, Social and Political Science, Education, Mathematics, Natural Science

(continued)

Table 16.1 Continued

Country/territory	No. OUs	Target student body	Total enrollment	Types of programs offered	Percentage of OU enrollment to total HE enrollment	Courses offered
Malaysia	2	Lifelong learners; working Malaysians regardless of their educational, ethnic or socio-economic background	160,000 (2018)	Diploma; Bachelor's; PG degrees Bachelor's; PG degrees	1.1%	Business and Management, Applied Sciences, Educational and SS, Digital Technology
Myanmar	1	All students within the country including those residing in border areas	<1000	Bachelor's degrees	0.009%	Business and Administration, Psychology, Education, SS
Philippines	1	Marginalized sectors of the society	4,000 (2020)	Associate; Bachelor's; Graduate Certificates and Diplomas; PG degrees	0.019%	Education, Information and Communication
Thailand	2	Working adults; young students who cannot pass national entrance examination for normal universities	800,000 (2018)	Bachelor's; PG degrees	2.4%	Agriculture, Art, Communications, Economics, Education, Health sciences, Liberal Arts, Management, Nursing, S&T
Vietnam	2	Open to all people; including students who scored too low in the high school exams to be admitted to regular universities	132,000 (2018)	Certificate, PG degrees. Bachelor's, Master's	0.47%	Economics, Finance, Management, IT, Law, Biotechnology, Civil Engineering, Languages, SS
South Asia						
Bangladesh	1	Rural disadvantaged groups like rural women, agricultural workers, unemployed youths, uneducated adults, adults busy with family or work	650,000 (2017)	Bachelor's; Master's; Non-formal courses	1.6%	Agriculture and Rural Development, Business, Education, SS, Humanities & Languages, S&T

Pakistan	2	Marginalized social groups: prisoners; visually impaired persons; dropout girls; and the transgender community	1.275 million	Undergraduate; PG degrees; Associate; Diploma; Bachelor's; PG degrees	6.7%	Arabic & Islamic Studies, Education, Sciences, Humanities & SS
Sri Lanka	1	Adult population unable to access learning opportunities otherwise	40,000 (2017)	Certificate; PG degrees	0.6%	Education, Engineering S&T, Health Sciences, Humanities & SS, Natural Sciences, Management

Source: Information gathered from various sources including university websites and published articles/literature about the university.

4. AN ALTERNATIVE
TO CONVENTIONAL UNIVERSITIES

Open universities in the region offer a wide range of academic degree programs at the Bachelor, Master's, and doctoral level and can be considered an alternative system to conventional universities in accessing tertiary education across a range of disciplines. The degrees that most of the OUs provide are in education, economics, business and finance, and the social sciences. Many universities also provide courses in agriculture and IT-related fields.

However, degree programs which require more hands-on or skills-based training, are not as prevalent in OUs compared to their more traditional counterparts. In some countries, such as India, engineering degrees cannot be undertaken through distance learning (Supreme Court of India, 2017). However, several OUs do offer courses in medical fields, engineering, and the natural sciences. The OUM Malaysia offers nursing degrees from the undergraduate to doctoral level in online as well as blended modes (combining online study with face-to-face tutorials/seminars) demonstrating the flexibility some OUs can offer to students. More recently, immersive technologies are making such disciplines possible through distance education modalities. The Open University of Japan (The OUJ) has explored training students in required skills for chemistry by using computational chemistry simulation environments as a virtual laboratory (The OUJ, 2019).

In addition to traditional degree programs, there are some OUs that offer specific vocational education streams. OUs in India offer a range of vocational diploma and certificate-level courses from certification in ICT, motor-cycle repair, poultry farming, to food and nutrition and even dental hygiene/mechanic certifications (OUs in India and ODL Courses, n.d.). Meanwhile, all OUs in China have non-degree education departments or training centers offering a range of vocational training programs (OUC Education and Training Center, n.d.).

Table 16.1 lists the number of OUs in Asia,[9] by country/territory, using a single-distance mode of teaching (37 in total), their target student bodies as indicated in their respective mission and vision statements, total enrollment figures, the types of academic programs offered, and the percentage of OU enrollment to total higher education per country. The enrollment figures can be indicative of the portion of society who may not have the opportunity to access higher education if the OU system was not available.[10]

---

[9] As both Australia and New Zealand offer dual mode teaching, they are not included in this table.

[10] It should be noted that these enrollment figures may not have much impact on the country's Gross Enrollment Rate (GER) since usually, students of an Open University system are already beyond the age range at the tertiary level usually included in a country's GER. As described, most of the students of Open University systems are adult learners and those who want to have a "second chance" of getting a college degree.

The percentage of higher education students enrolled in OUs to total student enrollment in universities appears higher in countries in East Asia and relatively lower in South Asia (although Pakistan is an outlier in that region). This might be due to several factors including the way OUs are funded in the country; whether they are incorporated in educational and career frameworks, for example, whether they serve as an opportunity to climb the career ladder; or whether they are perceived as an appropriate alternative to conventional universities. Governmental policies towards OUs, the length of time OUs have been in a particular country; and the number of OUs in the country would also be factors to consider. While the scope of the present chapter does not allow diving deeper into this analysis, this is an important direction for future research that can contribute to the understanding of the perspectives and challenges of OUs in the Asia-Pacific region.

5. Challenges and Opportunities for the Open University System

5.1 Measuring Quality

There is a perception that distance education, which characterizes most of the OU system, is generally of lower quality than that of a conventional university. With the advent of the internet, many OUs added online learning as another mode of teaching from the 1990s (Qayyum and Zawacki-Richter, 2018; Zawacki-Richter and Qayyum, 2019), Still, this perception has continued with some scholars noting that "online learning carries a stigma of being lower quality than face-to-face learning, despite research showing otherwise" (EDUCAUSE, 2020). Some of this research has indicated that student performance is independent of the mode of instruction. (Ni, 2013), while other scholars contend that the distance education mode of instruction has been long-established with equal quality practices to its conventional counterparts (Stella and Gnanam, 2004).

At the national level, degree programs and credit courses offered by OUs in the Asia-Pacific region are subject to the same approval processes that govern residential universities. For example, the OUs in Malaysia are accredited by the Malaysian Qualifications Agency; in India, the Distance Education Council assesses the IGNOU and provides oversight on the quality of distance education in the country; the Universitas Terbuka, Indonesia, must adhere to the same quality standards and regulations applicable to HEIs in the country, including the submission of semester-based self-assessment reports to the Ministry of National Education; the OUJ is covered by the policy that all HEIs have to be reviewed and accredited every seven years by one of three QA agencies approved by the Ministry of Education, Culture, Sports, Science and Technology; and in South Korea, all universities offering four-year programs, including KNOU, must conduct self-evaluations at least once every two years and submit their findings to the Korean Council for University Education (Jung et al., 2011).

To further enhance the quality of delivery of education, OUs have adopted a range of models and quality frameworks, such as a Quality Circle framework. At UPOU, this takes the form of a multiple-expert review mechanism (subject matter experts, peer reviews, course designers, and media specialists) to ensure course packages are relevant, up-to-date, and pedagogically appropriate for its distance learners, as well as providing learner support and assessments (Bandalaria, 2007; Lumanta and Garcia, 2020). Other efforts to improve quality of service delivery by OUs center around implementation of different QA frameworks. A review of 12 QA frameworks implemented by distance education and technology-enabled instructions found 10 domains of quality relevant to OUs ranging from institutional leadership and teaching and staff qualifications to course content, delivery, and design, as well as IT infrastructure. However, not all QA systems are equal. Research by Jung et al. (2011) on QA frameworks across 11 countries/territories in Asia found the level of policy integration to respective national higher education QA systems varied considerably, posing challenges for OUs, HEIs, and governments to ensure quality graduates for the job market (Jung et al., 2011).

One goal of OUs is to provide greater access to marginalized groups, including women who for financial, social, or cultural reasons, and/or due to geographical distances, are not able to access higher education. While there does not appear to be region-level data on the gender balances of students who attend OUs in Asia-Pacific, limited information available at the national level does indicate that females comprise the majority of distance education users—64 percent (in 2020) and 63 percent (in 2013) of enrolled students were females at the National Open University, Taiwan (NOU) and UPOU respectively (NOU, 2020; Secreto, 2013). Given the large numbers of females who attend OUs, it is of note that research conducted on learners' perceptions of distance education in the region found that "even though DE has contributed to widening access to education and reducing gender disparity in education, there still exists a lack of gender-considerate supports [sic] in Asian DE" (Jung, 2012, p. 7).

5.2 Retaining Students to Be Fit for Purpose

Another indicator of quality for any university is the retention of its students. Researchers report poor retention and high dropout rates amongst open and distance learning (ODL) students are significantly higher than those from conventional universities (Fozdar and Kumar, 2007; Musingafi et al., 2015). Open universities in Asia-Pacific are not so different. Unfortunately, while openly recognized as an issue, there is currently no data available of retention rates of OUs across the region, with research in this area focused on the institution or country level. By way of one example, statistics from 2008 show the KNOU faced dropout rates as high as 39.4 percent for new students in their first semester (Lim et al., 2019)—there are also variations in retention between courses in the same institution (Fozdar et al., 2006; Fozdar and Kumar, 2007; Zulin et al., 2011). A cross-section of recent research indicates OUs in the region are conducting studies on how best to improve quality of delivery and increase student retention rates (see Zuhairi et al., 2020 on OUs in Taiwan and Indonesia; Au et al., 2018 on the OU of Hong Kong; or Sembiring, 2017 on Universitas Terbuka, Indonesia). Findings indicate that student retention would be improved with proactive and robust student support and better course design (linking study to student work and more flexibility in course design) (Au et al., 2018). Open universities that utilize mobile technologies to improve communication and learning could also help address the issue (Fozdar and Kumar, 2007) while using social media as a form of communication to motivate and support learners could also be used (UN-APCICT, 2014).

Just like any university, one of the basic functions of an OU is to produce graduates with relevant qualifications needed by industry. For those that do graduate, one indicator of quality education is employer satisfaction with the performance of their employees who are graduates of an OU system. Studies to measure are, again, mainly conducted at the individual institution level while some collaborative research in this area has also occurred. One study by OUM showed a 98.4 percent overall satisfaction rating by employers of OUM graduates, implying that ODL is a viable option in providing or teaching students with employable competencies required by major industries.[11] Another study conducted by the UPOU revealed that most respondents were willing to hire and recommend graduates from ODL, with no preference between ODL and residential graduates (Lumanta et. al., 2019). More broadly, a collaborative study of four OUs from Malaysia, Indonesia, Vietnam, and Thailand examined employers' perception of the sets of skills important in their workplaces, generally finding satisfaction with the performance of OU graduates for the skills the employers considered most important (Sungsri et al., 2017). While not a region-wide analysis, these studies do indicate a level of satisfaction by industry of the perceived quality of degrees and certifications acquired through the OU system.

6. Sustainability and Continued Relevance of Open Universities in Asia and the Pacific

6.1 The Role of ICTs in Shaping Open Universities

From the 1990s, most, if not all, OUs became more attuned to advancements in ICTs, including how access through the internet and utilization of ICTs could be maximized to deliver quality education.

UPOU, for instance, started integrating online components to its teaching and learning environment, mostly tutorial sessions, from 2001, and became fully online in

---

[11] The study involved 290 employer-respondents from various sectors like education, healthcare, service, manufacturing, hospitality, agriculture, and construction (Lim et al., 2011).

2007. This enabled the university to expand its student base by accepting students from around the globe to its degree programs. Following the KNOU model of offering courses online, the internet also enabled the establishment of 17 Cyber Universities and Colleges in South Korea by private organizations[12] (Lim et al., 2019). The internet further afforded a higher level of ubiquity or anytime-anywhere-any-gadget-access to instructional content as exemplified by the Virtual University, Pakistan's first cyber university, with the delivery of instructional content using free to air satellite television broadcasts and the internet to allow access regardless of a learner's physical location (Virtual University, n.d.). This flexibility in delivering instructional content has enabled the university to reach over 100 cities in the short span since its opening in 2002, including Pakistani students residing overseas in several other countries of the region.

The internet gave impetus to the acceleration of the open education movement, with the ultimate articulation of openness concretized by Open Educational Resource (OER) (from 2002), MOOCs (from 2008), and others. Another OU model that came about in 2011 was the OER universities (OERu)—a platform for students to obtain free education but with pathways to obtain credit towards academic qualifications at affordable cost (OERu, n.d.). The flexibility of many OUs in the region enabled them to adapt to these changes. To remain competitive, several OUs in the region added OERs and MOOCs to own their programs, thereby expanding access for existing and future learners (UNESCO, 2015). Further, member institutions of the Asian Association of Open Universities (AAOU) (discussed below), created their own Asian MOOCs portal, offering a range of free online courses.

However, while the internet enabled more access to higher education for many, the uneven development of, and access to, ICTs within countries, particularly for rural and marginalized communities, magnified the very social inequalities OUs sought to address. The digital divide or exclusion remains a major barrier for many in the Asia-Pacific region as far as modern ICT-enabled education is concerned, with only 65 percent of the region's population having access to the internet, while in specific countries this is below 35 percent (Statista, 2020). Even though the number of mobile internet users is predicted to increase to 61 percent of the population by 2025 (48 percent in 2020) (GSMA, 2020), suggesting greater accessibility for potential learners of OUs, issues remain including uneven internet penetration and poor connectivity at the local level, prohibitive costs of internet access and ICT equipment, as well as unreliable ICT infrastructure. This prevents OUs from fully embracing the use of the internet as the primary mode of education delivery (UN-APCICT, 2014; Kanwar et al., 2016). To address this reality, many OUs have implemented a range of blended strategies for instruction comprising different combinations of offline and online technologies for delivering instruction. Printed modules or course packages which are mailed to students are still dominant features of many OUs, like Universitas Terbuka, Indonesia, while others distribute USBs in their learner course packs which contain video materials and podcasts (Digital Review of Asia Pacific, n.d.). Various configurations of offline technologies,

---

[12] These cyber universities and colleges offer admission only to qualified persons, and the number of new students is decided by the Ministry of Education, unlike in KNOU, where anyone who graduates from high school can be admitted (Lim et al., 2019).

including the ability for teachers and students to access learning management systems and course materials on their computers, smart phones and laptops while offline, have also been developed to address internet access issues (Lumanta and Garcia, 2020). Other OUs have created learning centers located across their countries to allow access to teachers in regular, offline classrooms closer to the learners' homes (UN-APCICT, 2014).

6.2 Openness through the Culture of Sharing Ideas

Aligned with the development of ICTs, another pillar of the openness framework is in sharing of ideas among OUs, including the sharing of research results as well as best practices and lessons learned. For example, the AAOU, founded in 1987, is a non-profit organization of higher learning institutions primarily concerned with promoting ODL using a variety of media including publications, workshops, and conferences. The *AAOU Journal* is a peer-reviewed, open access journal for academics and scholars in the ODL field to share their research, expertise, and best practices including on QA frameworks, quality of instruction, student satisfaction, and utilization of upcoming ICT tools in teaching. Asian OUs are also members of the International Council for Open and Distance Education (ICDE) and the Commonwealth of Learning (COL) where ideas and best practices are also shared.

Although the culture of sharing appears strongly embedded in the philosophy of OUs, there are some constraints. Some studies have found barriers to greater sharing of knowledge, ideas, and resources at the institutional level including: confusion and lack of awareness regarding copyright protection and intellectual property right policies of an institution which inhibit greater sharing; a lack of open platforms or mechanisms for knowledge exchange; and an absence of a strong institutional culture promoting the sharing of knowledge, ideas, and resources among educators and their networks (Santosh and Panda, 2016).

6.3 Impact of Future Trends in Higher Education on OUs in Asia-Pacific

Historically, OUs have been at the forefront of distance education delivery and incorporating communication technology in their teaching. However, new challenges, including the COVID-19 pandemic of 2020, have highlighted the need for even more adaptable, agile, inclusive, and quality assured educational delivery to students. Current and future trends in the delivery of higher education include:

- Online learning which can be scaled to enhance teaching and learning experiences through the use of algorithms or artificial intelligence (AI) and analytics-driven support or through cloud-based learning platforms to expand access, data, and resource storage. Such automated services can more efficiently grade assignments, deliver personalized learning through adaptive content and assessments, and assist with administrative procedures such as managing enrollment and course deadlines, reducing the costs of faculty labor.

- Strengthened cooperation among universities to combine courses and program offerings that meet the knowledge and skills demands of industry. For example, the UPOU partnered with the country's leading telecommunications provider to develop an open online course on mobile applications (Bandalaria, 2018).
- A growing shift to online, digital credentials which focus on certificates and certifications that summarize achievement, skills, or competencies (Chakroun and Keevy, 2018). This trend, which is also a feature of the micro-credentials offered by major MOOC providers like Coursera and edX, is being driven by employers and industry certification programs, working in partnership with academic institutions—and is central to the "unbundling" of degrees into shorter-form micro-credentials that can stack into a larger lifelong curriculum. In the Asia-Pacific region, OUA has partnered with the OpenLearning platform to promote and deliver micro-credentials (OUA, 2020).

These emerging trends and predictions as to the future of higher education can be both a threat and an opportunity for OU systems. The integration of modern ICTs to the teaching and learning process demonstrates that access through the distance mode of instruction has been adopted by conventional or traditional universities, even more so since the COVID-19 pandemic. Since traditional universities now offer access to MOOCs in the same democratic terms of access as OUs, they pose a real threat to the existence of OUs. This will become a growing threat with the increasing number of MOOC certification programs (nano degrees; micro masters) and micro-credentialing offered by traditional universities in the near future. Asian countries account for 20–25 percent of enrollments in Coursera, edX, and Udacity MOOCs.[13] One way to directly address these challenges is for OUs in the region to integrate some of the same features (e.g., micro-credentialing towards a degree) in their own programs.

Open universities could also promote the unique advantages which distinguish themselves from their competitors. Most MOOCs from traditional universities are conducted in English and face similar issues of internet accessibility and the consequent digital divide. Open universities in the region could capitalize on their local strengths and outreach and their capacity to customize programs to the local context, as well as their experience in providing blended learning materials. In fact, OUs in Asia are developing MOOCs in languages spoken in Asian countries (AAOU, 2020). Open universities in the region should actively promote their message of openness for all, including to disadvantaged groups, as a distinguishing characteristic.

The funding of OUs has changed significantly over the last few decades. Initially funded mostly by national and state governments, OUs in the region are now largely funded by a combination of public funds, student fees, private grants, and charges

---

[13] See Farley's Chapter 17 in this volume.

for other non-degree learning and training. Allocation across these funding streams, however, varies at the institutional level and has also changed over time, particularly as demand for higher education has led many governments to reduce, sometimes drastically, their funding (Guri-Rosenblit, 2019). For example, IGNOU was almost entirely subsidized by its central government in 1985–1986, whereas by 2019 this contribution decreased to 15 percent, with 75 percent coming from student fees (Panda and Garg, 2019). For some OUs their fee structures are often lower than for conventional (including public) universities in their countries (Zuhairi et al., 2020). This lower comparative cost has been an added advantage for OUs in being able to offer higher education to those learners who are otherwise financially constrained. However, in some instances this advantage has also been eroded as competition for students has increased from the expansion of other distance education models and competition from conventional universities offering online programs. The KNOU, for example, has seen a steady decline in its enrollment numbers at the very same time that the cyber universities in the country have seen their numbers increase each year (Lim et al., 2019). In China, there are now as many as 68 online colleges in conventional universities offering online and distance education degrees and professional diplomas, in direct competition to the six single DTUs in the country (Guri-Rosenblit, 2019). To address these funding issues and reduced student numbers, OUs may need to consider expanding their future target audience including those who want to upgrade their professional skills, as well as follow the trend of younger students who in some high schools can complete degree course work concurrent with their final years of study (Guri-Rosenblit, 2019).

The COVID-19 pandemic has further accelerated the demand for traditional or conventional universities to quickly adapt to online learning worldwide, foretelling even greater competition to be faced by OUs in the region in the future. Open universities in Asia and the Pacific could enter into collaborative relationships with these other universities, emphasizing their strength as a partner with a lengthy history and experience of teaching through these distance education modalities. Further, OUs can partner with industry and leverage on the integration of modern technologies (e.g., immersive technologies) and even address the learning needs of gig workers who are increasing in number with the rise of the gig economy. Finally, as rapid modernization of ICTs shapes industry development, the resulting fast-changing work environments mean employees require continuous upskilling and reskilling to remain relevant, productive, and employable. As a result, the importance of, and demand for, lifelong learning opportunities has become widely recognized, something that is at the core of the OU system.

7. Conclusion

The long history of OU systems across the globe highlights the different articulations of the philosophy of open learning. It also defines their specific role in the framework of tertiary education systems in catering to non-traditional learners who cannot participate in more conventional modes of education. This chapter has highlighted the niche that OU systems occupy in higher education by examining how OUs are operationalized, defined, and distinguishable from their contemporary counterparts. A broad analysis of the OUs across the Asia-Pacific region, which has seen the most active development of OUs in recent decades, reveals institutions at the forefront of seeking to provide equal access to tertiary education, through lower costs, open admissions, and flexibility in educational delivery, all with governments at the helm of supporting these institutions. Open universities in the region have filled a gap in tertiary education systems, as evidenced by the many millions of learners who enroll with these institutions.

However, OUs must also contend with a range of competitors to maintain and in-crease enrollment levels, while not foregoing the quality of their educational deliverables. The emergence of MOOCs, OERs, and other "open" platforms finds OUs with more competitors than ever, not only nationally but also internationally. This has been further exacerbated by the COVID-19 pandemic which has forced many traditional and conventional universities to extend their teaching modalities, further blurring the lines between conventional universities and OUs. It can be expected that conventional universities will continue on this path, possibly maintaining some manner of hybrid or blended learning in the future. To remain competitive, OUs will need to continue innovating and maximizing the advantages of modern ICTs by offering a range of open teaching modalities, especially those which address the needs of the current breed of learners. These may include micro-credentialing through MOOCs, bridges and pathways to get a college degree, or further integrating AI into the teaching and learning processes that will enhance the quality of education in this mode of instruction.

This will also mean investing in resources to adequately train faculty and other uni-versity staff in these new possibilities and opportunities. Partnerships with businesses and industry could result in an expansion of target student bodies and may also help with funding and other resource limitations.

For OUs to remain relevant in the Asia-Pacific region, they will need to be agile and adept and continue to carve out their specialized areas, centered around their acces-sibility to those who would otherwise have no access to tertiary education, while also ensuring the skills of their graduates to meet industry expectations. They can empha-size their traditional strengths through their long history of providing distance educa-tion and create opportunities for establishing collaborations with other universities in the future—which is likely to see the emergence of new teaching models quite different from the current model of dual teaching universities. Open universities are well placed to respond to the call of the Paris Message for "online, open and flexible" education as well as the attainment of SDG 4.3, even beyond 2030. With the recognition that inclu-sive lifelong learning is necessary to keep pace with the fast-changing world of work, OUs can capitalize on their adaptability, flexibility, and innovativeness to better meet the challenges at the higher education level in the coming years.[14]

[14] The authors would like to thank Guzel Ishkineeva and Shengchi Ma for their research assistance on this chapter.

References

Ahmad, A. S., & Fadzil, M. (2002). *Distance Learning Developments in Malaysia*. https://core. ac.uk/download/pdf/298086521.pdf

Ali, A., Fadzil, M., and Kaur, A. (2006). *Open and Distance Education in Malaysia*. http://library.oum.edu.my/repository/204/1/Open_distance_education_in_Malaysia.pdf

Aoki, K. (2010). "The Challenges of ICT applications in distance Higher Education in Japan." *Asian Journal of Distance Education*, 8/2, 29–39.

Asia Development Bank (ADB) (2011). *Higher Education Across Asia: An Overview of Issues and Strategies*.https://www.adb.org/sites/default/files/publication/29407/higher-education-across-asia.pdf

Asia eUniversity (n.d.). https://aeu.edu.my/

Asian Association of Open Universities (AAOU) (2020). *Annual Report 2019*. https://www.aaou.org/annual-reports/

Au, O., Li, K., and Wong, T. (2018). "Student persistence in open and distance learning: Success factors and challenges." *Asian Association of Open Universities Journal*, 13/2, 191–202.

Awan, S. (2015). "Open learning system in Pakistan: A reappraisal." *Journal of the Punjab University Historical Society*, 28/2, 265–277. http://pu.edu.pk/images/journal/HistoryPStudies/PDF-FILES/19-samina_V28_no2.pdf

Baggaley, J. and Belawati, T. (eds.) (2010). *Distance Education Technologies in Asia*. New Delhi: Sage Publications India.

Bandalaria, M. dP. (2007). "Impact of ICTs on open and distance learning in a developing country setting: The Philippine experience." *International Review of Research in Open and Distributed Learning*, 8/1. https://doi.org/10.19173/irrodl.v8i1.334

Bandalaria, M. dP. (2018). "Open and distance e-learning in Asia: Country initiatives and institutional cooperation for the transformation of higher education in the region." *Journal of Learning for Development*, 5/2, 116–132.

Bandalaria, M. dP. (2020). "Universal access in online distance education: A case study from the Philippines." In S. L. Gronseth and E. M. Dalton (eds.), *Universal Access through Inclusive Instructional Design: International Perspectives on UDL*. New York: Routledge, 187–196.

Bangladesh Open University (n.d.). https://www.bou.edu.bd/

Beijing Open University (n.d.). https://www.bjou.edu.cn/

Belawati, T. and Bandalaria, M. dP. (2018). "Distance education in Asia: Indonesia and Philippines." In M. G. Moore and W. C. Diehl (eds.), *Handbook of Distance Education* (4th edition). New York: Routledge, 557–573.

Caliksan, O. (2012). "Design thinking in urbanism: Learning from designers. "Urban Design International", 17, 272–296.

Chakroun, B. and Keevy, J. (2018). *Digital Credentialing: Implications for the Recognition of Learning across Borders*. Paris: UNESCO.

Contact North (2018). https://teachonline.ca/tools-trends/universities

Cunningham, S., Tapsall, S., Ryan, Y., Stedman, L., Bagdon, K., and Flew, T. (1997). *New Media and Borderless Education: A Review of the Convergence between Global Media Networks and Higher Education Provision*. Canberra: Australian Government Publishing Service.

Daniel, J. S. (1996). *The Mega-Universities and the Knowledge Media*. London: Kogan Page.

Daniel, J. S. (2019). "Open Universities: Old concepts and contemporary challenges." *International Review of Research in Open and Distributed Learning*, 20/4, 195–211.

DeVries, I. J. (2019). "Open Universities and open educational practices: A content analysis of Open University websites." *International Review of Research in Open and Distributed Learning*, 20/4, 167–178.

Digital Review of Asia Pacific (n.d.). https://digital-review.org/themes/48-distance-education.html?start=2

Educationdata.org (2021). *Average Cost of College & Tuition*. https://educationdata.org/average-cost-of-college

EDUCAUSE (2020). https://er.educause.edu/articles/2020/3/the-difference-between-emergency-remote-teaching-and-online-learning

Fozdar, B. I. and Kumar, L. S. (2007). "Mobile learning and student retention." *International Review of Research in Open and Distance Learning*, 8/2, 1–18.

Fozdar, B., Kumar, S. A., and Kannan, S. (2006). "A survey of a study on the reasons responsible for student dropout from the Bachelor of Science programme at Indira Gandhi National Open University." *International Review of Research in Open and Distance Learning*, 7/3, 1–15.

Fraser, S. and Deane, E. (1997). "Why Open Learning?" *Australian Universities Review*, 1, 25–31

GSMA (2020). *The Mobile Economy Asia Pacific*. https://www.gsma.com/mobileeconomy/wp-content/uploads/2020/06/GSMA_MobileEconomy_2020_AsiaPacific.pdf

Gu, J. (1983). "The population and economic problems of South Asia." *Renkou Yanjiu*, 29/4, 49–53 (in Chinese). https://pubmed.ncbi.nlm.nih.gov/12313019/

Guiton, P. and Smith, M. (1984). "Progress in partnership: External studies in Western Australia." In K. Smith (ed.), *Diversity Down Under in Distance Education*. Toowoomba: Darling Down Institute Press, 83–87.

Guri-Rosenblit, S. (2019). Open Universities: Innovative past, challenging present, and prospective future. *International Review of Research in Open and Distributed Learning*, 20/4, 179–194.

ICEF Monitor (2015). *Is Asia Ready to be the Next Higher Education Superpower?* http://monitor.icef.com/2015/06/is-asia-ready-to-be-the-next-higher-education-superpower

International Association of Universities (2020). "The impact of COVID-19 on higher education around the world: IAU Global Survey Report."

Jones, C., Aoki, K., Russman, E., and Schlusmans, K. (2009). "A comparison of three open universities and their acceptance of technology enhanced learning." Paper presented at the 23rd ICDE World Conference on Open Learning and Distance Education, June 7–10, Maastricht, The Netherlands. http://libeprints.open.ac.uk/20657/1/Final_paper_081jones.pdf

Jung, I. (2012). "Asian learners' perception of quality in distance education and gender differences." *International Review of Research in Open and Distributed Learning*, 13/2, 1–25.

Jung, I., Wong, T. M., Li, C., Baigaltugs, S., and Belawati, T. (2011). "Quality assurance in Asian distance education: Diverse approaches and common culture." *International Review of Research in Open and Distributed Learning*, 12/6, 63–83.

Kanwar, A., Mishra, S., and Cheng, R. (2016). "Open education in Asia: Changing perspectives." Paper presented at the 30th Annual Conference of the Asian Association of Open Universities (AAOU), Manila, Philippines. http://oasis.col.org/bitstream/handle/11599/2444/2016_KanwarA_Open-Education-Asia_Transcript.pdf?sequence=1&isAllowed=y

Kaushik, M. and Dhanarajan, G. (2018). "Governance of open universities: A few observations on trends in Asia." *Journal of Learning for Development*, 5/3, 245–262.

Kember, D. and Murphy, D. (1990). "A synthesis of open, distance and student centred learning." *Open Learning*, 5/2, 3–8.

Latchem, C. (2018). "Australia." In A. Qayyum and O. Zawacki-Richter (eds.), *Open and Distance Education in Australia, Europe and the Americas: National Perspectives in a Digital Age*. Singapore: Springer, 9–24.

Lewis, R. (1990). "Open learning and its relevance to higher education." *Higher Education*, 19/2, 259–269.

Li, W. and Chen, N. (2019). "China." In O. Zawacki-Richter and A. Qayyum (eds.), *Open and Distance Education in Asia, Africa and the Middle East: National Perspectives in a Digital Age*. Singapore: Springer, 7–22.

Lim, C., Lee, J., and Choi, H. (2019). "South Korea." In O. Zawacki-Richter and A. Qayyum (eds.), *Open and Distance Education in Asia, Africa and the Middle East: National Perspectives in a Digital Age*. Singapore: Springer, 87–100.

Lim, T., Fadzil, M., Latifah, A. L., Goolamally, N. T., and Mansor, N. (2011). "Producing graduates who meet employer expectations: Open and distance learning is a viable option." Proceedings, ICLLL.

Lumanta, M. F. and Garcia, P. G. (eds.) (2020). *Quality Initiatives in an Open and Distance E-Learning Institution: Towards Excellence and Equity*. UPOU Networks – Multimedia Center, Philippines.

Lumanta, M. F., Lagaya, M. P., Villanueva, L., and Ortiguero, I. R. (2019). "Employers' perception of and attitude towards open and distance e-learning (OdeL) and hiring practices of Philippine industries." Proceedings of the 33rd Annual Conference of the AAOU https://aaou2019.vu.edu.pk/pages/ConferenceMaterials.aspx

Maxwell, L. (1995). "Integrating open learning and distance education." *Educational Technology*, 35/6, 43–48.

Musingafi, M. C., Mapuranga, B., Chiwanza, K., and Zebron, S. (2015). "Challenges for open and distance learning (ODL) students: Experiences from students of the Zimbabwe Open University." *Journal of Education and Practice*, 6/18, 59–66.

National Open University, Taiwan (n.d). *Facts and Figures*. https://www106.nou.edu.tw/~eng/facts_figures/A1091.pdf

Ni, A. (2013). "Comparing the effectiveness of classroom and online learning: Teaching research methods." *Journal of Public Affairs Education*, 19/2, 199–215.

OERu (n.d.). https://oeru.org/

Open Blockchain (n.d.). https://blockchain.open.ac.uk/

Open Universities Australia (2020). "Open Learning and Open Universities Australia work together to deliver new development grant and holistic microcredentials solution for universities." https://www.open.edu.au/about-us/media-centre/news-and-media-releases/2020/07/12/23/07/press-release-page-openlearning-and-open-universities-australia-work-together-to-deliver-new-development-grant-and-holistic-microcredentials-solution-for-universities

Open Universities in India and ODL Courses (n.d). http://indiaeduinfo.com/openuniversity.htm

Open University Kaohsiung (n.d.). https://www.ouk.edu.tw/english/AboutUsEN/a06.htm

Open University Malaysia (n.d). https://www.oum.edu.my/about-us/

OUC Education and Training Center (n.d.). http://www.ouchn.edu.cn/training/index.html

Panda, S. and Garg, S. (2019). "India." In O. Zawacki-Richter and A. Qayyum (eds.), *Open and Distance Education in Asia, Africa and the Middle East: National Perspectives in a Digital Age*. Singapore: Springer, 27–42.

Perris, K. (2015). "Comparing the Open University systems of China and India: Origins, developments and prospects." *Frontiers of Education in China*, 10/2, 274–305.

Qayyum, A. and Zawacki-Richter, O. (eds.) (2018). *Open and Distance Education in Australia, Europe and the Americas: National Perspectives in a Digital Age*. Singapore: Springer.

Santosh, S. and Panda, S. (2016). "Sharing of knowledge among faculty in a mega open university." *Open Praxis*, 8/3, 247–264.

Secreto, P. (2013). "Gender equality in online learning: The case of UP Open University." *Procedia – Social and Behavioral Sciences*, 103, 434–441.

Sembiring, M. G. (2017). "Exploratory study of academic excellence associated with persistence in ODL setting." *Asian Association of Open Universities Journal*, 12/2, 125–136.

Shurville, S., O'Grady, T. B., and Mayall, P. (2008). "Educational and institutional flexibility of Australian educational software." *Campus-Wide Information Systems*, 25/2, 74–84.

Statista (2020). *Internet Penetration in Asia as of June 2020, by Country or Region*. https://www.statista.com/statistics/281668/internet-penetration-in-southeast-asian-countries/#:~:text=Across%20the%20Asia%20Pacific%20region,in%20the%20past%20few%20years

Stella, A. and Gnanam, A. (2004). "Quality assurance in distance education: The challenges to be addressed." *Higher Education*, 47/2, 143–160.

Stevens, K., and Tate, S. (1994). "The changing nature of distance education in New Zealand 1992-93: Some strategic considerations." *New Zealand Annual Review of Education*, 3, 319–334.

Sungsri, S., Subramaniam, T. T., Rokhiyah, I., and Tuyet, H. (2017). "Employers' perception on the importance and the satisfaction level of identified set of skills among Open University undergraduates." *Proceedings of the 31st Annual Conference of the AAOU*, pp. 231–239.

Supreme Court of India, Civil Appellate Jurisdiction (2017). Civil Appeal Nos 17869–1787/2017, November 3. https://www.ugc.ac.in/pdfnews/3251872_judgement_03-Nov-2017.pdf

Surbhi, S. (2021). *Difference Between Amalgamation and Absorption*. https://keydifferences.com/author/author2

Tait, A. (2008). "What are Open Universities for?" *Open Learning*, 23/2, 85–93.

Tait, A. (2018). "Open Universities: The next phase." *Asian Association of Open Universities Journal*, 13/1, 13–23.

Thailand Higher Education (n.d.). https://education.stateuniversity.com/pages/1529/Thailand-HIGHER-EDUCATION.html

The Open University of Japan. (2019). News. FY 2019. *The 33rd AAOU Annual Conference in Lahore, Pakistan*. https://www.ouj.ac.jp/eng/global/2019.html

Tianjin Open University (n.d.). http://www.tjrtvu.edu.cn/

UN-APCICT (2014). *Open and Distance Learning in Asia and the Pacific*. http://sdghelpdesk.unescap.org/sites/default/files/2019-05/UN-APCICT%20ODL%20Case%20Study.pdf

UNESCO (2015). *Five Asian Open Universities Adopt Open Licensing and MOOCs*. https://en.unesco.org/news/five-asian-open-universities-adopt-open-licensing-and-moocs

UNESCO (n.d.-a). *The 2030 Agenda for Sustainable Development*. https://sdg4education2030.org/the-goal

UNESCO (n.d.-b). *Open Educational Resources (OER)*. https://en.unesco.org/themes/building-knowledge-societies/oer

Virtual University (n.d.). https://www.vu.edu.pk/AboutUs/AboutVU.aspx

White, M. (1982). "Distance education in Australian higher education: A history." *Distance Education Journal*, 3/2, 255–278.

Yaumi, M. (2007). "The implementation of distance learning in Indonesian higher education." *Lentera Pendidikan: Jurnal Llmu Tarbiyah dan Keguruan*, 10/2, 196–215. https://www.academia.edu/12837322/IMPLEMENTATION_OF_DISTANCE_LEARNING_IN_INDONESIAN_HIGHER_EDUCATION

Zadorozhna, T. and Kryms'ka, N. (2012). "Distance learning: Historical approaches." http://eir.nuos.edu.ua/xmlui/bitstream/handle/123456789/1521/Zadorozhna.pdf?sequence=1&isAllowed=y

Zawacki-Richter, O. and Qayyum, A. (eds.) (2019). *Open and Distance Education in Asia, Africa and the Middle East: National Perspectives in a Digital Age*. Singapore: Springer.

Zuhairi, A., Hsueh, A. C. T., and Chiang, I. C. N. (2020). "Empowering lifelong learning through open universities in Taiwan and Indonesia." *Asian Association of Open Universities Journal*, 15/2, 167–188.

Zulin, Z., Lei, B., Xinan, Q., Ying, L., Yanyan, C., and Yang, S. (2011). "The mining analysis on the dropout rate of modern distance education: Based on the data collected from 1999 to 2009 in Anhui Province of China [J]." *Journal of Distance Education*, 4, 18–26.

CHAPTER 17

··

MOOCS IN ASIA

Promise Unfulfilled or Promise Realized?

··

HELEN FARLEY

1. INTRODUCTION

THE Asia-Pacific is a diverse region encompassing two continents with both developed and developing economies. It is characterized by extremes of climate and geography with a staggering array of religions, dogmas, and ideas about gender, sexuality, and age. Accounting for less than a third of the Earth's land mass, Asia alone accounts for nearly 60 percent of its population. Australia and New Zealand add to the complexity of this region but by way of contrast, are relatively sparsely populated and despite their proximity to Asia, are more culturally aligned to the United Kingdom and United States. For sustained economic activity in the Asia-Pacific, inequalities must be minimized, and economic advancement prioritized for everyone (Annan-Diab and Molinari, 2017). Participation in higher education will be crucial in ensuring that there are the skills needed for continued growth and the capacity to solve the challenges arising from climate change, inequality, and most recently, a global pandemic. Existing and planned campus-based higher education institutions will be unable to accommodate the expected influx of learners, so governments are investigating ways to make education more accessible (Chapman and Sarvi, 2017).

The internationalization of higher education and the rapid socio-economic changes of the past two decades have placed great pressure on institutions to compete for worldwide rankings and funding. Across much of the region, higher education institutions are viewed as essential to the economic and social progress of developing countries. As a result, governments are providing financial investment and resources for enhancing graduate degree enrollments and research output (UNESCO, 2014). These factors together with the increasing importance of technology and a focus on delivering personalized learning experiences has resulted in more Asia-Pacific universities experimenting with new forms of instructional delivery (Asian Development Bank, 2011).

A willingness to embrace emerging technologies is a prominent characteristic of the peoples of the Asia-Pacific region, not purely from the perspective of the widespread adoption of smart technologies and dispersed populations, but because of the impact on modern youth of growing up in digitally enabled environments. In more developed countries such as Australia, Singapore, and South Korea, smartphones have become integral to everyday life and a large proportion have access to the internet, particularly in metropolitan areas. However, even in these regions, the inequality of access is significant and concerns about the emergence of a "digital divide" feature frequently in discussions about education policy. In less developed countries such as Vietnam and Laos, the dichotomy between those who have access to technology and connectivity and those who do not is more pronounced. Research focused on the youth in these regions has revealed an equal enthusiasm for new media in common with their global counterparts, becoming heavy users of inexpensive and low-end technologies including low-end mobile devices sold at reduced prices, and relying heavily on short message services (Tao and Donald, 2016).

This widespread acceptance of emerging technologies has facilitated changes in both formal and informal learning. With little evidence as to their efficacy and reach, Massive Open Online Courses (MOOCs) were viewed as the means by which the masses could access high-quality learning, alleviating the pressures on formal, face-to-face institutions. Appearing from 2008, they provided online learning that could be accessed after a free registration (McAuley et al., 2010). If the learner required certification, he or she paid a relatively modest amount after successfully passing the assessments (Zhu, et al., 2020). Educators and learners could interact, irrespective of geography, gender, or income. Indeed, some of the first MOOCs were offered by prestigious institutions such as Stanford University and MIT (Moe, 2015). However, when researchers investigated who enrolled in MOOCs, they found that mostly these learners were already in higher education (Lim et al., 2017). Most enrollments came from developed nations including the United States and Canada (Schmid et al., 2015). There was also a strong gender bias, particularly in developing nations. Recent research showed that 63 percent of participants were male and in China, that number stretched to 79 percent (Ruipérez-Valiente et al., 2020). The rhetoric of MOOCs making education available for all was not being realized. Rather than recruiting new learners, MOOCs primarily served learners within existing systems (Reich and Ruipérez-Valiente, 2019).

Despite the growing number of publications on the MOOC phenomenon, up until 2015, 82 percent of published papers were from North America and Europe. Just 8 percent came from Asia and most of those were from China (Veletsianos and Shepherdson, 2016). However, by 2019, Chinese authors ranked second only to authors from the United States. Between 2012 and 2017, more than 6,000 MOOC-related academic articles were published in China (Jiao and Fan, 2020). However, the number of papers from other Asian nations remained small. As most authors predominantly wrote about MOOCs in their own countries (Zhu et al., 2020), it can reasonably be assumed that the growth in literature about MOOCs in Asia reflected their growing prominence in the region.

Though Asian nations remain committed to achieving the United Nations Sustainable Development Goals, including Goal 4 to "Ensure inclusive and equitable quality education and promote lifelong learning opportunities for all" (United Nations General Assembly, 2015), many will struggle to do so. One of the challenges faced by developing countries is the urgent need to equip their people with the skills needed in a global economy. There was a maturing recognition by policymakers that existing systems, structures, and processes would not be adequate (Venkatataman and Prabhakar, 2020). It is within this context that MOOCs are gaining traction in the Asia-Pacific in a more urgent and supported way than elsewhere in the world.

In this chapter, the emergence of MOOCs is examined in six nations across Asia. It is not an exhaustive list: There are other Asian countries that have developed or use MOOCs that are not discussed here, and there are other MOOCs and MOOC platforms in these countries. Though MOOCs have emerged in both Australia and New Zealand, close cultural ties to both the United Kingdom and the United States mean that the factors driving their adoption are more closely aligned to those of the West. For this reason, they are not considered in any depth here. This examination of MOOCs in Asia is informed by the available literature in English. Thus, it is very likely to have inadvertently excluded academically relevant literature not drafted in English.

2. The Emergence of MOOCs in the Asia-Pacific

Massive Online Open Courses are just the latest incarnation of distance education (Alcorn et al., 2015), made possible with the widespread adoption of technologies and increased connectivity. Distance education has long been making education accessible to a greater number of people. It allows students to remain in their communities, and removes the tyranny of geography. Emerging technologies including learning management systems, synchronous online classrooms, social media and videoconferencing, facilitate the kind of interaction and synchronous communication usually associated with face-to-face models of formal education (Xiao, 2018). In Asia, as with the rest of the world, higher education institutions are increasingly turning to distance education and MOOCs have emerged in those countries where it is well established (Zhang et al., 2020). Their potential to rapidly scale at low cost has led to claims that MOOCs have an almost limitless potential to reach those people without access to higher education. By 2013, around one in five enrollments with Coursera, edX, and Udacity MOOCs were from Asia (Chen, 2013); a fifth of all enrollments were from India (Trehan et al., 2017) and by 2016, enrollments from India lagged only behind those from the U.S. and Brazil, and just ahead of enrollments from China (Shi and Yu, 2016). Further, the data showed that the general characteristics of the Asian MOOC learner (e.g., age, gender, and education) were not significantly different from those from other regions (Chuang and Ho, 2016).

2.1 China

Being the world's most populous country, it is unsurprising China boasts the largest open and distance learning system in the world. In the early 1970s, Vice Premier Deng Xiaoping met with UK Prime Minister Sir Edward Heath, to discuss the UK's Open University. The Vice Premier recognized the potential to reach more learners with this model and in response founded the Radio and TV Universities Network. Though born of worthy ideals, the Radio and TV Universities Network became synonymous with second-class education (Zhang, 2019). Even so, from these, the Open Universities network emerged and became the supplier of distance education, initially through the distribution of hard-copy materials. Changing with the increased penetration of ICTs and internet connectivity, these institutions were increasingly in competition with traditional campus-based universities (Li and Chen, 2019).

Building on this increased acceptance of open and distance learning, CORE (China Open Resources for Education) was founded in 2003, following an MIT OpenCourseWare Conference in Beijing. CORE was a non-profit consortium of 44 China Radio and TV Universities and 26 International Engineering Technology (IET) universities, aiming to provide universities with access to global open education resources. It folded just ten years later, coinciding with Tsinghua University and Peking University leveraging edX, the platform provided by MIT and Harvard University, under the auspices of the Ministry of Education Research Center for Online Education (Li and Chen, 2019). By May 2016, the platform had attracted 2.7 million learners and by the end of the year had enrolled 6 million users from 126 countries across 400 courses. By 2017, there were 9.3 million registered users (Jiao and Fan, 2020), making it the third biggest MOOC provider behind Coursera and edX, and the biggest in a developing country (Belawati, 2020). With this vast experience, Tsinghua University organized academic seminars for MOOC researchers and offered MOOC training for higher education institutions across China (Trehan et al., 2017). Launched in 2014, the next significant Chinese MOOC development was CNMOOC. By the end of 2018, it had released 817 courses in partnership with 93 universities and institutions. The third platform, also launched in 2014, was icourse163 built by Higher Education Press and an internet technology company, NetEase. In collaboration with 270 universities and institutions, icourse163 offered 2,204 MOOCs across disciplines including philosophy, science, and education (Jiao and Fan, 2020).

In April 2015, the Chinese Ministry of Education released "Opinions and Suggestions for Promoting the Construction, Application and Management of MOOCs," which created the necessary environment for the development and deployment of MOOCs in China. It was an aspirational plan to strengthen the construction, use, and management of MOOCs (Li and Chen, 2019). Just three years later in 2018, the Chinese government selected 490 courses as exemplars of the best open online courses with a goal to offer 3,000 to the public by 2030. The government provided funding and resources for the creation and delivery of these courses (Zhang et al., 2020). This alleviated the challenges associated with accessing foreign MOOCs which included the network firewall, language barriers, and cultural misunderstandings (Tang and Carr-Chellman, 2016).

In China, MOOCs are specifically targeted to university students as a means for improving "equity in higher ed." Learners are able to complement their formal offline learning with online course content. This is particularly useful for those in regions with limited access to quality course resources. The Chinese government has set targets for how many high-quality MOOCs should be produced. In 2019, there were more than 12,500 MOOCs across more than 10 different platforms (Schaffhauser, 2019). The number of learners enrolled in MOOCs approached one million in 2015, but by 2016 had exceeded 10 million (Zhou, 2020).

2.2 India

Distance education has featured in India since 1961, when correspondence courses were developed after Indian independence in 1947. Radio supplemented the paper-based resources with television gaining prominence from 1975 with SITE (Satellite Instructional Television Experiment). From 1984, the University Grants Commission developed the Countrywide Classroom television series, which was broadcast through the government national television network, Doordarshan. In 1985, an Act of Parliament enabled the Indira Gandhi National Open University (IGNOU) to be established, serving as a regulator to promote, coordinate, and accredit distance education in India. IGNOU also drove the development of learning materials that could be accessed via a national open educational resource repository. As of 2019, there were 15 Open Universities specifically offering distance education in India, though many others also offer it as an adjunct to their face-to-face delivery (Panda and Garg, 2019).

India's first MOOC was delivered in 2012 by Dr. Gautam Shroff of Tata Consultancy Services with faculty from the Indian Institute of Technology (IIT) in Delhi. IIT Kanpur developed the mooKIT platform with the Commonwealth of Learning in 2014. While not attracting the same number of enrollments as some of the international MOOCs, this first mooKIT course had much higher completion rates than those MOOCs (Venkatataman and Prabhakar, 2020). Also launching in 2014, IIT BombayX was an adaptation of the edX platform. "Blended MOOCs," where educators enrolled in a MOOC and delivered it in a blended mode at their own institutions, were delivered through IIT BombayX. This format allowed high-quality content from IIT to be used by smaller institutions, supposedly removing the need for highly trained faculty. Even so, a stable MOOC platform with enrollments beyond 100,000 learners in a course was yet to be developed in India, in spite of the large numbers seeking higher education (Trehan et al., 2017).

India's Ministry of Human Resource Development (MHRD) released guidelines for the development and implementation of MOOCs in 2016. In response, the SWAYAM (Study Webs of Active Learning for Young Aspiring Minds) platform was launched by the government in 2017 to provide free, online courses on a variety of topics and in local languages (Sharma, 2019).

With India's greater participation in the world economy, there has been an increased demand for specialized knowledge and skills. In 2015, India had 27 percent of the population engaged in higher education, amounting to 35 million students, with 16 percent participating in distance education (Pushpanadham, 2015). MOOCs have supplemented traditional higher education, rather than replacing or extending it. Around 40 percent of Indian MOOC learners were also enrolled in formal higher education as an undergraduate or as a postgraduate student (Alcorn et al., 2015). With English being widely spoken in India, most learners who enroll in MOOCs do so through the big MOOC platforms such as EdX, Coursera, and FutureLearn, rather than in homegrown offerings (Trehan et al., 2017).

2.3 South Korea

Distance education in the Republic of Korea (South Korea) started in 1972 with the founding of the Korea National Open University (KNOU), largely through the distribution of hard-copy materials (Lim et al., 2019). It was a means for those who had failed to gain entry to the competitive traditional universities to access higher education (Jung, 2019). While the KNOU vision and mission was consistent with the purpose of MOOCs, the way their programs were offered resembled MOOCs (Lee, 2015). First established by private organizations in 2001, cyber universities also offered ICT-focused programs at a distance on technical topics including information security management or design engineering (Lim et al., 2019).

South Korea also leveraged television and radio for the dissemination of learning in the decade until 1994. The Korea Distance Education Association was launched in 1990, with its journal launched a year later to mark a deliberate move into research (Lim et al., 2019). In 2007, the Korea Education and Research Information Service (KERIS) started a pilot Open CourseWare (OCW) project. It ran KOCW which was a public OCW repository. The Korea OCW Consortium (KOCWC) was founded in 2008 with 91 university members. By 2010, there were already 1,300 OCW courses available (Chen, 2013). Korea was providing video lectures developed by domestic universities and specialized institutions through the service (Kim et al., 2020).

In 2013, the Seoul National University offered its CourseWare via edX (Lim et al., 2019), and the Korea Advanced Institute of Science and Technology became a member of Coursera. From 2015, the Korean Ministry of Education started offering K-MOOCs (for Korean MOOCs) by NILE (National Institute for Lifelong Education) to provide more options around distance education (Lee, 2015). In the first instance, around 20 courses were offered from ten prestigious universities (Kim et al., 2020). As of 2017, KMOOCs had attracted some 4.74 million visitors, and claimed about 228,000 registered members (Kim et al., 2020). In more recent times, access to these MOOCs has generally been via mobile devices rather than personal computers.

The Ministry of Education, Science, and Technology has created a policy and funding environment that has facilitated the swift expansion of distance education in partnership with universities (Jung, 2019). Even though some 80 percent of high school graduates enroll in higher education, they rarely do so via distance education. Most enrollments are from those who are already established in their careers, with more than half of those pursuing a postgraduate qualification (Lim et al., 2019).

2.4   The Philippines

The University of the Philippines Open University (UPOU) was established in 1995 by the Commission of Higher Education. Established to be the national center of excellence in open learning and distance education for the Filipino people, its stated mission was to provide increased access to good quality higher education (Gervacio, 2015). More recently, in alignment with this aim, the Philippines government adopted a strategic position to skill its population via MOOCs and similar offerings (Bandalaria and Alfonso, 2015). The first MOOC, "Developing Mobile Apps Using the Android Platform," was delivered in 2013 by UPOU in conjunction with Smart Communications, Inc. The MOOC was launched on the Moodle-based platform, Massive Open Distance eLearning (MODeL), and was designed to equip students with the skills and knowledge to develop apps for Android devices, the predominant platform in the Philippines at that time (Gervacio, 2015).

The enactment of the Open Distance Learning Act in 2014 provided the signal that the government recognized the relevance of open and distance learning in the Philippines. In response, MOOC projects were supported by the government through UPOU in collaboration with private institutions under the Public–Private Partnership Program the following year. Regional and international organizations like the German development agency Deutsche Gesellschaft für Internationale Zusammenarbeit and UNICEF have partnered with the UPOU to offer MOOCs related to their missions using the MODeL platform. The UPOU and UNICEF have offered eight MOOCs related to Child Rights Protection (Jung et al., 2020).

The Technical Education and Skills Development Authority (TESDA) has also made MOOCs available since 2015. This government agency was created to maximize the participation of the Filipino workforce in MOOCs, to build their technical-vocational skills, enhance their competence, and instill positive work values. TESDA made extensive use of ICT, launching e-TESDA, a MOOC platform developed to improve the technical skills of the workforce at a modest cost. The e-TESDA program's target audience included students, out-of-school youths, unemployed adults, workers, professionals, and expatriate Filipino workers. An evaluation of the e-TESDA MOOCs revealed that nearly all felt the information gained would be useful in their work. While UPOU

MOOCs catered to a particular profession, the e-TESDA MOOCs boosted knowledge in the technical and vocational fields (Gervacio, 2015).

2.5 Sri Lanka

Though English is only spoken by around a quarter of the Sri Lankan population, it is widely spoken in education and business, and is the first language of about 75,000 people living in urban areas. Consequently, many learners engage in English language MOOCs offered by the major providers (Warusavitarana et al., 2014). Generally speaking, this engagement augments formal higher and tertiary education offerings.

To date, there have been very few regional Sri Lankan MOOCs developed. A suite of Continuing Professional Development (CPD) MOOCs have been developed at the Open University of Sri Lanka with the sponsorship of the Commonwealth Educational Media Center for Asia in New Delhi, India. This initiative was designed to raise awareness on the potential of Open Educational Resources (OER) and Open Educational Practice (OEP) among practitioners. The initiative involved four CPD MOOCs featuring carefully crafted learning scenarios that reflected the sorts of issues and challenges that practitioners were likely to face in their environments with the use of OER (Naidu and Karunanayaka, 2020).

2.6 Thailand

The first MOOC-like online course, titled "e-Learning Professional Development," was launched in Thailand in 2006 by the Thai Cyber University (TCU) using their Open CourseWare. TCU went on to introduce an Open edX-based platform called Thai MOOC in 2017. It partnered with MOOC developers via the Thai University Network which as of 2019, had created 261 courses (Thammetar and Jintavee, 2020). Other Thai universities have successfully delivered MOOCs using a combination of learning management systems and other platforms. Sukhothai Thammathirat Open University, a national distance learning university, was one of the leaders in offering several MOOCs listed on the Asian Association of Open Universities' MOOC site (Jung et al., 2020). Yet others including Assumption University and Chulalongkorn University, had signed up to Apple's iTunesU platform (Nasongkhla et al., 2015).

Released in 2016, the Thailand 4.0 Model in the Educational Development Plan of the Ministry of Education (2017–2021) explicitly stated its intention to promote the development of digital technology for education. The aim was to facilitate continuous learning throughout the lives of the Thai people by providing technology to access formal, nonformal, and informal education including MOOCs (Thammetar and Jintavee, 2020). In common with learners in many English language MOOCS, over half of Thai MOOC participants already had an undergraduate degree (Jung et al., 2020).

3. Regional Collaboration

Indonesia, Malaysia, the Philippines, Thailand, and Vietnam have formed strong collaborations through organizations including the Association of Southeast Asian Nations (ASEAN) and Southeast Asian Ministers of Education Organization (SEAMEO). Sharing a common location and similar challenges, they communicated knowledge about best practices, collaborated on open education initiatives, and shared innovations in MOOCs through events such as summits and conferences. The Southeast Asia MOOCs Network was recently established by the SEAMEO Regional Open Learning Centre, one of 24 centers that looked at open and distance learning in the region. The primary purpose of the Network is to build capacity among the MOOC providers by establishing a community of practice (Jung et al., 2020).

Founded in 1987, the Asian Association of Open Universities (AAOU) is a non-profit consortium of higher education institutions that promote open and distance learning through a journal, conferences, workshops and white papers. It also hosts a website that promotes the MOOCs of its members. The Asian Learning Portal served as AAOU's official MOOC platform which could be used by those member universities without the capacity for hosting their own MOOCs (Bandalaria, 2018). These services played a crucial role in ensuring the delivery of MOOCs and open education to those people who would struggle to access education in another way (Jung et al., 2020).

3.1 Why MOOCs in the Asia-Pacific Are Different

Unlike MOOCs in the United States, United Kingdom, and Europe, governments of many Asian countries, including China, Malaysia, the Philippines, South Korea, and Thailand were very active in initiating and supporting MOOC initiatives (Kim et al., 2020). Often these countries offered branded MOOCs such as K-MOOCs (in South Korea), Thai MOOCs, and Malaysia MOOCs. Recognizing their potential, the governments of these countries have aspired to use them to increase access to higher education, promote lifelong learning, or to reform current systems of higher education. The exception to this is Japan, where JMOOCs (Japan MOOCs) were the product of a consortium of academic organizations, government institutes, corporates, and universities. The biggest question concerns sustainability: How sustainable are these MOOC platforms given they are offered without cost? This question remains pertinent, especially given the big MOOC platforms such as Coursera and edX remain largely financially reliant on their home universities. Sustainability relies on establishing a means to ensure financial stability independent of government subsidies (Kim, 2015). In countries such as India, this could take the form of public–private partnerships (Pushpanadham, 2015).

Another point of difference lies in the fact that many MOOCs from Asian countries have become integral to formal education systems, with successful completion conferring credit towards a formal qualification (Jung et al., 2020). This has only been possible with support from governments and the implementation of specific policies relating to both open education and MOOCs. By way of example, Indian learners may earn up to 20 percent of their undergraduate degree through participation in SWAYAM MOOCs. In this way, India increased its Gross Enrollment Ratio (GER) in higher education from 24.5 percent in 2015–2016 to 25.8 percent in 2017–2018. The Indian government aspires to raise GER to 30 percent by 2021 (Zhang et al., 2020).

4. Challenges to the Adoption of MOOCs in Asia

Though there is great potential for MOOCs to deliver higher education to those who would otherwise miss out, the challenges to their adoption are considerable. Though this list is not exhaustive, it does articulate the main barriers to the wider adoption of MOOCs in Asia.

4.1 Poor Reputation of Distance Learning

In many areas, distance education has been viewed as a poor relation to traditional face-to-face modes of delivery (Xiao, 2018), though this is beginning to change. For example, this attitude was shared in India by government bodies such as the University Grants Commission, the Indian higher education regulator. Until recently, this body had banned postgraduate degree programs being offered at a distance (Qayyum and Zawacki-Richter, 2019). However, more recently, the National Education Policy 2020 reflected a modified stance saying that Master's and PhD programs in core areas such as AI (Artificial Intelligence) could be offered through digital platforms such as SWAYAM (Ministry of Human Resource Development, 2020). Chinese learners are also open to the benefits of distance learning even though academics hold more conservative views (Li, Chen, and Gong, 2017). Even so, there is evidence that the attitude of the government is shifting towards acceptance. The emergence and widespread availability of MOOCs had caused the Chinese government to become more receptive to online learning including degree programs.

Even among employers there are differing levels of recognition of the skills gained in MOOCs. In Australia and New Zealand, those skills are seen as an "add on" rather than a viable substitute for formal education. In fact, in these countries most employers were unfamiliar with this form of education. This attitude was also seen in other parts of the region. For example, employers in Indonesia generally did not value the skills and knowledge gained through MOOCs and the emphasis remained on skills obtained through traditional, face-to-face modes of education (Kurniasari et al., 2018). The knowledge gained through MOOCs is likely to be viewed more favorably when it is complementary to a formal qualification, rather than instead of such learning. Even so, some MOOC providers have actively worked to address this prejudice. In Taiwan, the MOOC provider eWant provided a QR code so that employers could verify the certificate. In addition, they also listed the curriculum on the back of the certificate so that employers could determine what knowledge the potential employee had gained (Chew et al., 2017).

4.2   eLearning Capability of Instructors

Educators who design MOOCs need to recognize they need a particular set of skills to adequately meet the needs of a diverse and distant cohort. To make these courses engaging, there needs to be sufficient interactivity as well as learning materials presented in a logical way. Learners are not able to ask questions of instructors if they have difficulties understanding the materials. Assessments must be designed so that they are rigorous but without being too onerous to mark. Asian educators, in common with their counterparts around the world, are often focused on their area of expertise, rather than on sound online pedagogies. This is especially true in countries where poor ICT infrastructure precludes the widespread use of distance learning. An educator in a developing country will likely require a solid induction into the world of online teaching (Venkatataman and Prabhakar, 2020), and second, specifically into the pedagogies of MOOCs.

A recent survey of educators in 33 Malaysian higher education institutions revealed they felt ill-equipped to design effective MOOCs. These educators also voiced their concerns about balancing two modes of delivery, MOOCs and traditional face-to-face, especially as the MOOCs were credit compulsory making the stakes high (Kumar and Al-Samarraie, 2018). In Thailand, Thaipisutikul and Tuarob (2017) reported on the resistance of conservative instructors in sharing teaching techniques and content on public platforms yet sharing is integral to the philosophy of MOOCs, which were born from the OER, OCW, and OEP movements.

4.3   Access to ICT and Internet

MOOCs are accessed in an online environment. Educators, usually located at a distance to their learners, create resources and activities locally that are widely and digitally distributed. To be able to access these resources, learners must have access to a computer or a mobile device, and they must have access to the internet. To make distance education viable, there must be robust ICT infrastructure in place and some countries have prioritized this more than others. For example, in South Korea the digitization of education was a development goal more than a decade ago (Zawacki-Richter and Qayyum, 2019).

Conversely, many countries in the region have poor connectivity in rural areas (Fadzil et al., 2015). In Sri Lanka, internet penetration is restricted to urban areas and a lack of reliable electricity further compounds this disconnection (Liyanagunawardena and Adams, 2014). Similar issues plague India, Indonesia, the Philippines, and Thailand. A lack of connectivity was not just the product of a difficult geography and economic resourcing, access for women is often more restricted. Fearing for their safety, women would often go to public libraries in preference to internet cafes (Laurillard and Kennedy, 2017). These limitations on connectivity inhibit the widespread uptake of MOOCs in many developing countries (Pushpanadham, 2015). In addition, when internet was available, it was frequently prohibitively expensive (Naidu and Karunanayaka, 2020).

Censorship is a significant problem across some countries in the Asia-Pacific, perhaps none more so than China. The Great Firewall is the name given to the extensive and sophisticated internet filtering system that prevents its citizens from looking at certain websites hosted on foreign servers. It is not clear on what basis access is restricted but even those foreign websites that are not blocked perform poorly because of the Great Firewall (Lee, 2018). It is likely that those learners who want to access MOOCs hosted outside of China will not have access to the full range of courses available or will be disinclined to access them because of their poor performance. With the Chinese government tightening its grip, the emphasis shifts from personal ambition towards China's collective ambitions and place in the world (Law, 2020).

Myanmar and Vietnam were among the most restrictive regimes with a particular focus on the restriction of independent media, material that could be considered to be politically sensitive, pertaining to human rights or political reform. Vietnam had sophisticated and effective filtering systems that resembled those of China. It is important for educators to understand the extent to which internet censorship could impact on MOOCs in Vietnam. Social networks, for example, are often used in learning scenarios to encourage collaboration and sharing of information. In Vietnam, however, local authorities partially or wholly blocked access to sites such as Facebook (Farley and Song, 2015).

Though not all learners can access computers, increasing numbers of people across Asia are adopting inexpensive smartphones with the capability of accessing the internet. In 2017, 27 percent of people could access internet-capable smartphones. This number is expected to rise to 36 percent by 2023 (Belawati, 2020). Even so, these technologies are not evenly distributed throughout the population. Around 1.7 billion women in low- and middle-income countries do not own cell phones (Laurillard and Kennedy, 2017). Most growth in smartphone ownership in Asia is among young people and those already well-educated. For example, nearly all Japanese people under 35 own a smartphone (96 percent), while only around 40 percent of those over 50 do (Taylor and Silver, 2019).

There are two ways that MOOCs can be accessed on a cell phone. First, platforms can be "mobile responsive," that is they can be adapted to display effectively on a small screen, rather than just appear as a very small website. Second, dedicated "apps" can enable all of the functionality on a mobile device that is typically accessed via a computer. The most common MOOC platforms including Coursera and edX have apps for both Android and Apple devices.

As the global COVID-19 pandemic continues, countries across the Asia-Pacific are scrambling for ways to ensure the continuity of education. An inability to adapt could lead to decreased lifetime earnings for workers and skills shortages for countries. In the first instance, governments turned to relatively low-tech solutions such as radio and television to ensure continuity or shifted from blended modes of learning to entirely online modes. In the longer term, there is likely to be a bolstering of technological infrastructure along with the provision of personal technologies (Panth and Xu, 2020). As universities shed staff to mitigate financial losses as a result of the pandemic, there will be a wider examination of alternative modes of education and it could be that learners will increasingly turn to MOOCs to ensure currency of skills and knowledge.

4.4 English Language Delivery

Only one-fifth of the world's population speaks English, yet more than 75 percent of the MOOCs worldwide are delivered in that language. English is the third most spoken language, trailing Mandarin and Spanish (Stratton and Grace, 2016). Those learners who speak English already have better access to quality higher education. Those learners who are not able to speak English well are significantly disadvantaged when enrolling in an English-language MOOC (Chen, 2013). Interestingly, regional MOOCs are often delivered in English. At KNOU, through eLIC, an international educational exchange arm of KNOU, almost all courses are delivered in English with a view to encouraging international collaboration (Lee, 2015). In Malaysia and the Philippines, most of the MOOCs were offered in English to encourage international enrollments. While this difference reflects each country's aspirations in offering MOOCs, the demographics of the actual participants should be closely examined to ensure providers are not at cross purposes (Jung et al., 2020).

Though Mandarin is the language spoken by most people in the world, most MOOCs are non-Chinese, causing a barrier to Chinese learners (Liu et al., 2010). To overcome this, there have been several attempts at localizing MOOCs to accommodate Chinese-speaking participants. There are several Chinese platforms offering MOOCs to Chinese learners in their native language (Che et al., 2016). There have also been non-Chinese MOOCs that have been designed to also be delivered using Chinese language. The German MOOC platform OpenHPI.de offered a version of one of their MOOCs in Chinese.

The dominance of English-language MOOCs presents a challenge to other cultures. Already Western paradigms are dominant across the globe, relentlessly eroding the distinctiveness of regional cultures and language. Further inroads through English-language MOOCs may accelerate this change. Cultures are never static but always shifting in response to outside influences and situations (Chen, 2013). Language barriers increase the possibility of miscommunication and misunderstanding between learners and educators. Learners may develop a sense of marginalization and sometimes alienation often resulting in decreased engagement and unsatisfactory course outcomes (Tang and Carr-Chellman, 2016).

4.5 Different Cultures Have Different Needs

When designing MOOCs, educators make assumptions about the capacities and the demographics of their learners. One of the main purposes of MOOCs is to spread the reach of education. Once a MOOC is online, it is theoretically accessible from anywhere by anyone with an internet connection. This can make educators be less mindful about the needs of their cohort, and to assume their learners are homogeneous; the reality is far different. Their learners are different from each other and different from the educator. Different learner characteristics will impact how each will experience the MOOC and how they will decipher the information presented. The disparity between courses and local cultures has been one of the impediments to the success of MOOCs in developing countries (Nkuyubwatsi, 2014).

Though delivery in a learner's own language is powerful, it is not sufficient. It is also necessary to ensure that resources and examples in a MOOC are relevant to the local community and that they make sense to the learners in that context (Zhang et al., 2020). MOOCs delivered to learners across many cultures should be flexible enough for cross-cultural relevance. Without this, meaningful learning is reduced. Recognizing this, in 2013, the World Bank signed an agreement with Coursera to provide MOOCs tailored to learners in developing countries (Nkuyubwatsi, 2014). In 2016, it launched its Open Learning Campus to provide learning in a variety of formats, partnering with regional organizations while maintaining its connection with Coursera (Jagannathan, 2017). The Open Learning Campus continues to provide learning through WBx Talks, WBa Academy, and WBc Connect.

There are similarities and differences within and between countries. Malaysia, Indonesia, and Brunei border each other, share a similar language, and are majority Muslim nations. Other Asian countries have different languages, cultural practices, histories, and aspirations for education (Abas, 2015). Even within the same country, there can be several indigenous and non-indigenous cultures that are markedly different to each other. For example, India is a country of many religions and cultures (Pushpanadham, 2015) and with its vast size and population, China is similar. This need for cultural relevance is recognized by governments in many countries who have supported the development of regional MOOCs to specifically cater for their own populations. In Malaysia, this was done by sourcing locally relevant subject matter, course resources and examples, but there is still room for improvement. Sharing of curricula between institutions and the formation of strategic university–industry partnerships would make this easier to achieve (Fadzil et al., 2015).

An effective way to address the cognitive dissonance would be to support the creation of local study groups to facilitate collaborative learning (Blom et al., 2013). Study groups could make learning difficult concepts tolerable and discussion within the group could help to clarify problematic content areas (Li et al., 2014). The efficacy of study groups has been demonstrated with learners enrolled in MOOCs at the École Polytechnique Fédérale de Lausanne. Similar groups were also formed to good effect by various cohorts of learners in Coursera courses (Nkuyubwatsi, 2014).

5. Pedagogical Approach

With the increased prominence of pedagogy as a focus of research, social and student-centered learning approaches have been gaining traction in North American, European, and Australian learning contexts. Though not universal, there has been a shift away from the "sage on the stage," content-focused approaches towards more "guide on the side" styles. In stark contrast, the first generation of MOOCs that came out of the United States replicated the didactic approach to learning and teaching (Romiszowski, 2013). The majority still take this form, with written materials or video content distributed to participants and assessed with self-marking quizzes. Discussion forums are available, but not mandated. So, despite their promises of good pedagogical practice, MOOCs have failed to democratize learning (Naidu and Karunanayaka, 2020). MOOCs in the Asia-Pacific region are no different. For example, Malaysia MOOCs use a teacher-focused, content-driven model that has failed to incorporate collaborative elements (Taib et al., 2017). This is problematic when learners are conditioned to be passive spectators in their own education. In China, the expert educator generally stands at the front, and the learners passively absorb that expert knowledge. When Chinese learners are required to participate in discussion forums or other collaborative activities, they struggle (Jiao and Fan, 2020). This was also the case with MOOC learners at the Ho Chi Minh City Open University of Vietnam, who were so used to educator-led teaching that they passively absorbed written and video materials at the expense of engagement with other learners on the forums (Dang et al., 2017).

The enculturation of learners in teacher-centered practice in Asia presents a formidable barrier to their full participation in those MOOCs presenting opportunities for community building and collaborative activity (Dang et al., 2017). To ensure the quality of the learning of those engaged with MOOCs and to promote learner engagement and retention, educators should use those approaches that place the learner at the center, and which do not rely on the dispassionate dissemination of content (Fladkjær and Otrel-Cass, 2017). Authentic, student-centered approaches mimic the messiness of real-world problems. This evidence-based approach ensures that the learner becomes familiar with the subject matter, and learns to apply it in an authentic context. This prepares the learner for the work environment but this should not be confused with workplace learning or work-integrated learning. This alternative approach starts with the context and not the content (Naidu and Karunanayaka, 2020). In a similar manner, a greater use of user-generated content would ensure greater engagement and better learning outcomes for MOOC learners (Jiao and Fan, 2020).

6. CONCLUSION

It is difficult to assess how effective MOOCs have been in extending access to higher education in the Asia-Pacific. There is still much work to be done to reach that population currently excluded from higher education and to increase the diversity of participants (Zhou, 2020). Though there have been some excellent initiatives by governments, higher education institutions, and corporates, the impact cannot be said to be uniform across Asia. MOOCs have been most successful where there has already been strong investment in technological infrastructure, and a robust and coherent policy environment. Of course, the infrastructure is poorest in those regions where access to education is most needed, in those regional areas where people are already remote from those institutes of learning that might facilitate their escape from poverty. Those regions are usually not well populated and the incentives for business to drive development are not there. Access to technology and connectivity will improve given time but may not keep pace with global developments sufficiently to address inequality.

In line with other areas of education, learners will raise their expectations around the design and delivery of MOOCs. As social media and mobile technologies become ever more personalized, educational designers will scramble to reflect those developments in their offerings. Learners will vote with their feet and unresponsive platforms will fail to thrive or survive. The analysis of the big data generated by massive enrollments could give MOOC providers clues as to how to personalize courses or provide just-in-time support for the struggling learner. However, there are challenges to be overcome including selecting the right data, storing that data, and interpreting it in a useful way. Along with the use of any personal data comes a whole raft of ethical and legal conundrums that are yet to be resolved (Yamada, 2015).

Education providers will continue to look for efficiencies as the cost of recruitment and competition from other institutions continues to grow. Almost certainly, providers will make greater use of AI to inform their decision-making as the sector becomes ever more complex (Kim and Lee, 2020). AI could also be front facing, incorporated into MOOC platforms to be used as an intelligent tutor. The Chinese government is already looking to bring AI into its classrooms to support its learners when human tutors become too expensive or too scarce (Jing, 2017). Udacity has recently partnered with a chatbot technology provider, Passage AI, to help learners select courses, answer questions, and guide them as they navigate through their course. Udacity's goal is to provide learners with an experience like talking to their tutors (Dickson, 2018). The ways in which AI can be leveraged to maximize learning while generating efficiencies are still being discovered. The spoils will almost certainly go to the MOOC platform that continues to innovate; that can provide a personalized experience that addresses not only the academic needs of the learner and community, but also his or her cultural, spiritual, and social needs. In this way, the promise of MOOCs to broaden access to higher education will finally be realized.

References

Abas, Z. W. (2015). "The glocalization of MOOCs in Southeast Asia." In C. J. Bonk, M. M. Lee, T. C. Reeves, and T. H. Reynolds (eds.), *MOOCs and Open Education Around the World*. New York: Routledge, 234–242.

Alcorn, B., Christensen, G., and Kapur, D. (2015). "Higher education and MOOCs in India and the Global South." *Change: The Magazine of Higher Learning*, 47/3, 42–49.

Annan-Diab, F. and Molinari, C. (2017). "Interdisciplinarity: Practical approach to advancing education for sustainability and for the Sustainable Development Goals." *The International Journal of Management Education*, 15/2, Part B, 73–83.

Asian Development Bank (2011). *Higher Education Across Asia: An Overview of Issues and Strategies*. Manila: ADB. https://www.adb.org/sites/default/files/publication/29407/higher-education-across-asia.pdf

Bandalaria, M. dP. (2018). "Open and distance elearning in Asia: Country initiatives and institutional cooperation for the transformation of higher education in the region." *Journal of Learning for Development - JL4D*, 5/2, 116–132.

Bandalaria, M. dP. and Alfonso, G. A. (2015). "Situating MOOCs in the developing world context: The Philippines case study." In C. J. Bonk, M. M. Lee, T. C. Reeves, and T. H. Reynolds (eds.), *MOOCs and Open Education Around the World*. New York: Routledge, 243–254.

Belawati, T. (2020). "Massive Open Online Courses: The state of practice in Indonesia." In K. Zhang, C. J. Bonk, T. C. Reeves, and T. H. Reynolds (eds.), *MOOCs and Open Education in the Global South: Challenges, Successes, and Opportunities*. New York: Routledge, 63–71.

Blom, J., Verma, H., Li, N., Skevi, A., and Dillenbourg, P. (2013). "MOOCs are more social than you believe." *eLearning Papers*, 33, 1–3.

Chapman, D. and Sarvi, J. (2017). "Widely recognized problems, controversial solutions: Issues and strategies for higher education development in East and Southeast Asia." In K. H. Mok (ed.), *Managing International Connectivity, Diversity of Learning and Changing Labour Markets*. Singapore: Springer, 25–46.

Che, X., Luo, S., Wang, C., and Meinel, C. (2016). "An Attempt at MOOC Localization for Chinese-Speaking Users." *International Journal of Information and Education Technology*, 6/2, 90–96.

Chen, J. C.-C. (2013). "Opportunities and challenges of MOOCS: Perspectives from Asia." Paper presented at the IFLA World Library and Information Congress, Singapore. http://library.ifla.org/157/1/098-chen-en.pdf

Chew, S. W., Cheng, I.-L., and Chen, N.-S. (2017). "Yet another perspectives about designing and implementing a MOOC." In M. Jemni and K. M. Kinshuk (eds.), *Open Education: From OERs to MOOCs*. Berlin: Springer, 117–133.

Chuang, I. and Ho, A. (2016). "HarvardX and MITx: Four years of open online courses – fall 2012–summer 2016." https://papers.ssrn.com/sol3/papers.cfm?abstract_id=2889436

Dang, T. T., Watts, S., and Nguyen, T. Q. (2017). "Massive Open Online Course: International experiences and implications in Vietnam." Paper presented at the InSITE 2017: Informing Science + IT Education Conferences, Ho Chi Minh City. https://www.informingscience.org/Publications/3745?Type=journalarticles

Dickson, B. (2018). "How AI could help improve the education enrollment process." *Venture Beat*, March 8. https://venturebeat.com/2018/03/08/how-ai-could-help-improve-the- education-enrollment-process/

Fadzil, M., Latif, L. A., and Munira, T. A. (2015). "MOOCs in Malaysia: A preliminary case study." In B. Kim (ed.), *MOOCs and Educational Challenges around Asia and Europe.* Seoul: KNOU Press, 65–85.

Farley, H. and Song, H. (2015). "Mobile learning in Southeast Asia: Opportunities and challenges." In J. A. Zhang (ed.), *Handbook of Mobile Teaching and Learning: Design, Development, Adoption, Partnership, Evaluation and Expectation.* Berlin: Springer-Verlag, 403–419.

Fladkjær, H. F. and Otrel-Cass, K. (2017). "A cogenerative dialogue: Reflecting on education for co-creation." In T. Chemi and L. Krogh (eds.), *Co-Creation in Higher Education: Students and Educators Preparing Creatively and Collaboratively to the Challenge of the Future.* Rotterdam: Sense Publishers, 83–98.

Gervacio, J. L. M. (2015). "MOOCs in the Philippines." In B. Kim (ed.), *MOOCs and Educational Challenges around Asia and Europe.* Seoul: KNOU Press, 103–120.

Jagannathan, S. (2017). "Exploring the future of development learning: The open learning campus." *Internal Journal of Advanced Corporate Learning (iJAC)*, 10/2, 96–105.

Jiao, J. and Fan, Y. (2020). "Current state of practice and research on MOOCs in mainland China: A critical review." In K. Zhang, C. J. Bonk, T. C. Reeves, and T. H. Reynolds (eds.), *MOOCs and Open Education in the Global South: Challenges, Successes, and Opportunities.* New York: Routledge, 28–40.

Jing, M. (2017). "China wants to bring artificial intelligence to its classrooms to boost its education system." *South China Morning Post* (Science & Research, October 14). https://www.scmp.com/tech/science-research/article/2115271/china-wants-bring-artificial-intelligence-its-classrooms-boost

Jung, I. (2019). "South Korea—Commentary." In O. Zawacki-Richter and A. Qayyum (eds.), *Open and Distance Education in Asia, Africa and the Middle East: National Perspectives in a Digital Age.* Singapore: Springer, 101–104.

Jung, I., Mendoza, G. A. G., Fajardo, J. C., Figueroa Jr., R. B., and Tan, S. E. (2020). "MOOCs in six emerging APEC member economies: Trends, research, and recommendations." In K. Zhang, C. J. Bonk, T. C. Reeves, and T. H. Reynolds (eds.), *MOOCs and Open Education in the Global South: Challenges, Successes, and Opportunities.* New York: Routledge, 199–211.

Kim, B. (2015). "What do we know about MOOCs?" In B. Kim (ed.), *MOOCs and educational challenges around Asia and Europe.* Seoul: KNOU Press, 3–6.

Kim, P. and Lee, K. (2020). "Evolution of online learning environments and the emergence of intelligent MOOCs." In K. Zhang, C. J. Bonk, T. C. Reeves, and T. H. Reynolds (eds.), *MOOCs and Open Education in the Global South: Challenges, Successes, and Opportunities.* New York: Routledge, 329–341.

Kim, Y., Kim, O. T., and Shon, J. G. (2020). "A historical journey into K-MOOCs leading to possible collaborations with North Korea." In K. Zhang, C. J. Bonk, T. C. Reeves, and T. H. Reynolds (eds.), *MOOCs and Open Education in the Global South: Challenges, Successes, and Opportunities.* New York: Routledge, 17–27.

Kumar, J. A. and Al-Samarraie, H. (2018). "MOOCs in the Malaysian higher education institutions: The instructors' perspectives." *The Reference Librarian*, 59/3, 163–177.

Kurniasari, F., Jusuf, E., and Gunardi, A. (2018). "The readiness of Indonesian toward MOOC system." *International Journal of Engineering & Technology*, 7/3, 1631–1636.

Laurillard, D. and Kennedy, E. (2017). "The potential of MOOCs for learning at scale in the Global South." https://www.researchcghe.org/perch/resources/publications/wp31.pdf

Law, W.-W. (2020). "The role of the state and state orthodoxy in citizenship and education in China." In A. Peterson, G. Stahl, and H. Soong (eds.), *The Palgrave Handbook of Citizenship and Education*. Cham: Palgrave Macmillan, 297–314.

Lee, J.-A. (2018). "Great firewall." In B. Warf (ed.), *The SAGE Encyclopedia of the Internet*, vol. 2. London: Sage, 407–410.

Lee, T. (2015). "A case study of MOOC at KNOU: KNOU MOOC for knowledge sharing." In B. Kim (ed.), *MOOCs and Educational Challenges around Asia and Europe*. Seoul: KNOU Press, 49–64.

Li, N., Verma, H., Skevi, A., Zufferey, G., Blom, J., and Dillenbourg, P. (2014). "Watching MOOCs together: Investigating co-located MOOC study groups." *Distance Education*, 35/2, 217–233.

Li, W. and Chen, N. (2019). "China." In O. Zawacki-Richter and A. Qayyum (eds.), *Open and Distance Education in Asia, Africa and the Middle East: National Perspectives in a Digital Age*. Singapore: Springer, 7–22.

Li, X., Chen, Y., and Gong, X. (2017). "MOOCs in China: A Review of Literature, 2012–2016." In W. Ma, C. K. Chan, Kw Tong, H. Fung, and C. Fong (eds.), *New Ecology for Education — Communication X Learning*. Singapore: Springer, 21–32.

Lim, C., Lee, J., and Chio, H. (2019). "South Korea." In O. Zawacki-Richter and A. Qayyum (eds.), *Open and Distance Education in Asia, Africa and the Middle East: National Perspectives in a Digital Age*. Singapore: Springer, 87–100.

Lim, V., Wee, L., Teo, J., and Ng, S. (2017). "Massive Open and Online Courses and Open Education Resources in Singapore." *Southeast Asian Ministers of Education (SEAMEO) Journal*, 1, 1–13.

Liu, X., Liu, S., Lee, S. H., and Magjuka, R. J. (2010). "Cultural differences in online learning: International student perceptions." *Journal of Educational Technology & Society*, 13(3), 177–188.

Liyanagunawardena, T. R. and Adams, A. A. (2014). "The impact and reach of MOOCs: A developing countries' perspective." *eLearning Papers, Special Edition 2014*, 38–46. http://centaur.reading.ac.uk/38250/

McAuley, A., Stewart, B., Siemens, G., and Cornier, D. (2010). "The MOOC model for digital practice: Digital ways of knowing and learning." https://www.academia.edu/download/43171365/MOOC_Final.pdf

Ministry of Human Resource Development (2020). *National Education Policy 2020*. https://www.education.gov.in/sites/upload_files/mhrd/files/NEP_Final_English_0.pdf

Moe, R. (2015). "The brief & expansive history (and future) of the MOOC: Why two divergent models share the same name." *Current Issues in Emerging eLearning*, 2/1, Article 2. https://scholarworks.umb.edu/ciee/vol2/iss1/2

Naidu, S. and Karunanayaka, S. P. (2020). "Orchestrating shifts in perspectives and practices about the design of MOOCs." In K. Zhang, C. J. Bonk, T. C. Reeves, and T. H. Reynolds (eds.), *MOOCs and Open Education in the Global South: Challenges, Successes, and Opportunities*. New York: Routledge, 72–80.

Nasongkhla, J., Thammetar, T., and Chen, S.-H. (2015). "Thailand OERs and MOOCs country report." In B. Kim (ed.), *MOOCs and Educational Challenges around Asia and Europe*. Seoul: KNOU Press, 121–135.

Nkuyubwatsi, B. (2014). "Cultural translation in Massive Open Online Courses (MOOCs)." *eLearning Papers*, 37, 1–10.

Panda, S. and Garg, S. (2019). "India." In O. Zawacki-Richter and A. Qayyum (eds.), *Open and Distance Education in Asia, Africa and the Middle East: National Perspectives in a Digital Age.* Singapore: Springer, 27–42.

Panth, B. and Xu, J. J. (2020). "Blending education and technology to help schools through the pandemic." In B. Susantono, Y. Sawada, and C.-Y. Park (eds.), *Navigating COVID-19 in Asia and the Pacific.* Manila: Asian Development Bank, 179–181.

Pushpanadham, K. (2015). "Universalizing university education: MOOCs in the era of knowledge based society." In B. Kim (ed.), *MOOCs and Educational Challenges around Asia and Europe.* Seoul: KNOU Press, 21–33.

Qayyum, A. and Zawacki-Richter, O. (2019). "The state of open and distance education." In O. Zawacki-Richter and A. Qayyum (eds.), *Open and Distance Education in Asia, Africa and the Middle East: National Perspectives in a Digital Age.* Singapore: Springer, 125–140.

Reich, J. and Ruipérez-Valiente, J. A. (2019). "The MOOC pivot: What happened to disruptive transformation of education?" *Science*, 363/6423, 130–131.

Romiszowski, A. J. (2013). "Topics for debate: What's really new about MOOCs?" *Educational Technology*, 53(4), 48–51.

Ruipérez-Valiente, J. A., Jenner, M., Staubitz, T., Li, X., Rohloff, T., Halawa, S., … Reich, J. (2020). "Macro MOOC learning analytics: Exploring trends across global and regional providers." Paper presented at the 10th International Learning Analytics & Knowledge Conference, Frankfurt. doi:10.1145/3375462.3375482

Schaffhauser, D. (2019). "MOOCs on the rise in China." *Campus Technology.* https://campustechnology.com/articles/2019/11/21/moocs-on-the-rise-in-china.aspx

Schmid, L., Manturuk, K., Simpkins, I., Goldwasser, M., and Whitfield, K. E. (2015). "Fulfilling the promise: Do MOOCs reach the educationally underserved?" *Educational Media International*, 52/2, 116–128.

Sharma, R. C. (2019). "India—Commentary." In O. Zawacki-Richter and A. Qayyum (eds.), *Open and Distance Education in Asia, Africa and the Middle East: National Perspectives in a Digital Age.* Singapore: Springer, 43–45.

Shi, X. and Yu, S. (2016). "The rising of China's MOOC: Opportunities and challenges to the HEIs." *Current Politics and Economics of Northern and Western Asia*, 25/1, 61–89.

Stratton, C. and Grace, R. (2016). "Exploring linguistic diversity of MOOCS: Implications for international development." Paper presented at the 79th ASIS&T Annual Meeting: Creating Knowledge, Enhancing Lives through Information & Technology, Copenhagen. https://asistdl.onlinelibrary.wiley.com/doi/pdf/10.1002/pra2.2016.14505301071

Taib, T. M., Chuah, K.-M., and Aziz, N. A. (2017). "Understanding pedagogical approaches of UNIMAS MOOCs in encouraging globalised learning community." *International Journal of Business and Society*, 18/S4, 838–844.

Tang, H. and Carr-Chellman, A. (2016). "Massive Open Online Courses and educational equality in China: A qualitative inquiry." *Journal of Educational Technology Development and Exchange (JETDE)*, 9/1, 49–66.

Tao, L. and Donald, S. H. (2016). "Migrant youth and new media in Asia." In L. Hjorth and O. Khoo (eds.), *Routledge Handbook of New Media in Asia.* Abingdon: Routledge, 28–38.

Taylor, K. and Silver, L. (2019). "Smartphone ownership is growing rapidly around the world, but not always equally." https://www.pewresearch.org/global/wp-content/uploads/sites/2/2019/02/Pew-Research-Center_Global-Technology-Use-2018_2019-02-05.pdf

Thaipisutikul, T. and Tuarob, S. (2017). "MOOCs as an intelligent online learning platform in Thailand: Past, present, future challenges and opportunities." Paper presented at the 10th

International Conference on Ubi-Media Computing and Workshops (Ubi-Media), Pattaya. doi:10.1109/UMEDIA.2017.8074143

Thammetar, T. and Jintavee, K. (2020). "Promoting open education and MOOCs in Thailand: A research-based design approach." In K. Zhang, C. J. Bonk, T. C. Reeves, and T. H. Reynolds (eds.), *MOOCs and Open Education in the Global South: Challenges, Successes, and Opportunities*. New York: Routledge, 140–155.

Trehan, S., Sanzgiri, J., Li, C., Wang, R., and Joshi, R. (2017). "Critical discussions on the Massive Open Online Course (MOOC) in India and China." *International Journal of Education and Development using Information and Communication Technology*, 13/2, 141–165.

United Nations Educational, Scientific and Cultural Organization (UNESCO) (2014). *Higher Education in Asia: Expanding Out, Expanding Up. The Rise of Graduate Education and University Research*. Montreal: UNESCO Institute for Statistics. http://www.uis.unesco.org/Library/Documents/higher-education-asia-graduate-university-research-2014-en.pdf

United Nations General Assembly (2015). *Transforming Our World: The 2030 Agenda for Sustainable Development* (A/RES/70/1). https://undocs.org/A/RES/70/1

Veletsianos, G. and Shepherdson, P. (2016). "A systematic analysis and synthesis of the empirical MOOC literature published in 2013–2015." *International Review of Research in Open and Distributed Learning*, 17/2, 198–221.

Venkatataman, B. and Prabhakar, T. V. (2020). "Responsive innovations in MOOCs for development: A case study of AgMOOCs in India." In K. Zhang, C. J. Bonk, T. C. Reeves, and T. H. Reynolds (eds.), *MOOCs and Open Education in the Global South: Challenges, Successes, and Opportunities*. New York: Routledge, 300–309.

Warusavitarana, P. A., Dona, K. L., Piyathilake, H. C., Epitawela, D. D., and Edirisinghe, M. U. (2014). "MOOC: A higher education game changer in developing countries." Paper presented at the Rhetoric and Reality: Critical Perspectives on Educational Technology conference, ascilite, Dunedin. https://www.ascilite.org/conferences/dunedin2014/files/fullpapers/321-Warusavitarana.pdf

Xiao, J. (2018). "On the margins or at the center? Distance education in higher education." *Distance Education*, 39/2, 259–274.

Yamada, T. (2015). "MOOC phenomena in Japan: JMOOC and OUJ-MOOC." In B. Kim (ed.), *MOOCs and Educational Challenges around Asia and Europe*. Seoul: KNOU Press, 35–48.

Zawacki-Richter, O. and Qayyum, A. (2019). "Introduction." In O. Zawacki-Richter and A. Qayyum (eds.), *Open and Distance Education in Asia, Africa and the Middle East: National Perspectives in a Digital Age*. Singapore: Springer, 1–6.

Zhang, J. (2019). "China—Commentary." In O. Zawacki-Richter and A. Qayyum (eds.), *Open and Distance Education in Asia, Africa and the Middle East: National Perspectives in a Digital Age*. Singapore: Springer, 23–25.

Zhang, K., Bonk, C. J., Reeves, T. C., and Reynolds, T. H. (2020). "MOOCs and open education in the Global South: Successes and challenges." In K. Zhang, C. J. Bonk, T. C. Reeves, and T. H. Reynolds (eds.), *MOOCs and Open Education in the Global South: Challenges, Successes, and Opportunities*. New York: Routledge, 1–14.

Zhou, M. (2020). "Public opinion on MOOCs: Sentiment and content analyses of Chinese microblogging data." *Behaviour & Information Technology*. https://doi.org/10.1080/0144929X.2020.1812721

Zhu, M., Sari, A. R., and Lee, M. M. (2020). "A comprehensive systematic review of MOOC research: Research techniques, topics, and trends from 2009 to 2019." *Educational Technology Research and Development*, 68/4, 1685–1710.

PART VI

....

COSTS

Who Pays?

....

CHAPTER 18

....

PUBLIC FINANCING

....

XI WANG AND W. JAMES JACOB

1. Introduction and Overview of Public Financing of Higher Education in Asia

....

As the rapid growth and increasing demand for higher education exists in many Asian countries, government higher education (HE) funding has seen steady competition for increasingly limited resources. Alternative funding streams have helped supplement government shortages, most notably in tuition increases and loan schemes. Several governments have noted goals to position their HE presence on international ranking systems by elevating their premier institutions to recognized world-class status. These institutions generally obtain financial preference over other government-supported higher education institutions (HEIs). But the notion of every Asian country establishing at least one HEI among the top 100-ranked HEIs worldwide is in many ways unrealistic, given the disproportionate funding capacity of the powerhouse countries compared to others. China's ability to invest heavily in its top-tier HEIs has enabled it to project multiple universities into the top-tier global rankings, but other countries have fallen short on this score. Still, according to John A. Douglass and other scholars, top-tier government-supported HEIs remain prominent *flagship universities* in their respective national and regional contexts (see, for instance, Douglass, 2016; Wang et al., 2020). Even in this limited resource/hyper-competitive context, several leading Asian universities have made significant gains in global rankings. In 2019 there were roughly 24 Asian HEIs ranked by the top three global ranking systems, compared to only 13 in 2004.[1]

---

[1] These trends are based on data from the three most prominent global university ranking systems—Shanghai Jiao Tong University Academic Ranking of World Universities (ARWU), *Times Higher Education (THE)*, and Quacquarelli Symonds (QS).

Another justification for channeling significant government funding toward research-intensive HEIs is the need for greater research output as recognized by number of documents produced in international academic journals and citations (see Table 18.1).

Several Asian countries leapfrogged others in global rankings, most notably China coming in at 2nd in 2018 (up from 6th in 1998), India at 5th in 2018 (up from 13th), Iran at 16th (up from 51st), and Indonesia at 24th (up from 63rd). Both Iran and Indonesia had 5,000 percent research output increases during the 20-year period highlighted in Table 18.1. Government investment in HE research has paid off for many countries. These figures are often linked to gauging national innovation and research and development capacity (Bornmann et al., 2015; Mathews and Hu, 2007; Hu and Mathews, 2008). As a result of increasing government funding with a focus on developing research programs in science, technology, engineering and math (STEM) fields, it is worth noting that when restricting the publications to STEM fields, all four Asian countries listed in the

Table 18.1 Journal citation ranking and documents produced by country, 1998, 2008, and 2018

Country	1998 Global rank (GR)	Documents[a]	2008 GR	Documents	2018 GR	Documents
Australia	11	27,309	11	58,392	10	106,228
China[b]	6	48,600	2	276,469	2	622,933
India	13	23,065	10	60,550	5	171,356
Indonesia	63	612	64	1,572	24	32,456
Iran	51	1,224	22	20,006	16	60,268
Japan	2	97,591	5	123,275	6	131,198
Korea	16	14,192	12	51,471	13	85,725
Malaysia	49	1,241	41	8,083	23	33,295
New Zealand	33	5,553	34	10,859	41	17,150
Pakistan	52	1,187	45	5,278	38	20,548
Russia	9	34,292	15	37,431	11	99,099
Singapore	36	4,012	32	13,043	34	22,495
Taiwan	20	12,358	16	35,128	19	36,691
Thailand	46	1,634	40	8,097	40	17,943
Vietnam	78	314	65	1,526	50	8,837

[a] The term *documents* refers to the number of published documents contained in Elsevier's Scopus database.

[b] China rankings and figures include data from China, Hong Kong, and Macao.

Source: Created by the authors with data from Scimago Lab (2020).

top 12 improve their publication output ranking in 2018 (i.e., China from 2nd to 1st, India from 5th to 3rd, Japan from 6th to 5th, and Korea from 13th to 9th) (NSB, 2019).

The average expenditure on tertiary education as percentage of the total expenditure on education is 19.1 percent (see Table 18.2). This regional average increased from 18.0 percent in 2003. Macao (37.1 percent), Taiwan (34.0 percent), and Bangladesh (33.3 percent) spent the greatest percentage of their education expenditure on tertiary education compared to Kyrgyzstan (4.6 percent), Cambodia (6.1 percent), and Mongolia (6.4 percent), which spent the least.

Powerhouse economies like China, Japan, Korea, and Taiwan each have sustained government funds to help sustain their respective HE sub-sectors. Other emerging economies like India, Indonesia, and Vietnam have also seen substantial increased investment in their HE sub-sectors, especially compared to 20 years ago.

Government expenditure on HE varies widely throughout the region. In many countries public funding far outweighs private funding for HE (see Figure 18.1). Governments contributed 76.1 percent and 63.9 percent of all tertiary funding in Indonesia and Russia respectively, compared to only 32.4 percent in Japan, 36.1 percent in Korea, and 37.8 percent in Australia. Figure 18.1 shows a global pattern that for those high-income countries such as Japan, Korea, and Australia, the private sector contributes a larger share of tertiary education expenditure than exists in the low-middle-income countries (such as China and Indonesia). As the trend of diversifying HE funding sources continues across the world, the private sector will most likely continue to increase its share of tertiary education expenditure among less developed countries.

Government expenditure on education as a percentage of GDP also varies across Asian countries (see Figure 18.2). This number allows for a comparison of countries' expenditures relative to their capacity to finance education. In 2016, the world average government expenditure on education as a percentage of GDP was 4.49 percent. Of the selected 15 Asian countries, Bhutan reported the highest government expenditure on education to GDP (6.64 percent in 2018), followed by Nepal (5.16 percent in 2018), and Korea (4.59 percent in 2016). The country with the lowest percentage was Myanmar (1.97 percent in 2018). A high percentage of GDP usually suggests a high priority for public spending on education.

However, where government expenditure appears lower as a share of GDP does not necessarily mean the country spends less on education. For example, of those more economically developed countries such as Japan, Singapore, and Korea, their public expenditure per tertiary student is essentially above that of other Asian countries. On one hand, they have a higher GDP than those developing countries. On the other hand, a majority of their students attend private HEIs, so the private funding has a larger share of total funding for HE. The expansion of private HEIs increased the general access to tertiary education without increasing the demand for public funds. As a result, we can see that Japan, Korea, and Singapore are positioned at the top of the list with governments spending the most on per enrolled tertiary student in recent years (see Figure 18.3). The government expenditure per tertiary student was 21,529 USD in Singapore in 2017 followed by Japan at 8,325 USD in 2016. In contrast, while Nepal had a higher share of

Table 18.2 Public tertiary funding trends as a percentage of government expenditure on education, 2003 to the latest year available

Country/jurisdiction	2003	2008	2013	Latest year available
Afghanistan	–	9.0[n]	11.8	16.0[s]
Australia	22.2[i]	22.5	26.0	26.8[t]
Bangladesh	9.1	13.3	14.7[p]	33.3[t]
Bhutan	14.1[i]	19.4	18.2	10.3[r]
Cambodia	5.0[e]	6.3[m]	6.1	–
China	30.2	30.0	28.0	26.0[v]
Hong Kong (China)	30.4[h]	30.9	38.9	29.4[v]
Fiji	13.6[f]	15.9[h]	22.6	–
India	20.1	36.5[m]	28.5	–
Indonesia	12.8[k]	11.0	16.4	15.8[s]
Iran	17.1	20.7	22.9	28.2[v]
Japan	16.8	18.9	20.0	19.8[t]
Kazakhstan	13.1[f]	13.9	15.3[s]	9.4[v]
Korea	13.5[c]	13.9	15.6[p]	20.4[t]
Kyrgyzstan	19.9	16.4	12.8	4.6[r]
Laos	12.6[f]	23.2[m]	14.1	13.8[r]
Macao (China)	41.1	36.6	44.9	37.1[u]
Malaysia	35.0	33.0[k]	30.5	21.3[v]
Mongolia	15.5[f]	6.7[n]	16.4	6.4[u]
Nepal	10.3	13.5	11.3	10.8[s]
New Zealand	24.9	28.9	25.3	23.7[t]
Pakistan	11.9[b]	–	32.2	22.8[s]
Philippines	13.2	10.4	12.0[m]	–
Russia	18.5	23.1	21.9	21.6[t]
Sri Lanka	12.2[a]	18.2[m]	21.1	14.2[t]
Taiwan	34.3[f]	36.6	34.2	34.0[u]
Tajikistan	7.8	14.2	11.2[p]	9.9[s]
Thailand	20.6[h]	21.2	15.6	–
Vietnam	9.2[h]	22.2	15.0	6.1[s]

Notes: [a]1996, [b]1997, [c]1999, [d]2000, [e]2001, [f]2002, [g]2003, [h]2004, [i]2005, [j]2006, [k]2007, [l]2008, [m]2009, [n]2010, [o]2011, [p]2012, [q]2013, [r]2014, [s]2015, [t]2016, [u]2017, [v]2018.

Source: Created by the authors with data from UIS (2020), World Bank (2020a), World Bank (2020b), Republic of China Ministry of Education (2019), National Bureau of Statistics (2020), China Educational Finance Statistical Yearbook (2013) People's Republic of China Ministry of Education (2019).

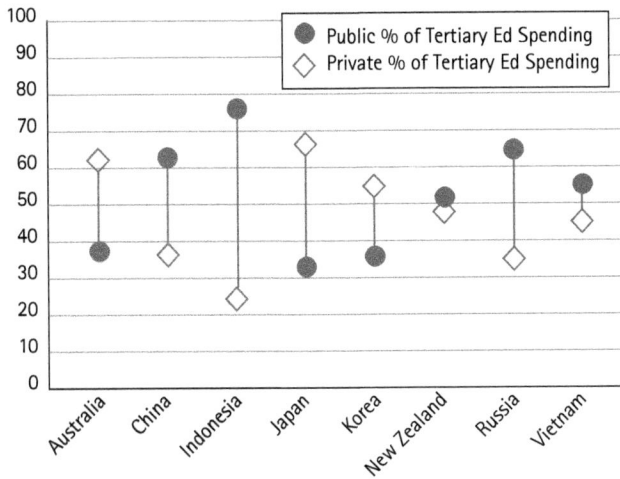

FIGURE 18.1 Public vs. private percentage of spending on tertiary education, latest year available

Sources: Created by the authors with data from OECD (2020), Fang and Liu (2018), and Vietnam Ministry of Education and Training and UIS (2016).

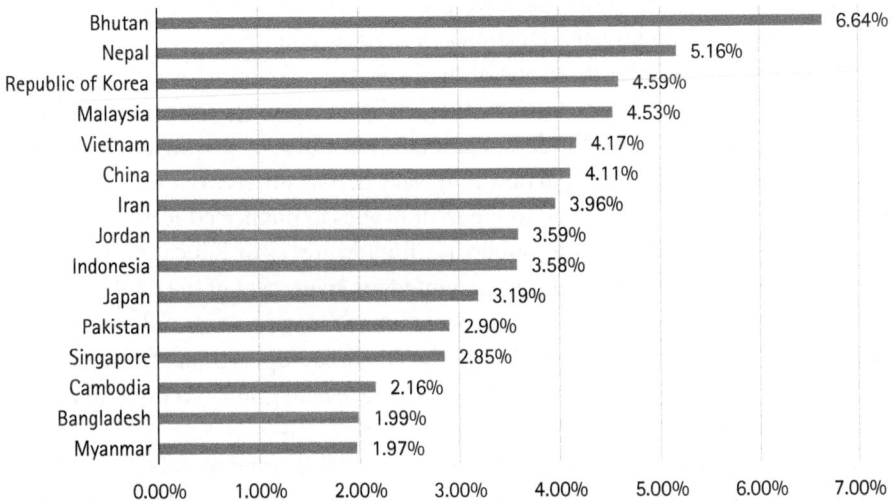

FIGURE 18.2 Government expenditure on education as a share of GDP in selected Asian countries in 2018

Note: All data refer to the year of 2018, except for Singapore (2013), Indonesia (2015), Japan (2016), Republic of Korea (2016), and Pakistan (2017), with latest year available.

Sources: Created by authors with data from UNESCO UIS (2020), Ministry of Education of PRC (2019a).

Country	Value
Nepal (2015)	609
Myanmar (2018)	1030
Bangladesh (2016)	1105
Vietnam (2013)	1798
Indonesia (2015)	2298
Jordan (2018)	2368
India (2013)	2419
China (2018)	3187
Pakistan (2017)	3346
Bhutan (2014)	4003
Iran (2017)	4868
Republic of Korea (2016)	5580
Malaysia (2018)	7530
Japan (2016)	8325
Singapore (2017)	21529

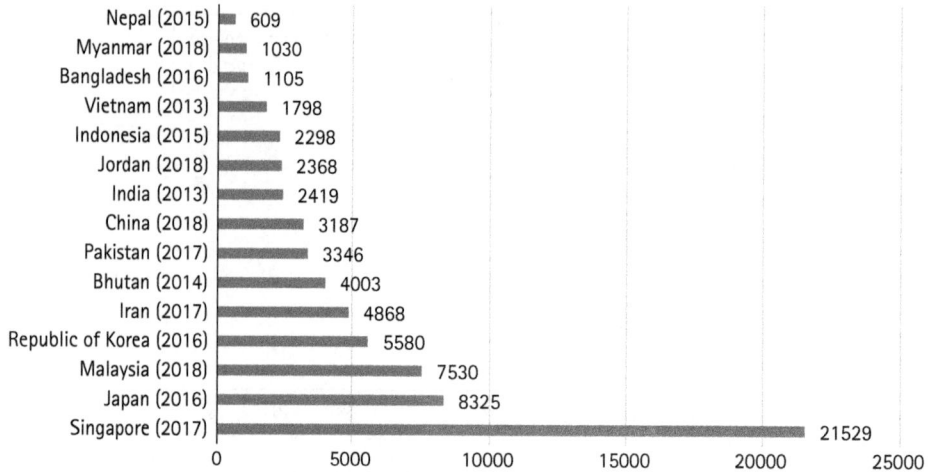

FIGURE 18.3 Government expenditure per tertiary student in selected Asian countries (PPP$), latest year available

Sources: Created by authors with data from UNESCO UIS (2020) and Ministry of Education of PRC (2019a).

government expenditure on education, the per tertiary student expenditure in 2015 was only 609 USD, which was among the lowest countries in the region.

Public expenditure on higher education across Asian countries can mainly be divided into several categories: education operational fees (i.e., personnel wages and benefits, maintenance, and other expenses for HEIs' daily operation); educational construction fee; research and project funds; student aid; subsidies for private universities; and other fees. Each category's proportion may vary across different countries, however, the largest part of funding devoted to HE mainly goes to finance education operational costs. According to the People's Republic of China Ministry of Education (PRC MOE) data, educational operations expenses accounted for 80 percent of the total government expenditure on HE in 2017, educational construction was 3 percent, and research funds accounted for another 3 percent. In Japan, the education operational funds accounted for 63 percent of total expenditure on HE in 2015, research grants accounted for 13 percent, and student financial aid another 6 percent.

Public HEIs primarily receive education operational income mainly as block grants from governments based on a statutory formula. This formula is calculated primarily on the basis of the number of enrolled students, the number of employees, the size of campus and other indicators. However, this statutory formula approach caused many HEIs to blindly expand their enrollments and offer new disciplines and majors without simultaneously expanding sufficient funding for teaching, which in turn impairs instruction quality and impedes operational efficiencies.

In terms of research and project funds, there is a trend shifting from basic grants to competitive grants in the region. Research and project funds are increasingly evaluated and granted competitively through a peer review process. However, even with rigorous assessment and peer review, many governments tend to allocate more funds toward top universities with concentrations on STEM disciplines rather than supporting research in humanities and social science.

When considering the public expenditure on higher education across levels of government, most Asian countries today rely heavily on local governments instead of their respective national governments to fund HE. For example, in China there are more than 2,900 HEIs across the country. Only approximately 4 percent of these institutions are affiliated with central-level ministries, which receive funding support directly from the national government. The majority of Chinese HEIs are managed by local governments, thus receiving local funding, albeit some of them also receiving research grants from the central government. Taking Jiangsu Province as an example, central government funding toward HE was 30.37 percent in 2015, while local government funding accounted for 69.63 percent. Similarly, in Vietnam, local governments allocated 64 percent of total spending in tertiary education in 2013. The national government contributed 12 percent and households contributed 24 percent (UIS, 2020). In Japan, university corporations[2] were the largest funding source for HE (51.4 percent in 2003), followed by the national government (41.7 percent), and local governments (7 percent) (MEXT, 2011).

Such funding mechanisms supported by national and local governments resulted in the unbalanced development of HE in different regions. In China, there is a large expenditure disparity between HEIs funded by the national government (and directly administrated by PRC MOE) and those HEIs financed by local sources. For example, in 2019, the top two universities with the highest national government expenditure allocation were Peking University and Tsinghua University, which received roughly six times the amount of overall funding received by many other large universities. In addition, due to unequal regional economic development, the local government expenditure on HE differs substantially across provinces (Jacob, 2004). The HE spending is higher in the eastern coastal regions of the country (where local economies are largely better developed) compared to the middle and western regions of China. For instance, the total government expenditure on education at all levels in Guangdong Province was more than 491.8 billion RMB in 2019 (DOEGDP, 2020). Whereas Qinghai Province spent only 28.9 billion RMB on education in the same year (DOEQH, 2020), which was 17 times lower. Inevitably, local government expenditures exacerbate HE financing inequality issues in China (Hawkins et al., 2009).

---

[2] In April 2004, all national universities were transformed into "National University Corporations." With this reform, each national university was separated from the central government as a public corporation (juridical public body) and possesses greater autonomy in terms of internal operations (Oba, 2005).

2. COUNTRY CASE STUDY EXAMPLES OF PUBLIC HIGHER EDUCATION FINANCING

In this section, we begin by providing some global innovative public financing examples to illustrate outside budgetary support to HE elsewhere. In addition, we provide more in-depth country case study examples of public HE financing in China, Japan, and Vietnam. Examples of how these countries finance public HE are addressed as well as how they provide financing for some of the most disadvantaged groups of people in their respective contexts. Also included are specific public financing policies and practices related to helping ethnic minority, indigenous, refugee, and low socio-economic status groups access and pay for HE.

2.1 Global Innovative Public Financing Examples

2.1.1 *Land-Grant Universities in the United States*

Under the first Morrill Act, which was passed by the US Congress in 1862, each state in the United States was granted 30,000 acres of federal land for each member of Congress representing that state. The lands were sold, and the proceeding funds were used to es-tablish and endow land-grant universities or colleges. The original mission of these institutions was to teach agriculture and mechanical arts with the aim of increasing college access and cultivating students' practical skills to meet the rapidly industrializing nation. The Second Morrill Act (1890) provided additional endowments for all land-grant universities and prohibited grant funding to universities that featured racial dis-crimination in admission policies. As a result, there is at least one land-grant university in each state in the United States. Some of the best-known land-grant universities include Ohio State University, Pennsylvania State University, the University of California, and so on. Moreover, some well-known private universities are also land-grant universities including Cornell University and Massachusetts Institute of Technology. In 2017, there were 1.7 million students enrolled across 109 land-grant universities. In 2019, the USDA National Institute of Food and Agriculture (NIFA) discretionary appropriations to partner land-grant universities for education and research had reached 1.47 billion USD (CRS, 2020).

2.1.2 *Income Forgone*

As federal and state governments continue to cut funding for HE, raising private support has become crucial for the development of HEIs. Governments implement various tax deduction policies to bring in charitable donations to universities and colleges. The en-dowment funds from taxpayers may be able to deduct the value of their contribution from income subject to tax. According to Sherlock et al. (2018), in FY2017, the total tax provisions that directly benefit education institutions was approximately 15.7 billion USD, including deductions for charitable contributions to educational institutions; private activity tax-exempt bonds for non-profit educational institutions; and the share of general obligation tax-exempt bonds benefits to public HEIs.

As Asia's wealth rises, there is increased charitable contributions to HE. Educational institutions are the largest beneficiaries of philanthropic donations in Asia. However, some major concerns pointed out by philanthropists include a trust deficit due to uncertain political support, lack of transparency, scandals at non-profit organizations, and the confusing term "non-governmental organization" (Shapiro, 2018). Therefore, it is crucial to increase donation transparency and to encourage tax regulations and policies on giving and receiving of donations for HEIs in Asia.

2.1.3 *Guaranteed Student Loan Programs*

Student loan programs are adopted by many countries to meet HE costs. Secured financing of student loans largely increased HE enrollments especially in private HEIs. In the United States, the federal government began guaranteeing student loans to help finance students' college education in 1965. These loans are different from private student loans in that they are guaranteed by the government. They are administered by approved private lending organizations. Should a borrower default on a guaranteed loan, the federal government pays approximately 97 percent of the principal balance to the lender and owns the right to collect payments on the loan (DOE, 2014). Private lenders would assume no risk should the borrowers ultimately default. However, owing to the arguments that the guaranteed student loan programs were more costly to the government, Congress ended the guaranteed loan programs in 2010. Thereafter, students could obtain a federal student loan under the direct student loan program, which is issued directly by the federal government to students. Nevertheless, due to millions of students who still owe money on guaranteed loans, these students are still paying down guaranteed loans issued before then.

Many Asian countries are also implementing various student loan programs to ease the financial burden on college students. In Japan (2017), South Korea (2010), and Thailand (2006), their respective governments have introduced an income-contingent loan (ICL) schema to help students from low-income households. In China, the Government-Subsidized Student Loans Scheme (GSSLS) was proposed in 1999 and experienced several modifications. Under GSSLS, four state-owned commercial banks are the loan lenders and the central and local governments subsidize half of the loan interest rate before students' graduation. Lending banks will be exempted from business tax on the student loans. However, certain difficulties have also been raised during the GSSLS implementation. For example, students enrolled in private HEIs are restricted from applying to the GSSLS and the maximum of loan coverage (6,000 RMB/year, which is around 857 USD) is generally insufficient to cope with student tuition, accommodation, and transportation fees, especially for those students enrolled in Medical and Art majors.

2.1.4 *University Bonds Market*

An increasing number of HEIs in the United States and the United Kingdom—including many elite universities such as Harvard, Yale, MIT, and Oxford—have issued bonds to help fill their current financial gaps. In most cases, the money is invested to build university infrastructure such as sport stadiums, libraries, and student residences. A majority of US universities choose municipal bonds, which usually have a lower cost of capital, fixed-rate interest, and a long-term maturity date. In 2017, the University of Oxford raised £750 million with a 100-year bond, which was the longest in the history of university bonds in the United Kingdom. However, a recent article reported around half of the bonds have been sold as taxable corporate bonds as they are experiencing historically low interest rates under the global COVID-19 pandemic and feature fewer restrictions on how the funds are allocated (Moran, 2020).

In addition to investing in infrastructure services, some university bonds target improving social services. For example, in 2015, Israel launched its first social impact bond (SIB) in HE, aiming to reduce the dropout rate of computer science students and extend their studies. By decreasing the dropout rate, Israeli universities will benefit from added revenue; it also leads to long-term positive impacts in developing a stronger IT-oriented economy for the nation. Several Latin American countries have also considered the implementation of social impact bonds to generate funds to improve the quality and effectiveness of social services to vulnerable populations. However, university bonds seem still new to a lot of Asian countries. In 2020, the Japanese government eased the requirements to allow national university corporations to issue their own bonds. The University of Tokyo decided to issue bonds worth 100 billion yen with a 30-year maturity period. This innovative fund-raising example will likely be implemented by more high reputation universities in Asia. However, certain difficulties also exist in Asia's context. For example, a lack of transparent and accurate data will make the bonds much riskier. In addition, legal and regulatory barriers prevent universities from issuing their own bonds, especially those universities which are owned and operated by the public sector.

2.1.5 *Off Budget Public Financing*

In 2017, the Ministry of Human Resource Development (MHRD), Government of India, and Canara Bank jointly set up a Higher Education Financing Agency (HEFA), with a participation of 90.91 percent and 09.09 percent respectively. This new funding model aims to help India's top-ranked universities attain higher global rankings. It provides timely finance with low interest rates to improve HEIs' academic and infrastructure quality. The not-for-profit HEFA leverages funds from the market and supplements them with donations and Corporate Social Responsibility (CSR) funds for capital projects in tertiary education. HEFA is able to fund a larger number of institutions as compared to a grants-funding approach. When looking at current funding agencies and organizations that provide funds for HE in Asia, a majority of them offer a grants-format support. Under the registered non-profit organization Asia SEED, most funds to support HE between Japan and Asian countries come from the Government of

Japan. Certain HE projects are funded from Japan Bank for International Cooperation loans, such as the "Indonesian Professional Human Resources Development Program III (PHRDP-3)" and "The Support Program for Employment of Japanese Language Lecturers on the higher education support plan (IT sector) in Vietnam." However, all of these loans were used to support individual students, rather than providing funding at the institutional level.

India's off budget public financing outlined in the paragraph above may provide an innovative financing example for more Asian countries to follow.

2.2 Higher Education Expansion in China, Japan, and Vietnam

During the past several decades, there has been a clear trend towards expansion of HE across China, Vietnam, and Japan in both the number of HEIs and student enrollment. Among the three countries, China has achieved the largest increase in both relative growth and absolute number of general HEIs at 158 percent, from 1,032 in 1996 to 2,663 in 2018 (PRC MOE, 2018).

Despite all three countries having experienced a large expansion in HE, gross tertiary enrollment percentages (or HE participation rate) differ among the three selected countries. In Japan, the gross tertiary enrollment rate had passed 50 percent in 2002 and reached to 63.4 in 2014 (Knoema, 2020). In contrast, the percentage of gross tertiary education in both China and Vietnam has increased much more sharply from 1995 to 2016, from 4.4 percent to 48 percent in China, and 2.8 percent to 28.5 percent in Vietnam (World Bank, 2020a). With the world's largest enrollment in HE in China, the participation rate, however, had only reached to 50.6 percent in 2018. Vietnam's HE participation rate is still low compared to the world average gross tertiary education rate at 37.4 percent in 2016 (World Bank, 2020a).

Large unmet demand for HE seems to exist within China and Vietnam compared to most developed countries in the world. Nevertheless, their gross enrollment rate (GER) at the tertiary level is much higher than when developed countries were at their same level of GDP per capita. For example, the GDP per capita in China in 2019 was 10,262 USD. This number is roughly equal to GDP per capita in Japan back in 1983 (10,425 USD). However, the gross tertiary enrollment rate in Japan was 29.7 percent in 1983, which was much lower than the GER in China in 2018. The massification of HE that occurred in those lower-income-level Asian countries has exacerbated the public financing problem of tertiary education.

2.3 The Role of Government in Funding Higher Education

Public financing trends in HE across the three countries exhibit both similarities and differences. The rapid development of HE in recent decades has made sole dependence on government funding difficult for HEIs in all three countries. Indeed, there is a clear trend of shifting from a dominant reliance on state funding to a cost-sharing model across all three countries. The governments of China, Vietnam, and Japan have developed policies to diversify funding streams to include other sources, including parents, businesses, philanthropists, and other donors. In addition, owing to increasing tuition fees in all three countries, all three central governments have provided more student scholarships and student loan programs to promote equality in access to HE of those students from disadvantaged groups (Sheridan, 2010; JASSO, 2019; PRC MOE, 2019a). Furthermore, public HEIs in the three countries have become more privatized, rely on more diverse funding sources (including increasing tuition fees), and have achieved increased administrative independence (Sanyal and Johnstone, 2011).

Regarding the funding differences, China and Vietnam have a larger share of government funding when compared to Japan. In 2013, government funds accounted for 60.3 percent of Chinese HEIs revenues, and another 34 percent came from tuition, miscellaneous fees, donations, and other auxiliary revenues (Jacob et al., 2017). In contrast, as private enrollment is larger in Japan than in other two countries, private sources accounted for 70 percent of HE funding, including 53 percent from households and 17 percent from other private entities. Only 30 percent of HE expenditures in Japan came from public sources in 2016 (OECD, 2019).

3. Public Higher Education Financing Policies in China

Following implementation of the Higher Education Law on January 1, 1999, Chinese HE has experienced noticeable expansions in the number of HEIs and in student enrollment. Regular student entrants at HEIs numbered nearly 1.6 million, an increase of 513,000 students or 47.4 percent from 1998 (Figure 18.4). During this period, the number of regular HEIs also increased sharply from 1,071 in 1999 to 2,305 in 2009 (Figure 18.5). As of 2018, the number of regular HEIs had reached 2,663. More than 45.2 million

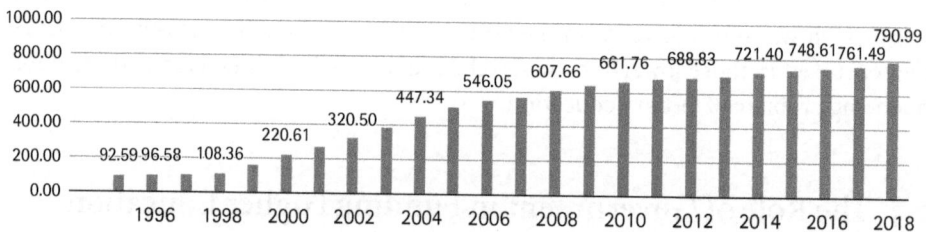

FIGURE 18.4 General higher education institution student entrants in 1995–2018 (unit: ten thousand)

Source: PRC MOE, *National Educational Development Statistical Yearbook* (in Chinese).

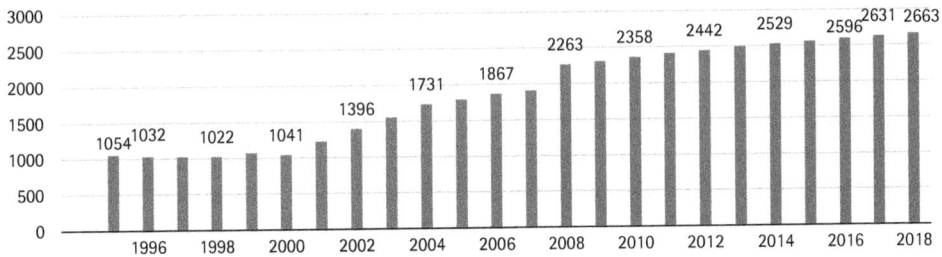

FIGURE 18.5 Number of general higher education intuitions in 1995–2018

Source: PRC MOE, *National Educational Development Statistical Yearbook* (in Chinese).

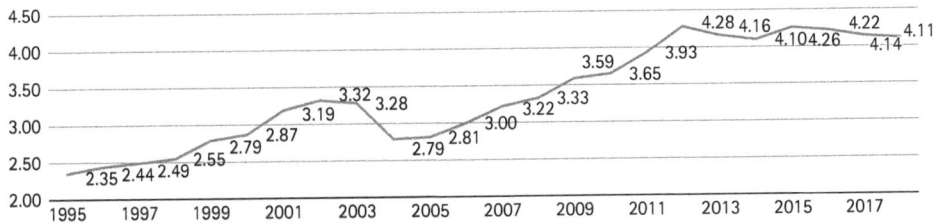

FIGURE 18.6 Governmental expenditure on education as percentage of GDP

Source: National Bureau of Statistics of China (2019).

students were enrolled in various types of HE programs and institutions, and a rate of 50 percent of tertiary gross enrollment has been reached (PRC MOE, 2018).

In addition, tuition and miscellaneous fee also increased notably from 37 billion yuan (5.2 billion USD) in 1998 to 529.3 billion yuan (75 billion USD) in 2017 (NBSC, 2019). Since 2000, tuition and miscellaneous fees have covered more than 20 percent of the total operating budgets of Chinese HEIs (Jacob et al., 2017). Governmental expenditure on education as a percentage of GDP has increased modestly since 1998. An expenditure goal of 4 percent GDP was achieved in 2012 (see Figure 18.6). Government expenditure on tertiary education as a percentage of GDP was 1.4 percent in 2019. HE funding sources have shifted from sole dependence on the government to a cost-sharing model, where government, individuals, and society share the financial responsibilities for HE.

4. Policies and Practices Supporting Disadvantaged Students

The Chinese government has also taken various actions to give support to disadvantaged groups of students to ensure that they could enjoy equivalent financial aid, and develop supports such as student loans, scholarships, and grants. The Education Law of the People's Republic of China effective in 1995 indicated in its Article 56: "The State Council and the local people's governments at the county level or above shall establish specific funds for education to be used mainly for assisting outlying and poverty-stricken areas and areas inhabited by minority ethnic groups in enforcing compulsory education there" (PRC MOE, 1995).

In 2002, the central government first set up its "National Scholarship" program, which granted 200 million yuan (28 million USD) to 45,000 economically disadvantaged undergraduate students each year. Students who receive this scholarship are exempted from all tuition fees for that year. In 2012, this scholarship expanded to master's and doctoral students (PRC MOE, 2019a).

In 1998, Tsinghua University first established the "Green Passage" program to help those admitted but financially disadvantaged students to successfully access HE. In 2000, the central government required all HEIs to adopt the "Green Passage" program to enable new students from poor families to proceed through admission procedures and to receive proper subsidies (PRC MOE, 2019a).

According to the *China Student Aid Development Report 2017*, nearly 42.76 million college and university students received financial aid totaling over 105.07 billion yuan (14.17 billion USD) in 2017, an increase of 9.93 percent from 2016 (China Daily, 2018).

5. Public Higher Education Financing in Japan

Since World War II, Japan has continuously developed a diverse HE system. In April 2004, all national universities were transformed into "National University Corporations." With this reform, each national university was separated from the central government as a public corporation (juridical public body). Although universities are still subject to government regulations regarding enrollment size and tuition fees, they now possess greater autonomy in terms of internal operations (Oba, 2005).

Before 2004, more than 90 percent of the national universities' funding came from the central government allocation. Beginning with the incorporation of both national universities and public universities in 2004, government expenditures on national university corporations have decreased consistently by 1 percent annually since then. For example, the government management expenses grants for national university corporations have decreased consistently from 1.24 trillion JPY (11.6 billion USD) in 2004 to 1.09 trillion JPY (10.2 billion USD) in 2016 (RIHE, 2016).

Given the relatively large proportion of HE in Japan that is private, public expenditure on HE is lower in Japan than in most of the OECD countries (Huang, 2018). According to OECD (2019) data, Japan's public expenditure on tertiary education in 2016 was 1.38 percent of its 4.93 trillion USD GDP, which came to around 64 billion USD. Similarly, the cost-sharing trend in HE will likely continue with further shifting from public to private financing sources (Kobayashi and Armstrong, 2017).

In 2003, 60 percent of all HEI expenditures were met by private sources, and the remaining 40 percent came from public ones (Newby et al., 2009). The trend of relying heavily on private funding has continued since then. In 2016, private sources accounted for 70 percent of HE expenditures, of which 53 percent came from households and 17 percent was from private entities. Thus, only 30 percent of HE expenditures came from public sources in 2016 (OECD, 2019).

Owing to this decrease in government funding for public HE sectors, national and public university corporations have been given more freedom to diversify their funding sources. At the same time, the tuition at national universities has maintained a continuous rise over the past decade (Kyodo, 2019). According to *Education at a Glance*, Japan belongs to one of the one-third of OECD countries that charge high tuition fees to national students. During the 2017/18 academic year, tuition at public HEIs in Japan was, on average, 5,200 USD per year for bachelor's programs (OECD, 2019). However, the increased tuition and student loan burden have affected the equality of access to HE (Kobayashi and Armstrong, 2017). However, the government has also increased new types of competitive research grants to expand HEI funding and to promote scientific research of all kinds. For example, the "Grants-in-Aid for Scientific Research," awarded by the Japan Society for the Promotion of Science (JSPS) under the Ministry of Education, Culture, Sports, Science, and Technology (MEXT), has increased consistently from 183 billion JPY (1.7 billion USD) in 2004 to 232 billion JPY (2.2 billion USD) in 2015 (RIHE, 2016).

With regard to funding disadvantaged students, the Japanese government, and the Japan Student Services Organization (JASSO), an independent organization affiliated with MEXT, have implemented various types of scholarships and student services for HE in Japan since 2004. One example is the "Scholarship Programs for Japanese Students," which aims to increase access to HE for students with financial barriers. This includes both Scholarship Loans, which must be repaid, and Scholar Grants, which are not repaid. JASSO has also expanded the scope of scholarship loans. The total amount of loans has reached approximately one trillion JPY (9.27 billion USD) going to a total number of 1.3 million annual recipients, meaning that one in 2.7 students at Japanese universities accessed JASSO's scholarship loan programs in fiscal year FY2018 (JASSO, 2019). Since 2017, public grants have first been offered to undergraduate students in Japan (Kobayashi and Armstrong, 2017). In addition, new legislation passed in 2019 indicated that university tuition fees will be waived for students from low-income families from 2020. HE students who come from households with annual incomes of 2.7 million JPY (25,000 USD) or less, are eligible for this new aid program, which does not require repayment (Kakuchi, 2019).

6. Public Financing of Higher Education in Vietnam

HE in Vietnam has made impressive progress during the country's rapid and sustained economic growth over the last three decades. To meet the needs of the country's industrialization in a global economy, the central government has reformed educational policies to increase HE enrollment and advance human capital development (WES, 2017). For example, the "Fundamental and Comprehensive Reform of Higher Education in Vietnam 2006–2020" policy (also known as the Higher Education Reform Agenda, or HERA) of 2005 included many goals for reforming HE (Nghi and London, 2010). One of these was to decentralize HE administration to local authorities. Furthermore, Decree 43/2006/ND-CP in 2006 further decentralized budgeting and encouraged schools to expand their own sources of income (UIS, 2016).

Government expenditure on education as a percentage of GDP in Vietnam remained above 4.1 percent between 2008 and 2018. This ratio increased steadily from 4.9 percent in 2008 to 5.7 percent in 2013, before decreasing to 4.2 percent (or 10 billion USD) in 2018 (World Bank, 2020a). Government expenditure on HE as a percentage of the entire education budget decreased from 22 percent in 2008 to 14 percent in 2009 and rose slightly to 15 percent in 2013 (World Bank, 2020a) (see Figure 18.7).

While the share of government expenditure on education as a percentage of GDP is relatively high, financial support has only represented a modest expenditure and produced modest results as Vietnam's GDP is relatively low (Anh and Hayden, 2017). Furthermore, government budget reductions led to the implementation of "education socialization," which requires the government, parents, and other sources to collectively fund the HE (Pham and Vu, 2019).

The Decree No. 86/2015/ND-CP, issued by the government in 2015, granted public HEIs more financial and managerial autonomy. Public HEIs and self-financing facilities can collect the tuition fees sufficient to cover training costs under this decree. However, the government also regulated the maximum tuition fees according to the area of study, academic year, and whether public HEIs exercise financial autonomy (Table 18.3). The tuition cap for the 2020–2021 academic year for a full-time bachelor's degree in financial-autonomous public HEIs is approximately twice that of tuition for students in non-autonomous HEIs that focus on social or nature sciences. Disparities in tuition rates are even larger in medicine and pharmacy (GSRV, 2015). It has been suggested that these differences may create even larger gaps in learning opportunities and outcomes among students from economically disadvantaged and minority groups (Doan et al., 2020).

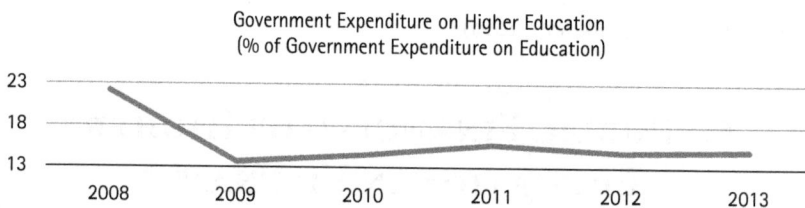

FIGURE 18.7 Expenditures on tertiary education as a percentage of government expenditures on education in Vietnam, 2008–2013

Source: World Bank (2020a).

Table 18.3 Maximum tuition fees at public HEIs according to every discipline from academic years 2015 to 2021 in Vietnam (unit: VND 1,000/month/student)

Discipline	From 2015/2016 to 2017/2018		From 2018/2019 to 2019/2020		Academic year 2020/2021	
	Exercise financial autonomy	Do not exercise financial autonomy	Exercise financial autonomy	Do not exercise financial autonomy	Exercise financial autonomy	Do not exercise financial autonomy
1. Social science, economics, law, agriculture, forestry, and aquaculture	1,750	610–740	1,850	810–890	2,050	980
2. Natural sciences, engineering and technology, physical education and sports, art, hotel and tourism	2,050	720–870	2,200	960–1,060	2,400	1,170
3. Medicine and pharmacy	4,400	880–1,070	4,600	1,180–1,300	5,050	1,430

Source: Government of Socialist Republic of Vietnam (GSRV), 2015. Decree No. 86/2015/ND-CP on Mechanism for Collection and Management of Tuition Fees.

To ease the financial burden on students from disadvantaged groups, the Vietnamese government provides tuition fee exemptions or rebates and merit scholarships to support students with financial difficulties. Universities are expected to devote 15 percent of their tuition fee income towards merit scholarships (Sheridan, 2010). In addition, the central government introduced student loan programs to assist students with financial difficulties. However, Sheridan (2010) argued that awarding scholarships may be less successful if universities have reduced incentives to fund scholarships by spending their own tuition income. Similarly, high interest rates and limited coverage of student loans also suggest loans may be insufficient to support the growing numbers of students from low-income families (Chapman and Liu, 2013). Therefore, strategic remedies are needed, such as increased numbers of tuition waivers, reserving places for ethnic minority "nominated students," encouraging endowment funds to cover scholarships, and establishing effective loan schemes that encourage students from disadvantaged backgrounds to gain access to HE (Sheridan, 2010; Doan et al., 2020).

7. CONCLUSION AND RECOMMENDATIONS

Government HE funding policies vary widely throughout Asia. In some instances, policies dictate that tuition remain equal for all citizens. In others, choice is provided to students to pursue their own destiny, and if they have the means, they can pay for their HE trajectory regardless of whether they gain admittance through national examinations. Some national HE systems in Asia have a robust private sector that rivals the public sector. Others are dominated by the public sector. Regardless of national contexts, the overall costs of HE operations and delivery are increasing.

The general global trend of tuition increases is also found throughout Asia, albeit some governments have legislated to counter this trend (Jacob et al., 2012). In many cases, tuition increases far outpace inflation, and thus seem to have embarked on an unsustainable trajectory. These tuition trends also further exacerbate inequalities that exist between students from low, middle, and high socio-economic backgrounds, urban and rural backgrounds, and dominant majority versus many ethnic minority groups. An overreliance on growing HE tuition costs not only shifts the responsibility away from governments, it also exposes vulnerabilities when too much reliance is placed on students. These financial vulnerabilities move to center-stage during national economic, natural disaster, political, and health crises (e.g., the COVID-19 pandemic).

HEIs that have both robust operating financial platforms and optimal delivery models are best able to cope with the dynamic changes required to meet student needs. Being able to navigate between when to offer traditional, hybrid, or entirely online courses to students is a key factor that HEIs face. HEIs which remain rigid in offering only traditional delivery formats will not be able to weather the financial fallout that inevitably arises when students are unable to attend campuses due to one or more of these crises.

Technology shifts alone are unable to provide the financial stability required to satisfy optimal business and delivery models. And technology shifts traditionally far outpace the ability of HEIs to adapt (Hershock et al., 2007). Professional development and training of staff members at all levels is a requirement to better prepare and empower faculty members, staff, and administrators with the necessary knowledge and skills for optimal delivery. ICT is at a critical junction in HE globally and in Asia. Leveraging ICT for optimal HE business and delivery models requires incorporating appropriate content management systems (CMS), software as a service (SaaS), and course delivery platforms. This leveraging process can help HEIs realize greater financial efficiencies only offered through such technologies (Jacob and Gokbel, 2020). ICT, along with professional development and training, enables HE stakeholders to focus on quality, efficiency, and simplicity. All these factors are essential in helping HEIs to cope with the financial challenges they are currently facing and will undoubtedly face in the future.

The advent of the COVID-19 pandemic has wreaked havoc on public financing of HE in Asia most notably through enrollment shifts, with student and staff mobility grinding to a halt for much of 2020 and 2021. While on-campus and in-person classes have drastically diminished, the disruptive shift to online delivery remains a challenge and will most likely remain so well into the foreseeable future. Thus, many students will not be able to attend in person their HEI of choice due to closures and coursework limitations online and other factors. But, importantly, students will most likely have a say in which HEIs survive and thrive in the post-COVID-19 era, as the weakest ones may well be swept away, with few tears shed (Mitchell, 2020). In many ways the pandemic has accelerated the necessary shift to more nimble and sustainable financial models and optimal delivery models as advocated by Clayton M. Christensen (Christensen and Eyring, 2011) and other scholars (Jacob and Gokbel, 2018, 2020). The expected long-term financial implications of COVID-19 require HEIs to diversify funding sources and increase collaboration with organizations and private companies to gain innovative technology and digital training. Academic programs which are best aligned with workforce needs and twenty-first-century skills are those that will most likely be able to sustain enrollments and weather the aftermath of financial disruptions (Sutin and Jacob, 2016; Jacob and Sutin, 2018).

The ongoing COVID-19 pandemic has precipitated HEIs in most Asian countries into both immediate and long-term financial challenges. Universities are expected to have large income losses. As social welfare and health sectors require even higher portions of government funding, governments' capacity to fund public HEIs will be more constrained. Affected by the pandemic, the income of many households has been seriously reduced or even lost. Both Japan and Indonesia's university students requested tuition reductions from their respective governments. Students will need to save on both tuition and dorm fees in order to remain solvent themselves. Moreover, as most universities have transitioned to online learning, HEIs have had to spend more on online learning infrastructure including both its technological aspects and pedagogical aspects in an effort to allow students and teachers to engage in online learning. However, educational inequality may also rise due to the unequal development as between countries with better internet infrastructure such as Japan, Korea, Singapore, and Taiwan, and countries with less internet infrastructure such as Cambodia and Vietnam.

REFERENCES

Anh, L. T. K. and Hayden, M. (2017). "The road ahead for the higher education sector in Vietnam." *Journal of International and Comparative Education*, 6/2, 77–89.

Bornmann, L., Wagner, C., and Leydesdorff, L. (2015). "BRICS countries and scientific excellence: A bibliometric analysis of most frequently cited papers." *Journal of the Association for Information Science and Technology*, 66/7, 1507–1513.

Chapman, B. and Liu A. Y. C. (2013). "Repayment burdens of student loans for Vietnamese higher education." *Economics of Education Review*, 37, 298–308.

China Daily (2018). *China Student Aid Development Report 2017*. http://www.chinadaily.com.cn/a/201803/14/WS5aa887dda3106e7dcc141903_4.html, accessed March 24, 2020.

China Educational Finance Statistical Yearbook (2013). *National Education Expenditure*. http://data.cnki.net/yearbook/Single/N2017120223, accessed March 25, 2020.

Christensen, C. M. and Eyring, H. J. (2011). *The Innovative University: Changing the DNA of Higher Education from the Inside Out*. San Francisco, CA: Jossey-Bass.

Congressional Research Service (CRS) (2020). *The U.S. Land-Grant University System: An Overview*. CRS Report Prepared for Members and Committees of Congress. https://fas.org/sgp/crs/misc/R45897.pdf, accessed July 10, 2020.

Department of Education (DOE) (2014). *Student Loan Overview: Fiscal Year 2014 Budget Proposal*. https://www2.ed.gov/about/overview/budget/budget14/justifications/s-loansoverview. pdf, accessed July 12, 2020.

Department of Education of Guangdong Province (DOEGDP) (2020). *Report on the Statistics of Education funding in Guangdong Province in 2019*. http://edu.gd.gov.cn/gkmlpt/content/3/3148/post_3148231.html#1660, accessed June 9, 2020.

Department of Education of Qinghai (DOEQH) (2020). *Report on the Statistics of Education in Qinghai Province in 2019*. http://jyt.qinghai.gov.cn/gk/cwgk/jyjf/202012/P020201207620568226367.pdf, accessed June 9, 2021.

Doan, D., Kang, J., and Zhu, Y. (2020). "Financing higher education in Vietnam: Student loan reform." Centre for Global Higher Education Working Paper Series, No. 51. https://www.researchcghe.org/perch/resources/publications/final-working-paper-51.pdf, accessed April 2, 2020.

Douglass, J. A. (2016). *The New Flagship University: Changing the Paradigm from Global Ranking to National Relevancy*. New York: Palgrave Macmillan.

Fang, F. and Liu, Z. (2018). "The changing and reflection of Chinese higher education financing from 2005–2015." *Chinese Higher Education Research*, 4, 78–85.

Government of Socialist Republic of Vietnam (GSRV) (2015). "Decree No. 86/2015/ND-CP Fee Exemption and Reduction and Financial Support from Academic." https://vanbanphapluat.co/decree-no-86-2015-nd-cp-fee-exemption-and-reduction-and-financial-support-from-academic, accessed April 6, 2020.

Hawkins, J. N., Jacob, W. J., and Li, W. (2009). "Higher education in China: Access, equity, and equality." In D. B. Holsinger and W. J. Jacob (eds.), *Inequality in Education: Comparative and International Perspectives*. Hong Kong and Dordrecht: CERC/Springer, 215–239.

Hershock, P. D., Mason, M., and Hawkins, J. N. (eds.) (2007). *Changing Education: Leadership, Innovation and Development in a Globalizing Asia Pacific*. Dordrecht: Springer.

Hu, M.-C. and Mathews, J. A. (2008). "China's national innovative capacity." *Research Policy*, 37/9, 1465–1479.

Huang, F. (2018). "Higher education financing in Japan: Trends and challenges." *International Journal of Educational Development*, 58, 106–115.

Jacob, W. J. (2004). "Marketization, demarketization, and remarketization: The impact of the economic market on higher education in China." Doctoral dissertation, Graduate School of Education & Information Studies, University of California, Los Angeles.

Jacob, W. J. and Gokbel, V. (2018). "Global higher education learning outcomes and financial trends: Comparative and innovative approaches." *International Journal of Educational Development*, 58/1, 5–17.

Jacob, W. J. and Gokbel, V. (2020). "Global higher education financial trends." *International Association of Universities (IAU) Horizons*, 25/1, 23–25.

Jacob, W. J., Mok, K. H., Cheng, S. Y., and Xiong, W. (2017). "Changes in Chinese higher education: Financial trends in China, Hong Kong and Taiwan." *International Journal of Educational Development*, 58, 64–85.

Jacob, W. J. and Sutin, S. E. (2018). "Global trends in higher education financing." *International Journal of Educational Development*, 58/1, 1–4.

Jacob, W. J., Wang, Y., Pelkowski, T. L., Karsidi, R., and Priyanto, A. D. (2012). "Higher education in Indonesia: A trends analysis of current challenges and opportunities." In W. Bruneau and H. G. Schuetze (eds.), *Reform of University Governance: Policy, Fads, and Experience in International Perspective*. New York: Palgrave Macmillan, 225–240.

Japan Student Service Organization (JASSO) (2019). *JASSO Outline 2019–2020*. https://www.jasso.go.jp/en/about/organization/__icsFiles/afieldfile/2019/07/12/e2019_a4_0702s.pdf, accessed March 28, 2020.

Kakuchi, S. (2019). "Mixed reaction to tuition waivers for low-income students." *University World News*. https://www.universityworldnews.com/post.php?story=20190726144908732, accessed March 28, 2020.

Knoema (2020). *Japan: Gross Enrolment Ratio in Tertiary Education*. https://knoema.com/atlas/Japan/topics/Education/Tertiary-Education/Gross-enrolment-ratio-in-tertiary-education, accessed April 9, 2020.

Kobayashi, M. and Armstrong, S. (2017). "Financing higher education in Japan and the need for reform." AJRC Working Paper 02/2017. Australia-Japan Research Centre, Crawford School of Public Policy, The Australian National University. https://ajrc.crawford.anu.edu.au/sites/default/files/publication/ajrc_crawford_anu_edu_au/2017-10/financing_higher_educatio_in_japan_and_the_need_for_reform.pdf

Kyodo (2019). "Who should pay for higher education in Japan? The public, parents or students themselves?" *The Japan Times News*. https://www.japantimes.co.jp/news/2019/05/21/national/pay-higher-education-japan-public-parents-students/#.Xn4cui2cYUs, accessed March 24, 2020.

Mathews, J. A. and Hu, M.-C. (2007). "Enhancing the role of universities in building national innovative capacity in Asia: The case of Taiwan." *World Development*, 35/6, 1005–1020.

Ministry of Education, Culture, Sports, Science, and Technology (MEXT) (2011). *III Expenditure on Education*. https://www.mext.go.jp/component/english/__icsFiles/afieldfile/2011/03/07/1303013_007.pdf, accessed July 20, 2020.

Mitchell, N. (2020). "Students to decide which institutions survive COVID-19." *University World News*. https://www.universityworldnews.com/post.php?story=20200507135847614, accessed May 7, 2020.

Moran, D. (2020). "Elite colleges join bond-market boom by seizing on low rates." *Bloomberg*. https://www.bloomberg.com/news/articles/2020-05-21/elite-colleges-join-bond-market-boom-by-seizing-on-low-rates, accessed July 15, 2020.

National Bureau of Statistics of China (NBSC) (2019). *China Statistical Yearbook, 2019*. Beijing: China Statistics Press. http://www.stats.gov.cn/tjsj/ndsj/2019/indexch.htm, accessed March 24, 2020.

National Bureau of Statistics of China (NBSC) (2020). *Chinese Education Expenditure and Higher Education Expenditure from 2000–2018*. http://data.stats.gov.cn/easyquery.htm?cn=C01, accessed May 25, 2020.

National Science Board (NSB) (2019). *Publications Output: U.S. Trends and International Comparison*. Science and Engineering Indicators. https://ncses.nsf.gov/pubs/nsb20206/publication-output-by-region-country-or-economy, accessed July 15, 2020.

Newby, H., Weko, T., Breneman, D., Johanneson, T., and Maassen, P. (2009). "OECD Review of Tertiary Education: Japan." https://www.oecd.org/japan/42280329.pdf, accessed March 25, 2020.

Nghi, P. T. and London, J. D. (2010). "The higher education reform agenda: A vision for 2020." In G. Harman, M. Hayden and P. T. Nghi (eds.), *Reforming Higher Education in Vietnam*. Higher Education Dynamics, Volume 29. Dordrecht: Springer, 51–64.

Oba, J. (2005). "The incorporation of national universities in Japan: Initial reactions of the new national university corporations." *Higher Education Management and Policy*, 17/2, 931–1070.

Organisation for Economic Co-operation and Development (OECD) (2019). *Education at a Glance 2019: Japan*. Paris: OECD. https://www.oecd.org/education/education-at-a-glance/EAG2019_CN_JPN.pdf, accessed March 25, 2020.

Organisation for Economic Co-operation and Development (OECD) (2020). *Spending on Tertiary Education (Indicator)*. Paris: OECD. https://www.oecd-ilibrary.org/education/spending-on-tertiary-education/indicator/english_a3523185-en, accessed March 25, 2020.

People's Republic of China Ministry of Education (PRC MOE) (1995). *Education Law of the People's Republic of China*. http://old.moe.gov.cn/publicfiles/business/htmlfiles/moe/moe_2803/200905/48457.html, accessed March 23, 2020.

People's Republic of China Ministry of Education (PRC MOE) (2018). *National Educational Development Statistical Yearbook, 1995–2018* (in Chinese). http://www.moe.gov.cn/jyb_sjzl/sjzl_fztjgb/, accessed March 22, 2020.

People's Republic of China Ministry of Education (PRC MOE) (2019a). *Funding Support to Chinese Students in 70 Years*. http://www.moe.gov.cn/jyb_xwfb/s5147/201909/t20190924_400640.html, accessed March 23, 2020.

People's Republic of China Ministry of Education (PRC MOE) (2019b). *Statistical Announcement on the Implementation of National Education Finance in 2018*. http://www.moe.gov.cn/srcsite/A05/s3040/201910/t20191016_403859.html, accessed May 25, 2020.

People's Republic of China Ministry of Education (PRC MOE) and National Bureau of Statistics of China (2009). *China Education Expenditure Statistics Yearbook, 2009*. Beijing: China Statistics Press.

Pham, H.-H. and Vu, H.-M. (2019). "Financing Vietnamese higher education: From a wholly government-subsidized to a cost-sharing mechanism." In N. T. Nguyen and L. T. Tran (eds.), *Reforming Vietnamese Higher Education: Global Forces and Local Demands*. Singapore: Springer, 75–89.

Republic of China Ministry of Education (2019). *Statistical Yearbook of the Republic of China 2018*. Taipei: Ministry of Education.

Research Institute for Higher Education (RIHE) (2016). *Statistic of Japanese Higher Education. School Basic Survey*. Hiroshima University. https://rihe.hiroshima-u.ac.jp/en/statistics/synthesis/, accessed March 25, 2020.

Sanyal, B. C. and Johnstone, D. B. (2011). "International trends in the public and private financing of higher education." *Prospects*, 41/157, 157–175.

Scimago Lab (2020). *Scimago Journal & Country Rank*. Amsterdam: Elsevier.

Shapiro, R. A. (2018). "Philanthropists in Asia: What do they want? What do they get?" In R. A. Shapiro, M. Mirchandani, and H. Jang (eds.), *Pragmatic Philanthropy*. Singapore: Palgrave Macmillan, 85–100.

Sheridan, G. (2010). "Preparing the Higher Education Sector Development Project (HESDP): Developing new model universities (NMU) in Vietnam." Vietnam Higher Education Sector Analysis. https://www.adb.org/sites/default/files/project-document/63092/42079-01-vie-tacr-03.pdf, accessed April 6, 2020.

Sherlock, M. F., Gravelle, J. G., Crandall-Hollick, M. L., and Hughes, J. (2018). *College and University Endowments: Overview and Tax Policy Options*. Congress Research Service Report. https://fas.org/sgp/crs/misc/R44293.pdf, accessed July 15, 2020.

Sutin, S. E. and Jacob, W. J. (2016). *Strategic Transformation of Higher Education: Challenges and Solutions in a Global Economy*. Lanham, MD: Rowman & Littlefield.

UNESCO Institute for Statistics (UIS) (2020). *Expenditure on Tertiary Education as a Percentage of Government Expenditure on Education, 2000–2019*. Montreal: UIS.

Vietnam Ministry of Education and Training (MOET) and UNESCO Institute for Statistics (UIS) (2016). *Education Financing in Vietnam, 2009-2013*. Hanoi and Montreal: MOET and UIS. http://uis.unesco.org/sites/default/files/vietnam-nea-report.pdf, accessed April 3, 2020.

Wang, X., Jacob, W. J., Blakesley, C. C., Xiong, W., Ye, H., Xu, S., and Lu, F. (2020). "Optimal professional development ICT training initiatives at flagship universities." *Education and Information Technology*, 25, 4397–4416.

World Education News (WES) (2017). "Education in Vietnam." *World Education News + Reviews*. https://wenr.wes.org/2017/11/education-in-vietnam, accessed April 4, 2020.

World Bank (2020a). *Education Statistics, 2000–2020*. Washington, DC: World Bank.

World Bank (2020b). *Improving the Performance of Higher Education in Vietnam: Strategic Priorities and Policy Options*. Higher Education Sector Report. Washington, DC: World Bank. https://openknowledge.worldbank.org/bitstream/handle/10986/33681/Improving-the-Performance-of-Higher-Education-in-Vietnam-Strategic-Priorities-and-Policy-Options.pdf?sequence=1&isAllowed=y, accessed June 25, 2020.

CHAPTER 19

....

PRIVATE PHILANTHROPY IN HIGHER EDUCATION IN ASIA

....

SWEE-SUM LAM

1. INTRODUCTION

....

THIS is an exploratory study on the impact of private philanthropy in higher education in Asia and the Pacific.[1] Private philanthropy is generally defined as the giving of monies, time, resources, and talents whether from individuals, family offices, foundations, or corporates. For the purpose of exploring the role and impact of philanthropy in higher education, this study considers only the amount of philanthropic monies donated to higher education institutions in Asia and the Pacific.

Higher education enrollment increased globally from 50 million in 1980 to 224 million students in 2018, representing a growth of 350 percent (UNESCO, 2020). In the same period, Asia and the Pacific saw an increase of higher education enrollment from 13.8 million in 1980 to 131.1 million in 2018, an increase of 850 percent.[2] However, this increase was unevenly distributed within Asia and the Pacific. For the two most populous countries in Asia, higher education enrollment in China has risen dramatically from 1 million to 45 million (4,400 percent) and in India from 3 million to 34 million (1,033 percent) over the same period. China and India accounted for 63.8 percent of the total increase in higher education enrollment from 1980 to 2018 (74.8 million out of 117.3 million).

---

[1] Higher education refers to all types of education (academic, professional, technical, artistic, pedagogical, long-distance learning, etc.) provided by universities, technological institutes, teacher training colleges, etc. Higher education is offered to students who have completed a secondary education, and whose educational objective is the acquisition of a title, a grade, certificate, or a diploma of higher education (OECD, 2022).

[2] In this study, the region Asia and the Pacific refers specifically to Asia (excluding Central Asia and the Middle East) as well as Australia and New Zealand in the Pacific.

This rapid growth in higher education enrollment in Asia and the Pacific saw it more than double its share of global enrollment from 27.5 percent in 1980 to 58.6 percent in 2018 (UNESCO, 2020).[3] This phenomenon is driven by both demand and supply factors. On the demand side, demographic, economic, cultural, and political factors have been driving the increase in higher education enrollment; while on the supply side, the increase in higher education opportunities was driven by capacity expansion of both the public and private higher education sector (Sanyal and Johnstone, 2011).

Key to the driving of demand is the cultural and traditional value Asian societies place on education and scholarship. This motivation is reinforced by economic returns, as higher education is key to better jobs, increased lifetime income and quality of life (e.g. Carnoy et al., 2012; World Bank, 2012; Johnstone, 2015), and access to greater opportunities, status, and social/political influence (Sanyal and Johnstone, 2011). Therefore, families in Asia are willing to invest a significant portion of their household income on education (Marginson, 2011). Demand is further created by increasing household income in Asia and the Pacific which, in turn, means that more families can now afford to facilitate the pursuit of higher education.

To cater for this increase in demand for higher education, the number of colleges and universities in Asia and the Pacific has surged. Governments across Asia and the Pacific have planned for this significant surge in demand for higher education (Asian Development Bank, 2011) by allowing the private higher education sector to expand. Governments across Asia recognize that higher education can generate more highly skilled labor that can unleash innovation that leads to global competitiveness and economic growth (Asian Development Bank, 2012).

These strategies have led to the massification of higher education in Asia and the Pacific. Instead of it being only for the elite, higher education is now perceived as a pursuit of the masses. The enrollment ratio in higher education has increased more than twofold from 12.4 percent in 1980 to 38 percent in 2018 globally (UNESCO, 2020).[4] Except for Central Asia, all the other parts of Asia have seen an even more rapid increase in higher education enrollment. In East Asia alone, the increase was more than tenfold, with higher education enrollment growing from 4.4 percent to 51.4 percent in the same period. In South Asia, the increase was close to fivefold, with enrollment growing from 4.5 percent to 25.8 percent.

This surge in higher education enrollment is accompanied by gaping funding needs in higher education institutions. Traditionally, in many Asian countries, government grants provide the main source of funding for higher education (Tan and Mingat,

---

[3] See also in this Handbook, Chapter 2: "From Elite Higher Education to Massification" and Chapter 5: "Access."

[4] The enrollment ratio is the number of students enrolled in each level of education, regardless of age, expressed as a percentage of the official school-age population corresponding to the same level of education. For the tertiary level, the population used is the 5-year age group starting from the official secondary school graduation age.

1992). The surge in higher education needs has thus put a huge financial strain on these governments.

To fund capacity growth and quality education, many universities have turned towards diversification of funding sources and increased funding from student fees, philanthropic dollars, investment incomes from endowment funds, and consultancy fees. Some universities in Asia have changed their admissions policies to allow private fee-paying students and introduced fee-based training courses, such as adult education and executive leadership courses. For example, the Cambodian government introduced tuition fees in 1996, public universities in Indonesia were empowered to introduce cost-recovery measures after becoming legal entities in 1999, and universities in Vietnam have been allowed full control of their own budgets since 2005 (UNESCO, 2014).

Moreover, many governments in Asia have allowed and encouraged the expansion of private higher education to channel self-paying students away from the heavily subsidized public sector. For example, private universities can operate in Cambodia since 1997, Malaysia since 1996, China since 2002, Thailand since 2003, and Vietnam since 2005. These private higher education institutions can set and charge full tuition fees. They provide greater post-secondary access without increasing the demand for public funds (UNESCO, 2014).

This introduction sets out the challenge of escalating funding needs in the higher education sector in Asia. In this chapter, we explore two research questions: (1) What role can private philanthropy play in addressing the growing funding needs in higher education in Asia and the Pacific? (2) What is the possible impact of philanthropic funding on higher education? To help address these questions, we next lay out the landscape, motivations, and trends of philanthropy in Asia. These insights lead us into a discussion on the role of philanthropy in higher education and its possible outcome and impact. Specifically, we discuss how philanthropic giving may affect the quality of education and the financial sustainability of the funded program or university.

2. PHILANTHROPY IN ASIA: LANDSCAPE

Beyond growing the pool of student fees, an increasing number of higher education institutions, particularly those in Asia, have started to actively seek out philanthropic largesse to supplement their receipts. The success and the amount of philanthropic dollars received are driven by many factors including the regulatory, socio-economic (Standley and Roodman, 2006), and cultural landscape for philanthropy, the professionalism of fundraising efforts (Siobhan, 2013), the reach and depth of the institutional alumni network, and the prestige of the institution (Bélanger et al., 2007; Breeze et al., 2011).

The regulatory, socio-economic, and cultural landscape for philanthropy can be evaluated by a country's economic, social, cultural, and tax conditions that influence the amount of philanthropic dollars that higher education institutions can raise, whether locally or cross-country. The Global Philanthropy Environment Index by Indiana University provides comprehensive information about the philanthropic environment in 79 countries and economies around the world using a standard instrument completed by country-based experts. It scores each country on a scale of 1 to 5 on five factors:

- Ease of operating a philanthropic organization—regulations for philanthropic organization formation, operation, and dissolution;
- Tax incentives—laws and regulations governing fiscal incentives and disincentives for giving and receiving donations domestically;
- Cross-border flows—laws and regulations governing fiscal incentives and disincentives of giving and receiving donations across borders;
- Political environment—governance and relations between government and philanthropic organizations; and
- Socio-cultural environment—cultural philanthropic traditions, public trust, and awareness of the importance of philanthropic organizations within a country (Indiana University Lilly Family School of Philanthropy, 2018).

In the countries with high overall scores, there are enabling conditions for philanthropic funds to flow. For example, governments support philanthropic organizations through tax incentives and policies that promote volunteering and partnerships that distribute public goods (Indiana University Lilly Family School of Philanthropy, 2018). In Asia, as well as Australia and New Zealand, the Index rated Singapore as having the most favorable philanthropic environment, followed by Japan and Korea (see Table 19.1).

Tax incentives play an enabling role for corporate, institutional, and individual donors as this lowers the price of donations (Gilbert, 2005; Standley and Roodman, 2006). In some countries like Singapore, Australia, New Zealand, and Hong Kong, donors can claim tax deductions for qualified donations. Giving towards higher education is either legislated or perceived as a charitable cause in many Asian countries.

In Singapore, the government legislated generous tax incentives and matching schemes to encourage giving. Donors that give to qualified charities such as public universities are allowed tax deductions at 250 percent of donated dollars until December 31 2021 (Ministry of Finance, n.d.). There have also been conscious efforts to push autonomous universities in Singapore to grow their own endowment funds. For newer universities with smaller endowments, the Singapore government matches three dollars for every dollar they raise. For more established universities the government provides a matching grant that ranges from $1 to $1.50 for every dollar raised (Teng, 2019). This policy supports the redistribution of philanthropic dollars towards less endowed universities. As a result, Singapore has one of the most if not the most favorable government schemes of support for philanthropic dollars in Asia.

Similarly, the government of the Hong Kong Special Administration Region has supported seven rounds of the Matching Grant Scheme to help the higher education sector diversify its funding sources since 2003. The most recent seventh Matching Grant Scheme that concluded in July 2019 was dedicated to supporting self-financing

Table 19.1 Asia and the Pacific countries in the Global Philanthropy
Environment Index

Economy	Ease of operating	Tax incentives	Cross-border flows	Political environment	Socio-cultural environment	Overall score
Singapore	4.83	4.8	3.9	4.75	3.8	4.42
Japan	4.83	4.25	4.5	4.25	4	4.37
Korea	4.67	4.4	4.2	4.1	4.5	4.37
New Zealand	4.67	4.7	4.1	4	4.2	4.33
Hong Kong	4.83	4.25	5	3	4	4.22
Australia	4.33	4	4.5	4	4	4.17
Philippines	4	3.75	4.25	4.5	4	4.1
Taiwan	4.5	4	3.5	4.25	4	4.05
Kazakhstan	3.63	3.9	4	3.8	3.8	3.83
Pakistan	3.67	3.5	3	3.5	4	3.53
India	3.33	3.5	2.7	3.5	3	3.21
Kyrgyz Republic	4.17	3.25	3	3	2.5	3.18
Indonesia	3.33	2.75	2.75	3	4	3.17
Thailand	3.5	3	3	3	3	3.1
Myanmar	2.83	2	2.5	3	4	2.87
China	2.2	2.4	2.4	2.75	4	2.75
Vietnam	2.67	2.1	2.1	3.2	3.5	2.71
Nepal	3	2.75	1.5	2.75	3	2.6

Source: Indiana University Lilly Family School of Philanthropy, 2018 Global Philanthropy
Environment Index.

degree-awarding institutions. Matching grants were made on a first-come, first-served
basis and disbursed to each institution on a dollar-for-dollar matching basis, up to the
floor amount of HKD$12 million, beyond which HKD$1 was matched for every HKD$2
donation, up to a grant ceiling of HKD$100 million (The Government of the Hong Kong
Special Administration Region, n.d.).

Some reputed Asian and Australasian universities that have sizable international
alumni networks, such as the University of Melbourne, National University of Singapore,
and Chinese University of Hong Kong, take fundraising a step further by also seeking
overseas donations and leveraging them through foreign countries' tax incentives,
such as the United States and Canada which provide tax deductions to their citizens for
qualified overseas giving. Therefore, these universities set up trusts, foundations, and/or
other legally structured tax vehicles to facilitate raising philanthropic dollars from their
alumni and donors in these host countries (Chinese University of Hong Kong, 2020a;

NUS America Foundation, n.d.; The University of Melbourne, n.d.). Foreign-sourced philanthropic giving could also be motivated by geopolitical and business interests.[5]

The philanthropic funding raised from alumni, corporates, bequests, foundations, or public donors can be used to support a variety of purposes, including faculty research, specific programs, scholarships, and other financial assistance to students. Philanthropic dollars can be used to meet an immediate funding gap in operating or program expenses. They can also be used strategically to seed or fund an endowment. Endowments are restricted funds with donor-specified uses. Donors give to endowments to grow program sustainability. That is, endowed dollars are invested to yield investment incomes that go to fund scholarships and financial aid, research grants and program expenses on an ongoing basis while the capital is preserved.

In China, this has been encouraged by the government. Since the introduction of the Higher Education Law in 1998 which provided that "the state encourages the investment in higher education by enterprises, institutions, social groups, other social organizations, and individuals," universities in China have gradually launched fundraising campaigns and started registering and establishing education foundations to collect donations. Some have also established alumni associations, development committees, school boards, foundations, and other organizations to raise funds (Chen and Feng, 2016).

Some universities in the Asia-Pacific region especially those of Australia, New Zealand, Singapore, and Hong Kong have taken this further and systematically and aggressively pursued philanthropic dollars through development offices, hiring professional fundraisers, and establishing endowments. This approach is modeled on universities in the developed West, particularly universities in the United States, that are at the forefront of fundraising. Since setting up its development office in 2003, the Chinese University of Hong Kong (2020b) has one of the largest endowments among Hong Kong universities at HK$3.9 billion. In Singapore, the National University of Singapore (NUS) has the highest endowment at S$6.3 billion as of March 2019 (Charity Portal, 2020).

In other parts of Asia such as India, higher education institutions are just starting on their fundraising journey. The Indian Institute of Technology (IIT) Delhi became the first institute in India to establish an endowment fund in 2019. According to the director of the institute, the fund will "bring in more financial freedom to conduct research, start new centers of excellence and hire scholars" (Sharma, 2019). The fund already has an initial commitment of Rs 250 crore from its alumni and nearly 20 corporate leaders who were alumni of the institute. Following the example from IIT Delhi, the Indian government has given its go-ahead to a policy that would see all centrally funded technical

---

[5] A recent example of foreign-sourced giving that is driven by business interests would be the $300 million endowment funded by American investor Stephen A. Schwarzman from his Schwarzman Foundation. Schwarzman has had extensive business dealings in China since 2007, and his private-equity firm, Blackstone, opened its Beijing office in 2008. Schwarzman seeded the Schwarzman Scholars Program at Tsinghua University in 2016.

institutions (e.g. Indian Institutes of Technology, the Indian Institutes of Management, the National Institutes of Technology) establish their own endowment funds in 2020. The funds will be powered by donations from alumni, industry, and philanthropists, and will be used for purposes like scholarship, infrastructure development, and establishment of chairs that will further research in specific fields (Sharma, 2020). As discussed elsewhere in this volume, high-quality private universities, such as Ashoka and Jindal, have emerged over the past 15 years. In Indonesia, Universitas Ciputra is a good example of strategic philanthropy in higher education. Rather than writing a check or establishing an endowment fund, the late philanthropist, Dr. Ir Ciputra, set up Universitas Ciputra in Surabaya in 2006 to fulfill his vision to bring forth a generation of educated entrepreneurs to help alleviate poverty in Indonesia.[6]

Nonetheless, the successes of Asian universities in raising philanthropic dollars trail behind the fundraising performance of top universities in the United States. Large university endowments are an American phenomenon driven by the culture of philanthropy as well as aggressive fundraising by universities. According to the Study on Endowments done jointly by the National Association of College and University Business Officers (NACUBO) and the Teachers Insurance and Annuity Association of America (TIAA) in 2019, 774 educational institutions across the United States accumulated $630 billion in total endowment assets as of June 2019. The top 10 universities with the biggest endowments, including Harvard, Yale, Princeton, and Stanford, each possesses well over $10 billion in endowment while the median endowment had approximately $144.4 million, and about 300 educational institutions had endowments of $101 million or less (NACUBO, 2019). This suggests that the fundraising ability of American universities is diffused. Prestigious institutions that already enjoy financial sustainability and high repute are more likely to raise further donations in an ongoing cycle of "accumulative advantage" (Merton, 1968) and continue to attract a disproportionate share of donations. As such, universities with the largest endowments tend to be the higher-ranked universities such as Harvard, Yale, Princeton, and Stanford.

The University with the Largest Endowment

Harvard University has an enviable $40.9 billion endowment as of 2019, the largest in the United States. In 2018, the university applied a $1.9 billion investment income from the endowment to fund about 35% of the school's annual operating budget. The $1.9 billion investment income was distributed as follows: 24% is used for professorships, 19% for scholarships and student support, 7% for research, 4% for program support, 4% for library and museums, 2% for faculty and teaching, 1% for capital and construction, 9% for other costs, and 30% for flexible spending (Hess, 2019).

---

[6] See Lam et al. (2016).

3. Philanthropy in Asia: Motivations and Trends

3.1 Motivations

Higher education philanthropy in Asia and the Pacific is driven by several factors and motivations, including a sense of social responsibility (John et al., 2013), gratitude and a desire to give back to society (Jansons, 2015), personal affiliation as university alumni or emotional ties with their alma mater, and the desire to drive change in society (Tan and Lam, 2018a, 2018b). Moreover, major religions in Asia, namely, Islam, Hinduism, Buddhism, Confucianism, and Christianity, encourage giving and may play an influential role in humanitarian attitudes (Spero, 2014). Lastly there are givers motivated by personal prestige and status and the desire to be held in high regard by their peers (Bekkers and Wiepking, 2011).

Philanthropy in Higher Education in India and China

India's "Golden Age of Indian Philanthropy" saw India's height in philanthropic giving in the pre-independence period, 1892–1947 (Sundar, 2000). Some of the most enduring trusts and foundations established include the Aligarh Muslim University, Banaras Hindu University, Jamia Millia Islamia University, Annamalai University, and Indian Institute of Science (Kapur and Mehta, 2008). Kapur and Mehta, however, show "that all three areas of higher education provision in India—state, private, and non-profit—suffer from severe distortions" (Kapur and Mehta, 2008, p. 121). A crisis of governance has persisted in Indian higher education; this is "most visibly manifest in the acute shortage of qualified faculty" (Kapur and Mehta, 2008, p. 142). There have been attempts to address this crisis in more recent years. A number of private universities in India are funded and/or started collectively by philanthropists, e.g., Ashoka University, Indian School of Business, and Krea University. Others such as Tata Institute of Social Sciences, Azim Premji University, and Jio Institute each has a prominent philanthropist or foundation backing hem (Pathak, 2019).

As an example of some of the funding structures, the Azim Premji University is supported by the Indian tech billionaire Azim Premji who was the chairman of Wipro. In 2019, Premji gave away shares worth US$7.6 billion to his education-focused Azim Premji Foundation. This increased his total donation to the foundation to at least US$21 billion since 2001 (Chung, 2019). The university was set up by the foundation to develop outstanding professionals in education and other related areas of human development (Ani, 2019). Premji strongly believes that "to whom much has been given, much should be expected" (Chung, 2019).

In China, many philanthropists such as Jack Ma, Hui Ka Yan, Chen Yidan, Robin Li, and Yeung Kwok Keung are contributing to higher education. The largest single donation thus far made to a Chinese university was by the real estate billionaire Yeung Kwok Keung who, motivated by his desire to repay society and contribute to the country, committed US$318 million (2.2 billion yuan) to Tsinghua University over 10 years to help foster talent and research into advanced technology in 2018 (Tsinghua University, n.d.).

3.2 Trends

Philanthropy in Asia has been growing in tandem with recent stellar economic growth in the region (until interrupted abruptly by the coronavirus epidemic of 2020 at the time of writing). A rapidly growing middle class, a growing number of high and ultra-high net worth individuals, an increasing awareness of socio-economic disparities, and a growing pressure on better-off families and corporations to support sustainable development are fueling philanthropic endeavors (Sciortino, 2017). The education sector, including the higher education sector, is a significant beneficiary of this philanthropic growth as education has been traditionally one of the top causes that philanthropists favor (Shapiro, 2018).

In China, giving general donations has increased from US$6 billion in 2009 to US$23.4 billion in 2017 (see Figure 19.1). Giving in China is dominated by corporations, followed by individuals and other types of organizations such as government agencies and public institutions. Education is the top cause supported particularly among the most generous of Chinese philanthropists (Cunningham, 2015; Hurun, 2019), though many prefer to give to their alma mater, directing their giving towards the expansion of university facilities including libraries, research labs, and scholarships (Chu and Wang, 2018).

In Singapore, total philanthropic giving registered by the Commissioner of Charity in Singapore has grown from S$1.8 billion in 2008 to S$2.7 billion in 2017. This giving consists of tax deductible and non-tax deductible donations. Religious giving was the top cause. However, when it comes to tax deductible donations, education is the top cause. Based on tax deductible donations in 2018, the education sector received the highest amount and share of total donations. It represented 46 percent of donations from corporations and 13 percent of donations from individuals (see Figure 19.2) (Ministry of Culture, Community and Youth, Charities Unit, 2019).

4. Philanthropy in Higher Education: Outcome and Impact

Given the tradition of philanthropic giving that is often associated with academic excellence in well-reputed private universities, e.g., Princeton, Harvard, Yale, and Stanford, one may hypothesize that a possible outcome of philanthropy on higher education is quality education through building excellence in both education and research (Burlingame, 2004; Thelin and Trollinger, 2014; Kerr, 2019). Public universities also benefit from an overall improvement in quality of education when private philanthropic funds complement those of government to underwrite growing and new program costs, subsidize tuition fees, and provide access to needy students. Strategic philanthropists and philanthropic organizations, like the Rockefeller Foundation, the Bill & Melinda

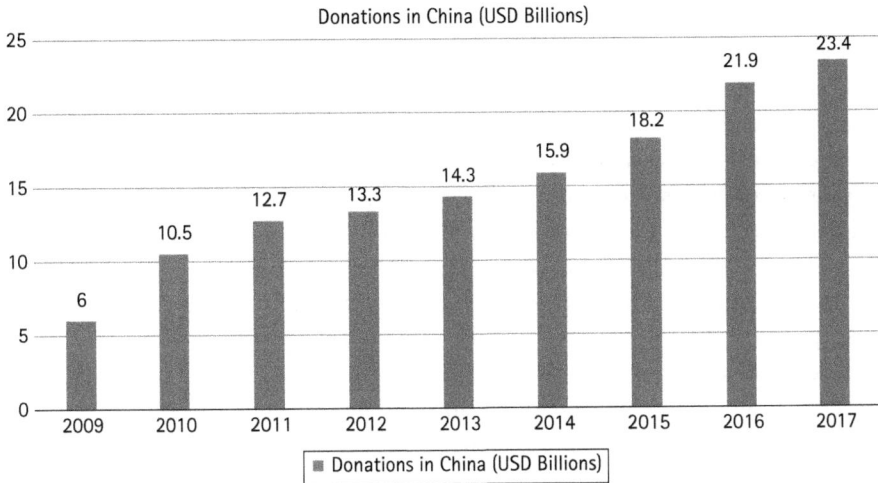

Donations in China (USD Billions)

- Donations in China (USD Billions)

FIGURE 19.1 Donations in China (in billions of US dollars)

Source: Chu and Wang (2018).

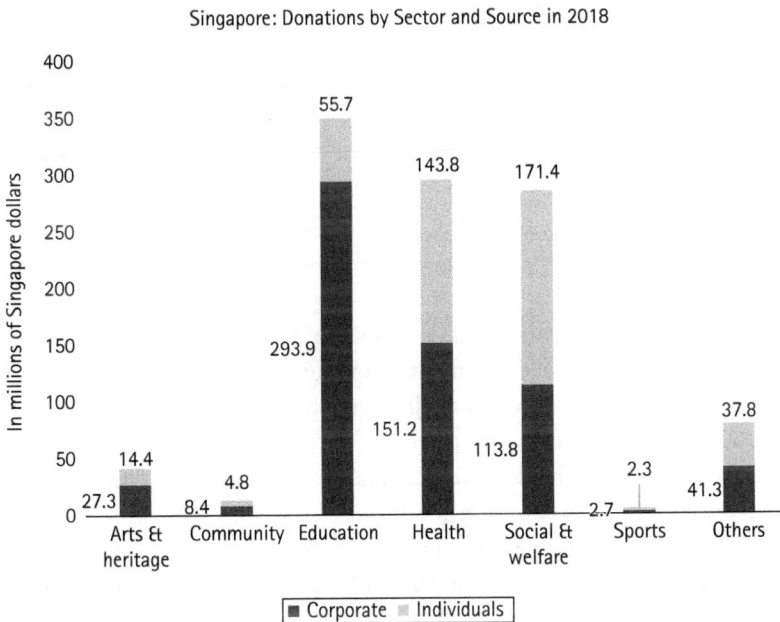

Singapore: Donations by Sector and Source in 2018

- Corporate - Individuals

FIGURE 19.2 Donations by sector and source in Singapore, 2018 (in millions of Singapore dollars)

Source: Ministry of Culture, Community and Youth, Charities Unit (2019).

Gates Foundation and the William and Flora Hewlett Foundation, have invested in education and research programs that strategically address targeted social and environmental challenges. For example, the Bill & Melinda Gates Foundation has programs that seek to address the challenge of K-12 and post-secondary success in public education in the United States (Bill & Melinda Gates Foundation, n.d.). Others have funded chaired professorships and research fellowships to spur scholarship and research excellence, providing resources for faculty and researchers to do outstanding work in research, clinical work, and teaching (National University of Singapore, n.d.).

There is a recent trend in strategic philanthropy and international development work to incorporate impact assessment as part of the funded programs (Brest and Harvey, 2018; Independent Evaluation Group, 2020). Here, philanthropic organizations and international development agencies collaborate with grantees early in the grant process to design and make an operational theory of change to engender specific outcomes and impact (Imas and Rist, 2009). Grantees conduct performance measurement throughout and even after the end of the funded programs to account for the targeted outcomes and impact. For example, one impact which may be of interest to strategic philanthropists would be the impact of the funding on the sustainability of the university or its funded program and asking what is the effect that the funding has on the grantee's ability to sustain itself or the funded program into the future? (The Center for Effective Philanthropy, 2012).

We next explore the possible outcome and impact of philanthropy on academic excellence and sustainability in Asian higher education.

5. QUALITY OF EDUCATION

Unlike philanthropic support that builds sustainability of core offerings and student financial aid, investing in excellence in education and research is often an arena where philanthropists are the actors of choice because they can afford to take risks in their giving or social investing. Such investments, if successful in yielding breakthroughs in education and research or in addressing a persistent gap in unmet needs, can raise the quality of education that is a common good.

In an exploratory study, we attempted to evaluate if philanthropy explains the quality of education. While there is a general tendency to equate university rankings with quality of education, there is a lack of consensus on what these rankings measure. Many believe that these rankings tend to value primarily research excellence rather than teaching quality. Others contend that these rankings do not measure the real and full impact of a university. Therefore, for lack of more satisfactory results and impact measures of higher education, findings using university world ranking metrics would best be interpreted as tentative or preliminary.

In this study, we drew our preliminary findings from the Quacquarelli Symonds (QS) World University Ranking, which provides one of the leading sources of comparative

Table 19.2 Top 10 ranked Asia–Pacific Universities in the QS world university ranking 2020

World ranking	Institution name	Country
11	Nanyang Technological University (NTU)	Singapore
11	National University of Singapore (NUS)	Singapore
16	Tsinghua University	China
22	Peking University	China
22	The University of Tokyo	Japan
25	University of Hong Kong (HKU)	Hong Kong
29	Australian National University (ANU)	Australia
32	The Hong Kong University of Science and Technology (HKUST)	Hong Kong
33	Kyoto University	Japan
37	Seoul National University (SNU)	South Korea

Source: QS (2020).

data on university performance. QS data, including ranking, overall score, as well as component scores for six constructs[7] were collected from 2014 and 2018. Based on the 2020 QS World University Ranking, six countries/city-states were identified from their representation (see Table 19.2). The top 10 ranked universities in Asia and the Pacific were located in six countries or city-states, namely Singapore, China, South Korea, Japan, Hong Kong, and Australia.[8] For each of these six countries/city-states represented, its top five QS-ranked universities were sampled. This generated a sample of 30 universities across the six Asia-Pacific region countries. Data on donations, endowment, expenditure, and revenue of these 30 universities in the six Asia-Pacific countries were then collected from the annual reports of each university for the period 2014 to 2018. The data were lagging as universities had different financial year end dates and data for financial year 2018 were the latest available for most universities.

---

[7] In QS methodology, the ranking of universities is aggregated from six constructs: Academic Reputation (40 percent), Employer Reputation (10 percent), Faculty/Student Ratio (20 percent), Citations per Faculty (20 percent), International Faculty Ratio (5 percent), and International Student Ratio (5 percent). Retrieved April 30, 2020 from https://www.topuniversities.com/qs-world-university-rankings/methodology.

[8] Of these six countries or city-states, China is a developing country by conventional definition in spite of its large economy and influence, while Hong Kong is a developed economy according to the World Economic Outlook database. China's two top-ranked universities, Tsinghua University and Peking University, belong to the C9 League—an official alliance of nine universities in China set up by the Chinese Central Government to promote the development and reputation of higher education in China. In terms of reputation and quality of education, the C9 League is the Chinese equivalent of the Ivy League in the United States.

Using the QS dataset, we used the overall score and academic reputation score as proxies for quality of education. The overall score is an aggregated score of the six component scores. It captures, for example, the faculty–student ratio, providing a weighted measure of student access to faculty guidance in learning. The academic reputation score is a more specific measure of expert opinions on the teaching and research quality of a university.

In our ordinary least square regression analysis, we attempted to identify what factors explained the quality of higher education. Firstly, we evaluated whether the proportion of a university's annual expenditure that was funded by philanthropic sources explains the quality of its offerings.[9] Secondly, we accounted for country fixed effects[10] to evaluate if variation in the socio-economic, cultural, and regulatory landscape of philanthropy across these six countries/city-states matters for the quality of higher education in that country.

Results from the regression analysis[11] suggest that the proportion of a university's annual expenditure that was funded by philanthropic dollars alone does not explain the quality of its education offerings. However, country fixed effects turn out to be statistically significant individually in explaining the quality of higher education in that country, as measured by academic reputation score.[12] Therefore, the results of this exploratory study suggest that the appropriate regulatory, socio-economic, and cultural landscape may play a significant catalytic role in spurring quality higher education in a country.[13] Future studies could explore what specific factors may contribute to these country fixed effects, whether these be governance, transparency of disclosures, corruption, etc.[14] However, such future studies would need to draw from a large sample of quality data for

[9] In our robustness tests, we evaluated both the contemporaneous and lagged effects of philanthropic dollars on the QS and Times Higher Education (THE) World University Rankings and their subcomponents as proxies of quality of education. The need for comparative data across the ten universities has limited the time series accessible for this study. It is acknowledged that any impact of philanthropic giving (including that on quality of education) may have long lags in its effects. Therefore, it is reasonable to expect that no significant effects be found in this study even if there were actual outcomes on quality of education—that is, sampling constraints are expected to lead to a downward bias on the impact on the quality of education even if there were statistically significant explanatory effects in this regression analysis.

[10] Country fixed effects are variables that are constant for a specific country. These allow for a study on whether any variation across countries is due to factors specific to a country.

[11] The regression results are available from the author upon request.

[12] Five countries (Singapore, Australia, Japan, China, and South Korea) have fixed effects that are statistically significant at 1 percent significance level, while Hong Kong's fixed effects are significant at 5 percent. The adjusted R-square is 0.20.

[13] We obtain similar findings for our robustness tests using the THE World University Ranking dataset. While philanthropic funds do not significantly explain academic excellence (measured by citation count in the THE World University ranking metrics), country fixed effects are statistically significant at 5 percent significance level for China, and they are significant at 1 percent for the other five countries—Australia, Singapore, Hong Kong, Japan, and South Korea. The adjusted R-square is 0.42.

[14] For example, Kapur and Mehta argue that the most acute weakness in India's higher education is "a crisis of governance, both of the system and of the individual institutions," resulting in market failure where "the bad drives out the good" (2008, pp. 141–142).

any robust comparative analysis of philanthropic giving across Asia and the Pacific to be done.

6. SUSTAINABILITY

A possible impact of philanthropy on higher education is building financial sustainability in higher education. Evidence of a growing trend in private philanthropy in the higher education sector across major Asian and Pacific countries suggests that private philanthropic dollars can complement government funding and student fees to sustain and even grow core programs in higher education (Tan and Lam, 2018b). That is, the state can leverage private philanthropy to meet growing public higher education needs. Historically, many alumni and philanthropic organizations fund scholarships and financial aid for needy students to help families break out of the poverty trap.[15] For this reason, higher education tends to receive a proportionately higher share of philanthropic giving in many countries. However, the question remains: does philanthropy help build sustainability into the higher education sector and, to what extent?

In this part of the study, we derive a gauge for a university's sustainability from the proportion of a university's annual expenditure that may be funded by investment incomes from a university's endowment. The proportion of the annual expenditure that is not funded by investment incomes would have to be sourced from a mix of student fee income, expendable donations (as opposed to those made towards an endowment), and the government, if this is a state-funded institution. Therefore, the sustainability of a university would depend on the sustainability of its various funding sources. However, accessibility to such private information is often a challenge to researchers and the public.

To the best of our ability, we construct a parsimonious measure of a university's sustainability from public information. We assume a spending rate of 5 percent on a university's endowment assets. We assume that a typical university allocates from its annual investment incomes an amount up to 5 percent of its endowment assets to fund its annual operating expenditure. This represents a relatively conservative rate of return for educational endowments. According to the 2019 NACUBO-TIAA Study of Endowments that looks at close to 800 educational endowments in the United States, the average return in the fiscal year 2019 was 5.3 percent while the average 10-year endowment return was 8.4 percent (NACUBO, 2019). Return on endowment depends on several factors including the investment environment, the investment mandate of the endowment, and the competence of the investment team managing the endowment portfolio. In some universities, the endowment is managed by professional fund managers.

---

[15] See United Nations Sustainable Development Goals. Goal 1 is "No Poverty." Retrieved April 29, 2020 from https://www.un.org/sustainabledevelopment/poverty/.

We attempted to estimate this sustainability measure for the same sample of 30 universities drawn from the six countries. However, there proved to be uneven disclosure on university endowment across these countries (and perhaps also across institutions). Given the data constraint, we abstracted a limited dataset of financial information from the annual reports of 13 universities drawn from five of the top six ranked countries/city-state (see Table 19.3). Here, we tabulated each university's endowment in the fourth column and our parsimonious measure for its sustainability in the last column.

In this small dataset, the National University of Singapore has the largest endowment at US$4.7 billion in 2019. Tsinghua University was last reported to have an endowment

Table 19.3 Some Asia–Pacific universities and their endowments

Country	Year	University	Endowment (US$ millions)	Imputed investment income (@ 5% of endowment value as percentage of annual expenditure)
SG	2019	National University of Singapore	4,650.5	12.1%
CN	2016	Tsinghua University	3,169.4	8.0%
SG	2019	Nanyang Technological University	1,492.8	5.9%
AU	2018	University of Sydney	1,400.7	4.3%
SG	2019	Singapore Management University	733.4	12.7%
AU	2018	The University of Melbourne	644.1*	1.7%
HK	2018	The Chinese University of Hong Kong	497.9	2.4%
HK	2018	University of Hong Kong	293.7	1.4%
AU	2018	University of Queensland	158.3	0.6%
HK	2018	The Hong Kong University of Science and Technology	147.8	1.3%
JP	2018	Kyoto University	113.9	0.3%
JP	2016	The University of Tokyo	99.2	0.2%
HK	2018	The Hong Kong Polytechnic University	47.5	0.3%

Note: * The endowment figure was based on the trusts with a sub-portfolio value of AU$914.1 million as at December 31, 2018 (The University of Melbourne, 2019). Note that the report stated that the sub-portfolio represented 33.5% of the university's total investment assets and did not explicitly state the endowment value. As the total investment assets might include university reserves, only the trusts' sub-portfolio value was taken for the endowment. This value represented a conservative estimate of the endowment portfolio.

Source: Annual Reports of sampled universities.

of US\$3.2 billion in 2016. The Nanyang Technological University, University of Sydney, and Singapore Management University trailed with endowments of US\$1.5 billion, US\$1.4 billion, and US\$0.7 billion in 2019, 2018, and 2019, respectively. When the sampled universities are ranked by the sustainability measure (in the last column of Table 19.3), the Singapore Management University ranked first—its imputed investment income covers up to 12.7 percent of its annual expenditure.[16] The National University of Singapore now ranked second, with a sustainability measure at 12.1 percent. Tsinghua University is ranked third with its imputed investment income able to fund 8.0 percent of its annual expenditure. However, these universities are the exceptions rather than the norm in Asia. Most Asian universities have small endowments, whose investment income would be able to fund less than 5 percent of their annual budgeted expenditure.

Apart from these outliers, there is no significant evidence that philanthropic giving has significantly contributed to a university's financial sustainability in Asia-Pacific. Nevertheless, financial sustainability that comes from growing endowment assets remains a long-term goal for most Asia-Pacific universities. With the growing trend of philanthropy in higher education, coupled with concerted strategies to raise philanthropic financial support, Asia-Pacific universities have the potential to systematically grow their financial sustainability.

7. CONCLUSION

Private philanthropy in higher education is an emerging trend in Asia. In this exploratory study we evaluated the possible strategic role, outcome, and impact of philanthropy. We explored philanthropic giving to higher education, quality of education, and financial sustainability in a small sample of Asia-Pacific countries. Through a series of regression analyses, we found that philanthropy in higher education in these Asia-Pacific countries does not explain quality education—philanthropy does not have significant contemporaneous or lagged effects on the academic reputation of a university. Notwithstanding, we do find some evidence that philanthropy is building sustainability into education and research offerings in a couple of the top-ranked public universities in these Asia-Pacific countries. Endowment is a funding strategy that possibly impacts the ability of a university or a funded program to sustain itself financially into the future. We are beginning to see anecdotal examples of Asia-Pacific universities building capacity and competency to fundraise and build up their endowments to diversify away from government funding. However, given the limited and uneven access to reliable information on university endowments, funding sources, and expenditure numbers, this

---

[16] We note that Singapore Management University is relatively young; it was established as a specialist university in 2000.

exploratory study may at best generate hypotheses for future research on the potential impact of private philanthropy on higher education in Asia and the Pacific.

Nonetheless, findings of this exploratory study do point to the influential role that socio-economic, cultural, and regulatory conditions play in affecting the academic reputation of a country's higher education. Future case studies can evaluate how a government, like the Singapore government, could play a catalytic role in helping its higher education sector build its academic reputation. Finally, a government can also facilitate the development of a philanthropic and non-profit eco-system by helping the various actors build capacity and reinforce sustainability in the higher education sector.

References

Ani (2019). "Azim Premji Foundation to set up university in north India." *Business Standard*, March 14. https://www.business-standard.com/article/news-ani/azim-premji-foundation-to-set-up-university-in-north-india-119031400410_1.html, accessed June 29, 2020.

Asian Development Bank (2011). *Higher Education Across Asia*. https://www.adb.org/sites/defa ult/files/publication/29407/higher-education-across-asia.pdf, accessed April 23, 2020.

Asian Development Bank (2012). *Counting the Cost: Financing Asian Higher Education for Inclusive Growth*. https://www.adb.org/publications/counting-cost-financing-asian-higher-education-inclusive-growth, accessed April 23, 2020.

Bekkers, R. H. F. P. and Wiepking, P. (2011). "A literature review of empirical studies of philanthropy: Eight mechanisms that drive charitable giving." *Nonprofit and Voluntary Sector Quarterly*, 40/5, 924–973.

Bélanger, C. H., Syed, S., and Mount, J. (2007). "The make up of institutional branding: Who, what, how?" *Tertiary Education and Management*, 13/3, 169–185.

Bill & Melinda Gates Foundation (n.d.). *Awarded Grants*. https://www.gatesfoundation.org/how-we-work/quick-links/grants-database#q/program=US%20Program, accessed April 30, 2020.

Breeze, B., Gouwenberg, B., Schuyt, T., and Wilkinson, I. (2011). "What role for public policy in promoting philanthropy?" *Public Management Review*, 13/8, 1179–1195.

Brest, P. and Harvey, H. (2018). *Money Well Spent: A Strategic Guide for Smart Philanthropy* (2nd edition). Stanford, CA: Stanford University Press.

Burlingame, D. (2004). *Philanthropy in America: A Comprehensive Historical Encyclopedia*. Santa Barbara, CA: ABC CLIO.

Carnoy, M., Loyalka, P., Androushchak, G. V., and Proudnikova, A. (2012). "The economic returns to higher education in the BRIC countries and their implications for higher education expansion." HSE Papers No. WP BRP 02/EDU/2012. Moscow: Higher School of Economics Research.

Charity Portal (2020). Financial Information. https://www.charities.gov.sg/, accessed April 10, 2020.

Chen, X. and Feng, Q. (2016). "Donor behaviour, donation income, and Chinese higher education institutions." In C. Hongjie and W. J. Jacob (eds.), *Trends in Chinese Education*. Abingdon: Routledge, 229–249.

Chinese University of Hong Kong (2020a). *Gifts from the U.S. and Canada*. https://www.oia.cuhk.edu.hk/eng/giving_to_cuhk/gifts-from-the-us-and-canada, accessed April 22, 2020.

Chinese University of Hong Kong, (2020b). Office of Institutional Advancement *About Us*. https://www.oia.cuhk.edu.hk/eng/about-us, accessed April 10, 2020.

Chu, P. and Wang, O. (2018). *Philanthropy in China*. Singapore: AVPN.

Chung, G. (2019). "Asia's 2019 heroes of philanthropy: Catalysts for change." *Forbes*, December 2. https://www.forbes.com/sites/gracechung/2019/12/02/asias-2019-heroes-of-philanthropy-catalysts-for-change/#1b322b3e6d98, accessed June 29, 2020.

Cunningham, E. (2015). *China's Most Generous: Understanding China's Philanthropic Landscape*. Ash Center for Democratic Governance and Innovation. https://chinaphila nthropy.ash.harvard.edu/uploads/files/7f1fc24e-caae-4f71-acc3-3435171   3a9ab-china-philanthropy-report.pdf, accessed April 23, 2020.

Gilbert, N. (2005). "The 'enabling state'? From public to private responsibility for social protection: Pathways and pitfalls." https://www.oecd-ilibrary.org/social-issues-migration-health/the-enabling-state-from-public-to-private-responsibility-for-social-protection_010142814 842, accessed April 23, 2020.

Hess, A. (2019). "Harvard's endowment is worth $40 billion—here's how it's spent." *CNBC*, October 28. https://www.cnbc.com/2019/10/28/harvards-endowment-is-worth-40-billionheres-how-its-spent.html, accessed April 23, 2020.

HKUST (2019). *Financial Statements*. https://archives.ust.hk/dspace/bitstream/9999/47742/1/coun-03-a029.pdf, accessed April 23, 2020.

Hurun Research Institute (2019). *Hurun China Philanthropy List 2019*. https://www.hurun.net/EN/Article/Details?num=93E8C4B53DE6, accessed April 23, 2020.

Imas, L. G. M. and Rist, R. C. (2009). *The Road to Results: Designing and Conducting Effective Development Evaluations*. Washington, DC: International Bank for Reconstruction and Development/The World Bank.

Independent Evaluation Group (2020). *Annual Report FY19: Transforming Evidence into Better Outcomes*. Washington, DC: The World Bank.

Indiana University Lilly Family School of Philanthropy (2018). *The Global Philanthropy Environment Index*. https://globalindices.iupui.edu/environment/index.html, accessed April 23, 2020.

Jansons, E. (2015). "The business leaders behind the foundations: Understanding India's emerging philanthropists." *VOLUNTAS: International Journal of Voluntary and Nonprofit Organizations*, 26/3, 984–1006.

John, R., Tan, P., and Ito, K. (2013). *Innovation in Asian Philanthropy*. Asia Centre for Social Entrepreneurship & Philanthropy, NUS Business School.

Johnstone, D. B. (2015). *Financing Higher Education in the Asia-Pacific Region: The Quest for Quality, Capacity, Affordability, and Equity*. Working Papers Series No.6/2015. Singapore: The Head Foundation.

Kapur, D. and Mehta, P. B. (2008). "Mortgaging the future: Indian higher education." In S. Bery, B. Bosworth, and A. Panagariya (eds.), *India Policy Forum 2007/08*. Los Angeles, CA: Sage, 101–158.

Kerr, E. (2019). "10 Universities with the Biggest Endowments." *US News*, September 24. https://www.usnews.com/education/best-colleges/the-short-list-college/articles/10-unive rsities-with-the-biggest-endowments, accessed April 23, 2020.

Kyoto University (2019). *Kyoto University Financial Report*. https://www.kyoto-u.ac.jp/en/about/publications/financial-report/documents/2018/01.pdf, accessed April 23, 2020.

Lam, S. S., Ang, A., and Jacob, G. H. (2016). "Universitas Ciputra: A philanthropist's vision for entrepreneurship in Indonesia." Case Centre Reference No. 816-0092-1. Singapore: Asia

Centre for Social Entrepreneurship and Philanthropy. https://www.thecasecentre.org/main/products/view?id=137415, accessed April 23, 2020.

Marginson, S. (2011). "Higher education in East Asia and Singapore: Rise of the Confucian model." *Higher Education*, 61, 587–611.

Merton, R. K. (1968). "The Matthew effect in science: The reward and communication systems of science are considered." *Science*, 159/3810, 56–63.

Ministry of Culture, Community and Youth, Charities Unit (2019). *Commissioner of Charities Annual Report.* https://www.charities.gov.sg/Publications/Pages/Publications.aspx, accessed April 23, 2020.

Ministry of Finance (n.d.). *Tax Deduction for Donations.* https://www.mof.gov.sg/policies/tax-policies/personal-income-tax/tax-deduction-for-donations, accessed April 23, 2020.

NACUBO (2019). "U.S. educational endowments report 5.3 percent average return in FY19." https://www.nacubo.org/Press-Releases/2020/US-Educational-Endowments-Report-5-3-Percent-Average-Return-in-FY19, accessed March 30, 2020.

National University of Singapore (n.d.). *NUS Giving. Fund Research Activities.* https://inetapps.nus.edu.sg/odp/Public/FundsList.aspx?BCID=16,Fund+research+activities, accessed April 30, 2020.

NUS America Foundation (n.d.). *NUS America Foundation.* http://www.nusamerica.org/, accessed April 22, 2020.

OECD (2022). Spending on tertiary education (indicator). doi: 10.1787/a3523185-en. https://data.oecd.org/eduresource/spending-on-tertiary-education.htm, accessed February 24, 2022.

Pathak, K. (2019). "Azim Premji raises philanthropy bar with $21 billion total pledge." *Live Mint*, March 13. https://www.livemint.com/companies/people/azim-premji-raises-philanthropy-bar-with-21-billion-total-pledge-1552500208294.html, accessed June 29, 2020.

QS (2020). *QS World University Rankings.* https://www.topuniversities.com/university-rankings/world-university-rankings/2020, accessed March 30, 2020.

Sanyal, B. and Johnstone, D. B. (2011). "International trends in public and private funding of higher education." *Prospects*, 41, 157–175.

School of Economics and Management Tsinghua University (2018). *2017–2018 Annual Report.* http://mis.sem.tsinghua.edu.cn/ueditor/jsp/upload/file/20180830/1535625979072048243.pdf, accessed April 23, 2020.

Sciortino, R. (2017). "Philanthropy in Southeast Asia: Between charitable values, corporate interests, and development aspirations." *Austrian Journal of South-East Asian Studies*, 10/2, 139–163.

Shapiro, R. A. (2018). "Philanthropists in Asia: What do they want? What do they get?" In R. A. Shapiro, M. Mirchandani, and H. Jang, *Pragmatic Philanthropy*. Singapore: Palgrave Macmillan, 85–100.

Sharma, K. (2019). "Fundraisers who helped Harvard, Stanford could now work for IIT-Delhi endowment fund." *The Print*, November 1. https://theprint.in/india/education/fundraisers-who-helped-harvard-stanford-could-now-work-for-iit-delhi-endowment-fund/314514/, accessed April 23, 2020.

Sharma, K. (2020). "Now, all IITs, IIMs will launch endowment funds to tap successful alumni for donations." *The Print*, March 3. https://theprint.in/india/education/now-all-iits-iims-will-launch-endowment-funds-to-tap-successful-alumni-for-donations/374137/, accessed April 23, 2020.

Siobhan, D. (2013). "Philanthropy, the new professionals and higher education: The advent of directors of development and alumni relations." *Journal of Higher Education Policy and Management*, 35/1, 21–33.

Spero, J. (2014). *Charity and Philanthropy in Russia, China, India, and Brazil*. New York: Foundation Center.

Standley, S. and Roodman, D. (2006). "Tax policies to promote private charitable giving in DAC countries." *SSRN Electronic Journal*. doi:10.2139/ssrn.984021.

Sundar, P. (2000). *Beyond Business: From Merchant Charity to Corporate Citizenship*. New Delhi: Tata McGraw-Hill.

Tan, J. P. and Mingat, A. (1992). *Education in Asia: A Comparative Study of Cost and Financing*. Washington, DC: The World Bank.

Tan, P. and Lam, S. S. (2018a). *Impact Investments by Foundations in Singapore and Hong Kong*. Singapore: Asia Centre for Social Entrepreneurship & Philanthropy, NUS Business School.

Tan, P. and Lam, S. S. (2018b). *Philanthropic Foundations in Asia: Insights from Singapore, Myanmar and China*. Singapore: Asia Centre for Social Entrepreneurship and Philanthropy, NUS Business School.

Teng, A. (2019). "Parliament: Younger universities get double the government funding in matching grants of older counterparts." *Straits Times*, January 15. https://www.straitstimes.com/politics/parliament-younger-universities-get-double-government-funding-than-older-counterparts, accessed April 23, 2020.

The Center for Effective Philanthropy (2012). *Grantee Perception Report for The William and Flora Hewlett Foundation*. Cambridge, MA.

The Chinese University of Hong Kong (2019). *Financial Report 2018–2019*. https://www.cuhk.edu.hk/fno/eng/financial_info/1819_financial_report_cuhk.pdf, accessed April 23, 2020.

The Government of the Hong Kong Special Administration Region (n.d.). *Results of Seventh Matching Grant Scheme*. https://www.info.gov.hk/gia/general/201909/18/P2019091800270.htm, accessed April 22, 2020.

The Hong Kong Polytechnic University (2019). *Financial Report 2018/2019*. https://www.polyu.edu.hk/fo/FO_Web/index.php?page=2&subpage=fr1819e, accessed April 23, 2020.

The University of Hong Kong (2018). *Financial Report 2018*. http://www.feo.hku.hk/finance/information/annualreport/publications/2018/HTML/6-7/index.html, accessed April 23, 2020.

The University of Melbourne (n.d.). *Giving Overseas*. https://www.alumni.unimelb.edu.au/give/giving-overseas, accessed April 22, 2020.

The University of Melbourne (2019). *Trusts Investment Report 2019*. https://www.unimelb.edu.au/__data/assets/pdf_file/0006/2800878/Trusts-Investment-Report-2018_FINAL.PDF, accessed April 23, 2020.

The University of Queensland (n.d.). *Endowments*. https://marketing-communication.uq.edu.au/files/4942/Endowment-final.pdf, accessed April 23, 2020.

The University of Sydney (2019). *Investment and Capital Management Investment Report 2018*. https://www.sydney.edu.au/content/dam/corporate/documents/engage/giving/investment-and-capital-management-annual-report.pdf, accessed April 23, 2020.

The University of Tokyo (2017). *Financial Report Including IR-DATA 2016*. https://www.u-tokyo.ac.jp/content/400071492.pdf, accessed April 23, 2020.

Thelin, J. and Trollinger, R. (2014). *Philanthropy and American Higher Education*. New York: Palgrave Macmillan.

Tsinghua University (n.d.). "Guangdong Guoqiang Public Welfare Foundation makes donation to Tsinghua University." https://news.tsinghua.edu.cn/en/info/1002/7960.htm, accessed April 23, 2020.

UBS (2011). *UBS-INSEAD Study on Family Philanthropy in Asia.* UBS Philanthropy Services, INSEAD.

UNESCO Institute for Statistics (2014). *Higher Education in Asia: Expanding Out, Expanding Up. The Rise of Graduate Education and University Research.* Montreal: UNESCO Institute for Statistics.

UNESCO Institute for Statistics (2020). *Education* [Data File]. http://data.uis.unesco.org/.

World Bank (2012). *Put Higher Education to Work.* Washington, DC: The World Bank.

....

CHAPTER 20

STUDENT LOANS IN PRACTICE

Benefits and Pitfalls of Loans Schemes in Asia

....

ADRIAN ZIDERMAN

STUDENT loans schemes are prevalent in university financing systems worldwide and no less so in Asian countries. Some 15 Asian countries have been identified as currently exhibiting state-sponsored loans schemes for university students. Many of these schemes are well established and of long standing: introduced in Australia in the late 1980s; in New Zealand, Thailand, Malaysia, and Vietnam in the 1990s; and various schemes in the Philippines as early as the mid-1970s. A list of these and a synoptic description are provided in Appendix Table 20.A.1.

Why have these particular forms of student finance been widely adopted in Asian countries? What purposes are they intended to serve? And how successful have they been in meeting stated objectives? The much-publicized shortcomings, and consequences, of student loans regimes in the United States have cast a dark shadow on discussions concerning the efficacy of student loan finance in other country settings. Are these ill effects—such as crippling debt obligations often leading to repayment default, repayment hardship resulting from sub-standard qualifications with poor labor market prospects—also present in Asian schemes? If so, can they be avoided by appropriate reform in both the design of the loans scheme and its operation? The chapter probes these issues in the context of loans schemes that currently are in place in Asian counties. It draws heavily on the author's past writings on student loans, both worldwide and in Asia (Ziderman, 2002, 2004, 2013; Shen and Ziderman, 2009).

1. BACKGROUND

Across Asia, university systems differ in the relative size of public and private university enrollment. The percentage of private university enrollment exceeds 75 percent in Japan, South Korea, and the Philippines and stands at about 60 percent in India and Indonesia; in contrast, the public sector is dominant in Australia, New Zealand, and Singapore. Other countries have mixed systems. While the extent of state control on the operations of public sector universities varies across countries, it typically includes a strong influence on the level of tuition fees, which are set at low levels. Such highly subsidized tuition fees, together with improved earnings and enhanced career prospects, have led to substantial increases in university enrollments in recent decades. Private universities, where tuition fees are more substantial, are seen also as a sound pathway to better career prospects and higher lifetime earnings. While the graduate may look forward also to a range of non-earnings benefits—including better health, social success, greater achievement in the civil sphere, and improved life chances—the present discussion focuses on lifetime earnings enhancement, which can be substantial. As an example, recent results for Indonesia indicate that the median earnings of four-year college graduates are about 60 percent higher than those of secondary school leavers, overall.

University study may be seen as a form of investment, from which the graduate may expect to receive enhanced lifetime earnings, representing a return on the costs incurred during study. The comparison of earnings benefits against costs can be expressed, in summary form, as a rate of return on this investment. Rates of return estimates for a number of Asian countries that have introduced student loans schemes are presented in Table 20.1. All reported rates of return are in excess of (or close to) 10 percent, and in some cases exceed 20 percent. These rates of return are generally in excess of returns available from other, alternative, private investments. The high profitability of investing in university education can be expected to create a high demand for university study; however, this may be curtailed in practice by difficulties in meeting the costs of education and/or by a reluctance to embark on higher education by those socio-economic groups who are unfamiliar with the nature or potential benefits of university study.

At the macro level, Asian universities, recognizing the importance of securing additional educated talent for economic and social development, of the need to provide greater university access particularly for less advantaged groups, and of increasing the availability of particular categories of trained manpower to avoid skilled bottlenecks, have responded positively to calls for expansion. But in the public university sector, this expansion has not been matched by necessary state funding, resulting in pressure on university budgets, buttressed by rising unit costs, both threatening academic standards. Where the response has been (state approved) tuition fee hikes to augment income, university access becomes beyond the reach of large sections of non-rich, aspiring students. While private universities are, in principle, able to ease pressures on university admissions, the high tuition fee levels are beyond the reach of the less well-off, potential student.

These conditions should create a demand for commercial loans from the banking system to see the student through the period of study, to meet tuition fees and, perhaps,

Table 20.1 Private rates of return to higher
education: selected Asian countries
with loans schemes

Estimate year	Rate of return (%)	Country
2010	14.1	Australia
2009	20.8	India
2010	11.5	Indonesia
2007	9.0	Japan
2010	22.0	Malaysia
2011	23.2	Philippines
1998	10.7	Singapore
2009	14.1	Sri Lanka
2010	12.7	South Korea
2011	17.2	Thailand

Source: Montenegro and Patrinos (2014).

living expenses too. But, given the risky employment outcome of university study, the requirement of collateral, and high market interest rates, such loans are affordable only by the well-off. This lacuna may be filled by a state-sponsored student loans scheme.

The chapter is structured as follows: The intended central purpose of any given loans scheme is of central importance for an understanding of its design, operation, outcomes, and degree of success; this issue is addressed in section 2. The main elements of loans scheme operation are presented in section 3, in terms of funding source, allocation and borrower selection, repayment regimes and mechanisms for repayment collection, and measures to contain repayment default; the section concludes with a consideration of debt repayment. Loans scheme financial outcomes are the focus of section 4, with discussions of their financial viability and justification of loan subsidies where appropriate. Section 5 probes the efficacy of loans schemes in Asia in successfully meeting the needs of the student population; the concluding section draws general conclusions, looking toward future change. A postscript is added on the effects of COVID-19.

2. Central Purpose and Justification

2.1 Loans Scheme Objectives

Government-sponsored student loans schemes in Asia differ widely in the central objective pursued. In an earlier paper, the author identified no fewer than 11 separate objectives that have underscored loans schemes around the world (Ziderman, 2002).

For purposes of the present comparative analysis, we restrict our focus to the four more pervasive purposes of loans schemes: budgetary objectives (including cost-sharing), social targeting, manpower needs, and general student support. Table 20.2 provides a matrix mapping the central purpose of a number of Asian loans schemes, against their coverage (whether they cover tuition fees or living expenses or both). Some schemes have additional, secondary objectives; these are shown in italics in the table.

2.1.1 Budgetary Objectives

Worldwide, public universities are underfinanced. Constrained government allocations to universities have resulted from a combination of ongoing increases in unit costs, policies favoring support for lower levels of education, as well as overall parsimony in state budgets. The result has been a growth in student numbers unmatched

Table 20.2 Loans scheme objective and coverage

Loans scheme coverage	Loans scheme objective			
	(1) Budgetary objectives (including cost-sharing)	(2) Social objectives	(3) Manpower needs	(4) General student Support
Tuition fees	Australia Japan Type 2 Singapore	Mongolia Philippines Indonesia (closed) Korea (ICL)	Korea (MoE – Engineering) *Japan Type 1+* *The Philippines +*	*Australia+* Hong Kong NLS* India (ELS scheme) Kazakhstan Other Korean schemes Singapore Thailand – former TICAL Uzbekistan
Living expenses		Hong Kong LSFS** Korea (MoE)		
Tuition fees and living expenses	New Zealand	China subsidized scheme (GSSL) Japan Type 1 Pakistan Thailand -SLS Vietnam India (NLSS- closed)	Brunei – priority fields	China – commercial scheme Malaysia

Notes:

* Hong Kong: non-subsidized scheme

** Hong Kong: main scheme: subsidized

+ Secondary objective of the loans scheme (*shown in italics*)

by commensurate government funding. The response has been the tapping of other sources of funding, through the sharing of costs with the beneficiaries; the main thrust has been the introduction, or increase, of student payments for tuition and/or provided living services. Such student fees are rendered both politically and socially acceptable by the introduction, in parallel, of state-sponsored student loans schemes.

While this model is found largely in Western countries, where the public university sector is dominant (such as in the United Kingdom and the Netherlands), it seems to have been adopted only in richer Asian countries. In Singapore, the 1988 university tuition fee rises were accompanied by subsidized loans equivalent to about half the value of the new tuition fees and the much-discussed Australian loans scheme was introduced in tandem with the imposition of university tuition fees in 1989.

2.1.2 Social Objectives

In most countries, raising the relatively low enrollment of the poor, minorities, and disadvantaged groups in non-compulsory levels of education has become a major element in educational and social policy; this is true of universities too. A major barrier to access is clearly a financial one. A regime of means tested state grants has long been regarded as the most effective means of enhancing the access of these disadvantaged groups. However, a widespread grants scheme is likely to impose an overly heavy burden of state funds. A student loans scheme, targeted on the poor, offers the dual benefit of increasing access and of reducing, or at least containing, public expenditures, as loan repayments build up. However, loans take-up by target groups will be contingent on the generosity of the terms on which loans are made available, thus providing a justification for extensive loans subsidies.

2.1.3 Manpower Needs

Loans schemes can constitute a tool for achieving other social and economic objectives, by encouraging students to enter fields of national priority. These would include easing of skill shortages (such as engineers or mathematics teachers) or working in areas of societal importance (e.g., doctors or teachers serving remote rural areas). Thus, the Korean Ministry of Education provides loans and scholarships restricted to engineering students, while special loans are available in the Philippines for students enrolling in "priority" courses.

2.1.4 General Student Support

National social and economic considerations provide a more general rationale for student loan provision. These stem from the importance accorded to the encouragement of youngsters to invest in their human capital, both to enhance their life chances and to contribute their acquired knowledge and skills to overall national economic and social investment. Removing or lowering financial barriers to university access is seen as a vital element of these policies, of which readily available student loans, on a broad front, play a part. However, in many of these schemes the needs of less advantaged social and economic groups are not ignored. Thus, while loans remain generally available to all potential students, for those emanating from disadvantaged sections of the population affirmative action policies offer them preferential treatment, even though social objectives are not the primary concern of these schemes. In Malaysia, superior loan terms are offered to the poor: loan size eligibility is positively related to family income, as is the length of the repayment horizon. While in India, under the current Educational Loans Scheme, loans are provided by banks on commercial lines, a government-funded interest payment "moratorium" is provided for students from low-income backgrounds during study and the year following.

2.2 Appropriate Scheme Coverage

The preceding discussion on loans scheme objectives has relevance to the policy issue of whether it is appropriate to restrict state-subsidized loans to particular student groups or to make them available to all those wishing to enroll.

2.2.1 Loans for Students at Private Universities?

Where the underlying objective of a loans scheme is social, manpower needs, or general student support, the public–private sector divide should not constitute a barrier to access. As noted, in many Asian university systems, the share of private university enrollment is high and in some it is dominant. In many cases where public and private universities coexist, disadvantaged groups face barriers to enrollment in the more prestigious (highly subsidized) public sector universities; they trend towards enrollment in the private sector where tuition fees are dramatically higher. Malaysia constitutes a case in point, where ethnic Chinese and Indian students are more highly represented in private universities. In these cases, and particularly where private universities are partially state funded, loans are justifiably available to students in these institutions.

However, where loans schemes have been introduced to facilitate cost-sharing in the public sector through higher fees, thereby easing pressure on government budgets, a prima facie case can be made for excluding students at private universities. But even in many country schemes where relatively few students are enrolled in private universities, loans are extended to students in both the public and private sectors. This is the case in Singapore (where private enrollment is about 15 percent) and even in Australia and New Zealand (only some 7 percent). This may seem surprising for these countries, where it might be expected that loans availability would be confined to public university students since, as noted, loans schemes are often introduced to facilitate cost-sharing in the public sector. However, student loans, by enhancing demand in private institutions and thus stimulating private sector growth, can contribute to an easing of the budgetary burden on the state in providing public higher education, as well as easing barriers to access.

2.2.2 Selective Coverage?

Apart from the issue of public sector eligibility, should all students be otherwise eligible for loan support? In principle, the three objectives of cost-sharing, manpower shortages, and general student support all justify the general availability of student loans to all segments of the population, regardless of need or ability. This is clearly not the case, however, for loans schemes with predominantly social objectives which aim, more narrowly, at easing university entry for the poor, minorities, and other disadvantaged groups. In order to reach out effectively to these populations, it is necessary that there be available a reliable means of ascertaining loans eligibility (especially of the poor) and that an effective system of proactive targeting to these populations be put in place. How far these outcomes are achieved in practice is probed in section 5.

While loans (for other than social purposes) should be made available to all students, in practice funding paucity may require some form of loans rationing. Thus, a distinction needs to be made between the deliberate targeting of the poor and the use of targeting as a rationing mechanism given limited loans funds. In the latter case, criteria need to be formulated if selection is not to be arbitrary (as on a "first come, first served" basis). While priority is often given to poor students, these are also higher-risk borrowers, with a greater propensity for repayment default. Targeting may be based on income, as in the New Zealand cost-sharing scheme. Selecting students on the basis of academic ability enhances the internal efficiency of the scheme, but these groups may not be regarded as the most deserving. Thirdly, preference may be given to students committing to work in outlying regions, in the public sector, or those enrolling in defined "priority" fields, such as loans schemes in Japan (Type 1) and in the Philippines.

3. Main Elements of Loans Scheme Operation

State-sponsored loans schemes are operated in differing institutional settings: from within a government department (usually the Ministry of Education, as in some Korean and Philippines schemes), as an independent national loans agency (Hong Kong, Malaysia, Thailand), or by the banking system (China, India). There are considerable differences across schemes in both organizational structure and administrative procedures, but operative responsibilities also differ widely. Few central bodies are charged with responsibility for all aspects of the scheme: initial and recurrent loan capital; individual loan conditions, loan size and eligibility; loan allocation to applicants and disbursement; and repayment collection. Usually, administrative responsibilities for particular aspects of the scheme are assigned to various external institutional players.

3.1 Funding Source

The major funding sources are the state budget and banking system (Table 20.3).

In a number of government-sponsored student loans schemes in Asia, initial loan capital is supplied from the state budget, usually to a national student loan agency

Table 20.3 Loans scheme funding source and loans allocation

Country – loans scheme	Source of funding		(3) Allocation institution
	(1) Current	(2) Formerly	
Australia	State	–	Central loans agency
China – GSSL	Commercial banks	–	Commercial banks
Hong Kong region	Government	Pension funds	Central loans agency
India	Banks	State	Banks
Japan	Banks Bonds Government		
Kazakhstan	Banks	State	
Korea – Ministry of Education – government employees	Banks State	– Pension fund	Higher education institutions Loans scheme
Malaysia	Capital market borrowing State pension funds	State	Higher education institutions
New Zealand	State		
Pakistan	Banks		Banks
The Philippines – SNPL – COE, Region 5	State	Financial institutions	Higher Education Commission – regional offices Higher education institutions
Singapore – TFL – CPF	State Central Provident Fund		Banks CPF
Thailand – Current scheme - TICAL	State State + Bonds	–	Higher education institutions Higher education institutions
Vietnam	State + (Bonds)	–	Bank of Social Policies (centralized scheme)
Uzbekistan	Banks		–

(Australia, Thailand). It is often assumed, mistakenly, that the need for continued state funding will cease over time; funding will continue at a diminishing rate, as it is gradually replaced by loan repayments. Then a revolving fund, which will finance new student loans, would result as final repayments are secured from the first cohort of borrowers. But, in practice, accumulated repayments will fall short of total borrowings because of interest subsidies and repayment default, implying the need for the continuation of state funding over the longer term. In addition, growing student enrollments will add to the need for continued, additional, state support. Such funding levels may not be available.

Governments can avoid these expenditures if the scheme is funded by external institutions, though such student loans generally remain subsidized and government guaranteed. In principle, external financing can be supplied in two main ways: through banks (and other financial institutions) which finance student loans from their own funds, or through recourse to a process of borrowing from financial institutions or the capital market.

The use of the banking system as the major source of loans is in place in such diverse settings as China (state commercial banks), India, Korea (the Ministry of Education scheme), and Pakistan. A major problem with this approach is the availability of state guarantees against payment default; this may considerably reduce incentives for lending banks to seek out recalcitrant borrowers and enforce repayment, resulting in high default rates. On the other hand, in response to growing default rates, banks may respond by screening-out higher-risk, often lower-income and poor, students; this has occurred in the case of the Indian loans scheme, as discussed below.

A third option is the financing of loans from an existing fund or quasi-government financial institution, such as from a national insurance fund. In Malaysia, the National Higher Education Fund (PTPTN), a statutory body managing the disbursement and repayments of student loans, was initially funded by government grants. When these ceased in 2003, the PTPTN began to fund student loans by borrowing from the two state-owned major pension funds; subsequently, borrowing was executed from commercial banks by the issue of bonds. However, given that the bond rate is far in excess of loan interest rates, the scheme is financially non-viable and relies on state support via government guarantees. In parallel to PTPTN loans, individuals can borrow from their accounts with the Employees Provident Fund to fund university access. In Singapore, too, savings from a Central Provident Fund can be accessed to finance undergraduate tuition fees for family members (CPF scheme). Alternatively, recourse may be made to the Ministry of Education Tuition Fee Loans scheme (TFL).

But such arrangements have not always worked well. The Korean loans scheme for government employees was financed in its early years by borrowings from their pension fund. Since the scheme is highly subsidized (loans are provided free of interest), overall loans recovery is low, thus weakening the financial robustness of the pension scheme. After temporary suspension in 1999, loans were resumed with the government as capital provider. In the case of the Study Now Pay Later scheme in the Philippines, an obligation was imposed in its initial years on various financial institutions (including the Government Service Insurance System) to fund the scheme. Given the high level of loans subsidy and resulting agency losses, these agencies were reluctant to disperse funds for student loans. With the disengagement of these agencies from the scheme, the government assumed the role of providing loan capital.

In principle, a student loans agency can tap the private financial markets by selling large bundles of student loans agreements to a secondary lender (such as a bank or insurance company), at a discount. In this way, the loans agency receives the stream of future repayment as an upfront payment (minus the discount to cover the risk borne by the secondary lender). In India, in an effort to contain non-repayment, commercial banks sell delinquent loans to asset restructuring companies. In some national loans schemes (mainly outside Asia) the central student loans agency finances student loans activities through borrowing from the money and capital markets. Government-guaranteed, fixed interest bonds, tradable on the stock exchange, are issued by the agency; in this process of "securitization" the bonds are secured by the future stream of loans repayments. Jasso, the Japanese loans agency, partially finances Type 2 loans through the regular issue of bonds. In planning the (short-lived) TICAL scheme in Thailand, securitization was officially examined, though not adopted, as an alternative to government as a funding source. However, securitization is unlikely to be appropriate for loans schemes that are highly subsidized, in particular those with strong social objectives.

Finally, an alternative to student loans for financing higher education has been developed in the United States, albeit somewhat experimentally, in terms of income share agreements (ISAs). An ISA is a contract between an individual student and an investor (usually, but not necessarily, the university), in which funding is received in exchange for the borrower's obligation to repay a specified percentage of income over a defined time period. The student could end up repaying a sum that is in excess of, or less than, the loan received, depending on the future earnings profile. Likewise, the investor could face losses if the ISA was taken out with a student whose earnings turned out to be low. There seems to be an incentive, particularly for a non-university investor, to identify and finance only those students with better earnings prospects. ISAs do not seem to have been adopted for university funding in Asia.

3.2 Loans Allocation and Borrower Selection

A mechanism must be developed through which loans funding reaches the student applicants. While practice varies considerably across loans schemes (Table 20.3, column 3), we may identify three main variants. In the few more centralized systems, applications are made directly to the central loans agency, which allocates loans to applicants; the Hong Kong Student Financial Assistance Agency (SFAA) operates in this way. Similarly, where the loans scheme is decentralized and run individually by various banking institutions, as in the Chinese commercial scheme, the Korean schemes, and in India, loan applications are serviced directly by these institutions. In the more usual, "top-down" allocation, universities act as intermediary institutions. Students make loan applications to their university, which allocates a loans budget among applicants; the university's loans budget is received from a central loans funding source, usually government.

There are two main advantages to loans allocation in centralized schemes. One is administrative simplicity; the other is that they foster horizontal equity, as loans are allocated across-the-board on the basis of standard, objective criteria. This may be lacking in the two other loans allocation systems.

In schemes financed and managed by commercial banks, loans applications are serviced on an individual basis. Incentives may be present to favor better-off students, who would be seen as less default-prone than those from lower-income backgrounds; this is exemplified by the Indian experience in recent years.

Under the prevailing Educational Loans Scheme (ELS), Indian public and private sector banks float student loans on a commercial basis within a framework developed by the Indian Banks' Association, though schemes differ slightly from bank to bank. Educational loans are officially designated as a loans priority sector for public banks, along with 13 other sectors. The benefit of open eligibility has been compromised in recent years given that banks essentially regard their operations as a business activity. Thus, while total loan disbursements have increased apace (by more than a third over a recent five-year period), the number of loan recipients has shrunk by a quarter. Average loan size has increased; increasingly banks have shunned the provision of smaller size loans which, being taken up mainly by less advantaged families, are more risky and exhibit higher default rates (see Table 20.4). They have preferred to concentrate on dispersing larger, more profitable, loans to the better-off segments of society. Since banks operate loans allocation on purely commercial lines, the loans scheme shares few of the features associated with schemes in other Asian countries or with the government-operated, zero-free National Loans Scholarship scheme which it replaced.

Top-down allocation through intermediaries, normally higher education institutions, may result in horizontal inequities among loan recipients. This is strongly illustrated by practice in Thailand. The central objective of the Thai scheme is to ease financial burdens and increase educational opportunity of poor students; thus, only those from low-income families are formally eligible. Since university loans budgets are determined by university enrollment size rather than the number of low-income students, some universities with large numbers of economically disadvantaged students receive too few funds to provide loans for all in need. Other universities, often in the private sector and with fewer very deserving students, are able to offer loans to less disadvantaged, yet still eligible, applicants. The issue is compounded by the autonomy granted to universities in deciding on the size of individual loans, up to the legally permitted maximum.

3.3 Alternative Repayment Regimes

Much controversy surrounds the scheduling of loan repayment, whether this should be income-related (as in the Australian model) or pre-fixed in terms of equal periodic installments over a defined time horizon (mortgage-type loans).

In mortgage-type loans (sometimes referred to as "time-based repayment loans"), repayment is made over a specified time period, usually in fixed periodic repayments; a designated interest rate and a maximum time horizon are employed to calculate the fixed periodic repayments. The higher the rate of interest that is set and the shorter the repayment period, the greater is the monthly sum required in repayment. Mortgage-type loan repayment is the common standard for loans schemes in most countries, as it

Table 20.4 Measures and sanctions against default

Loans scheme	Measure/sanction	Comments
China Subsidized scheme	Students' individual credit Moral pressure: publish defaulter list	
China Non-subsidized	Family co-signatures / pledge assets as collateral	Effective, but restricts loans to better-off students
Hong Kong Subsidized scheme	Loan guarantor	Serious and prolonged defaulters are referred to the Department of Justice for legal recovery
India NSLS (closed) ELS	Parental guarantee Various types of parental security/ guarantee; no collateral required for low-income households	Differs from bank to bank
Japan – Type 2	Penalties against delinquent loan repayments: Delinquent fees – 5% annually (10% from 2014)	Harsh loan collection measures: calls by collection servicers to urge repayment - report to credit information agencies, - legal action, such as seizure of bank deposits, attachment of earnings
Korea Ministry Education scheme	Joint surety (parents); Loan insurance; Moral pressure: publish defaulter list; Bar access to further credit if in default	Serious and prolonged defaulters are referred to the Department of Justice
Korea Government employees	Joint surety (parents); Moral pressure: publish defaulter list; Bar access to further credit if in default	
Malaysia	Blacklisted in the Central Credit Reference Information System (CCRIS), database system that stores financial records of Malaysian borrowers Passport renewal and travel abroad prohibited Legal action (rarely practiced)	These measures are neither fully implemented nor effective. Default = 45%+
Philippines National scheme	Loan guarantor	Ineffective: guarantors not required to pay off "bad" loans Virtually no loans repayment
Philippines (Reg.5)	None	

Table 20.4 Continued

Loans scheme	Measure/sanction	Comments
Philippines (COE)	Loan guarantor	
Singapore	-	
- TFE	One guarantor	
- CPF	No guarantor	
Thailand	Loan guarantor	Ineffective: reluctance to turn to guarantors Now taking serious offenders to court Civil servants' salaries deducted to pay repay debts
Vietnam	Parents/guarantors responsible for repayment	Not the borrower

is in Asian loans schemes (Table 20.5, column 3). Pioneered in Australia, income contingent loans schemes (ICL) entail periodic loan repayment obligations that are not pre-fixed but determined as a percentage of the graduate's income in each period; collection is usually entrusted to the income tax authorities because information on individual incomes is required. There is no set repayment horizon; this is dependent on the size of the initial loan and the graduate's annual income.

There are major practical differences between the two repayment regimes. With mortgage-type loans, the size and time horizon of monthly payments are known to the borrower at the outset. However, the *loan burden*—the proportion of monthly income that must be assigned to loan repayments—is not. This may result in a heavy repayment burden in the years following graduation, for those with low earnings. With ICL repayments, the repayment percentage out of monthly income (the loan burden) is fixed at the outset and can be set at levels that will avoid repayment burdens, particularly for low-income recipients.

There is now a sizable literature on the relative merits of the two approaches, the upshot of which is to argue for the superiority of ICL systems on theoretical grounds. Indeed, these findings are echoed in a number of recent studies probing, positively, the introduction of comprehensive ICL regimes in various Asian countries: China, Japan, Indonesia, and Thailand. However, these studies are essentially technical exercises in outcome simulations and they remain largely silent on underlying factors on the ground militating against implementation; these include political resistance and organizational and administrative weaknesses in these countries.

It may be asked why there are few ICL schemes in Asian countries? Possible explanations would include institutional lethargy of policymakers and vested interest of loans scheme practitioners in long-established mortgage-type schemes. However, there are two, more practical, reasons for this lacuna.

Table 20.5 Loan repayment: collection alternatives and repayment mechanisms

Type of collection		Country examples	
	(1) Collecting institution	(2) Country	(3) Repayment mechanism
Self-collection	National loans agency	Hong Kong	Mortgage
		Malaysia	Mortgage
	Banks	Korea (MOE)	Mortgage
		China	Mortgage
		India (ELS)	Mortgage
		Pakistan	Mortgage
		Singapore TFL	Mortgage
		Vietnam	Mortgage
	Universities	Philippines (Centers of Excellence, Region 5)	Mortgage
	Ministry of Education	Philippines (SNPL)	Mortgage
Agency collection	Banks	India (NLSS) – now closed	Mortgage
		Thailand (SLS)	Mortgage
	Taxation authorities (via employers – PAYE)	Australia	ICL
		Malaysia (borrowers registered with Inland Revenue Board)	Mortgage
		New Zealand	ICL
		South Korea – partial ICL coverage	ICL
		Thailand (TICAL) – now closed	ICL
		Japan Type 1, partial ICL option	ICL

First, the two necessary conditions for successfully implementing a system of income contingent repayment are usually lacking: information on graduates' current income and the institutional capacity to effect repayment collection, usually by tax authorities. ICLs can work only if there is a sufficiently large formal sector where individuals are within the tax ambit. Thus, these mechanisms are insufficiently well developed or too over-burdened in many Asian countries. However, over the longer term, the advance of big data and personal identification systems may facilitate a design whereby the loan repayment is automatically added to the tax payments due. But the introduction of ICL schemes, even where feasible, may come up against powerful treasury opposition. The short-lived Thai Income Contingent Allowance and Loans scheme (TICAL), fashioned on the Australian model, was discontinued in 2006, with a change in government, after only a year of operation. A major factor in its demise was the unwillingness of the powerful income tax authority to collect an income contingent loan.

Second, it is seen that initial funding and loan collection functions are undertaken by the banking system in many Asian loans schemes (Table 20.3). ICL repayment may not be compatible with accepted banking procedures. Banks usually base repayments on installment schemes that are not income contingent. The bank has two limitations with respect to ICL repayment; they do not have access to data on income nor do they usually enter lending agreements that resemble shareholder rights as with ICL schemes. Therefore, where banks constitute the lending vehicle, a system of mortgage-type repayments is the natural choice.

3.4 Collection

How are loan payments collected over the lengthy repayment horizon?

As indicated in Table 20.5, the body allocating loans also generally retains responsibility for collection ("self-collection"). Self-collection by bodies such as autonomous public student loan institutions, government ministries, or universities might work well (as in Hong Kong and the Korean Government Employees' Scheme). But, while such institutions may possess comparative advantages in identifying student need and selecting loan recipients, their capacity or will for effective repayment collection is less evident. Similarly, over-reliance by these self-collection loan organizations on government budgetary support may undermine the incentive to follow up on delinquent borrowers (as in the Philippine Study Now Pay Later (SNPL) scheme where collection is virtually non-existent); loan bodies may tend to rely largely on public funds to supply new loans rather than stepping up efforts to secure repayment to finance loans for new borrowers. Banks, however, usually have the necessary infrastructure and expertise that these other bodies may lack. Thus, self-collection by commercial banks (which also supply the loan capital), may be expected to be effective. However, it is not sufficient for banks to have a comparative advantage in collection; they must have also an incentive to collect proactively. But this may be undermined by public policy; a full government guarantee on loans may encourage private or public banks to collect the guarantee from the government rather than repayment due from the debtor. Thus, a less-than-full government guarantee may be advisable, with commercial banks assuming a small part of the risk (as in the Korean Ministry of Education scheme).

The outsourcing of repayment collection ("agency collection") is rare in Asian loans schemes, apart from ICLs. These schemes, by definition, rely on the tax authority because of its access to information on individual incomes and ability to require current repayment obligations by employers, via "pay as you earn" arrangements. Since repayment collection by tax authorities is also partially employed in Malaysia (confined to debtors with sufficient earnings for registration with the Inland Revenue Board), this mode of collection is seen as not confined to ICL schemes; in principle, they could be used for mortgage-type schemes too, if PAYE systems are comprehensive and effective (as in Hong Kong). The Thailand loans agency, exceptionally, employs a public bank (Krung Thai Bank) to administer loans collection and defaulter follow-up; the arrangement seems to work effectively.

3.5 Containing Repayment Default

Repayment default is rife in Asian loans schemes; repayment is virtually non-existent in the Philippines SNPL scheme and default approaches 50 percent in Malaysia. There may be three main causes underlying borrowers' failure to make repayments: they cannot repay; they may not be sufficiently pressed to repay; and they may not want to repay (repayment evasion).

The first cause, relating to weighty repayment burdens, is considered in section 4. In the second case, while loans schemes do employ a wide range of measures to ensure timely repayment (see Table 20.4 for a synoptic listing), these are not always effective or implemented. The measure that is most common is the co-signature of a guarantor (usually a family member), but little more than lip service has been paid to this provision in many cases (Thailand, the Philippines); those most in need of loans may be least able to provide effective guarantees. However, given the increasingly precarious financial situation facing many loans schemes, punitive measures are being adopted more widely and enforced. These include legal action, listing in credit agencies, and publication of defaulter lists. Some institutions, particularly commercial banks, do press defaulters hard for repayment. For example, the default rate on Type 2 loans in Japan is under 2 percent, partly because of stiff penalties and harsh loan collection measures. Nevertheless, it appears that in many countries there is neither sufficient incentive nor political will to strictly enforce repayment obligations. This, in turn, may encourage negative attitudes towards repayment on the part of working debtors, leading to overt repayment evasion. While measures to inculcate more positive attitudes towards debt repayment can be developed, or strengthened, these may be tantamount to changing established socially acceptable norms; such changes are not readily secured even over the longer term.

4. FINANCIAL VIABILITY

4.1 Repayment and Recovery

Almost all student loans schemes in Asia, as worldwide, fail to recover fully the loan sums outlaid and are, essentially, financially non-viable. There are two elements underlying this shortfall: the design of the loans scheme and effectiveness in its administration.

Repayment conditions in virtually all student loans schemes are, by design, "softer" than those on regular commercial loans. This difference represents a subsidy received by the student, in the sense that the borrower is not required to repay the full value of the loan received. The main factor leading to the less-than-full loan repayment is the low interest rates charged on the borrower: zero or below-market interest rates during repayment and also zero interest during study or grace periods following graduation. The effect of these built-in subsidies is amplified when the amortization period is long. A notable exception is the non-means tested loans scheme (NLS) in Hong Kong, which operates on a full cost recovery basis; a "no gain, no loss" rate of interest is charged, which includes a risk-adjustment element to cover the loan agency's risk in disbursing unsecured loans.

Interest rates are zero in many Asian loans schemes, including those in Japan (Type 1), New Zealand (for graduates remaining in the country), Pakistan, Sri Lanka, and, formerly, in Vietnam; they are set at only 1 percent in the Thai and Malaysian schemes. The extent of repayment shortfall resulting from these built-in interest subsidies can be surprisingly large.[1] For example: the *repayment ratio* (ratio of required repayments to loan size received) stands at about 85 and 77 percent, respectively, even in the well-designed Japan Type 2 and Singapore schemes; at some 65 percent in the Hong Kong subsidized scheme, the central Philippines and Japan Type 1 schemes; it is as low as 30 percent in the Thai scheme. These shortfalls represent, effectively, a "hidden grant" to the student who takes out the loan.

The repayment ratio relates to the perspective of the individual student. However, even if student loans were not subsidized and the individual student was required to repay in full, not all of the total outlays by the loan body would be recouped. The shortfall would depend on the effectiveness with which the scheme is run and, particularly, the success in minimizing repayment default. This *loan recovery*, then, focuses more widely on the scheme as a whole rather than on the individual borrower. The overall loan recovery ratio can be considerably lower than the individual repayment ratio as it takes account both of subsidies and default. Whereas in the Japan Type 1 scheme, the individual repays 65 percent of the loan, the scheme as a whole recovers only some 50 percent. An extreme example is afforded by the SNPL scheme in the Philippines; while the repayment ratio stands at about 66 per cent, a lack of effort at repayment collection results in the scheme showing an annual recovery loss, overall, of some 20 percent. The implication for this case, and for other schemes funded by the state, is the need for a continued influx of state funding, which is generally forthcoming. The consequences of low overall recovery are more severe in schemes drawing on funding from the capital market. The Malaysian scheme borrows from the capital market at between 4 and 5 percent but charges only 1 percent on student loans; with a 30 percent subsidy rate and over 50 percent non-repayment overall, recovery is only about a third. Since these losses can be recouped only through additional capital market borrowing, the system has accumulated a massive debt; the underlying business model in the Malaysian scheme is neither rational nor sustainable.

---

[1] The following estimates are derived from various sources and not necessarily fully up to date. But their general magnitude will not have changed substantially.

4.2 Loans Scheme Subsidies

In many schemes, attempts are ongoing to reduce, or at least contain, financial viability. However, the design elements (particularly interest subsidies) that lead to extensive loans scheme subsidization, remain in place. How far are these substantive built-in loan subsidies justifiable? In general, near full loan recovery should be the underlying aim of a well-designed student loans scheme; it is difficult to present a rationale for the extensive interest subsidies incorporated into most loans schemes in Asia. In the more extreme cases, the root cause is political populism, rather than an objective analysis of appropriate loans scheme design.

However, two of the four alternative loans scheme objectives discussed above may justify loan subsidy. Where loans are generally available, the manpower needs objective may indicate the need to offer softer loan conditions to encourage enrollment in these priority fields. The social objective presents a stronger case for subsidization. To be effective in increasing university access of the poor and disadvantaged, loans may need to be substantially subsidized through generous terms, including low interest rates, long repayment periods, and even repayment exemption in times of temporary hardship. But such subsidies, as noted above, implying a low repayment ratio and low recovery overall, will entail considerable budgetary costs. Since a grant offers a stronger and more direct incentive for access than does a (partially) repayable loan, the apparent advantage of loans over grants is less clear-cut. This highlights a central conundrum in loan policy: at what level of built-in loan subsidy would a grant be a more cost-effective instrument for helping the poor than a highly subsidized loan (containing a substantial hidden grant)? This suggests that, in country settings where state budgets are constrained, a more appropriate financial aid program for the poor is likely to involve a combination of both loans and grants, with a relatively larger overt grant element for the very poor. This is the practice in the subsidized Hong Kong scheme.

5. Do Loans Schemes Meet Students' Needs?

The discussion thus far has been directed to aspects of the loans scheme as a whole—objectives, operation, and financial viability. But focusing now on the individual student: How far do loans schemes meet the needs of the student population to whom, ultimately, the loans schemes are addressed? Three central issues are discussed. First, reach: loans should reach all of the student population for whom they are intended. Second, loan size: loans should be sufficiently sizable to adequately meet defined expenditure needs. And third: the borrower should not be beset by unduly heavy hardship over the period of repayment.

5.1 Reach

The appropriate reach of a loans scheme will depend very much on the underlying objectives of the scheme. In the case of cost-sharing and general student support schemes, loans should be available for all students who potentially would benefit from them, to achieve an impact nationally. In the case of schemes with social objectives, loans eligibility should be restricted to the target population of the poor and disadvantaged; but they should be readily available to all such students in need.

These ideals are not met in practice. A major reason for this shortfall is that the supply of loans funding is constrained. Some schemes, particularly in more economically developed countries, are well endowed—such as in the Australian and the non-subsidized Hong Kong schemes—and reach is substantial. The two Japanese schemes combined reach some 50 percent of student enrollments. But reach is limited in many other schemes, particularly those that are state financed; low loan recovery, together with growing demand for loans from expanding university enrollment, place an increasing financing burden on the state, which cannot be met.

The problem of reach is particularly prevalent in many schemes aimed at increasing access for the poor and disadvantaged groups. The Chinese subsidized scheme, the Korean Ministry of Education schemes, and all of the schemes in the Philippines are aimed at the poor; yet the percentage of poor students that are covered in practice is low. Under-provision of budgetary support may stem from inadequate planning in defining the size and location of the target population and the extent of loans take-up. A comparison between the subsidized Hong Kong and Thailand schemes, both aimed at the poor, is instructive. While the former scheme is well financed, providing adequate loan support for over a third of student enrollment, the no less extensive Thai scheme suffers from inadequate state budgeting and a lack of proactive targeting, thus limiting the reach of the scheme—many potential borrowers remain outside.

Finally, some schemes that were set up with limited coverage have remained small due to a lack of political will in acquiring sufficient budgeting for a larger scheme with national impact. Thus, the veteran SNPL scheme in the Philippines has always operated on a very limited scale, reaching only a few thousand new students each year. Similarly, both the earlier Vietnam and Brunei schemes are negligible in scale, the former reaching only some 3 percent of student enrollment while the Brunei scheme reaches a maximum of a few hundred.

5.2 Loan Size

For those students who are in receipt of a loan, is it sufficiently large to meet designated needs? This is clearly the case in those many schemes that fully meet a common standard tuition fee. However, students may find the tuition loan to be inadequate in systems where tuition fees vary across institutions and disciplines; this is the case in the Chinese subsidized scheme and in tuition loans for private university students in Thailand. A cash flow crisis in Malaysia in the recent past led to a reduction in the size of a new loan by 5 and 15 percent, respectively, for borrowers in the public and private sectors. In the budget-deficient central Philippines scheme, the maximum amount prescribed by outdated legislation falls short of current fee levels. The problem is more severe for loans to meet living expenses; in the Vietnam case, the loan provides only up to a quarter of the sum needed to live in the major cities, where most students are enrolled. There is frequently an information gap with regard to the loan size required, which is likely to rise over time. The Hong Kong case succeeds in providing an adequate level of student assistance, since loan size for living expenses is updated periodically, based on student expenditure surveys and the compilation of a student price index. In the Thai scheme, living cost loan size ceilings are set, seemingly, with little account taken of available student expenditure surveys. Moreover, in the Thai and Philippine schemes, loans for living expenses are not updated periodically to reflect ongoing inflation, so their real value falls over time.

5.3 Debt/Repayment Burdens

Perhaps the one issue associated with student loans that has attracted most attention in public discourse (notably in relation to loans schemes in the United States) is the burden imposed on the individual borrower by the large size of student debt. This concern, however, is misplaced, as can be shown by analogy with housing loans. Here, the householder rejoices in a larger mortgage (debt) but is wary of payment difficulties imposed by high mortgage repayments over time in relation to current and expected earnings. Similarly, with student loans, attention should not be focused on the total size of accumulated debt with which the borrower is "saddled," but rather on whether repayment obligations are unduly large in relation to income, thus both imposing repayment hardship and fostering repayment default.

A central advantage of ICL repayment schemes is that the repayment percentage out of income is defined in the scheme and constant over the years of repayment. If this ratio is set at a reasonable size, a burden of repayment is largely obviated. This stands at 9 percent in the partial ICL option in Japan Type 1 loans and 10 percent in the New Zealand scheme, a rate which might be regarded as borderline in terms of constituting a repayment burden.

Repayment burdens are more readily associated with mortgage-type repayment schemes. The repayment burden will decline over the life cycle, given the fixed periodic repayments and rising incomes over time; however, repayment may constitute a particular burden for the lower paid during the years immediately following graduation. In the Vietnam case, with a stringent maximum four-year repayment period, the lowest paid 20 percent would find it impossible to meet required repayments for the first three years, because repayment equals or is in excess of earnings. More generally, since repayment will constitute a burden when required repayments are large in relation to income, the size of both the numerator and the denominator in the repayment/income ratio are relevant. In many schemes in Asia, the extensive in-built subsidies—low interest, period of "grace" following graduation, and long repayment time horizons—result in a low value for the numerator. In the case of the highly subsidized Thai scheme, borrowers, on average, repay only 3–4 percent overall, out of their income. The problem, then, may often lie more in low income size (the denominator) than in any heavy repayment obligation imposed by the loan.

Which sections of the graduate population are prone to low earnings and, therefore, subject to a sizable loan repayment burden? We may identify four such potentially vulnerable groups. First, there are those who have completed courses of study for which labor market prospects are not high. This can arise in two ways. The academic quality of the institution may be mediocre; this can be a serious issue in systems where most students attend private institutions of varying quality. Or, where students enroll in more esoteric, popular disciplines with scant market relevance, some loans schemes respond by restricting eligibility to STEM or priority fields.

A second group comprises those who complete professional studies in fields that are of high societal value but not well paid (often in the public sector), such as social workers. Apart from easing repayment obligations, other compensating measures may be made available, such as housing subsidies and health benefits. A third, and far more significant, group consists of graduates whose low earnings are due to adverse conditions in the labor market. While they may possess otherwise marketable skills, market demand is low either because of a prolonged general downturn in the economy or because of an oversupply of these skills, relative to demand. Periodic unemployment or working in lower-skilled jobs may be the only options. While the loans scheme authorities are not well placed to influence the employment and earnings of graduate borrowers, they can provide information and guidance on career and earnings prospects associated with alternative courses of university study. Or more draconian measures may be adopted, in limiting loan eligibility to students entering study disciplines with good earnings prospects and/or national need, a practice already recognized in some loans schemes.

6. A Summing Up

It is not possible to draw clear-cut conclusions on the efficacy of loans schemes in Asia, generally, given the considerable diversity in objectives, design, practice, and outcomes, across schemes. While most loans schemes may be found wanting in some aspects of their operation, they may record success in others. A loans scheme offering general student support may be deemed successful if student coverage is substantial; but the sheer size of the scheme may result in bureaucratic inefficiencies, leading to substantial repayment default. A more conservative, limited, scheme with loans supply falling short of demand, may register an excellent repayment record from the relatively few students who benefit. And an overly subsidized scheme, with a relatively light repayment burden, may compromise the financial integrity of the scheme. Given multiple yardsticks for success, policymakers will need to weigh carefully concurrent, often conflicting, effects in appraising the efficacy of a given loans scheme.

Overall, our findings do indicate the need for policymakers to revisit the workings of their loans scheme(s) and to ponder the desirability for change. But what direction should change take? Three different ways forward present themselves.

The first approach calls for the replacement of the current scheme by one based upon a loans scheme from another country setting, which is widely acknowledged to work well. A frequently suggested candidate in this regard is the well-oiled Australian HECS scheme. But even HECS has its limitations: for example, the repayment ratio is high but still stands at some 75 percent and the lack of necessary institutional framework in many, less-developed, Asian countries would render the emulation of a HECS-type scheme to be inappropriate, except perhaps over the longer term. Indeed, institutional imitation across countries does not provide a panacea, as it is not possible to identify any single "best practice" loans scheme.

A second, less radical, approach indicates a path of substantial internal reform. This entails a learning process based on international experience in the operation of loans schemes, leading to the adoption of elements that work well and shunning those that do not. This approach should involve a carefully planned and executed process of internal reform of the current system, which is long overdue in many schemes in the region.

A third approach, which may be complementary to the other two, is to identify policy initiatives that may constitute alternative pathways to achieving loans scheme objectives. A loans scheme may not always constitute the most appropriate instrument for achieving these different goals. A few examples present themselves. Low-income students might be better served through simple scholarships such as tuition waivers, which are both less costly and easier to administer than loans, particularly so where repayment default and loan subsidies are substantial. More flexible study program regimes could enable students to engage in part-time work, thus reducing the need for living expense loans; provision of student employment opportunities on campus would be a complementary measure. Loan debt relief could be introduced for each year of national or community service for, say, up to five years (prior to or following university study), thus securing societal benefits in exchange for loan forgiveness; alternatively, tuition waivers could be made available, thus lowering the demand for student loans. And cost-sharing could be extended to the employers of university graduates, thus lightening the tuition fee and consequently, the loan burden. In sum, careful and open-minded scrutiny of alternatives is a prerequisite for sound policy reform.

It is not possible at present to release a general clean bill of health for loans schemes in Asia. However, the positive, albeit indirect, contributions they have made to economic and societal development in many Asian countries should not be underrated. And at the level of the student beneficiaries themselves, student loans have promoted university education of the poorer and other disadvantaged sections of the community, they have eased student financial difficulties during study, and they have helped to open up, for the younger generation, a window of opportunity to improve life chances. These, indeed, are no mean achievements.

7. POSTSCRIPT: EFFECTS OF COVID-19

The near completion of this chapter has coincided with the onslaught of the COVID-19 epidemic. We conclude with some thoughts on possible implications for loans schemes in Asia, distinguishing between outcomes in the short run and, more briefly, over the longer term.

The most immediate effect of the virus is likely to fall on loan repayment obligations. Borrowers must face a contraction in the labor market, with widespread employment shutdowns, layoffs, and reduced earnings. These will have their effect in increasing the burden of loans repayment. Curtailed graduate recruitment will bear particularly heavily on recent graduates; for example, job offers for graduates in Japan have dropped by over 15 percent. As a consequence, measures are underway in many countries to lighten the increased burden of student loan repayments. Under Bank of India regulations a six-month moratorium on loans repayment (including education loans) for those undergoing financial challenges due to COVID-19, can now be extended for two years. A one-year suspension of loans repayment and interest has been introduced for government loans in Singapore. The Malaysian government's agreement to put off PTPTN loan repayment for a nine-month period has been extended for another three months for eligible borrowers. In New Zealand, graduates struggling to make loan repayments can propose a suitable repayment installment arrangement.

A number of expected effects may follow where increased repayment default is substantial. For state-funded loans schemes, the reduction in incoming repayments will either require additional budgetary support (which may not be forthcoming) or lead to a cutback in loan approvals. In bank-financed schemes, banks may be more selective, channeling loans to potentially safer, middle-class borrowers, with a consequent reduction in loans availability for lower-income applicants.

The emerging free tuition movement, seen worldwide in such diverse settings as New Zealand, Chile, Ontario (Canada), and the United States may signal the demise of student tuition loans programs in these countries. However, progress is likely to fall victim to the macroeconomic downturn, engendered by COVID-19. The implementation of comprehensive free tuition policies would be excessively costly to governments. Given increasing government budgetary parsimony, emphasis is likely to be placed on economic recovery and health rather than on free tuition in the higher education sector.

Over the longer term, a tardy economic recovery, with continued unemployment and limited new job openings, would create an air of uncertainty regarding the efficacy of embarking on university studies and of taking up the student loans they finance.

COVID-19 could also lead to a dramatic change in the norms of university course provision, with implications for student loans. With the university campus in shutdown across Asian countries, universities increasingly have extended or introduced online courses to replace, temporarily, on-campus classes. Many commentators see a continuation of this development beyond COVID-19, with online provision assuming a more central role. We may speculate that these developments could result in lower university costs overall, leading to tuition fee reductions and a fall in individual loan size.

Table 20.A.1 Asian loans schemes: general description

Loans scheme(s)	Country
The Higher Education Contribution Schemes (HECS), 1989. Broadly based scheme, provides subsidized tuition loans for private and public sector university students. Pioneered income contingent loans.	Australia
Education Loan Assistance scheme: very limited, government funded scheme, available for fields that are priority for Brunei's needs. Only a few hundred borrowers a year.	Brunei
Two national schemes, operated by the banking system. The major scheme, aimed at the poor, is subsidized by government. The second, open to all students, operates on commercial lines. Limited coverage but growing.	China
Veteran, centralized loans scheme (part of a comprehensive framework, providing grants and subsidized loans to poor and non-subsidized loans for non-poor students). Broad regional coverage.	Hong Kong
The Indian Banks' Association (IBA) formulated a comprehensive model educational loans scheme for adoption by all banks aimed at providing financial support from the banking system to deserving/meritorious students for pursuing higher education.	India
Closed. Short-lived scheme: 1998–2001.	Indonesia
The Japan Student Services Organization (JASSO) operated two parallel mortgage-type schemes covering some 50% of university students. A third of loans are Type 1, interest free, based on merit and need; an ICL option introduced in 2017. Type 2, low interest loans for those with economic need, now extended to middle-class students.	Japan
Introduced in 2005. Loans through banks. Very small scheme, with fewer than 1,000 borrowers to date.	Kazakhstan
National Higher Education Fund (PTPTN), a statutory body managing the disbursement and repayments of student loans, funds student loans by borrowing through commercial banks issuing bonds, backed by government guarantees. In parallel, individuals can borrow from accounts with the Employees Provident Fund to fund university access.	Malaysia
Interest free (formerly 5%) tuition loans. Meets only some 50% of the student need for loans. Currently, some 25,000 recipients.	Mongolia
ICL loans scheme, introduced in 1992. Zero interest for graduates remaining in New Zealand.	New Zealand
National Bank of Pakistan loans scheme operated in partnership with major commercial banks. Loans limited to meritorious students with financial constraints. Interest free, repayment over 10 years.	Pakistan

Table 20.A.1 Continued

Loans scheme(s)	Country
State-funded Study Now Pay Later (SNPL) scheme—very small, long-established national loans scheme. Complemented with two new schemes (regional and high-level institutions). Aimed at poor but the schemes are marginal in total size and impact.	Philippines
Loans can be accessed from savings accounts in the Central Provident Fund, to finance undergraduate tuition fees for family members. Alternatively, recourse may be made to the Ministry of Education Tuition Fee Loans scheme.	Singapore
A number of separate state-funded schemes, each run independently and designed to meet the needs of different target populations. The largest, Ministry of Education scheme, is aimed at the poor.	South Korea
Loans available for tuition fees at non-state higher education institutions, for those qualified but unable to secure placement at state universities. Zero interest; loan repayable over 8 years.	Sri Lanka
Highly subsidized, with broad national coverage; aimed at the poor, but badly targeted. Loans available for students in upper secondary and tertiary level institutions. Low financial viability. Temporarily replaced by TICAL (ICL) scheme.	Thailand
Established in 2001, open to all students. Loans provided by banking system. Ten years maximum repayment period, including years of study. Interest free loans for orphans and disabled, 50% discount for low-income families.	Uzbekistan
Credit Fund, established in 1998, but, reaching only 3% of students. Interest free, repayable over 15 years, poorly designed, New centralized scheme, established in 2017, run by the Bank of Social Policies; 6.8% interest rate; broad student coverage.	Vietnam

References

Montenegro, C. E. and Patrinos, H. A. (2014). *Comparable Estimates of Returns to Schooling Around the World.* Policy Research Working Paper No. 7020. Washington, DC: The World Bank. https://openknowledge.worldbank.org/handle/10986/20340

Shen, H. and Ziderman, A. (2009). "Student loans repayment and recovery: International comparisons." *Higher Education,* 57/3, 315–333.

Ziderman, A. (2002). "Alternative objectives of national student loans schemes: Implications for design, evaluation and policy." *Welsh Journal of Education,* 11/1, 37–47. Reprinted in: *Peking University Education Review,* 2 (2004) (in Chinese).

Ziderman, A. (2004). *Policy Options for Student Loan Schemes.* Paris: International Institute for Educational Planning, UNESCO. Vietnamese edition, UNESCO, Hanoi, 2006. Chinese edition, Peking University, 2010.

Ziderman, A. (2013). "Student loans schemes in practice: A global perspective." In D. E. Heller and C. Callender (eds.), *Student Financing of Higher Education: A Comparative Perspective.* International Studies in Higher Education series. Abingdon: Routledge, 32–60.

PART VII

CONSEQUENCES
AND CHALLENGES

CHAPTER 21

....

RETURNING TALENT

....

RENNIE J. MOON

1. INTRODUCTION

....

GLOBALLY and in the Asia-Pacific (hereafter, Asia) region, the continuing expansion of higher education has been accompanied by an increasing number of students studying or working abroad. The number of foreign students grew from 2 million in 1998 to 5.3 million in 2017, growing at an average annual rate of 5 percent among OECD countries and 6 percent among non-OECD countries. The most recent statistics available show that among OECD countries, there were 3.7 million international or foreign students in 2017, 6 percent more than in 2016 (OECD, 2019a).

One of the major concerns related to greater student mobility is the phenomenon of return migration and the impact of returnees on home country development. These concerns are especially relevant for countries in the Asian region, whose citizens constitute a major source of the world's student migrants.

This chapter first presents an overview of the major patterns of student flows from Asia. Next, it presents a framework based on previous research on the factors affecting return migration, followed by a discussion of the impact of returning talent on home country development. Lastly, it reviews the various policy approaches used by countries in Asia to encourage migrants to return home. The chapter ends with a discussion of the main conclusions from this literature and reflects on the implications of some recent developments, including growing geopolitical rivalries and the ongoing COVID pandemic, on the prospects for return migration.

2. GLOBAL AND STUDENT FLOWS
OUT OF ASIA

....

The most recent United Nations *International Migration* report (2019) indicates that regions in Asia continue to be major net sending (negative net migration)

Table 21.1 Net number of immigrants per period by development group and region, 1950–2020 (thousands)*

Development group/region	1950–60	1960–70	1970–80	1980–90	1990–00	2000–05	2005–10	2010–15	2015–20
More developed	271	5,965	13,109	12,812	23,767	16,452	16,945	14,527	14,010
Less developed	-271	-5,965	-13,109	-12,812	-23,767	-16,452	-16,945	-14,527	-14,010
Europe	-4,637	-131	3,856	3,984	8,130	9,179	8,643	6,890	6,805
Northern America	4,111	4,182	7,863	7,981	14,791	6,385	6,751	6,199	5,982
Oceania	832	1,225	379	964	674	508	1,186	957	781
N. Afr. & W. Asia	-240	-1,114	-1,573	201	-2,617	151	4,010	1,950	225
Sub-Saharan Africa	-531	-825	-1,270	-2,978	-2,002	-955	-1,344	-2,485	-1,566
LAC	-1,612	-3,818	-6,188	-7,460	-8,972	-5,331	-3,793	-2,830	-2,607
E. & SE Asia	742	-177	-1,101	313	-2,546	-4,762	-5,634	-2,311	-2,850
Ce. & S. Asia	1,336	659	-1,939	-3,005	-7,459	-5,176	-9,819	-8,370	-6,770

Note: * Figures reflect only movements from or to countries located outside the region or group.
Source: United Nations (2019, p. 22).

regions.[1] For the 2015–2020 period, Central and South Asia was the largest sending region in the world, followed by East and South-East Asia. Both regions have generally experienced negative net migration since the 1970s (Table 21.1). The top sending countries during the 2000–2020 period for East and South-East Asia were China (372,000 per annum), the Philippines and Myanmar (around 200,000 each) while for Central and South Asia, they were India (478,000), Bangladesh (445,000), Nepal (179,000), and Pakistan (162,000).

International students from Asia also form the largest group enrolled in tertiary education programs at all levels, totaling 2.1 million and 56 percent of all mobile students across the OECD in 2017. Two-thirds of Asian students study abroad in a narrow range of destination countries: Australia, Canada, Japan, the United Kingdom, and the United States. Between 2013 and 2016, Asia also experienced the largest growth rate (26 percent) in the emigration of tertiary-level students, relative to other regions (OECD, 2019b).[2]

---

[1] Net migration refers to the difference between the number of immigrants and the number of emigrants, irrespective of citizenship.

[2] Japan is the preferred Asian destination among OECD and partner countries, with 164,000 international students, just above China with 157,000 foreign students: they each have a share of 4 percent in the international education market in OECD and partner countries and about 3 percent globally in 2017 (OECD, 2019a).

Projections estimate that China and India, which together accounted for 40 percent of the OECD-G20 pool of tertiary-educated young adults in 2015, should keep their overall rank in 2030. While China's contribution is likely to fall by 4 percentage points in the next decade, mainly due to its decreasing population, India's will significantly increase (OECD, 2019a).

The top countries of origin of international students in the United States has changed significantly over time. In 1949–1950, Canada, Taiwan, India, and several European and Latin American countries were the major sending countries. When national-origin quotas were eliminated following the Immigration Act of 1965, students from Asian countries began to predominate (Zong and Batalova, 2018). Students from China have consistently comprised the largest numbers over the past decade (International Institute of Education, 2019).

For the Asian source countries, a central concern is how many and how long their students stay abroad, since this may be considered a significant loss of human capital. The most recent available data on international student stay rates in the United States in science and engineering shows that a high percentage of doctoral recipients with temporary visas—ranging between 64 and 71 percent between 2003 and 2017—stayed in the United States five years after obtaining their degree. Those from China and India, however, saw a decline in their stay rates from 93 percent and 90 percent, respectively, in 2003, to 84 percent and 85 percent, respectively, in 2013. From 2013 to 2017, the rates remained stable. This shows that while China and India still have the highest stay rates, they have decreased gradually over time. In general, countries such as Taiwan, South Korea, and Japan have had below-average stay rates throughout the 2000s. South Korea, unlike China and India, shows more fluctuations over time—its five-year stay rates increased from 2003 to 2007 (36 percent to 58 percent), decreased from 2007 to 2011 (58 percent to 42 percent), then increased again to 57 percent in 2017 (Finn, 2014; National Science Board, 2020).

3. FACTORS AFFECTING RETURN MIGRATION

Given the large outflow of students from Asia, much research has examined the factors that influence student stay rates. A possible framework for understanding these relationships might consist of various personal, professional, and societal variables, each acting as either a push or pull factor in the decision to stay or leave:

Duration. Short-term stay rates are much higher than medium-term stay rates (Finn, 2014).

Level of study. In general, medium- to long-term stay rates of doctoral students and researchers tend to be higher than those of undergraduate students. That is, those with more advanced degrees tend to have higher stay rates (Wang, 2012). Not only do international students comprise a much larger percentage of enrollments at the doctoral level

(22 percent) than at the bachelor's level (6 percent) (OECD, 2019a), but those doctoral students are also more likely to stay.

Field of study. Stay rates of international students enrolled in the natural sciences or in a technical field tend to be higher than for those enrolled in the social sciences and humanities. In 2017, doctoral recipients in the social sciences had a significantly lower stay rate (52 percent) than the average across all fields (71 percent). Stay rates have been especially higher in the field of life sciences (Finn, 2014) and these patterns have changed over time. In the United States, for example, stay rates for biology majors underwent a dramatic reversal, with very low stay rates in the 1980s and the highest in the 2000s, due to national policy and funding shifts (Kim et al., 2011).

Economic and political conditions in the country of origin. Students from less developed countries tend to display higher stay rates than their peers from developed countries (Vasiljeva, 2014). Chinese and Indian international students, for example, as mentioned earlier, are usually among those with the highest stay rates (Wang, 2012). Altbach (1991) argued that return rates for Taiwanese and South Koreans only began to increase as economic development took off in those countries in the 1980s and 1990s. Periods of economic or political crises can also act as push/pull factors that contribute to changes in stay rates. For example, as a result of the Asian financial crisis in 1997–1998, the Korean labor market for PhDs declined and stay rates for Korean PhDs in the United States increased (Freeman et al., 2008). Chinese students remained abroad following times of political crises such as Tiananmen Square and the transfer of Hong Kong's sovereignty (Zweig and Changgui, 1995).

Mode of financing. Receiving a fellowship, employer support, or foreign government financial assistance as the primary source of funding lowers stay rates significantly since students are usually required to return home to work for the funding body upon graduation. Receiving a teaching assistantship in the host country, however, increases stay rates (Kim et al., 2011).

Gender. Female international students tend to have higher stay rates than their male counterparts (Kim et al., 2011; Finn 2014), perhaps due to the availability of more degree-relevant job opportunities for women in the host country than the home country. The more hierarchical the society in the home country, the more likely males return home, suggesting that male students self-select to return home where they can secure relatively high social positions (Vasiljeva, 2014).

Continuing generation status. International students with doctoral degrees with parents who had received undergraduate or advanced degrees were more likely to stay than first-generation international students (Kim et al., 2011). More educated families may be more supportive of their children pursuing educational opportunities and academically related careers either at home or abroad.

Receipt of undergraduate education in the host country. International doctorates who received their bachelor's degrees in the host country are twice as likely to stay. In the case of the United States, Chinese, Indian, and Korean students were always much more likely to stay (compared to the Canadian reference group) (Kim et al., 2011). Studying in the host country at an earlier age enhances greater embeddedness in, acculturation to, and identification with the host country that can influence stay rates.

Family formation. Married students are more likely to stay than single students.

Securing employment. Securing a job increases stay rates of international students (Bijwaard and Wang, 2016).

Non-economic host country characteristics. Non-economic host country characteristics such as linguistic or cultural similarities with the home country, the presence of a larger diaspora in the host country, and increasing geographical distance between the home and host countries are all correlated with higher stay rates of international students.

Economic differences between home and host countries. Earnings increases in the host country increase long-term stay rates while both higher degrees of income inequality in the home country and higher returns to education in the home country decrease stay rates (Bratsberg, 1995). Similarly, Rosenzweig (2008) showed that if the skill price in the source country doubles, the stay rate decreases by 32 to 41 percent. Foreign students from Asian countries were in general less likely to stay in the United States after they completed their study program, but they were also found to react more sensitively to changes in skill prices.

In addition to understanding the factors that affect stay rates, perhaps the most important question is whether the best students and researchers are more likely to stay. The evidence indicates that this is indeed the case. Those within the highest category of productivity (measured as number of publications weighted by publishing journals' impact factors) were approximately twice as likely to stay in the United States (Van Bouwel and Veugelers, 2012; Gaulé, 2014). For Chinese scientists with foreign doctoral degrees, the higher the ranking of the institution from which they received their doctorates, the more likely those scientists stayed abroad (Tian, 2013).

4. Empirical Evidence of Return Migration

If students do not stay, do they return home? Reliable return migration statistics in the country of origin are less abundant, but case studies suggest that substantial numbers of students and researchers in some country contexts do in fact return home. For example, between 1950 and 1998, 3,337,174 Taiwanese students went abroad to study and one-fifth (20 percent) returned, comprising about 30 percent of masters and doctorates in the country during this period (Tsay, 2003). Largely due to aggressive government policies and measures incentivizing return, the share of returnees in the total stock of masters and doctorates in the country was 31, 28, and 32 percent in the 1970s, 1980s, and 1990s, respectively. Between 1950 and 1994, male returnees comprised a much higher percentage (62.9 percent) than female returnees (37.1 percent). Also, the share of returnees with doctorate degrees declined over time from 28 percent in 1976–1979 to 16 percent in 1980–1995 to 13 percent in 1996–1998. The share of returnees specializing in the fields of science and technology dropped from around 40 percent in the 1980s to 34 percent or lower in the 1990s. However, engineering majors increased substantially from 46.6 percent in 1975–1979 to 70 percent in 1990–1995, reflecting the process of Taiwan's economic development during this time period.

In the case of South Korea, there was a dramatic reversal between the 1960s and 1980s. Over 80 percent of those who received their PhDs in science and engineering in the 1960s chose to stay in the United States where they had studied; by 1987, almost two-thirds of those who had received their PhDs in the 1980s chose to return (Song, 1997). However, the evidence also indicates that most of these PhD returnees only stayed in Korea temporarily, moving back (mostly to the United States) after a short stay.

In the case of China, between 1978 and 1998, 110,000 out of the 320,000 Chinese government-sponsored students who went to study abroad returned and among those who studied abroad in the United States (53 percent), the return rate was only 18.8 percent (Keren et al., 2003). In 2014, as many as 459,800 Chinese students studied abroad while as many as 364,800 returned home, showing a sharp increase since 2008 (Hao et al., 2017). Tian (2013) estimates that over 2.2 million, or 79.9 percent of Chinese overseas students who had completed their tertiary or postgraduate studies had returned to China by the end of 2015. In 2017, the Ministry of Human Resources and Social Security claimed to have attracted 50,000 returnees through various programs and in 2018, reported there to be around 500,000 returnees (versus about 650,000 students studying abroad) (Zwetsloot, 2020).

Despite the impression these statistics provide of a "reverse Chinese brain drain," stay rates in talent-receiving countries remain high. For example, stay rates for US-trained Chinese AI doctorates remained stable at around 90 percent from 2014 to 2018 (Zwetsloot et al., 2019). Also similar to South Korean PhD returnees, many Chinese PhDs have been noted to be *guihai*, or "returning overseas," staying in China only temporarily (Kennedy, 2019). This mixed picture suggests that a combination of economic and non-economic push/pull factors are at work, as noted in the framework above, such as the country's rising levels of wealth as well as perceived discrimination, politicization of universities and companies in China, lower quality of colleagues, internet censorship, and unattractiveness of a network-based (rather than a merit-based) system.

5. CONSEQUENCES OF RETURN MIGRATION

Another major area of research has focused on the consequences (or, seen another way, contributions) of returnees to home country growth and development after acquiring skills from abroad. Case studies for Asian countries are well documented.

For example, in the case of Taiwan, by 1987, 20 percent of the executives of large Taiwanese firms were former migrants and returnees became important investors and entrepreneurs, particularly in the design sector (Kenney et al., 2013). In the case of China, returnee entrepreneurs working in China's high-tech firms created significant spillover effects that promoted innovation in other local high-tech firms (measured as patents per employee of a firm) (Filatotchev et al., 2011). Similarly, several studies have documented the significant role of Indian returnees in building the Indian information technology (IT) industry that took place since the 1990s (Nanda and Khanna, 2010).

In the higher education sector, returnees have contributed to areas such as academic leadership, research productivity, and international research collaboration. For example, Welch and Hao (2013) point out that returnees comprise as high as 78 percent of presidents of public universities, 63 percent of PhD holders, and 72 percent of directors of research labs. A more recent study by Ma and Pan (2015) found that 25 of the 39 presidents of the prestigious "985" group of universities were returnees.

Murakami (2014) found a positive relationship between Japanese researchers returning from the United States and the number of international co-publications with American researchers. Similarly, a recent study by Jiang and Shen (2019) demonstrates that Chinese PhD returnees trained in European institutions had co-authored with their advisors and continued to maintain academic research ties with them following their return. A few studies, though, such as that by Shin et al. (2014) who examine the cases of Malaysia, Hong Kong, and South Korea, present contradictory results, suggesting that returnees who are foreign degree holders tend to be less productive in research than their colleagues with domestic degrees.[3]

The evidence discussed so far assumes that returnees contribute to their home countries through permanent return migration. More recent work on "brain circulation," however, recognizes that migrants can also contribute their skills and expertise while living abroad, whether it be in the country where they received their education or in other transit countries where they moved upon graduation. Even though citizens of a country may not return home at all or decide to leave their home country for a second time after a temporary return, their ties and networks with their home country can contribute less tangible but equally important benefits, such as enhanced trust and cooperation, information sharing, improved access to market information, fostering trade and capital flows, influencing home country institutions, norms, and values, and inducing further migration flows.

This represents a significant shift in conceptualizing talent flows, from one that was largely based on the value of human capital, to an expanded view that also encompasses the value of social capital. While the conventional human capital approach considered the movement of talent as a zero-sum game in which the host country receives a net inflow of human capital from the home country, enhancing the competitiveness of the host country at the home country's expense (or vice versa), the emerging approach emphasizes mutually beneficial ties between home and host countries,

---

[3] Research productivity in this study was measured as the number of refereed journal articles and authored or edited books and book chapters published in the past three years (see Shin et al., 2014, p. 471).

creating a win–win, positive sum situation for both sides. Under a social capital logic, contributions of non-returnees who engage with their home country can be just as valuable as the contributions of returnees.

However, major data constraints and caveats associated with talent migration statistics still need to be addressed to better understand the contributions of returnees. The first constraint is simply the frequent lack of available data on return rates. There may be good-quality data on stay rates in the country of study, but data on return rates in the country of origin are lacking. This is true of many developing countries, but even of economically advanced ones (e.g., Singapore does not have any publicly available data on return rates).

In terms of quality, there is a need for more fine-grained data and better indicators. For example, measuring different skill levels of returnees (and their impact) is often a key variable in return migration studies, but most studies use educational attainment to distinguish between low and high skilled due to data availability reasons, which only offers a rough differentiation of skill levels. Additional measures, such as occupational attainment and/or income levels of returnees, are often unavailable, compelling researchers to rely on the same set of indicators.

More fine-grained, consistent, systematic data on the educational and professional career trajectories of returnees over time (not just whether or not they return and static characteristics) would also be helpful to advance current debates on the extent of returnee impact (both short- and long-term). Due to these and other limitations, the findings on the consequences of returning talent vary due to uneven data and data sources across countries, the specific group being studied, the field/level of study, the combination of host and source countries being studied, and the time period under investigation.

6. Policies for Return Migration in Asia

Historically, strong state intervention played an important role in shaping return migration policies in Asia. In the 1960s and 1970s, for example, when Taiwan was a developing nation suffering from severe outmigration and very low return rates of its scientists and engineers, the government played an active role in fostering the development of the semiconductor and electronics industries through the creation of public industrial research institutions and parks in the 1980s. Throughout the 1990s, many US-educated Taiwanese engineers began to return home, through active government recruitment and opportunities created by such infrastructures, resulting in higher return rates. In 1980, there were less than 100 returnees employed in the Hsin-Chu Science-based Industrial Park established by the National Science Council, but this number rapidly increased to

3,000 in 1998 and 5,000 in 2000. The proportion of returnees among total employees was less than 1 percent in the 1980s but reached 5.2 percent in 2000s (Tsay, 2003).

Similarly, in the case of South Korea, large numbers of highly educated Koreans left South Korea throughout the 1950s and 1960s, with very few returning home. In 1967, the percentages of non-returning students were as high as 87, 97, and 91 percent among Korean engineers, natural scientists, and social scientists, respectively. As in the case of Taiwan, a weak industrial base, poor R&D infrastructure, and the limited capacities of higher education institutions offered neither employment opportunities nor incentives for return. In the 1970s and 1980s, however, the South Korean government, with strong industry development strategies, targeted premier R&D institutes to support specific industries, and hence aimed to recruit the best to return home. Through such concerted government efforts, South Korea was able to recruit back many ethnic Korean scientists living in industrialized countries, especially in the United States.

In China, increasingly low rates of return of overseas students and scholars (*liuxuesheng*) since the 1990s prompted the government as well as various institutions to implement a series of return programs in an effort to attract overseas Chinese academics back to China. Throughout the 1990s, the Chinese government established a number of science parks (e.g., the Zhong Guan Cun Science Park) and R&D zones to attract returnees. The majority of the programs initiated in the 1990s and 2000s were primarily designed to encourage eventual permanent return, including for example, the Cheung Kong Scholars Program (which appoints outstanding scientists to professorships at Chinese universities), the National Science Fund for Distinguished Young Scholars (awards research grants to promising scientists), and the Hundred/Thousand/Ten Thousand Talents programs (awards research grants to produce outstanding Chinese researchers). Yet, despite such efforts, studies suggest that while these programs have triggered higher return rates overall, they have largely failed to achieve a reverse brain drain of the best and the brightest, top-tier talent (Zweig and Wang, 2013).

Countries throughout Asia have adopted other variations of return migration policies. While not as aggressively as countries in East Asia, India's return migration policies have also encouraged Indian academics abroad to return to work as faculty or scientists in India through grants and fellowships (e.g., the Ramalingaswami Fellowship). Another example is Malaysia's Returning Expert Program (REP), implemented in 2011, which offered fiscal incentives and legal benefits to its high-skilled Malaysian diaspora to return to work in Malaysia. A recent impact assessment of the program finds that the REP has been effective in attracting migrants to fill Malaysia's skill needs and there are large net benefits to the program when measured in fiscal terms.

Both "Contact Singapore" (established in 1998) and the SkillsFuture (established in 2015) initiatives partly aimed to attract back Singaporeans living overseas. Other initiatives have targeted Singaporean graduate students abroad through financial inducements and relaxing restrictions for foreign degrees. Such direct financial incentives, however, may be problematic in certain respects because they may have simply subsidized individuals who were likely to return anyway, or may backfire by arousing resentment among non-migrants (as in the case of Singapore) or by encouraging more people to emigrate in order to receive these benefits upon return.

Return migration continues to be a major policy agenda for Asian countries, especially for those countries that have a preference for ethnic returnees rather than attracting foreigners. However, attracting top talent through return migration policies alone remains challenging, suggesting that factors that are more difficult to change such as the social, cultural, educational, and environmental factors discussed earlier, may need to be addressed more seriously. For example, students from countries characterized by large gender gaps and hierarchical values have been shown to positively impact stay rates (Vasiljeva, 2014).

Since top talent often hesitates to return home permanently, countries such as China and South Korea have also initiated short-term, temporary stay programs in recent years. For example, China increasingly stresses that its overseas citizens "serve the country" over "returning to serve the country" and its Thousand Talents short-term programs reflect this expansion in the character of its policies.

An interesting observation is that given that most countries in Asia are not countries of immigration, policies for talent recruitment tend to be limited in scope and set specific targets (recruiting high-performing academics or offering professorships to select individuals, for example), in contrast to the comprehensive points-based (Australia and Canada) or employment-based (United States) migration regimes of traditional destination countries. It may also be possible to distinguish between an "East Asian, developmental, state-driven model" versus a largely "market-driven model" of return migration policies. Due to their legacies as development states, the return migration policies adopted by countries in East Asia continue to be largely government-led. This is in stark contrast to the market-driven approach adopted by countries such as Australia and India.

7. Conclusions

Countries in the Asia-Pacific region continue to be a major source of the world's student migrants. For the Asian source countries, a central concern is the extent and nature of those students who decide to stay abroad versus return home, since a large net outflow of students (a trend that is likely to continue) may be considered a significant loss of human capital investment. The factors that influence return migration are multiple and complex, and vary across national contexts and over time. Countries in Asia also vary widely in their choice of policies to encourage return migration, depending on their level of development, specific needs, and availability of resources.

It is worth noting that as geopolitical tensions intensify, there may be significant implications for outbound student mobility from and return migration to, the Asian region. Policy conversations in major receiving countries around the national security implications of talent and technology transfer, including the United States, Australia, Canada, Britain, Netherlands, and Japan, have been taking place over the last few years. For example, the Australian government created the University Foreign Interference Taskforce in 2019, which published guidelines on incorporating security into assessments of foreign research collaborations. The United States has presented a string of unfriendly policies and rhetoric since 2018 towards international students, including suspending visas for Chinese graduate students, conducting federal investigations of researchers suspected of working on behalf of government agencies, and enhancing scrutiny of STEM students from China and Chinese talent programs such as the Thousand Talents Program due to national security concerns—actions that will likely discourage students from studying abroad. These students may either choose to stay at home and attend international programs or consider alternative study abroad destinations (such as Britain or Australia) that provide attractive options such as a shorter schooling period for achieving graduate degrees, a friendlier immigration experience, and longer post-study leave periods for international students. At the same time, students and workers already residing abroad are likely to return home or move elsewhere if they continue to face hostility in the host country. President Trump's suspension of issuance of new H-1B and other work-related visas and extended restrictions on new green cards, for example, was and may continue to be felt most strongly among Asian skilled workers, especially Indian and Chinese nationals, who make up more than half of the 85,000 H1-B visa holders each year, perhaps resulting in more overseas talent returning home over time.

Lastly, fears about and practical constraints related to the coronavirus pandemic may possibly influence the volume and pattern of student flows. Uneasiness regarding sudden changes in visa, travel restrictions and university policies, general health concerns, and uncertainty about the future may encourage more students to take gap years or modify their study abroad plans altogether, significantly reducing outbound student mobility from Asia. These students may instead choose to study abroad in more accessible and nearby countries, perhaps resulting in increased intra-regional student flows, especially to popular Asian study abroad destinations such as Japan or South Korea.

References

Altbach, P. (1991). "Impact and adjustment: Foreign students in comparative perspective." *Higher Education*, 21/3, 305–323.

Bijwaard, G. and Wang, Q. (2016). "Return migration of foreign students." *European Journal of Population*, 32, 31–54.

Bratsberg, B. (1995). "The incidence of non-return among foreign students in the United States." *Economics of Education Review*, 14/4, 373–384.

Filatotchev, I., Liu, X., Lu, J., and Wright, M. (2011). "Knowledge spillovers through human mobility across national borders: Evidence from Zhongguancun Science Park in China." *Research Policy*, 40/3, 453–462.

Finn, M. G. (2014). "Stay rates of foreign doctorate recipients from U.S. universities, 2009." Oak Ridge, TN: Oak Ridge Institute for Science and Education.

Freeman, R., Stephan, P., and Trumpbour, J. (2008). "Career patterns of foreign born scientists and engineers trained and or working in the US" (Workshop Report). http://www.nber.org/*sewp/Workshop.Report.November.2007.pdf, accessed July 21, 2020.

Gaulé, P. (2014). "Who comes back and when? Return migration decisions of academic scientists." *Economics Letters*, 124/3, 461–464.

Hao, X., Yan, K., Guo, S., and Wang, M. (2017). "Chinese returnees' motivation, post-return status and impact of return: A systematic review." *Asian and Pacific Migration Journal*, 26/1, 143–157.

International Institute of Education (2019). "Number of international students in the United States hits all-time high." https://www.iie.org/Why-IIE/Announcements/2019/11/Number-of-International-Students-in-the-United-States-Hits-All-Time-High#:~:text=The%20total%20number%20of%20international,total%20U.S.%20higher%20education%20population, accessed July 8, 2020.

Jiang, J. and Shen, W. (2019). "International mentorship and research collaboration: Evidence from European-trained Chinese PhD returnees." *Frontiers of Education in China*, 14/2, 180–205.

Kennedy, A. (2019). "China's rise as a science power: Rapid progress, emerging reforms, and the challenge of illiberal innovation." *Asian Survey*, 59/6, 1022–1043.

Kenney, M., Breznitz, D., and Murphree, M. (2013). "Coming back home after the sun rises: Returnee entrepreneurs and growth of high tech industries." *Research Policy*, 42/2, 391–407.

Keren, L., Guo, F., and Ping, H. (2003). "China: Government policies and emerging trends of reversal of the brain drain." In R. Iredale, F. Guo, and S. Rozario (eds.), *Return Migration in the Asia Pacific*. Cheltenham, UK and Northampton, MA, USA: Edward Elgar Publishing, 88–111.

Kim, D., Bankart, C., and Isdell, L. (2011). "International doctorates: Trends analysis on their decision to stay in the US." *Higher Education*, 62, 141–161.

Ma, Y. and Pan, S. (2015). "Chinese returnees from overseas study: An understanding of brain gain and brain circulation in the age of globalization." *Frontiers of Education in China*, 10/2, 306–329.

Murakami, Y. (2014). "Influences of return migration on international collaborative research networks: Cases of Japanese scientists returning from the US." *The Journal of Technology Transfer*, 39/4, 616–634.

Nanda, R. and Khanna, T. (2010). "Diasporas and domestic entrepreneurs: Evidence from the Indian software industry." *Journal of Economics & Management Strategy*, 19/4, 991–1012.

National Science Board (2020). *2020 National Science Board Science & Engineering Indicators: The State of U.S. Science & Engineering*. NSB-2020-1.

OECD (2019a). *Education at a Glance 2019: OECD Indicators*. Paris: OECD Publishing. https://doi.org/10.1787/f8d7880d-en.

OECD (2019b). *International Migration Outlook 2019*. Paris: OECD Publishing. https://doi.org/10.1787/c3e35eec-en.

Rosenzweig, M. R. (2008). "Higher education and international migration in Asia: Brain circulation." In J. Y. Lin and B. Pleskovic (eds.), *Higher Education and Development*. Washington, DC: The World Bank, 59–84.

Shin, J. C., Jung, J., Postiglione, G. A., and Azman, N. (2014). "Research productivity of returnees from study abroad in Korea, Hong Kong, and Malaysia." *Minerva*, 52/4, 467–487.

Song, H. (1997). "From brain drain to reverse brain drain: Three decades of Korean experience." *Science, Technology and Society*, 2/2, 317–345.

Tian, F. (2013). "Skilled flows and selectivity of Chinese scientists at global leading universities between 1998 and 2006." *Journal of Science and Technology Policy in China*, 4/2, 99–118.

Tsay, C. (2003). "Taiwan: Significance, characteristics and policies on return skilled migration." In R. Iredale, F. Guo, and S. Rozario (eds.), *Return Migration in the Asia Pacific*. Cheltenham, UK and Northampton, MA, USA: Edward Elgar Publishing, 112–135.

United Nations, Department of Economic and Social Affairs, Population Division (2019). *International Migration 2019: Report* (ST/ESA/SER.A/438).

Van Bouwel, L. and Veugelers, R. (2012). "An 'elite brain drain': Are foreign top PhDs more likely to stay in the U.S.?" Working Paper, Faculty of Business and Economics, Katholieke Universiteit Leuven, Belgium.

Vasiljeva, K. (2014). "On the importance of macroeconomic factors for the foreign student's decision to stay in the host country." Economics Working Papers, No. 2014-17, Aarhus University, Denmark.

Wang, H. (2012). *China's Competition for Global Talents: Strategy, Policy and Recommendations*. Research report. Asia Pacific Foundation of Canada.

Welch, A. and Jie, H. A. O. (2013). "Returnees and diaspora as source of innovation in Chinese higher education." *Frontiers of Education in China*, 8/2, 214–238.

Zong, J. and Batalova, J. (2018). *International Students in the United States*. Migration Policy Institute. https://www.migrationpolicy.org/article/international-students-united-states, accessed July 7, 2020.

Zweig, D. and Changgui, C. (1995). *China's Brain Drain to the United States*. Berkeley: University of California's Institute of East Asian Studies.

Zweig, D. and Wang, H. (2013). "Can China bring back the best? The Communist Party organizes China's search for talent." *The China Quarterly*, 215, 590–615.

Zwetsloot, R. (2020). *China's Approach to Tech Talent Competition: Policies, Results, and the Developing Global Response*. Washington, DC: Center for Security and Emerging Technology.

Zwetsloot, R., Dunham, J., Arnold, Z., and Huang, T. (2019). *Keeping Top AI Talent in the United States*. Washington, DC: Center for Security and Emerging Technology.

CHAPTER 22

ASIA AS A PRODUCER OF KNOWLEDGE

YOUNGSUK CHI AND JOHN VAN ORDEN

1. INTRODUCTION

IN today's hyper-competitive, global knowledge economy, research institutions play a key role in creating innovation and defining future job growth, particularly in the context of country or regional strategies for smart specialization. The generation of knowledge and its economic and societal benefits has long been viewed as a critical component for the modern development of any country or region. In order to discuss this topic in the Asian context, however, it is important to first clarify precisely what is meant by knowledge production. Knowledge manifests in many forms, but this chapter will primarily focus on knowledge transfer from two different viewpoints—scholarly research publications and patents.

Sections 2 and 3 will be centered on scholarly publications, and the various metrics that the scholarly research community uses to track the quantity and impact of publications, collectively known as bibliometrics. Section 4 will focus on knowledge translation by the business sector, an important contributor to research and development initiatives. In examining knowledge production in Asia through these two lenses, we hope to capture a snapshot of where different parts of Asia participate in the knowledge-based economy.

2. SETTING THE STAGE

Asia is a large and diverse continent, and its many countries, regions, and territories approach knowledge production with different policies, priorities, and levels of resource commitment. In the following sections, general trends that hold true across the entire region are discussed where possible, but country-level case studies are also required to highlight the many differences between knowledge producers in Asia.

Throughout this chapter, 46 countries and regions were analyzed by drawing upon, filtering, and examining bibliometric and patent statistics from Elsevier's Scopus database as well as LexisNexis PatentSight. For selected analyses, these 46 countries and regions are broken down into four broad groupings to discuss regional differences in knowledge production within Asia: East Asia, South-East Asia, South Asia, and Australia and New Zealand (The World Bank, 2020a).[1]

These 46 countries and regions have vastly different economies, populations, and geographies. They range from low-income economies such as the Democratic People's Republic of Korea (commonly referred to as North Korea) to high-income economies like Singapore (The World Bank, 2020a), and represent land-locked countries, island nations, net importers, net exporters, and many different cultures, languages, and people. Their governing structures vary from presidential republics to single party leadership.

The purpose of this chapter is not to discuss these many differences, but nonetheless a study of knowledge production within Asia cannot be effective without keeping in mind the political, social, and economic context that drives research and development policy and efficacy across Asia.

One of the largest influencing factors on knowledge production is a country or region's allocation of money to be spent on research and development. Gross Expenditure on Research and Development (GERD) includes money spent funding academic research as well as money spent by private companies on their own internal research and development. GERD varies from less than 0.5 percent of GDP to nearly 4.5 percent of GDP in different parts of Asia, according to data from UNESCO (2020) as well as the OECD (2020).[2] Because it is such an important driver of research and development, many of the trends in knowledge production can be explained through differences in GERD.

---

[1] The 46 countries and regions are those classified by The World Bank (2020a) as part of "East Asia & Pacific" and "South Asia." For this chapter, it was decided the "East Asia & Pacific" category should be further broken down into East Asia, South-East Asia, and Australia and New Zealand in order to analyze and compare these regions' differences in knowledge production. China data includes Hong Kong and Taiwan, but Hong Kong and Taiwan are plotted and discussed individually in this chapter as well. The four groupings are as follows:

East Asia: China, Hong Kong (Semi-Autonomous Region (SAR), China), Japan, Democratic People's Republic of Korea, The Republic of Korea, Macao (SAR, China), Mongolia, and Taiwan (Province of China).

South Asia: Afghanistan, Bangladesh, Bhutan, India, Sri Lanka, Maldives, Nepal, Pakistan.

South-East Asia: American Samoa, Brunei Darussalam, Cambodia, Fiji, French Polynesia, Guam, Indonesia, Kiribati, Lao PDR, Malaysia, Marshall Islands, The Federated States of Micronesia, Myanmar, Nauru, New Caledonia, Northern Mariana Islands, Palau, Papua New Guinea, Philippines, Samoa, Singapore, Solomon Islands, Thailand, Timor-Leste, Tonga, Tuvalu, Vanuatu, Vietnam.

Australia and New Zealand: Australia and New Zealand.

[2] In this chapter, a combination of OECD (2020) and UNESCO (2020) data was used to collect GERD. Where values were missing between supplied data points, these were estimated using interpolation to find the intermediate point or points between supplied data. The interpolation assumes

Figures 22.1a and 22.1b plot GDP vs. GERD for ten countries and regions in Asia.[3,4]

One of the main indicators of economic growth is the rise of GDP. One might expect that GERD will grow with GDP as well, and this is exactly what we find in many cases within Asia (Figures 22.1a and 22.1b). China, for example, is not only the largest economy in Asia, but it has also exhibited large growth in GDP from 2009 to 2018. That growth has been accompanied by a growth in GERD, as the two increased in lock-step over the decade. This means that GERD as a percentage of GDP has remained roughly constant over time in China.[5] This is also the case in many other places in Asia, including Japan, New Zealand, and Hong Kong, where GERD as a percentage of GDP has remained relatively constant since 2009.[6]

Like China, India too has seen increases in its GDP in recent years, although India's GDP is not as large—at $9.3 trillion USD compared to China's $22.1 trillion USD in 2018—and has not grown as much as China's.[7] However, while China's GERD has increased with its GDP, India's GERD shows relatively little growth, resulting in a more horizontal trajectory in Figure 22.1a. This means that as a percentage of GDP, GERD in India has actually fallen since 2009 from 0.7 percent to 0.6 percent in 2018, suggesting that the importance of R&D investment has decreased in India over this time period relative to other programs and priorities.

Conversely, South Korea and Malaysia have both seen growth in GERD outpace their growth in GDP. That means that as a percentage of GDP, GERD has increased over the years. In fact, as of 2018, South Korea has grown its GERD to represent 4.5 percent of its GDP, the highest as a percentage of GDP in Asia, and the second highest in the world only after Israel's 4.94 percent (OECD 2020).

It is also worth noting Japan's contribution of GDP to GERD. In 2009, Japan had almost the same GERD as a percentage of GDP as South Korea, 3.2 percent. While South Korea's GERD grew faster than its GDP since then, Japan's grew in step with its GDP. This has led to consistently high GERD in Japan, at 3.3 percent of GDP in 2018—the second highest GERD as a percentage of GDP in Asia.

The outcome of the different levels of investment in GERD will become clearer as we examine bibliometric and patent data in these different countries and regions. In

---

that the change between two values is linear. If the most recent values were missing, the linear growth rate of the data available for earlier years was extrapolated to estimate a forecast.

[3] Throughout this chapter, the eleven largest knowledge producers by publication output are compared, in addition to the four country groupings (East Asia, South Asia, South-East Asia, and Australia and New Zealand). The 11 largest knowledge producers are: China, India, Japan, Australia, South Korea, Taiwan (Province of China), Malaysia, Singapore, Hong Kong (SAR, China), and Indonesia.

[4] GERD data for Indonesia is unavailable, so it is not included in Figure 22.1.

[5] In fact, China's GERD as a percentage of GDP has grown slightly from 1.7 percent in 2009 to 2.2 percent in 2018.

[6] GERD as a percentage of GDP among these countries and regions in 2009 and 2018 respectively is: Japan (3.2 percent, 3.2 percent), New Zealand (1.3 percent, 1.4 percent), and Hong Kong (0.7 percent, 0.7 percent)

[7] China's GDP grew by 96 percent from 2009-2018. Its GERD grew by 158 percent. India's GDP grew by 84 percent, while its GERD grew by only 41 percent.

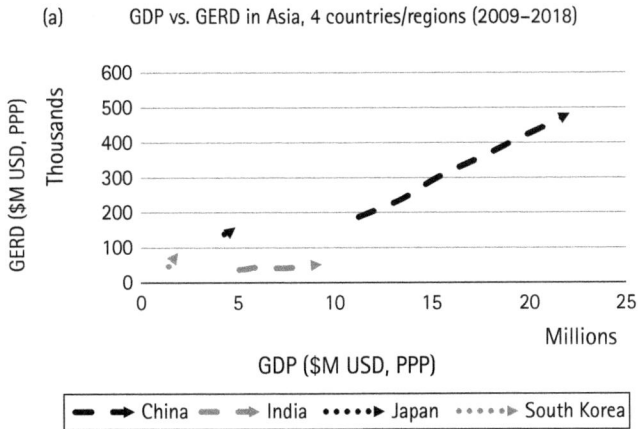

(a)   GDP vs. GERD in Asia, 4 countries/regions (2009–2018)

FIGURE 22.1A GDP vs. GERD in Asia, four countries/regions, 2009–2018

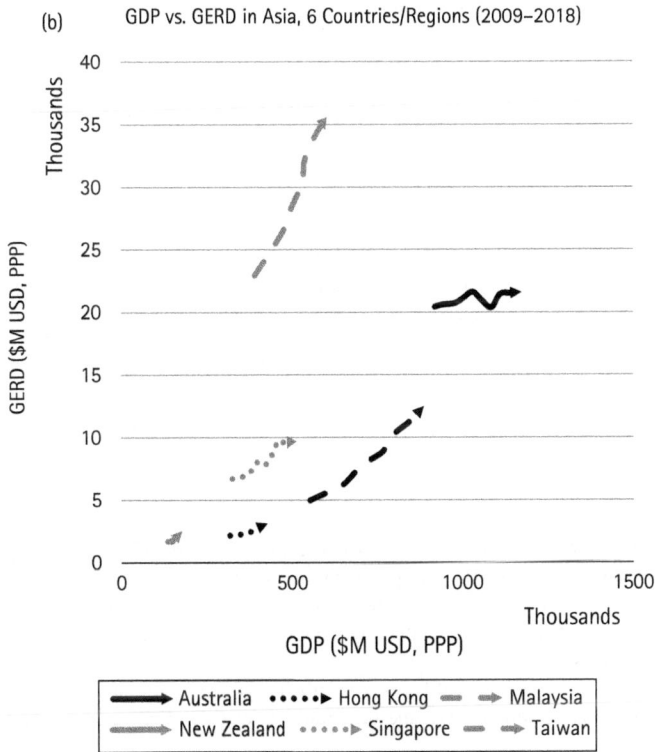

(b)   GDP vs. GERD in Asia, 6 Countries/Regions (2009–2018)

FIGURE 22.1B GDP vs. GERD in Asia, six countries/regions, 2009–2018

particular, as GDP grows, GERD tends to grow along with it in many cases, with the notable exception of India as discussed above. As GERD grows, then, one may expect that more investment in research and development will lead to more knowledge production in the form of scholarly research. As we will see in the coming sections, this is often, but not always, the case.

3. BIBLIOMETRICS

Although publishers were once predicted to be the very first victims of the internet (Hayes, 1995), some have capitalized on the digital revolution of the 1990s to create citation graphs, enabling the quantitative representation of research around the world. This has led to the wide adoption of bibliometrics to assess the quantity and, in cases, the scholarly impact of the knowledge produced. Today, we can leverage this information to look both more holistically and more granularly at the state of scientific research in Asia. This section will aim to provide readers with meaningful insight into these metrics through analyses and interpretation.

A standard and frequently used indicator with which to begin this journey is arguably one of the most measurable metrics of knowledge—publications.[8] But before attempting to say anything specific about the publication output of Asia, it is useful to first establish the relative size of each country's contribution.

The top 11 producers of scientific research publications in Asia can be seen in Figures 22.2a and 22.2b.[9,10]

As we will see throughout this chapter, China has the highest research production, nearly doubling its annual output from 309,000 publications in 2009 to 605,000 publications in 2018. The data shown in Figures 22.2a and 22.2b are based on whole counting methods—that is, if a paper has been co-authored by one author in China and four authors in Malaysia, then that paper counts equally towards the publication count of both countries as one publication for China and one publication for Malaysia. In contrast, by fractional counting methods, in the above example, the paper would count as 0.2 publications for China and 0.8 publications for Malaysia. In fact, using fractional

---

[8] For the purposes of this discussion, we will use the standard definition of a publication from SciVal (2020), a visualization and analytics platform built on Scopus (Scopus, 2020) data from Elsevier, which includes articles, conference papers, reviews, book chapters, notes, editorials, letters, articles in press, short surveys, errata, books, conference reviews, business articles, abstract reports, retracted publications, and reports.

[9] The dip in Chinese research output from 2014 to 2015 is due to a methodological change in Scopus indexing, resulting in cessation of coverage of a number of titles that did not meet Scopus quality standards.

[10] Here and for all other plots and data unless otherwise specified, the source is Elsevier's Scopus database (Scopus, 2020).

(a)

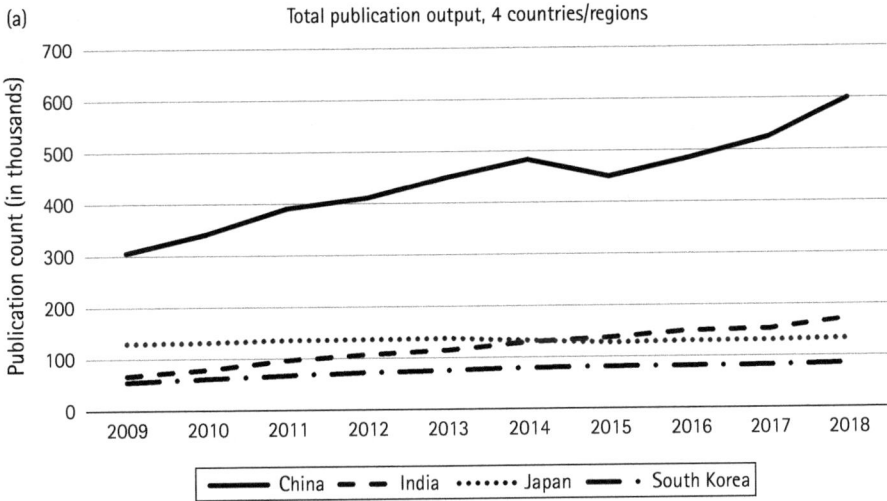

FIGURE 22.2A Total publication output, four countries/regions, 2009–2018

(b)

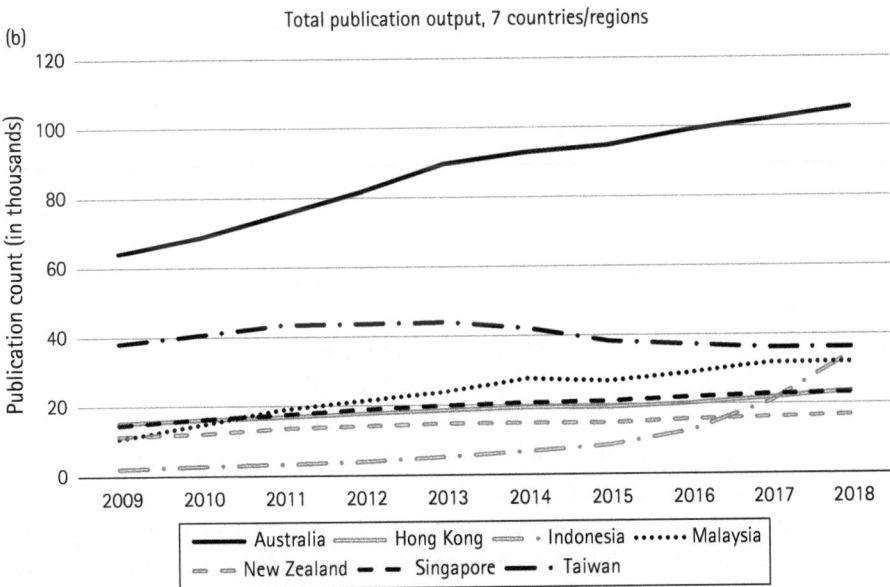

FIGURE 22.2B Total publication output, seven countries/regions, 2009–2018

counting to track research output, China has become the world's number one producer of scientific knowledge as of 2018, the first country to surpass the United States (National Science Foundation, 2018).

But the boom in research output is not a success story only China has earned the right to tell, nor is that growth shared equally throughout all parts of Asia. India has also seen its scientific output surge by 156 percent, and Indonesia and Malaysia have exhibited strong gains of 1,523 percent and 190 percent respectively, all as a percentage increase from 2009 to 2018. Meanwhile, much has been made of Japan's apparent stagnation in scientific research output, as well as its attempts to reignite the levels of growth not seen in the science and technology sector since the late 1990s (National Research Council (US), 2010). An interesting and possibly unique case within Asia, Japan will be re-examined in section 4 for a detailed look at private sector knowledge production.

Lastly, while this chapter focuses primarily on the years 2009–2018 for analysis to ensure the discussion is as up to date and relevant as possible, it is worth noting in broad strokes how publication output has evolved prior to this period in Asia. The Scopus database reliably covers research as far back as 1996. From 1996 to 2009, Asia also saw strong growth in publications almost across the board. This was led by China, India, and South Korea, but reached every country in Asia.[11] More moderate but still significant growth over this time period occurred elsewhere, such as in Australia, New Zealand, Japan, and South-East Asia.[12]

Now that we have looked at publication output across Asia, it is a good time to combine our earlier discussion of GERD with our recent examination of publication output. Plotting the two against each other reveals that there is indeed a strong correlation between the two variables, as seen in Figures 22.3a and 22.3b.

It is difficult to measure the impact of GERD on a region's knowledge production because of the vast number of variables that would need to be controlled for in such a model, however the largest factor is GERD that is spent directly on academic research. While GERD supports everything from research infrastructure, lab assistants, experimental equipment, travel and collaboration costs, and more (OECD, 2020), if GERD is spent on activities that directly lead to publications, we might expect the kind of strong correlation between GERD and publication output that is seen in Figures 22.3a and 22.3b.

One way to interpret this result then, is that countries that fall far above or below the regression line in Figures 22.3a and 22.3b allocate their GERD in different ways. In other words, the data suggests that in some countries and regions, GERD is spent more often on activities resulting in publications, while in other places GERD is not as frequently used to directly drive publication output.

Another angle from which we can approach the question of how GERD affects knowledge production in different parts of Asia is by looking at publication output normalized by two common drivers of scientific research. Of particular interest is (1) monetary investment (GERD), which fuels the development of infrastructure and (2) the researchers themselves, who drive the production of research. Normalizing

[11] China: 33,261 (1996) to 309,427 (2009), India: 21,819 (1996) to 68,587 (2009), South Korea: 10,603 (1996) to 54,997 (2009). None of the 11 largest producers of knowledge saw a decrease in publication output over this time.

[12] Australia: 25,978 (1996) to 63,931 (2009), New Zealand: 4,999 (1996) to 11,536 (2009), Indonesia: 582 (1996) to 2,138 (2009), Philippines: 465 (1996) to 1,239 (2009), Japan: 94,567 (1996) to 129,315 (2009).

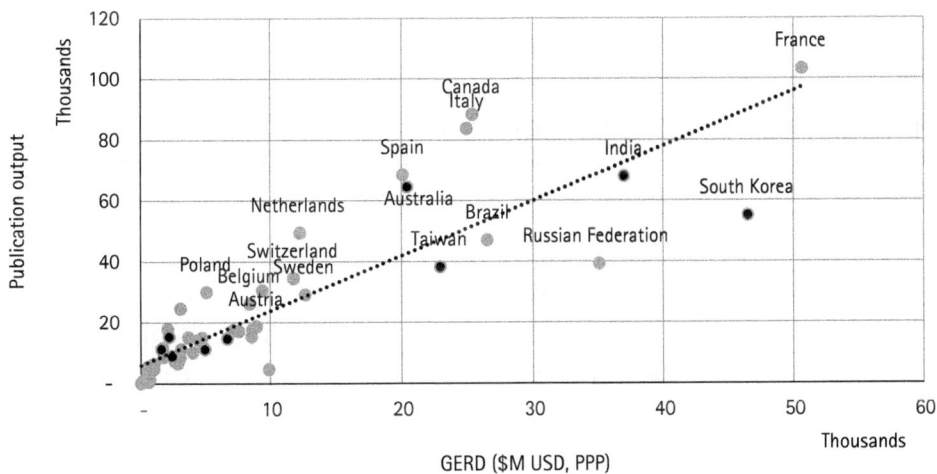

(a) GERD vs. publication output, 61 global countries/regions (2009)

FIGURE 22.3A GERD ($M USD, PPP) vs. publication output, global countries/regions, 2009

Note: Countries and regions in Asia are colored black, while the rest of the world is colored gray.

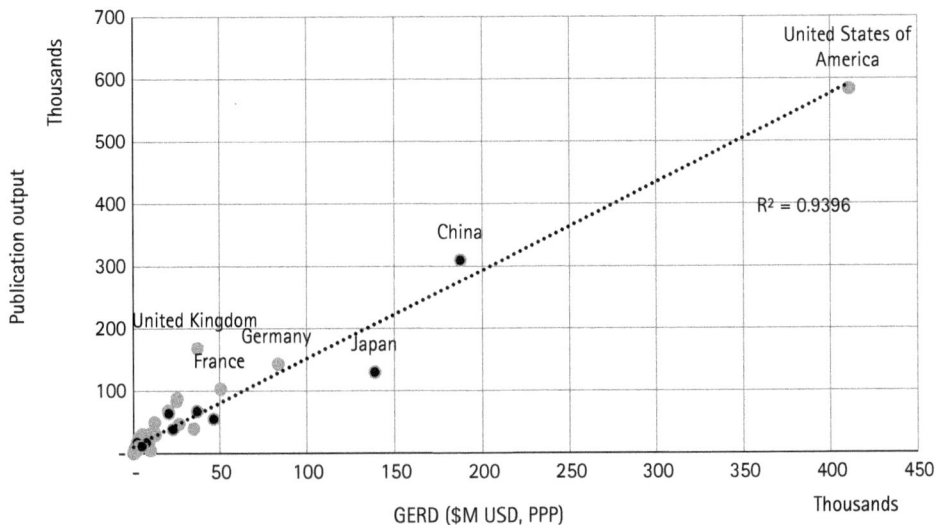

(b) GERD vs. publication output, 56 global countries/regions (2009)

FIGURE 22.3B GERD ($M USD, PPP) vs. publication output, global countries/regions, 2009

Note: Countries and regions in Asia are colored black, while the rest of the world is colored gray.

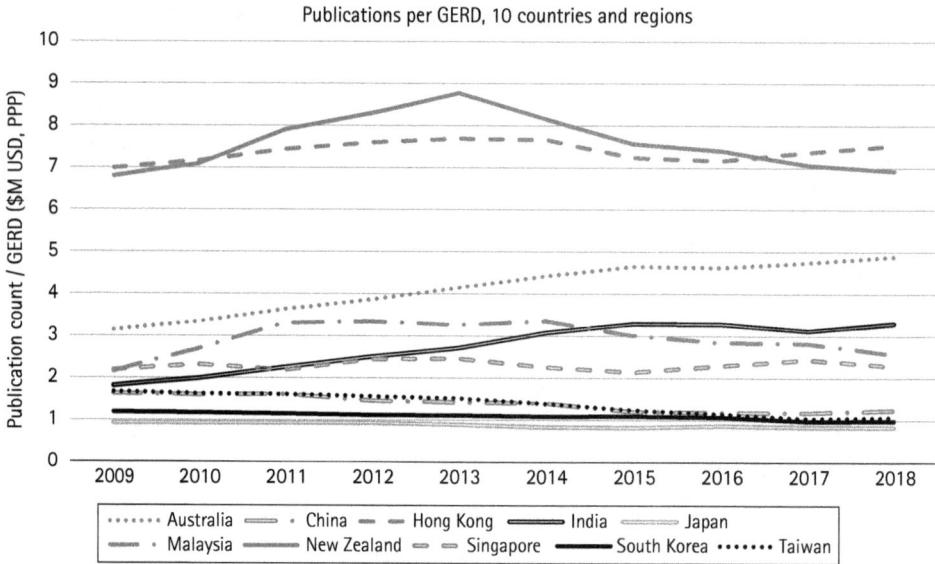

FIGURE 22.4 Publications per GERD ($M USD, PPP) from 2009–2018

publications by GERD and by number of researchers can reveal interesting similarities and groups irrespective of total publication output among countries and regions, as well as provide a better sense of the "efficiency" of their research systems.

3.1 Research Efficiency: Asia's Publications per GERD

Let's begin with publications per $M GERD. As previously mentioned, research investments beget new equipment, fund collaborative research, support research work-flow tools, finance researchers' salaries, and most importantly, provide scientists with the resources they need to design and follow-through with high-quality studies and experiments with long life cycles.

At the high end in terms of publications per $M GERD (Figure 22.4),[13,14] New Zealand and Hong Kong produce the most publications per investment dollar in re-search and development. The reasons for these stand-outs could be anything from government policy to pressure to publish, but the largest factor is likely that these two

---

[13] OECD (2020) data uses 2010 PPP dollars as a baseline, while UNESCO (2020) uses 2005 PPP dollars as a baseline. Elsevier performed comparisons and found that the difference does not make a material difference to trends or rankings, and thus for the purposes of this chapter we will consider this data comparable, despite the different base years.

[14] Data for Indonesia were incomplete or unavailable.

regions tend to spend more of their GERD on activities that relate directly to publishing scholarly research, relative to their peers in Asia.

Meanwhile, despite Japan and South Korea ranking among the top countries in Asia in terms of their GERD as a percentage of GDP, they conversely rank among the lowest in terms of publication output per $M GERD, likely because their GERD is being invested in ways that do not directly lead to the publication of scientific research. The Organisation for Economic Co-operation and Development (OECD) splits GERD into Business Enterprise R&D (BERD), Higher Education R&D (HERD), Government R&D (GOVERD), and Other. In 2014, Japan and South Korea HERD represented only 6.9 percent and 9.0 percent respectively of their total GERD (stats.oecd.org, n.d.). This is the lowest among OECD comparators, including the UK (26.1 percent), US (14.9 percent), China (12.6 percent), and Germany (17.3 percent). In terms of BERD, Japan and Korea have the highest research investment among these same comparators, with 77.3 percent and 78.2 percent BERD respectively.[15] Not only do these values show that Japan and Korea have particularly large private sector investment in R&D compared to higher education investment, but they also remind us that BERD is actually the single largest component of GERD in any country.

Japan and Korea's high BERD may explain the low publication output per $M GERD in both countries. Research in the private sector focuses on different outcomes than higher education research, and private sector researchers also have different incentive schemes and policies that are driven by the nature of the economic and business sector they work within. BERD as a percentage of GERD in Australia was 56 percent in 2013 and 53 percent in 2015, 20 percentage points lower than in Korea and Japan, and Australia has the third most publications per $M GERD in Asia. BERD simply may be utilized to fund R&D that does not as often contribute to publication output as other kinds of R&D.

Conversely, India stands apart from Japan and Korea in its very low BERD, which some have argued is a reason for India's general stagnation in GERD (Ministry of Finance India, 2018) overall (see Figure 22.1a). Much of the GERD in India is direct Government Spending on R&D (GOVERD), making it challenging to compare India directly to other countries where the primary components of GERD are BERD and HERD.[16] Nonetheless, Figure 22.4 seems to indicate that some of India's GOVERD is being dedicated to research that results in publications, with India having the fourth highest publications per GERD in the countries surveyed here.

---

[15] 2014 BERD for comparators: UK (64.4 percent), US (71 percent), China (77.8 percent), and Germany (67.9 percent).

[16] In 2015, India's BERD was approximately 40 percent of GERD, about half of China, Korea, and Japan's BERD as a percentage of GERD. However, India's GOVERD was almost 55 percent of GERD, compared to China's 18 percent, Korea's 12 percent and Japan's 10 percent.

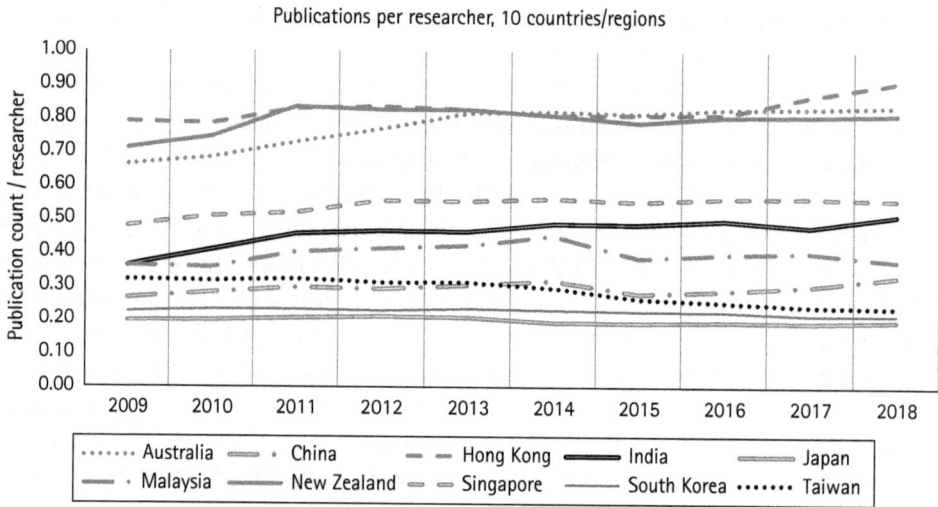

FIGURE 22.5 Publications per researcher in Asia, 2009–2018

Note: Data for Indonesia were incomplete or unavailable.

3.2 Research Efficiency: Asia's Publications per Researcher

Another measure of the efficiency of research is publications per researcher.[17] In Figure 22.5, we can see that when normalized against the number of researchers, New Zealand, Hong Kong, and Australia have a particularly high publication output. In contrast, the number of publications in Japan and South Korea is again the lowest among large knowledge producers in Asia. One possible explanation for this is the different priorities, pressures, incentives, and career progression schemes that may lead researchers in some regions to publish more often, an effect commonly referred to as "publish or perish."

However, there are many other factors that could contribute to the patterns we see in publications per researcher. Because researcher count includes those in the private sector, it is possible that Australia, New Zealand, and Hong Kong have higher numbers of researchers in academia relative to private sector researchers. Because academia tends to prioritize publication, having more researchers in academia would lead to more publications on a per researcher basis. Similarly, because the private sector does not prioritize publications as much as in the academic sector, countries and regions with higher BERD and more private sector researchers would have a lower publication count per researcher. In addition, as many researchers could attest to, the demands on their time include varied activities not necessarily related to publishing, including education,

---

[17] Here the term researcher is defined as any person who carries out academic or scientific research in laboratories, organizations, universities, institutions, etc.

peer review, team management, editorial responsibilities, speaking opportunities, conference attendance, and more, all of which can contribute to researchers publishing more or less often.

A final consideration that may be a factor in the trends visible in Figure 22.5 is language. In order to be indexed in Elsevier's Scopus database, which was the basis for the bibliometric analyses done in this chapter, a publication must meet certain quality standards and have an English title and abstract. While there are no requirements that the publication itself be in English, there are many non-English journals and publications in the world that are not captured by Scopus because they do not have an English language abstract or title.

There is no way of knowing how many publications *are not* in Scopus due to language but we can see that the number of non-English publications in Scopus varies widely by country or region. Five countries and regions have more than 1 percent of publications in a language other than English, but per Figure 22.6, China clearly stands out with nearly 1 in 5 publications being published in Chinese with an English title and abstract. The data in Figure 22.6 suggest that not capturing non-English papers may lead to the under-counting of publications, thereby decreasing the publication count per researcher and GERD.

Unfortunately, to definitively say which of these or other factors lead some countries to contribute higher publication outputs per GERD and per researcher would require more detailed study which is outside the confines of this chapter. However, we hope this question can be investigated in more detail by others in the future.

In conclusion, it is clear that Asian publication output has seen strong growth over the last decade. But what factors might explain these observed trends? First, the impact of funding must be reiterated. GERD is the driving motor of knowledge production and is strongly correlated with knowledge output across the world. In Asia, as with elsewhere, GERD is linked to GDP, and the growth in GDP of many Asian countries and territories

Percentage non-English publications, 2009–2018

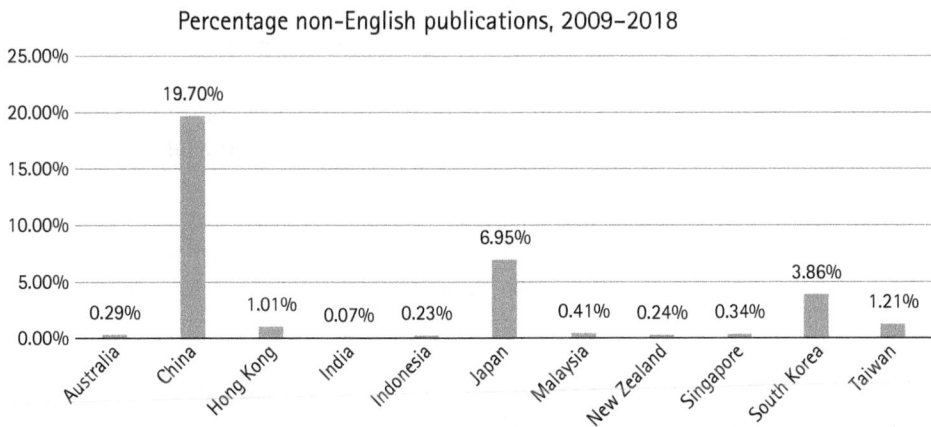

FIGURE 22.6 Percentage of publications from 2009 to 2018 written in a language other than English in each country/region

since 2009 has led to growth in GERD as well. In fact, GERD in East Asia and South Asia grew 280 percent from \$179.3B USD in 1996 to \$680.8B USD in 2018.[18] Chinese GERD alone grew 6,150 percent from \$4.86B USD in 1996 to \$304B USD over the same period (The World Bank, 2020a). Such an enormous increase in funding plays a significant role in driving research output and has led to a growth in publications from Asia, expanding Asia's contribution to the global publication count from 31 percent in 2009 to 41 percent of global output in 2018.[19]

Second, for decades researcher incentives were heavily aligned with publication output. Beginning with Nanjing University's release of its influential Science Citation Index (SCI) in the late 1980s, the emphasis on the number of publications produced became a key factor in determining faculty promotions, awards, and funding applications (Shuo, 2020b). This "publish or perish" pressure has dramatically affected researchers' behavior across Asia, and is still codified in policies across the region. As just one example, take the University Grants Commission's Academic Performance Indicator in India, established in 2010, which puts heavy emphasis on the number of publications for researcher promotion (Das and Chattopadhyay, 2014).

Recently however, many institutions and countries are beginning to recognize the downsides of a quantity focused approach to research, and have begun emphasizing the need for alternative metrics when evaluating researcher performance (Patwardhan, 2019). In 2015, Australia published its National Innovation and Science Agenda (NISA), which began to discourage frequent publishing in favor of collaboration with industry (Department of Industry, Science, Energy, and Resources of Australia, 2015), while Chinese universities are also now being encouraged to reduce their dependence on the SCI metric when evaluating researcher performance (Shuo, 2020a). Although it is too soon to know the impact of such a policy change, a shift to alternative metrics in the future could alleviate the pressure to publish many researchers still face today.

A third possible explanation for the growth in Asian research is the rise of international university rankings produced by organizations like Times Higher Education and QS. It is not uncommon for countries to launch programs to accelerate their universities into the "top 100 globally," at least as defined by these lists. As just two examples, take Japan's Top Global University Project, launched in 2014 (Ministry of Education, Culture, Sports, Science and Technology, Japan, 2014), or Indonesia's plan to enter the top 100 list by hiring foreign rectors, launched in 2019 (The Jakarta Post News Desk, 2019).

It has become clear that university rankings often act as proxies by which many universities show their achievements on the global stage, and a major component of such rankings at institutions like THE (Times Higher Education, 2020) and QS (QS

---

[18] East Asia GERD grew from \$176B to \$658B, or 273% growth, and South Asia GERD grew from \$3.3B to \$22.8B, or 590 percent between 1996 and 2018. (Dollars in 2020 USD.)

[19] Asia (as defined by the 46 countries and territories in this chapter) had 724,796 publications in 2009 and 1,299,105 publications in 2018. Worldwide, there were a total of 2,342,927 publications in 2009 and 3,179,643 publications in 2018.

Quacquarelli Symonds, 2019) is typically the research performance of the institution. More research with higher impact can lead to higher rankings, which in turn can lead to more marketing materials to attract new researchers, more funding, new collaboration opportunities, etc. Ultimately the pressure to increase publication output and quality falls upon researchers, whether this was the initial intention or not.

Within China, rankings have been emphasized at least since the governments launch of the 211 Project in 1995 (Lixu, 2004), which was intended to construct 100 universities for the twenty-first century. This was followed by the 985 Project in 1998 (Zhang, et al., 2013), aimed at creating world first-class universities in China. Today's Double First-Class University system is more dynamic and focused on the disciplinary level (Ministry of Education, Ministry of Finance, National Development and Reform Commission, China, 2017; Department of Education, Skills, and Employment, Australia, 2017) than its predecessor programs, as institutions can be added or removed from the government's classifications. This means internal competition to perform at the level mandated by the government continues to play a role in developing China's university system. As a proxy metric for progress towards government goals, interest in global university rankings continues to grow in China and across Asia, growing publication output and impact with it.

Penultimately, one should take into account changes in human resources—researchers, scientists, lab technicians, etc.—as a key driver in Asia's booming research output. In China, it begins with the opening up and reforms in the last quarter of the twentieth century, during which government restructuring allowed for greater resources and opportunities to flow to China's education, science, and technology sector (Kobayashi et al., 1999). This set the stage for a new generation of talented researchers to grow, creating the basis of human capital to drive scholarly output in China. More recently, the first two decades of the twenty-first century saw not only an emphasis on international collaboration within science that carried over from previous decades, but a new focus on the return to China of researchers abroad. According to one study, in the year 2000, 39K researchers went abroad and 23.4 percent returned home. By 2017 this has risen to 5.2M abroad with an 83.7 percent return rate (Cao et al., 2019).

And China has not been alone in its development of Science and Technology human resources in Asia. South Korean researchers in R&D grew from 99K in 1996 to 412K in 2018—a 316 percent increase in researchers (The World Bank, 2020b) compared to a 13 percent increase in the overall population during the same period. Meanwhile, India and the Philippines have also launched or increased support for programs such as the Visiting Advanced Joint Research Faculty (VAJRA) (Department of Science and Technology, India, 2017) and Balik Program (Department of Science and Technology, Philippines, 2018) respectively to entice researchers abroad to return home and pursue critical scientific issues in Asia.

Finally, the inflow and outflow of researchers in Asia can be viewed as one component of the larger theme of international collaboration. Using co-authorship of research publications, it can be shown that international collaboration in Asia runs the gamut from as high as 52 percent in New Zealand to as low as 17 percent in India (Scopus,

2020). Interestingly, Asia tends to have lower international collaboration rates than countries in Africa, the Middle East, and Europe (Hu et al., 2020). The reasons for this likely include:

(1) A lack of major pan-Asian funding bodies to encourage international collaboration, compared especially to countries in Europe and organizations like Horizon Europe.

(2) Critical levels of investment in research, population, technology adoption, and education that allow many countries in Asia to collaborate effectively within themselves, without needing to search for international research partners.

(3) Language barriers, both between Asian countries and between the English-speaking world of international science, that continue to impact the efficacy of international collaboration.

(4) National funding bodies and policies in many countries that have historically favored applied research because it leads to more immediate economic benefits than basic research. This means there is often a nationalistic slant to research grants awarded by national funding bodies that can hinder international partnerships, as each country views its research investments as a way to drive economic growth (Bentley et al., 2015). Although this phenomenon is not unique to Asia, it may play a role in contributing to lower international collaboration rates.

What effect these lower international collaboration rates have on publication output and publication impact is difficult to quantify, partly because the lost synergies normally generated through international collaboration varies based on collaborating partners, resources, number of authors, and many other factors. Nonetheless it is reasonable to conclude that the lower level of international collaboration may be one of the few factors that is *detracting* from the growth of both publication output and publication quality in Asia.

Taken alone, no single explanation, whether economic, political, or cultural, can explain the explosive growth in Asian knowledge production. But taken together and aligned towards a common goal, these factors could effectively launch Asian research production on such a strong upward trajectory in the first two decades of the twenty-first century that we have observed.

3.3 Research Impact

So far in this discussion, the focus has primarily been on the quantity of knowledge production—publication output. However, of equal importance to researchers and the institutions that fund their work is the quality of knowledge production. Unfortunately, there is no method by which we can objectively measure a subjective trait such as quality. Instead, a common approach used by funders and research managers is to examine the citations received by publications to estimate the academic impact of the research.

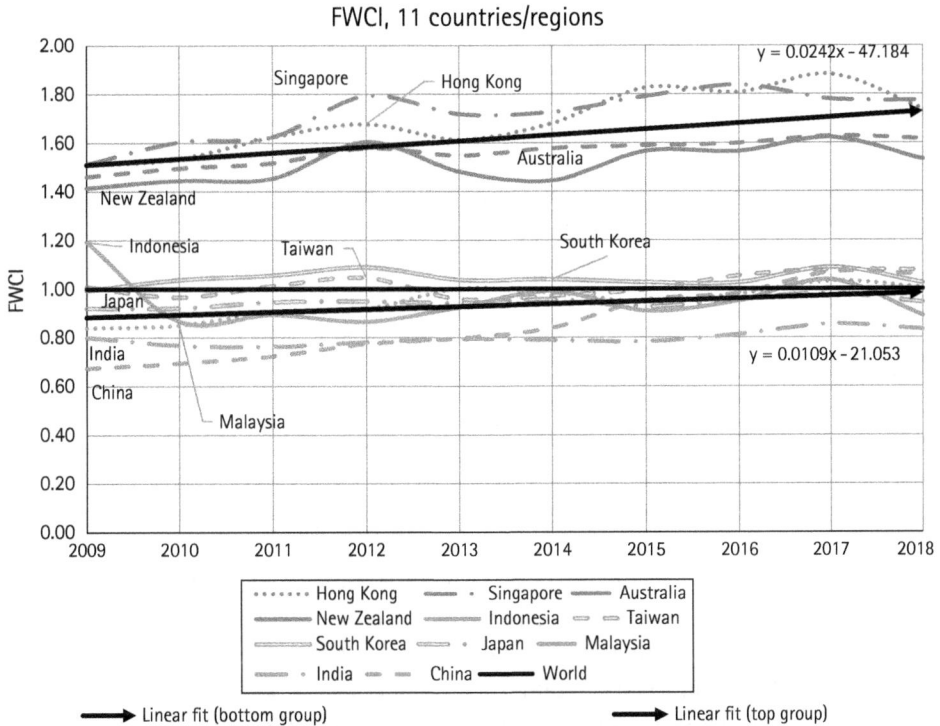

FIGURE 22.7 Field-weighted citation impact of top Asian knowledge producers, 2009–2018

The Field Weighted Citation Impact (FWCI) is an often used proxy for the scholarly impact of a piece of research, and is calculated as the number of citations received by a given paper, normalized by the average number of citations received by all papers of the same year of publication, type of publication, and subject area. The average FWCI across all publications from a country or region provides a means of assessing the influence of a country's research based on citations relative to global levels. Thus, an FWCI of 1.0, the baseline for all publications across all subjects at the global level, is exactly of average "impact" by this metric, while an FWCI greater than 1 means more citations than average, and thus a higher scholarly impact (Elsevier, 2019).

Examining the FWCI of top knowledge producers in Asia from 2009 to 2018 in Figure 22.7 reveals an interesting bifurcation. The top cluster of regions (Hong Kong, Singapore, Australia, and New Zealand) have all individually maintained an FWCI over 1.4 and have also, on average, improved the FWCI of their scientific literature by +0.0242 units per year.[20]

Looking more closely at this top group of four, it is interesting to note that they also represent the top four most efficient regions in terms of publications on a per

---

[20] FWCI of publications in Hong Kong, Singapore, Australia, and New Zealand were averaged for each year, and a linear trendline was applied. The slope of the trendline has units of FWCI units per year.

researcher basis (see Figure 22.5) from 2009 to 2018. Three of the four regions in this group (Australia, New Zealand, and Hong Kong) also represent the three most efficient regions in terms of publications per $M GERD over this time frame (see Figure 22.4). Taken together, the high FWCI and high publication output per researcher and per $M GERD may indicate these regions place a particularly high value on scholarly research.

The lower group of 7 countries and regions in Figure 22.7 are clustered with an FWCI ranging from 0.7 to 1.1 over the same time period, but on average have shown much less FWCI growth at only +0.011 units per annum.[21] This group also includes China, which boosts the FWCI growth due to its large improvement in FWCI since 2009. Remove China from the group and the change in FWCI becomes +0.005 units per year. Although India and Malaysia showed FWCI improvement of 4.0 percent and 19.8 percent[22] from 2009 to 2018 respectively, China's large gain in FWCI is the main exception within this group and is significant enough to warrant a closer look.[23]

China's average FWCI has grown from 0.7 in 2009 to 1.1 in 2018, a 52.5 percent improvement. At the same time, China represents fully 45 percent of all publications in Asia and 16 percent of the publications in the world during the period 2009–2018. Because China's increase in citations has brought up the world average, the normalized nature of the FWCI metric leads to a decline in FWCI in other parts of the world, including the US (-6.7 percent) and Europe (-2.5 percent). Of course, China is not the only place to see growth in FWCI (Stahlschmidt and Hinze, 2018)—South America (2.4 percent), the Middle East (16.1 percent), and Africa (16.5 percent) have all also grown their FWCI since 2009 and contributed to the decline in FWCI in the US and Europe (Stahlschmidt and Hinze, 2016).[24]

As we explored in section 3, Asia is growing the number of publications it produces in most places. Whether or not Asia's growth in publications and FWCI is an early indicator of the rise of Asia more broadly to replace the United States and Europe as the center of science and technology globally is an open debate, but the resources and opportunity for growth in Asia do indicate—at least from this narrow bibliometric perspective—that the possibility exists over the coming decades (Xie et al., 2014).

Before concluding our discussion of these two important metrics however, let us plot FWCI against publication output for top knowledge producers in Asia (Figures 22.8a and 22.8b).

Three of the top 11 knowledge producers show consistent year-to-year growth in both FWCI and publication outputs: China, Malaysia, and Australia. India stands out for its surge in publication output, as mentioned in section 3, but growth in FWCI in India has

---

[21] FWCI of publications in Indonesia, Taiwan, South Korea, Japan, Malaysia, India, and mainland China were averaged for each year, and a linear trendline was applied. The slope of the trendline has units of FWCI units per year.

[22] FWCI percentage increase from 0.75 (2009) to 0.8 (2018) in India and 0.91 (2009) to 0.96 (2018) in Malaysia.

[23] From 2009–2018 the change in FWCI of the other members of this group was: Indonesia (-31.3%, an inflated decrease because 2009 was an outlier year with Indonesia's highest FWCI ever at 1.1), Taiwan (-1.7%), South Korea (0.4%), Japan (0.2%), and China (52.5%).

[24] FWCI as reported by SciVal (2020) in 2009 and 2018.

Publication output vs. FWCI, 11 countries/regions (2009–2018)

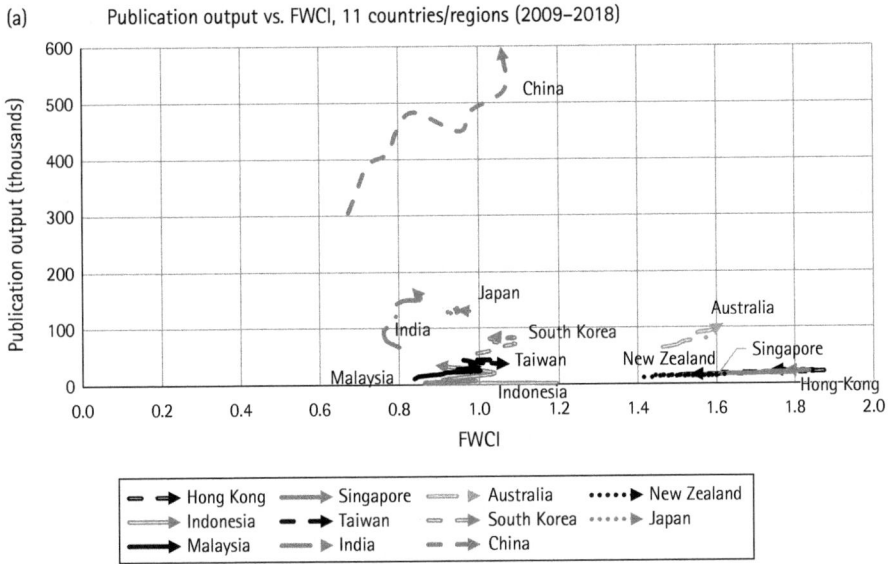

FIGURE 22.8A Change in publication output and FWCI, 2009–2018 (arrowhead indicates 2018)

Publication output vs. FWCI, 6 countries/regions (2009–2018)

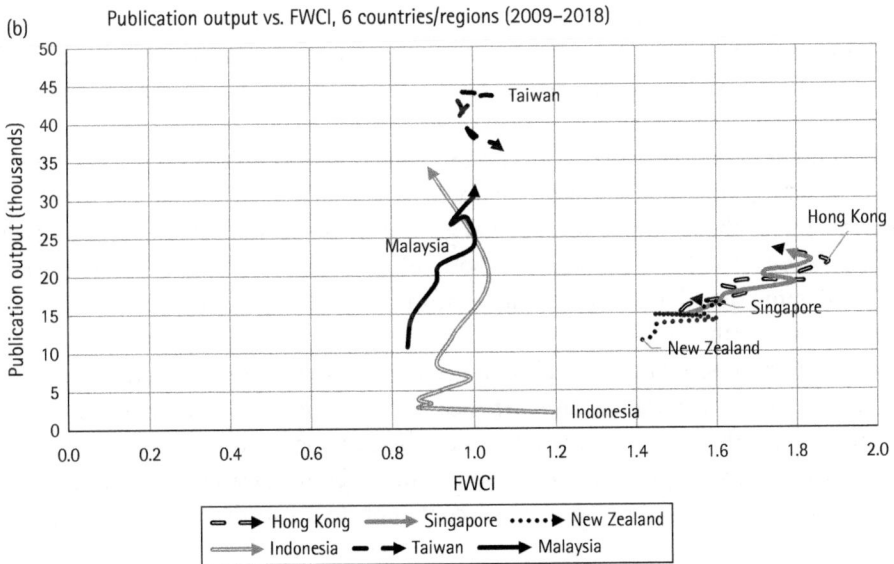

FIGURE 22.8B Change in publication output and FWCI, 2009–2018 (arrowhead indicates 2018)

been relatively small over this time frame. Finally, in the bottom right of Figure 22.8b are the cluster of New Zealand, Singapore, and Hong Kong. All three have had a stable FWCI and publication output during the 10-year time span with an FWCI that remains within a narrow range, and small growth in publication output since 2009 compared to other knowledge producers in Asia.

As we have seen, in aggregate, Asia's publication output is growing as is its global share of citations, raising the region's FWCI. But Figures 22.8a and 22.8b serve as a reminder that much of this growth in publications and FWCI is driven by the large gains in China, and on a case-by-case basis, other parts of Asia have been developing their research and publication ecosystems at different speeds and in different ways between 2009 and 2018.

3.4 Research Impact Across Disciplines

Just as FWCI and publication output vary across Asia, so do differences in research disciplines arise between different countries and regions. One way to approach these regional specializations and research priorities is to examine research output as broken down by six categories of research disciplines: Agricultural & Veterinary Sciences, Engineering & Technology, Humanities & the Arts, Medical & Health Sciences, Natural Sciences, and Social Sciences (OECD, 2015, pp. 57–59). These categories are drawn using classifications from SciVal, and are based on the classification of the source title (i.e., journal) that the publication appears in. It is important to note that publications can be counted towards more than one category—an interdisciplinary publication can be classified as, for example, both Engineering & Technology and Natural Sciences within SciVal.

In addition, SciVal uses citation-based modeling to generate Topics and Topic Clusters (Elsevier, n.d.), which are collections of documents with a common focused intellectual interest. Topics change over time and can grow, shrink, or be newly created as new research areas evolve. There are nearly 96,000 unique Topics in SciVal that can be used to look with more specificity at how certain research areas change and are contributed to in different parts of the world.[25]

Research managers can use Topics to discover pockets of well-funded research, top performing researchers, and areas where peers and competitors are currently active. For the purposes of this chapter, we will focus on this last application of Topics to compare regional differences in publication activity within different research Topics across Asia.

To begin, how do different parts of Asia contribute to the six disciplinary categories in terms of publication output?

To answer this question, the Relative Activity Index (RAI) was used. The RAI is the proportion of the publication output of a region in a certain discipline (for example, 69 percent of publications in East Asia were in the Natural Sciences from 2009 to 2018) divided by the global proportion of publications in that same discipline over the

[25] There are nearly 96,000 as of May 2020.

same time period (for example, 54 percent of global publications were in the Natural Sciences). Thus, a value of 1.00 indicates that a region is similarly focused in that subject as the rest of the world, while above 1.00 represents an outsized focus.

With the notable exception of Australia and New Zealand, most regions in Asia do not tend to publish heavily in the humanities. As discussed previously, this is potentially another situation where language has an impact on results. Because Scopus does not capture many non-English publications, and various sectors of the humanities are by nature regional, geographic, or cultural studies tied to a particular language or area, these papers are less likely to be written in English than more global disciplines such as physics or medicine. Australia and New Zealand have an RAI of 1.08 in Humanities & the Arts, just above 1.00 and much higher than the rest of Asia, possibly because local language is not a consideration limiting indexing in the Scopus database there.

It is worth noting that the Humanities & the Arts are the smallest disciplinary category of the six in Figure 22.9. Across Asia, it saw only 142,307 publications between 2009 and 2018, compared to 1.5 million publications in total during these years.[26] Globally,

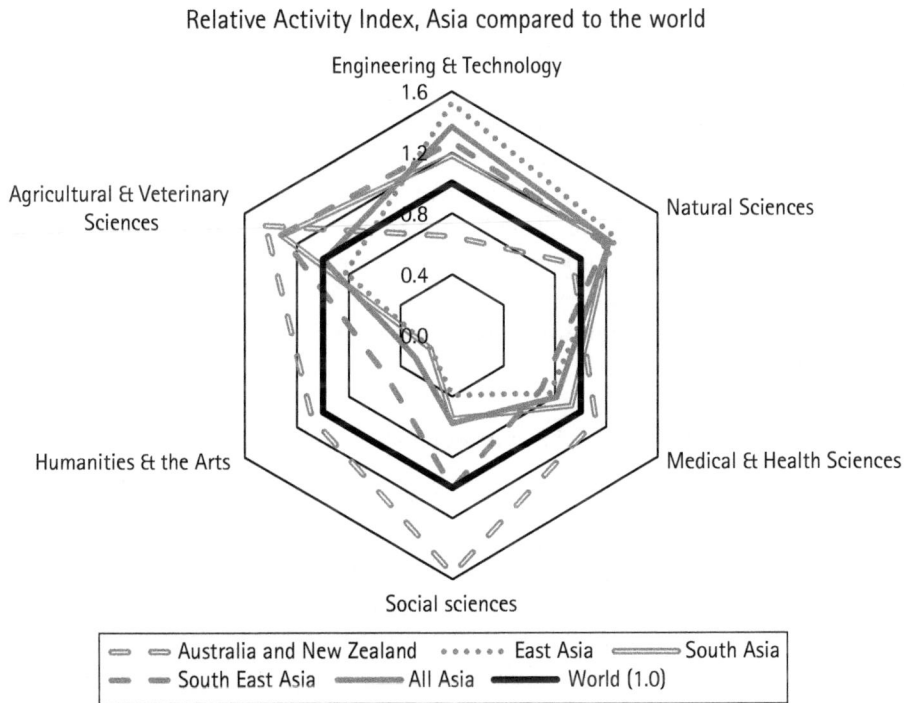

FIGURE 22.9 Comparing Asian regions' relative activity by discipline, 2009–2018

[26] Total publication count in Asia for each discipline: Engineering & Technology (4,063,950), Natural Sciences (6,703,946), Medical & Health Sciences (2,638,921), Agriculture & Veterinary Sciences (626,456), Social Sciences (830,965), and Humanities & Arts (142,307). These numbers are larger than the output discussed in section 3 because publications are classified in multiple disciplines.

Humanities & the Arts publications account for only 5 percent of all publications in this time frame, or 1,384,737 out of 28,160,070 publications in total.

With the exception of Australia and New Zealand, all regions in Asia have a similar shape on Figure 22.9, indicating they tend to publish in disciplines with similar emphasis or proportion of publications relative to the world. There are only three regions where disciplines have an RAI above 1.40: Australia and New Zealand in the Social Sciences (225,838 publications, representing an RAI of 1.56) and Agriculture & Veterinary Sciences (90,874 publications, representing an RAI of 1.44), and East Asia in Engineering & Technology (3,111,684 publications, representing an RAI of 1.53). Because it is by far the largest, let us discuss this last item.

With China, Japan, and South Korea all as contributors, East Asia publishes 77 percent of all Engineering & Technology research in Asia, higher than the 69 percent share East Asia has of all research in Asia. The larger share and RAI could be a result of government policy, funding schemes, business enterprise contributions, or other factors that would promote the publishing of more papers in this discipline relative to the world.

Topics within Engineering & Technology also often tend to have high prominence, which might lead to more interest in researching them. From 2009 to 2018, of the five Topics in Engineering & Technology that East Asia had the highest publication output in, three of the five have a prominence of 100 percent, while the other two have a prominence well above 99 percent. While these five Topics only represent a few of the 96,000 Topics identified by SciVal, it is clear that there are specialized, high prominence, trending areas of research that East Asia is a global leader in. As we can see in Table 22.1, East Asia contributed 85 percent or more of all publications in the world to these particular Topics.

By total output, East Asia produces the vast majority of its research in the Natural Sciences (72 percent) and Engineering (77 percent), with its highest FWCI in the Natural Sciences at just under 1.1.[27] However, if we look at the FWCI of all six disciplines in East

Table 22.1 Top engineering and technology Topics by publication count, East Asia, 2009–2018

Engineering and Technology Topic	Publication count	Percent of global contribution	Prominence
Methylammonium lead; perovskite; solar cells	6536	87.61	100.00%
Asymmetric supercapacitors; nanosheets; capacitance	6398	85.57	100.00%
Organic photovoltaics; solar cells; fullerenes	5793	89.01	100.00%
Secondary building; organometallics; ligands	5490	92.36	99.93%
Containment control; control; multi agent systems	5406	94.81	99.74%

[27] As noted previously, publications can and often are counted multiple times in different categories; 72 percent and 77 percent sum to more than 100 percent, and suggest there is a significant amount of overlap between the two categories.

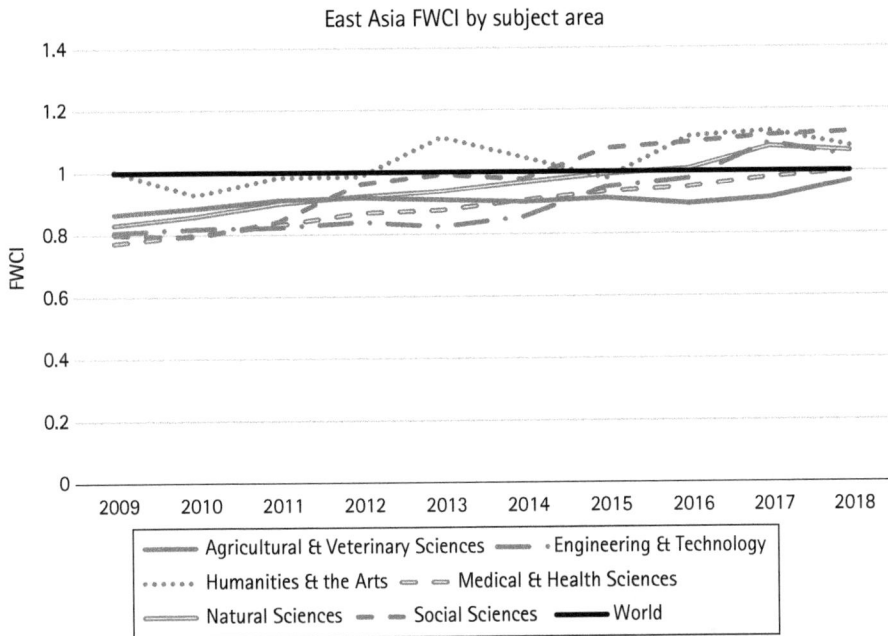

FIGURE 22.10 Breakdown of East Asia's FWCI by subject area, 2009–2018

Asia since 2009, growth is not limited to any particular area. Despite East Asia's higher RAI in Engineering & Technology and its highest FWCI in the Natural Sciences from 2009 to 2018, it has consistently improved in all disciplines in the past decade (see Figure 22.10).

China has only very recently reached the end of its ambitious National Science and Technology Plan (The National Medium- and Long-Term Program for Science and Technology Development (2006–2020)) and the early results indicate that the plan has benefited all research disciplines fairly uniformly, pushing FWCI from well below 1.0 in 2009 to above 1.0 in all categories except Agriculture & Veterinary Sciences in 2018.

Taking a step back from global comparators, it is also possible to calculate the RAI of different regions in Asia relative to Asia as a whole. Doing so allows us to compare different parts of Asia more directly than by using the entire world as a base in the calculation.

We can still see some of the trends in Figure 22.9, many of which are emphasized in Figure 22.11. However, it is clearer how much more Australia and New Zealand focus on Social Sciences and Humanities. South-East Asia follows, still greatly surpassing East and South Asia in these two disciplines.

East and South Asia are fairly well balanced in Figure 22.11, especially compared to the other two regions. Because they are the largest regions in terms of publication output in Asia, they have the largest influence on what represents an RAI of 1.0 for all Asia. Partly as a result of this, all of their RAI are within a relatively narrow range of 0.6 to 1.3, suggesting they do not tend to very heavily favor one discipline over another, relative to other parts of Asia. For comparison, Australia and New Zealand and South-East Asia

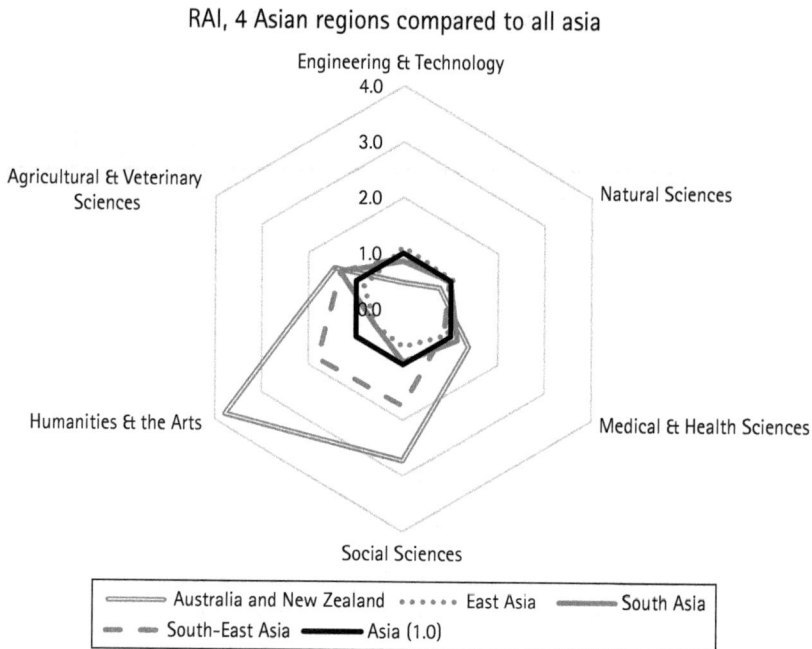

FIGURE 22.11 Comparing Asian region's Relative Activity Index (RAI) by discipline, 2009–2018

have an RAI range of 0.5 (Engineering) to 4.0 (Humanities) and 0.9 (both Engineering and Medicine) to 1.8 (Humanities) respectively—a wider spread that suggests more specialization.

South Asia's RAI of 1.3 in Agriculture & Veterinary Sciences as well as 1.2 in Medical & Health Sciences are both the second highest in those categories. Led by India, South Asia has seen large growth in publication output across all disciplines from 2009 to 2018 (see Figures 22.2a and 22.2b). However, despite its higher RAI in Agriculture & Veterinary Sciences and Medical & Health Sciences, their FWCI has not improved much in the last decade. In fact, in 2018, these were the two disciplines with the lowest FWCI in South Asia, at 0.7 and 0.8 respectively (see Figure 22.12).

Since 2009, the FWCI of output across all research fields in South Asia has grown 8.4 percent, and across disciplines it has changed by as much as 39 percent (Humanities & the Arts) to as little as -3 percent (Medical & Health Sciences). For its part, Engineering & Technology in South Asia has only improved its FWCI by 0.6 percent, but it has remained above the FWCI of all other disciplines. Compared to East Asia (Figure 22.10) however, South Asia does not show equally large FWCI growth in any of the six disciplines.

By now, we have seen how publication output and FWCI varies across Asia, as well as some of the differences that exist in terms of research efficiency (publications normalized by researcher count and financial investment in Research and Development) and research disciplines. Now that we have established these trends, it is time to look

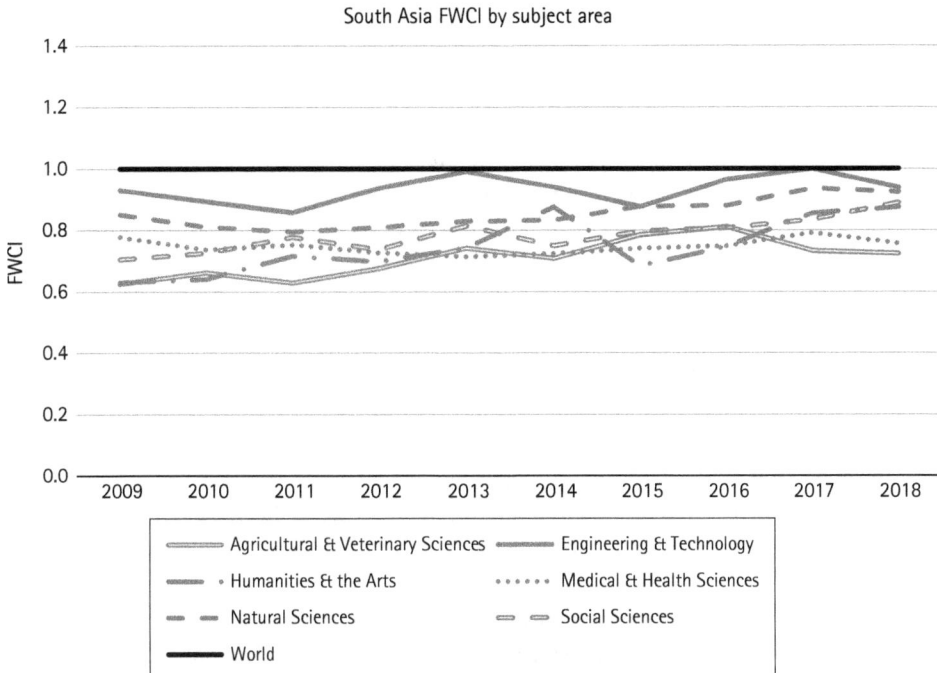

FIGURE 22.12 Breakdown of South Asia's FWCI by subject area, 2009–2018

specifically at knowledge production in the private business sector, primarily through an examination of patents and patent citations.

4. ECONOMICS: CORPORATE KNOWLEDGE PRODUCTION

"I love to be free to explore, research, and evolve." These are not the words of a theoretical physicist, anthropologist, or some great polymath. Instead, they are from Japanese fashion designer Issey Miyake, an industry leader who is known for his technology-driven approach to design. We enjoy this quote for two reasons. First, it reminds us that research is not just the domain of university professors and trendy college innovation spaces. Yes, research is developed through the nurturing environment of universities, but it is also given space and investments to grow at private corporations, like Miyake's firm. And furthermore, this quote serves to remind us that research is not just for giant pharmaceutical multinationals in the private space. Research benefits many different industries, from aviation to fashion.

No assessment of knowledge production can be contained within an academic setting. By investigating some economic and private sector metrics—namely patent citations and patent applications—this section aims to provide an overview of Asian knowledge production through the lens of applied research and business.

Representing 40 percent of global exports and 36.9 percent of global imports in 2019 (ESCAP, 2020), and with 25,000 publicly listed domestic companies (The World Bank, 2020c) in 2018, Asian business is a significant contributor to knowledge production, through direct internal research and development (IR&D), partnerships, grants, and economic development. Oftentimes that economic investment in IR&D results in a patent or some other less-quantifiable form of intellectual property.

4.1 Patent Citations

Section 3 discussed many important aspects of publications themselves, but did not venture into how publications support knowledge translation as reference sources for patents. To begin our discussion of knowledge production in the private sector, let's shift from examining all publications in Asia to only those that were cited by a patent, as in Figure 22.13.

It is possible to count both the citations and the number of patents filed by different countries and regions thanks to data from different patent offices around the world. Patents that are expected to have a high value are often filed in more than one patent office, so for the purposes of this chapter we will limit our focus to this kind of patent. In particular, we will use triadic patents, which are defined as patents filed at the European Patent Office (EPO), the United States Patent and Trademark Office (USPTO), and the Japan Patent Office (JPO). Because filing a patent requires time and resources, patents that are filed in all of these three major patent offices are likely anticipated to be of higher value by the filer.

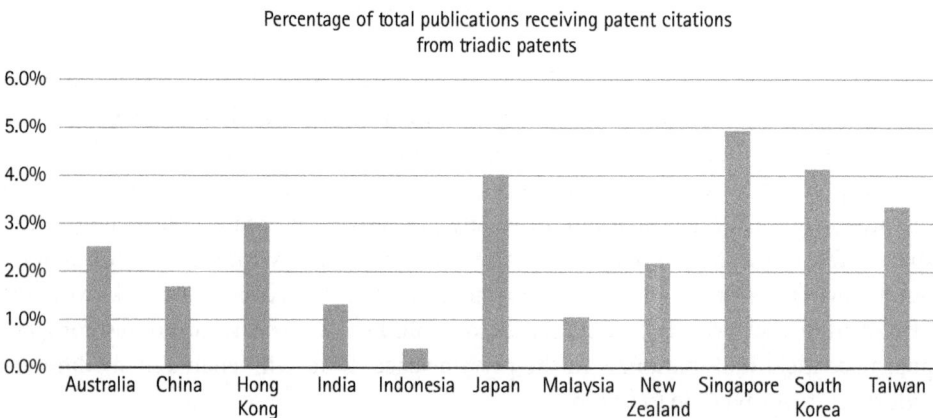

FIGURE 22.13 Percentage of total publications receiving patent citations, 2009–2018 (EPO, JPO, USPTO)

When a patent is filed, it will often include citations to previous patents or academic research. One important difference between these citations in patents and citations in publications discussed in section 3, is that patent citations are suggested by both the author and the examiner at the patent office receiving the patent application. The practice of citing in patents also varies from patent office to patent office. Comparing patent citations to academic research in several patent offices gives a sense of how much a country or region's research is being translated into applications.

Japan, Singapore, South Korea, and Taiwan all have smaller total publication outputs when compared to China or India, but assessing the percentage of publications with patent citations in each country or region shows that between 3.3 percent and 4.9 percent of research published in these four countries/regions receives a patent citation. This means that larger percentages of publications, produced by both the private sector and academia in these countries/regions are being leveraged to support patents in these parts of Asia. For comparison, 4.1 percent of US publications and 2.6 percent of European publications received patent citations over the same time period.

Figure 22.14 shows the number of patent citations to publications from the 11 major knowledge producers in Asia broken down by publication discipline. The Natural Sciences, Engineering & Technology, and Medical & Health Sciences tend to dominate patent citation counts due to the wide applicability of these fields. In the case of Medical & Health Sciences, Australia in particular has a high patent citation count. This is in addition to Australia and New Zealand's Relative Activity Index of 1.1 in the Medical & Health Sciences (see Figure 22.11) as well as very high average FWCI of 1.7, indicating a possible specialization in this discipline.[28]

Here, similar to the case with patent counts, we see hints of Japan leading on knowledge production. As discussed, many have commented on the decline of scientific research in Japan. While much of this is based on reasonable assessment of scholarly literature, it neglects other forms of knowledge production such as the strong Japanese private sector research ecosystem.

To emphasize this last point, we look at the sectors driving patent applications through citations. Any given research paper can be classified based on the affiliation of the authors as being the result of efforts by different sectors—for example, publications may be the result of authors in the academic sector, corporate sector, or the collaboration between academic and corporate sectors (AC). Figure 22.15 narrows our analysis of Figure 22.14 further to include only the four countries whose publications received the most patent citations: China, Japan, South Korea, and Australia. It then breaks down the patent citation based on whether the citation was to an academic, corporate, or AC publication.

Figure 22.14 shows that among these four countries (and thus in Asia), Japan receives the most or second-most patent citations across all disciplines and sectors. In particular

---

[28] 1.7 is the highest FWCI of any of the 11 countries or regions examined in this chapter in a particular discipline.

Total patent citations (2009–2018)

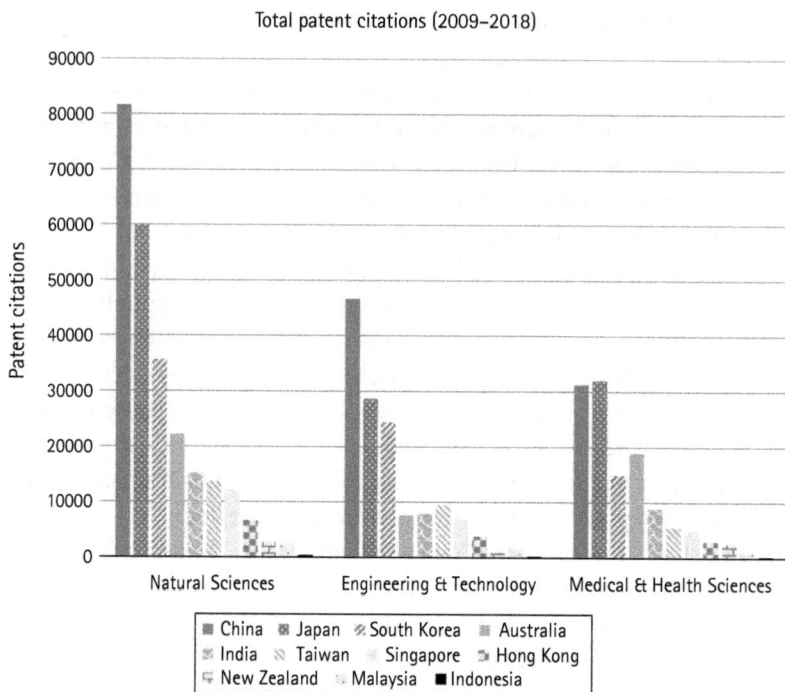

FIGURE 22.14 Total patent citations accrued by research from the top Asian knowledge producers, 2009–2018 (EPO, JPO, USPTO), disaggregated according to publication field of research

Patent citations received by four countries by sector

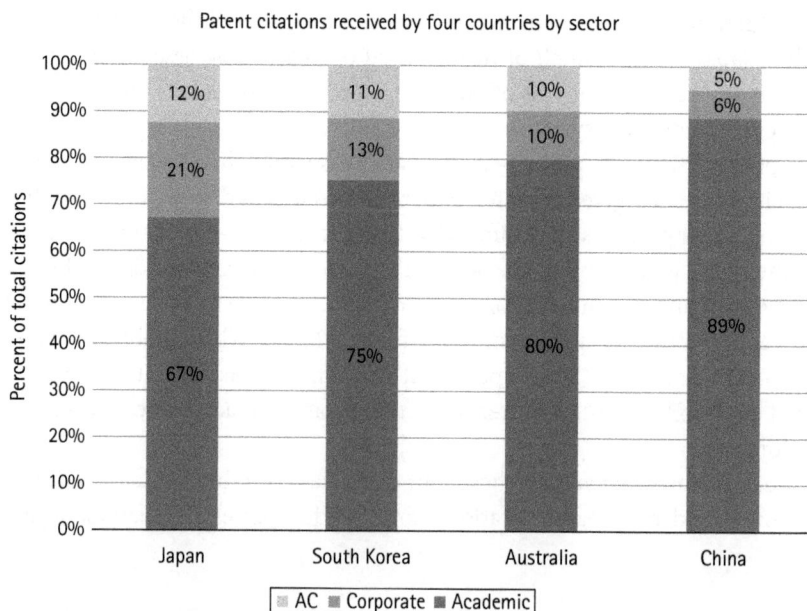

FIGURE 22.15 Percentage of patent citations to publications from each country by sector of publication authors, 2009–2018 (EPO, JPO, USPTO), all six disciplines included

however, Japanese corporate research is heavily cited by individuals and institutions filing patents. Among all patent citations received by Japanese publications from 2009 to 2018, fully 33 percent were to a publication with at least one corporate author, while 67 percent were purely academic papers (Figure 22.15). In China, only 11 percent, or one-third the amount seen in Japan, of patent citations went to a paper with a corporate author. It is clear that the private sector in Japan is heavily contributing to Japan's strong count of both patents and patent citations in Asia, further suggesting that GERD in Japan is often used to finance knowledge transfer through patent applications.

Of course the private sector in Japan is not working entirely alone; 67 percent of all patent citations to Japanese papers are still to papers with only academic authors, indicating that the majority of patents still rely on academia as reference sources. However, this 67 percent is the lowest among all of the 11 top knowledge producers in Asia.[29] Typically, AC publications receive more views, downloads, citations, and thus impact because the combined resources and different strengths of researchers in academia and the private sector tend to enrich and improve any given research effort. For example, from 2009 to 2018 the University of Hong Kong produced 47,785 publications. Of those, 46,648 of these papers were academic collaborations only and collectively had an FWCI of 1.56. The 1,137 publications that had at least one corporate author however had an FWCI of 9.08.

4.2 Patent Count

In the context of a chapter on knowledge production, it may be helpful to think of publications as a means to disseminate knowledge, while patents are meant to protect knowledge as intellectual property. Both are equally important components of a knowledge economy. We have thus far examined publications and citations to publications extensively, so let us now shift to counting patent output in different parts of Asia (Figures 22.16a and 22.16b).[30]

Immediately, Japan stands out in Figure 22.16a with many times more triadic patents filed than the second largest filer in Asia, China. Japan's particular strength with respect to patent data is a common theme that will arise and be discussed in more detail throughout this section.

---

[29] Seventy-nine percent of patent citations to Japanese publications are to publications with at least one academic author. For other knowledge producers, this is: Australia (89 percent), China (94 percent), Hong Kong (91 percent), India (92 percent), Indonesia (90 percent), Malaysia (96 percent), New Zealand (88 percent), Singapore (88 percent), South Korea (87 percent), and Taiwan (92 percent)

[30] For readers less familiar with the patent filing process, a patent often takes many years from when it is filed until it is actually approved. Only once a patent is approved does it appear in these data, and that is why beginning in 2016 or 2017 the plots in Figure 22.14 begin to decline. This is simply the lag between the filing and approval date of patents.

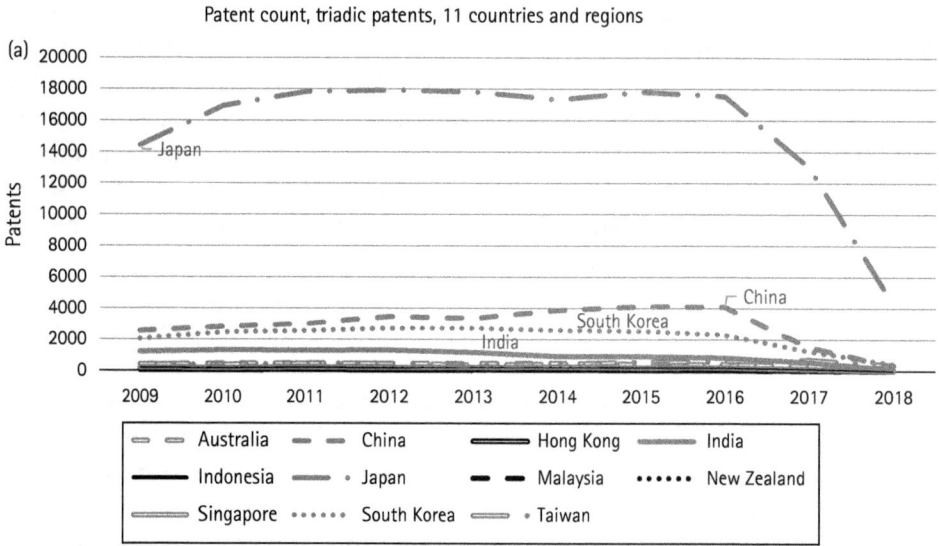

Patent count, triadic patents, 11 countries and regions

FIGURE 22.16A Triadic patent count among top Asian knowledge producers, 2009–2018 (USPTO, EPO, and JPO), all six disciplines included

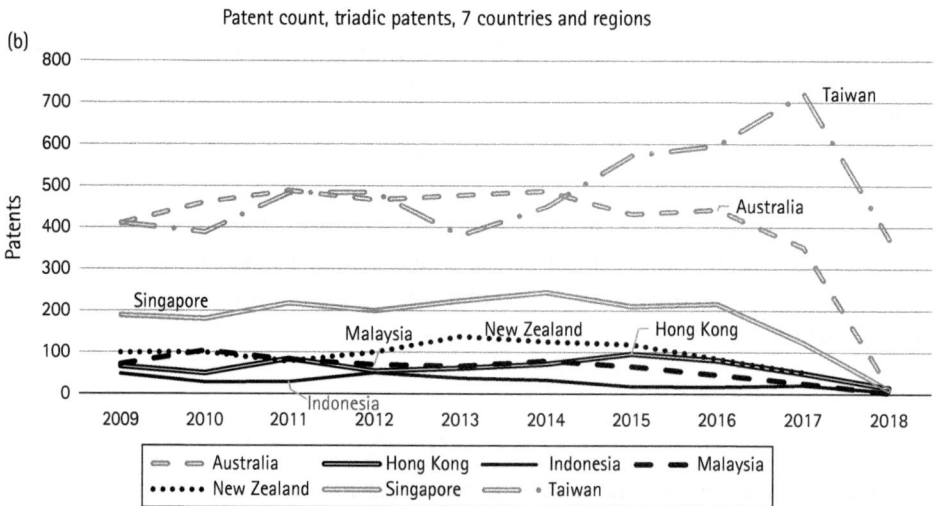

Patent count, triadic patents, 7 countries and regions

FIGURE 22.16B Triadic patent count among top Asian knowledge producers, 2009–2018 (USPTO, EPO, and JPO)

South Korea also stands out with the third most patents filed annually after Japan and China. Recall from section 3 that Japan and Korea both had the highest GERD as a percentage of GDP, highest BERD as a percentage of GERD, and lowest publications per GERD ($M USD) and per researcher counts in Asia.

HERD is most likely to result in publications, so in cases where GERD is high but publication output is low, this low apparent efficiency may be because a high amount of GERD is from BERD. BERD is more likely to result in patents as the private sector attempts to secure intellectual property rights that can be leveraged for financial gain, rather than publications that may not be directly linked to any immediate economic benefit. With higher BERD than their Asian peers, Japan and Korea did indeed have particularly high patent output from 2009 to 2018.

An additional consideration when discussing patents is the quality of the patents themselves. Similar to how FWCI allows us to use publication citations to get a sense of the impact of scholarly research, so too can we leverage patent citations to get a sense of the impact or relevance of patents. The Technology Relevance metric (LexisNexis, 2020) accomplishes this by examining forward citations received by patents, and normalizing the number of citations received by patents by time-dependence, patent office, and technology field.[31] Technology Relevance assesses the potential impact of patents by calculating how often patents are cited in later patents, an indicator that the original patent is a driver of knowledge transfer. This metric has been developed by Lexis Nexis' PatentSight and is part of the calculation for a second metric, the Patent Asset Index (LexisNexis, 2020).[32]

While most countries and regions in Figure 22.17 have a Technology Relevance between 2.0 and 2.5, Japan's is only 1.6. Although Japan dominates in portfolio size (number

---

[31] Technology Relevance is based on forward citations. Technology Relevance measures whether a patent has been more often cited than other patents from the same technology field and year, while also considering that international patent offices follow different citation rules. The total number of patent citations received not only depends on the technology field of the patented invention, but also on the time that has passed since the patent was published. Patents only recently published tend to have received much fewer citations than older patents. The time-dependency of citations is corrected by dividing the number of citations received by a patent by the average number of citations received by all patents published in the same year.

Technology Relevance also considers that international patent offices follow different citation rules. Therefore, the number of patent citations is corrected for age, patent office citation practice, and technology field. It is a relative measure comparing one patent to other patents. A value of 2 means that the patent is twice as relevant for subsequent developments as an average patent in the same technology field and of the same age.

[32] Patent Asset Index is calculated by combining Technology Relevance with Market Coverage. Market Coverage is defined as the total size of the worldwide markets for which patent protection exists. The more patents firms own in important markets, as indicated by high Market Coverage values, the more valuable the patents are because innovators spend more on multi-market protection via patents if they believe an invention is more valuable. Thus, the scope of international patent protection is an important indicator of patent value. Market Coverage is calculated based on granted and pending, hence valid patents per country adjusted for each market's size. The size of each market is estimated using the countries' gross national incomes relative to the US gross national income as the largest global economy. Alternatively, Market Coverage may also be calculated based on industry-specific market size data.

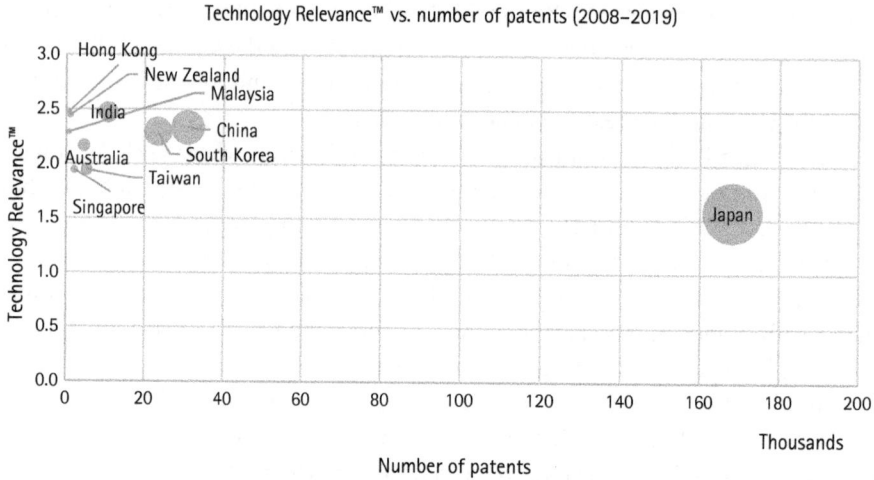

FIGURE 22.17 Number of patents vs. technology relevance, 2008–2019 (Triadic patents filed at EPO, USPTO, and JPO) (bubble size indicates Patent Asset Index)

of patents), in terms of impact and relevance these patents lag behind the rest of Asia. Part of Japan's large portfolio is due to the inclusion of the Japanese Patent Office in triadic patent counts. However, it still may be that some form of "patent or perish" exists within the Japanese knowledge economy, pushing a large number of patent applications to be filed there, with these patents receiving relatively few citations.

Together, the data above paint an interesting picture of knowledge transfer in Japan. Despite the fact that Japan does not rely as much on the academic sector to generate knowledge that is cited in patents, 4 percent of its papers are cited by patents (Figure 22.13), it still produces the most patents overall (Figure 22.16a), it has the second-most patent citations to its research, after China (Figure 22.14), and the corporate sector supports patents through research publication more in Japan than it does anywhere else in Asia (Figure 22.15).

4.3 A Note on the Role of Foreign MNCs

As has been discussed throughout this section, the filing of patents and their relationship with scholarly research allows us a window through which to view the impact of research on knowledge transfer. In many cases, the development of patents is also closely linked to investment from R&D centers of multinational corporations (MNCs), as Business Expenditure on Research and Development drives private sector application of fundamental research from academic partners.

This link is becoming increasingly apparent when looking at R&D expenditure by US majority-owned foreign affiliates in Asia (National Science Foundation, 2018), which has grown from just $1.9B USD in 1997 to $12.6B USD in 2014, with especially rapid growth in India and China (National Science Foundation, 2018). In a 2019 paper by Branstetter, Glennon and Jensen, it is shown that from 1989 to 2014, US MNC investment abroad fell from a 74 percent concentration in 5 countries (UK, Germany, Japan, France, and Canada) to only 43 percent, noting "Many of these new hubs have only recently graduated from the ranks of developing countries, and two of the most important new destinations for US MNC R&D, China and India, still have relatively low per capita incomes" (Branstetter et al., 2019). This rapid growth in foreign MNC R&D investment has played a role in driving patent production. Examining patents assigned to MNCs in which all inventors list China as their country as well as patents assigned to MNCs with inventors from both China and abroad, we see that these two categories grew from close to zero patents in 1990 to over 5,000 by 2011 (Jaffe and Jones, 2015).

The role of such foreign MNC investment likely continues to be significant in its impact on and acceleration of patent generation in the region and therefore contributes to the observed trends and projected forecast of trends, and this complex and evolving topic should be explored in much greater detail outside the confines of this chapter. However, for now we will return to the lens of bibliometrics to conclude our discussion of knowledge production in Asia.

5. Conclusion

Knowledge production in Asia is a complex topic that is influenced by everything from individual researcher behaviors to macroeconomic policy and much more in between. But these complexities aside, we can say with confidence that in some places knowledge production in Asia is booming. Collectively, Asia has rapidly grown its publication output from 31 percent to 41 percent of global publications between 2009 and 2018, with an accompanying increase in FWCI from 1.0 to 1.1. But we must keep in mind that the gains are not uniform, and the surge of growth in China can partly mask trends in other parts of Asia.

Asia also invests in knowledge production in very different ways. Some countries have heavier investment in academic research, while others have higher investment in business enterprise research. In particular, Japan and Korea fall into the latter category. As a result, they tend to have fewer publications per dollar invested in research, but far more patents. These countries seem to have particular emphasis on business sector research as well as leveraging all research, both academic and corporate, to support patents.

Of course, no review of knowledge production is complete without lastly considering the future of collaboration in the context of geopolitical tensions, particularly between the United States and China. Threats by both countries to curb or ban technologies produced by the other have the potential to disrupt the free and open communication that is critical for the strong development of science.[33] In fact, political tension has already begun to spill into the world of scientific research, with limitations on Chinese visas to the US, increased surveillance on Chinese researchers in the US, and the US National Institute of Health (NIH) instructing over 10,000 research organizations to not share NIH grant data with overseas parties due to security threats (Lee and Haupt, 2020a). The challenges posed by any potential US–China decoupling are made graver by the limited global mobility and recent dependence at all stages of the scientific process on virtual communication due to the COVID-19 pandemic. International research conferences, visiting professors, and even graduate and undergraduate students now must contend with the potential consequences of a nationalist approach to science and technology development within these two global superpowers.

Will US-Sino tension shift the trends we currently see of increasing scholarly output and impact (FWCI) in Asia? One thing is clear: scientific collaboration between the two countries is at an all-time high, with each country firmly established as the other's top international research partner. From 2015 to 2019, China published 2.8M scholarly articles and the United States published 3.4M articles. An impressive 260K articles were co-authored by researchers from both countries. The size of this collaboration cannot be overstated. China's next largest international research partner is the UK, with 66K co-authored publications (Scopus, 2020), four times smaller than the magnitude of collaboration with the United States (Lee and Haupt, 2020b).

On one hand, it would take an enormous effort to dismantle this pre-existing level of deeply established collaboration. On the other hand, political changes could limit the growth potential in terms of research output that China has seen in recent years as partnerships with and funding from the US come under pressure. With enormous financial and human resources at its disposal, China may be able to maintain strong growth in research output by shifting towards more inter-regional and domestic collaboration. However, such a shift would likely affect the FWCI of Chinese research, which as we have seen in this chapter has risen sharply in recent years, but benefits greatly from large numbers of citations to internationally collaborative research.

In the end, much is still left unsaid on the topic of Asia as a producer of knowledge. How Asia collaborates internally and externally, as well as how it consumes knowledge are just two areas worth investigating further to better understand this topic. However, one thing remains clear—Asia has seen large growth since 2009 and has become a powerful engine of research, development, and knowledge production on the world stage.

---

[33] As only a few examples, take US President Donald Trump's 5/15/19 Executive Order banning Huawei (US Department of Commerce, 2019), his 8/6/20 Executive Order banning TikTok downloads in the United States (Trump, 2020a), and his 8/6/20 Executive Order banning WeChat downloads in the United States (Trump, 2020b).

References

Bentley, P. J., Gulbrandsen, M., and Kyvik, S. (2015). "The relationship between basic and applied research in universities." *Higher Education*, 70/4, 689–709.

Branstetter, L. G., Glennon, B., and Jensen, J. B. (2019). *The Rise of Global Innovation by US Multinationals Poses Risks and Opportunities*. Washington, DC: Peterson Institute for International Economics. https://www.piie.com/system/files/documents/pb19-9.pdf

Cao, C., Baas, J., Wagner, C., and Jonkers (2019). "Returning scientists and the emergence of China's science system." *Science and Public Policy*, 47/2, 172–183.

Das, D. N. and Chattopadhyay, S. (2014). "Academic performance indicators: Straitjacketing higher education." *Economic and Political Weekly*, 49/50, 68–71.

Department of Education, Skills, and Employment, Australia (2017). *Implementation Measures Released for China's New World-Class University Policy*. https://internationaleducation.gov.au/News/Latest-News/Pages/Implementation-measures-released-for-China%E2%80%99s-new-world-class-university-policy.aspx

Department of Industry, Science, Energy, and Resources of Australia (2015). *National Innovation and Science Agenda Report*.

Department of Science and Technology, India (2017). *VAJRA India | SERB*. https://dst.gov.in/vajra

Department of Science and Technology, Philippines (2018). *Balik Scientist Program*. https://bspms.dost.gov.ph/

Elsevier (2019). *Research Metrics Guidebook*. https://www.elsevier.com/?a=53327

Elsevier (n.d.). *Topic Prominence in Science – Scival*. https://www.elsevier.com/solutions/scival/features/topic-prominence-in-science

ESCAP (2020). *Trade and Goods Outlook in Asia and the Pacific 2020/2021*. https://www.unescap.org/resources/trade-goods-outlook-asia-and-pacific-20202021#

Hayes, J. (1995). "The internet's first victim." *Forbes*, December 18.

Hu, Z., Tian, W., Guo, J., and Wang, X. (2020). "Mapping research collaborations in different countries and regions: 1980–2019." *Scientometrics*, 124/1, 729–745.

Jaffe, A. B. and Jones, B. F. (2015). "The rise of international coinvention." In A. B. Jaffe and B. F. Jones (eds.), *The Changing Frontier: Rethinking Science and Innovation Policy*. Chicago: University of Chicago Press, 135–168. https://www.nber.org/system/files/chapters/c13028/c13028.pdf

Kobayashi, S., Baobo, J., Sano, J., and Sakura Institute of Research Inc. (1999). "The 'three reforms' in China: Progress and outlook." *Japan Research Institute RIM*, 45/1. https://www.jri.co.jp/english/periodical/rim/1999/RIMe199904threereforms/

Lee, J. J. and Haupt, J. P. (2020a). *The "China Threat" and the Future of Global Science*. https://blogs.scientificamerican.com/observations/the-china-threat-and-the-future-of-global-science/

Lee, J. J. and Haupt, J. P. (2020b). "Winners and losers in US–China scientific research collaborations." *Higher Education*, 80, 57–74.

LexisNexis (2020). *PatentSight Patent Asset Index*. Patentsight.com. https://www.patentsight.com/patent-asset-index#:~:text=PatentSight%C2%AE%20Technology%20Relevance%20is

Lixu, L. (2004). "China's higher education reform 1998–2003: A summary." *Asia Pacific Education Review*, 5/1, 14–22.

Ministry of Education, Culture, Sports, Science and Technology, Japan (2014). *Top Global University Project*. https://tgu.mext.go.jp/en/

Ministry of Education, Ministry of Finance, National Development and Reform Commission, China (2017). "Announcement of the list of world-class universities and first-class discipline construction universities and disciplines." http://www.moe.gov.cn/srcsite/A22/moe_843/201709/t20170921_314942.html

Ministry of Finance India (2018). *Economic Survey.* https://mofapp.nic.in/economicsurvey/economicsurvey/pdf/119-130_Chapter_08_ENGLISH_Vol_01_2017-18.pdf

National Research Council (US) (2010). *S&T Strategies of Six Countries: Implications for the United States.* Washington, DC: National Academies Press.

National Science Foundation (2018). *Science and Engineering Indicators 2018.* Chapter 4. Research and Development: US Trends and International Comparisons. https://www.nsf.gov/statistics/2018/nsb20181/report/sections/research-and-development-u-s-trends-and-international-comparisons/u-s-business-r-d

OECD (2015). *Frascati Manual 2015: Guidelines for Collecting and Reporting Data on Research and Experimental Development.* Paris: OECD Publishing.

OECD (2020). *Gross Domestic Expenditure on R&D by Sector of Performance and Type of R&D.* https://stats.oecd.org/Index.aspx?DataSetCode=GERD_TORD, accessed April 7, 2020.

Patwardhan, B. (2019). "Why India is striking back against predatory journals." *Nature,* 571/7763, 7.

QS Quacquarelli Symonds (2019). *Top Universities Methodologies.* QS World Rankings. https://www.topuniversities.com/qs-world-university-rankings/methodology

SciVal (2020). *SciVal.* https://www.scival.com/, accessed April 1, 2020.

Scopus (2020). *Scopus.* https://www.scopus.com/, accessed April 1, 2020.

Shuo, Z. (2020a). "Research evaluation challenged." *China Daily.* http://www.chinadaily.com.cn/a/202002/25/WS5e546e83a310128217279fd0.html

Shuo, Z. (2020b). "University's grad students no longer have to publish to earn their master's." *China Daily.* https://global.chinadaily.com.cn/a/202008/07/WS5f2ca549a31083481725ec6d.html

Stahlschmidt, S. and Hinze, S. (2016). "How does the scientific progress in developing countries affect bibliometric impact measures of developed countries? A counterfactual case study on China." In *Proceedings of the 21st International Conference on Science and Technology Indicators.* Universitat Politècnica de València, 1250–1256.

Stahlschmidt, S. and Hinze, S. (2018). "The dynamically changing publication universe as a reference point in national impact evaluation: A counterfactual case study on the Chinese publication growth." *Frontiers in Research Metrics and Analytics,* 3.

The Jakarta Post News Desk (2019). "Indonesia opts to recruit foreign academics." *The Jakarta Post.* https://www.thejakartapost.com/news/2019/07/31/indonesia-opts-to-recruit-foreign-academics.html

The National Medium- and Long-Term Program for Science and Technology Development (2006–2020). https://www.itu.int/en/ITU-D/Cybersecurity/Documents/National_Strategies_Repository/China_2006.pdf

The World Bank (2020a). *World Bank Country and Lending Groups – World Bank Data Help Desk.* https://datahelpdesk.worldbank.org/knowledgebase/articles/906519-world-bank-country-and-lending-groups, accessed March 16, 2020.

The World Bank (2020b). *Researchers in R&D (per million people) – Korea, Rep. | Data.* https://data.worldbank.org/indicator/SP.POP.SCIE.RD.P6?locations=KR, accessed May 10, 2020.

The World Bank (2020c). *Listed Domestic Companies, total – South Asia, East Asia & Pacific | Data*. https://data.worldbank.org/indicator/CM.MKT.LDOM.NO?locations=8S-Z4, accessed May 10, 2020.

Times Higher Education (2020). *THE World University Rankings 2021: Methodology*. Times Higher Education (THE). https://www.timeshighereducation.com/world-university-rankings/world-university-rankings-2021-methodology

Trump, D. J. (2020a). *Executive Order on Addressing the Threat Posed by TikTok*. https://trumpwhitehouse.archives.gov/presidential-actions/executive-order-addressing-threat-posed-tiktok/

Trump, D. J. (2020b). *Executive Order on Addressing the Threat Posed by WeChat*. https://trumpwhitehouse.archives.gov/presidential-actions/executive-order-addressing-threat-posed-wechat/

UNESCO (2020) *Science, Technology and Innovation: Gross Domestic Expenditure on R&D (GERD), GERD as a Percentage of GDP, GERD Per Capita and GERD Per Researcher*. http://data.uis.unesco.org/index.aspx?queryid=74, accessed April 7, 2020.

US Department of Commerce (2019). *Securing the Information and Communications Technology and Services Supply Chain*. https://www.federalregister.gov/documents/2019/11/27/2019-25554/securing-the-information-and-communications-technology-and-services-supply-chain

Xie, Y., Zhang, C., and Lai, Q. (2014). "China's rise as a major contributor to science and technology." *Proceedings of the National Academy of Sciences*, 111/26, 9437–9442. https://www.ncbi.nlm.nih.gov/pmc/articles/PMC4084436/

Zhang, H., Patton, D., and Kenney, M. (2013). "Building global-class universities: Assessing the impact of the 985 Project." *Research Policy*, 42/3, 765–775.

CHAPTER 23

....

ASIAN HIGHER EDUCATION AS SOFT POWER?

....

JACK T. LEE

HIGHER education in Asia has witnessed profound changes following World War II as the region's demography and economy transformed in dramatic ways. In Confucian societies with a deep reverence for education beyond the human capital logic, heavy investments in learning, both privately and publicly, are particularly striking (Marginson, 2011a). Demands for social mobility, political emancipation, and modernization in Asia continue to exert pressure on higher education institutions to respond and demonstrate relevance. Burton Clark's pioneering comparative research identified three important pivots in the coordination of higher education: the academy, the state, and the market (Clark, 1986). Not only is this triumvirate evident in many contexts, but it also serves as a powerful heuristic device to compare higher education developments over time and across different societies. However, the discourse of coordination and change in higher education focuses on individual and societal gains. Whether the discourse entails a historical review or an imagination of higher education's future, stakeholders expect universities to contribute locally in tangible ways. In essence, Clark's triumvirate is a guardian of domestic affairs.

With the rise of globalization and growing interdependence among nation-states, analyses of higher education's developments must extend beyond the local and national scale to examine universities' participation in international relations. While higher education institutions are often cast as cultural anchors in many civilizations, they are also the catalytic engines of globalization. A nation's outward engagement with the world extends beyond the hard power of trade and security—the conventional chambers of international politicking. The spirited interactions between nations through education, sports, performative arts, and humanitarian aid all constitute public diplomacy (Cross and Melissen, 2013). More specifically, nation-states jostle in "winning the hearts and minds" of foreign audiences to leverage public diplomacy as soft power (Nye, 2004). Higher education plays a key role in public diplomacy as a platform for cultural interactions and knowledge exchange. Through teaching, personnel training, technical assistance, and collaborative research, a country's higher education can cultivate important allies. For example, the British Council and the Germany Academic Exchange Service (DAAD) are both very active in promoting the higher education systems of their respective countries as well as in congregating international actors to discuss key issues that affect higher education. The DAAD also provides scholarships for international students to study in Germany and promotes German language education overseas. Similarly, the United States' Fulbright program has sponsored generations of visiting foreign scholars and dispatched Americans around the globe to forge links between American universities and foreign scholars.

This chapter will examine higher education as a soft power resource by drawing on examples from Asia. How are Asian states embedding and leveraging higher education in their foreign policies? What constraints and challenges stymie the use of higher education as a soft power resource? The chapter will first provide a theoretical discussion on soft power and clarify some common misconceptions. Section 2 will highlight soft power initiatives that draw on higher education from four states: Singapore, Taiwan, Japan, and China. Section 3 will reflect on the challenges and contradictions of exercising soft power in the context of contemporary politics and the global pandemic.

This chapter focuses on the role of the state even though public diplomacy entails an array of non-state actors (Nye, 2004; Lee, 2011). Universities, museums, media conglomerates, sports teams, and performance arts can all contribute to a country's public diplomacy. The decision to focus on the state is both theoretical and empirical. From Clark (1986) to Neave and van Vught (1991) to Marginson (2011b), the role of the state remains a timeless subject of inquiry in the research on higher education. Moreover, in many parts of Asia, the state plays a prominent role in steering the development of higher education via policymaking and regulatory oversight. Foreign policy is even more embedded in statecraft than education when issues of national security and global competition mediate international relations. Therefore, the chapter takes an explicit state-centric perspective of soft power even though this is not necessarily true elsewhere in the world.

Furthermore, this chapter does not dwell on higher education's involvement in hard power. Some universities have pursued research, openly and covertly, that accrued economic and military advantages for the host country. Higher education's complicity in building a military-industrial complex is well documented in the United States and the former Soviet Union. While the Cold War has ended, fields such as engineering, nanotechnology, robotics, and artificial intelligence continue to forge advances in telecommunication, surveillance, space exploration, and weaponry. The intimate link between higher education and the military in the United States can be traced back to the Morrill Land-Grant College Act of 1862, which stipulated that higher education institutions must provide training for the military when reaping benefits from the sale of federal land. Furthermore, Vannevar Bush, a prominent American civil servant, inventor, and former vice president of MIT, reformed research funding in the United States in the 1940s in such a way that the federal state became an outsized benefactor and beneficiary of university research. These arrangements have unequivocally contributed to America's military prowess and economic vitality over many generations. While some academics and universities in Asia have also engaged in similar research for hard power, the scale of operation and level of institutionalization in the United States are unique.

1. Muddling Theory, Policy, and Practice

A brief overview of soft power as a concept is essential to clarify many misconceptions and theoretical shortcomings. While American political scientist Joseph Nye is often credited with coining the term "soft power" in the 1990s, the intellectual origins pre-date Nye. Power has been a core concept in the field of international relations since its inception. Steven Lukes' influential volume *Power: A Radical View* (1974) mapped out three dimensions of power: decision-making, non-decision-making, and ideo-logical. Born out of a dissatisfaction with the behavioral focus of power analyses, Lukes argued that power can operate in covert ways to bring about compliance without visible disagreements or conflicts. He later clarified this *third dimension* (ideological) of power:

> To say that such power involves the concealment of people's "real interests" by "false consciousness" evokes bad historical memories and can appear both patronizing and presumptuous, but there is, I argue, nothing inherently illiberal or paternalist about these notions, which, suitably refined, remain crucial to understanding the third dimension of power. (Lukes, 2005, p. 13)

Reviewing Lukes' extensive body of work is beyond the scope of this chapter, but his theorization established a foundation that is later echoed by Nye in differentiating soft power from deception. Similarly, international relations giant Kenneth Waltz (1979) recognized that material strengths (realism) may not always be effective even though anarchy is an eternal malaise in international politics.

Building on these ideas, Nye (2004) identified three sources of soft power that a country can possess:

(1) Culture—when certain elements are attractive to others.
(2) Political values—when one lives up to these values at home and abroad.
(3) Foreign policies—when these are seen as legitimate and moral.

Higher education exemplifies culture as foreign audiences gravitate toward the quality, prestige, and success of a higher education system (Lee, 2015b). In particular, elite universities with distinguished histories and research track records generate a spillover effect that uplifts the reputation of an entire higher education system. For example, the Ivy League and Russell Group institutions of the United States and United Kingdom, respectively, radiate a powerful glow that elevates other institutions in the same country even though the quality of education and research vary significantly. While undergraduate programs attract large numbers of students, graduate programs led by renowned researchers and supported by generous resources command international attention. Provisions such as MOOCs, interdisciplinary programs, double and joint degrees do not appear to generate significant traction when compared to the research metrics touted by global rankings. Scholarship funding can also attract talented international students and cultivate lasting transnational ties. Many international students gain a positive view of the host country through academic exchanges and even instigate reforms that mimic the ideologies of their host countries upon return to their home countries (Richmond, 2003; Atkinson, 2010).

In operationalizing Nye's conceptual framework, three misconceptions are notable in both policy discourse and research. First, many advocates and critics assume that attraction automatically results in acquiescence (Bislev, 2017; Lomer, 2017). For example, a strong attraction to American music and American higher education should generate sympathetic views toward the United States—a fallacy that Nye has debunked repeatedly. A country may possess significant soft power resources but struggle to convert ideational capital into beneficial international relations:

> Attraction does not always determine others' preferences, but this gap between power measured as resources and power judged as the outcomes of behavior is not unique to soft power. It occurs with all forms of power. (Nye, 2004, p. 6)

The Soft Power 30, an oft-cited annual global index, claims to operationalize Nye's framework by integrating objective and subjective data to determine a country's attractiveness. Objective metrics include a country's levels of human development, violence in society, international students, tourism, and music production. The subjective data relies on large opinion polls to gauge outsiders' views of a country's trust, welcoming nature, cuisine, and even luxury goods among other things. In essence, these variables are entirely about power resources and national branding rather than anything remotely behavioral or ideological as conceived by Nye and Lukes.

Second, many skeptics dismiss soft power as a concept because there is limited evidence of its existence let alone effectiveness. Not only is the power source difficult to define and measure, but the behavioral outcome is even more complex to assess (Hall and Smith, 2013). Even if these constructs were well established, impact studies demand longitudinal data collection to ascertain a cause-and-effect relationship. While these methodological concerns are justified, the inability to prove existence or effectiveness does not suddenly annul policy discourses and practices. The large body of sociological research on education policy demonstrates that policymakers pursue myriad ideas and aspirations without clear evidence of effectiveness (Ball, 1993; Rizvi and Lingard, 2010; Steiner-Khamsi, 2014). For example, there is no consensus on how to evaluate teaching effectiveness; yet, policies and practices on improving teaching continue to proliferate.

Therefore, repudiating the antidote (policies and practices) due to scant evidence of efficacy (behavioral outcomes) ignores the ailment (power dynamics) entirely. The phenomenon of unequal power dynamics in international relations persists regardless if social scientists can properly study them.

Third, many observers conflate soft power with propaganda and exploitation. This confusion exists among both critics and some advocates of soft power. Nye admits that politicians abuse this confusion; however, these are not interchangeable concepts because soft power relies on persuasion and an exchange of information while propaganda depends on deception and censorship.[1] Most would agree that propaganda is depraved while the pursuit of self-interest is not inherently immoral. Studies that treat persuasion and manipulation equally under the pretext of soft power raise questions about construct validity. In short, assumptions and misplaced expectations contribute to the confusion and skepticism over soft power.

Although Nye does not weigh the three sources of soft power differently, he does acknowledge that unappealing political values and foreign policies can negate the effects of cultural attraction. While scholarships may attract international students, there is limited evidence that such beneficiaries behave in ways that support the host country after graduation (Papatsiba, 2005; Atkinson, 2010). Negative experiences in a host country such as encountering racism can also jeopardize the positive relational gains through academia (Mulvey, 2019; Fan et al., 2020). Similarly, political values that violate human rights and aggressive foreign policies that incite war can quickly squander all notions of cultural attraction. Ultimately, higher education's ability to exert soft power cannot be reduced to simply the intellectual enterprise of teaching, learning and research—this is a simplistic view that Nye's conceptual framework never promoted. Therefore, analyses of higher education as soft power must recognize both the complexity of attraction as well as the methodological challenges in studying behavioral outcomes. Studies that focus on the relationship between higher education and behavioral outcomes often adopt a reductive framework akin to the design of behavioral psychology experiments. Ironically, many of these studies utilize qualitative methods but adopt a positivist worldview that seeks causal relationships for the purpose of generalization. While outcomes are important in international relations, the ideological nature of soft power is inherently social and constructivist.

2. HIGHER EDUCATION AS SOFT POWER

Given Asia's large geographic expanse and sharp differences in both political economy and higher education development, any generalization risks simplifying a complex

---

[1] Nye (2008, p. 142) states bluntly, "Educating the public is not the same as indoctrinating the public with propaganda. There is an important difference of degree between Roosevelt's fireside radio broadcasts and Hitler's elaborately staged Nuremberg rallies."

phenomenon. Rather than attempt to evaluate educational soft power across the region, this section will highlight the policies and practices among four different states. The case selections are purposeful to showcase states with power differentials in the international arena: a dynamic small power (Singapore), a constrained power (Taiwan), a classic middle power (Japan), and an emerging superpower (China). The purpose of this section is not to identify best practices or success stories but rather to examine the different motivations and approaches in leveraging higher education as a soft power resource. Nye's work has been criticized for focusing heavily on superpowers like the United States and the former Soviet Union (Lee, 2011). Research into soft power must also consider the contexts of small and middle powers to fully appreciate the complexities in international relations. Using power as a variable across four cases allows an analytical generalization that contributes to theory building rather than a statistical generalization to characterize a population (Yin, 2010).

2.1 Singapore: The Dynamic Small Power

Singapore is often described as a small state that "punches above its weight" as its spectacular history demonstrates (Heng and Aljunied, 2015). From an impoverished state without a reliable source of drinking water in the 1960s to its lofty position as one of the wealthiest and most advanced countries in the world today, Singapore's engagement with power intrigues international relations experts and economists alike. Without natural resources or a large military, this city-state has relied on ingenuity to minimize its vulnerabilities and advance its interests abroad (Lee, 2000). Economic power and soft power are both critical to Singapore's foreign policy (Jayakumar, 2011).

Singapore's higher education system is carefully planned to align with national interests just like many other parts of its society that operate on strategic pragmatism (Schein, 1996). Singapore hosts some of the best universities in Asia through steady investments, raw ambition, and an active recruitment of global talent that mirrors its approach to staffing corporations and government agencies. In 2002, the government put forth an ambitious proposal to turn the city-state into an education hub. Widely known as a haven for international trade, Singapore saw an opportunity to brand itself as an international education hub with geopolitical clout (Lee, 2015a). By elevating standards, subsidizing international branch campuses, funding laboratories, and recruiting international students, higher education emerged as a source of soft power. This initiative extended far beyond teaching to include high profile research partnerships (e.g., with MIT and Rolls Royce), leadership training for Asian corporations and governments, and a specialization in intellectual property laws.

Today, the education hub initiative seldom appears on policy agendas in Singapore. However, the ambition and activities that characterize this narrative remain visible. The recruitment of international students has waned in the last few years as locals grapple with rising population density, soaring living costs, and widening social inequities. The fervor of building international branch campuses has subsided. However, Singapore recognizes that its quality universities can attract international students and project an enlightened image of the country. In practice, internationally oriented academic programs and advanced laboratories with funded doctoral posts attract neighboring Malaysians and other foreigners. Unlike many countries that recruit international students largely for short-term financial gains, Singapore is keen to convert international students into skilled immigrants in order to mitigate the effects of an aging workforce and declining birth rate. Singaporean universities also advise education providers overseas (institutions and governments). Undoubtedly, Singapore's own impressive development and peaceful rise provide credibility when imparting lessons to foreign audiences who wish to emulate the city-state or collaborate for mutual benefits.

2.2 Taiwan: The Constrained Power

Taiwan's spectacular rise as an economic powerhouse, technology hub, and democratic beacon in Asia provides a fascinating study on soft power particularly in light of its protracted conflict with China. Unlike Singapore, Taiwan does not enjoy the full liberty of international engagement given its exclusion from many international organizations such as the United Nations and the World Health Organization. Despite decades of lobbying by the Taiwanese government for international recognition as a sovereign state, China's persistent international campaign to curtail the island state presents a bleak future for Taiwan's foreign policy. While Taiwan is not internationally known for its higher education, generations of Chinese Malaysians have flocked to the island to pursue degrees when marginalized by Malaysia's race-based affirmative action. Taiwan also attracts many purist Sinophiles who value the country's preservation of the traditional Chinese text and Chinese art while the mainland weathered socio-cultural destruction during the Cultural Revolution and adopted the simplified text.

In 2016, Taiwan launched a bold new foreign policy to reduce its economic dependence on China: the New Southbound Policy. This initiative aims to actively engage with the 18 nations of South-East Asia in trade, investment, agriculture, and education. The number of students from South-East Asia studying in Taiwan rose sharply by 85 percent from 2014 to 2018 (Wu, 2019). In 2018, more than 50,000 students from Southbound Policy countries were studying in Taiwan (ICEF, 2019). The government even designated some Taiwanese universities as partner institutions of specific South-East Asian countries for student exchange, community development projects, and research collaborations. While Taiwanese universities and society are still learning how to welcome these students and support their aspirations, the country's pivot towards South-East Asia explicitly positions higher education as a foreign policy instrument that seeks bilateral exchange rather than just a unilateral projection of a national image. Interestingly, the restricted space that Taiwan operates in as a "non-sovereign state" has reified soft power as a critical diplomatic tool. Many foreign policy instruments that are available to a conventional sovereign state are simply not available to Taiwan. Without membership in the United Nations, Taiwan is excluded from many international fora and occasionally permitted as a passive observer at best. Likewise, Taiwanese universities and researchers must also operate with a *persona non grata* overcast when international politics diffuse into academic spaces such as conferences and research collaborations. Ironically, Taiwan's preservation of Chinese culture, rapid economic development, and remarkable democratization exhibit strong soft power potential by any definition, but global power dynamics restrict its ability to act and benefit from productive foreign relations.

2.3 Japan: The Classic Middle Power

Japan's history as a colonial power and economic titan provides a fascinating backdrop for a study on soft power. Its military terrorized many parts of Asia in the twentieth century and left a legacy of animosity and distrust for generations to come. Its economic transformation between the 1960s and 1980s drew attention to the developmental state model, which later inspired the Asian Tigers (Taiwan, Singapore, Hong Kong, and South Korea). However, economic stagnation in the last few decades coupled with a sacrosanct constitution that enshrines pacifism and restricts military fortification has forced Japan to embrace soft power as a key plank of its foreign policy (Lee, 2011; Heng, 2017). Watanabe and McConnell (2008) even called Japan a "soft power superpower."

While post-war Japan has democratized, flourished through international trade, and contributed actively to global governance, its higher education system is in fact very insular with an imperceptible international footprint. Despite being the first country in Asia to achieve mass higher education, Japanese education is generally known for its achievements at the primary and secondary level rather than higher education (Hayhoe, 2008). In the 1980s, Japan began to experiment with educational soft power through the creation of international branch campuses, development of programs taught in English, and recruitment of international students. However, these strategies have produced limited success because most universities remain very Japanese and inaccessible to international students and academics (Yonezawa, 2008).

To evaluate Japanese higher education as a soft power asset, one must look beyond the traditional remit of universities. Specifically, the interface between higher education and international development provides some evidence of Japanese soft power. Prior to the 1990s, Japanese participation in education aid focused on higher and vocational education based on the logic that assistance at these levels was less intrusive than at basic education, which is a domain for nation-building and civic orientation (Kuroda and Hayashi, 2015). Furthermore, Japanese presence in basic education overseas may conjure up painful memories of its colonial past because Japanese language and education ethos were propagated throughout its vast empire (Kuroda and Hayashi, 2015). In the 1990s, Japan began to dedicate its Official Development Assistance (ODA) to basic education as part of the global movement to support *Education for All*. By the end of the decade, the government returned to higher education aid and created several research centers on international development within universities (e.g., Hiroshima, Nagoya,

Tokyo, and Tsukuba). Since 2002, the Japan International Cooperation Agency (JICA) has been courting university involvement at the institutional level rather than at the individual level of academics. For example, JICA launched its "Science and Technology Cooperation on Global Issues" to promote research collaborations between Japanese and foreign universities and spur capacity building activities. Through JICA's support, the Open University of Japan offers lectures (Development Studies Program) on Japan's modernization experience to foreign audiences. JICA also funds collaborations between 14 Japanese universities and 26 South-East Asian universities to promote engineering education (JICA, 2016). While all these activities are largely channeled through the prism of development aid, they do reflect Japanese higher education's contributions to the country's soft power agenda. Sharing Japan's modernization experience, conducting research on development, and promoting engineering education all tap into the country's strengths for public diplomacy.

2.4 China: The Emerging Superpower

The concept of soft power appeared in many Chinese foreign policies soon after Nye circulated his ideas in the late 1990s. Nye's work also echoes the teachings of ancient Chinese intellects on strategic alliances and benevolent leadership by military general Sun Zi and philosopher Mencius, respectively (Wang and Lu, 2008). As China's economic and military powers continue to scale new heights, soft power projections become even more important to reassure outsiders of China's peaceful rise (Kurlantzick, 2007; Pan, 2013). In Chinese policies and academic literature, soft power appears explicitly as a literal translation or in a slight variation as *soft authority*.[2] Wang and Lu (2008) insightfully note that Chinese usage of "soft power" is broader than Nye's framework. Specifically, Chinese use this concept to characterize not only projections from nation-states but also from organizations and individuals as well as a state's domestic behavior to enhance its benevolence and legitimacy among its citizens.

In conceiving culture and higher education as soft power resources, China has enthusiastically built a network of institutions around the globe: the Confucius Institutes. Founded in 2004, these institutes provide Chinese language education, promote Chinese culture, and assist foreigners who wish to connect with China for professional purposes (e.g., business interactions). Currently there are over 300 Confucius Institutes located in over 100 countries. Most of these institutes are housed on university campuses. Astutely, the Chinese government generously funds each institute and pairs each with a Chinese university to deepen collaborations in higher education.[3] For

---

[2] According to Wang and Lu (2008), Chinese discourse uses *ruan li liang* (软力量), *ruan shi li* (软实力), and *ruan quan li* (软权力),

[3] Each institute reportedly costs US$1 million to set up and over US$200,000 per year to operate (Kralev, 2010).

example, the Confucius Institute of Chulalongkorn University, Thailand, is partnered with Peking University.

The role of the Chinese state in creating and coordinating this network of Confucius Institutes on a global scale has attracted suspicion and even protests that led to several closures recently (Legerwood, 2020; Myklebust, 2020). Concerns over academic freedom, propaganda, espionage, and human rights abuses have unfortunately tarred an institution that was created for cultural diplomacy. While these charges are grave, critics also exaggerate the role of the Chinese state in overseeing Confucius Institutes (Yang, 2010; Hubbert, 2019). Yang (2010) reports unfettered operation at most institutes and even the inclusion of speakers and Taiwanese politicians who are critical of Chinese policies at events hosted by Confucius Institutes. In the wave of censure on Confucius Institutes, an undertone of xenophobia is also palpable because other state-sponsored cultural institutions have thrived for decades without being subjected to such scrutiny and condemnation (e.g., British Council, Goethe Institute, and Alliance française). Is the uproar over the Confucius Institutes about the role of the state in cultural diplomacy or about China's rise as a superpower?

Beyond the Confucius Institutes, Chinese higher education is also active in development aid. In Africa, Chinese universities contribute to capacity building, personnel training, and even the formation of new institutions with local partners (e.g., the Ethio-China Polytechnic College established in 2009 in Kenya). Chinese higher education's involvement in Africa began well before Confucius Institutes were conceived. Kenneth King's unique volume *China's Aid and Soft Power in Africa* (2013) provides many accounts of international engagements by Chinese universities. Increasingly, many African students are also studying in China through Chinese scholarships (Mulvey, 2019). Chinese scholars have affirmed that the Chinese government is keen to use higher education as a platform for soft power (Fang and Wu, 2016; Zheng and Ma, 2016; Chan and Wu, 2020).

3. POLITICS, PANDEMIC, AND THE LIMITS OF SOFT POWER

The soft power strategies deployed by Singapore, Taiwan, Japan, and China in leveraging their higher education institutions vary widely from the traditional practice of recruiting international students to the large-scale construction of cultural centers around the world. Asia's extensive experience in economic transformation and modernization in the last 50 years frankly provides more credibility in development assistance than the prescriptions from the Global North, which may come across as clinical and uninformed. Countries such as Japan, Korea, and Taiwan can also draw on their experiences in democratization after emerging from authoritarianism. The four cases profiled in this chapter are instructive on many levels, but a broader recognition of contemporary politics and the current pandemic is necessary because neither higher education nor soft power operates in a vacuum.

First, recruiting international students and academics for the sake of forging positive relationships with the host country is not a new practice. Many established examples of state-funded programs to attract international scholars already exist: the American Fulbright Program, Colombo Plan, Commonwealth Scholarship, Canada Research Chairs, and China's Thousand Talents plan. One may question the sincerity and effectiveness of these schemes, but they are nevertheless policy instruments that explicitly target foreign audiences for joint pursuits in higher education. While many studies of soft power focus on inbound international students as the most visible captive audience, the cases in this chapter demonstrate that international academic relations are not confined to teaching or the sovereign territory of the host country. Research, training, and technical assistance also exert soft power. Sometimes these activities are conducted overseas far away from the host country. Therefore, a broader conception of soft power is essential in providing more comprehensive analyses of higher education as a source of soft power.

Second, repugnant political values and foreign policies can quickly squander the goodwill that higher education attracts as a cultural platform. When the Confucius Institutes reverberate Chinese political values and foreign policies, international audiences are understandably alarmed. Concerns over academic freedom, human rights abuses, and proselytizing of Chinese governance are legitimate when foreign host universities value an open space for intellectual inquiries. China's crackdown on grassroots movements in Xinjiang and Hong Kong and assertions in the Spratly Islands dispute have dominated international headlines in the last few years and elicited condemnation. Similarly, Singapore faces the same challenge when restricted civil liberties and democratic participation at home contradict its use of higher education as soft power. Japan's periodic recognition of its wartime figures (e.g., Yasukuni Shrine) and inclination towards military armament in the face of a rising China and threatening North Korea (Smith, 2019) also illustrate the detrimental impact of unappealing political values and hard power. Even in the United States and United Kingdom, where higher education remains an enduring reservoir of soft power with global recognition, rising nationalism and populist politics generate anxiety among international students and academics. Foreign academics who are abandoning the United Kingdom due to Brexit and leaving China due to a restrictive climate represent not only a brain drain but also an erosion of public diplomacy. Such shocks to a system may require years of intense diplomacy to recover the soft power that is squandered. In short, soft power begins to tread on the slippery slope of insincerity and even propaganda when hypocrisy and intolerance metastasize to the viscera of diplomacy.

Third, despite the genuine efforts to attract talent through higher education and cultivate personal connections to a host country, the wider society may be unwelcoming or unprepared to provide a positive experience. Immigrant countries such as the United States and Australia may be more adept at providing a cosmopolitan environment in large metropolises, but small towns and conservative regions may present a severe culture shock for international students and academics. Similarly, while Taiwan is generally an open society, many communities retain traditional values and remain impenetrable for someone who does not speak Mandarin or Taiwanese. Japan, renowned for its insular society, recently blocked its foreign residents from re-entering the country during the COVID pandemic even though its citizens continued to travel freely. Long-term foreign residents are now beginning to question their future in Japan as well as the country's commitment to become a leading destination in Asia for talent and capital (Dooley, 2020). Therefore, deeply embedded societal views, inadequate services, and discriminatory measures may alienate outsiders even if higher education institutions managed to impress.

Finally, the current pandemic has introduced many disruptions to higher education and challenged many forms of international engagement. How viable are international student mobility and academic conferences when travel restrictions appear periodically without advance warning? Can elite universities with global recognition rely on their reputations by timidly adopting online learning? How can international development projects and collaborative research continue when higher education institutions face more imminent problems such as viral transmission on campus and financial bankruptcy? In this period of crisis and hardship, trust and compassion may in fact accrue far more soft power with a lasting impact than the prosaic metrics of research. If states wish to continue their pursuit of educational soft power, the safety and welfare of international students and colleagues should be paramount. What are the limits of higher education as a soft power resource when a country's political values and foreign policies repudiate all notions of shared humanity? These reflections, coupled with a persistent eye on developments in Asian higher education, can hopefully bring greater clarity to the theories, policies, and practices in soft power projections.

References

Atkinson, C. (2010). "Does soft power matter? A comparative analysis of student exchange programs 1980–2006." *Foreign Policy Analysis*, 6/1, 1–22.

Ball, S. J. (1993). "What is policy? Texts, trajectories and toolboxes." *Discourse: Studies in the Cultural Politics of Education*, 13/2, 10–17.

Bislev, A. (2017). "Student to student diplomacy: Chinese international students as a soft-power tool." *Journal of Current Chinese Affairs*, 46/2, 81–109.

Chan, W. K. and Wu, X. (2020). "Promoting governance model through international higher education: Examining international student mobility in China between 2003 and 2016." *Higher Education Policy*, 33/3, 511–530.

Clark, B. R. (1986). *The Higher Education System: Academic Organization in Cross-National Perspective*. Berkeley: University of California Press.

Cross, M. K. D. and Melissen, J. (eds.) (2013). *European Public Diplomacy: Soft Power at Work*. New York: Palgrave Macmillan.

Dooley, B. (2020). "Japan's locked borders shake the trust of its foreign workers." *New York Times*, August 5.

Fan, Y., Pan, J., Shao, Z., and Xu, Y. (2020). "How discrimination increases Chinese overseas students' support for authoritarian rule." 21st Century China Center Research Paper No. 2020-05. University of California San Diego. https://ssrn.com/abstract=3637710, accessed February 21, 2021.

Fang, B. and Wu, Y. (2016). "On changing trends of China's foreign students of higher education: An analysis of statistic data of the past 15 years." *Journal of Higher Education*, 39/2, 19–30 (in Chinese).

Hall, I. and Smith, F. (2013). "The struggle for soft power in Asia: Public diplomacy and regional competition." *Asian Security*, 9/1, 1–18.

Hayhoe, R. (2008). "Philosophy and comparative education: What can we learn from East Asia?" In K. Mundy, K. Bickmore, R. Hayhoe, M. Madden, and K. Madjidi (eds.), *Comparative and International Education: Issues for Teachers*. Toronto: Canadian Scholars' Press, 23–48.

Heng, Y.-K. and Aljunied, S. M. A. (2015). "Can small states be more than price takers in global governance?" *Global Governance*, 21/3, 435–454.

Hubbert, J. A. (2019). *China in the World: An Anthropology of Confucius Institutes, Soft Power, and Globalization*. Honolulu: University of Hawai'i Press.

ICEF (2019). "Taiwan's foreign enrolment getting a boost from Southeast Asia." *ICEF Monitor*, February 20. https://monitor.icef.com/2019/02/taiwans-foreign-enrolment-getting-a-boost-from-southeast-asia/, accessed October 27, 2020.

Jayakumar, S. (2011). *Diplomacy: A Singapore Experience*. Singapore: Straits Times Press.

JICA (2016). ASEAN University Network Southeast Asia Engineering Education Development Network (AUN SEED-Net) Project. https://www.jica.go.jp/indonesia/english/office/topics/160820.html, accessed October 27, 2020.

King, K. (2013). *China's Aid and Soft Power in Africa: The Case of Education & Training*. Rochester, NY: James Currey.

Kralev, N. (2010). "China 60, U.S. 0: Culture centers in other's country." *The Washington Times*, April 8. https://www.washingtontimes.com/news/2010/apr/8/china-60-us-0-culture-centers-in-others-country/, accessed October 27, 2020.

Kurlantzick, J. (2007). *Charm Offensive: How China's Soft Power Is Transforming the World*. New Haven, CT: Yale University Press.

Kuroda, K. and Hayashi, M. (2015). "Japan's educational cooperation policies and its implications for a post-2015 world." In I.-H. Cheng and S. J. Chan (eds.), *International Education Aid in Developing Asia: Policies and Practices*. Singapore: Springer, 39–56.

Lee, J. T. (2015a). "The regional dimension of education hubs: Leading and brokering geopolitics." *Higher Education Policy*, 28/1, 69–89.

Lee, J. T. (2015b). "Soft power and cultural diplomacy: Emerging education hubs in Asia." *Comparative Education*, 51/3, 353–374.

Lee, K.-Y. (2000). *From Third World to First: The Singapore Story 1965–2000*. New York: HarperCollins.

Lee, S.-W. (2011). "The theory and reality of soft power: Practical approaches in East Asia." In S. J. Lee and J. Melissen (eds.), *Public Diplomacy and Soft Power in East Asia*. New York: Palgrave Macmillan, 11–32.

Legerwood, R. (2020). "As US universities close Confucius Institutes, what's next?" *Human Rights Watch*. https://www.hrw.org/news/2020/01/27/us-universities-close-confucius-institutes-whats-next, accessed October 27, 2020.

Lomer, S. (2017). "Soft power as a policy rationale for international education in the UK: A critical analysis." *Higher Education*, 74/4, 581–598.

Lukes, S. (1974). *Power: A Radical View*. London: Macmillan.

Lukes, S. (2005). *Power: A Radical View* (2nd edition). New York: Palgrave Macmillan.

Marginson, S. (2011a). "Higher education in East Asia and Singapore: Rise of the Confucian model." *Higher Education*, 61/5, 587–611.

Marginson, S. (2011b). "Imagining the global." In R. King, S. Marginson, and R. Naidoo (eds.), *Handbook on Globalization and Higher Education*. Cheltenham, UK and Northampton, MA, USA: Edward Elgar Publishing, 10–39.

Mulvey, B. (2019). "International higher education and public diplomacy: A case study of Ugandan graduates from Chinese universities." *Higher Education Policy*, 33/3, 459–477.

Myklebust, J. P. (2020). "Confucius institutions close as China relations deteriorate." *University World News*, May 16. https://www.universityworldnews.com/post.php?story=2020051309 2025679, accessed October 27, 2020.

Neave, G. and van Vught, F. (eds.) (1991). *Prometheus Bound: The Changing Relationship between Government and Higher Education in Western Europe*. Oxford: Pergamon Press.

Nye, J. S. (2004). *Soft Power: The Means to Success in World Politics*. New York: Public Affairs.

Nye, J. S. (2008). *The Powers to Lead*. Oxford: Oxford University Press.

Pan, S. Y. (2013). "Confucius Institute project: China's cultural diplomacy and soft power projection." *Asian Education and Development Studies*, 2/1, 22–33.

Papatsiba, V. (2005). "Student mobility in Europe: An academic, cultural and mental journey? Some conceptual reflections and empirical findings." In M. Tight (ed.), *International Relations* (International Perspectives on Higher Education Research, Volume 3). Bingley: Emerald Group, 29–65.

Richmond, Y. (2003). *Cultural Exchange and the Cold War: Raising the Iron Curtain*. University Park: Pennsylvania State University Press.

Rizvi, F. and Lingard, B. (2010). *Globalizing Education Policy*. London: Routledge.

Schein, E. H. (1996). *Strategic Pragmatism: The Culture of Singapore's Economic Development Board*. Boston: MIT Press.

Smith, S. A. (2019). *Japan Rearmed: The Politics of Military Power*. Cambridge, MA: Harvard University Press.

Steiner-Khamsi, G. (2014). "Cross-national policy borrowing: Understanding reception and translation." *Asia Pacific Journal of Education*, 34/2, 153–167.

Waltz, K. N. (1979). *Theory of International Politics*. New York: Addison-Wesley.

Wang, H. and Lu, Y.-C. (2008). "The conception of soft power and its policy implications: A comparative study of China and Taiwan." *Journal of Contemporary China*, 17/56, 425–447.

Watanabe, Y. and McConnell, D. L. (eds.) (2008). *Soft Power Superpowers: Cultural and National Assets of Japan and the United States*. Armonk, NY: M. E. Sharpe.

Wu, F. (2019). "Southeast Asian student enrollment up 85% in Taiwan." *CommonWealth*. https://english.cw.com.tw/article/article.action?id=2376, accessed October 27, 2020.

Yang, R. (2010). "Soft power and higher education: An examination of China's Confucius Institutes." *Globalisation, Societies and Education*, 8/2, 235–245.

Yin, R. (2010). "Analytic generalization." In A. J. Mills, G. Durepos, and E. Wiebe (eds.), *Encyclopedia of Case Study Research*. Thousand Oaks, CA: Sage, 21–23.

Yonezawa, A. (2008). "Facing crisis: Soft power and Japanese education in a global context." In Y. Watanabe and D. L. McConnell (eds.), *Soft Power Superpowers: Cultural and National Assets of Japan and the United States*. Armonk, NY: M. E. Sharpe, 54–74.

Zheng, G. and Ma, L. (2016). "The Belt and Road Initiative and education for overseas students in China: An analysis on data between 2004 and 2014." *Education and Economy*, 4, 77–82 (in Chinese).

CHAPTER 24

....

HIGHER EDUCATION AND NATIONALISM IN THE ASIA-PACIFIC

....

CHRISTOPHER D. HAMMOND

THIS chapter explores some of the dynamics and tensions between higher education and nationalism in the context of the Asia-Pacific. "Nationalism" is an evocative term that has re-emerged in public discourse in recent decades, contextualized by and often juxtaposed with the sweeping forces of neoliberal globalization. The meaning of the term and its implications have evolved over time, with recent iterations in many contexts evoking populist themes, hostility toward perceived enemy "others" either internal or external to the nation, and a refutation of globalism. In many parts of the Western world, a wave of anti-globalist sentiment has emerged among selected populations, spurring a rise of populist, right-wing political parties and politicians claiming to represent these disaffected groups. Notable examples include the anti-immigration nationalist discourses of "England for the English" which has provided fuel for the UK's "Brexit" from the European Union (Vickers, 2017), and slogans advocating to "Build the Wall," put "America First," and "Make America Great Again," which became synonymous with the Trump presidency in the United States. Declines in the number of international students heading to these traditionally popular higher education destinations—the majority of whom hail from Asia-Pacific countries—points to one way in which nationalism and global higher education intersect. The rise of nationalism in the Western world can indeed have worldwide effects, but there are numerous examples of homegrown forms of nationalism intersecting with and impacting higher education within the Asia-Pacific as well. These intersections are considered below.

Nationalism and national identity have been widely studied, debated, and defined (see for example Anderson, 2006; Hobsbawm, 2012; Smith, 2010; Triandafyllidou, 1998). The chapter thus begins with a brief survey of some of the key debates and proposes a working typology of nationalism for the purposes of the subsequent analysis. The challenge of addressing a topic as complex as nationalism is compounded by its analytical application to the contested geographies of the "Asia-Pacific," a regional entity comprising numerous countries and societies and unparalleled political, cultural, and linguistic diversity. As such, justifying the selection of particular nation-states as case studies that can somehow be representative of the "Asia-Pacific" is especially problematic.

Connected to this, the propensity for social researchers to take the nation-state as a primary unit of analysis has itself become critiqued as a form of "methodological nationalism" (Dale, 2005; Wimmer and Glick Schiller, 2002). I endeavor to avoid this methodological approach, but inevitably the topic of contemporary nationalism entails making reference to the policies and practices of particular nation-states. Thus, while I do draw on a purposive set of examples of nationalism manifesting in selected Asia-Pacific contexts, I attempt to frame these phenomena from the unifying analytical perspective of higher education.

1. Conceptualizing Nationalism

Of the multiple meanings of "nationalism," Anthony D. Smith posits the term most often refers to the language and symbolism, socio-political movements, and ideologies developed on behalf of the nation (Smith, 2010, pp. 5–6). Smith argues it is the *ideologies of nationalism* that have the most salience, as it is ideology that "gives force and direction to both symbols and movements" (Smith, 2010, p. 8). He offers the following working definition:

> An ideological movement for attaining and maintaining autonomy, unity and identity for a population which some of its members deem to constitute an actual or potential "nation." (Smith, 2010, p. 9)

Smith's definition is quite general and abstract, and serves as an umbrella concept that can include a wide range of nationalist ideologies. This wide range can be understood in various ways, but one helpful contrast is to delineate *civic* and *ethnic* types. Civic nationalism is organized around the idea of an inclusive, diverse community of "equal rights-bearing citizens, united in patriotic attachment to a shared set of political practices and values" (Ignatieff, 1993, p. 6). A key element of this type of community is its acknowledgment of "voluntarism," in that one can *choose* to be a member and adopt a particular national identity. By contrast, ethnic nationalism entails that a community is bound together by an inherited ethnicity and culture. In this case, one is born as a member of an ethno-cultural national community, and has little choice in the matter. Arguably, civic nationalism is more conducive to democracy while ethnic nationalism aligns with more authoritarian regimes (Ignatieff, 1993, p. 6), but in actuality, things are more complex. These two types of nationalism should be considered as ideal-types positioned on two ends of a spectrum, with manifestations in reality including some combination of the two and complicated further by additional factors such as language, religion, colonial histories, and political economic ideologies. Nevertheless, these ideal-types serve as a useful analytical tool through which to explore and juxtapose various forms of nationalism.

Nationalism as a discursive concept has evolved over time, with contemporary usage of the term frequently associated with xenophobic, extremist, and authoritarian forms. Arguably a more banal but similar concept is "patriotism," which connotes a positive feeling of love and support for one's country. Figure 24.1 posits a conceptualization of the various forms and types of nationalism, acknowledging that nations and actors within them may embody different intersecting combinations of these ideal-types at different points in a nation's history and across different subgroups within a nation-state.

Nationalism as a term did not initially have a negative connotation. It was originally seen as a force of progress and development, and as a tool of resistance against imperialism. Members of colonized societies who envisioned themselves as part of a national community were better able to unite in resistance against their colonizers and demand independence. Independence movements fueled by nationalistic ideologies first took place in Latin America, then Eastern Europe, and finally Asia and Africa after World War II. During this era, nationalism was championed by many progressive intellectuals, poets, and artists (Etzioni, 2019).

However, once independence was gained, many of those in power in newly formed nation-states recognized how important inculcating national identities was to maintain control and legitimacy both at home and abroad. Ruling powers have long utilized education as a political tool, employing civic, history, and moral education curricula in an attempt to instill in their citizenry unquestioning beliefs in national mythologies, often bound up with a glorification of the state in order to legitimatize its existence. In many

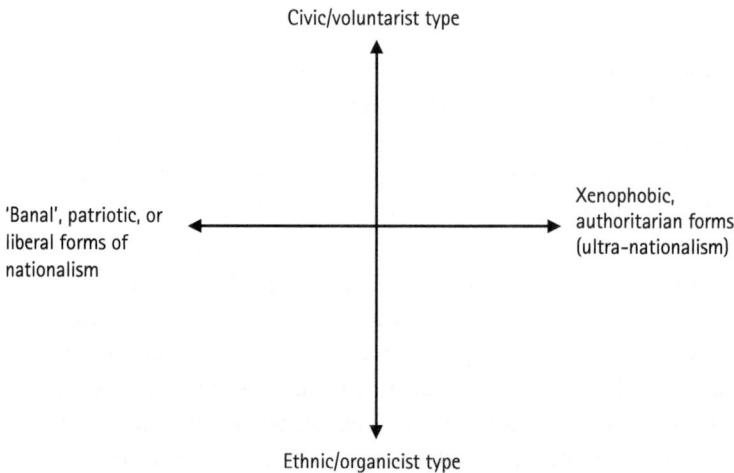

FIGURE 24.1 A conceptualization of forms and types of nationalisms

Source: Adapted from Smith (2010).

cases, demagogues and other ruling elites utilized xenophobic forms of nationalism in order to deflect criticism away from themselves, placing blame on enemy "others" outside (or sometimes inside) national borders (Morris et al., 2015). The practice of "othering" in some form is arguably an essential component of national identity formation. Triandafyllidou (1998, p. 593) posited that only through distinguishing and differentiating the nation from other nations or ethnic groups does the idea of a national community become meaningful. While often benign, this sense of "us versus them" is a volatile element of nationalistic thinking that has the potential to lead to extremist and violent forms.

Nationalism is not always exercised as a tool for political control by ruling elites of a nation-state, however. At times it emerges organically, from the bottom up, and serves as a force to challenge those in power. This often manifests in sub-regions of an existing nation state, where a community of people understands their own communal identity to be different from and unrepresented by the nation state in which it exists. These forms of nationalism align with early manifestations that emerged as resistance against colonialism, and are often the fuel for independence movements seen in places like Spain's Catalonia and the Basque country. This grassroots form of nationalism has arguably been emerging in Hong Kong as well, and is discussed in more detail below.

Depending on the context, the various forms of nationalism can be conceived as both bottom-up, grassroots, and populist manifestations and top-down influences that can mutually reinforce one another (Figure 24.2). As populist upwellings of nationalist sentiment emerge, political leaders claiming to represent these constituencies become legitimized and empowered. Once in positions of authority, they can exercise their influence to foment nationalist sympathies, further solidifying their power.

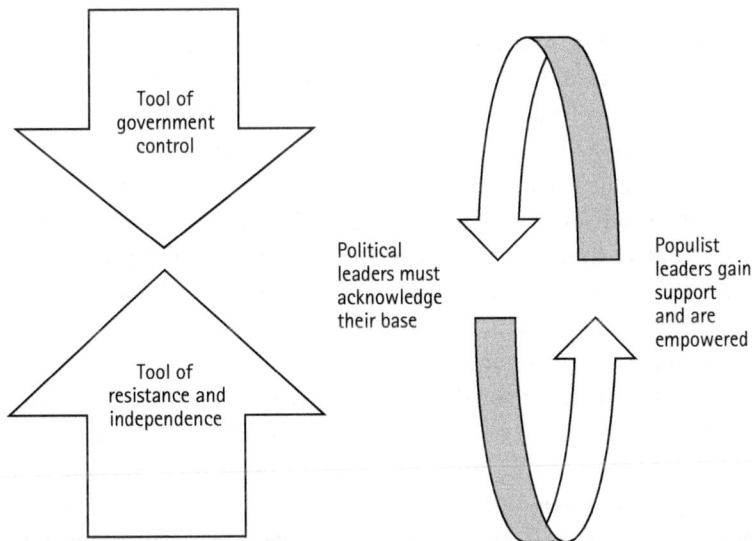

FIGURE 24.2 Top-down and bottom-up nationalism

Having presented a basic framework for understanding nationalism, the chapter now turns to a discussion on the relationship between nationalism and higher education. To frame this discussion I draw on ideas from Clark Kerr, who describes the inherent tensions between higher education's cosmopolitan DNA and its relationship to the nation-state. Following this I posit six ways that nationalism and higher education can intersect, drawing on examples from a number of Asia-Pacific contexts.

2. COSMOPOLITAN HIGHER EDUCATION IN A WORLD OF NATIONS

> Knowledge, as Socrates would have it, is the "only one good" and is universal in value; but knowledge, as Bacon would have it, is also power, and power is particularised and those with the power may not want to share it. Which to serve: the universal truth or the particularised power? (Kerr, 1990, p. 6)

In 1990, Clark Kerr wrote that "universities are, by nature of their commitment to advancing universal knowledge, essentially international institutions, but they have been living increasingly in a world of nation states that have designs upon them" (Kerr, 1990, p. 5). This commitment to universal knowledge has a long history. Institutes of higher learning can be traced back thousands of years to places such as ancient Greece, Persia, India, and China. Modern-day universities most closely emulate the medieval universities of Europe, which predate the formation of nation-states by centuries. Universities from this period were characterized by self-governing guilds of scholars who were free from state control, and education was available to all who were capable of traveling to these locations and undertaking study in Latin. In this sense, contemporary higher education has cosmopolitan DNA, and it has only been since the emergence of the Westphalian system of nation-states that universities have found themselves increasingly tied up with constraining objectives of the states in which they reside (Kerr, 1990). Nevertheless, prestigious institutions with long-standing commitments to academic freedom, the universality of knowledge, and liberal education have persisted and been influential on modern higher education systems worldwide. Western higher education models, primarily from the United Kingdom, France, Germany, and the United States, have been alternatively exported, imposed, copied and adapted by various countries, including many in the Asia-Pacific.

The tensions inherent in higher education's international ethos and its relationship to the state are described by Kerr as "conflicting laws of motion" that shape universities in the contemporary age. Hawkins (2012) discusses a similar phenomenon in relation to cross-border regional cooperation of higher education in East Asia, using the concepts of *centripetal* and *centrifugal forces* that push university activities beyond national borders and pull them back from achieving forms of higher education regionalization found in other world regions like Europe. Consideration of these forces or laws of motion helps to conceptualize the ways higher education and nationalism intersect. Of the varied ways these forces manifest in national and institutional strategies, policies and practices, I focus below on what I consider to be the most important intersections in the age of globalization and global competition, drawing on salient examples from Asia-Pacific contexts.

3. INTERSECTIONS OF NATIONALISM AND HIGHER EDUCATION IN ASIA-PACIFIC CONTEXTS

The various intersections presented below can be examined as isolated examples of how nationalism can be expressed in relation to higher education, but I endeavor to present them in a logical order that reflects the conceptualizations of nationalism discussed above. The first four intersections represent the "top-down" policies and practices of the state in its attempt to shape and constrain the activities of universities. This segues to the fifth intersection which explores the "bottom-up" influence of student-led activism and the utilization of university campuses as physical spaces for mobilizing social change, activities which are frequently tied up either in support of or opposition to various nationalist causes. The final intersection looks to cyberspace, and the issues surrounding the rise of misinformation and targeted nationalist extremism that has implications for university educators and policymakers. In the various Asia-Pacific examples presented below, nationalism can be seen to manifest in a range of civic, ethnic, banal and extreme forms.

3.1 Nation-Building

National education systems are frequently utilized by states as a powerful platform for the mass inculcation of national identities. However, things become more complex at the higher education level, in large part due to the various elements of higher education that transcend national borders.

In the context of the Asia-Pacific, modern higher education systems are a relatively recent phenomenon, and coincide with the industrialization and colonization of the modern world by European powers. As such, many Asia-Pacific countries were colonized and had their systems of higher learning imposed upon them by their colonizers. While constraints on academic freedom were often imposed in attempts to curtail anti-colonial sentiment, colonial universities were often sites where resistance movements emerged. Philip Altbach writes:

> University-based indigenous intellectuals in country after country in Asia were re-
> sponsible for the growth of nationalist ideas, of cultural renaissance movements
> and of modernizing ideas in general. In a sense, the colonial universities were the
> seedbeds of the downfall of colonialism and of the emergence of independent
> nations. University-trained intellectuals were the key nationalist leaders virtually
> everywhere. (Altbach, 1989, p. 17)

While many Asia-Pacific countries utilized higher education as a tool to resist colonization, non-colonized nations such as Japan saw higher education as a tool to "catch up"
with the industrialized nations of the West. Higher education in this context was primarily seen as a means to achieve economic growth for the nation, and centralized government steering entailed an emphasis on producing graduates to meet this end. In the
early Meiji period, Japan sent its elites out into the world to acquire modern scientific
knowledge; a study abroad tour undertaken for primarily nationalistic purposes. The
degree to which various academic disciplines are emphasized is also connected to the
nation-building project. While the humanities indeed have their place in universities
across Japan, since the beginning, and particularly at the level of the national research-
intensive universities, higher education has had a strong focus on producing the
bureaucrats, economists, scientists, and engineers needed to facilitate the construction
of a modern industrialized nation.

Scholars have argued that Japan's early adoption of Western ideas of modernity
contributed to the development of a unique sense of positioning within Asia, fueling
an ethno-nationalist worldview which served to rationalize the nation's imperialist project in the region (Kim, 2016). South Korea and Taiwan were influenced by Japan's role
as a colonizer, and while the peoples of these and other occupied territories colonized
by Japan were subjected to inhumane oppression and violence, they also experienced
an expansion of educational infrastructure under Japanese rule that subsequently
augmented development in those societies. The "catch up" mentality that has served to
propel Japan into the ranks of industrialized nations has been influential in other Asian
nations as well, some of which have looked to Japan's education system as a model to
emulate. Singapore is one such example, whereby a highly centralized developmental
state utilizes its universities for manpower planning, continually recalibrating the aims
of higher education to augment Singapore's capacity to contribute to the global economy
(Lee and Gopinathan, 2003).

While the era of colonialism has passed, forms of Western domination can still be
found worldwide, including in higher education. Communicative globalization and
the emergent global dimension of higher education has enabled expanded access to
knowledge and increased cross-border collaboration and mobility, but the global
system is stratified with UK and US universities dominating global rankings and the
top scientific journals requiring publication in English (Marginson, 2021). In this context, universities and systems existing outside the Anglosphere must conform and as-
similate in order to compete. With the rise of Asian higher education the application of
this "center/periphery" model is called into question, and forms of resistance emerge

that could arguably be called "academic nationalism." Here the emphasis is not on publishing in English but in the national language, and attempting to develop a prestigious indigenous higher education tradition. For example, in South Korea, the influence of the United States on higher education has spurred many academics to seek out PhD degrees at American universities, returning to Korea upon completion of their doctoral programs. However, recent years have seen a push to cultivate a more prestigious and effective domestic system utilizing the Korean language (Tang, 2014).

Japan, too, has long remained insular and nationally oriented, particularly in the social sciences and humanities, with Japan-specific academic societies and relevant publications published in Japanese. While there are arguably merits to this approach, access to knowledge produced becomes limited to those who can comprehend local languages, and international faculty trying to build careers in places like Japan can report feeling marginalized from the "mainstream" academic culture (Brotherhood et al., 2020).

3.2 National "Brand" Promotion and Soft Power

Another related intersection is the utilization of higher education for soft power diplomacy (Nye, 2017). In this respect, universities are used as tools to promote the national "brand" (Kingston, 2017). A salient example from the Asia-Pacific is the over 1000 Confucius Institutes that the Chinese government has installed in partnership primarily with universities (and some K-12 schools) worldwide (Green-Riley, 2020). These institutes provide Chinese language and culture classes, research grants to selected faculty, and pay yearly dues to host universities (Kingston, 2017). However, Confucius Institutes have come under scrutiny in some contexts for perceived encroachment on academic freedom and censorship of subjects the Chinese Communist Party deems politically sensitive (Green-Riley, 2020). In 2020, the US State Department designated the Confucius Institute US Center (CIUS) as a "foreign mission" of the Chinese government involved in advancing "Beijing's global propaganda" on US campuses and in classrooms (Green-Riley, 2020), despite empirical evidence highlighting how Confucius Institutes largely emphasize traditional Chinese culture and present an apolitical version of China to global audiences (Hartig, 2018). Nevertheless, in light of these debates and under conservative political pressure a number of universities have closed down their Confucius Institutes (Green-Riley, 2020).

Another physical manifestation of national brand promotion can be found in the proliferation of transnational higher education through the establishment of branch campuses, twinning programs, and forms of program and provider mobility. Here universities export their offerings for degrees and their associated status to lucrative international markets. China has proven to be one such market, with over 1,000 programs and institutions approved by the Chinese government in recent decades (Fang, 2012; Montgomery, 2016). Transnational education is also used as a tool to augment national competitiveness in the host country. Singapore, for example, initiated a plan after the Asian Financial Crisis to bring in 10 world-class universities to Singapore within 10 years, to help boost the nation's innovation productivity[1] (Sanders, 2018). Transnational higher education is not always motivated by the goals of national brand promotion; however; at times the impetus is purely profit-driven and concerns institutional-level brand promotion.

A third example of soft power diplomacy can be found in the realm of cross-border research collaboration. Termed "science diplomacy" by policymakers, this approach aligns the aims of scientific research with those of the nation-state. For example, the Council for Science, Technology and Innovation (CSTI) in Japan describes science diplomacy in the following way:

> the international competitiveness of science and technology systems is improved by using science and technology for diplomacy and using diplomacy for science and technology promotion to contribute to solving common global issues to all mankind and at the same time to *increase the wealth and power of the nation* ... (Cabinet Office, 2015, emphasis added)

This strategic approach to the steering of STI priorities highlights another, more political orientation to the notion of competitiveness in higher education research. Not only is Japan concerned with advancing knowledge and innovation to enhance economic competitiveness, but it sees STI cross-border research as a political tool for achieving its goals in the international relations arena, to "enhance the power of the nation." This strategic and political approach to the support of research has implications for academic freedom and institutional autonomy, as projects that do not align with the diplomatic goals of the government may be deemed ineligible for funding opportunities. I will return to the tensions between nationalism and academic freedom below.

The above examples highlight how higher education can be utilized as a tool of the state and geared towards national purposes. But within many of these cross-border nation-building activities lie the tensions alluded to by Kerr, which become evident upon an investigation of policies and practices of higher education internationalization.

3.2 Nationalism and Internationalization

Both nation-building and soft power diplomacy are connected to internationalization of higher education. The internationalization of higher education has expanded dramatically since Kerr wrote of the opposing laws of motion, and so too has the global

---

[1] As part of the "Global Schoolhouse" initiative, efforts to establish world-class universities in Singapore have been beset with obstacles, including foreign universities withdrawing due to financial difficulties, quality assurance issues, and increasing restrictions on Singapore's liberal immigration policy (Tan, 2016).

competition among nation-states to develop the most successful higher education systems and institutions. While "success" can be interpreted in different ways, higher education internationalization has largely evolved in line with the broader neoliberal project and has increasingly been characterized in many contexts by marketization, commodification, and corporatization. University enrollment has dramatically increased worldwide, and when domestic demand is not met due to supply issues or perceived lack of quality, many students who can afford it are increasingly studying outside their home countries. Estimated to be a US$300 billion industry (Altbach and de Wit, 2020), a massive global market has emerged that seeks to attract these fee-paying students to universities, with the US, UK, and Australian higher education sectors taking particularly aggressive approaches.

There is also a global job market for academics, with many universities actively recruiting international faculty. Research has shown that international diversity among academics can have dramatic effects on research output (Mahroum, 2000; Mamiseishvili and Rosser, 2010) and thereby augment the global competitiveness of universities and the nations in which they reside (Altbach and Yudkevich, 2017). In the Asia-Pacific, the presence of international faculty is uneven across higher education systems. In countries like Malaysia and Japan, the low proportion of international faculty has led to concerted efforts to augment their recruitment at many universities (Huang, 2021; Muftahu et al., 2021). By contrast, Hong Kong has a relatively high proportion of international faculty, while in Singapore the high proportion of foreign academics has given rise to anxieties about the lack of a Singaporean "core" (L. Kong, personal communication, July 11, 2020).

International mobility has been on the rise, particularly from (and within) Asia. But tensions have also arisen as these various forms of internationalization meet with xenophobic nationalism. Recent years in particular have witnessed a rise in anti-immigration sentiment in destination countries like the United Kingdom and the United States, and some discourses have spilled over into discussions of potential threats to national security, with Chinese international students being viewed with suspicion by some for being possible spies (Basken, 2018). In Australia, reports of violence and racism against students and other immigrants of South Asian descent have sparked international media coverage and protests (Perry, 2009). Xenophobic nationalism has further melded with racism and hate crimes against students of East Asian descent during the emergence of the COVID-19 pandemic that reportedly originated in China. International students made headlines again when the Trump administration attempted to forbid international students from residing in the United States (under threat of deportation) if their universities planned to only offer online tuition due to the pandemic, a policy that was quickly overturned due to fierce opposition from many American universities (Jordan and Hartocollis, 2020).

While it may appear that universities serve as social institutions that resist nationalism, research has also pointed to more banal expressions of nationalism emerging *from* internationalizing universities both in the West and in Asia. Friedman (2018) describes how "everyday" forms of nationalism are embedded within conceptualizations and strategies for internationalization at elite Western universities through an analysis of the views of university administrators (Friedman, 2018, p. 248). In Asian contexts, studies have shown how internationalization policies in Japan are bound up with efforts to inculcate and export strong Japanese national identities (Hammond and Keating, 2017; Yonezawa, 2014), while efforts at cross-border research collaboration are at times impeded by nationally oriented competition among research teams (Hammond, 2019). This work complicates notions that internationalizing universities inherently stand in opposition to the forces of nationalism, and highlights how the opposing laws of motion can manifest not only in response to external pressures, but also as internalized ideas about a university's institutional identity and its relationship to the nation. External pressures can serve to reinforce these internalized ideas however, and these pressures have arguably become more acute in recent decades as a result of the expansion of the global system of university rankings.

3.4 Global Rankings and Status Competition

The growing prominence of global rankings has created another intersection of higher education and nationalism. Stratified national systems are no longer solely judged for prestige and reputation in isolation: they are now compared against world-class universities on a global scale. With the twenty-first century termed the "Asian Century" by some (Woetzel and Seong, 2019), many universities and higher education systems in Asia-Pacific countries are moving up in the league tables. This has led to intense competition both within and across Asia-Pacific countries. Japan, which was long recognized as the higher education forerunner in the twentieth century, now finds itself in stiff competition with mainland China, South Korea, Singapore, and Hong Kong. China in particular has consistently invested substantially in higher education and R&D (rising 18 percent per year between 2000 and 2012) (Marginson, 2016), and has now surpassed the United States in the quantity of scientific papers published (Tollefson, 2018). Similar investments by the government of Malaysia have led to increases in research productivity and improved rankings of Malaysian universities, which in turn serves to attract more international students, faculty and researchers (Bloomberg, 2019).

In addition to investment in national systems, cross-border co-authorship and collaborative research also continues to rise, and at the government level international cooperation in higher education is often framed as a means to augment national competitiveness. This emphasis on competition can hinder collegial forms of cooperation in various ways, particularly when internationally cooperating research teams find significant overlap in their areas of expertise and each have pressure by their respective governments to publish and be awarded patent rights (Hammond, 2020). The various forms of pressure put on institutions and researchers to conduct applied research and enhance national competitiveness also have implications for another key intersection of higher education and the state: the role of universities as public spaces for exercising and safeguarding academic freedom.

3.5 Constraints on Academic Freedom

Academic freedom entails autonomy to conduct and share research without interference from the state, one's own institution, or others in positions of power. This includes the ability to research and be critical of the government and other forms of authority in society. Governments and other actors can constrain academic freedom in overt and subtle ways. These techniques can include the selective funding of research, unofficial marginalization and discrimination of dissenting voices, and the outright forbidding and punishment of criticism and dissent.

Overt cases of constraint on academic freedom can be found in Asia-Pacific contexts like India and China. In the populous Indian state of Uttar Pradesh, a law was passed in 2019 that effectively forbade "anti-national activities" at all private universities (Jangid, 2019). What this means in practice is unclear, but Jangid suggests that the ordinance could have wide-ranging implications. He writes:

> What that activity might be is not defined so any interpretation by politicians or bureaucrats can turn critical thinking into anti-nationalism. For example, a historian's talk about medieval India and the Mughal period might be questioned if it does not concur with a right-wing narrative against Muslim rulers. Any public gathering of students on campus can be termed as anti-national if it is about human rights in Kashmir or the burning of copies of Manusmriti, the legal text of some Hindu laws, by the Dalits who have a problem with this book as it codifies and legitimises the caste system. (Jangid, 2019)

In China, crackdowns on academic freedom have been highlighted as worsening in recent years, with a comprehensive study conducted by New York University-based group Scholars at Risk describing the situation in stark terms:

> In mainland China, state and university authorities have employed a range of tactics to intimidate, silence, and punish academics and students. They include limits on internet access, libraries, and publication imports that impair research and learning; orders to ban discussion and research on topics the Party-state deems controversial; surveillance and monitoring of academic activity that result in loss of position and self-censorship; travel restrictions that disrupt the flow of ideas across borders; and the use of detentions, prosecutions, and other coercive tactics to retaliate against and constrain critical inquiry and expression. (Scholars at Risk, 2019, p. 4)

Restrictions on academic freedom in China can have spillover effects in collaborating countries as well, as was evidenced by the detention in 2019 of a Japanese academic who was conducting research in China and was arrested for possession of what was termed a "forbidden book" (Kakuchi, 2019). The arrest was met with surprise and disapproval by the academic community in Japan, with many scholars canceling research trips to China and arguing the move cast a shadow on future possibilities for collaboration (ibid.). A similar controversy unfolded with regard to a journal published by Cambridge

University Press, which initially complied with a Chinese government request to block access to over 300 articles in the renowned *China Quarterly* which were deemed objectionable (Phillips, 2017), before reverting their decision under international pressure.

Beyond research, academic freedom can also encompass the activities of students and faculty, many of whom utilize their time at university and the physical spaces of university campuses to organize and demonstrate for social change. It is here too in these physical and organizational spaces that higher education intersects, and at times clashes with, nationalism.

3.6 Campuses as Spaces of Activism

An important intersection where higher education meets nationalism is in the physical spaces of many university campuses. A salient example can be found at UC Berkeley in the United States. In the mid-1960s Berkeley was the epicenter of the Free Speech Movement.[2] More recently, images of "alt-right" white nationalist groups can be found brandishing "Free Speech" banners reproduced utilizing the same typeface used in the original Berkeley protests, in an attempt to conceal what has widely been recognized as anti-immigrant hate speech under the guise of the more palatable Free Speech Movement. These extreme nationalist groups have clashed with counter-protesters, at times violently with anti-fascist groups. University campuses across the United States have become sites for similar battles where student-led groups protest against organized speeches on campuses by speakers accused of inciting hate. A number of university campuses in the Asia-Pacific, too, have emerged as sites for contestation and struggle, although the issues and intersections with nationalism tend to differ in these varied contexts. Arguably the most globally recognizable student-led movement in Asia is the pro-democracy protests that took place in Beijing's Tiananmen Square in 1989, which were suppressed by the Chinese military at the behest of China's leader at the time, Deng Xiaoping (Kingston, 2017). Rejecting the possibility of a pluralistic and democratic system of governance, the ruling CCP has since utilized pervasive "patriotic education" curricula to inculcate national identities across China, conflating notions of *aiguo* ("love of country") with a recognition of the legitimacy of CCP rule (Zhao, 1998).

A more contemporary example can be found in Hong Kong, with student and academic-led groups like Scholarism emerging to challenge the growing encroachment of mainland China and pro-Beijing local politicians. At the time of writing, the most recent manifestation had been the massive protests against a bill that allowed for the extradition of Hong Kongers to the mainland for trial and the subsequent perceived overreaction of the Hong Kong police attempt to quell the protests. Many of these clashes have played out on university campuses, with the Chinese University of Hong Kong and

---

[2] Incidentally, Clark Kerr was the President of the University of California at this time, and his relatively forgiving position on the student protests ultimately led to his dismissal by the Board of Regents under political pressure from then governor of California, Ronald Reagan (Hechinger, 2003).

Hong Kong Polytechnic University in particular emerging as sites for battle between students who occupied the campus and the police. The tensions between Hong Kongers and mainland Chinese have also played out globally on campuses at universities world-wide, as international students from different domestic education traditions encounter one another's opinions for the first time.

The tensions in Hong Kong extend beyond higher education, and connect to the perceived steady encroachment of mainland China into the lives of Hong Kongers in recent years. One in seven residents is a mainlander who arrived after 1997 and pre-pandemic Hong Kong reportedly saw 40 million mainland tourists each year. Furthermore, an influx of money from mainland China's rapidly growing economy has had dramatic effects. Many newly rich mainland Chinese have been investing heavily into local real estate, which has driven up the cost of living and triggered a housing crisis (Fisher, 2019). As a result, Hong Kong's traditionally dominant social class of educated, white-collar professionals have been hit hard, with stalling or declining wages leading locals to become less well-off than their parents had been. Some joined Hong Kong's lo-calist movement, which advocated political autonomy and cultural distinctiveness from mainland China (Fisher, 2019). This combination of demographic change and economic dislocation has led people to reshape their identities and politics around a sense of us-versus-them, spurring the development of a grassroots nationalism. The sense of dis-affection coupled with longing for the creation of a liberal democratic political system create the conditions for social activism, movements largely populated and often led by university-age students. Beijing has shown no indication of softening its stance on the Special Administrative Region, however, and the future is sure to be wrought with challenges as the peoples from the mainland and Hong Kong struggle within a frame-work scholar Brian Fong has termed "One country, two nationalisms" (Fisher, 2019).

A dire situation has emerged on university campuses in India. India is home to a minority population of over 200 million Muslims (out of a total population of ap-proximately 1.3 billion), an expansive group that has experienced a dramatic rise in discrimination, hate crimes, and outright violence since the rise of right-wing Hindu nationalism aligning with the party of Prime Minister Narendra Modi. Modi himself was a member of a Hindu nationalist volunteer organization called the RSS, a group that has been described as an extremist and paramilitary group whose members have engaged in anti-Muslim violence (Kingston, 2017). Upon the re-election of his party in 2019, the Modi administration revoked the special status of Jammu and Kashmir, and enacted a controversial Citizenship Amendment Act which has been criticized for discriminating based on religion and excluding Muslims (Schultz, 2019). Passage of the legislation provoked widespread protests country wide, many of which took place on university campuses.

A backlash to these protests also ensued at a number of universities. A masked, armed mob that some argue was part of a student organization associated with Modi's BJP stormed onto campuses such as New Delhi's Jawaharlal Nehru University, attacking students and academics, injuring scores of people (Niazi and Sharma, 2020). A similar attack occurred at Jamia Millia Islamia some months earlier when baton-wielding police came onto the campus and attacked students who were reportedly protesting the new Citizenship law (Niazi, 2020). Clashes such as these among university students and scholars and nationalist groups are not limited to the physical spaces of university campuses, but are increasingly manifesting in online spaces as well.

3.7   Globalization of Nationalism in Cyberspace

The final intersection considers the roles of universities and educators in equipping learners with the critical thinking and media literacy skills necessary for informed "civic reasoning" in an age characterized by what *The New York Times* has termed the "globalization of nationalism" (Becker, 2019). Recent years have witnessed growing patterns of disinformation strategically disseminated online by state and non-state actors with the intention of fomenting social divisiveness, xenophobia, and far-right nationalist extremism. In this new context, I argue that it is imperative for university educators and policymakers, including those in massifying Asian higher education systems, to recognize the importance of equipping learners with the awareness and tools to engage critically with the quality and credibility of the information they encounter.

While many may assume that the younger generations are digital natives with an ingrained tech awareness, a recent study conducted by education researchers at Stanford University found that large percentages of youth were unable to distinguish online news articles from advertisements, critically engage with imagery from dubious sources, or logically evaluate the credibility of statistical information presented in a tweet on Twitter (Stanford History Education Group et al., 2016). In the executive summary to their report they write:

> When thousands of students respond to dozens of tasks there are endless variations. That was certainly the case in our experience. However, at each level—middle school, high school, and college—these variations paled in comparison to a stunning and dismaying consistency. Overall, young people's ability to reason about the information on the Internet can be summed up in one word: *bleak*. (Stanford History Education Group et al., 2016, p. 4)

In the contemporary period, extremist nationalists often take to the internet where they find strength in numbers, and proceed with harassing and intimidating critics (including journalists) and spreading false information. An international disinformation machine has emerged designed to foment division in Western democracies, devoted to the cultivation, provocation, and amplification of far-right, anti-immigrant passions and political forces. Governments and politicians too have become overtly involved in the spreading of false information for political gain both at home and abroad, evidenced by the interference in the US election system by Russian hackers (Abrams, 2019), and the frequent spreading of maligning disinformation by former President Trump on Twitter, much of it directed at China. A salient example emerging from the Trump White House was the discriminatory references to the novel coronavirus as the "China Virus," which has been linked to subsequent rises in anti-Asian Twitter content in parallel with the rise in Asian hate crimes in the United States (Reja, 2021).

I argue that these developments in cyberspace pose both a challenge and a call to arms for educators at universities, including those in the Asia-Pacific. It is imperative that higher education provides an opportunity to engage critically with the range of online media, and teaches the younger generation to become increasingly tech-savvy in order to identify fake news, deep-fake videos, and other misinformation. Today, many young people are increasingly adopting extremist worldviews based on online misinformation, with platform algorithms recommending users to explore dangerous rabbit holes of increasingly extremist content. Educators and universities must become aware of this reality and should make a concerted effort to educate for media literacy and high-quality information and literature searching as a component of citizenship education curricula. Approaches to education for citizenship vary considerably across national contexts, and an emphasis on collective responsibilities and social duty may prevail over a focus on potentially disruptive individual rights in some Asia-Pacific societies. Nevertheless, it is arguably beneficial to cultivate a basic skillset for navigating the internet among the citizenry of any country, including an independent critical awareness and natural skepticism when interpreting information online.

4. Concluding Remarks

Nationalism in various forms has intersected throughout the historical development and ongoing evolution of higher education in the Asia-Pacific and presents educators, students and policymakers with a range of pressing challenges. The international DNA of higher education finds its avenues for expression increasingly constrained by the demands of the nation-state, including high expectations for global competitiveness and the use of science as a tool of soft power diplomacy. Governments and funding bodies exert varying degrees of pressure on academic freedom, and nationalistic crackdowns can have spillover effects on the global dimension of higher education. The local, physical spaces of universities also serve as sites where people engage with a range of social causes, many of which address to some degree the tensions between the local, national, international and global phenomena shaping modern life. Perhaps most volatile of these is the new means of accessing information through the internet, which has become awash with misinformation and requires new pedagogical approaches to equip student-citizens with skills to navigate it responsibly.

All of these developments have relevance in Asia-Pacific countries and societies, especially as the region is recognized by many to be on the cusp of assuming a leading global role in the twenty-first century. The intersections and examples from Asia-Pacific contexts introduced above highlight some of the salient ways nationalism and higher education are intertwined, but there is room for further consideration and more rigorous empirical analysis. The vastness and differentiation of the Asia-Pacific entails that detailed case studies could be made of any of the countries that make up the region, and it is my hope that this chapter may provide some analytical lenses that could aid in these future endeavors.

REFERENCES

Abrams, A. (2019). Here's What We Know So Far About Russia's 2016 Meddling. *Time.* https://time.com/5565991/russia-influence-2016-election/

Altbach, P. G. (1989). Twisted roots: The Western impact on Asian higher education. *Higher Education*, 18/1, 9–29. https://doi.org/10.1007/BF00138959

Altbach, P. G., & de Wit, H. (2020, March 14). COVID-19: The internationalisation revolution that isn't. *University World News.*

Altbach, P. G., & Yudkevich, M. (2017). Twenty-first Century Mobility: The Role of International Faculty. *International Higher Education*, 90, 8–10. https://doi.org/10.6017/ihe.2017.90.9743

Anderson, B. (2006). *Imagined Communities: Reflections on the Origin and Spread of Nationalism.* Verso.

Basken, P. (2018, November 13). FBI warns US universities of "threat" from Chinese nationals. *Times Higher Education.*

Becker, J. (2019). The Global Machine Behind the Rise of Far-Right Nationalism. *The New York Times.* https://www.nytimes.com/2019/08/10/world/europe/sweden-immigration-nationalism.html

Bloomberg. (2019). Malaysia's R&D Investment Paying off with Higher Research Productivity and Improved University Ranking. *Bloomberg.* https://www.bloomberg.com/press-releases/2019-11-05/malaysia-s-r-d-investment-paying-off-with-higher-research-productivity-and-improved-university-ranking

Brotherhood, T., Hammond, C. D., & Kim, Y. (2019). Towards an actor-centered typology of internationalization: A study of junior international faculty in Japanese universities. *Higher Education.* https://doi.org/10.1007/s10734-019-00420-5

Cabinet Office - Government of Japan. (2015). *Council for Science, Technology and Innovation brochure.* https://www8.cao.go.jp/cstp/english/panhu/index.html

Dale, R. (2005). Globalisation, knowledge economy and comparative education. *Comparative Education*, 41(2), 117–149. https://doi.org/10.1080/03050060500150906

Etzioni, A. (2019). "Good" vs "Bad" Nationalism in Asia. *The Diplomat.* https://thediplomat.com/2019/09/good-vs-bad-nationalism-in-asia/

Fang, W. (2012). The development of transnational higher education in China: A comparative study of research universities and teaching universities. *Journal of Studies in International Education*, 16(1), 5–23. https://doi.org/10.1177/1028315311410607

Fisher, M. (2019, September 27). "One Country, Two Nationalisms": The Identity Crisis Behind Hong Kong's Turmoil. *The New York Times.*

Friedman, J. Z. (2018). Everyday nationalism and elite research universities in the USA and England. *Higher Education*, 76(2), 247–261. https://doi.org/10.1007/s10734-017-0206-1

Green-Riley, N. (2020). The State Department labeled China's Confucius programs a bad influence on U.S. students. What's the story? *The Washington Post.*

Hammond, C. D. (2019). Dynamics of higher education research collaboration and regional integration in Northeast Asia: a study of the A3 Foresight Program. *Higher Education*, 78(4), 653–668. https://doi.org/10.1007/s10734-019-00363-x

Hammond, C. D. (2020). *Regional cooperation in Northeast Asia: an analysis of policy ideas across institutions and disciplines in Japanese higher education* [University of Oxford]. https://ora.ox.ac.uk/objects/uuid:0fb04803-666d-4288-bd3e-5fa51bc002cb

Hammond, C. D., & Keating, A. (2017). Global citizens or global workers? Comparing university programmes for global citizenship education in Japan and the UK. *Compare: A Journal of Comparative and International Education, 7925*(September), 1–20. https://doi.org/10.1080/03057925.2017.1369393

Hartig, F. (2018). China's Global Image Management: Paper Cutting and the Omission of Politics. *Asian Studies Review, 42*(4), 701–720. https://doi.org/10.1080/10357823.2018.1511684

Hawkins, J. N. (2012). The Challenges of Regionalism and Harmonization for Higher Education in Asia. In J. N. Hawkins, K. H. Mok, & D. E. Neubauer (Eds.), *Higher Education Regionalization in Asia Pacific: Implications for Governance, Citizenship and University Transformation* (pp. 177–189). Palgrave Macmillan US. https://doi.org/10.1057/9781137311801_11

Hechinger, G. (2003, December 3). Clark Kerr, Leading Public Educator and Former Head of California's Universities, Dies at 92. *The New York Times.* https://www.nytimes.com/2003/12/02/us/clark-kerr-leading-public-educator-former-head-california-s-universities-dies-92.html

Hobsbawm, E. J. (2012). *Nations and nationalism since 1870: Programme, myth, reality* (2nd ed.). Cambridge University Press.

Huang, Futao. (2021). International Faculty at Japanese Universities: Main Findings from National Survey in 2017. In Futao Huang & A. R. Welch (Eds.), *International Faculty in Asia: In Comparative Global Perspective.* Springer Nature Singapore.

Ignatieff, M. (1993). *Blood and belonging: Journeys into the new nationalism.* Viking.

Jangid, K. (2019, July 27). "No anti-nationalism" clause threatens critical thinking. *University World News.*

Jordan, M., & Hartocollis, A. (2020). U.S. Rescinds Plan to Strip Visas From International Students in Online Classes. *The New York Times.*

Kakuchi, S. (2019, December 4). China research trips cancelled over scholar spy charge. *University World News.*

Kerr, C. (1990). The internationalisation of learning and the nationalisation of the purposes of higher education: two "laws of motion" in conflict? *European Journal of Education, 25*(1), 5. https://doi.org/10.2307/1502702

Kim, T. (2016). Internationalisation and development in East Asian higher education: an introduction. *Comparative Education, 52*(1), 1–7. https://doi.org/10.1080/03050068.2016.1144309

Kingston, J. (2017). *Nationalism in Asia: A History Since 1945.* Wiley Blackwell.

Lee, M. H., & Gopinathan, S. (2003). Centralized decentralization of higher education in Singapore. In *CERC Studies in Comparative Education* (Vol. 13).

Mahroum, S. (2000). Highly skilled globetrotters: mapping the international migration of human capital. *R and D Management, 30*(1), 23–32. https://doi.org/10.1111/1467-9310.00154

Mamiseishvili, K., & Rosser, V. J. (2010). International and citizen faculty in the United States: an examination of their productivity at research universities. *Research in Higher Education, 51*(1), 88–107. https://doi.org/10.1007/s11162-009-9145-8

Marginson, S. (2016). *The role of the state in university science: Russia and China compared* (No. 9; Issue 9). http://www.researchcghe.org/publications/the-role-of-the-state-in-university-science-russia-and-china-compared/

Marginson, S. (2021). Globalisation of HE: the good, the bad and the ugly. In *Center for Global Higher Education working paper series* (Issue 66).

Montgomery, C. (2016). Transnational partnerships in higher education in China: The diversity and complexity of elite strategic alliances. *London Review of Education*, 14(1), 70–85. https://doi.org/10.18546/LRE.14.1.08

Morris, P., Shimazu, N., & Vickers, E. (2015). East Asian images of Japan: An overview. In P. Morris, N. Shimazu, & E. Vickers (Eds.), *Imagining Japan in Post-War East Asia*. Routledge.

Muftahu, M., Wan, C. D., & Sirat, M. (2021). Retaining and Integrating International Faculty into Malaysian Universities: Issues and Challenges. In F. Huang & A. R. Welch (Eds.), *International Faculty in Asia: In Comparative Global Perspective*. Springer Nature Singapore.

Niazi, S. (2020, January 14). Call for JNU's VC to be removed after campus attacks. *University World News*.

Niazi, S., & Sharma, Y. (2020). Angry campuses become more volatile after JNU attack. *University World News*. https://www.universityworldnews.com/post.php?story=20200106220359163

Nye, J. (2017). Soft power: the origins and political progress of a concept. *Palgrave Communications*, 3, 17008. https://doi.org/10.1057/palcomms.2017.8

Perry, M. (2009). Australian PM condemns attacks on Indian students. *Reuters*. https://www.reuters.com/article/idUKSYD134541?edition-redirect=uk

Phillips, T. (2017, August 20). Cambridge University Press censorship "exposes Xi Jinping's authoritarian shift." *The Guardian*.

Reja, M. (2021). Trump's "Chinese Virus" tweet helped lead to rise in racist anti-Asian Twitter content: Study. *ABC News*.

Sanders, J. S. (2018). National internationalisation of higher education policy in Singapore and Japan: context and competition. *Compare: A Journal of Comparative and International Education*, 7925, 1–17. https://doi.org/10.1080/03057925.2017.1417025

Scholars at Risk. (2019). *Obstacles to Excellence: Academic Freedom & China's Quest for World Class Universities*. https://www.scholarsatrisk.org/resources/obstacles-to-excellence-academic-freedom-chinas-quest-for-world-class-universities/

Schultz, K. (2019). Modi Defends Indian Citizenship Law Amid Violent Protests. *The New York Times*.

Smith, A. D. (2010). *Nationalism: Theory, Ideology, History*. Polity Press.

Stanford History Education Group, Wineburg, S., McGrew, S., Breakstone, J., & Ortega, T. (2016). Evaluating information: The cornerstone of civic online reasoning. In *Stanford Digital Repository*. http://purl.stanford.edu/fv751yt5934

Tan, J. (2016). Singapore's "Global Schoolhouse" Aspirations. *International Higher Education*, 87, 9–10. https://doi.org/10.6017/ihe.2016.87.9501

Tang, H. H. (2014). Academic Nationalism and Academic Internationalism in East Asia: Findings and Implications from Hong Kong and South Korea Professoriates. *ASAA 20th Biennial Conference*.

Tollefson, J. (2018). China declared world's largest producer of scientific articles. *Nature: News*. https://www.nature.com/articles/d41586-018-00927-4

Triandafyllidou, A. (1998). National identity and the "other." *Ethnic and Racial Studies*, 21(4), 593–612. https://doi.org/10.1080/014198798329784

Vickers, E. (2017). All quiet on the eastern front? Populism, nationalism and democracy in East Asia. *Georgetown Journal of International Affairs*, 18(2), 59–68.

Wimmer, A., & Glick Schiller, N. (2002). Methodological nationalism and beyond: nation-state building, migration and the social sciences. *Global Networks*, 2(4), 301–334. https://doi.org/10.1111/1471-0374.00043

Woetzel, J., & Seong, J. (2019). We've entered the Asian Century and there is no turning back. *World Economic Forum.*

Yonezawa, A. (2014). Japan's challenge of fostering "global human resources": Policy debates and practices. *Japan Labor Review*, *11*(2), 37–52. http://www.jil.go.jp/english/JLR/documents/2014/JLR42_yonezawa.pdf

Zhao, S. (1998). A State-led Nationalism: The Patriotic Education Campaign in Post-Tiananmen China. *Communist and Post-Communist Studies*, *31*(3), 287–302.

CHAPTER 25

LIFELONG LEARNING AS A GLOBALLY DIFFUSED POLICY DISCOURSE IN ASIA

HONGXIA SHAN AND ZHENG REN

1. INTRODUCTION

LEARNING throughout life is likely an ancient wisdom for all peoples from all nations. As an educational policy discourse though, it was around the 1990s that lifelong learning (LLL) started attracting global attention. Despite its relative recency, LLL has become a policy mantra in many parts of the world, including Asia, which makes it a most successful case of policy diffusion (Zapp and Dahmen, 2017). The goal of this chapter is to introduce the development of LLL as a globally diffused policy discourse in Asia. Policy diffusion in its broadest sense refers to the spread and the sequential adoption and adaptation of policies, practices, programs, institutions, ideas, and ideologies across places (Stone, 2017). The term "policy discourse" is employed, rather than policy alone, to denote all these "matters" of diffusion. The term "diffusion" is used here rather than "transfer" to avoid the impression of a unilateral movement of LLL as a fixed policy object from the West to the rest. It is also in recognition that adoption of any global policy in a local place might not be an entirely rational project. Rather, it is perhaps more of a "contagious process" with its unique mechanism (Stone, 2017, p. 57). By treating LLL as a globally diffused policy discourse, this chapter also speaks to how the development of LLL in Asia converges and diverges from LLL as a dominant discourse in the West.

The chapter begins by introducing the rise of LLL in the West. It then shares the context of Asia, before it reviews the development of LLL in Asia, including the problems that LLL is intended to address, the kind of society being imagined through the introduction of LLL, the general trends of development in LLL, and the main drivers of LLL. The chapter ends with a discussion of the promises, problems, and politics associated with the diffusion of LLL in Asia.

2. THE RISE OF LIFELONG LEARNING AS A GLOBAL POLICY DISCOURSE

In the 1960s and 1970s, industrialized countries in the West were faced with a massive economic downturn, as well as intense social unrest. These are perhaps some of the woes the Western world experienced while transitioning from a modern to a postmodern society—the former is characterized by industrialization, mass production, lifelong employment, and a degree of stability and predictability in life; the latter is associated with the rise of a service-based economy, customized production, non-standard employment, and a loss of certainty and social security. Amid all the crises, it was determined that the formal education system designed for modern times had failed to meet the needs of a fast-changing world. In response, a multitude of educational ideals emerged, including the notions of a learning society, lifelong education, and lifelong learning.

In the 1970s, UNESCO formally introduced the ideal of a learning society, which was initially a utopian vision that sought to redefine a society by its capacity to afford lifelong education to all. Core to this vision is the cultivation of a democratic, scientific, and humanistic culture (Wain, 2004) in which an individual is positioned as "agent of development and change, promoter of democracy, citizen of the world, author of his own fulfillment," and indeed a lifelong pursuer of "the ideal of the complete man [sic]" (Faure, 1972, p. 158). This original version of a learning society, however, failed to capture the attention of policymakers. In the 1990s, the notion of a learning society made a strong comeback, under the auspices of international organizations such as the OECD, the World Bank, and the International Monetary Fund (IMF). The ascendance of learning society as a global discourse is marked by a pronounced shift from lifelong education to lifelong learning at its core (Wain, 2004). This shift is far from semantic. It dovetails well with the global spread of neoliberalism. It places the onus of transformation on individuals, who are expected to become entrepreneurial, and take responsibility for their own wellbeing in the midst of vicissitudes brought about by technological changes and globalized capitalism. The "leftist" agenda associated with the original vision of the learning society is thus superseded by a predominant interest in vocational skills and the pursuit of knowledge economies. The neoliberal, utilitarian, and individualist thrusts of LLL have been criticized and yet normalized in the literature.

Lifelong education and learning have given rise to an expansive literature and a field in the making. In the 1976 UNESCO *Recommendation on the Development of Adult Education*, the term lifelong education and learning is used to reference "an overall scheme aimed both at restructuring the existing education system and at developing the entire educational potential outside the education system." The 2015 *Recommendation on Adult Learning and Education* (UIL, 2015) orients people's attention to three specific domains of adult education and learning. These are (1) literacy and basic skills, (2) vocational skills through continuing education and professional development, and (3) active citizenship skills through liberal, popular, and community education. Notably, this typology is largely exclusive of higher education, which as shown in this chapter, is nonetheless influenced by the introduction of LLL in many places.

3. The Context of Asia

Asia is the world's largest and most populous continent. Economically, vast differences exist among and within Asian countries. In addition to Australia and New Zealand, two main Oceanian countries that are culturally and institutionally more aligned with Anglo-Saxon countries, seven Asian countries, along with the three special administrative zones, are classified as High-Income Countries (HICs) (UN, 2019). Nine countries are classified as the Least Developed Countries (LDCs) (UN, 2019). Among the nine, four are in South Asia, i.e., Afghanistan, Bangladesh, Bhutan, and Nepal, four in South-East Asia, i.e., Cambodia, Laos, Myanmar, and Timor-Leste, and one in West Asia, i.e., Yemen (UN, 2019). In the last two decades, Asia as a whole has experienced some rapid economic growth. Yet, South Asia still has a large share of the global poor, which increased from 27.3 percent in 1990 to 33.4 percent in 2013 (SAAPE, 2019). Further, the economic gap between the rich and the poor is glaring in many countries. In South-East Asia, a report by the ASEAN Post (2018) states: "The richest one percent in Thailand controls 58 percent of the country's wealth ... In Indonesia, the four richest men there have more wealth than the poorest 100 million people ... In Vietnam, 210 of the country's super-rich earn more than enough in a year to lift 3.2 million people out of poverty." Often economic disparity is exacerbated by issues such as the urban and rural divide, gender, and ethnic and religious group status. These economic and social disparities across countries constitute the major contexts as well as problems that LLL policies and programs address.

Demographically, Asia is a relatively young continent, with the exception of Australia and New Zealand, where the count of the older people, i.e., people aged 65 and above, has surpassed 50 percent of the entire populations (UN, 2019). The share of the older population is relatively low in Central and South Asia, staying at 6 percent in 2019 (UN, 2019). It is, however, much higher in East and South Asia, where the percentage goes up to 11.2 percent. In China, older people account for 11.5 percent of the population (UN, 2019). In South Korea, the percentage of the older generation was 13.8 percent, and in Japan, it was more than 27 percent in 2018 (Hori et al., 2018). Between 2019 and 2050, it is projected that South Korea will see the largest increase in the share of older people in the world, followed by Singapore, Taiwan, Macao, Maldives, Thailand, and Hong Kong (UN, 2019). The varying demographic backgrounds may explain why many countries and areas have drawn attention to older people as a special group of learners.

Education is crucial for improving a nation's social and economic conditions. Notably, as part of the global movement of Education for All (EFA), for which high-income countries such as Australia and Japan provided financial aids, all regions in Asia have made significant progress in universalizing primary education and increasing access to secondary education (UNESCO, 2015). All regions have also seen significant improvement in adult literacy rates (UNESCO, 2017). Between 1990 and 2016, adult literacy rates rose from 46 percent to 72 percent in South Asia, from 64 percent to 81 percent in North Africa and West Asia, and from 82 percent to 96 percent in East and South-East Asia. Yet, Asia is still home to more than half of the world's illiterate adults; South Asia alone accounted for 49 percent of the world's illiterate adults in 2016 (UNESCO Institute for Statistics, 2017). Further, educational benefits out of the EFA movement are not evenly distributed, especially when it comes to women from impoverished families and in rural areas. To give an example, in Nepal, education was reserved for the social elites. It was not until 2005, that the percentage of primary school enrollment started increasing dramatically, reaching 97.2 percent in 2017–2018 (UNESCO Office in Kathmandu, 2017; UNESCO Institute for Statistics, 2020). Literacy rates in the country also increased to 64 percent for people aged 15 years and above—75.3 percent for men and 54.2 percent for women—in 2015/16 (UNESCO Office in Kathmandu, 2017). Yet, according to the Annual Household Survey 2014/15, only 30 percent of Nepalese women living in poverty were literate, and, among those in rural areas, just under half were literate. Even among the richest, women's literacy rates were substantially lower than men's, 75 percent versus 93 percent (UIL, 2019).

4. DEVELOPMENT OF LIFELONG LEARNING IN ASIA

The movement towards LLL is uneven in Asia, with HICs heading the policy movement and debates. Japan is perhaps the first to enter the discourse of lifelong education and then lifelong learning. Following UNESCO's publication of the Faure report in 1972, Japan started working towards the recommendations of the report. In 1990, the country passed the Lifelong Learning Promotion Law (Ogden, 2010). In South Korea, state responsibility for lifelong education was specified in the Constitution in 1980, and in 1999, in the aftermath of the Asian financial crisis, the country implemented the Lifelong Education Act (OECD, 2020). Interestingly, in Australia, whereas the ideal of lifelong learning entered the policy realm in the 1970s, the country does not have an overarching LLL policy per se. Instead, the language of LLL, accompanied with strategy recommendations, has been introduced to all educational sectors within the existing learning system, inter alia, school-based education, vocational education, adult and community education and higher education (Chapman et al., 2005; OECD, 2019). For New Zealand, the discourse of LLL was introduced in the 1990s and it is said to have disrupted the progressive tradition of adult community education (Tobias, 2004). Singapore, acclaimed for its remarkable rise to economic prosperity and educational achievement after its separation from Malaysia in 1965 (Lee and Morris, 2016), might be a bit late in taking up the LLL discourse, compared to other HICs. Yet, it has launched a series of LLL initiatives, including the Lifelong Endowment Fund Act in 2001, and the national movement of SkillsFuture in 2015 (Tan, 2017).

The language of LLL has also found its entrance to the policy realms in other Asian countries. Upper-middle- and lower-middle-income countries, such as China, Thailand, Indonesia, the Philippines, and Malaysia, introduced LLL policies and legislations prior to the commencement of the new millennium (Singh, 2002; Shan, 2017). In the LDCs, inter alia, Nepal and Laos, LLL did not enter the national agenda until 2015 (Regmi, 2015). Regardless of their stages of development, the (emerging) LLL systems typically build on the history and tradition of adult education particular to the country, which may emphasize variously adult and community education, literacy education, social education, vocational education, and/or worker education. There are, however, also cases, where countries, inter alia, Australia, New Zealand, Singapore, and Myanmar, have also mobilized the LLL discourse to reorganize or reorient the existing education system. In most cases though, as a UIL report (Yorozu, 2017) of South-East Asia points out, the language of LLL policy is often "inspiring, ambitiously broad and optimistic" (Yorozu, 2017, p. 15), and the financial resources committed tend to be limited, which is reportedly also the case for HICs such as Australia and New Zealand (Amundsen, 2020; Golding, 2020). To map the development of LLL in Asia, this section reviews the range of problems that LLL policies are positioned to address, the kinds of society being imagined through the adoption of LLL, the general patterns of movement towards LLL, and the international drivers of the movement of LLL.

4.1 Issues LLL Posed to Address

Across countries, LLL is framed foremost to address a shortage of skills and human capital, and to meet the needs of technological change and global competition. It follows that the building of the LLL system across countries involves a heightened emphasis on vocational skills training, including continuing education and professional development (Govinda, 2017; Yorozu, 2017; UIL, 2019). This orientation towards vocational and employment skills is evident in all countries, regardless of development levels. For instance, in Han's study (2001) of South Korea, Japan, Hong Kong, Singapore, Thailand, and the Philippines, it is shown that the growth of the LLL system largely follows the "business mind" of global capitalism. Similarly, in Malaysia, lifelong learning is identified as the third pillar of a human capital development system in the pursuit of the knowledge economy (Yorozu, 2017). In China, the goal of educational reform is to achieve socialist modernization and the country has proclaimed a will to shift from, through educational reform, "made in China," i.e., a manufacture-based economy, to "created in China," i.e., a knowledge-based economy (Shan, 2017).

Literacy is another major issue that countries in Asia continue to address through the implementation of LLL policies and mechanisms. Notably, the LLL systems in countries such as Afghanistan, Bangladesh, Thailand, and the Philippines, have retained the previous adult and non-formal education systems with a focus on basic literacy (Govinda, 2017). In some other countries, Nepal and India for instance, while the language of lifelong learning is employed in governmental documents, policy priority remains with literacy education (Singai et al., 2016). Within literacy education though, enhanced attention has been paid to issues such as gender disparity and social inequity. Literacy movements and programs often target women, ethnic communities, religious minorities, indigenous populations, people living in impoverished rural areas, and other socially disadvantaged groups. Meanwhile, basic literacy education has expanded to include other social, vocational, and economic goals. In Afghanistan, for instance, its Education Law promotes literacy and basic education to enable people to acquire vocational skills and to engage in continuous education (Govinda, 2017). In Indonesia, related policies stress, among others, the importance of upgrading "literacy learning integrated with life skills (personal, social, academic and vocational), so learners have a chance to increase their income or gain a dignified profession" (Govinda, 2017, p.19). In India, the Saakshar Bharat Mission, an initiative to increase women's literacy and to foster lifelong learning within communities, was designed to link literacy learning with income-generating activities (Hanemann, 2015).

In addition to vocational skills and adult literacy, LLL has also been posed to address a wide range of other issues, including but not limited to aging, quality of life, citizenship education, environmental protection, natural disaster risk reduction, promoting intercultural dialogue, preserving cultural heritage, and prevention of violent extremism. Not all these issues are foci within the traditional educational systems; to some extent, LLL has been used as a panacea for all social problems. The emphasis of these issues, however, varies from country to country, depending on the context and the capacity of the actors. For instance, where an aging demographic may pose a challenge to the capacity of the welfare system, seniors have become a special target group for LLL policies. This is the case in countries such as Australia, China, Japan, New Zealand, South Korea, Singapore, and Thailand. In Thailand, for instance, strengthening LLL among senior citizens is a priority of the Second National Plan on the Elderly (2002–2021), which focuses on enabling seniors to receive lifelong education. These LLL programs for seniors do not necessarily address issues of employment. Instead, they are designed to mainly promote active aging. In Central Asia, UNESCO has worked with the national governments of Kazakhstan, the Kyrgyz Republic, Tajikistan, and Uzbekistan to identify areas of development priorities. Given the resurgence of Islamic extremism and terrorism in the region, these countries have developed a range of formal and non-formal programs to address, among other issues, the spread of violent extremism and sustainable development (UNESCO Office Almaty, 2018).

4.2 Societies Imagined through LLL

How countries take up the discourse of LLL also reflects how they (re)imagine themselves as nation-states. In many countries, particularly the developing ones, where there is a clear articulation of LLL, there is often an aspiration to become modernized states. This is accompanied by a desire to prepare for the "knowledge age," or to succeed in the global "knowledge economy." The ideal of a knowledge economy is clearly articulated by high-income countries and areas such as South Korea, Japan, Singapore, Hong Kong (Han, 2001; Tan, 2010), rising economic powers such as China (Shan, 2017) and India (Singai et al., 2016), other developing countries such as Malaysia, Thailand, and the Philippines (Han, 2001), as well as some of the LDCs such as Myanmar (Ministry of Education Myanmar, 2012). There is, however, rarely any mention of where the country is structurally in relation to the prospect of a knowledge economy. If knowledge economy is defined by the expansion of the knowledge-intensive sectors, characterized by digitalization, automation, and artificial intelligence, there has to be a structural leap that many countries have to make to enter this utopia. In other words, knowledge economy might be more of a mantra in many contexts, unaccompanied by clear and attainable plans. Yet, by promoting this ideal, LLL is easily mobilized in various countries "to re-engineer the relationship between education and economic development" (Lee and Fleming, 2012, p. 349).

In addition to serving as a pathway to a knowledge economy, LLL is also considered a building block of a learning society. There is rarely any explanation of what a learning society means. It is perhaps literally taken as a society within which people learn. Of note, the image of a learning society is often coupled with some national agendas. In the case of Myanmar, the Ministry of Education (2012, p. 1) declared that its vision is to "create an education system that will generate a learning society capable of facing the challenges of the Knowledge Age," and its motto is to "build a modern developed nation through education." In countries that have been influenced by Confucianism, inter alia, China, Japan, and South Korea, the generic image of a learning society is coupled with the desire for social harmony (Yang and Yorozu, 2015; Osborne and Borkowska, 2017). In China, for instance, LLL is believed to be the foundation of and bridge to a learning society at the same time that it should serve the country's desire for a harmonious society, through improving the educated quality of its people (Shan, 2017).

Finally, there is a trend for different countries to adopt, in their LLL policies and reports, the language of equity, inclusivity, and increasingly, sustainability, as part of their imagined future. Countries in Asia have committed themselves, policy wise, to breaking down barriers for socially disadvantaged groups to access education and learning opportunities. In China, terms such as social justice and equity, and education for socially disadvantaged groups have become frequently used in national educational policies, as part of the nation's vision statements about lifelong education since 2001 (Shan, 2017). In Laos, LLL is believed to be creating "opportunities for Lao citizens to access education, improve livelihoods and bring about sustainable development" (Khammang, 2017, p. 7). In a project between UNESCO and the Southeast Asian Ministers of Education Organization (SEAMEO), it is recommended that inclusive teaching and practice need to be upheld as a building block of lifelong learning in the region, and that regulations should be in place to move towards Sustainable Development Goals 4 and 5, i.e., quality education and gender equity (UIL, 2017). Apparently, the ideal of lifelong learning has been coupled with progressive discourses that address issues of social justice.

4.3 Major Trends and Patterns of Development

There are some converging trends of development of LLL in Asia. First, across countries, there has mushroomed a *multitude of non-formal and informal learning opportunities*— non-formal learning occurs through structured training programs outside of the educational system, and informal learning takes place beyond structured training and educational programs. For instance, in Japan, LLL comprises not only school-based education, but also social education, i.e., non-degree-related training, as well as learning that takes place through sports, cultural activities, recreational, and volunteer activities (Ogden, 2010). In South Korea, the adult learning system comprises two pillars. One focuses on employment skills, and the other on recreational or civic and life enrichment education that prioritizes personal enjoyment and development (OECD, 2020). In Singapore, the SkillsFuture movement is geared towards equipping individuals with the skills needed for the future economy, as well as enabling Singaporeans to pursue their own interests and self-fulfilling programs (Tan, 2017). In general though, most LLL opportunities focus on vocational, literacy, numeracy, and computer skills, with some involving civic and citizenship education, and not all countries have connected LLL to personal interests, leisure, and recreational needs of individual citizens.

Notably, LLL policies and systems often build on local adult education traditions. In East Asia, this means the retention of social education, traditional adult education practices as well as expansion to address liberal education and community building (Choi and Han, 2019). Some of the modules of learning are introduced from outside Asia. The University of the Third Age (U3A) is one example. Originating in Europe in the 1970s, U3A has developed swiftly in Asia. In China for instance, whereas there was one U3A in 1983, the number has jumped to 49,000 in 2017 with an enrollment of 7 million seniors (Zhao and Chui, 2019). The model of U3A, however, may not be easily adaptable across contexts. In Thailand, Ratana-Ubol and Richards (2016) identify a number of reasons why local seniors resisted the concept of U3A. Among others, they suggest that the term "university" in U3A might invoke the image of modernist education that is credential-based, formalized, and structured, whereas seniors tend to associate lifelong learning with their needs to stay healthy and connected with families and communities, as well as local and traditional wisdom.

Second, the expansion of non-formal and informal learning is accompanied by *systematic changes of the education system*. In some countries, this means the expansion of the formal education sector. In the case of New Zealand, for instance, with the regulation of the Tertiary Education Commission, the country has merged non-formal and formal education into one formal sector. Unfortunately, as part of the reorganization, adult and community education has narrowed its goal from equity and empowerment to employment skill preparation (Amundsen, 2020). In Singapore, the introduction of LLL policies, particularly the launch of the SkillsFuture movement in 2015, entails an enhanced emphasis on the vocational dimension within the formal education system. Among others, SkillsFuture has made a professional core course a requisite in public schools and higher learning institutions. It also extended enhanced internships and work-study programs to students in polytechnic and technical institutions (Tan, 2017). SkillsFuture also comprises a credit program, which allocates an opening credit of 500 Singapore dollars (SGD) for people aged 25 and above to register for training courses, with a guaranteed additional one-off SGD 500 top-up (Tan, 2017).

For some countries, the move towards LLL has disrupted the traditional image of a linear educational pathway from primary to higher education with age as a normative reference point for progression. Singapore, for instance, introduced subject-based banding in primary schools in 2008, which means that students could pursue different subjects at different levels. In some countries the introduction of LLL involves building alternative and iterative pathways for people to access formal education. In Myanmar, the National Education Strategic Plan 2016–2021 (Ministry of Education, 2016) specifies both formal and alternative education pathways that individuals may follow for career and lifelong learning. Given the need to build articulation among different forms of learning, various countries have started developing qualification recognition frameworks in reference to traditional academic qualifications (Singh and Duvekot, 2013). South Korea, for instance, has implemented an academic credit bank system, which is a degree-granting institution of the last resort that allows students to earn a degree by accumulating credits from different sources. The challenge, however, is to have this system well accepted by the larger society, and particularly, by employers (Usher, 2014).

Third, national governments often take a lead in constructing *overarching visions and overall policy frameworks for LLL* (Govinda, 2017). Meanwhile, the actual building of LLL systems often involves decentralized governance and the participation of multiple stakeholders. While traditionally, education across countries is the responsibility of the education ministries, the movement towards LLL has devolved the power of educational policymaking. Today, the building of an LLL system often involves inter-ministerial collaboration and horizontal and vertical integration of governmental functions. The design, delivery, and promotion of LLL programs and initiatives in practice also require the participation of multiple stakeholders, including for instance, educational institutions, families, neighborhood houses, community learning centers, the private sector, voluntary associations, and individuals. Given the need to bring multiple stakeholders on board in the design and delivery of LLL initiatives, the development of LLL policies and programs has been uneven within countries. To give the example of Australia, only half of its states and territories had funded adult education systems, and by early 2020 many of them had become much diminished (Golding, 2020). To mobilize various stakeholders, mass movements such as building learning cities have been adopted in a number of countries. As well, there has been an increase in the number of learning cities in countries such as China, South Korea, and Japan. Of note, while the ideal of a learning city in the dominant (Western) LLL discourse is associated with individual self-directedness and entrepreneurism, the drive towards learning cities in Asia is more likely to be based on a community relation model and speak more of a collective ethos (Han and Makino, 2013; Osborne and Borkowska, 2017).

Fourth, the mobilization of civil society for LLL involves the *mobilization of community learning centers* (CLCs) in many countries. There has been an upsurge in the number of CLCs in Asia, including in the less developed and lower-middle-income countries such as Bangladesh, Bhutan, Cambodia, Nepal, the Philippines, and Thailand (UIL, 2017). In Cambodia, for instance, the number of CLCs increased from 57 in 2006 to 347 in 2015 (Kingdom of Cambodia, 2016). These CLCs have played a role in reaching rural, remote, and underserved populations. CLC is not entirely an imported idea from outside Asia. Communities are the traditional vectors of adult learning in many countries, known for their capacities to address local needs. Yet, CLC goes beyond communities being sites of learning. Within an LLL system, CLC is typically employed as a model that allows various stakeholders to participate in the structuring of CLCs and in the design and delivery of activities through CLCs. In a study of 27 CLCs in Thailand, Charungkaittikul and Henschke (2014) point out a number of features common to these centers. Among others, the CLCs share a respect for local wisdom and leaders, and an emphasis on democracy and good governance. In other words, CLCs potentially offer a space for the local communities to build capacity for participation in local governance.

Finally, the development of LLL involves an *increased use of open and distance education, and information and communication technology* (ICT). In all countries, barriers—economic and geographical among others—exist that inhibit people, particularly those who are socially disadvantaged, from accessing learning and education opportunities. The use of open and distance learning and ICT has been promoted as a means to overcome these barriers. According to Bandalaria (2018), more than 20 Asian countries have distance education institutions, also known as Open Universities. These institutions may operate as standalone institutions or as part of traditional academic institutions. They range from residential universities to offering instruction fully online. Some of them are mega Open Universities, with an enrollment of more than 200,000 people. The largest one is Indira Gandhi Open University in India, which had an enrollment of more than 3 million people in 2017 (Bandalaria, 2018). In China, distance education was initially offered as correspondence education and then through broadcasting and television. In 1998, the Ministry of Education announced the Modern Distance Education Project, seeking to build upon the open educational network to establish a system of lifelong learning. It then approved the plan for four universities to construct online education colleges as a pilot project. Today, 67 other universities have joined this pilot project (Liu and Zhang, 2018). The reliance on ICT to provide learning opportunities is promising and challenging at the same time. There is a consensus that ICT has the potential to promote inclusion by improving access to learning. Yet, while the development of digital technology is swift in some countries and areas, there are still persistent digital divides in others. For example, in 2017, while the internet coverage in urban India was 65 percent, it was only 20 percent in rural India (Madangopal and Madangopal, 2018). ICT is important also because it may lend itself to more student-centered learning and respond to local needs. Yet, education in Asian countries is traditionally associated with teachers having high degrees of control over the learning and teaching process. To move from a predominantly teacher-centered to student-centered mode of teaching requires educators to rethink a host of issues at the core of education, including but not limited to curriculum design, delivery, assessment, what is valued as knowledge, as well as pedagogical engagement (see also Noor-UI-Amin, 2013).

4.4 International and Regional Drivers of LLL

The development of LLL in Asia is propelled through international and regional conversations, conferences, collaboration and partnership in which international organizations, intergovernmental organizations, and other organizations and institutions have played a role. The UNESCO Institute for Lifelong Learning (UIL) and its predecessor, the Institute for Education, have promoted policy and practice in life-long education and lifelong learning for more than four decades. They have influenced the diffusion of adult learning and education (ALE) discourses through a multitude of activities, e.g., organizing global ALE conferences, partnering with regional, national and local governments and organizations to pilot initiatives, publishing policy frameworks, and conducting research and producing reports on the progress of ALE around the world. UIL conducted the first most comprehensive global report on adult learning and education in 2009, which became the basis of the Belém Framework for Action (BFA) and the BFA has subsequently provided guidance for the global development of adult literacy and adult education (UIL, 2009). In addition to UNESCO, OECD is another core institution proactive in the diffusion of LLL. Although without financial power, Rubenson (2015) points out, the OECD has become a kind of "eminence grise" in educational policymaking. With its capacity for knowledge creation and policy recommendation, OECD is instrumental in turning LLL into "common sense." The danger, however, is that what is not accepted by the economists at the OECD as knowledge gets filtered out of the kind of policies that it promotes, which have a predominant economic interest.

In addition to UNESCO and OECD, a multitude of global financial institutions, intergovernmental organizations, and interest-based organizations—private and public— are instrumental in creating an environment of policy learning across nations. The World Bank for instance is a major donor and/or loaner that financially incentivizes development projects. The Commonwealth of Learning, a legacy of the British Empire, is devoted to the promotion and development of distance education and open learning across 54 countries, including eight in South and South-East Asia. Livelihoods Funds, started by Danone Group, a world food company together with the Ramsar Convention, funds projects that benefit rural farming communities. No organization operates in singularity. Not only do they necessarily involve local partners in order for various projects to take root locally, but they often work across sectors, in partnership and through networks to maximize impacts. For instance, UIL, OECD, and the World Bank have worked directly with regional and national partners to develop educational policies and initiatives. There are at least three ways for these organizations to exercise power and control over the formation of LLL policies and practices in local contexts. The first is to select best examples for others to follow. The second is to offer training and capacity-building activities for government officials, private businesses, and not-for-profit organizations so that they take leadership in local initiatives. The third is to set the funding criteria. In other words, these international organizations constitute major bodies in the transnational governance of LLL through creating the space and conduits for policy learning and diffusion.

5. CONCLUSIONS

By adopting LLL as part of the arsenal of educational policies, Asian countries seek to address a range of social and economic issues, among which vocational skills and adult literacy are the top priorities. The turn to LLL also demonstrates a desire for developing countries to become modernized states, and for all countries to enter and thrive in the global knowledge economy and to become learning societies. Although a knowledge economy and learning societies are perhaps aspirational rather than descriptive of where many countries are structurally, they help rationalize the move towards LLL. In practice, the discourse of LLL has seen an expansion of non-formal and informal learning opportunities, as well as a reorganization, in some countries, of the formal education system. The development of the LLL system is characterized by central policy guidance, as well as decentralized governance, given the need to mobilize multiple stakeholder groups, in the design and delivery of LLL programs. It has also been facilitated through the use of distance education and ICT although challenges around digital divides, local relevance of learning, and pedagogical innovation are real.

It would have been ideal to make some general observations about the measurable outcomes of LLL in Asia. This is however a challenge, given the vast differences across and within Asian countries. That said, there are at least three ways for researchers to look at outcomes of LLL policies in Asia. The first is to examine country-specific results of the Programme for the International Assessment of Adult Competencies, which may offer some insights into the progress different countries have made periodically. A second way is to reference the global reports on ALE produced by UIL, although UIL (2019) has acknowledged that, with notable exceptions, data on ALE participation outside of EU and OECD countries are typically limited and sketchy. The third and most desirable approach is to gather and examine evaluation reports locally produced for local programs and initiatives, which would provide more insights into how LLL policies work at particular places.

The policy movement of LLL in Asia is promising and problematic at the same time. It is promising not merely because of all the learning opportunities it has presented to people of all ages. It is also because countries have demonstrated more sensitivity to the needs of marginalized groups. Most importantly, the movement of LLL seems to have opened up or democratized the opportunity for more people to participate in the public space. This is evident, for example, in the ways individuals and communities are involved in the building of learning cities and CLCs, which may help expand people's participatory capacity in the public. If the building of CLCs and learning cities is indeed grounded in community knowledge and local wisdom, LLL may eventually work to democratize the process of policymaking as well as knowledge making. This process of grounding, however, could be the core challenge that LLL policies, programs, and practitioners need to grapple with. In the contexts of Australia and New Zealand, for instance, researchers have pointed to the problematic nature of navigating the Western worldview on the one hand, and the indigenous worldview on the other hand when trying to be inclusive of indigenous learners (Mlcek, 2011). Ideally, the LLL policy discourses could be further expanded to address issues around competing knowledge systems.

Despite all these promises and possibilities associated with LLL, caution should be taken not to place the hope and burden of national futures squarely on enhancing the participatory parity and capacity of individuals, groups, and communities. The rhetoric around inclusion in the grand visions of LLL is largely a neoliberal approach towards social equity. The ideal is that once individuals and communities build their participatory capacity in the public space, they will be able to achieve equity for themselves. The LLL discourse in Asia is largely silent on structural inequality, with little reference to the critical tradition of ALE, which would have allowed critique of existing social, cultural, and economic structures that (re)produce marginalization. For instance, where the knowledge economy is highlighted as an ideal, rarely is attention directed towards the marginality some of the countries have experienced in the global economic system. Nor is there much consideration of the structural leap that many countries have to make to become a knowledge economy. Similarly, it is inspiring to see the discourse of LLL coupling itself with progressive ideals such as sustainability. Supposedly, the introduction of the discourse of sustainability to LLL should rein in the global quest for unfettered economic growth. Yet, there is rarely any discussion of how this quest of accelerated economic growth may conflict with the pursuit of sustainability.

Of note, structural inequality may have become more salient at this time of the COVID-19 pandemic, which has amplified the social and economic disparities across and within nation-states. During this pandemic, policymakers across countries look to health research and border control to minimize the impacts of the pandemic. Adult learning and education has hardly been the center of policy concern, or public and media attention. The prolonged pandemic has instead witnessed adult and community learning centers and institutions shutting down their physical spaces. Yet, the success of managing this crisis depends on adults, educators, communities, and organizations who learn on the go as they respond to the extraordinary circumstances. Institutions and organizations providing training and education have also moved their activities online or started providing services remotely. Adult learning and education is clearly in action during this pandemic and at the heart of a resilient society. We might have accumulated vast experiences with online learning, and digital strategies that can be amassed and leveraged to further promote LLL in the future.

Finally, while charting the movement towards LLL in Asia, it is also important to note the power dynamics involved for the diffusion of LLL as a policy discourse. Often countries with more economic power have more control and autonomy over how LLL may take root. In the case of China, de Jong (2013) uses the image of institutional bricolage to suggest selectiveness, gradualism, and in our view pragmatism as the government pulled together domestic and foreign policies. Singapore is also deliberate in how it adopts the most beneficial policies that are promulgated in the global educational market (Tan, 2010). In contrast, in Cambodia, the educational policy trajectory has shifted from a politics of rebelling, i.e., resisting the policies imposed by former colonizers, to the politics of compelling, as it is obligated to accept and implement policy forms as one of the conditions of foreign aid (Tan, 2010). If there is a better recognition of the politics of policy diffusion, there is a better chance to ensure that the LLL movement builds on the culture, traditions, worldviews, and will of the people in different countries.

References

Amundsen, D. (2020). "Sixty years of adult learning in Aotearoa New Zealand: Looking back to the 1960s and beyond the 2020s." *Australian Journal of Adult Learning*, 60/3, 444–466.

Bandalaria, M. (2018). "Open and distanced eLearning in Asia: Country initiatives and institutional cooperation for the transformation of higher education in the region." *Journal of Learning for Development*, 5/2, 116–132.

Chapman, J., Gaff, J., Toomey, R., and Aspin, D. (2005). "Policy on lifelong learning in Australia." *International Journal of Lifelong Education*, 24/2, 99–122.

Charungkaittikul, S. and Henschke, J. A. (2014). "Strategies for developing a sustainable learning society: An analysis of lifelong learning in Thailand." *International Review of Education*, 60, 499–522.

Choi, S. and Han, S. (2019). "Adoption of lifelong learning policies and reterritorialization of adult education in East Asia." *New Directions for Adult and Continuing Education*, 162, 125–137.

de Jong, M. (2013). "China's art of institutional bricolage: Selectiveness and gradualism in the policy transfer style of a nation." *Policy and Society*, 32/2, 89–101.

Faure, E., Herrera, F., Kaddoura, A.-K., Lopes, H., Petrovsky, A. V., Rahnema, M., and Ward, F. C. (1972). *Learning to Be: The World of Education Today and Tomorrow*. Paris: UNESCO.

Golding, B. (2020). "Getting serious: The national 'vision splendid' for adult education 60 years on." *Australian Journal of Adult Learning*, 60/3, 365–398.

Govinda, R. and UIL (2017). *CONFINTEA VI Mid-term review 2017: The status of adult learning and education in Asia and the Pacific. Regional Report*. Hamburg: UNESCO Institute for Lifelong Learning. https://unesdoc.unesco.org/ark:/48223/pf0000259722

Han, S. (2001). "Creating systems for lifelong learning in Asia." *Asia Pacific Education Review*, 2/2, 85–95.

Han, S. and Makino, A. (2013). "Learning cities in East Asia: Japan, the republic of Korea and China." *International Review of Education / Internationale Zeitschrift für Erziehungswissenschaft / Revue Internationale de l'Education*, 59/4, 443–468.

Hanemann, U. (2015). *The Evolution and Impact of Literacy Campaigns and Programmes 2000–2014*. Hamburg: UNESCO Institute for Lifelong Learning.

Hori, S., Choi, I., and Park, J. (2018). "A comparative study of older adult learning in Korea and Japan: Focusing on learning after 70 years old." *Educational Gerontology*, 44/5–6, 354–367.

Khammang, O. (2017). "Towards a lifelong learning policy in Lao PDR." *Newsletter: Lifelong Learning and Non-formal Education in Lao PDR and Southeast Asia*, 4, 6–7. https://issuu.com/dvvinternationalsouth-andsoutheasta/docs/newsletter_4-2017-en

Kingdom of Cambodia, Ministry of Education, Youth and Sport (2016). *Mid-Term Review Report in 2016 of the Education Strategic Plan 2014–2018 and Projection to 2020*. https://www.globalpartnership.org/sites/default/files/2016-11-cambodia-mid-term-review-education-sector-plan.pdf

Lee, M. and Morris, P. (2016). "Lifelong learning, income inequality and social mobility in Singapore." *International Journal of Lifelong Education*, 35/3, 286–312.

Lee, W. and Fleming, J. (2012). "The institutionalisation of lifelong learning in Australia, Hong Kong and the United States: A bridge to the community or a competitor to the university?" In D. N. Aspin, J. Chapman, K. Evans, and R. Bagnell (eds.), *Second International Handbook of Lifelong Learning*. London: Springer, 349–374.

Liu, J. and Zhang, H. (2018). "MOOCs in Chinese education." In H. A. Spires (ed.), *Digital Transformation and Innovation in Chinese Education*. Hershey, PA: IGI Global, 39–59.

Madangopal, D. and Madangopal, M. (2018). "ICT in education: The rural challenge." Centre for Communication and Development Studies. https://digitalequality.in/ict-in-education-the-rural-challenge/

Ministry of Education, the Government of the Republic of the Union of Myanmar (2012). *Education for All: Access to and Quality of Education in Myanmar. Conference on Development Policy Options with Special Reference to Education and Health in Myanmar, Nay Pyi Taw*. https://yangon.sites.unicnetwork.org/files/2013/05/Education-for-All-in-Myanmar-Final-2012-FEB-2.pdf

Ministry of Education, the Government of the Republic of the Union of Myanmar (2016). *National Education Strategic Plan 2016–21*. http://www.moe.gov.mm/en/?q=content/national-education-strategic-plan

Mlcek, H. S. (2011). "Competing knowledges in lifelong education." *International Journal of Lifelong Education*, 30/6, 815–829.

Noor-Ul-Amin, S. (2013). "An effective use of ICT for education and learning by drawing on worldwide knowledge, research, and experience." In *ICT as a Change Agent for Education*. India: Department of Education, University of Kashmir, 1–13.

OECD (2019). *Getting Skills Right: Future-Ready Adult Learning Systems*. Paris: OECD Publishing.

OECD (2020). *Strengthening the Governance of Skills Systems: Lessons from Six OECD Countries*. Paris: OECD Publishing.

Ogden, A.C. (2010). "A brief overview of lifelong learning in Japan." *The Language Teacher* 34/6, 5–13.

Osborne, M. and Borkowska, K. (2017). "A European lens upon adult and lifelong learning in Asia." *Asia Pacific Education Review*, 18/2, 269–280.

Ratana-Ubol, A. and Richards, C. (2016). "Third age learning: Adapting the idea to a Thailand context of lifelong learning." *International Journal of Lifelong Education*, 35/1, 86–101.

Regmi, K. D. (2015). "Lifelong learning and post-2015 educational goals: Challenges for the least developed countries." *Compare: A Journal of Comparative and International Education*, 45/2, 317–322.

Rubenson, K. (2015). "Framing the adult learning and education policy discourse: The role of the Organisation for Economic Co-operation and Development." In M. Milana and T. Nesbit (eds.), *Global Perspectives on Adult Education and Learning Policy*. Basingstoke: Palgrave Macmillan, 179–193.

Shan, H. (2017). "Lifelong education and lifelong learning with Chinese characteristics: A critical policy discourse analysis." *Asia Pacific Education Review*, 18/2, 189–201.

Singh, M. (2002). *Institutionalising Lifelong Learning: Creating Conducive Environments for Adult Learning in the Asian Context*. Hamburg: UNESCO Institute for Education.

Singh, M. and Duvekot, R. (eds.) (2013). *Linking Recognition Practices and National Qualifications Frameworks: International Benchmarking of Experiences and Strategies on the Recognition, Validation and Accreditation (RVA) of Non-Formal and Informal Learning*. UNESCO Institute for Lifelong Learning. https://unesdoc.unesco.org/ark:/48223/pf0000 224694

Singai, C., Gioli, G., Riemer, E., Regmi, K. D., Mastrokoukou, S., and Singh, S. (2016). "Knowledge economy and demographic change: Comparative case study of Europe and South Asia." In R. Egetenmeyer (ed.), *Adult Education and Lifelong Learning in Europe and Beyond*. Frankfurt am Main: Peter Lang, 67–86.

South Asia Alliance for Poverty Eradication (SAAPE) Secretariat (2019). *Growing Inequality in South Asia: South Asia Inequality Report 2019*. Kathmandu, Nepal: S. B. Printer and Publication. https://www.globaltaxjustice.org/sites/default/files/South%20Asia%20Inequality% 20Report%202019.pdf

Stone, D. (2017). "Understanding the transfer of policy failure: Bricolage, experimentalism and translation." *Policy & Politics*, 45/1, 55–70.

Tan, C. (2010). "Educational policy trajectories in an era of globalization: Singapore and Cambodia." *Prospects*, 40, 465–480.

Tan, C. (2017). "Lifelong learning through the Skills Future movement in Singapore: Challenges and prospects." *International Journal of Lifelong Education*, 36/3, 278–291.

The ASEAN Post Team (2018). "Southeast Asia's widening inequalities." July 17. https://theaseanpost.com/article/southeast-asias-widening-inequalities

Tobias, R. (2004). "Lifelong learning policies and discourses: Critical reflections from Aotearoa, New Zealand." *International Journal of Lifelong Education*, 23/6, 569–588.

UN (2019). *World Population Prospects 2019. Volume 1: Comprehensive Tables*. New York: United Nations.

UNESCO (1976). Recommendation on the development of adult education, Nairobi, UNESCO https://uil.unesco.org/fileadmin/keydocuments/AdultEducation/Confintea/en/Nairobi% 20Recommendation_Eng.pdf

UNESCO (2015). *Status, Trends, and Challenges of Education for All in South Asia (2000–2015): A Summary Report*. New Delhi: UNESCO New Delhi Cluster Office. https://unesdoc.unesco.org/ark:/48223/pf0000234967?posInSet=1&queryId=46958b60-d960-4e7d-abc6-43d40d9ca14d

UNESCO (2017). *Reading the Past, Writing the Future: Fifty Years of Promoting Literacy*. Paris: UNESCO. https://unesdoc.unesco.org/ark:/48223/pf0000247563?posInSet=1&queryId=def739e5-docf-4e4c-8e3d-fe1ab69187a6

UNESCO Institute for Lifelong Learning (UIL) (2009). *Global Report on Adult Learning and Education*. Hamburg, UIL. https://unesdoc.unesco.org/ark:/48223/pf0000186431

UNESCO Institute for Lifelong Learning (UIL) (2015). *Recommendation on Adult Learning and Education*. Paris: UIL.

UNESCO Institute for Lifelong Learning (UIL) (2019). *The 4th Global Report on Adult Learning and Education (GRALE)*. Paris: UIL. https://uil.unesco.org/system/files/grale_4_final.pdf

UNESCO Institute for Statistics (2017). *Literacy Rates Continue to Rise from One Generation to the Next*. Fact Sheet 45, September. http://uis.unesco.org/sites/default/files/documents/fs45-literacy-rates-continue-rise-generation-to-next-en-2017_0.pdf

UNESCO Institute for Statistics (2020). *School Enrolment, Primary (% gross) – Nepal*. https://data.worldbank.org/indicator/SE.PRM.ENRR?end=2019&locations=NP&start=1990

UNESCO Office Almaty (2018). *UNESCO Sub-Regional Strategy for Kazakhstan, the Kyrgyz Republic, Tajikistan and Uzbekistan, 2018–2021*. Kazakhstan: UNESCO Office Almaty. https://unesdoc.unesco.org/ark:/48223/pf0000368265?posInSet=1&queryId=c8423118-8596-4edb-860f-3767b8cc02a9

UNESCO Office in Kathmandu (2017). *Literacy and Lifelong Learning*. Kathmandu: UNESCO. https://en.unesco.org/node/317362

Usher, A. (2014). *The Korean Academic Credit Bank: A Model for Credit Transfer in North America?* Toronto: Higher Education Strategy Associates.

Wain, K. (2004). *The Learning Society in a Postmodern World: The Education Crisis*. New York: Peter Lang.

Yang, J. and Yorozu, R. (2015). *Building a Learning Society in Japan, the Republic of Korea and Singapore*. Hamburg: UNESCO Institute for Lifelong Learning.

Yorozu, R. (2017). *Lifelong Learning in Transformation: Promising Practices in Southeast Asia*. UIL Publications Series on Lifelong Learning Policies and Strategies, 4. Hamburg, UNESCO Institute for Lifelong Learning. https://unesdoc.unesco.org/ark:/48223/pf0000253603

Zapp, M. and Dahmen, C. (2017). "The diffusion of educational ideas among international organizations: An event history analysis of lifelong learning, 1990–2013." *Comparative Education Review*, 61/3, 492–518.

Zhao, X. and Chui, E. (2019). "The development and characteristics of Universities of the Third Age in Mainland China." In M. Formosa (ed.), *The University of the Third Age and Active Ageing: European and Asian-Pacific Perspectives*. Cham: Springer, 157–168.

PART VIII

COUNTRY STUDIES

CHAPTER 26

CHINA

Historical and Contemporary Development of Higher Education

WENQIN SHEN AND WANHUA MA

CHINESE civilization is one of the oldest in the world. There is no doubt that the inheritance and maintenance of this civilization depends on the system of higher education, that is, a system that transfers higher learning. For a long time, the main function of the Chinese higher education system was to serve the imperial examination system (*Ke Ju*) to select government officials. The integration of the higher education system and the state is still a prominent feature of contemporary Chinese higher education. Since the second half of the nineteenth century, China has gradually established a local university system on the basis of learning from the Western university system, integrating teaching and scientific research. After more than a century of development, China's higher education system has become the largest system in the world. Although the development of higher education in China benefits from Western experience, it is also deeply rooted in its own historical traditions. This chapter will review the historical background of the development of higher education in China, as well as contemporary developments since 1949, including significant reform and internationalization strategies. Further, the chapter will examine the dual structure of private and public higher education, higher education finance, the World Class University Movement, and the massification of higher education in China.

1. HISTORICAL BACKGROUND OF HIGHER EDUCATION IN CHINA

1.1 Higher Education in Ancient China

China is a country with a long tradition of higher education. The existence of some kind of a "school" dates back to the early second millennium during the Shang dynasty (about 1800–1050 BCE), but little is known about how schools operated during this time period. In the Western Zhou dynasty (1046–771 BCE), school education was mainly for the aristocratic class, and its main purpose was to cultivate talent to serve the king (Lee, 2000). During the life of the famous Chinese philosopher, Confucius, in the fifth century BCE (551–479 BCE), it is said that Confucius had up to 3,000 disciples to whom he imparted knowledge as a form of education. In the Warring States period (483–221 BCE), Confucius and most other thinkers were private teachers who taught in a nomadic setting so institutionalized schools were not needed.

As time passed, the rulers realized that a permanent brick-and-mortar school was necessary to disseminate higher learning. The national ruler of Qi established an institution of higher education (Jixia Academy) in about 360 BCE, which existed for more than a century. Duke Huan and subsequent rulers invited various scholars (including Confucian and Taoist thinkers) to teach and debate at the school. At its height, there were more than 10,000 scholars and students at the school (Lee, 2000). During the Western Han dynasty (202 BCE to 8 CE), rulers of the Han dynasty established the highest institution of the country—the Imperial College (Taixue) in 124 BCE—marking the beginning of official institutionalized higher education in China. The Imperial College was an education system set up to recruit intellectuals, especially sons from gentry families, to fill civil service posts in the imperial government to become political elites. The main content of the teaching in the Imperial College was Confucian classics.

Around the tenth century, the first non-governmental academies (Shu-yuan) were established by the gentry, supported by private funding. Over the next thousand years, these academies would become the foundation of China's private higher education institutions (Chen and Shen, 2012). Compared with official higher educational institutions, these non-governmental academies permitted more intellectual freedom, thus attracting more intellectuals to conduct their research there. But non-governmental academies did not operate with complete autonomy from government influence as they still largely served imperial examinations for top government positions (Lee, 1985; Walton, 1999).

1.2   Higher Education in China between the End of the Nineteenth Century and 1949

Although China has a long tradition of higher education, the emergence of modern universities in China was the result of imitation of the West (Hayhoe, 1986; Shen, 2014). By the end of the nineteenth century, the first group of Western-influenced universities in China was established, including Northern University (predecessor of Tianjin University) in 1895 and Capital Metropolitan University (predecessor of Peking University) in 1898. As the first national comprehensive university, Capital Metropolitan University was also the national administration body, equivalent to the Ministry of Education. In addition to these universities, Western religious authorities established a number of Christian colleges in China. Among them were Saint John's College founded in 1879, Soochow University founded in 1900, Jinling College founded in 1915, and Yanjing University founded in 1919.

In 1905, the Qing government finally abolished the imperial examination system which had lasted for more than 1,300 years as the officials in power believed that a modern school system could not be established concurrently with an imperial examination system. As a result, the traditional education system which perpetuated an esteemed social class of bureaucratic elites ended. The next generation of would-be elites, bitter that they were being deprived of a channel to power, turned to revolutionary activities and accelerated the demise of the Qing Empire (Bai and Jia, 2016). With the collapse of the Qing dynasty in 1912, the Republic of China was formally established, ending over 2,000 years of imperial rule. Under the leadership of the first Minister of Education of the Republic of China, Cai Yuanpei, a series of modern education laws and regulations were established, laying the foundation for the development and emergence of modern higher education. In 1917, he took up the post of president of Peking University. President Cai followed the European university system, especially the German system, to promote academic freedom, pure academic research, and to transform Peking University into a modern research university (Chen, 2002).

Inspired by the German example of "saving the country from poverty through scholarship" (学术救国), the Chinese government increased funding for higher education while the emerging middle class provided a stable supply of students who could afford expensive tuition. Over the next 30 years, higher education developed rapidly despite a weak economic foundation and political instability. By 1949, 205 higher education institutions were established in China, including 124 public universities, 60 private higher education institutions, and 21 religious colleges and universities. According to estimations, there were a total number of 255,000 university graduates between 1911 to 1949 (Huo, 1999). It is worth noting that the foundation of China's elite universities was laid during this period. Out of China's 42 "double first-class" universities (an initiative by the Chinese government in 2017 which aims to foster 42 universities, of which 36 have been identified as "world-class" with "world-class" academic disciplines, and 6 having the potential to be "world-class" with "world-class" academic disciplines), 33 such elite universities were established before 1949.

1.3 Higher Education in China between 1949 and 1976

At the establishment of the People's Republic of China in 1949, there were 205 higher education institutions in the country, with 116,504 college students. Between 1950 and 1957, China undertook significant reorganization and reform of colleges and universities in accordance with the Soviet model, which classified universities into three categories: comprehensive, industrial, and specialized. The disciplines of comprehensive universities include humanities and sciences, and industrial universities focus on disciplines in the engineering field, while specialized universities mainly focus on a single discipline, such as agriculture, medicine, law, mining, and so on. While the numbers of comprehensive universities were greatly reduced from 55 in 1950 to 14 in 1957, the number of industrial universities and specialized universities increased significantly to meet the needs of industrialization. During this period, the number of university admissions doubled from 58,330 to 105,581. Between 1957 to 1959, during the Great Leap Forward, the number of higher education institutions more than tripled from 229 to 841, and the number of students admitted to universities increased from 105,581 to 274,143, peaking at an enrollment rate of 962,000 students in 1960. By 1966, the total number of college graduates in Chinese universities reached 1,673,704 (DPFMEPRC, 1984).

Higher education was severely damaged during the Cultural Revolution from 1966 to 1976. During the first four years of the revolution from 1966–1970, teaching and scientific research work was severely curtailed and all universities in the country were forced to stop enrolling students. The number of college students dropped sharply from 534,000 in 1966 to 48,000 in 1970. Between 1970 and 1976, universities were permitted to resume enrollment of "worker-peasant-soldier" students (Chinese students who were children of workers, peasants, or soldiers). Colleges and universities gradually resumed teaching and scientific research, and the number of college students increased steadily from 83,000 in 1971, to 565,000 in 1976 (DPFMEPRC, 1984, pp. 20–23).

1.4 Higher Education in China after 1977

With the fall of the Gang of Four in 1976, the Cultural Revolution came to an end. Reformists regained power and proposed that science and education were the keys to modernization. In 1977, under the instruction of the then-leader of the People's Republic of China, Deng Xiaoping, the college entrance examination system was restored. In 1980, a three-cycle academic degree system (BA–MA–PhD) based on the Anglo-Saxon model was introduced into the Chinese higher education system.

During China's period of economic reforms, including its "open-door" policies in the late 1970s and early 1980s, China began to send a large number of students and teachers to developed Western countries such as the United States, Japan, the United Kingdom, and Germany (Lampton et al., 1986). There were also frequent international exchanges with foreign universities. As China gradually adopted marketization principles, universities were permitted to charge tuition fees and set up university-run enterprises (Eun et al., 2006). By the mid-1990s, some high-tech enterprises established by universities had gained significant national influence, such as Peking University's Founder Group Corp and Tsinghua University's Tsinghua Unigroup, both of which are among China's largest technology conglomerates. These university-run enterprises generally return part of their income to the university. Before the implementation of the "985 Project" in 1998, income from the Founder Group was an important and stable financial source for Peking University.

Due to the success of China's economic reform policies, the fiscal revenue of the Chinese government reached a surplus in the early 1990s. In 1995, the government launched the "211 Project" aimed at building a number of key disciplines in approximately 100 universities, and in 1998, the government launched the "985 Project" to build "world-class" universities (Chen, 2011).

In 1999, China started its higher education expansion plan (Wan, 2006). The gross enrollment rate of higher education in China exceeded 15 percent by 2002, entering the stage of mass higher education as defined by Martin Trow. The rate of expansion far exceeded policy expectations.

Around 2000, China undertook further major reforms in higher education. Universities that were originally affiliated with different state departments, for example, the Ministry of Finance, Ministry of Machinery Industry, and Ministry of Coal Industry, obtained independent status. Furthermore, specialized universities dominated by a single subject were considered outdated and counterproductive. Many universities in the same city were requested to merge to build comprehensive universities and enhance universities' capacity to accommodate more students. By the end of the 2000s, there had been more than 400 mergers in China (Cai and Yang, 2016).

Between 1998 and 2005, the Chinese government issued a series of policies to support the development of higher vocational colleges in order to achieve two goals. The first was to meet the needs of the fast-growing economic system for highly skilled people, and the second was to achieve the goal of higher education massification. Under this policy context, many vocational colleges were established or upgraded from secondary professional schools over a short period of time. By 2019, China had 1,423 vocational colleges, of which 1,047 were newly built or upgraded after 1999.

Another fundamental change in Chinese universities after 2000 was the dramatic increase in research and development funding from government and industry. Elite universities have been able to gradually change from teaching universities to research universities. However, as the scale of higher education became larger and larger, it was no longer possible for the government to manage higher education meticulously. Therefore, it turned to governing higher education institutes through evaluation tools, such as the China Discipline Ranking (CDR) initiated in 2002 (similar to the British Research Excellence Framework in some respects) and the undergraduate teaching evaluation launched in 2003.

After China joined the World Trade Organization in 2001, its economy increasingly integrated into the world economic system, along with the internationalization of its higher education programs. Among them, Sino-foreign cooperation universities developed rapidly.

By 2010, China's higher education enrollment reached 31.05 million students and the gross enrollment rate of higher education reached 26.5 percent. In this context, the Chinese government also began to pay more attention to improving quality and innovation capabilities of higher education. In 2012, the Ministry of Education issued two policy documents targeting the quality of higher education: "Opinions on Implementing the Innovation Capability Improvement Plan of Higher Education Institutions" and "Several Opinions on Comprehensively Improving the Quality of Higher Education." With the support of these two policies, a large number of scientific research centers in universities have received public funding to promote interdisciplinary and university–industry scientific research cooperation. The latter policy document also proposes a gradual increase in public funding per student for colleges and universities to ensure the quality of teaching.

In 2015, the State Council of China issued the "Overall Plan for Promoting the Construction of World-Class Universities and World-Class Disciplines," which proposed that the number and strength of world-class universities and world-class disciplines would be among the top in the world by the middle of the twenty-first century. This project, called the "Double First-Class Project," replaced the previous "211 Project" and "985 Project."

2. THE INTERNATIONALIZATION OF CHINA'S HIGHER EDUCATION

During the Cultural Revolution from 1966 to 1976, the Chinese higher education system existed in isolation from the rest of the world. Chinese scholars did not publish papers in international journals and there were very few international exchanges of students and teachers. This changed under Deng Xiaoping's leadership beginning in 1978, as he sought to send large numbers of students abroad to learn advanced foreign technology and bring back the knowledge to accelerate China's modernization. From October 7–22, 1978, a Chinese education delegation led by the President of Peking University, Zhou Peiyuan, visited the United States and signed an informal agreement with the US State Department, National Science Foundation, Department of Health, Education and Welfare, National Security Council and others, under which the United States would agree to accept 500–700 undergraduate students, graduate students, and visiting scholars from China in 1978–1979. Between 1979 and 1986, the State Education Commission of China signed similar agreements with the United Kingdom, Egypt, Canada, the Netherlands, Italy, Japan, Federal Germany, France, Belgium, Australia, and several other countries. Since then, China has continued to send large numbers of students to Western countries (Shen et al., 2016). Furthermore, China has increased its research capacity through publications in international journals while searching for more collaborative opportunities to undertake international scientific research.

In 2007, China's Ministry of Education and Ministry of Finance jointly established a program called the "National Development High-Level University Public-Sponsored Postgraduate Student Scheme." This program aimed to "implement the state's strategies of achieving national prosperity with science, education, and talents, and expedite the training of high-level talents" (Jiang & Shen, 2019). As of June 2014, approximately 44,000 individuals, including 18,000 degree-seekers and 26,000 visiting doctoral students, were accepted into the scholarship program. This program has played an important role in improving the quality of Chinese doctoral training and promoting international scientific research cooperation (Shen, 2018).

In addition to sending a large number of students abroad, the Chinese government has also issued various policies to encourage students to return to the country, including the "Hundred Talents Program of the Chinese Academy of Sciences" in 1994, the "Changjiang Scholars Program of the Ministry of Education" in 1999, and the "thousand-talent program" under the responsibility of the Central Organization Department in 2008. These programs provide applicants with generous salaries and advanced scientific research infrastructure to promote "reverse brain-drain" and attract high-level talents to return to the country. China's economic prosperity and the increasing difficulty of getting a good job in the West are also the main reasons for the rapid increase in returnees. In 2018, there were 662,100 students studying abroad and the returnees reached 519,400 in the same year (MOE, 2019a).

Chinese universities have also been trying to improve the quality of higher education by cooperating with Western universities since the mid-1980s to form new synergies and adapt to international standards. The earliest cooperation was mainly at the program level. In 1984, Dalian University of Technology and the State University of New York in Buffalo jointly organized an MBA program, which was the earliest transnational higher education program (TNHE) in China. Sino-foreign cooperative education programs catered to the growing middle class's demand for international education, and at the same time brought significant economic benefits to participating universities. For the government, this has been a way to solve people's educational needs without public investment. These factors have combined to stimulate the development of TNHE. As seen in Figure 26.1, the number of Sino-foreign cooperative education programs increased rapidly between 2000 and 2004, with another period of growth between 2009 and 2014.

The establishment of the University of Nottingham Ningbo in 2004 marked a new model of international cooperation as the first Sino-foreign cooperative university to be established in China. Since then, 12 other Sino-foreign cooperation universities have been built or are under construction in China.

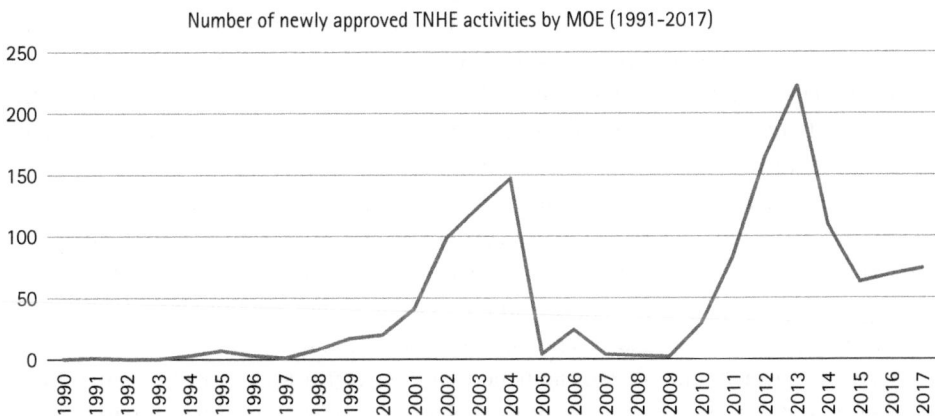

FIGURE 26.1 Number of newly approved TNHE activities

Source: MOE (2016), calculated by the authors (2018).

The Chinese government acknowledges the use of higher education as a tool to convey a nation's culture and soft power (Shambaugh, 2013). In order to increase international influence in the past decade, the Chinese government has been vigorously trying to attract international students to study in China. In September 2010, the Ministry of Education enacted the "Program of Studying in China" with a goal of attracting 500,000 foreign students to study in mainland universities. This target was almost achieved in 2018, with 492,185 overseas students from 196 countries studying in China (MOE, 2019a).

3. THE RISE OF PRIVATE HIGHER EDUCATION AMID THE STRONGHOLD OF PUBLIC HIGHER EDUCATION IN CHINA

3.1 Private Higher Education in China

Before the creation of the People's Republic of China in 1949, 79 private universities existed. However, they were ultimately abolished in 1952 during the Chinese Revolution as "privatization" was deemed to be against the prevailing principles of socialism at the time. This ideological barrier was finally lifted when China adopted economic reform in a series of "open-door" policies in the 1970s and 1980s. As stipulated in the 1982 Constitution of the People's Republic of China, the state encouraged collective economic organizations, state enterprises and institutions, and other social forces to run educational institutions. With these new reforms, private higher education institutions (*Minban* universities) began to reappear in China. China's first Minban higher education institution of this era, Zhonghua Shehui University, was established in March 1982 (Yang, 2004).

Further promotion of the development of private institutions ensued with the promulgation of a series of laws by the Chinese government: the *Provisional Regulations on the Establishment of Private Higher Education Institutions* in 1993; the *Education Law of the People's Republic of China* in 1995; *Regulations of Education Run by Social Forces* in 1997; and *Law on Promotion of Privately-Run Education* in 2002. Each of these laws propose that the development of Minban higher education should encourage and protect the legitimate rights and interests of Minban higher education institutions, giving investors and stakeholders reassurance of government support for private institutes. The 2002 law further guarantees that private colleges will hold the same legal status as public colleges and have complete autonomy in terms of president election, internal management, strategic planning, finance, and other related matters.

When the government officially launched a higher education expansion plan in 1999, it found that it did not have sufficient financial resources to support the massification of higher education. As a result, the government began to encourage private capital to support the development of private higher education institutions. Foreign investment was also permitted but with some limitations (Zhang, 2003). The success of these policies in attracting investment in private higher education institutes is evident, with the establishment of 757 private colleges and universities in China by 2019, of which 614 (approximately 80 percent) were created after 2000. In 2018, Westlake University, one of the first research universities approved by the government to engage in doctoral education among private universities in China after 1949, was established. In its first year, Westlake University officially admitted 120 doctoral students. These doctoral students are jointly trained by Westlake University, Zhejiang University, and Fudan University. Since Westlake University has not yet obtained the power to grant doctorate degrees, students will receive their doctorate degrees from Fudan University or Zhejiang University.

From the late 1990s, the Chinese government encouraged another type of private higher institute, independent *colleges* (Duli Xueyuan), otherwise known as "second-tier colleges." Independent colleges are completely self-funded, financed mainly through partnerships or directly from the private sector, and are able to charge enrollment fees and tuition fees from students in line with government stipulations. By 2018, there were 265 independent colleges and universities with a total enrollment of 6,496,000 students, accounting for 16.95 percent of national enrollment (MOE, 2019b).

It is noteworthy that while the total enrollment in private colleges and universities reached 6.28 million in 2017, there was a drastic shortage of teachers in private colleges and universities. Based on 2017 figures, there were only 316,174 full-time faculty and staff at private colleges and universities (Department of Strategic Planning, 2018), giving a student–teacher ratio of 19.86:1. This exceeded the 18:1 ratio set by the government. Several reasons explain the shortage of teachers in private colleges and universities, including the lack of status and prestige associated with China's private universities. In China, long-standing public universities are coveted by top students, thus private universities tend to admit the overflow of students who generally have lower test scores in college entrance examinations. They also lack government funding, are heavily reliant on tuition fees for operational costs, and have various government restrictions in the development of postgraduate education.

3.2 The Critical Advantage of the Public Higher Education System

Although China's private higher education has gained development opportunities in the process of massification to become an increasingly integral part of China's higher education system, China's public higher education system still occupies an unalterably dominant position.

Out of the two types of higher education in China (four-year higher education institutions and three-year vocational or technical institutions), there are 1,265 four-year higher education institutions, among which 831 are public (65.69 percent), and 1,423 vocational or technical institutions, among which 1,101 are public (77.37 percent). Separately, there are also 756 adult higher learning institutions.

In terms of student enrollment, public higher education colleges and universities are the predominant providers of mass higher education. In 2019, there were 40.02 million students in higher education nationwide, of which 32.93 million were in public universities, accounting for 82.28 percent (Ministry of Education, 2020).

Similar to the German and Japanese higher education systems, China's best universities are public due to their more prestigious status and ability to attract quality educators and students, and more favorable government support and funding to be able to facilitate advanced research capabilities. Until 2011, private higher education institutions in China were not even allowed to offer graduate education programs and could only provide "associate" degrees. Since 2011, five private colleges—Beijing City University, Xijing University, Hebei Institute of Communications, Heilongjiang Oriental College, and Jilin Huaqiao Foreign Languages Institute—have received permission to engage in graduate education, though the share of private higher education in graduate education remains small. In 2018, there were only 1,490 postgraduates enrolled in private colleges and universities nationwide, accounting for 0.05 percent of the country's total.

At present, no private university in China is qualified to independently train doctoral students. The dominant position of the public higher education system stems from the government's protective policies on the one hand, and the large amount of financial investment on the other. Since the government's support for the "Double First-Class Project" does not include private education institutions, the status of private higher education in China may remain in an increasingly disadvantaged position.

4. HISTORICAL CHANGES IN HIGHER EDUCATION FUNDING

As seen in Table 26.1, government investment in higher education rapidly increased after the Chinese government launched the "985 Project" in 1998. However, private funding of higher education revenue has remained consistently low, peaking at 4.73 billion yuan in 2016.

While elite research universities have been trying to raise funds from the private sector, this effort has not resulted in much success. In 2017, revenue from private donations was only 4.64 billion yuan, accounting for only 0.42 percent of the total income of Chinese colleges and universities that year. This may be due to the fact that private fundraising in public higher education is still a relatively new concept. It was only after 2008 that a few Chinese universities set up foundations to raise funds (interview

Table 26.1 Structure of higher education funding source, 1994–2017

	Total income	National financial education funding (billion yuan)	Private university organizer investment (billion yuan)	Social donations (billion yuan)	Tuition and fees (billion yuan)
1994	24.8	17.7	–	0.30	3.29
1998	58.7	28.9	–	1.18	8.55
2002	152.7	67.6	–	2.80	42.6
2006	305.8	130.3	–	1.95	90.6
2011	562.9	296.5	2.70	3.00	172.5
2014	869.4	526.3	1.92	4.04	202.6
2015	951.8	593	2.81	4.82	205.8
2016	1012.5	628.8	4.73	4.72	217.7
2017	1110.8	689.9	3.79	4.64	233.2

Source: MOE & National Bureau of Statistics of China. (1994-2017). *China educational finance statistical yearbook.* Beijing: China Statistics Press.

with a University Foundation staff member, March 2020). As a result, Chinese colleges and universities are still highly dependent on government funding.

According to official statistics for 2017, 62.11 percent of funding at public institutions of higher education came from central and local governments while 20.1 percent came from tuition and other fees (Department of Strategic Planning, 2018). HEIs received 126.5 billion RMB in funding for R&D from the government, industry, and other sources. By comparison, all 71 public R&D institutions and central government departments (e.g., the institutes of the Chinese Academy of Sciences, Ministry of Science and Technology, Ministry of Industry and Information Technology, Ministry of Agriculture, etc.) received 243.5 billion RMB, nearly two times as much as the universities. Among the 71 public R&D institutions and central government departments, the Chinese Academy of Sciences received the most R&D funding of 44.3 billion RMB (National Bureau of Statistics, 2018).

5. From the 985 Project to the Double First-Class Program: China's World Class University Movement

Since 1949, China has faced problems in developing higher education to achieve the goal of modernization. Due to insufficient financial resources of the government, it was a realistic policy decision to build a few elite universities first. In 1954, China decided to focus on building six key universities. This expanded to 16 key universities in 1959, of which only three were newly established universities, namely the Renmin University of China (1950), Beijing University of Aeronautics and Astronautics (1952), and University of Science and Technology of China (1958). By the end of 1981, 96 universities had been designated as key universities.

However, in the 1980s, even key national universities faced serious problems of in-sufficient funding. In an interview in 1988 Ding Shisun, the then-president of Beijing University, explained that he was an active supporter of increased government funding, which he believed was the only real way to solve the problem. In support of his argu-ment, he stated that all 36 universities under the direct management of the National Education Commission should have an annual grant of 1,800 yuan per student. Some provincial universities receive grants from local governments and some also receive local subsidies, bringing the total grant for each student up to 2,300 yuan on average. In other words, the financial support received by key national universities was not even as much as that of local universities (Pepper, 1990, p. 146). Even in the early 1990s, after China had already adopted market economy policies, higher education still faced great financial difficulties resulting in low wages for teachers and insufficient research funding. As a result, approximately 27 percent of young teachers recruited since 1981 (many of whom were considered "promising" or "core" members of their department) left by 1991 for other career tracks (Cao, 1998).

In 1995, the Chinese government renewed its ambitions to foster "world-class" universities by launching the "211 Program," which aimed to improve the capabilities and competitiveness of some 100 universities in education, research, management, and social services. In 1998, coinciding with the 100-year anniversary of Peking University, the "985 Project" was officially launched to build "world-class" universities by improving scientific research capabilities of universities and establishing the Chinese version of research universities. Between 1996 and 2008, about US$6.2 billion was distributed to over 100 key universities (Li, 2004; Huang, 2015). Empirical research shows that the rate of growth in publications for Chinese universities as a whole increased rapidly after the implementation of the "985 Project" (Zhang et al., 2013). However, while world-class university programs have greatly increased the research output of Chinese universities, in general, Chinese universities are still catching up to international standards (Horta and Shen, 2020). Despite gaining an affiliation with top Chinese universities, Chinese scientists still lag behind Western countries in original contribution.

From 1978 to 1980, 2,457 SCI articles were published by Chinese scholars. By global standards, this figure was much lower than that of India (35,322) and America (407,726). A turning point occurred in 1990, when the number of SCI articles increased to 7,607, narrowing the gap between China and India to 10,327 articles (Zhong, 1998; Oleksiyenko, 2014). In 2005, the number of high-citation articles surpassed that of Japan, and by 2009, the number of SCI publications was comparable to those from the UK and Germany (Xie et al., 2014). However, despite the great achievements of Chinese scholars in scientific publications since 1978, critics believe that the development of

Chinese universities is already hitting a ceiling in terms of quality and breakthrough research (Altbach, 2016). For example, a leading scholar in the field of computer science pointed out that "our originality is still low ... We now have a lot of papers, and the number exceeds that of the United States, but 90% of the true original ideas still comes from other countries" (interview with top computer scientist, 2018). So far, in mainland China, there has only been one Nobel Prize winner. Chinese scholars have been publishing more international papers in the field of humanities and social sciences, but these papers still lack global influence (Liu et al., 2015).

With the improvement in quality scientific research in recent years, more Chinese universities have risen in university rankings. In the QS and THE rankings in the last ten years, Peking University and Tsinghua University have both ranked in the top 50. This has led to further discussion about the existing Chinese university model (Deng, 2016), although there is no consensus on the characteristics and value of the Chinese model of higher education development.

Since the Chinese government launched the "Double First-Class" university program in 2016, replacing the previous "985 Project," 42 universities have been identified as "world-class" (or "first-class" as known in China) and another 95 universities have begun to receive funding to build at least one "world-class" discipline. Government investment of 110 billion yuan has been planned for 2016 to 2020, equivalent to twice the total of the "985 Project" and "211 Project" combined. However, universities that have not been included in the "Double First-Class" university program are still to a greater or lesser degree facing problems of insufficient financial investment.

It can be seen that while key university policies since the 1950s have enabled a small number of elite universities to obtain sufficient investment, other universities have been left to suffer from underinvestment. As a result, an institutional hierarchy exists. Compared with non-elite universities, graduates from elite universities earn higher incomes and have easier access to elite jobs (Hu and Vargas, 2015). For students from the working class and peasantry who are lucky enough to enter elite universities, higher education is a ladder of social mobility, but at the same time higher education, especially elite higher education, has become a tool for social stratification.

6. The Expansion of the Chinese Higher Education System

In 1978, when China was just beginning its economic reform and opening up to the rest of world, China's gross higher education enrollment rate was only 2 percent of the population (Ji and Wu, 2018). Over the decades, with a multitude of higher education expansion policies, the gross enrollment rate reached massification (15 percent) in 2002 as defined by Martin Trow, and universalization (50 percent) in 2019.

Today, there are 2,688 colleges and universities, including 257 independent colleges, 1,265 four-year universities, and 1,423 vocational colleges. The total enrollment of higher education has reached 40.02 million, of which 2,863,700 are graduate students (Ministry of Education, 2020). Currently, China has the largest higher education system in the world.

The process of massification of higher education in China is paralleled with a process of system differentiation of higher education. Private higher education, higher vocational education, and adult higher education have all expanded through the same process (Lai, 2014). In the process of massification, a hierarchical structure consisting of elite research universities, local applied universities, private universities, independent colleges, higher vocational colleges, and adult higher education institutions has gradually formed. The non-elite higher education sector has developed rapidly with the number of higher education institutions increasing from 1,942 in 1999 to 2,663 in 2018. Partly inspired by the German model of a dual higher education system, the Chinese government hopes that all teaching universities will develop in the direction of applied universities. Applied universities also hope to obtain funds through more research activities to generate revenue and enhance the reputation of the university. Therefore, the phenomenon of academic drift in the European university system has also appeared in China (Gellert, 1993).

6.1 The Trade-offs between "Access" and "Quality"?

Whether the expansion of higher education will affect the quality of teaching in universities is a matter of recent concern in China. Some studies have pointed out that because the quality of university teachers and financial investment lags behind the speed of expansion, there are problems with the quality of teaching in some universities. Since 2005, revenue from tuition fees in colleges and universities has been declining, causing colleges and universities to raise funds from multiple channels. It is worth noting that local and private colleges and universities, in particular, are still highly dependent on tuition fees, which form a very large part of university income (up to 86.96 percent) (see Figure 26.2). Therefore, if tuition fees remain low, the quality of teaching in local universities and private universities will be difficult to guarantee. These universities will face great difficulties in recruiting new teachers and updating teaching facilities without sufficient financial sources.

6.2 The Opportunity for Equity in the Expansion of Higher Education

The expansion of higher education in China has provided opportunities for higher education to groups who did not previously have the privilege of attending university,

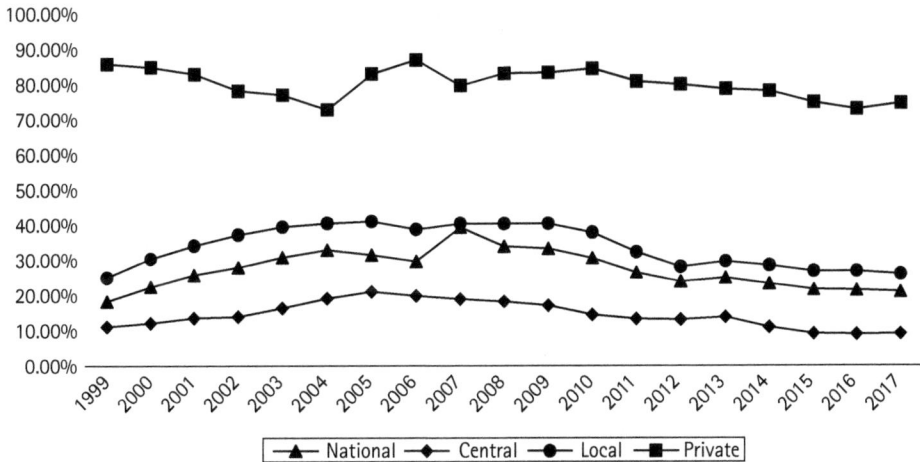

FIGURE 26.2 The ratio of tuition to overall revenue in different colleges and universities and its changes (%)

Note: National refers to national average level; central refers to public universities supervised by central government; local refers to public universities supervised by local government.

increasing their earning capacity by 40 percent as a result of attaining a higher education qualification (Ma et al., 2016). Expansion of higher education has also increased women's access to education. In 1978, the proportion of female students in the higher education system was only 24 percent. By 1999, this proportion was close to 40 percent. In 2009, the number of female college-level students in China surpassed male students for the first time (Development Planning Department, Ministry of Education, People's Republic of China, 2010) and only shortly after in 2010, the proportion of female students in master's programs surpassed male students (Department of Development Planning, Ministry of Education, People's Republic of China, 2011).

However, wealth and social inequality in China remains an issue affecting overall access to Chinese higher education (Hannum et al., 2019). The expansion of the higher education system has not solved the problem of unfair access to higher education. Compared to students from the lower socio-economic class, students from the middle and upper class have obvious advantages in the merit-based college entrance examination due to their cultural capital advantage and their economic ability to purchase shadow education. Therefore, they are more likely to get access to elite universities (Ye, 2015; Liu and Wan, 2019; Zhang, 2020).

In addition, the sudden expansion of higher education in China has made it increasingly competitive for college students to find employment (Li et al., 2014; He and Mai, 2015; Mok and Qian, 2018). With millions of graduates each year across all disciplines, the government must now focus on ensuring quality education that rewards graduates with commensurate pay in industry without overvaluing degrees.

7. The Regulation of the Higher Education System through Evaluation Tools after the mid-1990s

With the growing number of higher education institutions since the mid-1990s, the central government has turned to regulating and managing higher education institutes through evaluation mechanisms. At the beginning of 1994, the State Education Commission of China launched an evaluation of undergraduate teaching. Subsequently, in 2002, the Ministry of Education officially introduced an evaluation scheme for both undergraduate training and postgraduate education and research activities that runs on five-year cycles, called the China Discipline Ranking (CDR).

During the first round of CDR in 2002, 80 disciplines, known as first-level disciplines in China, were assessed, including philosophy, sociology, geography, basic medicine, civil engineering, geophysics, etc. Although taking part in CDR is not mandatory, a total of 229 universities across the country participated in the first CDR. Since then, CDR evaluation has been successfully conducted roughly every five years in 2006, 2012, 2016, and 2020.

CDR ranking has grown in importance for Chinese universities as many provincial governments reward disciplines that achieve a high CDR ranking with additional funding. In research universities, managers also allocate funds for the "985 Project" based on their CDR ranking. Because of this, CDR has had a profound impact on the management behavior of universities. University administrators have formulated various performance indicators and quantitative methods to evaluate faculty members' research (Shen et al., 2021). Meanwhile, universities, as well as the national government, have begun to take notice of world rankings. In 2003, Shanghai Jiaotong University published its first World University Rankings which will have a huge impact on the global higher education system (Liu et al., 2015). Since then, China's elite universities have shown considerable commitment to improving their rankings through various reforms and have become more accepting of government regulations.

Although the central government claims to provide more autonomy to universities, especially top universities, Chinese universities are still largely governed the same way as administrative departments by two government bodies—the party committee and the administration (Ngok, 2008). However, the division of labor between the two systems is unclear and often prone to conflict (Shen et al., 2020). Furthermore, presidents and party secretaries of "double first-class" universities are appointed directly by the government. While they have great autonomy in many respects, such as recruitment and teaching reform, they are still bound by certain restrictions, such as setting tuition fees. In addition, presidents of research universities, like government officials, are required to retire at the same age as civil servants (normally 63 years old). Therefore, they tend to have short tenures (normally four to eight years) which makes it difficult to implement and oversee their own policy agendas. Some scholars remain concerned that while the changing nature of government–university relations has resulted in greater procedural autonomy for institutions, it has actually led to a narrowing of substantive autonomy (Yang et al., 2007).

8. Conclusion: The Continual Rise of Chinese Higher Education and the Challenge Ahead

Despite the impressive growth and development of China's universities, China's higher education sector still faces many challenges. First of all, the problem of brain drain is still very serious. While China's research infrastructure and university teachers' salaries have greatly improved, many Chinese scholars who have obtained doctorate degrees abroad are still reluctant to return to China, indicating that major problems in the local academic culture persist. For example, relationship-building (*guanxi*) still plays an important role in seeking opportunities and funding, which is widely criticized in Western standards as a form of nepotism. All this shows that China is still in a relatively peripheral position in the global academic system.

Secondly, although a good governance structure is considered to be one of the key factors in building a world-class university, excessive government intervention has long been considered a major drawback in the governance of Chinese universities. Since the 1980s, China has been exploring reforms in university governance, aiming to achieve a delicate balance between increasing university autonomy and maintaining government control. Furthermore, China's higher education system needs to achieve a better balance in the array of disciplines and higher education structure. Since the 1950s, the Chinese government has been implementing a development strategy of prioritizing science and technology, leaving social science and humanities underfunded and underprioritized.

Another challenge remains in the serious funding shortage of local and private universities. This exacerbates the Matthew effect of accumulated advantage of China's higher education system which has an unfortunate impact on the equality of higher education (Hu and Vargas, 2015). Surely, a quality higher education system cannot be supported by just a few elite universities. In addition, as pointed out above, although private higher education has increased in quantity, it remains extremely weak in scientific research and graduate education. Private Chinese universities should make use of the increasingly abundant private capital to vigorously develop private higher education, building a structure where public higher education and private higher education compete with each other.

Finally, and most importantly, Chinese universities need to resolve the tension between cultural traditions and Western models. China's higher education tradition, rooted in an imperial college system (Taixue) and academies (Shu Yuan), emphasizes intellectual authority and the application of knowledge. This still has a great impact on organizational behaviors in Chinese universities and colleges today. Chinese universities retain a similar structure to government departments in terms of administration and governance, which are quite different from their Western counterparts. Both Chinese higher education researchers (Yan, 2009) and foreign observers (for example, see Douglass, 2012) agree that one of the major obstacles in the development of Chinese higher education is the excessive role of government intervention. Chinese universities that wish to develop and internationalize further will need to integrate Western academic values. Integration of the East and the West will be key to the rise of Chinese universities.

References

Allen, R. M. (2017). "A comparison of China's 'Ivy League' to other peer groupings through global university rankings." *Journal of Studies in International Education*, 21/5, 395–411.

Altbach, P. G. (2016). "Chinese higher education: 'Glass ceiling' and 'feet of clay'." *International Higher Education*, 86, 11–13.

Bai, Y. and Jia, R. (2016). "Elite recruitment and political stability: The impact of the abolition of China's civil service exam." *Econometrica*, 84/2, 677–733.

Cai, Y. and Yang, X. (2016). "Mergers in Chinese higher education: Lessons for studies in a global context." *European Journal of Higher Education*, 6/1, 71–85.

Cao, X. (1998). "The strategic role of faculty development and management." In M. Agelasto and B. Adamson (eds.), *Higher Education in Post-Mao China*. Hong Kong: Hong Kong University Press, 29–58.

Chen, H. (2002). *The Classical German University Idea and its Influence on Chinese Universities*. Beijing: Peking University Press (in Chinese).

Chen, H. and Shen, W. (2012). "Toward general education in the global university: The Chinese model." In A. R. Nelson and I. P. Wei (eds.), *The Global University: Past, Present, and Future Perspectives*. New York: Palgrave Macmillan, 177–188.

Chen, X. F. (2011). "Ideal-oriented policymaking: An analysis of the 985 project policy process." *Chinese Education & Society*, 44/5, 8–18.

Deng, W. (2016). "Chinese higher education model in change: Negotiation with Western power." In C. P. Chou and J. Spangler (eds.), *Chinese Education Models in a Global Age*. Singapore: Springer, 121–132.

Department of Planning and Finance, Ministry of Education of the People's Republic of China (DPFMEPRC) (1984). *Statistics on Educational Achievements in China (1949–1983)*. Beijing: People's Education Press.

Department of Strategic Planning, Ministry of Science and Technology (2018). *China Science and Technology Statistics Yearbook 2018*. Beijing: China Statistics Press.

Development Planning Department of the Ministry of Education of the People's Republic of China (2010). *China Education Statistics Yearbook 2009*. Beijing: People's Education Press.

Development Planning Department of the Ministry of Education of the People's Republic of China (2011). *China Education Statistics Yearbook 2010*. Beijing: People's Education Press.

Douglass, J. A. (2012). China futurisms: Research universities as leaders or followers? *Social Research: An International Quarterly*, 79/3, 639–668.

Education Yearbook Compilation Committee of the Ministry of Education (EYCCME) (1948). *The Second China Education Yearbook*. Shanghai: Commercial Press

Eun, J. H., Lee, K., and Wu, G. (2006). "Explaining the 'university-run enterprises' in China: A theoretical framework for university–industry relationship in developing countries and its application to China." *Research Policy*, 35/9, 1329–1346.

Gellert, C. (1993). "Academic drift and blurring of boundaries in systems of higher education." *Higher Education in Europe*, 18/2, 78–84.

Hannum, E., Ishida, H., Park, H., and Tam, T. (2019). "Education in East Asian societies: Postwar expansion and the evolution of inequality." *Annual Review of Sociology*, 45, 625–647.

Hayhoe, R. (1986). "Penetration or mutuality? China's educational cooperation with Europe, Japan, and North America." *Comparative Education Review*, 30/4, 532–559.

Hayhoe, R. (2017). "China in the center: What will it mean for global education?" *Frontiers of Education in China*, 12/1, 3–28.

He, Y. and Mai, Y. (2015). "Higher education expansion in China and the 'ant tribe' problem." *Higher Education Policy*, 28/3, 333–352.

Horta, H. and Shen, W. (2020). "Current and future challenges of the Chinese research system." *Journal of Higher Education Policy and Management*, 42/2, 157–177.

Hu, A. and Vargas, N. (2015). "Economic consequences of horizontal stratification in postsecondary education: Evidence from urban China." *Higher Education*, 70/3, 337–358.

Huang, F. (2015). "Building the world-class research universities: A case study of China." *Higher Education*, 70/2, 203–215.

Huo, Y. (1999). *Higher Education in Modern China*. Shanghai: East China Normal University Press.

Ji, Y. and Wu, X. (2018). "New gender dynamics in post-reform China." *Chinese Sociological Review*, 50/3, 231–239.

Jiang, J., & Shen, W. (2019). International mentorship and research collaboration: Evidence from European-trained Chinese PhD returnees. *Frontiers of Education in China*, 14/2, 180–205.

Lai, Q. (2014). "Chinese adulthood higher education: Life-course dynamics under state socialism." *Chinese Sociological Review*, 46/3, 55–79.

Lampton, D. M., Madancy, J. A., and Williams, K. M. (1986). *A Relationship Restored: Trends in US–China Educational Exchanges, 1978–1984*. Washington, DC: National Academies Press.

Lee, T. H. (1985). *Government Education and Examinations in Sung China*. Hong Kong: Chinese University Press.

Lee, T. H. (2000). *Education in Traditional China: A History*. Leiden: Brill.

Li, L. (2004). "China's higher education reform 1998–2003: A summary." *Asia Pacific Education Review*, 5/1, 14–22.

Li, S., Whalley, J., and Xing, C. (2014). China's higher education expansion and unemployment of college graduates. *China Economic Review*, 30, 567–582.

Liu, L. and Wan, Q. (2019). "The effect of education expansion on intergenerational transmission of education: Evidence from China." *China Economic Review*, 57, 101327.

Liu, W., Hu, G., Tang, L., and Wang, Y. (2015). "China's global growth in social science research: Uncovering evidence from bibliometric analyses of SSCI publications (1978–2013)." *Journal of Informetrics*, 9/3, 555–569.

Ma, B., Cai, H., and Yao, X. (2016). "College enrollment expansion and changes in the rate of return to college education: An empirical study based on CGSS data." *Economic Theory and Economic Management*, 6, 45–57 (in Chinese).

MOE & National Bureau of Statistics of China. (1994–2017). *China educational finance statistical yearbook*. Beijing: China Statistics Press.

Ministry of Education (2019a). "The number of study abroad students reaches 662.1 thousand in 2018" (in Chinese). http://www.gov.cn/xinwen/2019-03/27/content_5377428.htm, accessed April 24, 2019.

Ministry of Education (2019b). *Statistical Communiqué on National Education Development in 2018* [EB/OL]. http://www.moe.gov.cn/jyb_sjzl/sjzl_fztjgb/201907/t20190724_392041.html

Ministry of Education (2020). *2019 National Educational Development Statistical Bulletin* [EB/OL]. http://www.gov.cn/xinwen/2020-05/20/content_5513250.htm

Mok, K. H. and Qian, J. (2018). "Massification of higher education and youth transition: Skills mismatch, informal sector jobs and implications for China." *Journal of Education and Work*, 31/4, 339–352.

National Bureau of Statistics (2018). *China Science and Technology Statistical Yearbook 2018*. Beijing: China Statistics Press.

Ngok, K. (2008). "Massification, bureaucratization and questing for 'world-class' status." *International Journal of Educational Management*, 22/6, 547–564.

Oleksiyenko, A. (2014). "On the shoulders of giants? Global science, resource asymmetries, and repositioning of research universities in China and Russia." *Comparative Education Review*, 58/3, 482–508.

Pepper, S. (1990). *China's Education Reform in the 1980s: Policies, Issues, and Historical Perspectives*. Berkeley, CA: Institute of East Asian Studies.

Shambaugh, D. L. (2013). *China Goes Global: The Partial Power*. Oxford: Oxford University Press.

Shen, W. (2014). "Foreign influence, nationalism, and the founding of modern Chinese universities." *International Higher Education*, 77, 19–21.

Shen, W. (2018). "Transnational research training: Chinese visiting doctoral students overseas and their host supervisors." *Higher Education Quarterly*, 72/3, 224–236.

Shen, W., Huang, Y., and Fan, W. (2020). "Morality and ability: Institutional leaders' perceptions of ideal leadership in Chinese research universities." *Studies in Higher Education*, 45/10, 2092–2100.

Shen, W., Mao, D., and Lin, Y. (2021). "Measuring by numbers: Bibliometric evaluation of faculty's research outputs and impact on academic life in China." In A. Welch and J. Li (eds.), *Measuring Up in Higher Education: How University League Tables and Rankings Are Reshaping Knowledge Production in the Global Era*. Cham: Palgrave Macmillan, 203–227.

Shen, W., Wang, C., and Jin, W. (2016). "International mobility of PhD students since the 1990s and its effect on China: A cross-national analysis." *Journal of Higher Education Policy and Management*, 38/3, 333–353.

Walton, L. A. (1999). *Academies and Society in Southern Sung China*. Honolulu: University of Hawai'i Press.

Wan, Y. (2006). "Expansion of Chinese higher education since 1998: Its causes and outcomes." *Asia Pacific Education Review*, 7/1, 19–32.

Xie, Y., Zhang, C., and Lai, Q. (2014). "China's rise as a major contributor to science and technology." *Proceedings of the National Academy of Sciences*, 111/26, 9437–9442.

Yan, F. (2010). "The academic profession in China in the context of social transition: An institutional perspective." *European Review*, 18, S99–S116.

Yan, G. (2009). "The construction of the Chinese academic system: Its history and present challenges." *Frontiers of Education in China*, 4/3, 323–342.

Yang, R. (2004). "Toward massification: Higher education development in the People's Republic of China since 1949." In J. C. Smart (ed.), *Higher Education: Handbook of Theory and Research*. Dordrecht: Kluwer, 311–374.

Yang, R., Vidovich, L., and Currie, J. (2007). "'Dancing in a cage': Changing autonomy in Chinese higher education." *Higher Education*, 54/4, 575–592.

Ye, H. (2015). "Key-point schools and entry into tertiary education in China." *Chinese Sociological Review*, 47/2, 128–153.

Zhang, H., Patton, D. and Kenney, M. (2013). "Building world-class universities: Assessing the impact of the 985 Project." *Research Policy*, 42/3, 765–775.

Zhang, W. (2020). "Shadow education in the service of tiger parenting: Strategies used by middle-class families in China." *European Journal of Education*, 55/3, 388–404.

Zhang, X. (2003). "Private universities open up new channels for overseas financing." *China Investment*, 3, 42–44 (in Chinese).

Zhong, W. (1998). "Chinese scholars and the world community." In M. Agelasto and B. Adamson (eds.), *Higher Education in Post-Mao China*. Hong Kong: Hong Kong University Press, 59–77.

CHAPTER 27

ELITE UNIVERSITIES IN CHINA

LAN XUE, ZHEN YU, AND ZHOU ZHONG

1. INTRODUCTION: CONCEPTUALIZING ELITE UNIVERSITIES IN CHINA

1.1 The Concept of Elite Universities

THE concept of "elitism" often denotes an elite/mass dichotomy in social stratification which enables a small group of individuals to exert their position of superiority and exercise power and authority over the masses. "Elitism" is an enduring theme in human existence, guarded by a sense of exclusivity in membership and determined by societal rules and expectations of any given time period, including the ability to be born, and restrictions on being bred, into the highest social class. Beyond the embodiment of "elitism" within a social hierarchy, the term "elitism" can also be used more broadly to define a group of top-performing individuals in their particular industry and practice. In the latter definition, elitism is gained on the basis of merit, whether this requires physical and mental strength or endurance, or intellectual prowess, and depends less on social hereditary factors. The question posed in this chapter is whether "elite universities" are a meritocracy characterized by academic excellence as top performers in education, or institutions created by and for the social "elites," or a matter of both as institutions based on meritocracy but realistically mostly reserved for social elites.

The term "elite university" builds upon the idea of elitism at an institutional level and can be so classified if it comprises three elements. The first element of an elite university refers to an ideal academic and social institution in pursuit of truth, excellence, and common welfare. The second element of an elite university refers to the creation of a prestigious brand for academic excellence that is fostered by its related community including students, scholars, and alumni of that university, as well as the broader university community and key stakeholders. The third element of an elite university refers to its influential identity based on the physical location of its founding campus, unique disciplinary strengths that meet national needs, and a symbiotic relationship with the surrounding community.

A more popular way to identify elite universities has been through various kinds of university rankings. The growing popularity of university league tables to compare institutional performance over the past two decades has driven universities to compete for national or international status against a small number of narrowly defined quantitative measures. Despite controversies, the pecking order of universities creates, or perhaps reflects, social desire for elite university status by promoting academic rankings or social standing in an age of proliferating higher education in our increasingly globalized world.

The conceptualization of the elite university varies in different contexts. Unlike the US and the UK higher education systems, most universities in modern China are public and rely on financial input from the government to support their operations. Realizing the important role of elite universities in the knowledge economy, the Chinese government has launched several national elite university projects (e.g., Project 211 and Project 985) to foster world-class universities. The selected universities in these projects are usually recognized as elite universities in China. The majority of these universities are selected based largely on their academic performance and reputation, but some universities are selected because of the government's political strategy to serve national interests such as balancing regional development and promoting economic growth (e.g., agriculture and national defense). Chinese families work hard to send their children to these elite universities as a symbol of social status, and for better future job prospects. This zeal has largely directed the attention of Chinese society to a few elite universities.

In this chapter, we provide an overview of the history of China's elite universities (section 1), review China's world-class university policies since the 1950s (section 2), and discuss the current status of China's elite universities in terms of their academic performance, funding situations, international collaboration, and global impact (section 3). Finally, we conclude the chapter with the authors' reflections on how to advance China's world-class university efforts.

1.2 Fundamental Issues of Elite Universities

In the context of the aforementioned triadic concept of elite universities, elite institutions are able to safeguard academic excellence by managing tensions between meritocracy and social mobility, and between diversity and stratification. These tensions have grown ever more significant over the past three decades as higher education systems in many countries including China have upgraded to mass and universal systems.

Both meritocracy and mobility are closely related to the function of the university in educating the elite. First, meritocracy refers to a highly selective process of cultivating, evaluating, and recognizing a chosen few by awarding opportunities, power, and resources based on talent, effort, and achievement, rather than inherited socio-economic status. Although there have been various critiques of meritocracy (e.g., Sandel, 2020), it is deeply rooted in Asian culture and social fabric. Second, mobility refers to the movement of individuals or groups of people within or between social strata which changes one's social position. According to the French sociologist Bourdieu, "state nobility" arises from "a set of carefully selected chosen people" distilled out of highly competitive examinations, which they succeed in, empowered by elite education from high school onwards in many cases, and in all cases at graduate level. Thus, the process of examination and education becomes "a legitimate form of election" and "gives rise in and of itself to symbolic capital that increases the degree of restriction and exclusivity of the group so established" (Bourdieu, 1996, p. 79).

Societal stratification occurs when institutional division develops and labor diversifies as the higher education sector expands to build capacity for mass and universal accessibility. According to Trow (2007), a national higher education system develops through three modes in turn, each mode classified by a distinctive educational purpose which is reflected in gross tertiary enrollment rate (GTER): (1) the elite mode (GTER below 15 percent) aims to shape the mind and character of the ruling class and prepare for broad elite roles in government and the learned professions, (2) the mass mode (GTER above 15 percent but below 50 percent) aims to enhance skills and knowledge transmission and prepare for a broader range of technical and economic elite roles, and (3) the universal mode (GTER reaching 50 percent or above) aims to maximize the adaptability of the "whole population" to rapid social and technological changes. Consequently, in the mass or universal higher education system, two or three types of higher education institutions (HEIs) coexist: elite universities, mass-access HEIs, and universal-access HEIs. Each type has a distinctive way in which the institution is structured, governed, and evaluated and how students are selected, taught, and organized (Trow, 2007). Moreover, elite universities rely on a differentiation strategy with increasing openness and inclusiveness to raise academic selectivity and socio-cultural diversity to safeguard excellence and promote welfare.

1.3   The Development of Universities in China

The Chinese concept of a higher learning institution or "university" was first articulated by Confucius' disciple Zengzi (505–435 BCE) over two millennia ago:

> The Way of Great Learning lies in enlightening the virtues, perfecting the people, and achieving ultimate goodness (大学之道,在明明德,在亲民,在止于至善); the individual can and should obtain Great Learning as integration of being, to knowing and doing through investigating the world to acquire genuine knowledge

and understanding (格物致知), examining one's sincerity to rectify one's heart (诚意正心), cultivating the body and mind (修身), managing one's family and kinship (齐家), governing the state (治国), and achieving Great Harmony for all under the Heaven (平天下). (Zhu, 2011, p. 4)

Zengzi's "Way of Great Learning" has been studied as one of the prime texts in Confucianism by generations of scholars throughout Chinese history and describes the holistic and transcendent purpose of higher learning for achieving reciprocal self-perfection and to serve the common good. Chinese classics have accounts about institutions for "Great Learning" from time immemorial, so Zengzi's idea is both an inheritance and a new articulation of indigenous forms of Chinese universities "太学" which date back to 124 BCE when Emperor Hanwu (circa 156–87 BCE) established an imperial university and endowed chairs for doctors to teach the five classics of Confucianism.

It was not until the late nineteenth and early twentieth century that China established modern universities with a national system of education. China experimented with a variety of reference frameworks, shifting from Japanese until the 1900s to European and American until the 1940s, then Soviet in the 1950s and 1960s (Zhong, 2014). Since the mid-1980s China has embarked on continuous domestic reforms while opening up to learn from the rest of the world in higher education and education in general.

It is important to understand China's university development in terms of the crucial symbiosis between elite universities and state examinations. The two are both complementary and conflicting. This is because Chinese institutions are in control of students' progress and resource allocation throughout their education while state examinations define the caliber of the vast majority of students in the university sector. However, the continuous negotiation between elite universities and state examinations has become increasingly difficult with China's rapid higher education expansion. While elite universities have maintained a largely stable level of undergraduate student intake over the past two decades, the state examination system has to cope with a rapidly expanding number of people—from 3.8 million in 2000 to 10.7 million in 2020—taking China's annual National Unified Examination for Admissions to Universities and Colleges (*Gaokao*).

Moreover, there is also a distinctive cultural momentum in sustaining the symbiosis of Chinese elite universities and state examinations. China has a long history of using state examinations to legitimize and confer the status of state nobility to scholars regardless of social background. China's traditional state examination, the imperial civil servant examination, lasted 1,300 years from the late sixth century to 1905. *Gaokao* has operated since 1952 to determine admission into undergraduate education. Often seen as a single-log bridge, *Gaokao* serves as the only fair way to regular higher education in China for the vast majority of Chinese students. An individual's *Gaokao* score is calculated from the performance of five or six academic subjects in upper secondary school and streams students into the strata of HEIs in China. In this way, elite universities in China attract students with only the highest *Gaokao* scores.

Gaokao as a social institution has undergone reform in response to changing social needs, as well as long-standing criticism such as high stress, rigidity in standard, content, and method, emphasis on rote learning, and growing reliance on expensive commercial cramming programs outside schools. In parallel with the *Gaokao* system, China also has a state examination system at regional levels for competitive entrance into general upper secondary schools. A major criticism in recent years has extended to "elite upper secondary schools," which comprise a small number of highly selective schools that monopolize the best teachers and students, and therefore access to elite universities. Both elite universities and most of their feeding schools are public institutions. In recent years, the crucial link between the two has attracted growing debate over educational quality and equity and also issues of wider social dynamics such as mobility and accountability.

2. EVOLUTION OF ELITE UNIVERSITY POLICIES IN CHINA SINCE THE 1950S

2.1 National Key Universities

After the founding of People's Republic of China in 1949, China Sovietized the entire higher education system, about 200 HEIs, to accelerate industrialization in 1952. All comprehensive universities were restructured and most of them were downsized by losing several academic departments to other institutions. The restructuring created a large number of small and specialized HEIs in engineering, agriculture, medicine, normal education, political science and law, finance and economics and also a large number of narrowly defined academic subjects. The restructuring produced a strong emphasis on engineering. About three-quarters of all science and engineering departments and colleges were removed from their home universities to be either merged into other institutions or to form new institutions (Ma and Dong, 1998). Since then, about one-third of Chinese students in higher education have studied engineering. Moreover, most Chinese elite universities, such as Tsinghua, have sustained a distinctive engineering strength. China de-Sovietized the higher education system through reverse restructuring in the 1990s, by merging specialized HEIs into big comprehensive universities. Many elite universities, such as Nanjing University and Zhejiang University, suffered from department closures in 1952 until they acquired several colleges in the 1990s.

The contemporary Chinese idea of elite universities began with the National Key University (NKU) policy which prioritized investment in a small, selective group of high-performing universities in 1954 (MOHE, 1954). The first batch of national key universities had six candidates (Peking University, Tsinghua University, Renmin University of China, Harbin Institute of Technology, Beijing Medical College, and China

Agricultural University). These institutions were made into exemplars of Sovietization and were pioneers of close collaboration with the Soviet Union. Given the severe resource scarcity in China after emerging from a century of intermittent international and civil wars, the NKU policy enabled China to spearhead the development of a small number of universities to serve strategic national needs, including preparing engineers, government cadres, university faculty, and other professionals for the country's economic and social development.

From the early 1950s to the early 1990s, all university resources were centrally planned and allocated by the government, including, among others, funding, number of faculty, staff and students, structure and scale of academic disciplines, and campus infrastructure. Moreover, China developed key secondary schools at regional and municipal levels across the nation which became the feeder schools for key universities. These focused policies represented China's way of tackling educational quality versus quantity and elitism versus equity conflicts in complex, large-scale educational development in a nation with a significant population, severe resource scarcity, and marked regional disparities.

The NKU policy evolved under different names but the intention of the policy has remained the same. As the Chinese education system developed steadily over the years, the number of national key universities increased from 6 in 1954 to 99 in 1981. It is worth noting that after the decade-long education stagnation during the Cultural Revolution, China resumed the NKU policy in 1978 as one of its top priorities. Two other top priorities were reestablished, *Gaokao* and study-abroad national scholarships programs, both of which served to benefit elite universities more than other universities.

In 1985, China introduced comprehensive reforms to break away from the Soviet model of education and research systems[1] by implementing the National Key Discipline policy alongside the NKU policy to introduce competition through performance-based measures to invigorate the university sector. The new policy redefined elite universities as it provided a new opportunity for non-elite universities to move up the reputation ladder based on merit. As a result, this policy generated a middle tier of universities between elite and non-elite universities.

2.2 World-Class Universities 1.0: Project 211 and Project 985

Initiated by the State Council in 1995, Project 211 had the objective of permitting "some Chinese universities and disciplines [to] approach or achieve advanced international level."[2] Project 211[3] aimed to build about 100 prestigious universities for the twenty-first

---

[1] Decision of the CPC Central Committee on the Reform of the Education System, 1985 (中共中央关于教育体制改革的决定).

[2] The overall construction plan of project 211, 1995 ("211工程"总体建设规划).

[3] The name of "211 project" came from 21 (21st century) and 1 (100) universities.

century by prioritizing key disciplines, investing infrastructure to support education and research, and building a network of national libraries and laboratories.

On May 4, 1998, China's then-President Jiang Zemin called for a few world-class universities (WCU) in his remarks at the centenary celebration of the establishment of Peking University. Following this statement, the State Council approved the *Action Plan for Revitalizing Education for the 21st Century* and officially launched Project 985.[4] Project 985 prioritized reform in institutional governance and management, and the development of key disciplines through enhanced faculty welfare and building multi-disciplinary academic platforms to create departmental or college-level centers of excellence in arts and sciences, respectively.[5]

China's elite universities, as beneficiaries of Project 211 and Project 985, have enjoyed two decades of continuous support from the government for WCU development. The ambition to achieve WCU status has served as a vital alignment of the elite university, the state, and the market to drive China's higher education development. Elite universities first proposed the idea of WCU to set themselves new strategic goals and to persuade the government for increased support and societal contribution through fundraising efforts. The central government has promoted the WCU idea to raise aspirations of the entire higher education sector in China and co-create innovative policy measures with WCU members to reform higher education. Regional governments have also committed to achieving WCU as leverage to require universities to enhance responsiveness while bargaining with the central government and industry for more investment in regional education infrastructure. As a result, aspirations towards WCU status in China have exerted a multiplier effect from strategic planning to raising standards, mobilizing resources, and creating checks and balances to maintain meritocracy.

The dynamics of WCU membership are such that there is a relatively stable core of elite universities while the door is kept open for small-scale new membership recruitment. Project 211 began with 16 universities in 1995, and 112 universities by 2011 with membership being approved in five batches. Project 985 began with 2 universities in 1998 and 39 universities by 2011 with membership being approved in three batches. Since Project 985 members also enjoyed Project 211 membership and neither project had a membership withdrawal mechanism, there was inevitable inertia among elite universities due to their "taken-for-granted status, as well as a lack of alignment and competition" (State Council, 2015).

2.3 World-Class Universities 2.0: DWC Policy

Between 1999 and 2015, China's GTER grew 3.8 times from 10.5 percent to 40.0 percent. Its total higher education enrollment grew 3.5 times from 10.5 million to 36.5 million,

---

[4] The name 985 came from 98 (the year 1998) and 5 (the month of May).
[5] Action Plan for Revitalizing Education for the 21st Century, 1999 (面向21世纪教育振兴行动计划).

and the number of higher education students per 100,000 people grew nearly eight times from 328 to 2,524 (MOE, 2016a). This rapid growth in higher education participation took place within the context of rapid economic development and major demographic transition. Up to 2015, China was the world's fastest-growing major economy with growth rates averaging 10 percent in 1985–2015 (World Bank, 2017). Meanwhile, the size of China's 18–24 age cohort fell from 176 million in 1990 to 129 million in 2015 (NBS, 2016).

In 2015, the Double-World-Class (DWC) policy was introduced to integrate and replace the previous two projects (Project 211 and Project 985). The DWC policy aimed to build some universities and disciplines to a level of world-class excellence, while manifesting Chinese characteristics. The DWC policy conceptualized the WCU as "an engine in knowledge discovery and science and technology innovation, a fountain of advanced thought and excellent culture, a base for fostering all kinds of high-caliber talent, and a significant player in driving national innovations, advancing economic and social development, promoting traditional Chinese culture, fostering socialistic core values and promoting quality-driven development in higher education" (State Council, 2015). This conceptualization echoes that of Project 985 which stated that WCU embodied the five attributes of excellence in talent cultivation, knowledge discovery and application, cultural development, and international exchange.

The DWC plan also encapsulates the idea of WCU with "Chinese characteristics" within a socialist flagship university capable of strengthening the leadership of the Communist Party of China (CPC), supporting and developing Chinese socialism through continuous reform and opening, honoring the country's traditional culture, bringing innovations to Chinese culture, and committing to building the world-class universities and disciplines simultaneously in the long-run (MOE et al., 2017). This set of DWC ideas is embodied in a 35-year timeline with rather ambiguous goals in line with China's macro development planning cycles. The DWC plan states that by 2020, several universities and a group of disciplines will be esteemed as world-class, and several disciplines will be in leading positions; by 2030, more universities and disciplines will be esteemed as world-class; several universities will be esteemed as world-leading; and China will be in the leading position in more disciplines. By 2050, the number and quality of world-class universities and disciplines are hoped to be among the best in the world.

The DWC policy provides flexible membership on a five-year basis, subject to renewal through regular reviews. The criteria for DWC membership reflect the value system that underpins Chinese higher education: a university's current capacity and potential in terms of institutional goals, academic profile, stage of development, and differentiated value proposition (MOE, MOF & NDRC, 2017a). A total of 140 universities with 465 world-class disciplines were selected in 2017 as the first group of DWC candidates, comprising 42 WCU candidate universities (39 Project 985 members and 3 Project 211 members) and 98 "World-Class Discipline" candidate universities (the rest of the Project 211 members and 25 non-Project 211 members) (MOE, MOF & NDRC, 2017b). The high concentration of Project 985 and Project 211 members in the DWC group demonstrated the sustainability of the WCU efforts.

Furthermore, the DWC Plan has developed new accountability mechanisms for promotion and demotion of DWC membership based on their performance evaluation at disciplinary, institution, and system levels (State Council, 2015). In this way, the DWC plan introduced fair competition to boost commitment and confidence in the new era of China's WCU building. The MOE conducted a comprehensive evaluation of the first five-year DWC phase (2016–2020) of the DWC in 2021, then put forward a new list of candidates for the second phase (2021–2025) in February 2022. In the new list, there are 147 universities and 433 disciplines as DWC candidates, including seven new universities and 58 new disciplines (MOE, MOF & NDRC, 2022). A special note is that both Tsinghua University and Peking University were granted autonomy to set their own list of DWC candidates for the second phase, and they would announce their respective list later. Moreover, 15 universities received formal warnings from the MOE as not meeting the DWC building requirement. Those universities were required to submit a re-evaluation in 2023 to remove their warning or to be removed from the DWC list.

While the DWC policy provides standardized concepts and frameworks, it leaves room for the individual universities and regions to exert indigeneity in formulating their DWC strategies. The central government plays a key role in platform orchestration for DWC development. The process of implementing the DWC plan entails a process of individual universities developing their institutional DWC strategies and aligning multi-stakeholder views and multi-functional strategies at institutional, local, regional, and national levels. After several rounds of feedback and revisions, all 140 DWC universities completed their institutional strategies and obtained approval from their host regional governments and central government by mid-2018. Subsequently, the MOE, Ministry of Finance (MOF), and National Development and Reform Commission (NDRC) jointly issued a DWC Guideline (2018) to accelerate DWC implementation by appreciating and aligning diverse regional and institutional initiatives into a synergistic new framework. As an open platform innovation, the DWC policy contains a regulated space to maintain its core requirements while leveraging a creative space to enable both individualized interpretations from current participants and conditioning potential participants.

3. The Status of DWC Universities in China

3.1 Characteristics and Performance

Most WCU candidate universities are characterized by strong academic performance, high-quality education, and a high level of social recognition. While three universities were selected due to consideration for regional balance, the remaining 39 universities are those bearing cumulative advantages from the previous Project 985. In terms of global reputation, China is rising quickly in global university rankings. From 2015 to

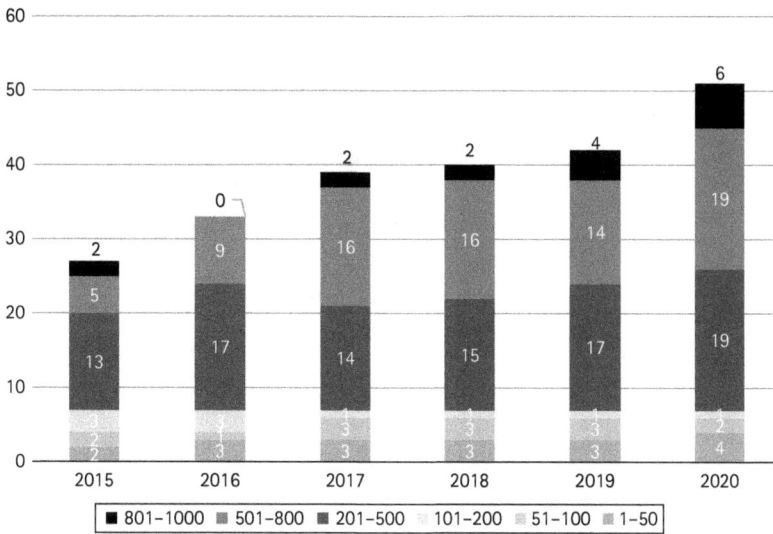

FIGURE 27.1 Number of China's universities in QS top 1000 ranking

Source: Compiled by the authors.

2020, China's number of QS Top 1000 universities almost doubled from 27 to 51 (Figure 27.1). However, most of the increase occurred in the lower ranks (top 1000–top 200), and only 7 universities managed to squeeze into the top 200. In 2020, among the 51 universities listed in the Top 1000, 35 are WCU candidate universities, but in the top 500, 23 of 26 are WCU candidate universities.

From a spatial perspective, DWC universities are unevenly distributed in China (Figure 27.2). As the cultural and educational center of China, Beijing has a remarkably large number of candidate universities in both the WCU project (8) and the World-Class Discipline project (33), accounting for more than a fifth of the total candidate universities. Eastern regions such as Jiangsu (15) and Shanghai (13) also show a clear advantage in the number of DWC universities. In middle and western China, only Shanxi (8), Hubei (7), and Sichuan (7) have a relatively large number of DWC universities. Although most western provinces are not part of the more prestigious WCU project, almost every province has at least one university involved in the World-Class Discipline project. This illustrates the nation's sustained effort to tackle regional disparities in higher education through coordinated long-term planning. Yunnan University and Xinjiang University, for instance, were selected mainly due to the consideration to promote equal access to quality education for China's less prosperous areas.

DWC universities regard world-class discipline development as the key driver of building WCUs. China's DWC universities have put more emphasis on developing hard sciences or practical disciplines as world-class. Among the current 456 World-Class disciplines, science and engineering account for 49 percent, medical science, agriculture, and forestry together represent 22 percent, whereas humanities and social science only have a share of 11 percent and 18 percent respectively. Some disciplines with

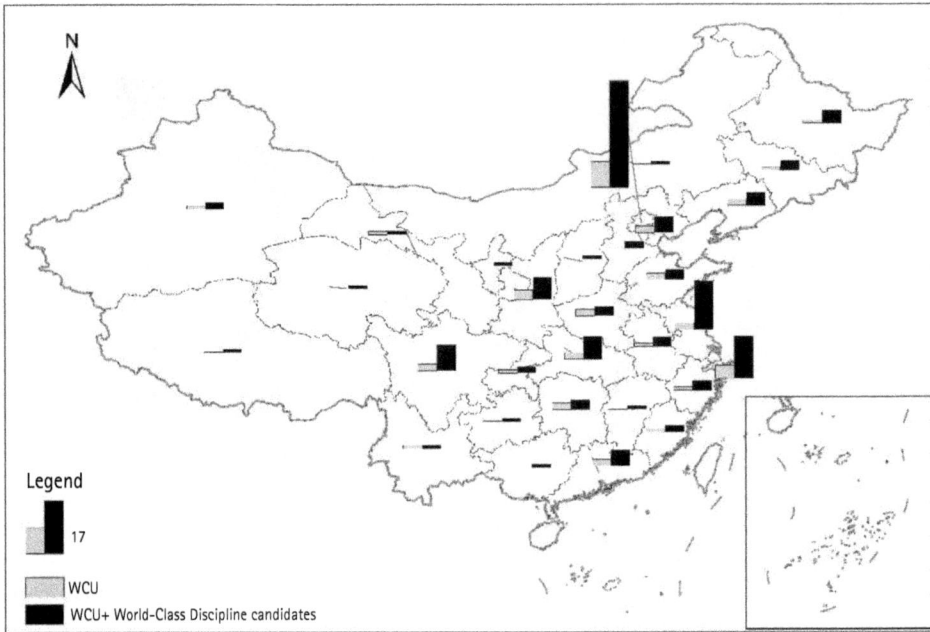

FIGURE 27.2 Spatial distribution of China's DWC universities

Source: Compiled by the authors.

Chinese characteristics such as Chinese medicine and Marxism studies are encouraged to be enlisted in the World-Class Discipline project. Inevitably, however, there are some reflections that the World-Class Discipline project may drive universities to concentrate limited resources on existing competitive disciplines at the cost of other disciplines, leading to an unbalanced academic structure (Liu, 2018).

3.2 Funding Situation

In Project 211 and Project 985, the central government channeled funds to universities directly administered by the MOE and other ministries, while local authorities were responsible for financing selected local universities. This is now changing, particularly among top universities. When the DWC initiative was implemented in 2017, it was expected that DWC universities would actively seek more financial support from society to diversify their financial sources. Still, fiscal input from both central and local government plays an important role. While the fiscal input from the central government has not increased much, local governments are very enthusiastic about matching funds to selected DWC universities in their jurisdictions. Together, it was reported that there would be RMB 40 billion public funds allocated for DWC universities. As the DWC initiative is an open scheme that allows new universities to be involved every five years, local governments are competing to have more universities listed in the initiative.

Yet, for elite universities to build WCUs, fiscal appropriation from the government is far from enough. In 2017, according to the budget information released by 75 universities under the MOE, most of the universities' annual income is lower than the annual budget. Top universities are striving to increase their income from other sources to cover their world-class-level research and education. In China's top 10 universities by income, operations income accounts for a larger share than government appropriation. On average, operations income represents 43.5 percent of these universities' total accounts, surpassing that from fiscal appropriation (37.7 percent). Operations income of a university refers to the revenue acquired from teaching activities (e.g., tuition fees) and scientific research (e.g., technology transfer). Meanwhile, income from other sources such as donation, investment, bank deposit interest, and rent is rising (EOL, 2019). Nonetheless, compared to top US universities, philanthropic income remains a very small part of Chinese universities' total income. From 1980 to 2017, the total donation to mainland China's universities reached RMB 92.7 billion, of which alumni donation accounted for 34.5 percent. In 2019, only six DWC universities received philanthropic donations of more than RMB 100 million each.

3.3 International Partnerships

Opening-up to the world in education as learning from the world through cross-border engagement for exchange and collaboration has been an essential feature of China's modernization since the late nineteenth century. Today, the principle of opening-up has been enshrined in China's constitution (NPC, 1982). The higher education sector, especially the elite universities, serve as a national pillar of China's opening-up. The DWC plan has made international exchange and collaboration one of ten essential tasks of WCU building. For example, typical forms of international partnerships are Sino-foreign joint-run programs and institutions offering degree-awarding undergraduate and postgraduate education (MOE, 2021). The joint institutions involve either a sub-university unit, such as a college or school hosted by a Chinese university, or a joint-venture university as an independent legal entity.

By May 2021, the 42 WCU candidates had developed 102 joints programs, 28 joint sub-university institutions and three universities. All of them offered predominantly on-shore programs, while many of them also had offshore options for sending students to overseas partner universities for a period of time. Among the 102 joints programs, about one-third were in science, engineering, and medicine, two-thirds in social science, particularly business administration, accounting, finance, and management studies. The partners of those joint ventures were mainly developed countries, especially the United States and the United Kingdom. The three joint-venture universities are partnerships involving Chinese and foreign universities and also municipal governments that hose the campuses. They are the Shanghai New York University by East China Normal University, New York University, and Shanghai government, Duke Kunshan University by Wuhan University, Duke University, and Kunshan municipal government, and Xi'an

Jiaotong-Liverpool University by Xi'an Jiaotong University, Liverpool University, and Suzhou government. All of them started enrollment in 2012–2014. They are all clustered in or around Shanghai, which is the most prosperous and densely populated region of China. Altogether those joint-venture programs and institutions have not only provided Chinese students with onshore access to international higher education, but have also pioneered many higher education reforms and innovations in China.

3.4 Striving for Global Impact

The DWC plan, the Educational Action Plan for the Belt and Road Initiative (MOE, 2016b), and the China Modernization Strategy 2035 (CCCPC & SC, 2019) have reinforced each other to prioritize international strategies. The latest national policy in deepening the DWC building efforts forward in February 2022 stated the following tasks in enhancing global impact (MOE, 2022b): developing foreign affairs administration in order to achieve high-level educational opening-up, innovating mechanisms to support two-way studying abroad in collaboration with high-level universities in the world, developing mutual recognition of academic credit and joint- and double-degree programs, developing platforms for promoting Sino-foreign educational and cultural collaboration, improving management of international students studying in China, expanding international student enrollment in high-quality degree programs, developing demonstration courses taught in English for international students, and enhancing holistic quality in degree programs for international students.

Tsinghua University is a unique case as a born-global in China. Since its founding it has embraced internationalization as learning process of building world-class excellence (Zhong, 2021). Tsinghua was founded 1911 as a preparatory school for selecting the best Chinese students to study abroad in 1911 on national scholarship. Today, Tsinghua has become a leading comprehensive research university. In 2021, it hosted over 57,000 students and 16,000 faculties and staff in 21 schools and 59 departments, including over 3,300 international students from 130 countries and over 300 full-time international faculty and staff (Tsinghua, 2021). It has partnerships with about 300 universities and institutes worldwide and has established over 100 exchange programs and 50 dual and double-degree programs with world-renowned institutions (Tsinghua, 2022). Tsinghua ranked 17th and the 16th respectively in the QS and THE world university rankings in 2022. Tsinghua set its first WCU goal in 1985, 14 years before China adopted WCU strategy as a national strategy in 1998. It adopted the "open university" model to build academic and institutional excellence, that is, a university opening to the whole society with proactive engagement with the world through expanded scale and scope of international exchange and collaboration (Tsinghua, 1996). In striving for having Tsinghua recognized as a world-class university at its centennial in 2011, Tsinghua regarded strengthening international collaboration as a fundamental strategy for long-term and comprehensive development for the university in 2006 (Tsinghua, 2006). Tsinghua put forward its first global strategy in 2016 with the goal to become a world-leading university by 2050 (Tsinghua, 2016), then a global strategy 2030 in 2021 to restate the commitment to global engagement through developing students of global competence, faculties of global excellence, and a university of global impact (Tsinghua, 2021a).

Guided by its global strategy, Tsinghua has developed overseas centers to strengthen partnership building in education, research, innovation, and service. Tsinghua established the Global Innovation Exchange (GIX), in Seattle, in partnership with the University of Washington, USA in 2015, the China–Italy Design Innovation Hub in Milan, Italy, in partnership with Polytechnic University of Milan in 2017, and Tsinghua University Southeast Asia Center in Indonesia and Tsinghua University Latin America Center in Chile both in 2018. Moreover, Tsinghua has also initiated several international alliances, including the China–UK Association for the Humanities in Higher Education in 2016, the Asian Universities Alliance in 2017 with 14 prestigious Asian universities, the Global Alliance of Universities on Climate in 2019 with 11 universities including MIT, Cambridge, Sciences Po, and the University of Tokyo, and the Global MOOC and Online Education Alliance in 2020.

In the meantime, Tsinghua has developed comprehensive internationalization at home. As a flagship program in Tsinghua's international drive, the Schwarzman Scholars Program aims to cultivate future global leaders who can bridge China and the world. The program is a fully-funded, one-year master's degree and leadership program in global affairs mainly taught at Tsinghua's main campus in Beijing. From 2016 to 2021, the program graduated over 600 scholars from over 70 countries, including 20 percent from China, 40 percent from the USA, and 40 percent from the rest of the world. Moreover, Tsinghua opened its Shenzhen International Graduate School (SIGS) in 2019 by integrating the Tsinghua Shenzhen Graduate School established in 2001 and the Tsinghua-Berkeley Shenzhen Institute established in 2014.

Several other Chinese elite universities have also established overseas presence and international schools at home. For example, Xiamen University has developed an international campus in Malaysia since 2013. Zhejiang University has developed an international campus near its China main campus since 2013 to host joint institutes with partner universities such as the University of Edinburgh, the University of Illinois at Urbana-Champaign, and Imperial College London. Both Xiamen and Zhejiang received the first batch of students on their international campuses in 2016. Moreover, Peking University HSBC Business School opened a branch campus at Oxford, UK, in 2017.

In the context of China's opening-up strategy and growing role in global affairs, Chinese elite universities have made a sustained effort in internationalization in order to learn from and with the world, stimulate domestic reform and innovation through transnational exchange and collaboration, participate in and contribute to global development, tap the education market for talent cultivation for increasingly more Chinese and international students, develop institutional differentiation by benchmarking their global competitiveness, and build a global network of educational engagement in service to public diplomacy (Zhong, 2021).

4. Conclusions and Future Development

Overall, modern Chinese higher education has grown from a humble base since the late nineteenth century into the world's largest system on many fronts today. In higher education development, China has adopted an ambidextrous strategy of WCU building alongside enrollment expansion since 1999. When China adopted the DWC policy in 2015, Chinese higher education had already evolved into a huge system with over 36 million students. By 2020, China's GTER has reached 54.4 percent.

Although the number of Chinese universities rose from 1,071 in 1999 to 3,005 in 2020, the number of publicly recognized elite universities remains stable as during the Project 985 period. The DWC initiative is largely designed to break this identity lock-in, but the previous WCU projects have shown strong resilience, and many parts of society still judge a university by whether it was previously a Project 985 or Project 211 university. This consideration applies not only to students and their parents in choosing universities, but is also relevant among researchers looking for academic positions, and employers hiring graduates. Although many new universities in China are now catching up quickly in rankings and academic performance, few enjoy the reputation of historical elite universities. This demonstrates how government projects affect the social construction of elite universities in China. Given the small number of WCU candidate universities, competition to get access to elite universities is very intense in China. In 2020, when 10.7 million students took *Gaokao*, only 6 percent of them (0.64 million) were admitted to the 137 DWC universities, and 1.9 percent of them (0.2 million) succeeded in getting into the more prestigious Project 985 period universities.

The pursuit of equity is one of the main characteristics of China's elite university system. As public-owned HEIs, China's elite universities shoulder significant responsibilities beyond scientific research and talent training: they are also expected to play important roles in regional economic and social development. As mentioned, several Project 211, Project 985, and DWC universities were designated deliberately to provide good-quality education to less advanced regions and minority groups. The *Gaokao* system, though it suffers from continuing criticism, is still considered the only way to provide equal opportunities for millions of students from lower social classes to gain access to elite universities and change their fates.

Meanwhile, elite universities are striving for more autonomy in recruiting students through autonomous admission processes, which can put more weight on the holistic quality of students rather than the *Gaokao* score. Though students with special talents in science, arts, or sports may enjoy a lower requirement on the *Gaokao* score in some universities, *Gaokao* cannot be avoided in any case. Enrollment in this way still involves a small proportion of overall recruitment, but the trade-off between quality and equity is subtly affected. There are concerns that student family income and background may play a role in differentiating those with better special talent performance.

It is clear that China's elite universities are catching up in global university rankings and have played an important role in China's socio-economic development through talent cultivation, scientific research, and entrepreneurial activities. It is expected that many of these universities will benefit from this momentum and finally join the list of WCU as China's economy continues to grow. And we very much hope that more Chinese elite universities will become more active in addressing global sustainable development challenges.

However, there is a hard reality behind this blueprint that China needs to take into account while forging ahead. First, the Chinese government and universities should seriously reflect on what constitutes a world-class university, or the label of world-class could be framed in misleading ways (Liu, 2018). Climbing up university rankings is only a narrow goal. Can elite universities in China also attract global top talents from all over the world as do Harvard, MIT, Oxford, and Cambridge? Can academic talents trained by Chinese universities demonstrate high levels of competence in top foreign universities? Can there be more genuine contributions (e.g., at the Nobel Prize level) to human knowledge arising from within Chinese universities rather than only rising numbers of scientific publications? Evidently, the answer is "no" for now.

At the moment, there are a handful of exceptions such as the Schwarzman Scholars Program in Tsinghua University, which can attract the best and brightest from around the world. The fact that an increasing number of middle-class families in China still prefer to send their children to Western universities shows that there is still a long way to go for China's elite universities to become truly world-class universities.

A related issue is concerned with the ecosystem made up by Chinese universities. A healthy ecosystem constitutes a vibrant and diverse set of institutions involving large comprehensive universities, small and specialized colleges, excellent teaching institutions, great research institutions, and so on. Such a system will not only meet the diversified social needs better, it will also provide students with many more choices and better learning environments. A mature national higher education system needs all-round champions and champions in specialized fields as well. Throughout the history of China's higher education system, there have been many excellent small and specialized universities and colleges that can be considered as elite institutions in their own categories. However, in the rush to become WCUs, many of them were merged into larger universities or were left out. There is a need to think about how to leave some space for the development of these specialized institutions.

In addition, how to deal with the tensions between top-down directives and bottom-up initiatives also needs further attention. In the DWC initiative, the central government channels the political will to develop world-class universities in the national interest (e.g., involving considerations of education equity, regional balance, and economic development) through specific selection criteria, in guiding the selection process, and in deciding what universities and disciplines should be accredited in the DWC system. However, continued excellence in global higher education requires academic autonomy at the institutional level and regulated competition among institutions, and this needs to be reconciled with the top-down directives of the DWC effort.

Finally, one should never forget that it is China's reform and open-door policy initiated in 1978 that has brought about the tremendous changes we witness today. In the past 40 plus years, Chinese universities have benefited hugely from their interaction with their international peers, and vice versa. Recent geopolitical tension has cast some shadow over these interactive processes and some countries have even begun to constrain these linkages. No matter how long these short-sighted policies may last, China's experience over the past 40 years has shown that leading universities all over the world can only thrive in an atmosphere of open competition and simultaneous intense cooperation against a backdrop of more general peaceful competition and mutual respect.

Based on the progress made by Chinese universities over the last four decades, it is reasonable to believe that elite universities in China will continue to navigate through various challenges and maintain their unique position in both the Chinese and global higher education landscapes, but can only do so against the backdrop sketched immediately above. The healthy development of Chinese elite universities will generate not only huge benefit for China, but also great contributions to the world in a virtuous circle with sister institutions abroad.

REFERENCES

Asian Universities Alliance (AUA)(2017). Mission Statement. Asian Universities Alliance.

Bourdieu, P. (1996). *The State Nobility: Elite Schools in the Field of Power*. Cambridge: Polity Press.

CCCPC & SC (General Office of the Central Committee of the Communist Party of China and State Council) 2019. China Education Modernisation 2035. 23 February 2019.

EOL (2019). "Building double first-class universities: Where is the money from, and where to go?" ("双一流"高校的钱从哪里来，到哪里去？), September 19. https://www.eol.cn/news/uni/201909/t20190919_1683628.shtml

Liu, X. (2018). "The 'Double First-Class' initiative under top-level design." *ECNU Review of Education*, 1/1, 147–152.

Ma, Y. and Dong, B. (1998). "Restructuring and Chinese engineering higher education." *Tsinghua Journal of Education*, 4, 65–69.

MOE (2021). List of Sino-foreign joint-run programs and institutions. Ministry of Education of China. 20 May 2021. https://www.crs.jsj.edu.cn/index/sort/1006

MOE (2016a). *2015 National Statistical Bulletin on the Development of Education*. Ministry of Education of China. July 6, 2016.

MOE (2016b). Educational Action Plan to Promote the One Belt and One Road Initiative. Ministry of Education of China. July 15, 2016.

MOE, MOF & NDRC (Ministry of Education, Ministry of Finance, and National Development and Reform Commission) (2022a). The list of Universities and Disciplines for the Second Phase of the Development of World-class Universities and Disciplines. February 9, 2022.

MOE, MOF & NDRC (Ministry of Education, Ministry of Finance, and National Development and Reform Commission) (2022b). Opinions on the Development of World-class Universities and Disciplines. January 16, 2022. 关于深入推进世界一流大学和一流学科建设的若干意见》

MOE, MOF & NDRC (Ministry of Education, Ministry of Finance, and National Development and Reform Commission) (2017a). Tentative Measures for Implementing the Development of World-class Universities and Disciplines. January 27, 2017.

MOE, MOF, and NDRC (2017b). *Implementation Measures for Promoting the Construction of World-Class Universities and World-Class Disciplines (Tentative)*. /统筹推进世界一流大学和一流学科建设实施办法（暂行）.

MOHE (1954). Resolution of the Ministry of Higher Education on the Scope of Work of Key Institutions of Higher Education and Experts. August 3. 关于重点高等学校和专家工作范围的决议.

NBS (2016). *Yearbook of Chinese Demographic Statistics*.

Sandel, M. (2020). *The Tyranny of Merit: What's Become of the Common Good?* New York: Penguin Books.

State Council (2015). "Notice on the overall plan for the construction of world-class universities and world-class disciplines." /国务院关于印发统筹推进世界一流大学和一流学科建设总体方案的通知.

Trow, M. (2007). "Academic standards and mass higher education." *Higher Education Quarterly*, 41/3, 268–292.

Tsinghua University (1996). Tsinghua University Nineth Five-Year Plan (1996–2000). Beijing: Tsinghua University.

Tsinghua University (2006). Tsinghua University Eleventh Five-Year Plan (2006–2010). Beijing: Tsinghua University.

Tsinghua University (2016). Tsinghua University Global Strategy. Beijing: Tsinghua University.

Tsinghua University (2021a). Tsinghua University Global Strategy 2030. Beijing: Tsinghua University. December 2021.

Tsinghua University (2021b). Facts and figures, as of 31 August 2021. Tsinghua University.

Tsinghua University (2022). Overview: International Students. Tsinghua University. [Accessed on 26 February 2022].

World Bank (2017). *World Development Indicators 2017*. Washington, DC.

Zhong, Z. (2014). "China: An overview." In J. Hsieh (ed.), *Education in East Asia*. London: Bloomsbury Academic, 1–28.

Zhong, Z. (2021). "Opening-up as entrepreneurial internationalisation in Chinese higher education", *International Journal of Comparative Education and Development*, 23/3, 175–192. https://doi.org/10.1108/IJCED-04-2021-0035

Zhu, X. (2011). *Notes to Chapters and Sentences in the Four Books*. Beijing: Zhonghua Book Company. 朱熹, 四书章句集注 , 2011, 中华书局.

CHAPTER 28

INDIA

History and Thrust of Overall Higher Education and Research Patterns

NIRAJA GOPAL JAYAL

THE genesis of the modern university in India lies in the colonial requirement of a system for testing the eligibility of individuals for government employment. Modeled on the then University of London, the first three universities set up in India in 1857 were essentially examining and certifying bodies, with the teaching being conducted in affiliated colleges.[1] Many of the distinguishing features of Indian universities today, including their character as affiliating institutions, but especially their structures of governance and their regulatory impulses, have their origins in the colonial framework. The most enduring legacy has been the resilience of the idea that the sole purpose of universities is certification and their singular value credentialization. Other than the attachment of a small elite to the ideals associated with Western universities, the purpose of higher education is not a subject that has elicited much philosophical deliberation or policy debate in India.

1. WHAT IS A UNIVERSITY FOR?

Any publicly funded system of higher education has both intrinsic and instrumental value. The intrinsic value of education is typically seen to lie in the intellectual and

---

[1] Affiliating universities were a source of vexation for colonial administrators from the late nineteenth century onwards. This has persisted into the post-independence period, from the first University Education Commission Report (1948–1949) identifying these as the single most harmful type of institution in Indian higher education to the most recent National Education Policy 2020, which proposes to encourage affiliated colleges to become autonomous degree granting institutions or else to be phased out over the next 15 years (Government of India, 2020: 37)

emotional qualities it fosters: minimally, self-awareness, the ability to use to their highest potential the human faculties of reason, intellect, and argument, on the one hand, and the cultivation of the imagination and emotions such as compassion and empathy, on the other. Above all, other background conditions being conducive, such education affords an individual the chance of leading the kind of life she wishes to lead and of being the kind of person she wishes to be. Of course, these individual qualities also have social benefits insofar as they encourage public-spirited civic behavior, and foster practices of democratic citizenship.

In terms of instrumental value, higher education provides an important avenue of social mobility. For a first-generation university-goer, the realization of a professional ambition is not just a personal achievement; it is also a way of eroding inherited social and economic inequality. Similarly, when women acquire an education, this has empowerment consequences that enhance female workforce participation and reduce fertility rates.

While several societies have wrestled with the question of what a university is for, the circumstances of the arrival of the modern university in India meant that the purpose of the university was inextricably tied to the purposes of the colonial state and to the social classes that sought to benefit from it. The literary and humanistic bias of education in colonial India may be explained by the fact that historically it was "the traditionally literate castes" (Basu, 1982, p. 17) that sought and found easy access to education. These were the upper caste elites who craved government employment, or professions like medicine and the law. Though India had relatively few technical institutions (Japan had 25 times more), the number of engineering graduates exceeded the number of available jobs, as industrial development was stunted and even superintending engineers for government works were recruited in Britain (Basu, 1982, p. 17).

The idea of the intrinsic value of higher education found eloquent expression in the first official report after independence, with universities being seen as sites of "intellectual adventure" and education as advancing the ideals of democracy, justice, liberty, equality, and fraternity (Government of India, 1949 Chapter II). However, a combination of the embedded governmentalized practices in this field, and the need to educate the young for the economic development of a newly independent nation, meant that this remained paper idealism. The governmental approach to higher education as a site of control and the private sector view of it as a source of enormous revenue potential, tended to occlude even a debate on the issue. Alongside the difficult nature of the struggle for wider access, this ensured that the primary purpose of the university remained credentialization, and the idea of the university as a site of critique or of the germination of new knowledge, let alone intellectual adventure, did not take root.

This is reflected in the early separation of teaching and research. After independence, Jawaharlal Nehru's own predisposition and respect for specialist expertise resulted in the establishment of research institutes in several fields, from statistics to atomic energy to economic growth. Consequently, universities remained largely teaching institutions, bereft of any impetus for cross-fertilization with research. If the original mistake was the delinking of research from teaching, the subsequent massification of higher education in India ensured that the commitment to research remained superficial and tokenistic. The next section briefly maps this massification through an account of the evolution and expansion of higher education in independent India.

2. Mapping the Landscape of Higher Education in India

From 1857 to 1947, the year in which India attained independence, the number of universities had increased from 3 to 25 of which just 6 were exclusively teaching institutions, with the remainder being affiliating or federative, the total enrollment in 1947 being approximately 250,000 students.[2] The number of colleges of general education had increased from 21 in 1857 to 496 in 1947, while those of professional education had increased from 13 to 130 over the same period. These included 116 law colleges, 36 engineering colleges, 24 medical colleges, and 17 agricultural colleges.

The years following independence witnessed a substantial expansion, and a further acceleration following the liberalization of the Indian economy in 1991. Since independence, the number of degree-awarding universities has increased 52 times, the number of colleges has increased approximately 84 times, and student enrollment has gone up 178 times.[3]

India now has 45 Central Universities, established by Acts of Parliament, of which 40 are under the administrative control of the Ministry of Human Resource Development.[4] There are also 409 State Universities, established by or incorporated in an Act of a State legislature, ineligible for receiving grants from the Central Government or the UGC.[5] In addition to these, there are 349 private universities, spread across 24 states of the federation. These may be established through an Act of Parliament or a State legislature, but sponsored by a body such as a society or trust or company.

In addition to Central and State public universities and private universities, there is a category of "Deemed-to-be Universities," essentially institutions whose performance is viewed as being almost on par with a proper university.[6] Finally, there are Institutions of National Importance, usually established by an Act of Parliament and there are 95 such,[7]

---

[2] Government of India (1949).

[3] University Grants Commission, Annual Report 2018–19.

[4] The precise numbers for different types of universities in India are not consistent as between the University Grants Commission (UGC) Annual Report (2018–2019), the website of the Ministry of Human Resource Development (MHRD), and the Report of the All India Survey on Higher Education (AISHE) for 2018–2019 of the same Ministry. The latter data are based on self-reporting by institutions, some of whom do not even respond. The figures used here are from the MHRD website, also the most recent (February 2, 2020)

[5] The UGC figure for Central Universities is 51 while that of the AISHE is 46. The UGC figure for State Universities is 397 while that of the AISHE is 371.

[6] These get the appellation from the Central Government under Section 3 of the UGC Act.

[7] The UGC lists 126 Institutes of National Importance, and the AISHE lists 127.

including several All India Institutes of Medical Sciences; 23 Indian Institutes of Technology (IITs); 20 Indian Institutes of Management (IIMs); 23 Indian Institutes of Information Technology (of which only 5 are entirely publicly funded); 31 National Institutes of Technology; the National Institute of Design across three campuses; 7 Indian Institutes of Science Education and Research, and several others. There are also similar institutes created by State legislatures and at the level of the state.[8]

India has a total number of 41,901 colleges with an additional 10,726 stand-alone colleges, that include polytechnics and institutions providing teacher training as well as training in nursing, paramedical training, hotel management, and so forth. An overwhelming percentage (78 percent) of HEIs offering professional degrees in engineering, pharmacology, hotel management, architecture, business management, etc., are in the private sector (Agarwal, 2006, p. 47). Between 2000 and 2001, and 2013–2014, the average increase in the number of colleges was as high as 40 new colleges per week. "In 2013–14 alone, 2,467 new colleges opened – nearly seven per day (including weekends!)" (Kapur and Mehta, 2017, p. 3).[9]

The gross enrollment ratio (GER) for India has increased almost threefold in the last two decades, up from 8.1 percent in 2000–2001 to 26.3 percent in 2018–2019, with the total enrollment of students standing at 37.39 million. Approximately 80 percent of the students in higher education are enrolled at the undergraduate level, and less than 0.5 percent at the PhD level. The male–female ratio is almost the same in gross enrollment, but dips dramatically for women at the level of the PhD, with 23,765 men being awarded PhDs as compared to 17,048 women. The share of female students is the lowest in Institutes of National Importance and in private universities.

The distribution of enrollment across different fields of education varies greatly by level. The enrollment at the undergraduate level is much higher for both men and women in general courses in the arts, humanities, and social sciences (33.73 percent), less in science (16.28 percent), commerce (14.92 percent), and engineering/technology (12.84 percent), with education, medicine, and information technology accounting for less than 10 percent of the total. But while the largest number of undergraduates are enrolled in arts and humanities courses, at the postgraduate level, it is the sciences that account for higher enrollment, indicating that the bachelor's degree is the terminal qualification for most students in the arts and humanities (Government of India, 2019a).

---

[8] Possibly unique to India, there is an additional category of universities, with a dedicated page on the website of the University Grants Commission, that of "Fake Universities." This is a list of 25 universities as of November 2019.

[9] These numbers do not include the coaching industry that prepares students for competitive examinations for entry into engineering, medicine, management, and law. The phenomenal rise in this sector over the last decade testifies to the intense competition for access to coveted places in professional education, as also to the popular perception of education as purely an avenue of social mobility. The value of this completely unregulated industry is estimated at USD7.5 billion ("Prepare for an entrance," *India Today*, New Delhi, July 5, 2019. https://www.indiatoday.in/magazine/guest-column/story/20190 715-prepare-for-an-entrance-1561843-2019-07-05, accessed September 10, 2020.

Although they account for 78 percent of HEIs, and for 67 percent of the total enroll-ment in higher education, private colleges and universities are chiefly providers of first degrees, and contribute little or nothing to the production of knowledge. Enrollment in the PhD program is less than 0.4 percent of the total enrollment in tertiary education. In 2018, with 37.4 million students enrolled in HEIs, the number of PhDs awarded was 40,813 (Government of India, 2019a, p. 3). In percentage terms, the PhDs awarded con-stitute 0.071 percent of the total enrollment. Moreover, 70 percent of all PhD enrollments are in public sector institutions: state public universities, central public universities, and Institutes of National Importance. Only 12.66 percent of all PhD enrollments are in pri-vate deemed universities and 6.5 percent in private universities in the states. Although PhDs are overwhelmingly produced in the public sector, there are many problems with both the quality of doctoral theses as well as worrying practices of corruption, cronyism, and even contract cheating.

Cumulatively, these data point to an unprecedented rate of expansion of higher educa-tion institutions in India. The frequent bemoaning of the under-supply of tertiary edu-cation can be attributed to the fact that the enrollment of 37 million students obscures from sight the 45 million young people of the same age demographic who lack access to any form of tertiary education, even of the vocational type, and the consequences of this for the future of work.

The expansion that has occurred has not been an unmitigated good. If the biggest advantage of this massification has been the increase in access to higher education, its biggest casualty has been a precipitous decline in the already modest quality of education provided, arguably undermining the gains of access. While access has been enormously expanded both in terms of numbers, and in particular in enhanced opportunities for women and members of historically disadvantaged groups, several distortions have crept in. The most frequently cited, in the quarter-century since economic liberaliza-tion and globalization, is the mismatch between education and employability as in the estimates that anywhere between 75 and 90 percent of engineering graduates are un-employable (Kapur, 2018, p. 376). This may in turn be accounted for by other, arguably more fundamental, distortions that include low funding and poor infrastructure; regu-latory failure and the mushrooming of dubious institutions; the constrictive governance of public universities; and the bureaucratized over-regulation of both these as well as the better private universities. The consequences of all these for the quality of education are significant.

The idea that the demands of expansion needed to be balanced with those of quality was signaled in the Kothari Commission Report (1964–1966) which recommended that public spending on education should be 6 percent of the GDP and also sought to nur-ture a few institutions of excellence. The actual expenditure on education has remained in the region of 3 percent. Despite repeated acknowledgment of the fact that a third of India's population is between 15 and 24 years of age, higher education, as a proportion of the total budget of the Government of India, has stagnated at around 1.47 percent, for a decade. There is also a distributive imbalance in that approximately 60 percent of the central government's budget goes to the IITs, IIMs, and central universities while

94 percent of India's students attend state universities or other institutions. Meanwhile, the fund allocation for the UGC has been steadily declining, from Rs. 9315.45 crore in 2015–2016 to Rs. 4922.7 crore in 2017–2018, to 4722.7 crore in 2018–2019.

An analysis of these issues calls for a brief description of the architecture of governance in the higher education sector. The Indian Constitution placed the power to legislate on education in the State List. In 1976, education was moved to the Concurrent List which allows both the center and the states to legislate though, in case of a conflict, it is the Central law which prevails. The chief governing institution for the higher education sector is the UGC established by an Act of Parliament in 1956. Belying its name, the *primary* purpose of the UGC is defined as being "the promotion and coordination of University education and … the determination and maintenance of standards of teaching, examination and research in Universities" (UGC Act, 1956, III.12). It is *in order* to perform these functions that the Commission "may" allocate and disburse grants to specified categories of universities. In addition to the UGC, there are over a dozen professional bodies—such as the All India Council for Technical Education, the Bar Council of India, the Medical Council of India, the Indian Council of Medical Research, the Institute of Chartered Accountants—that are statutorily empowered to determine standards for education imparted in different fields. The most powerful of these is the All India Council for Technical Education (AICTE), established in 1945 and given statutory status in 1987, with powers to accord recognition to technical institutions, far in excess of those enjoyed by the UGC. In 1994, in response to the concerns about the deteriorating quality of higher education, the government established the National Assessment and Accreditation Council (NAAC), which conducts a periodic evaluation of Indian universities that volunteer to be evaluated. Its formal status—that of an autonomous body under the UGC, which partially finances it—casts doubts on its neutrality in addition to eroding the power of the UGC.

The controversies surrounding engineering and medical education illustrate the high costs of the fragmented nature of governance in this sector. With its extensive statutory powers to license private technical and management institutions, set quality standards, and stipulate the fees that can be charged by them, the AICTE came to oversee a much larger number of institutions than those over which the UGC exercised oversight, with the predictable incentives for arbitrary decision-making and rent-seeking behavior. The farcical quality of inspections was a public secret, with both faculty and equipment moving from a just-inspected college to the one next in line to be inspected, and with the connivance of the vendors who "loaned" equipment and books that would impress the inspection team (Ayyar, 2017, p. 261). A major corruption scandal led to the imprisonment of several senior staff.[10]

---

[10] In 2008–2009, 20 senior staff of the AICTE had police file First Information Reports (FIRs) against them. Seven of the most senior staff members, including the Chairman himself, were imprisoned on corruption charges, essentially for approving the creation of new colleges for kickbacks (Mehrotra, 2016, p. 262).

A similar racket in granting "recognition" to medical colleges led to the arrest, in 2010, of the president of the Medical Council of India on charges of bribery and corruption. Subsequently, the taint of corruption reached the judiciary, with even High Court judges being accused of having manipulated judicial orders relating to institutions that had first been denied recognition. The reform of medical education became a priority and in August 2019, Parliament passed the National Medical Commission Act that has been widely criticized for effectively handing medical education over to the private sector, and diminishing the role of the state governments in favor of the central government.

We shall return to the regulation of universities in a later section of this chapter, but before doing so it is important to note that the emergence of the private sector, *in the particular form it assumed*, was a significant development in the evolution of higher education in India, and its propensity to expand access while diluting quality.

3. The Public and the Private in Indian Higher Education

Contrary to popular belief, the emergence of the private sector in higher education is not a recent phenomenon in India. Indeed, the concerns relating to the late twentieth-century boom in private institutions, especially engineering colleges, are intriguingly prefigured in the heated debates, in colonial policy circles in the 1880s, on the issue of government devolving responsibility to private entities. The chief imperative for the encouragement given to private colleges by colonial policy in the late nineteenth century was cost-cutting. The indiscriminate founding of colleges dependent on fees rather than government subsidy led to concerns that it had resulted in a decline in standards along with a rise in the numbers of educated unemployed.[11] However, more idealistic indigenist initiatives also emerged, in the early twentieth century, animated by the vision of a "national" education, as an alternative to Western education, with funds mobilized by nationalist leaders like Madan Mohan Malaviya for the Banaras Hindu University and Gandhi himself for the Jamia Millia Islamia. At least some of these have retained their standing as they transition into the twenty-first century.

After independence, the emergence of politician-entrepreneurs in the 1960s was a response to demands for the expansion of higher education that came to be intensely politicized with colleges being founded by territorial, caste, and religious communities. Given the widespread association between higher education and the desire for status,

[11] The policy of devolving responsibility to private agencies was inaugurated by the Indian Education Commission of 1882. The huge expansion in the numbers of students and a lax regulatory regime led to the founding of large numbers of poorly equipped and low-quality affiliated colleges running on fees rather than government subsidy. This was one of the chief targets of Lord Curzon's attention when he became Viceroy of India in 1899.

wealth, and power, political representatives saw their personal political fate resting partly on satisfying such demands. As Lloyd and Susanne Rudolph wrote in 1972, the ordinary legislator was not concerned with how that demand was satisfied, and not concerned either with the quality of education provided, if doing so in any way obstructed his search for political support and influence (Rudolph and Rudolph, 1972, p. 34). As colleges and universities became primarily a political resource for politicians, educational goals were displaced by organized political interests of caste, religion, and locality. Even the appointments of Vice-Chancellors got enmeshed in such competition, and extra-educational interests subsumed educational goals. This form of politicization grew exponentially in subsequent decades, becoming so normalized as to elicit neither surprise nor disapproval. As time went on, politicians themselves became investors in HEIs, setting up professional colleges commanding high fees, and using their political capital to overcome the obstacles of licensing and subsidized land that other private entrepreneurs would face.

After the liberalization of the economy in the 1990s, large numbers of so-called self-financing engineering (and medical) colleges emerged, many of them owned by politicians and governed like family-owned firms. A major impetus for this was the demand generated by India's newly successful Information Technology industry. The state of Andhra Pradesh, for instance, had 107 engineering colleges in 2001. By 2013, with the enhanced demand for engineering graduates following the IT boom, these had multiplied to 700 colleges. In 2008, the state government announced the "fee reimbursement scheme" which enabled poorer students to access professional colleges, without paying any fees, with the government paying the colleges directly for their education. This became an incentive for the establishment of engineering colleges by politicians and businessmen with access to capital (Upadhya, 2014, p. 13). Over time, the AICTE, the IT industry, and "self-financing" engineering colleges, got locked in a happy and mutually beneficial embrace. In Andhra Pradesh, Chief Minister N. Chandrababu Naidu persuaded Microsoft to set up offices in Hyderabad, simultaneously facilitating the establishment of engineering colleges, which went from 20 when he assumed office to 220 by the time he completed his tenure. Being a coalition partner of the ruling party at the center meant that he could prevail upon the central government and the AICTE to assist him in getting the requisite permissions (Matthew, 2017, p. 4).

In Uttar Pradesh, local authorities allotted thousands of acres of land (extorted from farmers at a very low price) to politicians for setting up colleges, often under charitable trusts because this mode affords opportunities for tax exemption as well as money-laundering. Around the town of Meerut alone, 350 private colleges were set up within a decade, without proper infrastructure or qualified faculty, often without even the semblance of academic life, but guaranteeing certification in exchange for fee revenue (Singh, 2017). However, such certification requires an arrangement with a recognized university, so that the degrees awarded to students by institutions of indifferent quality bear the names of universities created by state legislation. The Chaudhary Charan Singh University in Meerut (Uttar Pradesh), is one of many such umbrella institutions. Founded in 1965 and describing itself as one of India's premier HEIs, this university lists as many as 68 Aided/Government Colleges, apart from 342 Self-Financing Colleges and Institutes, of which 126 are Law Colleges.[12]

Altogether distinct from such institutions, a handful of credible private universities, often modeling themselves on liberal arts colleges in the United States, have in recent years emerged through the route of state legislation. Not having their origins in clientelist politics, they have often found themselves subject to unreasonably constrictive regulation by the UGC. One example of this is the withdrawal of permission for the four-year undergraduate program (the standard Indian practice is three years). The University of Delhi had in 2013 launched a four-year undergraduate program, but political pressure from students and the minister for Human Resource Development led the UGC to rescind this decision in 2014. Private universities that had introduced similar degree programs were compelled to conform. The National Education Policy (NEP) of August 2020 promises flexibility in this regard.

4. The Regulation and Governance of Higher Education

The assumption that higher education would be an instrument of national transformation, of social progress and of economic development is reflected in the report of every major commission on education, seeking to harness universities to the state project of the day—constitutional values and nation-building in the 1950s, promoting socio-economic mobility in the following decades, and most recently the creation of a twenty-first-century knowledge society.

As previously mentioned, the UGC in India was given wide and encompassing powers not only to channel funding to universities, but also to take steps "for the determination and maintenance of standards of teaching, examination and research in Universities" (UGC Act, 1956: Ch. III, Sec. 12). But the UGC is not the only regulator in the field of higher education. It was initially lethargic in coordinating higher education in accordance with its legislative mandate, failing to discipline universities that violated its own norms and even fake universities.[13] Its role as a junior partner of the Ministry; its statutory limitations in the matter of setting up new colleges and universities compared to those of the AICTE; and the establishment of the NAAC to perform its inspectional role, contributed to the charge that "the UGC has made a virtue of leaving the universities to act on their own. Not only that, non-intervention has been elevated into

---

[12] https://www.ccsuniversity.ac.in/ccsu/colleges/combine-list-Self-Finacnce-All-course.pdf.

[13] The UGC publishes annually a list of fake universities that it identifies. The fine levied on such universities remained a paltry Rs. 1000 for decades. In 2018, the UGC mooted a proposal to increase the fine to Rs. 50,00,000 along with a 10-year jail term for the promoter. It is not clear if the UGC Act has been amended in respect of the punishment.

a principle" (Singh, 2004, pp. 45–46). This changed over the last decade and a half with a steady, and somewhat inadvertent, accretion of power in the UGC.[14] From its earlier inertia and incapacity to even implement its own regulations it got transformed into a formidable and powerful leviathan that universities could resist only at their own peril. In recent years, the UGC has displayed a considerable appetite for exacting conformity and even unquestioning obedience from universities, and for imposing centralized, homogenizing bureaucratic control over their day-to-day functioning. Characterizing this as "sarkarikaran" (governmentalization), Pankaj Chandra compares the UGC to a prison warden rather than a regulator, as its debilitating control "hampers the main activity of the University – that is, learning" (Chandra, 2017, p. 100).

The "New UGC" (Ayyar, 2017, p. 313) is a very powerful regulator, exercising disciplinary and punitive powers over both public and private universities. Along with, and as an obedient junior partner of, the MHRD, the UGC—through both its earlier non-interventionist phase, and in its current proactively interventionist phase—has been one of the primary sources of the erosion of university autonomy. It formulates model syllabi to create curricular uniformity across the country; exercises considerable powers in the licensing of new programs and the suspension of existing ones; conducts a centralized examination for doctoral research funding and a standardized qualifying examination, the National Entrance Test, to determine eligibility for candidates applying for an Assistant Professorship; and has moved towards an audit culture by developing quantifiable matrices for evaluating the quality of faculty across the country to judge fitness for recruitment and promotion.

This bureaucratization finds acceptance because of the assumption that, their salaries being publicly funded, academics in public universities are identical to civil servants. Faculty recruitment, security of tenure, and pay-grades along with leave rules and mechanisms for promotion in the academic hierarchy, are all governed by the same principles as those for civil servants. A recent UGC notification with potentially deleterious consequences for academic autonomy, even states that wherever the rules of their own institutions are silent, teachers in central universities will be governed by Civil Service Conduct Rules. At its most absurd, this could mean requiring official permission even to publish books and articles!

In independent India, 70 years after independence, the government continues to select and appoint Vice-Chancellors of public universities and heads of research

---

[14] The inadvertent accretion of power in the UGC came about when, like several other states, Chhattisgarh enacted a law for establishing private universities and notified as many as 97 universities in less than a year. Many of these were later found to be one-room outfits, essentially offering spurious degrees for sale. Encouraged by the MHRD, the UGC issued a set of regulations called the UGC (Establishment of and Maintenance of Standards in Private Universities) Regulations, 2003. Ruling on a writ petition (*Yash Pal and Another v. State of Chhattisgarh and Others*, 2005), the Supreme Court upheld the UGC's new regulations as the appropriate framework for setting up a private university. This has been interpreted as having "marked the metamorphosis of the UGC from an ineffective regulatory organization into a powerful [sic] whose regulations bind even State Legislatures and State Governments, not to speak of universities" (Ayyar, 2017, p. 312).

institutions, and since the choice is determined less by academic or leadership credentials and more by political fealty, the individuals selected are typically either ideo-logically aligned to the government or willing to be guided by it in the matter of uni-versity appointments and award of contracts. In central universities, it is the Ministry of Human Resource Development (recently renamed the Ministry of Education) that finalizes the appointments of Vice-Chancellors that are then approved by the President of India as Visitor. The President is today the Visitor of over a hundred such institutions, in which capacity s/he also nominates chancellors and members to the governing bodies of universities, such as the Court, the academic council, the executive council, as well as nominees to selection panels for faculty recruitment. In state universities, it is the Governor of the state government who plays this role. Here, Vice-Chancellors' appointments are often intensely politicized and manipulated, in some places even secured through corrupt means. The T. S. R. Subramanian Committee records that it was informally told about the "going rate" for Vice-Chancellorships (Government of India, 2016, p. 134).

Patronage, nepotism, and even corruption are thus common features of university appointments, especially in state universities which account for the overwhelming ma-jority of the total number of publicly funded universities in the country. Here, even the recruitment of teachers for government colleges is done—if and when it is done at all, given the large numbers of vacant positions—directly by state public service commissions who use their punitive powers of disciplining teachers by treating them as transferable employees. Little wonder, then, that the higher education sector is plagued by litigation.[15]

The large numbers of vacant teaching positions are frequently attributed to the lack of availability of qualified faculty. The total number of vacancies in central and state universities is 77,912. A third of teaching positions are vacant in 42 central universities, and a third of other university staff likewise. A Parliamentary Committee report of March 2020 shows that more than 6,688 positions out of a total of 18,243 sanctioned teaching posts, and 12,323 non-teaching positions out of a total of 34,928, have not been filled (Parliament of India, Rajya Sabha, 2020, p. 7). Vacancies in other pre-mier institutions range from 22 percent in the IIMs to 41 percent in the IITs. Outside of these relatively privileged institutions, the level of vacancies is considerably higher. Meanwhile the annual numbers of PhDs produced in Indian universities (disregarding for the present the question of their quality) is approximately 40,000. The University of Delhi has approximately 5,000 teachers without tenure (called ad hoc teachers or guest lecturers, similar to adjuncts in the United States). They are fully qualified to teach, and

[15] In their study of Supreme Court cases on higher education, Devesh Kapur and Madhav Khosla have analyzed the trends in a list of 507 judgments delivered between 1950 and 2009. They estimate that, in the first three decades after independence, the Supreme Court adjudicated 1.5 cases annually related to higher education; in the decade 2000–2009, this had increased to 20.6 cases annually (Kapur and Khosla, 2017, pp. 209–210). These figures of course do not account for the (literally) innumerable cases in the High Courts and district courts across the length and breadth of India.

are employed under the most precarious conditions, sometimes for as long as a decade or two in the same college. In such cases, the much-vaunted shortfall in faculty is not entirely attributable to the non-availability of adequately qualified teachers, but rather to the tendency towards adjunctization and casualization.

Over and above this are the well-known but incomputable phenomena of political interference and rigged markets in academic jobs. In recent years, the politicization of the academic profession has taken on a more egregious and damaging form. This is reflected in the tendency to fill vacancies based on ideology, even at the expense of qualifications. Academic integrity is strained not only when jobs are up for sale but also when they are based on ideological affiliation. Both are arguably forms of corruption, and both are facilitated when universities surrender academic autonomy, whether voluntarily or by coercion.

5. AUTONOMY AND ACADEMIC FREEDOM

Autonomy has always been a beleaguered idea in the Indian academy. The control of government over appointments, whether those of Vice-Chancellors or of members of university senates, is a colonial legacy that has been fortified and strengthened. In its most benign form, the relationship between the state and the university has been one of mutual benefit, as governments have sought legitimacy from academics as public intellectuals while academics have been willing to perform this role as they seek government patronage for the advancement of their careers. In recent years, however, this nexus has assumed a more malevolent form, with appointments not only aligned to a divisive right-wing and majoritarian ideology but accompanied also by the complicity of partisan academics in the clamp down on dissent and academic freedom in all of the three canonical senses specified in the famous Declaration of Principles of the American Association of University Professors in 1915. The first of these, freedom to research and publish, has been threatened by court cases against scholarly works on the grounds that they are "anti-Hindu" or "anti-national." An example of the egregious form this can take is the directive of the Government of Gujarat to all the universities in the state, prescribing a set of 82 seriously puerile topics for PhD theses.[16] Inside and outside the classroom, secondly, freedom is curtailed by the use of goon squads, who prevent students and faculty from speaking on controversial political issues or staging plays on themes like sexual violence. Academics have been suspended from universities simply for speaking up on issues that offend the Hindu right. Finally, the targeting by the police

---

[16] The topics included: "Comparative study of Sardar Patel Awas Yojana and Indira Awas Yojana"; "Gujarat: Good governance for growth, scientific management and development – A critical study of existing pattern [sic] and future course – a policy suggestions [sic]"; and "Mutual cooperation among states' action plans and comparative analysis of strategies for development – a Gujarat model" (*Times of India*, April 26, 2016).

of professors doing research in areas of Maoist insurgency or protesting discriminatory citizenship law is a clear restraint on extra-mural freedom. The cumulative effect of these developments has been chilling and even encouraging of self-censorship, thus inhibiting scholarship.

In 2018, the government announced its decision to award "autonomy" to 60 institutions of higher education that had maintained high academic standards. These universities would be given "graded autonomy," determined by their performance as evaluated by NAAC and their ranking under the national ranking framework. The announcement led to an outcry, not from the hundreds of universities that were denied this honor, but from those that were part of the eligible pool. This reaction is not baffling when the governmental meaning of the term autonomy is considered: chiefly the freedom to launch new courses, and the freedom to hire foreign faculty at differential salaries, within the ambit of, but not funded by, the UGC. In other words, the raising of independent resources is a precondition for the exercise of autonomy, and opens a pathway to privatization. Indeed, implicit in the ministerial offers of autonomy as an inducement to universities to become "world class," is the premise that not all universities are deserving of autonomy and, by implication, that autonomy is not an essential requirement for a thriving academic life. Controversially, autonomy also brings with it exemption from compliance with constitutional provisions of affirmative action.

6. The Limits of Access

Publicly funded education, combined with affirmative action, has long been a normative commitment of educational policy in India, for its promise of access and social mobility. Quotas were constitutionally guaranteed for members of the Scheduled Castes (SC) and Scheduled Tribes (ST), and later extended for other groups such as Other Backward Classes (OBCs) and Persons of Disability. These have subsisted within a highly subsidized system of public education along with provisions for scholarships. Such expansion of access as has occurred is indeed largely due to the provisions for quotas. Even so, the GER of the Scheduled Castes and Scheduled Tribes, at 23 percent and 17.2 percent respectively, though it has undoubtedly narrowed over time, is considerably lower than the national average of 26.3 percent (Government of India, 2019a). An analysis of the recently released National Statistical Office Report on Education (2017–2018) shows that those at the lower end of the socio-economic ladder are more likely to be studying humanities than professional courses like law. Students who do not belong to the SC/ST/OBC groups are six times more likely to be studying management than a student belonging to the Scheduled Tribes. Students from these groups, as also women, are less likely to be studying in the English medium (Kishore and Jha, 2020).

Of the groups that are not eligible for quotas, access for Muslims (unless they are OBCs and entitled to reservation), at 5.24 percent, remains much lower than their proportion in the population, though an increase of 0.76 percent between 2014 and 2015 and

2018–2019 yielded an increase of 27.73 percent in absolute numbers. The GER for women (26.4 percent), on the other hand, is very slightly higher than that for men (26.3 percent). In Distance Education courses, which account for 11 percent of the total enrollment, female enrollment stands at 42 percent.

To the extent that faculty recruitment depends crucially on the supply of trained academics, the extent of diversity in university faculty is also a reflection on the success or otherwise of initiatives for providing access to disadvantaged groups. Faculty composition remains much less diverse in terms of caste, tribe, and religion, though reasonable in terms of gender. On the all-India level, SC, ST, and OBC teachers are at 8.7 percent, 2.36 percent, and 32.1 percent respectively, with states like Andhra Pradesh, Maharashtra, and Telangana showing higher SC representation. The share of Muslim teachers in faculty, including teaching departments in universities as well as affiliated and constituent colleges is 4.86 percent, with the gap between male and female Muslim teachers widening at the higher level of university departments. Women constitute 42.15 percent of all teachers, though the proportion varies hugely across states: Bihar has only 21.3 percent female teachers, while Kerala, Punjab, Haryana, and Goa have more female than male teachers. For SC/ST/OBCs, affirmative action is a requirement for faculty hiring, and the large numbers of vacancies are often attributed to the non-availability of suitable candidates from these groups. It would not be far-fetched to assume that the absence of such groups, as also of women, is more pronounced as one moves up the academic ladder.

The sad fact is that, notwithstanding the expansion of access, members of disadvantaged groups have, in testimonies ranging from suicide notes to interviews with researchers, affirmed the persistence of the everyday practices of discrimination they encounter even in the best institutions, which consequently fail to enable more than token "inclusion."[17] In the 1990s and again in the 2000s, the bogey of merit was raised to protest the expansion of quotas to include other categories of "backward classes" (castes). The debate has typically been framed pitting access against merit, the latter category speaking to the exclusion of supposedly "meritorious" members of non-disadvantaged groups as a result of quotas for the disadvantaged.[18] It is this argument that insulated the IITs and IIMs from affirmative action requirements in faculty composition, resulting in a huge diversity deficit in these institutions, with the SCs, STs, and OBCs accounting for just 9 percent of the total faculty in the IITs, and 6 percent in the IIMs.[19] Many of these institutes have absolutely no SC or ST faculty.

[17] Undoubtedly the most tragic incident of this kind was the suicide of the brilliant young doctoral student of the University of Hyderabad, Rohith Vemula. For interviews with Dalit students in Delhi, see Deshpande (2011).

[18] This argument has obviously not been used in the context of the recently introduced quota for Economically Weaker Sections. According to the Parliamentary Committee Report (2020), the number stands at 9.15 lakhs for 2018–2019, going up to 11.33 lakhs for 2019–2020 and to 12.28 lakhs for 2020–2021.

[19] Kritika Sharma, "Diversity deficit in IIMs, IITs – just 23 STs and 157 SCs in 9,640 faculty posts." *The Print*, February 13, 2019. https://theprint.in/india/education/diversity-deficit-in-iims-iits-just-23-sts-and-157-scs-in-9640-faculty-posts/191246/.

Education is as much an instrument of the social reproduction of elites, as it is an instrument of social mobility. Historically, it was elite classes and upper castes that grasped the opportunities for acquiring a Western education, in the English language, offered by university education under colonial rule. That combination of caste, class, and language has continued to structure access to the world of higher education, because despite being heavily subsidized by the state, the scarcity of quality institutions has ensured that access has effectively been limited to elites with the requisite social and cultural capital. Such gatekeeping has tended to reproduce inherited inequality and to inhibit possibilities of social mobility for the vast numbers excluded from it. Needless to say, the fact of access is no guarantee of access to an education of decent let alone good quality. The problem of mass credentialization without attention to standards contributes to high levels of unemployability.

7. Education and Employability

Policy documents on higher education in India, since at least the 1960s, have urged the synchronization of tertiary education with the requirements of the economy, about 95 percent of which remains in the unorganized sector. The failure to simultaneously plan for education and employment is, however, squarely attributable to policy inertia rather than to any deeply apprehended philosophical dilemma between the intrinsic and instrumental value of higher education.

The mismatch between the employment market and college degrees leads to farcical, even tragic, situations like that of the recruitment, advertised in 2017, of 62 messengers in the Uttar Pradesh police, for which the required qualification was fifth grade schooling and the ability to ride a bicycle. Some 28,000 people with postgraduate qualifications applied, 3,700 of whom held PhDs. In 2018, over 200,000 people (including doctors, lawyers, and engineers) applied for 1,100 positions of constables in the Mumbai police. In Rajasthan, in December 2017, 129 engineers, 23 lawyers, and 1 chartered accountant were among the 12,453 people interviewed for 18 jobs of delivery boys.[20] Curiously, however, this was not what made the incident scandalous, but rather the fact that one of those selected was the son of a ruling party legislator, who had passed the tenth grade school examination. These facts are an indication not just of the scarcity of job opportunities, but also of the dismal quality of the degrees held by these ostensibly overqualified individuals. This has much to do with the relaxation of the licensing regime and the mushrooming of unregulated for-profit private colleges.

Engineering education offers a good example of this problem. In 2011, the Kakodkar Committee Report estimated that:

---

[20] https://economictimes.indiatimes.com/news/politics-and-nation/over-93000-candidates-includ ing-3700-phd-holders-apply-for-peon-job-in-up/articleshow/65604396.cms?from=mdr.

more than 500,000 graduates who come out of our engineering colleges annually ... have not met the expectations in terms of quality. This has resulted in a large
number of the graduates coming out of these colleges being found unemployable
needing training even while there is an acute shortage of capable engineers and
technologists to meet the requirements of industry and other segments. (Kakodkar
Committee Report, 2011, p. 33)

At this time, the IITs accounted for the production of only 0.5 percent of the 500,000
engineers who graduated every year, down from 10 percent in the 1970s and early 1980s
(Kakodkar Committee Report, 2011, p. vi). More recent figures suggest that 100,000
engineering and management places were added every year from 2000 onwards, in
institutions under the AICTE, accounting for the 1.5 million engineers who graduate
annually. However, large numbers of unfilled places remained and since 2011, there has
been a progressively increasing trend towards the closure of engineering colleges as well
as private business schools. This is due less to a contraction in the market for engineers
and managers per se, and more to the indifferent quality of the graduates produced,
leading to many engineering colleges choosing the option of "progressive closure." In
2018, based on its examination of the student intake of colleges over a five-year period,
the AICTE announced its decision to shut 800 engineering colleges across India from
the following academic year.[21] At the same time, the fact that hundreds of thousands
of aspirants continue to appear for the competitive entrance to the IITs, suggests that
the demand for engineering education persists, as indeed does the market demand for
engineers, but that engineering colleges have neither been able to fulfill this demand nor
enabled their graduates to be employable.

On the other hand, those engineers who receive a quality education prefer
occupations that fetch more money or prestige than an engineering job. Since managers
in companies are generally better remunerated than engineers, IIT graduates frequently
seek to enhance their career prospects by doing a postgraduate degree in business.
Many others succumb to the enduring (and arguably colonial) lure of the civil service.
Approximately half of those who pass the combined civil services examination are
engineers. In 2017, engineers accounted for 19 of the 20 toppers of this examination, and
between 2014 and 2016, for between 30 and 40 percent of the entrants into the generalist
Indian Administrative Service.[22]

[21] The National Employability Report Engineers 2019, by the company Aspiring Minds, documents
what it calls "Stubborn Unemployability." It estimates that 80 percent of engineers are unemployable
for any job in the knowledge economy, and attributes this to the failure to develop relevant curricula.
Not uncontroversially, it argues that the increase in the quantity of educational institutions is inversely
affecting the average quality of education in these. https://www.aspiringminds.com/blog/research-artic
les/why-are-indian-engineers-unemployable/.

[22] https://theprint.in/india/governance/majority-of-ias-recruits-are-engineers-or-graduates-not-
domain-experts/169224, accessed September 11, 2020.

The fragmented architecture of governance for this sector makes it near impossible to have a coordinated policy approach to the question of higher education, let alone forward and backward linkages between education and the economy.

8. THE SEARCH FOR EXCELLENCE: RESEARCH, PUBLICATIONS, AND THE WORLD-CLASS UNIVERSITY

The early delinking of teaching and research, bolstered by spurious matrices of measuring research output, has had deleterious effects on the production of knowledge. The establishment of research councils like the Indian Council of Social Science Research (ICSSR) (and similar bodies for historical and philosophical research) was intended to promote research by channeling funds for it. However, the bulk of ICSSR funding goes towards maintaining 30 stand-alone research institutes, paying their maintenance and development costs including faculty salaries, with research per se commanding only a small percentage of its resources. Over the last five years, 121 PhDs—averaging less than one per year across the Institutes—have been produced here. Even a decade and a half ago, the Fourth Review Committee of the ICSSR had noted the "conspicuous reluctance to support open, independent research in social sciences" and the abysmally low allocations for social research except on operational or policy issues (ICSSR, 2007, p. 21).

Subsequently, the acquisition of research degrees got an impetus in the competition for an expanding cadre of college and university teachers. Regrettably, this served only to motivate research for purposes of credentialization, rather than the desire for the pursuit of or contribution to knowledge. The failure to build up a research culture, or even a culture of objective peer evaluation, was compounded by India's version of quality assurance through the introduction of audit culture in the form of an Academic Performance Index, as the basis for recruitment and promotion. The pressure to have quantifiable research outputs generated a race-to-the-bottom academic market in publications and conference papers. Twenty-seven percent of the world's predatory journals in the world are published in India, which is the single largest source of such journals and has also spawned a predatory conference circuit, to game the API system.

India's research output is only 4.8 percent of the world's total, the corresponding figures for China and the United States being around 18 percent (Kapur, 2020, p. 83). This is not surprising when we consider that R&D expenditure in India is about one-tenth of those two countries, and less than 3 percent of global R&D expenditure (Government of India, 2019b). Almost entirely public expenditure, this has stagnated at between 0.6 and

0.7 percent of GDP for two decades, much lower than the 3 percent that the country's scientists have been asking for, and much lower also than the corresponding figures for the United States (2.8), China (2.1), Israel (4.3), and Korea (4.2). Two of the three biggest spenders are atomic energy and space (Government of India, 2019b, p. 8). Moreover, not just in the United States but even China, two-thirds of R&D expenditure comes from the private sector, while in India it is less than half (Kapur, 2020, p. 82). The NEP 2020 acknowledges the fact that India's spending on research is only 0.69 percent of GDP, which compares unfavorably to that of the United States, Israel, and South Korea. It recommends the establishment of a National Research Foundation, without, however, offering any concrete commitment as to funding.

Meanwhile, in 2016, the government established the Higher Education Funding Authority, a joint venture of the Ministry of Human Resource Development and the Canara Bank, tasked with mobilizing money through market borrowings to make interest-free loans to universities for research infrastructure and R&D with a view to making them globally competitive. Rs. 22,450 crores have already been borrowed. Even if interest is waived, the principal of the loan needs repayment from "internal resource generation" through research earnings (sources of which are negligible) and students' fees. Being as cash-strapped as universities are, they would have no choice but to commodify education to raise revenue. Already student agitations around fee hikes, transferring the burden for privatized facilities and hostel maintenance to students, have indicated the direction. In at least one premier university, the budget for security has gone up fourfold, even as journal subscriptions have been slashed. This hardly bodes well, even for the government's aspiration for Indian universities to figure in global rankings.

In 2017, the government announced its intention of establishing 20 world-class universities, called Institutions of Eminence, 10 each in the public and private sector, which would enjoy complete autonomy in academic, administrative, and financial matters. In the first round, eight public and three private universities were selected, apart from one "greenfield" project existent only on paper, funded by India's biggest corporation. The process in this round was vitiated by a lack of transparency, failing to confer this coveted status on any of the universities (excluding IITs) that have figured in the top 10 of the government's own national rankings. The fate of these under the NEP 2020, which envisages the creation of Multidisciplinary Education and Research Universities "to attain the highest global standards in quality education" (Government of India, 2020, p. 38) is unclear.

9. CONCLUSION

The multiple crises of funding, governance, and quality that beleaguer the public university in India make the policy choice offered by Kapur's "iron triangle of education"—that any country can choose only two of the three options of scale, cost, and quality—challenging (Kapur, 2020). Empirically, all three currently elude India. Funding, for infrastructure and research, has been steadily declining for most, with only a handful of institutions receiving enhanced support for the vanity project of the world-class university. Autonomy too is reserved for these institutions, with the vast majority being deemed worthy only of stringent policing, both as minor departments of state and as sites of ideological conformism. To these ends, the stranglehold of the state over university governance is strengthened. What remains for universities to do is just credentialize, regardless of the quality of education on offer. This vitiation of the quality of education affects all, including and especially those who have managed to gain access to it after generations of struggle. The achievements of social justice are undermined by the manifest injustice of poor-quality teaching and learning. Higher education remains the pre-eminent source of credentialization fulfilling, however minimally, the criterion of instrumental value. The intrinsic value of education, even as an ideal, remains as elusive as the idea of the university itself.

References

Agarwal, P. (2006). "Higher education in India: The need for change." Working Paper No. 180. New Delhi: Indian Council for Research on International Economic Relations.

Ayyar, R. V. V. (2017). *History of Education Policymaking in India 1947–2016*. New Delhi: Oxford University Press.

Basu, A. (1982). *Essays in the History of Indian Education*. New Delhi: Concept Publishing Company.

Chandra, P. (2017). *Building Universities That Matter: Where Are Indian Institutions Going Wrong?* Hyderabad: Orient BlackSwan.

Deshpande, A. (2011). *The Grammar of Caste: Economic Discrimination in Contemporary India*. New Delhi: Oxford University Press.

Government of India (1949). *The Report of the University Education Commission (December 1948–August 1949)*. Volume I. New Delhi: Ministry of Education.

Government of India (2016). *National Policy on Education 2016: Report of the Committee for Evolution of the New Education Policy*. Chairman: T. S. R. Subramanian. New Delhi: Ministry of Human Resource Development.

Government of India (2019a). *All India Survey on Higher Education 2018–19*. New Delhi: Ministry of Human Resource Development.

Government of India (2019b). *R&D Expenditure Ecosystem: Current Status and Way Forward*. New Delhi: EAC-PM (Economic Advisory Council to the Prime Minister).

Government of India (2020). *National Education Policy 2020*. New Delhi: Ministry of Human Resource Development. https://www.mhrd.gov.in/sites/upload_files/mhrd/files/NEP_Final_English_0.pdf

Indian Council for Social Science Research (2007). *Restructuring the Indian Council of Social Science Research: Report of the Fourth Review Committee*. https://icssr.org/sites/default/files/important_notice/finalreport.pdf

Kakodkar Committee Report (2011). *Taking IITs to Excellence and Greater Relevance*. Report of Dr. Anil Kakodkar Committee Appointed by MHRD to Recommend Autonomy Measures to Facilitate IITs Scaling Greater Heights.

Kapur, D. (2018) "Indian Higher Education." In Charles T. Clotfelter, (ed.) *American Universities in a Global Market*. Chicago: University of Chicago Press.

Kapur, D. (2020). *Liberalization sans Liberalism: The Dilemmas of Higher Education in India*. [PowerPoint slides]. Personal Communication, March 16, 2020.

Kapur, D. and Khosla, M. (2017). "The Supreme Court and private higher education: Litigation patterns and judicial trends." In D. Kapur and P. B. Mehta, (eds.), *Navigating the Labyrinth: Perspectives on India's Higher Education*. Hyderabad: Orient BlackSwan, Chapter 8.

Kapur, D. and Mehta, P. B. (2017). "Introduction." In D. Kapur and P. B. Mehta, (eds.), *Navigating the Labyrinth: Perspectives on India's Higher Education*. Hyderabad: Orient BlackSwan, 1–37.

Kishore, R. F. and Jha, A. (2020). "Mapping education inequalities." *Hindustan Times*, New Delhi, August 1. https://www.hindustantimes.com/india-news/mapping-education-inequalities/story-xhTIlYty7kF7MNqxnOyGtO.html, accessed August 22, 2020.

Matthew, A. (2017). "Andhra's fee reimbursement scheme: Intended and unintended impact of higher education in A.P. and Telengana." *College Post*, April–June.

Mehrotra, S. (2016). "The employability of tertiary-level graduates in India." In N. V. Varghese and G. Malik (eds.), *India Higher Education Report 2015*. New Delhi: Routledge, 251–274.

Parliament of India, Rajya Sabha (2020). *Three Hundred and Thirteenth Report of the Parliamentary Standing Committee on Human Resource Development of Rajya Sabha*. Demands for Grants 2020–21 (Demand No. 59) of the Department of Higher Education. Presented to both Houses of Parliament on March 5, 2020.

Rudolph, L. I. and Rudolph, S. H. (1972). *Education and Politics in India: Studies in Organization, Society and Policy*. Delhi: Oxford University Press.

Singh, A. (2004). *Fifty Years of Higher Education in India: The Role of the University Grants Commission*. New Delhi: Sage Publications.

Singh, S. (2017). "How Indian universities become profit machines." *Global Dialogue* (Magazine of the International Sociological Association), 7/2, June.

University Grants Commission (2002). *The University Grants Commission Act, 1956 (modified up to 20th December, 1985)*. New Delhi: University Grants Commission.

Upadhya, C. (2014). "Engineering mobility? The 'IT craze', transnational migration, and the commercialisation of education in coastal Andhra." Provincial Globalisation Working Paper No. 7. Bangalore: National Institute of Advanced Studies and Amsterdam Institute of Social Science Research.

CHAPTER 29

PRIVATE UNIVERSITIES IN INDIA

New Dawn or False Dawn?

PRATAP BHANU MEHTA

1. INTRODUCTION

INDIA has, over the past four decades, seen such a rapid expansion of private higher education that it is well on its way to being one of the most privatized higher education systems in the world. According to the All India Survey on Higher Education (AISHE) Report 2019–2020, produced by the Ministry of Human Resource Development, 78.6 percent of all colleges in India are private colleges; 65.2 percent of colleges are private unaided colleges, which means they receive no government assistance. India now has 396 private universities, out of a total of 1,043. The Program for Research on Private Higher Education estimates that 59 percent of students in India are enrolled in a private institution. In comparative terms this figure is quite high (Table 29.1). The New Education Policy (NEP) adopted by the Government of India in 2020 calls for even more private philanthropic investment in education. India was well on its way to private dominance of the higher education sector since the beginning of the 2000s and even more so today (Kapur and Mehta, 2008).

Yet there is still an air of ambivalence about this privatization. This is captured in a remark once made by a public regulator that in India "all education is public; private education is simply public education financed by private money." There may be a rhetorical exaggeration in this remark. But it does capture very well the paradoxical nature of this de facto privatization in India—the fact that private education is still very much embedded in state power in several ways.

The first embedding is simply legal. Article 19(1)(g) of the Indian Constitution guarantees a right to "practice any profession or to carry on any occupation, trade or business." This right might seem like a propitious basis for establishing private education institution. But the Supreme Court of India has argued that education is not a trade or

Table 29.1 Private enrollments in selected countries

Country	Percentage of enrollment in private higher education (%)
India	58.3
US	27.5
Brazil	72.7
China	19.6
Japan	78.6
Indonesia	58.2
South Korea	80.7
Iran	44.9
Philippines	60.8
Russian Federation	14.7

Source: Program for Research on Private Higher Education. Countries listed in order of total number of students in private higher education, 2017 (http://www.prophe.org/en/global-data/country-dimension-tab les/ten-largest-systems%E2%80%99-individual-and-aggregated-priv ate-shares/).

business or a profession (*Unnikrishnan v. State of A.P.*). One consequence of this stipulation is that private education cannot be "for profit." In a series of cases the Supreme Court has granted that the fee structure of private education institutions can be different from that of public institutions. But it has stipulated that the freedom to charge higher fees must not, "from the standpoint of the interest of the general public" lead to the *commercialization* of higher education. Institutions are allowed to generate reasonable surpluses, but these can be used only for the benefit of the education institution. Profits cannot be given to shareholders or in any way diverted for personal gain or any other business or enterprise (*Islamic Academy v. State of Karnataka*). This prohibition on commercialization has two consequences. First, it still gives the state in principle the right to regulate fees of all private institutions. These fees are subject to negotiation. Although in recent times states have got more liberal and allowed private institutions to set high fees, private institutions have to be mindful of what the state finds acceptable. Second, the requirement that fees be benchmarked to generating a reasonable surplus, means, in effect, that many education entrepreneurs make money, not by transparently declaring profit, but by extracting surplus through inflating costs and creating complicated contractual arrangements for providing services to the institution that allow profits to be extracted (Kapur and Khosla, 2017).

The second sense in which private education is embedded in state power is regulatory. Higher education was one of the last bastions of the license permit raj, where in principle any aspect of education was subject to severe governmental regulation. Admissions policies, the internal organization of the institution, course structures, qualification of teachers, nomenclature of departments, and degree structures were all subject to heavy regulation by myriad regulators. The very act of setting up an institution requires active support from government. There are several regulatory pathways to creating private higher education institutions. Universities can be created through either an Act of Parliament or an Act of State Legislature. As things stand, the University Grants Commission (UGC) can grant "Deemed to be a University Status" to institutions. Some states have an enabling Private Universities Act that authorizes the state governments to notify the creation of private universities. The Government of India has now created an enabling mechanism to approve what it calls "Institutions of Eminence" which are selected on the basis of proposals submitted by interested parties. In the case of colleges, they require cooperation of the public university with which they are affiliated for degree granting purposes. Different states can impose different requirements for setting up an institution. Recognition by the UGC requires placating the Commission. In practice, the degree of control exercised by the state has varied considerably. Competition amongst states to attract private investment in higher education is forcing states to create State Acts that are more propitious for attracting private investment (see Table 29.2). For example, the Haryana Government Private Universities Act or the recently passed Tamil Nadu Private Universities Act, 2019, are premised on granting institutions more autonomy. For instance, they have fewer (barely one or two) government representatives on the governing body of the university. Even the informal culture of some state governments has become more respectful of the administrative autonomy of private institutions. But the state still retains considerable regulatory power. It can set the fees, it can provide administrative oversight, and use its municipal powers over land, zoning, and construction to exercise leverage over state universities. If it chooses, it can still exercise immense *discretionary* power in allowing institutions to be set up, or in the form in which they are regulated and assessed. This places them at the mercy of the state.

Both of these stipulations—that private institutions be not for profit and they be properly regulated—give private institutions in India a formally public purpose in the way in which the official quoted above was hinting. But what is the broader vision that lies behind India's embrace of private education?

2. Historical, Economic, and Political Context for Privatization

India has had, in some ways, a long history of private higher education. India had a glorious tradition of universities like Nalanda, Vikramshila, and Taxila that housed tens of thousands of students and were zones of cosmopolitan cultural, scientific, and intellectual exchange (Apte, 1961; Sankalia, 1972). Much can be said about the curriculum of these universities, but in organizational form they were pioneers. Many of these universities were sustained by land grants or gifts from various monarchs. But the most important point about them was that, for the most part, they retained autonomous control over their assets which allowed them to survive the ebbs and flows of different

Table 29.2 Requirements for setting up private universities: three examples

	Project proposal	Requirements	Setting up
Uttar Pradesh	The project report needs to explain the objectives of the university, types of programs of study, deed of the institution (whether a trust/society/non-profit entity under Section 25 of the Companies Act, or is being run by one), fee structure, admissions format, composition details of board of governors, availability of academic research and training facilities, building plan and land deed, etc.	Land requirements are as follows: (i) That the university possess a contiguous land of minimum 20 acres of land in urban areas and 50 acres of land run rurally. (ii) Invest a minimum of Rs. 2 crore in developing infrastructure and further earmark 6 crore to be invested in the next five years. (iii) Purchase books worth Rs. 10 lac every year for the library.	If the government is satisfied that it is advisable to establish the university, it may issue a letter of intent where it will seek to scrutinize whether the sponsoring body has complied with the requirements laid down in the Act.
Tamil Nadu	The project report needs to include the details of the sponsoring body along with copies of its registration certificate under the Indian Trusts Act, 1882 (Central Act 2 of 1882) or the Tamil Nadu Societies Registration Act, 1975 (Tamil Nadu Act 27 of 1975) or the Companies Act, 2013 (Central Act 13 of 2013) as the case may be, along with objectives of the university, types of programs of study etc.	(i) Possess contiguous land of not less than 100 acres earmarked for the private university. (ii) While there is no requirement of a fixed deposit, under section 5 of the Act, fees charged by private universities have been limited to Rs. 25 lakh.	After considering the recommendation of the Expert Committee (the state government has the right to accept or reject its report), the state government shall establish the university by way of amendment to the Schedule after satisfying that the sponsoring body has fulfilled the conditions of Letter of Intent.
Haryana	Similar in its approach to UP's.	Land requirements are as follows: (i) a minimum of 202 acres of land outside the municipal limits; or (ii) a minimum of 20 acres of land within the municipal limits; (iii) a minimum of 5 acres of land within the municipal corporation limits. In addition to this, the sponsoring body will have to have an endowment fund with a minimum amount of five crores rupees which shall be pledged in the form of Fixed Deposit Receipt in original in favor of the Higher Education Commissioner, Haryana, Panchkula.	If the government is satisfied that it is advisable to establish the university, it may issue a Letter of Intent and ask the sponsoring body to comply with requirements such as: (i) construct a minimum of 10,000 square meters of covered area for administrative and academic purposes. (ii) purchase books and journals of at least 20 lac rupees. (iii) develop immovable assets and infrastructure facilities worth 20 lac rupees, etc.

Indian monarchs. In fact, these universities were, arguably, the first *endowment*-based universities in the world. There is a Sanskrit term used to describe their financial structure, *akshay nidhi*, which literally translated means "that wealth which is indestructible." The central conceptual point is that it was widely recognized that a university, in order to retain its autonomy, and endure over time, had to have financial autonomy. Quite why these universities declined after seven to eight centuries is a matter of historiographical debate. Some scholars attribute it to Turk and Mughal invasions (Chandra, 2004) while others contest the claim (Jha, 1989). The net result was that India's tradition of creating large independent universities declined.

In the nineteenth century there were elements of a revival in private higher education in India. But the nature of this revival, in some senses, set the pattern for the form in which private education was permitted. By the 1880s, India had four universities and 67 colleges. Much of the funding for these colleges came from Indian private sources. The colonial government set the regulatory tone, where colleges were privately funded, but public institutions controlled the degree granting functions. The University of the Punjab in Lahore was set up as a teaching university in 1882. But for most universities the teaching function was overshadowed by the degree granting function, whereby they conducted degree exams for a large number of colleges. In some ways this was a reproduction, at a totally inappropriate scale, of the Oxford/Cambridge model, where teaching happened in the colleges, but the university conducted the examinations. Some universities, like Calcutta University, decided to break this mold, by converting themselves into research universities. This is reflected in a powerful speech given by Sir Ashutosh Mukherjee, one of India's great Vice-Chancellors and the founder of Calcutta University. He asked:

> They have from time to time asked what a University is and found themselves at sea. Is it a set of fine buildings? Is it an education institution which has beneficent patrons and has secured the gift of a million? Is it an aggregate of the Four Faculties? Is it a scholastic guild? Is it a society of masters? Is it an assembly of students? Is it an examining body authorized to grant degrees? Is it a corporation of individuals who investigate the unknown, but neither teach nor test? Is it an association of teaching institutions without a curriculum? Must it possess any or all of these characteristics? (Mukherjee, 1918)

In the beginning of the twentieth century most Indians would have associated a university with "an examining body authorized to grant degrees." But this structure, where private players set up colleges, which were then subject to examination by a public university, set the template for private higher education in India. Many of the great public universities of the time, including Delhi University, had this structure. They were mostly a federation of private colleges, united by a common examination structure given by a public university. There were some exceptions like Calcutta University that were inspired more by the German Humboldtian model of a university. They tried to transform themselves into research universities, with the help of private philanthropy (Manjapara, 2014). This historical pattern set a precedent for the form in which private investment in education could take place. It was easier to set up colleges and affiliate with an existing public university for degree granting purposes. Consequently, the structure of private higher education in India retains a threefold classification:

(a) Private universities that have degree granting power.
(b) Colleges that are affiliated with existing universities and grant their degrees through them.
(c) Standalone independent institutions that do not have the power to grant degrees, but may grant diplomas, usually in fields like management, or vocational engineering.

It is fair to say that from the period of 1947 to the 1970s almost any expansion in private higher education was through the creation of colleges. India hardly created any new private universities till the turn of the twenty-first century. According to the UGC Annual Report, 2018–2019, India had 51 Central Government Universities, 397, State Public Universities, 334 Private Universities, and 126 Institutions that were Deemed to be Universities. But the remarkable story is that in 2000 India had one private university. By 2010 it had 80, and by 2018 it had 334. Or just to illustrate how dramatic the recent growth in private higher education is, consider the following statistic. According to AISHE, of the 1,147 colleges established in 2017, 941 (82 percent) were private colleges, out of which 834 are private unaided and 107 are private aided. Whereas only 206 (18 percent) are government colleges.

But the second, unintended, consequence of this system where colleges were private but affiliated to degree granting universities was this. It actually led to the creation of several mega universities, where a university like Mumbai or Delhi would have over a hundred affiliated colleges, with a few hundred thousand students. It ended up creating the worst of both worlds, where private colleges did not have pedagogical autonomy. But the public universities became unwieldy and rigid in their structure because any curricular reform had to satisfy a large number of constituent colleges. This was one of the reasons why it was harder to reform public universities.

This institutional backdrop is essential to understanding the move towards creating space for private institutions in India. The drivers of the push towards privatization of higher education were the failures of the state, rather than a considered ideological project. But in the late 1970s and early 1980s, public higher education in India was beginning to face a dead end. On the one hand, India's demography was creating demand for higher education. On the other hand, the state was not able to cater to this demand for a variety of reasons. The first was financial: the state could not generate the financial resources that would be required for a high-quality expansion. It was doubly constrained. The share of public expenditure on higher education remained relatively stagnant around 1.5 percent of GDP (Tilak, 2013). But there were also severe political constraints on raising fees and other forms of revenue in public universities. A second reason was that Indian universities were increasingly overregulated and subject to greater bureaucratic and political control. The enforcement of more homogeneous administrative norms was beginning to erode the autonomy of these universities. This combination of financial constraints and political control was choking their ability to supply good-quality education.

But the structural dilemma that higher education faced came largely from what is known as "massification." How can one expand the education system and yet deliver quality education? It is important to remember that higher education in India was always the preserve of a very tiny elite. In 1950, India had only 0.4 million students enrolled in higher education. This number grew to only 2.75 million in 1980, and 8.4 million in 2000. But between 2000 and 2015 this number shot up to almost 24 million, a tripling of the enrollment, in a mere 15 years. Total enrollment in higher education was 38.5 million in 2019–20 (Government of India, 2019). This is a staggering growth. Or to put it another way, in 2017 India was opening roughly three new colleges per day.

What is the nature of this massification? The push towards mass higher education by increasing gross enrollment ratios (GERs) was driven by economic growth. The liberalizing of the economy in 1991 had clearly created more space for the private sector in India more generally. The period between 2000 and 2010 is also the golden period of economic growth, where it was easier to see plausible returns to education. The Indian economy on an average grew close to 8 percent a year during this period.

But there were other pressures as well. You could attribute India's slow expansion of higher education to the slow expansion of education in general. India reached 100 percent school enrollment only in 2006. So as school education expanded, it was inevitable the demand for higher education would grow. At first glance India seems to be following a pattern that was first laid out in a well-known paper by Martin Trow that examined three stages of higher education: (1) elite—shaping the mind and character of a ruling class and preparation for elite roles; (2) mass—transmission of skills and preparation for a broader range of technical and economic elite roles; and (3) universal—adaptation of the "whole population" to rapid social and technological change (Trow, 2007). It was a small exclusive preserve till the 1980s. Then, when India experienced a growth spurt, and a turn to the IT industry under Rajiv Gandhi, higher education slowly began to expand with engineering and medical education. And now the expansion of higher education may be driven by a rights-based commitment to universal access to higher education. India's population does have a right to education, but not a right to education beyond grade eight. But increasingly, the rights-based story has become part of political discourse, persuading politicians to commit to higher GERs.

In the Indian context, Trow's story might need to be nuanced in two ways. The first is the question of universalization. That there is greater normative and political pressure to make higher education available to all is beyond doubt. What is interesting in the case of India is that demand for higher education is always a demand for a degree. For instance, in India vocational education is largely seen as a supplement to help school dropouts. Vocational education is regarded as an inferior form of education, so the pressure for universalization will always be borne by the university system, not by the creation of alternative channels of higher education.

The second nuance is this. India's massification story is somewhat paradoxical. The real growth in massification in India occurred in the 1990s and early 2000s. But the governance challenges faced by Indian universities were probably at their peak in the 1960s and 1970s when student strikes and unrest were common (Altbach, 1968). What this suggests is that while massification posed a challenge to the Indian education system, the decline in the university system cannot be attributed entirely to massification, but was the result of financial, administrative, and political decisions. While the massification at the turn of the century posed great challenges for improving quality, the critical factor in producing quality still remains governance. (For these governance issues see Chandra, 2017.)

3. Legal, Regulatory, and Institutional Framework for Private Education

It was South India that first decided to give private higher education a push. South India was generally ahead of the rest of India in school enrollment as well, so it is not surprising the first pressures emanated there. The motive was less to enhance the quality of education, but to ease the pressure on the public system. The initial wave was focused largely on professional schools because there was an effective demand for professional degrees. These could therefore command high fees. But the process of creating new private colleges did not require great regulatory changes. This expansion could happen largely through the mechanism of affiliating colleges. But politicians soon discovered the enormous rents to be extracted in the process of facilitating the entry of private colleges. The demographics were favorable to the point where private colleges were likened to ATM machines: you just had to put them there to generate cash. But there were also rents to be collected through exercising the discretionary power of the state. So only particular kinds of entrepreneurs, those who could get the necessary permissions, entered the education space. As it turned out these were largely politicians themselves, or political brokers. In southern states almost two-thirds of private colleges had active politicians as part of the governance structure if not ownership of the colleges. Between a quarter and a third of elected legislators are involved in running colleges. For instance, in Uttar Pradesh 30 percent of elected officials run private colleges (Varma, 2020).

This expansion had three consequences. On the positive side, this expansion coincided with the early boom in the Indian IT industry, which combined with an expanding demand for health care provided a stock of engineering and medical graduates. Even though quality was not high, it arguably helped supply enough graduates to sustain India's nascent economic boom. Some of these institutions, like Manipal and Vellore, developed good reputations over time. But on the negative side, they helped create a political economy where politicians had less interest in supporting good public institutions; it was in fact in their interest to run them down.

This wave of privatization of higher education in India that lasted till the early 2000s had the following features. First, it was concentrated on professional education, largely on engineering, medical, and law colleges. In 1950 only 15 percent of engineering seats, for example, were in private colleges By 2003, 85 percent of engineering seats were in private colleges. Second the financing model was entirely revenue based, with relatively little genuine philanthropic commitment. Third, it did not require, for the most part, the development of full-fledged private universities, so a whole range of disciplines were not well served. Fourth, the focus was largely on easing the supply constraints in the public system largely for India's upper and middle classes who could afford private education. But there was no inbuilt dynamic that would enhance the average quality of Indian higher education. The focus was largely on quantity. Finally, there was a sociology to the relationship between the public and private sectors in higher education where the private education was, in numbers becoming more and more indispensable, but the legitimacy of private institutions was still under question. They were, in some ways, now considered guilty of a crime worse than profiteering; they were sly profiteering: maintaining the façade of non-profit institutions, while enriching their owners.

4. Governance Challenges

By the early 2000s, private Indian higher education was being looked upon to play a different and more ambitious role (Kumar, 2018). Four developments helped catalyze this new role. Partly as a result of India's economic boom and greater liberalization of norms, more Indians were now able to consume foreign higher education. The number of Indians going abroad for higher education began to rise dramatically increasing from 59,112 in 1998 to 375,055 in 2018 (UNESCO Institute for Statistics). According to RBI (2021) data, outward remittances under the Liberalised Remittance Scheme (LRS) for resident individuals for study abroad was $3.6 billion in 2018–2019 and $5 billion in 2019–2020. Of course, this is a baseline number since expenses can come from other sources as well. Therefore, India is spending more in the range of $10 billion a year on consumption of higher education abroad. In a way India's greater integration into global education markets did two things. One, it changed the quality benchmarks where more parents from the middle classes were beginning to look for a broader based, high-quality liberal education. The state began to realize that India was losing a great deal of revenue, with the privileged classes in some ways seceding from Indian institutions and going abroad. Second, liberalization more generally helped create an ideological climate where private sector participation was more acceptable. This was evidenced in a remarkable fact that there were at least three committee reports the government commissioned from leaders of Indian industry to outline the case for private higher education. The Ambani-Birla Report recommended the introduction of the user pay principle in higher education and establishment of private universities in the country. In 2012, the Planning Commission released the Narayana Murthy Committee report on Corporate Sector Participation in Higher Education. The Committee recommended possibilities and 15 modalities for the corporate sector participation in expansion of higher education and research in India. In 2013, the FICCI brought out a vision document which also made a similar case. There was still some skepticism about private higher education (see Yashpal Committee Report), but the ideological tide was turning. Thirdly, in 2005 there was great expansion of affirmative action in central universities with the extension of quotas for Other Backward Castes to these institutions. In part, the appetite for private institutions came from the increasing shortage of general category seats, and the cynical desire to have private institutions where there would be affirmative action requirements that were less onerous. So various private institutions are subject to some quota requirements, depending on the state. But they are not nearly as demanding as those faced by public institutions. Finally, and perhaps most importantly a decade of almost 7 percent growth from 1999 to 2009, made available surpluses with Indian capital that allowed the possibility of thinking of universities not as money minting ATMs but as genuinely philanthropic investments. In the first phase of the expansion of private colleges, the promoters were largely living *off* education; in this new phase it was expected that they would contribute *to* education.

But change was still slow. In the wider political economy there were two contradictory sources of resistance to the privatization of higher education. The first was the old crony private education entrepreneurs who did not want high-quality competition, and wanted to reap the rents from an artificially created scarcity. The second was a worry that the privatization of education might make educational institutions less inclusive spaces. After all, they were self-consciously being subject to fewer affirmative action requirements. And in the latest iteration, of a special category of institutions called Institutions of Eminence, the institutions can self-design their affirmative action criteria, which are advisory in any case. An old worry is that if access to education is a function of class, then education, rather than being a leveler, will reproduce social inequality. Public institutions, for all their other weaknesses, had produced socially inclusive universities even if at low quality. It is in some senses a pity that while there was pressure on these universities to be inclusive, there was little corresponding commitment to support them in enhancing their quality.

There were several legislative attempts to create a lighter regulatory structure for private universities at the central level (Agrawal, 2009). But these legislative efforts did not garner enough support, so the regulatory action shifted to the states, and state after state enacted legislation enabling the creation of private universities. This process was not linear and was fraught with great uncertainty. It had been taken for granted till 2002 that all private universities needed approval from the UGC. But the government of Chhattisgarh in 2002 enacted a Private Universities Act creating 108 universities in one go. There was immense backlash against this legislative largesse. Prompted by the Supreme Court the UGC once again established supervisory superintendence of universities created by state legislatures. Broadly speaking it has led to an arrangement where the states can create private universities through their legislatures. But these have to conform to some basic requirements laid down by the UGC. There is also greater oversight of these institutions through accreditation and ranking processes which are conducted by the UGC. In effect, there is now a co-regulatory model where the states can freely exercise their right to create universities. But these have to be subject to accreditation and ranking processes that are operated by the UGC.

The UGC also created special mechanisms to allow the entry of private players. The latest in this effort was the introduction of a scheme called Institutions of Eminence that would allow selected public and private universities to be exempt from heavy regulation. The details of the scheme are not important. What is important is the new ambition it signaled for Indian universities. For private universities it envisaged that a university would invest close to 1.5 billion dollars over 10–15 years. But the net result of state legislative action, and changes in UGC regulation was the creation of over 200 private universities since 2005.

What is different about this new wave of private institutions? There are a number of issues. For one thing, the scale of *ambition*. Universities were no longer supposed to simply pick up the slack from the public sector. They are, in a new ideological framing, supposed to be world class. Indeed, the Institutions of Eminence Criteria stipulate that the university must demonstrate a pathway to be in the top of the Global Rankings over the next 15 years. So, in principle, the promise of private universities will be redeemed by their global excellence. This also fitted with the idea that one of the rationales for these universities is to reduce the need for Indian students to go abroad.

The second way in which the new universities are different is that they will all be *full-fledged universities*. This is part of a larger ideological shift that emphasizes breadth, multidisciplinarity, and choice in curricula. Even the elite IITs are being turned into full-fledged universities, representing the entire range of subjects. The Institution of Eminence Criteria clearly emphasized multidisciplinarity. Even private professional universities are being encouraged to broaden into liberal arts universities. The implicit model of undergraduate education is shifting from the British model to the American one. Instead of early streaming into particular disciplines, the new model places greater emphasis on a choice-based credit system.

The third difference was *financing models*. The expansion of private colleges was largely premised on almost the entire financing and generation of reasonable surplus being generated by revenue. In the new model, it was recognized that it is impossible to create a top-class, socially inclusive university without a significant philanthropic commitment. This is particular true of research universities, where the capital costs of building research infrastructure, and the imperatives of providing financial aid, make a purely revenue-based university prohibitively expensive. In the older model of private colleges, there was no expectation that faculty would do research. This was a double saving in so far as the institution did not have to invest in top-class talent or infrastructure. It also allowed institutions to maintain higher student–teacher ratios, since faculty were expected to only teach. The new generation of universities are expected to produce research, and run full-fledged graduate programs. In this sense, these universities are meant to provide the public good of research and also be a training ground for the next generation of university professors. It is for this reason that the higher end of the new private universities is being held to globally benchmarked student–teacher ratios of between one to ten and one to fifteen.

But there are significant obstacles to financing. Although India was historically a pioneer of endowment-based universities, even in the new model most universities are not endowment based. This is for two simple reasons. First, it takes a long time to build a viable endowment. An annual expenditure of 3–5 million dollars would require an endowment of close to 80 million dollars. Under Indian tax law, there are severe restrictions on where endowments can invest. Most often, they invest in fixed deposits, bonds, or government securities where the rates of return on endowments are also quite low. As such, universities remain dependent on revenue or annual financial grants for their viability. The typical model is for philanthropic commitments to cover the capital costs of the university, while revenue covers operations costs. But given that these universities remain dependent on revenue, their likely fees structure is going to remain relatively high in the Indian context.

Can private universities receive public funding? This is technically a tricky question. Central government funding for universities is largely disbursed by the UGC. Under section (12)B of the UGC Act, 1956, universities are declared eligible for government funding. In principle, private institutions can be included under this section that would make them eligible for public funding. But to date only eight, rather obscure private institutions have been included in this category and the support the UGC gives is limited to salary support and scholarships for students. The government is reluctant to give public money to private institutions, perhaps for understandable political reasons. But there is no legal bar to doing so.

Private universities can also receive other kinds of public funds, but only indirectly. For example, private universities were not eligible for receiving institutional grants from the Department of Science and Technology. Unlike in the United States, where a substantial amount of research grants to private universities comes from the federal government, private institutions in India cannot receive such grants. But given that private institutions dominate the landscape, the New Education Policy (2020) has recommended that private institutions also be made eligible for government research funding. This will greatly help private institutions strengthen their position in STEM fields. It is not clear whether this will be implemented. But in the meantime, the government has allowed individual scientists working in private universities to apply for competitive grants that are given to individual researchers, rather than institutional development grants.

But the one significant departure in financing models is this. Older private institutions were largely driven by single promoters whose name the institution carried. Among the new institutions there are many where a single promoter dominates and the university is named after them. The naming and governance rights of the university are a function of philanthropic gifts. But the real innovation has been in universities that have a model of collective philanthropy. Ashoka and KREA are two good examples. Under this model, no one proprietor or a small set of proprietors "owns" the university. In the last few years there is beginning to emerge a new organizational form for a private university. This organizational form is relatively new to India. It is based on *collective philanthropy*. New universities like Ashoka and KREA are the nascent products of this organizational form. The collective philanthropy model has a few advantages. It ensures that the university is not an extension of the will of one or two proprietors. It ensures that governance processes in the university have to be relatively strong since attracting new donors requires credibility in process. Ashoka has demonstrated some early success with this model and has quickly gone on to become India's leading liberal arts university. But it is still an open question whether the cultural and political preconditions exist for such a model to acquire widespread currency. This model requires a widespread culture of relatively "dispassionate" philanthropy. There is a new generation of philanthropists—largely first-generation entrepreneurs, with strong experience of American universities—who are willing to go down this path. Given that the minimum scale of a viable research university in India requires at least 200–300 million dollars in philanthropic commitments per university as a starting point, it is not clear how many projects of this kind can take shape.

Fourth, there is a new model of *governance*. In principle, an ideal organizational form should allow the university a degree of insulation from both the state and immediate commercial considerations. But internally the governance structure of universities also needs to craft the right relationship between the trustees and the academics. In almost all of the top 500 institutions in the world, securing both an independent Board of Trustees and the independence of faculty from them in academic matters, is a vital institutional consideration. One of the dismal failures of private universities was this. Since they were revenue based, they did not shield the university from commercial considerations. In the older model, because of the adverse selection of entrepreneurs, the governing structure of the university had little interest in academic excellence. While the government overregulated and under-governed private institutions, proprietors also exercised undue influence on academic matters. In the new generation of private universities, these governance deficits are being addressed. There is more of an insistence on credible, independent boards, though the blunt truth is that in single proprietor-dominated universities, the universities still remain at the mercy of the proprietor. The fate of the university in some ways depends on the virtues of the proprietor more than the formal structures of governance. In universities based on collective philanthropy there is a higher likelihood of better governance practices taking hold, since they have an incentive to be process driven rather than be dominated by the will of single proprietors. In a vast majority of India's private universities there is still a risk that academics will not enjoy the right degree of autonomy in relation to the proprietors or the trustees. This will be the single biggest constraint in enhancing the quality of the institutions. A few institutions are beginning to break this trend, but it is too early to tell how decisive this governance revolution will be. This will probably be the single most critical determinant of the success of the new private university revolution.

Fifth, there is a different kind of sociology to the promoters and entrepreneurs of the new universities. Prior to independence, private philanthropy was the norm in Indian higher education. Over the next few decades, it withered as the state expanded its control over all aspects of the economy. Private higher education re-emerged in the 1980s, as the economy began to gradually liberalize, but many of the promoters of this generation of private colleges were brokers, and politicians. That continued for about two decades, but gradually a new generation of promoters began entering the education sector. These entrepreneurs (like Shiv Nadar, Ashish Dhawan, and Sanjeev Bikhchandani) typically have the following characteristics. They are first-generation entrepreneurs who have made the transition from the middle class to being industry leaders. Their sensibilities tend to be rooted in middle-class ideals of education. They mostly have technology or finance backgrounds and their biggest asset is their own education. They have personal exposure to education in the United States. And because of their technology and finance backgrounds they are less invested in the older ways of Indian capital that relied on brokering state power. One ought not to exaggerate the degree of autonomy of these new entrepreneurs, but their businesses were in parts of Indian capitalism that were considered relatively clean. Finally, because of their own professional background they brought a different level of managerial and institutional skills to the building of these universities. They were, in some ways, much more professional than their counterparts.

All these developments have made India more cautiously optimistic about the possibility of some private universities breaking the mold of mediocre private universities. In some ways India could even pitch its ambitions higher. It could not just create a number of global-class universities, but also become a global hub for high-quality education. India should be a high-quality, low-cost alternative to the West. Depending on how one estimates costs, top universities (in the West?) estimate that the cost per student varies between 100,000 and 150,000 dollars per student per year. It should be quite possible for India to offer a competitive education at cost structures of 20,000 to 25,000 dollars a year. But will this nascent private revolution in India allow it to become a global education hub?

There are formidable obstacles to this outcome. In part, education systems flourish with country reputations. If India's democracy becomes corroded, its growth story falters, and the general living environment remains unattractive it will be difficult for its universities to compete globally. There are still a significant number of challenges facing Indian universities. This chapter will flag four challenges.

The first, and perhaps most complicated challenge is the continued legitimacy of private universities. In a poor country, marked by deep social and economic inequality, the "legitimacy" of elite universities is always open to question. The state was mindful of the social location of universities. A higher education system would be "tolerated" only in so far as it provides a means of social mobility and is not simply the site of the reproduction of social inequality. Arguably, this is an area of concern globally. Much of the "political" backlash against elite universities is fueled by the sense that these are not socially inclusive spaces. Often this backlash is experienced simply through exit; a large majority of citizens do not think these are universities where their children *belong*. The role of universities in reproducing rather than mitigating social distinction is a matter of global debate. Most universities recognize the importance of the issue. Affirmative action and diversity programs are designed to mitigate invidious forms of social exclusion that have marked universities. Yet it is hard to argue that universities, or the process to get to them, have been socially inclusive.

Should a society worry about elitism of universities? As Ashutosh Mukherjee, the great founding Vice-Chancellor of Calcutta University argued, intellectual elitism is, to a certain extent, inescapable in higher education. But he was sanguine that the ultimate worth of intellectual elitism can be redeemed by the fact that these institutions produce graduates who would be exemplars in thinking about the public good. The university would become socially inclusive through the actions of its graduates and their impact on society (Mukherjee 1918).

But societies do measure their universities on the scale of social inclusion. This was a truth that the democratic state in India recognized. Its answer was twofold. It introduced wide ranging reservations for historically marginalized groups, where the aim of the universities was to mirror the social composition of society. This affirmative action has been the subject of great political contention. But this was also one of the reasons why there was political pressure to keep *fees* low. One of the criticisms public universities faced was precisely that they were unable to mobilize resources or signal the value of education by not pricing it right. The effects of these of these policies can be debated. They often ended up giving massive subsidies to the middle class as much as they enabled marginalized groups. But they signaled the fact that the university had to be positioned as a socially inclusive institution.

The dilemma for India is this. As the space for "private" education opens up, will the university remain a socially inclusive space? New universities like Ashoka are committed to social inclusion, through financial aid programs and an outreach program that recognizes social disadvantage. But there are three major challenges. First, the amount of philanthropic commitment and cross-subsidy required to sustain a genuinely inclusive model is quite massive. Indeed, there is anecdotal evidence that socially inclusive private universities do not do badly in reaching out to socially marginalized groups with incomes under 500,000 rupees a year (about five times per capita income in 2019–2020): conscious outreach and targeting can help. They also do well with privileged groups. But it is the lower middle they miss out on, where the signal of a high price tag sends tends to socially deter these groups. If one were brutally honest about it, even a genuinely "needs blind" admission policy is sustainable only on the basis of prior inequality that is encoded into the admission and selection process. In a country like India a fully needs blind admissions policy would require forgoing almost 80–90 percent on the yield curve. Second, universities are built on the top of great inequality in school education and are yet expected to compensate for the inequality inscribed at the school level. The representation of the most marginalized groups in higher education is hobbled by the fact that the pipeline that funnel applicants coming from the school system gets narrower the lower down the social or class order one goes. Third, and finally, there is the challenge of the university as a social space. One of the challenges of elite universities is the fact that their culture is such that often students feel they don't belong there. Even if the university is financially inclusive, the challenge of creating a socially inclusive space remains. Imagine the challenges of creating a space where a first-generation Dalit student, whose parents are barely out of bonded labor, inhabits the same space as a fifth-generation millionaire. Even in democratic societies there is often a polite veil thrown over the fact that these spaces are *difficult* to create. Higher education is about intellectual distinction. But the social legitimacy of universities is measured by their social inclusiveness. This social inclusiveness is a pedagogic necessity; it is a requirement of justice. But it is also a prudential political requirement. A university has to be a public trust in this respect: it has to be place where everyone potentially belongs. This is easier to announce than it is to credibly realize.

The second challenge is the continued shadow of government. The New Education Policy has, for the first time, institutionalized the acceptance of private philanthropically based education. The government has also promised universities greater autonomy. To this end it has introduced a series of benchmarks. If universities meet those benchmarks, they will, in principle, be given more autonomy. The government is also proposing a new light touch regulation. But this is still a very uncertain and fraught process for two reasons. First, the broader environment for liberal thinking has deteriorated in India, and there is something incongruous about trying to build liberal arts universities as the country itself becomes less liberal. An ideological control or reorientation of the education system is very much a part of the ruling BJP's cultural agenda. In public universities there has been an astonishing clampdown of the freedom of expression of faculty and students (Sundar, 2020). How far private universities will remain insulated from this remains to be seen. There is already some evidence that the government is exercising its discretionary powers of regulation to even make private universities fall in line. Second, even with light touch regulation, the government still has the powers to regulate all aspects of university administration, from fees to admissions. There is currently great variance in how the state chooses to exercise these powers; some states have been more liberal than others. But liberal regulation is not yet embedded enough in state practice for one to be entirely confident of this liberal regulatory environment continuing. This may not necessarily impede the creation of good universities in STEM and professional fields. After all Russia and China created top-class universities under conditions of severe repression. But it does suggest that private universities will not be entirely protected from the pressures of politicization.

The third challenge is simply capacity. Raising the quality of private universities will require continual philanthropic commitment. A lot of the investments we are currently seeing in this sector are a consequence of India's spectacular growth in the early 2000s. But as growth slows, and the returns to education diminish, the financial pipeline for private education is likely to be hit as well. Both philanthropic commitment, and the ability to pay high fees will diminish. There has been the entry of a significant number of philanthropists in this area. But in proportion to what is possible the levels of philanthropic commitments are still disappointing. In principle, there are at least 20–30 billionaires in India who could single-handedly create world-class universities. But we are still looking only at three or four new projects that are genuinely new and exciting.

5. Conclusion

There is little doubt that private higher education will continue to dominate Indian higher education. It is now deeply institutionalized, despite formidable ideological and political economy obstacles. But its future success will depend on two things. First, it will depend a great deal on the broader growth of the Indian economy. This is a sector that flourishes when there is optimism about the economy, and confidence about returns to education. In a growing economy, not only does the demand for education expand, so does the willingness to invest. If, however, economic growth slows then the legitimacy of the sector might come under greater scrutiny especially if private education is seen as reproducing existing inequalities not mitigating them. Second, India has the institutional and intellectual sophistication to become a global powerhouse in higher education. What has kept it back is not lack of resources, or the challenges of mass education. It has been held back by deliberate political and administrative choices. There has been some learning from India's past mistakes; the fact that private education has been allowed to expand and new experiments are being encouraged is testament to that. But there are also signs that as broader governance norms in Indian democracy are challenged, the erosion of these norms will reverberate on Indian universities as well. Indian public universities continue to suffer. But whether Indian private universities will buck this trend is an open question.

References

Agrawal, P. (2009). *Indian Higher Education: Envisioning the Future*. New Delhi: Sage Publications.

Altbach, P. G. (ed.) (1968). *Turmoil and Transition: Higher Education and Student Politics in India*. New York: Basic Books.

Apte, D. G. (1961). *Universities in Ancient India*. Baroda: Sayajirao Gaekwad University Press.

Chandra, P. (2017). *Building Universities That Matter: Where Are Indian Institutions Going Wrong?* Hyderabad: Orient BlackSwan.

Government of India (2019). *All India Survey on Higher Education 2018–19*. New Delhi: Ministry of Human Resource Development.

Kapur, D. and Khosla, M. (2017). "The Supreme Court and private higher education: Litigation patterns and judicial trends." In D. Kapur and P. B. Mehta, (eds.), *Navigating the Labyrinth: Perspectives on India's Higher Education*. Hyderabad: Orient BlackSwan, Chapter 8.

Kapur, D. and Mehta, P. B. (2008). "Mortgaging the future? Indian higher education." *Brookings-NCAER India Policy Forum*, 4, 101–157.

Kumar, C. R. (ed.) (2018). *The Future of Indian Universities*. Delhi: Oxford University Press.

Manjapara, K. (2014). *The Age of Entanglement*. Cambridge, MA: Harvard University Press.

Mukherjee, A. (1918). "Convocation address to University of Mysore." *Dacca Review*, 8/17, 10–20.

Program for Research on Private Higher Education (2017). "Ten largest systems' individual and aggregated private shares, 2017." http://www.prophe.org/en/global-data/country-dimension-tables/ten-largest-systems%E2%80%99-individual-and-aggregated-private-shares/

RBI Bulletin (2021). "Outward remittances under the Liberalised Remittance Scheme (LRS) for resident individuals." https://www.rbi.org.in/scripts/BS_ViewBulletin.aspx?Id=20179

Sankalia, H. D. (1972). *The University of Nalanda*. New Delhi: Oriental Publishers.

Sundar, N. (2020). *Academic Freedom in India: A Status Report*. New Delhi. https://indianculturalforum.in/wp-content/uploads/2020/09/ICF-Academic-Freedom-.pdf

Tilak, J. B. G. (ed.) (2013). *Higher Education in India: In Search of Equality, Quality and Quantity*. New Delhi: Orient BlackSwan.

Trow, M. (2007). "Reflections on the transition from elite to mass to universal access: Forms and phases of higher education in modern societies since WWII." In J. J. F. Forest and P. G. Altbach (eds.), *International Handbook of Higher Education*. Dordrecht: Springer, 243–280.

University Grants Commission (n.d.). *Annual Reports* 2016–2017; 2017–2018. New Delhi: University Grants Commission.

Varma, R. (2020). "Politicians will pose the biggest challenge to NEP." *Hindustan Times*, August 10.

CHAPTER 30

JAPAN

The Changing Role of Higher Education for Nation-Building

AKIYOSHI YONEZAWA

1. INTRODUCTION

JAPAN was among the first countries in Asia to develop a modern higher education system based on Western higher education models. Until the mid-nineteenth century, Japan had relatively limited influence from Western civilization due to its prohibition on private trade with foreign countries. Japanese trade with Western countries was monopolized by the Netherlands until 1858, when the Treaty of Amity and Commerce with the United States was signed, opening up private trade with the United States and other Western countries (Yonezawa et al., 2017).

Under the Meiji government that was newly established in 1868, Japan began radical Westernization reform through voluntary policy borrowing (Nakayama, 1989). The slogans widely used in the Meiji period—such as *fukoku kyohei* (a wealthy nation and a strong army), *shokusan kogyo* (encouraging industry) and *bunmei kaika* (civilization and enlightenment)—were used to promote the building of a modern nation through the active adoption of various aspects of modern Western civilization (Low, 2005). The education system, including higher education, was considered a core instrument for absorbing and realizing what was considered to be the most advanced form of civilization development. While the ideas of both "nation-states" and "universities" changed significantly over the next 150 years, education continues to play an important role in nation-building and has defined higher education policy in Japan (Institute for International Cooperation, 2004).

The higher education system in Japan is a highly mature system that can absorb the basic demands of higher learning for the domestic population as well as provide well-developed education and research directed towards both national and international communities. Particularly in recent years, however, many inside and outside the country have critiqued its response to the changing global context (e.g., Nature Index, 2019). Demographic changes, especially the decreasing youth population, are leading to an oversupply of university education (Yonezawa, 2020a). While the Japanese government and Japanese universities are struggling to improve the quality of education and research in order to enhance the country's global competitiveness and attractiveness, it is becoming apparent that higher education in Japan is losing its international presence in the face of a rapidly changing global and domestic environment. The result is a lost opportunity to develop a highly-skilled labor force that will support and contribute to the rise of Asia as an important region in the knowledge economy.

Higher education institutions in Japan are divided into four categories: universities, junior colleges, colleges of technology, and professional training colleges. Universities provide four- to six-year undergraduate programs, and some provide postgraduate programs. The other three categories mainly provide two- to three-year programs that lead to associate degrees or diplomas. As seen in neighboring higher education systems such as South Korea, Taiwan, and the Philippines, private universities and higher education institutions are dominant, especially at bachelor, associate degree, and diploma programs in terms of the number of institutions and student enrollment. There is a growing tendency among youth to prefer bachelor programs over associate degree and diploma programs (Table 30.1).

Recent arguments regarding higher education policies in Japan focus on the structural problem of pursuing education reforms, especially university reforms. Education reform is widely used as both an academic term and to refer to educational policy

Table 30.1 Higher education institutions and student enrollment, 2020

	Universities *Daigaku*	Junior colleges *Tanki daigaku*	Colleges of technology *Koto senmon gakko*	Professional training colleges *Senshugakko senmon katei*
Institutions				
National	86		51	9
Local public	94	17	3	184
Private	615	306	3	2 612
Total	795	323	57	2 805
Students				
National	598,881		51,217	299
Local public	158,579	5,548	3,800	23,293
Private	2,158,145	102,048	1,957	580,823
Total	2,915,605	107,596	56,974	604,415

and practices. There is wide consensus on the timing of Japan's first education reform, namely, the implementation of a modern, Western-style education system as part of the drastic Westernization movement after the Meiji Restoration. The second education reform is understood as the profound transformation of the education system under the supervision of the Allied forces after Japan's defeat in World War II in 1945, which led to the massive expansion of Japan's higher education system. Since then, Japan's education system, including its higher education system, has experienced challenges in terms of policies and practices for three-quarters of a century. Discussions have focused on further education reforms, but these new reforms have not been clearly defined (Kariya and Rappleye, 2020).

Reforms have been proposed and implemented based on the idea that social problems are caused by the poor design of the education system and education policies, and therefore, educational reform has the potential to solve such social problems. The second education reform, which occurred after World War II, is a typical example of this idea; it was implemented based on the assumption that the pre-war education system had led Japanese society and citizens to support the military regime (Tsuchimochi, 1993).

Regarding university reforms, there has been more active and continuous discussion since the beginning of the 1980s, when the national government and society in general recognized the need to adjust to the new global trends that were leading to the knowledge economy. However, these university reforms, which have not resulted in visible and substantial improvement in terms of learning and research achievements, are now perceived in a skeptical manner (Sato, 2019).

This chapter discusses the history, current profile, and future of Japanese higher education within the Asian and global contexts. Section 2 outlines the historical development of Japan's higher education system in relation to the policy of nation-building. Section 3 explains the current conditions of Japanese higher education, focusing on its background and current challenges. Section 4 discusses future perspectives, including how Japan's universities and higher education institutions have developed relationships with other Asian higher education systems, especially as a result of the "new normal" caused by the COVID-19 pandemic and its aftermath.

2. Japan's Higher Education and Its Associations with Nation-Building

2.1 Adoption of Western Higher Education Systems

In the mid-nineteenth century, Japan sent national delegations and future young leaders to Europe and North America to study various aspects of Western civilization at universities and other higher education institutions. During the Meiji Restoration which began in 1868, the Japanese government opened the country to Western trade and set up a national plan and legal framework for the systematic development of its higher education system as a nation-building project. Information about various foreign higher education systems was meticulously collected and translated into Japanese for the Japanese government and university leaders to fully understand the merits of various higher education systems around the world before they designed a higher education system suitable for Japan. The resulting higher education system was based on a combination of different types of Western philosophies and higher education models with long existing intellectual traditions (e.g., studies of Chinese classics and Japanese thought combined with Western knowledge, mainly from the Netherlands) (Nakayama, 1989). This differed greatly from the implantation of Western systems in other Asian countries colonized by Western countries as the Japanese government and university leaders had autonomous decision-making powers regarding which models and traditions they applied to the new higher education system. The establishment and development of Japan's higher education system and national Japanese-language academic communities were also closely linked with universities' role in the development of highly-skilled talent for nation-building and improvements in science, technology, and civilization (Institute for International Cooperation, 2004). This concept of nation-building was borrowed from Western higher education systems such as the University of Berlin and French imperial universities (Ben-David, 2017).

In 1877, the University of Tokyo was established as the first university in Japan, with affiliated faculties in law, medicine, letters, and natural sciences, through the amalgamation of pre-existing public higher education institutions. In 1886, the University of Tokyo added the faculty of engineering and became the first imperial university. In 1897, the second imperial university was established in Kyoto, followed by other imperial universities in Tohoku in 1907, Kyushu in 1911, Hokkaido in 1918, Osaka in 1931, and Nagoya in 1939. In addition, Keijo Imperial University was established in Seoul in 1924, and Taipei Imperial University was established in Taipei in 1928. These two imperial universities in colonized territories were occupied mainly by Japanese faculties and students, and did not serve the autonomous development of local societies until these territories gained independence and new flagship universities were established under their own ownership (i.e., Seoul National University in 1946 and National Taiwan University in 1945) (Kim, 2018). Various polytechnics (*semmon gakko*) for professional higher education were also established, some of which had become leading universities by the end of World War II, including Tokyo Institute of Technology (engineering) and Hitotsubashi University (commerce).

Throughout the development of the university and higher education system described above, the ideas of academic freedom and university autonomy have also developed in complex ways; partly through the interaction between the national government and the university faculties, as well as the accumulated dialogues on the ideas of universities and nation-states referring to various foreign models. In this process, the university faculties strengthened autonomous power to select their own university leaders, while facing limitations in academic activities especially under the military regime from the 1930s to the end of World War II (Terasaki, 2020).

2.2 Absorbing Mass Demand through Non-Governmental Resources

Japan's higher education system has developed not only through public investment by the national government but even more so, through the engagement of local communities and private stakeholders (Altbach and Umakoshi, 2004). Before the Meiji Restoration, Japan had various types of local public higher education institutions, called *hanko* (clan schools), and private higher education institutions, called *shijuku* (e.g., Keio Gijuku).

Throughout the modernization process, leaders in the private sector with various attitudes and ambitions towards Western and Eastern civilization and intellectual traditions donated to, founded, and developed universities and higher education institutions in both the public and private sectors. For example, Yukichi Fukuzawa, who founded Keio Gijuku (the current Keio University) in 1858, was known for his support for Japan's direction of "leaving Asia and entering Europe" (Narsimhan, 1999). By contrast, Shigenobu Okuma, who founded Tokyo Senmon Gakko in 1882 (the current Waseda University), later revealed his support for the idea of integrating Western and Eastern civilizations (Lebra-Chapman, 1973; Yonezawa et al., 2017).

By 1919, some of these institutions were officially authorized as private universities by the national government, responding to the demand by private firms and industry for highly-skilled human resources with a university education (Itoh, 2002). Universities, including imperial universities, started to admit female students; Tohoku University began to do so in 1913 and is the first such case. However, the number of female students remained very low. Some women's higher education institutions, such as Tokyo Women's Christian University, were founded and called "universities" or "colleges," although they were not officially authorized as such by the national government until the end of World War II. National and local public universities and higher education institutions, including imperial universities, also accepted large-scale support from local communities and private financial groups for the establishment of institutions and the addition of faculties. In 1945, there were 48 universities, 309 polytechnics, 33 higher schools (*koto gakko*; gymnasiums for higher education level general education prior to university education), 142 normal schools (*shihan gakko*), and other miscellaneous schools for teacher training. Except for teacher training institutions, private higher education has taken a significant role in terms of both the number of institutions and the number of students as shown in Table 30.2 (Terasaki, 2020; Itoh, 2021).

After World War II, Japan experienced drastic reformation of its higher education system under the supervision of the Allied powers (Tsuchimochi, 1993; Itoh, 2002). This was the beginning of a new education system with a simplified structure (i.e., six-year primary, three-year junior secondary, three-year upper secondary, and four-year undergraduate education) that emulated the US system. By merging existing universities and higher education institutions, at least one comprehensive national (public) university was established in each of the 47 prefectures. Unlike the state higher education systems in the United States, however, these new public universities remained "national

Table 30.2 Higher education institutions and student enrollment, 1945

	Universities Daigaku	Higher schools Senmon gakko	Polytechnics Semmon gakko	Normal schools and other miscellaneous schools Shihan gakko
Institutions				
National	19	26	90	142
Local public	2	3	56	
Private	27	2	163	
Total	**48**	**33**	**309**	**142**
Students				
National	44,283	17,372	70,612	76,188
Local public	1,305	1,535	18,301	
Private	34,550	2,780	124,039	
Total	**80,138**	**21,687**	**212,952**	**76,188**

Source: Terasaki (2020, p. 282).

universities" that were directly established and operated by the national government. Aside from these, various local public universities were established by municipal authorities, and private universities were operated by non-profit and non-governmental school corporations with the authorization of the national government. Although local public and private universities existed in the pre-war system, many universities were either newly established or upgraded from higher and secondary education institutions. All national and local public and private universities were given equal status as institutions that could issue bachelor's degrees and, in some cases, master's and doctoral degrees (Terasaki, 2020). The accreditation of the universities was first introduced as the non-governmental quality assurance by Japan University Accreditation Association in 1947, following the US accreditation model. However, the Ministry of Education (Monbusho) introduced a standard for the establishment of universities in 1956; this regulatory system authorizes the establishment of universities through the assessment of the expert committee under the Ministry.

The Japanese economy had mostly recovered from the damage of World War II by the beginning of the 1960s. At the same time, the first generation born after World War II reached the age of entering higher education; the 18-year-old population rapidly changed from 2.0 million in 1960, to 1.4 million in 1964, and to 2.49 million in 1966 (see Figure 30.1). It became apparent that further expansion of higher education was necessary to absorb the demands for higher learning of these "first baby boomers" born after the war, as well as for rapid economic development and highly-skilled human resources in industrial sectors from the mid-1950s to the beginning of the 1970s. In particular, the private higher education sector contributed to the realization of mass higher education by the 1970s by absorbing the massive demand resulting from universal secondary

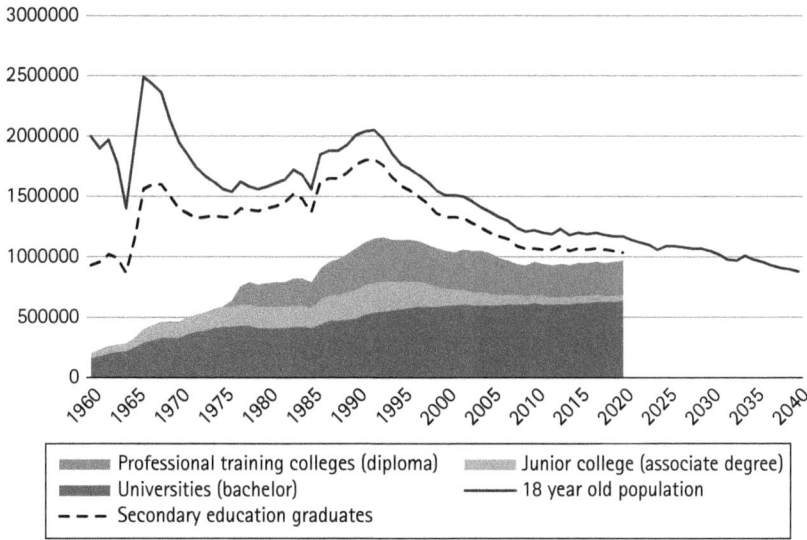

FIGURE 30.1 Number of newly enrolled students in higher education, graduates from secondary education (1960–2020) and 18-year-old population (estimated 1960–2040)

Source: Central Council for Education (2018), MEXT School Basic Survey.

education which automatically qualified secondary school graduates to apply for higher education programs (Yonezawa, 2013). In the post-war education system, faculty members of universities were given a high level of autonomy, and academic freedom was assured in the new constitution and acts enacted after World War II.

The private higher education sector expanded mainly as a result of the limited financial capacity of the national government to provide sufficient quality education to meet the massive increase in demand for higher education. The national government was somewhat reluctant to expand the national higher education sectors, as it wanted higher education institutions to maintain their education and research standards. In addition, the tuition fees of national and local public universities remained nominal and did not reflect the cost of education in the 1970s. Instead, the government allowed private universities to increase enrollment to absorb the demand for mass higher education and charge tuition fees from students, which constituted their main source of income.

Together with the Philippines, South Korea, and Taiwan, Japan was one of the earliest examples of the expansion of higher education through partial reliance on the demand-absorbing functions of private higher education, a model that would be widely adopted in East and South-East Asia (Altbach and Umakoshi, 2004).

2.3 Hierarchical Differentiation Based on Student Selectivity

Sparked by student activism, which initially started as resistance against tuition rises among private universities in the mid-1960s, the national government introduced a partial public subsidy for the operational expenditure of private universities and higher education institutions to discourage the hike of tuition fees in 1970. At the same time, the government introduced strict control of the student enrollment under the national higher education plan in 1976, with a quota of the student number allowed to be enrolled for each university and college program, even private institutions. This was partially intended to control the effect of a public subsidy for private universities; if the number of students at private universities continued to grow, the government would have to increase the subsidy without limits.

However, the governmental policy for support and control of private higher education led to an unintended consequence (Yonezawa, 2013). The government control and support led to an overdemand in the student market because the demand for higher education continued to grow under the restriction of student enrollment numbers. This in turn meant that the private universities could once again raise tuition fees partly because of less resistance from the student movement, but also because of an overdemand for higher learning accelerated by the government policy controlling student enrollment. The tuition fees of national and local public universities also started to rise, reflecting the change in governmental policy from nominal pricing as a commission fee to partial cost-sharing of educational expenditures with students. However, the tuition fee levels of selective private universities, especially in the field of social sciences, remained at a relatively reasonable level to compete with top national universities in attracting elite students. By the end of the 1970s, the top private universities were able to achieve a high selectivity rate based on academic achievement (which was assessed mainly through entrance examinations), almost equal to that of competitive national universities (Geiger, 1986).

In a 1971 national policy paper, the government revealed its idea to categorize the functions of universities and higher education institutions—from research and elite universities to mass and universal higher learning institutions (Itoh, 2002). This idea of "functional differentiation" has been continuously discussed and developed up until today. In 1976, the government launched non-university postsecondary education through "professional training colleges." In 2019, some of these were upgraded to a new category: "professional universities" (Yonezawa and Inenaga, 2017). The professional universities provide vocational-oriented educational programs such as arts and culture, tourism, fashion, informatics, digital entertainment, animation, food services management, rehabilitation, etc.

Although the legal status of universities ensures that they are, in principle, equal, a de facto hierarchical structure based on their historical background and student selectivity has been widely recognized throughout the history of Japan's modern higher education system (Yonezawa and Huang, 2018). This structure has led to a preference for prestigious higher education institutions and undergraduate programs among both students and employers. Overreliance on the selectivity of universities by students, universities, and society in general based on prestige has been severely criticized as a social problem termed "diploma disease" (Dore, 1976).

2.4 Further Participation in the Context of Population Decline

Participation in bachelor's programs has increased over the last three decades partly as a result of a supply-side factor, namely, the capacity of student enrollment provided by the universities has increased. In a movement supported by the government, higher education institutions, especially junior colleges were upgraded to four-year universities to seek market opportunities for meeting the demand of further higher learning especially among females.

Traditionally, female students tended to choose junior colleges rather than universities, mostly because of the clear preference of employers for male graduates in the traditionally patriarchal Japanese society until a shift began to occur in the 1980s, culminating in the Equal Employment Law for Men and Women in 1985. Since then, the enrollment of female students in universities and job opportunities for female university graduates have increased (see Figure 30.2), albeit unevenly across fields of studies (Yamamoto, 2019). From the mid-1980s, partly through the guidance of the Japanese government, junior colleges, which were characterized as a short education track for women, were upgraded and transformed into, in most cases, co-education universities with four-year undergraduate programs and, in some cases, postgraduate programs.

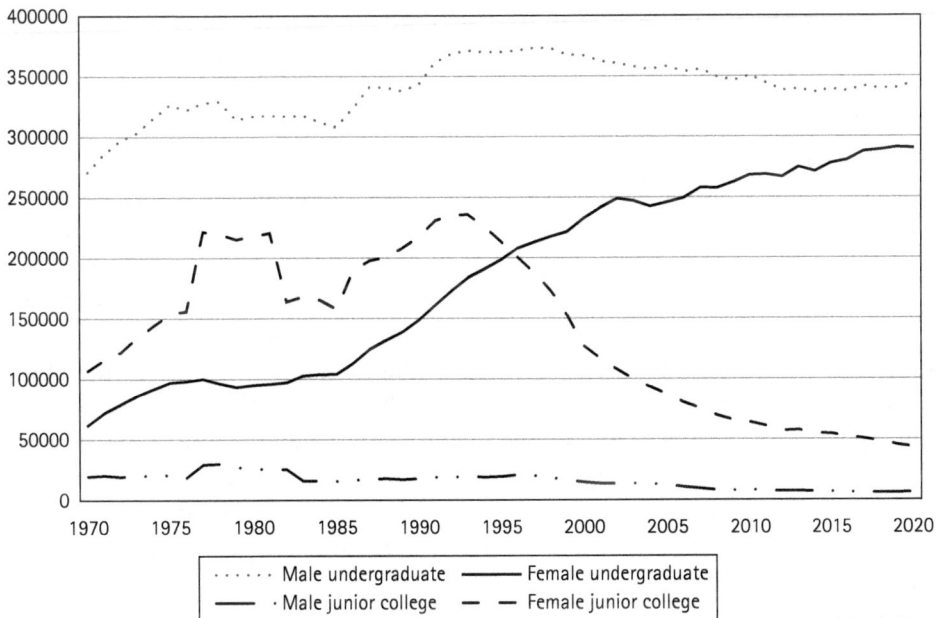

FIGURE 30.2 Number of newly enrolled students by gender (four-year undergraduate and junior colleges, 1970–2020)

Source: MEXT School Basic Survey.

Today, however, female graduates continue to face challenges in employment and promotion in the Japanese labor market. These challenges include employment conditions that disadvantage female participation such as rigid working hours that do not accommodate the needs of family life and a preference for internal promotion systems based on seniority. Inevitably, this has led to a limited proportion of women among senior leaders (Kosugi, 2017).

In the 1990s, the Japanese government enacted a policy to develop postgraduate programs to foster human resources with the skills and knowledge necessary to participate in the knowledge economy in the fields of science, technology, and innovation. However, compared to other countries with advanced economies, postgraduate education in Japan has developed at a rather slow pace, especially in science and technology doctoral programs and professional graduate education in social science fields. This is mainly because Japanese firms continue to rely on in-house training and a rigid wage system that does not differentiate between undergraduate and postgraduate degree holders. In other words, there is no clear incentive for learners to pursue postgraduate degrees for their career development, and Japanese companies in general are relatively reluctant to recruit doctoral degree holders because their expertise may be too narrow and may not fit well with work requirements in the real world. In the last decade, the government has tried to encourage the reform of graduate education to make it more suitable for non-academic careers. Since then, the supply of postgraduate programs has increased the learning opportunities of adult learners (Fujimura, 2015). However, mainly because of the slow change in recruiting behaviors and decreased spending power in research and development in Japanese companies, the total number of doctoral students which once reached to 75,365 in 2006 has stagnated and was 75,345 in 2020 (Hamanaka, 2015).

Japan's higher education enrollment rate is modest compared with both advanced and emerging economies (i.e., 49.9 percent compared with the OECD average of 58.9 percent at the ISCED 6 [bachelor's] level in 2016[1]). However, the literature also identifies characteristics seen in mature economies, such as the long-established tendency for static socio-economic status rather than upward mobility, related stagnation in the spending power of both families and the public budget, and the socio-economic divide between metropolitan urban and rural areas in terms of social expectations and job opportunities as a result of higher learning (Hozawa, 2016; Matsuoka, 2015, 2019). Oversupply in the undergraduate market amid a decreasing youth population since the end of the twentieth century has caused a substantial number of universities to cease selective practices and adopt de facto open admissions strategies.

---

[1] See p. 277 of the *International Labor Databook 2019* by the Japan Institute for Labor Policy and Training (https://www.jil.go.jp/kokunai/statistics/databook/2019/08/d2019_T8-01.pdf).

3. LOST IN GLOBALIZATION

By the 1980s, Japan had gained a leading economic status in the international context. The Asian "tigers" (South Korea, Taiwan, Hong Kong, and Singapore) and the Association of Southeast Asian Nations (ASEAN) countries also experienced rapid economic expansion, and China adopted market economy policies. These changes have contributed to the increasing importance of higher education in East and South-East Asia following the collapse of the Soviet Union in 1991 (Mok, 2012).

These changes in the global economy had a significant impact on higher education systems in this region, especially leading universities in East Asia which have attracted international attention (Marginson, 2011). At the end of the 1990s, the Hong Kong-based magazine *Asiaweek* issued a ranking of Asia's best universities, which was dominated by Japanese national universities with research profiles, such as the University of Tokyo, Tokyo Institute of Technology, and Tohoku University. In the 2000s, global university rankings, such as the Academic Ranking of World Universities, the Times Higher Education ranking and the Quacquarelli Symonds (QS) ranking, became influential. At first, Japanese universities, especially the University of Tokyo, achieved top status among Asian universities based on their impressive research achievements and long-standing reputations. However, as the Japanese economy started to stagnate from the mid-1990s on, its top universities—and the higher education system as a whole—gradually lost their primacy in Asia and salience in the world, except in certain natural science disciplines and medical research (Yonezawa et al., 2002; Yonezawa, 2016). This declining trend in Japanese academic prominence intensely irritated leading politicians, leading to frequent interventions and pressure described as "university reforms." However, these efforts have not led to an increase of financial support for the higher education sector because the Japanese government has faced financial constraints with huge governmental debts. This produced a chicken and egg effect; the stagnation of public and private investment in higher education led to slow internationalization (which is a means for universities to improve their ranking) as fewer Japanese students study abroad, and fewer foreign students seek to study in Japan. Under these conditions, the Japanese government and university leaders have committed to continuous university reforms in various aspects of university management and governance without clear prospects of the increase of resources necessary to attract talents from all over the world (Yonezawa, 2019). To date, there has been a gradual decline of Japanese universities' positions in international and Asian rankings.

3.1 Stagnation in Higher Education Investment

In the mid-1970s, partial public subsidies for private universities and higher education institutions were introduced. At the end of the 1970s, the percentage of public subsidies to the total income of private universities reached almost 30 percent. However, in the 1980s, due to the termination of welfare state policies, the ratio of public subsidy to total income of private universities dropped to around 10 percent by the end of the decade (Yonezawa, 2013). As a consequence, the operational budget for national universities stagnated, while project-based research funding increased based on the governmental policy to stimulate competition for performance in public funding. Indeed, partly responding to a campaign by leaders of national universities and academic communities, the Basic Act on Science and Technology was enacted in 1995, strengthening project-based research funding. This resulted in an overall increase in the revenues of national universities, but their financial stability was undermined due to the increased share of mostly research-related, project-based funding (Asonuma, 2002).

In 2004, all national universities that were operated directly by the national government through a special account in the national budget became incorporated (Yamamoto, 2004). The earmarked budget system, which was mainly based on the number of chairs, academic positions, and students, was transformed into a lump-sum budget that gave universities autonomous decision-making power over internal financial allocations (Yamamoto, 2010). At the same time, the government cut the total operational budget for national universities by 1 percent annually for 10 years. In addition, local public universities have occasionally faced stronger pressure to make budgetary cuts by municipal governments that are not necessarily knowledgeable in higher education policy trends. Nonetheless, most national universities, especially the leading research universities, modestly increased their total revenue through diversification of financial resources, such as research collaborations with industry. This trend, however, led to instability in the employment of early-career researchers hired with fixed-term project funding. Research performance in middle-range national universities was more severely damaged than in top national universities through a series of national policies to concentrate resource allocation to top universities (Toyoda, 2019).

Tuition fees have not been a promising income source for further development, either. Since the Japanese economy entered a period of long-term stagnation and deflation in the 1990s, the standard tuition fees set by the national government for all national universities stopped increasing from 2005 onwards. Local public universities have followed this standard. The 18-year-old population once increased to 2.05 million in 1992, when the "second baby boomers," the generation whose parents are "first baby boomers" born after World War II, started to enroll in higher education. However, after that, the 18-year-old population declined to 1.17 million in 2020, and is expected to decline to 0.88 million in 2040 (see Figure 30.1; Central Council for Education 2018). Facing a continuous decline in the youth population, private universities have found it difficult to raise tuition fees due to the increased supply of programs.

Students can make use of the public loan scheme provided by the Japan Student Service Organization (JASSO, a governmental organization) if they meet the required standard for grade point average and household income. The share of full-time undergraduate students utilizing the JASSO loan scheme and other loans and fellowships reached a high of 52.5 percent in 2012. However, the rate gradually decreased to 47.5 percent in 2018, with a growing concern that the repayment of these loans after graduation would become a heavy financial burden especially if they are not able to get high-income jobs (Armstrong et al., 2019). In 2020, the government started a system of fellowship grants to undergraduate students and a new income contingent student loan program as the targeted financial support for students from low-income families and graduates with no or less earnings (Kobayashi, 2020).

It could be argued that the recognition of and responses to the advent of the knowledge economy in the 1980s and the investment into research and innovation started relatively early in Japan. However, this has not progressed much because of limitations in social and individual investments in higher education. In short, Japan has failed to realize further investment in its education and research activities after entering the twenty-first century, in contrast to the significant increase in public and private investment in Asia and the rest of the world.

3.2 Slow Internationalization

Japan has a rather long history of policy attempts to internationalize higher education. Japanese universities and higher education institutions have actively accepted neighboring Asian students and researchers since the beginning of public and private higher education in Japan. At the same time, occasional tensions, including the colonization of Asian neighbors by the Japanese military, have influenced student and academic exchanges. After World War II, official university exchanges were mostly inactive. This was partly because of the Cold War and partly because of the struggle for decolonization among newly established countries, which involved eliminating the influence of Japan as a former colonizer. That having been said, collaborations on official development aid projects in the higher education sector were implemented under the terms of war reparation, technology transfer, and collaboration schemes. Such schemes led to, for example, the construction of the University of Indonesia and the establishment and development of King Mongkut's Institute of Technology Ladkrabang in Thailand.

In the 1980s, the Japanese government intentionally strengthened its policy of promoting internationalization of higher education. Based on the country's rapid economic development and renewed ties with socialist states (e.g., China, Vietnam), by the beginning of the 1980s, linkages with various universities and higher education institutions through Asia had dramatically deepened and widened. In 1983, Japan announced a plan to accept 100,000 international students by the end of the twentieth century. This number was reached in 2003 by accepting an absolute majority of foreign students from within Asia, over half of whom were from China. Another plan was implemented in 2008 to accept 300,000 international students by 2020. This plan has been realized mainly by accepting students at Japanese language schools, who come from countries with linguistic similarities (e.g., China and South Korea) as well as from other countries in Asia including Vietnam, Nepal, and Sri Lanka. The increase of students without a linguistic background closer to Japanese is creating pressure to increase English medium instruction that is still highly limited among universities in Japan. While many of these students work part-time during their study and seek job opportunities in Japan after graduation, higher learning in Japanese language requires a high level of linguistic command especially in humanities and social sciences.

It should be noted that Japan has not realized its own economic development objectives through the internationalization of higher education (Ota, 2018). The causal relationship is almost the opposite. When Japan's economic development—the most rapid in East Asia—was realized by the beginning of the 1980s, few non-Japanese citizens were students and academic staff at Japanese universities. The economic success of Japan, however, attracted attention as a model for the industrialization of Asian countries, and Japan was willing to accept more international students from Asia. Some of these students settled in Japan and later became teaching and research staff at Japanese universities. Despite this, most faculty members at Japanese universities acquired their final degrees in Japan, and the proportion of those who received overseas degrees is limited compared with Japan's Asian neighbors, such as South Korea, Taiwan, Hong Kong, and Singapore (Yonezawa et al., 2016).

Moreover, the acceptance and provision of cross-border education has been limited. In the 1980s, the Japanese government made an agreement with the US government to host US universities in Japan, and since then, it has hosted around 40 overseas branches and programs from US institutions, mostly state universities, to attract mainly Japanese youth seeking a university education from the United States. However, a very limited number of programs have survived, mostly because of the mismatch with the demands of Japanese youth, who perceive study abroad experiences as opportunities for language training and intercultural experiences rather than overseas job opportunities and migration. While there are social demands for "global" human resources with language and intercultural skills, as of 2015, only 13 percent of enterprises recruit Japanese students with study abroad experiences, and the reward system for these international competencies is mostly underdeveloped (Kainuma, 2018).

The self-contained nature of university academics in Japan has led to a slow process in internationalization. In 2004, the Japanese government began to officially recognize campuses and programs hosted by non-Japanese universities and permitted Japanese universities to host overseas campuses and programs. However, there has been no official establishment of full-scale campuses by Japanese universities overseas. The Ministry of Education, Culture, Sports, Science and Technology (MEXT) set up an official authorization process for joint degree programs for promoting quality education collaboration with international partners, which prefer joint degree programs over double degree programs. However, the authorization process imposes a heavy administrative burden.

The rapid improvement in overall academic quality and performance in Asia, especially at top universities, has led to a more mutual exchange of academics and students (albeit often for short stays rather than full degree programs). These networks of Asian researchers have been partially developed by those who have studied in North America, Europe, and Oceania. The connection with global research networks through English as the medium of instruction has become an advantage for countries such as Singapore, South Korea, and Malaysia. Japan is also becoming more open to English-language programs and classes, particularly at the graduate level, which may facilitate further participation in international research networks to a greater extent.

However, inside Japan, tensions between leading national universities and the national government are increasing because Japanese universities are losing their prestige compared with other top Asian universities. The stagnation and, in some cases, decline in the globally visible performance of the top Japanese universities has been discussed as a result of slow university reforms; slow internationalization due to self-contained training and recruitment of academics and students; and constraints on public investment in higher education, at least compared to top universities in other Asian countries. Indeed, research performance, especially in the fields of science and technology, is linked to financial investment. The national policy for science and technology has become more focused on universities' contribution to the industrial economy through innovation, and research universities have tended to be unable to afford the wide range of daily research activities that could improve their visible performance in focused research areas and attract international attention.

To invest in human resource development, in 2011 the Japanese government launched a policy of fostering "global human resources" to lead in the global economy (Yoshida, 2017). This policy included the creation of a plan to increase the number of Japanese students studying abroad while enhancing campus internationalization through the active acceptance of international students. However, this scheme unfolded against a sustained backdrop of economic nationalism, and the policy is aimed more at providing the internationalized human resources required by Japanese enterprises than at attracting global capital.

3.3 University Reforms without a Prospective Future Vision

The stagnation in public and private investment and slow process of internationalization are evident not only in the higher education sector but also in Japan's industry and society as a whole. The pressure caused by an aging population is becoming a heavy burden on Japan's economy and its ability to sustain and develop the national higher education system and society as a whole.

As mentioned in the introduction to this chapter, in Japan, the term "university reform" is mostly embedded in an inherently national context (i.e., universities are used actively and efficiently to further national development). Until the 1970s, many universities in Japan had experienced turmoil due to radical student movements advocating for the suspension of tuition increases and, later, improvements to the organization of universities (Krauss, 1988; Osaki, 1999). The economic boom in Japan and policy changes (such as the introduction of market mechanisms) among the leading socialist states (the USSR and China) in the 1980s discouraged radical activism among students and academics as well as the communist and socialist parties and movements in general. Under these conditions, in 1984, the national government enacted a policy in which a future vision of education would be developed through discussions by a Provisional Council for Education, which was to be operated directly under the Cabinet Office.

Kariya (2018) argues that, in general aspects—economic growth, welfare, science, technology and civilization—Japan achieved its goal of nation-building to "catch up" with advanced Western countries by the end of the 1980s, but then it lacked a clear policy direction. The Provisional Council under then Prime Minister Yasuhiro Nakasone anticipated the advent of a society based on information and technology and identified systemic reform of universities as a path towards further development of Japanese society as well as the active contribution of Japan to the world in terms of cultural and knowledge diplomacy.

Influenced by international policy trends, neoliberal ideas were actively discussed when formulating the higher education policy vision. Higher education was understood as a knowledge industry and a supplier of highly-skilled human resources and intellectual property in collaboration with industry and the government. Public investment in higher education became more focused on advanced research and technology, and education became more reliant on private funding (Yonezawa, 2019).

By the beginning of the 1990s, it had become clear that the focus of Japan's higher education policy had changed from quantitative expansion to qualitative improvement. In this transformation process, two different ideas were introduced to policy debates about higher education: the idea that the function of education was to provide skills and knowledge and the idea that new public management is a way to apply business and/or commercial management tools and strategies in the public sector including higher education (Kudo, 2003). These two ideas were intertwined in a university reform policy that involved planning and assessment to improve the quality and performance of universities' education, research, and social contribution.

In contrast with the much-admired basic and secondary education of Japan, universities and higher education faced harsh criticism, even as Japan was receiving global praise for its successful development in the 1980s (US Department of Education, 1987). The nation-wide tendency of students and employers to consider only the selectivity of universities as an indicator of prestigiousness produced negative side effects on both students' and employers' appreciation of the benefits of graduate study, which are widely recognized in other countries. Consequently, the national government and university leaders came to recognize a developing crisis in the sector, and university reforms were placed on the agenda in response to neoliberalism, new public management ideas, and, eventually, globalization (Eades et al., 2005).

The government attempted to strengthen the quality assurance system of higher education in the 1990s to ensure the quality of education in the saturated market (Yamamoto, 2010). An interesting combination of US accreditation and UK quality assessment was introduced. Since 2004, all national and local public and private universities have been requested to undergo pass–fail institutional-level quality assurance (accreditation) evaluations every seven years, while professional postgraduate programs must be accredited every five years. In addition, national universities must publish six-year mid-term plans, in which they must aim for improvements in their measurable performance through more efficient use of resources. These planning exercises seem to have produced few tangible positive results (Yamamoto, 2009).

However, the tendency to consider the selectivity of higher education institutions over the quality of education remains strong among both students and employers. In addition, the high graduation rate of all universities and higher education institutions tends to stimulate distrust among employers regarding the skills and competencies of university graduates.

At the beginning of the 2020s, industrial actors still generally prefer to recruit young graduates from prestigious universities without work experience. Japanese enterprises, especially large, established ones, display strong confidence in their tradition of in-house training and career promotion through their internal labor market (Yoshida, 2020). While the preference for master's degree holders in the science and technology fields increased by the end of the twentieth century, doctoral and MBA programs have not been as popular as in other industrial and middle-income countries. Industry leaders are aware of the limitations of the traditional labor market and development practices, and they are engaging in more comprehensive dialogue and collaboration with universities and the government to meet the needs of the globalized knowledge economy (Keidanren, 2020).

Overall, university leaders and staff are required to commit to university reforms, and dialogues among higher education stakeholders have multiplied and deepened. However, the call for university reforms has not been linked to significant and visible improvements and achievements. As a result, university stakeholders are experiencing accumulating stress, and tensions between universities and wider society are becoming more sharply defined.

4. CONCLUSION

Historically, Japan's higher education has been regarded as a model linking higher education with nation-building, especially from East and South-East Asian neighbors. Its early and continuous development since the latter half of the nineteenth century as part of the national education system has given it a strong national identity. This identity includes usage of the Japanese language for instruction and research, focused public investment in science and technology in terms of both research and human resource development, and the nationally self-contained formation of academic professions.

Overall, these characteristics functioned positively to aid Japan in "catching up" with the advanced economies of the West. However, once the country had caught up to some degree, the Japanese higher education system tended to lose sight of its goal for reform and further development. Thus, there remains pressure to carry out reforms for further improvement. At the beginning of the twenty-first century, Japan attempted to strengthen equal partnerships in higher education with its Asian neighbors, taking into account changes in the region in terms of both economy and knowledge. However, these attempts have not reached successful outcomes, mostly because of unstable diplomatic relationships at the national level.

In the last three decades, the presence of higher education systems in the Asian region increased significantly, mainly due to the rapid socio-economic development of East Asia and South-East Asia as well as the dynamic regional frameworks to accelerate international academic and student mobility in both education and research (Chao, 2014; Lo, 2016; Chou and Ravinet, 2017). However, Japan has lost its distinguished position in this region.

The COVID-19 pandemic is drastically changing the environment surrounding Japanese higher education. The suspension of cross-border mobility among students and academics, and the possible shift to online or remote transnational education and research, will have both positive and negative impacts (Yoshimi, 2020). Compared with leading economies, especially English-speaking ones, the financial impact on higher education due to the loss of incoming international students will be relatively modest. However, Japan lacks international competitiveness in transnational education, and its international presence in research, especially in the humanities and social sciences, is becoming increasingly vulnerable.

The growing geopolitical tension between the United States and China and their increasing national and systemic control of academic activities is another concern, especially considering the ambivalent position of Japan's higher education and academic community; it is heavily linked with both the United States and China, while somewhat independent from both in terms of its academic tradition.

The rise of Asian higher education may ultimately lead to the question of whether universities in Japan and its Asian neighbors share a common identity with universities in the West, as the academic community based on the values of autonomy and freedom for pursuing universal knowledge creation (Yonezawa, 2020b). It is critical for academic communities in Japan and Asia to determine whether they can maintain and develop academic and student exchanges and dialogues at the grassroots level across universities and higher education systems in the region and across the regions.

REFERENCES

Altbach, P. G. and Umakoshi, T. (2004). *Asian Universities: Historical Perspectives and Contemporary Challenges*. Baltimore, MD: Johns Hopkins University Press.

Armstrong, S., Dearden, L., Kobayashi, M., and Nagase, N. (2019). "Student loans in Japan: Current problems and possible solutions." *Economics of Education Review*, 71, 120–134.

Asonuma, A. (2002). "Finance reform in Japanese higher education." *Higher Education*, 43/1, 109–125.

Ben-David, J. (2017). *Centers of Learning: Britain, France, Germany, United States*. Abingdon: Routledge.

Central Council for Education (2018). *2040 nen ni muketa Koto Kyoiku no Grand Design* [A Grand Design for Higher Education in 2040]. MEXT.

Chao, R. Y. (2014). "Pathways to an East Asian higher education area: A comparative analysis of East Asian and European regionalization processes." *Higher Education*, 68/4, 559–575.

Chou, M. H. and Ravinet, P. (2017). "Higher education regionalism in Europe and Southeast Asia: Comparing policy ideas." *Policy and Society*, 36/1, 143–159.

Dore, R. (1976). *The Diploma Disease: Education, Qualification and Development*. London: Allen & Unwin.

Eades, J. S., Goodman, R., and Hada, Y. (eds.) (2005). *The "Big Bang" in Japanese Higher Education: The 2004 Reforms and the Dynamics of Change*. Melbourne: Trans Pacific Press.

Fujimura, S. (2015). "Daigakuin kakujū seisaku no yukue" [Issues of Japanese graduate education after the politics of expansion]. *Research in Higher Education*, 47, 57–72.

Geiger, R. L. (1986). *Private Sectors in Higher Education: Structure, Function, and Change in Eight Countries*. Ann Arbor: University of Michigan Press.

Hamanaka, J. (2015). "Daigakuin kaikaku no airo: Hihan no haigo ni aru kigyō jin no mikeiken" [Barriers to graduate school reform in Japan]. *Japanese Journal of Higher Education Research*, 18, 69–87.

Hozawa, Y. (2016). *Kōtō kyōiku kikai no chiiki kakusa* [Local Disparities in Higher Education Opportunities]. Tokyo: Toshindo.

Institute for International Cooperation (2004). *The History of Japan's Educational Development*. Tokyo: Japan International Cooperation Agency.

Itoh, A. (2002). "Higher education reform in perspective: The Japanese experience." *Higher Education*, 43, 7–25.

Itoh, A. (2021). *Senjiki Nihon no Shiritsu Daigaku* [Private Universities in Wartime Japan]. Nagoya: Nagoya University Press.

Kainuma, T. (2018). "Ryugaku no kyaria, koyo ni kansuru inpakuto" [Impact of study abroad experience on career and employment]. In M. Yokota, H. Ota, and Y. Shimmi (eds.), *Ryugaku ga kyaria to jinsei ni ataeru inpakuto* [Impact of Study Abroad Experience on Career and Life], Tokyo: Gakubunsha, 211–235.

Kariya, T. (2018). Daigaku seiakusetsu' ni yoru mondai kōchiku to iu < mondai > [Problem construction based on "university innate evilness" <Problem>. In Sato, I. (ed.) *50-Nen-me no 'daigakukaitai' 20-nen-go no 'daigaku saisei' ["University dismantling" in the 50th year "University revitalization" 20 years later]*. (pp. 47–104.) Kyoto: Kyoto University Press.

Kariya, T. and Rappleye, J. (2020). *Education, Equality, and Meritocracy in a Global Age: The Japanese Approach*. New York: Teachers College Press.

Keidanren (2020). *Society 5.0 Ni muketa daigaku kyōiku to saiyō ni kansuru kangaekata* [Perspectives on University Education and Recruitment for Society 5.0]. Keidanren.

Kim, T. (2018). *Forming the Academic Profession in East Asia: A Comparative Analysis*. New York: Routledge.

Kobayashi, M. (2020). "International comparison of higher education cost sharing and Japanese challenges." *Japan Labor Issues*, 20/4, 29–44.

Kosugi, R. (2017). "Daisotsu-sha no shigoto no hen'yō" [Changes in graduates' employment]. *Japanese Journal of Higher Education Research*, 20, 71–92.

Krauss, E. S. (1988). "The 1960s' Japanese student movement in retrospect." In G. L. Bernstein and H. Fukui (eds.), *Japan and the World* (pp. 95–115). London: Macmillan.

Kudo, H. (2003). "Between the 'governance' model and the policy evaluation act: New public management in Japan." *International Review of Administrative Sciences*, 69/4, 483–504.

Lebra-Chapman, J. (1973). *Okuma Shigenobu: Statesman of Meiji Japan*. Canberra: Australian National University Press.

Lo, W. Y. W. (2016). "The concept of greater China in higher education: Adoptions, dynamics and implications." *Comparative Education*, 52/1, 26–43.

Low, M. (2005). *Building a Modern Japan: Science, Technology, and Medicine in the Meiji Era and Beyond*. Dordrecht: Springer.

Marginson, S. (2011). "Higher education in East Asia and Singapore: Rise of the Confucian model." *Higher Education*, 61/5, 587–611.

Matsuoka, R. (2015). "Gearing up for university entrance examinations: Untangling relationships between school tracking, high school seniors' educational expectations, and their efforts." *Waseda Institute for Advanced Study Research Bulletin*, 7, 29–40.

Matsuoka, R. (2019). *Kyōiku kakusa* [Educational Disparity]. Tokyo: Chuko Shinsho.

Mok, K, H. (2012). "The quest for innovation and entrepreneurship: The changing role of university in East Asia." *Globalisation, Societies and Education*, 10/3, 317–335.

Nakayama, S. (1989). "Independence and choice: Western impacts on Japanese higher education." *Higher Education*, 18/1, 31–48.

Narsimhan, S. (1999). *Japanese Perceptions of China in the Nineteenth Century: Influence of Fukuzawa Yukichi*. New Delhi: Phoenix Publishing House.

Nature Index (2019). Nature Index Japan [Special issue]. *Nature Index*, 567/7748.

Osaki, H. (1999). *Daigaku Kaikaku 1945–1999* [University Reform 1945–1999]. Tokyo: Yuhikaku.

Ota, H. (2018). "Internationalization of higher education: Global trends and Japan's challenges." *Educational Studies in Japan*, 12, 91–105.

Sato, I. (2019). *Daigaku kaikaku no meiso* [The Vagaries of University Reform]. Tokyo: Chikuma Shobo.

Terasaki, M. (2020). *Nihon Kindai Daigaku Shi* [History of Modern Japanese Universities]. Tokyo: University of Tokyo Press.

Toyoda, N. (2019). *Kagaku rikkoku no kiki: Shissoku suru Nihon no kenkyū-ryoku* [Crisis of Science-Based Nation Crisis: Japan's Stagnating Research Power]. Tokyo: Toyo Keizai Shimpo.

Tsuchimochi, G. H. (1993). *Education Reform in Postwar Japan: The 1946 US Education Mission*. Tokyo: University of Tokyo Press.

US Department of Education (1987). *Japanese Education Today*. Washington, DC: US Department of Education.

Yamamoto, K. (2004). "Corporatization of national universities in Japan: Revolution for governance or rhetoric for downsizing?" *Financial Accountability & Management*, 20/2, 153–181.

Yamamoto, K. (2010). "Performance-oriented budgeting in public universities." *Journal of Finance and Management*, 7, 43–60.

Yamamoto, K. (2019). "Daigaku shingaku josei ni okeru senkō bun'ya tayō-ka no kaisō-teki haikei: SSM chōsa dēta ni yoru bunseki" [Who studies in non-traditional fields? An analysis of the relationship between female graduates' choice of field of study and their social background]. *Forum Gendai Shakaigaku*, 18, 88–101.

Yamamoto, S. (2009). "Quality assurance and higher education in Japan." In T. W. Bigalke and D. E. Neubauer (eds.), *Higher Education in Asia/Pacific* (pp. 111–120). Basingstoke: Palgrave Macmillan.

Yonezawa, A. (2013). "The development of private higher education in Japan since the 1960s: A reexamination of a center–periphery paradigm." In A. Maldonado-Maldonado and R. M. Bassett (eds.), *The Forefront of International Higher Education: A Festschrift in Honor of Philip G. Altbach* (pp. 189–200). Dordrecht: Springer.

Yonezawa, A. (2016). "Can East Asian universities break the spell of hierarchy? The challenge of seeking an inherent identity." In C. Collins, M. N. N. Lee, J. N. Hawkins, and D. E. Neubauer (eds.), *The Palgrave Handbook of Asia Pacific Higher Education* (pp. 247–260). London: Palgrave Macmillan.

Yonezawa, A. (2019). "National university reforms introduced by the Japanese government: University autonomy under fire?" In C. Wan, M. N. N. Lee, and H. Loke (eds.), *The Governance and Management of Universities in Asia* (pp. 81–93). Abingdon: Routledge.

Yonezawa, A. (2020a). "Challenges of the Japanese higher education amidst population decline and globalization." *Globalisation, Societies and Education*, 18/1, 43–52.

Yonezawa, A. (2020b). "Do we share a common university identity?" *International Higher Education*, 100, 4–5.

Yonezawa, A., Horta, H., and Osawa, A. (2016). "Mobility, formation and development of the academic profession in science, technology, engineering and mathematics in East and South East Asia." *Comparative Education*, 52/1, 44–61.

Yonezawa, A., Hoshino, A., and Shimauchi, S. (2017). "Inter- and intra-regional dynamics on the idea of universities in East Asia: Perspectives from Japan." *Studies in Higher Education*, 42/10, 1839–1852.

Yonezawa, A. and Huang, F. (2018). "Towards universal access amid demographic decline: High participation higher education in Japan." In B. Cantwell, S. Marginson, and A. Smolentseva (eds.), *High Participation Systems of Higher Education* (pp. 418–438). Oxford: Oxford University Press.

Yonezawa, A. and Inenaga, Y. (2017). "The consequences of market-based mass postsecondary education: Japan's challenges." In P. G. Altbach, L. Reisberg, and H. de Wit (eds.), *Responding to Massification: Differentiation in Postsecondary Education Worldwide* (pp. 89–98). Rotterdam: Sense Publishers.

Yonezawa, A., Nakatsui, I., and Kobayashi, T. (2002). "University rankings in Japan." *Higher Education in Europe*, 27/4, 373–382.

Yoshida, A. (2017). "'Global human resource development' and Japanese university education: 'Localism' in actor discussions." *Educational Studies in Japan*, 11, 83–99.

Yoshida, W. (2020). "Kokunai Daikigyo no Shinsotsu Saiyo ni Okeru Gakkoreki no Ichizuke" [How large Japanese firms regard college selectivity when hiring new graduates: A quantitative analysis of firm-level data on new hires]. *The Journal of Educational Sociology*, 107, 89–109.

Yoshimi, S. (2020). "Online university, pandemics and the long history of globalization." *Inter-Asia Cultural Studies*, 21/4, 636–644.

CHAPTER 31

JAPAN

Challenges in Internationalization of its Higher Education Sector

MIKI SUGIMURA AND SHINOBU YUME YAMAGUCHI

INTERNATIONALIZATION of higher education includes promoting flows of students and researchers, cultivating innovative international programs such as joint or double degrees, and promoting collaboration with foreign or other international higher education institutions. This chapter focuses on internationalization policies and implementation for higher education in Japan since the 1980s which primarily aim to attract international students by improving admissions systems and creating a supportive environment to integrate international students into Japanese higher education systems. These policies reflect Japan's strategy of positioning the country as a network hub for knowledge exchange in Asia.

While the government reached its target in 2019 of attracting 300,000 international students in Japan, there has been negligible progress, however, on increasing the number of outbound Japanese students studying abroad. This chapter assesses the outcomes of internationalization policies for higher education in Japan, including their positive influence on the establishment of a diverse range of programs, and limitations and challenges to implementation; and considers future prospects for internationalization in the context of regional and global educational mobility.

1. THE EVOLUTION OF JAPANESE HIGHER EDUCATION POLICY FOR INTERNATIONALIZATION

1.1 Early Stages: Policies Focused on Attracting International Students

The current policy of the government of Japan for international students originated from the country's post-war strategy for higher education, which was developed through recommendations of the Japanese National Commission for UNESCO and the Science Council of Japan. In 1954, the Ministry of Education (MOE) established a government scholarship system for international students in higher education institutions in Japan, supporting 23 out of a total of 111 students who arrived during the year. The number of international students remained low and stable during the 1960s and 1970s (Kudo, 2001). After Japan joined the Organisation for Economic Co-operation and Development (OECD) in 1964, a visit from an OECD Education Research Team in 1970 urged Japan to increase its commitment to international cooperation (Tojo, 2010). The Science Council of Japan (SCJ) and the Central Council for Education (CCE) recommended that the government prioritize the identification of core international research fields, and establish a dedicated system for accepting international students. The recommendations also emphasized the importance of financial support for universities to develop international collaboration on education and research.

During the 1980s in Japan, internationalization was considered an important keyword across the economy, politics, and education. In 1983, the government announced a comprehensive policy to promote international students studying in Japan, as a contribution to international understanding and cooperation. It also aimed to advance human resource capacity building for developing countries. Specifically, the government laid out the Recommendation on International Student Policy for the 21st Century – 100,000 International Student Plan. The policy was unprecedented in setting a quantitative target for inbound international students. It was based on recommendations by the Council Committee (1983), reflecting the growing trend towards expansion of international student exchange in France, Germany, the United Kingdom, and the United States. An analysis by Takeda (2006) identified two main reasons for the adoption of the plan. First, it was a political decision by the late Prime Minister Yasuhiro Nakasone, who recognized that Japan's higher education sector lacked competitiveness compared to other developed countries. Second, as Japan was facing intense trade friction with leading countries, the business community urgently needed to exchange human resources with foreign countries. This was evident in the creation of a foundation by business leaders which established the International University of Japan (IUJ) in Niigata, with postgraduate programs aiming to develop professionals who will help to internationalize Japanese enterprises.

During this period the government focused on attracting international students to study in Japan. When the 100,000 International Students Plan was launched in 1983, there were only 10,482 international students (Ministry of Education, Culture, Sports, Science and Technology [MEXT], 2008). Its initial period (1983–1992) prioritized establishing basic infrastructure for international students, to facilitate an accelerated increase in numbers during the latter period (1993–2000). For each international student cohort, the plan aimed for a ratio of 6:3:1 between undergraduate students, postgraduate students, and those studying at specialized language institutions. Private universities and colleges were encouraged to admit more international students, with the goal of accounting for double the number of those studying at national universities. Further, higher education institutions throughout Japan were expected to enroll international students, avoiding concentration in major urban areas. (Ministry of Education [MOE], 1985).

A team of experts analyzed the multiple issues that Japanese higher educational institutions were facing at the time. These included a lack of international recognition for Japanese universities, absence of systematic procedures for admitting international students, difficulty in acquiring Japanese language ability, and insufficient financial support for international students (MOE, 1986). Reflecting this analysis, the government's policy encouraged (i) attracting quality students through an expansion of government scholarships; (ii) establishing proper systems to admit international students; (iii) strengthening Japanese language education; and (iv) improving accommodation facilities for international students. Accordingly, the MOE budget related to international students increased from USD8 million in 1983 to USD34.6 million in 1993. According to the results of an interim evaluation on the implementation of the policy, while a steady increase in the number of international students was recognized, it identified residual problems including regional imbalance due to slower growth in private and prefectural universities and colleges, aging facilities of campus buildings and dormitories, and financial difficulties faced by privately funded students. This report indicated that the four measures laid out in 1983 had not yet been fully implemented (MOE, 1993, pp. 49–64).

During this period, a number of unique research and educational institutions were established, as part of a new approach to internationalizing higher education in Japan. The National Graduate Institute of Policy Studies (GRIPS) was established in Tokyo in 1997, with a focus on hosting postgraduate students from overseas to enhance the quality of their research to an internationally competitive level. In the early 2000s, both Ritsumeikan Asia Pacific University (APU) in Kyushu and Akita International University (AIU) in Tohoku were founded, with the aim to develop and implement international education curriculums for undergraduate students. As mentioned earlier, the IUJ was established in 1982 in Niigata, providing postgraduate programs in response to the urgent need of the business community for globally competitive professionals. Further, the Office of the Prime Minister led the development of a globally competitive research institute in Okinawa in 2001. The Okinawa Institute of Science and Technology Graduate University (OIST) was founded in 2012, with more than half of its faculty members from overseas. OIST has become recognized as a highly competitive postgraduate school, with international students comprising over 80 percent of the total cohort. The acceptance rate was less than 1 percent in 2020 (Advanced Academic Agency, 2020).

In 2003, the number of international students in Japan reached 109,508 (Figure 31.1), of which 10 percent were supported by Government of Japan scholarships. Regarding regional distribution, over 90 percent were from Asian countries, with 80 percent coming from China, the Republic of Korea, and Taiwan. The majority of the international students were in degree programs, while 6.2 percent (6,750) were students on short-term programs. Overall, 48 percent (52,981) belonged to undergraduate programs and 26 percent (28,305) were in postgraduate programs, while 19 percent were

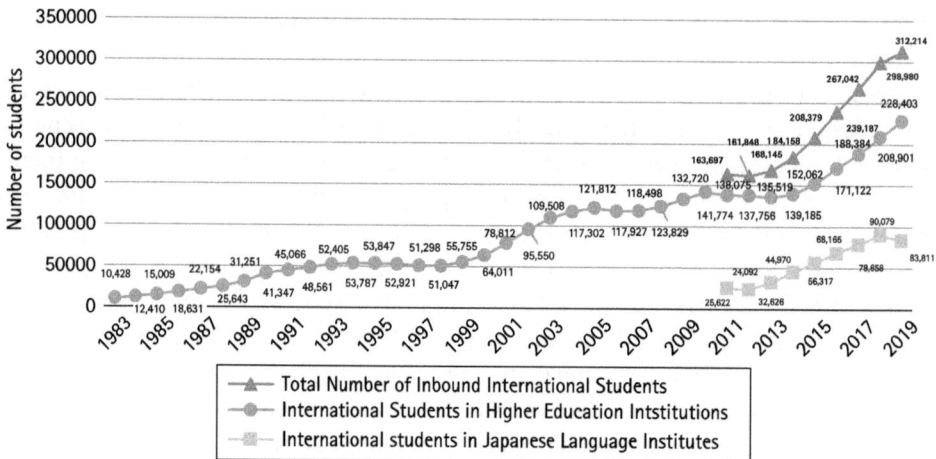

FIGURE 31.1 Number of inbound international students to Japan, 1983–2019

Source: Ministry of Education, Culture, Sports, Science and Technology (MEXT) (2020).

Note: The statistics from 2011 onwards consists of three categories: (1) the number of Japanese language institutes, (2) higher education institutes, and (3) total number of inbound international students. Because the two kinds of visa "studying at universities (Ryugaku)" and "leaning Japanese language and culture at Japanese language institutes (Shugaku)" were unified into one type of visa called "Ryugaku" from 2011, both have been included.

engaged in studies at specialized schools. Private institutions accounted for 70 percent of international students (78,451), while 26 percent (28,305) belonged to the national universities and 2.5 percent (2,707) to prefectural universities.

The number of international students studying in Japan during this initial (20-year) period is closely related to the immigration policies of Japan (Shiraishi, 2006). During the first ten years (1983–1992), the number increased steadily, reaching 48,561 in 1992. This was mainly because Japanese language schools received more international students in preparation for degree studies at universities and colleges. The Ministry of Justice allowed international students to work as part-time employees as the country's economy was growing rapidly. Over the next seven years, however, the number of international students only increased to 52,755 (1999). One of the reasons was a stricter immigration policy with greater controls on entry procedures and more restrictive criteria, as the government considered an increase in illegal employment as a problem. Between 2000 and 2003, the number of international students increased again from 64,011 (2000) to 109,058 (2003). This increase was achieved by relaxing the criteria for student visas after a recommendation from the Report of the Advisory Committee on International Students Policy (1999) recognized international students as an "intellectual contribution to the international society."

Although the target of 100,000 students was achieved in 2003, an evaluation of the initial period of internationalization of higher education in Japan by CCE found several quantitative and qualitative issues. Reflecting the rapid growth of the global economy and international trends in education, the number of international students studying in 50 leading countries for international student exchange programs increased by

170 percent in a ten-year period (1988–1998) from 940,000 to 1.6 million. This saw non-English speaking countries in Europe, including France and Germany, achieving significant increases in inbound international students in line with their national strategies. In Japan, however, international students continued to constitute a small share (2.6 percent) of students in higher education compared to other OECD countries such as France (7.6 percent). The CCE further analyzed this trend and identified two main issues: the financial burden of living in Japan for international students, and the inadequate support system in place at universities and colleges in Japan that host international students. In this analysis, regional imbalance in the home countries of international students was again emphasized. Eighty percent of international students were from China, reflecting the country's rapid economic growth. Simplification of immigration procedures and improved services for foreign residents also advanced this trend. Although the original policy objective of building human capacity in developing countries was achieved, the regional imbalance remained a crucial issue.

Multiple concerns were also raised from a qualitative perspective. These included the quality of international students, insufficient academic and administrative support systems, illegal employment of international students beyond permitted hours, and limited job opportunities at Japanese enterprises upon graduation.

Based on the CCE's evaluation and recommendations, the MOE introduced further policies in 2004 to promote Japanese higher education programs beyond the country's borders. This authorized foreign universities to establish campuses located in Japan, and branches of Japanese universities to be set up overseas. Starting in 2007, universities and colleges were granted flexibility in their academic calendars, and encouraged to start their academic programs in the autumn semester to align with the international academic standard. Further, a quarter system was approved in 2013 to accommodate flexible enrollment of students from overseas.

Despite the efforts of the government and higher education institutions between the 1980s and the early 2000s, there was little international recognition of reforms in Japanese higher education. For example, in a comparison by Altbach and Knight (2007) of achievements in internationalization of higher education across the globe, Japan was omitted from a set of influential examples in Asia and the Pacific.

1.2 Internationalization of Higher Education in the Context of Japan's Revitalization Strategy

In the mid-2000s, the then-Prime Minister Abe presented his grand plan of positioning Japan as a bridge between Asia and the world. In 2007, the Asian Gateway Initiative was launched as a key strategy to revitalize Japan through mobilizing people, products, funds, culture, and information (Council for Asian Gateway Initiatives, 2007). It aimed to strengthen links between Japan and the growing economy of Asia, and emphasized that Japan should serve as a platform for intellectual exchange and communication.

In this context, higher education was featured as one of the top seven areas of focus. Two specific goals were identified: (i) improving the global competitiveness of Japanese higher education through mutual exchange of young people; and (ii) fostering a networked hub of high-achieving students in the region.

Experts on educational reform have highlighted the unique features of strategies related to internationalization of Japanese higher education during this period (Ninomiya, 2008; Sugimura, 2015a). First, international exchange programs were elevated as an important element of national strategy for the first time. Accepting international students was no longer considered part of Official Development Assistance (ODA) for developing countries. Instead, increasing the number of international students in Japan was seen as a vital investment for building a network of human resources, and recognized as an important step towards creating an attractive environment for foreigners through collaboration with industry and local communities. Second, the policy introduced an ambitious commitment to attracting 5 percent of the world's international students to Japan annually. This was an epoch-making decision, adopting the concept of a relative goal in the context of the international student market, as opposed to a static quantitative target. Third, to increase opportunities for Japanese youth to study abroad, short-term programs including offshore programs were highly encouraged through incentives and subsidies. Fourth, the importance of career development for international students was emphasized through increased support by Japanese businesses and enterprises.

In 2007, Japan's long-term strategic principle, Innovation 25, was endorsed by the Cabinet. It highlighted the further importance of international student strategy for creating an international network of human resources. In 2008, the then-Prime Minister Yasuo Fukuda announced the 300,000 International Students Plan to be achieved by 2020. The policy was supported by five concrete measures: (i) creating a one-stop service for academic and admissions procedures; (ii) improving entrance examination systems by providing on-site interviews overseas; (iii) establishing degree programs taught in English; (iv) connecting international students with local communities and enterprises; and (v) assisting international students with career development in Japan (MEXT, 2008).

After this plan was adopted, Japanese higher education policy became more strategic and reforms of university governance were undertaken. For example, the Global 30 Project launched in 2009 provided funding to 13 selected core universities to promote an international academic environment, including degree programs conducted entirely in English (MEXT, n.d.). These universities were expected to enhance inter-university networks for sharing educational resources by establishing overseas offices that can be jointly used by all Japanese universities. The project supported innovative activities, leading to the creation of more courses and curriculums in English, ranging from environmental science to East Asian culture and society. It also improved admissions systems by providing on-site interviews at overseas locations for international students, provided more opportunities for cooperation with industry for career development, and expanded academic networking and sharing of resources between universities. Further, to attract international students strategically, shared overseas offices for universities were established in eight cities across seven countries, serving as liaison offices for studying in Japan.

During the same period, positive steps were taken to encourage Japanese students to study abroad. The Go Global Japan project launched in 2011 provided financial support for Japanese students studying abroad. The Council on Promotion of Human Resources and Globalization Development was established in collaboration with multiple government ministries. With the experience of the Great East Japan Earthquake in March 2011, the government was compelled to foster a new generation of creativity, developing "global talent" for the twenty-first century with strong communication skills, problem-solving skills, foreign language proficiency, and other global competencies. The government also initiated the Inter-University Exchange Project to develop international cooperation and exchange programs, taking advantage of the strengths of each university. The main purpose of the project is promoting international student exchange programs with partner universities in target countries and regions,[1] with a special focus on quality assurance.

1.3 Internationalization and University Governance Reform

The government's most recent policy initiative is the Top Global University Project (TGU project), launched in 2014—a decade-long program engaging 37 Japanese universities to lead internationalization through innovative practices and university reforms. Its objective is to position Japanese higher education to lead the country's growth by attracting talented researchers and students. It aims to improve the standing of Japan's higher education sector in global rankings, and cultivate skills in students and faculty so they can effectively use problem-solving and cross-cultural communication. To achieve these goals, strengthening and improving the structure and organizational culture of participating universities is seen as necessary to increase their global competitiveness (MEXT, 2014). As part of this effort, the project encourages Japanese universities to establish specific linkages with leading universities overseas.

Importantly, the TGU project urges participating universities to implement university governance reforms. Sugimura (2015b) analyzed the important difference between this project and previous initiatives. In the past, internationalization initiatives such as Global 30 focused on tangible outcomes such as increasing the number of incoming and outgoing students, as well as establishing new curriculums taught in English. In contrast,

---

[1] The target countries and regions were: (i) Japan/China/Republic of Korea's "Campus Asia" and the USA (FY 2011), (ii) ASEAN (FY 2012), (iii) ASEAN International Mobility for Students (AIMS) program (FY 2013), (iv) Russia and India (FY 2014), (v) Latin America and Turkey (FY 2015), (vi) the second Campus Asia and ASEAN countries (FY 2016), (vii) Russia and India (FY 2017), (viii) USA (FY 2018), (ix) the European Union (FY 2019), (x) Africa (FY 2020), and (xi) the Third Campus Asia and ASEAN countries (FY 2021).

the new project focuses on the decision-making mechanisms within universities that enable implementation of internationalization, as a part of long-term governance reform. The need for governance reforms in Japanese universities have already been highlighted in the Central Council on Education Report (1995), which called for the heads of universities to have greater decision-making authority. Specifically, the Japan Association of Corporate Executives (2012) and the CCE (2014) criticized the heavy reliance on faculty meetings within university governance structures and recommended assigning more authority to the head of each higher education institution. In 2015, revisions of the School Education Law and the National University Corporation Law recognized the role of the faculty council as a consultative body to support the management of each institution.

The TGU project also mandated several specific requirements for the universities, including an annual salary system, a tenure track system for faculty mobility, an active international recruitment system, an evaluation system in line with international standards, international recruitment, and the involvement of external experts as advisory board members (MEXT, 2014). These measures were introduced to the Japanese universities with the intention of responding to international standards reflecting the overseas employment system.

The number of foreign faculty members has increased slightly in recent years with the progress of internationalization. According to MEXT (2008), before the Global 30 project there were 5,760 foreign faculty members (approximate figure) at Japanese universities, accounting for 3.4 percent of the total of 167,600 in 2007. Along with promoting international mobility for students, the CCE recommended appointing foreign faculty members and provided financial support for this through the Global COE Program and the Global 30 Project. Further, the Foreign Research Fellowship Project was launched to recruit prominent faculty members and young foreign researchers from overseas. However, as of 2019 there were still only 8,800 foreign faculty members (approximate figure), 4.7 percent of the total of 187,800 (MEXT, 2020). This ratio is extremely small compared to other countries in Europe and North America.

2. Issues and Opportunities for Internationalization of Higher Education in Japan

2.1 Issues for Internationalization Policy and Implementation in Higher Education

With the implementation of the 300,000 International Students Plan, the total number of inbound international students in Japan reached 312,214 in 2019 (Figure 31.1).

Approximately 73 percent of students belonged to higher education institutions, while the rest were students of Japanese language institutes (MEXT, 2020).

While recognizing the achievement of the quantitative target, MEXT (2018) identified a number of issues requiring further attention. On the first objective of improving global competitiveness of Japanese higher education, uneven implementation at the undergraduate level across the universities remained prevalent, particularly for private universities and institutions located outside urban areas. Further, no improvements were made on the lack of strategic recruitment of high school students from overseas.

Considering the plan's contribution to developing human resources in Asia and beyond, it has been successful in promoting exchange of students between Japan and Asia, with 94.6 percent of international students coming from countries in the region (as of 2020). While this balance has remained stable for the last two decades, the countries of origin have diversified. In 2000, when the total number of international students was about 64,000, the top five countries and regions were China (50.5 percent), the Republic of Korea (20.1 percent), Taiwan (6.5 percent), Malaysia (2.9 percent), and Indonesia (2.1 percent). However, in the 2010s, the number of students from Nepal and Vietnam started to increase. In 2020, the top five countries and regions were China (43.6 percent), Vietnam (22.3 percent), Nepal (8.6 percent), The Republic of Korea (5.6 percent), and Taiwan (2.5 percent) (JASSO, 2001, 2021). One of the reasons for this, as shown in Figure 31.1, was the unification of student visas in 2011, which categorized all students attending Japanese language schools as international students. The future plan of MEXT is to encourage student exchange with diverse regions of the globe. MEXT highly recommends taking advantage of the network of graduates of Japanese higher education institutions, including the effective use of social networks. Further, looking at trends in the gender balance of international students between 2000 and 2020, male students were between 51 percent and 56 percent of the total while female students remained between 44 percent and 49 percent (JASSO, 2001, 2021). Further investigation is required, including the gender balance in different fields of study.

The implementation of policies for internationalizing Japanese higher education over four decades has created a growing imbalance between inbound students in Japan and outbound Japanese students overseas. As shown in Figure 31.2, in 2020 there were 115,146 Japanese students studying overseas, while the number of inbound students reached over 300,000 in 2019. Of the Japanese students studying abroad, 66 percent (76,464) belonged to short-term programs (less than one month in duration), in a total of 32 different countries. Eighty percent of outbound Japanese students were located in North America and Europe, with 60 percent in North America.

The Go Global Japan project mentioned above contributed to an increasing number of Japanese students studying abroad. It should be noted, however, that fewer Japanese students are now enrolling in degree courses in the United States which was historically the most popular destination of Japanese students. Several studies have asserted that this is due to Japanese students' inward orientation, influenced by long-lasting economic stagnation (Yokota and Kobayashi, 2013; Ota, 2014; Kojima et al., 2015; National Institute for Youth Education, 2019). These studies explain that the younger generation

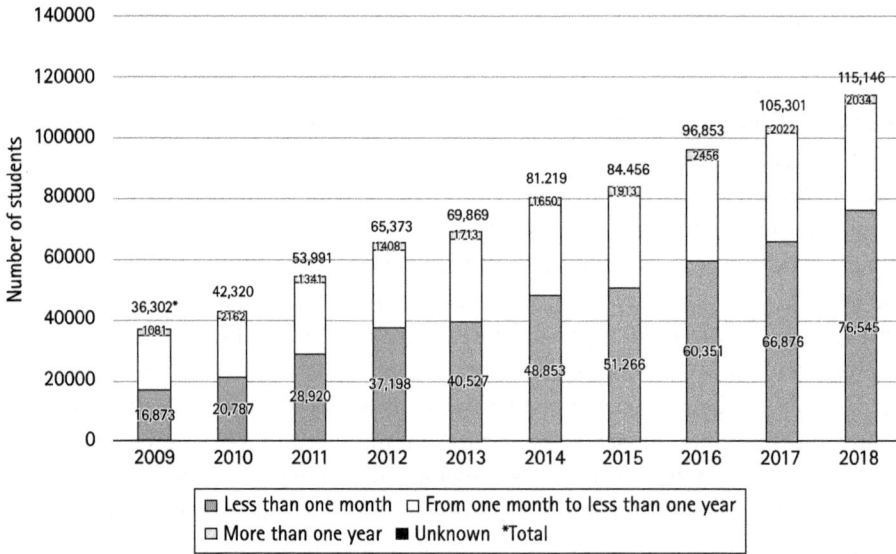

FIGURE 31.2 Short-term outbound students from Japan, 2009–2018

Source: Created by the Authors from "Research on Outbound Students from Japan," JASSO.

tends to be satisfied with student life in Japan and considers studying abroad a risky choice. In addition, Japan's private sector recruitment system no longer favors foreign degrees, and thus, there is less incentive for Japanese students to study abroad. Further, the current rigid credit transfer system of Japanese universities is considered a barrier to studying abroad.

In analyzing the achievement of internationalization of higher education, support from the private sector community has also been vital (CCE, 2014). In 2016, as part of the Japan Revitalization Strategy, the government announced a goal of raising the employment rate for international students with degrees from Japanese universities to 50 percent. As of 2018, however, it remained at 35 percent, including both undergraduate and postgraduate international students. It is evident that employment opportunities in Japanese enterprises are an attractive proposition for international students considering studying in Japan. Close collaboration between academia and the business sector will continue to be vital in attracting young people with high potential to choose Japan as their study destination.

Further, the Prime Minister's Office of Japan announced specific measures to strengthen support for highly skilled foreign nationals (Prime Minister's Office, 2021). This reflects the need to accelerate innovation and the productivity of the Japanese economy in a highly competitive international market, by welcoming foreign experts. In addition, this strategy aims to help cope with Japan's demographic challenges of an aging society and decreasing population. These measures will support foreign experts in cooperation with Japanese companies and local communities, seeking to create an environment to promote their active contribution to Japanese society. Specifically, in

2020, the Foreign Resident Support Center (FRESC) was established in Tokyo to promote recruitment of foreign students by Japanese companies, including through internship opportunities and other employment-related initiatives. Other measures include support for foreign entrepreneurs, including startups, in cooperation with the Japan External Trade Organization (JETRO). For example, Kyoto Overseas Business Center is collaborating with Doshisha University, a local university, to connect their MBA students to local business and enterprises.

2.2 Diversification of International Programs

Despite the multiple issues analyzed above, one area in which internationalization of Japanese higher education has clearly made a significant contribution is the development of joint degree and double degree programs. In 2014, the Central Council for Education of Japan proposed the Guidelines for Building International Joint Diploma Programs, providing an effective mechanism for Japanese universities to develop programs to confer degrees jointly with foreign universities. Since the government granted permission for universities to establish such programs in 2014, a range of unique initiatives has been developed, mobilizing the strengths, resources, and networks of each university.

Between 2008 and 2018 the number of Japanese universities offering double degree programs doubled from 82 to 170 (Figure 31.3). During the same period, the number of international students accepted under these programs increased nearly nine times. This shows that in the process of internationalizing higher education, various types of educational programs were developed to meet the demand for transnational programs. Greater attention was also paid to quality assurance of the programs, including strengthening the current credit transfer system.

Along with such collaboration, the Government of Japan encouraged faculty collaboration in research and education. In 2018, Japan was one of the 15 highest-producing countries of internationally coauthored articles in science and engineering (National Science Foundation, 2019). However, compared with the top two countries, China and the United States, Japan has fallen far behind in both the absolute number of such articles produced, and its relative share of the total. Aiming to address this, in 2019 MEXT included faculty exchange as an important component of its support, with a budgetary commitment, as part of further enhancing inter-university development initiatives with the EU.

Another key development has been the emergence of a new model of international cooperation in higher education during the last decade. Since 2010, in promoting integration of research into education, collaboration through research-oriented consortiums has been supported by MEXT. Specifically, three joint universities have been established through agreements between the Government of Japan and host countries: the Egypt–Japan University of Science and Technology (E-Just) located in Alexandria (2010), the Malaysia–Japan International Institute of Technology (MJIIT) in Kuala Lumpur (2012),

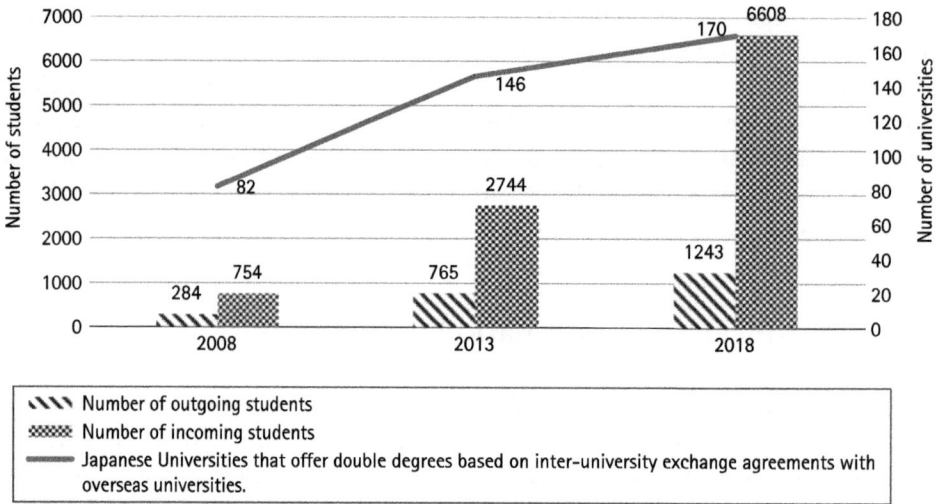

FIGURE 31.3 Number of Japanese universities offering double degree programs and number of outgoing and incoming students participating in double degree programs

Source: Created by the authors from "Status of reform of educational content at universities" (MEXT, 2008, 2013, 2018).

and Vietnam–Japan University in Vietnam (2016). In each case multiple Japanese universities dispatched faculty members to develop joint programs in collaboration with local researchers and professionals. For example, one-third of the faculty members located at MJIIT are from a consortium of 23 Japanese universities. The initiatives aim to promote mobility of students, researchers, and faculty members.

The scheme has been facing some challenges, including coordination between the Japanese universities to effectively develop joint curriculums. With the onset of the COVID-19 pandemic in 2020, some personnel were forced to return home to Japan, and all research and academic activities have been conducted online in coordination with local faculty members. The success of these programs will depend on their ability to cope with this unexpected situation while maintaining quality and the motivation of the students and faculty members.

2.3 The Emergence of "Internationalization at Home"

In the course of developing international programs and schemes, Japanese universities have also created programs through which students can learn and gain experiences with international partners without going overseas. Examples range from diversifying incoming international student groups, to introducing joint online courses with foreign universities, to actively involving students on campus to participate in project-based learning activities with overseas students. Such programs promoting "internationalization at home" aim to connect learners to each other by creating an innovative and collaborative learning environment. While such initiatives are by no means equivalent to living abroad—particularly in the rich cultural and social experience it provides students with, and how it broadens their perspectives—they have become a popular topic in the higher education sector in Japan. Internationalization at home is defined as "the purposeful integration of international and intercultural dimensions into the formal and informal curriculum for all students within domestic learning environments" (Beelen and Jones, 2015, pp. 68–69). Some of the key features of this approach include offering students global and intercultural perspectives, and making purposeful use of cultural diversity in the classroom for inclusive learning, teaching, and assessment practice. It fosters purposeful engagement with international students, and can include virtual mobility through online work with partner universities (Jones and Reiffenrath, 2018). Several initiatives for collaborative online international learning (COIL) have been developed, following the example of Kansai University, which create platforms with financial support from MEXT. For example, a COIL initiative on international health connecting Japan (Sophia University and the University of Shizuoka), the United States (the University of Portland), and Mongolia (Dornogovi Medical School) provided multifaceted and multicultural learning. This initiative promotes critical thinking through collaborative learning among the students of nursing departments who often have limited opportunities to study abroad due to rigid curriculums. Some short-term international courses in Japan illustrate good examples, showing how learners with different cultural backgrounds can effectively discuss social and environment issues with comparative perspectives (Suematsu et al., 2019; Sakurai et al., 2020).

3. THE INFLUENCE OF GLOBAL NETWORKS ON INTERNATIONALIZATION OF HIGHER EDUCATION

3.1 Regional and Global Networks Promoting Student Mobility

During the last two decades, student mobility in higher education has been promoted as a strategy in different parts of the world to increase economic and political competitiveness. The successful European Community Action Scheme for the Mobility of University Students (ERASMUS) was an example of best practice for other nations in terms of promoting educational mobility in the 1990s. In 2000, over 2,700 institutions in Europe participated in the program, which mobilized 110,000 students and 12,000 faculty members within the region.

Taking into account different environments for promoting student mobility in different regions, the question of quality assurance has gained attention in the international community. For example, UNESCO and the OECD have jointly published guidelines on Quality Provision in Cross-Border Higher Education in 2005. This has further contributed to establishing the International Standard Classification of Education (ISCED, 2011)—a comprehensive framework for organizing education programs and qualifications by applying uniform and internationally agreed definitions to facilitate comparisons of education systems across countries.

In Asia and the Pacific, the UNESCO Regional Convention on the Recognition of Qualifications in Higher Education (Tokyo Convention) was adopted unanimously by 26 member countries in 2011 in Tokyo (UNESCO, 2011). It came into effect in 2018, promoting education mobility among higher educational institutions of participating countries (UNESCO Bangkok Asia Pacific Regional Bureau of Education, 2018). The convention aims to support recognition of qualifications, including through effective credit transfer systems, while holding participating institutions accountable for the quality of their programs. In accordance with the Tokyo Convention, the National Information Center for Academic Recognition Japan (NIC) was established in 2019. The NIC's mission is to ensure the credibility of Japanese higher education qualifications and to facilitate recognition of qualifications between Japan and countries in the Asia-Pacific, as well as those of other regions.

Such a movement to support student mobility encourages universities to explore new collaboration and substantive international programs with partner universities and research in Asian regions and the rest of the world. Coupled with the financial support of the Japanese government, it has resulted in an increased number of double degree programs in the last ten years.

3.2 Influence of Regional Networks and Prospects of Internationalization of Higher Education in Japan and Asia

In the context of growing regional and global networks in higher education, the participation of Japanese universities in new intra-regional student mobility programs has become more active and evident since 2010. For example, students have been mobilized between East Asian countries through the Collective Action for Mobility Program of University Students in Asia (CAMPUS Asia) program. This initiative was supported by the second China–Japan–Republic of Korea Summit Meeting in 2009. Ten universities in Japan collaborate with their partner universities in China and the Republic of Korea, creating specific mobility programs for students focusing on their areas of expertise. This has stimulated the interest and motivation of students for participating in diverse research and educational experiences in East Asian countries. The program covers areas ranging from political science and East Asian studies to engineering and environmental science. It is unique in that the university provides students with career development guidance and overseas internships in collaboration with the career's office and outside organizations.

Another example is the ASEAN International Mobility for Students (AIMS), created by the Southeast Asia Ministers of Education Organization – Regional Center for Higher Education and Development (SEAMEO-RIHED). It provides opportunities for Japanese universities to play an active role in regional higher education development beyond the country's borders. This scheme promotes credit transfer systems for universities in Japan and ASEAN countries while focusing on quality assurance. This was in line with Japan's Revitalization Policy, aiming to increase interdependence among countries in Asia as part of socio-economic regionalization.

While many of these university networks are focused on higher education in general, others in the region have formed in relation to specific topics of teaching and research. In 2008, as an initiative of the United Nations University, the Promotion of Sustainability in Postgraduate Education and Research Network (ProSPER.Net) was established. This network is an alliance of leading universities in the Asia-Pacific region that are committed to integrating the principles of sustainable development into postgraduate courses, curriculums, and research. The network also mobilizes knowledge and innovation for substantive joint research projects on a diverse range of sustainability issues, including studies on the impacts of climate change, how to position disaster risk reduction in higher education curriculums, and human–nature coexistence for a sustainable society at the local and regional levels. As of December 2020, ProSPER.Net comprises 50 member universities located in 16 different countries across the region.

Such diverse implementation of regional programs across countries provides evidence of unique initiatives of cross-border collaboration in the region. It illustrates the growing international programs in higher education evolving from quantitative increase of international students to substantive research and leadership training maximizing the strengths of participating institutions.

4. Conclusion

This chapter explored a series of policies promoting internationalization of higher education in Japan, and their implementation. The approach has become more active and strategic since the 1980s, reflecting the changing economic and political position of Japan in Asia and the world. Japan's initial internationalization policy focused on quantitative targets for increasing international students. While two major targets for accepting diverse students from abroad were achieved, several implementation issues have been identified.

Trends in international student mobility have changed significantly over the last three decades, and there is an urgent need to rethink the direction of internationalization of higher education in Japan. The increasing number of transnational and cross-border programs, along with the rapidly changing environment in Asia and the Pacific and beyond, has presented new models for studying abroad. To further consolidate the strength of Japanese higher education in providing high-quality programs that are attractive to international students, as well as to motivate more Japanese students to study abroad, there is a need to carefully analyze the positioning of higher education within national strategy. The first step should be to move beyond education programs focused on increasing the number of international students. Instead, efforts should focus on creating a learning environment involving all kinds of participants, including Japanese and international students, as well as learners from the business sector and local communities. In particular, quality programs need to be developed at the undergraduate level so that young people can learn from each other in a unique learning environment. Japanese universities must carefully analyze the strengths and distinct characteristics of each institution so as to develop attractive education and research environments, together with effective and accessible administrative support. The government of Japan must identify the most relevant positioning of Japanese higher education to increase its competitiveness in the Asia-Pacific region and in the world. Further, the gender composition of international students will need to be carefully considered in the context of promoting diversity.

Moreover, while instruction in English has become more widespread, many important academic subjects including Japanese literature and linguistics, and legal affairs continue to be taught in Japanese, which provides a unique competitive advantage for Japanese universities. Indeed, some inbound international students are eager to study their specific subjects in Japanese. This illustrates that internationalization should go beyond providing programs taught in English, to encompass the creation of more meaningful and quality programs for students. It is also important to widely disseminate information on studying abroad in Japan, including Japanese language education programs as well as employment opportunities after graduation. Japanese universities should take concerted action to recruit high-achieving students from overseas high schools utilizing their recruitment systems, including overseas offices in different parts of the regions of the world.

The future of higher education of Japan needs to be discussed in the context of the Society 5.0 concept, including the "super-smart society" (CCE, 2018). The fourth industrial revolution represents the unprecedented influence of information technology on society, including the use of big data, the internet of things (IOT), artificial intelligence (AI), and augmented robotics. As we shift from a labor-intensive economy to a knowledge-intensive economy, the meaning of higher education needs to be revisited. There is a need for educational opportunities beyond national borders, and more open and collaborative initiatives. Further, higher education will be expected to play a key role in developing future generations that can cope with unexpected and unprecedented situations. This must be reflected and incorporated in the internationalization of higher education as it continues to progress and evolve, in particular through advancing student-centered learning and continuing education opportunities.[2]

---

[2] The views expressed in this chapter are those of the authors and do not necessarily reflect the views of the United Nations University.

References

Advanced Academic Agency (2020). "Attracting world class human resources to OIST." Interview article, *Innovative Learning Online*, October (in Japanese). https://www.sentan kyo.jp/articles/37a698ae-72c4-43fd-aa1e-bb1de6b3af25, accessed January 3, 2021.

Advisory Committee on International Students Policy (1999). *Development of Intellectual International Contribution and New Policy of International Students: International Students Policy after the year of 2000.*

Altbach, P. G and Knight, J. (2007). "The internationalization of higher education: Motivations and realities." *Journal of Studies in International Education*, 11/3–4, 290–305.

Beelen, J. and Jones, E. (2015). "Redefining internationalization at home." In A. Curaj, L. Matei, R. Pricopie, J. Salmi, and P. Scott (eds.), *The European Higher Education Area: Between Critical Reflections and Future Policies* (pp. 59–72). Dordrecht: Springer.

Central Council for Education (2003). "Development of new international education policy: Expansion and improvement of quality of international students exchange." December ("Arata na Ryugakusei Seisaku no Tenkai ni Tsuite: Ryugakusei Koryu no Kakudai to Shitsu no Kojo wo Mezashite") (in Japanese). https://www.mext.go.jp/b_menu/shingi/chukyo/chukyoo/toushin/03121801/009.pdf, accessed March 7, 2020.

Central Council for Education: Working Group on the Internationalization of Universities, Japan (2014). "Guidelines for building international joint diploma programs including double and joint degree programs." https://www.mext.go.jp/component/b_menu/shingi/toushin/__icsFiles/afieldfile/2015/04/17/1356863_1.pdf

Central Council for Education: Working Group on University System and Education Reform (2018). "International students policy and post-accepting 300,000 international students policy." https://www.mext.go.jp/b_menu/shingi/chukyo/chukyo4/043/siryo/1404629.htm, accessed November 29, 2020.

Council for Asian Gateway Initiatives (2007). *Asian Gateway Initiative.* May. http://japan.kantei.go.jp/gateway/index_e.html, accessed March 7, 2020.

Council Committee to the Prime Minister focusing on the International Students Policy of Japan towards the 21st Century (1983). "Proposal on the international students policy of Japan towards the 21st century." August ("21 Seiki eno Ryugakusei Seisaku ni Kansuru Teigen") (in Japanese).

Japan Society for the Promotion of Science (JSPS) (2014). https://www.jsps.go.jp/english/e-tgu/outline.html, accessed April 18, 2020.

Japan Student Services Organization (JASSO) (2001 and 2021). "Statistics of international students in Japan 2000/2020." https://www.studyinjapan.go.jp/ja/statistics/zaiseki/index.html, accessed May 2, 2021.

Japan Student Services Organization (JASSO) (2019). "International students in Japan 2018." https://www.jasso.go.jp/en/about/statistics/intl_student/__icsFiles/afieldfile/2019/04/19/data18_brief_e.pdf, accessed April 18, 2020.

Jones, E. and Reiffenrath, T. (2018). "Internationalisation at home in practice." European Association of International Education (EAIE) website https://www.eaie.org/blog/internationalisation-at-home-practice.html, accessed April 19, 2020.

Kojima, N. et al. (2015). "Inward-oriented Japanese students and international exchange." *Sogo Hoken Kagaku*, 31, 35–42. Health Service Center, Hiroshima University.

Kudo, S. (2001). *Transformation of International Student Exchange and Current Status.* Tokyo: The Asian Students Cultural Association.

Ministry of Education (MOE) (1985). "Development of Japan's international student exchange – 100,000 International Student Plan." *Monthly Journal of Education*, 1301, 34–39 (in Japanese).

Ministry of Education (MOE) (1986). "Second report on education reform by Council of Education." *Monthly Journal of Education*, 1309, 17 (in Japanese).

Ministry of Education (MOE) (1993). "Current status of international student exchange and policy implementation." *Monthly Journal of Education*, 1397, 44–51 (in Japanese).

Ministry of Education, Culture, Sports, Science and Technology (MEXT) website on Global 30 Project (n.d). https://www.mext.go.jp/en/policy/education/highered/title02/detail02/sdetail02/1373894.htm, accessed March 10, 2020.

Ministry of Education, Culture, Sports, Science and Technology (MEXT) (2008). *Outline of the Student Exchange System: Study in Japan and Abroad*. https://www.mext.go.jp/a_menu/kou tou/ryugaku/081210/001.pdf, accessed March 10, 2020.

Ministry of Education, Culture, Sports, Science and Technology (MEXT) (2008, 2013, 2018). *Status of Reform of Educational Content at Universities*. https://www.mext.go.jp/a_menu/koutou/daigaku/04052801/005.htm, accessed January 17, 2021.

Ministry of Education, Culture, Sports, Science and Technology (MEXT) (2008, 2020). *Statistics Handbook* [Monbukagakusho Tokei Yoran]. https://warp.ndl.go.jp/info:ndljp/pid/11293659/www.mext.go.jp/b_menu/toukei/002/002b/mokuji20.htm, accessed May 21, 2021. https://www.mext.go.jp/b_menu/toukei/002/002b/1417059_00003.htm, accessed May 21, 2021.

Ministry of Education, Culture, Sports, Science and Technology (MEXT) (2009). *On the International Collaborative Program Scheme* [Daigaku ni okeru Kyouikukatei no Kyodo Jisshi Seido ni kansuru Shitsugioutojikou]. https://www.mext.go.jp/a_menu/koutou/dai gakukan/1258058.htm, accessed April 18, 2020.

Ministry of Education, Culture, Sports, Science and Technology (MEXT) (2014). *Top Global University Project Application Guidelines*. http://www.jsps.go.jp/j-sgu/data/download/01_s gu_kouboyouryou/pdf, accessed March 15, 2019.

National Institute for Youth Education (2019). *Report on the Secondary School Students' Orientation to Studying Abroad: A Comparative Study among Japan, USA, China and Republic of Korea*.

National Science Foundation (2019). *Science and Engineering Indicators*. Publication Output: U.S. Trends and International Comparisons. https://ncses.nsf.gov/pubs/nsb20206/international-collaboration, accessed May 3, 2021.

Ninomiya, A. (2008). "Strategies for foreign students designed by the council for the Asia gateway initiative and the roles of UMAP: focusing on a possible 'regional students mobility program'." *Ajia Kenkyu*, 54(4). 56–69. (Azia Geitowei Senryaku Kaigi ga Egaku Ryugakusei Senryaku to UMAP no Yakuwari: "Ikinai Ryugaku Kouryuu Keikaku" no Kanousei wo Tyushin toshite) (in Japanese).

Ota, H. (2014). "A study on the inward-looking of Japanese students: Revisiting students' international mindset with exiting data." *Ryugaku Kouru*, 40. July. Japan Students Services Organization (JASSO) (Nihonjin Gakusei no Uchimuki Shiko ni Kansuru Ichikousatsu: Kizon no Deeta ni yoru Kokusai Shikosei Saikou) (in Japanese).

Prime Minister's Office of Japan (2021). *Promoting Active Engagement of Foreign Experts* (in Japanese). https://www.kantei.go.jp/jp/singi/keizaisaisei/portal/foreign_talent/, accessed April 28, 2021.

Sakurai, K. et al. (2020). *Practices and Issues of Short-Term In-Country International Courses.* Sophia University Press [Nihon de Deau Sekai: Kokunai de Jitsugen suru Tanki Syutyugata Kokusai Kenshu] (in Japanese).

Shiraishi, K. (2006). "Transition of number of international students and policy of accepting 100,000 international students from the view point of Japanese immigration policy." *ABK Ryugakusei Mail News*, 61, 1–6. [Ryugakuseisu no Hensen to Nyukan Shisaku kara miru Ryugakusei Juumannin Keikaku] (in Japanese).

Suematsu, K. et al. (2019). *International Collaboration Learning.* Toshindo. [Kokusai Kyodo Kyoushu: Bunkateki Tayousei wo Ikashita Jugyo Jissen heno Apurochi] (in Japanese).

Sugimura, M. (2015a). "Circulation brains, challenges for higher education." In R. Mouer (ed.), *Globalizing Japan: Striving to Engage the World* (pp. 70–92). Balwyn North: Trans Pacific Press.

Sugimura, M. (2015b). "The mobility of international students and higher education policies in Japan." *The Gakushuin Journal of International Studies*, 2, 1–19.

Takeda, S. (2006). "Transition of the roles of Japans international education policy – from foreign aid to global citizenship." *The Nippon University Graduate School of Social and Cultural Studies Journal*, 7, 77–88.

Tojo, K. (2010). "A review on internationalization of Japanese higher education." In *Search for the Rationale: The Osaka Women's College Summary*, 7.

UNESCO (2011). "Asia-Pacific Regional Convention on the Recognition of Qualifications in Higher Education 2011." http://portal.unesco.org/en/ev.phpURL_ID=48975&URL_DO= DO_TOPIC&URL_SECTION=201.html, accessed March 15, 2020.

UNESCO Bangkok Asia Pacific Regional Bureau of Education (2018). "Cross-border mobility in Asia-Pacific higher education gets major boost as Tokyo Convention comes into force." January 19. https://bangkok.unesco.org/content/cross-border-mobility-asia-pacific-higher-education-gets-major-boost-tokyo-convention-comes, accessed April 19, 2020.

Yokota, M. and Kobayashi A. (eds.) (2013). *Internationalization of Japanese Universities and the International Mindset of Japanese Students* [Daigaku no Kokusaika to Nihonjin Gakusei no Kokusaishikosei]. Gakubunsha.

CHAPTER 32

....

HIGHER EDUCATION IN THE REPUBLIC OF KOREA

....

JANG WAN KO

1. INTRODUCTION

....

OVER the past seven decades, the Republic of Korea (hereafter South Korea) has achieved dramatic economic growth and educational development. Rebuilding from the 1950–1953 Korean War, South Korea had recovered to become the eleventh largest economy in the world by 2015. Education has been considered the most important driving force behind the country's stunning economic development. The desire to achieve high levels of education was explored immediately following independence. Since then, the government has established a series of policies to meet the people's educational needs. Society's demand for education and the government's policy of fostering a highly skilled economic workforce through education propelled South Korea's dramatic economic growth. In education, South Korea has become one of the highest-performing countries in student enrollment and academic achievement. The student enrollment ratio in primary education increased from 54 percent to 99.9 percent between 1945 and 2019 (Ministry of Education, National Institute for International Education, 2016; Ministry of Education, 2019a). In terms of academic achievement, South Korea is ranked among the world's top nations in the OECD's PISA test for 15-year-old students and consistently scores in the top percentiles in mathematics, science, and reading since the exam was developed in 2003.

Higher education in South Korea has also experienced dramatic transformations. The massive expansion of higher education institutions (HEIs) and student enrollment represent the first significant change. Through several transformational stages, many South Korean universities have now become top performers in international rankings. With strong government intervention and policy initiatives, higher education development in South Korea has expanded access for all students to meet growing demand, and enhance national competitiveness. The former is related to college admission and enrollment quota policies, higher education financing, and tuition issues. The latter is related to economic development and collaboration with the private sector, and internationalization. This chapter discusses the South Korean higher education system, including its historical development, policies on access and financing, internationalization, and current policy initiatives.

2. HISTORICAL DEVELOPMENT AND BACKGROUND

The first type of HEI in Korea, *Taehak*, was established in 372 during the Goguryeo era and provided Confucian education and military instruction and training for the elite. The HEI changed its title several times during the *Korea* dynasty, and the first *Sungkyunkwan* was established in Gaesung in 1362 at the end of the dynasty. The *Joseon* dynasty, the last dynasty on the Korean peninsula, was established in 1392 and moved the nation's capital from Gaesung to Hansung (now Seoul). *Sungkyunkwan*, the foremost educational institution to promote Confucian scholarship, was established in Hansung in 1398. For several hundred years until the end of the nineteenth century, Sungkyunkwan was the nation's highest educational institution, dedicated to cultivating national leaders and scholars. Although Sungkyunkwan's status weakened during the Japanese colonial period, it reopened as a general higher education institution, Sungkyunkwan University, in 1946.

At the end of the nineteenth century, in the late *Joseon* dynasty, also known as the Enlightenment period, various forms of educational institutions began to emerge in Korea. During this period, the government attempted to introduce Western culture and establish a new educational system. Accordingly, the government implemented policies to enhance the national education system and introduced a foreign education curriculum, including English. In particular, many Korean visionaries actively promoted the establishment of private schools to foster national leaders and activists to restore national power and promote the anti-Japanese movement through educational practice. As a result, by 1910, thousands of private educational institutions had been established. In addition, foreign Christian missionaries, mostly from the United States, used education and medical care to promote Christian ideas, establishing missionary schools and medical institutions. Although no foreign Christian missionaries intended to support the establishment of an HEI in Korea (Kim, 2008), several missionary schools effectively became dedicated to higher education after liberalization. During this period, HEIs were not Western-style universities, but rather professional schools that provided advanced training to technicians and professionals to develop technocrats in diplomacy, military, medicine, law, and education (Kim, 2008).

The Japanese occupation of the Korean Empire from 1910 to 1945 is considered the country's dark age of education. Japanese authorities suspended all levels of education, including the closure of professional schools, which were considered post-secondary education institutions in 1911. Although the Japanese rulers allowed a few professional schools to open after 1915, they were either sponsored by the Japanese government or owned by Christian missionaries. In 1919, as the independence movement began to spread throughout the country, demand grew for higher education to cultivate national leaders. In response to the independence movement, Japan implemented various appeasement policies to weaken the burgeoning national consciousness and quell internal and external criticism of Japanese rule. As part of this appeasement policy, Japanese authorities revised the Korean Education Decree in February 1922 to expand educational opportunities for Koreans. The Japanese policy permitting HEIs led to the establishment of several professional schools by Korean visionaries; by 1945, more than 20 such professional schools had been established or reopened. Nevertheless, the Japanese continued to suppress these educational institutions. Although the colonial powers founded Kyungsung Imperial University in 1924 to appease demands by Korean visionaries to establish a Western-style university, Korean admission was restricted. The institution was not publicly accessible, but rather a university to train local colonial officials (Kim, 2008).

After independence from Japan in 1945, the Korean peninsula was divided into the two nations of South and North Korea, and the US Military Government ruled South Korea until 1948. The South Korean higher education system and primary and secondary education were remodeled during the interim US Military Government (Chae and Hong, 2009). Seoul National University was founded, forming the basic framework of South Korea's current higher education system. Nevertheless, the 1950s was considered a laissez-faire period with minimal government intervention on higher education; the government's top priority was primary and secondary education to meet educational demand and rebuild the nation. With limited capacity to support higher education, the government encouraged the private sector to establish HEIs, which became the root of private-led development in South Korea.

Between 1962 and 1981, the government initiated four Five-Year National Economic Development Plans (FNEDPs), which sought to boost skilled workers into the labor force. The First and Second FNEDPs (1962–1966, 1967–1971) focused on "labor-intensive industries centered on light industry," while the Third and Fourth FNEDPs (1972–1976, 1977–1981) concentrated on "fostering capital-intensive heavy and chemical industries." The government accordingly had to shift its emphasis from primary and secondary education to vocational high school and higher education, especially with respect to setting up Junior Colleges to produce high-level technicians.

As a result of the series of FNEDPs, the number of college students dramatically increased from 141,636 to 647,505 during the 1960s and 1970s, including the number of junior college students from 23,159 to 165,051 between 1965 and 1980 (see Table 32.1). Because the government had insufficient resources to establish public HEIs to meet and support demand for higher education, private constituencies were allowed to open HEIs to increase access to higher education and produce highly skilled graduates for national development. As a result, private HEIs increased from 47 in 1960 to 147 in 1980, while the number of national and public tertiary institutions increased from 34

Table 32.1 Historical development of the number of HEIs and student enrollment

Year	Total		Two-year colleges*		Four-year universities*		Graduate schools	
	HEIs	Students	HEIs	Students	HEIs	Students	HEIs	Students
1965	162	141,636	48	23,159	114	114,635	0	3,842
1970	168	201,436	65	33,483	103	161,313	0	6,640
1975	205	318,683	101	62,866	104	241,947	0	13,870
1980	237	647,505	128	165,051	109	448,515	0	33,939
1985	262	1,451,297	120	242,117	142	1,141,002	0	68,178
1990	265	1,691,681	117	323,825	148	1,280,693	0	87,163
1995	327	2,343,894	149	574,239	178	1,655,819	0	113,836
2000	372	3,363,549	159	914,347	196	2,219,765	17	229,437
2005	419	3,548,728	161	856,564	224	2,409,939	34	282,225
2010	411	3,644,158	149	772,509	222	2,555,016	40	316,633
2015	431	3,608,071	158	769,403	226	2,505,190	47	333,478
2019	430	3,326,733	157	692,214	228	2,315,279	45	319,240

* Note: Two-year colleges includes all 2-year or less than 4-year programs and four-year universities includes all 4-year programs.

Sources: Ko (2018); Ministry of Education and Korean Educational Development Institute (2019a).

to 67 over the same period. By 2005, the number of private HEIs continued to soar to 301 while public HEIs declined to 59. Between 1960 and 2005, student enrollment in private HEIs also rose from approximately 65,000 to over 2,374,000, while enrollment in national and public institutions increased from 42,000 to 552,000 (Ko, 2018). As of 2019, there were 755,750 students (22.7 percent) in national and public HEIs, compared to 2,570,983 students (77.3 percent) in private institutions (Ministry of Education and Korean Educational Development Institute, 2019a).

In 1969, the government abolished middle school entrance exams to reduce primary school students' academic load and unhealthy competitive stress, and to boost middle school enrollment. Subsequently, however, competitive access shifted to entry into high school, resulting in the high school equalization policy in 1974. These demographic and policy changes led to calls for expanded access to higher education. In response to this pressure, the military-led government, which had recently taken power, initiated major higher education reform in the 1980s by abolishing entrance exams for individual universities, replacing these with nationwide exams managed by the government, and establishing a Graduation Quota System (GQS). In addition, the government included students' academic achievement scores in high school as a key element for entrance evaluation, with the aim of minimizing the influence of private tutoring and reducing excessive private expenditure.

The government introduced the GQS, which allowed universities to recruit 130 percent numbers of students but eliminate the extra 30 percent at the end of typically four-year degree courses. The initial idea of GQS policy was not about increasing the number of university students. However, the government met with strong resistance from students and parents and eventually gave up controlling the number of graduates. Thus, the policy resulted in an unintended consequence, which was the expansion of the number of university students. As a result, the enrollment quota for four-year universities increased and the total number of students in HEIs doubled between 1979 and 1983 (Chae and Hong, 2009). Table 32.1 shows a 100 percent increase in student enrollment from 1980 to 1985.

Several social and political changes in the late 1980s and early 1990s also influenced the higher education landscape in South Korea. The demand for democracy increased significantly at the end of the 1980s and a new democratic civil administration was launched in 1993. Koreans had high expectations and aspirations for the new government which set educational development as one of its key priorities. A Presidential Council on Education Reforms was established to tackle two key challenges: preparing students for globalization, informatization, and knowledge socialization in the twenty-first century; and resolving major educational problems such as intense competition in the college entrance exams and the heavy burden of private education expenses.

On May 31, 1995, the government enacted a major education policy widely known as the *5.31 Education Reform*. To this day it is still considered one of the most comprehensive higher education reforms in Korea's history and is recognized as the most important framework followed by all administrations regardless of their ideological character or policy orientation (Ahn and Ha, 2014).

The Council developed a New Education Plan with five major goals: an open education system, student-centered education, autonomous education, diversification and specialization, and informatization.[1] To achieve these goals, the 5.31 Education Reform included reform policies in nine areas: the establishment of an open society and life-long education system; diversification and specialization of universities; creation of a democratic and autonomous school community; curriculum design focusing on the humanities and creativity; reform of the university admission system; diversification of educational programs for learners' needs; establishment of a new school evaluation system; cultivation of competent teaching and remodeling of teacher training programs; and an increase in educational expenditure to 5 percent of the gross national product by 1998 (Ahn and Ha, 2014).

Of the many educational initiatives in the 5.31 Education Reform, two policies— the Deregulation of Student Enrollment Quotas and the University Establishment Regulations—contributed directly to the expansion of higher education. Historically, the government controlled HEIs through various measures, including regulating

---

[1] Informatization here refers to a process or strategy that uses ICT as a means to become an information-based society.

enrollment quotas. In 1994, the new government announced a strategic plan to deregulate enrollment quotas with the goal of increasing college access and meeting social
demands, allowing HEIs to set their own enrollment quota, starting from universities
and colleges in non-Seoul metropolitan areas. As a result, the enrollment quota rose
to 15,965 in 1996 and 16,465 in 1997. By the end of 1997, the total enrollment quota had
increased to 22,935 in 76 HEIs (Jang, 2007). In 2004, a plan for the promotion of university autonomy was established and student enrollment quotas were abolished and left to
universities to decide, save for national universities and universities in the Seoul metropolitan area.

The University Establishment Regulations introduced in 1996 greatly reduced the establishment criteria, standards, and requirements of higher education institutes, leading
to the establishment of various types of HEIs that barely met the minimum standards
and requirements set by the government. Forty-two four-year universities and 36
graduate universities[2] were established in the first 10 years after these regulations were
introduced (Im, 2008). Consequently, the University Establishment Regulations have
been criticized for encouraging the mass introduction of sub-par HEIs, resulting in the
abolishment of that regulation in 2014. The government introduced a new regulation to
establish an HEI requiring a certain level of human resources, educational programs,
and facilities in 2015.

The demographic change in Korea influenced the development of higher education in two ways. Firstly, demographic change had mostly affected national colleges
and universities. For example, between 2010 and 2019 the overall number of students
decreased by 9.4 percent (239,737) at four-year universities and by 10.4 percent (80,295)
at two-year colleges. However, the rates of decline at private institutions were only 5.2
(four-year universities) and 9.5 (two-year colleges) compared to that of 18.9 (four-year
universities) and 41.4 (two-year colleges) at public institutions (Ministry of Education
and Korean Educational Development Institute, 2010, 2019a). Partly because of that, the
government has controlled the size of public institutions tightly by implementing a restructuring policy over the public sector from 2004.

Secondly, it also narrowed the gender gap in higher education participation. The
number of female students in higher education increased sharply by about 9.3 times,
from only 26.8 percent in 1985 to 42.0 percent in 2019, while the growth of male students
during the same period was only about 3.7 times (Ministry of Education and Korean
Educational Development Institute, 2019a). In terms of degree subjects, female students
now outnumber men in medicine (60.2 percent), education (58.9 percent), humanities
(57.1 percent), and arts/physical education (55.1 percent). Nonetheless, men are still
dominant in science and engineering. For example, female participation is 45.1 percent
in natural science and only 19.7 percent in engineering.

---

[2] A new type of university established further to the 5.31 Education Reform of 1995. Graduate
universities, unlike graduate schools in four-year universities, offer only graduate programs. There were
44 graduate universities in 2019.

The government made special efforts to improve the ratio of female academics in higher education institutions. In 2003, the government amended the Education Civil Service Act to improve gender equality at national universities. However, the plan without coercion did not make any practical difference (Park and Park, 2019). In 2015, the government brought the Framework Act on Gender Equality forward to promote gender-equal employment in the education sector for a second time. The government aimed at improving the ratio of female academics from 15.4 percent in 2016 to over 18 percent by 2022. The government also revised the Decree on the Appointment of Education Public Officials in 2020 to secure at least 25 percent of employment for female academics by 2030 (Ministry of Education, 2020b). Despite continued efforts, nonetheless, the proportion of female professors at national universities has not improved significantly.

3. Types of Higher Education Institutions

The Higher Education Act lists seven types of HEIs in South Korea:[3] Universities (regular four-year universities), Industrial Universities, Universities of Education, Junior Colleges, Distance Learning Universities, Technical Universities, and Miscellaneous Schools (Ko, 2018). Each type of HEI has a specific mandate. For instance, Universities of Education, which include ten national universities, are for students who want to be elementary school teachers. Industrial Universities train industrial personnel, while Technical Universities are for those seeking to upgrade their skills. At present, South Korea has only two Industrial Universities and one Technical University. Among the seven types of HEIs, the leading ones are Universities and Junior Colleges (which educate the technical workforce through two- to three-year programs). In 2019, there were 191 universities in total—35 national and public universities and 156 private universities. The 137 Junior Colleges comprise nine national and public Junior Colleges and 128 private colleges (Ministry of Education, 2019b). Junior Colleges account for 78.7 percent of all HEIs.

Higher education in South Korea is primarily a private sector venture. National universities and colleges established and operated by the central government and public HEIs run by regional municipal governments account for just 22.7 percent (755,750 students) of all students. Private HEIs are managed by institutional foundations, and the

---

[3] In addition, there are 31 HEIs, not regulated by the Higher Education Act but regulated by other special laws. For instance, some featured HEIs include four Institutes of Science and Technology established by the South Korea Advanced Institute of Science and Technology Act, thirteen HEIs established and operated based on the Lifelong Education Act, and nine Polytechnic Colleges established by the Workers Vocational Skills Development Act.

term "private" refers to not-for-profit because for-profit private HEIs are not allowed by law in Korea. As of 2019, there were 2,570,983 students (77.3 percent of total) in 372 private universities and colleges (Ministry of Education and Korean Educational Development Institute, 2019a). These figures show that private HEIs dominate the higher education sector in both the number of institutions and the number of enrolled students, which is a unique feature of Korean higher education compared to other countries. For instance, private HEIs account for 56.3 percent of all HEIs, while 78.6 percent of students are enrolled in public HEIs in the United States (Hussar et al., 2020), and in Singapore, private HEIs account for 82.4 percent of all HEIs and only 58.5 percent of students are enrolled in private HEIs (Ministry of Education, Singapore, 2020). Only Japan is close to Korea, with 73.7 percent of students enrolled in private HEIs (MEXT, 2019).

Other than public and private universities, a third kind of HEIs—incorporated universities—have also been established since the government granted independent legal status to some national universities. Although the basic concept was outlined in the 5.31 Educational Reform of 1995, it was not until the mid-2000s that the government enacted reform of national universities to enhance their institutional autonomy and managerial accountability. At that point, the autonomy of national universities in South Korea was rated at the lowest level among OECD member countries. As state institutions, national HEIs were controlled by government regulations with respect to budget, accounting, procurement, organization, and personnel. This arrangement resulted in rigid organizational, personnel, and financial management, which made it difficult for national HEIs to secure accountability for operation and performance while simultaneously carrying out teaching and research functions to fulfill their mandate to create and transfer world-class knowledge (Chun et al., 2008). Thus, the government sought to eliminate management inefficiencies by ensuring autonomy and accountability through privatization. Although debate on transforming national universities into corporate universities had been going on for many years, there was strong opposition from existing national universities. They argued that privatization would reduce direct financial support from the government and the loss of retirement age and benefit guarantees for faculty members and university employees. Thus, the government decided to establish the first corporate university, Ulsan National Institute of Science and Technology (UNIST), in 2007. Later, Seoul National University also became a corporate university in 2011, followed by Incheon National University in 2013.

Despite greater autonomy, regulations dictate that Seoul National University and Incheon National University must be subject to annual performance evaluations by the Ministry of Education. The performance evaluation should ensure the autonomous operation of national university corporations to enhance the efficiency of university management. The evaluation results are disclosed publicly and are used to adjust performance goals and indicators, as well as to develop annual strategic plans. The government also determines financial incentives for the national university corporations based on the performance evaluation. According to the government's evaluation report, Seoul National University's annual performance since becoming a corporation has been rated "excellent (80–89% satisfactory)" for the past eight years, from 2012 to 2019 (Ministry of Education and Korean Educational Development Institute, 2020).

4. FINANCING HIGHER EDUCATION

The total budget of the Ministry of Education in 2019 was 74.9 trillion Korean Won (KW) (about USD64.3 billion), accounting for 18.7 percent of the total government budget (Ministry of Education, 2019c). Higher education was earmarked 10,081 billion KW, about 13.5 percent of the total budget of the Ministry of Education while the K-12 education received about 59,383 billion KW (79.3 percent) and lifelong education received 743 billion KW. Although HEIs have sources of funding external to government ministries and agencies, debate on increasing higher education funding, especially from government and public sector entities, continues to be a major point of contention. In fact, the expenditure on HEIs as a percentage of gross domestic product (GDP) was 2.2 percent (1 percent from public sources, 1.2 percent from private) in 2015 (OECD, 2019). Although the percentage was higher than the OECD average of 1.6 percent, the expenditure from private sources of funds in South Korea was much higher than the OECD average of 0.5 percent. This means that private individuals and organizations in South Korea spend more on higher education than the public sector. Moreover, the total expenditure on educational institutions per full-time equivalent student was USD10,109, which is about 64.6 percent of the OECD average (USD15,656) in 2015. Those two indicators—more expenditures from private sources and relatively low expenditure per student—have been a contentious issue for many years in the higher education sector

Higher education in South Korea is financed by the government in three ways: an operating budget for national and public HEIs, national scholarships, and a general subsidy. The operating budget is only for national, public universities and private universities established through majority government funding for special purposes. National scholarships are awarded directly to students based on family income, except in a few cases of merit-based scholarships. The general subsidy is distributed directly to HEIs.

Funding sources for HEIs vary by institution type. In 2017, for example, the major funding source of national and public universities was the state. Central government funding for national HEIs accounts for 50.6 percent of their total budget while the other 49.4 percent is derived from intramural profits. For private HEIs, however, their major source of income was from students' tuition and fees, accounting for 53.2 percent of their total operating budget, followed by government support, accounting for 15.3 percent. The Higher Education Corporation supported just 4.5 percent of the total operating budget, while other income (15.4 percent) and external donations (2.3 percent) are negligible (Park, 2018).

One of the biggest policy changes to expand access to higher education in South Korea has been the introduction of a new student financial aid system in 2012. The government established the South Korea Student Aid Foundation (KOSAF) to manage the National Scholarship Funds. National student aid programs consist of National Scholarships, Student Loans, and Talent Development Programs (South Korea Student Aid Foundation, 2013). While the national grant and scholarship programs consist of several sub-programs based on need- or merit-based scholarships, two major scholarship programs (as measured by monetary value and the number of recipients) are the National Scholarship Types I and II. Types I and II are based solely on students' family income levels, mainly focusing on the lowest or lower income levels. Type II, in addition to student's income level, varies according to institutional efforts and willingness to provide additional funding matched with the national scholarship. During its first year of operation, the government provided 1.5 trillion KW in scholarships directly to students (Type I) and distributed about 750 billion KW more through institutions (Type II). Thus, the total amount of student financial aid increased from 438.8 billion KW in 2010 to 2.25 trillion KW in 2012. This kind of national scholarship distribution is especially important to HEIs because, to receive the Type II scholarship, HEIs have to match the government's contribution. While the government intentionally includes the Type II program to maximize the amount of scholarships, many HEIs have criticized the programs because of the additional financial burden placed on them.

Figure 32.1 presents trends of national scholarships since 2005, clearly showing the dramatic increase in scholarships in 2012. As of 2019, the total amount of student aid reached about 3.61 trillion KW (Ministry of Education, 2020a), accounting for 33.4 percent of the total higher education budget.

The general subsidy is now distributed directly to HEIs. Since 2018, however, the general subsidy had been distributed mainly through the project-based funding system, meaning that individual HEIs have to submit proposals for projects to get money. The

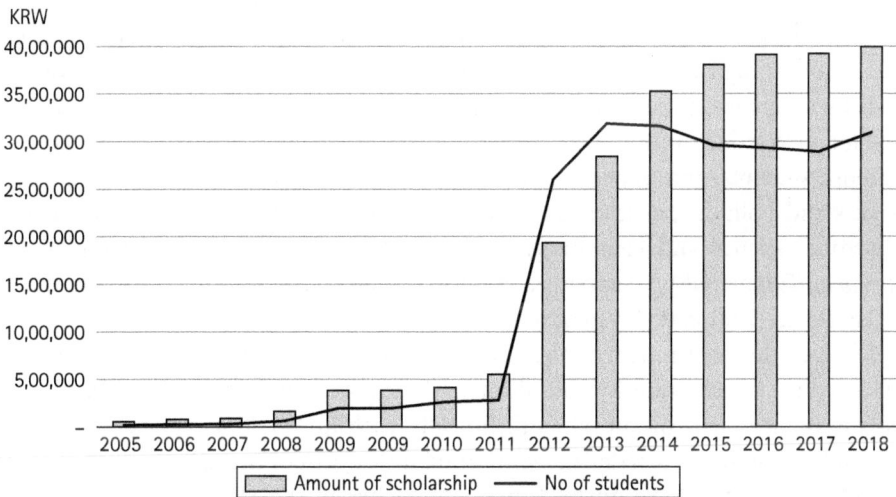

FIGURE 32.1 Trends of national scholarship

Source: Author created based on Public Data Portal (2020).

government then selects a designated number of HEIs, based on its evaluation of the institution's performance (Ko, 2018). Major project-based funding programs include the University for Creative Korea, Brain Korea 21, the Advancement of College Education (ACE) projects, the Initiative for a College of Humanities Research and Education (CORE), the Program for Industrial needs-Matched Education (PRIME), and the Leaders in Industry–University Cooperation (LINC+). These funding programs are multi-year projects and the amount of funding varies by project, from 50.1 billion to 272.8 billion KW in 2017 (Hwang, 2017). Since 2018, the government has introduced a new funding system, integrating many existing funding projects such as ACE+, CORE, and PRIME projects into one funding system, while maintaining a couple of existing projects, such as LINC+. A new funding model, the Basic University Competency Evaluation system, basically intends to provide a general subsidy to HEIs and to re-spect institutions' autonomous management (Ministry of Education, 2019d). HEIs are classified into four categories based on the evaluation of institutional performance and management and only HEIs in the first category receive full funding and enjoy insti-tutional autonomy. The total budget for the Basic University Competency Evaluation system in 2019 was about 817.6 billion KW.

5. Tuition Issues

High college tuition and fees (hereafter tuition) have been a critical issue for several decades. When HEIs took advantage of their autonomy in setting tuition fees, the cost of tuition increased far quicker than the inflation rate. Between 2000 and 2008, college tuition increased 8.1 percent for national HEIs and 6.3 percent for private HEIs annually, more than two times higher than the inflation rate (Ban, 2008). The tuition level was the second-highest in the world (OECD, 2009) and many students and parents suffered because of the high costs. However, government support for higher education was rela-tively low compared to primary and secondary education and the HEIs did not take ser-ious action to reduce tuition costs. These problems became a social issue as stakeholders (parents, students, and public interest groups) protested for change. Policy decision-makers and political parties soon joined in the debate. As a result, the Ministry of Education, Science, and Technology tried to control college tuition by introducing the *Half-price Tuition Policy* in 2007 as a political campaign promise, and officially enacted the Half-price Tuition Policy in 2011.

However, the government's control over tuition costs became a thorny issue in the higher education community and ultimately, the government could not directly force HEIs to reduce their tuition rates. Technically, each university has the right to set its own tuition rates, albeit with increases limited to 1.5 times the inflation rate over the preceding three years. So, instead, two approaches to the Half-price Tuition Policy were taken to help reduce student tuition burdens: (1) keeping tuition at current levels; and (2) providing significant student financial support. The government had already initiated a new student financial aid system at that time, awarding a large number of national scholarships directly to students through the South Korea Scholarship Foundation. With strong administrative power over HEIs, the government linked institutional tuition increases to their performance evaluation when giving financial support. As a result, the government has successfully restrained college tuition increases over the past ten years despite the HEIs' constant criticism of the Half-price Tuition Policy. This policy has had two main effects: (1) reducing students' tuition burden by lowering tuition rates; and (2) increasing national scholarships. But it also exacerbated the financial difficulties faced by HEIs, especially private HEIs, due to a decrease in revenue. There has been increasing concern about the deterioration in the quality of education caused by the drop in educational costs per student.

6. Internationalization

It was not until the 1990s that South Korea contemplated comprehensive internationalization policies when the government tried to respond to the pressures of the World Trade Organization to open the Korean higher education market. The government announced the New Plan for HEIs in 1996, which involved a series of initiatives including allowing joint operations of educational programs in 1997, partially allowing the establishment of foreign universities in 1998, and expanding the scope of authorization to establish foreign universities in South Korea in 1999 (Lee, 2007). Several other factors also contributed to the internationalization of higher education (Lee, 2007; Byun and Kim, 2011). For instance, the 5.31 Educational Reform introduced market mechanisms and global competition into the higher education system and consequently pushed for both the government and HEIs to adopt more active internationalization policies. Further, the financial crisis of the late 1990s called for more balanced financial expenditures between in-bound and out-bound students. At the time, there were far more South Korean students going abroad than foreign students entering the country, and this deficit in the balance of study abroad persisted for a long time. Following the national financial crisis, the deficit in the balance of study abroad increased from USD1.06 billion in 2001 to USD1.84 billion in 2003 (Ministry of Education and Human Resource Development, 2004). In response, the government shifted its policy to recruit more international students for balanced student flows and spending. Finally, demographic changes also impacted internationalization policy. As South Korean society aged due to an increase in the elderly population, its school-age population simultaneously began to decrease as a result of falling birth rates. For instance, the school-age population (aged 6–21) decreased from 14.4 million in 1990 to 7.4 million in 2020. Further decreases to 6.1 million by 2030 and to 4.6 million by 2050 are expected. Likewise, the population aged 18–21 (920,000 in 1990) decreased to 508,000 in 2020 and a further decrease to approximately 321,000 by 2050 is also predicted (National Statistics Bureau, 2006). Both the government and universities realize the serious implications of this demographic shift: from the government's perspective, it would be difficult to meet the demands of the labor force, while universities are concerned about their financial stability due to declining student enrollments in the future.

The government initiated a series of policies on the internationalization of higher education. These include the Comprehensive Strategies for Internationalization of Higher Education of 2006, which addresses the integration of higher education reforms across 11 ministries, and the Higher Education Internationalization Strategy of 2012, which introduces ten major internationalization policies dealing with the shortage of domestic college students, enhancing international competitiveness, and improving the quality of higher education programs.

Since internationalization policies in higher education mainly focus on the mobility of students and academic professionals, the total number of foreign students in South Korea has increased dramatically from 16,832 in 2004 to 160,165 in 2019 (Figure 32.2). The first policy to recruit international students, the Study South Korea Project, was launched in 2004. This project aimed to recruit 50,000 international students by 2010. Since the goal was accomplished earlier than expected, it was revised in 2008 with a new target of recruiting 100,000 foreign students by 2012 (Ko, 2018). In early 2012, the government further expanded the initiative with an expanded target of 200,000 foreign students by 2020 (Ministry of Education, Science and Technology, 2012). However, this

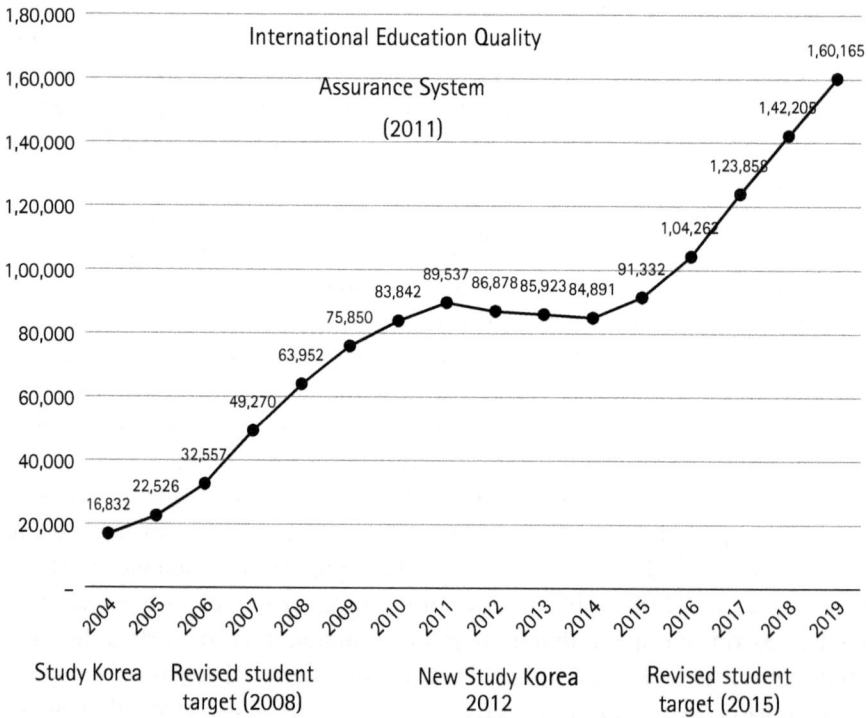

FIGURE 32.2 Internationalization policies and the number of international students in Korea

Source: Author.

goal was harder to achieve since the number of international students started to drop from 89,537 in 2011, to 86,878 in 2012 (Ministry of Education, 2019b).

One of the possible reasons for this decline is the introduction of a new quality control policy for international student recruitment. In 2011, the government implemented the International Education Quality Assurance System (IEQAS) to improve the quality management of international education and to attract high-quality foreign students by accrediting and evaluating education programs in South Korean HEIs. As the number of international students started to drop, in 2015 the government extended the deadline for recruiting 200,000 international students to 2023. As of 2019, there were 160,165 foreign students in South Korea, of which 100,215 (62.6 percent) were in degree programs (Ministry of Education, 2019b). Of these, 65,828 (65.7 percent) were undergraduate students, 23,605 (23.6 percent) were master's students, and 10,782 (10.8 percent) were doctoral students.

The most dramatic change in the international student demographic occurred in doctoral programs (Table 32.2). The number of international students in doctoral programs rose from 3,811 in 2010, to 10,782 in 2019—an increase of nearly 183 percent. The trend is similar in master's programs as international students can receive financial support from research projects, which may include research funds and funds from national R&D programs such as Brain Korea 21 (BK21).

Of the 59,950 international students (37.4 percent of all students) in non-degree programs in 2019, 44,756 are enrolled in language programs, a significant increase from 17,064 in 2010. Language institutes in HEIs are considered to be a pathway to universities and colleges. HEIs have expanded language programs and aggressively recruited international students since the government lowered the college admission criteria for international students from Test of Proficiency in Korean Level 3 to Level 2 when students enroll in language programs.

There have been many issues surrounding the internationalization of higher education in South Korea, including the need to recruit *talented* and diverse students in terms of origin or nationality, the language of instruction, the capacity of HEIs to support international students, and discrimination against international students (Ko, 2018). The need to recruit talented international students has been one of the controversial issues. In the early stages of the internationalization process, HEIs in South Korea recruited *any* foreign student with minimal qualifications, not necessarily *talented* foreign students as the government expected. The primary goal of HEIs was not only to make up for the shortage of domestic students, but also to receive better scores in the university performance evaluation from the government. The higher the number of international students at HEIs, the higher the government evaluation. Although the government introduced IEQAS for HEIs to maintain international students, the performance indicators have not changed. As more international student recruitment is important for HEIs, a number of measures have been recommended, including promoting globalization of individual universities, expanding scholarships for international students, and expanding employment opportunities for international students after graduation (Ihm et al., 2015). Nevertheless, policy discussions on international

Table 32.2 The number of international students by degree programs

Year	Total	Degree programs				Non-degree programs		
		Subtotal	AS/BA	MA	Doctoral	Subtotal	Language programs	Other
2019	160,165	100,215	65,828	23,605	10,782	59,950	44,756	15,194
	(100.0)	(62.6)	(41.1)	(14.7)	(6.7)	(37.4)	(27.9)	(9.5)
2018	142,205	86,036	56,097	21,429	8,510 (6.0)	56,169	41,661	14,508
	(100.0)	(60.5)	(39.4)	(15.1)		(39.5)	(29.3)	(10.2)
2017	123,858	72,032	45,966	18,753	7,313 (5.9)	51,826	35,734	16,092
	(100.0)	(58.2)	(37.1)	(15.1)		(41.8)	(28.9)	(13.0)
2016	104,262	63,104	38,944	17,282	6,878 (6.6)	41,158	26,976	14,182
	(100.0)	(60.5)	(37.4)	(16.6)		(39.5)	(25.9)	(13.6)
2015	91,332	55,739	32,972	16,441	6,326 (6.9)	35,593	22,178	13,415
	(100.0)	(61.0)	(36.1)	(18.0)		(39.0)	(24.3)	(14.7)
2010	83,842	60,000	43,709	12,480	3,811 (4.5)	23,842	17,064	6,778
	(100.0)	(71.6)	(52.1)	(14.9)		(28.4)	(20.4)	(8.1)

Source: Ministry of Education (2019b).

student employment are limited although the government provides basic employment services to international students. Considering the declining population in general and the decrease in the labor force in particular, the government needs to develop pro-active policies to support international talent to live and work in Korea.

In terms of the diversity of international students, in 2019, 91.0 percent of international students were from Asian countries (Ministry of Education, 2019b). Chinese students dominated the international student cohorts, making up 44.4 percent, followed by students from Vietnam (23.4 percent) and Mongolia (4.6 percent). The proportion of Asian students has remained steady for the past 10 years—91.2 percent in 2010 and 90.0 percent in 2019. However, the percentage of Chinese students has decreased from 71.0 percent to 44.4 percent even though the total number of international students rose from 59,490 to 71,067 during this period. The proportion of Vietnamese students has dramatically increased from 2.3 percent to 23.4 percent, but this cohort is mostly enrolled in non-degree programs. Higher education communities and the government believe that it is important to recruit more international students from other regions of the world, especially from Europe, the Americas, and Africa to realize *true* internationalization.

Although most international students are from Asian countries, international faculty tends to come from Western countries. According to the Ministry of Education (2019c), there were 5,126 international faculty in South Korea in 2019, down by 5.8 percent from 5,441 in 2018 (Table 32.3). Of this number, 40.8 percent of international faculty were from the United States (2,092), followed by Canada (649, 12.7 percent) and China (460,

Table 32.3 Top five countries of origin for international students and faculty, 2019

International students			International faculty		
Country	Number	Percentage	Country	Number	Percentage
Total	160,165	100.0	Total	5,126	100.0
China	71,067	44.4	USA	2,092	40.8
Vietnam	37,426	23.4	Canada	649	12.7
Mongolia	7,381	4.6	China	460	9.0
Japan	4,392	2.7	UK	310	6.0
USA	2,915	1.8	Japan	266	5.2
Other	36,984	23.1	Other	1,349	26.3
Top 5 total	123,181	76.9	Top 5 total	3,777	73.7
Asia	145,747	91.0	Asia	1,242	24.2

Sources: Ministry of Education (2019b); Ministry of Education and Korean Educational Development Institute (2019b).

9.0 percent). The number of international faculty from the top five counties accounted for 73.7 percent of the total international faculty in South Korea. While about 90 percent of international students were from Asian countries, international faculty from Asian countries accounted for only 24.2 percent. English-speaking countries accounted for 62.5 percent of international faculty. International faculty came from the United States, Canada, United Kingdom, Australia, New Zealand, and the Republic of South Africa. This demonstrates how English has been emphasized in the internationalization of higher education in Korea. Using English as a medium of instruction in tandem with the increasing number of international students is encouraged, and local professors have been using English as a means of communication to collaborate with international scholars to increase their research productivity.

7. Quality Assurance in Higher Education

Quality assurance (QA) in higher education mainly comprises two systems: National Accreditation Systems and internal institutional QA arrangements (Ko, 2018). Institutional accreditation focuses on QA of university education and emphasizes student learning outcomes. Two agencies, KCUE (Korean Council for University Education) for all four-year universities and KCCE (Korean Council for University

College Education) for all two- and three-year colleges, were each recognized as an Institutional Recognition Agency by the government. The evaluation criteria for four-year universities consist of 30 criteria in five categories, including six key evaluation criteria, which are mandatory evaluation items that must be met (Korean University Accreditation Institute, 2019). The first two criteria involve a quota of full-time faculty and the number of facilities which are considered essential educational conditions to be satisfied among the four basic requirements for establishing a university according to regulations. The next two criteria, new student enrollment rate and retention rate, are related to student demand and satisfaction. The last two criteria, ratio of educational expenditure to tuition and ratio of scholarships to tuition, are related to the institution's financial soundness and student support. HEIs must meet these six criteria to be accredited.

Individual HEIs have established institutional-level recognition systems for their internal quality management. One of the most popular systems is the new graduation requirement that students must complete a certain number of additional curricula or programs offered by universities to graduate. Although there was some debate when first introduced about whether this was a redundant requirement in addition to the required number of credits, it has been widely implemented in most universities. Recently, four-year universities have introduced the "major program accreditation system" to maintain high educational quality at the department or program level. The evaluation criteria vary by institution and differ from department to department, although universities have tended to adopt the major program accreditation system.

8. Collaboration with Private Sector

Although HEIs in South Korea have cooperated with the private sector for several decades, two major collaborative approaches between HEIs and private sector firms have been initiated since the 2000s. The first approach is to establish education programs—either degree or non-degree—in HEIs with the private company providing financial support. This is a common type of collaborative arrangement based on the individual needs of an HEI and industry. For instance, LG Electronics established an "Embedded Software" program for a master's degree program at the South Korea Advanced Institute of Science and Technology (KAIST) in 2009 to secure high-quality manpower in the software sector. KAIST provides the education programs, and LG Electronics provides full tuition and other financial support to students, in addition to guaranteeing student employment in LG Electronics after graduation. The semiconductor company Hynix and Samsung also provide these kinds of collaboration programs. Another well-known example is the collaboration between Samsung and Sungkyunkwan University (SKKU). Samsung established the Samsung Institute of Technology (SSIT) in 1989, which became the first in-company HEI after being recognized by the government in 2001. With strong collaboration with SKKU, SSIT is the only in-company educational institution to grant four-year degrees in South Korea. In addition, SKKU and Samsung founded the Semiconductor Systems Engineering Department at SKKU to "foster advanced technology personnel customized for semiconductors to lead the academic development of the high-tech semiconductor field and actively meet the technological needs of the semiconductor industry" (Sungkyunkwan University, 2020). The Department offers various tailored education programs and courses to train highly-advanced technicians in semiconductors, and also offers practice-oriented education to provide opportunities for researchers with PhDs at Samsung to teach courses and for students to take internships and field practice at Samsung. Samsung covers all costs of running the program, including student tuition and additional scholarship funds, and guarantees student employment at Samsung. Currently, this program is considered the best professional education program in the semiconductor field in the world.

Another approach is government involvement in encouraging HEI–private company collaborations. The government initiated several projects to support academic–industry partnerships, including the Fostering Regional Hub Research Group in University (2004–2011), the Human Resource Development Project of Leading Industries in Great Economic Areas (2009–2011), and the Hub University for Industrial Collaboration (2004–2011). However, the government later launched a new comprehensive project by integrating these previously existing initiatives. The Leaders in Industry–University Cooperation (LINC) project, first initiated in 2012 to promote academic–industry partnerships, encourages HEIs to reform their existing system and/or programs to better meet workforce needs and ultimately lead the development of local communities through cooperation with local industries (Ministry of Education, 2018, 2019a). The LINC project has provided over 1 trillion Korean Won to 57 four-year universities and 30 junior colleges and has made a significant contribution to improving industry–academic ties, as well as helping HEIs be more cooperation-friendly with the private sector (Lee, 2017). Hence, in 2017, the government initiated a new LINC+ initiative, which is another major project to promote industry–university collaboration. As the successor to the LINC project, LINC+ aims to establish various Industry-Academic Cooperation Leading models based on institutional autonomy and expanding the scope of industry–academic collaborations to include not only industry, but also local communities, and to support not only engineering and the natural sciences, but also social sciences, humanities, and cultural fields (Ministry of Education, 2018). This project currently supports 75 universities and 59 junior colleges.

9. The Restructuring of Higher Education

Restructuring HEIs is a critical issue in ensuring the sustainability of higher education in South Korea. Although higher education had expanded for several decades, HEIs have recently experienced a shortage of students due to a decline in the school-age population. Demographic trends in terms of low birth rates have impacted higher education enrollment rates. For many years now, South Korea has seen a steady decline in the school-age population, resulting in a decline in the number of college students. The total number of students in HEIs reached a peak of 3,735,706 in 2011, but dropped to 3,326,733 in 2019 (Ministry of Education, 2019b).

To respond to the shortage of college students and to prevent problems such as financial difficulties for HEIs, the government has initiated a new intervention program. The Higher Education Restructuring Promotion Plan was introduced in 2014 (Ministry of Education, 2014) to reduce college student enrollment based on the performance evaluation of HEIs. This plan categorized HEIs by five tiers, and HEIs classified as Level 2 and below will be ordered to cut their enrollment quotas. According to the plan, restructuring will take place in three cycles: college student enrollment will be reduced by 40,000 in the first cycle (2014–2016), 50,000 in the second cycle (2017–2019), and 60,000 in the third cycle (2020–2022). The government's goal in the first cycle was met, as the total enrollment quota decreased by about 44,000. Because it was criticized from its outset, the new government, which came to power in 2018, abandoned this intervention policy in 2019.

The new policy retains the main features of previous policy frameworks, but has moved from direct intervention to voluntary participation. Maintaining university autonomy and alleviating the burden of evaluation, the new policy allows HEIs to choose whether or not to participate in the government performance evaluation program. However, if HEIs want to receive financial support from the government, they must take part in the program and meet the criteria. In addition, the government still provides some HEIs with limited financial support, including student financial aid from the government. Because the decline in the school-age population is expected to continue in the next decade and the government has both accountability over higher education and the power to control HEIs, government intervention will likely persist.

10. CONCLUSION

Higher education in Korea has continued to develop. The government has constantly intervened in response to people's enthusiasm for education and national development goals. These interventions have sometimes emerged in the form of controls and sometimes as support for HEIs. Under the government's control and support policies, each university has actively complied with government policies to find a way to survive and pursue development strategies. As a result, Korea's higher education has improved significantly in terms of access and international competitiveness.

Nevertheless, two recent trends pose a new challenge to higher education in Korea. The decline in the number of students is the biggest challenge. The results of college admissions in 2021 were somewhat shocking to many universities in non-metropolitan areas. Despite the government's continued efforts to prepare for the decline in the school-age population, and despite the continuous efforts of individual universities to recruit college students, many HEIs, especially those in non-metropolitan areas, were unable to fill their admission quota. The demographic decline has become a reality, and universities must develop effective survival strategies to attract students.

The second challenge is related to the current outbreak of COVID-19. What kind of changes or transformations in higher education should be made in the post-pandemic era? University education in Korea has remained successful and uninterrupted during the COVID-19 pandemic due to strong government controls and the active response of the government and universities. The government has relaxed various regulations related to online classes, and universities have provided the necessary educational and training programs to enhance students' and professors' virtual teaching and learning capabilities. However, many challenges, including effective online teaching and learning, university management, and financial issues remain, and appropriate measures are necessary for higher education in the post-pandemic era.

REFERENCES

Ahn, B. Y. and Ha, Y. S. (2014). *Education Reform in Korea: Evaluation and Challenges*. Korean Educational Development Institute.

Ban, S. J. (2008). "Higher education finance and tuition & fee, what's the problem?" *Journal of Korean Social Trend and Perspective*, 77, 102–137.

Byun, K. Y. and Kim, M. (2011). "Shifting patterns of the government's policies for the internationalization of Korean higher education." *Journal of Studies in International Education*, 15/5, 467–486.

Chae, J. E. and Hong, H. K. (2009). "The expansion of higher education led by private universities in Korea." *Asia Pacific Journal of Education*, 29, 341–355.

Chun, Y. et al. (2008). *A Study on the Promotion Plan of National University Incorporation*. Ministry of Public Administration and Security.

Hussar, B., Zhang, J., Hein, S., Wang, K., Roberts, A., Cui, J., Smith, M., Bullock Mann, F., Barmer, A., and Dilig, R. (2020). *The Condition of Education 2020* (NCES 2020-144). Washington, DC: US Department of Education, National Center for Education Statistics.

Hwang, C. (2017). "Improvement of government financial support programs on universities in Korea." *Journal of Educational Development*, 33/2, 69–88.

Ihm, C., Ko, J., Han, K., Lee, K., and Kim, Y. (2015). *Measures to Improve the Internationalization Capacity of Higher Education and Support Organizations*. Sejong: Ministry of Education.

Im, Y. K. (2008). "A study of the impact analysis of university establishment regulations." *The Journal of Educational Administration*, 26/4, 147–167.

Jang, S. (2007). "An analysis of university enrollment quota policy since civilian government." *The Journal of Educational Administration*, 25/4, 389–412.

Kim, K. (2008). *A Study on Korean Higher Education*. Seoul: Kyoyookbook.

Ko, J. W. (2018). "Higher education system and institutions in Korea." In J. C. Shin and P. Teixeira (eds.), *Encyclopedia of International Higher Education Systems and Institutions*. Dordrecht: Springer. https://doi.org/10.1007/978-94-017-9553-1_509-1

Korean University Accreditation Institute (2019). *2020 Handbook on University Accreditation in KOREA*. Seoul: Author.

Lee, K. (2007). *Diagnosis and Improvement Plan for Internationalization Strategy of Higher Education*. Policy document for state audit.

Lee, Y. (2017). "Promote social-customized Leaders in Industry-University Cooperation (LINC+) project. *The HRD Review*, 20/1, 84–91.

Ministry of Education, Culture, Sports, Science and Technology (MEXT) (2019). *Statistics Handbook*. Tokyo: Author.

Ministry of Education (2014). *Announcement of Higher Education Restructuring Plan*. Seoul: Author.

Ministry of Education (2018). *Education in Korea*. Sejong: Author.

Ministry of Education (2019a). *Education in Korea*. Sejong: Author.

Ministry of Education (2019b). *2019 Basic Statistics of Education*. Sejong: Author.

Ministry of Education (2019c). *Budget of 77.3871 trillion 3871 won for fiscal year 2020 confirmed*. Sejong: Author.

Ministry of Education (2019d). *A Plan for Basic University Competencies Evaluation in 2021*. Sejong: Author.

Ministry of Education (2020a). *Basic Plan for National Student Aid, 2020*. Sejong: Author.

Ministry of Education (2020b). Press report, July 13. Sejong: Author.

Ministry of Education and Human Resource Development (2004). *Comprehensive Plan to Recruit International Students* (Study South Korea Project). Seoul: Author.

Ministry of Education and Korean Educational Development Institute (2010). *An Analysis of Educational Statistics: Higher Education, 2010*. Seoul: Author.

Ministry of Education and Korean Educational Development Institute (2019a). *An Analysis of Educational Statistics: Higher Education, 2019*. Sejong: Author.

Ministry of Education and Korean Educational Development Institute (2019b). *Education Statistics Yearbook, 2019*. Sejong: Author.

Ministry of Education and Korean Educational Development Institute (2020). *2018 Performance Evaluation Report on Seoul National University*. Sejong: Author.

Ministry of Education, National Institute for International Education (2016). *Education in Korea*. Seongnam: Author.

Ministry of Education, Science and Technology (2012). *Higher Education Internationalization Strategy*. Seoul: Author.

Ministry of Education, Singapore (2020). *Education Statistics Digest*. Author.

National Statistics Bureau (2006). *Population Projections (2001 ~ 2050)*. Seoul: Author.

Organisation for Economic Co-operation and Development (OECD) (2009). *Education at a Glance*. Paris: OECD Publishing.

Organisation for Economic Co-operation and Development (OECD) (2019). *Education at a Glance*. Paris: OECD Publishing.

Park, K. (2018). *Financial Status and Improvement Plan for Private Universities*. Seoul: South Korea Higher Education Research Institution.

Park, N. G. and Park H. W. (2019). "A study on the low rates of female professors in South Korea." *The Women's Studies*, 100/1, 161–189.

Public Data Portal (2020). *South Korea Student Aid Foundation National Student Aid Information*. https://www.data.go.kr/data/3060496/fileData.do, accessed August 29, 2020.

South Korea Student Aid Foundation (2013). *KOSAF at a Glance*. Seoul: Author.

Sungkyunkwan University (2020). Department of Semiconductor Systems Engineering. https://skb.skku.edu/semi/intro/intro.do, accessed November 2020.

CHAPTER 33

....

SINGAPORE

*The Making of Higher Education in
an Asian Education Hub*

....

S. GOPINATHAN AND MICHAEL H. LEE

1. INTRODUCTION

SINGAPORE is characterized as a "developmental state," which, according to Castells (1992), refers to its ability to gain legitimacy through promoting and sustaining socio-economic development. Since its independence in 1965, the Singapore government has consistently and strongly emphasized development strategies to promote economic growth; a consequence has been a significant presence of foreign direct investment in Singapore's export-oriented economy. The reasons for Singapore becoming one of the most impressive destinations of foreign direct investments from developed economies like the United States, Europe, and Japan, can be attributed to the availability of a sufficient stock of educated and skilled human resources and the state's capacity to promote and utilize high-quality research and development (R&D).

Singapore's higher education policy development over the past five decades has been characterized by, firstly, a cautious and incremental expansion with an increase of universities leading to a gradual rise of the cohort participation rate since the 1990s but without compromising the quality of higher education; secondly, a significant increase in state spending on R&D as universities have been tasked to become more research intensive; thirdly, a more noticeable presence of international institutions in the provision of higher education in partnership with local private education institutions (PEIs), such as Singapore Institute of Management Global Education, PSB Academy, and Ngee Ann Academy, and by other overseas institutions of higher learning with their offshore campuses in Singapore such as Curtin Singapore, James Cook University Singapore, and ESSEC Asia Pacific, Singapore; and fourthly, a firm commitment by the government to develop Singapore as a regional education hub by strengthening international links and hosting several world-renowned institutions of higher learning which offer both collab-oration and competition opportunities (Gopinathan and Lee, 2011). More recently, amid increasing concerns over rising inequality and slowing social mobility, the government has stressed the importance of higher education in promoting upward social mobility and upholding academic and talent meritocracy (Lee, 2019).

This chapter examines the changing context of higher education policy and devel-opment in Singapore and analyzes how the island-state tackles internal and external challenges facing the higher education system with reference to major policies since the mid-1990s. It will also shed light on policy lessons to be learnt from Singapore's ex-perience of developing and reforming higher education. Apart from the introductory section, there are four sections in this chapter. The first section provides a brief review of the historical development of higher education in Singapore. The next section examines, in the face of internal and external challenges, how the development of higher educa-tion in Singapore has been affected by the five main policy issues/directions mentioned in the preceding paragraph. The penultimate section discusses the policy lessons to be learnt from the Singapore case. The concluding section ends with some observations about the implications for the future evolution of higher education in Singapore.

2. HISTORICAL REVIEW OF HIGHER EDUCATION DEVELOPMENT IN SINGAPORE

The British Straits Settlements government set up King Edward Medical College in 1905 and the Raffles College of Arts and Sciences in 1919, both of which became the founding colleges of the University of Malaya (UM) in 1949. With the independence of Malaya in 1957, UM was then divided into two campuses, one in Singapore and one in Kuala Lumpur. In 1962 the Singapore campus separated from UM and was renamed the University of Singapore (SU). While SU was a publicly funded, English-medium univer-sity, there also existed a private Chinese-medium university which had been set up by the Chinese community known as Nanyang University (Nantah) in 1955.

In the late 1970s, following the recommendations of Lord Dainton, then Chancellor of Sheffield University in the United Kingdom, the two universities were merged to form the National University of Singapore (NUS) in 1980 (Dainton, 1979). The Nantah campus was turned into Nanyang Technological Institute (NTI). In the late 1980s, when the Singapore economy had moved towards high-technology industries and the under-graduate population of NUS and NTI collectively reached 20,000, Dainton was once again invited by the Singapore government to review and recommend policies to cope with the needs of economic restructuring and the growing demand for increased access to university education. Dainton recommended the formation of a second university which was achieved by upgrading NTI to full university status. NTI was subsequently renamed Nanyang Technological University (NTU) (Dainton, 1989; Goh and Tan, 2008).

In 1996, the Singapore government announced in a "Boston of the East" speech by then Prime Minister Goh Chok Tong that both NUS and NTU would be supported to become world-class institutions of higher education (Goh, 1996). This also marked the beginning of a wide range of significant changes and reforms of higher education in Singapore, ranging from massification to quality assurance, and the granting of greater autonomy to public universities for greater accountability. With higher education expanding significantly in the 1990s, more stringent systems of student admission, academic recruitment, and quality assurance were put in place to ensure that the quality of higher education would not be compromised (Selvaratnam, 1994).

In 1997, an International Academic Advisory Panel (IAAP) was established to evaluate the performance of the university sector and advise on its future development. Apart from recognizing both universities' bid to become world-class universities, IAAP also recommended the establishment of a third university to meet the growing demand for higher education. In 2000, Singapore Management University (SMU) was established to specialize in disciplines including business management, law, and social sciences (Goh and Tan, 2008). Distinct from NUS and NTU, SMU was established through a partnership with the Wharton Business School of the University of Pennsylvania. This not only signified a new approach to developing Singapore higher education by providing a pathway to internationalization, it also followed a more American approach to the higher education system. In 2012, a fourth university, Singapore University of Technology and Design (SUTD) was similarly established through a partnership with two overseas universities, namely the Massachusetts Institute of Technology and Zhejiang University to provide undergraduate studies, before moving on to postgraduate studies and research (Magnanti, 2018; Fisher, 2020). The Singapore Institute of Technology (SIT) was the fifth university to be established in 2009 to provide alternative access to university education for polytechnic graduates, partly based on collaboration with overseas universities in offering undergraduate programs. The sixth university, the Singapore University of Social Sciences (SUSS), formerly UniSIM (SIM University), a privately run institution by the Singapore Institute of Management (SIM) until 2017, was made an autonomous university, enabling it to receive public funding similar to the other five degree-awarding institutions. SUSS specializes in applied research primarily in social sciences and caters to the needs of working adults in lifelong learning.

3. HIGHER EDUCATION POLICIES

Policies derived from the vision of Singapore as the "Boston of the East" assured strong leadership and funding to ensure that Singapore's universities would be regarded as "world class." Higher education has been considered highly instrumental in enhancing Singapore's competitive edge, positioning it as a regional education hub to attract and retain local and foreign talents and also to expand its market share of global education for students (Gopinathan and Lee, 2011).

In the more unpredictable and complex socio-economic context facing higher education, policy responses and reforms have varied; but, in general, universities have been called upon to maximize effective value for public money invested in the sector, in line with the principles of public management and accountability. There has also been a general paradigm shift of higher education provision moving towards more market-based principles of choice and competition, one in which institutions of higher learning are, in turn, allowed greater operational freedom and autonomy for the sake of managerial efficiency and research innovation. In response to these changes and challenges, five major characteristics of higher education policy and development can be identified in Singapore. The first is the massification of higher education, done cautiously and incrementally, without sacrificing education quality. The second is a strong emphasis and heavy investment in R&D to develop cutting edge innovation. The third is the increased role of the private sector in higher education provision in Singapore. The fourth is the internationalization of higher education with the development of Singapore as a regional education hub. The fifth is concerned with the importance of higher education in securing upward social mobility and thus addressing the problem of social inequality. This section examines the development of higher education in Singapore from these five perspectives.

3.1 Cautious and Incremental Massification

Before the 1980s, higher education in Singapore was an elite system catering for a very low percentage of the age cohort to receive university education. A majority of students who completed secondary education would proceed to polytechnic education or vocational training deemed necessary during the early stage of industrialization which focused on manufacturing and electronic industries in the newly independent nation. Significant change happened around the mid-1980s when Singapore underwent its first ever economic depression which was partly caused by the sudden drop of prices in electronic goods in the global market. This triggered the government to conduct a thorough review of the future directions and strategies for developing Singapore's economy. The review recommended that more emphasis be put on high value-added industries, including technological and service industries. This, in turn, required the qualitative growth and diversification of higher education. In order to achieve a competitive edge for the Singapore economy, the government also decided to expand opportunities in the skills sector via expanding vocational and polytechnic education (Ministry of Trade and Industry, 1986).

In Singapore, the participation rate of university education, which is calculated as a percentage of Primary One cohort, has grown significantly since the 1980s. It has increased from a mere 3 percent in 1980 to 8 percent in 1985, then reached 15 percent in 1990, and subsequently 23, 30 and 37 percent in 2003, 2013, and 2018 respectively (Singapore Department of Statistics, 2002, 2019). Prime Minister, Lee Hsien Loong, announced in his National Day Rally speech of 2011 that by 2020, 40 percent of each school cohort would receive university education with a total of 16,000 places of full-time degree programs offered by the six publicly funded universities yearly. In 2015, 14,000 publicly funded full-time degree places were planned for Singapore with a cohort participation rate (CPR) of 30 percent (Ministry of Education, 2012). The goal of 40 percent pre-employment training, publicly funded university CPR was reached in 2020. Additionally, another 10 percent of working adults pursue publicly funded continuing education and training degree programs (Davie, 2020).

Even though Singapore's higher education system has expanded substantially since the mid-1980s, the process of massification was planned and implemented cautiously to avoid the negative impacts of excessive expansion on education quality, institutional reputation, and resource allocation. The expansion of the student population and universities has been kept at a modest pace; it took 40 years to raise the cohort participation rate of universities from 3 to 40 percent and to increase the number of universities from one to six. Moreover, unlike other developed countries such as Britain and Australia, the Singapore government did not follow these countries' footsteps to upgrade polytechnics to universities in order to provide more university places within a short period of time. Instead, a binary system comprising universities and polytechnics was developed and maintained to serve more diversified needs of education and training in response to changes in the labor market. For the higher education sector in Singapore, the process of massification is concerned not only with quantitative expansion, which implies a considerable increase of students and universities, but also qualitative consolidation with an emphasis on quality assurance and managerial efficiency. Rather than just focusing on the "quantity" aspect, it is more concerned about the "quality" aspect that universities use more stringent criteria and mechanisms for recruiting academics, incentives for improving teaching quality, financial resources for promoting academic and scientific research, and more institutional autonomy for greater accountability (Selvaratnam, 1994; Ministry of Education, 2000). These measures, together with the rational use of public funding on higher education, which has been increased continuously over the past two decades, are essential for universities to achieve both goals of delivering quality education and world-class standards amidst the process of gradual and incremental massification.

3.2 R&D and Higher Education

The shift in Singapore's economy towards high value-added and technologically oriented industries, and more professionalized service sectors, requires more active engagement in R&D activities, which are essential for improving the technical and technological efficiency of industries as well as management skills and business efficiency. Universities are widely expected to serve as vital agents for enabling post-industrial economic growth and upgrading the workforce with the most up-to-date knowledge and skills developed and adopted in new niche areas such as artificial intelligence, biomedical technology, digital economy and technology, cell therapy manufacturing, and sustainable urban food production (Heng, 2019).

The other newer universities have been developing their own research niches and areas of excellence, such as in management, social sciences, and computing in SMU; and engineering, and design and technology in SUTD. SIT and SUSS have been focusing on applied research in technology and social sciences so as to promote the practicability and relevance of academic research in the industrial and social settings. These developments are, without doubt, reflective of the Singapore government's determination to adopt highly proactive and supportive policies in promoting R&D to serve the needs of economic restructuring throughout the process of economic disruption and the Fourth Industrial Revolution.

The need for a policy on R&D first surfaced in the Economic Committee Report in 1986 that reviewed Singapore's economic strategies following the first ever economic downturn since independence in the mid-1980s (Ministry of Trade and Industry, 1986). Subsequently, in 1991, the National Science and Technology Board (NSTB) was established to facilitate and coordinate R&D activities in accordance with the First National Science and Technology Five-Year Plan. A*STAR, established in 2001, is now responsible for developing the national research agenda, building up the national pool of researcher-scientists, and attracting foreign researchers. In 2006, the National Research Foundation (NRF) was set up to set the direction of R&D by developing policies, plans, and strategies for research, innovation, and enterprise (RIE) activities, funding strategic initiatives, and building up R&D capabilities by nurturing research talent so as to make Singapore a vibrant R&D hub and a knowledge-intensive, innovative, and entrepreneurial economy.

Singapore's gross expenditure on R&D (GERD) as a percentage of GDP increased considerably from 0.85 percent in 1990 to 2 percent in 2017 (A*STAR, 2016, 2018). The decade of the 2010s saw further enhancement. Between 2011 and 2020, the amount of government research spending increased by S$35 billion (US$25 billion) (Lee, 2016). According to Lee, Singapore's long-term aim is to be among the most research-intensive, innovative, and entrepreneurial economies in the world in order to create high value-added jobs and economic prosperity for Singaporeans. Research and innovation underpin the competitiveness of Singapore's industries and catalyze new growth areas.

One indicator of the success of the government's strategy is that Singapore regained the top spot as Asia-Pacific's most innovative nation in the latest global innovation index (Yip, 2020). Tan (2020) notes that today, NUS and NTU have several research groups that could be regarded as among the best in the world in fields like material science, engineering, and chemistry.

As illustrated in Table 33.1, while the private sector remains the highest spender on Singapore's R&D activities, the higher education sector's proportion of R&D spending has increased more significantly from 12 to 18 percent from 1999 to 2018. In other words, universities and public research institutes such as A*STAR have been playing a more significant role in contributing to R&D in Singapore.

Table 33.1 Distribution of R&D spending in Singapore, 1999–2018 (S$
million)

	1999	2009	2018
Private sector	1,670 (63%)	3,694 (61.4%)	5,638 (60.7%)
Higher education sector	310 (11.7%)	854 (14.2%)	1,651 (17.8%)
Government sector	304 (11.4%)	683 (11.3%)	1,069 (11.5%)
Public research institutes	370 (13.9%)	780 (13%)	923 (9.9%)
Total	2,656	6,012	9,282

Source: Singapore Department of Statistics, https://www.tablebuilder.singstat.gov.sg/publi
cfacing/createDataTable.action?refId=14600.

Further, apart from R&D in science and technology, the Singapore government recently also acknowledged the importance of research in social sciences and humanities, including disciplines such as business, management, law, and accountancy. The Social Sciences Research Council (SSRC) was established in 2016 to promote and support research, and to develop capabilities and partnerships and develop relevant human capital. Following the establishment of the SSRC, the Ministry of Education set aside S$350 million during 2016–2020 to fund research in these areas, a 40 percent increase from 2011 to 2015.

The increased emphasis on academic research productivity will have several consequences. Teaching will likely be seen as less important in research-intensive universities; while academics, concerned with the impact of their work, may focus on citation indexes and other indices as these are well-established indicators of research quality. One consequence of this substantial investment in R&D has been that both NUS and NTU have enhanced their reputation and prestige internationally (see Table 33.2).

As noted earlier, the Singapore government plays a prominent role in higher education finance and development. The six universities, together with the five polytechnics and ITE, in the higher education sector, are all publicly funded. The higher education sector is also heavily subsidized by the government, which supports 75 percent of the cost of university education at the undergraduate level, and 85 percent of the cost of polytechnic education (Teng, 2019). Moreover, the government has also increased its spending and investment in higher education to cater for the continuous growth of student enrollments and research capacity of publicly funded institutions of higher learning concomitantly, with an increasing demand for private higher education provision and financial input. Tables 33.3 and 33.4 show that the Singapore government increased incrementally the public expenditure on university education from S$537.4 million (US$376 million) in 1998 to S$3.2 billion (US$2.3 billion) in 2018 or the public expenditure on university education per student from S$12,580 (US$8,990) in 1998 to S$22,192 (US$15,870) in 2018. The relatively lower growth rate of per student expenditure can

Table 33.2 International rankings of Singapore universities, 2016–2021

	NUS		NTU	
	QS Global ranking	THES	QS Global ranking	THES
2021	11	25	13	47
2020	11	25	11	48
2019	11	23	12	51
2018	15	22	11	52
2017	15	24	13	54
2016	22	26	39	55

Note: QS: QS World University Rankings; THES: Times Higher Education Supplement World University Rankings.

Table 33.3 Government recurrent expenditure on higher education, 1998–2018 (S$ thousand)

	Publicly funded diploma courses (polytechnics)	Publicly funded degree courses (universities)
2018	1,274,614	3,254,804
2008	946,113	1,808,987
1998	419,673	537,450

Source: Singapore Department of Statistics, https://data.gov.sg/dataset/government-recurrent-expenditure-on-education?view_id=c9e16c77-eab2-4ad5-a8be-0926b375158d&resource_id=0db9f5fb-7b87-43e1-9e5d-78404e57b79d.

Table 33.4 Government recurrent expenditure on higher education per student, 1998–2018 (S$)

	Publicly funded diploma courses (polytechnics)	Publicly funded degree courses (universities)
2018	16,408	22,192
2008	13,479	19,664
1998	8,144	12,580

Source: Singapore Department of Statistics, https://data.gov.sg/dataset/government-recurrent-expenditure-on-education-per-student?view_id=d54d133c-c8ee-4eed-a74e-4b7e61c93b66&resource_id=1b84f2f7-b11e-4705-af17-82b67f050b85.

be explained by a significant growth of total student enrollments in publicly funded universities from 32,000 in 1998 to 70,000 in 2018 (Ministry of Education, 2003, 2019).

We noted earlier the government's goal to ensure academic excellence and relevance in the higher education sector. Adequate resourcing was a key strategy. Apart from investing heavily in the higher education sector, the Singapore government is also very much concerned about the importance of raising the quality of higher education so that its universities would be transformed to world-class higher education institutions to develop Singapore as Asia's premier higher education hub. Instead of imposing direct control over the management and operation of universities, the state sees its role as the planner and facilitator of long-term development and improvement of higher education in Singapore. In this state-centered model of development, the state's capacity for making appropriate and effective policies has been a critical factor affecting how well higher education is and will continue to be relevant. For instance, massification has been implemented incrementally in order to avoid causing negative effects on the quality of higher education while at the same time ensuring that it could meet the increasing demands for university education. Another example was the government's decision in 2000 to allow universities to have more autonomy to govern and allocate resources themselves so that they would be more accountable for their performance which is subject to close scrutiny by the Ministry of Education through various means of quality assessment and evaluation (Ministry of Education, 2000). This movement of institutional autonomy and accountability resulted in the conversion of publicly funded universities into autonomous universities (Ministry of Education, 2005). While the government retains its authority over issues related to tuition fees, the university's degree structure, targeted student enrollments, and funding allocation, universities are given autonomy over the design and delivery of education, its research portfolio, and its internal management (Magnanti, 2018). Tan (2020) contends that corporatization has allowed Boards of Trustees to play a central role in steering institutional goals signaling that the university belongs to its stakeholders, thus fostering institutional pride and ownership.

3.3 Development of Private Higher Education in Singapore

In recent years, the government has been aware of the growing importance of the private sector in the provision of university education for working adults and polytechnic graduates who have strong aspirations to pursue further studies in local and overseas universities. These increasing demands are being met by a two-pronged approach. With the enactment of the Private Education Act, the Committee for Private Education was set up under SkillsFuture Singapore in 2016 to establish the quality assurance framework for uplifting standards of the PEIs in Singapore. With the aim of raising the university participation rate to 50 percent in order to cater to the needs of mature learners or working adults who want to pursue higher qualifications (Davie, 2020), local and overseas private education institutions are expected to further increase their student enrollments. An exemplary example is the conversion of Singapore's privately run, not-for-profit Singapore Institute of Management University (UniSIM), which received a degree-granting license from the Ministry of Education and is now Singapore's sixth publicly funded autonomous university. In 2017, it was established as the Singapore University of Social Sciences (SUSS). One of the main responsibilities of SUSS is to support the SkillsFuture policy by encouraging lifelong learning among mature learners and working adults with a special focus on social sciences and applied learning (Tan, 2018).

3.4 Internationalizing Universities in an Asian Education Hub

Internationalization as a strategy for developing higher education was initiated by then Prime Minister, Goh Chok Tong, in 1996 to make Singapore the "Boston of the East" and to transform local universities into world-class institutes of higher learning (Goh, 1996). The aim was to develop Singapore as a global city and also an Asian education hub. The main strategy for internationalizing university education has been to develop the public universities, in particular NUS and NTU into world-class institutions comparable to other renowned higher education institutions in the United States and Europe. As a part of the internationalization strategy, several high-end partnerships and collaborations have been forged between local universities and overseas institutions of higher learning, such as MIT, Yale, and Imperial College over the past two decades. Moreover, some renowned universities and institutions such as INSEAD were also encouraged by the Singapore government to set up offshore campuses or run degree and postgraduate programs in Singapore.

According to then Prime Minister, Goh Chok Tong, the government's vision was for NUS and NTU to become world-class universities in the twenty-first century with three goals:

> First, they must provide excellence in teaching and a good, all-round education. They must not only develop professional knowledge and skills, but also nurture future generations of leaders in all areas of national life. Second, they must become hubs of research and intellectual exchange in Asia ... They should also promote greater intellectual understanding between Asia and the West in politics, society and culture. Third, they must each develop a community of alumni with strong bonds among each other and strong attachments to their alma mater. (Goh, 1996)

A World Class Universities (WCU) programme was launched in 1998, to be followed later by the Global Schoolhouse project. Their objectives were to develop Singapore's education industry "as an engine of economic growth, capability development and talent attractions for Singapore" (Economic Review Committee, 2003). Subsequently, the vision for the "Boston of the East" was reiterated by then Minister for Education, Teo Chee Hean, in his speech in 2000:

> Our vision ... is to become the Boston of the East. Boston is not just MIT or Harvard. The greater Boston area boasts over 200 universities, colleges, research institutes and thousands of companies. It is a focal point of creative energy, a hive of intellectual, commercial and social activity. We want to create an oasis of talent in Singapore: a knowledge hub, an ideas-exchange, a confluence of people and idea streams, an incubator for inspiration. (Teo, 2000)

The WCU programme led to the University of Pennsylvania, MIT, Duke, and Johns Hopkins, among others, either establishing or strengthening their presence in Singapore. The partnerships of SMU–Wharton, SUTD–MIT–Zhejiang, Duke–NUS, Yale–NUS and NTU–Imperial College London demonstrate Singapore's strong ability to attract institutions, academics, and students internationally, based on the city-state's reputation for academic standards and education quality. In 2009, the government also established the Singapore Institute of Technology, partnering with reputable overseas universities, such as Newcastle University and Technical University of Munich to provide polytechnic graduates opportunities to pursue a university education. Through a range of collaborative arrangements and partnerships with Singapore's universities, the government aims to create a robust higher education sector which is sustainable and characterized by high-quality graduates (Ng, 2010).

While there is much to admire in the ways that Singapore has achieved internationalization and massification, it has come with some "costs." With the consistent growth of foreign academics in Singapore's universities, there is now widespread concern about whether there is a lack of a Singaporean academic core in local universities as foreign academics have grown in numbers. There are also similar concerns over whether internationalization would bring about an influx of international students at the expense of local Singaporean students' opportunities to study in local universities. These are issues that need to be addressed carefully. Moreover, there have been some setbacks facing the process of internationalization. For instance, Warwick declined to accept the government's invitation to set up an offshore campus in Singapore in 2005 due to worries about academic freedom and affordability issues; the Division of Biomedical Sciences of Johns Hopkins Singapore was requested by A*STAR to shut down in 2007 because the institute could not meet its agreed goals in research and education; and University of New South Wales Asia closed in 2007 because of financial issues and lower than expected student enrollments (Lee and Gopinathan, 2007). Further in August 2021, NUS announced that Yale-NUS College would close in 2025 and be merged with NUS's University Scholars Program to form the NUS College. This college would be organized as an interdisciplinary honors college. This move was met with concern and disappointment, especially from students and parents. Notwithstanding the above, in general, we believe that Singapore's internationalization policies in higher education have been successful.

3.5 Affordable Higher Education for Social Mobility

Higher education in Singapore's development model is underpinned by the state's commitment to meritocracy. Singapore seeks to identify and select elites through meritocracy impartially for effective governance. The government has consistently argued that meritocracy provides equal opportunities to all in a non-discriminatory manner, regardless of socio-economic background. Those who perform well academically in the education system are rewarded with scholarships, university places, and eventually lucrative careers, both in the well-regarded civil service and business. However, meritocratic elites, once successful, will likely invest heavily in their children's education in a bid to place them in a more advantageous position to succeed in the competitive education system, and thus, contribute to a cycle of social stratification across generations (Tan and Dimmock, 2015). Moreover, the recognition of growing income inequality and social stratification in developed economies has drawn attention to Singapore as well. Questions are now being asked as to how well meritocracy works, especially in the education system.

In 2006, then Prime Minister, Goh Chok Tong, used the term "compassionate meritocracy" to urge those who benefit from the meritocratic system to contribute more to society by assisting the less able and less fortunate (Anwar, 2015). As shown in a survey conducted by the Institute of Policy Studies in 2013, most people in Singapore were in favor of a less competitive, more holistic education system which is also more inclusive, thus enabling students to learn with others of different abilities and backgrounds (Amir, 2013).

Additionally, widespread concerns remain on how to improve the education performance of Malay students. A Council for the Development of Malay Education (Mendaki) was established in 1981 to provide additional financial and educational support to Malay students (Kamaludeen et al., 2009; Mutalib, 2011). Although the educational performance gap between Malays and other races has narrowed in primary and secondary education since the 1980s, the extent of Malay underachievement in higher education remains significant. In 1999, the percentage of Primary One cohort admitted to universities was 25 percent Chinese, 4.2 percent Malay, and 10 percent Indian (Tan, 2007). In 2000, as shown in the population census, ethnic representation at the universities was 92.4 percent Chinese, 2.7 percent Malay, and 4.3 percent Indian; while Malays and Indians constitute 14 percent and 8 percent of the population respectively (Tan, 2004). The existing gap between Malays and other ethnic groups is also reflected by the percentage of highest qualification attained: 5.1 percent of Malays attained university qualification in 2005, increasing to 6.8 percent in 2010. The percentage for non-Malays was higher at 22.4 percent in 2005, rising to 28.3 percent in 2010 (Association of Muslim Professionals, 2012). It is also the case that these figures mask an even greater disparity as a larger percentage of Chinese are in private post-secondary institutions in Singapore or are studying abroad (Gopinathan, 2015).

With higher education considered essential to promoting upward social mobility, it is important for the government to ensure a level playing field enabling all capable students, regardless of their socio-economic backgrounds, to succeed in accordance with the fundamental principle of meritocracy in Singapore. In 2019, Prime Minister Lee Hsien Loong announced in his National Day Rally speech that university tuition fees would be lowered together with a significant increase in bursaries to be given to students, especially those from lower income families. He announced that:

> MOE (Ministry of Education) will lower the annual fees for the full-time general degree programmes in SIT and SUSS, from around S$8,000 (US$5,700) now, to S$7,500 (US$5,400) … MOE will significantly enhance government bursaries. For university courses, we will increase government bursaries from up to 50 per cent of general degree fees today, to up to 75 per cent … Similarly, for polytechnic diploma programmes, we will increase the bursary coverage from up to 80 per cent of the fees today, to up to 95 per cent. (Lee, 2019)

Further, in order to encourage lower-income students to study medicine in NUS and NTU, government bursaries for attendance at medical schools will be substantially enhanced. As a result of increased government bursaries, lower-income medical school students will now need to pay a tuition fee of S$5,000 (US$3,500) instead of the original fee ranging between S$29,000 and S$35,000 (US$20,600–25,000) (Lee, 2019). While these are important steps to tackle the issue of social and educational inequality, it remains to be seen how much change there will be in the socio-economic composition of students. While affordability is one factor, qualifying to enter medical school is still impacted by opportunities and quality of education received in the K-12 education sector.

4. Lessons from Singapore's Experience

Singapore's higher education system has gone through significant changes and steady growth, especially in the last three decades as a consequence of five main policy directions as discussed in the previous section. Strong state leadership, and timely and sustained investment in education as a whole, especially in post-secondary education, has ensured a strong link between post-secondary education and manpower needs in the economy to help Singapore establish a high-quality higher education system. The case of Singapore demonstrates that the strong developmental state is without doubt a crucial factor contributing to the relative success in both education quality and international standing. This section will shed light on policy lessons learnt from the island-state.

4.1 Strong Developmental State and Higher Education Development

As a "developmental state," which gains legitimacy through its ability to promote and sustain socio-economic development, Singapore has concentrated its efforts in bringing about modernization and industrialization since its independence in 1965 (Castells, 1992). Similar to other East Asian developmental states such as Japan and South Korea, Singapore's main economic policy direction focuses on export-oriented industrialization, capital accumulation, as well as R&D capacity. Government agencies, including EDB and A*STAR, also adopt a pragmatic approach to strengthening the Singapore economy by maximizing the potential of niche areas where Singapore enjoys comparative and competitive advantages, such as in education quality and R&D. Moreover, R&D has been made a core strategy of economic development, concentrating resources and efforts in several niche areas such as biomedical science, advanced manufacturing, and sustainable food science.

In Singapore, higher education serves to support economic and human capital development and facilitate equitable social outcomes so that economic growth and social stability can be sustained (Woo, 2018). This coincides with a key strategy adopted by Singapore as a developmental state in that education and training policies are designed to boost stocks of human capital. The steady expansion of higher education has served to enhance labor productivity and raise innovation capacity in Singapore, where a strong emphasis is placed on science and technology at all levels in the system, together with expansion of polytechnic and vocational education. The state has achieved a tight coupling of education and training systems with state-determined economic policies. Moreover, it has managed to create a centrally planned, universally available, standardized, and state-driven education system to cater to the state's modernization project. The state's strong commitment to and heavy investment in higher education and R&D is justified by significant returns on investment, with high skills development, high wages, and thus higher standards of living (Gopinathan, 2007). This development journey clearly explains why universities are treated as vital state assets and are well-resourced (Loke et al., 2017).

As the world becomes more volatile, uncertain, complex, and ambiguous (VUCA) with economic disruption affecting most countries around the world (Giles, 2018; Chua, 2019), the state needs to be even more decisive to make and effectively implement timely and effective policies to cope with risks and opportunities to maintain its competitiveness in the global economy. The developmental state in Singapore may be characterized as effective and visionary, planning proactively in a range of areas, including higher education. Moreover, it enjoys strong performance legitimacy which is largely a result of its strong performance in socio-economic development that is endorsed by voters through regular parliamentary elections and thus, in comparative terms, has a high level of trust from the populace.

While planning is no doubt essential, it cannot take into account the many variables that must be considered. Traditionally, the basics have been demand for university places, the state's ability to fund to meet demand, tempered by the needs of the economy. The question is not if there is a mismatch but how serious the problem is. Planning is going to be even more difficult in the post-COVID era. When will national and global economies recover, how will economies be restructured, can accurate estimates be made of numbers going overseas to study and size of foreign students in Singapore? These are questions for which there are no easy answers and which planners have to contend with.

4.2 Getting Rid of "Over-Academized" Higher Education

The rise of global market competition, the emergence of the Fourth Industrial Revolution, and, more recently, the COVID-19 pandemic, are crucial determinants in how the higher education system will evolve in the twenty-first century. While universities have to refer to the state for policy directions and financial assistance, they also need to be highly adaptive to an uncertain and unpredictable external environment. Studies on the changing nature and character of universities over the past two decades have introduced such concepts as adaptive universities, entrepreneurial universities, enterprise universities, and academic capitalism, all focused on the changes universities should make in order to remain relevant. Universities are urged to equip themselves with strong leadership and effective management to cope with more rapid, unpredictable, and complex changes. Students are also expected to be educated and nurtured with relevant skills and knowledge, as well as possess an entrepreneurial spirit by integrating academic learning and work. Singapore's universities corporatization strategy can be seen as a response to these needs in that within a state-dominated system, universities have autonomy and flexibility to respond quickly.

Another response to these challenges is the effort by many higher education institutions to more closely integrate academic study with work experience. The call to rethink the role and nature of university education has recently been made by Senior Minister Tharman Shanmugaratnam, who served as Minister for Education in Singapore between 2003 and 2008. He questioned whether university education around the world has been "over-academized." He was of the view that universities and other institutes of higher learning should help students develop both hard and soft skills, together with creativity, team skills, and cross-cultural skills. University education in the future should go far beyond attaining academic excellence as shown in key performance indicators and international rankings. What is more important is to ensure students are equipped with skills necessary to stay competitive in the global employment market. It is also necessary to address the problem of inefficiencies in higher education: "a massive mismatch of the demand and supply of the skills as well as a mismatch between abilities of students and the type of pathways that they are proceeding on at the tertiary level" (Lim, 2019). One response to the above challenge is the effort to create diversified learning pathways for students to learn and accumulate the most relevant and updated skills and knowledge to cope with the needs of the marketplace and thus improve their employability.

While "lifelong learning" has been promoted for decades, Singapore's SkillsFuture initiative breaks new ground. SkillsFuture, first announced in the Finance Minister's 2015 budget, is a cross-ministry program for lifelong learning and skills training for the Singapore economy. It stemmed from the view that low worker productivity was hampering economic growth and transformation. The government decided that an expansion of university places would be conditional on internships being made central to the curriculum, and that the degree programs would be well-tuned to job shortages in the economy. This highlights the issues of employment and employability and their relation to university education which have taken center stage in government planning for higher education (Loke and Gopinathan, 2016).

At the core of SkillsFuture is a vision of collaboration between government, employers, employees, and training providers for instilling "skills mastery" among Singaporeans from their schooling years to retirement. The government announced that every Singaporean citizen aged 25 and above would receive $500 worth of SkillsFuture credit that can be used towards courses recognized by the government. Its aim was to enable learners to strike a better balance between knowledge and skills pursuits as well as between academic and competency accomplishments. Newly established universities like SIT and SUSS provide alternative pathways focusing on applied degree programs for polytechnic graduates and working adults for their career development (Ministry of Education, 2012; Tan, 2018; Davie, 2020). In order to promote lifelong learning within the SkillsFuture framework, all six publicly funded universities take part in providing alternative qualifications in the form of short courses or modules, or short-term certificate programs, which can be stacked towards degrees, student immersion programs, and apprenticeship degrees (SkillsFuture Work-Study Degree) (Loke and Gopinathan, 2016; SkillsFuture Singapore, 2019). These professional and continuing education institutions are offered at universities including the NUS School for Continuing and Lifelong Education (2016), SMU Academy (2017), SITLEARN Professional Development (2017), SUTD Academy (2018), NTU Centre for Professional and Continuing Education (2019), and Institute of Adult Learning in SUSS (2019).

The latest initiative by the government is the "70-70 target," as announced in the 2020 budget by Deputy Prime Minister and Finance Minister, Heng Swee Keat, to provide financial incentives to allow 70 percent of graduates of universities, polytechnics, and ITEs to attain overseas exposure or international experience through internship, exchange programs, service learning, or study trips, particularly in ASEAN countries, China or India (Cheong, 2020; Heng, 2020). While diversification and better integration between study and work are set to be among the major trends of higher education development in the coming years, it is not yet clear if COVID-19 and geopolitical tensions between major powers will affect the desire and ability of students to study abroad. Singapore's universities have, at short notice, provided additional places to students unable to travel to US and UK universities.

4.3 Pursuing Global Rankings or Serving Society

Even while acknowledging the shortfalls of rankings, the high rankings attained by the two research-oriented comprehensive universities, NUS and NTU, in THES and QS rankings, suggest that Singapore's higher education system is performing well internationally. These universities have been able to use these rankings to recruit high-quality students and academics, and to draw in donations. Nevertheless, there are concerns about whether universities are too obsessed with international rankings by concentrating too much of their efforts in boosting certain key performance indicators such as research publications in top international peer-reviewed journals and citation index data, as opposed to paying attention to the things that matter more broadly. This is especially true given the many pitfalls of some of the international rankings, whose methodology is often questioned for their employment of subjective criteria addressing institutional reputation, the failure to measure the quality of teaching and students' experiences, and the unfavorable rankings for smaller and more specialized institutions (Coclanis, 2020).

Lim and Pang (2018) have pointed out that the pursuit of international rankings by universities would undermine good university governance in Singapore as the higher education system in Singapore is currently skewed towards hiring academics unwilling or unable to engage with important public policy research. This relates to the hiring and promotion of academic staff on the basis of how much research they have published and if they had published in top-ranked journals which are more likely to favor research of theoretical significance and universal applicability in the fields of science, technology, engineering, mathematics, and medicine. They contend that Singapore scholars who pursue local research in fields such as humanities, social sciences, business and law, and on public policy issues such as poverty, inequality, and social mobility are disadvantaged. While the setting up of Singapore's SSRC in 2016 is a step in the right direction to promote locally relevant scholarship and research, it is even more important to overcome the institutional constraints and mindsets which limit the development of local scholars and local research when the publicly funded universities are swayed by international academic rankings.

It was reported by Singapore newspaper *Today* that some arts and humanities academics quit NUS and NTU in response to their pursuit of rankings and the lack of transparency in the performance criteria used for granting promotion and tenure (Ng, 2019). That *Today* article was eventually taken down. Both universities asserted that faculty are not promoted based on rankings but on peer review (Jaschik, 2019). Then Minister for Education Ong Ye Kung referred to the view of the IAAP that current international rankings rely too much on research indicators and overlook areas like experiential learning and entrepreneurship. Ong made it clear that:

> If there is a change I wish for ... it will be to evaluate the effectiveness of a university in collaborating with the world outside of academia – industries, society, communities, government – and delivering impact in all these sectors. This will go way beyond publications and citations, which are the easiest to measure today and we may have relied on quite a lot. (Teng, 2018)

He suggested that international university rankings should not just focus on publications and citations but also take into account how universities work with industry, society, community, and government (Teng, 2018). Singapore universities understand the need for universities to strike the right balance between pursuing global rankings, presently a mark of academic excellence, and serving the interests of nation-building and socio-economic development in Singapore.

5. CONCLUSION

With regard to universities, both massification and internationalization strategies were carefully planned for. The government also made large-scale investments in R&D which benefited universities and contributed to transforming a port-based trading economy into one characterized by advanced manufacturing, financial, and other services. Singapore's small size and performance-oriented model of governance enabled it to seize opportunities in the spread of globalization and onset of the Fourth Industrial Revolution. At least two of Singapore's six universities are regarded as among the best in Asia and highly regarded globally.

Singapore's post-secondary system now faces major challenges. Singapore's globalized opportunities and allure are beginning to diminish and become replaced by economic nationalism and unilateralism. The most recent push for a "Singapore core" over the hiring of nationals in place of foreigners will have impact on internationalism in universities. The onset of the COVID-19 pandemic in 2020 has also caused massive disruptions to post-secondary education. While Singapore has a robust system of post-secondary education, in the COVID-19 context it will need to reimagine university education. While campus-based, in-person learning is an integral part of university education, how will social distancing be managed in classrooms and hostels? The pandemic has brought international student mobility to an abrupt halt and caused a drop of foreign students in Singapore's universities.

Policymakers now argue that the pandemic has presented an opportunity to rethink curriculum, pedagogy, and assessment. In response, some pedagogical and curriculum changes have been initiated by universities. They have adopted a blended learning model featuring a combination of online teaching and traditional face-to-face classroom instruction, and they are planning for an interdisciplinary curriculum with greater emphasis on experiential and lifelong learning together with Singapore's SkillsFuture programs. In December 2020, NUS launched an interdisciplinary college, the College of Humanities and Science, which admitted its first cohort of students in August 2021 (Teng, 2020). While commitment and resources are available, it will also be necessary for academics to adjust their mindsets to promised new curriculum and pedagogical changes.

In a major policy speech in early February 2021, then Education Minister Lawrence Wong stressed:

1. the importance of universities providing for more holistic learning and more interdisciplinary and cross domain knowledge via internships and service-based learning,

2. that, in order to promote lifelong learning, universities will need to make provision for multi-entry points along both age distribution and the entire skills spectrum, and that

3. universities must continue to play an important role in Singapore's socio-economic development by successfully innovating to meet future changes and opportunities (Wong, 2021).

In conclusion, with a strong and competent government committed to financing and developing higher education, Singapore's universities have managed to maintain high quality while catering to growing demands from students and working adults. Singapore's universities clearly have to stay relevant to changing manpower and economic needs. While stressing academic excellence they have paid due attention to improving graduates' employability. Singapore could well become a trendsetter in showing how other higher education systems can chart new and resilient pathways in the post-COVID era.

REFERENCES

A*STAR (2016). *National Survey of Research and Development in Singapore 2015*. Singapore: Agency for Science, Technology and Research.

A*STAR (2018). *National Survey of Research and Development in Singapore 2017*. Singapore: Agency for Science, Technology and Research.

Amir, H. (2013). "Singaporeans want 'compassionate meritocracy'." *Today*, August 26.

Anwar, N. (2015). "Negotiating Singapore's meritocracy: A subtle shift?" *RSIS Commentary*, 30, February 12. Singapore: S. Rajaratnam School of International Studies.

Association of Muslim Professionals (2012). *The Next Decade: Strengthening Our Community's Architecture*. Third National Convention of Singapore Muslim Professionals. Singapore: Association of Muslim Professionals.

Castells, M. (1992). "Four Asian tigers with a dragon head: A comparative analysis of the state, economy, and society in the Asian Pacific Rim." In R. Appelbaum and J. Henderson (eds.). *State and Development in the Asian Pacific Rim* (pp. 33–70). Thousand Oaks, CA: Sage Publications.

Cheong, D. (2020). "A leg-up for youth and securing nation's future." *The Straits Times*, February 19.

Chua, M. (2019). *Singapore, Disrupted*. Singapore: The Straits Times Press.

Coclanis, P. (2020). "QS university rankings: Quite subjective?" *The Straits Times*, June 27.

Dainton, F. (1979). *Report on University Education in Singapore, 1979*. Singapore: Government Printer.

Dainton, F. (1989). *Report on University Education in Singapore, 1989*. Singapore: Government Printer.

Davie, S. (2020). "Planning for uni places needs rethink." *The Straits Times*, January 28.

Economic Review Committee (2003). *New Challenges, Fresh Goals: Towards a Dynamic Global City*. Singapore: Ministry of Trade and Industry.

Fisher, D. R. (2020). *Education Crossing Borders: How Singapore and MIT Created a New University*. Cambridge, MA: MIT Press.

Giles, S. (2018). "How VUCA is reshaping the business environment, and what it means for innovation." *Forbes*, May 9.

Goh, C. B. and Tan, W. (2008). "The development of university education in Singapore." In S. Lee, C. B. Goh, B. Fredriksen, and J. Tan (eds.), *Toward a Better Future: Education and Training for Economic Development in Singapore since 1965* (pp. 149–166). Washington DC: The World Bank.

Goh, C. T. (1996). "Vision for National University of Singapore (NUS) and Nanyang Technological University (NTU) in the 21st century." Speech by Prime Minister Goh Chok Tong at the National University of Singapore (NUS) Alumni Day and Exhibition at NUS Multi-purpose Hall on September 21. Singapore: Prime Minister's Office.

Gopinathan, S. (2007). "Globalisation, the Singapore developmental state and education policy: A thesis revisited." *Globalisation, societies and education*, 5, 53–70.

Gopinathan, S. (2015). *Singapore Chronicles: Education*. Singapore: The Straits Times Press.

Gopinathan, S. and Lee, M. H. (2011). "Challenging and co-opting globalisation: Singapore's strategies in higher education." *Journal of Higher Education Policy and Management*, 33, 287–299.

Heng, J. (2019). "Three areas singled out for bumped-up R&D funding after govt review." *The Business Times*, March 28.

Heng, S. K. (2020). *Budget 2020: Budget Speech – Advancing as One Singapore*. Singapore: Ministry of Finance.

Jaschik, S. (2019). "Are global rankings damaging universities?" *Inside Higher Ed*, January 28.

Kamaludeen, M. N., Pereira, A., and Turner, B. (2009). *Muslims in Singapore: Piety, Politics and Policies*. London and New York: Routledge.

Lee, H. L. (2019). "PM Lee Hsien Loong delivered his National Day Rally speech on 18 August 2018 at the Institute of Technical Education College Central." Singapore: Prime Minister Office.

Lee, M. H. and Gopinathan, S. (2007). "Internationalizing university education in Singapore: Future directions." *Higher Education Forum*, 4, 87–112.

Lee, U. (2016). "Record S$19b set aside for R&D until 2020." *The Business Times*, January 9.

Lim, J. (2019). "Tertiary education has been 'over-academised': Applied education also important: Tharman." *Today*, October 18.

Lim, L. and Pang, E. F. (2018). "How Singapore's obsession with university rankings only serves to hurt it." *South China Morning Post*, December 21.

Loke, H. Y., Chia, Y. T., and Gopinathan, S. (2017). "Hybridity, the developmental state and globalisation: The case of Singapore's universities." *Studies in Higher Education*, 42, 1887–1898.

Loke, H. Y. and Gopinathan, S. (2016). "The policy and politics of the cohort participation rate in universities: The case of Singapore and 'SkillsFuture.'" *International Journal of Chinese Education*, 5, 209–225.

Magnanti, T. (2018). "Building a new academic institution: The Singapore University of Technology and Design." In P. Altbach, L. Reisberg, J. Salmi, and I. Froumin (eds.), *Accelerated Universities: Ideas and Money Combine to Build Academic Excellence* (pp. 103–127). Leiden: Brill Sense.

Ministry of Education (2000). *Fostering Autonomy and Accountability in Universities: A Review of Public University Governance and Funding in Singapore*. Singapore: Ministry of Education.

Ministry of Education (2003). *Education Statistics Digest 2003*. Singapore: Ministry of Education.

Ministry of Education (2005). *Autonomous Universities: Towards Peaks of Excellence*. Singapore: Ministry of Education.

Ministry of Education (2012). *Report of the Committee on University Education Pathways beyond 2015: Greater Diversity, More Opportunities*. Singapore: Ministry of Education.

Ministry of Education (2019). *Education Statistics Digest 2019*. Singapore: Ministry of Education. Ministry of Trade and Industry (1986). *The Singapore Economy: New Directions*. Singapore: Ministry of Trade and Industry.

Mutalib, H. (2011). "The Singapore minority dilemma." *Asian Survey*, 51, 1156–1171.

Ng, E. H. (2010). "Speech by Dr Ng Eng Hen, Minister for Education and Second Minister for Defence at the Grand Opening of the NUS Business School's Mochtar Riady Building." Singapore: Ministry of Education.

Ng, K. (2019). "Opaque policies, fixation with KPIs, rankings: Why arts and humanities academics quit NUS, NTU." *Today*, January 6.

Selvaratnam, V. (1994). *Innovations in Higher Education: Singapore at the Competitive Edge*. Washington, DC: The World Bank.

Singapore Department of Statistics (2002). *Yearbook of Statistics, Singapore 2002*. Singapore: Singapore Department of Statistics.

Singapore Department of Statistics (2019). *Yearbook of Statistics, Singapore 2019*. Singapore: Singapore Department of Statistics.

SkillsFuture Singapore (2019). "More work-study opportunities for Singaporeans." Press Release, July 12. Singapore: SkillsFuture Singapore.

Tan, C. (2007). "Narrowing the gap: The educational achievements of the Malay community in Singapore." *Intercultural Education*, 18, 53–64.

Tan, C. and Dimmock, C. (2015). *Tensions between Meritocracy and Equity in Singapore: Educational Issues in Preparing a Workforce for the Knowledge-Based Economy*. Singapore: The Head Foundation.

Tan, E. C. (2020). "World class universities." In T. Koh (ed.), *Fifty Secrets of Singapore's Success*. Singapore: Straits Times Press.

Tan, J. (2004). "Singapore: Small nation, big plans." In P. Altbach and T. Umakoshi (eds.), *Asian Universities: Historical Perspectives and Contemporary Challenges* (pp. 175–200). Baltimore, MD: Johns Hopkins University Press.

Tan, J. (2018). "University governance and management in Singapore: The case of the Singapore Institute of Management University (UNISIM)." In D. Chang, M. N. N. Lee, and H. Loke (eds.), *The Governance and Management of Universities in Asia: Global Influences and Local Responses* (pp. 112–118). London: Routledge.

Teng, A. (2018). "Rankings need to evolve and evaluate wider impact of unis: Ong Ye Kung." *The Straits Times*, September 27.

Teng, A. (2019). "Parliament: Newer universities get double government funding in matching grants." *The Straits Times*, January 17.

Teng, A. (2020). "NUS launches new interdisciplinary College of Humanities and Science." *The Straits Times*, December 8.

Teo, C. H. (2000). "Education towards the 21st century: Singapore universities of tomorrow." Address by RADM (NS) Teo Chee Hean, Minister for Education and Second Minister for Defence at the Alumni International Singapore (AIS) Lecture. Singapore: Ministry of Education.

Wong, L. (2021). "Opening Remark by Mr Lawrence Wong, Minister for Education at The Straits Times Education Forum 2021 'Reimagining universities, post-COVID,'" February.5, Singapore: Ministry of Education.

Woo, J. J. (2018). "Educating the developmental state: Policy integration and mechanism re-design in Singapore's SkillsFuture scheme." *Journal of Asian Public Policy*, 11, 267–284.

Yip, W. Y. (2020). "Singapore remains Asia-Pacific's most innovative nation." *The Straits Times*, September 4.

CHAPTER 34

HIGHER EDUCATION IN HONG KONG

Recent Developments and Challenges

JIN JIANG

1. INTRODUCTION

ON July 1, 1997, the sovereignty of Hong Kong was officially transferred from the United Kingdom to the People's Republic of China. Hong Kong was renamed a Special Administrative Region (SAR) of China with the promise of semi-autonomous status for 50 years with certain economic and political guarantees under a "One Country, Two Systems" principle. These guarantees include autonomy in the administration of the Hong Kong government, the higher education sector, and respect for academic freedom. As a result of its history and political status, Hong Kong has great potential to leverage its uniquely "privileged position" as a bridge connecting the international academic community to mainland China (Lo and Ng, 2015, p. 518). With long-standing higher education institutions that are well-recognized for their international standing and reputation, the Hong Kong government has been supportive in developing Hong Kong's higher education system into an education hub in the Asia-Pacific region (Cheng et al., 2016a) and more broadly, towards transforming Hong Kong into a "world-class" city with "world-class" education (University Grants Committee of Hong Kong SAR Government (UGC), 2004, p. 3).

Against the background outlined above, this chapter discusses recent developments and challenges for the higher education sector in Hong Kong. The first section begins with an overview of the current higher education system in Hong Kong and structural changes in recent decades. The second section focuses on marketization and diversification strategies of higher education in Hong Kong and the governance of public universities and private higher education institutions. The third section discusses the expansion of higher education and challenges in social equality, with a focus on educational inequality in university admissions, graduate employment, and social mobility.

The fourth section draws upon internationalization strategies and policies in Hong Kong. Finally, the conclusion reflects on the development of Hong Kong as a regional education hub.

1.1 Current Higher Education System in Hong Kong

Hong Kong has 22 degree-awarding higher education institutions (HEIs), of which nine are publicly funded by the Hong Kong government and 13 are self-funded (see Table 34.1). Among the nine publicly funded HEIs, eight are funded by the University Grants Committee (UGC) (these universities are thus called UGC-funded universities). The

Table 34.1 Degree-awarding HEIs in Hong Kong

Nature		HEIs	QS Rankings 2021
Publicly funded (9 HEIs)	UGC-funded	City University of Hong Kong (CityU)	48
		Hong Kong Baptist University (HKBU)	264
		Lingnan University (LU)	571–580
		The Chinese University of Hong Kong (CUHK)	43
		The Education University of Hong Kong (EDUHK)	n.a.
		The Hong Kong Polytechnic University (PolyU)	75
		The Hong Kong University of Science and Technology (HKUST)	27
		The University of Hong Kong (HKU)	22
		Hong Kong Academy for Performing Arts	n.a.
Self-funded (13 HEIs)		Caritas Institute of Higher Education	n.a.
		Centennial College	n.a.
		Chu Hai College of Higher Education	n.a.
		Gratia Christian College	n.a.
		HKCT Institute of Higher Education	n.a.
		Hong Kong Nang Yan College of Higher Education	n.a.
		Hong Kong Shue Yan University	n.a.
		Technological and Higher Education Institute of Hong Kong, Vocational Training Council	n.a.
		The Hang Seng University of Hong Kong	n.a.
		The Open University of Hong Kong	n.a.
		Tung Wah College	n.a.
		UOW College Hong Kong	n.a.
		Yew Chung College of Early Childhood Education	n.a.

Sources: Education Bureau (Hong Kong) (2019a); Quacquarelli Symonds (QS) World University Rankings 2021 (QS, 2021).

remaining one HEI, the Hong Kong Academy for Performing Arts (HKAPA), is funded directly by the Hong Kong government (Education Bureau (Hong Kong), 2019a).

UGC is a non-governmental committee which acts as an independent professional advisor to the Hong Kong government on the development and funding of HEIs. Its primary responsibility is to distribute an allocation of public funds to HEIs, evaluate the effectiveness of such funds, and provide advice to the Hong Kong government on the strategic development of higher education (UGC, 2018). Thus, UGC serves as an intermediary between the government administration and UGC-funded universities to protect the institutional autonomy of universities and academic freedom.

Hong Kong is home to several "world-class" universities in terms of excellence in teaching and research with five UGC-funded universities, namely, HKU, HKUST, CUHK, CityU, and PolyU, among the top 100 universities in the QS World University Rankings 2021 (QS, 2021) (see Table 34.1). In fact, HKU, HKUST, and CUHK have been "long-standing" performers in top 100 universities in the QS ranking in the last ten years, while CityU and PolyU have become top 100 universities since 2015 and 2018, respectively.

The Hong Kong government respects and supports the differentiated roles and missions among universities to achieve international competitiveness (UGC, 2004, pp. 2–4). For example, LU has a particular focus on liberal arts and PolyU emphasizes teaching, professional training, and applied research (UGC, 2004, p. 11).

While HEIs in Hong Kong may offer various programs and different teaching and learning experiences, fundamentally, the role of higher education in Hong Kong serves three main missions: teaching, research, and knowledge transfer (KT). UGC defines KT as "systems and processes by which knowledge, including technology, know-how, expertise and skills are transferred between higher education institutions and society" (UGC, 2019e). In addition to educating students and pursuing academic excellence, universities are expected to engage in KT as a priority over technology transfer in the emergent knowledge society (Mok, 2012). More importantly, the purpose of KT is to enact innovative, profitable, economic, or social improvements (UGC, 2019e). Therefore, HEIs in Hong Kong are expected to be entrepreneurial in transferring research and knowledge to the wider community and society, and to be proactive in promoting industry–university, community/society–university collaboration (Mok and Jiang, 2018a) and cross-border collaboration (Kang and Jiang, 2020).

1.2 Structural Changes to Accessing Higher Education in Hong Kong

Before 1997, access to higher education in Hong Kong was modeled after the "5+2" system used by the British education system (Shek, 2019) which comprised of five years of secondary education (Form 1–Form 5) and two years of matriculation education (Form 6 and Form 7). Students were required to take two public examinations—the

Hong Kong Certificate of Education Examination (HKCEE) in Form 5 and the Hong Kong Advanced Level Examination (HKALE) in Form 7 (Shek, 2019; Education Commission (Hong Kong), 1988, pp. 18–19). At that time, HEIs provided three-year undergraduate degree courses after Form 7 except for one university offering four-year undergraduate degree courses after Form 6 (Education Commission (Hong Kong), 1988, pp. 18–20, 100). Recognizing that different opportunities for entry into higher education were creating extra pressure on Form 6 students to study for their first attempt into a university and inflating competition among universities, the Education Commission sought to standardize the admission process and the duration of undergraduate degree courses across universities (Education Commission (Hong Kong), 1988, pp. 18–21).

In 2009, the Education and Manpower Bureau (Hong Kong) (2005) announced the implementation of a new academic structure called "334," comprising three years of junior secondary education, three years of senior secondary education, and four years of an undergraduate program at university. The new academic structure encourages students to complete six years of the secondary education curriculum[1] and the previous two exams (HKCEE and HKALE), taken at the end of Form 5 and Form 7, were integrated into only one examination (i.e., the Hong Kong Diploma of Secondary Education (HKDSE)) at the end of Form 6 (Hong Kong Examinations and Assessment Authority, 2015). This new academic structure in Hong Kong aligns with other educational systems around the world including mainland China and the United States and helps to facilitate the mobility of students in Hong Kong to participate in global academic systems.

1.3 The Pathway to Post-Secondary Education

Upon taking the HKDSE, students have the option to apply for undergraduate (four-year bachelor degree) programs at local universities through the Joint University Programs Admission System (JUPAS) (Education Bureau (Hong Kong), 2019b). Students may apply to UGC-funded programs at relatively low cost, self-financed full-time bachelor degree programs offered by OpenU, or subsidized full-time bachelor degree programs for designated professions offered by self-funded HEIs.[2]

---

[1] In Hong Kong, students are entitled to 12 years of free primary and secondary education. Upon the completion of the first three years of secondary education (lower secondary education), students may opt for a secondary vocational program instead of a mainstream upper secondary education. Since 2008, the government has provided full subvention for full-time vocational programs offered by the Vocational Training Council (VTC) for Secondary 3 school leavers. Holders of the diploma of vocational education can apply for higher diploma programs. For details, see the government's website (https://www.gov.hk/en/about/abouthk/factsheets/docs/education.pdf) and the VTC website (https://www.vtc.edu.hk/admission/en/programme/overview/s3/diploma-of-vocational-education/).

[2] See details about the JUPAS scheme from its official website: https://www.jupas.edu.hk/en/about-jupas/introduction/. Local students holding an academic qualification (e.g., international qualifications, such as International Baccalaureate Diploma, GCE A-level) other than HKDSE can submit application to a university through the direct application (non-JUPAS) route. See details about the admission of students outside JUPAS from the government's website: https://www.info.gov.hk/gia/general/201401/08/P201401080457.htm.

Further studies (including postgraduate diploma, master's degree, and doctoral degree programmes) or employment		Employment
Four-year bachelor's degree programme	Top-up degree programme (4th year)	
	Top-up degree programme (3rd year)	
	Sub-degree programme (including associate degree (AD), higher diplomas and diplomas (HD) (2nd year)	
	Sub-degree programme (associate degree (AD), higher diplomas and diplomas (HD) (1st year)	
Hong Kong Diploma of Secondary Education (HKDSE) / Diploma Yi Jin (DYJ)		
Six-year secondary education		

FIGURE 34.1 Pathway to post-secondary education

Sources: Figure adapted from the Education and Manpower Bureau (Hong Kong) (2005, p. 11)
and Hong Kong FSTE (2016).

In the academic year of 2012/2013, the Diploma Yi Jin (DYJ) was introduced to provide a pathway for Form 6 school leavers and adult learners to earn a qualification comparable with obtaining five subjects in HKDSE level 2, which could be used as credit towards further educational qualifications (Federation for Self-Financing Tertiary Education (FSTE) (Hong Kong), 2016). As an alternative pathway for students to gain an academic qualification and access to higher education, the DYJ received positive evaluations from students (Wong and Yeung, 2004). Wong and Yeung (2004) find that students who completed the program have better opportunities for further study or employment, compared with those who failed to do so.

Apart from bachelor degree programs, sub-degree programs, including associate degrees and higher diploma programs, offer students further education opportunities beyond secondary education. Sub-degree programs generally prepare students for employment in management positions at an entry-level or could be used as a foundational course earning credit for articulation towards a bachelor degree (Hong Kong SAR Government, 2017). After obtaining a bachelor degree, graduates have the option to enter the workforce or continue with further studies, including pursuing a postgraduate diploma, a master's degree, or a doctoral degree (Figure 34.1).

2. Who "Pays" for Higher Education?

2.1 Public Universities

Before the 1980s, Hong Kong only had two universities, HKU and CUHK, with a very low enrollment rate of around 2 percent (Jung and Postiglione, 2015; Lee, 2016). To meet the growing demand for socio-economic development and labor market needs arising from the knowledge economy, the Hong Kong government made serious attempts to

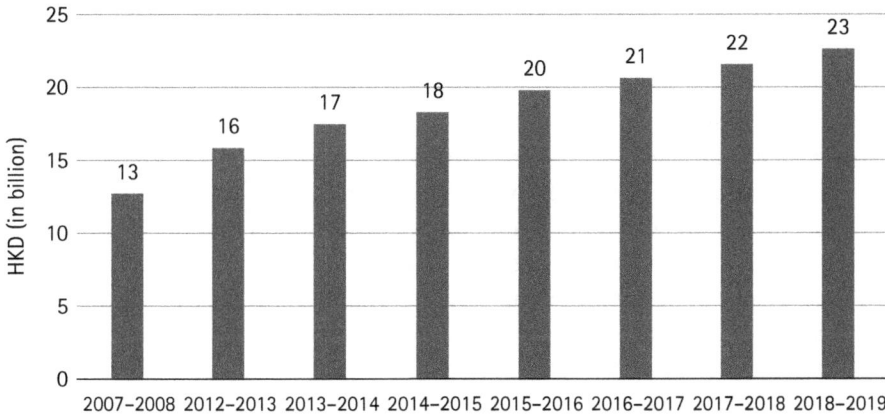

FIGURE 34.2 Recurrent government expenditure on post-secondary education in Hong Kong, 2007–2019

Source: Education Bureau (Hong Kong) (2020).

increase its investment in higher education to expand student enrollment. Figure 34.2 shows the rising trend of government expenditure on post-secondary education since the academic year of 2007/2008. Specifically, government expenditure increased from HKD 12.7 billion (approximately USD1.6 billion) in 2007/2008 to HKD22.6 billion (approximately USD2.9 billion) in 2018/2019, indicating an approximate 80 percent growth in the last ten years.

As mentioned in section 1.1 above, the Hong Kong government's funding for HEIs is mainly given to eight publicly funded universities through UGC with the exception of the Hong Kong Academy for Performing Arts (HKAPA) which is funded directly by the Hong Kong government (Education Bureau (Hong Kong), 2019a). UGC-funded institutions have autonomy to use recurrent grants for "UGC-fundable activities,"[3] though are required to adhere to an approved quota of students for UGC-funded programs (UGC, 2015, 2019a).

2.2 Changing Funding Policies: Changes in Funding Allocations and the Importance of Teaching and Research

In general, UGC plans funding for UGC-funded universities in a triennial cycle. Funding is generally allocated to three components, namely, teaching (approximately 75 percent), research (approximately 23 percent), and professional activity (approximately 2 percent) (UGC, 2019a). To encourage all public institutions to consider

---

[3] UGC-fundable activities include activities associated with teaching, research, and institutional support that are allowable and funded by UGC. Whereas non-UGC activities are generally associated with self-financing activities, non-UGC-funded research activities and others (UGC, 2015).

strategic development and to enhance their international competitiveness, UGC has adopted a competitive allocation mechanism for publicly funded degree places since the planning for the 2009–2012 triennium. Except for disciplines that involve manpower planning (such as medicine, health science, and education), a small proportion of first-year, first-degrees (FYFD) are redistributed among universities based on UGC's assessment of comparative merit among these universities (UGC, 2019a).

The government has also adopted a Research Assessment Exercise (RAE) to assess the research performance of UGC-funded universities since 1993. Results of the RAE have been used to inform the allocation of research funding from the UGC Block Grant to universities (UGC, 2019b). In the previous five RAEs of 1993, 1996, 1999, 2006, and 2014, the research assessment was based on research outputs submitted by each university. In addition to the research outputs,[4] RAE 2020 is the first evaluation cycle to include research impact to encourage universities to conduct research that can provide "demonstrable contributions, beneficial effects, valuable changes or advantages that research qualitatively brings to the economy, society, culture, public policy or services, health, the environment or quality of life" (UGC, 2017a, 13).

2.3 Marketization and Diversification of Higher Education

Hong Kong's higher education system has experienced marketization and diversification in recent years (Mok, 1999). Although public universities in Hong Kong receive funding from the government, they have increasingly turned to additional sources for support to cope with rising operating costs and development (Jacob et al., 2018). For example, there is a growing demand for new facilities to cope with increasing enrollment rates. Public HEIs have thus changed their tuition income model by adopting a "user-pay principle" (charging students tuition fees to cover a proportion of costs); as well as offering fully "self-financed" courses, especially for postgraduate programs (Mok, 1999).[5] Program tuition fees account for a substantial proportion of income for universities. Universities also raise funds from non-government sectors, such as receiving sponsorship from trust funds and industries and earning income from providing services in consultancy, business, and other commercial activities (Mok, 1999).

HKU, for example, is a comprehensive UGC-funded university and receives the largest amount of funding among the eight UGC-funded universities. In the 2018/2019 academic year, HKU received 50 percent of its funding from government subventions, a decrease from the 64 percent it received in 2003/2004 (see Table 34.2).

[4] In the RAE 2020, three elements are assessed (the respective weighting listed in parentheses): research outputs (70 percent), impact (15 percent), and environment (15 percent) (UGC, 2017a, p. 3).
[5] For example, the tuition fee in 2021–2022 for UGC-funded bachelor degree programs is HKD42,100 (approximately USD5,423), and the tuition fees for self-financed bachelor degree programs range from HKD78,120 (approximately USD10,063) to HKD98,100 (approximately USD12,636). See details from https://www.jupas.edu.hk/en/page/detail/529/.

Table 34.2 The funding sources of HKU, 2018–2019 and 2003–2004 (in thousand HKD, percentage of total funding in parenthesis)

	Government subventions	Tuition, programs, and other fees	Donations and benefactions	Auxiliary services	Other income	Interest and/or investment income	Total
2018–2019	5,304,526 (50%)	3,116,399 (29%)	442,324 (4%)	423,033 (4%)	863,818 (8%)	520,235 (5%)	10,670,335 (100%)
2003–2004	3,056,538 (64%)	713,559 (15%)	378,574 (8%)	112,534 (2%)	222,442 (5%)	289,415 (6%)	4,773,062 (100%)

Sources: HKU (2004, 2019a).

Meanwhile, tuition, programs, and other fees accounted for 29 percent of HKU's funding in 2018/2019, almost double that from 2003/2004. Similarly, income from auxiliary services and other income streams in 2018/2019 also doubled in figures from 15 years prior. Such changes demonstrate that sources for private funding, particularly tuition and other program fees, have become increasingly important to government-funded universities.

In the Hong Kong government's Policy Address in 2000 (Hong Kong SAR Government, 2000, p. 22), it was announced that the proportion of high school graduates receiving post-secondary education would double to 60 percent within 10 years to meet the needs of the gradual progress of Hong Kong towards a knowledge-based economy and to keep up with the level of other advanced economies. Since government funding alone would be insufficient to achieve this policy objective, the Hong Kong government encouraged non-government stakeholders to be involved in establishing HEIs to broaden opportunities and choices for students (Jacob et al., 2018). As shown in Table 34.1, Hong Kong currently has 12 self-funded degree-awarding institutions. Except for the Open University of Hong Kong and Hong Kong Shue Yan University which registered as an approved post-secondary institution in the 1970s and 1980s, respectively, other self-funded institutions were approved as degree-awarding institutions in more recent decades after 2004. The mobilization of market forces in the provision of higher education by the private sector reveals the Hong Kong government's policy intent to diversify higher education provision and funding (Mok, 1999).

Although private HEIs operate on a self-funded basis, the Hong Kong government has provided a series of funding schemes to support self-funded HEIs for sustainable development, such as the start-up loan scheme in 2001, the research endowment fund in 2009, the self-financing post-secondary education fund in 2011, the qualifications framework fund in 2018, and the student financial assistance schemes (Legislative Council Panel on Education, 2020, pp. 17–20).

2.4 Is There a Dominant Model?

Since the 2001/2002 academic year, the self-funded higher education sector has expanded rapidly. Not only have new private self-financed HEIs been established but publicly funded HEIs have also set up self-financed departments with encouragement from the Hong Kong government to promote the "parallel development" of the publicly funded and self-financed higher education sector (Task Force on Review of Self-Financing Post-Secondary Education (Hong Kong), 2018). Although self-financing has become an increasingly popular strategy for universities, the reputation and ranking of publicly funded universities continue to attract the majority of students (Figure 34.3).

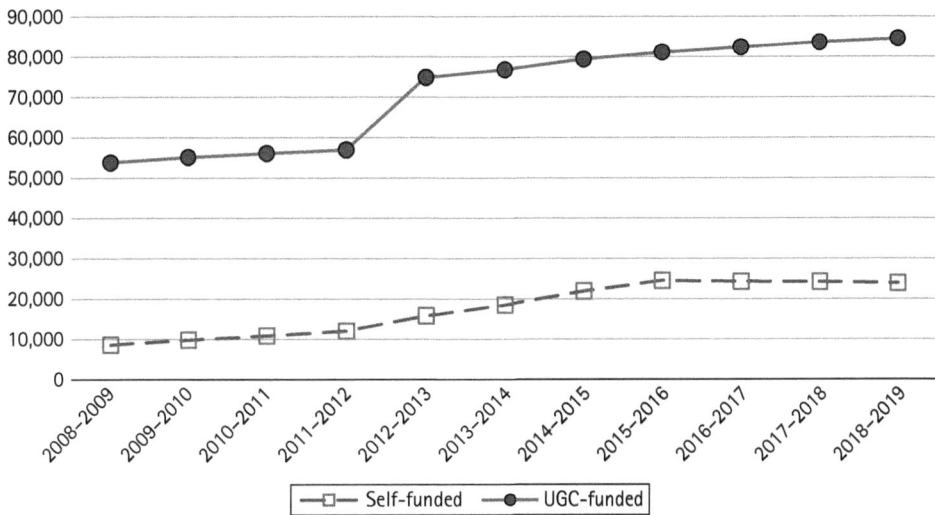

FIGURE 34.3   Number of full-time undergraduate students, 2008–2019
Sources: Committee for Self-Financing Post-Secondary Education (2019) and UGC (2020a).

3. HIGHER EDUCATION EXPANSION AND SOCIAL INEQUALITY

3.1 From Elite to Mass: The Expansion of Higher Education

In recent decades, societies in East Asia and the Pacific have witnessed massive expansion in the higher education sector (Neubauer et al., 2017). Hong Kong is not an exceptional case. The Hong Kong government recognizes that low levels of tertiary graduates will not be able to provide a sufficiently well-educated workforce for the transformation of the economy from manufacturing to a knowledge-based society (Kember, 2010, p. 170). By mobilizing both public and private sectors to offer learning opportunities, the higher education system in Hong Kong has experienced massification in recent years (Jung and Postiglione, 2015).

Figure 34.4 shows the gross enrollment ratio of higher education in Hong Kong, the average of East Asia and the Pacific, and the world average. The gross enrollment ratio is measured by the number of students enrolled in higher education as a percentage of the total population of the corresponding age group. In the 1970–1980s, the gross enrollment ratio of higher education was less than 15 percent. However, it gradually increased in the 1990s and has dramatically increased since the 2000s. By 2018, the enrollment ratio was 77 percent, more than twice that in 2016 (34.5 percent). According to the three different development stages defined by Trow (1974), the development of higher

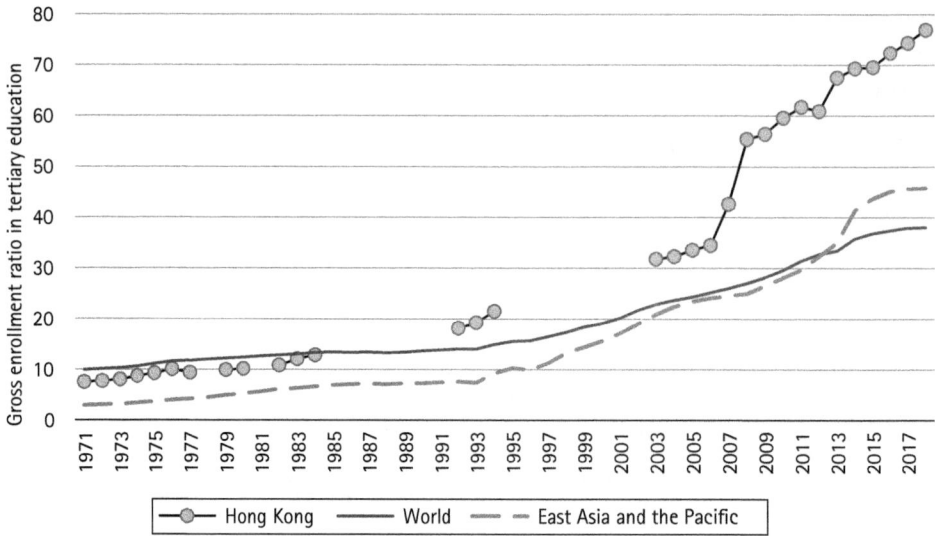

FIGURE 34.4 Expansion of higher education in Hong Kong, East Asia and the Pacific, and the world

Note: The gross enrollment ratio of higher education is the total enrollment in higher education expressed as a percentage of the total population of the corresponding age group.

Source: UNESCO (2021) database, http://data.uis.unesco.org.

education in Hong Kong has experienced a transformation from the elite stage (with an enrollment ratio of up to 15 percent) to the mass stage (up to 50 percent) from the 1990s to mid-2000s, and finally to the universal stage (exceeding 50 percent) since 2008.

3.2 Challenges for Equality of Educational Opportunity and Social Mobility

The expansion and marketization of higher education are two concurrent changes happening in Hong Kong which have created challenges in ensuring equality in educational opportunity and social mobility for individuals and maintaining autonomy in university governance.

Existing studies on higher education expansion and access to education have documented rising inequality in university admission despite higher education expansion in East Asian societies (Hannum et al., 2019). A similar situation is occurring in Hong Kong. Expanded opportunities in university degree programs have increasingly been dominated by young adults from rich families (Lee, 2016). Based on an analysis of Hong Kong census data, Chou (2013) found that the undergraduate enrollment rate of young people from the top 10 percent of the wealthiest families in Hong Kong accounted for 48.2 percent in 2011, whereas the rate of those living in poverty (i.e., at or below 50 percent of the median household income) was only 13 percent. The difference in enrollment rate between the rich and poor was 3.7 times in 2011, much wider than the gap of 1.2 times in 1991.

Although the government offers financial assistance schemes to support students studying either publicly funded programs or self-financed programs in the form of a grant or loan,[6] gloomy prospects of graduate employment are a major concern for students from underprivileged families pursuing higher education. In recent years, a university degree no longer guarantees good prospects of employment. Young adults are now frequently encountering unemployment, precarious work (Mok and Jiang, 2018b), and a decreasing earnings premium for graduates with a college degree relative to those without a degree (Lui and Suen, 2005). Lui and Suen (2005) suggest that the shrinking earnings premium for college degree holders in Hong Kong is due to the declining quality of university graduates that comes with higher education expansion. Additionally, the provision of higher education expanded dramatically in the private sector, creating a cohort of graduates from self-financed programs who are vulnerable to ongoing debt while facing uncertain employment prospects and low wages (Lee, 2016).

Further, it remains doubtful whether the expansion of higher education in Hong Kong enhances the upward social mobility of young people in the city. Drawing on 1996, 2006, and 2016 Hong Kong Population By-census, Peng et al. (2019) find that the intergenerational economic transmission among high-earners has been strong, and they suggest that there are other factors in addition to education that are important when accounting for the intergenerational transition. Indeed, a youth survey of graduate employment and social mobility in Greater China revealed that approximately 80 percent of Hong Kong young adults in the survey strongly agreed or agreed that "the opportunities for upward social mobility among college students were decreasing" (Mok and Jiang, 2018b). Although it is not a representative survey, the results reveal the pessimistic view of some Hong Kong young adults on their prospects of upward mobility.

3.3 Challenges for Higher Education Governance

In addition to challenges at an individual level, higher education expansion and marketization have also affected higher education governance, specifically in quality assurance and accountability of HEIs.

3.3.1 *Quality Assurance*

Several committees govern the quality assurance of HEIs in Hong Kong. UGC plays an important role in administering a series of quality assurance systems for UGC-funded universities that link fund allocation directly to the performance of universities. The Quality Assurance Committee (QAC) was established under UGC in April 2007 to

---

[6] Further details of Hong Kong government higher education grants and/or loans are available from the official website of the Student Finance Office of the government: https://www.wfsfaa.gov.hk/sfo/en/postsecondary/index.htm.

assist the UGC in assuring the quality of all programs at each degree level offered by UGC-funded universities (UGC, 2017b).

As discussed in section 2.2 above, RAE has also been adopted since 1993 to assess the research performance of UGC-funded universities, and consequently, to inform funding allocation (UGC, 2019b). Further, the Teaching and Learning Quality Process Review (TLQPR) and the Management Review (MR) administered by UGC serve as important mechanisms in promoting the self-assessment and self-enhancement of universities to assure teaching and learning quality (Postiglione and Wang, 2012). The recent TLQPRs were conducted from 2011 to 2013 with emphasis on the review of teaching and learning quality assurance process of the UGC-funded universities instead of the quality of teaching and learning per se.[7] The MRs were conducted in the 1998–2001 triennium to examine each UGC-funded university's roles, missions, academic objectives, resource allocation, planning, and financial process mechanisms.[8] However, the results of TLQPR and the MR are not directly related to resource allocation (Postiglione and Wang, 2012).

To better assure the quality of teaching and learning at UGC-funded universities, the UGC initiated the quality audits of these universities. The first two rounds of the quality audits covering the first-degree program or above offered by each UGC-funded university were completed by the QAC in 2011 and 2016. And the audits of sub-degree operations of these universities were completed in 2019 (UGC, 2020b). In the audit process, the audit panel of QAC examines the submission of the institution's self-review on student learning, and conducts a visit to the respective university and prepares for an audit report with commendations on good practice and recommendations for improvement.[9]

In addition, UGC adopted the University Accountability Agreements (UAA) in 2016 to establish duties and responsibilities associated with public funding and performance indicators for universities. The UAA for each UGC-funded university includes sector-wide performance indicators and institution-specific performance measures, covering quality of teaching, learning, research performance, and research postgraduate experience; knowledge transfer; wide engagement; internationalization; financial health and institutional sustainability (UGC, 2019c). These performance indicators are publicized on the UGC website and serve as instruments to assure the quality and performance of universities. The practices of quality assurance stress accountability and performance of universities by incorporating a "corporate governance" model (Mok, 2019). "Corporate governance" places emphasis on the performance of the university and management authority centralized in institutional governance to achieve enhanced performances and efficiency (Mok, 2019, pp. 165–166).

---

[7] For details, see the official website of UGC about the TLQPR: https://www.ugc.edu.hk/eng/ugc/about/press_speech_other/press/2000/pren000412.html

[8] See the UGC report about the MR for details: https://www.ugc.edu.hk/minisite/ugc_report/trienniu m98-01/E_3_5.HTM.

[9] See the Audit Manual by QAC for details: https://www.ugc.edu.hk/doc/eng/qac/manual/auditman ual.pdf.

The rapid expansion of private HEIs and self-financed programs in Hong Kong has raised concerns about the quality of teaching and learning. The Hong Kong Council for Accreditation of Academic and Vocational Qualifications (HKCAAVQ) was established in 1990 as an independent statutory body to perform academic accreditation of non-self-accrediting post-secondary institutions and provide authoritative advice on academic standards of sub-degree and degree programs offered by these HEIs (Education Bureau (Hong Kong), 2008). The establishment of this body shows that the government plays an important role in quality control instead of leaving the development of the private sector of higher education solely to market forces.

4. INTERNATIONALIZATION OF HIGHER EDUCATION

Over the decades, internationalization of higher education has been enriched by a comprehensive process-based approach instead of a narrow activity-based or technical approach (Cheng et al., 2016b, pp. 3–5). Internationalization of higher education is "the process of integrating an international, intercultural or global dimension into the purpose, functions or delivery of postsecondary education" (Knight, 2003, p. 2).

Cheng et al. (2016b, pp. 3–6) claim that the purpose or motive of internationalization of higher education includes the following: educational and academic motives, such as developing the global competencies of students and staff, international benchmarking and building a world-class academic capability; economic motives, such as developing economic and financial competitiveness and generating income; political motives, such as the enhancement of regional diplomatic influence and national soft power; and social and cultural motives, such as societal transformation facilitation and multicultural adaptations.[10] Given the complicated, dynamic, and multidimensional nature and motives of internationalization of higher education and the unique characteristics of Hong Kong, this section focuses on the educational and academic motives of internationalization.

4.1 Internationalization of Students in Hong Kong: Strategies and Policies

Attracting and retaining academically gifted students from different parts of the world can address the manpower needs and enhance the competitiveness of Hong Kong's economy. Therefore, the Hong Kong government has made significant efforts to

[10] See detailed discussions on the internationalization of higher education in Hong Kong in the edited book by Cheng et al. (2016b).

formulate supportive policies and measures, such as increasing the admission quota of non-local students, setting up the HKSAR Government Scholarship Fund, and allowing non-local students to stay in Hong Kong without limitation for one year after graduation under the Immigration Arrangements for Non-local Graduates (IANG) scheme (Immigration Department (Hong Kong), 2012).

To attract meritorious non-local students and local students to advance their study in Hong Kong, the government allocates funds to publicly funded HEIs to enable them to offer scholarships to both local and non-local applicants. The scholarship grants eligible local students HKD40,000 (approximately USD5,159.50) and non-local students HKD80,000 (approximately USD10,319) per academic year (Education Bureau (Hong Kong), 2019c). Since 2013, more than 800 students have been awarded a government scholarship every year, though official statistics do not provide a breakdown of local and non-local recipients. The latest UNESCO statistics (2021) show that in 2018, students from abroad comprise of 14.3 percent of total enrollment in tertiary education in Hong Kong.

Further, to attract high-quality research talent for PhD studies in Hong Kong, the Hong Kong PhD Fellowship Scheme was established to provide an annual stipend of HKD309,600 per student (approximately USD39,700).[11] Candidates, irrespective of their country of origin, prior work experience, and ethnic background, are eligible to apply. The selection criteria are the applicants' academic excellence, research ability and potential, communication and interpersonal skills, and leadership ability (Research Grant Council (Hong Kong), 2020).

4.2 Development of Internationalization: Student Mobility and Curriculum

The strategies and policies outlined above have attracted high-quality talent worldwide to enhance the internationalization of the higher education sector in Hong Kong. As Figure 34.5 shows, the number of non-local students has increased in both UGC-funded and self-financed programs.

According to the latest UNESCO statistics (2021), 36,420 Hong Kong students studied abroad for tertiary education in 2018, of whom 45 percent went to the United Kingdom, 26 percent to Australia, and 19 percent to the United States. The phenomenon of students studying abroad is symptomatic of increased competition for tertiary education in Hong Kong due to local enrollment quotas. While international student mobility is a global trend, some scholars fear that the trend may intensify the "brain drain" phenomenon in Hong Kong, especially when students graduating from overseas universities decide to stay abroad to pursue careers and residences (Cao, 2008). Nevertheless, recent

---

[11] This value is the latest amount as of 2020, and it may be adjusted by the Hong Kong government.

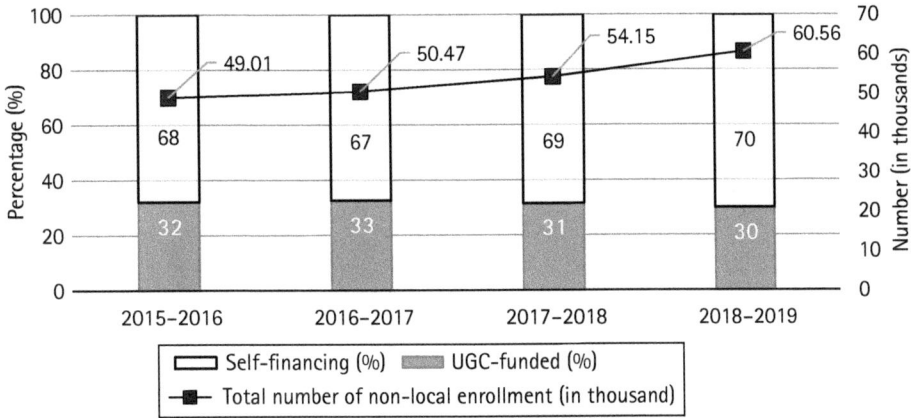

FIGURE 34.5 Non-local enrollment of self-financed and UGC-funded programs from 2011/12 to 2018/19

Sources: Committee for Self-Financing Post-Secondary Education (2015–2019) and UGC (2015–2019).

studies suggest that a positive effect of the "brain drain" phenomenon may arise as a result of these students establishing social and cultural networks overseas and the potential to create transnational synergies, otherwise known as "brain circulation" or "brain bridging" (Shin and Choi, 2015).

International mobility enabled by student exchange is also an important factor of internationalization. Hong Kong universities have long been actively promoting short-term student exchange. Of outgoing exchange students from UGC-funded universities in 2017/18, 15 percent went to the United States and 15 percent to the United Kingdom, constituting the two most popular study-abroad destinations. In the same year, among incoming exchange students, 20 percent came from the United States, accounting for the largest proportion by place of origin, followed by mainland China (12 percent) and the United Kingdom (11 percent) (UGC, 2019d, p. 60).

4.3 Internationalizing Staff

In addition to the active expansion of the non-local student body in the higher education sector, the academic staff of Hong Kong universities are also highly internationalized. Hong Kong universities have long been attracting overseas faculty members; for example, 64 percent of HKU's professoriate staff come from overseas (HKU, 2019b). Universities have also built an international network that fosters academic visits, academic exchange, and research collaboration (Fok, 2007). As the medium of instruction in universities in Hong Kong is English (except for some programs, such as studies in Chinese), international staff can integrate easily into Hong Kong universities. Additionally, as English is one of the official working languages in Hong Kong, local academic staff are generally proficient in English and can contribute to international publications. Such advantages not only attract global talent, but also give university graduates a significant advantage in employment and global competition.

5. Conclusion

The Hong Kong government has recognized the importance of developing Hong Kong as a regional education hub. In 2007, it recommended exploring ways to "attract more non-local students to study in Hong Kong and to develop Hong Kong into a regional education hub" (Hong Kong SAR Government, 2007, 38) and identified the education service as one of the six economic areas for further development in Hong Kong (Task Force on Economic Challenges (Hong Kong), 2009).

As Cheng et al. (2016a) suggest, to be a successful education hub, the higher education system in Hong Kong must meet several requirements. These include the ability to attract and support international students, uphold strong research capacity, and comprehensive quality assurance. Hong Kong needs to focus on building world-class soft power rather than marketing for income generation (Cheng et al., 2016a, 2016b). Policies and strategies should be developed to enhance the city's international competitiveness and world-class soft power to meet the emerging needs for high-quality postsecondary education in the region.

More importantly, the development of Hong Kong as an education hub is affected by education demand in the region and internal dynamics or even political tension within and surrounding Hong Kong. As an international city with a well-recognized high education system, Hong Kong's future success in its continued development as a prominent education hub in the Asia-Pacific region will depend on how it addresses its strengths and limitations. For example, the Hong Kong government's management of the pandemic and post-pandemic crisis will profoundly influence student mobility and employment in the coming years, and impact Hong Kong's ability to position itself as a safe education hub.

Finally, Hong Kong remains uniquely positioned with its geographic proximity and close relationship with mainland China to serve as a bridge for the international community to develop a strong education hub that incorporates the synergies of Eastern and Western systems (Li and Bray, 2007). How Hong Kong should build such a bridge through various initiatives will be one of the core concerns of higher education stakeholders, including higher education providers and policymakers. Importantly, the credibility of Hong Kong's ability to develop an education hub may rest on its ability to preserve its rigorous quality assurance mechanism that warrants academic freedom (Cheung et al., 2008).

References

Cao, C. (2008). "China's brain drain at the high end: Why government policies have failed to attract first-rate academics to return." *Asian Population Studies*, 4/3, 331–345.

Cheng, Y. C., Cheung, A. C. K., and Yuen, T. W. W. (2016a). "Developing Hong Kong as a regional education hub: Functions, modes, and requirements." In C. Crisan-Mitra and A. Borza (eds.), *Internationalization of Higher Education* (pp. 21–42). Singapore: Springer.

Cheng, Y. C., Cheung, A. C. K., and Ng, S. W. (eds.) (2016b). *Internationalization of Higher Education: The Case of Hong Kong.* Singapore: Springer.

Cheung, A., Yuen, W. W., and Yuen, Y. M. (2008). "Exporting Hong Kong's higher education in Asian markets: Strengths, weaknesses, opportunities, and threats." *International Journal of Educational Reform,* 17, 308–326.

Chou, K. L. (2013). "HKIEd study: Disparity in higher education attainment is widening between rich and poor." *HKIEd News.* https://www.eduhk.hk/aps/hkied-study-disparity-in-higher-education-attainment-is-widening-between-rich-and-poor-by-prof-chou-kee-lee/

Committee for Self-Financing Post-Secondary Education (2015–2019). "Key statistics on post-secondary education." https://www.cspe.edu.hk/resources/pdf/en/postsec_keystat.pdf

Committee for Self-Financing Post-Secondary Education (2019). "Statistic: 7. Number of enrolments of full-time locally-accredited self-financing post-secondary programmes." https://www.cspe.edu.hk/tc/Statistics.page#

Education Bureau (Hong Kong) (2008). "Performance indicators for Hong Kong schools 2008 and revised school self-evaluation tools." Education Bureau Circular Memorandum no. 82/2008. https://www.edb.gov.hk/attachment/en/sch-admin/sch-quality-assurance/circulars-letter/edbcm2008_082e_6469.pdf

Education Bureau (Hong Kong) (2019a). "Local higher education institutions." Institutions. https://www.edb.gov.hk/en/edu-system/postsecondary/local-higher-edu/institutions/index.html

Education Bureau (Hong Kong) (2019b). "Post-secondary education: Overview." https://www.edb.gov.hk/en/edu-system/postsecondary/index.html

Education Bureau (Hong Kong) (2019c). "HKSAR Government Scholarship Fund." https://www.edb.gov.hk/en/edu-system/postsecondary/local-higher-edu/publicly-funded-programmes/scholarship.html

Education Bureau (Hong Kong) (2020). "Government expenditure on education." https://www.edb.gov.hk/en/about-edb/publications-stat/figures/gov-expenditure.html

Education Commission (Hong Kong) (1988). "Report no. 3: The structure of tertiary education and the future of private schools." https://www.e-c.edu.hk/doc/en/publications_and_related_documents/education_reports/ecr3_e.pdf

Education and Manpower Bureau (Hong Kong) (2005). "The new academic structure for senior secondary education and higher education action plan for investing in the future of Hong Kong." https://334.edb.hkedcity.net/doc/eng/report_e.pdf

Federation for Self-Financing Tertiary Education (FSTE) (Hong Kong) (2016). "Multiple pathways for post-secondary education." https://www.fste.edu.hk/en/study-paths/multiple-pathways-for-post-secondary-education/

Fok, W. K. (2007). "Internationalisation of higher education in Hong Kong." *International Education Journal,* 8/1, 184–193.

Hannum, E., Ishida, H., Park, H., and Tam, T. (2019). "Education in East Asian societies: Postwar expansion and the evolution of inequality." *Annual Review of Sociology,* 45, 625–647.

Hong Kong Examinations and Assessment Authority (2015). "Recognitions of Hong Kong Examinations and Assessment Authority (HKEAA)'s exams." http://www.hkeaa.edu.hk/en/about_hkeaa/

Hong Kong SAR Government (2000). "Policy address 2000." https://www.policyaddress.gov.hk/pa00/epa2000.pdf

Hong Kong SAR Government (2007). "Report on Economic Summit on China's 11th Five-Year Plan and the development of Hong Kong." http://www.info.gov.hk/info/econ_summit/eng/pdf/tb_aa.pdf

Hong Kong SAR Government (2017). "Flexible and multiple pathways available for secondary school graduates." https://www.info.gov.hk/gia/general/201705/06/P2017050500289.htm?fontSize=1

Immigration Department (Hong Kong) (2012). "Immigration arrangements for non-local graduates (IANG)." https://www.immd.gov.hk/eng/services/visas/IANG.html

Jacob, W. J., Mok, K. H., Cheng, S. Y., and Xiong, W. (2018). "Changes in Chinese higher education: Financial trends in China, Hong Kong and Taiwan." *International Journal of Educational Development*, 58, 64–85.

Jung, J. and Postiglione, G. A. (2015). "From massification towards the post-massification of higher education in Hong Kong." In C. S. Jung, G. A. Postiglione, and F. T. Huang (eds.), *Mass Higher Education Development in East Asia*. Cham: Springer International, 119–136.

Kang, Y. and Jiang, J. (2020). "Revisiting the innovation systems of cross-border cities: The role of higher education institution and cross-boundary cooperation in Hong Kong and Shenzhen." *Journal of Higher Education Policy and Management*, 42/2, 213–229.

Kember, D. (2010). "Opening up the road to nowhere: Problems with the path to mass higher education in Hong Kong." *Higher Education*, 59/2, 167–179.

Knight, J. (2003). "Updated definition of internationalization." *International Higher Education*, 33, 2–3.

Lee, S. Y. (2016). "Massification without equalisation: The politics of higher education, graduate employment and social mobility in Hong Kong." *Journal of Education and Work*, 29/1, 13–31.

Legislative Council Panel on Education (2020). "The revamp of the Committee on Self-Financing Post-Secondary Education and the proposed enhancement and start-up grant scheme for self-financing post-secondary education." https://www.legco.gov.hk/yr19-20/english/panels/ed/papers/ed20200306cb4-363-1-e.pdf

Li, M. and Bray, M. (2007). "Cross-border flows of students for higher education: Push-pull factors and motivations of Mainland Chinese students in Hong Kong and Macau." *Higher Education*, 53, 791–818.

Lo, W. Y. W. and Ng, F. S. K. (2015). "Trends and developments of higher education research in Hong Kong: In pursuit of a cosmopolitan vision." *Higher Education Policy*, 28/4, 517–534.

Lui, H. K. and Suen, W. (2005). "The shrinking earnings premium for university graduates in Hong Kong: The effect of quantity or quality?" *Contemporary Economic Policy*, 23/2, 242–254.

Mok, K. H. (1999). "Education and the market place in Hong Kong and Mainland China." *Higher Education*, 37, 133–158.

Mok, K. H. (2012). "The quest for innovation and entrepreneurship: The changing role of university in East Asia." *Globalisation, Societies and Education*, 10/3, 317–335.

Mok, K. H. (2019). "Governance, accountability and autonomy in higher education in Hong Kong." In D. S. Jarvis and K. H. Mok (eds.), *Transformations in Higher Education Governance in Asia* (pp. 153–169). Singapore: Springer.

Mok, K. H. and Jiang, J. (2018a). "Questing for entrepreneurial university in Hong Kong and Shenzhen: The promotion of industry–university collaboration and entrepreneurship."

In D. Neubauer, K. H. Mok, and J. Jiang (eds.), *The Sustainability of Higher Education in an Era of Post-Massification* (pp. 115–133). Abingdon: Routledge.

Mok, K. H. and Jiang, J. (2018b). "Massification of higher education and challenges for graduate employment and social mobility: East Asian experiences and sociological reflections." *International Journal of Educational Development*, 63, 44–51.

Neubauer, D. E., Mok, K. H., and Jiang, J. (eds.) (2017). *The Sustainability of Higher Education in an Era of Post-Massification*. Abingdon: Routledge.

Peng, C., Yip, P. S. F., and Law, Y. W. (2019). "Intergenerational earnings mobility and returns to education in Hong Kong: A developed society with high economic inequality." *Social Indicators Research*, 143/1, 133–156.

Postiglione, G. A. and Wang, S. (2012). "Hong Kong: Government and the double-edged academy." in W. Locke, W. K. Cummings, and D. Fisher (eds.), *Changing Governance and Management in Higher Education: The Perspectives of the Academy* (pp. 343–368). Dordrecht: Springer.

Quacquarelli Symonds (QS) (2021). "QS World University Ranking, 2021." https://www.topuniversities.com/university-rankings/world-university-rankings/2021

Research Grant Council (Hong Kong). (2020). "Hong Kong PhD Fellowship Scheme." https://cerg1.ugc.edu.hk/hkpfs/index.html.

Shek, D. T. (2019). "Development of the new 4-year undergraduate program in Hong Kong." In D. T. L. Shek, G. Ngai, and S. C. F. Chan (eds.), *Service-Learning for Youth Leadership* (pp. 1–17). Singapore: Springer.

Shin, G. W. and Choi, J. N. (2015). *Global Talent: Skilled Labor as Social Capital in Korea*. Stanford, CA: Stanford University Press.

Task Force on Economic Challenges (Hong Kong) (2009). "Six economic areas identified by Task Force on Economic Challenges for further development." http://www.fso.gov.hk/tfec/eng/press.html

Task Force on Review of Self-Financing Post-Secondary Education (Hong Kong) (2018). "Consultation document." https://www.gov.hk/en/residents/government/publication/consultation/docs/2018/TF_SFPE.pdf

Trow, M. (1974). "Problems in the transition from elite to mass higher education." In *Policies for Higher Education* (pp. 55–101) from the General Report on the Conference on Future Structures of Post-Secondary Education. Paris: OECD.

University Grants Committee of Hong Kong SAR Government (UGC) (2004). "Hong Kong higher education to make a difference to move with the times." https://www.ugc.edu.hk/doc/eng/ugc/publication/report/policy_document_e.pdf

UGC (2015). "Cost allocation guidelines for UGC-funded and non-UGC-funded activities." https://www.ugc.edu.hk/doc/eng/ugc/note/CAGs.pdf

UGC (2015–2019). "Key statistics on UGC-funded universities (2015–2019)." https://cdcf.ugc.edu.hk/cdcf/searchStatSiteReport.action

UGC (2017a). "Framework for Research Assessment Exercise (RAE) 2020." https://www.ugc.edu.hk/doc/eng/ugc/rae/2020/framework.pdf

UGC (2017b). "About the Quality Assurance Council." https://www.ugc.edu.hk/eng/qac/about.html

UGC (2018). "About the UGC." https://www.ugc.edu.hk/eng/ugc/about.html

UGC (2019a). "Recurrent funding." https://www.ugc.edu.hk/eng/ugc/faq/q2.html

UGC (2019b). "Research assessment exercise." https://www.ugc.edu.hk/eng/ugc/activity/research/rae.html

UGC (2019c). "University accountability agreement for the -22 triennium." https://www.ugc.edu.hk/eng/ugc/activity/university_acc_agree.html

UGC (2019d). "Annual Report 2018–2019." https://www.ugc.edu.hk/doc/eng/ugc/publication/report/AnnualRpt1819/full.pdf

UGC (2019e). "Knowledge transfer." https://www.ugc.edu.hk/eng/ugc/activity/knowledge.html

UGC (2020a). "Student enrolment by university, level of study, mode of study and sex 2008–2019." https://cdcf.ugc.edu.hk/cdcf/searchStatSiteReport.action

UGC (2020b). "Quality audits of UGC-funded universities." https://www.ugc.edu.hk/eng/qac/quality/first_degree.html

UNESCO (2021). *Global Flow of Tertiary-Level Students.* http://uis.unesco.org/en/uis-student-flow#slideoutmenu

University of Hong Kong (HKU) (2004). "The University of Hong Kong, QuickStats 2003–2004." https://www.cpao.hku.hk/qstats/files/Archive/2005e.pdf

University of Hong Kong (HKU) (2019a). "The University of Hong Kong, Annual Report 2018–2019." http://www.feo.hku.hk/finance/information/annualreport/publications/2019/HTML/12-13/index.html#zoom=z.

University of Hong Kong (HKU) (2019b). "Staff profiles." https://www.cpao.hku.hk/qstats/staff-profiles

Wong, E. K. P. and Yeung, A. S. (2004). "Project Yi Jin: An alternative route to lifelong education in Hong Kong." *International Journal of Lifelong Education*, 23/4, 351–366.

CHAPTER 35

···

AUSTRALIA

History versus Geography in an Evolving
National System

···

ANTHONY WELCH

1. INTRODUCTION

···

FOR tens of thousands of years, sophisticated forms of higher learning were practiced among Australia's indigenous population. Shaped by both the local environment and deeply held, integrated spiritual cosmologies, the process of an individual's induction into the highest levels of culture and kinship encompassed oral forms of both spiritual and practical learning, that were lifelong (Hart, 1974; Berndt and Berndt, 1988; Welch, 1996, pp. 26–27; Marett, 2005; Welch et al., 2015).

But it was not until the mid-nineteenth century that the first university was established. Ignoring the rich array of diverse cultures and languages that made up indigenous Australia, the constitution of each of the earliest universities reflected the fact that white Australia had been established as a series of British colonies. Hence, the earliest Australian universities were "part of the transplantation of British settlers, values and culture of Empire" (Horne and Sherington, 2013, pp. 284–285). Nowhere was this intellectual and institutional obeisance to the Oxbridge tradition expressed more clearly than in the Latin motto of the very first such institution, the University of Sydney (1850): *Mens Sidere, Eadem Mutato* (broadly, The Same Mind, Under Different Stars).[1] The origins of the overwhelmingly male staff of these early institutions were also almost entirely British: "The German, French and American universities seem to have been beyond the pale" (Smith, 2001, p. 4; see also Sherington, 2019; Welch, 2021a). At the University of Sydney, until around World War I, a selection committee based in the

---

[1] The Universities of Queensland, and Western Australia, however, rejected the Oxbridge model as unsuitable for their conditions, where populations were more rural and dispersed.

UK made recommendations regarding Chairs. It was not until around the same time that any Australians were appointed to Chairs (and largely on the basis of qualifications gained overseas). Further imperial ties, including schemes such as the Rhodes scholarship, also connected Australian scholars to the "mother country" and later to the (British) Commonwealth of Nations (Pietsch, 2010, 2013; Horne and Sherington, 2013).

At a time when, at Federation in 1901, Australia's population totaled a mere 3,788,100, no more than 2,652 university students (0.07 percent of the population) were enrolled across the country. Almost all were men. Rather like the United Kingdom, women did not gain entry to universities until the 1870s (despite attempts by the University of Adelaide (1874), for example, that were disallowed by the British government), although by the 1920s, the proportion of women in higher education was already a little higher than in the United Kingdom, and from a broad set of socio-economic backgrounds (Bowen, 1985; Horne, 2016). Teaching was the main activity at the time: research was not a core function, and the first home-grown PhDs were not awarded until 1948 (CBCS, 1952; Dobson, 2012). At the onset of World War II, by which time the national population reached 6,967,754, of a total university enrollment of 14,236, fewer than 100 were higher degree candidates.

2. INSTITUTIONAL FORMS

The dominant institutional model continues to be the comprehensive public university. Among these, the top-tier Go8 category, which broadly parallels the United Kingdom's Russell Group, or the American Association of Universities, leads most performance indicators, albeit less so than previously. Of Australia's 43 universities, only three smaller private institutions exist (Bond, Notre Dame, and the recently accredited University of Divinity), although there are, in addition, one or two small outposts of US-based private universities (Carnegie Mellon University Australia, and Torrens[2]). This apparently public profile, however, ignores two elements. First is the increasing privatization of public universities, whose dependence on fee income, notably from international students, is exceptionally high, relative to other countries, and which arguably impinges on their public standing, and which has also been criticized for leading them to behave more like enterprises (Marginson and Considine, 2000). While, on average across the OECD, around 32 percent of total expenditure on tertiary institutions is sourced from the private sector, in Australia, the proportion is almost double, at 62 percent (Guardian, 2018; OECD, 2019).

Second is the proliferation of smaller, private higher education (niche) providers, some of which provide high-level, specialist professional education, others a mix of vocational and higher education offerings, while still others are religious and

---

[2] Torrens forms one of the Laureate International chain.

denominational in form. While mostly small in size, there are now more than 120 such private higher education providers registered (TEQSA, 2020). Of the 43 universities, 6 are dual-sector higher education institutions (HEIs), that provide both mainstream higher education qualifications, as well as some lower-level technical qualifications (Reforming, 2019; Swinburne University, 2019).

3. Governance and Management

The governance and management of Australian universities has been an arena of significant change over recent decades. Governance here refers to the authority to develop organizational models, policies, and plans and decisions, and account for their probity, responsiveness, and cost-effectiveness. Management refers to the achievement of goals through assigning responsibilities and resources, as well as monitoring their efficiency and effectiveness (Gallagher, 2001, p. 49).

For public universities, patterns of governance relate to the federal form of the Australian polity: with only two exceptions, all universities were established via legislative Acts of individual state parliaments.[3] Yet, although state parliaments were important in the early decades of university establishment, their influence is now somewhat vestigial. In practice, unlike all other education sectors, higher education is governed by federal, rather than state, authority, and related agencies. Key federal agencies include the Tertiary Education Quality and Standards Agency (TEQSA), which is responsible for higher education quality assurance, and Excellence in Research Australia (ERA) which collects, analyzes, and monitors research output and quality (see, inter alia, Welch, 2015, 2016, 2019a, 2019b).

While some of the regulatory architecture still reflects its origins in the British system, much has changed. Despite repeated allusions to contemporary managerial mantras like "steering from a distance," the overall result has been more steering, and less distance. In the name of quality assurance, ever-increasing, and more detailed demands for performance data now consume substantial amounts of institutional time and resources. Vice-Chancellors' complaints about the burden imposed at institutional levels is contradicted by their enthusiastic implementation of detailed regulatory apparatus internally. Institutional enlargement (a number of universities now have enrollments of 60,000+), has further accelerated the trend towards more corporate, line-management forms of governance, and the associated proliferation of senior, high-salaried positions, responsible for governing one or other aspect of institutional performance, and all ultimately responsible to the Vice-Chancellor. Reveling in titles such as Vice-President, Deputy Vice-Chancellor, Pro Vice-Chancellor, and Provost, each is in turn supported

---

[3] The two exceptions are the Australian National University (ANU) and Charles Darwin University (sited in the Northern Territory, a federally administered region).

by a growing number of appointees. Such salaries are very high relative to those of academics, whose wages have largely stagnated in recent years (except for a few "star" performers) (Welch, 2012a).

A key site to observe changes to institutional governance patterns is seen in the evolution of the role of faculty Dean, who is now regarded as part of the executive management team, rather than the earlier, and more collegial, *primus inter pares*. Resistance by academics, including to further corporatization and managerialism now tends to be seen as inhibiting effective management, and a form of recalcitrance, rather than an instance of democratic dissent. Systematic differences regarding the importance of collegiality, and centralized control now distinguish management from academic staff (Marginson and Considine, 2000, pp. 64–66). It has been argued that an audit culture now governs most aspects of academic work and performance (Welch, 2016).

4. Financing Higher Education

The growth of the Australian higher education system to over 1.5 million students has been sustained by a changing mix of both public and private funding. Over the decade 1996–2006, the share of funds from the federal government fell, meaning that the share of funding from private sources, particularly from student fees, rose appreciably. By the turn of the century, OECD data showed private contributions to higher education in Australia, at around 46 percent of total funding, higher than most comparable countries, while the proportion of gross domestic product (GDP) devoted to higher education had also fallen, and was low, relative to most other OECD countries (Productivity Commission, 2002, pp. 32, 34). By 2016, OECD data shows private expenditure had increased to 62.2 percent of the total (OECD, 2019) (Figure 35.1).

Over recent years, the massification of Australian higher education has been driven by two principal financial elements: the demand-driven system, and the national income-contingent loans scheme. The first was a government scheme that, over the years 2012–2017, provided universities a fixed sum of money for teaching. Effectively, this ensured that universities could enroll as many Australian undergraduate students as they wished (other than in medicine), since funding was assured. The aim of the scheme was to boost overall participation in higher education, as well as boost access for under-represented groups in society. Evidence revealed that participation increased significantly, and many of the non-traditional students succeeded in their studies, although students with lower literacy and numeracy backgrounds, fared less well: "By age 23 years, 21 percent of the additional students had left university without receiving a qualification, compared with 12 percent of other students" (Productivity Commission, 2019, p. 2, see also p. 9). In order to reduce such inequities, modest additional funds were provided to universities under the Higher Education Participation and Partnerships Program (HEPPP) to raise aspirations of disadvantaged children and to provide additional support services.

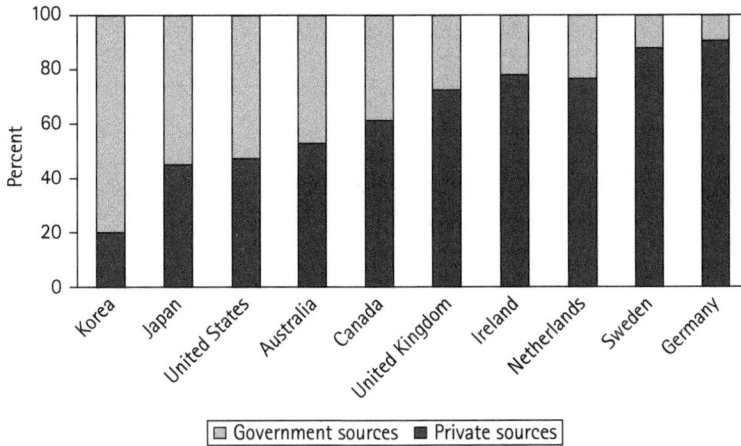

FIGURE 35.1 Public and private expenditure on higher education, selected countries, 1999

Note: Under OECD definitions, student contributions via the government's
Higher Education Contribution Scheme (HECS) are included as private funding for Australia.

Source: Productivity Commission (2002, p. 32), based on OECD data.

The demand-driven system replaced the supply-driven, or "block-grant" scheme, whereby the government provided a block amount of funding to universities (for which they were required to deliver a certain number of places), and then decided on how many places, and how much funding was to be applied to each university. While this rather bureaucratic system was parodied by some as the equivalent of "Moscow on the Molonglo,"[4] it did deliver an additional loading, for example, to students at regional universities, in the interests of equity (Carrington and Pratt, 2003).

But in response to the substantial rise in funding that was needed to sustain the demand driven system, it was substantially amended. Faced with a 50 percent rise in funding in real terms over the period 2008–2017, the government froze undergraduate funding in late 2017, with the proviso that universities meeting specified performance criteria might have their funds adjusted from 2020 to take account of changes in populations (DEST, n.d.). Effectively, this meant a return to block funding, albeit minus enrollment targets (Norton, 2019). Universities were able to reduce the number of places. But pressure on the system is scheduled to increase in the early 2020s, as the number of school leavers rises to its highest level ever.

Australia's innovative income-contingent loans scheme has been the other important pillar of higher education funding. Widely seen as a success, versions have now been adopted in a number of countries. The system allows universities to set fees within three bands. These bands, and associated fees, vary according to discipline, with the highest levels (medicine, dentistry) reflecting highest income potential. The current three bands reflect such disciplinary differences, as seen in Table 35.1.

---

[4] The Molonglo is the name of a river near Canberra, the nation's capital.

Table 35.1 Student fees by disciplinary band, 2020

Band 3: Law, dentistry, medicine, veterinary science, accounting, (business) administration, economics, commerce	$0–$11,155
Band 2: Computing, built environment, other health, allied health, engineering, surveying, agriculture, mathematics, statistics, science	$0–$9,527
Band 1: Humanities, behavioral science, social studies, education, clinical psychology, foreign languages, visual and performing arts, nursing	$0–$6,684

Source: Study Assist (2020).

Unlike mortgage-type student loans such as exist in the United States, the interest-free income-contingent loan does not become repayable until three specific conditions have been met: graduation, employment, and an earned income above the threshold (set at $45,881 in 2018–2019). Once these conditions have all been met, the loan is repaid over time, via the tax system, with graduated repayment rates, according to incomes. Students who do not meet the three conditions are not required to repay the loan. The Australian government, as well as each university, makes some scholarships available to postgraduate scholars, both domestic and international, while a range of countries, including China, Saudi Arabia, Chile, and Brazil, provide research scholarships that are tenable in Australia (among a number of countries). A domestic PhD scholarship is currently valued at A$30,000, tax free.[5]

5. Participation and Equity

Australia is a high-participation system, reflecting the government policy target to reach a rate of 40 percent of those aged 25–34 holding a degree by 2025. Of a total population of a mere 25 million, overall higher education enrollments had reached 1,562,520 by 2018, including a 30 percent increase at the undergraduate level over the years 2009–2015 (Czarnecki, 2018, p. 502; Norton, 2019). As indicated, the Go8 HEIs stand out to an extent, revealing a more comprehensive profile, a more selective intake, and higher salaries postgraduation. These are largely older institutions; newer universities reflect a stronger equity profile. It is still the case that having parents with a university-level education and/ or a professional occupation are the best predictors of the likelihood of university graduation (Lee, 2014; Czarnecki, 2018). Other research shows that class also differentiates the choice of institution, field, or discipline, with lower socio-economic status families tending to choose lower-status fields, and HEIs. The process of entrenching class

---

[5] At the time of writing around US$20,000.

Percent of age cohort, domestic students

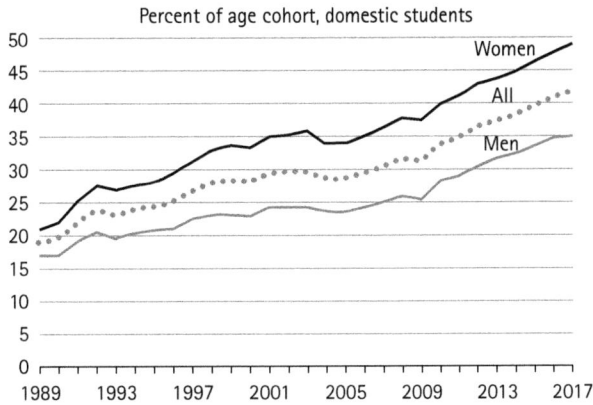

FIGURE 35.2 Participation rates by gender, 1989–2017

Source: Norton (2019).

divisions begins well before higher education, and deepens throughout schooling: data from the Universities Admissions Centre show that, at the end of the secondary school stage, 1.3 percent of lowest SES (socio-economic status) students gain an admission score of 90 (of a possible 100), compared to 9.4 percent of pupils from the highest SES. Australia's large private secondary higher education sector, particularly the elite, high-fee schools, are also disproportionately represented among university students (Marginson, 2016). Other things being equal, coming from a middle-class family, and/ or going to the "right school" is an advantage. A survey in 2016 revealed that, whereas 25 percent of children of skilled and unskilled laborers were either attending university or held a degree, the rate for children of managers and professionals was 61 percent (Norton, 2019).

As seen Figure 35.2, women now outnumber men in higher education, albeit there is still work to be done to lift rates of female participation in key STEM (Science, Technology, Engineering, and Mathematics) fields. By 2010, overall gender parity had been reached, including at the doctoral level: the proportion of all PhDs awarded to women, including in science disciplines, had reached 50 percent (AAS, n.d.-a; Dobson, 2012, p. 95). This did not mean however, that parity obtained in all such disciplines. Women are still overrepresented in fields such as education, and social work (and social sciences and humanities more generally), but remain underrepresented in engineering. Overall differences in participation are seen in Figure 35.3.

In effect, while total enrollments by indigenous and rural and remote students have increased recently, all equity groups remain significantly underrepresented in Australian universities. Unsurprisingly, some research relates this to lower school achievement levels, which also positions such individuals less well, when entering university. Together with higher rates of participation in part-time work, it results in higher dropout and non-completion rates (Productivity Commission, 2019, p. 13). Although there are limitations to the data regarding indigenous higher education participation

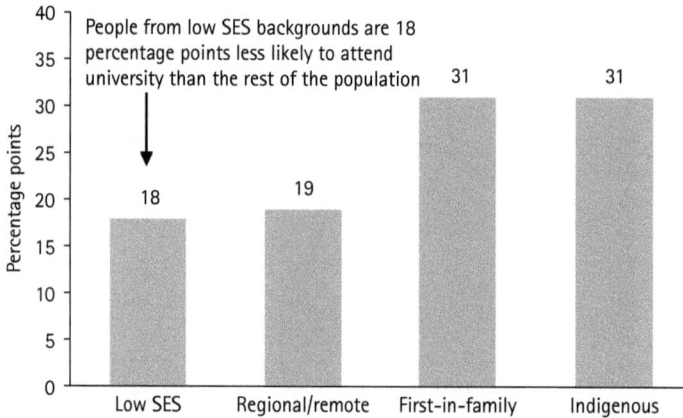

FIGURE 35.3 Higher education participation rates, by equity group, 2016

Source: Productivity Commission (2019).

(Wilks and Wilson, 2015), Figure 35.3 demonstrates that, of all equity groups, indigenous students, and first-in-family, are by far the most disadvantaged, with rates of higher education participation a full 31 percent lower than the rest of the population. The Behrendt report of 2012 on indigenous education outlined major disparities: despite forming 3.3 percent of the overall population, Aboriginal and Torres Strait Islander students made up a mere 1.4 percent of all enrollments in university, with women outnumbering men. The report outlined three key factors in maintaining such patterns of persistent disadvantage: inadequate respect by non-Aboriginal Australians; the dependence of higher education success on achievements in lower levels of education; and a related need for major improvements in health, housing, and financial hardships. The legacy of colonialism, long-standing racism, and the lingering effects on the Stolen Generation,[6] must also be acknowledged as further factors (Behrendt et al., 2012, p. 8; Welch et al., 2015). While recent schemes such as the Indigenous Scholars Success Programme provide scholarships to numerous indigenous higher education students, much remains to be done to undo decades of disadvantage (NIAA, n.d.).

It is important to acknowledge that gender disparities are not limited to students: although women now comprise over half of all PhD graduates and early career researchers, including in the science area, representation among senior academic ranks still lags, at less than 20 percent (Carrington and Pratt, 2003; AAS, n.d.-a). Overall, 44 percent of academic staff in Australia are female, yet women are underrepresented above Senior Lecturer level and in leadership positions: only 25 percent of university Vice Chancellors, for example, are women (Jarboe, 2016, p. 16). Among university staff, a mere 1.0 percent of total full-time equivalent university staff were indigenous in 2010; and just 0.8 percent of academic staff (Behrendt et al., 2012).

---

[6] The term "Stolen Generation" refers to Aboriginal people forcibly removed from their families, who often grew up with little or no knowledge of their family's whereabouts, or their own origins.

6. Internationalization

As a long-standing country of migration, with settlers from 200 countries, it should be no surprise that Australian student and staff cohorts are both very diverse (Sheehan and Welch 1996; Welch 1999, 1996; Oishi, 2017; Welch, 2021a, 2021b). But the character of this international profile has changed substantially, from the narrowly British, to vibrantly global, with a growing Asian influence, that again reflects the fact that some 40 percent of Australian migrants now originate from Asia, and that hundreds of thousands of international students, largely from the region, secured Permanent Residence (PR), and then citizenship. Of 1.6 million international students who enrolled between 2001 and 2014, 16 percent gained PR and a pathway to citizenship, although in recent years the process has become more protracted (APH 2012, Mares, 2016; Hurley, 2020).

Together with generally competitive salaries (Welch, 2012b), this has helped generate significant (Asian) knowledge diasporas in the Australian higher education system, of which the Chinese is the largest, with Indian and Vietnamese also prominent. Current scholarship schemes are also strongly regional, and reflect Australia's growing regional engagement (Welch, 2014). Australia Awards support select developing country students at Australian universities, while the New Colombo Plan provides both short-term mobility programs and scholarships, to Australian students, tenable at 40 Asia-Pacific locations (DFAT, n.d.-a, n.d.-b, n.d.-c).

The New Colombo Plan takes its name from the earliest major scheme to offer scholarships to international students. The Colombo Plan offered degree-level education at Australian universities to students from developing countries in the region. Established in 1950, in the aftermath of World War II, it was both a recognition that the British Empire no longer guaranteed Australia's security, and that more attention needed to be paid to the region, and Australia's Asian neighbors in particular. Cold War tensions bounded much international scholarly mobility, including the Colombo Plan (Oakman, 2004, pp. 43–44). A third, contradictory element was the persistence of an explicitly racist immigration policy, the so-called "White Australia Policy,"[7] that was not finally abandoned until the early 1970s, and was the source of much resentment among Australia's neighbors. Research networks also expanded in the post-war years: "university research was constructed more through international networks ... beyond ... older attachment to Britain and Empire" (Baker et al., 1993, Horne and Sherington, 2013, p. 285).

Colombo Plan students from the region studied programs in fields such as public administration, agriculture, and engineering, but had to promise to return home after graduation. The aims were to reduce poverty in the region, boost levels of human

---

[7] Somewhat like the United States and Canada at much the same time, Australia's Immigration Restriction Act of 1901 sought to restrict the right to immigrate to Australia, by banning Asian and other migrants, in an effort to keep Australia "British." The Act was widely termed and critiqued as the "White Australia Policy."

capital, and contribute to goodwill, although the plan has also been characterized as "a complex mix of self-interest, condescension and humanitarianism" (Oakman, 2004, p. 4; see also Megarrity, 2007). Even at the time, however, private international students were part of the mix: indeed, in 1955, just 23 percent of international students were from the Colombo Plan, and in 1965, this had fallen to 16 percent. Among recipients, students from ASEAN (Association of Southeast Asian Nations) member states figured strongly: in 1974–1975, for example, of a total of 2,780 awardees, Indonesia accounted for 428 Australian scholarships, Malaysia 455, Singapore 224, Thailand 331, and South Vietnam 422—a subtotal of 1,860 or 67 percent (Welch, 2014, p. 153). A notable exception at the time was Vietnam, a product of a Cold War mentality, that saw students from communist countries excluded. Although having originally joined in 1951, the Socialist Republic of Vietnam withdrew in 1978, and was only added again, in 2004, after joining ASEAN a decade earlier, in 1995. Then, as now, private students from ASEAN were an important cohort of Australia's international student intake, as seen in Table 35.2.

But an important change to Australia's rationale for international higher education occurred in the mid-1980s, with the simultaneous publication, in 1984, of the Goldring, and Jackson reports, each of which drew opposite conclusions (Goldring, 1984; Jackson, 1984). The former favored a continuing cap on the number of subsidized international students, while the latter argued the existing system should be overhauled. Calling for the existing Overseas Student Charge (OSC) to be steadily increased, such that by the mid-1990s overseas students would pay the full costs of their education, Jackson's view ultimately prevailed, marking the beginning of the development of international higher education as an industry.

As a result, international student numbers mushroomed, from 84,000 in 1993, to almost 160,000 in 1999 (of which higher education occupied more than half). Branch campuses were established by a number of Australian universities, in Vietnam, South Africa, and Malaysia, and, in addition, growing offshore enrollments at Australian

Table 35.2 ASEAN private overseas post–secondary and higher education students, 1976–1984

Country	1976	1977	1978	1979	1980	1981	1982	1983	1984
Indonesia	490	538	514	488	423	365	371	593	943
Malaysia	3,139	3,094	3,123	3,580	4,001	4,619	5,353	6,016	7,341
Philippines	28	28	27	23	17	18	17	26	30
Thailand	258	270	257	241	214	191	170	151	152
Viet Nam	n.a.	n.a.	n.a.	n.a.	n.a.	n.a.	n.a.	n.a.	n.a.
Other Asia	396	361	345	394	366	419	428	449	559
National TOTAL	5,486	5,852	6,004	6,745	7,383	8,103	9,125	10,656	13,047

Source: Welch (2014, p. 154).

Table 35.3 International student enrollments, higher education, 2002–2019

	2002	2011	2019
Higher education	124,992	241,440	442,219
English language programs (ELICOS)	58,435	94,853	156,880
Non-award	23,518	27,568	48,217
Total	206,945	363,861	647,316

Note: Some universities maintain their own English-language training facility, others use outside organizations.

Source: Department of Education, Skills and Employment (DESE) (2020).

universities were fueled by the development of online education (MacDonald 2006). By 2011, international higher education enrollments totaled 242,351, with China accounting for more than a quarter of that total. A stark contrast was revealed in the meagre number of outbound students, with a mere 11,000 Australian students studying abroad, and no ASEAN member state among the top five destinations. By 2019, international enrollments had skyrocketed, with numbers of universities becoming overly dependent on international student fee income to sustain operations, particularly in research (Table 35.3).

Although some scholars had long pointed to the problem (Altbach and Welch, 2011; Welch, 2012c; Babones, 2019), the vulnerability of this international profile was dramatically underscored in 2020, as the coronavirus (COVID-19) spread worldwide. The substantial decline in per-student funding (see above) that had long afflicted Australian universities had spurred them to energetically seek to diversify sources of income, most particularly via fee-paying international students. By far the largest cohort were mainland Chinese, numbering around 150,000 in 2019, hence not merely was the overall proportion of international students (25 percent) extremely high by comparison with other higher education systems, but mainland Chinese students comprised almost 40 percent of all onshore international students (Babones, 2019). At a small number of universities, Chinese students accounted for two-thirds of all international enrollments in 2017, with the University of Sydney alone earning $752 million from international student fees in 2017[8] (Audit Office, 2018; SMH, 2018a). Hence, when travel bans on returning from China were instituted in early 2020, many thousands of mainland students who had returned home for Spring Festival, or to undertake fieldwork for their degrees, were unable to return to Australia to resume their studies.

---

[8] All figures are expressed in Australian dollars. Substantial fluctuations in the exchange rate with the US$, over time, make conversions to that currency misleading. Recognition of the over-dependence on Chinese students led many universities to attempt to diversify intake, especially to increase students from South and South-East Asia.

This created a profound disruption to their study routines. But it also had systemic economic effects, threatening the bottom line of virtually all Australian universities, especially the Go8 which had by far the highest number and proportion of mainland students enrolled, and in the two most populous states, New South Wales and Victoria. The extent of risk was obvious: of the eight Go8 institutions, at least four earned around a third of their total income from international students (SMH, 2019). While, at the time of writing, it was not possible to be certain how long the travel bans would remain in place, it was estimated that the net loss to universities around the country might well total an initial $4.6 billion, with at least two universities claiming they could well each lose $600 million in 2020 alone.[9] Universities Australia modeling projected overall job losses of 21,000 and income losses of $23 billion over following years (UWN, 2020). In response, immediate plans were instituted to suspend and/or reduce capital expenditure, project spending, contractors and consultants, international travel, and staff recruitment (VC Email, 2020). Some universities moved quickly to institute staff redundancy procedures; others were slower. The federal government's initial stimulus package, announced in March 2020, and designed to mitigate the economic fallout from COVID-19, largely resisted taking account of the pronounced effects on university budgets. Some universities were more affected than others, but the longer-term effects, including of worsening China–Australia relations, had become clearer by 2022 (Marginson 2019, Welch 2022).

But changing student flows are by no means the whole story. Australian universities' staff profile reveals a rich mix of both academic and administrative personnel, from a wide range of countries. The dominance of UK academics in Australian universities began to break down after World War II, initially due to an unexpected influx of European Jewish refugees post-war (numbers of whom were highly qualified and went on to be "notable contributors to that nation's scientific, business, academic and cultural communities") (BBC, 2010). The gradual dismantling of the White Australia Policy, that was finally ended in the early 1970s, also opened up the system (Sherington, 1990; SMH, 2018b; Welch, 2021a). Current estimates are that the proportion of overseas-born academics in Australian universities is 45 percent, much higher than in the overall Australian population (26.8 percent) (Oishi, 2017, p. 11),[10] and much higher than the equivalent in almost all other academic systems.

While the aging of the Australian professoriate is one factor, of greater importance is the rise of Asia, most notably the two giants of China and India, each of which, and particularly the former, are making significant contributions to the Australian higher education system.[11] Not only are Asian Australians now almost 15 percent of the population,

---

[9] The Australian academic year, unlike the northern calendar, begins at the beginning of March. All amounts are expressed in Australian dollars.

[10] Although, if it were to include individuals with one overseas born parent, the proportion would be around 50 percent.

[11] Of Australia's total population of 25 million, around 1.2 million are now of Chinese heritage, while settlers from India tripled over the decade 2006–2016.

but OECD research showed Australia to have the highest net brain gain among member countries, in part due to its emphasis on high-skilled migrants (OECD, 2007; Welch and Zhang, 2008a, 2008b; Yang and Welch, 2010, 2012). International studies of the academic profession show the country to be one of the most diverse worldwide, with the proportion of academics born in Asia having grown by over 50 percent during 2005–2015, from 10 percent to 15.4 percent overall (Oishi, 2017). Figure 35.4 illustrates the diverse composition of Australian academic staff, particularly the origins and proportions of Asian-born staff.

The rising numbers of Asian-born academic staff has led to the creation of substantial knowledge diasporas, of which the Chinese and Indian are the most notable (Hao and Welch, 2012; Welch and Hao, 2015; Hao et al., 2016). A 2015 survey of Asian academics in the system revealed that the most common countries of birth were, in descending order, China (32.1 percent), India (15.8 percent), Malaysia (8.5 percent), and Sri Lanka (6.3 percent). This has yielded not merely a rich array of cultural and linguistic capital, but extensive, and persistent, ethnic-based intellectual networks, both national and international. Fields such as engineering, IT, and business had the highest proportions of Asian-born staff, with agriculture and environment (5.6 percent), education (5.3 percent), and creative arts (5.3 percent) featuring much lower ones.

Significantly, more than three-quarters (76.1 percent) of Asian-born academics have collaborated with scholars from an Asian country; indeed, survey results showed

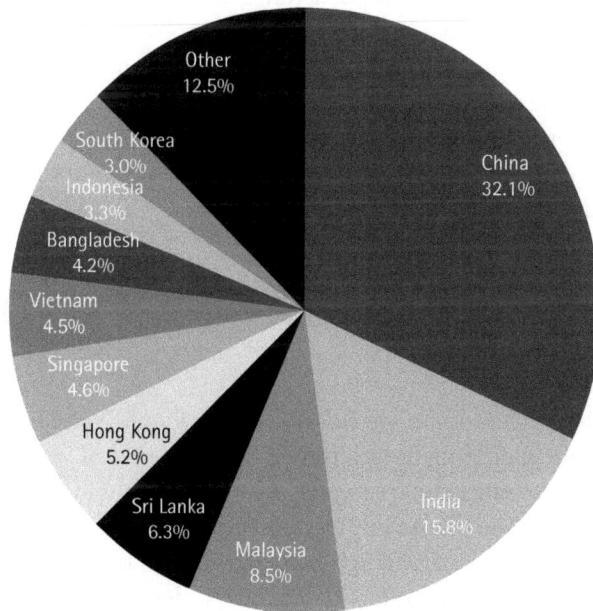

FIGURE 35.4 Asian-born academics, Australian universities, by place of birth, 2015

Note: If Hong Kong's reversion to China in 1997 were to be included in the above, it would further increase the Chinese contribution.

Source: Department of Education and Training data (2016), cited by Oishi (2017, p. 16).

two-thirds (66.3 percent) reported working on joint research projects. Among such international partnerships, national origin was particularly important: 34.6 percent had helped to develop exchange programs with their country of origin (Oishi, 2017, p. 18). China, in particular, is now one of Australia's key knowledge partners, with active research collaborations across a range of fields, both in the natural and applied sciences, and social sciences and humanities (Chief Scientist, 2013). The US–China trade war, however, now recognized as a Tech War and even Culture War, has crimped bi-lateral cooperation (Marginson 2019, Welch 2022).

But the growing presence of Asian-born academics in Australian universities did not always translate into equivalent recognition, with respondents often reporting feelings that their contributions were not always acknowledged and that, at times, their cultural background constituted a disadvantage: "I often feel that I am non-existent in meetings. People don't even see my face or talk to me" (Oishi, 2017, p. 38). Gender could constitute a double disadvantage, with gender gaps evident across numerous fields. The same survey revealed that Asian-born women academics held 4.8 percent of engineering posts, for example (their male peers held 28.5 percent). In IT, gender disparities were almost as large: female Asian-born academics occupied 9.4 percent of the total, relative to their male peers at 25.1 percent. Asian-born academics were also underrepresented at the more senior academic levels. One in four of the lowest staff tier (Level A) were found to be Asian-born, but only one in ten at Level E (Professor), and less than one in 30 at Deputy Vice Chancellor level (Oishi, 2017, p. 30).

The problem is not isolated to the academic profession, but arguably reflects wider patterns of power and privilege in Australian society: "Asian Australians account for 9.6 percent of the Australian population but only 3.1 percent of partners in law firms, 1.6 percent of barristers, and 0.8 percent of the judiciary" (AHRC, 2019). Less than 2 percent of members of the federal parliament are from an Asian cultural background, leading some to argue the presence of a "bamboo ceiling" confronting Asian Australians (Soutphommasane, 2014).

7. CONCLUSION: A MIXED PICTURE

The Australian higher education system, now 170 years old, reveals both continuities and change. Anyone wandering the grounds of the University of Sydney could not help but be reminded of its institutional fountainhead, Oxbridge. At the same time, the original and singular function of teaching (again reflecting Oxbridge at the time) has now been widely supplanted by a major emphasis on research performance, albeit often with a view to boosting institutional ranks on an ever-wider range of national and international league tables (Welch, 2016).

The fact that a far-flung, modest-sized academic system, remote from the major knowledge centers of Europe and North America, boasts six universities among the top 100 worldwide, is, prima facie, a sign of success. A string of Nobel prizes, and other achievements, adds to this picture (AAS, n.d.-b). A further strength is the rich cultural diversity evident among both academic and administrative staff, although much still remains to be done to dismantle long-standing disadvantage and racism in the system, most particularly with respect to indigenous Australians, but also affecting Asian Australians and women (Yosso, 2005; Walker, 2019; Welch, 2019c). Schemes such as the New Colombo Plan offer hope of further extending academic relations between Australia and its Asian neighbors, on a much more reciprocal basis than the earlier scheme (DFAT, n.d.-b, n.d.-c).

But league tables, and diverse student and staff profiles, cannot be the only measures of success. The increased size of many universities (some of which enroll more than 60,000 students), has helped fuel a steep rise in managerialism, a proliferation of administrative staff, and a widening fissure separating academic staff and management. Wholesale casualization has divided academic staff into two tiers, and led to significant exploitation (Welch, 2012b; Fathi and Megarrity, 2019). Long-standing, significant inequities still persist in rates of student participation, while the enduring government underfunding of the system has driven an entrepreneurial approach to international student recruitment. Universities have become too dependent on international student fees to sustain their operation, most particularly research performance. While there is much to celebrate in the evolution and accomplishments of Australian higher education, much remains to be achieved.

References

Altbach, P. and Welch, A. (2011). "The perils of commercialism: Australia's example." *International Higher Education*, 62, 21–23.

Audit Office (NSW) (2018). "Universities 2017 audits." June 8, 21. https://www.audit.nsw.gov. au/our-work/reports/universities-2018

Australian Academy of Science (n.d.-a). "Gender equity." https://www.science.org.au/ supporting-science/diversity-and-inclusion/gender-equity

Australian Academy of Science (n.d.-b). "Nobel Australians." https://www.science.org.au/education/history-australian-science/nobel-australians

Australian Human Rights Commission (2019). *Breaking the Bamboo Ceiling*. https://www.humanrights.gov.au/about/news/breaking-bamboo-ceiling

Babones, S. (2019). "The China student boom and the risks it poses to Australian universities." Sydney Centre for Independent Studies. https://www.cis.org.au/app/uploads/2019/08/ap5.pdf

Baker, M., Robertson, F., and Sloan, J. (1993). *The Role of Immigration in the Australian Higher Education Labour Market*. Canberra: Australian Government Publishing Service.

BBC (2010). "The Dunera Boys – 70 years on after notorious voyage." https://www.bbc.com/news/10409026

Behrendt, L., Larkin, S., Griew, R., and Kelly, P. (2012). *Review of Higher Education Access and Outcomes for Aboriginal and Torres Strait Islander People Final Report*. Canberra: Australian Government. http://www.innovation.gov.au/HigherEducation/IndigenousHigherEducation/ReviewOfIndigenousHigherEducation/Pages/default.aspx.

Berndt, R. M. and Berndt, C. H. (1988). *The World of the First Australians*. Canberra: Aboriginal Studies Press.

Bowen, J. (1985). "University admission and women's aspirations: A century of class conflict in Australia." *Discourse: Studies in the Cultural Politics of Education*, 5/1, 1–13.

Carrington, K. and Pratt, A. (2003). "How far have we come? Gender disparities in the Australian higher education system." https://www.aph.gov.au/About_Parliament/Parliamentary_Departments/Parliamentary_Library/Publications_Archive/CIB/cib0203/03CIB31

Chief Scientist (2013). *Partners in Influence: How Australia and China Relate through Science*. Canberra: Australia Centre on China and the World. https://www.chiefscientist.gov.au/wp-content/uploads/Australia-China-speech.pdf

Commonwealth Bureau of Census and Statistics (CBCS) (1952). *University Statistics*. Part 2: Degrees Conferred, Universities 1947 to 1952 (Table 3). Canberra: CBCS.

Czarnecki, K. (2018). "Less inequality through universal access? Socioeconomic background of tertiary entrants in Australia after the expansion of university participation." *Higher Education*, 76, 501–518.

Department of Education, Science and Training (DEST) (n.d.). *Performance Based Funding for the Commonwealth Grant Scheme*. https://www.education.gov.au/performance-based-funding-commonwealth-grant-scheme

Department of Education, Science and Training (DEST) (2002). *Setting Firm Foundations: Financing Australian Higher Education*. http://hdl.voced.edu.au/10707/109882

Department of Education, Skills and Employment (DESE) (2020). *International Student Data*. https://internationaleducation.gov.au/research/International-Student-Data/Pages/default.aspx

Department of Foreign Affairs and Trade (DFAT) (n.d.-a). *Australia Awards*. https://www.dfat.gov.au/people-to-people/australia-awards/Pages/australia-awards

Department of Foreign Affairs and Trade (DFAT) (n.d.-b). *New Colombo Plan*. https://www.dfat.gov.au/people-to-people/new-colombo-plan/pages/new-colombo-plan

Department of Foreign Affairs and Trade (DFAT). (n.d.-c). *About the New Colombo Plan*. https://dfat.gov.au/people-to-people/new-colombo-plan/about/Pages/about.aspx

Dobson, I. (2012). "PhDs in Australia, from the beginning." *Australian Universities Review*, 54/1, 94–101.

Fathi, R. and Megarrity, L. (2019). *You Matter: The Australian Historical Association's Casualisation Survey*. https://researchnow.flinders.edu.au/en/publications/you-matter-the-australian-historical-associations-casualisation-s

Gallagher, M. (2001). "Modern university governance: A national perspective." In *The Idea of a University. Enterprise or Academy?* (pp. 49–57). The Australia Institute, Discussion Paper 39.

Goldring, J. (1984). *Mutual Advantage: Report of the Committee of Review of Private Overseas Student Policy*. Canberra: AGPS.

Guardian (2018). "Private education spending in Australia soars ahead of other countries." https://www.theguardian.com/australia-news/2018/sep/11/private-education-spending-in-australia-soars-ahead-of-other-countries

Hao, J. and Welch, A. (2012). "A tale of sea turtles: Job-seeking experiences of *Hai Gui* (high-skilled returnees) in China." *Higher Education Policy*, 25/2, 243–260.

Hao, J., Wen, W., and Welch, A. (2016). "When sojourners return: Employment opportunities and challenges facing high-skilled Chinese returnees." *Asian and Pacific Migration Journal*, 25/1, 22–40.

Hart, M. (1974). *Traditional Aboriginal Education: Kulila*. Sydney: Australian and New Zealand Book Company.

Horne, J. (2016). "The final barrier: Australian women and the nineteenth century public university." In L. Panayotidis and P. Stortz (eds.), *Women in Higher Education, 1850–1970: International Perspectives* (pp. 76–96). London: Routledge.

Horne, J. and Sherington, G. (2013). "Dominion' legacies: The Australian experience." In D. Schreuder (ed.), *Universities for a New World: Making a Global Network in International Higher Education, 1913–2013* (pp. 284–307). London: Sage Publications.

Hurley, P. (2020). "International students vital to coronavirus recovery." https://www.vu.edu.au/sites/default/files/issues-brief-international-students-covid.pdf

Jackson, R. (1984). *Report of the Committee to Review the Australian Overseas Aid Programme.* Canberra: AGPS.

Jarboe, N. (2016). *Women Count. Australian Universities 2016.* https://www.universitiesaustralia.edu.au/wp-content/uploads/2019/06/WomenCount-Autralian-Report_ARTWORK-1.pdf

Lee, J.-S. (2014). "The attainability of university degrees and their labour market benefits for young Australians." *Higher Education,* 76/4, 501–518.

Macdonald, I. (2006). "Offshore university campuses: Bonus or baggage." *Proceedings of HERDSA Conference 2006* (pp. 207–215).

Mares, P. (2016). *Not Quite Australian: How Temporary Migration is Changing the Nation.* Sydney: Text Publishing.

Marett, A. (2005). "Dreaming songs: Sustaining tradition." In *Songs, Dreamings and Ghosts: The Wangga of North Australia* (pp. 39–46). Middletown, CT: Wesleyan University Press.

Marginson, S. (2016). *Higher Education and the Common Good.* Melbourne: Melbourne University Press.

Marginson, S. (2019). "How should universities respond to the new Cold War?" *University World News.* https://www.universityworldnews.com/post.php?story=20191112103413758

Marginson, S. and Considine, M. (2000). *The Enterprise University: Power, Governance and Reinvention in Australia.* Cambridge: Cambridge University Press.

Megarrity, L. (2007). "Regional goodwill, sensibly priced: Commonwealth policies towards Colombo plan scholars and private overseas students, 1945–1972." *Australian Historical Studies,* 38/129, 88–105.

National Indigenous Australians Agency (NIAA) (n.d.). *National Indigenous Success Program.* https://www.niaa.gov.au/indigenous-affairs/education/indigenous-student-success-program

Norton, A. (2019). "Demand-driven funding for universities is frozen. What does this mean and should the policy be restored?" *The Conversation.* https://theconversation.com/demand-driven-funding-for-universities-is-frozen-what-does-this-mean-and-should-the-policy-be-restored-116060

Oakman, D. (2004). *Facing Asia: A History of the Colombo Plan.* Canberra: Pandanus Books.

Oishi, N. (2017). *Workforce Diversity in Higher Education: The Experiences of Asian Academics in Australian Universities.* Asia Institute, University of Melbourne. https://arts.unimelb.edu.au/__data/assets/pdf_file/0012/2549496/AA-Report_Final-Copy_Web_5Nov.pdf

Organisation for Economic Co-operation and Development (OECD) (2007) International Migration Outlook 2007. https://www.oecd-ilibrary.org/social-issues-migration-health/international-migration-outlook-2007_migr_outlook-2007-en

Organisation for Economic Co-operation and Development (OECD) (2019). *Spending on Tertiary Education.* https://data.oecd.org/eduresource/spending-on-tertiary-education.htm

Parliament of Australia (APH) (2012). *Temporary Migration and its Implications for Australia.* Papers on Parliament, No. 57. https://www.aph.gov.au/About_Parliament/Senate/Powers_practice_n_procedures/~/~/link.aspx?_id=06B96F584FD0483D9F369F0B5186C6A9&_z=z

Pietsch, T. (2010). "Wandering scholars? Academic mobility and the British world, 1850–1940." *Journal of Historical Geography*, 36, 377–387.

Pietsch, T. (2013). *Empire of Scholars: Universities, Networks, and the British Academic World 1850–1939.* Manchester: Manchester University Press.

Productivity Commission (2002). *University Resourcing: Australia in an International Context.* https://www.pc.gov.au/inquiries/completed/universities/report

Productivity Commission (2019). *The Demand Driven University System: A Mixed Report Card.* https://www.pc.gov.au/research/completed/university-report-card/university-report-card.pdf

Reforming Post-Secondary Higher Education in Australia: Perspectives from Australia's Dual Sector Universities (2019). https://static1.squarespace.com/static/5ca6919bfb1820665837baad/t/5cabdaf441920212c1ea4165/1554766595690/Reforming+Post-Secondary+Education+in+Australia_FINAL%5B2%5D.pdf

Sheehan, B. and Welch, A. (1996). "The academic profession in Australia." In P. Altbach (ed.), *The International Academic Profession* (pp. 51–96). Princeton: Carnegie Foundation for the Advancement of Teaching.

Sherington, G. (1990). *Australia's Immigrants 1788–1988.* Sydney: Allen & Unwin.

Sherington, G. (2019). *Alexander Mackie: An Academic Life in Education.* Sydney: Sydney University Press.

Smith, F. (2001). "Academics in and out of the *Australian Dictionary of Biography*." In F. Smith and P. Crichton (eds.), *Ideas for Histories of Universities in Australia* (pp. 1–15). Canberra, ANU Press.

Soutphommasane, T. (2014). "Are Asian Australians trapped under a bamboo ceiling?" *The Guardian.* https://www.theguardian.com/commentisfree/2014/jul/11/are-asian-australians-trapped-under-a-bamboo-ceiling

Study Assist (2020). *Student Contribution Amounts.* https://www.studyassist.gov.au/help-loans-commonwealth-supported-places-csps/student-contribution-amounts

Swinburne University (2019). "Dual Sector VCs call for more connection between two systems." https://www.swinburne.edu.au/news/latest-news/2019/04/dual-sector-vcs-call-for-more-connection-between-two-systems.php

Sydney Morning Herald (2018a). "Degrees of risk: Inside Sydney's extraordinary international student boom." *Sydney Morning Herald*, March 2. https://www.smh.com.au/interactive/2018/international-student-boom/

Sydney Morning Herald (2018b). "Dunera lives review: Another way of telling a troubling story." *Sydney Morning Herald*, July 27. https://www.smh.com.au/entertainment/books/dunera-lives-review-another-way-of-telling-a-troubling-story-20180719-h12wcg.html

Sydney Morning Herald (2019). "The universities which rely most on international students for cash." *Sydney Morning Herald*, August 25. https://www.smh.com.au/national/the-universities-which-rely-most-on-international-students-for-cash-20190823-p52k4m.html

Tertiary Education Quality Standards Agency (TEQSA) (2020). *National Register.* https://www.teqsa.gov.au/national-register/

University World News (2020). "Universities face disastrous fall in income due to COVID-19." https://www.universityworldnews.com/post.php?story=202004221408487

VC Email (2020). "Savings measures: Impact of COVID-19 on the University's financial out-look." University of Sydney, March 3.

Walker, D. (2019). "Significant other: Anxieties about Australia's Asian future." *Australian Foreign Affairs*, 5/2, 5–28.

Welch, A. (1996) *Australian Education. Reform or Crisis*. Sydney: Allen and Unwin

Welch, A. (1999). "The peripatetic professor: The internationalisation of the academic profession." *Higher Education*, 34/3, 323–345.

Welch, A. (2012a). "Academic salaries, massification and the rise of an underclass in Australia." In P. Altbach, L. Reisberg, M. Yudkevich, G. Androushchak, and I. Pacheco (eds.), *Paying the Professoriate: A Global Comparison of Compensation and Contracts* (pp. 61–71). London: Routledge.

Welch, A. (2012b). "Contributing to the Southeast Asian knowledge economy? Australian off-shore campuses in Malaysia and Vietnam." In A. R. Nelson and I. P. Wei (eds.), *The Global University: Past, Present, and Future Perspectives* (pp. 55–81). New York: Palgrave Macmillan.

Welch, A. (2012c). "Opportunistic entrepreneurialism and internationalisation of higher education: Lessons from the Antipodes?" *Globalisation, Societies and Education*, 10, 295–315.

Welch, A. (2014). "Richer relations? Four decades of ASEAN–Australia relations in higher education." In S. Wood and B. He (eds.), *The Australia-ASEAN Dialogue: Tracing 40 Years of Partnership* (pp. 145–166). New York: Palgrave Macmillan.

Welch, A. (2015). "The ties that bind: Federalism in Australian education." In M. Crossley, G. Hancock, and T. Sprague (eds.), *Education in Australia, New Zealand and the Pacific* (pp. 41–59). London: Bloomsbury.

Welch, A. (2016). "Audit culture and academic production: Re-shaping Australian social science research output 1993–2013." *Higher Education Policy*, 29/4, 511–538.

Welch, A. (2019a). "Management, leadership and governance in Australian higher education." In J. Jacob (ed.), *Bloomsbury Education and Childhood Studies: Higher Education*. London: Bloomsbury (Online series). https://www.bloomsbury.com/uk/discover/bloomsbury-digital-resources/products/bloomsbury-education-and-childhood-studies/

Welch, A. (2019b). "Research and knowledge in Australian higher education." In J. Jacob (ed.), *Bloomsbury Education and Childhood Studies: Higher Education*. London: Bloomsbury (Online series). https://www.bloomsbury.com/uk/discover/bloomsbury-digital-resources/products/bloomsbury-education-and-childhood-studies/

Welch, A. (2019c). "Globalization in Australian higher education." In J. Jacob (ed.), *Bloomsbury Education and Childhood Studies: Higher Education*. London: Bloomsbury (Online series). https://www.bloomsbury.com/uk/discover/bloomsbury-digital-resources/products/bloomsbury-education-and-childhood-studies/

Welch, A. (2021a). "International academics in Australian higher education: People, process, paradox." In F. Huang and A. Welch (eds.), *International Faculty in Asia: Comparative Global Perspective* (pp. 115–134). Dordrecht: Springer.

Welch, A. (2021b). "The shift to the east, and the changing face of internationalization." In J. Thondhlana et al. (eds.), *The Bloomsbury Handbook of the Internationalization of Higher Education in the Global South* (pp. 148–160). London: Bloomsbury.

Welch, A. (2022) A plague on higher education? COVID, Camus and Culture Wars in Australian universities. https://onlinelibrary.wiley.com/doi/full/10.1111/hequ.12377

Welch, A. and Hao, J. (2015). "Global argonauts: Returnees and diaspora as sources of innovation in China and Israel." *Globalisation, Societies and Education*, 14/2, 272–297.

Welch, A., Königsberg, P., Rochecouste, J., and Collard, G. (2015). "Australia: Aboriginal education." In M. Crossley, G. Hancock, and T. Sprague (eds.), *Education in Australia, New Zealand and the Pacific* (pp. 91–110). London: Bloomsbury.

Welch, A. and Zhang, Z. (2008a). "Higher education and global talent flows: Brain drain, overseas Chinese intellectuals, and diasporic knowledge networks." *Higher Education Policy*, 21/4, 519–537.

Welch, A. and Zhang, Z. (2008b). "Communication networks among the Chinese knowledge diaspora: A new invisible college?" In R. Boden, R. Deem, D. Epstein, and F. Rizvi (eds.), *Geographies of Knowledge, Geometries of Power: Higher Education in the 21st Century. World Yearbook of Education 2008* (pp. 338–354). London: Routledge.

Wilks, J. and Wilson, K. (2015). "A profile of the Aboriginal and Torres Strait Islander higher education student population." *Australian Universities Review*, 57/2, 17–30.

Yang, R. and Welch, A. (2010). "Globalisation, transnational academic mobility and the Chinese knowledge diaspora: An Australian case study." *Discourse: Australian Journal of Educational Studies*, 31/5, 593–607.

Yang, R. and Welch, A. (2012). "Belonging from afar? Transnational academic mobility and the Chinese knowledge diaspora: An Australian case study." In N. Bagnall and E. Cassity (eds.), *Education and Belonging* (pp. 123–137). New York: Nova Science Publishers.

Yosso, T. (2005). "Whose culture has capital? A critical race theory discussion of community cultural wealth." *Race, Ethnicity and Education*, 8/1, 69–91.

CHAPTER 36

EDUCATION FOR ALL?

Higher Education at a Crossroads in Aotearoa New Zealand

KATHRYN A. SUTHERLAND AND
STEPHEN J. MARSHALL

1. INTRODUCTION

> No greater mistake can be made than to suppose that universities are
> intended only for people of private means and learned desire. The true
> function of a modern university I take to be, to give to all – men and
> women alike – who wish to avail themselves of it every facility for higher
> education in whatever branch they choose for themselves. (Governor
> William Jervois, at the opening of the Auckland University College of
> the University of New Zealand in 1885, cited in Malcolm and Tarling,
> 2007, p. 84)

WHILE New Zealand is a young country, only having been inhabited by humans in the
last 800 years or so, it has a deep commitment to higher education, as evidenced by the
quotation with which we open this chapter, and an abiding goal that higher education be
accessible to many people. This generous aim is at risk, however, and arguably has never
really ever been achievable given the structural problems pervading the system in New
Zealand, from inadequate public funding to inequitable access.

Although the specific details may vary, many of the challenges facing the New
Zealand system are not unique to this country and are evident in their own way elsewhere (Marshall, 2018). Countries with a long tradition of university education are
struggling to evolve their higher education systems to sustain a meaningful place in society as costs continue to grow disproportionately (Vedder, 2004; Martin, 2011; Bowen,
2012) as the scale of demand and provision grows. Employment patterns are shifting
rapidly, and economies are seeing a growing divide between highly skilled employment

and very low-skilled service roles (Bialik, 2010; Coelli et al., 2012). Prestigious highly ranked universities are becoming even more elite over time, while others expand to the point of oversupply and overeducation (Chevalier and Lindley, 2009; Leuven and Oosterbeek, 2011), eroding the perceived value of their degrees.

Furthermore, technology is catalyzing and accelerating change by stimulating the development of new models of learning, but also challenging the norms and assumptions of the university. Technology has enabled powerful new opportunities by providing means for communication, collaboration, and greater availability of information for education and research, and increasing the potential power and influence of multinational commercial providers acting on unbundled services outsourced and disaggregated from universities (Czerniewicz and Morris, 2017; McCowan, 2017; Newfield, 2019).

Most recently, the COVID-19 pandemic and the disruption it has caused to the global economy has thrown into stark relief the fragility of higher education systems. It has taken only a brief disruption in the flow of international students to destabilize the finances of New Zealand universities and threaten their futures as public institutions (Leaman, 2020; Rutherford, 2020). The immediate impact the pandemic is having on the finances of universities is exacerbated by systematic decline in funding from the government, sharpened by a regulatory environment that combines the worst features of neoliberal markets with the worst features of bureaucratic central planning. The comparatively high level of dependence on (declining) public funds leaves universities with very few options other than international students for revenue growth.

Moreover, despite comparatively reasonable tertiary education[1] levels, many students in New Zealand fail to progress into higher education or high-skilled employment (Scott, 2005). Coupled with New Zealand's low-wage economy, the tertiary sector fails to provide a return on educational achievement equivalent to that of countries such as Australia (OECD, 2019). There is also substantial evidence of systematic inequality in the higher education system. Despite the Māori and Pacific populations growing significantly in recent decades, participation and success rates for both groups remain much lower than for other parts of New Zealand society (Ministry of Education, 2019).

Not all is doom and gloom, however. In this chapter, we first provide an overview of tertiary education in New Zealand, from the establishment of the University of New Zealand in the late 1800s through to the more expansive, publicly funded tertiary sector of the twenty-first century. Tertiary education in New Zealand is underpinned by a commitment to the principles of biculturalism and partnership in Te Tiriti o Waitangi (the Treaty of Waitangi), signed between the Crown and Māori in 1840. This commitment informs and provides considerable focus for the government's Tertiary

---

[1] New Zealand has a tertiary education sector, encompassing all post-high school education, including universities, polytechnics and institutes of technology, wānanga (Māori-focused institutions), and private training establishments. More on the composition of the tertiary sector and its funding body, the Tertiary Education Commission, is provided in the next section. In this chapter, we use "tertiary education" to refer to all post-school education and "higher education" in particular places to refer to degree-level and/or university education only.

Education Strategy, by which universities in New Zealand are funded and monitored. This history provides context for the challenges and prospects of a publicly funded tertiary system in a bicultural context *and* an increasingly globalized world. We outline the challenges of responding to the impact of increasing demand for and participation in tertiary education, as well as the pervasive influence of more recent neoliberal policies and marketization. We conclude by providing three options for taking New Zealand's tertiary education into a future that can hopefully sustain the idea of education remaining accessible for all who desire it.

2. BACKGROUND AND CONTEXT

New Zealand is an island nation of approximately five million people. Geographically isolated, the country was the last large, habitable place to be populated by humans. As young as the country is, higher learning and education has long played a vital role. Over many centuries, New Zealand's first inhabitants (Māori) engaged in vocational learning at schools that taught boat building, carving, and weaving, for example. There was also higher learning of esoteric and theoretical knowledge of lore, history, rituals, and traditions at whare wānanga, houses of knowledge (Best, 1934; Kidman, 1999). By the mid-1800s, when European settlement increased at pace, the need for accessible education for all inhabitants was identified, along with a need to train up school teachers to provide such education (Gardner, 1973).

In 1870, an Act of Parliament brought the University of New Zealand into existence as an examining and degree-granting body for what became four teaching institutions, two on the South Island and two on the North: Otago (already established as a university in 1869), Canterbury (1873), Auckland (1883) and Victoria (1899). As our opening quotation emphasizes, New Zealand's university system was founded on egalitarian principles, with the aim from the outset to provide relatively open access. Indeed, New Zealand was the first country in the Commonwealth to award a university degree to a woman (Kidman, 1999). There was also a focus on ensuring that part-time and distance study were available, and that evening classes were encouraged. While some proponents of the need for a New Zealand university were determined to "strike out a line of our own … [not] reproduce Oxford, Cambridge, or Edinburgh in New Zealand" (Veel, editor of the *Christchurch Press* in the 1870s, as cited in Gardner, 1973), the University of New Zealand was very tightly tied to its colonial roots. Examination scripts were sent back to England for marking until well into the 1940s, for example.

Post-World War II saw the mass return of service personnel seeking brighter futures through higher education, and the government boosted university finances with an injection of funding for research, as well as establishing a Grants Committee to provide greater financial support for universities. By the 1960s, the original four university colleges were recognized as full universities in their own right, along with two new universities (Waikato and Massey), and the University of New Zealand disbanded.

Universities received bulk-funding on a five-yearly basis from the University Grants Committee, a "buffer body" between the universities and government (Savage, 2000, p. 46). Decisions on how to spend the government funding, and other governance and curriculum decisions were made by each university's Council, which included professors, lay people, and government appointees.

All this changed in the 1980s and 1990s when universities were caught up in what has been described as "one of the most aggressive and extensive applications of neo-liberal market policies in the English-speaking world" (Robinson, 2006, p. 42). New Zealand's public sector underwent reforms that saw increasing privatization, competition, and marketization. Education became a commodity that could be sold and traded (Roberts, 2009), with more and more "customers" (students) now choosing their "product" (degree) from "providers" (universities), or from "competitors" (polytechnics, wānanga, and private training establishments) who aggressively branded themselves and marketed their offerings beyond their local regions (Sutherland, 2018). Vice Chancellors, rather than university Councils, became the employers of university staff; salaries were no longer decided by the national Higher Salaries Commission; degrees could be offered by providers other than universities; and weekly grants for all students were replaced by a student loan scheme. Tertiary education shifted from being viewed as a public good to a private benefit and students were expected to contribute to the cost of gaining this benefit by paying fees that, throughout the 1990s, increased on average by 13 percent per annum (Healey and Gunby, 2012).

As the types of providers increased, so too did participation in tertiary education through the 1990s and into the early 2000s. Wānanga were recognized in the Education Act as tertiary education organizations with a distinctly Māori focus. They provide education in (though not exclusively) te reo Māori (Māori language) and mātauranga Māori (Māori knowledge), among other subjects, and are founded on and driven by Māori tikanga (practices or protocols) and kawa (procedures or policies). Enrollments swelled in wānanga in the mid-2000s as thousands of people (Māori and non-Māori) took up opportunities to gain entry-level and degree qualifications.

Private training establishments (PTEs) also rose in prominence, offering a range of specialized post-school education opportunities from English language schools to religious education, aviation training, hairdressing, culinary, sports and leisure qualifications, and much more. Since the 2000s, students at PTEs have been able to get access to student loan funding. This opened up wider opportunities for tertiary qualifications to a broader range of students, something the government saw as important for enhancing New Zealand's workforce capabilities. Not all of this new provision was of high quality, however, and the government had serious concerns about funding tertiary education places for which they saw little or no return on investment.

Government priorities through the 2000s thus shifted much more towards aligning tertiary education offerings with workforce and industry needs. The Tertiary Education Commission came into existence and since 2002 has laid out a Tertiary Education Strategy every few years to which tertiary education organizations must align their own plans and priorities in order to guarantee continued government funding.

Demand-driven funding ceased, with providers instead required to identify targets for enrollments and stay within 3 percent either side of that target (Crawford, 2016). Institutions also had to report on education performance indicators aligned with the Tertiary Education Strategy, including course and qualification retention and completion rates. Graduate outcomes also became more prominently tied to economic factors, with an Occupation Outlook app introduced in 2016 that enabled prospective students to match potential qualifications to job prospects in that field, alongside qualification costs and potential earning capacity.

Also in the early 2000s, teaching and research funding were separated, with the introduction of competitive government research funding in the form of the Performance Based Research Fund (PBRF) and the establishment of ten Centers for Research Excellence (CoREs). As the OECD New Zealand country report from that time noted (Goedegebuure et al., 2008), all these reforms meant that the New Zealand tertiary education system bore little resemblance, either in size or shape, to that existing some 20 years ago. Now, in 2021, the system is again shifting in response to government reforms and external realities, as the next section of this chapter explains.

3. Participation in New Zealand's Tertiary Education Sector

As of December 2020, New Zealand's tertiary sector consists of eight public, government-funded universities, and one national institute of skills and technology (created early in 2020 from a merger of the 16 former institutes of technology and polytechnics). There are also three government-funded wānanga (Māori-focused institutions), and hundreds of private training establishments (many of which also receive a small share of government funding). Around half of all tertiary enrollments are in universities, about a third in polytechnics, and the rest in wānanga or private training establishments.

New Zealand is now recognized as operating in a highly marketized neoliberal public policy environment (Larner and Le Heron, 2005; Martens and Starke, 2008; Lewis and Shore, 2019). The country has been lauded internationally (and often derided locally) for the ambition and scope of the public sector reforms that were implemented in the 1980s. Education policy is dominated by the interests of employers and the economy overall. A pseudo-competitive marketplace has operated for some years in the provision of degree education with individual universities competing actively for domestic students through aggressive marketing campaigns and student recruitment efforts in schools and communities. A major issue distorting this market remains the reality that the majority of student funding is provided by the government through student loans and direct subsidies and so the government has an interest in controlling the operation of the market. These controls include limits on student numbers, constraints on fees and other charges for services, and performance measures aligned to specific policy priorities such as for school leavers, and Māori and Pacific participation and success.

The marketized model is also evident in the importance placed on international rankings by the New Zealand universities. As of February 2021, New Zealand's eight universities are all ranked in the 2020 Top 500 (QS) rankings (compared with 26 of 42 of Australian universities in the Top 500). The limitations of rankings are well acknowledged in the literature (Diver, 2005; Marginson, 2007; Hazelkorn, 2015) and their influence suggests a level of homogeneity in the operation of the universities. This in part reflects the importance of international students to the universities (see below) and the perception that rankings influence student choice.

4. PARTICIPATION IN TERTIARY EDUCATION

Overall enrollments in the wider tertiary sector in New Zealand have decreased steadily from a peak of nearly half a million (499,695) in 2005, which represented 12 percent of the population, to 388,730 in 2019, around 7 percent of the population. The bulk of this decrease is in the sub-degree certificate or diploma level, which has shifted from more than two-thirds (68 percent) of all enrollments just over a decade ago (Goedegebuure et al., 2008, p. 16) to less than half of all tertiary enrollments (42 percent) in 2019.

As well as now being at degree rather than sub-degree level, the bulk of enrollments in 2019 are in universities. This represents another significant flip from the mid-2000s, where the figures for polytechnics and universities were reversed (42 percent and 33 percent respectively). Given the inevitable bedding-in period of the newly-created Te Pūkenga, New Zealand Institute of Skills and Technology, and recent significant decreases in polytechnic enrollments (a 4.7 percent decrease between 2018 and 2019, for example), this trend may continue for some time. However, the current government is targeting a significant increase in student enrollments in trade training and apprenticeships post-COVID 19.

Another enrollment challenge facing tertiary institutions in New Zealand arises from a decrease in births at the turn of the century, meaning there will be fewer school leavers for the next few years (contrasting with a "baby blip" more than a decade earlier which led to an increase in enrollments in the mid-2000s). A projected decrease in the numbers of domestic students from 2016 onwards (driven by this 1–2 percent annual decrease in the number of school leavers) appears to have hit non-degree enrollments most, with universities less negatively affected.

Despite significant decreases across the overall tertiary sector, there are areas that continue to see growth. University enrollments, for example, have increased steadily—though not dramatically—since 2015 (from 172,050 to 177,905). However, all of the increase is attributable to sharp rises in international student enrollments (domestic numbers decreased in universities over the same period). In the next section, we describe the phenomenon of increasing international student numbers.

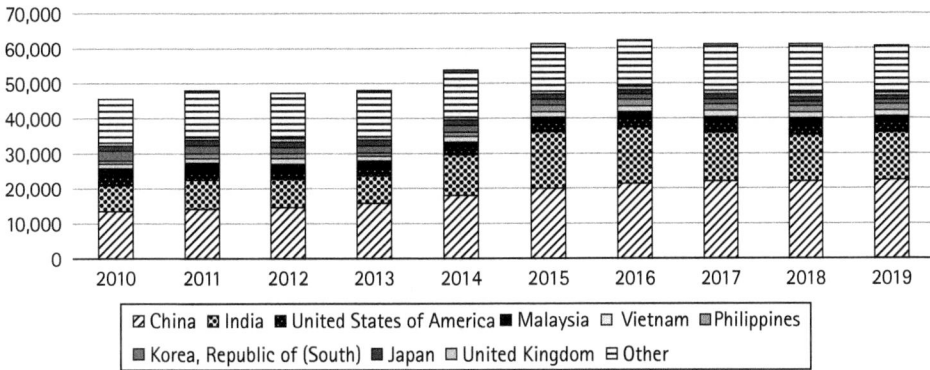

FIGURE 36.1 International students studying in NZ tertiary institutions by country of citizenship, 2009–2019

Source: Figure compiled from data available on the Education Counts website.

5. International Participation

New Zealand has one of the highest rates in the OECD of foreign-born people in the overall population, with a quarter of the population born outside New Zealand. At 25.1 percent, New Zealand ranks fourth highest for foreign-born, after only Luxembourg, Switzerland, and Australia (OECD, 2020). This high percentage in the overall population is reflected in a very high percentage of international academic staff—up to half of the academic staff in New Zealand universities (Sutherland, 2018)— and in one of the highest percentages of international students in the OECD, across all levels of education from primary schools and high schools through to universities and other tertiary providers. It is no surprise, then, that education was New Zealand's fourth largest export earner in 2015/16, behind dairy, tourism, and meat (Shannon et al., 2019, p. 79). International tertiary education contributed approximately US\$2.55 billion to the economy (Education New Zealand, 2019), with universities generating 45 percent of this, a significant complement to the US\$2.3 billion spent by the government on tertiary education (New Zealand Treasury, 2019).

According to the OECD (2019, p. 2), New Zealand has one of the highest shares of international students in tertiary education with 20 percent coming from abroad, compared to the OECD average of 6 percent. New Zealand Ministry of Education figures from the Education Counts website show that, in 2019, a total of 60,655 international students were enrolled at New Zealand tertiary providers, of which 60 percent were from China (37 percent) and India (23 percent) and the remaining 40 percent from more than 130 other countries (Figure 36.1).

Over half of the international students in New Zealand's public tertiary sector in 2019 were enrolled in universities (33,900), and this internationalization has a much stronger focus on Asia than on Europe (as in the past) or elsewhere (Shannon et al.,

2019). In New Zealand's universities, this is particularly pronounced with Chinese student enrollments increasing significantly from 29 percent of all international students in New Zealand universities in 2009 to a massive majority of 46 percent of all international university students in 2019. The percentage of Indian students in New Zealand universities has also increased from 6 percent in 2009 to 9.4 percent in 2019, leaping to second place as a source country and overtaking students from the United States (students from the United States made up 8 percent of all international students in New Zealand universities in 2019, a decrease from 11 percent in 2009) (Figure 36.2).

The percentage of international students in New Zealand is most obvious at the doctoral level, with nearly half (48 percent) of New Zealand's doctoral candidates coming from abroad. The recent OECD country note for New Zealand comments on this further:

> This is well above the total across OECD countries (22%) and also higher than other English-speaking countries such as Australia (32%) and the United Kingdom (42%). One factor influencing the high level of international doctoral candidates in New Zealand is the tuition fee which is the same for national and foreign students (US 4 739). In contrast, foreign doctoral students studying in Australia pay USD 16 187 for their degree. (OECD, 2019, p. 2)

The reliance on the Chinese market is less prominent in PhD enrollments, though still high. Chinese students make up 27 percent of all doctoral enrollments, followed by India (13 percent), Iran (11 percent), and the United States (8 percent).

We sounded a warning in earlier work (Marshall, 2019) about universities' reliance for income on international student enrollments, particularly from China as such a dominant market. China is a particular concern as international education by Chinese students is subject to significant regulation and control by the Chinese government and at risk of rapid changes as a consequence of unrelated political events.

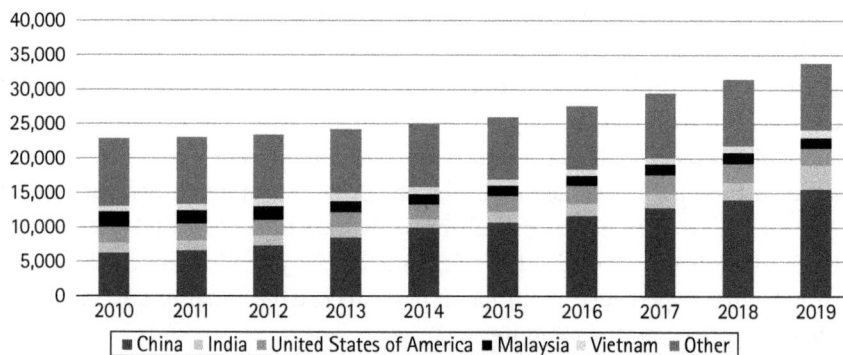

FIGURE 36.2 International students studying in NZ universities by country of citizenship, 2009–2019

Source: Figure compiled from data available on the Education Counts website.

A significant chunk of university income (at least 10 percent, if not as high as 20 percent) is at risk if this market fails as it did in 2002 when SARS affected international enrollments (Feast and Bretag, 2007) and in 2003 when two private providers collapsed causing massive reputational damage across the sector (Li, 2003). In 2020, we have seen this risky reality play out in response to COVID-19. If borders remain closed and international students continue to be barred from entering the country, that income will once again be threatened, and universities are rightly worried about this (Leaman, 2020; Rutherford, 2020).

6. COMPLETIONS

Complicating New Zealand's reliance on international student income is the challenge simultaneously faced in meeting government and societal expectations around tertiary participation *and* completions for local students. The proportion of adults in New Zealand with a degree is not high (34 percent), but it is on par with the OECD average of 30 percent. Yet, New Zealand has a much higher proportion (52 percent) with a level 4 qualification[2] or higher, significantly more than the OECD average (42 percent) (Ministry of Education, 2019, p. 4). So, a good proportion of people are completing sub-degree qualifications but not necessarily seeing the need—or having the opportunity—to carry on with further, degree-level study and qualifications. Furthermore, while New Zealand's completion rates for full-time study compare well with other countries, "compared with other countries the New Zealand system is characterised by very high levels of part-time, or part-programme study, which have lower qualification completion rates" (Ministry of Education, 2019, p. 4), as explained further below.

These phenomena—of high enrollments (but not necessarily high completions) in sub-degree tertiary programs, and correspondingly high levels of part-time enrollment—are particularly problematic when viewed in light of the government's long-expressed strategy to increase Māori and Pacific tertiary participation and success. Māori and Pacific students are more represented in sub-degree tertiary programs than in universities or other degree programs, and their overall participation rates are low compared with their representation in the wider population. These lower participation and completion rates have been ascribed to external barriers (family and community responsibilities, financial issues), institutional barriers (systemic racism, monocultural institutions with poor support systems, a lack of Māori and Pacific staff), and individual barriers (negative schooling experiences, lack of confidence/experience, inadequate

---

[2] New Zealand's qualification framework ranges across 10 levels, with levels 1–3 mostly completed in school, levels 4–6 corresponding with pre- or sub-degree level qualifications such as trade certificates and diplomas, and levels 7–10 being degree level (up to doctorates at level 10). More detail is available on the NZ Qualifications Authority website: https://www.nzqa.govt.nz/studying-in-new-zealand/understand-nz-quals/.

preparation, etc.) (Theodore et al., 2017). In an effort to "improve access, participation, and achievement of Māori and Pacific learners at higher levels of the tertiary education system" (TEC, 2020) the government now allocates more funding per Māori and/ or Pacific student at level 7 and beyond. The government has also targeted participation and completion rates that reflect the wider population representation: for Māori participation in degree-level study, they have a set a 2022 target of 17.9 percent. Given that in 2018, Māori participation in degree-level study was 14 percent, and only moved 0.4 percent from 2016 to 2018, this is an ambitious target. It is also problematic that the decrease in domestic enrollments has disproportionately affected Māori and Pacific students. For example, in 2018, domestic student enrollments decreased 2.3 percent overall, but for Māori this percentage was 4.9 percent and for Pacific students, 3.9 percent.

Despite proclamations from the government and the universities themselves (Universities New Zealand, 2019) about a desire to increase Māori and Pacific enrollment *and* completion rates, there is skepticism that such goals are achievable without addressing structural inequalities and without a radical shake up of the tertiary education workforce (Kidman and Chu, 2017, 2019; Naepi et al., 2017).

7. WORKFORCE INEQUITIES

New Zealand universities were established in colonial times and were predominantly staffed by white and male academics for many decades. The original four university colleges also clung to colonial traditions and curricula for a long time (Connell, 2017; Sutherland, 2018). Tully and Whitehead (2009) argue that actions such as sending exam scripts back to the UK for marking may have occurred because of a lack of trust in local standards/professors, a desire to impose controls, the need to meet standards with universities in the home country, or "a classic example of colonial 'cringe' or the fear of going it alone" (p. 36). This "cringe" mentality in New Zealand academia has been labeled a "shared [with Australia and Canada] inferiority complex" that "marginalizes local work" (Curtis, 2019, p. 196). Citing evidence from the New Zealand Performance Based Research Fund subject rankings, Curtis shows that higher-scoring subjects have a lower proportion of New Zealand-trained academics and argues that "research about New Zealand and by New Zealand-trained academics is undervalued in comparison to what is considered international" (Curtis, 2019, p. 197). This is particularly problematic for Māori academics whose research often focuses on local concerns (Ruckstuhl et al., 2019; Staniland et al., 2020). Exacerbating this tendency to speak and write "out" to the rest of the world, rather than developing national conversations about New Zealand's own specific issues and situations (Bell, 2017) is the reality that Māori and Pacific people are underrepresented in academia in general, and severely underrepresented in permanent and senior academic roles (Kidman and Chu, 2017, 2019; McAllister et al., 2019, 2020; Naepi, 2019; Naepi et al., 2019).

The proportion of academic staff in New Zealand universities who are employed full-time has decreased from 65 percent of the total university academic staff in 2012 to 54 percent in 2019, according to the latest data on the Education Counts website. At the same time, the "other academic staff" category has increased from 28 percent in 2012 to 34 percent in 2019. Within the "other academic staff" category, there is an increasing trend towards more precarious part-time employment, with 72 percent of "other academic staff" employed part-time in New Zealand universities in 2012 increasing to 82 percent in 2019. Compared with other ethnic groups, Māori academics in New Zealand universities continue to be employed in the lower ranks and in more precarious roles. The latest data show that the majority of Māori are employed in the "other academic staff" category (38 percent of all Māori academics compared with 32 percent of Pākehā/New Zealand European academics). At the other end of the academic scale, by contrast, 15 percent of all Pākehā/New Zealand European academics are professors, compared with just 8 percent of all Māori academics. Furthermore, as a recent paper investigating the "glass ceiling" in New Zealand academia for Māori and Pacific academics showed, Māori make up only 3.1 percent of all professors nationally and Pacific academics only 1 percent (McAllister et al., 2020) and both are less likely to get promoted or earn as much as their Pākehā/New Zealand European counterparts.

This induces negative flow-on effects for attempting to increase Māori and Pacific student participation and completion in tertiary education, creating a lack of role models and appropriate mentoring. Naepi et al. (2019) show a huge difference, for example, between Māori staff to Māori student and Pacific staff to Pacific student ratios, especially compared with Pākehā/NZ European staff to Pākehā/NZ European student ratios.

Considerable work is needed to improve New Zealand's tertiary curricula and institutional structures (such as hiring practices and promotion and reward systems) to better reflect the wide variety of cultures within the New Zealand population and to move more towards true bicultural partnership with Māori. Several scholars writing about the New Zealand tertiary education system (Kidman and Chu, 2017; Naepi et al., 2017, Bowl, 2018) often cite Sara Ahmed's influential work on diversity in the institution (2012), and proclaim that 'diversity' and 'inclusion' have become a means of appearing to address racism and colonialism in higher education, while in fact functioning to support their reproduction (Naepi et al., 2017, p. 84). More than lip-service through the box-ticking exercise of having an "equity and diversity" strategy is required—universities have had such strategies for the last decade or so, but increases in numbers of Māori and Pacific staff have been negligible.

Despite slow progress, some positive shifts towards biculturalism are evident, particularly in a physical sense on New Zealand university campuses. Te Herenga Waka Victoria University of Wellington built the country's first marae complex (Māori meeting space) in the 1980s and Adds et al. (2011) show how the marae has provided transformative learning experiences for Māori *and* non-Māori students. Students and staff both use the marae space to build relationships, understand Māori culture and heritage in relation to their own, and to teach and learn in innovative ways. All new staff are welcomed on to the marae and invited into the university whanau (family) at the beginning of each year, as are new international students. At Wellington city's other university campus, Peace and Shearer (2017) describe a project that aims to "explore the story of the [Massey University] Wellington campus from pre-colonial times to the present day" and which has created "learning and teaching resources that may be used in different disciplinary contexts as stimuli for projects, activities, and group actions" (p. 84). Massey has also announced itself as a Tiriti-led university (Massey University, 2018), and Victoria University of Wellington has declared itself a global-civic university with "our marae at our heart" and has added "Te Herenga Waka" (which translates as "the hitching post for all canoes" and is also the name of the marae) to its name in official university branding (THWVUW, 2020a). Most other New Zealand universities and many polytechnics now also boast marae complexes, and Auckland University also houses a large and very well-used Fale Pasifika (community meeting space, similar in concept to the Agora of Greece or Māori marae): "This iconic building is the spiritual home of the University's Pacific community, and an important social and performance space" (University of Auckland, n.d.). City council endorsement has also recently been given to explore the construction of a Pacific fale in downtown Wellington (THWVUW, 2020b). Without adequate funding, however, New Zealand universities will be unable to sustain increases in participation *or* in infrastructure.

8. Future Priorities

New Zealand's tertiary education system is at something of a crossroads. The government and the universities have been able to avoid making choices while international student revenue and a generally buoyant economy sustained a slightly uneasy complacency. Challenges such as the Christchurch (2010 and 2011) and Kaikoura (2016) earthquakes and the consequent massive disruption to Canterbury and Lincoln universities have distracted government, as has the financial collapse of the public vocational tertiary system which saw the majority of Institutes of Technology and Polytechnics operating at significant deficits in 2018 and projections of sector-wide shortfalls of nearly NZ$300 million by 2022 assuming no change in operating conditions (Tertiary Education Commission, 2018). The latter, resulting in a highly risky restructuring of the 16 polytechnics into a single centrally controlled New Zealand Institute of Skills and Technology (NZIST), is very clearly a warning shot to the universities of New Zealand. Similar financial challenges facing the universities as a result of government tight regulation of fees and domestic student numbers, combined with ongoing barriers to international student study caused by the pandemic response, mean that the sector's future is unclear. The system, and the government as the primary funder, and ultimately the arbiter of the system through its various agencies, has choices for the road ahead that include:

- Allowing the market to operate, forcing the closure of some universities and the commercial expansion of the remaining institutions under a much more profit-oriented model of operation.
- Combining the universities into a structured network modeled on coordinated systems such as the Californian State system under Clark Kerr's Master Plan (Marginson, 2016) or the college system under the University of London umbrella.
- Maintaining a publicly funded system of independent Humboldtian universities combining excellence in research and teaching with a wider social agenda aligned to the public good.

We now consider these from first to last as potential strategies.

A fully market-driven model may superficially seem to be a good fit given the policy disposition historically apparent in New Zealand, as discussed earlier. Fees would likely increase for some universities (as has happened in the United Kingdom for example). While economically successful, such a model would bring the risk of a significant increase in structural inequality as the government would likely quickly reduce its funding in the face of dramatic increases in student loan costs. This would foreseeably be accompanied by rapid political backlash as New Zealand communities would see affordability of university education decline dramatically, again as seen in the United Kingdom. Another challenge facing universities operating in a fully market-driven model is the relatively low investment by the private sector in education. The New Zealand economy has comparatively very few privately operated medium or large enterprises, instead being dominated by large public organizations, consortia of primary industry organizations such as the dairy cooperative, Fonterra, and very small private enterprises. None of these are typically large-scale investors in development or research, which is also similarly dominated by public funding. This means that any opportunity for growth from private sector funding is of limited scale and subject to significant competitive pressure. The low domestic base also makes international expansion harder with lack of funds for the level of risk and scale of investment needed for large-scale transnational education such as that achieved by some Australian and UK institutions in Asia and the Middle East.

Some form of coordinated network model (option two, above) seems attractive. The drivers for this are similar to those that saw the Californian Master Plan enacted in 1960 (Marginson, 2016), such as the desire to see public investment in tertiary education having a positive impact on reducing social inequality; coordination of activities to maximize scale and efficiency and to leverage collective power in negotiations with suppliers and other stakeholders; and prioritization of expensive and constrained resources that have the greatest impact on the public good. A reduction in competitive behavior would also drive savings in marketing and recruitment and increase the likelihood of collaboration in research and teaching, and in the development of significant infrastructure. The political appeal of aspects of this model is apparent, and has a strong alignment with the current government's restructuring of the vocational education system. There are, however, questions about the viability of this model given the decline and failure of it in the Californian context, where—despite being regarded as one of the best systems in the world—political expediency and funding pressure has seen the system start to break down and fragment into pieces that are either failing or acting in ways that are now reinforcing structural inequality and privilege (Mettler, 2014). The risk in having a coordinated national network might be that political influences and vested interests would see the accelerated emergence of a two-speed system as has happened in California. In New Zealand, this would likely see a small number (perhaps two or three) of elite universities providing comprehensive research-informed higher education to a minority of select students, while the remainder of the sector become teaching-focused institutions, potentially even positioned as large polytechnics and integrated also into the NZIST structure and systems. There would even be the possibility that all the New Zealand universities would go down this route with postgraduate and specialized higher education simply outsourced to the Australian system reflecting the dominating influence of that country on New Zealand's economic structure. Even if comprehensive research universities were maintained in this model, without a significant boost in government funding for tertiary education, the ongoing dependence on international student revenue would continue to exist, distorting the priorities of the universities and their offerings to those attractive to international markets rather than those aligned to local communities.

The increasing use of online delivery has suggested a modern alternative network structure, where individual universities might combine to offer a virtual "University of New Zealand" to the world through a common online platform such as that suggested for the national provision of vocational education by a new national institute of skills and technology. The problems of such a strategy are illustrated by the similar attempt a decade ago by the United Kingdom to create a national e-University (UKeU). Intended to offer a coherent and comprehensive national presence for online learning to the world, this effort failed in the face of inadequate funding, minimal student interest, and a failure to align success of the collaboration with factors recognizably driving success for the universities (House of Commons, 2005). The demographics of New Zealand mean that such a collaboration would always be framed around growing export education revenues and this flounders on the problem that international education is influenced by reputation and by immigration (Findlay et al., 2012), neither of which is enhanced through an online consortium model. Finally, as with the UKeU, relationships with commercial service-providers would be a significant influence and evidence already suggests that this unbundling and re-bundling process exacerbates inequality and further erodes the viability of public alternatives to private education (Czerniewicz and Morris, 2017; McCowan, 2017; Newfield, 2019).

The last of the options listed above, the maintaining of a publicly funded system of independent Humboldtian universities combining excellence in research and teaching with a wider social agenda aligned to the public good, is perhaps the most palatable to those comfortable with the status quo. Sadly, it is also the least likely to be viable in an economic environment further damaged by the global pandemic and prioritization of national policies towards actions which rebuild and repay the debt accrued in crisis mitigation responses. A major problem of such a model is in the way it removes market pressures driving competition in a world where reputation and rankings dominate national strategies for education (i.e., China), and a frequent consequence is the ongoing maintenance of structural inequality (i.e., South Korea and the United Kingdom) (Marshall, 2018). Economic and social realities mean that a Humboldtian university must either be the beneficiary of extreme wealth, or necessarily managed so that the scale of its operation is affordable and socially justifiable (Greenberg, 2018).

A major factor that would make a public-good framing of the universities viable for the future is the provision of effective alternatives such as that sought in the NZIST reforms. Countries like Germany (admittedly a wealthier country than New Zealand) have been able to sustain a large-scale free and public-good-oriented university system primarily as a result of having socially and economically viable alternatives that are heavily embedded into and subsidized by employers. Such a shift would see the viability of the university maintained by limiting the scale of the system's operation to that needed for New Zealand society and where investment in intellectual excellence addresses historical inequality as well as being oriented to the needs of modern and future New Zealand society. This can be realized, provided that the sector—including agencies responsible for funding policy and regulation—starts focusing on public-good and social success measures rather than on external rankings or the limited set of economic and inequality measures that constitute the current tertiary strategy.

References

Adds, P., Hall, M., Higgins, R., and Higgins, T. R. (2011). "Ask the posts of our house: Using cultural spaces to encourage quality learning in higher education." *Teaching in Higher Education*, 16, 541–551.

Ahmed, S. (2012). *On Being Included: Racism and Diversity in Institutional Life*. Durham, NC: Duke University Press.

Bell, A. (2017). "Working from Where We Are: A Response from Aotearoa New Zealand." *Higher Education Research & Development*, 36/1, 16–20.

Best, E. (1934). "'The Whare Wananga'. The Maori as he was: A brief account of life as it was in pre-European days." Wellington: Dominion Museum. http://nzetc.victoria.ac.nz/tm/scholarly/tei-BesMaor-c4-2.html

Bialik, C. (2010). "Seven careers in a lifetime? Think twice, researchers say." *The Wall Street Journal*, September 4.

Bowen, W. G. (2012). "The 'cost disease' in higher education: Is technology the answer?" Stanford University. http://www.ithaka.org/sites/default/files/files/ITHAKA-TheCostDiseaseinHigherEducation.pdf

Bowl, M. (2018). "Differentiation, distinction and equality – or diversity? The language of the marketised university: An England, New Zealand comparison." *Studies in Higher Education*, 43, 671–688.

Chevalier, A. and Lindley, J. (2009). "Overeducation and the skills of UK graduates." *Journal of the Royal Statistical Society: Series A*, 172, 307–337.

Coelli, M., Tabasso, D., and Zakirova, R. (2012). *Studying beyond Age 25: Who Does It and What Do They Gain?* Adelaide: NCVER and the Commonwealth of Australia.

Connell, R. (2017). "Southern theory and world universities." *Higher Education Research & Development*, 36, 4–15.

Crawford, R. (2016). "New Zealand Productivity Commission Research Note 2016/1: History of Tertiary Education Reforms in New Zealand." January. https://www.productivity.govt.nz/assets/Documents/65759a16ed/History-of-tertiary-education-reforms.pdf

Curtis, B. (2019). "The rise and rise of the performance-based research fund?" In S. Wright and C. Shore (eds.), *Death of the Public University? Uncertain Futures for Higher Education in the Knowledge Economy* (pp. 193–212). New York: Berghahn Books.

Czerniewicz, L. and Morris, N. (2017). *The Unbundled University: Researching Emerging Models in an Unequal Landscape.* https://unbundleduni.com/

Diver, C. (2005). "Is there life after rankings?" *The Atlantic*, November. http://www. theatlantic.com/magazine/archive/2005/11/is-there-life-after-rankings/304308/

Education New Zealand (2019). *2019 Value & Enrolments in International Education to New Zealand.* https://intellilab.enz.govt.nz/document/668-2019-economic-contribution-enrolments-infographic

Feast, V. and Bretag, T. (2007). "Responding to crises in transnational education: New challenges for higher education." *Higher Education Research & Development*, 24, 63–78.

Findlay, A. M., King, R., Smith, F. M., Geddes, A., and Skeldon, R. (2012). "World class? An investigation of globalisation, difference and international student mobility." *Transactions of the Institute of British Geographers*, 37, 118–131.

Gardner, W. J. (1973). "The formative years, 1873–1918." In N. C. Phillips (ed.), *A History of the University of Canterbury 1873–1973* (pp. 17–170). Christchurch: University of Canterbury.

Goedegebuure, L., Santiago, P., Fitznor, L., Stensaker, B., and van der Steen, M. (2008). *OECD Reviews of Tertiary Education: New Zealand.* http://www.oecd.org/education/skills-beyond-school/38012419.pdf

Greenberg, R. D. (2018). "Making universities grow: The New Zealand experience." In J. Valsiner, A. Lutsenko, and A. Antoniouk (eds.), *Sustainable Futures for Higher Education: The Making of Knowledge Makers* (pp. 99–107). Cham: Springer.

Hazelkorn, E. (2015). *Rankings and the Reshaping of Higher Education: The Battle for World-Class Excellence* (2nd edition). New York: Palgrave Macmillan.

Healey, N. and Gunby, P. (2012). "The impact of recent government tertiary education policies on access to higher education in New Zealand." *Journal of Educational Leadership, Policy and Practice*, 27/1, 29–45.

House of Commons (2005). *UK e-University.* Third Report of Session 2004–05 Report, together with formal minutes, oral and written evidence. London: House of Commons, Education and Skills Committee.

Kidman, J. (1999). "A people torn in twain: Colonial and indigenous contexts of university education in New Zealand." *Interchange*, 30/1, 73–91.

Kidman, J. and Chu, C. (2017). "Scholar outsiders in the neoliberal university: Transgressive academic labour in the whitestream." *New Zealand Journal of Educational Studies*, 52, 7–19.

Kidman, J. and Chu, C. (2019). "'We're not the hottest ethnicity': Pacific scholars and the cultural politics of New Zealand universities." *Globalisation, Societies and Education*, 17, 489–499.

Larner, W. and Le Heron, R. (2005). "Neo-liberalizing spaces and subjectivities: Reinventing New Zealand universities." *Organization*, 12/6, 843–862.

Leaman, A. (2020). "Coronavirus: NZ universities face 'huge' funding shortfall if Covid-19 border restrictions stay." *Stuff*, April 17. https://www.stuff.co.nz/national/education/

121010508/coronavirus-nz-universities-face-huge-funding-shortfall-if-covid19-border-restrictions-stay

Leuven, E. and Oosterbeek, H. (2011). "Overeducation and mismatch in the labor market." In E. Hanushek, S. Machin, and L. Woessmann (eds.), Handbook of the Economics of Education (Vol. 4, pp. 283–326). Amsterdam: Elsevier.

Lewis, N. and Shore, C. (2019). "From unbundling to market making: Reimagining, reassembling and reinventing the public university." *Globalisation, Societies and Education*, 17, 11–27.

Li, M. (2003). "Culture and classroom communication: A case study of Asian students in New Zealand language schools." Paper presented at the Australian Association for Research in Education and New Zealand Association for Research in Education conference, November 29–December 3, Auckland, New Zealand.

McAllister, T., Kidman, J., Rowley, O., and Theodore, R. F. (2019). "Why isn't my professor Māori? A snapshot of the academic workforce in New Zealand universities." *MAI Journal*, 8. https://doi.org/10.20507/MAIJournal.2019.8.2.10

McAllister, T., Kokaua, J., Naepi, S., Kidman, J., and Theodore, R. (2020). "Glass ceilings in New Zealand universities: Inequities in Māori and Pacific promotions and earnings." *MAI Journal*, 9. https://doi.org/10.20507/MAIJournal.2020.9.3.8

McCowan, T. (2017). "Higher education, unbundling, and the end of the university as we know it." *Oxford Review of Education*, 43/6, 733–748.

Malcolm, W. and Tarling, N. (2007). *Crisis of Identity: The Mission and Management of Universities in New Zealand*. Wellington: Dunmore Publishing Ltd.

Marginson, S. (2007). "Global university rankings: Implications in general and for Australia." *Journal of Higher Education Policy and Management*, 29/2, 131–142.

Marginson, S. (2016). *The Dream is Over: The Crisis of Clark Kerr's California Idea of Higher Education*. Berkeley: University of California Press.

Marshall, S. (2018). *Shaping the University of the Future: Using Technology to Catalyse Change in University Learning and Teaching*. Singapore: Springer

Marshall, S. (2019). "Are New Zealand universities underperforming? An analysis of international enrolments in Australian and New Zealand universities." *Compare: A Journal of Comparative and International Education*, 49, 471–488.

Martens, K. and Starke, P. (2008). "Small country, big business? New Zealand as education exporter." *Comparative Education*, 44/1, 3–19.

Martin, R. E. (2011). *The College Cost Disease: Higher Cost and Lower Quality*. Cheltenham, UK and Northampton, MA, USA: Edward Elgar Publishing.

Massey University (2018). https://www.massey.ac.nz/massey/maori/te-tiriti-o-waitangi/te-tiriti-o-waitangi_home.cfm

Mettler, S. (2014). *Degrees of Inequality: How the Politics of Higher Education Sabotaged the American Dream*. New York: Basic Books.

Ministry of Education (2019). "Evidence brief for the Tertiary Education Strategy." September 16. https://conversation.education.govt.nz/assets/TES/16-Sept-2019-Annex-2-Draft-Evidence-Brief-003.pdf.

Naepi, S. (2019). "Why isn't my professor Pasifika? A snapshot of the academic workforce in New Zealand universities." *MAI Journal*, 8. https://doi.org/10.20507/MAIJournal.2019.8.2.9

Naepi, S., McAllister, T. G., Thomsen, P., Leenen-Young, M., Walker, L. A., McAllister, A. L., Theodore, R., Kidman, J., and Suaaliia, T. (2019). "The Pakaru 'pipeline': Māori and Pasifika pathways within the academy." *The New Zealand Annual Review of Education*, 24, 142–159.

Naepi, S., Stein, S., Ahenakew, C., and Andreotti, V. de O. (2017). "A cartography of higher education: Attempts at inclusion and insights from Pasifika scholarship in Aotearoa New Zealand." In C. Reid and J. Major (eds.), *Global Teaching: Southern Perspectives on Teachers Working with Diversity, Education Dialogues with/in the Global South* (pp. 81–99). New York: Palgrave Macmillan.

New Zealand Treasury (2019). *Vote Tertiary Education – Education and Workforce Sector–Estimates2019/20*.https://www.treasury.govt.nz/publications/estimates/vote-tertiary-education-education-and-workforce-sector-estimates-2019-20-html

Newfield, C. (2019). "Unbundling the knowledge economy." *Globalisation, Societies and Education*, 17/1, 92–100.

OECD (2019). *Education at a Glance. Country Note: New Zealand.* https://www.oecd.org/education/education-at-a-glance/EAG2019_CN_NZL.pdf

OECD (2020). *Foreign-Born Population (Indicator)*. doi:10.1787/5a368e1b-en

Peace, R. and Shearer, F. (2017). "Puke Ahu: Articulating a place-based, university campus identity." *Kōtuitui: New Zealand Journal of Social Sciences Online*, 12, 83–94. https://doi.org/10.1080/1177083X.2016.1261909

Roberts, P. (2009). "A new patriotism? Neoliberalism, citizenship and tertiary education in New Zealand." *Educational Philosophy and Theory*, 41/4, 410–423.

Robinson, D. (2006). *The Status of Higher Education Teaching Personnel in Australia, Canada, New Zealand, the United Kingdom, and the United States.* Report prepared for Educational International, Universidade de Santiago de Compostela. http://firgoa.usc.es/drupal/files/ei_study_final.pdf.

Ruckstuhl, K., Amoamo, M., Hart, N. H., Martin, W. J. Keegan, T. T., and Pollock, R. (2019). "Research and development absorptive capacity: A Māori perspective." *Kōtuitui: New Zealand Journal of Social Sciences Online*, 14/1, 177–197. https://doi.org/10.1080/1177083X.2019.1580752.

Rutherford, H. (2020). "Universities warned travel ban was doing 'incalculable damage' to China relationship." *New Zealand Herald*, March 14. https://www.nzherald.co.nz/business/news/article.cfm?c_id=3&objectid=12316514

Savage, D. (2000). "Academic freedom and institutional autonomy in New Zealand universities." In R. Crozier (ed.), *Troubled Times: Academic Freedom in New Zealand* (pp. 1–225). Palmerston North: Dunmore Press.

Scott, D. (2005). "Retention, completion and progression in tertiary education in New Zealand." *Journal of Higher Education Policy and Management*, 27/1, 3–17.

Shannon, W., Doidge, M., and Holland, M. (2019). "A clash of internationalizations: New Zealand and the Bologna Process." *European Journal of Higher Education*, 9, 73–86.

Staniland, N. A., Harris, C., and Pringle, J. K. (2020). "'Fit' for whom? Career strategies of Indigenous (Māori) academics." *Higher Education*, 79, 589–604.

Sutherland, K. A. (2018). *Early Career Academics in New Zealand: Challenges and Prospects in Comparative Perspective.* Cham: Springer

Te Herenga Waka Victoria University of Wellington (THWVUW) (2020a). *Strategic Plan.* https://www.wgtn.ac.nz/about/governance/strategic-plan

Te Herenga Waka Victoria University of Wellington (THWVUW) (2020b). "Vote of support for Pasifika Fale Malae welcomed," March 9. https://www.wgtn.ac.nz/pasifika/our-community/news/vote-of-support-for-fale-malae-welcomed

Tertiary Education Commission (2018). *ITP Roadmap 2020: Sector Financial Modelling.* Wellington: Author.

Tertiary Education Commission (2020). *Funding and Payments.* https://www.tec. govt.nz/funding/funding-and-performance/funding/fund-finder/equity-funding/ funding-and-payments/

Theodore, R., Gollop, M., Tustin, K., Taylor, N., Kiro, C., Taumoepeau, M., Kokaua, J., Hunter, J., and Poulton, R. (2017). "Māori university success: What helps and hinders qualification completion?" *AlterNative: An International Journal of Indigenous Peoples*, 13, 122–130.

Tully, K. and Whitehead, C. (2009). "Audacious Beginnings: The Establishment of Universities in Australasia 1850–1900." *Education Research and Perspectives*, 36/2, 1–44.

Universities New Zealand (2019). *Building Māori and Pasifika Success.* https://www. universitiesnz.ac.nz/sector-research/building-māori-and-pasifika-success

University of Auckland (n.d.). *The Fale Pasifika.* https://www.auckland.ac.nz/en/on-campus/ life-on-campus/pacific-life/fale-pasifika.html

Vedder, R. (2004). *Going Broke by Degree: Why College Costs Too Much.* Washington, DC: American Enterprise Institute Press.

CHAPTER 37

INDONESIA

The Politics of Equity and Quality in Higher Education

CHIARA LOGLI AND HERMIN INDAH WAHYUNI

INDONESIA has one of the largest higher education systems in the world, with over 4,000 institutions serving eight million students (Ngo and Meek, 2019). Extended across the biggest archipelago on the planet, Indonesia is a forerunner in the challenge of bridging physical distance by providing learning experiences to its 6,000 inhabited islands. It also is home to the largest Muslim population in the world and its educational system has aimed to reconcile secular with religious demands since its independence in 1945. As the fourth most populated country, with over 270 million people of whom 43 percent are under the age of 24, Indonesia confronts the urgency of offering a valuable and access-ible tertiary education (UNESCO, 2021).

Despite membership in the G20 and being the tenth largest global economy, social inequality remains rampant in Indonesia—the GDP per capita is US$4,135 and the GINI Index is 38.2 (de Haan, 2017; World Bank, 2020). With the rest of the world, Indonesia faces the dilemma of how to achieve better access, equity, and quality across universities while also keeping public spending tamed (Wicaksono and Friawan, 2011).

The country has managed to expand tertiary education with limited governmental funding, but forgoing equity and quality. Despite its extraordinary growth, Indonesian universities remain out of reach for most youth, as the number of applicants widely exceeds the capacity provide by state investment. In addition, students who succeed in entering college often find questionable quality in teaching and research (Welch, 2011). This chapter examines recent developments in Indonesian higher education. It focuses on the efforts to establish and maintain equity and quality as they intersect with the dynamics of massification, internationalization, and governance. The chapter also contextualizes Indonesia within South-East Asia, with comparative attention given to the middle-income countries of the Association of Southeast Asian Nations (ASEAN).

1. Historical Overview

In the mid-nineteenth century, the Dutch colony opened a medical school and law school in Jakarta, an engineering institute in Bandung, and an agriculture center in Bogor, in order to compensate for the shortage of human resources (Buchori and Malik, 2004). With independence in 1945, those first four institutions expanded and new universities opened, beginning with the public secular Gadjah Mada University and the private Islamic University of Indonesia (Nizam, 2006). In 1961, Law No. 22 on Higher Education prescribed the establishment of at least one state university in each of the 34 provinces of Indonesia to intensify integration across the archipelago (Mason et al., 2001).

Since independence, the Indonesian educational system has aimed to advance knowledge, character, and religiosity in order to benefit the country as a whole (Soedijarto, 2009). The 1945 Constitution stipulates that the role of education is to "increase the level of spiritual belief, devoutness, and moral character" and to "advance science and technology with the highest respect for religious values and national unity." The Higher Education Law of 1961 is still in effect today and reiterates that education should embody the five principles of the Pancasila (i.e., monotheism, humanity, unity, democracy, social justice). The three original functions of Indonesian higher education (*Tridharma*) also remain teaching, research, and community service.

In the 1970s, American-educated faculty members gained leading positions in Indonesian universities and, largely through their influence, the dominant higher education model became Anglo-American—stressing standardization, autonomy, and efficiency (Moeliodihardjo, 2014). Subsequently, Indonesian higher education has come to absorb the dominant global paradigm of neo-liberalism, in which market-driven dynamics often de-emphasize human rights concerns, including matters of access, equity, and representation (Neubauer, 2007; Hawkins, 2011).

The national picture hides differences across provinces (OECD, 2020). The island of Java wields the majority of the political power in the nation while accounting for only 6 percent of land area, but 60 percent of the population, 75 percent of college students, and all of the prestigious universities (Hartanto, 2009). By contrast, the rest of the archipelago, especially the Eastern islands, faces a shortage of infrastructure, which severely limits both educational and economic opportunities. For instance, the gaps between Java and Eastern provinces affect all indicators, from the illiteracy rate (0.2 vs. 22 percent), to years of schooling (15 vs. 10 years), regional GDP (US$16,000 vs. US$1,500), unemployment rate (1.5 vs. 8.1 percent), and formal employment (70 vs. 25 percent).

In line with global trends, non-traditional students in Indonesia have less probability of getting into college, completing their degree, attaining the same knowledge, and experiencing relatively similar post-graduation lives compared to mainstream students (Farrell, 2007). The Indonesian Constitution stipulates the right of all citizens to obtain

Table 37.1 Indonesian higher education institutions in 2019

	Universities	Institutes	Colleges	Polytechnics	Academies	Total
Public	81 (14%)	65 (29%)	85 (3%)	124 (44%)	83 (8%)	438 (9%)
Private	518 (86%)	158 (71%)	2,467 (97%)	161 (56%)	992 (92%)	4,296 (91%)
TOTAL	599 (12%)	223 (5%)	2,552 (54%)	285 (6%)	1,075 (23%)	4,734

Source: Ngo and Meek (2019).

an education, but it does not specify the level of education and how this could be equally applied to the diversity that actually characterizes Indonesian students (Logli, 2015, 2016a, 2016b).

2. CURRENT LANDSCAPE

Rapid economic and demographic national growth has meant that Indonesian higher education has itself expanded over a relatively short time. University enrollment increased from 6,000 in 1950 to 805,200 in 1983 and 8 million in 2018 (Rais, 1987; Pardoen, 1998; Koning and Maassen, 2012; Brewis, 2019). Gross higher education enrollment has also expanded from 5 percent in the 1970s to 36 percent in 2018, placing it in relatively the same tier as its important regional comparatives, Malaysia at 45 percent and Thailand at 49 percent. In 2018, of those aged 25 years or older, 9 percent held a bachelor's degree, 0.6 percent held a master's degree, and 0.05 percent held a doctoral degree. The low enrollment in higher education springs from the overall limited national participation rate in secondary education as well as limited university availability.

Indonesian tertiary education encompasses public and private, secular and religious, academic and vocational, face-to-face and online institutions (Table 37.1). Indonesia records the highest enrollment in private tertiary education of all ASEAN countries, with the exception of Cambodia. Private higher education institutions count for over 90 percent of all universities and 57 percent of the students, and some are extremely small, admitting as few as 500 students. Contrary to their public counterparts, private institutions receive nearly no government oversight and assistance, and are often supported by domestic and foreign religious organizations.

Since the 1980s, the mushrooming of private higher education institutions has occurred primarily because the national budget cannot respond to the escalating demand for higher education across the archipelago. The oil price boom and the subsequent industrialization within the country led to an expansion of the middle class and a corresponding schooling attainment (Jamshidi et al., 2012). In addition, external pressures for more structural adjustments by the World Bank and other international agencies stirred the country towards privatization. According to the data from the Association of Indonesian Private Universities (APTISI), proposals for private universities have increased steadily, with an average of 200 applications per year since the 2000s. Private institutions generally rely on student tuition fees, which may be up to five times higher than those in public institutions. For example, the yearly cost carried by the students, including tuition and living expenses, ranges from IDR7 million (US$500) to IDR20 million (US$1,500) in public universities, but around IDR30 million (US$2,000) for private colleges.

Students may enroll in private universities because they did not qualify for public institutions, or they may prefer a private college closer to their hometown, so that they can save in living costs and remain in their cultural fabric. Such students are usually from families that can afford the tuitions, mainly from the new middle class of business owners. Yet, some private religious institutions offer substantial scholarships as well as excellent education. Compared to state universities, issues of quality and equity are generally aggravated in private colleges, as the sections below will unpack.

Indonesia has the largest Islamic tertiary education sector in the world. Islamic universities were originally private but the 1967–1998 Suharto regime started allowing public Islamic Institutes (IAIN) in a bid to gain the support of the Muslim majority (Hefner, 2000). Subsequent governments have continued in this vein, by adding public Islamic Universities (UIN). As a result, over 16 percent of total universities currently are Islamic, either private or public, and enroll 11 percent of total students (Jackson and Bahrissalim, 2007). These institutions have extensive freedom over their curricula, and range from religiously progressive to conservative content with all shades in between. Additionally, Catholic, Protestant, Hindu, and Buddhist universities also exist.

Academies and polytechnics are vocational institutions and lead to diplomas (D1–D4) after one to four years of study. Colleges, institutes, and universities are academic in designation and culminate in providing bachelor's degrees (S1) after four years of study, with a further two years for a master's degree (S2) and an additional three years for a doctorate (S3) (OECD and Asian Development Bank, 2015).

Distance education was initiated with the establishment of the public Open University (*Universitas Terbuka*) in 1984 (Soekartawi et al., 2012). The Open University is the only university in Indonesia that teaches entirely by means of distance education. It has 37 regional offices across the archipelago and provides four colleges—education, science, economics, and law. Enrolling approximately 650,000 students, it ranks as one of the top 10 mega-universities in the world (i.e., having more than 100,000 students). Approximately 95 percent of the students are working adults who cannot attend regular schooling because of their remote location, work schedule, or personal constraints.

High school seniors generally prefer applying for colleges offering in-person education and campus activities. High-performance universities like Gadjah Mada University started integrating online learning in 2017 through a limited number of professors in selected programs (Kafil, 2020). During the COVID-19 pandemic, the Open University benefited from its experience in distance learning, while all other colleges struggled to adapt to new demands. As the discussion below reveals, challenges and opportunities lay in the area of distance education in the post-2020 era.

Indonesia continues to experience positive rates of return to education at all levels, as measured by earnings, employment rate, and work status (Allen, 2016; OECD, 2020). In 2015, employees with a university degree had the highest monthly average salary at US$270, compared to senior and junior high school graduates at US$194 and US$90 respectively. In 2017, the unemployment rate was 5 percent for college graduates, compared to 7 percent for mid-high school graduates and 8 percent for primary graduates. Generally, as the average number of year of schooling increases, the returns to education tend to decrease—for example, the Indonesian rate was slightly higher in 1998 at 13.4 percent compared to 11.5 percent in 2010 (Montenegro and Patrinos, 2014).

However, the Indonesia Human Capital Index ranked 65th out of the 130 countries surveyed in 2017, below Malaysia, Thailand, Vietnam, and the Philippines (WEF, 2016 and 2017). In Indonesia, an estimated 51.5 percent of workers are under-qualified and 8.5 percent are over-qualified. The issue lies in the quantity as just 11 percent of employees have at least a university degree and university graduates run only 2 percent of small or medium manufacturing enterprises (Tambunan, 2019; World Bank, 2019). Many employers report difficulty filling high-skilled positions and managerial roles, due to the dearth of English and digital readiness. Yet, the issue also lies in the quality (Hanushek et al., 2017). Behind the rest of ASEAN, in Indonesia only 41 percent of the firms indicated that college graduates had met enterprises' needs but, at the same time, just 13 percent of firms offered training (ILO, 2014).

Data is limited on the linkage between women's graduation rates and employability. Of total highly educated workers, 6.7 million are women and 6.2 million are men (Woetzel, 2018). Yet, generic indicators remain problematic—50 percent of women participate in the labor force (among the lowest across ASEAN and consistent since the 1990s), the gender pay gap amounts to around 20 percent (compared to less than 15 percent in the OECD), and almost 40 percent of women are in low-paid work (compared to 20 percent for men) (ILO, 2017).

3. Equity Pressures

Regional, socio-economic, and ethnic disparities exacerbate the dearth of equity in Indonesian higher education, evidence of which exists at many levels. Firstly, students outside of Java are less likely to score highly on academically focused entrance exams, because of the generally weaker quality of secondary schools on their islands, especially in rural areas (Clark, 2014; Negara and Benveniste, 2014). Every year, more than 450,000 high school graduates take the national public university entrance examination to compete for 75,000 seats. The PISA findings also confirm the regional performance gap (OECD, 2018). In addition, among those who have any type of university education,

Table 37.2 Gross attendance ratio indicators in Indonesian higher education in 2017

	Total (%)	Urban (%)	Rural (%)
Poorest quintile	9.5	10.6	9.2
Second quintile	18.7	23.3	15.9
Middle quintile	24.3	24.7	23.9
Fourth quintile	37.6	35.9	41.7
Richest quintile	79.9	82.5	69.6

Source: UNESCO (2021).

25 percent are from the rural areas; at the master's and doctoral level, the percentage is 10 percent and 1 percent respectively.

Secondly, poorer students are less able to pay for education and possibly to relocate to Java (Table 37.2). A recent survey found that while 88 percent of high school seniors aspire to attend tertiary institutions, only those in the richer quintiles are financially able to do so. An average Indonesian household has to devote one-third of its annual expenditure to fund a family member in the most reasonably priced public university. In addition, students from wealthier families tend to gravitate to public universities, which are prized for the best reputation and the lowest tuition fees, while students with modest backgrounds are often left with the option of either a private institution or no college degree at all (Susanti, 2011; Sitepu, 2013).

Thirdly, with more than 700 languages spoken across the archipelago, many students are not native speakers in Indonesian, the language of instruction (Arifin, 2017). Female students remain a minority in the STEM fields, especially in engineering and information science (Table 37.3). However, overall females are more likely to graduate from higher education than males (59 percent and 41 percent, respectively) and all education-related Gender Parity Indexes are above 1.

Fourthly, in moments of crisis, pre-existing issues are exacerbated. A salient instance of this is that during the COVID-19 pandemic, the pressures for remote learning widened the equity gap (Paddock and Sijabat, 2020; Straits Times, 2020). In principle, online learning can provide flexibility and efficiency, as students can save time, energy, and money on transport and relocation across the archipelago. In practice, remote classes are inaccessible to many students due to inadequate mobile data quota, internet service, and network reception.

In 2020, only 56 percent of the Indonesia population had access to the internet, because of financial constraints, poor connection in rural areas, and limited electricity in some villages. Connectivity is still highly concentrated in Java. Most students lack computers and use cellphones operating with a small data plan. Some learners climb

Table 37.3 Graduation indicators in Indonesian higher education in 2018

	Graduates (%)	Graduates who are female (%)
Agriculture, Forestry, Fisheries, Veterinary	4.1	48.3
Arts, Humanities	5.2	58.9
Business, Administration, Law	18.3	57.9
Education	23.9	69.6
Engineering, Manufacturing, Construction	7.9	24.9
Health, Welfare	16.1	78.0
Information, Communication Technologies	8.3	34.7
Natural Sciences, Mathematics, Statistics	3.3	74.3
Social Sciences, Journalism, Information	12.9	50.6
Science, Technology, Engineering, Mathematics (STEM)	19.4	37.4

Source: UNESCO (2021).

trees, travel miles, and sit hours on the side of the road in search of a cell signal to complete their assignments. In addition, universities lack digitized platforms and the national examination still relies on pencil and paper. Some institutions responded to the COVID-19 crisis by training faculty, providing free data plans, and opening some online classes to the public but these were in the minority.

Over the past 20 years, a series of laws has attempted to increase equity in public higher education without much success. Overall, college recipients of government-based scholarships increased from 85,000 in 2018 to 400,000 in 2020, equivalent to 5 percent of the total 8 million students currently in tertiary education. Private scholarships are very limited. Targets for financial aid, setting tuition brackets, and increasing enrollment numbers among low-income and marginalized students have not yet been reached.

In 2003, Law No. 20 stipulated that students have the right to either a scholarship, based on both need and merit, or tuition fee waivers, based on need only. In 2012, Law No. 12 also obliged state universities to admit at least 20 percent of its intake from academically gifted students in the 3T category (i.e., disadvantaged, remote, and outermost areas). In addition, it standardized five categories of tuition fees based on parental income brackets, with students in the lowest groups paying between IDR500,000 (US$35) and IDR2 million (US$150) per semester. Public universities are able to admit students at a higher tuition rate, but are capped at 30 percent of the intake.

Furthermore, the law mandated that at least 20 percent of students should receive scholarships in state universities. The government-based program named Indonesian Smart Card (Kartu Indonesia Pintar)—previously known as Bidik Misi—provides scholarships mainly to students at public universities that have attained superior accreditation. This financial aid is based on a combination of academic merit and financial need as well as other special criteria, such as excellence in academic, athletic, and cultural competitions. It delivers the same amount to all universities that applied and qualified, with the objective to cover full tuition and a monthly stipend for living costs. Institutions with tuition rates higher than the scholarship need to fill the gap to ensure that students benefit from full assistance.

Despite the financial support, the selection criteria for entry into university are fundamentally problematic. The public awareness of funding opportunities is limited. In addition, the number of low socio-economic students from marginalized regions, who would actually qualify, is narrow. As a result, in 2016 the ministry introduced the ADIK Papua/3T scholarship, which allows students from West Papua province and other remote regions to apply to state universities through a separate admissions process and receive full coverage. The ADIK scholarship was more effective and reached 4,386 students in 2019, doubling the number from 2015.

4. ACADEMIC MATTERS

Massification has brought tremendous challenges in providing a satisfactory quality of education across the archipelago. Indonesian higher education suffers from weak intake from secondary schooling as well as a host of internal academic challenges with regard to faculty, research, and academic freedom. The 2018 PISA report showed that the Indonesian scores for reading (74), mathematics (73), and science (71) had declined and were below the rest of ASEAN (Kurniawati et al., 2018). These findings, however, need to be interpreted in the context of the vast strides that Indonesia has made in increasing enrollment in education over the past years—among 15-year olds, the PISA sample covered 46 percent in 2001 and 85 percent in 2018.

The standard for foreign languages also remains low in K-12, virtually cutting off Indonesian students from access to academic literature outside the country. Rather than adding more foreign languages, the 2013 curriculum reform removed English as compulsory in primary school and reduced the number of hours allocated for English lessons in junior high schools (four hours per week) and senior high schools (two hours per week) (Manara, 2014; Azmy, 2020). In 2014, the ministry also limited participation in international schools, for example excluding Indonesian children from Embassy schools (Sebastian et al., 2019).

In addition, limited faculty capability, research productivity, and intellectual freedom tarnish academic quality in higher education, although steps have been taken recently to redress these constraints. Firstly, qualified faculty teaching in public institutions are numerically scarce (Sayidah et al., 2019), while conditions in the private sector are even worse. In 2005, a new law prescribed that faculty hold at least a master's degree to receive enhanced remuneration. It also incentivized posts in marginalized regions (daerah khusus) in an attempt to distribute qualified faculty more evenly across the archipelago.

Governmental scholarships for graduate studies both domestically and internationally (Indonesia Endowment Fund for Education) skyrocketed from US$105 million in 2016 to US$3.2 billion in 2019 (Dilas et al., 2019; Dzulfikar, 2019).

As a result, the number of faculty holding graduate degrees, including from overseas programs, has been increasing. However, PhD holders continue to be a small minority among faculty members and they tend to gravitate to the few elite universities in Java. In 2019, only 14 percent of the total 293,775 faculty members had earned a doctoral degree, resulting in a low number of candidates eligible for full professorships, approximately 4,167. In addition, top universities have a tendency to hire their own graduates, exacerbating academic in-breeding and intellectual insularity (Rakhmani and Siregar, 2016; Rakhmani, 2021). Because of limited salaries, moonlighting is an extensive practice for faculty members who teach in multiple institutions to gain additional income and take on lucrative off-campus consultancies (Welch, 2012).

Secondly, limited research opportunities also negatively affect educational quality (Darmadji et al., 2018). In 2012, the ministry added the requirement for PhD candidates to publish a paper in English in an international journal in order to complete their degree (O'Connor et al., 2017). This new mandate has intensified the pressure on advisers, who also need research achievements as a prerequisite for their own career advancement (Gaus et al., 2017). From 1996 to 2019, Indonesia increased the number of published documents from 609 to 44,576, ranking 21st globally and 5th within Asia, ahead of all ASEAN members (SCImago, 2021).

Yet, publication quality remains problematic and international collaborations limited. In 2019, Indonesia produced 10,481 academic citations (ranking 46th globally and 12th within Asia) and 241 H-index articles (ranking 57th globally and 12th in Asia)—lagging behind Malaysia and Thailand as well Vietnam (for citations) and the Philippines (for H-index articles). It ranked last among its ASEAN counterparts in international collaboration on publications, scoring below 30 percent. Scholars in top Indonesian universities tend to produce publications with those institutions in advanced economies at which they earned their graduate degree, such as Australia, Japan, and the United States (Rakhmani, 2016; Pelupessy, 2017). As ASEAN strengthens its political support and scholarly capacity, Indonesia has also begun to expand its academic ties with Malaysia, Thailand, and Singapore.

Relatively heavy teaching workloads remain the key to gaining program accreditation and facilitating faculty promotion, despite a series of reforms meant to increase research incentives. A shortage of English-language skills, and lack of access to international publications and proper facilities also stand as barriers to the production of quality research. Beyond these factors, the brain drain phenomenon is an acknowledged concern, although limited empirical data are available to effectively monitor it. When queried, approximately 38 percent of Indonesians would choose to relocate to Singapore, followed by Europe (13 percent) and Malaysia (7 percent) (Khidhir, 2019). More than 2,000 Indonesian researchers work abroad, where wages are higher. For instance, researchers with the PhD can earn as little as US$300 monthly in Indonesia compared to US$3,000 in Malaysia (Business Updates, 2014).

Thirdly, academic freedom has regressed recently, a result of the overall decline in freedom of expression and democracy in Indonesia (Duile, 2017). While students and academics engage in petitions and protests supporting human and civil rights, hardline groups tend to have more political weight and subsequent effect (Permata and Abdil, 2017). Overall, campuses have become breeding areas for underground radical Islamic networks (Fox, 2004). Islamic extremist factions have succeeded in passing laws against blasphemy as a tactic to restrain knowledge and promote the arrest of non-radical Muslims, including a professor in Aceh who was teaching an interreligious course (Amnesty International, 2014).

In a further act of suppression of academic freedom, the government has confiscated books deemed "against national culture," including those on the 1965 anti-Chinese violence, leftist theories, and sexuality (Yulius, 2016). Several universities have cancelled events focused on controversial issues, such as land disputes, corruption, and human rights (Wiratraman, 2016). In 2019, a new law required that all research considered "dangerous"—threatening "social harmony" and "national security"—needed to be authorized by the central government after clearance by an ad hoc ethics committee. In 2019, the ministry threatened to sanction universities that "mobilize student movements" or are involved in protests against the government.

Because of these limitations, Indonesian universities struggle in the international ranking competition. According to the 2020 THE rankings, Indonesia falls behind Malaysia and Thailand. Similarly, the 2020 QS rankings listed nine Indonesian universities in the top 1,000 institutions globally. Three institutions ranked within the top 500—the University of Indonesia (296), Gadjah Mada University (320), and Bandung Institute of Technology (331)—and one private entity made a surprising entry for the first time, Bina Nusantara University in Jakarta.

5. Internationalization

Considerations of equity and quality also arise in relation to Indonesian efforts to internationalize higher education. Utilizing both outbound and inbound mobility as well as the opening of foreign campuses, Indonesian universities have made progress in exposing local students to global knowledge and experiences (Ratanawijitrasin, 2015). A general assessment of attitudes toward international education indicates that a significant majority of Indonesian students and faculty members generally prefer increased opportunities for campus internationalization, intercultural contact, and intellectual freedom.

Within ASEAN, Indonesia is the third-largest contributor of students' outbound mobility, after Vietnam and Malaysia (Table 37.4). The number of Indonesian students studying abroad has increased by 69 percent since 1999, but still accounts for only 0.6 percent of total enrollment, the second-lowest rate in ASEAN after the Philippines. The dearth of proficiency in foreign languages coupled with substantial financial

Table 37.4 International mobility in tertiary education in ASEAN middle-income countries in 2018

	2018 enrollment	Outbound mobility		2018 inbound mobility
		Year 1999	Year 2018	
Asia (Southeastern)	18,858,851	155,090	324,279	225,975
Cambodia	211,484	1,405	6,161	68 (e)
Indonesia	8,037,218	29,579	49,900	7,653
Lao PDR	105,439	1,600	6,558	451
Malaysia	1,284,876	54,785	61,904	124,133
Myanmar	932,199	1,485	10,277	100 (c)
Philippines	3,589,484 (a)	5,082	18,859	2,665 (d)
Thailand	2,410,713 (b)	22,102	32,912	31,571
Vietnam	2,307,361 (b)	8,080	108,527	5,624

Source: UNESCO (2021), (a) Year 2017, (b) Year 2016, (c) Year 2012, (d) Year 2008, (e) Year 2006.

aid need are among the leading causes for this low rate. Approximately 95 percent of Indonesian students abroad are self-funded and, given the high costs of living overseas, scholarships would play a vital role in boosting mobility.

Outgoing students prefer the Asia-Pacific region, North America, and Western Europe as well as the Arab States (Table 37.5). The top three destinations are consistently Australia, the United States, and Malaysia, which together make up over 50 percent of all outbound Indonesian students—11,040, 8,782, and 5,823 respectively in 2017. Yet, other estimates suggest higher numbers than the UNESCO data and indicate that China has gained popularity as an educational destination (ICEF, 2019; Syakriah, 2019).

The number of foreign students studying in Indonesia also increased from 2,026 in 2005 to 7,677 in 2018. Yet, it remains low compared to Malaysia and Thailand (Table 37.4). With many highly ranked universities in the region, international students are unlikely to turn to Indonesia as a preferred destination. Most incoming students are from the Asia-Pacific region and more than 50 percent of them are consistently from Malaysia, Timor Leste, and Thailand—1,745, 1,650, and 996 respectively in 2017 (Table 37.5). In Indonesia, foreign students tend to favor international programs in English at top universities, such as the University of Indonesia, where they constitute 11 percent of the total 41,170 full-time students (Times Higher Education, 2020). In all other institutions, foreign students account for fewer than 1,000 students, 1–4 percent of the total student body.

The first foreign campus in Indonesia, established by Monash University, is set to open in 2021 (Nott, 2021). The Indonesian government granted its approval based on Law No. 53 in 2018 and the Indonesia–Australia Comprehensive Economic Partnership

Table 37.5 International mobility in tertiary education in Indonesia in 2017

	Outbound mobility (Indonesian students abroad)	Inbound mobility (international students in Indonesia)
Arab States	4,290	279
Central and Eastern Europe	922	57
Central Asia	6	28
East Asia and the Pacific	22,999	5,849
Latin America and the Caribbean	16	145
North America and Western Europe	19,049	252
South and West Asia	304	994
Sub-Saharan Africa	10	140
Unknown regions		19
TOTAL	47,596	7,763

Source: UNESCO (2021).

Agreement in 2019. The legislation requires that foreign universities in Indonesia must be for non-profit, well-ranked, accredited in their home country, prepared to open at least two fields of study and to integrate in their curriculum the four compulsory Indonesian subjects (i.e., religion, Pancasila, civics, Indonesian). However, securing approvals is complex and the process is unclear, including around permitted locations in a "special economic zone" and the employment of foreign staff. For instance, Law No. 9 (2009) and Law No. 12 (2012) mandate that 80 percent of university employees shall be Indonesian citizens and that Indonesian educators are the only ones allowed to teach the four mandatory subjects. In 2019, the Minister of Higher Education announced plans to recruit foreign academics to boost university rankings, but some educational segments criticized that decision.

On one hand, international branch campuses can provide innovative content, technologies, funding opportunities, and global collaboration, all of which contribute significantly to both learning potential and rankings. Such attributes expand the range of educational choices that are available and reduce the flight of top students who, otherwise, seek prestigious brands abroad. With such resources, Indonesian students can keep their current jobs, live with their families, and enjoy higher-ranking universities at a fraction of the cost of going abroad. In a relevant regional comparison, Singapore, Malaysia, and Vietnam have admitted numerous foreign campuses since the 1990s.

On the other hand, some Indonesian scholars warn that these franchise universities are accessible to only a few students—those with robust English skills and the resources to afford international rates (Jacob et al., 2012). Although branch campuses charge about half of the tuition of their parent institutions, they are still more expensive than local universities. For instance, a master's degree at Monash Indonesia totals US$21,000–30,000 in tuition for 72–96 credit points. Other critics are concerned that foreign universities poach the best faculty members and students from local institutions because of their richer resource base (Pincus, 2015).

The internationalization of Indonesian higher education reflects long-lasting cooperation across borders, from ASEAN to Australia, China, and the Middle East. Founded in 1967, ASEAN stirred pioneering experiments in regionalization in higher education, especially around intra-regional tuning and quality assurance. It supports education ministers' meetings, a University Network, the Regional Institute for Higher Education and Development, and many initiatives, such as the Malaysia–Indonesia–Thailand Student Mobility Pilot Project in 2009 and the ASEAN International Mobility for Students Programme in 2012 (Kuroda et al., 2018).

Australia has also emerged as an important educational ally for Indonesia, a result of its geographical proximity, educational quality, and opportunity provided to Indonesians to master the English language. More recently, China has been solidifying its influence by increasing the full scholarships available for Indonesians from 15 in 2015 to 197 in 2017. Finally, the Middle East has a strong appeal for Indonesia's population, which comprises the greatest number of Muslim adherents in the world. These educational ties date back to the thirteenth century, when notable Indonesian men started to pursue advanced teaching at al-Azhar University in Cairo.

6. Quality Assurance

Indonesia has implemented accreditation systems to establish and uphold the quality of higher education, while facing the challenge of meeting standards and resisting corruption. Since 2012, the Ministry of Education has published over 17 regulations addressing quality assurance, from system-wide rules on management and curricula to specific guidelines for professional schools and distance education. For instance, Law No. 50 in 2014 and Law No. 44 in 2015 indicated that each institution must meet the National Higher Education Standards in teaching, research, and community service.

Indonesia took the lead in ASEAN in establishing an accreditation agency in 1994. The National Education Board for Higher Education (BAN-PT) is appointed by and reports to the Ministry of Education. It reviews and provides recommendations to undergraduate and graduate degree programs; and since 2011, it has also conducted institutional accreditation. This review involves a self-study through a standardized report, but site visits are rare due to budget constraints.

All public and private programs must be accredited to operate, but can operate while waiting for their review decisions. If accreditation is denied, they cannot produce certificates for their graduates and are subject to closure. A superior accreditation indicates that the institution has demonstrated excellence in all aspects of the university, from teaching to research, international recognition, student affairs, and administration

(Lubis et al., 2009; Akib and Ghafar, 2015; Yusri et al., 2019). For public universities, superior accreditation results in higher global rankings, national popularity, and financial aid allocation. For private institutions, it mainly affects their prestige and ability to leverage fundraising, since they receive few or no government subsidies. Private universities generally score lower than their public counterparts, due to less financial means for infrastructure and human resources. Reflecting this, in 2015, only 3 percent of private programs as compared with 22 percent of the public programs evaluated by BAN-PT achieved an "A" rating.

BAN-PT's limited annual budget allows for the accreditation of approximately 2,200 programs per year. By 2019, BAN-PT had accredited 39 percent of public programs and 8 percent of private programs. To expedite the process, Law No. 5 in 2020 ruled that accreditation renews automatically every five years. Accredited programs are required to maintain an annual tracer study submitted to the Online Higher Education Accreditation System (SAPTO) and apply for an extension six months prior to the accreditation expiration. BAN-PT monitors each university's tracer study and requires follow-up documentation if there are indications of declining quality, such as enrollment reduction over five years in a row. For instance, the Open University has introduced various standard operating procedures and improved support services to meet the requirements of accrediting agencies. Institutions can always apply for a new accreditation if they aim to improve their score.

Ensuring that the quality of educational programs meets local and international standards simultaneously has become a great challenge in Indonesia (Ryan, 2015). The regulatory efforts in higher education have been increasingly difficult to monitor because of increases in massification, private sector involvement, and geographical disparities. In addition, corruption remains problematic in Indonesia, which scored 37 out of 100 in the Corruption Perceptions Index in 2020 (Kubo, 2013; Transparency International, 2020). From 2015 to 2019, the Indonesia Corruption Watch found 202 corruption cases, including 20 cases in higher education, which caused an estimated US$6 million in state losses (Nurbaiti, 2020).

For example, a parliament member received bribes for approving a contract for laboratory equipment for 16 universities (Sutrisno, 2020). The rector and vice-rector of the University of Indonesia misused funding intended for the library and information technology (Rosser, 2019). The rector of the Jakarta State University appointed his relatives to campus positions and approved 327 doctoral candidates without due process, including the governor of the Southeast Sulawesi province, who plagiarized his dissertation.

In addition, the ministry's involvement in the election of state university rectors raises concerns as it exposes the process to possible favoritism and conflicts of interest (Jakarta Post Editorial, 2019). University officials have asked the Corruption Eradication Commission to safeguard rector elections; yet, the commission has also been facing criticism for low performance and credibility (Mulholland and Mochtar, 2021).

In most corruption cases, little is revealed to the public, leaders are suspended but not legally prosecuted, and their enabling entourage remains untouched. Corruption undermines credibility, public access, quality, and the values that should be upheld by educational institutions, such as transparency and accountability. There is a need for further auditing, enforcement, and protection for whistleblowers, who have been fired, transferred, or suspended, such as in the case of a law student at Semarang State University after he reported the rector for alleged graft (Aqil, 2020).

7. Governance Ambiguity

The root cause of the limitations in equity and quality in higher education is the government's blurred sense of responsibility in supporting advanced learning as a public good. Under the Ministry of Education and Culture, the Directorate General of Higher Education is responsible for general tertiary education (public and private), whereas the Ministry of Religious Affairs oversees mainly Islamic higher education institutions (public and private). However, many religious universities, such as Muhammadiyah and virtually all minority-religious institutions, fall under the Directorate General because they teach a standard curriculum, instead of acting as schools of theology. Additionally, various ministries, provinces, and cities supervise vocational education and training at either secondary or tertiary levels, including the Ministries of Education, Defense, Finance, Health, Labor, and National Development (Waluyo, 2018).

Since 2015, the government has started to investigate ways to streamline its super-vision of higher education. For instance, it has relocated the National Development University from the Ministry of Defense to the Ministry of Education. In addition, it has begun to deliberate how to incorporate well-established private universities under its state system, for example by merging several private colleges into one public university.

Private colleges have close to full independence in their own administration. Public universities can be completely under state control or enjoy partial autonomy. The 1996–2005 third plan by the Directorate General of Higher Education launched a "new paradigm" based upon five pillars of reform—autonomy, quality, account-ability, accreditation, and evaluation. The controlling premise was that more autonomy could generate greater competitiveness and therefore better quality in higher educa-tion. An avalanche of contradictory laws followed, generally with little guidelines for implementation.

Initially, Law No. 61 in 1999 granted financial, administrative, and executive powers to the so-called State Owned Legal Entities (BHMN). Autonomy status was granted to the four most established universities, which had "sufficient management capabilities" to accommodate the new responsibilities (i.e., University of Indonesia, University of Gajah Mada, Bandung Institute of Technology, and Bogor Agricultural University). Law No. 20 in 2003 expanded the autonomy model to other top state universities (Beerkens, 2002; Kusumadewi and Cahyadi, 2013; Sunarto, 2015).

In 2005, Law No. 23 re-calibrated the original autonomy plan, stressing financial ac-countability only. The law mandated that BHMN universities gained the new Public

Service Agency status (BLU). BLU entities are part of the government and within its bureaucratic purview, but follow business practices by earning the revenues from their activities. Twenty-one universities were classified as BLU. In 2008, Law No. 9 dictated that all state universities were to become autonomous, but the Constitutional Court revoked this law in 2010 due to tremendous public protests.

In 2012, Law No. 12 further downscaled previous autonomy legislation by declaring that universities could establish policies and procedures concerning teaching, research, and community service. It also renamed autonomous public universities as State University Legal Entities (PTNBH). In 2020, Law No. 4 stipulated that the autonomous status could be granted to universities that held at least 60 percent of their degree programs with a superior accreditation score and with students at any winning places in national or international competitions. The intent of these laws was a form of centralized decentralization, which cuts financial support while maintaining control of all influential functions, as the next two sections elaborate.

8. Financial Shortcomings

Inadequate public funding for universities is the most impactful illustration of the dearth of governmental accountability in Indonesia. In 2002 and 2003, Indonesian law mandated that 20 percent of the national budget be allocated to education, excluding salaries for teaching staff. This investment has yet to materialize, despite public funding for education increases every year.

The funding for the higher education sector is especially slim. For example, in 2013 the overall budget for tertiary education accounted for 0.5 percent of GDP, 2.8 percent of all public expenditures, and 16 percent of all educational expenditures. Across both private and public divides, personnel costs absorb more than 70 percent of an average university budget, leaving all other educational needs underserved. The funding allocation for research is perhaps the most abjectly inadequate, accounting for 0.25 percent of the GDP in 2019, behind Thailand (0.6 percent) and Malaysia (1 percent).

Private higher education receives 8–10 percent of the total budget for tertiary institutions. In public universities, approximately 60 percent of the budget comes from government transfers and 40 percent from tuition revenue. In comparison, autonomous state universities receive about one-fifth of their income from government and always face the threat of further financial cuts, as they are expected to become self-sustaining. Consequently, about 60 percent of their budget is dependent on the continuously rising tuition fees and student numbers. For instance, at the University of Indonesia, the share of public funding has decreased from 81 percent in 1994 to 20 percent in 2006, while tuition grew threefold and an additional admission fee was sought in certain disciplines, such as medicine and engineering.

As part of Law No. 61 in 1999, a particularly controversial strategy has been the Special Passage (Jalur Khusus 12) of admission for students who can pay higher fees, regardless of their entrance examination results. For example, at the Institute Technology Bandung's Engineering Department, ten places were offered at the cost of IDR200 million (US$15,000). In 2010, the Constitutional Court declared the charging of differential fees unconstitutional, but such practices persist due to insufficient governmental budgetary support.

Law No. 12 in 2012 and Law No. 55 in 2013 limited the proportion of the budget acquired from student tuition to 30 percent in any public university, with some flexibility for postgraduate and non-regular programs. However, public universities increasingly go above the tuition threshold as they scramble for funding. The government incentivizes universities to raise revenues though loans, investments, research grants, publishing, and provision of professional training, consultation, and asset management such as dormitories, cafeterias, parking, and bookstores. Yet, these sources of income are insufficient and mainly support universities in Java.

9. Centralized Autonomy

The restricted autonomy of state universities is the second area pointing to an ambiguous sense of obligation of the government toward tertiary education. While cutting funds for public higher education, the government maintains financial, organizational, staffing, and academic control. Firstly, it directs state universities through resource allocation and financial mechanisms. It enforces results-based monitoring by imposing financial sanctions when revenues do not meet the target. It also applies cumbersome regulations around loans and authorized revenues that universities can obtain. For instance, public research funding remains slim, the application process is convoluted, and the disbursement is clogged. Therefore, even if researchers succeed in receiving funding, they often have insufficient time to spend the funds while facing extensive reimbursement delays.

In addition, the ministry imposes heavily bureaucratized audit mechanisms, including two internal audits (i.e., by the Internal Control Unit of the parent ministry and the additional control unit inside each individual agency), two external audits (i.e., by the Financial Audit Boards and a Public Accounting Firm), and numerous reporting requirements. The increased demands for performance data, business methods, and discretionary funds are often unrealistic in a country where manual bookkeeping still exists, university administrators are not entrepreneurs, and few or no additional personnel or resources are available to respond to such requirements.

Secondly, the government controls public universities through structural steering. The rector holds administration and management powers only, according to Law No. 152 passed in 2000 and Law No. 66 in 2010. By contrast, the ministry approves the university bylaws, controls 35 percent of the votes in the election of rectors, and is represented on the Boards of Trustees, which oversee the general operations, budget, and appointment of the rector as well as making suggestions to the ministry regarding university management. Yet, governance bodies like the Oversight Unit, Advisory Board, and even the Boards of Trustees do not have enough external representation to ensure that tertiary education institutions are accountable to stakeholders and the public.

Thirdly, faculty recruitment and promotion in state universities remain very much within the purview of the government bureaucracy. Law No. 20 (2003) planned the reclassification of faculty and staff in public universities from governmental civil servants to university employees. Yet, the mandate never materialized and 88 percent of the employees of public universities are civil servants, and as such subject to the vicissitudes of their parent bureaucracies. The State Personnel Agency (BKN) handles matters of hiring, firing, and promotion according to existing teaching hours and the requirements of administrative projects, instead of academic merit and research productivity.

Faculty members receive lifetime tenure after two years and face long bureaucratic processes if they wish to move to another university. Termination is extremely rare, even for staff members whose performance is poor. In 2018, the ministry introduced a grant scheme to encourage professors to take sabbatical leave, but the civil servant regulations do not allow civil servants to use it.

Fourth, autonomy is limited with respect to the nature, content, and execution of academic programs in public universities. The ministry regulates the degrees that the university may offer, including the duration of their achievement and standards which govern them. For instance, universities cannot offer new degree programs or discontinue old ones without the ministry's permission, and the process for obtaining approval is sufficiently long and complicated that it discourages many institutions from trying to expand their academic offerings. Furthermore, despite numerous reports of irregularities and deficiencies, the ministry rarely uses its power to close problematic programs.

10. Conclusion

Indonesia continues to face challenges in finding a balanced pathway to reach equity, quality, and sustainable public spending in higher education. Despite their many efforts, Indonesian universities struggle to thrive against broader socio-economic issues, such as population, inequality, and globalization. Merely increasing schooling years and university availability, without focusing on the actual dynamics and content of learning, loses its causal relationships with any discernible types of patterned development.

Reducing the divide between Java and the rest of the archipelago requires an approach that accommodates place-based measures as the existing effects of centralization paralyze the country's potential. The government's uniform expectations in the realm of finance, capacity building, and internationalization are unrealistic when applied to the extraordinary diversity present across the country. Not all tertiary education institutions can be self-financed as well as have productive collaborations with stakeholders, international publications, and global exposure. In the aftermath of the COVID-19 pandemic, not all universities will be able to accommodate long-term online teaching across disciplines and student populations.

Realistically each university should have definable capacity to respond specifically to the problems it faces and develop layered strategies in line with existing conditions. For example, internationalization may be a priority for some universities, but capacity building may be more impactful for others. Depending on their geographical location, higher education institutes should most usefully focus on diverse specializations within their distinct capabilities. Online teaching can bring the archipelago closer together through selected programs, such as the Open University, that can commit to provide adequate technology and faculty capacity to support all students within proven capacity.

Further research on Indonesia higher education is urgent. The continuing dearth of publications in the field hinders the prospects for improvement across all matters, from quality to equity. More data- and theory-driven studies could expand the scope of possible resolutions to the current predicaments that are rife throughout the higher education system. Indonesian scholarship is needed to reframe the expressed purposes of higher education, the execution of educational policies, and the commercialization of learning with equity and quality in mind as guiding principles. Additional scholarship could also inform better educational policies, including those that seek to increase or maintain the value of education as the ability to adapt and thrive in a constantly changing environment. For example, it could advocate for the learning of foreign languages in K-12 and higher education, because learning multiple languages does not threaten regional values but rather benefits students in multiple ways, according to decades of evidence from cognitive science, cultural studies, and labor relations. Curricula should be framed in terms of "and/and" not "either/or," as youth needs to be supported from multiple angles to be able to contribute to society.

The main risk of not shifting strategies in the immediate future is that the public will perceive Indonesian higher education to be an ivory tower—exclusive and unattainable. In a best-case scenario, the Indonesian experience can be a source of learning for other countries that also have diverse populations spread across significant geographical boundaries. Their representation in higher education is vital as it influences the graduates' readiness to resolve predicaments throughout society, such as sustainable development and social leadership across the archipelago and around the planet.

References

Allen, E. (2016). *Analysis of Trends and Challenges in the Indonesian Labor Market.* Manila: Asian Development Bank.

Amnesty International (2014). *Prosecuting Beliefs: Indonesia's Blasphemy Laws.* London: Amnesty International.

Aqil, A. (2020). "University student suspended after reporting rector over alleged graft." *The Jakarta Post*, November 19.

Arifin, M. (2017). "The role of higher education in promoting social mobility in Indonesia." *European Journal of Multidisciplinary Studies*, 2, 233–241.

Azmy, K. (2020). "Examining the issue of abolishing English tuition in primary school in Indonesia." *Language Research Society*, 1/1, 47–57.

Beerkens, E. (2002). "Moving towards autonomy in Indonesian higher education." *International Higher Education*, 29, 24–25.

Brewis, E. (2019). "Fair access to higher education and discourses of development: A policy analysis from Indonesia." *Compare: A Journal of Comparative and International Education*, 49, 453–470.

Buchori, M. and Malik, A. (2004). "The evolution of higher education in Indonesia." In P. Altbach and T. Umakoshi (eds.), *Asian Universities: Historical Perspectives and Contemporary Challenges* (pp. 249–297). Baltimore, MD: Johns Hopkins University Press.

Business Updates (2014). "Indonesia's brain drain pains." *Global Business Guide Indonesia*, March 17.

Clark, N. (2014). "Education in Indonesia." *World Education News*, April 4.

Darmadji, A., Prasojo, L., Kusumaningrum, F., and Andriansyah, Y. (2018). "Research productivity and international collaboration of top Indonesian universities." *Current Science*, 115, 653–658.

De Haan, J. (2017). "Indonesia: Economic developments and future prospects." *Future Directions International*.

Dilas, D., Mackie C., Huang Y., and Trines, S. (2019). *Education in Indonesia*. New York: World Education Services.

Duile, T. (2017). "Reactionary Islamism in Indonesia." *New Mandala*, April 17.

Dzulfikar, L. (2019). "Welcoming foreign universities: Is it a good deal for Indonesians?" *The Conversation*, September 20.

Farrell, J. (2007). "Equality of education: A half-century of comparative evidence seen from a new millennium." In R. Arnove and C. Torres (eds.), *Comparative Education: The Dialectic of the Global and the Local* (pp. 129–150). Lanham, MD: Rowman & Littlefield.

Fox, J. (2004). "Currents in contemporary Islam in Indonesia." *Harvard Asia Vision*, 21.

Gaus, N., Sultan, S., and Basri, M. (2017). "State bureaucracy in Indonesia and its reforms: An overview." *International Journal of Public Administration*, 40, 658–669.

Hanushek, E., Schwerdt, G., Wiederhold, S., and Woessmann, L. (2017). "Coping with change: International differences in the returns to skills." *Economics Letters*, 153, 15–19.

Hartanto, W. (2009). *The 2010 Indonesia Population Census*. Jakarta: Biro Pasat Statistik.

Hawkins, J. (2011). "Variations on equity and access in higher education in Asia." In D. Neubauer and Y. Tanaka (eds.), *Access, Equity, and Capacity in Asia-Pacific Higher Education* (pp. 15–30). New York: Palgrave Macmillan.

Hefner, R. (2000). *Civil Islam: Muslims and Democratization in Indonesia*. Princeton, NJ: Princeton University Press.

ICEF (2019). *Recruiting from Indonesia in a Context of Increased Competition*. Bonn: International Consultants for Education and Fairs.

ILO (2014). *Survey of ASEAN Employers on Skills and Competitiveness*. Bangkok: International Labour Organization.

ILO (2017). *Indonesia Jobs Outlook 2017: Harnessing Technology for Growth and Job Creation*. Jakarta: International Labour Organization.

Jackson, E. and Bahrissalim (2007). "Crafting a new democracy: Civic education in Indonesian Islamic universities." *Asia Pacific Journal of Education*, 27, 41–54.

Jacob, J., Wang, Y., Pelkowski, T., Karsidi, R., and Priyanto, A. (2012). "Higher education reform in Indonesia: University governance and autonomy." In H. Schuetze, W. Bruneau, and G. Grosjean (eds.), *University Governance and Reform: Policy, Fads, and Experience in International Perspective* (pp. 225–240). New York: Palgrave Macmillan.

Jakarta Post Editorial (2019). "Corruption on campus." *The Jakarta Post*, August 8.

Jamshidi, L., Arasteh, H., Navehebrahim, A., Zeinabadi, H., and Rasmussen, P. (2012). "Developmental patterns of privatization in higher education: A comparative study." *Higher Education*, 64, 789–803.

Kafil, Y. (2020). "Mixed response but online classes to stay post COVID-19." *University World News*, May 14.

Khidhir, S. (2019). "Indonesia has a big problem." *The ASEAN Post*, July 24.

Koning, J. and Maassen, E. (2012). "Autonomous institutions? Local ownership in higher education in Eastern Indonesia." *International Journal of Business Anthropology*, 3, 54–74.

Kubo, A. (2013). "Indonesian education falls behind its economic growth." *Diplomat*, December 26.

Kurniawati, S., Suryadarma, D., Bima, L., and Yusrina, A. (2018). "Education in Indonesia: A white elephant?" *Journal of Southeast Asian Economies*, 35, 185–199.

Kuroda, K., Sugimura, M., Kitamura, Y., and Asada, S. (2018). *Internationalization of Higher Education and Student Mobility in Japan and Asia*. Paris: UNESCO.

Kusumadewi, L. and Cahyadi, A. (2013). "The crisis of public universities in Indonesia today." *Universities in Crisis: Blog of the International Sociological Association*.

Logli, C. (2015). "Higher education and the public good: Creating inclusive and diverse national universities in Indonesia in the era of globalization." In D. Neubauer and C. Collins (eds.), *Redefining Asia Pacific Higher Education in a Global Context* (pp. 24–40). New York: Palgrave Macmillan.

Logli, C. (2016a). "Cultural studies in education: Filming fluid subjectivities in Indonesian universities." *Pedagogy, Culture and Society*, 24, 177–190.

Logli, C. (2016b). "Higher education in Indonesia: Contemporary challenges in governance, access, and quality." In D. Neubauer, J. Hawkins, M. Lee, and C. Collins (eds.), *Handbook of Asian Higher Education* (pp. 561–582). New York: Palgrave Macmillan.

Manara, C. (2014). "'That's what worries me': Tensions in English language education in today's Indonesia." *International Journal of Innovation in English Language Teaching and Research*, 3, 21–35.

Mason, T., Arnove, R., and Sutton, M. (2001). "Credits, curriculum, and control in higher education: Cross-national perspectives." *Higher Education*, 42, 107–137.

Moeliodihardjo, B. (2014). *Higher Education Sector in Indonesia*. Jakarta: British Council.

Montenegro, C. and Patrinos, H. (2014). *Comparable Estimates of Returns to Schooling around the World*. Washington, DC: World Bank.

Mulholland, J. and Mochtar A. (2021). "Indonesia's Corruption Eradication Commission in dire straits." *East Asia Forum*, March 16.

Negara, S. and Benveniste, L. (2014). *Tertiary Education in Indonesia: Directions for Policy*. Washington, DC: World Bank.

Neubauer, D. (2007). "Globalization and education: Characteristics, dynamics, and implications." In P. Hershock, M. Mason, and J. Hawkins (eds.), *Changing Education:*

Leadership, Innovation and Development in a Globalizing Asia Pacific (pp. 29–62). Hong Kong: Springer.

Ngo, J. and Meek, L. (2019). "Higher education governance and reforms in Indonesia: Are the matrices of autonomy appropriate?" *Journal of International and Comparative Education*, 8, 17–26.

Nizam (2006). "Indonesia." In UNESCO, *Higher Education in South-East Asia* (pp. 35–68). Bangkok: UNESCO.

Nott W. (2021). "Monash reveals foreign campus in Indonesia." *The Pie News*, December 1.

Nurbaiti A. (2020). "KPK, not police, should investigate university graft case, ICW says." *The Jakarta Post*, June 4.

O'Connor, P., Raffiudin, R., Sukarno, N., Juliandi, B., and Rusmana, I. (2017). "Scientists publishing research in English from Indonesia." In M. Cargill and S. Burgess (eds.), *Publishing Research in English as an Additional Language: Practices, Pathways and Potentials* (pp. 33–54). Adelaide: University of Adelaide Press.

OECD (2018). *PISA Results*. Paris: OECD.

OECD (2020). *Employment and Skills Strategies in Indonesia*. Paris: OECD.

OECD and Asian Development Bank (2015). *Education in Indonesia: Rising to the Challenge*. Paris: OECD.

Paddock, R. and Sijabat, D. (2020). "When learning is really remote: Students climb trees and travel miles for a cell signal." *The New York Times*, September 5.

Pardoen, S. (1998). *Assessment of Investment in Private Higher Education in Indonesia: The CASE of Four Private Universities*. Jakarta: Atma Jaya Catholic University.

Pelupessy, D. (2017). "Indonesia races against its ASEAN neighbours, but science needs more collaboration." *The Conversation*, September 14.

Permata, Y. and Abdil, M. (2017). "How autonomous are Indonesian universities?" *Indonesia at Melbourne*, November 28.

Pincus, J. (2015). "For Indonesian higher education, it's time to grow up." *Nikkei Asian Review*, April 27.

Rais, A. (1987). "Muslim society, higher education and development: The case of Indonesia." In A. Sharom and S. Siddique (eds.), *Muslim Society, Higher Education and Development in Southeast Asia* (pp. 9–27). Singapore: Institute of Southeast Asian Studies.

Rakhmani, I. (2016). "Insularity leaves Indonesia trailing behind in the world of social research." *The Conversation*, February 3.

Rakhmani, I. (2021). "Reproducing academic insularity in a time of neo-liberal markets: The case of social science research in Indonesian state universities." *Journal of Contemporary Asia*, 51/1, 64–86.

Rakhmani, I. and Siregar, M. (2016). *Reforming Research in Indonesia: Policies and Practices*. New Delhi: Global Development Network.

Ratanawijitrasin, S. (2015). "The evolving landscape of South-East Asian higher education and the challenges of governance." In A. Curaj, R. Pricopie, J. Salmi, and P. Scott (eds.), *The European Higher Education Area* (pp. 221–238). Cham: Springer.

Rosser, A. (2019). "Big ambitions, mediocre results: Politics, power and the quest for world-class universities in Indonesia." In D. Jarvis and J. Mok (eds.), *Transformations in Higher Education Governance in Asia: Policy, Politics, and Progress* (pp. 81–100). Singapore: Springer.

Ryan, T. (2015). "Quality assurance in higher education: A review of literature." *Higher Learning Research Communications*, 5/4.

Sayidah, N., Ady, S., Supriyati, J., Winedar, M., Mulyaningtyas, A., and Assagaf, A. (2019). "Quality and university governance in Indonesia." *International Journal of Higher Education*, 8, 10–17.

SCImago (2021). *Journal and Country Rank*. Madrid: SCImago Research Group.

Sebastian, E., Rish, V., and Evans, K. (2019). *Stronger Education Partnerships: Opportunities for Australian Education and Training Providers in Indonesia*. Melbourne: Australia-Indonesia Centre.

Sitepu, I. (2013). "Competencies of higher education graduates: A case of Universitas Kristen Indonesia." PhD dissertation, Kassel University.

Soedijarto (2009). "Some notes on the ideals and goals of Indonesia's national education system and the inconsistency of its implementation: A comparative analysis." *Journal of Indonesian Social Sciences and Humanities*, 2, 1–11.

Soekartawi, S., Haryono, A., and Librero, F. (2012). "Great learning opportunities through distance education: Experiences in Indonesia and the Philippines." *Journal of Southeast Asian Education*, 3, 283–320.

Straits Times (2020). "Indonesian Internet users hit 196 million, still concentrated in Java: Survey." *Straits Times*, November 12.

Sunarto, K. (2015). "Corporatizing Indonesian higher education." *Global Dialogue*, 5.

Susanti, D. (2011). "Privatisation and marketisation of higher education in Indonesia: The challenge for equal access and academic values." *Higher Education*, 61, 209–218.

Sutrisno, A. (2020). "Corrupt at all levels? Indonesian higher education and the problem of corruption." In E. Denisova-Schmidt (ed.), *Corruption in Higher Education: Global Challenges and Responses* (pp. 132–137). Leiden: Brill Sense.

Syakriah, A. (2019). "Indonesia's higher education: A sleeping giant?" *The Jakarta Post*, August 19.

Tambunan, T. (2019). "Recent evidence of the development of micro, small and medium enterprises in Indonesia." *Journal of Global Entrepreneurship Research*, 9, 1–15.

Times Higher Education (2020). *World University Rankings*. London: The World Universities Insights.

Transparency International (2020). *Corruption Perceptions Index*. Berlin: Transparency International.

UNESCO (2021). *Institute for Statistics*. Montreal: UNESCO.

Waluyo, B. (2018). "Balancing financial autonomy and control in agencification: Issues emerging from Indonesian higher education." *International Journal of Public Sector Management*, 31/7, 794–810.

WEF (2016 and 2017). *Human Capital Index*. Cologny: World Economic Forum.

Welch, A. (2011). *Higher Education in Southeast Asia: Blurring Borders, Changing Balance*. New York: Routledge.

Welch, A. (2012). "The limits of regionalism in Indonesian higher education." *Asian Education and Development Studies*, 1, 24–42.

Wicaksono, T. and Friawan, D. (2011). "Recent developments in higher education in Indonesia: Issues and challenges." In S. Armstrong and B. Chapman (eds.), *Financing Higher Education and Economic Development in East Asia* (pp. 159–187). Canberra: Australian National University Press.

Wiratraman, H. (2016). "Academic freedom post-Soeharto: Not much better." *The Jakarta Post*, February 15.

Woetzel, J. (2018). *The Power of Parity: Advancing Women's Equality in Asia Pacific*. San Francisco, CA: McKinsey Global Institute.

World Bank (2019). *The World Bank Indonesia Skills Development Project: Program Information Document*. Washington, DC: World Bank.

World Bank (2020). *World Development Indicators*. Washington, DC: World Bank.

Yulius, H. (2016). "When books become threats: Preserving 'public order' in Indonesia." *Indonesia at Melbourne*, May 23.

CHAPTER 38

HIGHER EDUCATION IN MALAYSIA

CHANG DA WAN

1. INTRODUCTION

MALAYSIA is a multi-ethnic country, with Malays and indigenous people, known as Bumiputera, making up about 67 percent of the population; ethnic Chinese about 24 percent; ethnic Indians about 6 percent; with the remainder of the population comprising other ethnic minorities. While Bahasa Malaysia is the national language and the official medium of instruction in schools and public higher education institutions, English, Mandarin, and Tamil are widely spoken and offered in vernacular primary schools or independent secondary schools. Most private schools and higher education institutions teach in English. With a gross domestic product of USD358.58 billion and a per capita of USD11,383 in 2020, Malaysia is classified as an upper middle-income economy (World Bank, 2020), and continues to aspire to become a high-income economy and a developed nation.

Although a university existed in Malaysia prior to independence from the British in 1957, significant developments to the higher education landscape took place post-independence. The first official university, University of Malaya, was established in 1949 through the merger of King Edward VII Medical College of Medicine and Raffles College. The university was initially set up in Singapore, and in 1959, an autonomous campus was established in Kuala Lumpur, which effectively restructured the university into two autonomous campuses. By 1962, the two autonomous campuses separately became the University of Singapore and University of Malaya. It is important to note the parallel national development in this period: Malaya gained independence in 1957 from British rule, Malaysia was formed in 1963 comprising Malaya, Sabah, Sarawak, and Singapore until Singapore left Malaysia in 1965.

From one public university at the time Malaya gained independence, higher education has since grown leaps and bounds. Currently, the higher education system is made up of two equally sizable public and private sectors. In the public sector, there are 20 universities, 36 polytechnics, and 99 community colleges, while in the private sector, there are 48 universities, 10 international branch campuses, 33 university colleges, and 345 colleges (DOHE, 2019; MOE, 2019).

Apart from the remarkable quantitative expansion of higher education in Malaysia, this chapter charts the key phases of development of higher education from a historical perspective and explores critical issues including: gender and ethnicity underlying participation in higher education, the role of languages and medium of instruction, the notion of academic freedom and institutional autonomy, as well as the rapidly growing private higher education sector and the aspiration to become an international hub. These issues and how they evolved over key phases of development have collectively shaped higher education in Malaysia into its current state.

2. Key Phases of Higher Education Development

The six decades of higher education in Malaysia may be viewed in terms of four key phases of development: (1) the autonomous phase (1962–1975); (2) the nationalism phase (1971–1996); (3) the liberalization phase (1996–2007); and (4) the neoliberalism phase (2007–2020).

(1) The *autonomous* phase began with the establishment of the University of Malaya in Kuala Lumpur in 1962 and was a phase in which universities were permitted to be self-governed without direct interference from the government (see Wan, 2017). Among the key events that took place within this phase was the May 13 racial riot in 1969 that led to a state of emergency and subsequent introduction of the New Economic Policy (NEP), enactment of the Universities and University Colleges Act 1971 (Act 30), and the establishment of four public universities. The amendment made to Act 30 in 1975, that completely removed the autonomy of public universities, marked the end of this phase.

(2) The *nationalism* phase began with the enactment of the NEP in 1971 and the introduction of ethnic quotas across universities and all its programs. The emphasis and switch to the national language, expansion of public universities, as well as the monopolized authority of the government to provide higher education, characterized this phase until the amendment of various laws on higher education were adopted in the mid- to late-1990s that signified a relinquishment by the government on its monopoly in higher education.

(3) The *liberalization* phase was marked by legislative reforms in higher education between 1996 and 1998 which legalized the establishment of private higher education institutions and resulted in exponential growth in higher education. Other

key developments in this phase include the corporatization of public universities and the establishment of the Ministry of Higher Education.

(4) The *neoliberalism* phase was ushered in with the introduction of the National Higher Education Strategic Plan 2007–2020. It underlined an explicit shift of higher education expansion strategy in Malaysia towards neoliberalism, with intensification of managerialism in both public and private institutions under which key performance indicators became the norm, alongside an increased focus on university rankings, as well as internationalization.

These four key phases of higher education development in Malaysia have some overlap and serve as useful heuristic devices to guide discussions in a more systematic way in examining the various issues and topics relating to higher education in Malaysia in the following sections of this chapter.

3. ACCESS AND EQUITY: PARTICIPATION, ETHNICITY, AND GENDER

Equitable access has been one of the most contentious issues in Malaysian higher education, as it is not merely an educational issue, but has vast socio-political-economic ramifications. In the autonomous phase when there was only one public university, access was highly elitist and based entirely on merit. There were only 650 students enrolled in 1949 when the University of Malaya was operating in Singapore, and the autonomous campus in Kuala Lumpur started with 322 students in 1959–1960 (Abdul Majid, 1971; Khoo, 2005). By 1962 when the University of Malaya was established in Kuala Lumpur, 1,341 students were enrolled (Abdul Majid, 1971). In 1969, shortly after the May 13 racial riot, 6,672 students were enrolled in University of Malaya, and 57 students were enrolled as the pioneering batch in the first university that was established by the Malaysian government in Penang.

Driven by the need to create a skilled workforce, a decade later in 1980, Malaysia expanded its higher education system to five public universities with a gross enrollment ratio (GER) for tertiary education at almost 4 percent (UNESCO Institute of Statistics, 2020). GER for tertiary education is defined as formal post-secondary education that includes higher education, technical, vocational education and training (TVET) as well as skills training. By 1995, GER for tertiary education in Malaysia achieved 11 percent. Following the introduction of the Private Higher Education Institutions Act 1996 (Act 555) which legalized the establishment of private higher education institutions, GER for tertiary education rose to 22 percent in 1998. By then Malaysia had entered the "massification" stage in the typology of growth of higher education systems according to Trow (1973).

As of 2018, Malaysia had achieved a 45 percent GER for tertiary education with a total of 1.3 million students in Malaysian higher education institutions (see Table 38.1). A total

Table 38.1 Enrollment and number of institutions, 2008 and 2018

Status	Year		Type of institution	Student enrollment		Number of institutions	
	2008	2018		2008	2018	2008	2018
Public	521,696 (53.7%)	675,141 (50.2%)	University	419,334 (80.4%)	552,702 (81.9%)	20	20
			Polytechnic	85,280 (16.3%)	96,370 (14.3%)	27	36
			Community college	17,082 (3.3%)	26,069 (3.8%)	42	99
Private	450,576 (46.3%)	668,689 (49.8%)	University	136,864 (30.4%)	332,843 (49.8%)	37	48
			University college	73,959 (16.4%)	89,512 (13.4%)	18	33
			College	198,572 (44.1%)	218,768 (32.7%)	430	345
			International branch campus	41,181 (9.1%)	27,566 (4.1%)	4	10

Sources: MOE (2019); MOHE (2009).

of 552,702 students were enrolled across 20 public universities, 668,689 were enrolled across all private higher education institutions, and 96,370 and 26,069 were enrolled in polytechnics and community colleges respectively, which are institutions geared towards TVET.

However, two critical aspects of access require further scrutiny. The first is the infamous ethnic quota for student enrollment that was introduced by the Malaysian government in 1971 under the New Economic Policy in direct response to the May 13 racial riot in 1969. Prior to the introduction of the ethnic quota, the ethnic distribution among the student population was not reflective of the ethnic distribution in the country (Abdul Majid, 1971; Sato, 2007). In 1970, the ethnic composition in Malaysia was made up of 55.5 percent Bumiputera (Malays and indigenous people), 34.1 percent Chinese, and 10.4 percent Indian and other ethnicities. However, Bumiputera were significantly underrepresented at universities with less than 40 percent of students being Bumiputera (see Table 38.2). This was largely due to the inherent societal structure inherited from pre-independence days, where the majority of Bumiputera were disadvantaged and remained in poorer economic conditions living as peasants in rural areas with limited access to education.

The ethnic quota imposed a 55:45 Bumiputera to non-Bumiputera student enrollment requirement. This quota was not only for the overall student population of a university, but applicable to every course and program at public universities. The Centralized

Table 38.2 Ethnic proportion in Malaysian
public universities, 1966–2013
(percentage)

Year	Bumiputera	Chinese	Indian	Others
1966	28.8	56.5	14.7	
1970	39.7	49.2	11.1	
1985	63.0	29.7	7.3	
2002	68.9	26.4	4.7	
2003	62.6	32.2	5.2	
2013	74.3	19.0	4.4	2.3

Source: Aida Suraya et al. (2015).

Admission Unit in the Ministry of Education was subsequently set up to ensure compliance with the ethnic quota by managing admissions for public universities, and effectively removed the authority of a university to select its students. By 1985, only a decade later, the ethnic quota policy proved effective with the ethnic composition of student populations reflective of the ethnic demographic of Malaysian society at large.

The ethnic quota lasted for three decades until it was officially abolished in 2002. The effect of its removal can be clearly seen among those who were admitted in the following year in 2003; with a noticeable increase in the proportion of Chinese, Indian, and Others compared with previous years.

Although the ethnic quota has been removed, a two-track admission pathway into public universities was introduced in 2005 to improve Bumiputera access to higher education. In addition to admission through the Malaysian Higher School Certificate (STPM), which is a pre-university examination taken by students in public schools, the alternative Matriculation Program was introduced with an ethnic quota of 90:10 Bumiputera to non-Bumiputera. This Program admitted students into a one-year preparatory program in colleges with boarding facilities, which concurrently also consolidated and centralized different pre-university programs for Bumiputera in various public universities into a single national program. While STPM is a public examination organized by an independent body, the Matriculation Program is an internally coordinated examination within the Ministry of Education with the Matriculation colleges. Both examinations are considered of equal standing and enabled more Bumiputera to be admitted into public universities using a common framework (Lee, 2004b). Consequently, the proportion of Bumiputera surpassed 70 percent. A further point to note is that, out of the 20 public universities, the Universiti Teknologi MARA only admits Bumiputera students and this is arguably the largest university in Malaysia, enrolling almost 30 percent of all Bumiputera students.

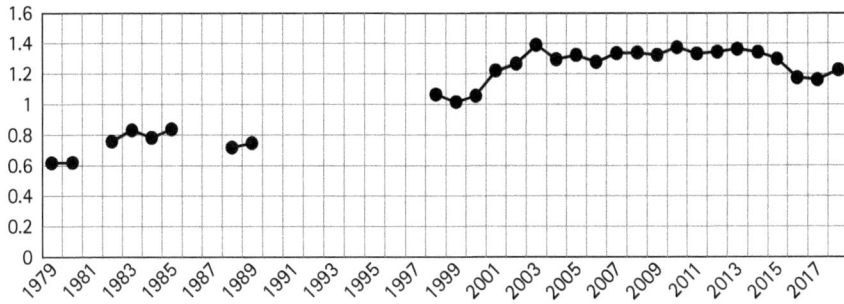

FIGURE 38.1 Gender Parity Index for tertiary education in Malaysia, 1979–2018

Source: UIS (2020).

The second critical issue relating to equitable access is the change in gender distribution over time. The Gender Parity Index illustrates the differences in enrollment between the two genders. An index of 1 reflects equal participation between male and female, while a number smaller than 1 underlines that there are more male than female students and vice versa. Figure 38.1 shows how gender parity has changed between 1989 and 1998. Until 1989, there were more males than females in tertiary education. After a period of data gaps since 1998, there have been more females than males in tertiary education without a reversal in sight.

There are two interesting trends worth exploring further with respect to the issue of gender equity (see Wan, 2018). On the one hand, there is a significant difference between the gender distribution in public and private higher education institutions. Within public institutions, there are more females than males, and as the type of institutions become more academically inclined, the proportion of females increases. On the other hand, within private institutions, gender seems to be more balanced as a whole.

However, gender distribution changes according to the type of institution and cost of education. As the estimated cost of study at an institution increases, the proportion of males also increases. This is because there is a cultural tradition for families to invest more in the education of their sons than daughters. Given that international branch campuses tend to be the most expensive among private institutions, expectedly, these institutions have the highest concentration of males compared to other private institutions.

Lastly, it is important to note that a crucial enabler to accessing higher education has been the creation of the National Higher Education Loan Fund (PTPTN) in the liberalization phase, alongside the legalization of private institutions. The PTPTN offers students a loan with fixed monthly repayment and negligible administrative charges. However, this loan arrangement has been plagued with issues of low repayment, sustainability of the funds, and flip-flop of policies under different governments. Notwithstanding the problematic issues, without doubt, PTPTN has been pivotal in ensuring equitable access whereby no Malaysian who qualifies for a placement in any recognized higher education institution in the country is denied the opportunity because of financial constraints (Wan et al., 2016; Russayani and Shaza Nawwarah, 2019).

4. Academic Freedom and Institutional Autonomy: Lost but Found?

From a governance viewpoint, the most significant issue for Malaysian universities has been institutional autonomy, particularly among public universities. In 2012, the then Minister of Higher Education announced that four public universities, after undergoing extensive good governance review and audit, would be granted autonomous status. All public universities were gradually bestowed autonomous status, with the last public university receiving it in 2018.

What exactly is "autonomous status" in the context of Malaysian universities? Autonomous status bestowed by the Ministry of Higher Education between 2012 and 2018 is operationalized in terms of four domains: institutional, financial, human resource, and academic (see Fauziah and Ng, 2015). However, without legislative and governance reforms, autonomous status currently has no impact on universities, academics, and students, and institutional autonomy remains a superficial and rhetorical concept.

Autonomous universities are not a new concept in Malaysia and date back to the first phase of development, labeled the "autonomous" phase. Institutional autonomy at that point in history was in fact guaranteed through legislation. The University of Malaya was established with its own Act of Parliament—the University of Malaya Ordinance 1949 which later became the University of Malaya Act 1961 (Act 44). Similar legislation was also drafted for the Universiti Sains Malaysia (then known as University of Penang) and the Universiti Kebangsaan Malaysia, but these draft laws were not tabled in Parliament due to the suspension of the August House between 1969 and 1971 following the racial riot and state of emergency. When Parliament resumed sitting, the Universities and University Colleges Act 1971 (Act 30) was tabled to provide the legal framework for respective legislation pertaining to individual universities to become university constitutions.

There is a striking similarity among the inaugural version of Act 30, Act 44, and the two draft laws, whereby the structure of governance for universities has insulated them from external influence on the university, including from the government. The most explicit illustration of such autonomy can be reflected by the fact that the Chairman of the Council of University of Malaya, the highest governing body in the university, was led by an opposition figure in Parliament. Interestingly, the university still received 80 percent of its operational expenditure from the government of the day (Wan, 2017). As further pointed out by the Chairman of the Cabinet Committees that drafted the legislation for two new universities in 1969, the laws were intended to ensure that universities "should be ... autonomous bod(ies) separate and apart from the Government" (Suffian, 1969, p. 1).

However, the legal provision for governance of universities as autonomous bodies was dismantled with an amendment to Act 30 in 1975. The Council of the University, previously composed of elected representatives of various interest groups from academics, alumni, and society, became the governing body with all its members appointed by the Minister of Education. The prerogative to appoint institutional leaders—Vice Chancellors—was transferred from the council to the *Yang di-Pertuan Agong* (the Monarch) on the advice of the Minister of Education (and subsequently to the Minister of Education in 1996) (Wan, 2019). The amendment to Act 30 in 1975 essentially revoked the university as an autonomous body and turned it into an entity directly under the authority of the Minister of Education.

In a situation where universities cannot be autonomous from the government, it will inevitably hinder their ability to provide a neutral space for academic freedom to be practiced. If institutional appointments are dictated by the government, universities must conform to the whims and fancies of politicians and bureaucrats. Furthermore, as institutions continue to rely financially, and almost exclusively, on the government for operational and capital expenditures, such reliance will not only further restrict the autonomy of universities but render them subject to strict financial enforcement of public service.

As public universities are classified as federal statutory bodies and receive funding for salaries for their academic and non-academic staff in the form of operational expenditure, this arrangement therefore requires all the staff to comply with the general framework of public service and the Statutory Bodies (Discipline and Surcharge) Act 2000 (Act 605). Compliance with Act 605 is one of the biggest impediments to academic freedom for academics in public universities (Wan, 2021). Under this Act, staff of statutory bodies have to adhere to many prohibitions, two of which contradict the very nature of academic work, specifically: not to make public statements either in speech or writing, and not to become an editor of publications external to their department. Fundamentally, not only have these prohibitions impinged on academic freedom, they effectively render a significant portion of academic work illegal, to say the least.

5. Language and Medium of Instruction

Language and medium of instruction in higher education has been a contentious issue in the development of higher education in Malaysia. Although Malaysia is a multi-ethnic and multilingual society, Malay is the national language upheld by Article 152 of the Federal Constitution of Malaysia. However, the same article also provides that "no person shall be prohibited or prevented from using, or from teaching or learning, any other language; and nothing in this clause shall prejudice the right of the Federal Government or of any State Government to preserve and sustain the use and study of the language of any other community in the Federation" (Article 152, Federal Constitution of Malaysia).

As the University of Malaya was inherited from the British, English was the official language and medium of instruction. The first change concerning language came with the enactment of the National Language Act 1963 (Act 32). While the University of Malaya unanimously recognized Bahasa Malaysia as the official language, the university initiated a two-stream admission based on English and Malay, as a way to enable students from the Malay-medium schools to enter university. The switch to the national language—the Language Policy Implementation Program (LPIP)—was only initiated in the middle of 1970, a year after the May 13 racial riot and seven years after Act 1963. According to the Report by the Committee Appointed by the National Operations Council[1] to Study Campus Life of Students of the University of Malaya, language barriers were a significant challenge in the university especially among the 1,050 undergraduates from the Malay-medium stream (Abdul Majid, 1971). Furthermore, the absence of implementing a single language for teaching purposes claimed to have divided students at the university based on ethnicity and language. In response to the language policy, the then Vice Chancellor issued a statement that articulated the need for a gradual implementation of LPIP and highlighted several fundamental issues that needed to be considered more carefully, among which was the change in criteria used for admission and graduation of students, as well as terms and conditions in hiring and promotion of academic staff. Without considering these issues, LPIP could have contributed to other challenges for the university in terms of fairness and academic quality. By 1972, Bahasa Malaysia became the official language and medium of instruction in universities.

An interesting challenge to the role of language in higher education came from a proposal to establish the Merdeka University. As mentioned earlier, there are vernacular schools in Malaysia that use Mandarin as the medium of instruction at the primary level, and at the secondary level, including private independent Chinese high schools. Inspired by the Nanyang University in Singapore which used Mandarin as its official medium of instruction between 1953 and 1980, the United Chinese School Committees Association and the United Chinese School Teachers Association jointly mooted the idea of a Chinese-speaking university called the Merdeka University, with the aspiration of establishing a Chinese-instruction institute in Malaysia (Tan and Teoh, 2015).

The proposal for Merdeka University was submitted as a petition to the *Yang di-Pertuan Agong* in 1978 for His Majesty's consideration to establish a private university through Act 30 on the basis that opportunities in higher education were insufficient for non-Bumiputera. The petition was challenged in the Federal Court, the highest court in

---

[1] The National Operations Council was the emergency administrative body in lieu of the elected government between May 1969 and February 1971 following the May 13 racial riot and suspension of Parliament. It was only dissolved with the restoration of Parliament.

the country, and it was decided by a verdict of 4 to 1 that universities were public bodies and therefore must use the national language as the language of instruction (*Merdeka University v. Government*, 1982). Consequently, Merdeka University was not allowed to be established.

However, there was an interesting twist to the language debate with the establishment of the International Islamic University of Malaysia (IIUM) in 1983. This was a university that was established jointly by the Malaysian government with the cooperation of members of the Organisation of Islamic Conference (OIC) (Kamal Hassan, 2019) through a minor amendment to Act 30 for this university to be set up as a company under the Companies Act 1965 (Act 125). The main justification provided by the Malaysian government to permit an amendment to Act 30 was that IIUM would not be solely owned by the Malaysian government but an international university with contribution from other nations of OIC. However, apart from the status of a public university established as a company limited by guarantee, the medium of instruction for this university is English and Arabic, and Bahasa Malaysia is the administrative language.

Fast forward to 1996, the enactment of Act 555 to enable the establishment of private higher education institutions, provided authority for the Minister of Education to give exemption for programs to be conducted in languages other than the national language. This exemption has effectively contributed to most private higher education institutions adopting English as their official language and medium of instruction.

Concurrently, while the official language and medium of instruction for public universities established under Act 30, with the exception of IIUM, is Malay, the practice in these universities has been mixed. Apart from the national university, Universiti Kebangsaan Malaysia, where the national language has been explicitly included in the constitution of the university, other public universities tend to use Malay and English interchangeably according to discipline and level of programs. Programs and courses in science and technology, as well as those of professional courses, tend to use English, while the social sciences and arts and humanities tend to use Malay. Variability also depends on individual academics as well as the composition of the class, especially where there are international students. Ironically, there is also regulation that forbids dissertations to be written in other languages apart from the national language, and this regulation even extends to courses like Chinese Studies and Tamil Studies. Overall, the policy and practice of language use in public universities is less clear and underlines a situation of competing interests in balancing the various factors, including nationalism and internationalism (Wan and Morshidi, 2018b).

6. The Private Higher Education Sector: Boon or Bane?

The enactment of the Private Higher Educational Institution Act 1996 (Act 555) marked the beginning of the liberation phase in the development of Malaysian higher education.

Prior to Act 555, the provision of higher education was solely the jurisdiction of the government and it was a legal offense for private institutions to be set up as a university.

Following the introduction of ethnic quotas in public universities, opportunities in higher education for non-Bumiputera were highly restricted and reduced. Many non-Bumiputera who could not gain admission into public universities pursued higher education abroad, especially in Australia, New Zealand, and the United Kingdom due to a shared colonial connection and the fact that higher education in these countries did not charge tuition fees at the time. It was estimated that in 1985, there were 68,000 Malaysian students studying in universities abroad, and another 15,000 in private institutions in Malaysia (Lee, 2004a). These figures made up 40 percent and 9 percent respectively of the total number of Malaysians in higher education, with the remaining 51 percent in public universities.

As the economy of Malaysia began to recover from a recession in the mid-1980s, the pressure to further increase access to higher education gained momentum. Yet, this was also a time when the economic ideology of neoliberalism began to exert its influence on higher education in Australia and the United Kingdom, whereby foreign students were charged tuition fees for the first time in 1992 and 1994 respectively. Hence, it became more expensive for Malaysian students to go abroad to pursue higher education. As a result of both domestic and foreign developments, private higher education institutions began to proliferate and offered access to higher education through creative means to circumvent the legal prohibition. This was also the era when private colleges were providing twinning programs, where a significant part of the program was taught locally and the remaining portion was completed abroad at a foreign university to earn a foreign degree. The invention of twinning programs globally—an innovative measure that resulted from straitened circumstances and increased leeway to experiment—can be attributed to Malaysia's higher education strategy.

By 1995, approximately 50,600 Malaysian students were studying abroad (about 14 percent of the student population), 130,000 Malaysian students were attending private institutions locally (about 35 percent of the student population), and the remaining 190,000 (51 percent) of Malaysian students were in public universities (Lee, 2004a). Thus, one of the motivations for the government to introduce Act 555 was to liberalize the higher education sector, to legalize the existence of private higher education institutions, as well as to provide order and control in a rapidly expanding private higher education sector.

The earliest official statistics by the Ministry of Education (n.d.) show that in 2002, seven years after enacting Act 555, there were 294,600 students enrolled across 534 private higher education institutions. Of these institutions, 11 were universities, 4 were international branch campuses, 1 was a university college, and 518 were colleges. This meant that more than 85 percent of students were enrolled in colleges and 11 percent were enrolled in universities including international branch campuses. There were 14,392 academics, of whom 767 (5.3 percent) had a doctorate and 3,919 (27 percent) had a master's degree, with the remaining majority holding either a bachelor's degree or diploma.

Fast forward to 2020, the private higher education sector has become a significant part of Malaysian higher education. Half of the students enrolled in higher education are in private institutions. The private higher education sector has also been recognized as an important economic sector for Malaysia. Citing reports from the Department of Statistics Malaysia, the former Director General of Higher Education claimed that the gross domestic product from private education in 2018 was MYR 16.62 billion and estimated to exceed MYR 30 billion when including investment into infrastructure and infostructure (Siti Hamisah, 2019).

Not only has private higher education contributed to the economic and social development of Malaysia, it has also been an important enabler for Malaysian higher education to strive towards becoming an international educational hub, with the branding of "Education Malaysia."

7. INTERNATIONALIZATION

The aspiration to become an international educational hub was first articulated in the National Higher Education Strategic Plan 2007–2020 (PSPTN). One of the goals of the strategic plan was to transform and establish Malaysia as an international hub of higher educational excellence. The emergence of internationalization in higher education in policy discourse coincides with the transition from the liberalization to the neo-liberalism phase.

Internationalization is not a new phenomenon in Malaysian higher education. However, what is new about internationalization efforts is the explicit articulation in PSPTN. Aspiration to be an international education hub has brought about a new focus on internationalization in policy discourse. The underlying motivations to internationalize have been both economic and a pursuit for prestige. In PSPTN, the goal of becoming an international education hub was predominantly about bringing in international students and the economic benefits associated with this (Knight and Morshidi, 2011). In striving towards this aspiration, Malaysian higher education embarked on the "Education Malaysia" branding. This was also the period where the craze for Malaysian universities to chase university rankings began, and positions in university rankings became a measure of success throughout PSPTN (Sarjit and Morshidi, 2010).

Apart from positioning in university rankings, the measure of internationalization in PSPTN as well as the succeeding Malaysia Education Blueprint 2015–2025 (Higher Education) (MEBHE) has been centered on the sheer ability to attract international students to Malaysia. The initial target was 100,000 international students by 2010, 150,000 by 2015, 200,000 by 2020, and 250,000 by 2025 (MOHE, 2007; MOE, 2015). However, as of 2018, there were only 39,099 international students in public universities and 92,415 in private higher education institutions, with another 5,650 students on mobility programs across both public and private institutions (MOE, 2019). With a total of only 131,514 international students in 2018, even the target set for 2015 has not been met.

Further examination of international students in Malaysia over the last decade or so shows that the bulk of international students in Malaysia came from neighboring countries in South-East Asia, China, South Asia, the Middle East, and sub-Saharan Africa. Conversely, Malaysian students who went abroad for higher education in 2017, regardless of whether they were self-financed or through scholarships, went mainly to the United Kingdom, Australia, and the United States. In total, 45,425 went to these three countries, making up 52 percent of total Malaysian students abroad (MOE, 2019).

In addition to international students, PSPTN also outlined a target of recruiting up to 15 percent of academics who were non-Malaysian citizens across the five public research universities by 2020. The MEBHE further elaborated on the need for global talent in the form of inspiring educators, accomplished researchers, entrepreneurial personalities, and transformational thought leaders in Malaysia's institutions to strive towards global prominence (MOE, 2015). As of 2018, there were 1,452 (4.6 percent) international academics across 20 public universities, and 3,010 (13.1 percent) in private higher education institutions (MOE, 2019). As Wan and Morshidi (2018a) point out, recruitment efforts for international academics in Malaysia have fallen short as issues and challenges of job security, economic uncertainty, as well as difficulty integrating into the academic community or undertaking key administrative positions in public universities due to language constraints, remain.

From three international branch campuses established in 2000, there are currently ten such institutions in Malaysia. Out of these, five are British institutions (Heriot-Watt, Newcastle, Nottingham, Reading, Southampton), three Australian (Curtin, Monash, and Swinburne) and one each from China (Xiamen) and Ireland (a partnership between two Irish institutions—the Royal College of Surgeons in Ireland and University College Dublin). Three of the British institutions are operating from EduCity, an educational hub located in the state of Johor, about a 30-minute drive from Singapore. The business model of international branch campuses has also changed, whereby those established in EduCity are wholly owned by the foreign university through establishing a holding company in Malaysia, as compared to others established earlier through joint ventures and partnerships between the foreign university and a local corporation (see Wan and Weerasena, 2018 for details of institutions in EduCity).

As mentioned, internationalization is not a recent phenomenon. It has taken different forms with different foci spanning across the different developmental phases of higher education in Malaysia. In the autonomous phase, the establishment of University of Malaya can be regarded as highly international. Addresses were read on the Foundation Day for the university in 1949 by representatives of universities from the United Kingdom, United States, Australia, New Zealand, Canada, Ireland, Hong Kong, Indonesia, Sri Lanka, and India (Khoo, 2005). The university throughout this phase also had significant numbers of academics who were non-Malaysian, and a large majority of Malaysian academics were sent abroad for postgraduate training.

Following the transition into the nationalism phase and the introduction of Malay language as the official medium of instruction in public universities, the number of international academics declined and were replaced by Malaysian academics who returned from their studies abroad. Internationalization in this phase was geared more towards gaining foreign support for capacity building and career development of local academic staff.

Conversely, the liberalization phase witnessed an intense growth of internationalization among private institutions through twinning programs. Such arrangements laid the foundation for the growth of the private higher education sector before Act 555 was enacted and continued for almost a decade. Partnerships with foreign universities, mostly with Anglo-speaking institutions in the United Kingdom and Australia, have projected the private sector as more international than public universities. This has been further strengthened by the fact that the official medium of instruction for private higher education institutions is English.

The announcement of the inaugural Times Higher Education University Rankings in 2004, where two Malaysian public universities (University of Malaya and Universiti Sains Malaysia) ranked among the top 200, has ignited a chase for international standing and heavily influenced policy discourse in higher education where such chase of prestige has been explicitly articulated in major policy documents like PSPTN and MEBHE.

8. Conclusion: Way Forward

Higher education in Malaysia is where it is today as a result of being shaped by social-political-economic influences from both within and outside of the country for more than six decades. Issues of access, language, recognition, and quality remain key areas for the future development of higher education. However, while the past development of higher education has focused primarily on the domestic and national front, this has changed significantly from internationalization and globalization. Furthermore, as motivation to become a global player in the form of an international educational hub was strongly driven by neoliberal and market forces, the craze for prestige and simple tangible measurables, such as university rankings, will continue to become a feature in the development of higher education in Malaysia.

Inevitably, the world is still struggling to come to terms with the COVID-19 pandemic and this has become the most disruptive issue that is likely to change the higher education landscape. The disruptions have also unearthed a significant implication in the transformation and expansion of higher education driven by market forces. While the role of higher education has evolved from an elitist form of capacity training for nation-building to becoming accessible to the Malaysian masses, the pandemic has forced a shift towards online and remote learning, revealing another stark reality between those who have and those who do not have the sufficient resources and access to technology, computing, and internet connectivity. Those who do not have sufficient resources have been further disadvantaged by the sudden change of mode in higher education learning, and this has exposed major implications to achieve equity and inclusiveness in a massified higher education system.

The pandemic has literally brought all international travel to a standstill, including the mobility of academics. The more skeptical commentators surmise that the extent of global academic mobility in the post-pandemic era will never reach the level of pre-pandemic, and more optimistic ones suggest a period of three to five years for academic mobility of students to re-intensify. Regardless, the status of an international educational hub in Malaysia that is relying on international students and its strength and comparative advantage, such as affordability, image of a moderate Islamic nation, political stability, as well as the diversity of cultures, needs to be leveraged as we enter the post-pandemic era of higher education.

Most importantly, the COVID-19 pandemic presents an opportunity for Malaysia's higher education system, as well as institutions to pause from the norm, take stock and strategize for the next phase of development. The initiative to recover from this disruption is an opportune moment to end the neoliberalism phase in the development of Malaysian higher education by putting a stop to the policies and strategies dictated by a culture of managerialism, measurables, and a craze for prestige.

What, then, should be the next phase of development? Perhaps the single most important lesson the COVID-19 pandemic has taught us is the supreme importance of life. Hence, in the context of higher education, it is time to re-humanize Malaysian higher education by bringing back the focus of the purpose, role, and function of education and academic research to the betterment of humankind.

REFERENCES

Abdul Majid, I. (1971). *Report of the Committee Appointed by the National Operations Council to Study Campus Life of Students of the University of Malaya*. Kuala Lumpur: Jabatan Chetak Kerajaan.

Aida Suraya, M. Y., Ibrahim, C. O., and Wan, C. D. (2015). "The transition from secondary education to higher education: Malaysia. In UNESCO, *The Transition from Secondary Education to Higher Education: Case Studies from Asia and the Pacific* (pp. 91–107). Paris: UNESCO and UNESCO-Bangkok.

Department of Higher Education (2019). *Senarai Daftar IPTS* [Private Higher Education Institutions Registration List, November]. http://jpt.mohe.gov.my/portal/ipts/institusi-pen didikan-tinggi-swasta/senarai-daftar-dan-statistik-ipts, accessed January 8, 2020.

Fauziah, M. T. and Ng, M. L. Y. A. (eds.) (2015). *Governance Reforms in Public Universities of Malaysia*. Penang: Universiti Sains Malaysia Press.

Kamal Hassan, M. (2019). "An Islamic university in the Malaysian context: Pursuing the mission of desecularisation, integration and Islamicisation of human knowledge." In C. D. Wan, S. Morshidi, and A. R. Dzulkifli (eds.), *Higher Education in Malaysia: A Critical Review of the Past and Present for the Future* (pp. 209–221). Penang: Universiti Sains Malaysia Press.

Khoo, K. K. (2005). *One Hundred Years: The University of Malaya*. Kuala Lumpur: University of Malaya Press.

Knight, J. and Morshidi S. (2011). "The complexities and challenges of regional education hubs: Focus on Malaysia." *Higher Education*, 62, 593–606.

Lee, M. N. N. (2004a). "Private higher education in Malaysia: Expansion, diversification and consolidation." In M. N. N. Lee (ed.), *Restructuring Higher Education in Malaysia* (pp. 19–35). Penang: School of Educational Studies, Universiti Sains Malaysia.

Lee, M. N. N. (2004b). "University admission in Malaysia: Quota or meritocracy?" In M. N. N. Lee (ed.), *Restructuring Higher Education in Malaysia* (pp. 77–89). Penang: School of Educational Studies, Universiti Sains Malaysia.

Merdeka University Berhad v. Government of Malaysia (1982). 2 MLJ 243: Federal Court.

Ministry of Education (n.d.). *Data Institusi Pengajian Tinggi Swasta (IPTS) 2002–2007* [Private Higher Education Institutions Data 2002–2007]. https://www.moe.gov.my/en/muat-turun/laporan-dan-statistik/pendidikan-tinggi/buku-perangkaan/2002-2007, accessed January 29, 2020.

Ministry of Education (2015). *Malaysia Education Blueprint 2015–2025 (Higher Education)*. Putrajaya: Ministry of Education Malaysia.

Ministry of Education (2019). *Higher Education Statistics 2018*. Putrajaya: Ministry of Education Malaysia.

Ministry of Higher Education (2007). *The National Higher Education Strategic Plan Beyond 2020*. Putrajaya: Ministry of Higher Education Malaysia.

Ministry of Higher Education (2009). *Higher Education Statistics 2008*. Putrajaya: Ministry of Higher Education Malaysia.

Russayani, I. and Shaza Nawwarah, Z. I. (2019). "Student loans: The National Higher Education Fund Corporation (PTPTN)." In C. D. Wan, S. Morshidi, and A. R. Dzulkifli (eds.), *Higher Education in Malaysia: A Critical Review of the Past and Present for the Future* (pp. 62–71). Penang: Universiti Sains Malaysia Press.

Sarjit, K. and Morshidi, S. (2010). "Going for global university ranking through the Accelerated Programme for Excellence (APEX) in Malaysia: Full throttle ahead." In K. Sarjit, S. Morshidi, and W. G. Tierney (eds.), *Quality Assurance and University Rankings in Higher Education in the Asia Pacific: Challenges for Universities and Nations* (pp. 194–217). Penang: Penerbit Universiti Sains Malaysia and National Higher Education Research Institute.

Sato, M. (2007). *Dilemmas of Public University Reform in Malaysia*. Clayton: Monash University Press.

Siti Hamisah, T. (2019). "Higher education as an industry." *The Star*, August 18. https://www.thestar.com.my/news/education/2019/08/18/higher-education-as-an-industry, accessed January 29, 2020.

Suffian, M. (1969). *Report of the Cabinet Committee on the Constitution of the University of Penang under the Chairmanship of the Honourable Mr Justice Suffian*. Kuala Lumpur: Jabatan Chetak Kerajaan.

Tan, Y. S. and Teoh, H. S. (2015). "The development of Chinese education in Malaysia, 1952–1975: Political collaboration between the Malaysian Chinese Association and the Chinese educationists." *History of Education Society*, 44/1, 83–100.

Trow, M. (1973). *Problems in the Transition from Elite to Mass Higher Education*. Berkeley: Carnegie Commission on Higher Education.

UNESCO Institute of Statistics (2020). *Education: Gross Enrolment Ratio by Level of Education*. http://data.uis.unesco.org/, accessed January 9, 2020.

Wan, C. D. (2017). *The History of University Autonomy in Malaysia*. Policy IDEAS No. 40. Kuala Lumpur: Institute for Democracy and Economic Affairs.

Wan, C. D. (2018). "Student enrolment in Malaysian higher education: Is there gender disparity and what can we learn from the disparity?" *Compare: A Journal of Comparative and International Education*, 48/ 2, 244–261.

Wan, C. D. (2019). "The Universities and University Colleges Act (AUKU) in Malaysia: History, contexts and development." *Kajian Malaysia*, 37/2, 1–20.

Wan, C. D. (2021). "Academic freedom in Malaysian public universities." *Kajian Malaysia* http://web.usm.my/km/earlyView_May2021/29_KM-OA-03-20-0050.R1.pdf.

Wan, C. D., Abdul Razak, A., and Russayani, I. (2016). "Equity in Malaysian higher education: Revisiting the policies and initiatives." In S. Paivandi and K. M. Joshi (eds.), *Equity in Higher Education: A Global Perspective* (pp. 83–96). Delhi: Studera Press, 83–96.

Wan, C. D. and Morshidi S. (2018a). "International academics in Malaysian public universities: Recruitment, integration, and retention." *Asia Pacific Education Review*, 19/2, 241–252.

Wan, C. D. and Morshidi, S. (2018b). "The development of Malaysian higher education: Making sense of the nation-building agenda in the globalisation era." *Asian Education and Development Studies*, 7/2, 144–156.

Wan, C. D. and Weerasena, B. (2018). "EduCity, Johor: A promising project with multiple challenges to overcome." *Trends in Southeast Asia*, 4.

World Bank (2020). *Country Profile: Malaysia.* https://databank.worldbank.org/views/reports/reportwidget.aspx?Report_Name=CountryProfile&Id=b450fd57&tbar=y&dd=y&inf=n&zm=n&country=MYS, accessed January 9, 2020.

CHAPTER 39

PRIVATIZED HIGHER EDUCATION IN THAILAND

In Pursuit of Legitimacy and Profitability

PRACHAYANI PRAPHAMONTRIPONG KANWAR AND FLORENCE LO

1. INTRODUCTION

THAILAND, with more than 70 million people, is the second largest economy in South-East Asia and has achieved many developmental indicators of well-being more successfully than its ASEAN neighbors (World Bank, 2019). The country's modernization has been a fascinating journey shaped by complex and often contradictory political, economic, and societal forces. These forces have often turned to the higher education system, which itself has transformed from elite to mass education, as a tool for technocracy, social transformation, and nation-building.

One of the key drivers of the expansion of Thai higher education is the country's economic growth. While Thailand grew by 7 percent between 1960 and 1985, and by 9.5 percent during the boom years between 1985 and 1995, its economic performance faltered after the Asian financial crisis. From 2005 to 2019 and even prior to the 2020 coronavirus (COVID-19) pandemic, Thailand's economic growth was approximately 3.4 percent, lagging other South-East Asian economies. The country's economy was hampered by domestic political uncertainty, drought, and US–China trade tensions. The COVID-19 pandemic further exacerbated the dip in growth, causing weak global demand, restricted international tourism and domestic mobility, and declining private investment (Sussangkarn and Nikomborirak, 2016; OECD, 2020; World Bank, 2021).

Nevertheless, the country is expected to rebound by 2022, and Thai higher education today is expected to cater to an innovation-driven economy as part of an effort to improve the country's economic liberalization and internationalization. The higher education system is driven by both privatization and marketization, which have increasingly blurred the boundaries between private and public higher education institutions (HEIs). As Thailand's higher education expands to meet the country's economic needs, it also faces critical challenges, including declining growth, academic quality control and financial constraints.

The Thai government's two intertwined policy initiatives, *the privatization of the public sector* and *the promotion of the private sector's growth*, are expected to elevate Thailand's higher education market toward international recognition. Within this framework, many leading universities are seeking more legitimacy based on their academic rigor and social acceptability, while other HEIs are focused on quantity and market-driven principles.

This chapter's scope is limited mostly to private and public HEIs under the oversight of the Thai Ministry of Higher Education, Science, Research and Innovation (MHESI), established in 2019. These HEIs play a major role in the country's labor market and social and economic development. Public community colleges and HEIs under other government agencies exist but contribute little to the country's labor force. Table 39.1 summarizes the various types of Thai HEIs.

2. The Dominating Public Sector and the Birth of Private Higher Education

Although Thailand has never been colonized by Western forces, Thai higher education, like many Asian institutions, has been influenced by various continental European models. The Thai higher education system echoes the French pattern of "Single Public System: Multiple Sectors" (Clark, 1983, pp. 54–55), where different types of HEIs (e.g., universities, teachers' colleges, technological colleges, and specialized colleges) fall under the state umbrella but report to different central bureaus. In Thailand, the government assumes sole responsibility for higher education, with MHESI overseeing the governance, finance, and function of private, and most public, HEIs.

As with many of Thailand's neighboring countries, Thailand's higher education has been led by the public sector under the French model of *grandes écoles* since the late 1800s, when access to public universities was limited to the ruling elite. While the private sector was forbidden to operate at a higher education level, private primary and secondary education, vocational training, Western medicine, and social welfare remained a crucial asset in Thailand.

As part of Thailand's political modernization after World War II (Darling, 1962; Fineman, 1997), public higher education began expanding regionally, although access remained restricted. It was not until the late 1960s that the Thai government started investing in private higher education, when increasing demands rose beyond the capabilities of the existing public universities.

Table 39.1 Types of HEIs in Thailand, 2020

Type of HEI	Legal form	Description	Number of institutions	Number of students
Public universities	Public	HEIs under state supervision and funding. Each institution is governed by its own Act, has a juristic person status, and functions as a government agency under MHESI.	7	94,301
Autonomous universities	Public	HEIs with a legal entity under state supervision. Each institution is governed by its own Act. While receiving the government funding, they have full autonomy in creating their own administrative structure and budgeting system.	26	529,408
Rajabhat universities	Public	HEIs under state supervision and funding. They are governed under the Rajabhat University Act, have a juristic person status, and function as a government agency under MHESI. They were initially founded as teachers' colleges across the country.	38	367,098
Rajamangala universities of technology	Public	HEIs under state supervision and funding. They are governed under the Rajamangala Universities of Technology Act, have a juristic person status, and function as a government agency under MHESI. They were initially established as regional technology and vocational colleges.	9	129,310
Open universities	Public	HEIs under state supervision and funding. Each institution is governed by its own Act, has a juristic person status, and functions as a government agency under MHESI. This is the only public HEI type that has an open admission policy.	2	163,957
Community colleges	Public	Colleges under state supervision and funding. They are governed under the Community Colleges Act, have a juristic person status, and function as a government agency under MHESI. They only offer baccalaureate degrees and diplomas based on local wisdom and needs.	20	12,761
HEIs under other government agencies	Public	Specialized training institutes under other ministries such as sports, transportation, military, etc.	N/A	25,144

(continued)

Table 39.1 Continued

Type of HEI	Legal form	Description	Number of institutions	Number of students
Private universities	Private	HEIs with a juristic person status under MHESI supervision. Governed by the Private Institution of Higher Education Act, they are expected to be comprehensive universities, offering all degree levels.	42	195,904
Private colleges	Private	HEIs with a juristic person status under MHESI supervision. Governed by the Private Institution of Higher Education Act, they are expected to offer specialized fields of study at all degree levels.	19	25,938
Private institutes	Private	HEIs with a juristic person status under MHESI supervision. Governed by the Private Institution of Higher Education Act, they are expected to offer only a few programs at all degree levels.	11	31,426
		Total	**174**	**1,575,247**

Source: Ratchakitchanubeksa (2020).

Despite the growing need for private higher education, the Thai government remained slow to embrace it. In 1969, the Private College Act was issued, granting "college" status to the first six private vocational schools, with rigid control over their academic programs. However, it was not until 1979 that the Thai government finally passed the Private Higher Education Act, which legalized private higher education in Thailand for the first time and enabled private universities to confer master's degrees. By the late 1990s, private HEIs were an established sector, growing parallel with public higher education. In 2001, private HEIs outnumbered public HEIs, which peaked at 68 percent of the higher education share (see Table 39.2).

The increasing demand for higher education during the 1990s was due, in part, to the government's efforts to achieve universal primary education. This commitment was declared at the World Conference on Education for All in Jomtien, Thailand in 1990 and was one of eight goals in the United Nations' Millennium Development Goals set in 2000. With increasing student participation in primary, and thus secondary, education, demand from high school graduates became a major impetus for the government to invest more in higher education.

The political influences on the higher education system were apparent during Thaksin's government in the early 2000s. As part of the government's populist policies, the nationwide education reform was put in place, causing a major shift in Thai higher education. Most notably, the government passed laws enabling public universities

Table 39.2 Comparison of private and public higher education growth in Thailand

Year	Total number of HEIs	Total number of public HEIs	Total number of private HEIs	Total private HEIs (percent)	Total number of HE enrollment	Total enrollment number in public HEIs	Total enrollment number in private HEIs	Total private HE enrollment (percent)
1972	17	11	6	35.29	67,848	63,823	4,025	5.93
1981	25	14	11	44.00	670,829	639,798	31,031	4.63
1991	46	21	25	54.35	629,498	518,956	110,542	17.56
2001	75	24	51	68.00	1,179,569	955,759	223,810	18.97
2011	133	77	56	42.11	2,056,978	1,758,684	298,294	14.50
2020	154	82	72	46.75	1,537,342	1,284,074	253,268	16.47

Note: Intervals of years are organized using the Thai B.E. year (starting from B.E. 2515). Data of public community colleges and HEIs under other ministries have been excluded.

Sources: Praphamontripong (2010); MHESI (2020) for years 2011 and 2020.

to become autonomous, transferring Rajabhat (teachers' colleges) and Rajamangala (technological colleges) from the Ministry of Education to the oversight of the Commission on Higher Education and upgrading them to public university status. This led to a drastic jump in the number of public universities from 24 institutions in 2001 to 77 institutions in 2011. The major drivers behind these laws include a series of national education acts, the national economic and social development plans, and higher education long-range plans. The government sought to ensure better access to Thailand's higher education by addressing capacity, equitable access, efficiency, internationalization, decentralization of management, accountability, quality assurance, academic freedom, and increasing government support for private providers.

Today, most of Thailand's private and public HEIs fall into one of three categories: identity (religious/gender/ethnic), semi-elite and non-elite (demand-absorbing/serious demand-absorbing) (Levy, 1986, 2019, forthcoming; Praphamontripong, 2010). *Identity* institutions founded upon faith-based/cultural missions and specialized programs serve particular religious and cultural niches.

Some public and private institutions claim the moniker of *semi-elite* and the academic prestige it bestows—based on their student and alumni socio-economic status, academic excellence, ability to produce leadership in niche and business-related fields, and accessibility to crucial employment networks for graduates. Only a handful of Thai private universities, such as Assumption, Bangkok and the University of the Thai Chamber of Commerce (UTCC), and flagship public universities, such as Chulalongkorn, Mahidol, and Thammasat, are considered semi-elite. The Asian Institute of Technology could be regarded as semi-elite, given its prominent alumni status, academic rigor (specifically in the STEM fields), and substantial funding from the Thai government and international interests.

Non-elite institutions typically offer low-cost programs in high-demand fields of study, such as business, accounting, and technology, and capitalize on the demand for higher education. By definition, non-elite institutions are *demand-absorbing* institutions that meet the educational demand that the existing institutions cannot, or will not, accommodate. While some institutions are dubious in their legitimacy and have heavily market-oriented behaviors, others, termed *serious demand-absorbing* HEIs, have elevated their academic esteem with specialized programs and a high placement rate in the job market. Approximately 70 percent of private HEIs and all public Rajabhat, Rajamangala, and open admission universities fall into the demand-absorbing category with only a few being regarded as serious (Praphamontripong, 2010). Non-elite demand-absorbing institutions, more than religious and semi-elite HEIs, struggle to balance academic quality with market-driven behaviors.

These three institutional categories embody different degrees of legitimacy and prestige in the Thai higher education marketplace. Legitimacy of an institution stems from three major external sources: the government, the market, and academia (Clark, 1983; Slantcheva and Levy, 2007) (see Figure 39.1). The perception of institutional legitimacy is stratified, ranking a handful of flagship public universities at the apex of the marketplace and a vast majority of non-elite, demand-absorbing private and public HEIs at the bottom. The bulk of private HEIs in Asia, including Thailand, are found at the bottom of the prestige hierarchy (Altbach, 2004). Thailand's higher education system reflects Trow's (1987) "Analysis of Status," where leading universities maintain their legitimacy in the market competition while new non-elite institutions—private or public—are unlikely to compete effectively or equally.

3. Key Public Policy Challenges

Thailand's two major policy directives—*privatization of public higher education* and the *promotion of private higher education*—aim to stimulate change within the higher education system and address the ongoing issues of access, quality control and financing.

3.1 Access: The Nexus of Demand and Supply

As in most countries, the Thai government endeavored to follow Adam Smith's (1776) idea of increasing productivity of manpower and free markets as fundamental to the development of higher education and the growth of the nation's wealth overall. Consequently, the government privatized public higher education by transforming public HEIs into autonomous institutions in 2003 and upgrading the status of public colleges to full-fledged universities between 2004 and 2005. This allowed public

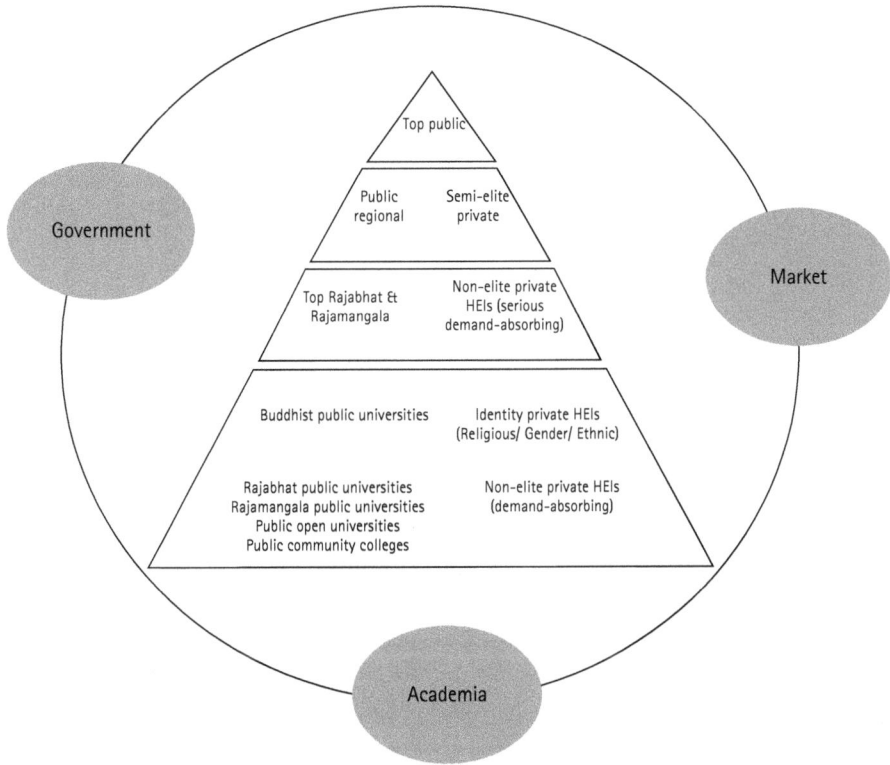

FIGURE 39.1 Legitimacy of private and public institutions in the Thai higher education marketplace

Sources: Clark (1983); Praphamontripong (2010); Slantcheva and Levy (2007).

universities the flexibility and freedom to adapt to market forces. The government also promoted the growth of private higher education through deregulation, which attracted more private investment and facilitated private expansion. As a result, higher education enrollment expanded threefold between 1995 and 2015, peaking at slightly more than 2 million students (see Figure 39.2).

Despite these expansion efforts, Thailand's population growth rate has been declining since the 1990s. The demographic structure has shifted to an aging society, and the working-age population has been declining since 2015, leading to labor shortages. By 2040, the 0-to-24 age bracket is projected to fall to just 20 percent of the population. Consequently, higher education enrollment has continued to drop every year since 2016 and now sits slightly above 1.5 million students.

The decreased demand in Thai higher education has led to aggressive recruitment strategies for HEIs vying for a dwindling number of qualified applicants. Some non-elite demand-absorbing private HEIs no longer require written exams, interviews, or TCAS, GAT-PAT, and O-NET scores and portfolios,[1] while others entice students with

---

[1] TCAS stands for Thai University Central Admission System. GAT/PAT stand for General Aptitude Test/ Professional and Academic Aptitude Test. O-NET stands for Ordinary National Educational Test.

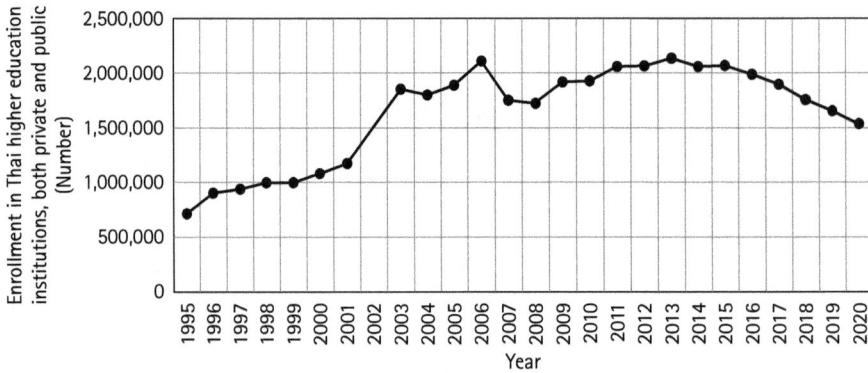

FIGURE 39.2 Thai higher education enrollment, both private and public, 1995–2020

Source: MHESI (2020).

discounts on tuition fees and free accommodation, uniforms, and textbooks. Likewise, open public universities have lowered their tuition fees by 40 percent per credit (Prachachat Dhurakij, 2020).

This competition creates a domino effect of non-coercive isomorphism where HEIs in any of the three categories voluntarily behave like one another to remain profitable and, if possible, gain academic prestige. While profit-seeking behaviors seem common among private institutions, especially non-elite demand-absorbing ones, demand-absorbing public universities can also behave as for-profit in "disguise." In this respect, the line between legitimacy and profitability becomes blurred.

3.2 Internationalization as a Survival Strategy

While Australia, the United Kingdom, and the United States are leading countries in international higher education, Asian countries such as Malaysia, Singapore, and Thailand have recently become major recruiters in the region as well, all claiming to be international education hubs (Wit et al., 2015). Thailand has invested in several policy initiatives that aim to recruit more foreign students—with the hope that they continue to work in Thailand after graduation.

Such *internationalization at home* (Knight, 2006) has been a driving force in the Thai private sector since the 1970s, especially for semi-elite universities striving to meet global standards and distinguish themselves. Although the private sector initially pioneered Thailand's internationalization of higher education in 1972, the public sector has made the strategy more widespread, both domestically and internationally. This is due, in part, to the fact that the public sector is much larger, and public universities are able to take advantage of the government's privatization initiative and their own credentials (seemingly more legitimate than private institutions) to arrange international programs and cross-border agreements.

As part of the ASEAN community, Thailand benefits from shared academics, students, and labor among member countries. Under the government's privatization initiative, in 2010, there were 2,720 active memorandum of understandings (MOUs) signed between Thai HEIs (mostly public) and foreign HEIs in more than 60 countries (Lao, 2015; Kanjananiyot and Chaitiamwong, 2018). Partnerships with HEIs abroad mostly benefit semi-elite and serious demand-absorbing private HEIs and flagship public universities that choose to launch qualified international programs, enhance collaborative research activities, or initiate exchange programs.

The skyrocketing number of international programs in relation to the withdrawal of government financial support for public universities and autonomous university policy marks a shift toward commercialization of Thailand's higher education where profit-seeking is the prime rationale (Lao, 2015). Many HEIs, particularly non-elite demand-absorbing, offer an international program that charges substantial tuition fees for a program that lacks the commensurate capacity and resources, including unqualified lecturers, questionable quality of the curriculum, and limited English proficiency of both faculty and students. Most international programs in Thailand are simply using the Thai curriculum (traditional content-based teaching) translated into English (Chalapati, 2007). Still, these programs are often more affordable than studying abroad for middle-class students, and they are also more affordable than Western programs for foreign students from neighboring countries.

Currently, almost 24,500 students from more than 160 countries are pursuing higher education in Thailand. The majority are from Asia, mostly China (48.80 percent), followed by Myanmar (10.02 percent) and Cambodia (6.03 percent) (MHESI, 2020). Of the total number of international students, 70 percent are studying at an undergraduate level, likely because Thailand still lags behind on international standards in academic research and innovation. Private HEIs (mostly demand-absorbing) attract more international students than their public counterparts because they usually have less strict admission requirements.

While leading flagship public universities tend to have international programs with well-established finances, prestigious faculty, and high student engagement, demand-absorbing public universities with limited funding and unqualified teaching staff may struggle to maintain their international programs. For example, academics are an increasing concern for Rajamangala public universities competing with their private counterparts to attract foreign students via international programs designed for specific nationalities (Prachachat Dhurakij, 2019). While they charge lower tuition and fees than the private HEIs—making them an attractive option for students—some do not have the resources to manage a quality international program (e.g., courses are designed by teaching staff without a background related to the courses; there are lower course requirements to ease the language barrier, etc.). Likewise, Rajabhat public universities changed their traditional objective of teacher training to comprehensive programs, forcing them into competition with other universities for research-oriented professors, students with academic potential, research facilities and research funds. This has raised concerns about their capability to produce quality research and fulfill higher education standards. Non-elite demand-absorbing private and public HEIs in Thailand rarely conduct research or innovation and, even when they do, the research is mostly applied science (Praphamontripong, 2010).

Outbound international mobility for higher education abroad has limited impact on the domestic demand for higher education in Thailand. In 2016, Thailand's outbound mobility ratio, of the total higher education enrollment, was only 1.28 percent, ranking close to India (0.94 percent) and Indonesia (0.63 percent) (UIS, 2016). For those who choose to study abroad, the top five host countries for Thai students, based on 2017 figures, are Australia, the United States, the United Kingdom, Japan, and Indonesia. Typically, students pursuing higher education abroad either come from families with a high socio-economic status, are recipients of a Thai government scholarship, or both. Thailand's scholarship students are contractually obligated to work for the Thai government upon returning from their studies abroad.

Thailand's internationalization efforts are paying off considerably, as graduates returning from international HEIs, especially from prestigious universities overseas, often assume leadership roles in various sectors of the workforce. Apart from technical expertise, overseas graduates from Western universities often pick up new social and cognitive skills in creative, independent thinking and problem-solving. Their exposure to new social paradigms helps break the cycle of traditional Thai learning that conforms with strict cultural norms of deference and power distance that can stifle creativity and innovation. Particularly for graduates from wealthy backgrounds who are often destined for positions with significant influence, international higher education experiences enable them to bridge the cultural gap in international relations and contribute significantly towards Thailand's political, economic, and social development.

Foreign investment in Thai higher education is another internationalization strategy with appreciable benefits. Because of dropping student enrollment, a majority of family-owned, private, demand-absorbing HEIs have been operating with a financial loss and lack of liquidity so critical that some are closing or selling to investors. Thailand witnessed the first two major acquisitions of private universities from Chinese investors in 2018 and 2019: Krirk University by Mingchang International Education (Prachachat Dhurakij, 2018) and Stamford International University (under the Laureate global network) by China Yuhua Education Corporation Limited (Royal Coast Review, 2019).

Foreign investments are helping to ease the financial deficits and may raise institutional quality to international standards. However, it is too soon to appreciate the challenges it may create for the Thai government struggling to maintain control over private HEIs and academic standards.

3.3 Academic Quality and Employability

Thailand's higher education is often described as a profitable and commercialized market with a lack of quality control. Quality indicators include both academics (student demographics, faculty training, curriculum, etc.) and graduates' employability.

Also, quality, together with legitimacy, is often used as an indicator of an institution's legal and social acceptability (Slantcheva and Levy, 2007).

The Thai government's privatization policies aim to improve the academic quality and efficiency of the system as a whole by making private and public HEIs more accountable to their constituencies (i.e., students, the labor market, and the government). They must be competitive and creative in the labor market to remain financially solvent.

Although privatization as a concept is a practical approach to handling larger enrollments and increasing funding (ADB, 2011b), in Thailand, it has been more beneficial to long-standing flagship public universities that are not struggling with quality control issues and are already known for their academic excellence, competitive students, reputable faculty, and substantial endowment.

Likewise, the government's increasing support for private institutions is particularly beneficial for semi-elite and serious demand-absorbing HEIs where academic esteem and specialization overrule profit motives. When the government keeps regulations minimal, these private institutions, striving for academic legitimacy and attributes commensurate with flagship public universities, are better equipped to offer quality education.

Thailand, nevertheless, has joined many other countries in confronting issues of dubious quality as the higher education market expands. Privatization often encourages profit-seeking activities, given that public HEIs can operate commercially and charge higher tuition fees similar to private HEIs. Most demand-absorbing private institutions take advantage of government deregulation by increasing enrollment and opening more programs that barely meet the government's quality standards or align with the market needs. Non-elite demand-absorbing institutions are "rife with abysmal quality and fraud" (Levy, 2019, p. 19), and academic quality suffers as institutions focus on their return on investments.

Despite the concern for quality higher education, privatization—and the profit-seeking behaviors it encourages—has yet to affect students' employability. According to the MHESI's 2019 report (see Table 39.3), employment rates for graduates of private colleges (85.45 percent), private universities (78.33 percent), and Rajabhat publics (62.48 percent) are encouraging. However, the report does not include information on starting salaries, employer demographics, or the correlation between fields of study and job descriptions. Still, data suggest that most students graduating from non-elite demand-absorbing institutions are responding well to the market demands, particularly for blue collar and service industries.

In contrast, public universities and colleges (mostly regional) and public autonomous universities, which produce the most graduates (60,137 and 26,989, respectively), have unemployment rates as high as 32.48 percent and 36.07 percent, compared with private colleges (10.94 percent) and universities (13.93 percent). Graduates from these top public universities are likely more selective in their job search, compensation, or office location compared with those graduating from non-elite institutions. Those from more financially secure backgrounds may also choose to rely on their parents' support or enroll in further education if they cannot find a job that matches their educational

Table 39.3 Graduates by employment status and type of HEIs, overall, 2018

HEIs	Currently employed		Currently employed & continuing further study		Currently unemployed		Continuing further study		Total
	Number	Percentage	Number	Percentage	Number	Percentage	Number	Percentage	Number
Private colleges	7,360	85.45	181	2.10	942	10.94	130	1.51	8,613
Private universities	19,905	78.33	417	1.64	3,540	13.93	1,551	6.10	25,413
Rajabhat public universities	11,500	62.48	277	1.51	6,310	34.28	318	1.73	18,405
Public universities & colleges	36,661	60.96	819	1.36	19,532	32.48	3,125	5.20	60,137
Rajamangala public universities of technology	15,524	60.42	286	1.11	9,478	36.89	404	1.57	25,692
Public autonomous universities	15,844	58.71	398	1.47	9,736	36.07	1,011	3.75	26,989
HEIs under other government agencies	244	58.51	2	0.48	158	37.89	13	3.12	417
Public Open Universities	3,527	50.54	20	0.29	3,110	44.57	321	4.60	6,978
Public community colleges	748	48.79	95	6.20	414	27.01	276	18.00	1,533

Note: The table is sorted by the highest percentage of currently employed graduates.

Source: MHESI (2019).

background. As for the private sector, semi-elite and serious demand-absorbing HEIs often tout strong connections to certain employers, and identity HEIs in particular produce graduates to serve their specific religious/cultural groups (Levy, forthcoming).

Analyzing employability is further complicated by the disconnect between the academics taught at HEIs and the skills sought by the labor market and high-tech industries. Thai employers often struggle to find new hires with the necessary basic and technical skills—a problem often shared by employers across Asia (ADB, 2011a).

While a majority of Thai graduates hold social sciences degrees, industries are increasingly seeking employees with science and technology educational backgrounds. Most new employees require skills training in digital literacy, English literacy, and functional competencies before they can actually work (Dumrongkiat, 2018).

To better align graduate qualifications with labor market demands, and to mitigate concerns about varying academic quality, the 2019 Higher Education Act mandates both internal and external quality assurances (QAs) for all Thai HEIs. These standards emphasize five dimensions: learners' achievement, research and innovation, academic services to community, preservation of Thai culture, and institutional management.

These QA policies have created institutional stratifications between private and public sectors and within the subsectors (Praphamontripong, 2011). While private HEIs have gained more legitimacy than in the past when private and public HEIs were held to different standards and regulations, some QA standards, such as research and innovation, have proven difficult to meet, especially for small non-elite demand-absorbing HEIs that are mostly teaching-oriented with limited resources and capacity. Only semi-elite private universities and leading flagship public universities tend to be comfortable with the existing QA policies.

Many HEIs also seek legitimacy by meeting international standards beyond the Thai QA policies. Although semi-elite private and public universities aspire to improve their international rankings (Lao, 2018), none of the flagship public universities are in the top 500 of the Times Higher Education (THE) World University Rankings 2020. Mahidol University, ranked first nationally, is between 601 and 800 in the rankings. Within Asia alone, Mahidol ranks 122nd with a high score on industry income but a low score on research.

Although 16 public universities are listed in the overall THE ranking, Thai private HEIs have yet to gain such international recognition. Three private universities (mostly semi-elite)—Bangkok, UTCC, and Siam—are working toward that goal and are in the QS Asia University Rankings 2020 (QS Quacquarelli Symonds, 2020). They all scored high on international aspects but were lacking, not surprisingly, on international research efforts.

3.4 Financing Disparities

Funding is a crucial component for any HEI, public or private, to maintain quality academics and remain a sustainable institution. In recent decades, critical budget constraints from overwhelming higher education demands have forced Thailand to adopt a "cost-sharing" model where other stakeholders and the private sector share the cost of higher education expansion via privatization and commercialization strategies (Johnstone, 2006; ADB, 2009; Levy and Kanwar, 2013). However, while the government has less financial burden, it also has less control over investor/owner motives. Many small, non-elite demand-absorbing private HEIs are driven to support themselves with minimum governmental aid, further entrenching the mindset of quantity over quality.

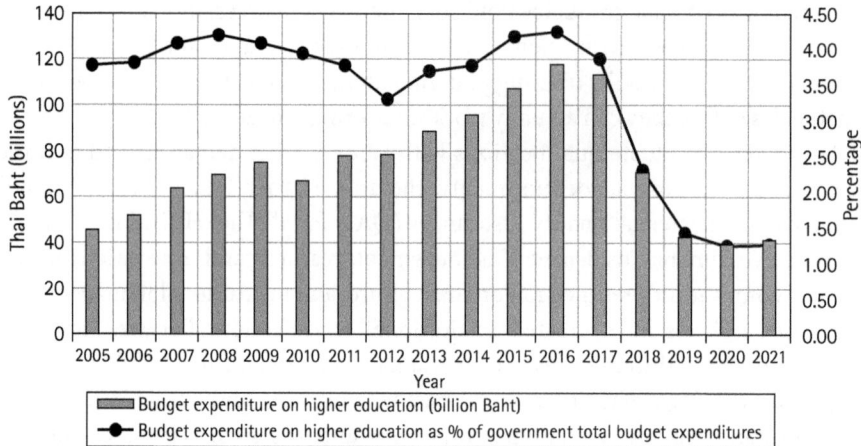

FIGURE 39.3 Government budget expenditure on higher education, 2005–2021

Note: Data only include budget expenditure for MHESI office and public HEIs under MHESI. Data on community colleges have been omitted.

Source: Budget Bureau (2020a).

The push for cost-sharing in Thai higher education began after the regional currency crisis in the late 1990s, and public HEIs started seeking incomes from nongovernment sources. Still, the government's expenditure on higher education between 2005 and 2016 has escalated, perhaps due to the populist policies of the Thaksin's and Yingluck's governments (Sagarik, 2014). Under the most recent General Prayut's government, public HEIs experienced significant scrutiny of government funding, as most public universities' annual budgets were cut by almost half (Thai Post, 2018). Figure 39.3 highlights government expenditure on higher education in relation to the total budget expenditures, which dropped from 3.87 percent in 2017 and 2.32 percent in 2018 to 1.26 percent in 2021. This was likely a strategic push for all public universities to become more financially self-supporting as per the cost-sharing policy initiative. Public universities whose graduates were unable to gain employment or programs that did not respond to the market needs were affected the most.

3.4.1 Direct and Indirect Subsidies

As part of a government agency, Thai public HEIs automatically receive a direct government subsidy as an annual block grant that they can freely manage according to their institutional priorities. However, discrepancies in the government subsidy allocation are apparent, and not all public institutions are funded equally, resulting in greater institutional stratification (Lao, 2018; Praphamontripong, 2010).

As illustrated in Figure 39.4, the autonomous university subsector—which includes all of the flagship public universities—has the largest budget. The top three universities with the most government funding in 2021 were Mahidol University (3bn Baht), Thammasat University (1.76bn Baht), and Kasetsart University (1.59bn Baht) (Budget

Bureau, 2020b). For the semi-elite public university, Mahidol, the government budget constitutes only about 20 percent of its income, while the government budget for Chaiyaphum, a demand-absorbing Rajabhat university, is equivalent to as much as 70 percent (Budget Bureau, 2018; Policy and Planning Bureau, 2019).

Rajabhat demand-absorbing institutions, although the largest group in the public sector, received only 16 percent of the total budget. This may be, in part, because they are teaching-only, rarely research oriented, and have low operating costs. In essence, the more established and prestigious the institutions, the greater their ability to secure funding and academic resources. Conversely, the less legitimate, the lower the income and the more quality aspects (students, faculty, teaching, etc.) will be affected. With limited financial and academic resources, demand-absorbing public HEIs face many challenges meeting the quality standards, financial responsibility, and accountability to their stakeholders.

Both private and public HEIs receive significant government aid in the form of Thailand's Student Loan Fund (SLF) policy. Revised in 1998 as part of the country's economic liberalization commitment to the International Monetary Fund, the policy aims to remove financial barriers to higher education by providing student loans with favorable repayment conditions (Ziderman, 2003).

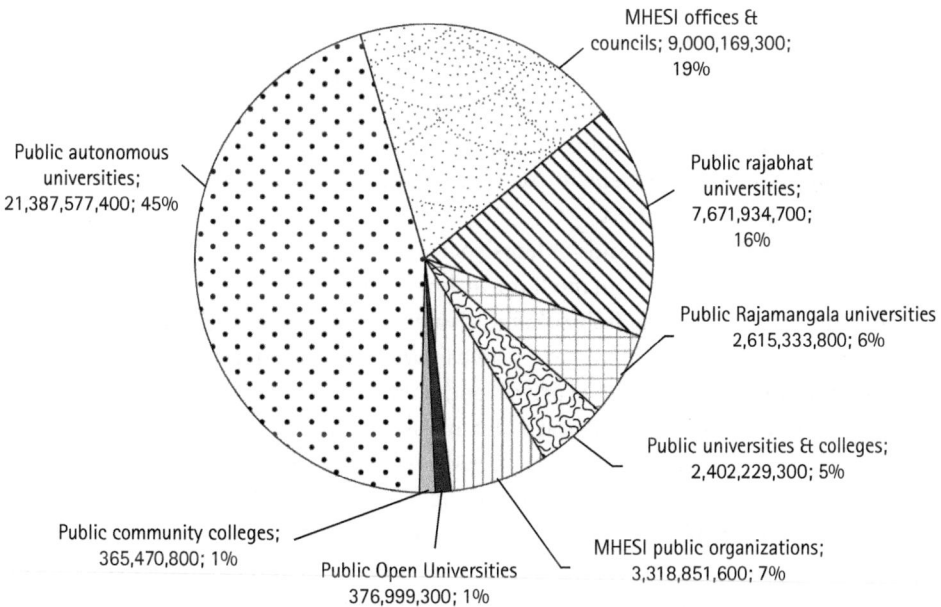

THE MHESI ANNUAL BUDGET EXPENDITURE BY TYPE
FISCAL YEAR 2021 (THAI BAHT; PERCENTAGE)

MHESI offices & councils; 9,000,169,300; 19%

Public autonomous universities; 21,387,577,400; 45%

Public rajabhat universities; 7,671,934,700; 16%

Public Rajamangala universities 2,615,333,800; 6%

Public universities & colleges; 2,402,229,300; 5%

MHESI public organizations; 3,318,851,600; 7%

Public community colleges; 365,470,800; 1%

Public Open Universities 376,999,300; 1%

FIGURE 39.4 The MHESI annual budget expenditure by type, fiscal year 2021 (Thai Baht; percentage)

Source: Budget Bureau (2020b).

The latest SLF (2020) specifies that eligible borrowers from both private and public sectors must be high school students, vocational education students, and baccalaureate and undergraduate students whose family's annual income is less than 200,000 Baht (US$6,165). Borrowers from both private and public HEIs receive similar loan amounts, yet the loan amount per annum varies by field of study, ranging from 60,000 Baht (US$1,850) for social science and 70,000 Baht (US$2,158) for engineering, science, and technology, to 200,000 Baht (US$6,165) for medicine, veterinary medicine, and dentistry (SLF, 2020). SLF also gives each borrower an extra 36,000 Baht (US$1,110) per annum for living expenses. In most cases, the loans sufficiently cover tuition fees for both private and public HEIs. For loan repayment, borrowers must begin paying back the loan amount starting two years after graduation. Students may enter into a mortgage plan of up to 15 years at a 1 percent annual interest rate to complete loan repayments.

While this policy has allowed access to higher education for a multitude of students, reaching almost 6 million borrowers across Thailand, less than a quarter of the total borrowers have successfully repaid their loans as of February 2021 (SLF, 2021). Approximately 60 percent of borrowers remain in a repayment process, while others have defaulted on their loans. Such a discrepancy between total loan disbursement and loan recovery is typical in Asia, where student loans are primarily subsidized by the government with softer lending conditions than commercial loans. Thai SLF was initially criticized for loan recovery rates of 40–50 percent, resulting in a burden on taxpayers but later started to show healthier re-collection rates as the SLF agency and commercial banks collaborated for a more robust repayment system (World Bank, 2012; Levy and Kanwar, 2013; Crocco, 2018).

For demand-absorbing private and public HEIs, SLF is a primary income source through tuition. Approximately 70–80 percent of students at demand-absorbing private HEIs are SLF borrowers, compared with 30 percent at semi-elite private universities (Praphamontripong, 2010). Still, public universities, especially demand-absorbing Rajabhat and Rajamangala, benefit from SLF as well; within the public sector, students from Rajabhat borrow the most.

An institution's legitimacy and students' socio-economic status are intrinsically linked with SLF funding. Students with medium-to-low socio-economic status who depend on SLF mostly enroll in demand-absorbing private HEIs and Rajabhat and Rajamangala public universities—which often have scarce financial and academic resources—if they are denied admission to semi-elite private and public universities. Presumably, students with low socio-economic status are at a higher risk of receiving a dubious education.

Thai private HEIs receive other indirect government subsidies as well, through government aids, a deduction and exemption of tax, and other academic privileges (Education Council, 2004). In particular, private HEIs receive governmental support through soft loans for infrastructure, faculty development, and laboratory equipment. For most private HEIs, these loans are essential for their operations, although the application process is cumbersome.

Private HEIs especially welcomed tax waivers since 2003 as a major form of financial relief. They are exempt from import tax for goods and equipment related to academia and research, and licensees and donors are exempt from income tax, specific business tax, and stamp duty for any land transfers and donations of non-movable property to private HEIs. Nevertheless, private HEIs have normally been required to pay an annual tax on property and donations—a bureaucratic burden for private universities with large campuses and those affiliated with religious foundations and philanthropic movements (Praphamontripong, 2010). The recent 2020 amendment to the tax law, however, now provides all private HEIs with a 90 percent reduction in their annual property tax. The change comes as welcome relief for many small non-elite private HEIs struggling during the current economic downturn resulting from the COVID-19 pandemic.

3.4.2 *Diversifying Income*

Both private and public HEIs in Thailand earn income from various sources beyond government aid. Tuition fees are an integral funding source, and they constitute the primary income for private HEIs, accounting for as much as 90 percent of the revenue stream. While tuition fees are capped for undergraduate Thai programs at public HEIs, some graduate and international programs at leading flagship public universities charge tuition fees equivalent to or even higher than most private institutions. Private HEIs have no caps on tuition fees.

Public universities are also encouraged to seek research grants/contracts from the business sector, commercialize university services and properties, campaign for donations/endowments, and charge fees for affiliated public healthcare facilities. For instance, both Mahidol University and Mae Fah Luang University have affiliated hospitals and other research businesses, while Chulalongkorn University owns 456 acres, 30 percent of which is zoned for commercial use (Chulalongkorn University, 2020).

Many private institutions now run profitable businesses that cater to the public, not just students and faculty: dormitory and sport facility rentals, publishing houses, private healthcare facilities, partnerships with business industries, the sale of goods, and public access to on-campus shopping malls and food plazas. Rangsit University, for example, owns RSU International Hospital and various healthcare centers; Assumption University has impressive residence halls, a laundry service, a gym, and a minimart; and both Dhurakij Pundit University and Dusit Thani College have their own hotels.

By law, public HEIs are not required to return all income and surplus to the state, and instead they often reinvest in different institutional funds. For all private HEIs—legally holding a "not-for-profit" status—70 percent of the profits must be reinvested in the institution while the remaining 30 percent are distributed to licensees and shareholders.

4. THE SLOW JOURNEY
TO INTERNATIONAL RECOGNITION

Thailand's higher education system continues to face significant challenges, including a declining population, stagnating enrollment, slow economic growth exacerbated by the COVID-19 pandemic, US–China trade tensions, domestic political uncertainty, and drought. The system risks stagnating, and it is imperative that Thai HEIs strive to improve quality and research capabilities to better compete with neighboring countries.

While the government's push to privatize public higher education and promote existing private higher education has created a burgeoning system with increasing institutions and student enrollment for overall growth, it has yet to improve academic quality and international recognition. Only a handful of leading flagship public universities show international academic potential and legitimacy, while most Thai HEIs are still non-elite demand-absorbing, with a strong perception that they lack academic integrity and research and innovation (Altbach, 2004; Slantcheva and Levy, 2007).

At a national level, the Thai government has taken steps to elevate its higher education quality into the international arena by establishing the MHESI to promote and support policies related to higher education, science, and research and innovation. Initiated in 2018, the government's Engineering, Technology and Innovation Workforce Development (KOSEN) project aims to strengthen collaboration among the government, industry, and academia to enhance national competitiveness and respond to the labor market demands for engineers and technicians (Vandeweyer et al., 2021). Partnering with Japan's National Institute of Technology, Thailand's KOSEN institutes were established at two flagship public universities (King Mongkut's Institute of Technology Ladkrabang and King Mongkut's University of Technology Thonburi), a few public vocational colleges, and the private serious-demand-absorbing Thai-Nichi Institute of Technology. In 2020, MHESI also adopted the Policy and Strategy for Higher Education, Science, Research and Innovation 2020–2027, which defined the objectives and key results for seven program management units for research and innovation grants (NXPO, 2020).

Along with research and innovation, the government's policy agenda to promote healthy higher education market competition should consider allowing the mechanisms of the higher education economies to work freely with minimal government intervention. To increase efficiency and success in higher education reform, Thailand needs better political stability and less overturn in leadership overseeing HEIs. The government must offer coherent regulations, policies, and laws that promote sustainable reform and development.

At an institutional level, to survive in this increasingly competitive market, both private and public HEIs must diversify their academic programs and funding sources beyond government aid. The current focus on the commercialization of institutional assets has proven a useful strategy, as has aggressive recruitment of international students. Further creation of specialized academic programs to better address the labor market demands may also be another useful strategy.

Under such competitive conditions, the survival of Thai HEIs in a privatized higher education marketplace depends critically on the institutions' ability to secure funding and academic resources. Semi-elite private universities and flagship public universities are adapting well to the competitive market, while other HEIs continue to struggle. Non-elite demand-absorbing private and public HEIs are the most vulnerable to competition, and any changes or uncertainty in governmental aid, especially SLF, will lead to closures, mergers, or sales.

Because Thai higher education has become an international endeavor, all HEIs must ultimately yield to an internationally recognized quality standard—not an easy task for non-elite demand-absorbing HEIs with limited academic and financial capabilities. The existing QA policy is useful but is only the beginning of a long and slow march toward international recognition.

Foreign investments in the Thai higher education market could remain a crucial answer to the financial challenges, as long as HEIs invest in effective quality control measures. Even so, Thailand should seek long-term solutions for its higher education financial sustainability without relying primarily on foreign support.

Ultimately, to promote a healthy and competitive higher education market, the current Thai higher education system—flooded with institutions with wide-ranging aspirations—requires more conformity, perhaps in the form of private–public partnerships (PPPs). These could reduce overcrowding in specific regions by allowing institutions to legally partner or merge to increase efficiency, share responsibility, and avoid redundancy. PPPs might also help demand-absorbing HEIs in both sectors focus on specialized programs for a niche market.

Despite many public policy challenges, Thailand's move to a privatized higher education system has brought welcome growth to the country. Ongoing initiatives and changing market forces continue to shape both private and public HEIs to better serve not only Thai students, but a growing number of international students, pushing Thailand's higher education offerings onto the world stage.[2]

References

ADB (2009). *Good Practice in Cost Sharing and Financing in Higher Education*. Mandaluyong City, Philippines: Asian Development Bank.

ADB (2011a). *Higher Education Across Asia: An Overview of Issues and Strategies*. Mandaluyong City, Philippines: Asian Development Bank.

ADB (2011b). *Improving Instructional Quality: Focus on Faculty Development. Higher Education in Dynamic Asia*. Mandaluyong City, Philippines: Asian Development Bank.

Altbach, P. G. (2004). "The past and future of Asian universities: Twenty-first century challenges." In P. G. Altbach and T. Umakoshi (eds.), *Asian Universities: Historical Perspectives and Contemporary Challenges* (pp. 13–32). Baltimore, MD: Johns Hopkins University Press.

[2] The authors are grateful for valuable comments from Distinguished Prof. Daniel C. Levy, Director of Program for Research on Private Higher Education (PROPHE), University at Albany, SUNY; Asst. Prof. Oliver S. Crocco, Louisiana State University; and Prof. Suchatvee Suwansawat, Chairperson of the Council of University Presidents of Thailand.

Budget Bureau (2018). *Akekasan Ngobpraman Chababtee Saam: Ngobpraman Raijai Porsor 2562 Mahawittayalai Mahidol* [Annual Budget Expenditure No. 3 Fiscal Year 2019 Mahidol University]. Bangkok: Prime Minister's Office.

Budget Bureau (2020a). *Praratchabanyat Ngobpraman Raijai Prajumpee* [Government Budget Expenditure Act]. Bangkok: Prime Minister's Office. http://www.bb.go.th/topic.php?gid= 543&mid=308, accessed April 2, 2021.

Budget Bureau (2020b). *Praratchabanyat Ngobpraman Raijai Prajumpee Ngobpraman Porsor 2564* [Government Budget Expenditure Act Fiscal Year 2021]. Bangkok: Prime Minister's Office.

Chalapati, S. (2007). "The internationalisation of higher education in Thailand: Case studies of two English-medium business graduate programs." Doctoral dissertation, School of Global Studies, Social Science and Planning Design and Social Context Portfolio, RMIT University, Australia. https://researchbank.rmit.edu.au/eserv/rmit:6630/Chalapati.pdf

Chulalongkorn University (2020). "Ownership of the land presented to the University by King Vajiravudh." *100 Stories of the Past Century*. Chulalongkorn University. http://www.cu100. chula.ac.th/story-en/630/, accessed June 27, 2020.

Clark, B. R. (1983). *The Higher Education System: Academic Organization in Cross-National Perspective*. Berkeley, CA: University of California Press.

Crocco, O. S. (2018). "Thai higher education: Privatization and massification." In G. W. Fry (ed.), *Education in Thailand: An Old Elephant in Search of a New Mahout* (pp. 223–255). Singapore: Springer.

Darling, F. C. (1962). "American policy in Thailand." *Western Political Quarterly*, 15/1, 93–110.

Dumrongkiat, M. (2018). "Universities, industry tackle labour market mismatch." *Bangkok Post*, February 21. https://www.bangkokpost.com/thailand/general/1415094/ universities-industry-tackle-labour-market-mismatch

Education Council (2004). *National Education Act B.E. 2542 (1999) and Amendments (Second National Education Act B.E. 2545 (2002))*. Bangkok: Ministry of Education.

Fineman, D. (1997). *A Special Relationship: The United States and Military Government in Thailand, 1947–1958*. Honolulu: University of Hawai'i Press.

Johnstone, D. B. (2006). *Financing Higher Education: Cost-Sharing in International Perspective*. Rotterdam: CIHE Boston College/Sense Publishers.

Kanjananiyot, P. and Chaitiamwong, C. (2018). "The internationalization of Thai higher education over the decades: Formidable challenges remain!" In G. W. Fry (ed.), *Education in Thailand: An Old Elephant in Search of a New Mahout* (pp. 271–321). Singapore: Springer.

Knight, J. (2006). *Internationalization of Higher Education: New Directions, New Challenges: 2005 IAU Global Survey Report*. Paris: International Association of Universities.

Lao, R. (2015). *A Critical Study of Thailand's Higher Education Reforms: The Culture of Borrowing*. New York: Routledge.

Lao, R. (2018). "Quality and autonomous universities: Policy promises and the paradox of leadership." In G. W. Fry (ed.), *Education in Thailand: An Old Elephant in Search of a New Mahout* (pp. 257–270). Singapore: Springer.

Levy, D. C. (1986). *Higher Education and the State in Latin America: Private Challenges to Public Dominance*. Chicago: University of Chicago Press.

Levy, D. C. (2019). "The family album inside the world's private higher education landscape." In P. G. Altbach, E. Choi, M. R. Allen, and H. de Wit (eds.), *The Global Phenomenon of Family-Owned or Managed Universities* (pp. 9–28). Leiden: Brill.

Levy, D. C. (forthcoming). *A World of Private Higher Education: A Global Analysis*.

Levy, D. C. and Kanwar, P. P. (2013). "Student finance in Asia: Privatization amid decisive inter-sectoral difference." In D. E. Heller and C. Callender (eds.), *Student Financing of Higher Education: A Comparative Perspective* (pp. 174–199). New York: Routledge.

MHESI (2019). "Rabob phawa karnmeengantham khong bundit" [Employment status of graduates]. Office of Higher Education Commission, MHESI. http://www.employ.mua.go.th/index.php/MTB8fG1haW4vZGV0YWlssc3ViMS8yNTYy, accessed July 9, 2020.

MHESI (2020). "Higher education statistics download." Ministry of Higher Education Science Research and Innovation. http://www.info.mua.go.th/info/, accessed February 10, 2020.

NXPO (2020). "NXPO, TSRI and 7 program management units unveil 2020 science, research and innovation budget." https://www.nxpo.or.th/th/en/4273/, accessed May 1, 2020.

OECD (2020). *OECD Economic Surveys: Thailand 2020: Economic Assessment.* Paris: OECD Publishing. https://doi.org/10.1787/ad2e50fa-en.

Policy and Planning Bureau (2019). *Ngobpraman Raijai Prajumpee Ngobpraman Porsor 2562 Mahawittayalai Rajabhat Chaiyaphum* [Annual Budget Expenditure Fiscal Year 2019 of Chaiyaphum Rajabhat University]. Chaiyaphum, Thailand: Chaiyaphum Rajabhat University.

Prachachat Dhurakij (2018). "Toon Chin Maosua Dhurakij Thai Hoob Mahalai Rongpayaban Condo" [Chinese investment buying Thai businesses: University, hospital, condo]. *Prachachat Online*, September 29. https://www.prachachat.net/property/news-226549, accessed April 23, 2020.

Prachachat Dhurakij (2019). "Longmahalaichin Book Rajamangala Funkhatoong Kumluksood Thai" [Rajamangala attracting Chinese students: Getting commissions, controlling the curriculum]. *Prachachat Online*, July 22. https://www.prachachat.net/education/news-351998, accessed April 26, 2020.

Prachachat Dhurakij (2020). "Mor Akekachon KangDu Sor Jengranao Reaanfree-Mapengang Dailodperm" [Private universities compete fiercely – potential closure – free tuition fee]. *Prachachat Online*, June 6. https://www.prachachat.net/education/news-474099, accessed July 18, 2020.

Praphamontripong, P. (2010). "Intra-sectoral diversity: A political economy of Thai private higher education." Doctoral dissertation, Educational Administration and Policy Studies, University at Albany, State University of New York.

Praphamontripong, P. (2011). "Government policies and institutional diversity of private higher education: Thailand in regional perspective." *Journal of Comparative Policy Analysis*, 13/4, 411–424.

QS Quacquarelli Symonds (2020). "QS Asia University Rankings 2020." https://www.topuniversities.com/university-rankings/asian-university-rankings/2020, accessed July 18, 2020.

Ratchakitchanubeksa (2020). "Thai laws." http://www.mratchakitcha.soc.go.th/index.html, accessed April 22, 2021.

Royal Coast Review (2019). "Chinese education investor purchases Stamford University." *Royal Coast Review Thailand*, July 1. https://royalcoastreview.com/2019/07/chinese-education-investor-purchases-stamford-university/, accessed April 26, 2020.

Sagarik, D. (2014). "Educational expenditures in Thailand: Development, trends, and distribution." *Citizenship, Social and Economics Education*, 13/1, 53–66.

Slantcheva, S. and Levy, D. C. (eds.) (2007). *Private Higher Education in Post-Communist Europe: In Search of Legitimacy*. New York: Palgrave Macmillan.

SLF (2020). *Types of Loans, Scope of SLF Lending, and Eligible Fields of Study Year 2020.* Bangkok: Student Loan Fund. https://www.studentloan.or.th/th/news/1578646950, accessed April 28, 2020.

SLF (2021). "Satithi kormoon kor yor sor" [SLF statistics as of February 28, 2021]. https://www.studentloan.or.th/th/statistics/1540900492, accessed April 26, 2021.

Smith, A. (1776). *An Inquiry into the Nature and Causes of the Wealth of Nations.* 1993 World's Classic edition. New York: Oxford University Press.

Sussangkarn, C. and Nikomborirak, D. (2016). "Thailand's long-term growth: Aspiration, reality and challenges." *Asian Economic Papers,* 15/2, 23–43.

Thai Post (2018). "Mahalai pawha big Tu aowjing tadngob" [Scared universities: Serious Big Tu's budget cut]. *Thai Post,* January 24. https://www.thaipost.net/main/detail/1684, accessed April 22, 2021.

Trow, M. A. (1987). "The analysis of status." In B. R. Clark (ed.), *Perspectives on Higher Education: Eight Disciplinary and Comparative Views* (pp. 132–164). Berkeley and Los Angeles, CA: University of California Press.

UNESCO Institute for Statistics (UIS) (2016). "Outbound mobility ratio by host region – all regions, both sexes (%)." http://data.uis.unesco.org/index.aspx?queryid=174#, accessed April 24, 2020.

Vandeweyer, M., Espinoza, R., Reznikova, L., Lee, M., and Herabat, T. (2021). "Thailand's education system and skills imbalances: Assessment and policy recommendations." OECD Economics Department Working Papers No. 1641. https://dx.doi.org/10.1787/b79addb6-en

Wit, H. de, Deca, L., and Hunter, F. (2015). "Internationalization of higher education: What can research add to the policy debate?" In A. Curaj, L. Matei, R. Pricopie, J. Salmi, and P. Scott (eds.), *The European Higher Education Area: Between Critical Reflections and Future Policies* (pp. 3–12). New York: Springer.

World Bank (2012). *Putting Higher Education to Work: Skills and Research for Growth in East Asia.* Washington, DC: International Bank for Reconstruction and Development/World Bank.

World Bank (2019). *World Development Indicators.* http://datatopics.worldbank.org/world-development-indicators/, accessed February 13, 2020.

World Bank (2021). *Thailand Economic Monitor: Restoring Incomes Recovering Jobs.* Washington, DC: International Bank for Reconstruction and Development/World Bank.

Ziderman, A. (2003). *Student Loans in Thailand: Are They Effective, Equitable, Sustainable?* Vol. 1 of *Policy Research and Dialogue: Student Loans Schemes in Asia.* Bangkok: UNESCO/IIEP.

CHAPTER 40

HIGHER EDUCATION IN MYANMAR

MARIE LALL, CAMILLE KANDIKO HOWSON, AND
AYE AYE TUN

1. INTRODUCTION: BACKGROUND AND HISTORY OF MYANMAR'S HIGHER EDUCATION SYSTEM

IN the early part of the twentieth century Myanmar had a strong and thriving higher education system, with Rangoon University (now the University of Yangon) being one of the top universities in Asia, recruiting students from across the Southeast Asian region. However, decades of underinvestment and civil strife over 70 years have resulted in the slow and steady decay of Myanmar's state education system, including higher education (Lall, 2016). In 1964, under the socialist regime, all private schools and universities were ordered to close. The students' anti-government protest of 1988 again led to the closure of all universities for two years. Another series of student strikes in 1996 and 1998 resulted in further periods of closures. In Yangon, the University of Yangon was closed for 10 out of 12 years. Students' engagement in pro-democracy movements politicized higher education and led to the government tightening control and limiting funding, curtailing higher education's ability to be an engine for economic and social change.

After the reopening of universities and colleges in 1999, the government relocated universities to different regions and undergraduate programs were moved to campuses far away from any urban center to avoid further student protests. This extreme version of domestic and international isolation has caused the quality of higher education to slip to dramatically low levels. Reforming universities became a government priority when the country started to open again after the 2010 elections with major education reforms commencing in 2012 (Kandiko Howson and Lall, 2020 Lall, 2021a). The reforms have been interrupted by a military coup on February 1, 2021. Myanmar's unique history of isolation and neglect continues to impact its higher education, and recent political events do not signal a clear trajectory for the future of higher education in the country.

2. The Size and Structure of Higher Education: Facts and Figures

Myanmar is amongst the least developed countries in the world (United Nations Development Programme, 2016) and universities operate on very low levels of government grant. The government allocated 1.92 percent of gross domestic product to education in 2018 and 1.93 percent in 2019 (MPF, 2018b; UNESCO, 2021).[1] There is little research on higher education in Myanmar and limited data in the public domain (Lall and South, 2014). The higher education system in Myanmar is highly centralized. Its 193 universities are under the jurisdiction of nine ministries (see Table 40.1) and fall into two broad categories: arts and sciences universities and the technical and professional universities. Teacher education colleges recently came under the remit of the Ministry of Education (MoE). Private higher education institutions in Myanmar are not permitted to identify themselves as universities, even if they are degree-awarding (Heslop, 2019).

According to UNESCO data, the total tertiary-level enrollment in Myanmar in 2018 was 932,901 of which 58.6 percent was female (2021). There is little structural diversity in the tertiary sector, with most degrees offered at the bachelor level. Only 3 percent of tertiary enrollments were in the short cycle level and less than 2 percent at the master's level, and only 2,785 enrollments at the doctoral level (2021). Mobility into the country is limited, with the total number of foreign students in the country at 425 in 2017–2018, alongside 176 foreign experts (MoE, 2019a, p. 54, fig. 2.6.5 and 2.6.6), with 62 percent from China (fig. 2.6.10) (see Table 40.2).

Myanmar's higher education gross enrollment ratio (GER) is low at 16 percent (UNESCO, 2019a). This is due to a weak secondary school structure. Baseline data collected before the start of the reforms in 2010/11 showed that from the around 1.1 million new entrants to Grade 1 each year, only around 300,000 reached Grade 11; two-thirds of which failed matriculation every year (Education Management and Information Systems study cited in Lall, 2021a). Entrance to university depends on students' scores in the matriculation exam, taken in Grade 11 at the age of 16.[2] Private schools are only recognized if they offer the government curriculum, which means

---

[1] Compared to other Southeast Asian countries this is very low: in 2018 Cambodia allocated 2.2 percent, Vietnam 4.2 percent, and Malaysia 4.5 percent (UNESCO, 2021).

[2] University entrance was being changed as part of the ongoing curricular and examination reforms process. It is unclear at the time of writing if the matriculation will be retained and what year they will be taken as the Myanmar schooling system was being changed to 12 years.

Table 40.1 Number and type of higher education institutions under the ministries

No.	Ministry	Type and number of HEIs	Total
1.	Education	32 Arts/Science universities; 5 Arts/Science degree colleges; 2 Arts/Science colleges; 2 universities of education; 3 universities of economics; 2 universities of foreign languages; 2 universities of distance education; 1 national academy of management; 2 universities of information and communication technologies; 25 education degree colleges	76
2	Health	5 universities of medicine; 2 universities of dental medicine; 2 universities of medical technology; 2 universities of pharmacology; 2 universities of nursing; 1 university of public health; 1 university of community health; 1 university of indigenous medicine	16
3	Agriculture, livestock breeding and irrigation	1 university of agriculture; 1 university of livestock breeding and veterinary science; 4 universities of cooperatives; 1 college of lacquerware art	7
4	Religious affairs and culture	2 national universities of culture and arts; 1 international university of Theravada Buddhism; 2 national universities of pariyatti sasana (i.e., propagation of Buddhist scriptures)	5
5	Natural resources and environmental preservation	1 university of forestry	1
6	Defense	1 national university of defense; 1 military academy; 1 Tatmadaw (Defense Services) university of medicine; 1 Defense Services university of technology; 1 Defense Services university of nursing and paramedical science; 1 Defense Services university of computer studies and technology	6
7	Border areas	1 university of the development of the national races of the union; 2 degree colleges of the development of the national races of the union	3
8	Transportation	1 maritime university; 1 mercantile maritime college	2
9	Science and technology	33 universities of technology; 27 universities of computer studies; 7 government technical colleges	67
	Total		183

Source: Presentation by Dr Aung Khin Myint, undated, http:// moe.gov.mm (accessed February 16, 2020) and http://www.most.gov.mm/ (accessed April 27, 2022).

that students who complete their basic education in the private sector generally cannot access Myanmar universities.

In 2017–2018, Myanmar had 13,610 teachers in higher education (MoE, 2019a). The government sent 1,546 staff on overseas study tours and 350 received Leadership and Management training from the National Institute for Higher Education Development (MoE, 2019a, p. 158). According to the government's Comprehensive Education Sector

Table 40.2 Students in higher education in Myanmar, 2017–2018

Institutional type	Number of students (undergraduate through to PhD programs)
Arts & Sciences Universities	266,833
Technological Universities, Universities of Computer Studies	75,455
Education Colleges	20,069
Sub-total	**362, 357**
Universities of Distance Education	515,002
Total	**877,359**

Source: MoE (2019a).

Review (CESR, 2013), 83 percent of academic staff and 60 percent of students in 2012 were female.[3]

2.1 Distance Education

Myanmar's distance education system has around 500,000 part-time students. Distance education offers access to the poorer sections of society, where students can study part-time whilst still working and living at home. It also received state support as a result of the 1988 and 1990 student protests—students who are not living together in university residences are less likely to get involved in national protests (Lall, 2021a). The current system is coordinated by two distance education universities, Yangon University of Distance Education for Lower Myanmar, and Mandalay University of Distance Education for Upper Myanmar. There are 19 bachelor-level courses delivered by 35 learning centers in day universities providing national coverage (Fawssett and Gregson, 2016, p. 3). However, teachers have not been trained to deliver courses appropriately through a distance learning pedagogy. Distance education arts students attend the day university twice a year, once to enroll, between January to March, the other time for 10 days to prepare for and sit the exam at the end of the academic year (October–November) for what is in effect a cramming session that covers the same material as what is usually delivered over four months for full-time students. Science students are additionally required to attend 12 weekends over the year for practical sessions.

There are no dedicated distance education staff. All sessions are delivered by university teachers mostly in Burmese—something done on top of their regular workload of teaching university students. Most people in Myanmar are aware of the low quality of

---

[3] The duration and funding source of the tours are not in the public domain.

the distance education system, yet interestingly research by the Open University found that employers (that were interviewed for that research) said they did not distinguish between distance education and full-time higher education degrees, rather employment depended on the skills of the candidates (Fawssett and Gregson, 2016).

2.2 Education College Reforms: Becoming Higher Education Institutions

As part of the reformation process, all two-year government Education Colleges (ECs) were to be transformed into four-year Education Degree Colleges (EDCs). These reforms have expanded the higher education sector and interface it with the basic education sub-sector.

There are 25 ECs across Myanmar, with at least one in each state or region, providing pre-service teacher education to prepare student teachers to teach at primary and lower secondary school levels in government schools.[4] ECs were previously Teacher Training Schools prior to their upgrade in 1998 (San Yee, 2017). In the 2019–2020 academic year the new four-year degree program started, and ECs admitted 3,343 first year student teachers (1,676 female and 1,667 male).[5] These numbers were lower than those for previous years, presumably to ensure manageability for ECs in the roll out of the four-year degree program. Teacher Educators are either former upper secondary schoolteachers with education degrees, usually with a bachelor or master's degree in education, or former university teachers or graduates in non-education specializations.[6] The medium of instruction is Burmese for all subject areas except English in the first and second years of the curriculum.[7]

The plan to upgrade ECs into EDCs in accordance with the National Education Strategic Plan (described in more detail below) initiated the subsequent shift of jurisdiction over them from the Department of Education Research, Planning and Training to the newly set up Teacher Education Section in the Department of Higher Education.[8] As part of preparations for EDCs, the organizational structure with new designations

---

[4] Pre-service education for upper secondary school teachers is provided by two Universities of Education, which is under a different section of the Department of Higher Education, that oversees also Universities of Arts and Sciences.

[5] Calculation of the numbers based on admission lists at http://www.moe.gov.mm/?q=ec-admission-2019 (in Myanmar language).

[6] According to informal conversations with EC staff, the previous curriculum distinguished between "methodology" and "subject knowledge." Hence, there are Teacher Educators with two different types of qualifications.

[7] The second year curriculum is being developed. It is very likely that the medium of instruction will be English for the third and fourth years.

[8] It is possible that English will be the medium of instruction in the third and fourth year curriculum as in other higher education institutions. However, English will pose a language barrier to both Teacher Educators and student teachers.

for faculty, which will be aligned with that of higher education institutions under the Department for Higher Education, was submitted to but has yet to be approved by the MoE.[9] ECs did join the higher education community through their representative principals who were engaging with the Rectors Committee (described below).[10]

Although preparations for transitioning of ECs to the EDCs started with the CESR, the actual implementation began in 2019, with the training of teacher educators on the new curriculum for the degree program and the introduction of the first-year curriculum.

The EC reforms were mainly supported by two projects: Strengthening Pre-Service Teacher Education Myanmar, implemented by UNESCO (DFAT, 2017; UNESCO, 2019b); and Towards Results in Education and English run by a British Council-led consortium (British Council, 2020). The former focused primarily on developing a Teacher Competency Standards Framework on which the new four-year EC curriculum is based; reviewing the existing EC curriculum and framework development for the new four-year curriculum; and capacity building of information and communications technology Teacher Educators through training, the installation of internet infrastructure in all ECs and the development of an e-portal. The Towards Results in Education and English project aimed to improve the quality of teaching by Teacher Educators and academic oversight of management staff in Teacher Education Institutions (Myanmar Teacher Education Working Group, 2019).

3. THE NATIONAL CONTEXT FOR EQUITY AND INCLUSION

Myanmar is a multi-ethnic country, divided into seven states (populated mostly by ethnic nationality communities[11]) and seven regions dominated by the majority Burman (*Bamar*) ethnic group. Demographic statistics remain contested, despite a census—the first in 31 years held in 2014—which calculated the population at 51.4 million people (Government of the Union of Myanmar, 2015). It is estimated that non-Burman communities make up around 30–40 percent of the population.[12] The official categories of 135 "national races" (*taingyintha*) recognized by the government are deeply problematic, representing arbitrary and often imposed identities (Cheesman, 2017). Under military rule, the Bamar majority used this diversity as an excuse to impose its language and culture, a process referred to as *Burmanization*, that started in the early 1960s after Ne

---

[9] According to informal conversations with EC staff.

[10] From informal conversation with an EC principal.

[11] Non-Burman ethnic communities reject the term "minorities" and prefer to be referred to as "ethnic nationality communities."

[12] Including Shan 9 percent, Karen 7 percent, Rakhine 4 percent, Chinese 3 percent, Indian 2 percent, Mon 2 percent, and other 5 percent (World Fact Book, 2020).

Win's military coup allegedly to keep the country united. Having to learn in Burmese rather than starting education in their mother tongue (through, for example, a mother tongue-based multilingual system) has meant that ethnic nationals often drop out of school, very rarely making it to university.

Those ethnic nationals who do stay in the education system are often unable to join university due to poorer matriculation marks, resulting in a cycle of lifelong disadvantage for the individual, their family, and the whole community. These research findings are borne out in the census data of 2014 that shows how children and families in ethnic states are less literate, access fewer schools, and are in the end less well-off than those living in the Bamar-dominated regions. This disparity is aggravated for those in rural areas, including remote and conflict-affected regions, where there are few, if any, Bamar residents and where government education often cannot reach. Despite this disparity, the main focus of "inclusion" in education for poorer sections of society has traditionally been through donations to monasteries to support monastic schools rather than notions of equality and equity. Issues of unequal access to education for different ethnic groups has been brought to the fore of the (incomplete) peace process in parallel with the wider education and other reforms (South and Lall, 2018; Lall, 2021a).

Currently, there is no ethnic breakdown of participation in higher education.[13] The CESR Phase 1 Report had already identified this gap, saying it was unclear how Myanmar's wide ethnic diversity was represented in higher education (Welch and Hayden, 2013, p. 1). There are, however, regional universities in ethnic states that operate quite differently from those in urban centers. For example, universities in ethnic states will often have local staff who will not be rotated as part of the national system. Based on her interviews, Heslop (2019) argues that setting up universities in ethnic states has been part of politically motivated integration efforts across conflict-affected regions.

But the inequities go beyond ethnicity. The CESR Phase 1 Report quotes that only 11 percent of Myanmar youth are able to access higher education (Welch and Hayden, 2013). Based on data from the 2014 census, there are higher urban rates of education completion, and much higher numbers of urban female than male students enrolled in higher education institutions. The feminization of higher education is in part due to low salaries, transfer orders, as well as not being strongly associated with routes of power, making it less attractive as a career for men. Wealth inequality is also vast: 68 percent of young people from the richest quintile (top 20 percent) attain education levels beyond secondary education versus only 1.2 percent from those from the poorest quintile going beyond secondary education (Government of the Union of Myanmar, 2015). Thus, there is very little access to higher education overall and hardly any for ethnic minorities, resulting in a missed opportunity for higher education to be a site of integration or social mobility.

---

[13] The Census (Government of the Union of Myanmar, 2015) shows the breakdown of people whose highest education attainment is post-secondary education by state, but not by ethnic group. In any case the percentage of those having completed tertiary education in ethnic states is lower than the national average of 9 percent (Government of the Union of Myanmar, 2015, p. 56).

3.1 Access and Inclusion Challenges in ECs

Recent policy changes in ethnic states suggest access to ECs appears now to be more equitable and inclusive. Student teachers in each township in EC catchment areas are selected on the basis of data on teachers needed in the township and ECs' capacity to accommodate student teachers. Therefore, applicants in remote, rural, ethnic, or poor townships do not have to compete with those in townships with better education and economic opportunities or with a predominantly Myanmar population.[14] ECs have also made some progress in inclusive access in terms of gender. According to the MoE (2019a, p. 48) the numbers of female student teachers who were awarded teacher certificates have far exceeded those of male student teachers from 2014–2015 to 2017–2018.[15] The gender ratio amongst student teachers was more balanced in 2019–2020.[16] Moreover, ECs have relaxed restrictions on disability and have begun to admit student teachers with minor disabilities.

4. Challenges of Autonomy, Quality, and Control

The military leaders never positioned higher education, or education in general as part of a strategy to boost economic growth (Lall, 2016), as has been the case in countries such as Thailand, Malaysia, and South Korea. To date, Myanmar's universities have operated under a centralized system, with each ministry responsible for the higher education institutions and their curriculum under it, leaving universities with hardly any autonomy.[17] The curriculum and the assessments are set by the MoE. The hiring of

---

[14] This new practice started in the 2017–2018 academic year. Previously, applicants from the Bamar majority could apply to ECs in ethnic areas. As many of them usually performed better in matriculation examinations than ethnic students did, they were admitted to ECs at the expense of ethnic applicants (information from informal conversations with teacher educators; see also MoE, 2019b, 2019c).

[15] 2,606 female and 124 male students in 2014–2015 and 39,249 female and 8,821 male students in the 2017–2018 academic year.

[16] Some EC staff believed that selection criteria for male applicants were relaxed in 2019–2020, in order to increase male teachers and improve the gender ratio among schoolteachers (see MoE, 2019b).

[17] "Universities have 'no authority on appointments, travel, research, promotion, curriculum development, disciplinary association conference, even the planning of a golden anniversary university conference' (Senior staff comment). Another rector noted that there was no authority to appoint even lower-order maintenance staff, even a window-cleaner. Everything had to go up 'through proper channels'. Even when a member of staff is invited to a prestigious conference in the region, the conference date may have passed before any decision is taken 'on high'. If someone is allowed to travel to a meeting, the passport has to be returned afterwards" (King, 2013, p. 16). "HEIs have been formally without financial autonomy since the 1970s. However, from 1998, there has been the possibility of a measure of income generation through what are termed Human Resource Development (HRD) courses in most if not all HEIs under the MOE. These often take place early in the day, before regular working hours, or after work. As the CESR notes, the scale and the income associated with what are in effect parallel courses are not well-known. But in at least one major university, the HRD numbers in masters and diploma courses are almost 50% of the entire university enrolment. Also, CESR notes that the total number of HRD courses are 195 as compared with regular courses which are 215" (King, 2013, p. 17).

staff is also coordinated by the government and most staff are rotated every two to four years to universities around the country, making the setting up of research teams almost impossible. The centralized "command and control" system has resulted in strict hierarchies with many senior academics worried about taking decisions that might be counter to the Ministry's wishes. Universities, therefore, have not been able to develop their own research programs. Reforms started only recently to engage with issues of access, quality, and the designing of independent curricula.

The main issues faced by the higher education sector are the quality of what is taught and the teaching methods, as academic teaching staff are not research active in an international sense and courses need updating to meet international standards. The teaching language is theoretically English; however, this is rarely the case because the academic staff (as well as students) do not necessarily speak English well enough. Quality of teaching and learning is poor with rote learning as the norm, outdated textbooks, lack of information technology infrastructure, high teacher–student ratios and salaries that are deemed "unattractive" (Welch and Hayden, 2013, p. 4). The system is under-resourced and lacking specialized teaching spaces such as laboratories.

The current heavily centralized system presents challenges to developing a quality higher education system, including:

- Excessive bureaucratization
- Precariousness of academic leadership
- Widespread passive attitude
- A system that does not inspire an "active culture of learning"
- Insufficient budget and financial allocation (CHINLONE, 2018).

Myanmar is ranked 145th out of 145 countries on the World Bank's Knowledge Economy Index when weighted by population, and its graduate employability is very low—the sign of a "poorly aligned higher education system" (CHINLONE, 2018).[18]

5. THE WIDER REFORMS

As described in the introduction, Myanmar was under military rule between 1962 and 2010. A pathway to change opened around 2005, with a new military-drafted Constitution in 2008 and elections in 2010. The Constitution reserves control of three key ministries as well as 25 percent of all seats in all parliaments for the Tatmadaw, the Myanmar military. The first civilianized government under President Thein Sein started a comprehensive reform process with three priorities: national reconciliation with the National League for Democracy (NLD) led by Daw Aung San Suu Kyi, ethnic peace with the (roughly) 20 ethnic armed groups, and economic reforms. Education reforms were

[18] Data from 2012 when Knowledge Economy Index last reported. https://knoema.com/aomssce/knowledge-economy-index.

added shortly after. Whilst democracy was not on offer (Lall, 2016), a new participatory system ensured that in 2015 the NLD won a majority of seats—as they did again in November 2020.

Between 2011 and 2020 (before COVID forced the country into lockdown), Myanmar went through a period of opening up and economic growth. This had a limited effect on the demand for higher education. From 2011–2012 to 2016–2017 the largest growth was seen in engineering and health subjects (Ministry of Labour, 2018, pp. 6–9, table 10). The total number of students enrolled increased by 14.5 percent from 2016–2017 to 2017–2018 (MoE, 2019a).[19] The enrollment for Distance Education also increased from 324,537 students in 2014 to 516,701 in 2017 (Ministry of Planning and Finance, 2018a, pp. 189–190).

In a forthcoming chapter on Myanmar's higher education, Mark Brown discusses how there is a mismatch between what education and training higher education offers and the skills required in the labor market. In the study conducted by Bernhardt et al. (2017) employers mention that the workforce is inadequately educated. This had already been concluded in a study by Boateng et al. in 2014. Brown cites that the unemployment rate amongst graduates is higher than the national unemployment rate (9.3 percent vs. 3.8 percent—Ministry of Labour, Immigration and Population, 2014, p. 5 cited in Brown, in press). He also explains how the job market is unlikely to provide adequate job opportunities, with graduates already competing for low-paid and unskilled jobs. The fault for this lies with the universities as the National Education Policy Commission chairman admits that curricula are not developed with industry in mind (Myo Kywe, 2020 cited in Brown, forthcoming).

6. Education Reforms and the National Education Strategic Plan

6.1 The Comprehensive Education Sector Review

Initiated by President Thein Sein's government in 2011–2012, the government started the CESR as part of wider socio-political and economic reforms, spearheaded by the MoE and supported by a range of international development partners including the Asian Development Bank, UNICEF, and national aid agencies including the United Kingdom and Australia. These reforms changed the education landscape dramatically and resulted in the creation of the five-year National Education Sector Plan, the guiding

---

[19] More recent data were not available.

document for the whole education sector that was renamed the National Education Strategic Plan (NESP) after the elections in 2015, but remained broadly accepted by the NLD government that subsequently took power after the 2015 elections (Lall, 2016).

The drafting of the National Education Law in 2014 was a major landmark. It attempted to address the key issues facing higher education in Myanmar, including the autonomy of universities, the right to form unions, and the right of universities to formulate their own curriculum (Kamibeppu and Chao, 2017). However, the law was not without controversy and believing that it did not go far enough, student protests rocked the streets of Yangon and other cities in Myanmar in 2014. Unlike with previous protests, government representatives met with the student leaders to discuss their demands. This resulted in minor concessions from the government and a re-issuing of the National Education Law in 2015.

Education, and higher education in particular, remained a key priority of the NLD government. The appointment of Dr Myo Thein Gyi, the former rector of West Yangon University and a hardliner during the 2014 student protests, as the Minister of Education in 2016, resulted in serious efforts towards delivering the priorities defined in the NESP. Under the leadership of Daw Aung San Suu Kyi, one of the key priorities was the restoration of the historical flagship University of Yangon to its former "glory" as one of Asia's leading universities (Esson and Wang, 2018).

As part of the broader reforms, undergraduate students were being reintegrated to the main campuses of urban universities. New government higher education coordinating bodies were created, such as the National Education Policy Commission[20] in 2011, the National Institute for Higher Education Development in 2017, and the Rectors Committee in 2018 (Lall, 2021a). The Policy Commission was designed to have an executive role in advising and coordinating higher education policy and legislation in the form of Myanmar's 30-year Long-term Education Development Plan, as well as coordinating with development partners (Channon, 2017).

6.2 The NESP's Higher Education Chapter Including Higher Education Priorities

The NESP (MoE, 2016) identifies three strategies for higher education reform based on the National Education Law and the CESR, namely: (1) to strengthen higher education governance and management capacity;[21] (2) to improve the quality and relevance of

---

[20] Called "National Education Committee" (NEC) at the time.

[21] Senior management teams (including rectors) from 11 universities (Myanmar's flagship university as well as three higher education institutions located in ethnic states) took part in a University College London-delivered Higher Education Leadership and Management Programme, set up in partnership with the Ministry of Education, the Irrawaddy Policy Exchange (IPE), and the British Council (BC). The co-designed program was based on the NESP Intermediate Outcomes to help train the NIHED trainers and strengthen higher education governance and management capacity.

higher education; and (3) to expand equitable access to higher education. Whilst the NESP promised to allow universities to gradually become more autonomous, the biggest hurdle remains in that the government controls the centralized budget and effectively does not allow individual institutions to make their own decisions. The granting of autonomy was tested by the University of Yangon and University of Mandalay in being allowed to select their students and, as of 2020, being allowed to hire some of their own staff as well.[22]

6.3 Mid Term Review of the NESP

In the summer of 2019, the NESP reached its mid-point and the MoE organized a mid-term review to establish if the reforms were "on track." The results were seen as mixed, with progress recorded, but the Review concluding that there was still some way to go to meeting the policy aspirations detailed in the NESP (Mid Term Review, 2020).

7. The Drivers for the Reforms

Myanmar's higher education reforms have been driven by three broad aspirations: (1) meeting Association of Southeast Asian Nations (ASEAN) regional benchmarks for higher education; (2) gaining a place in international league tables; and (3) the need for higher education and research to support post-conflict national development (Sansom and Barakat, 2016). The first two stem from a neoliberal discourse, influenced by international aid agencies and feelings of national pride, while the latter is based on notions of state-building (Kandiko Howson and Lall 2019).

7.1 ASEAN Benchmarking

Under the umbrella of the CESR Phase 1 Report, a technical annex on higher education was published in 2013 with a section entitled "Summary and Recommendations" (CESR, 2013, p. vi), which contextualized Myanmar's higher education reform within the ASEAN region. The report cites Myanmar's desire to adopt ASEAN standards as benchmarks for its own reform higher education goals. The current state of Myanmar's higher education system compares unfavorably with its neighbors in the region in

---

[22] This, of course, is bound to create a difference between locally hired staff attached to individual universities compared to staff hired by the Ministry of Education, who rotate and have government employee status. Whilst the universities are aware that this will create issues, at the time of writing, no solutions have as yet been proposed.

terms of investment in education, research output, knowledge economy indices, and enrollment ratios.[23] The CESR, Phase 2 Report (2014) summarized the overriding aspiration for higher education as an improvement in "systemic quality" that included employability, targeting the skills needs of the workplace, the expansion of the private sector, and internationalization. The need to approximate standards found elsewhere in ASEAN and internationally was explicitly recognized, as was the need for broader international collaborations and certification.[24] The National Education Policy Commission started to engage with the ASEAN standards framework before the military coup.

7.2 International League Tables

Evidence from the CESR and the NESP suggests that Myanmar wished to align its higher education system with its neighbors in the region and as a part of the reforms develop world-class higher education institutions that could enter the global university rankings. The NLD actively sought help in the form of aid money and experts from both Britain and Australia to support the (re)development of the University of Yangon as a leading higher education institution. In order to start to compete in international league tables, some flagship universities began to promote working towards international levels of research and publications.

As of 2018 research publications became part of the criteria for promotion and staff could apply to the ministry for small grants to help with research projects.[25] Research output has increased; approximately one in two research papers was published in international journals in 2018 (MTR, 2020, pp. 51–54), although research quality remains a concern. Many universities hoped that support from overseas universities would help them with the newly required standards. The MoE reported 102 Memoranda of Understanding/Agreement with foreign institutions in 2014–2015, falling to 51 and 29 in the subsequent two years (MoE, 2019a, p. 53, fig. 2.6.4), although as Heslop noted, most of these are inactive, small scale, and largely benefit foreign institutions, with details not publicly available.

7.3 Support Post-Conflict National Development

The drive towards the league tables, influenced by the World Bank and other international aid organizations (Lall, 2021a) was likely to be at the expense of developing

---

[23] It was not possible to show Myanmar in comparison to other ASEAN countries; only very limited data are available on Myanmar, with the officially reported statistics presented in this chapter. More detailed and comparative information is not robust or reported upon.

[24] The one relevant move in this direction was Myanmar taking part in SHARE, https://share-asean.eu/about-share.

[25] Interview with the DG for Higher Education in September 2018 in NPT. He explained that this might even be rolled out for Teacher Educators who were now seen as academic staff.

regional universities, leading to an increased stratification of the system by exacerbating the urban/rural divide. A neoliberal push for international collaboration with urban flagship universities is at odds with local needs for higher education to promote integration and social justice across ethnic regions and conflict-affected regions within the country due to chronic underfunding of the sector (Heslop, 2019).

In a 2018 national Higher Education Conference, a MoE representative's presentation on *Equity in Myanmar's Higher Education: Opportunities and Challenges*, emphasized that equity was still a major priority of Myanmar's higher education reform. He held that increased disparity would widen the social divide, gradually leading to social unrest, and conflict and chaos in society. Therefore "equity interventions" were needed to reduce disparities and include marginalized groups to ensure social justice, and facilitate social cohesion, peace, and prosperity of the whole society. He noted that one way forward was to establish more higher education institutions across the country to address the imbalanced distribution, reflected in too many students enrolling in low-quality distance education programs. The urban/rural divide was also seen in the allocation of resources, reflected in regional universities having much higher teacher–student ratios than urban institutions, with a teacher–student ratio of 1:5 in Yangon University but 1:29 in Kalay University in the west.

8. Internationalization of Higher Education

Although Myanmar received significant amounts of global aid after 2012, limited amounts have been spent on education, and higher education has only received a fraction (Heslop, 2019). Prior to the 2012 reforms, international aid and development agencies, apart from UNICEF and the Japan International Cooperation Agency, had virtually no role to play in the country (Lall, 2021a). A lack of information, economic sanctions, difficulties in obtaining student visas and permission to study abroad were the main reasons very few students chose to study abroad in the past. Students who could went to Japan on Japanese scholarships—mainly for PhDs and graduate-level engineering. However, they were required to return to Myanmar.[26]

After the opening up of the country in 2012, an estimated 1,600 students went abroad for higher education (Atherton et al., 2018). Due to the declining quality of the state education system, students and parents have been craving better qualifications and study opportunities outside of Myanmar. This is, however, only an option for the rich and upper class who can afford to send their children abroad.

Although official data are not available, it is estimated that there are now between 8,000 and 25,000 students from Myanmar studying abroad (Ashwill and Neopane, 2017;

---

[26] Interview with JICA official in Tokyo in 2018.

Atherton et al., 2018; UNESCO, 2021), with a majority studying in neighboring Thailand. According to Ashwill and Neopane's report, "other destinations in Asia are Singapore, Japan, China and Malaysia, hosting approximately 5,000, 3,500, 3,000, 1,000 students respectively. There are also students from Myanmar studying in India, Hong Kong and Korea." A further 2,200 students are estimated to be studying in Australia (Australian Government, 2020), 1,800 in the United States (Institute for International Education, 2019) and 600 in the United Kingdom (Higher Education Statistics Authority, 2020). These figures do not take into account ethnic students from areas controlled by ethnic armed groups in the north who access higher education in China and India. The Kachin Independence Organisation (KIO) also has its own postgraduate colleges on the China border in Laiza and Mai Ja Yang, including a nursing college.[27]

8.1 International Engagement in Myanmar

The donor community and international organizations were able to step up their support to education and wider reform processes in Myanmar since 2012, when President Thein Sein allowed development partners to, for the first time, play a significant role in influencing Myanmar's recent education policy texts (Lall, 2016, 2021a). As a result, the dominant neoliberal discourse found its way into policy texts, a classical policy borrowing phenomenon described in many other instances of education reform in developing countries (Steiner-Khamsi, 2016).

In the absence of government legislation regulating private and international higher education provision, several "university colleges" have established a small, but growing market in transnational education foundation and pathway qualifications. These appear to be dominated by UK institutional arrangements, offering sub-degree-level provision (Heslop, 2019).

9. Conclusion

As the reforms panned out, higher education in Myanmar was poised for a metamorphosis. Even though wider education reforms started in 2012 with the CESR, higher education remained quite closed from external influence until 2016. This had resulted in a different trajectory from other countries in the Asia-Pacific region. Myanmar still has much to catch up on both compared to the region and globally.

On February 1, 2021 the Myanmar military (Tatmadaw) conducted a coup timed so as to stop the newly elected parliamentarians from taking their seats. The coup surprised

---

[27] The KIO send their students for medical studies to universities in China. There is no medical training available in Laiza beyond the nursing college.

most, as it was widely believed that even in the midst of reforms, the Tatmadaw retained its key role at the heart of government.

Early in February, anti-coup protests started, led initially by the doctors, nurses, and students from government hospitals, which also include Myanmar's medical schools. University staff and students soon followed. The protests have coalesced around different groups, but the higher education sector is mainly involved in the civil disobedience movement where staff have walked off the job and institutions have shut. At first some revolting staff were punished by demotion or being sent to more remote universities. The MoE then issued a circular stating that promotions would be denied to those who had taken part in the civil disobedience movement. In May 2021, around 13,000 staff were suspended.[28] Staff have been asked to declare whether they support the protests and to identify those who do. Because higher education staff are government employees, protesting academics were evicted from campus housing. In urban areas the newly arrived Tatmadaw divisions that are usually stationed in ethnic conflict areas have taken over campuses as well as government hospitals to accommodate their soldiers.

The government announced that postgraduate and final year undergraduate teaching was to resume in May 2021 but given that most staff refuse to work or have been suspended and the universities are now army barracks, it is unclear how this has been working. Any other undergraduate teaching has been cancelled, mirroring the 1980s and 1990s when universities were closed for over a decade and a half and a whole generation of young people missed out on higher education (Lall, 2021b). At the end of May 2021, the new higher education sector bodies were disbanded. Only the National Curriculum Committee is left, tasked to complete the curricular changes of the reforms.

Students have been at the forefront of the revolt—although across the country many other groups have joined the demonstrations, including many government teachers who present themselves in their uniforms with the MoE's green flag. At first protests were peaceful, resembling festivals with fancy dress and humorous placards, some of which insulted the Tatmadaw. Police reaction to the increasing crowds escalated from water cannons to sound grenades and rubber bullets. At the time of writing the conservative estimate of protesters killed is over 800. Volunteer medical teams are also targeted by the soldiers when they try to help the wounded and many doctors have gone into hiding. Most hospitals and their medical schools remain closed. As of April 2021, young people, many of them students, left the cities to get military training in the border areas controlled by the Karen National Union.

The State Administration Council that is governed by the Chief of Staff General Min Aung Hlaing has increased the repression both of the civil disobedience movement and the protests. This includes lists of wanted people (including academic staff and student leaders) read out on television every night and nightly arrests. At the time of writing there have been over 4,000 people arrested.

---

[28] This represents around 45 percent of academic staff. https://www.universityworldnews.com/post.php?story=20210514110259910.

This is not the first time that the Tatmadaw has cracked down on protests (1962, 1988, 1990, and 2007). Students and the wider higher education sector have always suffered most with years of closure and academic repression. In the eyes of the military, higher education is not a necessary element of wider reforms. The education system should—in the view of the Tatmadaw—teach young people to respect the military and its position. Those who disrespect them are in revolt against the stalwarts of the nation. Despite the ASEAN summit in April 2021 that called for an end to violence, no one can be sure when or how the standoff is going to end. What is clear is that the higher education sector will again take a long time to recover and aspirations for developing a globally competitive higher education system remain a distant dream.

REFERENCES

Ashwill, M. and Neopane, D. (2017). "The professional in international education blog." July 7. https://blog.thepienews.com/2017/07/myanmar-burma-new-frontier-higher-education-international-student-recruitment/

Atherton, G. et al. (2018). *The Shape of Global Higher Education: Understanding the ASEAN Region*. London: British Council.

Australian Government (2020). Department of Education, Skills and Employment. *International Student Numbers*. https://internationaleducation.gov.au/research/Data Visualisations/Pages/Student-number.aspx

Bernhardt, T., Kanay De, S., and Mi Win Thida (2017). *Myanmar Labour Issues from the Perspective of Enterprises: Findings from a Survey of Food Processing and Garment Manufacturing Businesses*. Yangon: Centre for Economic and Social Development.

Boateng, B., Camara, A. M. B., Delaney, C., Harake, N., and Hosain, M. (2014). *Youth Employment in Yangon, Myanmar*. Capstone Report. Sandhi Governance Institute. https://sandhimyanmar.org/index.php/category/publication/

British Council (2020). *Towards Results in Education and English (TREE)*. https://www.british council.org.mm/TREE-project

Brown, M. (in press). "Higher education in Myanmar." In L. Pe Symaco and M. Hayden (eds.), *International Handbook on Education in Southeast Asia*. Singapore: Springer Nature.

CESR (2013). *Comprehensive Education Sector Review: Technical Annex on the Higher Education Subsector, Phase 1*. Nay Pyi Taw: Government of Myanmar. http://themimu.info/sites/themimu.info/files/documents/Report_CESR_Phase_1_Technical_Annex_on_the_Higher_Education_Subsector_Mar2013.pdf

CESR (2014). *Comprehensive Education Sector Review: Technical Annex of the Higher Education Subsector: Phase 2*. Nay Pyi Taw: Government of Myanmar.

Channon, D. (2017). "Exploring the dynamics of higher education curriculum change in Myanmar: A case study of internationalisation in an English department." EdD thesis, UCL Institute of Education.

Cheesman, N. (2017). "How in Myanmar 'national races' came to surpass citizenship and exclude Rohingya." *Journal of Contemporary Asia*, 47/3, 461–483.

Connecting Higher Education Institutions for a New Leadership on National Education (CHINLONE) (2018). *Myanmar's Higher Education Reform: Which Way Forward?* University of Bologna, https://site.unibo.it/chinlone/it/report

Department of Foreign Affairs and Trade (DFAT) (2017). *Review of the Strengthening Pre-Service Teacher Education in Myanmar (STEM) Project and Management Response.* https://www.dfat.gov.au/sites/default/files/myanmar-strengthening-pre-service-teacher-education-stem-project-review.pdf

Esson, J. and Wang, K. (2018). "Reforming a university during political transformation: A case study of Yangon University in Myanmar." *Studies in Higher Education,* 43/7, 1184–1195.

Fawssett, S. and Gregson, J. (2016). *Investigation of Myanmar's Distance Education Sector and Proposals for Strengthening.* Maidenhead: The Open University.

Government of the Union of Myanmar (2015). *The Union Report: Census Report.* Department of Population, Ministry of Immigration and Population. http://www.dop.gov.mm/moip/index.php?route=product/product&path=54_49&product_id=95

Heslop, L. (2019). "Encountering internationalisation: Higher education and social justice in Myanmar." Doctoral thesis, University of Sussex.

Higher Education Statistics Agency (HESA) (2020). *Non-UK HE Students by HE Provider and Country of Domicile.* Academic year 2018/19. https://www.hesa.ac.uk/data-and-analysis/students/where-from

IIE (2019). *Institute of International Education Open Doors 2019 Report.* https://www.iie.org/Research-and-Insights/Open-Doors/Data/International-Students/Places-of-Origin

Kamibeppu, T. and Chao Jr, R. Y. (2017). "Higher education and Myanmar's economic and democratic development." *International Higher Education,* 88, 19–20.

Kandiko Howson, C. and Lall, M. (2020). "Higher education reform in Myanmar: neo-liberalism versus an inclusive developmental agenda." *Globalisation, Societies and Education,* 18/2, 109–124.

King, K. (2013). *Policy Insights for Higher Education: Recommendations for HE Reform in Myanmar.* Yangon: British Council. https://www.britishcouncil.org/education/ihe/knowledge-centre/national-policies/policyinsights-he-recommendations-myanmar

Lall, M. (2016). *Understanding Reform in Myanmar.* London: Hurst.

Lall, M. (2021a). *Myanmar's Education Reforms: A Pathway to Social Justice?* London: UCL Press.

Lall, M. (2021b). "Myanmar higher education in light of the military coup." *International Higher Education,* 107, 37–39.

Lall, M. and South, A. (2014). "Comparing models of non-state ethnic education in Myanmar: The Mon and Karen national education regimes." *Journal of Contemporary Asia,* 44/2, 298–321.

Mid Term Review (2020). *Government of Myanmar. Mid Term Review NESP 2016–2021.* Nay Pyi Taw: Ministry of Education.

Ministry of Education (MoE) (2016). *National Education Strategic Plan 2016–2021.* Nay Pyi Taw: Government of Myanmar. http://www.moe.gov.mm/en/?q=content/national-education-strategic-plan

Ministry of Education (MoE) (2019a). *Annual Performance Review Report FY 2017–18: National Education Strategic Plan 2016–21.* Nay Pyi Taw: Ministry of Education.

Ministry of Education (MoE) (2019b). Government of Myanmar. "Education college admission in 2019." http://www.moe.gov.mm/?q=ec-admission-2019

Ministry of Education (MoE) (2019c). Government of Myanmar. "University entrance guideline update with sound 19 6 2019" (in Myanmar language). https://www.youtube.com/watch?v=A_UM682nHOY

Ministry of Labour (2018). *Handbook on Human Resources Development Indicators 2016–17.* Nay Pyi Taw: Government of Myanmar. themimu.info/sites/themimu.info/files/documents/Report_Human_Resource_Development_Indicators_2018.pdf

Ministry of Labour, Immigration and Population (MLIP) (2014). *Policy Brief on Labour Force. 2014 Myanmar Population and Housing Census*. Nay Pyi Taw: Ministry of Labour, Immigration and Population.

Ministry of Planning and Finance (MPF) (2018a). *2018 Myanmar Statistical Yearbook*. Nay Pyi Taw: Central Statistical Organization.

Ministry of Planning and Finance (MPF) (2018b). *Myanmar Sustainable Development Plan (2018–2030)*. Nay Pyi Taw: Ministry of Planning and Finance.

Myanmar Teacher Education Working Group (2019). "Towards results in education and English." https://docs.google.com/presentation/d/1mTHfHxCGbhsbjSYESV5KjcLASyHR8 9ME/edit#slide=id.p1

Myo Kywe (2020). *CEPR Education Newsletter*. Special Issue, July 2020. Interview with Dr. Myo Kywe by Thiri Nyo and Tint Sabei Soe Win. Yangon: Center for Education Policy Research. https://www.parami.edu.mm/newsletter

May San Yee (2017). "Upgrading of education colleges to four-year degree colleges." Presentation, Higher Education Forum. http://www.moe.gov.mm/ (in Myanmar language).

Sansom, M. and Barakat, S. (2016). "Higher education as the catalyst of recovery in conflict-affected societies." *Globalisation, Societies and Education*, 14/3, 403–421.

South, A. and Lall, M. C. (eds.) (2018). *Citizenship in Myanmar: Ways of Being in and from Burma*. Singapore: ISEAS – Yusof Ishak Institute.

Steiner-Khamsi, G. (2016). "New directions in policy borrowing research." *Asia Pacific Education Review*, 17/3, 381–390.

UNESCO (2019a). *Myanmar Participation in Education*. Montreal: UNESCO Institute of Statistics. http://uis.unesco.org/en/country/mm

UNESCO (2019b). *Strengthening Pre-Service Teacher Education in Myanmar (STEM) Phase II*. https://opendata.unesco.org/project/XM-DAC-41304-545MYA1000; https://opendata. unesco.org/project/XM-DAC-41304-529MYA1001; https://opendata.unesco.org/project/ XM-DAC-41304-545MYA1000

UNESCO Institute for Statistics (2021). Statistical data. https://www.data.uis.unesco.org

United Nations Development Programme (2016). *Myanmar Annual Report*. http://www. mm.undp.org/content/myanmar/en/home/library/poverty/UNDP_MM_Annual_ Report_2016.html

Welch, A. and Hayden, M. (2013). *Myanmar Comprehensive Education Sector Review (CESR) Phase 1: Rapid Assessment. Technical Annex on the Higher Education Subsector*. Myanmar: CESR. http://www.cesrmm.org/assets/home/img/cesr-phase%201_rapid%20 assessment_higher%20ed%20subsector_technical%20annex_26mar13_for%20distrib_cln_ newlogo.pdf

World Fact Book (2020). *Burma*. Central Intelligence Agency. https://www.cia.gov/library/ publications/the-world-factbook/geos/bm.html

CHAPTER 41

....

PHILIPPINE HIGHER EDUCATION
A Case for Public–Private Complementarity in the Next Normal

....

MARIA CYNTHIA ROSE BAUTISTA, VICENTE PAQUEO, AND ANICETO ORBETA JR.

1. HISTORICAL DEVELOPMENT (1565–1990S)

1.1 Elite to Mass Education

PHILIPPINE higher education (HE) gestated in the cocoon of a long colonial history—three centuries of Spanish rule (1565–1898) and half a century under the United States (1901–1946).

Higher education in the Spanish era began in 1626 with the royal authorization to confer degrees in the Jesuit University of San Ignacio (1626) and the Dominican University of Santo Tomas (Santiago, 1991, p. 135). Baccalaureate degrees were originally reserved for Spaniards but Filipinos from elite families broke the racial glass ceiling in 1690. By 1772, they were allowed to pursue a doctorate in sacred theology, philosophy, and law (Santiago 1991, p. 141). However, those who obtained post-secondary degrees during the Spanish era constituted a small minority. A few pursued advanced studies in Spain and launched the propaganda movement that culminated in the 1896 Philippine Revolution (Alcala, 1999, p. 117).

Had Spain's plan in the 1800s to establish an extensive public instruction system up to the tertiary level with Spanish as a medium of instruction been carried out (Alzona, 1932, p. 95), Filipinos might have been proficient in the Spanish language at the end of Spanish rule in 1898. However, when Spain ceded the Philippines to the United States after the Spanish-American war, basic education in the local languages was in the hands of religious congregations. There was only one university where Spanish-speaking children of the elite studied—the University of Santo Tomas, which, had the distinction of a royal decree declaring some degrees equivalent to those of Spanish universities in 1863 (Alzona, 1932, p. 59).

Confronted by Filipino armed resistance and intense debates at home over its imperialistic intents, the US colonial administration underscored education's role in instilling civic-mindedness and democratic values as well as developing a pool of Filipino professionals for self-rule. As soon as it established its colonial civil administration in 1901, the United States instituted a secular public school system, providing free primary education with English as the medium of instruction. It created the Philippine Normal School in 1901, the Philippine Medical School in 1905, the University of the Philippines (UP) in 1908 (Caoili, 1983, pp. 309–310), and several post-secondary vocational and trade schools (Cardozier, 1984, p. 193).

The establishment of UP satisfied the short-term needs of the colonial bureaucracy but its limited resources could not accommodate the growing social demand spurred by mass education (Alcala, 1999, p. 119). In response to this demand, enterprising Filipinos established 64 colleges and universities before 1938, adding to the Catholic institutions that flourished even after Spain's exit. The colonial government's openness to private educational initiatives led to the creation of more private higher education institutions (PHEIs) during the American regime. Under the 1906 Corporation Law, any group could establish a PHEI, grant diplomas, and confer degrees by forming a corporation with the Secretary of Public Instruction's approval (Alcala, 1999, p. 120).

The US colonial government adopted a *laissez-faire* attitude towards private educational initiatives (Gonzales, 1989, p. 119) for a practical reason. In 1932, the Commissioner of Private Education estimated that government would spend more than the total appropriations for the Bureau of Education and the University of the Philippines if students in private high schools were accommodated (Caoili, 1983, p. 316).

Interestingly, during the 1935 transition to self-rule, the Filipino Commonwealth government used the same "limited funds" argument to abolish Grade 7 in all public schools (Alcala, 1991, p. 121). It is worth noting that most private schools retained an educational system consisting of kindergarten, seven years of elementary, and four years of high school after 1946. However, many of them caved in to public pressure to abolish Grade 7 in the 1980s. Only in 2013, when the Aquino administration pushed the K to 12 law and added two years of Senior high school, did the usually populist Philippine government manage to thwart six long decades of multi-sectoral resistance in acquiescence to global standards.

1.2 Public–Private Complementarity

The number of PHEIs continued to rise after the Philippines gained political independence in 1946, with the "big explosion" occurring after World War II. In the early 1950s, 90 percent of students were enrolled in 294 PHEIs. Between 1946 and 1985, private institutions grew 70 percent with enrollees increasing 2,700 percent. By 1985, private sources had covered 70 percent of higher education costs and PHEIs shouldered half of the institutional costs (James, 1991, p. 192).

The PHEIs continued to grow, from 950 colleges and universities in 1995 to 1,729 in 2020. However, an increase in the number of State Universities and Colleges (SUCs) slowly reduced their enrollment share. The Philippine Normal School became a SUC in 1949 followed by eight other regional normal schools in the 1950s. More SUCs were legislated in the 1960s and 1970s, some of which met minimum requirements for upgrading by amalgamating four-year degree programs with trade/technical schools or scattered specialized schools (Cardozier, 1984, pp. 194–195).

2. Structural Features (2000–2020)

2.1 Composition and Types of Higher Education Institutions

Philippine higher education continues to be characterized by the substantial participation of the private sector. In academic year (AY) 2019–2020,[1] the country's HEIs numbered 2,396 of which 667 are public and 1,729 private (Table 41.1). SUCs dominated public HEIs while non-sectarian schools dominated PHEIs. In AY 2009–2010 there were 607 public HEIs, increasing to 667 in AY 2019–2020. Satellite campuses of SUCs and Local Colleges and Universities (LUCs) account for the increase in the number of public HEIs while non-sectarian schools contributed to the higher number of PHEIs in AY 2019–2020.

Public HEIs consist of SUCs, LUCs, and special HEIs such as the Philippine Military Academy. SUCs differ from LUCs in their provenance and mandates. They are created by law with the Commission on Higher Education (CHED) chairing their governing boards and academic governance norms guiding the selection and terms of presidents and deans. On the other hand, LUCs are created by local ordinance with local chief executives chairing their governing boards and LUC presidents serving at their pleasure.

Until 2016, LUCs sought neither recognition nor academic program approval from CHED, using the 1991 Local Government Code as the legal basis for their autonomy. Since SUC Charters lodge academic decision-making with their governing boards, SUCs also vehemently defended their autonomy from CHED until 2015. The reluctant openness of SUCs and LUCs to CHED's institutional and program review is an offshoot of internationalization which made a CHED-managed database of recognized HEIs necessary for purposes of academic exchange and labor mobility. CHED insisted

---

[1] The COVID-19 pandemic delayed the Commission on Higher Education's consolidation and release of higher education data for Academic Year 2020–2021.

Table 41.1 Composition and enrollment of higher education institutions

Number of HEIs	AY 2009–2010		AY 2019–2020	
	Number	%	Number	%
Total HEIs (including SUC satellite campuses	2,180	100.0	2,396	100.0
Public	607	27.8	667	27.8
State Universities and Colleges (SUCs)	109	5.0	112	4.6
SUC satellite campuses	389	17.8	421	17.6
Local Colleges and Universities (LUCs)	93	4.3	121	5.0
Ohers (include Special HEIs)	16	0.7	13	0.5
Private	1,573	72.2	1,729	72.2
Sectarian	322	14.8	339	14.2
Non-sectarian	1,251	57.4	1,390	58.0
Enrollment	2,774,368	100.0	3.408,425	100.0
Public	1,087,983	39.2	1,575,645	46.2
Private	1,686,385	60.8	1,832,780	53.8

Source: CHED as constructed by Ortiz et al. (2019).

on program compliance of SUCs/LUCs as a prerequisite for inclusion in its list of recognized programs.

Private HEIs in the Philippines may be sectarian (owned and operated by a religious organization) or non-sectarian (owned or operated by non-religious bodies). Non-sectarian PHEIs are further categorized into non-stock/non-profit or stock/for-profit/proprietary entities. The Philippines was among the first countries in the world to allow the operation of for-profit educational institutions under the 1906 Corporation Law. Although the 1982 Education Act reversed this policy, the Act was amended in 1994 to enable the creation of stock educational corporations provided that they operate in capital-intensive programs and are ineligible for government support.

In 2015,[2] for-profit PHEIs constituted 19 percent of all HEIs while 53 percent were non-profit. A comparison of CHED's 2015 data with the 1985 figures cited in James (1991) shows an increase in the for-profit PHEIs' share of total PHEIs, from 35 percent to 53 percent. This increase is attributed to the amendment of the 1982 Education Act and the profitability of responding to the global market demand for Filipino professionals and associate professionals (Yee, forthcoming).

---

[2] 2015 is the last year prior to the implementation of the K to 12 reforms. The analysis before the K to 12 transition reflects the development of PHEIs under normal conditions.

CHED recently allowed the sale, merger, or consolidation of PHEIs to strengthen the sector through the operation of more viable and better quality HEIs, among other objectives. In response, several large business corporations have ventured into higher education.

2.2 System Outputs and Outcomes

2.2.1 *Enrollment and Graduation*

The enrollment rate in Philippine higher education is on par with middle-income countries' average (Figure 41.1). In terms of the composition of graduates, the latest available statistics show that the share of STEM graduates to total graduates is comparable to that of Korea and Thailand (Figure 41.2).

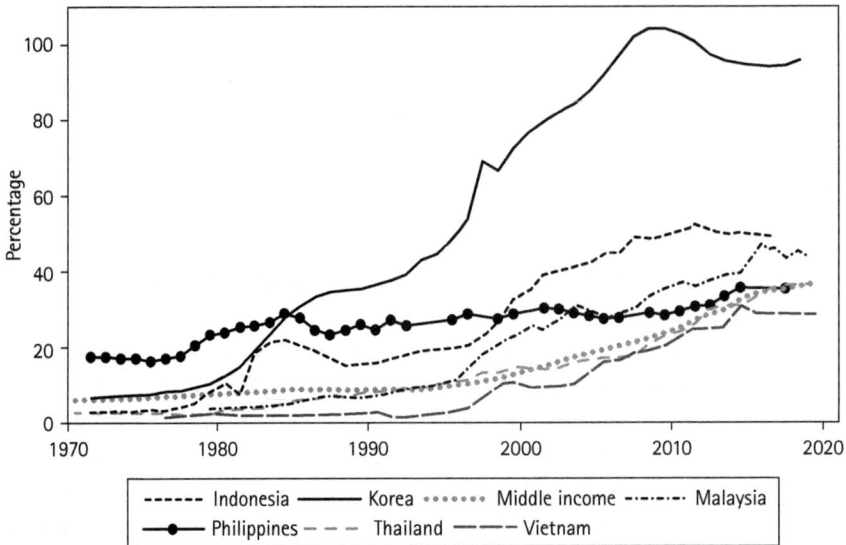

FIGURE 41.1 Higher education enrollment (%) comparison between the Philippines, regional peers and the average of middle-income countries

Source: World Bank.

2.2.2 *Quality*

- **Passing in professional board examinations (PBEs).** Passing professional board examinations (PBEs) is publicly acknowledged in the Philippines as a gauge of the quality of the outcome. Currently, there are 43 professional boards administering the PBEs. Table 41.2 provides the average passing rate in the last decade (2009–2018) for the PBEs. The passing rates hovered between 36 percent and 40 percent in the last 10 years. If only the first-time takers are considered, the passing rate

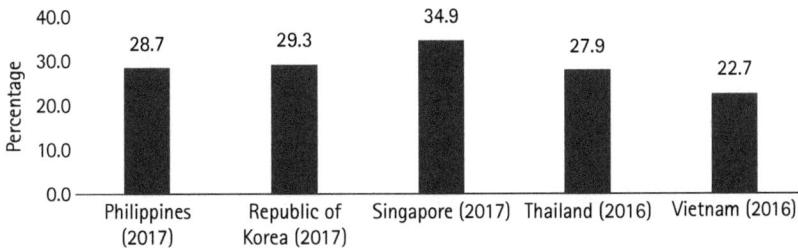

FIGURE 41.2 Percentage of STEM graduates in higher education, 2016

Source: UNESCO-IS.

Table 41.2 Some quality indicators

	2009	2010	2011	2012	2013	2014	2015	2016	2017	2018
Performance (% passing) in licensure examination										
Across all disciplines (overall takers)	36	34	36	43	39	40	39	38	37	38
Across all disciplines (first-time takers)	50	50	54	61	60	60	59	56	57	56
Faculty qualification										
% with graduate degrees	45	50	54	50	53	53	53	54	54	54
% with PhD	10	11	13	11	12	13	13	13	14	17
Accreditation										
% of HEIs with Accredited Programs	20	20	22	22	24	25	27	28	29	29

Source: CHED.

is a higher 50 percent to 61 percent, indicating either better training for newer graduates or obsolescence of professional knowledge for earlier graduates.

- **Faculty qualifications.** An important explanation for low passing rates in PBEs is training inputs. The foremost input is the quality of the faculty as indicated by proportion with graduate degrees—which appears to be improving slowly. Table 41.2 shows a gradual increase in the proportion of faculty with graduate degrees in the 2009–2018 decade from 45 percent in 2009 to 54 percent in 2018; while those with doctoral degrees increased from 10 percent in 2009 to 17 percent in 2018.

- **Quality assurance.** The achievement of desired student outcomes is also a function of the quality of the country's academic programs. The Philippines has a complex system of assuring the quality of higher education qualifications. CHED sets and monitors minimum standards; grants HEIs permits to operate; monitors compliance with standards; and recognizes quality beyond minimum standards by granting (1) autonomous and deregulated status to PHEIs based on program excellence and institutional quality and Level IV status to SUCs based on quality and relevance of instruction, research capacity and output, service to community, and resource management; and (2) Center of Excellence (COE) and Center of Development (COD) designations to less than 50 programs that continuously demonstrate excellent performance in instruction, research, publication, extension, linkages, and institutional qualifications.

Of the 1,729 PHEIs, only 5 percent are either autonomous (68) or deregulated (14) while 19 percent of SUCs, excluding the country's only national university, the University of the Philippines (UP), are at Level IV—the level roughly equivalent to autonomous/deregulated PHEIs.

There are now 199 COEs in the programs covered by the award, adding 82 COEs to the 117 COEs a decade earlier as reported in Tan (2011, p. 158). The number of CODs that are in the trajectory of becoming COEs also increased from 186 in 2009 to 233 in 2018. Due to the COVID-19 pandemic, the designation of COEs, CODs, and Level IV SUCs was extended until 2023.

CHED recognizes private accreditation bodies that accredit HEIs beyond minimum standards on a voluntary basis.[3] Five private accreditation bodies and two professional associations provide voluntary accreditation for HEI programs and institutions.

As to voluntary accreditation, a low proportion of programs passed voluntary accreditation—20 percent in 2009; 25 percent in 2014 (Conchada and Tiongco, 2015); and 29 percent in 2018 (Table 41.2).

3. Persistent Issues and Current Concerns

3.1 Inequitable Access to Higher Education

Equity of opportunities in Philippine higher education remains elusive. Figure 41.3 reveals the disparity in enrollment rates, with 49 percent of the richest decile enrolled in

---

[3] Until the draft of the Philippine Report on the Referencing of the Philippine Qualifications Framework to the ASEAN Qualifications Referencing Framework (AQRF, 2019) was critiqued by external reviewers from Australia and New Zealand and the AQRF Committee, quality assurance was commonly understood in the Philippines to refer to the voluntary accreditation of private accreditation agencies. In the ASEAN parlance, however, the accreditation process includes the government's grant of permits and compulsory regular monitoring of HEI compliance with standards.

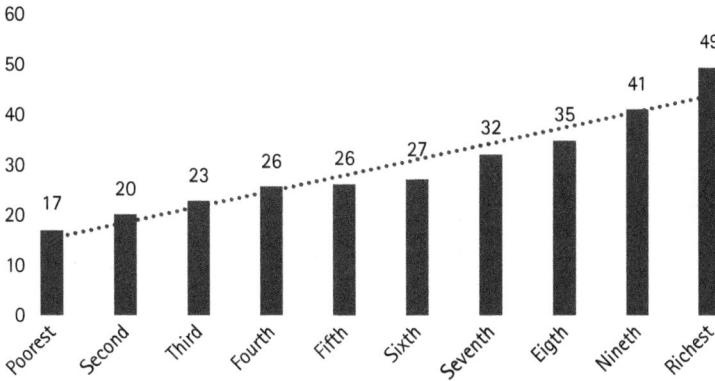

FIGURE 41.3 Net enrollment rate in higher education by income decile, 2019
Source: Authors' calculation using the country's 2019 Annual Poverty Indicators Survey (APIS).

Table 41.3 Participation rate of persons 17–24 years old in higher education: poorest vs. "richest," 1999, 2014, 2016, 2017, and 2019

	1999	2014	2016	2017	2019
Poorest	8%	10%	10%	12%	17%
Richest	63%	72%	64%	61%	50%

Source: Yee et al. (2019) for 1999 and 2014 and the authors' calculations for 2016 and 2017 using APIS 2016, 2017, and 2019. The 2019 figures are not comparable with earlier years.

higher education while only 17 percent in the poorest decile are enrolled. This disparity is expected because household income is the primary determinant of HE enrollment. It also highlights the well-known fact that most students from poor households drop out early in the education ladder. Yee et al.'s analysis (2019) shows little progress in providing the poor with chances to enroll in HE. Only 8 percent of the poorest decile enrolled in 1999, rising to 12 percent in 2017 (Table 41.3). The richest, on the other hand, have a steady above-60 percent enrollment rate reaching even to 72 percent in 2014. The 2019 figures from the same data source seem to suggest a significant increase in the enrollment share of the poorest decile but the change in the income indicator in 2019 renders these figures incomparable with those of earlier years.

The distribution of higher education enrollees in public HEIs by income decile is revealing. It shows that most of the students come from middle-income classes including a substantial proportion in the 8th and 9th income deciles (Figure 41.4a). The composition of enrollees in the private sector, on the other hand, is understandably dominated by students from higher-income classes (Figure 41.4b).

The year 2017 marked a major change in the financing of higher education. The Philippine Congress passed Republic Act 10931 making tuition (and other school fees)

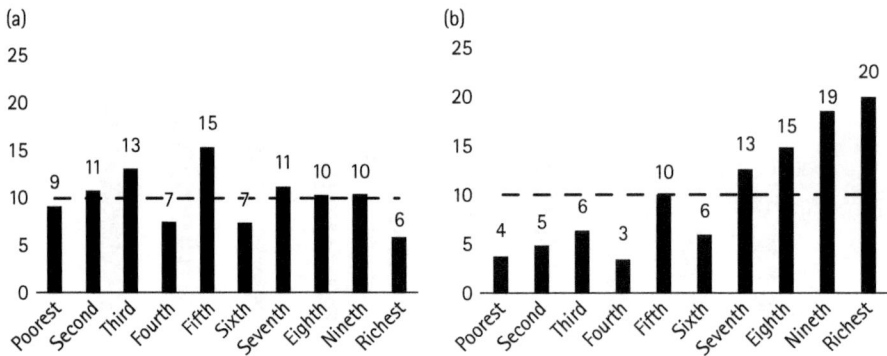

FIGURE 41.4 Distribution of enrollment in public and private HEIs, by income decile, 2019

in public universities and colleges free. In addition, it introduced the Tertiary Education Subsidy (TES) which provides financial assistance to cover tuition and living allowance of poor students in public and private HEIs. The law aims to prioritize academically deserving students from poor families.

Prior to 2017, the main instrument of public subsidy for higher education is funding public universities and colleges, which charge relatively low but varying levels of tuition, and some scholarships and grants-in-aid to support a limited number of students. Initial assessment of the law reveals "birthing pains." Even if its purposes appear to be well-understood by implementers, it is given a mixed review on whether its objectives are realistic and achievable (Ortiz et al., 2019). Untargeted financing like free tuition in public universities and colleges could exacerbate inequalities (Orbeta and Paqueo, 2017). Since the composition of enrollment for public universities favors middle classes including upper-middle classes, the impact of this law on equity will largely depend on the success of targeting the poor with the TES and providing funds for living allowance and other expenses.

3.2 Uneven Quality of HEIs

Philippine higher education institutions are of highly uneven quality (AQRF, 2019). That CHED has granted autonomous or deregulated status to only 5 percent of PHEIs deemed excellent or near excellent in 2019 and to 19 percent of SUCs in Level IV confirms that there is no critical mass of high-quality HEIs in the country.

While COEs rose by 70 percent over the last decade and 8 percent of all HEIs (excluding satellite campuses) have at least one COE, 57 percent of the COEs are concentrated in only two SUCs—UP (40 COEs) and Mindanao State University-Iligan Institute of Technology (8)—and 5 PHEIs—De la Salle University (DLSU-17); Ateneo de Manila University (ADMU-15); University of Santo Tomas (UST-12); Mapua University (MU-8); and Technological Institute of the Philippines (TIP-8).

The low number of high-quality HEIs may not be of much concern if the majority of Philippine HEIs meet the minimum quality standards that CHED's Technical Panels of experts update regularly to keep abreast with developments in their disciplines. Since only 29 percent of HEIs have gone for voluntary accreditation (Table 41.2) and consolidated results of CHED's HEI monitoring through quality assurance teams are not available, the passing rate of HEI graduates in the PBEs has been the common indicator in the literature of whether graduates of Philippine HEIs attain the desired learning outcomes and competences in their fields. The stark contrast between the very low average passing rates (36–40 percent) and the 90–100 percent passing rates of the few elite HEIs merely reflect the wide disparity in their quality.

The Philippines started out in the post-World War II era with a higher education system that was once touted as a model for many developing countries in terms of quantity and quality. In the 1960s, the proportion of the population enrolled in post-secondary education was second in the world, next only to the United States (Kim and Hunt, 1968, p. 412). By 2017, however, the country's gross tertiary enrollment ratio had been overtaken by the other Southeast Asian countries except for Lao PDR, Cambodia, and Myanmar (Licuanan, 2017). The quality of Philippine higher education was also presumably high until the early 1980s. Top Philippine universities provided graduate education to students from Southeast Asian countries—e.g., Indonesia and Thailand. In time, the early edge of the Philippines in graduate education eroded with the ASEAN economies and HEIs surpassing the country's economic and educational development.

The steep decline in the quality of Philippine higher education since its heyday in the 1960s/1970s is traceable to the government's populist education policies that supported the massification of higher education in a context of demographic expansion (Tan, 2011, p. 150). Since the implementation of the American colonial regime's mass education policy, the empirical evidence of intergenerational mobility attributed by Filipinos to college education created an increasing demand for higher education throughout the twentieth century and the first decades of the twenty-first century. Disdain for blue-collar occupations, discrimination against technical-vocational education, and the recruitment practices of employers in the Philippines and abroad—who until recently relied on a college degree as a screen even for jobs that don't require college-level competencies—further bolstered a pervasive cultural penchant for a college degree as key to social mobility.

In meeting populist needs, the higher education system effectively provided higher education to students with varying intellectual abilities (Gonzales, 1989, p. 139). Unlike ASEAN neighbors that funnel students into post-secondary technical or academic tracks based on aptitude, high school graduates in the Philippines, regardless of academic aptitude, are admitted to college, a fact that has undermined the development of the country's technical-vocational education sector.

The increasing demand for a college degree and the government's liberal policy towards the establishment of PHEIs—without levers to ensure that the market or the state can close poor-performing institutions—has resulted in the proliferation of PHEIs in the post-war years, some of dubious quality. Unlike the United States where the provision of student loans requires enrollment in accredited programs/institutions, thereby creating a compelling market for accreditation, the Philippines adopted the American system without a lever for quality control. Neither does CHED have the teeth to close/

phase out non-compliant PHEIs. Regional courts privileging the business interests of PHEIs with injunctions against CHED's closure orders and a public that patronizes non-compliant PHEIs for credentialing purposes undermine both the workings of a higher education market and CHED's regulatory function.

CHED has also had little control over the establishment of SUCs by populist politicians to serve parochial interests (Tan, 2011, p. 149). The Commission's control over the creation of LUCs, which are intimately linked to the politics of Local Government Units, is even more tenuous. Moreover, there is no mechanism for closing or phasing out established SUCs/LUCs except lobbying for their demise by legislation.

Despite this backdrop, a caveat is in order. An observer might be tempted to conclude that except for a few elite HEIs, most graduates of Philippine HEIs are not adequately prepared for domestic or foreign jobs. Yet, the higher education environment must be working somehow as evidenced by strong global demand for Filipino graduates not only in technical/associate professional jobs but as managers and professionals.

In 2018, the Philippine Statistical Authority registered 221,100 Filipinos working abroad in such occupations. Moreover, both domestic employers and international businesses operating in the Philippines interviewed by USAID's Science, Technology, Research and Innovation for Development (STRIDE) Program rated bachelor's and master's level personnel as technically capable and well trained, with those in the food industry asserting that their competent employees did not necessarily graduate from elite HEIs (USAID, 2014, p. 7).

3.3 Underdeveloped Innovation Ecosystem

In his assessment of the American impact on Philippine higher education, Gonzales (1989, pp. 119, 122) cited the failure of the US colonial government to establish a research tradition except in the University of the Philippines. The relative dearth of research in HEIs in the post-war decades, particularly scientific research, kept science and technology (S&T) degrees (except engineering) outside the radar of Filipino students. Accordingly, an underdeveloped labor market for S&T reinforced the predilection of students to pursue other professional careers.

Half a century later, the number of S&T programs in HEIs had increased alongside research units in government agencies. Moreover, the number of science majors had also increased in the 2000s—from 152,372 enrollees in 2005 to 219,171 in 2018 (Albert et al., 2019, p. 51). These positive developments, however, must be weighed against the broader role of research universities as platforms for "training the professionals, high-level specialists, scientists, and researchers needed by the economy and in generating new knowledge in support of national innovation systems."[4]

---

[4] Salmi (2016, p. 42, citing World Bank 2002, *Constructing Knowledge Societies: New Challenges for Tertiary Education*. Washington, DC: World Bank. Retrieved December 2, 2008, from http://go.worldbank.org/N2QADMBNI0).

The Philippines ranked 64th out of 141 countries on the 2019 Global Competitiveness Index, up from 65 in 2013 but significantly dropping from the previous year's rank of 56th out of 140 countries. However, it ranked 50th out of 131 countries and 5th in ASEAN on the Global Innovation Index (GII), up from 55th in 2018.

In 2014 and 2019, the USAID-funded STRIDE program, which aims to catalyze collaboration and research for innovation-led growth, assessed the Philippine innovation ecosystem using a model involving five processes: education/human capital development; research/knowledge creation; collaboration between universities and industry; intellectual property, protection, licensing, and commercialization of technology; and start-up companies based on technology innovation. With respect to education and human capital development, the program's respondents deemed training in science, technology, engineering, and mathematics (STEM) acceptable by global standards. However, they observed that the training is too focused on getting students to pass board examinations, with an outmoded curriculum that neither teaches students about new technologies nor exposes them to a research culture (USAID, 2019, p. 22).

STRIDE's 2019 assessment also flagged an oversupply of STEM graduates resulting in their migration and underemployment. Albert et al.'s (2019, p. 31) projection of the supply and demand for STEM graduates in the context of the Fourth Industrial Revolution (FIRe) corroborates this observation (see also Dadios et al., 2018).

That the supply of STEM graduates exceeds demand is ironic since the latest available comparative data (2015) show the Philippines as having only 106 researchers for every million population—below UNESCO's norm of 380, Thailand's 865, Malaysia's 2,308, and Singapore's 7,006 researchers in the same year.[5]

On research and knowledge creation, a common refrain among STRIDE's stakeholders is the lack of a highly developed research culture in the Philippines compared to some of its ASEAN peers. At least two factors account for this.

First, while government's support for research has increased significantly through the years—from P15.9M in 2015 to P60.4M in 2018—it is common knowledge in scientific circles that the ratio of the country's Gross Expenditure for Research and Development (GERD) to GDP (0.33) is still below UNESCO's standard of 1 percent and that of Malaysia (2018: 1.4 percent), Thailand (2017: 1.0 percent) and Singapore (2017: 1.94)[6]— albeit significantly higher than 0.13 percent in 2015.

Second, aside from research units of government, international agencies, and local/ multinational corporations, research in the Philippines rests on a small group of about 20 universities constituting the Philippine Higher Education Research Network (PherNET) with varying capacities for S&T research. Without exception, their academic researchers are saddled with heavy teaching load, limiting the pace of research, its

---

[5] data.uis.unesco.org/index.aspx?queryid=3830.

[6] https://data.worldbank.org/indicators/GB.XPD.RSDV.GD.ZS for the ASEAN countries; Department of Science and Technology for the Philippines.

translation to innovations and technologies, and the sustainability of strong academe–industry linkages.

Due to its relatively small research base, Killingley and Ilieva (2015, p. 26)—citing the 2015 research carried out by Elsevier—noted that the Philippines has the lowest quantity of publications among its peers in ASEAN. However, its citation impact was highest among the comparator group and 11 percent higher than the world average due to a relatively high proportion of international collaboration within the country's research output.

Overall, STRIDE noted an improvement in the Philippine innovation ecosystem from 2014 to 2019 but highlighted concerns that hold back the ecosystem's optimal contribution to economic growth. For one, concentration on teaching and publications in universities has constrained academe–industry partnerships, technology transfer processes in universities, and the number of technology-based start-up companies spinning off from research. Lack of intentionality in academe and government to align with industry; government's underspending for research; challenges to the creation and growth of enterprise; and barriers to collaboration, including lack of trust, are among the concerns cited (USAID, 2019, p. 49).

3.4 National Imperatives/Realities vis-à-vis Global Norms/Metrics

It is ironic that research infrastructure and support is palpably weaker in the Philippines than its ASEAN peers but it is also a research-related criterion in the Times Higher Education (THE) World University Rankings (WUR)—i.e., a citation score that is highest in ASEAN in the 2021 WUR and higher than the top 10 universities in the pre-clinical, clinical and health disciplines in 2020—that enabled the ranking of the University of the Philippines to rise from 800+ in 2017 to 401–500 in 2021.

The Filipino public expects its top universities to rank globally, accepting uncritically the annual results of WUR as a gauge of a university's improving or deteriorating quality and relevance. However, the multiple mandates of these HEIs in a society plagued by poverty and inequality nuance their perspective and resolve to fully align their strategies with the norms and metrics of research universities in the developed world.

As a case in point, a high ratio of doctoral to undergraduate students is not possible to achieve at this time given the imperatives of tuition-dependent private schools and the other mandates of SUCs, i.e., teaching, and public service. The case of UP is instructive. Its strategic planning workshops in the 1990s and 2000s articulated the vision of a research/graduate university with a much smaller undergraduate population. However, despite its mandate as the country's only national research university and the constraints posed by heavy teaching on faculty research productivity, UP shelved the vision in the face of its other mandate to educate future leaders in different branches of knowledge—especially the significant number of bright but poor undergraduates admitted through its rigorous admission system. The country's top private universities cannot absorb the number of these students while the top SUCs are not yet in a position to do so. Moreover, the country's uneven quality of undergraduate education has made it imperative to recruit UP's graduate students from among its best and brightest undergraduates.

Internationalization is another challenging global norm for Philippine HEIs. Although there is a well-articulated national strategy for it, the Philippines seems less open to internationalization compared to its peers in ASEAN as reflected in the lengthy and bureaucratic processing of student, academic, and employment visas; the 2019 law restricting ownership of transnational education ventures with local partners to 40 percent—rendering it unappealing to branded universities (Killingley and Ilieva, 2015, pp. 20–23); and its ambivalence towards financially supporting strategic research collaborations with foreign institutions.

Indicators of international outlook—e.g., international faculty/staff ratio—are particularly challenging for Philippine HEIs. Legally, public institutions are unable to grant tenure to foreign faculty. This impediment and low remuneration vis-à-vis other ASEAN universities make it difficult for foreigners to work in public HEIs. On the other hand, the financial resources of PHEIs limit the number of international faculty they can hire. Despite such limits and even without the same strategic focus on university rankings as other governments, two HEIs are in THE's list of ranked universities while 14 HEIs are in QS WUR in 2021.[7]

Many academics in the country's top universities agree that their standing in the WUR criteria neither defines their quality nor reflects their impact on Philippine society and humanity. But because public perception is real in its consequences and their current rankings reflect their strengths anyway, universities strive to sustain the work for which they have been ranked despite the constraints in meeting other WUR criteria. It is also notable that as of this writing, more universities are open to impact rankings towards the fulfillment of Sustainable Development Goals, albeit knowing that the metrics cannot capture many significant contributions.

As to other global education reforms, Philippine HEIs prior to the COVID-19 pandemic had begun the shift to a lifelong learning (LLL) paradigm with learning outcomes as a metric of qualifications; revising curricula in response to LLL and FIRe; and adopting appropriate pedagogies/assessments. These changes occurred later in the Philippines than in its ASEAN counterparts—i.e., the shift to lifelong learning began in 2007 for Malaysia and 2009 for Thailand[8] while CHED's policy was laid down in 2012.

---

[7] The ranked universities in the THE WUR are UP and DLSU. UP, ADMU, DLSU, UST, University of San Carlos Ateneo de Davao University, Mapua University, Mindanao State University-Iligan, Adamson University, Central Luzon State University, Central Mindanao University, Central Philippine University and Xavier University are in the QS WUR list.

[8] As shared by Prof. Zita Mohd Fahmi, Malaysian Qualifications Agency and Prof. Dr. Supachai Yabaprabhas, Chulalongkorn University in the Third EU-Support to Higher Education in the ASEAN Region (SHARE) National Workshop on Impact of Qualifications Frameworks and Learning Outcomes on Higher Education in ASEAN. Makati Diamond Residences, November 18, 2016.

3.5 Current Crisis of Private Education

The COEs, CODs, PherNET and ranked universities reflect a healthy mix of public and private HEIs. However, the significant increase in the number of public HEIs since the 1990s and the proliferation of their satellite campuses—exacerbated by the K to 12 reform which resulted in lost revenues for PHEIs from two cohorts of students; a wide salary gap between teachers in public and private HEIs due to government's salary standardization; free tuition and other fees in public HEIs; and more recently, the COVID-19 pandemic—is threatening the viability even of PHEIs of known quality. A few institutions and some widely recognized academic programs of reputable universities have closed for lack of enrollment, with students and faculty migrating to public HEIs.

The legislation in 2017 of RA 10931 (Universal Access to Quality Tertiary Education Act) is undermining the constitutional mandate of public–private complementarity and contributing significantly to the current crisis of private education. Interestingly, Congressional hearings prior to the legislation transpired in the months leading to the 2016 national elections, making politicians more susceptible to legislating a populist policy that resonates with the Filipino voters' penchant for a college education. In response to mounting pressure from private HEIs, Congress incorporated the Tertiary Education Subsidy (TES) program in the law as an afterthought. TES provides financial assistance in the form of vouchers to disadvantaged students who prefer to enroll in private schools of their choice.

In proposing the law, legislators claimed that the Philippines has the resources to simultaneously implement free universal higher education and meet all the funding requirements of quality basic education. While laudable, the intention of RA 10931 is built on a weak economic foundation.[9] It creates false hopes and distorts the allocation of resources. Taking about Php 30 billion from the approved basic education budget in 2019 to support enrollment in tuition-free public HEIs, which serve families with above-average incomes, is an example of resource allocation distortion. Another example is that the law, except for its TES and UniFAST provisions, reversed core provisions of the 2015 UniFAST law[10] before it could be implemented in earnest. In contrast to the approach of UniFAST, RA 10931's provision of increased subsidy is tied to SUCs, which are now obliged to enroll students applying for admission without passing a national examination.

Unlike the few advanced countries pursuing free higher education, the Philippines does not have the wherewithal to support its unrealistic higher education ambitions and at the same time ensure sufficient funding for basic education. Compared to

---

[9] Interestingly, the assumption that resources are not binding constraints has been completely demolished by the COVID-19 pandemic. The Philippine president signed the law over the objection of his economic team.

[10] RA 10867 (2015), An Act Providing for a Comprehensive and Unified Student Assistance System for Tertiary Education (UniFAST) Thereby Rationalizing Access Thereto, Appropriating Funds Therefore and For Other Purposes.

economically developed countries, it has yet to achieve universal access to quality basic education. This difference is crucial. Without good fundamental education for all, children from the poorest families will not qualify for higher education and benefit from its massification.

Other differences between the Philippines and countries with a free tuition policy like Germany are the lower demand for a college education in these countries because of a smaller population and well-developed technical education that enable the future employment of graduates of technical tracks in occupations that may be better compensated depending on their skills/competencies. In contrast, obtaining a college education is the goal of Filipino families because a degree rather than skills/competencies is still perceived to be the ticket to better-paying jobs in the country's less-developed economy. This perception and the reality that the Philippines is projected to have a young population in the next decades ensures sustained high demand for a free college education which the Philippines can ill afford in the long run.

Another consequence of free tuition is its adverse effect on the development of the country's technical-vocational education. In conferences convened by the Philippine Business for Education from 2013 to 2018 and countless meetings of its Academe-Industry Council, academic leaders, and CEOs of some of the country's top corporations forged a consensus to launch a campaign for the development of technical education as critical to Philippine economic growth, hoping to change a public mindset that considers a college degree a prerequisite to success. However, even before the campaign could be launched, the free tuition legislation further reinforced the Filipino's predilection for a college degree, making the campaign for technical education even more difficult to wage.

The proliferation of low-quality public HEIs is another likely consequence of free tuition. The rapid growth of SUCs and their satellite campuses—34 SUCs and 217 satellite campuses in the last two decades alone—attest to the possibility of even more proliferation in the future (Figure 41.5). Such proliferation accounts for prolonged under-investment in developing the country's top public and private universities into advanced institutions of higher learning that are authoritative sources of knowledge and expertise for the nation and enablers of cutting-edge research, innovations, and technologies to fuel the country's economy and provide solutions to pressing and anticipated problems.

In this regard, the reasoning behind the development of World-Class Universities (Salmi, 2016) and more specifically, new Flagship Universities (Douglass, 2016a)[11] is relevant to the Philippines. The argument: countries with limited resources are inefficiently using government's higher education budget by spreading it thinly over numerous publicly funded mediocre HEIs. These are unlikely to go very far in transforming the nation's ability to profit from advances in science and technology. Some of the funds allocated to mediocre HEIs are better spent on developing a few topnotch universities with a comprehensive range of capabilities that will help the Philippines transform its economy and move its people out of poverty.

---

[11] See also Douglass (2016b).

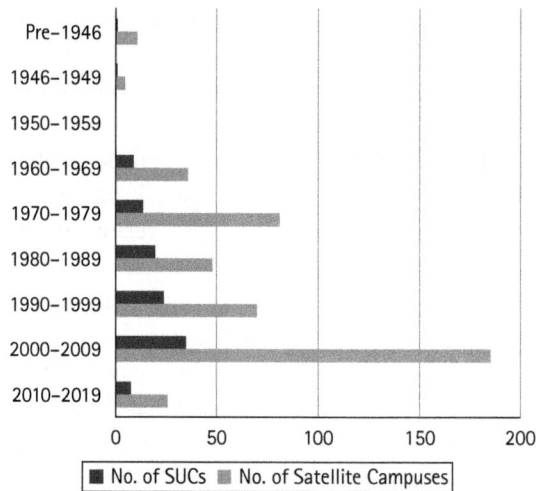

FIGURE 41.5 Number of SUCs established by year of legislation

Note: Satellite campuses of SUCs created before 1946 were established later.

Source: CHED.

The Flagship University (FU) concept is particularly useful given the nuanced political-economic context and circumstances of Philippine universities. Douglass (2016a, p. 1) describes the new FU—as opposed to its traditional referents in the US and other countries—as "an institution grounded in its historical purpose, but remarkably different in its devotion to access and equity, to the quality of its teaching, research, and public services mission, and to meeting national and regional socio-economic needs." The FU concept shifts the paradigm away from the idea of World-Class Universities that are associated with global university rankings. Narrowly focusing on research metrics (e.g., citations) and the reputation of universities, the current league tables do not reflect the FU's tripartite mission in the face of FIRe, climate change, and pandemics that include public service and community engagement.

The question is, how government can use its public and private resources strategically to develop a high-performing higher education system that is anchored on a few national Flagship Universities. This is a challenging question. From historical experience and the country's electoral politics, politicians in the legislature and local governments are likely to support SUCs/LUCs—regardless of quality—whose immediate benefits are palpable to their constituencies.

4. PUBLIC–PRIVATE EDUCATION COMPLEMENTARITY

The 1987 Philippine Constitution mandates the establishment of an integrated education system premised on the complementarity of public and private HE providers. Shortly thereafter, the Congressional Commission on Education (EDCOM) recommended reform measures—e.g., limiting graduate education to qualified universities through flagship/consortium arrangements—with the same presumption (Congressional Committee, 1993, p. 137).

Since 1987, however, the principle of public–private complementary has remained undefined. Having no authoritative articulation of the theory or logic behind the principle to guide its application, had the following consequences:

- a bureaucratic mindset that treats the national education system as consisting only of public HEIs and Department of Education (DepEd) schools;
- sidelined complementarity principle in policy debates at basic and higher education levels;
- inordinate government attention and support to public education to the detriment of private education;
- passage of laws/policies/measures that marginalize private education; and
- failure to fully capitalize on the comparative advantages of a government–private education partnership.

Clarifying the complementarity principle and developing a framework to guide its application is necessary to help create more opportunities for students to benefit from the advantages of government and PHEIs working together. The lack of a level playing field between public and private education has made it extremely difficult for an average PHEI to survive despite its relatively better learning outcomes than many public HEIs. Regulations that raise the cost and difficulty of providing private education tilt the balance even more against private education, thereby lowering system efficiency as students and resources are reallocated from private to public education despite the relatively lower cost-effectiveness of public HEIs.[12]

Arguably, there are resource reallocation inefficiencies resulting from a distortion of incentives—e.g., weakening of the drive and ability of segments of the private education sector to be innovative, adaptable, and responsive to advances in S&T and market conditions; and forgone financial support from non-tax revenues that parents are willing to pay for HE that can be mobilized to support more quality improvements.

The process of establishing an authoritative and coherent policy framework that clarifies public–private education complementarity and guides its application in future national education system reforms has begun with the Senate initiative to conduct public hearings on this issue.[13] While seemingly modest in its aims, it is fervently hoped that this Senate initiative would trigger a long overdue sequel to the Congressional Commission on Education (EDCOM) of the 1990s that successfully carved out from

---

[12] See Paqueo et al. (2020).

[13] Led by Sen. Sherwin Gatchalian under Senate Resolution. No. 302 (2020), Directing the Appropriate Senate Committee to Conduct an Inquiry, in AID of Legislation, on Strengthening the Complementary Roles of Public and Private Institutions in the Philippine Educational System and Formulating a Framework to Operationalize the Principle of Complementarity to Achieve Our National Objectives and Sustainable Development Goals in Education.

the huge bureaucracy of DepEd separate spaces for the technical-vocational and higher education sectors.

5. COVID-19, THE PRIVATE EDUCATION CRISIS, AND THE NEXT NORMAL

A notable consequence of the lack of complementarity between public and private HEIs is the latter's marginalization over time as reflected in the steady decline of the private sector's share in enrollment. The loss of two cohorts of enrollees due to K to 12—with the exception of a few enrollees from private high schools whose years of schooling and adjusted curricula rendered them eligible to enroll—triggered a marked decline in the first-year college enrollment share of both public and private HEIs in 2016 and 2017 (Figure 41.6). However, by 2019, public HEIs regained their pre-K to 12 first-year enrollment (112 percent) while private schools had only 69 percent of their 2014 enrollment.

If the HE game changer in the 2010–2019 decade is K to 12, the COVID-19 pandemic is the game changer of the 2020s for HEIs. Since mid-March 2020, lockdowns/community quarantine have compelled all HEIs to shift to synchronous and asynchronous learning for more than a year now. Poor internet connectivity, homes unconducive to teaching/learning, anxiety over the spreading SARS-CoV-2 virus/variants and loss of jobs, mental

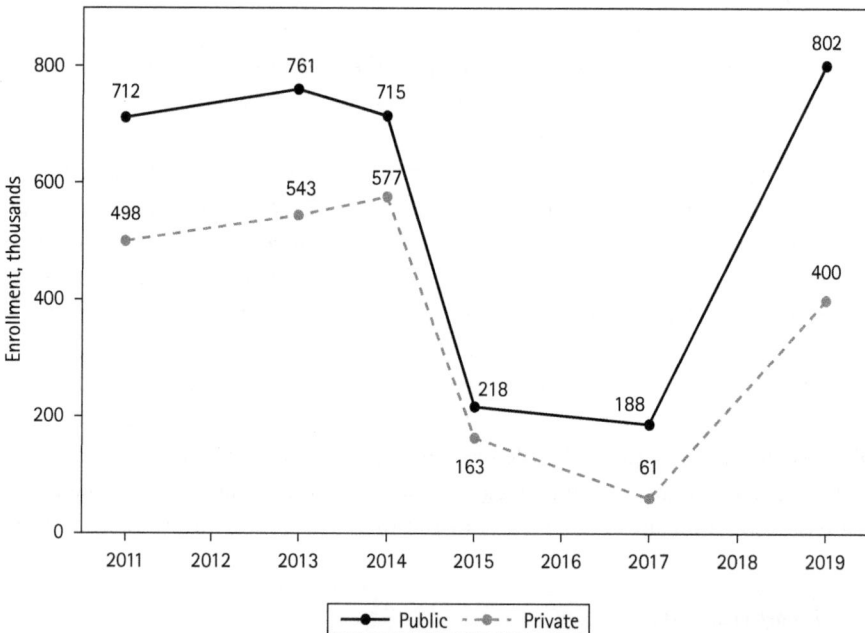

FIGURE 41.6 First year college enrollment in public and private HEIs, 2011–2019

Sources: Philippine Statistical Authority and APIS for various years as cited in Ortiz et al. (2019).

stress, overwhelming academic requirements, and faculty burnout from the close monitoring of learners are among the common challenges confronting all HEIs.

However, COVID-19 adversely affected PHEIs more than SUCs/LUCs. The Coordinating Council of Private Educational Associations (COCOPEA)—in its May 2021 letter to the Finance Secretary appealing the 25 percent tax on for-profit HEIs—argues that with the tax burden, many of these HEIs will be forced to suspend operations, as some have already done, and displace personnel or raise tuition at a time when Filipino families are reeling from the pandemic's employment impact.

During the pandemic, UP and other SUCs have been at the forefront of COVID-related research and innovations. While private HEIs also rendered COVID-related research and public service, most PHEIs are constrained from doing so by their enrollment crisis. Over 50 percent of respondents in the April 2021 Philippine Association of Colleges and Universities (PACU) survey, experienced a 10 to 50+ percent decline in enrollment in AY 2020–2021, with a corresponding drop in tuition income.

More than a year into the pandemic and with the hoped-for rollout of vaccinations, Philippine higher education has begun its transition to the next normal characterized by flexibility, interdisciplinarity, LLL opportunities, and a blend of face-to-face, virtual, and experiential learning, which the COVID-19 pandemic catalyzed.

The complementarity of public and private education is necessary for the next normal. If the private education sector is not supported to move out of its current crisis, the Philippines will not be able to optimize the benefits of government–private sector partnership in laying the groundwork for a better next normal. For this reason, it is imperative to open up a platform for reiterating the principle of public–private complementarity and rationalizing Philippine higher education, i.e., specifying the roles of government and the different types of public and private HEIs institutions; rethinking populist policies; curbing the increase in the number of SUCs and LUCs; and formulating policy options for greater inclusiveness while raising the ante for technical education within a lifelong learning framework; identifying flagship institutions among the top public and private universities and supporting their synergy in providing graduate degrees and producing cutting-edge research, and innovations; as well as strengthening the regulatory capacity of CHED to weed out non-compliant programs and institutions and its development function, among other imperatives.

Without rationalizing higher education, Philippine development will continue to lag farther behind its ASEAN peers.

References

Albert, J. R. et al. (2019). *The Future of S&T Resource Requirements in the Philippines*. Draft Final Report. Philippine Institute for Development Studies.

Alcala, A. (1999). "Higher education in the Philippines." *Philippine Studies*, 47/1, 114–128.

Alzona, E. (1932). *A History of Education in the Philippines, 1565–1930*. Manila: University of the Philippines Press.

AQRF Referencing Report of the Philippines (2019). https://pqf.gov.ph/Uploads/PH%20A
QRF%20Referencing%20Report%20Final.pdf, accessed December 22, 2020.

Caoili, O. (1983). "A history of higher education in science and technology in the Philippines."
Philippine Social Sciences and Humanities Review, 47, 302–303.

Cardozier, V. R. (1984). "Public higher education in the Philippines." *International Review of
Education*, 30, 193–208.

Conchada, M. and Tiongco, M. (2015). "A review of the accreditation system for Philippine
higher education institutions." *PIDS Discussion Paper Series No. 2015-30*. Quezon
City: Philippine Institute for Development Studies.

Congressional Commission on Education (1993). *Tertiary Education vol. 3. The Educational
Ladder*. Book 2: *Making Education Work*. Quezon City: Congressional Oversight Committee
on Education.

Dadios, E. et al. (2018). "Preparing the Philippines for the Fourth Industrial Revolution: A
scoping study." *PIDS Discussion Paper Series No. 2018-11*. Quezon City: Philippine Institute
for Development Studies.

Douglass, J. (2016a). "The evolution of flagship universities: From the traditional to the new."
University of California Center for Studies in Higher Education. Research and Occasional
Paper Series: CSHE.11.16.

Douglass, J. (ed.) (2016b). *The New Flagship University: Changing the Paradigm from Global
Ranking to National Relevancy*. London: Palgrave Macmillan.

Gonzales, A. (1989). "The Western impact on Philippine higher education." In P. G. Altbach and
V. Selvaratnam (eds.), *From Dependence to Autonomy* (pp. 117–141). Dordrecht: Springer.

James, E. (1991). "Private higher education: The Philippines as a prototype." *Higher Education*,
21, 189–206.

Killingley, P. and Ilieva, J. (2015). *Opportunities and Challenges in the Internationalization of the
Philippine Higher Education Sector*. Taguig: British Council.

Kim, C. I. E. and Hunt, C. (1968). "Education and political development: A comparison of
Korea and the Philippines." *The Journal of Developing Areas*, 2/3, 407–420.

Licuanan, P. (2017). "The state of Philippine higher education." Presentation at the Philippine
Higher Education Conference Private Education Assistance Committee, Pasay City,
November 28. https://peac.org.ph/wp-content/uploads/2017/12/LICUANAN-Philippine-
Education-Conference-ilovepdf-compressed.pdf, accessed December 22, 2020.

Orbeta, A. and Paqueo, V. (2017). "Who benefits and loses from an untargeted tuition subsidy for students in SUCs?" *Policy Notes No. 2017-03*. Quezon City: Philippine Institute for
Development Studies.

Ortiz, K., Melad, K., Araos, N., Orbeta, A., and Reyes, C. (2019). "Process evaluation of the
Universal Access to Quality Tertiary Education Act (RA 10931): Status and prospects
for improved implementation." PIDS DP 2019-36. https://pidswebs.pids.gov.ph/CDN/
PUBLICATIONS/pidsdps1936.pdf

Paqueo, V., Orbeta, A., and King, E. (2020). "Strengthening the complementarity of private
and public education: Towards greater inclusion, efficiency, and freedom of choice." Report
submitted to the Philippine Association of Colleges and Universities and Private Education
Assistance Committee.

Salmi, J. (2016). "Excellence strategies and the creation of world-class universities." In N. C. Liu,
Y. Cheng, and Q. Wang (eds.), *Matching Visibility and Performance: Global Perspectives on
Higher Education* (pp. 15–48). Rotterdam: Sense Publishers.

Santiago, L. (1991). "The beginnings of higher education in the Philippines, 1601–1772." *Philippine Quarterly of Culture and Society*, 19/2, 135–145.

Tan, E. (2011) "What's wrong with Philippine higher education?" *The Philippine Review of Economics*, XLVIII (1). June, 147–184.

USAID (2014 and 2019). *Science, Technology, Research and Innovation for Development. Philippine Innovation Ecosystem Assessment 2014 and 2019*. Manila: USAID.

Yee, K. M. (forthcoming). "The changing landscape of Philippine higher education: Going beyond the public and private debate". In F. dlC. Paragas. *Contemporary Issues in Philippine Higher Education*. Public Policy Monograph. University of the Philippines Center for Integrative and Development Studies Higher Education Research for Policy Reform Program.

Yee, K. M., Ducanes, G., and David, C. (2019). "Who serves the poor in Philippine higher education?" Presentation for the Higher Education Research and Policy Reform Program, University of the Philippines Center for Integrative and Development Studies, Quezon City.

Index

For the benefit of digital users, indexed terms that span two pages (e.g., 52–53) may, on occasion, appear on only one of those pages.

Note: Tables, figures, and boxes are indicated by an italic *t*, *f*, and *b* following the page number. The following abbreviations are used: GDP – gross domestic product; GERD – Gross Expenditure on Research and Development; HE – higher education; HEIs – higher education institutions; ICT – information and communication technologies; MOOCs – Massive Open Online Courses; PISA – Programme for International Student Assessment; R&D – research and development; STEM – science, technology, engineering, and mathematics; TVET – technical, vocational education and training

A

Abe, Shinzo 655–656
Abu Dhabi 322
academic freedom and autonomy 26–27
  China 589
  Hong Kong 714, 724
  India 603–604, 613–614, 624, 626–627
  Indonesia 777, 781–782, 783, 788–790
  Japan 632, 634–635, 640, 646–647
  Malaysia 799, 804–805
  Myanmar 844–845, 847–848
  nationalism 522, 524–526
  New Zealand 757–758
  Philippines 858–859
  Singapore 694, 695, 700, 702
  South Korea 674–675, 677–678, 679–681, 688
  Thailand 818–819, 823
Academic Freedom Index (AFI) 26n.11
academic nationalism 520–521
academic professionals
  Australia 735–736, 737–738, 742, 748–749
    internationalization 746–748, 747f
  China 561, 566, 569
    elite universities 578–579, 588
  gender 136f, 140–142, 768
  Hong Kong 719–720, 729–730

India 601, 602–604, 605, 608
  private universities 599–600, 622, 624
Indonesia 775, 779–780, 781–782, 784–785, 789, 791
Japan 632, 646
  internationalization 642–643, 658, 662
  professional education 235, 236
Malaysia 805, 806, 807, 810–811, 812
MOOCs 366
Myanmar 839–842, 843, 844–845
nationalism 523
New Zealand 757–758, 761, 764–766
Open Universities 350
Philippines 858, 861, 867–868, 869, 870, 874–875
professional education 228–229, 235, 236
returning talent 459, 460
Singapore 698, 702, 707–708, 709
South Korea 676, 684–686
Thailand 823–824
Academic Ranking of World Universities (ARWU) 13, 212, 213
  China 217
  Greater China 223–224
  indicator weights 214t
  Japan 639
  public financing 379n.1

access to HE 8–10, 70, 115–123, 130–131
  elite higher education to massification 55,
      56, 58, 59
  instruments to improve 123–128
    effectiveness 128–130
  rankings 13
  socio-economic status 69
accreditation see credentials
activism 1–2
  Hong Kong 101
  India 609, 618–619
  Indonesia 783
  Japan 631–632, 644
  Myanmar 837–838, 840, 847, 852–853
  nationalism 526–528
Adelaide, University of 35, 736
adult learning and education see lifelong
      learning
affirmative action 8–9, 123–124, 128–129,
      130–131
  gender 152
  India 604–605
    private universities 620–621, 625, 626
  student loans 427–428
Afghanistan
  access to higher education 122
  Education Law 538–539
  gender and socio-economic status 146t
  international students 269–270, 270t
  lifelong learning 536, 538–539
  public financing as percentage of total
      education spending 382t
Africa
  academic freedom 26
  Chinese universities' involvement in 509
  elite higher education to massification 61
  international students 16, 39–40, 684
  knowledge production 477–478, 480
  nationalism 516
  population growth 316
  urbanization 316
  see also North Africa; sub-Saharan Africa
age factors
  Australian academic professionals 746–747
  MOOCs 358–359
  Open Universities 333, 337, 342n.10,
      348–349
returning talent 454–455
  Singapore and lifelong learning 710
aging populations see demographics
Akita International University (AIU) 653
Allama Iqbal Open University (AIOU) 336,
      337, 338
Aligarh Muslim University 409b
All India Council for Technical Education
      (AICTE) 238, 597, 599, 600–601,
      607
All India Institute of Medical
      Sciences 594–595
Alliance française 509
American Association of University
      Professors 603–604
Andhra Pradesh Open University
      (APOU) 336
Android 367
Annamalai University 409b
Aotearoa see New Zealand
Apple 363, 367
Aquino, Benigno III 857
Arab countries
  enrollment rate 134
  hubs of HE 306, 314, 316
  international students
    from Indonesia 784, 785t
    to Indonesia 785t
  see also Middle East
Arimoto, Akira 22
Arkansas University 294
artificial intelligence (AI)
  employment and labor markets 74, 194
  future of higher education 40–41
  international students 294
  lifelong learning 539–540
  MOOCs 371
  Open Universities 347–348, 350
  STEM's importance 190
ASEAN (Association of Southeast Asian
      Nations)
  credentials 786
  cross-border cooperation 786
  employment and labor markets 74, 75–76,
      778
  enrollment rate 776
  Global Innovation Index 867

globalization 639
goals of higher education 106–107
Graduate Business and Economics
        Programme 275
innovation ecosystem 867, 868
international students 294–295, 783–784,
        784t, 869
    from Australia 744–745
    to Australia 743–744, 744t
    credit transfer scheme 295
    development assistance 275
    Thailand 823
journal publications 782
lifelong learning 869
MOOCs 364
Myanmar benchmarking 848–849
Myanmar protests 853
Philippines economic and education
        development comparison 865, 875
PISA scores 781
qualification frameworks 15
quality regulation 250
    national qualification frameworks 257
    Qualification References Framework
        (AQRF) 250, 862n.3
    quality assurance agencies 256, 256t
    Quality Assurance Network
        (AQAN) 294–295
Singapore's 70-70 target 707
STEM 194
well-being indicators 815
ASEAN Economic Community (AEC) 76
ASEAN International Mobility for Students
        (AIMS) 665
ASEAN Plus Three 275
ASEAN Qualifications Referencing
        Framework (AQRF) 250, 862n.3
ASEAN Quality Assurance Network
        (AQAN) 294–295
ASEAN university network (AUN) 275
ASEAN-China Business School Network 275
Ashoka University 407–408, 409b, 623–624,
        626
Asia eUniversity 336
Asia SEED 388–389
Asian Association of Open Universities
        (AAOU) 346, 347, 363, 364

Asian Cooperation Dialogue (ACD) 336
Asian Development Bank (ADB)
    access to higher education 121–122
    Asian University for Women,
        Bangladesh 181
    employment and labor markets 76, 82–84,
        88
    goals of higher education 94, 102
    innovation 318–319
    investment in higher education 67
    Myanmar 846–847
    poverty 69
    reports on higher education 3–4
Asian financial crisis 454, 521–522, 537, 815
Asian Institute of Technology 819–820
Asian Learning Portal 364
Asian Universities Alliance 587
Asian University for Women (AUW) 179–
        180, 181–182
Asia-Pacific Association of International
        Education 295
Asia-Pacific Economic Cooperation (APEC)
    Capacity Building Network (CBN) 77
    Education Network (EDNET) 77
    Education Strategy 2016–2030 76–77, 78,
        85, 87
    employment and labor markets 73, 87
    Framework on Human Resources
        Development in the Digital
        Age 77–78
    Human Resource Development Working
        Group (HRDWG) 77–78
    Kuala Lumpur Declaration (2020) 78
    Labour and Social Protection Network
        (LSPN) 77, 78
Asia-Pacific Quality Network
        (APQN) 294–295
Asia-Pacific Regional Convention on the
        Recognition of Qualifications
        in Higher Education see Tokyo
        Convention
Asiaweek 639
Association of American Colleges and
        Universities (AAC&U) 174–175,
        183–185
Association of Indonesian Private Universities
        (APTISI) 776–777

Association of Pacific Rim Universities
(APRU) 141
Association of Southeast Asian Nations *see*
ASEAN
Assumption University 363, 819–820, 831
Ateneo de Manila University 864
Auckland University 35, 755, 757–758,
765–766
Aung San Suu Kyi 845–846
Australia 748–749
access to higher education 117–118, 119
and China, tensions between 17, 746
Colombo Plan 743–744
cross-border cooperation 786
demographics 70t
economy 1, 68, 71t
elite HE to massification 6, 47, 51, 52, 54–55,
60–61
Japan comparison 58
Singapore comparison 59
employment and labor markets 75–76,
80–81, 82, 86
Excellence in Research Australia (ERA) 737
financing higher education 738–740, 739f
foreign-born population 761
gender 136–137, 147, 152
Go8 institutions 736, 740–741, 746
goals of higher education 5, 98
Goldring report 744
governance and management 737–738
Higher Education Contribution Scheme
(HECS) 444
Higher Education Participation
and Partnerships Program
(HEPPP) 738
highest educational attainment 72–73, 72t
history 5, 35, 37–40, 51, 735–736
hubs of HE 324–325
ICT readiness 139–140
Indigenous Scholars Success
Programme 741–742
Indonesian academic ties 782
influence on New Zealand's economic
structure 767–768
institutional forms 736–737
international academics in South
Korea 684–685

international branch campuses 15–16, 100,
312, 313n.2
Malaysia 321, 810
Singapore 321
international students
from China 294, 558
vs. domestic students 18t
from Hong Kong 728–729
from Indonesia 784
inward mobility rate 270–271, 270t
from Malaysia 808, 810
from Myanmar 850–851
numbers 269–270, 270t
from Thailand 824
wariness 21, 294
internationalization 2–3, 15, 17, 18–19, 73, 249,
271–272, 299t, 300t, 452, 743–748,
744t, 745t, 767, 822
commercial drivers 272–274
credentials and learning 167
development assistance 274
history 39–40
impacts on cities and regions 281–282
Malaysian partnerships 811
nationalism 522–523
postgraduate education 762
scholarships 298, 740
Tokyo Convention 296, 299
tuition fees 736
Jackson report 744
journal citations and documents
produced 380t
knowledge production 25–26, 465
bibliometrics 469f, 470, 472f, 473, 474–475,
474f, 475f, 476, 479–482, 479f, 481f,
483, 483f, 484, 485–486, 486f
GERD as percentage of GDP 467f
patent citations 488f, 489–491, 490f,
491n.29
patent count 492f, 494f
liberal arts and sciences 177–178
lifelong learning 536–537–, 539, 542, 545–546
living standards 68
MOOCs 356, 357, 358, 365–366, 370
Myanmar aid 846–847, 849
National Innovation and Science Agenda
(NISA) 476

New Colombo Plan 743, 748–749
Open Universities 332–333, 335, 336, 338,
  342n.9
Overseas Student Charge (OSC) 744
participation and equity 740–742, 741f,
  742f
polytechnics upgraded to universities 696
postgraduate education 95, 762
private HEIs 125f, 424, 736–737, 738, 743–
  744, 744t
private philanthropy 23, 405, 407, 414,
  416–417, 416t
  Global Philanthropy Environment
    Index 405, 406t
public financing of HE 125–126, 126t
  as percentage of private financing 381,
    383f
  as percentage of total education
    spending 382t
public HEIs 424, 736, 737
quality 54–55, 255–256, 262, 740–741
rankings 412–413, 413t
return on education 425t, 756
returning talent 460–461
soft power 510–511
student loans 24, 444
  description 446t
  funding source 429–431, 430t
  introduction 423
  objectives and coverage 426t, 427, 428,
    441
  repayment regime 433–435, 436, 436t
Tertiary Education Quality and Standards
  Agency (TEQSA) 737
University Foreign Interference
  Taskforce 460–461
Australia Awards 743
Australian National University (ANU) 413t,
  737n.3
autonomy see academic freedom and
  autonomy
Azim Premji University 409b

B

Banaras Hindu University 409b, 598
Bandung Institute of Technology 783, 788,
  789–790

Bangkok Convention 296, 297, 301, 302
Bangkok University 819–820, 827
Bangladesh 25
  access 122
  demographics 70t
  economy 71t
  employment and labor markets 82–83,
    148–149
  gender 135–136n.3, 136–137, 138–139,
    148–149
  highest educational attainment 72t, 73
  history 50, 335–336
  international academics in Australia 747f
  international students
    vs. domestic students 18t
    numbers 269–270, 270t
  internationalization 451–452
    commercial drivers 273
  liberal arts and sciences 179–180,
    181–182
  lifelong learning 536, 538–539, 543
  Open Universities 335–336, 339t
  private HEIs 14
  public financing
    per student 384f
    as percentage of GDP 383f
    as percentage of total education
      spending 381, 382t
Bank of India 445
Bar Council of India 597
Beijing 313
Beijing City University 562
Beijing Languages and Cultural University
  (BLCU) 294
Beijing Medical College 578–579
Beijing Normal University (BNU) 294
Beijing Radio and Television
  University 335–336
Beijing University 12, 564
  see also Peking University
Beijing University of Aeronautics and
  Astronautics 563–564
Belgium 320–321, 558
Bentinck, Lord William 32–33
Berlin, University of 631–632
Bharatiya Janata Party (BJP) 527–528,
  626–627

Bhutan
  access 122
  lifelong learning 536, 543
  public financing
    per student 384f
    as percentage of GDP 381, 383f
    as percentage of total education
      spending 382t
  Tokyo Convention 296
Bikhchandani, Sanjeev 624–625
Bill & Melinda Gates Foundation 410–412
Bina Nusantara University 783
Blackstone 407n.5
BLCU Tokyo College 294
BNU Cardiff Chinese College 294
Bogor Agricultural University 788
Bombay University 34
BombayX 360
bond markets 23, 388
Bond University 736
Boston city-region 310
Boston College, Center for International
    Higher Education 3
brain drain 24–25
  China 459, 569
  Hong Kong 728–729
  Indonesia 782
  Malaysia 9
  soft power 510
  STEM 189–190, 201–203, 206
branch campuses see international branch
    campuses
Brazil
  international students to Australia 740
  MOOCs 19, 358–359
  private HEIs 613t
bribery
  India 598
  Indonesia 787
British Council (BC) 167
  Myanmar 842, 847n.21
  soft power 500–501, 509
Brunei Darussalam
  access 122
  employment and labor markets 75–76
  gender 138–140
  goals of higher education 98

MOOCs 369
national qualification framework 258t
student loans 426t, 441, 446t
Buddhism
  history of HE 31–32, 34
  Indonesia 777
  private philanthropy 409
Burma see Myanmar
Bush, Vannevar 501–502
business models 17

C
Cai Yuanpei 555
Calcutta University 34, 616, 625
California, University of 386
Californian Master Plan 767–768
Cambodia
  access 118, 119, 121–122, 126, 127f
  economy 68
  elite HE to massification 52
  employment and labor markets 75–76, 83,
    83t, 150–151
  enrollment rate 776, 865
  gender 140, 146t, 147, 150–151
  goals of HE 98
  international students
    numbers 270t
    to Thailand 823
  internationalization 300t, 784t
  internet infrastructure 397
  lifelong learning 536, 543, 547
  national qualification framework 257, 258t
  private HEIs 14, 124–125, 125f, 404
  public financing
    as percentage of GDP 383f, 838n.1
    as percentage of total education
      spending 381, 382t
  STEM 194
  tuition fees 404
Cambridge University 51, 163
  Global Alliance of Universities on
    Climate 587
  influence of educational model 198–199
    Australia 735–736, 748
    India 616
  land portfolio 23
  talent attraction 589

Cambridge University Press 525–526
CAMPUS Asia 664
Canada
    employment and labor markets 84–85
    free tuition movement 445
    immigration policy 743n.7
    international branch campuses 313f
    international academics in South
            Korea 684–685, 685t
    international students 15, 73, 299t, 452, 453
        from China 558
    MOOCs 357
    private philanthropy 406–407
    public vs. private financing 739f
    Research Chairs 510
    returning talent 454–455, 460–461
    United States multinational
            corporations 495
Canara Bank 388–389, 609
Canterbury University 757–758, 766
Capital Medical University China 300–301
Capital Metropolitan University 554–555
Cardiff University 294
Caribbean 785t
Carnegie Mellon University Australia 736
Catholicism
    Indonesia 777
    Philippines 857
censorship
    Confucius Institutes 521
    India 603–604
    MOOCs 367
    nationalism 521, 525
    propaganda 504
    returning talent 456
Central Asia
    enrollment rates 116t, 403
    international students 451–452
        from Indonesia 785t
        to Indonesia 785t
    lifelong learning 536, 539
    quality assurance agencies 256t
Central Europe 785t
Central Universities, India
    affirmative action 620–621
    governance 601–602
    numbers 594, 617

postgraduate education 596
public financing 596–597
teaching vacancies 602–603
Chaiyaphum Rajabhat University 828–829
Chan-ocha, Prayuth 107
Charles Darwin University 737n.3
Chaudhary Charan Singh
        University 599–600
Chen Yidan 409b
Chicago, University of 11, 324
Chile
    free tuition movement 445
    international students to Australia 740
    Tsinghua University Latin America
            Center 587
China
    Academic Degrees Committee
            (ADC) 236–237
    academic freedom 26
    access 117–118, 119–120
        instruments to improve 124, 129–130
        international students 128
        scholarships 126, 127f
        study programs 121–122
    acquisition of Thai universities 824
    activism
        discouraged 644
        Tiananmen Square protests 454, 526
    and Australia, tensions between 17, 746
    Belt and Road Initiative 274, 295, 586
    C9 League 413n.8
    Cheung Kong Scholars Program 459
    continual rise of higher education and
            future challenges 569–570
    credentials and learning 11, 168–169
        examinations 162
        value 164
    cross-border cooperation 786
    demographics 18–19, 40, 69–70, 70t
    economic growth 1
    economy 68, 71t
    Education Law 391–392
    elite HE to massification 5, 6, 7f, 50–51, 53,
            54, 55–56, 60–61, 557, 562, 565–567,
            576, 580–581
        access/quality trade-offs 566
        equity 566–567

China (*cont.*)
  Hong Kong comparison 57
  India comparison 57
  private HEIs 560–561
  Singapore comparison 59
  Taiwan comparison 60
  elite HEIs 563–564, 565, 569, 588–590
    211 Project 556–557, 558, 564, 565, 575,
        579–580, 581, 584, 588
    985 Project 556–557, 558, 562, 564, 565,
        568, 575, 580, 581, 582–583, 584, 588
    characteristics and performance 582–
        584, 583*f*, 584*f*
    concept 574–575
    development 576–578
    Double First-Class Project 558, 562, 565
    Double-World-Class (DWC)
        policy 580–582, 584, 585, 586, 588,
        589
    funding 584–585
    global impact 586–587
    goals 105–106
    history 555
    international partnerships 585–586
    issues 575–576
    massification 566
    national key universities 578–579
    rankings 216–217, 222, 568
    research 557
  employment and labor markets
    future 75–76
    gender 148
    graduate work readiness 81
    lifelong learning 97
    overeducation 84–85
    technical, vocational education and
        training 82–83
  enrollment numbers 94, 95*f*, 390–391, 390*f*,
        402
  entrance examinations 9
  failure, academic 163
  funding of HE 562–563, 563*t*
  gender 145, 148
  Gender Gap Index 199–200
  geostrategic tensions 26–27
  globalization 639, 641–642
  goals of HE 5, 96, 98, 105–106, 108–109

  Green Passage program 392
  Higher Education Law 390–391, 407
  highest educational attainment 72*t*
  history 4–5, 31, 32, 33, 36, 37–40, 49, 50–51,
        105, 553
    Ancient China 553–554
    end of nineteenth century to
        1949 554–555
    1949–1976 555–556
    1977 onwards 556–558
  homogenization 290
  and Hong Kong
    relationship between 25, 26, 526–527, 730
    transfer 714
  hubs of HE 306–307
  Humboldtian universities 768–769
  influence of education model on Hong
        Kong 717
  international academics in Australia 746–
        748, 747*f*
  international branch campuses 290–291,
        293–294, 312, 313–314, 313*f*, 325
    Malaysia 810
    South Korea 684–685, 685*t*
  international research networks 20
  international students
    to Australia 740, 743, 744–745
    vs. domestic students 17–18, 18*t*
    to Hong Kong 729
    from Indonesia 784, 786
    to Japan 641–642, 653–655, 659
    to Malaysia 810
    from Myanmar 850–851
    to Myanmar 838
    to New Zealand 761–763, 761*f*, 762*f*
    numbers 269–270, 270*t*
    to South Korea 684, 685*t*
    to Thailand 823
    wariness about 21, 294, 523
  internationalization 16–17, 18–19, 73, 249,
        268–269, 271, 299*t*, 300*t*, 451–452,
        452n.2, 453, 558–560, 559*f*
    CAMPUS Asia 664
    credentials and learning 160, 164, 165–166,
        168
    cultural distance 272
    development assistance 274, 275

elite universities 579, 585–587
history 39–40, 556
impacts on cities and regions 280
importance 290–291
inward mobility rate 270t
Merdeka University proposal 806–807
modes of cross-border delivery 295
One Belt One Road policy 39–40
rankings 212, 216–217
researchers 278–279
soft power 21
Tokyo Convention 296, 299, 300–301, 302
journal citations and documents produced 380–381, 380t
knowledge production 465n.1, 495
bibliometrics 468–470, 468n.9, 469f, 472f, 473, 474f, 475f, 475–476, 477, 479f, 480–482, 481f, 484, 485
foreign multinational corporations 494–495
GERD as percentage of GDP 466, 467f
patent citations 488f, 489–491, 490f, 491n.29
patent count 491, 492f, 493, 494, 494f
liberal arts and sciences 176–177, 178–179
lifelong learning 536, 547
development 538, 539–540, 541, 542, 543–544
Ministry of Education (MOE) 251–252
Changjiang Scholars Program 559
China Discipline Ranking 568
Double-World-Class policy 582
funding 584–585
internationalization 558, 560
Modern Distance Education Project 543–544
MOOCs 359–360
Program of Studying in China 560
quality focus 557–558
Research Center for Online Education 359
Ministry of Finance (MOF) 558, 582
Ministry of Human Resources and Social Security 456
Modernization strategy 2035 586
MOOCs 20, 357–358

AI 371
censorship 367
cultural issues 369
emergence 358–360
language issues 368
pedagogical approach 370
regional collaboration 364
reputation of distance learning 365
National Development and Reform Commission (NDRC) 582
National Development High-Level University Public-Sponsored Postgraduate Student Scheme 558
National Key Discipline policy 579
National Scholarship program 392
National Science and Technology Plan 485
National Science Fund for Distinguished Young Scholars 459
nationalism
academic freedom, constraints on 525–526
activism 526–527
globalization of, in cyberspace 528–529
and internationalization 523
national brand promotion and soft power 521–522
rankings and status competition 524
numbers of HEIs 390–391, 391f
online learning 19
Open Universities 333n.5, 359
admission to 337
as alternative to conventional universities 342
future trends 348–349
history 335–336
single-teaching mode 335–336, 339t
private HEIs 125f, 404, 554, 555, 560–561, 562, 566, 569
percentage of enrollment 613t
private philanthropy 407, 409b, 414
endowments 416–417, 416t
Global Philanthropy Environment Index 406t
trends 410, 411f
professional education 229, 232–233, 236–237, 239–240, 241t, 242–243, 244
public financing 379, 390–391

China (*cont.*)
  categories 384
  disadvantaged student support 391–392
  expansion of higher education 389
  Government-Subsidized Student Loans
      Scheme (GSSLS) 387
  local governments 385
  per student 384*f*
  as percentage of GDP 383*f*, 391, 391*f*
  as percentage of private financing 381,
      383*f*
  as percentage of total education
      spending 381, 382*t*
  role of government 389–390
  public HEIs 561–562
  qualification frameworks, lack of 15
  quality 557–558, 562, 569
  diversified quality assurance
      system 260–261
  elite HE to massification 55, 566
  goals of HE 105–106
  internationalization 558, 559
  lead units 259*t*
  MOOCs 360
  neoliberalism 251–253
  Open Universities 359
  professional education 236–237, 240
  quality assurance and qualification
      frameworks as policy tool 257
  and repression 626–627
  Radio and TV Universities Network 359
  rankings 211, 216–217, 218, 220–221, 223–
      224, 412–413, 413*t*, 582–583, 583*f*
  China Discipline Ranking 223–224, 568
  elite HEIs 586
  power 221–222, 223
  professional education 237
  regulation of HE 568–569
  research 25
  collaboration 661
  output 608–609
  spending 608–609
  returning talent 559
  censorship 456
  consequences 456–457
  empirical evidence 456
  factors affecting 454–455

  Hundred/Thousand/Ten Thousand
      Talents programs 201–202, 459,
      460–461, 510, 559
  policies 459, 460
  Service-Learning Asia Network 182
  Singapore's 70–70 target 707
  soft power 504–505, 508–510, 521–522, 560
  State Council 558
  State Education Commission 558, 568
  STEM
  challenges and responses 201–203
  culture 197–198
  demand 191–194
  R&D spending 192–195, 193*t*
  student performance in science and
      math 196*t*
  student loans
  default measures and sanctions 434*t*
  description 446*t*
  funding source 430*t*, 431
  loans allocation and borrower
      selection 432
  objectives and coverage 426*t*
  operation 429
  reach 441
  repayment regime 435, 436*t*
  size of loan 441–442
  student numbers 566
  Taiwan conflict 506–507
  and the United States, tensions between
      495–496, 646, 815, 831–832
  University Alliance of the Silk Road 19
  urban population 316
  world class university movement 563–565
China Academic Degrees and Graduation
      Education Center (CDGDC) 237
China Agricultural University 578–579
China Discipline Ranking (CDR) 557, 568
China Open Resources for Education
      (CORE) 359
China Yuhua Education Corporation
      Limited 824
China–Italy Design Innovation Hub 587
China-Singapore Guangzhou Knowledge City
      (GKC) 313
Chinese Academy of Sciences 563
Chinese Communist Party (CCP)

Confucius Institutes 521
elite HEIs 581
international students 21
nationalism 525, 526
professional education 236
quality regulation 251–252
university charters 293–294
Chinese University of Hong Kong
(CUHK) 718–719
activism 526–527
history 50
private philanthropy 406–407, 416t
rankings 716
Christianity
China 554–555
Indonesia 777
International Christian University,
Japan 183
private philanthropy 409
South Korea 671–672
Chulalongkorn University 363, 508–509,
819–820, 831
Ciputra, Ir 407–408
CISCO 74
citizenship
goals of HE 8, 96–97, 98–99, 100–102, 108,
592–593
India 108, 592–593
liberal arts and sciences 183
lifelong learning 535–536, 539
nationalism 529
Singapore 100
City University of Hong Kong (CityU) 716
civic nationalism 515–516, 516f
class see socio-economic status
climate change
employment and labor markets 73
future of HE 40
international students 284
MOOCs 356
Philippines 872
CNMOOC 359
coaching 9
India 595n.9
codes of conduct 229, 233–234, 239–240,
241t
codes of ethics 229, 233–234, 239–240, 241t

Cold War
Australia 743
end of 314
Japan 641
Vietnam 744
collaborative online international learning
(COIL) 662–663
Collective Action for Mobility Program
of University Students in Asia
(CAMPUS Asia) 664
collective philanthropy, India 623–624
Colombo Plan 510
colonial legacy 2–3
Australia 741–742
goals of higher education 96
hubs of HE 307, 319
India 5, 592, 593, 603–604, 607
rankings 222
colonialism 32–35
Australia 735–736, 737–738, 743
credentials 164, 167, 168
elite HE to massification 49, 50, 53–54
end of 314
India 252–253, 592, 598
Indonesia 775
influence of education systems 199
Japan 507–508, 641
Malaysia 798, 808
nationalism 516, 517, 519–521
New Zealand 757, 764
Philippines 856–857, 865, 866
South Korea 671–672
Commonwealth Educational Media Center
for Asia 363
Commonwealth of Learning 347, 360, 544–545
Commonwealth Scholarship 510
Communist Party of China see Chinese
Communist Party
community learning centers (CLCs) 543,
545–546
competition
access 116, 123
China 582
goals of HE 8, 94, 103–104
Hong Kong 716–717, 719–720, 728–730
India 613–614, 621, 625
Indonesia 788

competition (*cont.*)
  internationalization 16, 269, 284
    importance 291
    modes of cross-border delivery 293
    researchers 278, 279
  Japan 103–104, 629–630
    globalization 639–640
    internationalization challenges 652, 653,
      655–656, 657, 659, 660–661, 665–666
    nation-building 636
  lifelong learning 538
  nationalism 21, 523–524
  New Zealand 759–760, 768–769
  Open Universities 346, 348–349, 350
  private philanthropy 403
  quality regulation 250–252
  rankings 12, 210–212, 215, 218–219, 220–221,
    223–224
    power 221–222
    prevalence 213
  returning talent 457–458
  Singapore 694–695, 705, 706
  soft power 501
  South Korea 670–671, 681–682, 688
  STEM 189, 190–191, 201–202, 203–204
  Taiwan 218–219
  Thailand 823–824, 832–833
Confucianism
  China 553–554
  elite HE to massification 52–54
  enrollment rate 95
  gender 145, 199–200
  history of HE 31, 32, 33, 49
  liberal arts and sciences 184
  lifelong learning 540
  private philanthropy 409
  soft power 500
  South Korea 671
  STEM 197–199, 205, 206
  Zengzi's "Way of Great Learning" 576–577
Confucius 553–554
Confucius Institutes 508–509, 510, 521
continuing education *see* lifelong learning
contract cheating 596
Convention on the Elimination of All Forms
    of Discrimination against Women
    (CEDAW) 124

Cornell Tech 321
Cornell University 321, 386
corporate universities, South Korea 677–678
correspondence learning 332–333, 334, 335–
    336, 543–544
  India 360
corruption
  India 596, 597–598, 602, 603
  Indonesia 786, 787–788
Coursera 19, 348, 358–359, 364
  apps 367
  China 359
  credentials 348
  cultural issues 369
  India 361
  lifelong learning 102
  South Korea 361–362
  study groups 369–370
COVID-19 pandemic
  APEC initiatives 78
  Australia 17, 745–746
  employment and labor markets 66, 78, 88
  future of HE 40, 41–42
  Hong Kong 730
  Indonesia 777–778, 779–780, 791–792
  internationalization 16–17, 21, 271, 272–274,
    282
  Japan 646, 662
  knowledge diplomacy 268–269, 283
  knowledge production 495–496
  lifelong learning 546
  Malaysia 811–812
  MOOCs 20, 277, 356, 368
  Myanmar 846
  nationalism 523, 528–529
  New Zealand 756, 760, 762–763, 766, 768–769
  online learning 283, 349, 396–397
  Open Universities 331, 347, 348, 350
  Philippines 858n.1, 862, 870, 870n.9, 874–875
  private philanthropy 410
  public financing 396–397
  rethinking universities 284
  returning talent 25, 461
  Singapore 705–706, 707, 709, 710
  soft power 509–511
  South Korea 689
  STEM investment 122

student loans 445–446
Thailand 815, 830–832
uncertainties 26–27
United States 17–18
university bonds market 388
credentials 159–161, 168–169
ASEAN 107
China 236–237
employment and labor markets 79, 88
history 38–39
Hong Kong 727
India 240, 592, 599–600, 606, 608, 609–
610, 621
Indonesia 786–787
international HE 159–161, 168–169, 291
value 164, 166–168
Japan 235, 236, 240, 633–634, 645, 664
and learning, relationship between 10–11,
159–49, 161–162, 165–166
liberal arts and sciences, relationship
between 11
lifelong learning 102, 542
MOOCs 275–276, 348, 357, 364–366
Myanmar 848–849
Open Universities 343, 345, 348, 350
Philippines 15, 862, 865–866
professional education 229–230, 233, 241t,
243–244
China 236–237
India 240
Japan 235, 236, 240
Taiwan 239, 240
quality regulation
diversified quality assurance
system 260–261
neoliberalism 252–253
quality assurance and qualification
frameworks as policy tool 254–255
upsurge of state control 260
South Korea 685–686
Taiwan 239, 240
value 164–165
credit institutions 23
credit transfer schemes 295
cronyism, India 596
Crowther, Lord 331–332
Culinary Institute of America 293

Curtin University
Malaysia 810
Singapore branch 100, 692–693
Curzon, Lord 598n.11

D
Dainton, Lord 693
Dalian 313
Dalian University of Technology 559
Danone Group 544–545
De la Salle University 864
debt, student see loans, student
Deemed-to-be Universities, India 594–595,
613–614, 617
Delhi University 336, 600, 602–603, 616–617
Democratic People's Republic of Korea see
North Korea
demographics 2
access to higher education 117–118, 128
China 580–581
COVID-19 pandemic 41
employment and labor markets 68, 69–70,
70t, 73, 75
future of higher education 40, 41
goals of higher education 98, 103–104, 107
hubs of HE 315
India 617–618, 619
Indonesia 774, 776, 791
international students 18–19, 39–40, 128,
271–272, 289–290
Japan 16–17, 103–104, 235, 629–630, 634–
635, 637–638, 639–640, 643–644
liberal arts and sciences 178–179
lifelong learning 536, 539
massification 6
MOOCs 368
Myanmar 842–843
New Zealand 760, 768
Open Universities 338
Philippines 865, 871
professional education 235
quality regulation 251
Singapore 505–506
South Korea 673, 675, 681–682, 683–684,
687–688, 689
STEM 191–192
Thailand 107, 821, 831–832

Deng Xiaoping 359, 526, 556, 558
Deutsche Gesellschaft für Internationale
        Zusammenarbeit 362
development assistance 274–275
Dhawan, Ashish 624–625
Dhurakij Pundit University (DPU) 831
digital divide
    Indonesia 777
    lifelong learning 543–544, 545
    Malaysia 811
    MOOCs 348, 357
    Open Universities 346–347
Ding Shisun 564
disability
    access 120
    India 604
    Myanmar 844
    Open Universities 333, 337
distance learning
    Indonesia 777–778, 786
    Myanmar 840–841, 846, 850
    see also correspondence learning; online
        learning
Divinity, University of 736
Dominican University of Santo Tomas 856
Dornogovi Medical School 662–663
Doshisha University 660–661
double degrees see joint/double degrees
dropouts
    Australia 741–742
    Israel 388
    Open Universities 344–345
dual-mode distance teaching Open
        Universities 334, 336
Dubai 292, 325
Dublin, University College 810
Duke Kunshan University 19, 585–586
Duke University Singapore 307, 320–321, 324,
        702
Duke-NUS Medical School 321
Dusit Thani College 831

E
East Asia
    access 128
    CAMPUS Asia program 664
    credentials and learning 161, 165–166, 168–169

demographics 18–19
developmental states 704–705
economic growth 1, 642, 646
educational meritocracy 162–163
elite HE to massification 6, 6f, 52–53, 54,
        723–725, 724f
enrollment rates 68, 115–116, 116t, 134, 251,
        403
    gender 134–135
expenditure on higher education 68
Gender Gap Index 199–200
globalization 639
history 36–37, 49
international students to and from
        Indonesia 785t
internationalization 18–19, 451–452
    development assistance 274
    researchers 278–279
    Tokyo Convention 299
knowledge production 465
    engineering and technology topics 484,
        484t
    Field Weighted Citation Impact 484–
        485, 485f
    GERD 475–476
    Relative Activity Index 482–483, 483f,
        484–486, 486f
liberal arts and sciences 176–177, 178–179, 184
lifelong learning 536–537, 541
nationalism 518–519, 523
nation-building, Japan 646
Open Universities 343
PISA scores 162–163
qualification frameworks 15, 257
quality regulation 250–251, 256t, 256, 257
researchers 152
returning talent 459, 460
returns to education 147–148
STEM 197–200, 205
East China Normal University 585–586
East India Company 32–33
Eastern Europe 516, 785t
École Polytechnique Fédérale de
        Lausanne 369–370
economic growth 1–2, 3–4
    access to HE 116, 122, 130–131
    Asian "tigers" and ASEAN countries 639

China 251–252, 559, 580–581, 589, 654–655
Confucianism 197
East Asia 642, 646
gender 134–135
goals of HE 5, 94, 106
Hong Kong 1
hubs of HE 323
India 593–594, 618, 620–621, 627–628
Indonesia 776
international students 272–273, 281
Japan 634–635, 641–642, 644
knowledge production 478
lifelong learning 546
Malaysia 844–845
Myanmar 844–845, 846
nationalism 520
Philippines 868
private philanthropy 403, 410
Singapore 106, 692, 696–697, 704–705
South Korea 1, 670, 844–845
South-East Asia 646
STEM 189–190
Thailand 815, 820–821, 833, 844–845
Vietnam 393–394
economy
    access to HE 123
    employment and labor markets 66–67,
        68–69, 70–72, 71t
        future 73–74
        graduate work readiness 80
    growth see economic growth
    hubs of HE 315
    international students 160
    returning talent 454, 455
    student loans 445
EDHEC 100
Edinburgh University 587
Education City Qatar 326
Education for All (EFA) 536–537
education hubs see hubs of HE
edX 19, 348, 358–359
    apps 367
    China 359
    credentials 348
    India 360, 361
    regional collaboration 364
    South Korea 361–362

Egypt 558
Egypt–Japan University of Science and
        Technology (E-Just) 661–662
elderly people 539, 541
e-learning see online learning
elite HEIs 6, 47, 48
    access 9, 115, 118, 123, 129–130
    China see China: elite HEIs
    future 60–62
    goals 8, 105–107
    history 5, 37, 49–51
    hubs of HE 320–321
    India 608–609, 625, 626
    Indonesia 782
    international students 2–3
    Japan 218, 636
    Malaysia 219
    New Zealand 755–756, 767–768
    Philippines 15, 856–857, 864–865
    present 52–60
    private philanthropy 23–24
    public financing 22–23, 379
    rankings 12, 210–211, 216–221, 222, 223–224
    Singapore 695
    social hierarchies 5
    South Korea 217
    STEM 203–204
    Taiwan 218–219
employability 81–82
    access to HE 121
    India 107–108, 596, 606–608
    Indonesia 778
    international students 280
    Myanmar 845, 848–849
    policy reform, need for 284
    professional education 243
    Singapore 706–707, 710
    strategic responses 85–86
    Thailand 824–827
    see also graduate work readiness
employment and labor markets 7–8, 66–67,
        78–82, 87–88
    AI 40–41
    China 56, 565, 567, 588
    credentials 10–11, 159–161, 165, 168
    diverse economies and
        demographics 68–73

employment and labor markets (*cont.*)
    elite HE to massification 53, 56, 57, 58, 59
    gender 9–10, 143–144, 147–151, 150*f*, 151*t*, 153
    Hong Kong 56, 57, 718, 725, 729–730
    hubs of HE 316–317
    India 58, 593
    Indonesia 775, 778
    international students 11, 272, 281–282
    Japan 16
        globalization 641–642, 644–645
        internationalization challenges 654,
            659–661, 666
        lifetime employment 103
        nation-building 636, 637–638
        part-time/short-term
            employment 103–104
    liberal arts and sciences 178
    lifelong learning 97
    mega trends 73–78
    MOOCs 365–366
    Myanmar 840–841, 846
    New Zealand 755–756, 758–760
    Open Universities 345
    overeducation 84–85
    Philippines 865, 866
    returning talent 454, 455, 458–459, 460
    Singapore 697, 703, 706–707
    South Korea 683–684, 686–687
    STEM 12, 189–191, 194, 199–202
    strategic responses to generating work-
        ready graduates 85–86
    student loans 442–443, 445
    Taiwan 59
    technical, vocational education and
        training 82–84
    Thailand 819–820, 822, 824, 832
    see also professional education; transitional
        labor markets; underemployment;
        unemployment
English language *see* language issues
English Proficiency Index 203–204
entrance examinations
    access 9, 129–130
    China 237, 553, 556, 567, 576, 577–578, 588
    credentials and learning 162–163
    India 238, 601
    Indonesia 778–780, 789–790

    Japan 103, 636
    Malaysia 802
    Myanmar 838–839
    Open Universities 337
    professional education 237, 238
    quality regulation 250
    regulations 14–15
    South Korea 673, 674
    STEM 197–198
    Thailand 821–822
entrepreneurs
    credentials 11
    graduate work readiness 86
    India 598–599, 612–613, 619, 621, 623–625
    Indonesia 407–408
    Japan 660–661
    liberal arts and sciences 183–184
    lifelong learning 535
    returning talent 456–457
    Singapore 706
equity/inequity
    access 116–123, 130–131
        instruments to improve 123–130
    Australia 118–739, 740–742, 748, 749
    China 55, 56, 565, 566–567, 569, 578, 579,
        583, 588
    elite HE to massification 6–7, 52–53, 55, 56,
        60
    employment and labor markets 67, 73, 75
    gender 134–153
    goals of HE 95–96
    Hong Kong 724–725
    India 604–606, 621, 625–626, 627–628
    Indonesia 774, 775, 777, 778–782, 779*t*, 783,
        788, 791–792
    international students 269, 276, 284
    Japan 637–638, 659
    liberal arts and sciences 182, 183
    lifelong learning 536–537, 538–539, 540,
        545–546
    Malaysia 800–804, 811
    MOOCs 276, 356, 357, 360, 366–367, 371
    Myanmar 842–844, 847–848, 849–850
    New Zealand 755, 756, 763–766, 767, 768,
        769
    Open Universities 333, 337–338, 344,
        346–347, 348

Philippines 862–864, 863f, 863t, 864f, 868
public financing 396
rankings 13
Singapore 692–693, 703–705
socio-economic status 162
South Korea 675–676
STEM 189–190, 199–201, 206
Taiwan 60
Thailand 818–819
ERASMUS 165–166
ESSEC Asia Pacific, Singapore 100, 325,
    692–693
Estonia 196t
e-TESDA 362–363
ethnic nationalism 515–516, 516f
ethnicity
access 9, 120–121, 124, 128–130
Australia 746–749
gender 144–145
goals of HE 96–97
lifelong learning 538–539
Malaysia 9, 798, 801–802, 802t, 806, 808
Myanmar 842–844, 845–846, 849–851,
    852
Open Universities 334
returning talent 460
Singapore 703
student loans 428
Vietnam 395
Europe
colonialism 32–35
economic growth 1
elite HE to massification 47, 48, 61
foreign direct investment in Singapore 692
gender 149n.12
high-skilled employment 316–317
history 49, 174
Indonesian academic ties 782
influence of education model
    China 577
    Japan 631–632
international academics 658
international students 2–3, 268–269, 453
    from Japan 659
    to New Zealand 761–762
    researchers 279, 827
    to South Korea 684

knowledge production 477–478, 480, 489
learning 165
liberal arts and sciences 174
MOOCs 357–358, 364, 370
nationalism 519
professional education 230, 243
quality of HE 39
rankings 39, 223–224
regionalization of HE 518–519
STEM 189–190
urbanization 316
see also Central Europe; Eastern Europe;
    Western Europe
European Commission 213–214
European Community Action Scheme for
    the Mobility of University Students
    (ERASMUS) 663
European Patent Office (EPO) 488
European Union (EU)
Brexit 510, 514
enrollment rate 134
hubs of HE 315
international students 290
lifelong learning 545
evening classes, New Zealand 757
eWant 365–366
examinations
credentials and learning 161–163, 168
entrance see entrance examinations
professional education 230, 235, 239
exploitation vs. soft power 504

F
faculty see academic professionals
failure, academic 163
fake news 528–529
Fake Universities, India 595n.8, 600–601
fees see tuition fees
fertility rates see demographics
Field Weighted Citation Impact (FWCI) 479–
    482, 479f, 481f, 484–485, 485f, 486–
    487, 487f, 495, 496
patent citations 489, 491
Fiji 382t
financial engineering 23
Finland 196t, 197t
flagship universities see elite universities

flexible learning
  Open Universities 331
    as alternative to conventional
      universities 342
    characteristics 332–333
    technologies 337–338
  part-time employment 444
foreign students *see* international students;
    internationalization
formal examinations *see* examinations
Fourth Industrial Revolution (4IR)
  employment and labor markets 66
    COVID-19 pandemic 88
    future 73, 75, 76
    TVET 82, 83–84, 83*t*
  future of higher education 40–41
  Japan 666
  Philippines 867, 872
  Singapore 697, 706, 709
  STEM 190
France
  elite HE to massification 7*f*, 51
  history 32, 34, 49
  influence of education model 199, 518
    Japan 631–632
    Thailand 816
  international branch campuses 313*f*
    Singapore 321
  international students 299*t*
    from China 558
    scholarships 298
    trends 652, 654–655
  private philanthropy 23
  professional education 229–230
  STEM 193*t*
  triangle of coordination 231–232
  United States multinational
      corporations 495
franchising 274, 293
Free Speech Movement 526
free tuition movement 445
freedom *see* academic freedom and autonomy
Fudan University 12, 293–294, 560–561
Fukuda, Yasuo 656
Fukuzawa, Yukichi 633
future of HE 40–42
  elite HE to massification 60–62

employment and labor markets 73–78
  APEC education strategy and associated
      initiatives 76–78
FutureLearn 361

G
G20 191–192, 453, 774
Gadjah Mada University 34, 775, 777–778,
    783, 788
Gandhi, Mohandas Karamchand 598
Gandhi, Rajiv 618
Gaokao see entrance examinations: China
Gatchalian, Sherwin 873n.13
gender 134–135, 151–153
  access 9–10, 116, 119–121, 123, 130–131
    affirmative action 124
    open and distance learning 127–128
    study programs 122–123
  Asian University for Women,
      Bangladesh 181–182
  Australia 735–736, 741–742, 741*f*, 748–749
  China 566–567
  educational sacrifices 161
  elite HE to massification 52, 60
  employment and labor markets 67, 70–72, 71*t*
  highest educational attainment 70–72, 72*t*, 73
  horizontal segregation in areas of
      study 138–140, 139*t*
  hubs of HE 307–308
  India 593, 595, 596, 604–605
  Indonesia 778, 779, 780*t*
  Japan 633, 637–638, 637*f*
  leaky pipeline in the academic
      profession 136*f*, 140–142
  lifelong learning 536–537, 538–539, 540
  Malaysia 803*f*, 803
  MOOCs 357, 358–359, 366–367
  Myanmar 838, 839–840, 841, 843–844
  New Zealand 757
  Open Universities 333, 344
  reasons for differences 142–151
  returning talent 454, 455–456, 460
  South Korea 675–676
  STEM 189–190, 199–201, 206
  Taiwan 60
  vertical progress in enrollment rates 135–138,
      136*f*, 137*f*, 138*f*

General Agreement on Trade in Services
        (GATS) 18, 292–293, 309, 320
George Mason University 320–321
Germany
    correspondence learning 334n.6
    free tuition 871
    history 33, 49
    Humboldtian universities 769
    influence of education model 199, 518
        China 555, 562, 566
        India 616–617
    international branch campuses 313f
    international students 299t, 652, 654–655
        from China 556, 558
    knowledge production 473, 473n.15
    massification 7f
    MOOCs 368
    public vs. private financing 739f
    R&D spending 193t
    Science Citation Index articles 564–565
    soft power 500–501
    United States multinational
        corporations 495
Germany Academic Exchange Service
        (DAAD) 500–501
Ghent University 320–321
gig economy 349
GINI Index 774
Global Alliance of Universities on
        Climate 587
Global Competitiveness Index 867
global financial crisis 53, 100
Global Innovation Exchange (GIX) 294, 321,
        587, 867
Global MOOC and Online Education
        Alliance 587
Global Philanthropy Environment
        Index 404–405, 406t
globalization 17–18
    elite HE to massification 49, 61
    employment and labor markets 66, 87
    history of HE 37–38
    hubs of HE 309
    India 238, 596
    Indonesia 791
    international students 290–291
    Japan 639–645

professional education 235
slow internationalization 641–643
stagnation in higher education
        investment 639–641
university reforms without a prospective
        future vision 643–645
liberal arts and sciences 173, 178–179
lifelong learning 535
Malaysia 811
models 322–323, 323f
nationalism 514, 518–519, 520–521, 528–529
professional education 235, 238
quality regulation 253
rankings 210, 215, 222, 575
Singapore 709
soft power 500–501
South Korea 674, 683–684
STEM 189, 191, 192–194, 202–203
goals of HE 5–6, 8, 93–98, 108–109
    China 105–106
    India 107–108
    Japan 102–104
    potential contradictions 98–102
    Singapore 106
    Thailand 106–107
Goethe Institute 509
Goh Chok Tong 694, 701, 703
Goodhart's Law 13
governance
    Australia 737–738
    China 105–106, 568–570
    goals of higher education 104, 105–106,
        108–109
    Hong Kong 724, 725–727
    hubs of HE 322
    India 592, 596, 597, 600–603, 608, 609–610
        private universities 613–614, 618–619,
        620–628
    Indonesia 788–789
    Japan 104, 108, 657–658
    lifelong learning 542–543
    Malaysia 804–805
    meritocracy 163
    Myanmar 847–848
    New Zealand 757–758
    Philippines 858–859
    private philanthropy 405

governance (*cont.*)
  quality regulation 263
    lead units 259*t*
    neoliberalism 250–254
    quality assurance and qualification
        frameworks as policy tool 255–256
    upsurge of state control 257–260
  rankings 213–214, 215, 219, 223
  Singapore 106, 108, 700, 703, 708, 709
government financing *see* public financing
graduate work readiness (GWR) 78–82, 87
  strategic responses 85–86
green economy 73
gross domestic product (GDP) 68
  enrollment rates 118, 118*f*
  GERD as percentage of 465–468, 467*f*,
    475–476
  goals of higher education 94
  government expenditure on higher
    education as percentage of 125–126,
    126*t*
  growth 1
  Indonesia 774, 775
  public financing as percentage of 381–384,
    383*f*
    China 391*f*, 391
    Japan 392
    Vietnam 394
  R&D spending as percentage of 192–194,
    193*t*
  research funding as percentage of 867
Guangzhou Knowledge City (GKC) 313

H
Hanwu, Emperor 577
Harbin Institute of Technology 578–579
Harvard Business School 102
Harvard University
  as elite 48
  MOOCs 359
  private philanthropy 408, 408*b*, 410–412
  professorial arrests 294
  public financing 388
  talent attraction 589
Hawawini, Gabriel 322–324
Heath, Sir Edward 359
Hebei Institute of Communications 562

Heilongjiang Oriental College 562
Heng Swee Keat 707
Heriot-Watt University 810
Higher Education Press 359
Hinduism
  history of HE 34
  India 527, 603–604
  Indonesia 777
  private philanthropy 409
history 4–5
  Australia 735–736
  China 553–558, 576–578
  colonialism and its legacy 32–35
  contemporary period 37–40
  distance learning 335–336
  elite higher education to
    massification 49–51
  India 598–599, 614–619
  Indonesia 775–776
  Japan 629, 631–632, 633–634
  liberal arts and sciences 174–176
  Malaysia 798–800
  Myanmar 837–838, 842–843, 845–846
  New Zealand 755, 756–758
  Philippines 856–858
  post-World War II 35–37
  precedents 31–32
  Singapore 693–694
  South Korea 671–676
  Tokyo Convention 296–297
Hitotsubashi University 632
HKSAR Government Scholarship
    Fund 727–728
Ho Chi Minh City Open University 370
Hokkaido University 632
Hong Kong 714–718, 730
  academic freedom 26
  access 117–118, 122, 716–717
  and China
    crackdown on grassroots
      movements 510
    relationship between 25, 26, 526–527, 730
    transfer of sovereignty 454
  credentials and learning 163–164, 168–169
  current system 715–716, 715*t*
  demographics 18–19, 40
  Diploma Yi Jin (DYJ) 718

economic growth 1
Education and Manpower Bureau 717
Education Commission 716–717
elite HE to massification 53–54, 56–57,
        723–724, 724*f*
    challenges 724–725
    Japan comparison 58
    Singapore comparison 59
employment and labor markets 81
English language 167
equality and social mobility
        challenges 724–725
failure, academic 163
funding
    dominant model 722
    marketization and diversification 720–722,
        721*t*
    policy changes 719–720
    public universities 718–719
globalization 639
goals of HE 101
governance challenges 725–727
    quality assurance 725–727
history 37–39, 49, 50
hubs of HE 306–307, 324
ICT readiness 139–140
international academics 729–730
    in Australia 747*f*
international branch campuses 293, 313
international students
    inward mobility rate 270*t*, 270–271
    from Myanmar 850–851
    numbers 269–270, 270*t*
internationalization 2–3, 15–17, 18–19,
        271–272, 642, 727–730
    commercial drivers 274
    cultural distance 272
    Immigration Arrangements for Non-
        local Graduates (IANG) 727–728
    learning 166
    strategies and policies 727–728
    student mobility and
        curriculum 728–729
Japan's developmental state model as
        inspirational 507
Joint University Programs Admission
        System (JUPAS) 717

knowledge production 25–26, 465n.1
    bibliometrics 469*f*, 472–473, 472*f*, 474–
        477, 474*f*, 475*f*, 479–482, 479*f*, 481*f*
    GERD as percentage of GDP 466, 467*f*
    patent citations 488*f*, 490*f*, 491n.29
    patent count 492*f*, 494*f*
liberal arts and sciences 177–178, 182
lifelong learning 536, 538, 539–540
nationalism 517, 523, 524, 526–527
non-means tested loans scheme
        (NLS) 438–439
Open Universities 336n.7, 339*t*
pathway to post-secondary education 717–
        718, 718*f*
PISA scores 162–163
private HEIs 57, 125*f*, 715–716, 715*t*, 722, 728,
        729*f*
    student numbers 723*f*
private philanthropy 405, 407, 414
    aggressive pursuit of 407
    endowments 416*t*
    Global Philanthropy Environment
        Index 406*t*
    Matching Grant Scheme 405–406
public financing as percentage of total
        education spending 382*t*
public HEIs 718–719
    funding 720–722
    internationalization 728, 729*f*
    student numbers 723*f*
quality 714, 716, 725, 730
    divergence between quality assurance
        and qualification framework 262
    diversified quality assurance
        system 260–261
    elite HE to massification 57
    lead units 259*t*
    quality assurance and qualification
        frameworks as policy tool 255–256
rankings 220, 223–224, 412–413, 413*t*
repayment regime 436*t*
Research Assessment Exercise (RAE) 720,
        726
returning talent 25, 454, 457
Service-Learning Asia Network 182
STEM 205–206
    challenges and responses 202–203

Hong Kong (*cont.*)
    culture 197
    demand 192
    R&D spending 194–195
    reform, need for 205
    student performance in science and
        math 196*t*, 197*t*
    Student Financial Assistance Agency
        (SFAA) 432
    student loans
        collection 437–438
        default measures and sanctions 434*t*
        description 446*t*
        funding source 430*t*
        loans allocation and borrower selection 432
        objectives and coverage 426*t*
        operation 429
        reach 441
        repayment and recovery 438–439
        size of loan 441–442
        subsidies 440
    University Grants Committee
        (UGC) 715–716, 715*t*
        funding 719–722
        internationalization 728, 729, 729*f*
        pathway to post-secondary
            education 717
        quality assurance 725–726
        University Accountability Agreements
            (UAA) 726
Hong Kong Academy for Performing Arts
    (HKAPA) 716, 719
Hong Kong Advanced Level Examination
    (HKALE) 716–717
Hong Kong Certificate of Education
    Examination (HKCEE) 716–717
Hong Kong Council for Accreditation
    of Academic and Vocational
    Qualifications (HKCAAVQ) 727
Hong Kong Diploma of Secondary Education
    (HKDSE) 717–718
Hong Kong PhD Fellowship Scheme 728
Hong Kong Polytechnic University
    (PolyU) 416*t*, 526–527, 716
Hong Kong Shue Yan University 722
Hong Kong University of (HKU) 718–719
    funding 720–722, 721*t*

history 50
    internationalization 729–730
    knowledge production 491
    private philanthropy 416*t*
    rankings 12, 413*t*, 716
Hong Kong University of Science and
        Technology (HKUST) 413*t*, 416*t*,
        716
Horizon Europe 478
Huan, Duke 554
Huawei 496n.33
hubs of HE 20, 306–308
    deep internationalization and articulated
        infrastructure 319–324
    definitions and patterns 309–314
    elite higher education to massification 54,
        59, 61
    Hong Kong 714, 730
    implications and critique 324–327
    India 625
    international students 249, 274
    Japan 651, 655–656
    Malaysia 219, 809, 810, 811, 812
    processes and structural change 314–319
    rankings 221–222
    Singapore 692–693, 700–472, 701–702
    soft power 505–506
    STEM 202–203, 206
Hui Ka Yan 409*b*
Human Capital Index (HCI) 86
    Indonesia 778
Human Development Index (HDI) 86
Humboldtian universities 767, 768–769
Hynix 686–687

I

icourse163 359
ICT
    gender 139–140, 153
    India 599, 618, 619
    lifelong learning 543, 545
    MOOCs 366–368
    Myanmar 845
    Open Universities 331, 345–348, 349, 350
    public financing 396
    South Korea 674, 686–687
    see also technological change

Illinois at Urbana-Champaign, University of 587
illiteracy *see* literacy/illiteracy
immigration policy
 Australia 743
 Hong Kong 727–728
 Japan 654
Imperial College (Taixue) 554
Imperial College London
 Singapore 320–321, 324, 701, 702
 Zhejiang University campus 587
Incheon 313, 320–321, 677–678
income share agreements (ISAs) 432
income-contingent loans (ICLs) 387, 433–437, 436*t*
 Australia 739–740
 collection 437–438
 debt/repayment burdens 442
incorporated universities, South Korea 677
India
 Academic Performance Index (API) 608
 access 117–118, 119, 120
  instruments to improve 123–124, 128–129
  limits of 604–606
  open and distance learning 127–128
  private universities 121
  scholarships 126, 127*f*
  study programs 122
 autonomy and academic freedom 603–604
 Citizenship Amendment Act 527–528
 Civil Service Conduct Rules 601
 demographics 69–70, 70*t*
 Department of Science and Technology 623
 Distance Education Council 343
 economy 68, 71*t*
 Educational Loans Scheme (ELS) 433
 elite HE to massification 5, 6, 7*f*, 53–54, 57–58, 596–597
  private HEIs 618–619
  purpose of HEIs 593–594
 employability 606–608
 employment and labor markets
  future 75–76
  graduate work readiness 81, 86
  labor force participation rates 70–72

  skill shortages 80
  TVET 82–83
 enrollment rates 94, 95*f*, 117–118, 402
 entrance examinations 9
 gender
  academics 141
  level of education 135–136n.3
  and socio-economic status 143, 144, 145, 146, 146*t*
  study programs 138–140, 139n.6
 goals of HE 5, 8, 96, 98, 101, 107–108
 governance crisis 414n.14
 Higher Education Financing Agency (HEFA) 388–389, 609
 highest educational attainment 72*t*, 73
 history 4–5, 31, 32–33, 34, 36, 37–40, 49, 50, 594
 homogenization 290
 informal sector 70–72
 international academics in Australia 746–747, 747*f*
international students
 to Australia 743
 vs. domestic students 18*t*
 inward mobility rate 270–271, 270*t*
 from Myanmar 850–851
 numbers 269–270, 270*t*
 to New Zealand 761*f*, 761–762, 762*f*
internationalization 73, 269, 271–272, 299*t*, 300*t*, 451–452, 453, 620–621, 824
 development assistance 275
 elite HE to massification 58
 entrepreneurs 624–625
 goals of HE 107–108
 history 39–40
 importance 290–291
 learning 166
 research networks 20
 Tokyo Convention 296
journal citations and documents produced 380–381, 380*t*
knowledge production
 bibliometrics 469*f*, 469–470, 472*f*, 473, 474*f*, 475*f*, 477–478, 479*f*, 480–482, 481*f*, 486
 foreign multinational corporations 494–495
 GERD as percentage of GDP 466, 467*f*

India (*cont.*)
  patent citations 488*f*, 489, 490*f*, 491n.29
  patent count 492*f*, 494*f*
  Kothari Commission Report 596–597
  liberal arts and sciences 176–177, 182, 184
  lifelong learning 538–540, 543–544
  loans scheme 24
  mapping the higher education
    landscape 594–598
  Ministry of Education 601–602
  Ministry of Human Resource Development
    (MHRD) 361, 388–389, 594, 601–602,
    601n.14, 609
    All India Survey on Higher Education
      (AISHE) 612, 617
  MOOCs 19
    access to ICT and internet 366–367
    cultural issues 369
    emergence 358–359, 360–361
    regional collaboration 364–365
    reputation of distance learning 365
  National Assessment and Accreditation
    Council (NAAC) 178, 252–253,
    600–601, 604
  National Board of Accreditation
    (NBA) 252–253
  National Education Policy (NEP) 365, 600,
    608–609
  National Loans Scholarship scheme 433
  National Medical Commission Act 598
  National Skills Qualifications Framework
    (NSQF) 252–253
  nationalism 525, 527–528
  New Education Policy (NEP) 612, 623, 626–627
  online learning 19
  Open Universities 360, 543–544
    admission to 337
    as alternative to conventional
      universities 342
    history 336
    quality measurement 343
    single-teaching mode 336
  poverty 69
  private HEIs 14, 124–125, 125*f*, 594, 595,
    596, 598–600, 612–614, 627–628,
    776–777, 781–782
    employability 606

    equity pressures 779
    financial shortcomings 789
    gender mix 595
    governance 620–627, 788
    historical, economic, and political
      context 614–619
    Institutions of Eminence 609, 613–614,
      621, 622
    legal, regulatory, and institutional
      framework 619–620
    percentage of enrollment 613*t*
    vs. public university enrollment 424
    quality assurance 786–787
    rankings 783
    regulations and governance 601, 601n.14
    requirements for setting up 615*t*
  private philanthropy 407–408, 409*b*
    Global Philanthropy Environment
      Index 406*t*
  professional education 229, 232–233, 237–238,
    239–240, 241*t*, 242–243, 244
  public financing 22
    off budget 388–389
    per student 384*f*
    as percentage of total education
      spending 381, 382*t*
  public HEIs 598–600
  purpose of universities 592–594
  quality 3, 251–253, 259*t*, 596, 597, 598–600,
    601, 609–610
    access 606
    elite HE to massification 58
    employability 607
    goals of HE 107–108
    international students 620–621
    private HEIs 618–619, 621, 622, 625,
      626–627
    professional education 238
  Ramalingaswami Fellowship 459
  rankings 222–224
  regulations and governance 600–603
  research 25
  return to higher education 425*t*
  returning talent 460–461
    consequences 456–457
    factors affecting 454–455
    policies 459, 460

Saakshar Bharat Mission 538–539
Satellite Instructional Television
        Experiment (SITE) 360
Science Citation Index articles 564–565
Service-Learning Asia Network 182
Singapore's 70-70 target 707
skill share 70–72
STEM 191–192, 199–202
    R&D spending 193t, 194–195
student loans
    COVID-19 pandemic 445
    default measures and sanctions 434t
    description 446t
    funding source 430t, 431–432
    loans allocation and borrower
        selection 432, 433
    objectives and coverage 426t, 427–428
    operation 429
    repayment regime 436t
University Grants Commission
        (UGC) 238, 240, 597, 600–601
    Academic Performance Indicator 476
    autonomy 604
    Countrywide Classroom 360
    funding 596–597
    MOOCs 365
    private HEIs 600, 613–614, 621–622,
        623
    urban population 316
    Visiting Advanced Joint Research Faculty
        (VAJRA) 477
Indian Banks' Association 433
Indian Council of Medical Research 597
Indian Council of Social Science Research
        (ICSSR) 608
Indian Institute of Science 409b
Indian Institutes of Information
        Technology 271, 594–595
Indian Institutes of Management
        (IIMs) 594–595
    access 605
    history 5
    private philanthropy 407–408
    public financing 596–597
    teaching vacancies 602–603
Indian Institutes of Science Education and
        Research 594–595

Indian Institutes of Technology (IITs) 237,
        594–595, 609
    access 605
    credentials 10–11
    employability 607
    full-fledged universities 622
    history 5
    international students 270–271
    MOOCs 360
    private philanthropy 407–408
    public financing 596–597
    quality 3
    teaching vacancies 602–603
Indian School of Business 409b
Indian Technical Education Quality
        Improvement Project 81
Indiana University 404–405, 406t
indigenous peoples
    Australia 735, 741–742, 742f, 748–749
    Malaysia 798, 801–802, 802t
    New Zealand 756, 758
        academic professionals 764–766
        completion rates 763–764
        history 757
        participation 759–760
Indira Gandhi National Open University
        (IGNOU) 336, 360
    admission to 337
    funding 348–349
    lifelong learning 543–544
    online learning 19
    quality measurement 343
    student numbers 338
Indonesia 774, 791–792
    academic freedom 26
    academic matters 781–783
    access 8–9, 117–118, 120
        scholarships 126, 127f
        study programs 122
    ADIK scholarship 781
    centralized autonomy 790–791
    Constitution 775–776
    cost-recovery measures 404
    current landscape 776–778, 776t
    demographics 69–70, 70t
    Directorate General of Higher Education
        Indonesia 257–260

Indonesia (*cont.*)
  economy 68, 71*t*
  elite HE to massification 7*f*, 52, 776, 781, 787
  employment and labor markets
    future 74, 75–76
    gender 148–149
    graduate work readiness 85–86
    labor force participation rates 70–72
    skill shortages 80
    TVET 83, 83*t*
    unemployment 80
  enrollment rates 95*f*, 860*f*
  equity pressures 778–781, 779*t*, 780*t*
  financial shortcomings 789–790
  gender 139–140, 143, 145, 148–149
  goals of HE 5, 96, 98
  governance ambiguity 788–789
  Higher Education Law 775
  highest educational attainment 72–73, 72*t*
  history 32, 34, 36, 38–39, 775–776
  international academics in Australia 747*f*
  international students
    to Australia 743–744, 744*t*
    vs. domestic students 18*t*
    to Japan 659
    numbers 270*t*
    to the Philippines 865
    from Thailand 824
  internationalization 300*t*, 783–786, 784*t*,
    785*t*, 792
    commercial drivers 273
    Tokyo Convention 296
  Japanese official development aid 641
  journal citations and documents
    produced 380–381, 380*t*
  knowledge production
    bibliometrics 469–470, 469*f*, 475*f*, 479*f*,
      480n.23, 481*f*
    patent citations 488*f*, 490*f*, 491n.29
    patent count 492*f*
  lifelong learning 536, 538–539
  Ministry of Education 788
    centralized autonomy 790–791
    Directorate General of Higher
      Education 750, 788
    quality assurance 786
  Ministry of Education and Culture 257–260

  Ministry of Education, Culture, Research
    and Technology 257–260
  Ministry of National Education 343
  Ministry of Religious Affairs 788
  Ministry of Research and Technology
    (MoRT) 257–260
  MOOCs 364, 365–367, 369
  National Education Board for Higher
    Education (BAN-PT) 786–787
  Open Universities 777–778, 787, 792
    admission to 337
    employer satisfaction with graduates 345
    history 336
    quality measurement 343
    single-teaching mode 336, 339*t*
  private HEIs 14, 124–125, 125*f*
    percentage of enrollment 613*t*
    vs. public HEIs enrollment 424
  private philanthropy 407–408
    Global Philanthropy Environment
      Index 406*t*
  public financing 22, 126*t*
    per student 384*f*
    as percentage of GDP 383*f*
    as percentage of private financing 381,
      383*f*
    as percentage of total education
      spending 381, 382*t*
    tuition fees 397
  public HEIs 776–777, 781–782
    centralized autonomy 790–791
    equity pressures 779, 780–781
    financial shortcomings 789
    governance 788–789
    quality assurance 786–787
  Public Service Agencies (BLU) 788–789
  quality 257–260, 258*t*, 259*t*, 774, 777, 778,
    781–782, 783, 786–788, 792
  rankings 476
  return to higher education 424, 425*t*
  Service-Learning Asia Network 182
  skill share 70–72
  State Owned Legal Entities
    (BHMN) 788–789
  State Personnel Agency (BKN) 791
  State University Legal Entities
    (PTNHB) 789

STEM 191–192, 194
student loans 426t, 435, 446t
Tsinghua University Southeast Asia
    Centre 587
Indonesia, University of
    corruption 787
    financial shortcomings 789
    governance 788
    international students 784
    Japan's role 641
    ranking 783
Indonesian Smart Card 780–781
Industrial Revolution 33
Industry 4.0 66, 73, 75–76
    TVET 83t
incquity see equity/inequity
informal economy 70–72, 71t
information and communication technologies
        see ICT
innovation see R&D
INSEAD 99, 100, 102, 322, 701
Institute for Teaching by Correspondence,
        Russia 334n.6
Institute of Chartered Accountants, India 597
Institutes of National Importance,
        India 594–595, 596
international branch campuses (IBCs) 273–274,
        290–291, 293–294, 311
    Australia 736, 744–745
    China 559, 585, 587
    deep internationalization and articulated
        infrastructure 320–321
    elite HE to massification 54
    geographies 312–314, 313f, 314f
    growth 19, 311–312, 312f
    implications and critique 324–326
    Indonesia 784–786
    Japan 505–506, 507, 632, 633, 642–643
    Malaysia 15–16, 803, 808, 810
    motivation for 295
    nationalism 521–522
    Singapore 100, 505–506, 692–693, 701, 702
    soft power 505–506, 507, 521–522
International Christian University (ICU),
        Japan 179–180, 182–183
International Conference on Globalism vs.
        Nationalism (November 2017) 38n.2

International Council for Open and Distance
        Education (ICDE) 347
International Islamic University of Malaysia
        (IIUM) 807
International Labour Organization
        (ILO) 66–67, 73, 74, 75–76
    automation of jobs 194
    COVID-19 pandemic 88
    gender 135, 149n.12
    high-skilled employment 316–317
    unemployment and
        underemployment 78–79
International Monetary Fund (IMF)
    COVID-19 pandemic 41
    learning society 535
    Thailand 829
International Standard Classification of
        Education (ISCED) 663–664
International University of Japan (IUJ) 652
internationalization 2–3, 15–21, 268–269,
        282–284, 303
    access 9, 128
    COVID-19 pandemic 41
    credentials 10–11, 159–161, 165–166, 168–169
        value 164, 165, 166–168
    diverse trends and legacies 269–277
        commercial drivers 272–274
        curriculum building 277
        development assistance 274–275
        online learning and MOOCs 275–276
    domestic vs. international students 17–18,
        18t
    elite HE to massification 54, 58, 61
    employment and labor markets 73
    future 27
    history 38–40
    impacts on cities and regions 280–282
    importance 289–292
    liberal arts and sciences 178–179
    modes of cross-border delivery 292–295
    MOOCs 368
    nationalism 514, 522–524
    quality regulation 249–250
    rankings 210–211, 212, 216–217
    researchers 277–279
    return see returning talent
    soft power see soft power

internationalization (*cont.*)

    STEM 201, 202–203

    Tokyo Convention 295–302

        history 296–297

        latent functions 301–302

        manifest functions 299–301

        Sustainable Development Goals
            297–299

    see also international branch campuses;
            under Australia; China; Hong
            Kong; India; Indonesia; Japan;
            Malaysia; Myanmar; New Zealand;
            Philippines; Singapore; South
            Korea; Taiwan; Thailand; Vietnam

internships

    China 237

    graduate work readiness 86

    international students 277, 664

    Japan 235

    professional education 230, 235, 237, 243

    Singapore 706–707, 709

    South Korea 686–687

Iran

    access 122

    international students to
        New Zealand 762

    journal citations and documents
        produced 380–381, 380*t*

    private HEIs 613*t*

    public financing

        per student 384*f*

        as percentage of GDP 383*f*

        as percentage of total education
            spending 382*t*

Ireland 96, 739*f*, 810

Irrawaddy Policy Exchange (IPE) 847n.21

Islam

    history of HE 34

    India 527, 604–605

    Indonesia 774, 777, 783, 786, 788

    lifelong learning 539

    Malaysia 807, 812

    private philanthropy 409

Islamic University of Indonesia 775

Israel 388, 466, 608–609

Italy 231–232, 299*t*, 558, 587

iTunesU platform 363

J

Jakarta State University 787

James Cook University Singapore 100,
    692–693

Jamia Millia Islamia University 409*b*, 527–528,
    598

Japan 629–631, 646–647

    academic freedom 26

    access 122–123, 128, 129

    Asian Gateway Initiative 655–656

    Central Council for Education (CCE) 651–652,
        654–655, 657–658, 661

    Certified Evaluation and Accreditation
        (CEA) revisions 261–262

    colonialism 671–672

    Council for Science, Technology and
        Innovation (CSTI) 522

    Council on Promotion of Human
        Resources and Globalization
        Development 657

    demographics 18–19, 40, 69–70

    developmental state 704–705

    economic growth 1

    economy 71*t*

    elite HE to massification 6, 7*f*, 51, 52, 53–54,
        58–59, 60–61

        nation-building 634–635, 636

    employment and labor markets 75–76, 81

    foreign direct investment in Singapore 692

    Foreign Research Fellowship Project 658

    Foreign Resident Support Center
        (FRESC) 660–661

    gender

        academic professionals 140–141

        employment and labor markets 149–151,
            150n.13

        Gender Gap Index 199–200

    Global COE Program 658

    globalization 639–645

        professional education 235

        slow internationalization 641–643

        stagnation in higher education
            investment 639–641

        university reforms without a prospective
            future vision 643–645

    goals of HE 8, 96, 98, 102–104, 108–109

    Great East Japan Earthquake 657

highest educational attainment 72–73, 72*t*
history 5, 31–32, 33, 35–36, 37–39, 49, 50, 51,
  58–59, 103, 629, 631–632, 633–634
ICT readiness 139–140
Indonesian academic ties 782
influence of education model on
  China 562, 577
Innovation 25: 656
international academics in South Korea 685*t*
international branch campuses 294, 313
international students
  from China 556, 558
  vs. domestic students 18*t*
  inward mobility rate 270*t*
  from Myanmar 850–851
  to New Zealand 761*f*
  numbers 269–270, 270*t*, 653–654, 654*f*,
   659, 660*f*
  to South Korea 685*t*
  from Thailand 824
internationalization 15–17, 18–19, 73, 249,
  268–269, 270–272, 299*t*, 300*t*, 452,
  452n.2, 453, 646–647, 651, 665–666
  100,000 International Student
   Plan 652–653, 654–655
  300,000 International Students
   Plan 656, 658–659
  CAMPUS Asia 664
  development assistance 274–275
  diversification 661–662
  Global 30 Project 656–658
  global networks 663–664
  Go Global Japan 657, 659–660
  impacts on cities and regions 280, 282
  importance 289–290
  "internationalization at home" 662–663
  Inter-University Exchange Project 657
  issues 658–661
  policy evolution 651–658
  rankings 639
  regional networks 663–665
  researchers 20, 278–279
  slow 641–643
  Tokyo Convention 299–301
internet infrastructure 397
journal citations and documents
  produced 380*t*

knowledge production 495
  bibliometrics 469–470, 469*f*, 472*f*, 473,
   474, 474*f*, 475*f*, 479*f*, 480n.23, 481*f*,
   484
  foreign multinational
   corporations 494–495
  GERD as percentage of GDP 466, 467*f*
  patent citations 488*f*, 489–491, 490*f*
  patent count 470*f*, 491–494
liberal arts and sciences 176–177, 178–179
  International Christian University 179–
   180, 182–183
lifelong learning 536–537, 538, 539–540, 541,
  542
Lifelong Learning Promotion Law 537
living standards 68
Ministry of Education (MOE)
  internationalization challenges 651–652,
   653, 655
  nation-building 633–634
Ministry of Education, Culture, Sports,
  Science and Technology
  (MEXT) 103–104, 393
  internationalization challenges 659,
   661–663
  joint degree programs 642–643
  Open Universities 343
  professional education 234–235
  quality regulation 252
Ministry of Justice 654
MOOCs 364, 367
National Information Center for Academic
  Recognition (NIC) 664
National Institute of Technology 832
National Institution for Academic Degrees
  and Quality Enhancement of
  Higher Education (NIAD-QE)
  professional education 235, 240
  quality regulation 261–262
nationalism
  academic freedom, constraints
   on 525–526
  and internationalization 523
  national brand promotion and soft
   power 522
  nation-building 520, 521
  rankings and status competition 524

Japan (*cont.*)
  nation-building
    absorbing mass demand through non-
      governmental resources 633–635
    adoption of Western higher education
      systems 631–632
    hierarchical differentiation based on
      student selectivity 635–636
    population decline 637–638
  Open Universities
    as alternative to conventional
      universities 342
    history 335
    quality measurement 343
    single-mode distance teaching
      universities 339*t*
  PISA scores 162–163
  postgraduate education 95
  private HEIs 14, 103, 124–125, 125*f*, 630
    globalization 639–640
    internationalization challenges 652–654,
      659
    nation-building 633–634, 635, 821–822
    percentage of enrollment 613*t*
    vs. public HEIs 424, 676–677
  private philanthropy 23, 414
    endowments 416*t*
    Global Philanthropy Environment
      Index 405, 406*t*
  professional education 229, 232–233, 234–
      236, 239–240, 241*t*, 242–243, 244
    graduate schools 234–235
    universities and junior colleges 235–236
  Provisional Council for Education 644
  public financing 125–126, 126*t*, 392–393
    categories 384
    expansion of higher education 389
    guaranteed student loans 387
    local governments 385
    off budget 388–389
    per student 381–384, 384*f*
    as percentage of GDP 381–384, 383*f*, 392
    as percentage of private financing 381,
      383*f*, 392–393
    as percentage of total education
      spending 381, 382*t*
    vs. private financing 739*f*

    role of government 389–390
    tuition fees 397
    university bonds market 388
  public HEIs
    globalization 640
    nation-building 633–634, 635, 636
  qualification frameworks, lack of 15
  quality 250, 629–630
    diversified quality assurance
      system 260–261
    globalization 643, 644, 645
    goals of HE 104
    input-based to output-based
      approach 261–262
    internationalization challenges 654–655
    lead units 259*t*
    nation-building 635
    neoliberalism 251–253
    professional education 235, 240
    quality assurance and qualification
      frameworks as policy tool 254–255,
      257
  rankings 12, 16–17, 211, 217, 218, 220, 412–
      413, 413*t*
    Top Global University Project 476
  research 22, 25–26
  return to HE 425*t*
  returning talent 457, 460–461
  Science Citation Index articles 564–565
  skill share 70–72
  soft power 504–505, 507–508, 509–511
  STEM 205–206
    challenges and responses 199–200, 202
    culture 197–198
    demand 191–194
    R&D spending 193*t*, 194–195, 205–206
    reform, need for 204–205
    student performance in science and
      math 196*t*, 197*t*
  student enrollment
    1945 634*t*
    2020 630*t*
    by gender 637–638, 637*f*
    trends 634–635, 635*f*
  student loans 24
    COVID-19 pandemic 445
    debt/repayment burdens 442

default measures and sanctions 434*t*

description 446*t*

funding source 430*t*, 431–432

objectives and coverage 426*t*, 429

reach 441

repayment and recovery 439

repayment default 438

repayment regime 435, 436*t*

technical institution numbers compared to India 593

Top Global University (TGU) project 657–658

University Council of Japan 234

Yasukuni Shrine 510

Japan Association of Corporate Executives 657–658

Japan Bank for International Cooperation 388–389

Japan External Trade Organization (JETRO) 660–661

Japan International Cooperation Agency (JICA) 507–508, 850

Japan ISI Corporation 294

Japan Patent Office (JPO) 488

Japan Revitalization Strategy 660

Japan Society for the Promotion of Science (JSPS) 393

Japan Student Services Organization (JASSO) 393, 431–432, 641

Japan University Accreditation Association (JUAA) 256, 633–634

Jawaharlal Nehru University 527–528

Jeju Global 324–325

Jervois, William 755

Jesuit University of San Ignacio 856

Jiang Zemin 580

Jilin Huaqiao Foreign Languages Institute 562

Jindal University 407–408

Jinling College 554–555

Jio Institute 409*b*

Jixia Academy 554

Johns Hopkins University (JHU) Singapore 307, 702

Johor Bahru 313

joint ventures

China 585–586

hubs of HE 321–322

joint/double degrees 293

Japan 651, 661, 662*f*, 664

Jordan 383*f*, 384*f*

K

Kachin Independence Organisation (KIO) 850–851

Kalay University 850

Kansai University 662–663

Kasetsart University 828–829

Kazakhstan

international students 299*t*

lifelong learning 539

private philanthropy 406*t*

public financing 382*t*

student loans 426*t*, 430*t*, 446*t*

Keijo Imperial University 632

Keio University 17n.6, 103, 633

Kerr, Clark 767

King Edward VII Medical College of Medicine 693, 798

King Mongkut's Institute of Technology

Ladkrabang 641, 832

Thonburi 832

knowledge diplomacy 268–269, 279, 283

knowledge production 464–468, 495–496

bibliometrics 468–487

efficiency of research 472–478

impact of research 478–487

corporate 487–495

foreign multinational corporations 494–495

patent citations 488–491

patent count 491–494

see also R&D

Koizumi government 104

Korea Advanced Institute of Science and Technology 361–362

Korea Distance Education Association 361

Korea Education and Research Information Service (KERIS) 361

Korea National Open University (KNOU) 336

dropout rates 344–345

enrollment numbers 348–349

ICT 345–346

MOOCs 361, 368

quality measurement 343

student numbers 338

Korea Open CourseWare Consortium
    (KOCWC) 361
Korean Council for University College
    Education (KCCE) 685–686
Korean Council for University Education
    (KCUE) 343, 685–686
Korean War 670
Krea University 409b, 623–624
Krirk University 824
Krung Thai Bank 437–438
Kuala Lumpur 313–314
Kuala Lumpur Education City (KLEC) 326
Kyoto Overseas Business Center 660–661
Kyoto University 17n.6, 23, 300–301, 413t,
    416t, 632
Kyrgyz Republic 381, 382t, 406t, 539
Kyungsung Imperial University 671–672
Kyushu University 632

L
labor markets see employment and labor
    markets
Lahore University of Management Sciences 2–3
land-grant universities 23, 386
language issues
    China 359–360, 586
    credentials 164, 167, 168
    elite HE to massification 54
    Hong Kong 729–730
    hubs of HE 315
    India 361, 606
    Indonesia 778, 779, 781, 782, 792
        internationalization 783–784, 785–786
    international students 16, 73, 271–272
        commercial drivers 273
        curriculum building 277
        importance 291–292
        inward mobility rate 270–271
        MOOCs 276
        Tokyo Convention 300–301
    Japan 646
        globalization 641–642
        internationalization 653, 656–658, 666
    knowledge production 475, 478, 483
    liberal arts and sciences 177, 178, 185
    Malaysia 798, 805–807, 811
        internationalization 810–811

MOOCs 20, 348, 359–360, 361, 363, 364,
    368–369
Myanmar 840–841, 841n.8, 842–843, 845
Open Universities 348
Philippines 856–857
rankings 13, 211–212, 216
research networks 643
scientific journals 520–521
South Korea 671, 684–685
Sri Lanka 363
STEM 203–204
Thailand 823, 826–827
Lao People's Democratic Republic
    access 118, 122, 127f
    digital divide 357
    economy 68
    employment and labor markets 75–76, 80
    enrollment ratio 865
    gender 135–136n.3, 144–145, 148–149
    goals of HE 98
    international branch campuses 294
    internationalization 296, 784t
    lifelong learning 536, 538, 540
    private universities 125f
    public financing 126t, 382t
Latin America
    academic freedom 26
    elite HE to massification 61
    enrollment rate 134
    international students 453
        to and from Indonesia 785t
    nationalism 516
    social impact bonds 388
    see also South America
league tables see rankings
learning and credentials 10–11, 159–49, 161–
    162, 165–166
    international HE 159–161, 165–169
    value 165
learning cities 542, 545–546
learning society 535, 540, 545
Lee Hsien Loong 695–696, 703–704
Lee Kong Chian School of Medicine 321
Lembaga Tabung Haji 326
LexisNexis 493
LG Electronics 686–687
Li, Robin 409b

Liber Hermods Institute, Sweden 334n.6
liberal arts and sciences 173–174
    emergence in Asia-Pacific 176–179, 177f
    history, core values, and
                philosophy 174–176
    Hong Kong unrest 101
    implications and challenges 183–185
    India 600, 622, 623–624, 626–627
    innovative examples 179–183
    learning 165–166
    quality of higher education 3
    and STEM, relationship between 11
    technological change 7–8
licensing 274
lifelong learning (LLL) 10, 534, 545–547
    APEC Education Strategy 2016–2030 76–77
    Asian context 536–537
    Australia 735
    China 566
    development 537–545
        international and regional
                drivers 544–545
        issues LLL is posed to address 538–539
        major trends and patterns 541–544
        societies imagined through LLL 539–540
    employment and labor markets 66, 76
    goals of higher education 93, 97–98, 101–102,
                103, 104, 106
    Japan 103, 104
    liberal arts and sciences 175–176
    MOOCs 275–276, 363, 364
    Open Universities 10, 350
    Philippines 869, 875
    rise as a global policy discourse 535–536
    Singapore 106, 694, 700–701, 706–707, 709,
                710
    South Korea 674, 678
    Sri Lanka 363
    Thailand 363
Lincoln University 766
Lingnan University (LU) 716
Lisbon Convention 15–16
literacy/illiteracy
    Indonesia 775
    lifelong learning 536–537, 538–539, 545
    Myanmar 843
    Open Universities 338

Livelihoods Funds 544–545
Liverpool University 585–586
living standards 68, 69–70
loans, student 14, 24, 423–425, 443–445
    Australia 739
    coverage 426t, 428–429
    COVID-19 pandemic 445–446
    forgiveness 444
    guaranteed loans 387
    Hong Kong 725
    Japan 393, 641
    Malaysia 803–804
    New Zealand 758, 759–760, 767
    objectives 425–428, 426t
    operation 429–438
        collection 437–438
        funding source 429–432
        loans allocation and borrower
                selection 432–433
        repayment default, containing 438
        repayment regimes 433–437
    repayment and recovery 438–439
    and student needs 440–443
        debt/repayment burdens 431
        reach 441
        size of loan 441–442
    subsidies 440
    Thailand 829–830, 832–833
    US 865–866
    Vietnam 395
London, University of 50, 334, 334n.6, 592
London Business School 102
Luxembourg 761

M
Ma, Jack 409b
Macao
    access 122
    gender 135–136n.3, 138–139
    international students 271
    lifelong learning 536
    public financing 381, 382t
    rankings 223–224
    STEM 196t
Madras University 34
Mae Fah Luang University 831
Mahidol University 819–820, 827, 828–829, 831

Malaviya, Madan Mohan 598
Malaya, University of (UM) 693
  history 34, 50, 798, 799, 800, 804–805, 806,
    810
  rankings 213–214, 220, 811
Malaysia 798–799, 811–812
  academic freedom and autonomy 804–805
  access 8–9, 117–118
    and equity 800–804, 801t, 802t, 803f
    instruments to improve 124, 128–129
    scholarships 127f
    study programs 121–122
  Code of Practice for Institutional Audit
    (COPIA) 261
  Code of Practice for Program Accreditation
    (COPPA) 261
  Constitution 805–806
  demographics 69–70, 70t
  Department of Community Colleges
    Education 257–260
  Department of Higher Education 260
  Department of Polytechnic
    Education 257–260
  development of HE 799–800
  economic growth 844–845
  economy 71t
  Education Blueprint (MEBHE) 253, 809,
    810, 811
  elite HE to massification 52, 53–54, 61, 776,
    800, 811
  Employees Provident Fund 431
  employment and labor markets
    future 74, 75–76
    gender 150–151
    graduate work readiness 81, 85–86
    labor force participation rates 70–72
    unemployment 80
  enrollment rates 95f, 860f
  gender
    academic professionals 141–142
    employment and labor markets 150–151
    level of education 135–136n.3
    study programs 138–139
  goals of HE 5, 96–97, 98
  highest educational attainment 72–73, 72t
  history 34, 37–39, 50, 693
  hubs of HE 306–307, 321, 326

  Human Capital Index 778
  Indonesian academic ties 782
  international academics in Australia 747,
    747f
  international branch campuses 290–291,
    294, 312, 313–314, 313f, 785
    Australia 744–745
    Xiamen University 587
  international students
    to Australia 743–744, 744t
    from Indonesia 784
    to Indonesia 784
    inward mobility rate 270t, 270–271
    to Japan 659
    from Myanmar 850–851
    to New Zealand 761f, 762f
    numbers 269–270, 270t
  internationalization 9, 15–16, 249, 271–272,
    300t, 783–784, 784t, 808, 809–811, 822
    commercial drivers 273–274
    cultural distance 272
    development assistance 274
    economic policy 160
    soft power 505–506
  journal citations and documents
    produced 380t
  journal publications 782
  knowledge production
    bibliometrics 468–470, 469f, 472f, 474f,
      475f, 479f, 480–482, 481f
    GERD as percentage of GDP 466, 467f
    patent citations 488f, 490f, 491n.29
    patent count 492f, 494f
  language and medium of instruction 167,
    805–807
  Language Policy Implementation Program
    (LPIP) 806
  lifelong learning 538, 539–540, 869
  Ministry of Education (MOE) 253, 257–260,
    261
    Centralized Admission Unit 801–802
    Matriculation Program 802
  Ministry of Higher Education
    (MOHE) 253, 257–260, 799–800,
    804
MOOCs
  cultural issues 369

eLearning capability of instructors 366
language issues 368
pedagogical approach 370
regional collaboration 364
National Higher Education Fund
        (PTPTN) 431, 445, 803–804
National Higher Education Strategic Plan
        (PSPTN) 253, 800, 809–810, 811
National Language Act 806
nationalism 523, 524
New Economic Policy (NEP) 799, 801
Open Universities
    admission to 337
    as alternative to conventional
        universities 342
    dual-teaching mode 336, 336n.7
    employer satisfaction with graduates 345
    quality measurement 343
    single-teaching mode 339t
private HEIs 9, 125f, 404, 798–799, 807–809
    access and equity 800, 803
    history 799–800
    internationalization 809, 810, 811
    language and medium of
        instruction 806–807
Private Higher Education Institutions
        Act 800, 807–808, 811
public financing 126t
    per student 384f
    as percentage of GDP 383f, 838n.1
    as percentage of total education
        spending 382t
public HEIs 798–799
    academic freedom and autonomy 804,
        805
    access and equity 800, 801–802, 802t, 803
    history 799–800
    internationalization 809, 810–811
    language and medium of instruction 807
quality 811
    divergence between quality
        assurance and qualification
        framework 262–263
    diversified quality assurance system 261
    lead units 259t
    national qualification framework 257,
        258t

neoliberalism 253
    upsurge of state control 257–260
rankings 211, 219, 221, 783
research funding 789, 867
research networks 643
researchers per million population 867
return to higher education 425t
Returning Expert Program (REP) 459
returning talent 457, 459
Singapore's separation from 537
Statutory Bodies (Discipline and Surcharge)
        Act 805
STEM 194, 195, 202–203
student loans
    collection 437–438
    COVID-19 pandemic 445
    default measures and sanctions 434t
    description 446t
    funding source 430t, 431
    introduction 423
    objectives and coverage 426t, 427–428
    operation 429
    repayment and recovery 439
    repayment default 438
    repayment regime 436t
    size of loan 441–442
Universities and University Colleges
        Act 804–805, 806–807
University of Malaya Act 804–805
Malaysia–Japan International Institute of
        Technology (MJIIT) 661–662
Malaysian Higher School Certificate
        (STPM) 802
Malaysian Qualifications Agency
        (MQA) 255–256, 261, 262–263, 343
Malaysian Qualifications Framework 255–
        256, 262–263
Malaysian Qualifications Register 255–256
Maldives 122, 536
Mandalay University 840, 847–848
Mandela, Nelson 334
Manipal University 619
Mann, Horace 8
Mapua University 864
Massachusetts Institute of Technology (MIT)
    Global Alliance of Universities on
        Climate 587

Massachusetts Institute of Technology
        (MIT) (*cont.*)
    land-grant university 386
    as model 198–199
    MOOCs 357, 359
    Open CourseWare Conference 359
    public financing 388
    research partnerships 505
    Singapore 320–321, 694, 701, 702
    talent attraction 589
Massey University 757–758, 765–766
massification 5–6, 6*f*, 14, 47, 48–49, 289–290
    access 115–117, 118, 123, 128, 129, 130
    Australia *see* Australia: elite HE to
        massification
    China *see* China: elite HE to massification
    and credentials 161
    demographic change 40
    financial aspects 22
    future 60–62
    gender 147
    history 5–7, 36–37, 49–51
    Hong Kong *see* Hong Kong: elite HE to
        massification
    hubs of HE 306–307, 315, 319
    income levels 6–7, 7*f*
    India *see* India: elite HE to massification
    Indonesia *see* Indonesia: elite HE to
        massification
    Japan *see* Japan: elite HE to massification
    Malaysia *see* Malaysia: elite HE to
        massification
    nationalism 528
    New Zealand *see* New Zealand: elite HE to
        massification
    Philippines *see* Philippines: elite HE to
        massification
    present 52–60
    private philanthropy 402–404
    public financing 389
    quality regulation 249, 250–251, 263
    rankings 210–211, 217
    Singapore *see* Singapore: elite HE to
        massification
    South Korea *see* South Korea: elite HE to
        massification
    STEM 191–192, 202–203, 205–206

    Thailand *see* Thailand: elite HE to
        massification
    Vietnam 52
Massive Open Distance eLearning
        (MODeL) 362
Massive Open Online Courses *see* MOOCs
Mauritius 86
McGill MBA Japan 293
Medical Council of India 597, 598
Melbourne 324–325
Melbourne University 23, 35, 406–407, 416*t*
men *see* gender
Mencius 508
Merdeka University 806
Microsoft 599
Middle East
    Asian University for Women,
        Bangladesh 181
    cross-border cooperation 786
    elite higher education to massification 61
    employment and labor markets 81
    history of higher education 49
    international students 273, 767
        from Indonesia 786
        to Malaysia 810
    knowledge production 477–478, 480
    see also Arab countries
Middlebury College, Center for Community
        Engagement 182
Milan, Polytechnic University of 587
Millennium Development Goals 22, 818
Min Aung Hlaing 852
Mindanao State University-Iligan 864
Mingchang International Education 824
missionaries, South Korea 671–672
MIT *see* Massachusetts Institute of
        Technology
Miyake, Issey 487
Modi, Narendra 527
Monash University
    Indonesia 784–786
    Malaysia 810
Mongolia
    collaborative international online
        learning 662–663
    gender 135–136n.3, 143, 150–151
    goals of HE 98

international students
    cultural distance 272
    numbers 270t
    to South Korea 684, 685t
    public financing as percentage of total
        education spending 381, 382t
    student loans 426t, 446t
MOOCs (Massive Online Open Courses) 19–
        20, 332, 346, 356–358, 371
    challenges 365–370
        access to ICT and internet 366–368
        cultural 369–370
        eLearning capability of instructors 366
        English language delivery 368–369
        reputation of distance learning 365–366
    credentials 348
    emergence 358–363
        China 359–360
        India 360–361
        Philippines 362–363
        South Korea 361–362
        Sri Lanka 363
        Thailand 363
    international students 18, 275–276, 277
    lifelong learning 102
        Open Universities 348, 350
    pedagogical approach 370
    regional collaboration 364–365
mooKIT 360
mortgage-type student loans 433–435, 436t,
        437, 740
    collection 437–438
    debt/repayment burdens 442–443
    Thailand 830
Muhammadiyah 788
Mukherjee, Sir Ashutosh 616, 625
Multidimensional Global Ranking of
        Universities (U-Multirank) 213–214,
        223–224
multinational corporations (MNCs) 494–495
multiversity 17
Mumbai University 617
Munich, Technical University of 702
Myanmar 25, 851–853
    academic freedom 26
    access 118, 119–120
        online learning 127–128
    scholarships 126, 127f
    study programs 122
    activism 2n.2
    autonomy, quality, and control
        challenges 844–845
    colonial legacy 2–3
    Comprehensive Education Sector Review
        (CESR)
        ASEAN benchmarking 848–849
        equity and inclusion 843, 847–848, 851
        rankings 849
    Constitution 845–846
    Department of Education Research,
        Planning and Training 841–842
    Department of Higher Education 841–842
    drivers for reforms 848–850
        ASEAN benchmarking 848–849
        national development 849–850
        rankings 849
    employment and labor markets 75–76
    enrollment rate 865
    equity and inclusion 842–844
        challenges in Education Colleges 844
    gender 135–136n.3, 138–140, 145, 146t,
        150–151
    goals of HE 98
    history 34, 837–838, 842–843, 845–846
    international students
        numbers 270t
        to Thailand 823
    internationalization 451–452, 784t, 838,
        848–849, 850–851
        cultural distance 272
    lifelong learning 536, 538, 539–540, 542
    Long-term Education Development Plan 847
    Ministry of Education (MoE) 838, 846–847
        activism 852
        autonomy, quality, and control
            challenges 844–845
        Education College reforms 841–842
        National Education Strategic
            Plan 847n.21, 848
    MOOCs 20, 367
    National Curriculum Committee 852
    National Education Law 847–848
    National Education Policy
        Commission 847, 848–849

Myanmar (*cont.*)
    National Education Strategic Plan
            (NESP) 542, 841–842, 846–848
        rankings 849
    National Institute for Higher Education
            Development 839–840, 847
    National League for Democracy
            (NLD) 845–847, 849
    Open Universities 339*t*
    private HEIs 838
    private philanthropy 406*t*
    public financing 126*t*, 381, 383*f*, 384*f*
    public HEIs 837–838
    quality 844–845, 847–848
        ASEAN benchmarking 848–849
        distance education 840–841
        history 837–838
        internationalization 850
    Rectors Committee 841–842, 847
    size and structure of HE 838–842, 839*t*, 840*t*
        distance education 840–841
        Education College reforms 841–842
    Strengthening Pre-Service Teacher
            Education Myanmar 842
    Teacher Competence Standards
            Framework 842
    Towards Results in Education and
            English 842
    wider reforms 845–846
Myo Thein Gyi 847

N

Nadar, Shiv 624–625
Nagoya University 632
Naidu, Nara Chandrababu 599
Nakasone, Yasuhiro 644, 652
Nalanda University 614–616
Nanjing University 476, 578
Nanyang Technological Institute (NTI) 693
Nanyang Technological University (NTU)
    Centre for Professional and Continuing
            Education 707
    history 693–694
    hubs of HE 324
    internationalization 701, 702
    joint venture with Imperial College
            London 321

    private philanthropy 23, 416–417, 416*t*
    R&D 697, 698
    rankings 413*t*, 699*t*, 707–708
    social mobility 704
Nanyang University (Nantah) 693, 806
national brand promotion 521–522
National Development University,
        Indonesia 788
National Graduate Institute of Policy Studies
        (GRIPS), Tokyo 653
national identity 96, 98–100, 516–517
    Japan 523–524, 646
National Institute of Design, India 594–595
National Institutes of Technology,
        India 407–408, 594–595
National Open University, Taiwan
        (NOU) 344
National Science Board (NSB) 191–192
National Science Foundation (NSF) 191–192
National Taiwan University 632
National University of Singapore (NUS)
    College of Humanities and Science 709
    credentials 10–11
    history 213, 693–694
    hubs of HE 321, 324
    internationalization 701, 702
    joint venture medical school 307
    private philanthropy 23, 406–407, 416–417,
            416*t*
    R&D 697, 698
    rankings 12, 413*t*, 699*t*, 707–708
    School for Continuing and Lifelong
            Education 707
    social mobility 704
nationalism 21, 514–515, 519–530
    academic freedom, constraints on 525–526
    campuses as activism spaces 526–528
    conceptualizing 515–518, 516*f*
    cosmopolitan higher education in a world
            of nations 518–519
    globalization of, in cyberspace 528–529
    goals of higher education 8
    and internationalization 522–524
    national brand promotion and soft
            power 521–522
    nation-building 21, 519–521
    rankings and status competition 524

Singapore 709
    top-down and bottom-up 517, 517*f*
nation-building
    elite HE to massification 51, 52–53
    goals of HE 8, 93–94, 95–96, 97, 98–99, 103,
        106, 107–108, 109
    India 107–108, 238
    Japan *see* Japan: nation-building
    Myanmar 848, 849–850
    nationalism 21, 519–521
    Singapore 106, 708–709
    Thailand 815
Ne Win 842–843
Nehru, Jawaharlal 593–594
Nepal
    academic freedom 26
    access 122
    demographics 69–70, 70*t*
    economy 68, 69, 71*t*
    employment and labor markets 70–72, 80
    gender 135–136n.3, 145, 146*t*, 148–149
    highest educational attainment 72*t*, 73
    history 31, 39–40
    international students
        in Japan 641–642, 659
        numbers 269–270, 270*t*
    internationalization 451–452
        history 39–40
        Tokyo Convention 296
    lifelong learning 536–537, 538–539, 543
    private philanthropy 406*t*
    public financing
        per student 381–384, 384*f*
        as percentage of GDP 381, 383*f*
        as percentage of total education
            spending 382*t*
    skill share 70–72
nepotism
    India 602
    Indonesia 787
NetEase 359
Netherlands
    colonialism 775
    history 32, 34, 49
    influence of education model on
        Japan 631–632
    international students from China 558

Japanese trade 629
    public vs. private financing 739*f*
    returning talent 460–461
    student loans 427
New South Wales Asia, University of 702
New York University (NYU) 17
    Abu Dhabi 19
    Shanghai 585–586
    Singapore 307
New Zealand 755–757
    access 117–118, 119
    background and context 757–759
    Centers for Research Excellence (CoREs) 759
    completions 763–764
    demographics 70*t*
    economic growth 1
    economy 71*t*
    elite HE to massification 47, 54, 61
    employment and labor markets 75–76, 80,
        81, 82–83
    free tuition movement 445
    future priorities 766–769
    gender 139–140, 147
    goals of HE 98
    highest educational attainment 72*t*, 72–73
    history 5, 35, 37–39, 40, 755, 756–758
    ICT readiness 139–140
    international academics in South
        Korea 684–685
    international branch campuses 312, 313n.2
    international students
        inward mobility rate 270–271, 270*t*
        from Malaysia 808
        numbers 269–270, 270*t*
    internationalization 2–3, 18–19, 271–272,
        300*t*, 760–763, 761*f*, 766
        commercial drivers 272–273
        COVID-19 pandemic 756
        future priorities 766, 767–768
        history 40
        impacts on cities and regions 281
    journal citations and documents
        produced 380*t*
    knowledge production 465
        bibliometrics 469*f*, 470, 472–473, 472*f*,
            474–475, 474*f*, 475*f*, 477–478, 479–482,
            479*f*, 481*f*, 483, 483*f*, 484, 485–486, 486*f*

New Zealand (*cont.*)
  GERD as percentage of GDP 466, 467*f*
  patent citations 488*f*, 489, 490*f*, 491n.29
  patent count 492*f*, 494*f*
  lifelong learning 536, 537–538, 539, 541–542,
    545–546
  MOOCs 356, 358, 365–366
  Open Universities 335, 336, 342n.9
  participation 759–760
  Performance Based Research Fund
    (PBRF) 759, 764
  private philanthropy 405, 407
    Global Philanthropy Environment
      Index 405, 406*t*
  private HEIs 125*f*, 758, 759
    vs. public HEIs 424
  public financing 125–126, 126*t*, 382*t*
  quality regulation 262
  research 25–26
  student loans 24
    COVID-19 pandemic 445
    debt/repayment burdens 442
    description 446*t*
    funding source 430*t*
    introduction 423
    objectives and coverage 426*t*, 428, 429
    repayment and recovery 439
    repayment regime 436*t*
  Tertiary Education Commission 758–759
  University Grants Committee 757–758
  Waitangi, Treaty of 756–757
  workforce inequities 764–766
New Zealand, University of 35, 757–818
New Zealand Institute of Skills and
    Technology (NZIST) 760, 766,
    767–768, 769
Newcastle University
  Malaysia 810
  Singapore 702
Ngee Ann Academy 692–693
Nigeria 299*t*, 316
Nobel Prize
  Australia 748–749
  China 564–565, 589
  rankings 222
  STEM 203–204
North Africa 273, 536–537

North America
  elite HE to massification 47, 49, 61
  gender 149n.12
  international academics 658
  international students
    from Indonesia 784, 785*t*
    to Indonesia 785*t*
    from Japan 659
    to South Korea 684
  internationalization 2–3, 268–269
    research networks 827
  learning 165–166
  liberal arts and sciences 177
  liberalism 53
  model of higher education 3
  MOOCs 357–358, 370
  rankings 39
  STEM 189–190
North Korea
  history 672
  knowledge production 465
  threat to Japan 510
North-East Asia 70–72, 203–204
Northern University 554–555
Notre Dame University 736
Nottingham University
  Malaysia 810
  Ningbo 325, 559

O

objectives *see* goals of HE
Odisha State Open University 336
off budget public financing 388–389
offshore campuses *see* international branch
    campuses
Ohio State University 386
Okinawa Institute of Science and Technology
    Graduate University (OIST) 653
Okuma, Shigenobu 633
older people 539, 541
Ong Ye Kung 708–709
online learning 19, 27
  access 127–128, 129
  Australia 744–745
  COVID-19 pandemic 283, 349, 396–397
  demand for 68
  elite HE to massification 48–49, 52

India 604–605
Indonesia 777–778, 779–780, 791–792
international students 275–276, 293
Japan 646, 662–663
lifelong learning 543, 544–545
Malaysia 811
New Zealand 768
Open Universities 331, 332–333, 334, 335–
   336, 343, 347–348
Philippines 874–875
Singapore 709
soft power 511
South Korea 689
student loans 445–446
see also MOOCs
Ontario 445
open education movement 346
open educational practice (OEP) 363, 366
Open Educational Resources (OERs) 332, 346
   China 359
   competition with Open Universities 350
   MOOCs 363, 364, 366
   Sri Lanka 363
Open Learning Campus 369
Open Universities (OUs) 330–331, 335–338,
   349–350
   access 10, 127–128, 129
   admission to 337
   as alternative to conventional
      universities 342–343
   characteristics 332–334
   China 586–587
   evolution 334
   future trends in higher education 347–349
   growth and development 338
   harnessing the potential of 331–334
   ICT 345–347
   Indonesia 777, 787, 792
   lifelong learning 543
   MOOCs 359, 360, 361, 362, 363, 364, 370
   online learning 19
   quality measurement 343–344
   retaining students 344–345
   sharing of ideas 347
   teaching modalities 335–336
   technology-enabled instruction 337–338
Open Universities Australia (OUA) 336, 348

Open University China (OUC) 337, 338
Open University Kaohsiung 337
Open University Malaysia (OUM) 336, 337–338,
   342, 345
Open University of Hong Kong (OpenU) 337,
   717, 722
Open University of Japan (OUJ) 337–338, 342,
   343
Open University of Sri Lanka 363
OpenCourseWare (OCW) 359, 361–362, 363, 366
OpenHPI.de 368
OpenLearning 348
Organisation for Economic Co-operation and
   Development (OECD)
   access to HE 119, 128
   autonomy of national universities 677
   completion rates 763
   Confucianism 197
   credentials and learning 163
   employment and labor markets 73–74, 78, 87
   enrollment rate 638
   goals of HE 94, 95–96, 102, 103–104
   hubs of HE 315
   international students 73, 160, 281, 451,
      452–453, 452n.2, 663–664
   Japan 651–652, 653–654
   knowledge production 465, 473
   learning society 535
   lifelong learning 535, 544–545
   meritocracy 162
   PISA *see* PISA
   private HEIs 124–125, 125*f*
   public financing of HE 678
      vs. private financing 736
   reports on higher education 3–4
   STEM 191–192, 200
   see also Programme for International
      Student Assessment
Organisation of Islamic Conference
   (OIC) 807
Osaka University 23, 632
Otago University 35, 757–758
overeducation
   employment and labor markets 79, 84–85
   India 606
   Indonesia 778
   New Zealand 755–756

overseas students *see* international students;
        internationalization
Oxford Economics 74
Oxford University
    as elite 48, 51
    failure, academic 163
    influence of educational model 198–199
        Australia 735–736, 748
        India 616
    land portfolio 23
    public financing 388
    talent attraction 589

P

Pacific region
    economy 70–72
    elite HE to massification 723–724, 724*f*
    employment and labor markets 78
    enrollment rates 68, 134, 251
        by gender 134–135, 135n.2
    expenditure on HE 68
    Gender Gap Index 199–200
    international students to and from
            Indonesia 785*t*
    quality assurance agencies 256, 256*t*
    researchers 152
    return to education 147–148
    STEM 199–200
    urban populations 318*f*
Pakistan
    access to higher education 118, 119, 122
        scholarships 127*f*
    demographics 69–70, 70*t*
    economy 71*t*
    employment and labor markets 70–72, 80
    gender 136–137, 145, 146*t*, 148–150
    Higher Education Commission 35
    highest educational attainment 72*t*, 73
    history 35, 37–38, 50
    international students 451–452
    journal citations and documents
            produced 380*t*
    Open Universities 336, 337, 339*t*, 343,
        345–346
    poverty 69
    private philanthropy 406*t*
    public financing 126*t*

    per student 384*f*
    as percentage of GDP 383*f*
    as percentage of total education
            spending 382*t*
    quality 2–3
    skill share 70–72
    STEM 195
    student loans
        description 446*t*
        funding source 430*t*, 431
        objectives and coverage 426*t*
        repayment and recovery 439
        repayment regime 436*t*
Palau 135n.2
Papua New Guinea 69, 145, 146*t*
Paris Message 330–331, 350
part-time education 52
    Myanmar 840
    New Zealand 757, 763–764
part-time employment 230, 281, 444, 765
Passage AI 371
Patent Asset Index 493, 494*f*
patent citations 488–491, 488*f*
patent count 491–494
patriotism 8, 516, 516*f*
patronage, India 602
Peking University
    985 Project 564
    credentials 10–11
    Double-World-Class policy 582
    Founder Group Corp 556
    history 554–555
    HSBC Business School 587
    international students 558
    MOOCs 359
    National Key University 578–579
    partnership with Confucius Institute of
            Chulalongkorn University 508–509
    public financing 385
    rankings 413*t*, 413n.8, 565
    see also Beijing University
Penang, University of 804
Pennsylvania State University 386
    Singapore 694, 702
per capita income (PCI) 6, 7*f*
Perry, Admiral 33
philanthropy 275

collective, India 623–624
private *see* private philanthropy
Philippine Higher Education Research
        Network (PherNET) 867–868
Philippine Medical School 857
Philippine Military Academy 858
Philippine Normal School 857, 858
Philippines 874–875
    access 117–118, 120, 121–122
        scholarships 127*f*
    Balik Program 477
    colonial legacy 2–3
    Commission on Higher Education
        (CHED) 362, 858–860, 875
        lifelong learning 869
        quality 861–862, 864–866
    composition and types of HEIs 858–860,
        859*t*
    Constitution 872–873
    Coordinating Council of Private
        Educational Associations
        (COCOPEA) 875
    Corporation Law 857, 859
    demographics 69–70, 70*t*
    economy 71*t*
    Education Act 859
    elite HE to massification 15, 52, 635, 856–
        858, 865, 870–871
    employment and labor markets
        future 74, 75–76
        graduate work readiness 85–86
        labor force participation rates 70–72
        TVET 82–83, 83*t*
    enrollment and graduation 860, 860*f*, 861*f*,
        874, 874*f*
    equity 862–864, 863*f*, 863*t*, 864*f*
    gender 139–140, 149–151
    Government Service Insurance System 431
    highest educational attainment 72–73, 72*t*
    history 33–34, 38–39, 856–858
    Human Capital Index 778
    innovation ecosystem 866–868
    international students
        to Australia 744*t*
        to New Zealand 761*f*
    internationalization 300*t*, 451–452, 783–784,
        784*t*, 865, 869

economic policy 160
    Tokyo Convention 296
Japan's higher education system
        comparison 630
journal publications 782
knowledge production 477
lifelong learning 538–540, 543
MOOCs
    access to ICT and internet 366–367
    emergence 362–363
    language issues 368
    regional collaboration 364
Open Distance Learning Act 362
Open Universities 339*t*
poverty 69
private HEIs 14, 124–125, 125*f*, 858, 859–860,
        872–875
    current crisis 870–872, 872*f*
    enrollment 424, 874, 874*f*
    equity 863–864, 864*f*
    history 857–858
    quality 861–862, 864, 865–866
    rankings 868–869
private philanthropy 406*t*
public financing 382*t*
public HEIs 858–859, 872–875
    crisis in private HEIs 870, 871, 872
    enrollment 874, 874*f*
    equity 863–864, 864*f*, 866
    rankings 868–869
public–private complementarity 857–858,
        872–874
qualification frameworks (QFs) 15
quality 15, 860–862, 861*t*, 864–866, 871, 873
    diversified quality assurance
        system 260–261
    lead units 259*t*
    MOOCs 362
    national qualification framework 258*t*
    uneven 864–866
rankings 868–869
return to higher education 425*t*
Service-Learning Asia Network 182
STEM 194–195
student loans
    default measures and sanctions 434*t*
    description 446*t*

Philippines (*cont.*)
  funding source 430*t*, 431
  introduction 423
  objectives and coverage 426*t*, 427, 429
  operation 429
  reach 441
  repayment and recovery 436*t*, 437, 438, 439
  size of loan 441–442
  Study Now Pay Later (SNPL) 431, 437, 438, 439, 441
  Technical Education and Skills Development Authority (TESDA) 362–363
  Tertiary Education Subsidy (TES) 863–864, 870
  UniFAST law 870
  Universal Access to Quality Tertiary Education Act 870
Philippines, University of the (UP)
  access 121
  COVID-19 pandemic 875
  history 857
  quality 862, 864
  rankings 868–869
PISA (Programme for International Student Assessment)
  gender 144, 151–152
  Indonesia 778–779, 781
  South Korea 670
  STEM 195–196, 196*t*, 205–206
    Malaysia 202
plagiarism, Indonesia 787
political stability, as HE goal 95–96
Portland, University of 662–663
Portugal 32, 33, 49
postgraduate education
  Australia 736, 740, 741
  China 237, 562
  goals 95
  Hong Kong 720, 728
  India 595–596, 602–604
  Indonesia 782
  Japan 234–235, 637–638, 645, 653–654
  Malaysia 810
  Myanmar 838, 850–851, 852
  New Zealand 762, 767–768

  Philippines 868–869
  professional education 234–235, 237, 243
  South Korea 675, 683
poverty 69
  Australia 743–744
  China 391–392
  Hong Kong 724–725
  India 599, 625, 626
  Indonesia 407–408, 779, 779*t*, 780–781
  Japan 393, 641
  lifelong learning 536–537, 538–539
  Malaysia 801
  MOOCs 371
  Myanmar 840, 843–844
  Open Universities 338
  Philippines 862–863, 863*f*, 863*t*, 868, 870–871
  private philanthropy 407–408, 415
  Singapore 703–704
  South Korea aid 678–679
  student loans 444–445
    loans allocation and borrower selection 433
    objectives and coverage 427–429
    reach 441
    subsidies 440
  Vietnam 394–395
Prayut Chan-o-cha 828
Premji, Azim 409*b*
Princeton University 198–199, 408, 410–412
private HEIs 6–7, 14
  access 121, 122, 124–125, 125*f*, 129
  elite HE to massification 51, 52, 57, 58, 61
  funding 22
  growth 404
  hubs of HE 307
  international students 274, 282
  liberal arts and sciences 173, 178–179
  loans schemes 24
  philanthropy 407–408, 410–412
  student loans 424, 428
  see also under Australia; China; Hong Kong; India; Indonesia; Japan; Malaysia; Myanmar; New Zealand; Philippines; Singapore South Korea; Thailand
private philanthropy 23–24, 402–404, 417–418

Asian University for Women,
        Bangladesh 181
    China 563t, 585–563
    India 612, 616–617, 619–621, 627
        private HEIs 622–625, 626–627
    landscape 404–408
    motivations 409
    outcome and impact 410–412
    quality of education 412–415
    sustainability 415–417
    tax deduction policies 386–387
    trends 410
professional bodies 244
    monitoring of higher education quality 231,
        233, 240
    triangle of coordination 232–233
professional education 228–229, 233–239, 244
    access 9
    Australia 736–737
    China 236–237
    conceptual frameworks 231–233
        comparison of models 239–242
    credentials 11
    emerging issues 242–244
    India 237–238, 619–620, 626–627
    Indonesia 786
    Japan 234–236, 632, 636, 638
    models and issues 13
    New Zealand 758
    Open Universities 333
    origins and development 229–231
    Philippines 860–861, 861t
    quality 3
    South Korea 671–672
    student loans 443
    Taiwan 239
    technological change 7–8
Programme for International Student
        Assessment see PISA
Programme for the International Assessment
        of Adult Competencies 545
project funds 384–385
Promotion of Sustainability in Postgraduate
        Education and Research Network
        (ProSPER.Net) 665
propaganda vs. soft power 504
Protestantism, Indonesia 777

protests see activism
PSB Academy 692–693
public diplomacy see soft power
public financing 14, 22–23, 379–389, 396–397
    Australia 738–739
    categories 384
    China 389, 390–391, 391f, 555, 558, 561–563,
        563t, 564, 565
        disadvantaged student support 391–392
        elite universities 579, 584–585
    elite HE to massification 53
        Hong Kong 57
        India 58
        Japan 58
        Singapore 59
    future 41–42
    guaranteed student loan programs 387
    Hong Kong 57, 715–716, 718–719, 719f,
        720–722
    hubs of HE 307
    income forgone 386–387
    India 58, 596–597, 599, 601–602, 609–610,
        617–618
        private universities 623
        R&D 608–609
    Indonesia 774, 776–777, 789–790, 791
    Japan 58, 103, 389, 392–393
        globalization 639–641, 644
        internationalization challenges 653,
            662–663, 664
        nation-building 633, 635–636
    Myanmar 838, 847–848, 849–850
    New Zealand 755–756, 757–760
        future priorities 767, 768–769
        indigenous peoples 763–764, 765–766
    off budget 388–389
    per student 381–384, 384f
    as percentage of GDP 381–384, 383f
        China 391, 391f
        Japan 392
        Vietnam 394
    as percentage of private financing 381, 383f
        Japan 392–393
    as percentage of total education
            spending 381, 382t
        Vietnam 394, 394f
    Philippines 863–864, 867, 870–871

public financing (*cont.*)
  role of government 389–390
  Singapore 59, 692–693, 709
    massification policy 696
    per student 699*t*
    policy context 695
    R&D 698–700
    recurrent expenditure 699*t*
    social mobility 703–704
  South Korea 670–671, 678–680
    historical development and
        background 674
    restructuring of higher education 688
    tuition issues 680–681
  student loans 424, 426–427
  Thailand 818, 819–820, 827–828, 828*f*
    internationalization 823–824
    subsidies 828–786
  university bonds market 388
  US land-grant universities 386
  Vietnam 389, 393–395
public HEIs 808
  access 129
  numbers by year of legislation 872*f*
  see also under Australia; China; Hong Kong;
        India; Indonesia; Japan; Malaysia;
        Myanmar; Philippines; Singapore;
        South Korea; Thailand
Punjab, University of the 616
purchasing power parity 1

Q

Qatar
  Education City 307–308
  hubs of HE 326
  international branch campuses 313*f*
Quacquarelli Symonds (QS) 13
  Asia University Rankings 223–224
    Thailand 827
  World University Rankings 212, 213, 220
    bibliometrics 476–477
    China 565, 582–583, 583*f*, 586
    graduate work readiness 81, 82
    Hong Kong 715*t*, 716
    indicator weights 214*t*
    Indonesia 783
    Japan 639

New Zealand 760
  private philanthropy 412–415, 413*t*
  public financing 379n.1
  Singapore 699*t*, 707–708
qualification frameworks (QFs) 15
  national 250, 256–257, 258*t*, 263
    quality assurance comparison 254, 254*t*
    quality assurance divergence 262–263
  regional 250
qualifications *see* credentials
quality
  access 116, 121
    instruments to improve 128–130
    online learning 127–128
  credentials and learning 167
  elite HE to massification 5, 6–7, 53
  employment and labor markets 67, 87
  history 38–39
  international students 2–3, 15, 17
  lifelong learning 540
  loans schemes 24
  MOOCs 275–276, 357, 362, 365–366, 368,
        370
  and national development 2
  and national economic prospects 2
  Open Universities 343–345, 350, 359
  private philanthropy 410–415
  professional education 13, 230, 231, 233,
        240, 241*t*, 243, 244
  regulation 14–15, 249–250, 263
    divergence between quality
        assurance and qualification
        framework 262–263
    diversified quality assurance
        system 260–261
    input-based to output-based
        approach 261–262
    neoliberalism 250–254
    quality assurance and national
        qualification frameworks as policy
        tool 254–257
    upsurge of state control 257–260
  soft power 502–503
  STEM 192
  student loans 442–443
  Sustainable Development Goals 22
  variance 2–3

see also elite universities; rankings; *under*
    Australia; China; Hong Kong;
    India; Indonesia; Japan; Malaysia;
    Myanmar; Philippines; Singapore;
    South Korea; Taiwan; Thailand
quality assurance (QA) 249–250, 255–256, 263
  agencies (QAAs) 15, 255, 256*t*
    divergence between quality assurance
      and qualification frameworks 262
    input-based to output-based
      approach 261–262
    lead units 259*t*
  Australia 737–738
  diversified system 260–261
  Hong Kong 725–727, 730
  India 608
  Indonesia 786–788
  input-based to output-based
    approach 261–262
  international students 295
    Tokyo Convention 296–297, 302
  Japan 645, 657, 661, 665–666
  Open Universities 343–344
  Philippines 861–862, 864–865
  qualification frameworks comparison 254,
    254*t*
  qualification frameworks divergence 262–263
  regional networks promoting student
    mobility 663–664, 665
  Singapore 694, 696
  South Korea 683, 685–686
  Thailand 818–819, 827, 833
  upsurge of state control 260
Queensland University 35, 335, 416*t*, 735n.1

R

R&D (research and development) 25–26
  access 122, 129–130
  Australia 736, 737, 740, 743, 744–745,
    747–748
  China 105–106, 217, 557–558, 562, 563,
    564–565
    elite HEIs 585–586
    history 555
    internationalization 558
    massification 566
    private HEIs 560–561

elite HE to massification 53–54
employment and labor markets 74
financial aspects 22
gender 150–151, 151*t*, 152
GERD
  patent applications 489–491
  patent count 493
  as percentage of GDP 465–468, 467*f*,
    475–476
    vs. publication output 470–472, 471*f*
  publications per 472–473, 472*f*
  publications per researcher 475
goals of HE 8, 93, 94, 103–104, 105–106,
  107–108
Hong Kong 719–720, 728, 730
hubs of education 307, 316, 318–319, 321
India 107–108, 593–594, 608–609, 616, 622,
  623–624
Indonesia 781–782, 789, 790
international students 277–279
Japan 103–104, 393, 629–630, 646
  globalization 218, 639–640, 641, 643, 644
  internationalization challenges 653, 660,
    661–662
  nation-building 636
  rankings 639
liberal arts and sciences 173, 174, 178–179
Malaysia 212
Myanmar 844–845, 849
nationalism 522–561
New Zealand 757–758, 759, 767–768
Open Universities 332, 350
Philippines 866–869, 875
public financing 380–381, 384–385, 393
  journal citations and documents
    produced 380–381, 380*t*
rankings 215, 216, 217, 218–219, 221–222
research networks 20, 277–279, 643, 743
returning talent 455, 457, 459
Singapore 106, 692–693, 709
  developmental state 704–705
  massification policy 696
  policy context 695, 696–700
  pursuing global rankings vs. serving
    society 707–708
  spending distribution 698*t*
South Korea 683

R&D (research and development) (*cont.*)
　spending by country 192–194, 193*t*
　STEM 189, 205–206
　　challenges and responses 199–202
　　culture 198–199
　　demand 192–194
　　importance 190
　　prioritization 194–195
　　reform, need for 203–204
　Taiwan 218–219
　Thailand 815–816, 823–824, 827, 832
　see also knowledge production
Raffles College 693, 798
Ramkhamhaeng University, Thailand 337
Ramsar Convention 544–545
Rangoon University 2n.2, 837–838
　see also Yangon University
Rangsit University 294, 831
rankings 8, 12–13, 210–212, 214–221, 223–224
　Australia 748–749
　China 216–217, 237, 565, 568
　　elite universities 575, 582–583, 583*f*, 589
　credentials and learning 159, 162–163,
　　　164–165, 168–169
　graduate employability 81
　history 38–39
　India 604, 609, 621, 622
　indicators weights 214*t*
　Indonesia 783, 785, 786–787
　Japan 16–17, 103–104, 218, 639, 657
　knowledge production 476–477
　liberal arts and sciences 178–179
　Malaysia 219, 809, 811
　Myanmar 848, 849–850
　nationalism 21, 523–524
　New Zealand 755–756, 760
　Philippines 868–869, 872
　power 221–223
　prevalence 212–214
　private philanthropy 412–415, 413*t*
　public financing 379–381, 388–389
　Singapore 699*t*, 706, 707–709
　soft power 502–503
　South Korea 217, 670–671
　STEM 202–204
　stratification initiatives, implication
　　　of 220–221

　Taiwan 218–219
　Thailand 827
Rashtriya Swayamsevak Sangh (RSS) 527
Reading University 810
Reagan, Ronald 526n.2
Regional Convention on the Recognition of
　　　Studies, Diplomas and Degrees in
　　　Higher Education in Asia and the
　　　Pacific *see* Bangkok Convention
regulations 14
　Australia 737–738
　China 236–237, 568–569
　cross-border delivery modes 293
　India 107–108, 238, 592, 596, 600–603
　　private HEIs 613–614, 617–618, 621–622,
　　　624, 626–627
　Indonesia 784–785, 786, 787, 789–791
　Japan 234–235, 392
　Malaysia 807
　New Zealand 756, 766
　Philippines 865–866, 873
　private philanthropy 292–405
　professional education 229, 232, 233, 240,
　　　241*t*, 242, 243–244
　　China 236–237
　　India 238
　　Japan 234–235
　　Taiwan 239
qualification frameworks 15
quality 249–250, 263
　divergence between quality
　　　assurance and qualification
　　　framework 262–263
　diversified quality assurance
　　　system 260–261
　input-based to output-based
　　　approach 261–262
　neoliberalism 250–254
　quality assurance and national
　　　qualification frameworks as policy
　　　tool 254–257
　state control over quality and
　　　accreditation impacts on
　　　institutions 257–260
Taiwan 239
Thailand 825, 832
university bonds market 388

Relative Activity Index (RAI) 482–486, 483f, 486f
    patent citations 489
Renmin University of China 293–294, 563–
        564, 578–579
Republic of Korea *see* South Korea
research and development *see* R&D
retention of students, Open
        Universities 344–345
returning talent 24–25, 451, 460–461
    China 559, 569
    consequences 456–458
    empirical evidence 455–456
    factors affecting 453–455
    global and student flows out of Asia 451–453,
        452t
    policies 458–460
    Thailand 824
Ritsumeikan Asia Pacific University
        (APU) 653
RMIT Vietnam 293
robotics 190
Rockefeller Foundation 410–412
Rolls Royce 505
Royal College of Surgeons, Ireland 810
Royal Melbourne Institute of Technology
        (RMIT) 335
rural populations
    access 8–9, 119–120, 121
    Australia 741–742, 742f
    China 129–130
    employment and labor markets 317
    gender 134–135, 139n.6, 147
        and socio-economic status 143, 144–145,
        144n.11
    Indonesia 777, 778–779, 779t
    Japan 638
    lifelong learning 538–539
    Myanmar 843, 844, 849–850
    Open Universities 333, 338, 346–347
Russia
    correspondence learning 334n.6
    geostrategic tensions 26–27
    hacking of US election system 528–529
    history 49
    international students 272, 299, 299t, 300t
    journal citations and documents
        produced 380t

    private HEIs 613t
    public financing 381, 382t, 383f
    quality 626–627
    STEM 192, 197t

S

sabbaticals, Indonesia 791
Saint John's College, China 560
Saint Paul's College, Goa 34
Samsung 686–687
Samsung Institute of Technology
        (SSIT) 686–687
Santo Tomas, University of 33–34, 864
Saudi Arabia 23, 137–138n.4, 299t, 740
Schneider, Carol Geary 175
Scholarism 526–527
scholarships
    access 126, 127f, 130
    Asian University for Women,
        Bangladesh 181
    Australia 740, 741–742, 743–744
    China 392, 509, 558, 579, 587, 589, 786
    Hong Kong 728
    India 604, 623
    Indonesia 777, 780–782, 783–784
    Japan 274–275, 393, 651–652, 653
    Myanmar 850
    private philanthropy 415
    Singapore 703
    soft power 500–501, 504, 509
    South Korea 678–679, 679f, 680–681,
        683–684, 685–686
    vs. student loans 444
    Sustainable Development Goals 298
    Thailand 824
    Vietnam 395
Schwarzman, Stephen A. 407n.5
Science Citation Index (SCI) 216, 220–221, 476
    China 217, 221, 223, 224, 564–565
Science Council of Japan (SCJ) 651–652
science, technology, engineering, and
        mathematics *see* STEM
Sciences Po 587
Semarang State University 787–788
seniors 539, 541
Seoul National University (SNU) 10–11, 413t,
        632, 672, 677–678

Service-Learning Asia Network (SLAN) 182
severe acute respiratory syndrome
        (SARS) 762–763
Shaanxi Normal University 293–294
Shah Alam 313
Shanghai 313–314, 325
Shanghai Jiaotaong University 39, 568
Shanghai New York University 585–586
Shanghai Ranking Consultancy 13
Shanghai-Vancouver Film School 293
Shanmugaratnam, Tharman 706
Shenzhen 313
Shenzhen International Graduate School
        (SIGS) 587
Shinawatra, Thaksin 800, 828
Shinawatra, Yingluck 828
Shizuoka, University of 662–663
Shroff, Gautam 360
Siam University 827
Singapore 692–693, 709–710
    70-70 target 707
    academic freedom 26
    access 117–118, 119, 122, 128
    Agency for Science Technology and
        Research (A*STAR) 202–203, 697,
        702, 704–705
    Central Provident Fund (CPF) 431
    Committee for Private Education
        (CPE) 255–256, 700–701
    Contact Singapore 459–460
    Council for the Development of Malay
        Education (Mendaki) 703
    credentials and learning 163
    demographics 18–19, 40, 70t
    economic growth 1
    economy 68, 70–72, 71t, 106
    Education Bureau (EDB) 704–705
    elite HE to massification 54, 61, 694, 702
        policy context 695–696, 700, 709
    employment and labor markets 74, 75–76,
        80–81, 86
    English language 167
    gender 150–151
    Global Schoolhouse 99–100
    globalization 639
    goals of HE 5, 8, 96, 98, 99–100, 106,
        108–109

    highest educational attainment 72t, 72–73
    history 34, 37–38, 49, 50, 59, 693–694
    homogenization 290
    hub of HE 20, 59, 306–308
        deep internationalization and articulated
            infrastructure 320–321, 324
        implications and critique 325
        INSEAD 322
        joint ventures 321
        processes and structural change 316
    ICT readiness 139–140
    Indonesian academic ties 782
    International Academic Advisory Panel
            (IAAP) 694, 708
    international academics in Australia 747f
    international branch campuses 290–291,
            312, 313f, 313–314, 785
    international students
        to Australia 743–744, 744t
        vs. domestic students 18t
        inward mobility rate 270t
        from Myanmar 850–851
        numbers 269–270, 270t
    internationalization 2–3, 15–17, 18–19,
            249, 268–269, 271–272, 300t, 642,
            701–702, 709, 822
        70-70 target 707
        commercial drivers 273, 274
        development assistance 274, 275
        economic policy 160
        Global Schoolhouse 99–100, 202–203,
            273, 307, 522n.1, 701–702
        goals of HE 99–100
        impacts on cities and regions 280,
            281–282
        importance 290–291
        policy 709
    internet infrastructure 397
    Japan's developmental state model as
            inspirational 507
    journal citations and documents
            produced 380t
    knowledge production 465
        bibliometrics 469f, 472f, 474f, 475f, 479f,
            479–482, 481f
        GERD as percentage of GDP 467f
        patent citations 488f, 489, 490f, 491n.29

patent count 492f, 494f
lessons from 704–709
  "over-academized" higher
      education 706–707
  pursuing global rankings vs. serving
      society 707–709
  strong developmental state 704–705
liberal arts and sciences 179–180, 184
Lifelong Endowment Fund Act 537
lifelong learning 536, 537–538, 539–540,
      541–542, 547
living standards 68
Malaysian history 537, 798, 800
Ministry of Education (MOE)
  goals of HE 106
  Higher Education Group 253–254
  quality 255–256, 700
  R&D 698
  social mobility 704
  Tuition Fee Loans (TFL) 431
MOOCs 357
National Research Foundation
      (NRF) 697
National Science and Technology Board
      (NSTB) 697
nationalism 520, 521–522, 523, 524
PISA scores 162–163
policy context 694–704
  affordable higher education for social
      mobility 703–704
  internationalization 701–702
  massification 695–696
  private higher education 700–701
  R&D 696–700
postgraduate education 95
private HEIs 125f, 692–693, 698, 700–701
  vs. public university enrollment 424
private philanthropy 23, 414, 418
  aggressive pursuit of 407
  endowments 416–417, 416t
  Global Philanthropy Environment
      Index 405, 406t
  tax incentives 405
  trends 410, 411f
public financing 125–126, 126t
  per student 381–384, 384f
  as percentage of GDP 381–384, 383f

public HEIs 676–677
quality 692–693, 709, 710
  developmental state 704–705
  elite HE to massification 59, 696, 700
  goals of HE 106
  internationalization 701, 702
  lead units 259t
  neoliberalism 253–254
  policy context 694
  pursuing global rankings vs. serving
      society 707–708
  quality assurance and qualification
      frameworks as policy tool 255–256
  R&D 700
rankings 220, 412–413, 413t
research 25–26
  funding as percentage of GDP 867
  networks 643
  researchers per million population 867
return to higher education 425t
returning talent 458, 459–460
skill share 70–72
SkillsFuture Singapore 81, 106, 459–460,
      537, 541–542, 700–701, 706–707,
      709
Social Sciences Research Council (SSRC) 698,
      708
soft power 504–506, 509–510
STEM 205–206
  challenges and responses 202–203
  culture 197
  demand 192–194
  as percentage of HE students 861f
  R&D spending 194–195, 205–206
  reform, need for 205
  student performance in science and
      math 196t, 197t
student loans
  COVID-19 pandemic 445
  default measures and sanctions 434t
  description 446t
  funding source 430t, 431
  objectives and coverage 426t, 427, 428
  repayment and recovery 439
  repayment regime 436t
World Class Universities (WCU)
      programme 701–702

Singapore Institute of Management
        (SIM) 694
    Global Education 692–693
Singapore Institute of Management University
        (UniSIM) 700–701
Singapore Institute of Technology (SIT) 694,
        697, 702, 704, 707
Singapore Management University (SMU)
        416t, 416–417, 694, 697, 702, 707
Singapore University 693, 798
Singapore University of Social Sciences
        (SUSS) 694, 697, 700–701, 704, 707
Singapore University of Technology and
        Design (SUTD) 694, 697, 702, 707
single-mode distance teaching
        universities 334, 335–336, 338, 339t,
        342, 348–349
SITLEARN Professional Development 707
SkillsFuture Singapore (SSG) 255–256
Smart Communications, Inc. 362
social class see socio-economic status
social impact bonds (SIBs) 388
social mobility
    China 56, 578
    credentials 159–160, 161
    elite HE to massification 56, 57, 61
    goals of HE 94–95, 96
    Hong Kong 57, 724, 725
    India 593, 604, 606, 625
    Japan 638
    Myanmar 843
    Philippines 865
    Singapore 692–693, 703–704
    student loans 444–445
Social Science Citation Index (SSCI) 216, 217,
        220–221, 223
social sciences 11–12, 122
Society 5.0 concept 666
socio-economic status (SES)
    access 69, 119–121, 129–131
    Australia 736, 740–741, 742f
    China 555, 559, 565, 567, 574, 575, 576, 589
    gender 134–135, 142–146, 146t
    goals of HE 95
    Hong Kong 57, 724–725
    India 593, 598–599, 604, 606, 619–621,
        624–625, 626

Indonesia 776–777, 779, 780–781
inequalities 162
international students
    commercial drivers 272–274
    Tokyo Convention 302
Japan 638
middle-class growth 1, 2
Myanmar 843, 850
Philippines 862–864, 863f, 863t, 864f
private philanthropy 410
professional education 243
return to higher education 424
STEM 199
student loans 427–428, 433
Thailand 823, 824, 830
see also poverty; social mobility
soft power 16, 21, 500–502, 504–511
    China 508–509, 560
    Hong Kong 730
    Japan 507–508
    nationalism 521–522, 529
    Singapore 505–506
    Taiwan 506–507
    theory, policy, and practice 502–504
Soft Power 30 index 503
Soochow University 554–555
    Laos 294
Sophia University 662–663
South Africa 334n.6, 684–685, 744–745
South Africa, University of (UNISA) 334, 334n.6
South America
    international students in South Korea 684
    knowledge production 480
    see also Latin America
South Asia
    colonial legacy 2–3, 34
    economic growth 1
    employment and labor markets 78
    enrollment rates 68, 116t, 134–135
    expenditure on higher education 68
    Field Weighted Citation Impact 486, 487f
    Gender Gap Index 199–200
    international students 451–452
        to Australia 745n.8
        from Indonesia 785t
        to Indonesia 785t
        to Malaysia 810

knowledge production 465, 475–476
   Relative Activity Index 483*f*, 485–486,
      486*f*
lifelong learning 536–537, 544–545
massification 6, 6*f*
Open Universities 338, 343
quality assurance agencies 256*t*
researchers 152
return to education 147–148
STEM 199–200
South Asia Association of Regional
      Cooperation 294–295
South Korea 670–671, 688–689
   5.31 Education Reform 674–675, 675n.2,
      677, 681–682
   academic freedom 26
   access 117–118, 119, 120, 121–122, 124, 128, 129
   Brain Korea 21 (BK21) 683
   credentials 161
   demographics 18–19, 40, 69–70, 70*t*
   Deregulation of Student Enrollment
      Quotas 674–675
   developmental state 704–705
   economic growth 1, 670, 844–845
   economy 68, 71*t*
   elite HE to massification 6, 7*f*, 51, 52, 53–54,
      60–61, 635, 670–671, 672–673, 674
     Japan comparison 58
     rankings 217
   employment and labor markets 75–76, 80,
      81
   English language 167
   enrollment rates 94, 95*f*, 100–101, 860*f*
   entrance examination 9
   financing higher education 678–680
   Five-Year National Economic Development
      Plans (FNEDPs) 672–673
   Fostering Regional Hub Research Group in
      University 687
   gender
     academic profession 140–141
     employment and labor markets 149–151,
      150n.13
     enrollment rate 136–137
     Gender Gap Index 199–200
     and socio-economic status 145
     study program s 144

globalization 639
goals of HE 5, 98, 100–101
Government Employees' Scheme 437
Graduation Quota System (GQS) 673–674
Higher Education Corporation 678
highest educational attainment 72–73, 72*t*
history 31, 36, 37–39, 49, 671–676, 673*t*
Hub University for Industrial
      Collaboration 687
hubs of HE 306–307, 320–321
Human Resource Development Project
      of Leading Industries in Great
      Economic Areas 687
Humboldtian universities 768–769
ICT readiness 139–140
international academics in Australia 747*f*
international branch campuses 313, 632
international students
   vs. domestic students 18*t*
   inward mobility rate 270*t*, 270–271
   to Japan 641–642, 653–654, 659
   from Myanmar 850–851
   to New Zealand 761*f*
   numbers 269–270, 270*t*, 684*t*
internationalization 15–16, 18–19, 268–269,
      270–271, 299*t*, 300*t*, 453, 642,
      681–685
   CAMPUS Asia 664
   Comprehensive Strategies for
      Internationalization of Higher
      Education 682
   countries of origin for international
      students and faculty 684–685, 685*t*
   cultural distance 272
   development assistance 274
   Higher Education Internationalization
      Strategy 682
   impacts on cities and regions 280
   International Education
      Quality Assurance System
      (IEQAS) 683–684
   rankings 217
   researchers 20, 278–279
   Study South Korea Project 682–683
   Tokyo Convention 296
   trends 682*f*
internet infrastructure 397

South Korea (*cont.*)
  Japan's developmental state model as
      inspirational 507
  Japan's higher education system
      comparison 630
  journal citations and documents
      produced 380*t*, 380–381
  knowledge production 495
  bibliometrics 469*f*, 470, 472*f*, 473, 474*f*, 474,
      475*f*, 477, 479*f*, 480n.23, 481*f*, 484
    GERD as percentage of GDP 466, 467*f*
    patent citations 488*f*, 489–491, 490*f*,
      491n.29
    patent count 492*f*, 493, 494*f*
  Leaders in Industry–University Cooperation
      (LINC/LINC+) projects 687
  liberal arts and sciences 176–177, 178–179,
      182
  Lifelong Education Act 537
  lifelong learning 536, 537, 538, 539–540, 541,
      542
  Ministry of Education, Science, and
      Technology
    budget 678
    cyber universities and colleges 346n.12
    Half-price Tuition Policy 680–681
    MOOCs 361–362
    student loans 437
  MOOCs 356, 357, 361–362, 364, 366
  National Institute for Lifelong Education
      (NILE) 361–362
  nationalism 520–521, 524
  New Education Plan 674
  New Plan for HEIs 681–682
  Open Universities 333, 336, 339*t*, 343,
      345–346
  PISA scores 162–163
  postgraduate education 95
  private philanthropy 414
    Global Philanthropy Environment
      Index 405, 406*t*
  private HEIs 14, 124–125, 125*f*, 676–677
    financing 678
    historical development and
      background 672–673, 675
    percentage of enrollment 613*t*
    vs. public university enrollment 424

  private sector collaboration 686–687
  public financing 125–126, 126*t*
    guaranteed student loans 387
    per student 381–384, 384*f*, 678
    as percentage of GDP 381–384, 383*f*, 678
    as percentage of private financing 381,
      383*f*
    as percentage of total education
      spending 381, 382*t*
    vs. private financing 739*f*
  public HEIs 676, 678
  qualification frameworks, lack of 15
  quality
    assurance 685–686
    regulation 250, 257
    internationalization 682
    tuition issues 680–681
  rankings 211, 217, 218, 220, 412–413, 413*t*
  research 25–26
    networks 643
    spending 608–609
  restructuring of higher education 687–688
  return to higher education 425*t*
  returning talent 454–455, 456, 457, 459,
      460, 461
  Service-Learning Asia Network 182
  skill share 70–72
  soft power 509–510
  STEM 205–206
    challenges and responses 199–200,
      201–202
    culture 197–198
    demand 191–194
    as percentage of HE students 860, 861*f*
    R&D spending 192–195, 193*t*, 205–206
    reform, need for 204–205
    student performance in science and
      math 196*t*, 197*t*
  student loans 24
    collection 437
    default measures and sanctions 434*t*
    description 446*t*
    funding source 430*t*, 431
    loans allocation and borrower
      selection 432
    objectives and coverage 426*t*, 427
    operation 429

reach 441
    repayment regime 436*t*
tuition issues 680–681
types of higher education
        institutions 676–678
University Establishment
        Regulations 674–675
South Korea Advanced Institute of Science
        and Technology (KAIST) 686–687
South Korea Student Aid Foundation
        (KOSAF) 678–679
Southampton University 810
South-East Asia
    access 121–122
    credentials 161
    demographics 18–19
    economic growth 1, 646
    economy 70–72
    employment and labor markets 78, 83
    enrollment rates 115–116, 116*t*, 865
    globalization 639
    highest educational attainment 72–73
    history 31, 33, 34, 36–37
    international students 269–270, 451–452,
        784*t*
        to Australia 745n.8
        cultural distance 272
        to Malaysia 810
    Japanese university collaborations 507–508
    knowledge production 465, 470
        Relative Activity Index 483*f*, 485, 486*f*
    learning 166
    legislation 15
    lifelong learning 536–537, 538, 544–545
    massification 6*f*, 6
    meritocracy 162
    nation-building, Japan 646
    Rangoon University 837
    Taiwan's New Southbound Policy 506–507
    Thai economy 815
Southeast Asia MOOCs Network 364
Southeast Asian Ministers of Education
        Organization (SEAMEO)
    lifelong learning 540
    MOOCs 364
    Regional Institute for Higher Education and
        Development (RIHED) 3, 665

South-West Asia 73, 78
Soviet Union/former Soviet Union
    activism discouraged 644
    collapse 639
    elite HE to massification 50, 51
    influence of education model on
        China 555–556, 577, 578–579
    military-industrial complex 501–502
    soft power 504–505
    Tokyo Convention 296
    triangle of coordination 231–232
Spain
    colonialism 856–857
    history 32, 33–34, 49
    international branch campuses 313*f*
    nationalism 517
Spratly Islands dispute 510
Sri Lanka
    access 118, 119, 122
        scholarships 127*f*
    gender 148–149, 150–151
    history 37–38
    international academics in Australia 747,
        747*f*
    international students
        to Japan 641–642
        Tokyo Convention 296
    MOOCs 363, 366–367
    Open University 339*t*, 363
    private HEIs 125*f*
    public financing 382*t*
    return to HE 425*t*
    student loans 439, 446*t*
Stamford International University 824
Stanford University innovation
        ecosystem 310
Stanford University 198–199, 357, 408,
        410–412
State Universities, India
    governance 601–602
    numbers 594, 617
    postgraduate education 596
    public financing 596–597
    teaching vacancies 602–603
State University of New York
    in Buffalo 559
    Incheon Global Campus 320–321

STEM 11–12, 189–190, 205–206
  access 9–10, 121–123, 128
  Australia 324–325, 741
  challenges and responses 199–203
  China 55–56, 569–570, 578
  cultural commonalities 197–199
  demand 191–194
  elite higher education to massification 52,
        55–56, 60
  employment and labor markets 74, 84–85
  gender 138–140, 139t, 143–144, 153
      access 9–10
      employment and labor markets 150–151,
          152
  goals of HE 100–101
  importance 190–191
  India 599, 606–607, 619–620, 623, 626–627
  Indonesia 779
  international students 21, 278, 294, 324–325
  Japan 638, 643
  and liberal arts, relationship between 11
  Myanmar 840
  Philippines 860, 861f, 866–868, 871, 873
  public financing 22, 380–381, 384–385
  quality 3
  R&D 194–195
  rankings 12
  reform, need for 203–205
  returning talent 454, 455–456, 458–459
  student loans 443
  student performance 195–196
  Taiwan 60
  technocratic sensibility 284
  Thailand 819–820, 826–827, 830, 832
student loans see loans, student
student retention, Open Universities 344–345
student unrest see activism
study groups, MOOCs 369–370
Study Webs of Active-Learning for Young
        Aspiring Minds (SWAYAM) 279,
        361, 365
sub-Saharan Africa 40, 785t, 810
Suharto 777
Sukhothai Thammathirat Open
        University 337–338, 363
Sun Zi 508
Sungkyunkwan University (SKKU) 671, 686–687

Sustainable Development Goals (SDGs) 331
  employment and labor markets 74
  lifelong learning 540
  MOOCs 358
  national qualification frameworks 257
  Open Universities 350
  public funding of HE 22
  R&D spending 194–195
  rankings 869
  Tokyo Convention 296–299
Suzhou 313–314
Sweden 231–232, 334n.6, 739f
Swinburne University 810
Switzerland 761
Sydney University
  Chairs 735–736
  history 35
  international student fees 745
  motto 735–736
  and Oxbridge 735–736, 748
  private philanthropy 416–417, 416t

T
Taipei Imperial University 50, 632
Taiwan
  academic freedom 26
  access 128
  China conflict 506–507
  demographics 18–19, 40
  economic growth 1
  economy 68
  elite HE to massification 51, 59–60, 635
  employment and labor markets 80–81,
        150n.13
  English language 167
  gender 150n.13
  globalization 639
  Higher Education Evaluation and
        Accreditation Council of Taiwan
        (HEEACT) 261–262
  history 38–39, 49, 50
  Hsin-Chu Science-based Industrial
        Park 458–459
  international branch campuses 632
  international students
      to Japan 653–654, 659
      numbers 269–270

internationalization 18–19, 268–269, 271–272,
        453, 642
    cultural distance 272
    development assistance 274
    impacts on cities and regions 280, 282
    importance 289–290
    learning 166
internet infrastructure 397
Japan's developmental state model as
        inspirational 507
Japan's higher education system
        comparison 630
journal citations and documents
        produced 380*t*
knowledge production 465n.1
    bibliometrics 469*f*, 472*f*, 474*f*, 475*f*, 479*f*,
        480n.23, 481*f*
    GERD as percentage of GDP 467*f*
    patent citations 488*f*, 489, 490*f*, 491n.29
    patent count 492*f*, 494*f*
liberal arts and sciences 176, 178–179
lifelong learning 536
Medical Accreditation Council 239
Ministry of Education (MOE) 257–260
    Department of Higher
        Education 257–260
    Department of Technical and Vocational
        Education 257–260
    professional education 239
Ministry of Examination 239, 240, 243
Ministry of Health and Welfare 239
MOOCs 365–366
National Science Council 458–459
nationalism 520
New Southbound Policy 506–507
Open Universities 337, 339*t*, 344
PISA scores 162–163
private philanthropy 406*t*
professional education 229, 232–233, 238–240,
        241*t*, 242–243, 244
public financing 381, 382*t*
qualification frameworks, lack of 15
quality 250
    diversified quality assurance system 260–261
    elite HE to massification 60
    input-based to output-based
        approach 261–262

lead units 259*t*
    neoliberalism 253
    professional education 239, 240
    quality assurance and qualification
        frameworks as policy tool 254–255, 257
    upsurge of state control 257–260
rankings 211, 218–219, 220, 221, 223–224
returning talent 454, 455–457, 458–459
soft power 504–505, 506–507, 509–511
STEM 205–206
    challenges and responses 201–202
    culture 197
    demand 191–192
    R&D spending 194–195, 205–206
    reform, need for 204, 205
    student performance in science and
        math 196*t*, 197*t*
Tajikistan 382*t*, 539
Taoism, China 554
Tata Consultancy Services 360
Tata Institute of Social Sciences 409*b*
taxation
    Australia 740
    India 599–600, 622–623
    private philanthropy 404–407, 410
    student loans 433–435, 436, 437–438
    tax deduction policies 386–387
    Thailand 830–831
Taxila University 614–616
Te Herenga Waka Victoria University of
        Wellington 757–758, 765–766
Te Pūkenga 760
Technical University of Munich 702
technical, vocational education and training
        see TVET
Technion–Israel Institute of Technology 321
technological change 27, 535, 538
    demand for higher education 2
    employment and labor markets 74–76, 87,
        139–140
    growth of HE 7–8
    hubs of HE 315
    MOOCs 20, 357
    New Zealand 756
    public financing 396
    see also artificial intelligence; ICT; online
        learning

Technological Institute of the Philippines 864

Technology Relevance 493–494, 494f

Telekom Malaysia Bhd. 326

Teo Chee Hean 701–702

Tertiary Education Quality and Standards
        Agency (TEQSA) 255–256

TH Properties Sdn Bhd. 326

Thai Chamber of Commerce, University of the
        (UTCC) 819–820, 827

Thai Cyber University (TCU) 363

Thai Income Contingent Allowance and
        Loans (TICAL) 431–432, 436

Thai University Network 363

Thailand 815–816
    access 117–118, 120, 121–122, 128, 820–822,
        822f
        scholarships 127f
    activism 2n.2
    Commission on Higher Education 818–819
    demographics 18–19, 40, 69–70, 70t
    dominating public sector and birth of
        private HEIs 816–820
    economic growth 815, 820–821, 833,
        844–845
    economy 71t
    elite HE to massification 7f, 52, 776, 815
    employment and labor markets 74, 75–76,
        86
    Engineering, Technology and Innovation
        Workforce Development
        (KOSEN) 832
    enrollment rates 95f, 860f
    financing disparities 827–831, 828f
        diversifying income 831
        subsidies 828–831
    goals of HE 5, 8, 98, 106–107, 108
    Higher Education Act 827
    highest educational attainment 72–73, 72t
    history 33–34
    Human Capital Index 778
    Indonesian academic ties 782
    international branch campuses 294
    international recognition, journey
        to 831–833
    international students
        to Australia 743–744, 744t
        to Indonesia 784

inward mobility rate 270t, 270–271
    from Myanmar 850–851
    numbers 269–270, 270t
    to the Philippines 865
internationalization 18–19, 271, 300t, 784,
        784t, 815–816, 818–819, 822–824,
        832, 833
    cultural distance 272
    development assistance 274
    Tokyo Convention 296
Japanese official development aid 641
journal citations and documents
        produced 380t
journal publications 782
lifelong learning 536, 538–540, 541, 543, 869
Ministry of Education 818–819
    Educational Development plan 363
Ministry of Higher Education, Science,
        Research and Innovation
        (MHESI) 816, 832
    annual budget expenditure by type 829f
    employability 825
    Policy and Strategy for Higher Education,
        Science, Research and Innovation 832
MOOCs 363, 364, 366–367
Open Universities 337–338, 339t, 345
Private College Act 818
private HEIs 6–7, 125f, 404, 815–820,
        832–833
    access 820–822
    financing disparities 827, 829–831
    growth vs. public HEIs 819t
    internationalization 822, 823–824
    legitimacy 820, 821f
    quality and employability 825–826, 826t,
        827
Private Higher Education Act 818
private philanthropy 406t
public financing 382t, 387
public HEIs 815–820, 832–833
    access 820–822
    financing disparities 827–829–, 831
    growth vs. private HEIs 819t
    internationalization 822–824
    legitimacy 820, 821f
    quality and employability 825–826, 826t,
        827

quality 815–816, 820, 824–827, 832, 833
  employability 824–827, 826*t*
  financing disparities 827
  goals of HE 106–107
  internationalization 823–824
  lead units 259*t*
  national qualification framework 257, 258*t*
rankings 783
research funding 789, 867
researchers per million population 867
return to higher education 425*t*
Second National Plan on the Elderly 539
Service-Learning Asia Network 182
skill share 70–72
STEM 194, 860, 861*f*
Student Loan Fund (SLF) 829–830, 832–833
student loans
  collection 437–438
  debt/repayment burdens 442–443
  default measures and sanctions 434*t*
  description 446*t*
  funding source 429–432, 430*t*
  introduction 423
  loans allocation and borrower
    selection 433
  objectives and coverage 426*t*
  operation 429
  reach 441
  repayment and recovery 439
  repayment default 438
  repayment regime 435, 436*t*
  size of loan 441–442
  types of HEIs 817*t*
Thai-Nichi Institute of Technology 832
Thammasat University 819–820, 828–829
Thein Sein 845–847, 851
Tianjin Hongzhuan Broadcast Correspondence
    University 335–336
Tianjin University 554–555
TikTok 496n.33
time-based repayment loans *see* mortgage-
    type student loans
Times Good University Guide 212
Times Higher Education (THE) World
    University Rankings 13, 212, 213, 220
  bibliometrics 476–477
  China 565, 586

indicator weights 214*t*
Indonesia 783
Japan 639
Malaysia 811
Philippines 868, 869
private philanthropy 414n.9, 414n.13
public financing 379n.1
Singapore 699*t*, 707–708
Thailand 827
Timor-Leste
  access 122
  economy 68, 69
  gender 146*t*
  international students 300*t*
    to Indonesia 784
  lifelong learning 536
  quality regulation 251
Tohoku University 17n.6, 632, 633, 639
Tokyo 313
Tokyo Convention 15–16, 291, 292, 295–296,
    303, 664
  history 296–297
  international students 19
  latent functions 301–302
  manifest functions 299–301
  Seoul Statement 296–297, 298, 302
  Sustainable Development Goals 297–299
Tokyo Institute of Technology 632, 639
Tokyo Senmon Gakko 633
Tokyo University 17n.6
  bonds market 388
  credentials 10–11
  Global Alliance of Universities on Climate 587
  history 632
  private philanthropy 416*t*
  rankings 413*t*, 639
Tokyo Women's Christian University 633
Toronto University 3
Torrens University 736
Toussaint and Langenscheidt Institute,
    Berlin 334n.6
transitional labor markets 78–79
transnational education zones *see* hubs of HE
Trends in International Mathematics and
    Science Studies (TIMSS) 151–152,
    196, 197*t*, 205–206
  Malaysia 202

triangle of coordination 231–233, 232f, 242, 242f
Trump, Donald 17–18, 460–461, 496n.33, 523
  nationalism 514, 523, 528–529
Tsinghua Shenzhen Graduate School 587
Tsinghua University 294, 586–587
  credentials 10–11
  Double-World-Class policy 582
  engineering 578
  Global Innovation Exchange 321, 587
  Latin America Center 587
  MOOCs 359
  National Key University 578–579
  private philanthropy 416–417, 416t
    Schwarzman Scholars Program 407n.5, 587, 589
    Yeung Kwok Keung 409b
  public financing 385, 392
  rankings 12, 223, 413t, 413n.8, 565
  Southeast Asia Center 587
  Tsinghua Unigroup 556
Tsinghua-Berkeley Shenzhen Institute 587
tuition fees
  Australia 736, 738, 808
    by discipline 739, 740t
    internationalization 744–745, 749
  Cambodia 404
  China 556, 561, 563, 563t, 568–569, 585
    ratio to overall revenue 566, 567f
  Hong Kong 720–722
  India 598–599, 612–613, 619, 622–623, 626–627
  Indonesia 776–777, 780–781, 785–786, 789–790
  Japan 393, 394, 395t, 635–636, 640, 644
  Malaysia 803
  New Zealand 758, 759–760, 762, 766, 767
  Open Universities 333–334, 348–349
  Philippines 863–864, 870, 875
  private HEIs 404
    vs. public HEIs 424
  public financing 393, 394, 395t, 396
  Singapore 700, 703–704
  South Korea 678
  subsidies 424
  Thailand 821–822, 823–824, 825, 830, 831
  UK 808

Turkey 296
TVET 82–84
  APEC Education Strategy 2016–2030 77
  Australia 736–737
  China 557, 562, 566
  graduate work readiness 81, 85
  Hong Kong 717n.1
  India 618
  Indonesia 777
  Japan 636
  lifelong learning 538
  Malaysia 800–801
  New Zealand 758, 759, 760, 766, 767–768
  Open Universities 342
  Philippines 857, 858, 865, 871, 873–874
  Singapore 695, 704–705
  South Korea 672, 676
  Thailand 818, 832
twinning arrangements 293

U
Udacity 19, 348, 358–359, 371
Ulsan National Institute of Science and Technology (UNIST) 677
underemployment
  goals of higher education 100–101
  graduate work readiness 78–79, 80
  Philippines 867
unemployment
  challenges 67
  COVID-19 pandemic 88
  elite HE to massification 55, 57
  goals of HE 100–101
  graduate work readiness 78–79, 80, 85, 86
  Hong Kong 57, 725
  India 598
  Indonesia 775, 778
  Myanmar 846
  overeducation 84–85
  rates 70, 71t
  Thailand 825–826
  trends 66–67
UNESCO
  access 119, 122–123
  Asian University for Women, Bangladesh 181
  Belém Framework for Action (BFA) 544

employment and labor markets 85–86, 87
gender 135, 152
    Gender Parity Index (GPI) 119
hubs of HE 315
Institute for Education 544
Institute for Lifelong Learning
        (UIL) 544–545
international students 249, 269–270,
        663–664
Japanese National Commission 651–652
knowledge production 465
learning society 535
lifelong learning 535–536, 537, 539, 540,
        544–545
quality regulation 257
research funding as percentage of GDP 867
researchers per million population 867
STEM 194–195, 197–198, 199–201
Strengthening Pre-Service Teacher
        Education Myanmar 842
Tokyo Convention 296–303, 664
UNICEF 362, 846–847, 850
United Arab Emirates (UAE)
    international branch campuses 290–291,
        313f
    international students 2–3, 300t
    see also Abu Dhabi; Dubai; Qatar
United Kingdom
    academic professionals in Australia 746
    Brexit 510, 514
    China–UK Association for the Humanities
        in Higher Education 587
    colonialism
        Australia 735–736, 737–738, 743
        Malaysia 798
        New Zealand 757, 764
        Singapore 693
    correspondence learning 334n.6
    cultural alignment with Australia and New
        Zealand 356, 358
    elite HE to massification 7f, 48, 51, 53–54, 58
    elite HEIs 575
    engineers recruited by India 593
    e-University (UKeU) 768
    failure, academic 163
    future of HE 41–42
    gender 137–138n.4, 736

goals of HE 96
history 32–33, 34, 35, 49, 50
Hong Kong's transfer to China 714
Humboldtian universities 768–769
influence of education model 199, 518
    Australia 735–736, 748
    Hong Kong 716–717
    India 622
    Indonesia 775
    Japan 645
international academics in South
        Korea 684–685, 685t
international branch campuses 15–16,
        290–291, 293, 294, 313f
    China 587
    Malaysia 321, 810
    Singapore 321
international students
    from China 556, 558
    from Hong Kong 728–729
    to Hong Kong 729
    from Malaysia 808, 810
    from Myanmar 850–851
    to New Zealand 761f
    scholarships 298
    from Thailand 824
    wariness 21
internationalization 15, 73, 249, 299t, 452,
        767, 822
    commercial drivers 274
    credentials and learning 166–167
    importance 290–291
    Malaysian partnerships 811
    postgraduate education 762
    trends 652
joint-venture universities 585–586
knowledge production 473, 473n.15, 496
land-grant universities 23
MOOCs 364
Myanmar aid 846–847, 849
nationalism 514, 522–523
Open University (UKOU) 331–332, 334,
        336, 359
PISA scores 162–163
polytechnics upgraded to universities 696
private philanthropy 23
professional education 233, 240

United Kingdom (*cont.*)
  public financing 388
    vs. private financing 739*f*
  quality regulation 255–256
  rankings 212, 520–521
  Research Excellence Framework 557
  returning talent 460–461
  Russell Group 502–503, 736
  Science Citation Index articles 564–565
  soft power 500–501, 510
  STEM 191–192
  student loans 427
  tuition fees 767
  US multinational corporations 495
United Nations (UN)
  2030 Agenda 296–297
  categories of tertiary education 135–136n.3
  employment and labor markets 78
  International Migration report 451–452
  Millennium Development Goals 22, 818
  sustainable development
      framework 283–284
  Sustainable Development Goals *see*
      Sustainable Development Goals
  Taiwan's exclusion 506–507
  Tokyo Convention 295–296, 297
  urbanization 316
United Nations University 665
United States
  access 122
  Americanization 290
  Association of American Universities 736
  Californian Master Plan 767–768
  and China, tensions between 495–496,
      646, 815, 831–832
  collaborative international online
      learning 662–663
  colonialism 856–857, 865, 866
  Confucius Institute US Center
      (CIUS) 521
  cultural alignment with Australia and
      New Zealand 356, 358
  economic growth 1
  elite HE to massification 6, 7*f*, 48, 49, 50, 51,
      53–54, 57, 60–61
  elite HEIs 413n.8, 502–503, 575, 872
  employment and labor markets 84–85

  enrollment rates 865
    gender 137–138n.4, 143n.9
  foreign direct investment in Singapore 692
  free tuition movement 445
  future of HE 41–42
  geostrategic tensions 26–27
  goals of HE 96, 97
  history 32, 35–37, 49–50
  hubs of HE 310, 321–322
  immigration policy 453, 743n.7
  Indonesian academic ties 782
  influence of education model 199, 518
    China 577
    Hong Kong 717
    India 600, 622
    Indonesia 775
    Japan 631–632, 633–634, 645
    Philippines 865–866
    Singapore 694
  international academics in South
      Korea 684–685, 685*t*
  international branch campuses 290–291,
      293, 294
    Incheon Global Campus 320–321
    Japan 642
    Singapore 321
  international students
    from China 294, 460–461, 556, 558
    to China 587
    from Hong Kong 728–729
    to Hong Kong 729
    from India 624–625
    from Indonesia 784
    from Japan 659–660
    from Malaysia 810
    from Myanmar 850–851
    to New Zealand 761–762, 761*f*, 762*f*
    numbers 270*t*
    to South Korea 685*t*
    from Thailand 824
    wariness 21, 294, 460–461
  internationalization 15, 73, 249, 271, 299*t*,
      452, 453, 822
    credentials and learning 165–167
    importance 290–291
    researchers 278–279
    soft power 21

STEM 201
  trends 652
Ivy League 413n.8, 502–503
and Japan, trade between 33, 629
joint-venture universities 585–586
knowledge production 468–469, 473,
    473n.15, 480, 489
land-grant universities 23, 501–502
liberal arts and sciences 174–175, 176–177,
    184–185
lifelong learning 97
military-industrial complex 501–502
missionaries to South Korea 671
MOOCs 19, 357–359, 364, 370
multinational corporations 494–495
National Institute of Health
    (NIH) 495–496
nationalism 514, 520–521, 522–523, 524, 526,
    528–529
popular degrees 11–12
private HEIs 125f
  percentage of enrollment 613t
  vs. public HEIs 676–677
private philanthropy 23, 406–407, 408,
    410–412, 415, 585
public financing 125–126, 126t
  guaranteed student loans 387
  land-grant universities 386
  vs. private financing 739f
  research grants to private HEIs 623
  university bonds market 388
quality 39, 253
rankings 211, 212, 222, 520–521
research 25–26
  collaboration 661
  output 608–609
  spending 608–609, 623
returning talent 460–461
  consequences 457
  empirical evidence 456
  factors affecting 454–455
  policies 458–459, 460
scholarships 16
  Fulbright Fellowship 16, 21, 500–501, 510
Science Citation Index articles 564–565
soft power 500–501, 503, 504–505, 510–511
South Korean Military Government 672

STEM
  brain drain 201
  China's Thousand Talents Plan 201–202
  demand 191–192
  gender 200–201
  importance 190–191
  international students 201
  pay levels 202
  R&D spending 193t
  student loans 423, 432, 442, 740, 865–866
  triangle of coordination 231–232
United States Patent and Trademark Office
    (USPTO) 488
Universal Declaration of Human Rights 115
universal HE 6, 47, 48, 49, 52
  access 115, 117–118, 119–120, 123
  China 565, 576
  Confucian heritage 52–53
  history 37
  India 618
  Japan 636
  Philippines 870
Universitas Ciputra 407–408
Universitas Terbuka 337, 343, 777–778
Universiti Kebangsaan Malaysia 804, 807
Universiti Sains Malaysia 804, 811
Universiti Teknologi MARA 802
University Alliance of the Silk Road (UASR) 19,
    295
university bonds market 388
University College London 3, 847n.21
University Mobility in Asia-Pacific
    (UMAP) 295
University of California Berkeley 526
University of California, Los Angeles
    (UCLA) 294
University of Chicago Booth School of
    Business 293
University of London college system 767
University of Science and Technology of
    China 563–564
University of Science Malaysia (USM) 219
University of the Philippines Open University
    (OPOU) 348
  admission to 337
  employer satisfaction with graduates 345
  ICT 345–346

University of the Philippines Open University
(OPOU) (*cont.*)
MOOCs 362
quality measurement 344
technology-enabled instruction 337–338
University of the Third Age (U3A) 541
unrest *see* activism
urban populations
access 119–120, 129–130
education hubs 315–316, 318–319
employment and labor markets 317
gender 134–135, 139n.6, 145
by geographic region 317*t*
Indonesia 779*t*
Japan 638
Myanmar 843, 849–850
urbanization 2
U.S. News & World Report 212
USAID STRIDE program 866, 867, 868
Utah, University of 320–321
Uzbekistan
lifelong learning 539
student loans 426*t*, 430*t*, 446*t*

V

validated programs 293
Vellore University 619
Vemula, Rohith 605n.17
Victoria University College 35
Victoria University of Wellington 757–758,
765–766
Vietnam 25
access 117–118
instruments to improve 124
scholarships 126, 127*f*
study programs 121–122
budgetary control 404
demographics 70*t*
digital divide 357
economy 71*t*
elite HE to massification 52
employment and labor markets
future 74, 75–76
graduate work readiness 81, 86
skill shortages 80
TVET 83, 83*t*
enrollment rates 860*f*

gender 143, 144–145, 147, 148
globalization 641–642
goals of HE 98
Higher Education Reform Agenda
(HERA) 393–394
highest educational attainment 72*t*
history 36, 37–38, 49
Human Capital Index 778
international academics in Australia 747*f*
international branch campuses 744–745,
785
international students
to Australia 743–744
vs. domestic students 18*t*
to Japan 641–642, 659
to New Zealand 761*f*, 762*f*
numbers 270*t*
to South Korea 684, 685*t*
internationalization 271, 299*t*, 783–784
commercial drivers 273–274
Tokyo Convention 296
internet infrastructure 397
journal citations and documents
produced 380*t*
journal publications 782
lifelong learning 536
MOOCs 20, 364, 367, 370
Open Universities 339*t*, 345
private philanthropy 406*t*
private HEIs 125*f*, 404
public financing
expansion of higher education 389
local governments 385
per student 384*f*
as percentage of GDP 383*f*, 392–394,
838n.1
as percentage of private financing 383*f*
as percentage of total education
spending 381, 382*t*, 394, 394*f*
role of government 389–390
quality regulation 258*t*, 259*t*
STEM 194, 195, 197, 861*f*
student loans
debt/repayment burdens 442–443
default measures and sanctions 434*t*
description 446*t*
funding source 430*t*

introduction 423
  objectives and coverage 426*t*
  reach 441
  repayment and recovery 439
  repayment regime 436*t*
  size of loan 441–442
Vietnam–Japan University 661–662
Vikramshila University 614–616
virtual learning *see* online learning
Virtual University, Pakistan 345–346
vocational education and training *see*
        technical, vocational education and
        training
Von Humboldt University 103

W

Waikato, University of 757–758
Warwick, University of 702
Waseda University 17n.6, 103, 335, 633
Washington University 294, 321, 587
Wawasan Open University 336n.7
WeChat 496n.33
West Asia
  international students to and from
        Indonesia 785*t*
  lifelong learning 536–537
  STEM 199–200
Westlake University 560–561
West Yangon University 847
Western Asia 116*t*
Western Australia, University of 35, 335,
        735n.1
Western Europe
  elite HE to massification 53, 61
  Gender Gap Index 199–200
  international students to and from
        Indonesia 784, 785*t*
Wharton Business School 102, 694, 702
William and Flora Hewlett
        Foundation 410–412
Wipro 409*b*
women *see* gender
Wong, Lawrence 709–710
work placements
  graduate work readiness 86
  international students 277
  professional education 230, 243

World Bank
  Asian University for Women,
        Bangladesh 181
  gender 135, 153
  Indian Technical Education Quality
        Improvement Project 81
  Indonesia 776–777
  Knowledge Economy Index 845
  learning society 535
  lifelong learning 535, 544–545
  MOOCs 369
  Myanmar 845, 849–850
  Pakistan's research environment 35
  rankings 212
  reports on higher education 3–4
  women's labor force participation 199
  World Development Report (2019) 68, 139–140
World Economic Forum (WEF)
  employment and labor markets 73, 75,
        78–79
  Gender Gap Index 199–200
  ICT 139–140
  STEM 190, 191–192
World Health Organization (WHO) 506
World Trade Organization (WTO)
  China 557
  cross-border delivery modes 292–293
  General Agreement on Trade in
        Services 18, 292–293, 309, 320
  South Korea 681–682
World War II 32, 35–36
  Australia 736
  Japan 633, 634–635
  New Zealand 757–758
Wuhan University 585–586

X

xenophobic nationalism 516–517, 516*f*, 523
Xiamen University Malaysia 273–274, 294,
        587, 810
Xi'an Jiaotong-Liverpool University 585–586
Xijing University 562
Xinjiang University 583

Y

Yale University 388, 408, 410–412
  Singapore 19, 179–180, 184, 701, 702

Yangon College 34
Yangon University 837, 847–848, 849, 850
    see also Rangoon University
Yangon University of Distance Education 840
Yanjing University 554–555
Yemen 536
Yeo, George 99
Yeung Kwok Keung 409*b*
Yunnan University 294, 583

Yunnan University of Finance and Economics
    (YUFE) Business School 294

Z

Zengzi 576–577
Zhejiang University 560–561, 578, 587
    Singapore 694, 702
Zhonghua Shehui University 560
Zhou Peiyuan 558